Brief Contents

Contents

Introduction to Using Financial Accounting Information

8e

Curtis L. Norton
ARIZONA STATE UNIVERSITY

Gary A. Porter
DRAKE UNIVERSITY

SOUTH-WESTERN
CENGAGE Learning

Australia • Brazil • Japan • Korea • Mexico • Singapore • Spain • United Kingdom • United States

SOUTH-WESTERN
CENGAGE Learning

Introduction to Using Financial Accounting Information, 8th International Edition
Curtis L. Norton, Gary A. Porter

Vice President of Editorial, Business:
Jack W. Calhoun

Editor-in-Chief: Rob Dewey

Executive Editor: Sharon Oblinger

Sr. Developmental Editor: Craig Avery

Editorial Assistant: Courtney Doyle

Marketing Manager: Natalie Livingston

Sr. Content Project Manager: Tamborah Moore

Media Editor: Jessica L. Robbe

Manufacturing Planner: Doug Wilke

Sr. Marketing Communications Manager:
Libby Shipp

Sr. Inventory Analyst: Terina Bradley

Production Service: LEAP Publishing Services, Inc.

Compositor: Cenveo Publisher Services

Art Director: Stacy Shirley

Internal Designer: Craig Ramsdell

Cover Designer: Patti Hudepohl

Cover Photo Credits:
B/W Image: Getty Images/Rubberball
Color Image: Shutterstock Images/oldm

Rights Acquisitions Director: Audrey Pettengill

Rights Acquisitions Specialist: Sam Marshall

Text Permissions Researcher:
Melissa Tomaselli/PMG

Image Permissions Researcher:
Sara Golden/PMG

Library of Congress Control Number: 2011944775

International Edition:
ISBN-13: 978-1-111-97217-2
ISBN-10: 1-111-97217-6

Cengage Learning International Offices

Asia
www.cengageasia.com
tel: (65) 6410 1200

Australia/New Zealand
www.cengage.com.au
tel: (61) 3 9685 4111

Brazil
www.cengage.com.br
tel: (55) 11 3665 9900

India
www.cengage.co.in
tel: (91) 11 4364 1111

Latin America
www.cengage.com.mx
tel: (52) 55 1500 6000

UK/Europe/Middle East/Africa
www.cengage.co.uk
tel: (44) 0 1264 332 424

Represented in Canada by
Nelson Education, Ltd.
www.nelson.com
tel: (416) 752 9100/(800) 668 0671

Cengage Learning is a leading provider of customized learning solutions with office locations around the globe, including Singapore, the United Kingdom, Australia, Mexico, Brazil, and Japan. Locate your local office at:
www.cengage.com/global

For product information: **www.cengage.com/international**
Visit your local office: **www.cengage.com/global**
Visit our corporate website: **www.cengage.com**

Printed in China
1 2 3 4 5 6 7 16 15 14 13 12

CHAPTER 6
Cash and Internal Control   292

CHAPTER 7
Receivables and Investments   330

CHAPTER 8
Operating Assets: Property, Plant, and Equipment, and Intangibles   376

To those who really "count":
Melissa
Kathy, Amy, Andrew

In memory of
Joel

Preface

Your Window into the World of Accounting

Norton/Porter 8e is your open window to success in business.
That's the goal of this revision, and our features have been crafted to help you learn accounting to get ahead in whatever field you choose for your career. Instead of an abstract approach to accounting, you will journey through real-world companies and their specific financial data and business strategies, view the real-life experiences of companies through their financial data, and learn how to make the same types of financial and business decisions you will face after college.

NEW: Chapter introductions focus on accounting's relevance— to You. "Why is accounting important to me?" "Why should I care about this chapter, this topic?" You ask these and similar questions every time you start a new section or begin to read a new chapter for class! So our chapter openers focus more on the importance of accounting and the value of the topics covered in the chapter to your study of accounting.

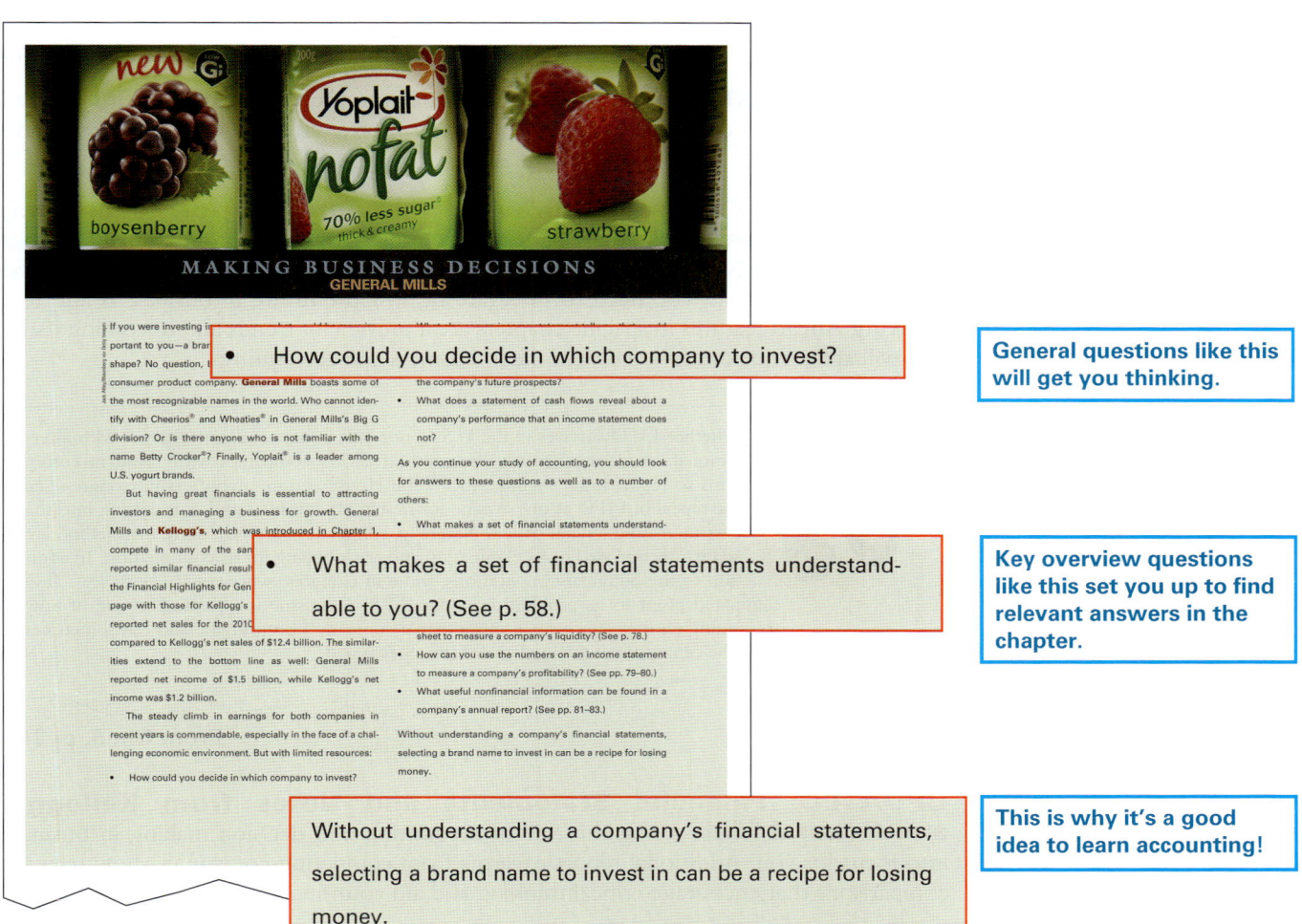

How could you decide in which company to invest?

General questions like this will get you thinking.

What makes a set of financial statements understand-able to you? (See p. 58.)

Key overview questions like this set you up to find relevant answers in the chapter.

Without understanding a company's financial statements, selecting a brand name to invest in can be a recipe for losing money.

This is why it's a good idea to learn accounting!

NEW: Spotlight interviews with business leaders in 9 of the 13 chapters show how actual managers, executives, accounting professionals, and analysts use accounting to get ahead in their careers. **Spotlights** profile real business professionals and their techniques, skills, business insights, and decisions to show how vital accounting is to their success—and will be for *yours.*

SPOTLIGHT
Reading Financial Statements Key to Successful Commercial Lending

Paul C. Stumb, Jr. is an Assistant Vice President at SunTrust Bank in Nashville, TN. According to Paul, the most important statements to review as a commercial lender are a company's balance sheet and income statement. Not only do these give an accurate picture of the current condition of a company (that is, year-to-date performance), but they provide the bank with an idea of how well the company is positioned to fare in future conditions. "If someone is seeking financing, we like to review at least three years of financial statement history. For existing clients, we generally receive monthly or quarterly financials to stay on top of what is going on in their company."

According to Paul, underwriting and credit analysis is an art, not a science. There are many factors that go into making an informed credit decision. For example, it is extremely important to have a complete understanding of a firm's operating cycle in order to make an informed lending decision. Financial analysis and accounting measures make up a large portion of what he does on a day-to-day basis.

For a bank to be comfortable lending money to a business or individual, it has to be comfortable with the quality and figures in the financial statements. You can't be successful in lending if you can't read the financial statements.

"**I have yet to meet a successful banker (in any field) that lacks a solid foundation in accounting. Accounting (especially financial accounting) is the root of lending.**"

Name: Paul C. Stumb, Jr.
Education: BS, Business Administration, Auburn University; MBA, Mississippi State University
College Major: Finance
Occupation: Commercial Banker
Age: 26
Position: Assistant Vice President, Commercial Banking Relationship Manager
Company Name: SunTrust Bank
See Paul Stumb's interview clip in CNOW.

From Ch. 2, p. 59

Additionally, **NEW Spotlight interview videos** to accompany the text are featured in CengageNOW's online study tools for Norton/Porter and also on the student companion web site.

NEW: Looking Ahead features help prepare you for accounting changes to come. Whether changes are on the horizon for International Financial Reporting Standards, for new and challenging financial statement formats, or due to the global economic crisis, you need to be aware of how the future of business is affected. **Looking Ahead** features in specific chapters are a preview of trends and upcoming issues that will affect your career—and your life in business and accounting.

LOOKING AHEAD

Whether LIFO survives in the U.S. is not only a matter of convergence with international standards. Because the method allows companies with rising inventory costs to report lower income, the White House and its supporters in Congress see the repeal of LIFO as one avenue for raising tax revenues and thus cutting into the ever-increasing federal deficit. Naturally, companies currently using the method are adamantly opposed to its elimination and are lobbying for its continuation. In addition to the budgetary implications, those in Congress who would like to see LIFO eliminated point to its prohibition under IFRS. This issue is a prime example of how accounting choices affect much more than a company's bottom line and can sometimes be at the center of national policy debates. Stay tuned.

Tetra Images/Getty Images

From Ch. 5, p. 246

UPDATED: Financial Statements and Notes from Kellogg's and General Mills bring the role of accounting and decision making in business into focus for you. Additional report excerpts from competing companies show relevant comparisons that encourage critical thinking and aid your financial decision making.

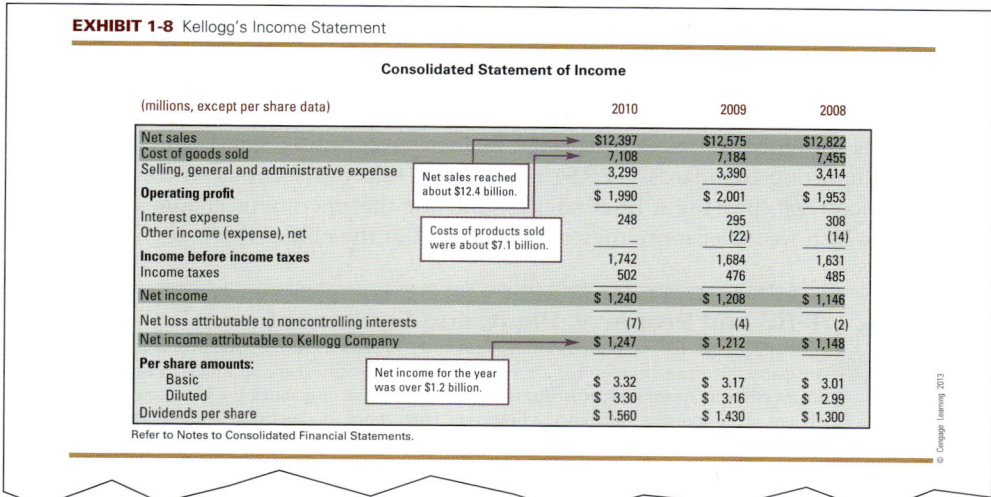

From Ch. 1, p. 21

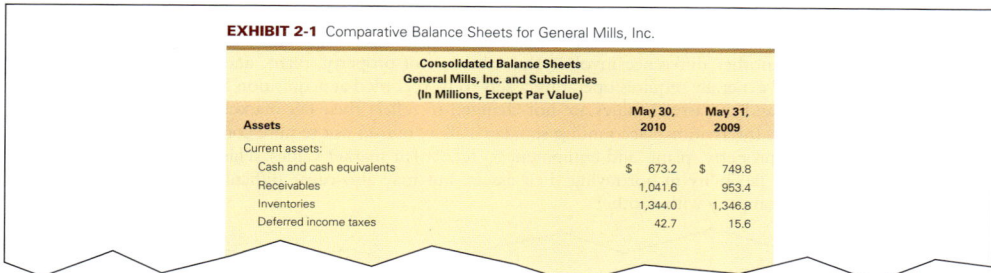

Excerpt From Ch. 2, p. 77

UPDATED: Real-World Financial Information. The text's **balance sheet organization** uses well-known companies such as Carnival Corporation & PLC, Nordstrom, Gap Inc., Sears Holdings, Apple Inc., Nike, Starbucks, The Coca-Cola Company, Southwest Airlines, Best Buy, and GameStop Corp. to help you apply accounting to the real world. Every chapter features a single company, complete with financial data and business strategy, along with assignments that ask you to dig deeper into the company's financials using the chapter concepts, ratio tools, and your growing analytical skills.

NEW and UPDATED: Hot Topics boxes in all chapters dive deeper into the latest issues and challenges of the chapter-opening company as of publication. This one is from Chapter 5.

> *I think the Norton/Porter text does an excellent job of integrating the real-world which is one of the stated objectives.*
>
> Patsy Lee
> *University of North Texas*

From Ch. 5, p. 225

UPDATED: Changes in Global Financial Standards. **Your future career will include changes to accounting standards that are already taking place due to the globalization of business.** In addition to the NEW Looking Ahead sections that preview upcoming regulatory, industry, and economic issues, **IFRS sections on selected topics** focus on global changes to specific financial accounting standards. International Financial Reporting Standards (**IFRS**) coverage in selected sections of the text, called out by an icon , provide a brief background for the upcoming changes in financial standards, which we cover more fully in Appendix A at the end of the text.

IFRS and Property, Plant, and Equipment

Generally, the Financial Accounting Standards Board's (FASB) standards concerning property, plant, and equipment are similar to the international accounting standards, and conversion to those standards should not impose great difficulties for U.S. companies. There are important differences, however. First, when depreciation is calculated, the international standards require that estimates of residual value and the life of the asset be reviewed at least annually and revised if necessary. If the estimate is revised, it should be treated as a change in estimate as we have described in this chapter. The FASB standards do not have a specific rule that requires residual value and asset life to be reviewed annually, so this is an instance where the international standards are more explicit than U.S. standards. The international standards also indicate that companies should determine the components of an asset and depreciate each component separately. For example, if a company buys a building, some parts of the building may be depreciated using one estimate of useful life and other parts may use a different estimate of useful life.

Another difference involves the valuation of property, plant, and equipment. The FASB generally requires operating assets to be recorded at acquisition cost, less depreciation, and the assets' values are not changed to reflect their fair market values, or selling prices. International accounting standards allow but do not require companies to revalue their property, plant, and equipment to reflect fair market values. This gives firms additional flexibility in portraying their assets, but may also cause difficulties in comparing one company with another.

From Ch. 8, p. 394

Decision Case 5-11 Write-Down of Obsolete Inventory   LO9

As a newly hired staff accountant, you are assigned the responsibility of physically counting inventory at the end of the year. The inventory count proceeds in a timely fashion. The inventory is outdated, however. You suggest that the inventory cannot be sold for the cost at which it is carried and that the inventory should be written down to a much lower level. The controller replies that experience has taught her how the market changes and she knows that the units in the warehouse will be more marketable again. The company plans to keep the goods until they are back in style.

Required

1. What effect will writing off the inventory have on the current year's income?
2. What effect does not writing off the inventory have on the year-end balance sheet?
3. What factors should you consider in deciding whether to persist in your argument that the inventory should be written down?
4. If you fail to write down the inventory, do outside readers of the statements have information that is a faithful representation? Explain your answer.
5. Assume that the company prepares its financial statements in accordance with IFRS. Is it necessary that the inventory be written down?

From Ch. 5, p. 291

UPDATED: IFRS Appendix A, "International Financial Reporting Standards" is a succinct overview of such topics as the reasons for a single set of standards, key differences between GAAP and IFRS, and the pace of change in the regulatory movement.

NEW: Daimler's balance sheet in Appendix A shows how financial statements for companies headquartered outside the United States sometimes differ in both the terminology used and the organization of the statements.

Real-World Decision Models

In addition to providing a wealth of real-world financial data, Norton/Porter strives to help you understand how to use such information for sound business decision making through a variety of models.

Financial Decision Framework. This **six-step process** illustrates how to apply financial information in business and investment decisions. The model will help you learn not only what accounting is, who makes the rules, and who uses financial information, but also how that information forms the basis for decision making.

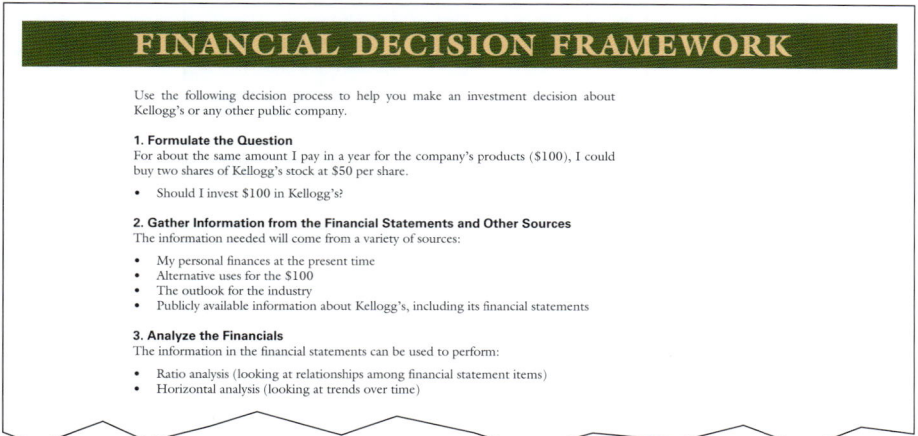

From Ch. 1, p. 13

Ratio Decision Model. Each time a new financial ratio is introduced, the **Ratio Decision Model** walks you through it step by step—from developing and using a financial ratio to financial statement excerpts that highlight ratio terms—helping you analyze and apply ratios most effectively.

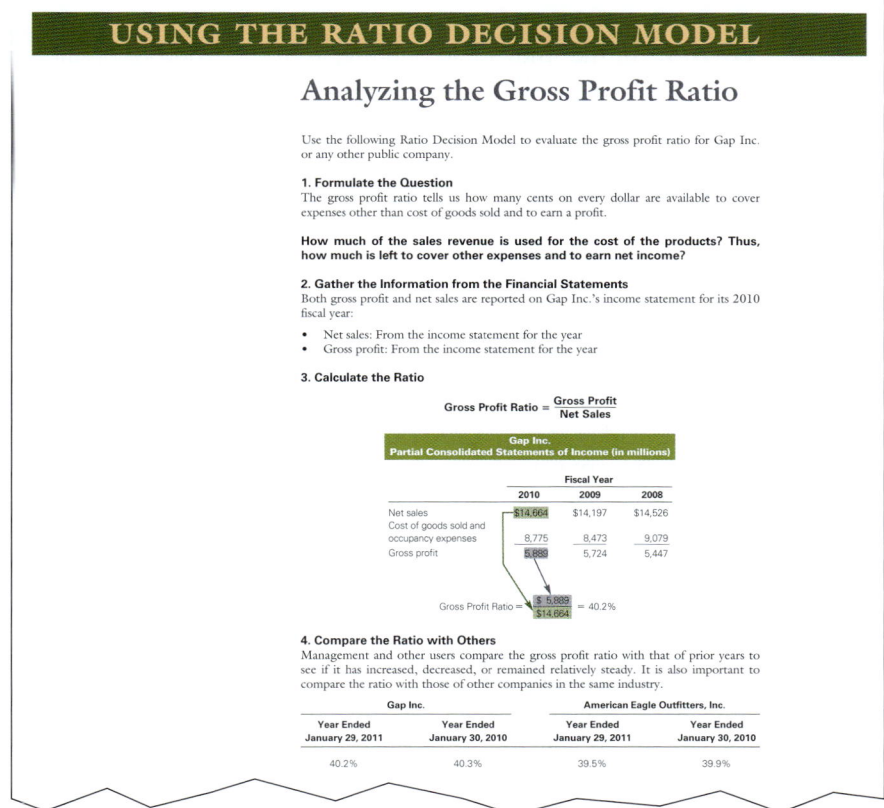

From Ch. 5, p. 234

> *[Accounting] is important for decision making regardless of your position within the organization.*
>
> Dolores Rinke
> *Purdue University Calumet*

Ethical Decision Model. Chapter 1 broadens the scope of business decision making to facilitate those involving the ethical dilemmas of our day. You will learn how to recognize ethical dilemmas in business, analyze key elements, determine alternatives, and select the best alternative.

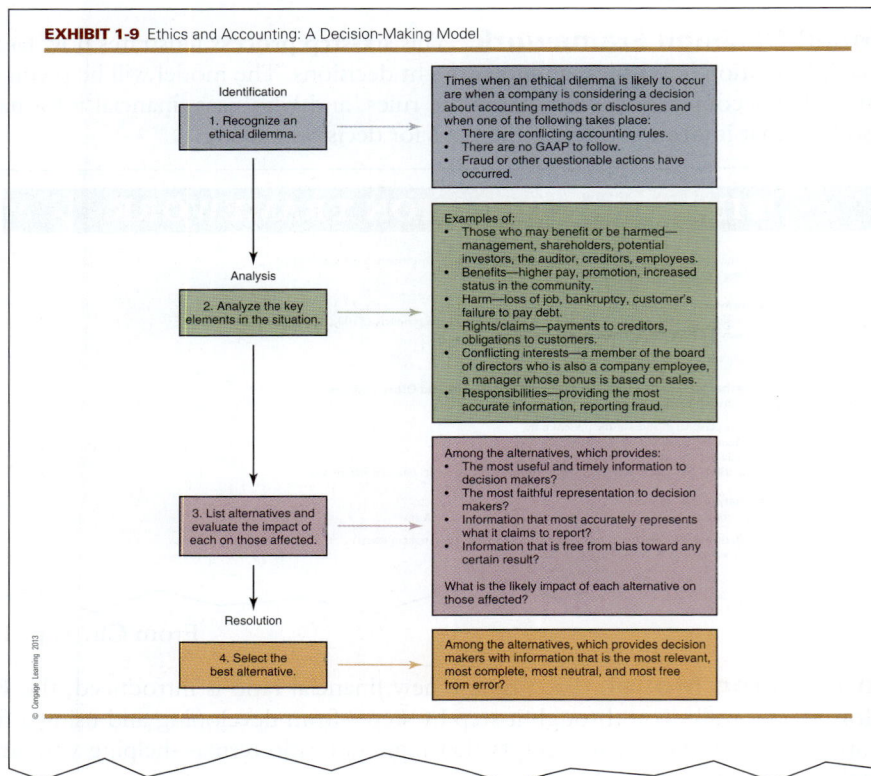

EXHIBIT 1-9 Ethics and Accounting: A Decision-Making Model

From Ch. 1, p. 28

Alternative Terms. In the study of accounting, as in the world of business, terms and terminology are very important. We present **Alternate Terms** at the end of each chapter that illustrate variations in financial accounting terminology that you may encounter.

These Key Features Will Help You Learn Accounting

Introduction to Using Financial Accounting Information provides **step-by-step learning models** that will help you **learn more, faster, and get better grades**. It is a complete learning experience with invaluable, informative chapter introductions, using actual companies; Looking Ahead features that preview the global future of business and accounting; Spotlight interviews with business leaders; and the latest news on chapter companies' financial and market status. In addition to the various decision and ethical models available for you to carry with you into your business future, the text contains a thorough learning system to help you learn, connect, and understand accounting concepts and skills, such as numbered Examples tied to end-of-chapter homework that encourage step-by-step learning; POD Reviews at the end of every section that provide instant feedback to help you master key concepts, and online tools like CengageNOW and Aplia™ that contain gradable, algorithmic homework activities and a wealth of study resources to provide the review and interaction you need to solidify learning.

Also key to your understanding of accounting is an intuitive system for notating transactions, so you'll understand immediately and clearly how each transaction affects the financial statements. Best of all, you can learn financial accounting using an integrated system of learning outcomes, section overviews, examples, review problems, and other learning aids to help you get on top of your reading, lectures, homework, and exams.

STUDY TIP

Ask your instructor about online homework options for your course.

Transaction Style How you view or "read" business transactions affects how you think about them. Each transaction in the text and the solutions manual is notated using a two-part element that focuses on the relationships between accounts, their increases and decreases, and the resulting articulation of the financial statements. This style makes it easier for you to think about the transaction, along with its effect on accounts and the financial statements, in one efficient process.

① **"Identify and Analyze"** This element shows how each transaction affects the income statement and the balance sheet, with key additional information in an active-learning format. Students learn to **Identify and Analyze**:
- The type of business **activity**—operating, investing, or financing.
- The **accounts** affected by the transaction.
- The **financial statement(s)** affected by the transaction—balance sheet, income statement, or both.

② **Transaction-Effects Equation** This element shows how each transaction affects the accounting equation, the balance sheet, the income statement, and stockholders' equity.

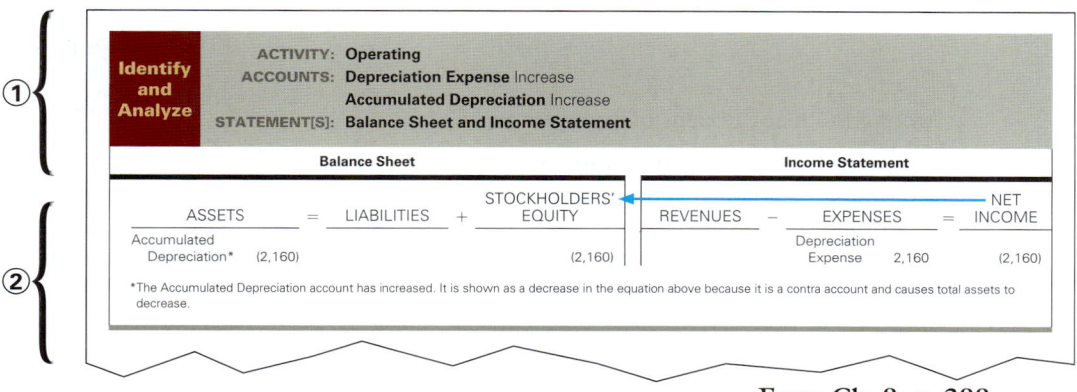

From Ch. 8, p. 388

In the **transaction-effects equation format**, we have a separate column for expenses and an arrow that leads from net income to stockholders' equity. When an expense increases, we show it as an increase in the Expense column. We also show the effect on net income and then show the effect on stockholders' equity via the arrow.

We believe that this form of notation has clear benefits for both students and instructors:
- It provides the clearest view of how transactions affect the balance sheet.
- Its **separation of balance sheet and income statement sides** differentiates these two equations and clearly shows how the income statement elements are affected.
- Its **arrow format** communicates the relationship between net income and stockholders' equity.
- This format **explains the difficult concept of contra accounts**. For example, if the account Accumulated Depreciation increased, we show it in the model as a decrease along with a note that says: "The Accumulated Depreciation account has increased. It is shown as a decrease because it is a contra account and causes total assets to decrease."

Examples Teach Key Concepts and Skills Students tell us that they refer to examples in the text with the goal of solving the homework. Thus, Exercises and Brief Exercises at the back of every chapter refer to the many numbered, step-by-step examples in each chapter. Numbered examples of key procedures, activities, or processes will help you focus on learning the important skills you will need for completing the homework.

This is good and would promote students' understanding of these concepts. Many of my students find the visuals more useful than reading more text.

Patsy Lee
University of North Texas

> **Example 5-2** Calculating Cost of Goods Sold
>
> The amounts shown below are taken from the Cost of Goods Sold section of Daisy's income statement as shown in Exhibit 5-4.
>
> | Description | Item | Amount |
> |---|---|---|
> | Merchandise on hand to start the period | Beginning inventory | $ 15,000 |
> | Acquisitions of merchandise during the period | + Cost of goods purchased | 63,000 |
> | Pool of merchandise available for sale during the period | = Cost of goods available for sale | $ 78,000 |
> | Merchandise on hand at end of period | − Ending inventory | (18,000) |
> | Expense recognized on the income statement | = Cost of goods sold | $ 60,000 |
>
> A $3,000 excess of ending inventory over beginning inventory means that the company bought $3,000 more than it sold ($63,000 bought versus $60,000 sold).
>
> Notice that ending inventory exceeds beginning inventory by $3,000. That means that the cost of goods purchased exceeds cost of goods sold by that same amount. Indeed, a key point for stockholders, bankers, and other users is whether inventory is building up, that is, whether a company is not selling as much inventory during the period as it is buying. A buildup may indicate that the company's products are becoming less desirable or that prices are becoming uncompetitive.

© Cengage Learning 2013

From Ch. 5, p. 227

Among the many dozens of examples are these:

Recording Depreciation (**Example 4-5**, pp. 170–171)
Determining Ending Inventory and Cost of Goods Sold Using Specific Identification (**Example 5-10**, pp. 238–239)
Preparing Comparative Statements of Cash Flow—Horizontal Analysis (**Example 13-3**, p. 682)

Homework Shows Cross-References to Key Examples beside the Exercises and Brief Exercises to help you review the related example material before completing the homework items.

> **LO3**
> EXAMPLE 5-1, 5-4, 5-6
>
> **Exercise 5-6 Purchase Discounts**
>
> Identify and analyze each of the following transactions of Buckeye Corporation. (All purchases on credit are made with terms of 1/10, n/30, and Buckeye uses the periodic system of inventory.)
>
> | July | 3: | Purchased merchandise on credit from Wildcat Corp. for $3,500. |
> | July | 6: | Purchased merchandise on credit from Cyclone Company for $7,000. |
> | July | 12: | Paid amount owed to Wildcat Corp. |
> | August | 5: | Paid amount owed to Cyclone Company. |

From Ch. 5, p. 270

NEW and UPDATED: Working-backward exercises have been added to end-of-chapter homework. Working-backward exercises generally give you a "result"—account balances, balance sheet or income statement presentations/amounts, or ratios. With this information, you are then asked to work backward to arrive at an answer to the exercise. **This type of problem solving is a test of your ability to think critically about key accounting concepts**.

It's great. Students seem to appreciate concise exhibits/illustrations rather than lengthy paragraphs.

Dolores Rinke
Purdue University Calumet

I like the book. I think it is well organized and easy to read/follow. For the students who do read the text, they will find good examples to help them work through the homework problems and fully understand the material being presented.

Kim Brickler
Lindenwood University

LO5 **Exercise 4-9 Working Backward: Depreciation**

EXAMPLE 4-5   Polk Corp. purchased new store fixtures for $55,000 on January 31, 2010. Polk depreciates assets using the straight-line method and estimated a salvage value for the machine of $5,000. On its December 31, 2012, balance sheet, Polk reported the following:

Property, plant, and equipment:		
Store fixtures	$55,000	
Less: Accumulated depreciation	15,000	$40,000

Required

1. What is the yearly amount of depreciation expense for the store fixtures?
2. What is the estimated useful life in years for the store fixtures? Explain your answer.

From Ch. 4, p. 195

> *Such an approach helps a student to learn concepts, not memorize numbers.*
>
> Gary Olsen
> *Carroll University*

The following are other examples of working-backward problems, which are found in seven key chapters of the text.

Exercise 5-10   Exercise 11-1*   Exercise 12-10
Exercise 6-3   Exercise 11-2*   Exercise 13-5
Exercise 7-10

*These items and others in Chapters 8–10 are labeled "Solving for Unknowns" for pedagogical reasons.

> *I like the fact that the authors are trying to reach a lot of the students' learning styles.*
>
> Jennifer LeSure
> *Ivy Tech Community College*

Overview sections at the start of each major head provide you with a summary of the concepts to be presented in that section. **Overviews provide a handy preview of concepts before you study the chapter**, as well as an additional chance to review concepts before tackling homework or taking an exam.

Analyzing the Effects of Transactions on the Accounting Equation

OVERVIEW: Some transactions affect just the balance sheet, and others affect both the balance sheet and the income statement. Regardless, as transactions are recorded, the accounting equation must remain in balance:

Assets = Liabilities + Stockholders' Equity

From Ch. 3, p. 108

> *I believe these brief overviews help students. Having this highlighted with a different color and type w[ill] help these students read at least this much.*
>
> Patsy Lee
> *University of North Texas*

Key Concept Highlights. More than ever before, the eighth edition highlights key concepts in the text using color, boldface, bulleting, and other design elements to help you zero in on key concepts you'll need to know for homework and tests.

Capital versus Revenue Expenditures

Accountants often must decide whether certain expenditures related to operating assets should be treated as an addition to the cost of the asset or as an expense. One of the most common examples involving this decision concerns repairs to an asset. Should the repairs constitute capital expenditures or revenue expenditures?

- A **capital expenditure** is a cost that is added to the acquisition cost of an asset.
- A **revenue expenditure** is not treated as part of the cost of the asset, but as an expense on the income statement.

Thus, the company must decide whether to treat an item as an asset (balance sheet) and depreciate its cost over its life or to treat it as an expense (income statement) of a single period.

The distinction between capital and revenue expenditures is a matter of judgment. Generally, the following guidelines should be followed:

- When an expenditure *increases the life of the asset or its productivity*, it should be treated as a capital expenditure and added to the asset account.
- When an expenditure *simply maintains an asset in its normal operating condition*, however, it should be treated as an expense.

The *materiality* of the expenditure must also be considered. Most companies establish a policy of treating an expenditure that is smaller than a specified amount as a revenue expenditure (an expense on the income statement).

LO7 Determine which expenditures should be capitalized as asset costs and which should be treated as expenses.

Capital expenditure
A cost that improves the asset and is added to the asset account.

Alternate term: Item treated as asset.

Revenue expenditure
A cost that keeps an asset in its normal operating condition and is treated as an expense.

Alternate term: Item treated as an expense of the period.

From Ch. 8, p. 389

Portable On-Demand (POD) Reviews give instant feedback to help you master key concepts. Appearing at the end of every major section in the chapter text, this review feature combines a summary of topics and a quick quiz to help cement what you've just read before reading on. **POD Reviews** are available to download onto electronic devices and in multiple formats.

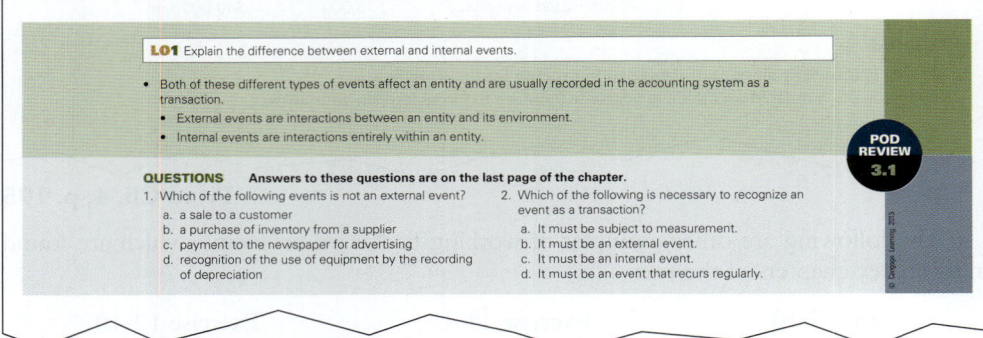

From Ch. 3, p. 107

Brief Exercises, tied to a single learning outcome, allow you to confirm what you've learned in the short run and develop the skills and confidence you need to effectively work more complex exercises and problems.

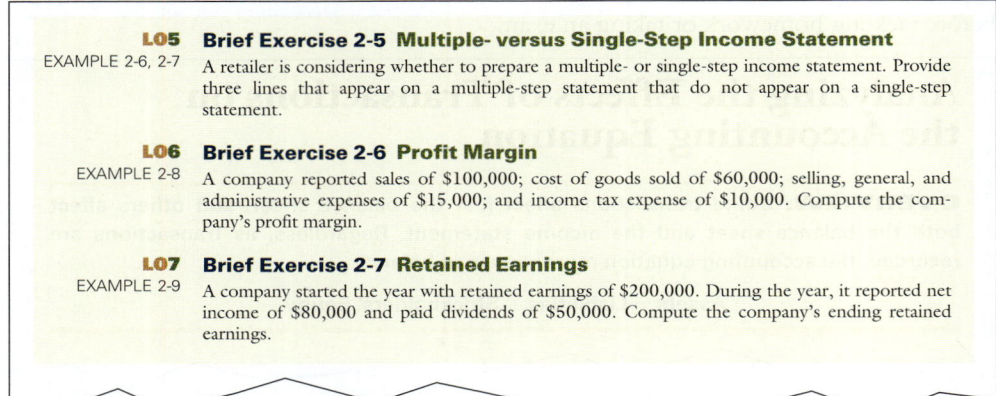

From Ch. 2, p. 88

Chapter-by-Chapter Changes

Chapter 1

1. Updated the chapter opener with the most current information available and replaced the financial statements from Kellogg's as the focus company for Chapter 1.
2. Introduced concept of *faithful representation* to reflect the new SFAC No. 8, *Conceptual Framework for Financial Reporting*.
3. Added new Spotlight featuring the CFO of a cruise line company.
4. Updated the Hot Topics feature showcasing Kellogg's as one of the world's most ethical companies.
5. Added a new Looking Ahead feature to introduce the FASB/IASB convergence project.
6. Updated end-of-chapter material: Warmup Exercise 1-3, P1-1, P1-7, P1-4A, DC1-2, DC1-3.

Chapter 2

1. Updated the chapter opener with the most current information available and replaced the financial statements from General Mills as the focus company for Chapter 2.
2. Revised the "Objectives of Financial Reporting" section to reflect the new SFAC No. 8, *Conceptual Framework for Financial Reporting*.
3. Revised the "What Makes Accounting Information Useful? Qualitative Characteristics" section to reflect the new SFAC No. 8, *Conceptual Framework for Financial Reporting*.
4. Updated the Hot Topics feature on General Mills' dividend decision.
5. Added a new Spotlight featuring the commercial loan officer of a regional bank.
6. Added a new Looking Ahead feature to introduce the FASB/IASB joint project on the format and presentation of financial statements.
7. Updated end-of-chapter material: P2-10, P2-10A, DC2-1, DC2-2.

Chapter 3

1. Updated the chapter opener with the most current information available and replaced the financial statements from Carnival Corporation as the focus company for Chapter 3.
2. Updated the Hot Topics feature on Carnival's financing options for its new ships.
3. Updated end-of-chapter material: DC3-1, DC3-2, DC3-3.

Chapter 4

1. Updated the chapter opener with the most current information available and replaced the financial statements from Nordstrom as the focus company for Chapter 4.
2. Added a new Spotlight featuring the founding partner in a CPA firm.
3. Revised the "Measurement" section to reflect the new SFAC No. 8, *Conceptual Framework for Financial Reporting*.
4. Updated the Hot Topics feature to highlight Nordstrom's same store sales reporting.
5. Added new end-of-chapter material: E4-9, E4-12, E4-13, E4-14, E4-18.
6. Updated end-of-chapter material: DC4-1, DC4-2, DC4-3.

Chapter 5

1. Updated the chapter opener with the most current information available and replaced the financial statements from Gap as the focus company for Chapter 5.
2. Added a new Spotlight featuring the margin control specialist for an automotive supply company.
3. Revised the Hot Topics feature on Gap's expansion to Italy and China.
4. Added a new Looking Ahead feature to highlight possible congressional repeal of LIFO.
5. Revised Exhibit 5-11, substituting a partial statement of cash flows for Kellogg's.
6. Revised E5-17, substituting amounts for Nordstrom.
7. Revised DC5-2, substituting inventory note for Walgreen Co.
8. Added new end-of-chapter material: E5-10, E5-16, E5-23, E5-24, E5-27.
9. Updated end-of-chapter material: E5-17, P5-2, P5-5, P5-7, P5-10, P5-2A, P5-5A, P5-7A, P5-8A, DC5-1, DC5-2, DC5-3.

Chapter 6

1. Updated the chapter opener with the most current information available and replaced the financial statements from Sears Holdings Corporation as the focus company for Chapter 6.
2. Updated the Hot Topics feature to highlight Sears' strategy to finance operating cash needs.
3. Added new end-of-chapter material: E6-3.
4. Updated end-of-chapter material: DC6-1, DC6-2.

Chapter 7

1. Updated the chapter opener with the most current information available and replaced the financial statements from Apple Inc. as the focus company for Chapter 7.
2. Added a new Spotlight featuring the CFO for a sign company.
3. Revised the Hot Topics feature on Apple's quarterly report filed with the SEC.
4. Added a new Looking Ahead feature to highlight possible changes in the statement of cash flows under the joint FASB/IASB project.
5. Revised P7-3A, substituting amounts for The Hershey Company and Kraft Foods, Inc.
6. Revised DC7-1, substituting amounts for Kraft Foods, Inc.
7. Added new end-of-chapter material: E7-2, E7-5, E7-7, E7-10, E7-16.
8. Updated end-of-chapter material: E7-6, P7-3, P7-3A, DC7-1, DC7-2, DC7-3.

Chapter 8

1. Updated the chapter opener with the most current information available and replaced the financial statements from Nike as the focus company for Chapter 8.
2. Revised the Hot Topics feature on Nike's intangible assets.
3. Added a new Spotlight focusing on the importance of operating assets to a lender.
4. Added coverage of the IFRS treatment of operating assets.
5. Updated end-of-chapter material DC8-1, DC8-2 for General Mills and Kellogg's.

Chapter 9

1. Updated the chapter opener with the most current information available and replaced the financial statements from Starbucks as the focus company for Chapter 9.
2. Revised the Hot Topics feature on Starbuck's contingent liabilities.
3. Altered the time value of money tables so that the table factors have five digits after the decimal. This major change was undertaken because, in the past, some students performed calculations using a calculator or a spreadsheet and got answers that differed from the suggested answers due to rounding issues. The new tables will result in more exact calculations, although rounding is still present in all time value of money problems. It will also allow our CNOW product to be more consistent with calculations in the text, solutions, and test bank.

4. Added a new Spotlight focusing on accounting issues for a small business owner.
5. Added a Looking Ahead feature on differences in accounting for contingent liabilities for U.S. GAAP and IFRS.
6. Revised all end-of-chapter items to be consistent with new five-digit time value of money tables.
7. Replaced DC9-3 with a case on Wal-Mart's contingent liabilities.
8. Updated other end-of-chapter material: P9-2, P9-3, P9-2A, P9-3A, DC9-1, DC9-2, DC9-4.

Chapter 10

1. Updated the chapter opener with the most current information available and replaced the financial statements from Coca-Cola as the focus company for Chapter 10.
2. Revised the Hot Topics feature on Coca-Cola versus Pepsi.
3. Altered all of the text discussion of bonds to be consistent with the five-digit time value of money tables in Chapter 9.
4. Added a new Spotlight featuring a bond trader's career advice.
5. Added a Looking Ahead feature on potential changes in the accounting for leases.
6. Revised all end-of-chapter items to be consistent with five-digit time value of money tables in Chapter 9.
7. Updated other end-of-chapter material with the most recent information: P10-9, P10-9A, DC10-1, DC10-2, DC10-3.

Chapter 11

1. Updated the chapter opener with the most current information available and replaced the financial statements from Southwest Airlines as the focus company for Chapter 11.
2. Revised the Hot Topics feature on the creation of shareholder value at Southwest Airlines.
3. Added a new Spotlight featuring a portfolio manager's use of accounting information.
4. Added a Looking Ahead feature on the accounting for comprehensive income.
5. Added E11-1 and E11-2.
6. Updated end-of-chapter material: P11-7, P11-7A, DC11-1, DC11-2.

Chapter 12

1. Updated the chapter opener with the most current information available and replaced the financial statements from Best Buy as the focus company for Chapter 12.
2. Revised Exhibit 12-1 to illustrate cash flow and net income differences.
3. Revised the Hot Topics feature on Best Buy's purchase of treasury stock.
4. Added a new Looking Ahead feature to highlight possible changes in the statement of cash flows under a joint FASB/IASB project.
5. Added new end-of-chapter material: E12-6, E12-10, E12-13, E12-21, E12-24.
6. Updated end-of-chapter material: DC12-1, DC12-2, DC12-3.

Chapter 13

1. Updated the chapter opener with the most current information available and replaced the financial statements from GameStop as the focus company for Chapter 13.
2. Revised the Hot Topics feature on GameStop's use of vertical analysis in its quarterly report.
3. Added a new Looking Ahead feature to highlight possible effects of the FASB/IASB joint project on financial statement presentation on statement analysis.
4. Added new end-of-chapter material: E13-5, E13-7, E13-8, E13-13, E13-16.
5. Updated end-of-chapter material: Review Problem, E13-1, E13-2, E13-6, E13-9, E13-12, DC13-1, DC13-2, DC13-3, DC13-4.

Supplements to Help You Learn—and Retain More and Faster for Homework, Quizzes, and Exams

CengageNOW
Where True Learning Takes Place

CengageNOW™ is a powerful course management and online homework tool that provides robust instructor control and customization to optimize the student learning experience and meet desired outcomes.

CengageNOW has the following advantages:

- **"Smart Entry"** ensures you get marked wrong only for being wrong and not for typos or formatting errors. It will also help you prepare for tests and quizzes.
- New levels of feedback and engaging student resources guide you through material and solidify learning.
- Blueprint problems bring concepts full circle and encourage critical thinking.
- A variety of study tools helps you review concepts. Check out the multimedia resources such as games, Spotlight videos, animated review problems, and more!

Personalized Study Plan CengageNOW will improve your performance. You can master key concepts and prepare for exams with CengageNOW's **Personalized Study Plan**—a diagnostic tool plus study plan—preloaded with an Integrated eBook and other multimedia resources to make learning more engaging! Take the Pre-Test to determine what you know right now. Next, the personalized study plan will automatically generate, pointing you to the resources that will help you focus on the areas where you need help the most. Finally, each time you take the Post-Test, the personalized study plan will be revised to help you continue to focus your study.

Aplia™ is a premier online homework product that successfully engages students and maximizes the amount of effort they put forth, creating more efficient learners.

Aplia has the following advantages:

- In addition to end-of-chapter homework, Aplia offers a separate, original problem set that complements the book to provide you with even more practice!
- Unique, detailed explanations and the full solution after each attempt is provided on many homework questions.
- "Grade It Now" allows you to see where you went wrong and enables feedback that will help you with the next attempt.
- "Smart Entry" helps eliminate common typos to help you truly learn the concept behind each answer.
- Blueprint problems bring concepts full circle and encourage critical thinking.

Ask your instructor about assigning CNOW or Aplia for your course!

Excel® Templates. Selected problems in each chapter may be solved on a Microsoft Excel spreadsheet to increase your awareness of basic software applications. Just download the Excel spreadsheets for homework items that are identified by icons in the text.

Student PowerPoint® Slides, by Cathy Lumbattis (Southern Illinois University) allow you to preview class lectures and review key concepts before exams. A smaller version of the Instructor PowerPoint Lectures, these slides allow you to get ready for upcoming lectures, quizzes, homework, and exams with core material you need for chapter study.

Web Resources. Chapter-by-chapter quizzes, topical discussions, updates on IFRS integration, POD Review audio downloads, and more are available for you to access. These items help reinforce and shed light on text topics. Discover more by logging into the text web site. Visit www.cengagebrain.com.

Instructor's Supplements

- The **Instructor's Manual**, by Sandra Augustine (Hilbert College), contains detailed lecture outlines, lecture topics, and suggestions for classroom activities. **NEW:** The chapter activities in the Instructor's Manual have been analyzed and assigned the same set of outcomes that are used in the Solutions Manual and the Test Bank. The Instructor's Manual is available online at login.cengage.com.
- The **Solutions Manual**, by the text authors, consists of solutions to all the end-of-chapter material keyed to learning outcomes and using the same Identify and Analyze and Transaction-Effects Equation form of transaction notation as found in the text. The Solutions Manual is available online at login.cengage.com.
- The **Test Bank**, by LuAnn Bean (Florida Institute of Technology), contains a comprehensive set of test items to meet every assessment need from brief exercises to problems and decision cases. The Test Bank in ExamView® is an easy-to-use test-creation program, making it simple to customize tests to your specific class needs as you edit or create questions and store customized exams. The Test Bank is available online at login.cengage.com.
- **Instructor PowerPoint Slides**, by Cathy Lumbattis (Southern Illinois University), are also included online at login.cengage.com.

Acknowledgments

Among those who have served as reviewers for the eighth edition are the following, to whom we are grateful for their insights:

Kim Brickler
Lindenwood University

Bowe Hansen
Virginia Tech University

Lisa Koonce
The University of Texas at Austin

Patsy Lee
University of North Texas

Jennifer LeSure
Ivy Tech Community College

Nathan C. Moore
Kaplan University

Tommy Moores
University of Nevada, Las Vegas

Gary Olsen
Carroll University

Dolores Rinke
Purdue University Calumet

W. Ron Singleton
Western Washington University

Greg Sommers
Southern Methodist University

William C. Stout
University of Louisville

Throughout the first seven editions, many other individuals have contributed helpful suggestions that have resulted in many positive changes. Although they are not cited here, we remain grateful for their assistance.

We also wish to thank several individuals whose help with supplements and verification have aided us in the revision: Sandra Augustine, *Hilbert College*, LuAnn Bean, *Florida Institute of Technology*, Jim Emig, *Villanova University*, Chris Jonick, *Gainseville State College*, and Cathy Lumbattis, *Southern Illinois University*. We are grateful to Malvine Litten, Peggy Shelton, and Erin Shelton at LEAP Publishing Services for their invaluable production assistance. Finally, we are grateful to the editorial, marketing, media, and production staffs at Cengage, primarily Matt Filimonov, Sharon Oblinger, Craig Avery, Natalie Livingston, Jessica Robbe, Stacy Shirley, and Tamborah Moore for their extensive help with the eighth edition and its supplements.

Curtis L. Norton
Gary A. Porter
December 2011

About the Authors

Curtis L. Norton is currently a Clinical Professor at Arizona State University. He is also a Professor Emeritus at Northern Illinois University in Dekalb, Illinois, where he has taught since 1976. He continues to teach in NIU's highly acclaimed CPA review program. Dr. Norton received his Ph.D. from Arizona State University and an M.B.A. from the University of South Dakota. Dr. Norton earned the University Excellence in Teaching Award at NIU and has published in *The Accounting Review, The Journal of Accounting Education, CPA Journal*, and other journals. A member of the American Accounting Association and Financial Executives International, he also consults and conducts training for private and governmental authorities, banks, utilities, and others.

Gary A. Porter is currently a Distinguished Lecturer at Drake University. He earned Ph.D. and M.B.A. degrees from the University of Colorado and his B.S.B.A. from Drake University. As Professor of Accounting, Dr. Porter served as Department Chair and taught at numerous universities. He has published in the *Journal of Accounting Education, Journal of Accounting, Auditing & Finance*, and *Journal of Accountancy,* among others, and has conducted numerous workshops on the subjects of introductory accounting education and corporate financial reporting.

Dr. Porter's professional activities include experience as a staff accountant with Deloitte & Touche, a participant in KPMG Peat Marwick Foundation's Faculty Development program, and a leader in numerous bank training programs. He has won an Excellence in Teaching Award from the University of Colorado and Outstanding Professor Awards from both San Diego State University and the University of Montana. He served on the Illinois CPA Society's Innovations in Accounting Education Grants Committee, the steering committee of the Midwest region of the American Accounting Association, and the board of directors of the Chicago chapter of Financial Executives International.

Dr. Porter currently serves on the National Advisory Council for Drake University's College of Business and Public Administration. He is a member of the American Accounting Association and Financial Executives International.

Accounting as a Form of Communication

1

AFTER STUDYING THIS CHAPTER, YOU SHOULD BE ABLE TO:

LO1 Explain what business is about.

LO2 Distinguish among the forms of organization.

LO3 Describe the various types of business activities.

LO4 Define accounting and identify the primary users of accounting information and their needs.

LO5 Explain the purpose of each of the financial statements and the relationships among them and prepare a set of simple statements.

LO6 Identify and explain the primary assumptions made in preparing financial statements.

LO7 Identify the various groups involved in setting accounting standards and the role of auditors in determining whether the standards are followed.

LO8 Explain the critical role that ethics plays in providing useful financial information.

STUDY LINKS

A Look at This Chapter Business is the foundation upon which accounting rests. After a brief introduction to business, we begin the study of accounting by considering what accounting is and who uses the information it provides. We will see that accounting is an important form of communication and that financial statements are the medium that accountants use to communicate with those who have some interest in the financial affairs of a company.

A Look at Upcoming Chapters Chapter 1 introduces accounting and financial statements. Chapter 2 looks in more detail at the composition of the statements and the conceptual framework that supports the work of an accountant. Chapter 3 steps back from financial statements and examines how companies process economic events as a basis for preparing the statements. Chapter 4 completes the introduction to the accounting model by considering the importance of accrual accounting in this communication process.

MAKING BUSINESS DECISIONS
KELLOGG COMPANY

Why is learning financial accounting important? Why should you care about learning to read the financial statements of a company?

To be frank, it's because successful companies generate jobs, and struggling companies shed jobs—and jobs affect the economy, which affects your future—how you live, learn, and work.

Also, the more you know about how successful companies work, the better are your chances of doing well in your chosen field. Whatever you plan to do, your knowledge of business and accounting helps you compete whether you invest, work for a company, or go into business for yourself.

Pick your favorite company. Maybe it is **Abercrombie & Fitch** because you buy clothes there. Or maybe it is **Google** because you use its search engine nearly every day. Or is it **Coca-Cola** because you like its commercials? Consider **Kellogg Company**. The Battle Creek, Michigan-based cereal company got its start over 100 years ago when two brothers by sheer chance discovered toasted flakes.

From a modest start, Kellogg Company has grown to the point that it employs nearly 31,000 people around the globe, manufactures its products in 18 countries, and markets those products in more than 180 countries. The company's brand names are among the most recognizable in the world, including such heavyweights as Kellogg's®, Keebler®, Rice Krispies®, and Special K®.

Kellogg Company has faced numerous critical decisions over the years. One of its most far-reaching decisions was made in 2001 when it acquired **Keebler Food Company**, a leading producer of cookies and crackers, for over $4 billion.

How does management of a company, its stockholders, and others interested in the financial well-being of a company know if the company is making good business decisions? Was Keebler "worth" the $4 billion that Kellogg Company paid for it? The numbers produced by an accounting system go a long way in assessing a company's financial performance. Consider the Financial Highlights shown on the next page as they appeared in Kellogg Company's 2010 annual report.

- The first chart shows that sales have exceeded $10 billion for the last six years, reaching a high of $12.8 billion in 2008.
- The second chart shows that earnings per share increased in 2010 for the ninth consecutive year, not coincidentally dating back to when Kellogg acquired Keebler.

Companies use this financial information in making decisions. When a stockbroker decides whether to recommend to a client the purchase of stock in a company, the broker needs information about the company's profits and its payment of dividends. When deciding whether to loan money to a company, a banker must consider the company's current debts.

Why do you need to study this chapter? Learning how accountants and other businesspeople assess a company's performance can work for you too as you prepare for your own competitive future:

- What is business? (See pp. 4–5.)
- What forms of organization carry on business activities? (See pp. 6–7.)
- In what types of business activities do those organizations engage? (See pp. 8–10.)
- What is revenue? How is it measured? (See p. 9.)

- What is net income? How is it measured? (See p. 16.)
- How do revenue and net income relate to a company's assets? (See pp. 15–16.)
- Where do the various items appear on a company's financial statements? (See pp. 15–18.)

Learning the answers to these questions—learning how accountants think and communicate—is just plain smart for everyone in today's job market.

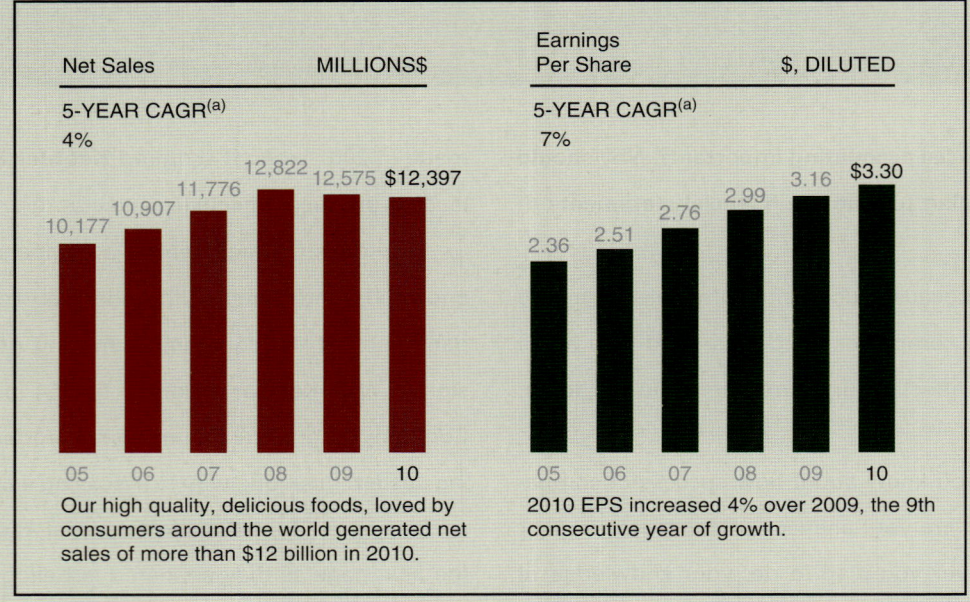

Net Sales   **MILLIONS$**

5-YEAR CAGR(a)
4%

10,177   10,907   11,776   12,822   12,575 $12,397

05   06   07   08   09   10

Our high quality, delicious foods, loved by consumers around the world generated net sales of more than $12 billion in 2010.

Earnings Per Share   **$, DILUTED**

5-YEAR CAGR(a)
7%

2.36   2.51   2.76   2.99   3.16 $3.30

05   06   07   08   09   10

2010 EPS increased 4% over 2009, the 9th consecutive year of growth.

Source: Kellogg Company's web site and its 2010 annual report.

What Is Business?

L01 Explain what business is about.

OVERVIEW: Businesses exist to provide members of society with goods and services. Product companies include manufacturers/producers, wholesalers, and retailers. Service providers are becoming increasingly important in today's economy.

Just as **Kellogg's** got its start over 100 years ago in Battle Creek, Michigan, your study of accounting has to start somewhere. All disciplines have a foundation on which they rest. For accounting, that foundation is business.

Business
All of the activities necessary to provide the members of an economic system with goods and services.

Broadly defined, **business** consists of all activities necessary to provide the members of an economic system with goods and services. Certain business activities focus on providing goods or products such as ice cream, automobiles, and computers. Some of these companies, such as Kellogg's, produce or manufacture the products. Other companies are involved in the distribution of the goods, either as wholesalers (who sell to retail outlets) or retailers (who sell to consumers). Other business activities, by their nature, are service-oriented. Corporate giants such as **Citigroup**, **Walt Disney**, **Time Warner**, and **United Airlines** remind us of the prominence of service activities in the world today. A broad range of service providers such as health-care organizations and Internet companies provide evidence of the growing importance of the service sector in the U.S. economy.

Example 1-1 Identifying Types of Businesses

To appreciate the kinds of business enterprises in our economy, consider the various types of companies that have a stake in the delivery of a box of cereal to the grocery store. First, Kellogg's must contract with various suppliers of the raw materials, such as grains, that are needed to produce cereal. Assume that Kellogg's buys grains from Wholesome Wheat. As a *manufacturer* or *producer*, Kellogg's takes the grain and other various raw materials and transforms them into a finished product. At this stage, a *distributor or wholesaler* gets involved. Assume that Kellogg's sells cereal to Duffy's Distributors. Duffy's Distributors, in turn, sells the products to many different *retailers*, such as **Albertsons** and **Safeway**. Although less obvious, any number of *service* companies are also involved in the process. Assume that ABC Transport hauls the grains to Kellogg's for production and others move the cereal along to Duffy's Distributors. Still others get the cereal to supermarkets and other retail outlets. Exhibit 1-1 summarizes the process.

EXHIBIT 1-1 Types of Businesses

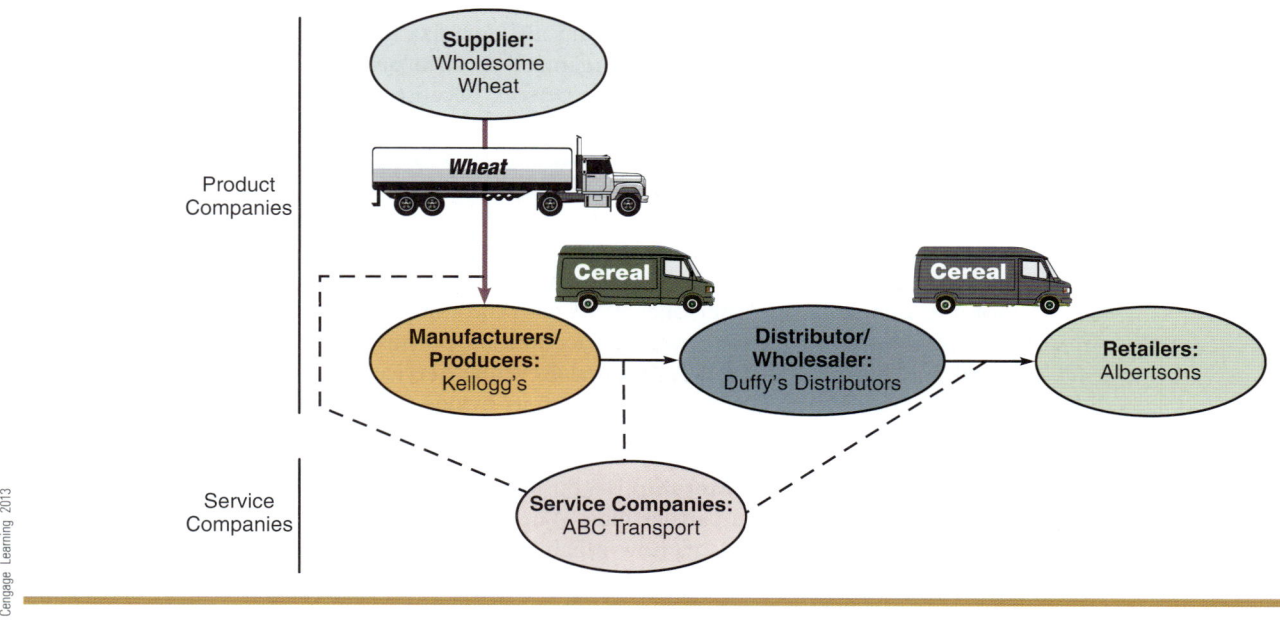

© Cengage Learning 2013

LO1 Explain what business is about.

- Business consists of all activities necessary to provide members of an economic system with goods and services. Suppliers, manufacturers, wholesalers, and retailers are examples of product companies.

QUESTIONS   Answers to these questions are on the last page of the chapter.

1. A department store is an example of a
   a. wholesaler.
   b. manufacturer.
   c. retailer.
   d. supplier.

2. An airline is an example of a
   a. service provider.
   b. retailer.
   c. supplier.
   d. producer.

© Cengage Learning 2013

Forms of Organization

LO2 Distinguish among the forms of organization.

OVERVIEW: Business entities are organized as sole proprietorships, partnerships, or corporations. Nonbusiness entities include government entities such as local, state, and federal governments and private organizations such as hospitals and universities.

There are many different types of organizations in our society. One convenient way to categorize the myriad types is to distinguish between those that are organized to earn money and those that exist for some other purpose. Although the lines can become blurred, *business entities* such as Kellogg's generally are organized to earn a profit, whereas *nonbusiness entities* generally exist to serve various segments of society. Both types are summarized in Exhibit 1-2.

Business Entities

Business entities are organized to earn a profit. Legally, a profit-oriented company is one of three types: a sole proprietorship, a partnership, or a corporation.

Sole Proprietorships This form of organization is characterized by a single owner. Many small businesses are organized as **sole proprietorships**. The business is often owned and operated by the same person. Because of the close relationship between the owner and the business, the affairs of the two must be kept separate. This is one example in accounting of the **economic entity concept**, which requires that a single, identifiable unit of organization be accounted for in all situations. For example, assume that Bernie Berg owns a neighborhood grocery store. In paying monthly bills such as utilities and supplies, Bernie must separate his personal costs from the costs associated with the grocery business. In turn, financial statements prepared for the business must not intermingle Bernie's personal affairs with the company affairs.

Unlike the distinction made for accounting purposes between an individual's personal and business affairs, the Internal Revenue Service (IRS) does not recognize the separate existence of a proprietorship from its owner. That is, a sole proprietorship is not a taxable entity; the business's profits are taxed on the individual's return.

Partnerships A **partnership** is a business owned by two or more individuals. Many small businesses begin as partnerships. When two or more partners start out, they need some sort of agreement as to how much each will contribute to the business and how they will divide any profits. In many small partnerships, the agreement is often just an

Business entity
An organization operated to earn a profit.

Sole proprietorship
A form of organization with a single owner.

Economic entity concept
The assumption that a single, identifiable unit must be accounted for in all situations.

Partnership
A business owned by two or more individuals; the organization form often used by accounting firms and law firms.

EXHIBIT 1-2 Forms of Organization

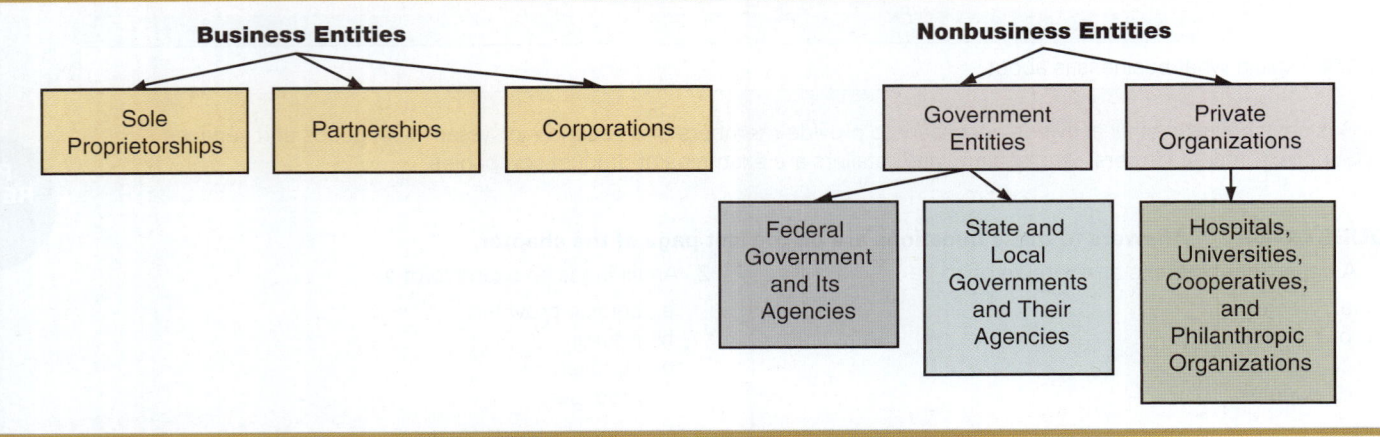

oral understanding between the partners. In large businesses, the partnership agreement is formalized in a written document.

Although a partnership may involve just two owners, some have thousands of partners. Public accounting firms, law firms, and other types of service companies are often organized as partnerships. Like a sole proprietorship, a partnership is not a taxable entity. Individual partners pay taxes on their proportionate shares of the business's profits.

Corporations Although sole proprietorships and partnerships dominate in sheer number, corporations control an overwhelming majority of the private resources in this country. A **corporation** is an entity organized under the laws of a particular state. Each of the 50 states is empowered to regulate the creation and operation of businesses organized as corporations in it. Even though Kellogg's is headquartered in Michigan, for legal reasons, it is incorporated under Delaware's laws.

To start a corporation, one must file articles of incorporation with the state. If the articles are approved by the state, a corporate charter is issued and the corporation can begin to issue stock. A **share of stock** is a certificate that acts as evidence of ownership in a corporation. Although not always the case, stocks of many corporations are traded on organized stock exchanges such as the New York and American Stock Exchanges. Kellogg Company stock is traded on the New York Stock Exchange.

Advantages of Incorporation What are the advantages of running a business as a corporation?

- **One of the primary advantages of the corporate form of organization is the ability to raise large amounts of money in a relatively brief period of time.** This is what prompted Kellogg Company to eventually "go public." To raise money, the company sold a specific type of security: stock. As stated earlier, a share of stock is simply a certificate that evidences ownership in a corporation. Corporations may also issue bonds. A **bond** is similar in that it is a certificate or piece of paper; however, it is different from a share of stock because it represents a promise by the company to repay a certain amount of money at a future date. In other words, if you were to buy a bond from a company, you would be lending it money. Interest on the bond is usually paid semiannually. You will learn more about stocks and bonds later.
- **The ease of transfer of ownership in a corporation is another advantage of this form of organization.** If you hold shares of stock in a corporation whose stock is actively traded and you decide that you want out, you simply call your broker and put in an order to sell. Another distinct advantage is the limited liability of the stock holder. Generally speaking, a stockholder is liable only for the amount contributed to the business. That is, if a company goes out of business, the most the stockholder stands to lose is the amount invested. On the other hand, both proprietors and general partners usually can be held personally liable for the debts of the business.

Nonbusiness Entities

Most **nonbusiness entities** are organized for a purpose other than to earn a profit. They exist to serve the needs of various segments of society. For example, a hospital provides health care to its patients. A municipal government is operated for the benefit of its citizens. A local school district meets the educational needs of the community's youth.

None of these entities has an identifiable owner. The lack of an identifiable owner and of the profit motive changes to some extent the type of accounting used by nonbusiness entities. This type, called *fund accounting,* is discussed in advanced accounting courses. Regardless of the lack of a profit motive in nonbusiness entities, they still need the information provided by an accounting system. For example, a local government needs detailed cost breakdowns in order to levy taxes. A hospital may want to borrow money and will need financial statements to present to the prospective lender.

Organizations and Social Responsibility

Although nonbusiness entities are organized specifically to serve members of society, U.S. business entities have become more sensitive to their broader social responsibilities.

Corporation
A form of entity organized under the laws of a particular state; ownership evidenced by shares of stock.

Share of stock
A certificate that acts as evidence of ownership in a corporation.

Bond
A certificate that represents a corporation's promise to repay a certain amount of money and interest in the future.

Nonbusiness entity
An organization operated for some purpose other than to earn a profit.

Because they touch the lives of so many members of society, most large corporations recognize the societal aspects of their overall mission and have established programs to meet their social responsibilities. Some companies focus on local charities, while others donate to national or international causes. The companies showcased in the chapter openers of this book have programs in place to meet their corporate giving objectives.

LO2 Distinguish among the forms of organization.

- Some entities are organized to earn a profit, while others are organized to serve various segments of society.
- The three forms of business entities are sole proprietorships, partnerships, and corporations.

POD REVIEW 1.2

© Cengage Learning 2013

QUESTIONS   **Answers to these questions are on the last page of the chapter.**

1. Kellogg's is organized as which of the following business entities?
   a. sole proprietorship
   b. partnership
   c. corporation
   d. none of the above

2. One of the advantages of the corporate form of organization is
   a. the ease of transfer of ownership.
   b. the limited liability of the stockholder.
   c. the ability to raise large amounts of capital in a relatively brief period of time.
   d. All of the above are advantages of the corporate form of organization.

The Nature of Business Activity

LO3 Describe the various types of business activities.

OVERVIEW: Businesses engage in three types of activities: financing, investing, and operating. Financing is necessary to start a business, and funds are obtained from both stockholders and creditors. These funds are invested in the various assets needed to run a business. Once funds are obtained and investments made in productive assets, a business begins operations, which may consist of providing goods or services or both.

Because corporations dominate business activity in the United States, this book will focus on this form of organization. Corporations engage in a multitude of different types of activities. It is possible to categorize all of them into one of three types, however: financing, investing, or operating.

Financing Activities

All businesses must start with financing. Simply put, money is needed to start a business. W. K. Kellogg needed money in 1906 to start his new company. The company found itself in need of additional financing later and thus eventually made the decision to sell stock to the public. Most companies not only sell stock to raise money but also borrow from various sources to finance their operations.

Accounting has unique terminology. In fact, accounting is often referred to as *the language of business*. The discussion of financing activities brings up two important accounting terms: *liabilities* and *capital stock*.

Example 1-2 Distinguishing Between Liabilities and Capital Stock

Liability
An obligation of a business.

A liability is an obligation of a business; it can take many different forms. When a company borrows money at a bank, the liability is called a *note payable*. When a company sells bonds, the obligation is termed *bonds payable*. Amounts owed to the government for taxes are called *taxes payable*. Assume that Kellogg's buys corn to produce Corn Flakes® and the supplier gives Kellogg's 30 days to pay the amount owed. During this 30-day period, Kellogg's has an obligation called *accounts payable*.

(Continued)

Capital stock is the term used by accountants to indicate the dollar amount of stock sold to the public. Capital stock differs from liabilities in one very important respect. Those who buy stock in a corporation are not lending money to the business, as are those who buy bonds in the company or make a loan in some other form to the company. Someone who buys stock in a company is called a **stockholder**, and that person is providing a permanent form of financing to the business. In other words, there is no due date when the stockholder must be repaid. Normally, the only way for a stockholder to get back his or her original investment from buying stock is to sell it to someone else. Someone who buys bonds in a company or in some other way makes a loan to it is called a **creditor**. A creditor does *not* provide a permanent form of financing to the business. That is, the creditor expects repayment of the amount loaned and, in many instances, payment of interest for the use of the money.

Capital stock
Indicates the owners' contributions to a corporation.

Stockholder
One of the owners of a corporation.
Alternate term: Shareholder.

Creditor
Someone to whom a company or person has a debt.
Alternate term: Lender.

Investing Activities

There is a natural progression in a business from financing activities to investing activities. That is, once funds are generated from creditors and stockholders, money is available to invest.

An **asset** is a future economic benefit to a business. For example, cash is an asset to a company. To Kellogg's, its buildings and the equipment that it uses to make cereal are assets. **An asset represents the right to receive some sort of benefit in the future.** The point is that not all assets are tangible in nature, as are buildings and equipment.

Asset
A future economic benefit.

Example 1-3 Identifying Assets

Assume that Kellogg's acquires from an inventor a patent that will allow the company the exclusive right to produce a certain product. The right to the future economic benefits from the patent is an asset. In summary, an asset is a valuable resource to the company that controls it.

At this point, you should notice the inherent tie between assets and liabilities. How does a company satisfy its liabilities, that is, its obligations? Although there are some exceptions, most liabilities are settled by transferring assets. The asset most often used to settle a liability is cash.

Operating Activities

Once funds are obtained from financing activities and investments are made in productive assets, a business is ready to begin operations. Every business is organized with a purpose in mind. The purpose of some businesses is to sell a *product*. Kellogg's was organized to produce and sell cereal. Other companies provide *services*. Service-oriented businesses are becoming an increasingly important sector of the U.S. economy. Some of the largest corporations in this country, such as banks and airlines, sell services rather than products.

Revenue is the inflow of assets resulting from the sale of products and services. When a company makes a cash sale, the asset it receives is cash. When a sale is made on credit, the asset received is an account receivable. Revenue represents the dollar amount of sales of products and services for a specific period of time.

Revenue
An inflow of assets resulting from the sale of goods and services.

We have thus far identified one important operating activity: the sale of products and services. However, costs must be incurred to operate a business.

- Kellogg's must pay its employees salaries and wages.
- Suppliers must be paid for purchases of inventory, and the utility company has to be paid for heat and electricity.
- The government must be paid the taxes owed it.

Those are examples of important operating activities of a business. Accountants use a specific name for the costs incurred in operating a business. **An expense is the outflow of assets resulting from the sale of goods and services.**

Expense
An outflow of assets resulting from the sale of goods and services.

EXHIBIT 1-3 A Model of Business Activities

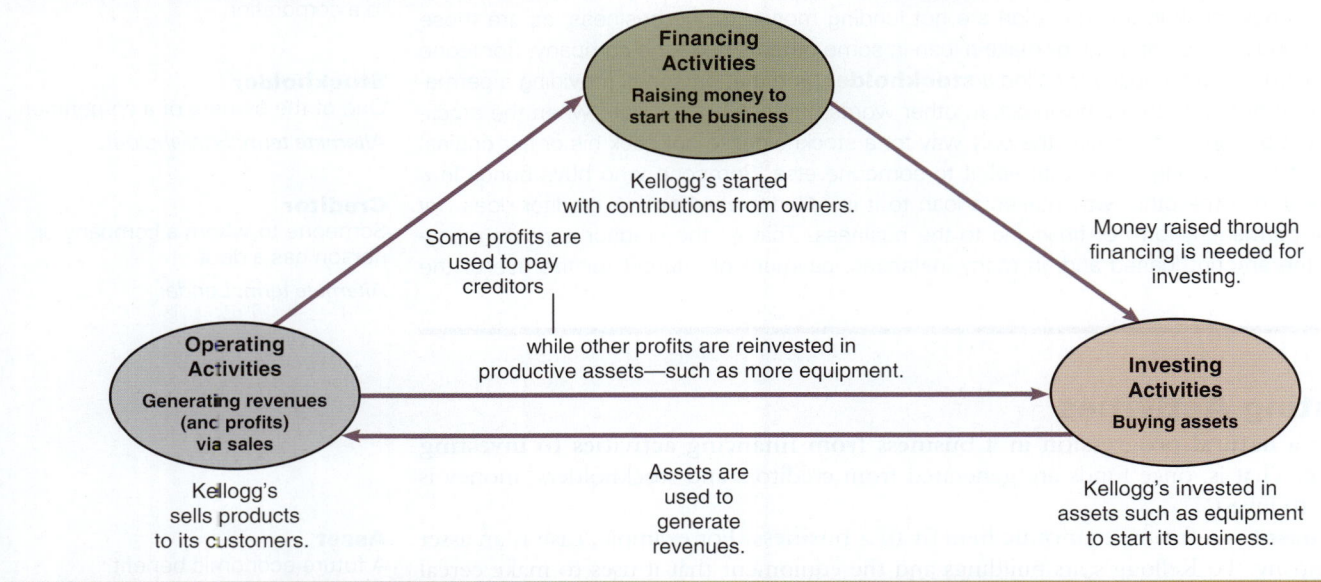

Exhibit 1-3 summarizes the three types of activities conducted by a business. The discussion and the exhibit present a simplification of business activity, but actual businesses are in a constant state of motion with many different financing, investing, and operating activities going on at any one time. Still, the model portrayed in Exhibit 1-3 should be helpful as you begin the study of accounting. To summarize, a company obtains money from various types of financing activities, uses the money raised to invest in productive assets, and then provides goods and services to its customers.

LO3 Describe the various types of business activities.

- All business activities can be categorized as operating, investing, or financing activities.
- Financing activities involve raising money from contributions made by the owners of a business as well as obtaining loans from outsiders.
- Companies invest the amounts raised from financing activities in various types of assets, such as inventories, buildings, and equipment.
- Once funds are obtained and investments are made in productive assets, a business can begin operations. Operating activities involve providing goods and services to customers.

POD REVIEW 1-3

QUESTIONS   **Answers to these questions are on the last page of the chapter.**

1. Capital stock as a form of financing differs from borrowing because
   a. stock has a due date.
   b. stock does not have a due date.
   c. borrowing is a permanent form of financing.
   d. There are no significant differences between the two forms of financing.

2. Which of the following is not an asset?
   a. accounts payable
   b. cash
   c. accounts receivable
   d. building

3. The inflow of assets resulting from the sale of products and services is called a(n)
   a. expense.
   b. asset.
   c. revenue.
   d. liability.

What Is Accounting, and What Information Do Users of Accounting Reports Need?

OVERVIEW: Accounting is the process of identifying, measuring, and communicating economic information to various users, including management of the company, stockholders, creditors, financial analysts, and government agencies.

LO4 Define accounting and identify the primary users of accounting information and their needs.

Accounting is not just a procedural record-keeping activity done by people who are "good at math." In fact, **accounting** is "the process of identifying, measuring, and communicating economic information to permit informed judgments and decisions by users of the information."[1]

Each of the three activities in this definition—*identifying*, *measuring*, and *communicating*—requires the judgment of a trained professional. Note that the definition refers to the users of economic information and the decisions they make. Who *are* the users of accounting information? We turn now to this important question.

Accounting
The process of identifying, measuring, and communicating economic information to various users.

Users of Accounting Information and Their Needs

It is helpful to categorize users of accounting information on the basis of their relationship to the organization. Internal users, primarily the managers of a company, are involved in the daily affairs of the business. All other groups are external users.

Internal Users The management of a company is in a position to obtain financial information in a way that best suits its needs. For example, if management of a Kellogg's production facility center needs to know whether the plant's revenues are enough to cover its operating costs, this information exists in the accounting system and can be reported. If the manager wants to find out if the monthly payroll is more or less than the budgeted amount, a report can be generated to provide the answer. **Management accounting** is the branch of accounting concerned with providing internal users (management) with information to facilitate planning and control. The ability to produce management accounting reports is limited only by the extent of the data available and the cost involved in generating the relevant information.

Management accounting
The branch of accounting concerned with providing management with information to facilitate planning and control.

External Users External users, those not directly involved in the operations of a business, need information that differs from that needed by internal users. In addition, the ability of external users to obtain the information is more limited. Without day-to-day contact with the business's affairs, outsiders must rely on the information presented by the company's management.

Certain external users such as the IRS require that information be presented in a very specific manner, and they have the authority of the law to ensure that they get the required information. Stockholders, bondholders, and other creditors must rely on *financial statements* for their information.[2] **Financial accounting** is the branch of accounting concerned with communication with outsiders through financial statements.

Financial accounting
The branch of accounting concerned with the preparation of financial statements for outsider use.

Stockholders and Potential Stockholders Both existing and potential stockholders need financial information about a business. If you currently own stock in Kellogg's, you need information that will aid in your decision either to continue to hold the stock or to sell it. If you are considering buying stock, you need financial information that will help in choosing among competing alternative investments. What has been the recent performance of the company in the stock market? What were its profits for the most recent year? How do these profits compare with those of the prior year? Did the company pay any dividends? One source for much of this information is the company's financial statements.

---

[1] American Accounting Association, *A Statement of Basic Accounting Theory* (Evanston, Ill.: American Accounting Association, 1966), p. 1.

[2] Technically, stockholders are insiders because they own stock in the business. In most large corporations, however, it is not practical for stockholders to be involved in the daily affairs of the business. Thus, they are better categorized here as external users because they normally rely on general-purpose financial statements, as do creditors.

Bondholders, Bankers, and Other Creditors Before buying a bond in a company (remember, you are lending money to the company), you need assurance that the company will be able to pay you the amount owed at maturity and the periodic interest payments. Financial statements can help you to decide whether to purchase a bond. Similarly, before lending money, a bank needs information that will help it determine the company's ability to repay both the amount of the loan and interest. Therefore, a set of financial statements is a key ingredient in a loan proposal.

Government Agencies Numerous government agencies have information needs specified by law. For example, the IRS is empowered to collect a tax on income from both individuals and corporations. Every year, a company prepares a tax return to report to the IRS the amount of income it earned. Another government agency, the Securities and Exchange Commission (SEC), was created in the aftermath of the Great Depression. This regulatory agency sets the rules under which financial statements must be prepared for corporations that sell their stock to the public on organized stock exchanges. Similar to the IRS, the SEC prescribes the manner in which financial information is presented to it. Companies operating in specialized industries submit financial reports to other regulatory agencies such as the Interstate Commerce Commission (ICC) and the Federal Trade Commission (FTC).

Increasingly, global companies must consider the reporting requirements in foreign countries where they operate. For example, a company might be listed on a stock exchange in the United States as well as in Tokyo or London. Additionally, companies often need to file tax returns in other countries.

Other External Users Many other individuals and groups rely on financial information. A supplier of raw material needs to know the creditworthiness of a company before selling it a product on credit. To promote its industry, a trade association must gather financial information on the various companies in the industry. Other important users are stockbrokers and financial analysts. They use financial reports in advising their clients on investment decisions. All of these users rely to a large extent on accounting information provided by management. Exhibit 1-4 summarizes the various users of financial information and the types of decisions they must make.

Using Financial Accounting Information

As stated earlier, financial accounting involves communication with external users. One of the primary external users of accounting information is a stockholder. The box on pages 13–14 contains a Financial Decision Framework that can be used to help make investment decisions with financial accounting information. Here you'll consider whether to buy a company's stock.

Let's say you have been eagerly awaiting an earnings announcement from Kellogg's. You have bought the company's products for a few years but never gave much thought to the financial side of its business.

EXHIBIT 1-4 Users of Accounting Information

Categories of Users	Examples of Users	Common Decision	Relevant Question
Internal	Management	Should we build another plant?	How much will it cost to build the new plant?
External	Stockholder	Should I buy shares of Kellogg's stock?	How much did the company earn last year?
	Banker	Should I lend money to Kellogg's?	What debts or liabilities does the company have?
	Employee	Should I ask for a raise?	How much are the company's revenues, and how much is it paying out in salaries and wages? Is the compensation it is paying reasonable compared to its revenues?
	Supplier	Should I allow Kellogg's to buy grain from me and pay me later?	What is the current amount of the company's accounts payable?

You log on to Kellogg's web site, and after clicking on the Investor Relations link, you begin to wonder . . . should I or shouldn't I buy stock in the company? Use the Financial Decision Framework below to help you make a decision.

LO4 Define accounting and identify the primary users of accounting information and their needs.

- The primary users of financial statements depend on the economic information conveyed in those statements to make decisions. Primary users may be broadly classified as internal and external users.
- Internal users are usually managers of a company.
- External users include stockholders, investors, creditors, and government agencies.

POD REVIEW 1.4

QUESTIONS   **Answers to these questions are on the last page of the chapter.**

1. Which of the following groups is not an external user of accounting information?

   a. stockholders
   b. bankers
   c. management
   d. All of the above are external users.

2. The branch of accounting that involves communication with outsiders through financial statements is

   a. management accounting.
   b. financial accounting.
   c. income tax accounting.
   d. none of the above.

FINANCIAL DECISION FRAMEWORK

Use the following decision process to help you make an investment decision about Kellogg's or any other public company.

1. Formulate the Question
For about the same amount I pay in a year for the company's products ($100), I could buy two shares of Kellogg's stock at $50 per share.

- Should I invest $100 in Kellogg's?

2. Gather Information from the Financial Statements and Other Sources
The information needed will come from a variety of sources:

- My personal finances at the present time
- Alternative uses for the $100
- The outlook for the industry
- Publicly available information about Kellogg's, including its financial statements

3. Analyze the Financials
The information in the financial statements can be used to perform:

- Ratio analysis (looking at relationships among financial statement items)
- Horizontal analysis (looking at trends over time)
- Vertical analysis (comparing financial statement items in a single period)
- Comparisons with competitors
- Comparisons with industry averages

4. Make the Decision

Taking into account all of the various sources of information, you decide either to:

- Use the $100 for something else
- Invest the $100 in Kellogg's

5. Interpret the Results

If you do decide to invest, you will want to monitor your investment periodically. Whether you made a good decision will be based on the answers to these two questions:

- Have I received any dividends on my shares?
- Has the price of the stock increased above the $50 per share that I paid?

A critical step in this framework is gathering information from the financial statements, the means by which an accountant communicates information about a company to those interested in it. We explore these statements in the next section. ■

Financial Statements: How Accountants Communicate

OVERVIEW: Accountants use financial statements to communicate important information to those who need it to make decisions. The balance sheet summarizes the assets, liabilities, and stockholders' equity at a specific date. The income statement summarizes revenues and expenses for a period of time. The statement of retained earnings reports the income earned and dividends paid over the life of a business. Finally, the statement of cash flows summarizes cash receipts and payments during the period from a company's operating, investing, and financing activities.

The primary focus of this book is financial accounting. This branch of accounting is concerned with informing management and outsiders about a company through financial statements. We turn now to the composition of the four major statements: balance sheet, income statement, statement of retained earnings, and statement of cash flows.

The Accounting Equation

The accounting equation is the foundation for the entire accounting system:

$$\text{Assets} = \text{Liabilities} + \text{Owners' Equity}$$

- The *left side* of the accounting equation refers to the *assets* of the company. Those items that are valuable economic resources and that will provide future benefit to the company should appear on the left side of the equation.
- The *right side* of the equation indicates who provided, or has a claim to, those assets. Some of the assets were provided by creditors, and they have a claim to them. For example, if a company has a delivery truck, the dealer that provided the truck to the company has a claim to the assets until the dealer is paid. The delivery truck would appear on the left side of the equation as an asset to the company; the company's *liability* to the dealer would appear on the right side of the equation. Other assets are provided by the owners of the business. Their claims to these assets are represented by the portion of the right side of the equation called **owners' equity**.

The term *stockholders' equity*, or *shareholders' equity*, is used to refer to the owners' equity of a corporation. **Stockholders' equity is the mathematical difference between a corporation's assets and its obligations, or liabilities.** That is, after the amounts owed to bondholders, banks, suppliers, and other creditors are subtracted from the assets, the amount remaining is the stockholders' equity, the amount of interest or claim that the owners have on the assets of the business.

LO5 Explain the purpose of each of the financial statements and the relationships among them and prepare a set of simple statements.

STUDY TIP

The accounting equation and the financial statements are at the heart of this course. Memorize the accounting equation and make sure you study this introduction to how the financial statements should look, how to read them, and what they say about a company.

© Cengage Learning 2013

Owners' equity
The owners' claims on the assets of an entity.

Stockholders' equity
The owners' equity in a corporation.
Alternate term: shareholders' equity.

Stockholders' equity arises in two distinct ways.

1. It is created when a company issues stock to an investor. As noted earlier, capital stock reflects ownership in a corporation in the form of a certificate. It represents the amounts contributed by the owners to the company.

2. As owners of shares in a corporation, stockholders have a claim on the assets of a business when it is profitable. **Retained earnings represents the owners' claims to the company's assets that result from its earnings that have not been paid out in dividends.** It is the earnings accumulated or retained by the company.

The Balance Sheet

The **balance sheet** (sometimes called the *statement of financial position*) is the financial statement that summarizes the assets, liabilities, and owners' equity of a company. It is a snapshot of the business at a certain date. A balance sheet can be prepared on any day of the year, although it is most commonly prepared on the last day of a month, quarter, or year. At any point in time, the balance sheet must be "in balance." That is, assets must equal liabilities and owners' equity.

For a company such as Kellogg's, real financial statements can be quite complex, especially this early in your study of accounting. Therefore, before we attempt to read Kellogg's statements, we will start with a hypothetical company.

Retained earnings
The part of owners' equity that represents the income earned less dividends paid over the life of an entity.

Balance sheet
The financial statement that summarizes the assets, liabilities, and owners' equity at a specific point in time.
Alternate term: Statement of financial position.

Example 1-4 Preparing a Balance Sheet

Top of the World owns and operates a ski resort in the Rockies. The company's balance sheet on June 30, 2012, the end of its first year of business, is presented below. As you study the balance sheet, note the description for each item to help you understand it better.

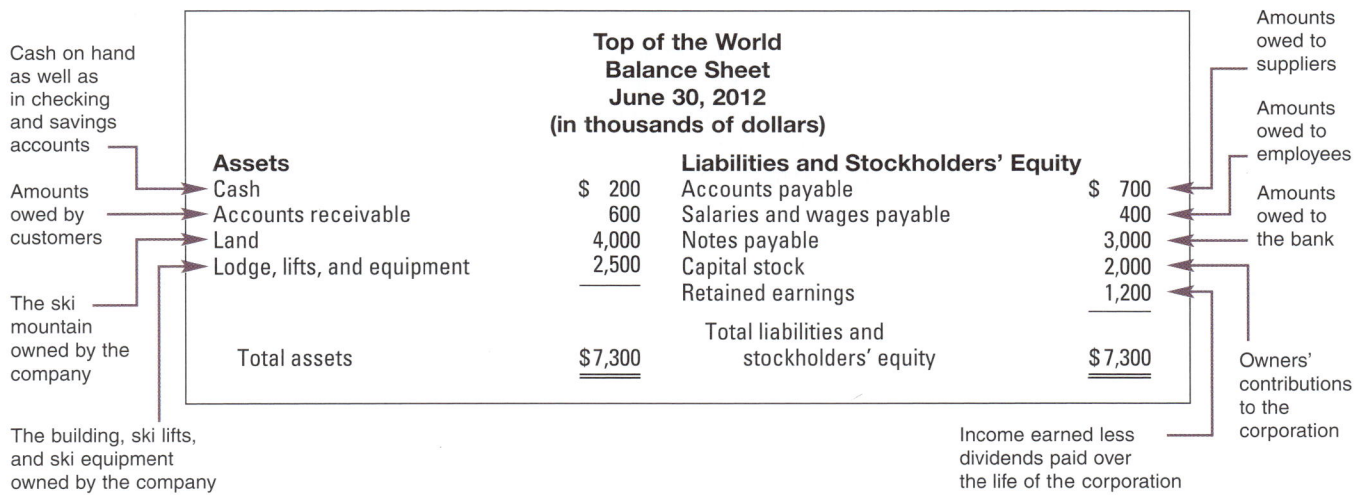

Two items should be noted in the heading of the statement. First, the company chose a date other than December 31, the calendar year-end, to finish its accounting, or fiscal, year. Although December 31 is the most common year-end, some companies choose a different year-end date. Often, this choice is based on when a company's peak selling season is over. For example, **Gap Inc.** ends its accounting year on the Saturday closest to January 31, after the busy holiday season. By June 30, Top of the World's ski season has ended and the company can devote its attention to preparing its financial statements. The second item to note in the heading of the statement is the last line: "in thousands of dollars." This means, for example, that rather than cash being $200, the amount is actually 1,000 × $200, or $200,000.

Exhibit 1-5 summarizes the relationship between the accounting equation and the items that appear on a balance sheet.

The Income Statement

An **income statement**, or statement of income as it is sometimes called, summarizes the revenues and expenses of a company for a period of time.

Income statement
A statement that summarizes revenues and expenses.
Alternate term: Statement of income.

© Cengage Learning 2013

EXHIBIT 1-5 The Relationship Between the Accounting Equation and the Balance Sheet

Assets	=	Liabilities	+	Owners' Equity

Economic resources	**Creditors' claims to the assets**	**Owners' claims to the assets**
Examples:	Examples:	Examples:
• Cash	• Accounts payable	• Capital stock
• Accounts receivable	• Notes payable	• Retained earnings
• Land		

Terminology Note: Exhibit 1-5 refers to Owners' Equity, while Example 1-4 refers to Stockholders' Equity. Remember, both are correct! *Owners' equity* is the general term by which we refer to ownership. "Stockholders' equity" refers only to ownership of a corporation by shareholders. Because we emphasize corporations in this book, we will use the term *Stockholders' equity*.

© Cengage Learning 2013

Example 1-5 Preparing an Income Statement

An income statement for Top of the World for its first year in business is shown below. **Unlike the balance sheet, an income statement is a *flow* statement.** That is, it summarizes the flow of revenues and expenses for the year. The top portion of the income statement makes it clear that the ski company has two distinct types of revenues: those from selling lift tickets and those from renting ski equipment. For example, if you paid the company $50 for a one-day lift ticket and another $30 to rent equipment for the day, each of those amounts would be included in Top of the World's revenues for the year. The expenses reported on the income statement represent all of the various costs necessary to run a ski resort. For example, a significant cost for such an operation is its payroll, as represented by salaries and wages on the income statement. Note that the amount reported for salaries and wages expense on the income statement is not the same amount that appeared as salaries and wages payable on the balance sheet. The expense of $2,000 on the income statement represents the total cost for the year, while the payable of $400 on the balance sheet is the amount owed to employees on June 30, 2012. We will have much more to say in later chapters about differences between balance sheet and income statement items. Finally, note that the excess of revenues over expenses, or **net income**, appears as the bottom line on the income statement. A company's net income is sometimes referred to as its profits or earnings.

Net income
The excess of revenues over expenses.

Alternate term: Profits, earnings.

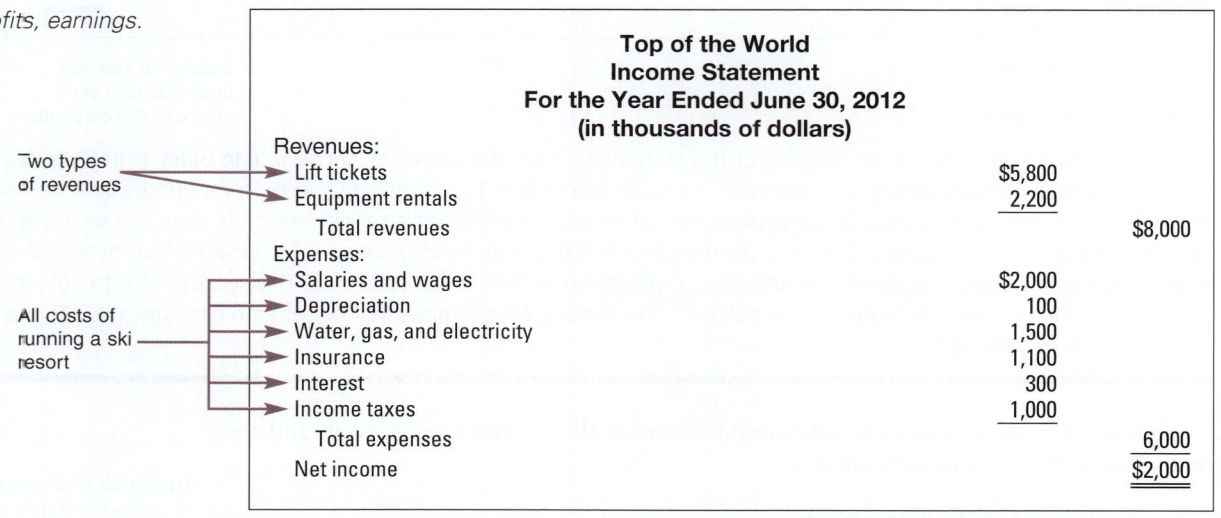

Two types of revenues

All costs of running a ski resort

Top of the World Income Statement For the Year Ended June 30, 2012 (in thousands of dollars)		
Revenues:		
Lift tickets	$5,800	
Equipment rentals	2,200	
Total revenues		$8,000
Expenses:		
Salaries and wages	$2,000	
Depreciation	100	
Water, gas, and electricity	1,500	
Insurance	1,100	
Interest	300	
Income taxes	1,000	
Total expenses		6,000
Net income		$2,000

© Cengage Learning 2013

The Statement of Retained Earnings

As discussed earlier, Retained Earnings represents the accumulated earnings of a corporation less the amount paid in dividends to stockholders. **Dividends** are distributions of the net income, or profits, of a business to its stockholders. Not all businesses pay cash dividends. Among those companies that do pay dividends, the frequency with which they pay differs. For example, most companies that pay dividends do so four times a year.

A **statement of retained earnings** explains the change in retained earnings during the period. The basic format for the statement is as follows:

Beginning balance	$xxx,xxx
Add: Net income for the period	xxx,xxx
Deduct: Dividends for the period	xxx,xxx
Ending balance	$xxx,xxx

Dividends
A distribution of the net income of a business to its owners.

Statement of retained earnings
The statement that summarizes the income earned and dividends paid over the life of a business.

Example 1-6 Preparing a Statement of Retained Earnings

A statement of retained earnings for Top of the World is shown below. Revenues minus expenses, or net income, is an increase in retained earnings, and dividends are a decrease in the balance. Why are dividends shown on a statement of retained earnings instead of on an income statement? Dividends are not an expense and thus are not a component of net income, as are expenses. Instead, they are a *distribution* of the income of the business to its stockholders.

Recall that stockholders' equity consists of two parts: capital stock and retained earnings. In lieu of a separate statement of retained earnings, many corporations prepare a comprehensive statement to explain the changes both in the various capital stock accounts and in retained earnings during the period. Kellogg's, for example, presents the more comprehensive statement of shareholders' equity.

Top of the World
Statement of Retained Earnings
For the Year Ended June 30, 2012
(in thousands of dollars)

Retained earnings, beginning of the year	$ 0
Add: Net income for the year	2,000
Deduct: Dividends for the year	(800)
Retained earnings, end of the year	$1,200

© Cengage Learning 2013

The Statement of Cash Flows

The **statement of cash flows** summarizes the cash flow effects of a company's operating, investing, and financing activities for the period. In essence, it shows the reader where a company got cash during the year and how it used that cash. (We will have more to say about this in Chapter 2.)

Statement of cash flows
The financial statement that summarizes a company's cash receipts and cash payments during the period from operating, investing, and financing activities.

Example 1-7 Preparing a Statement of Cash Flows

A statement of cash flows for Top of the World is shown on the next page. Note the three categories of cash flow: **operating, investing,** and **financing.** The one source of cash to the company from its operations was the cash it collected from its customers. After deducting cash payments for operating activities, the ski company generated $2,600 from its operations. During the period, the company spent $6,600 on various assets. The last category shows that the issuance of a note generated $3,000 of cash and the issuance of stock produced another $2,000. Finally, the company paid dividends of $800. The net increase in cash from these three categories is $200, and since the company was new this year, this number is also its ending cash balance.

(Continued)

Top of the World
Statement of Cash Flows
For the Year Ended June 30, 2012
(in thousands of dollars)

Cash flows from operating activities:		
Cash collected from customers		$ 7,400
Cash payments for:		
Salaries and wages	$ 1,600	
Water, gas, and electricity	1,500	
Insurance	400	
Interest	300	
Income taxes	1,000	
Total cash payments		4,800
Net cash provided by operating activities		$ 2,600
Cash flows from investing activities:		
Purchase of land	$(4,000)	
Purchase of lodge, lifts, and equipment	(2,600)	
Net cash used by investing activities		(6,600)
Cash flows from financing activities:		
Proceeds from issuance of long-term note	$ 3,000	
Proceeds from issuance of capital stock	2,000	
Dividends declared and paid	(800)	
Net cash provided by financing activities		4,200
Net increase in cash		$ 200
Cash at beginning of year		0
Cash at end of year		$ 200

Relationships Among the Financial Statements

Note the natural progression in the items from one statement to another. Normally, a company starts the period with balances in each of the items on its balance sheet. Because Top of the World is a new company, Exhibit 1-6 shows zero balances on July 1, 2011, the beginning of its first year in business. Next, the company operated during the year; the result was net income of $2,000 as shown on the income statement at the top of the exhibit. The net income naturally flows ❶ onto the statement of retained earnings. Again, because the ski company is new, its beginning retained earnings balance is zero. After the distribution of $800 to the owners in cash dividends ❷, ending retained earnings amounts to $1,200. The ending retained earnings number flows ❸ onto the ending balance sheet along with the other June 30, 2012, balance sheet items. Finally, the net increase in cash at the bottom of the statement of cash flows equals ❹ the amount shown on the June 30, 2012, balance sheet.

Looking at Financial Statements for a Real Company: Kellogg's

You would expect the financial statements of actual companies to be more complex than those for a hypothetical company such as Top of the World. Still, even this early in your study of accounting, there are certain fundamental points about all financial statements, real world or otherwise, that you can appreciate.

Kellogg's Balance Sheet

Balance sheets for Kellogg's at the end of two recent years are shown in Exhibit 1-7. For comparative purposes, the company reports its financial position at the end of the two most recent fiscal years. Because the company ends it fiscal year on the Saturday closest to December 31, the end of the 2010 fiscal year is January 1, 2011, and the end of the 2009 fiscal year is January 2, 2010. Also note the statement across from the headings for

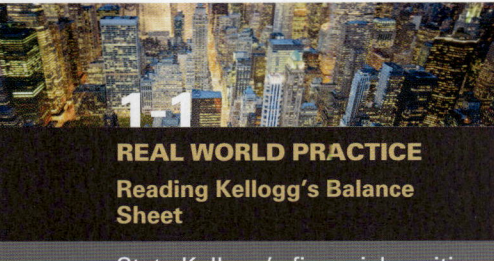

1-1

REAL WORLD PRACTICE

Reading Kellogg's Balance Sheet

State Kellogg's financial position at the end of the 2010 fiscal year in terms of the accounting equation. What amount do Kellogg's customers owe at the end of this year? What amount does Kellogg's owe its suppliers at the end of this year?

EXHIBIT 1-6 Relationships Among the Financial Statements

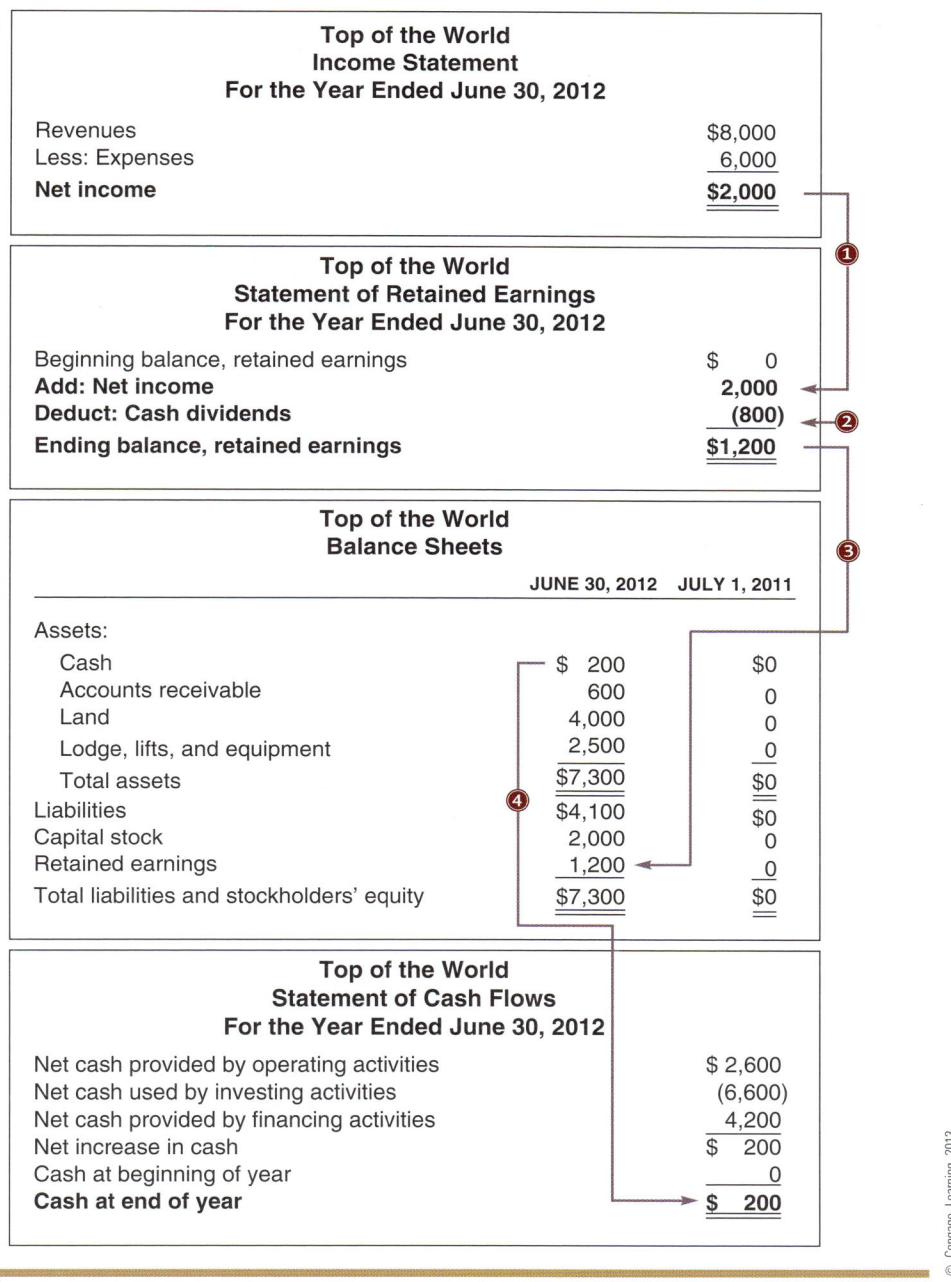

the two years that the amounts are in millions of dollars. For example, this means that Kellogg's had $11,847 × 1,000,000, or $11,847,000,000, of total assets at the end of 2010.

Total Assets: $11,847 × 1,000,000 = $11,847,000,000 = Nearly $12 billion!

A quick comparison of Kellogg's assets with those of Top of the World reveals one significant difference. Because the ski company is a service company, it does not have an Inventory account on its balance sheet. Conversely, "Inventories" of $1,056 million at the end of 2010 is a significant asset for Kellogg's. This account includes the various raw materials and products in various stages of production that have not yet been sold to customers.

EXHIBIT 1-7 Kellogg's Balance Sheet

Consolidated Balance Sheet

(millions, except share data)	2010	2009
Current assets A		
Cash and cash equivalents	$ 444	$ 334
Accounts receivable, net	1,190	1,093
Inventories	1,056	910
Other current assets	225	221
Total current assets	$ 2,915	$ 2,558
Property, net	3,128	3,010
Goodwill	3,628	3,643
Other intangibles, net	1,456	1,458
Other assets	720	531
Total assets	$11,847	$11,200
=		
Current liabilities L		
Current maturities of long-term debt	$ 952	$ 1
Notes payable	44	44
Accounts payable	1,149	1,077
Other current liabilities	1,039	1,166
Total current liabilities	$ 3,184	$ 2,288
+		
Long-term debt	4,908	4,835
Deferred income taxes	697	425
Pension liability	265	430
Other liabilities	639	947
Commitments and contingencies		
Equity SE		
Common stock, $.25 par value, 1,000,000,000 shares authorized		
Issued: 419,272,027 shares in 2010 and 419,058,168 shares in 2009	105	105
Capital in excess of par value	495	472
Retained earnings	6,122	5,481
Treasury stock at cost:		
53,667,635 shares in 2010 and 37,678,215 shares in 2009	(2,650)	(1,820)
Accumulated other comprehensive income (loss)	(1,914)	(1,966)
Total Kellogg Company equity	2,158	2,272
Noncontrolling interests	(4)	3
Total equity	2,154	2,275
Total liabilities and equity	$ 11,847	$ 11,200

Materials and goods in various stages of production account for over $1 billion of the assets.

Total assets of almost $12 billion.

Creditors' claims are about $9.7 billion.

Creditors' claims and equity is the same as total assets.

Refer to Notes to Consolidated Financial Statements.

© Cengage Learning 2013

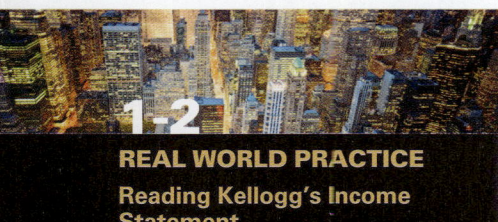

Various types of liabilities are reported on Kellogg's balance sheets, and we will return to look more closely at many of these in later chapters. For now, it is worth noting that total liabilities amount to $9,693 million at the end of 2010. This amount, when added to total equity of $2,154, equals $11,847, the same amount as total assets. (Note that Kellogg's uses the term "equity" rather than "stockholders' equity.")

Kellogg's Income Statement

Comparative income statements for three recent years are shown in Exhibit 1-8. As was the case for the balance sheet, you are not expected at this point to understand fully all of the complexities involved on the income statement of a real company. However, note the two largest items on the income statement: Net sales and Cost of goods sold. For now, it is sufficient for you to understand that the former is the revenue Kellogg's earned from selling its various products and the latter is the cost of these products. Net sales for

EXHIBIT 1-8 Kellogg's Income Statement

Consolidated Statement of Income

(millions, except per share data)	2010	2009	2008
Net sales	$12,397	$12,575	$12,822
Cost of goods sold	7,108	7,184	7,455
Selling, general and administrative expense	3,299	3,390	3,414
Operating profit	$ 1,990	$ 2,001	$ 1,953
Interest expense	248	295	308
Other income (expense), net	—	(22)	(14)
Income before income taxes	1,742	1,684	1,631
Income taxes	502	476	485
Net income	$ 1,240	$ 1,208	$ 1,146
Net loss attributable to noncontrolling interests	(7)	(4)	(2)
Net income attributable to Kellogg Company	$ 1,247	$ 1,212	$ 1,148
Per share amounts:			
Basic	$ 3.32	$ 3.17	$ 3.01
Diluted	$ 3.30	$ 3.16	$ 2.99
Dividends per share	$ 1.560	$ 1.430	$ 1.300

Net sales reached about $12.4 billion.

Costs of products sold were about $7.1 billion.

Net income for the year was over $1.2 billion.

Refer to Notes to Consolidated Financial Statements.

© Cengage Learning 2013

the most recent year amounted to about $12.4 billion, and Kellogg's cost to produce the goods sold was about $7.1 billion. Net income for the year amounted to over $1.2 billion after selling, general, and administrative expense; interest expense; and income taxes are taken into account.

LO5 Explain the purpose of each of the financial statements and the relationships among them and prepare a set of simple statements.

- Four major financial statements are covered in this chapter: balance sheet, income statement, statement of retained earnings, and statement of cash flows.
- The balance sheet is a snapshot of a company's financial position at the end of the period. It reflects the assets, liabilities, and stockholders' equity accounts.
- The income statement summarizes the financial activity for a period of time. Items of revenues, expenses, gains, and losses are reflected on the income statement.
- Ultimately, all net income (loss) and dividends are reflected in retained earnings on the balance sheet. The statement of retained earnings links the income statement to the balance sheet by showing how net income (loss) and dividends affect the Retained Earnings account.
- The statement of cash flows summarizes the cash flow effects of a company's operating, investing, and financing activities.

POD REVIEW 1.5

QUESTIONS Answers to these questions are on the last page of the chapter.

1. Which of the following financial statements summarizes the financial position of a company at a point in time?
   a. income statement
   b. balance sheet
   c. statement of retained earnings
   d. statement of cash flows

2. On a statement of retained earnings, how are net income and dividends treated?
   a. Net income is added, and dividends are deducted.
   b. Both net income and dividends are added.
   c. Both net income and dividends are deducted.
   d. Net income is deducted, and dividends are added.

3. Revenues are reported on which of the following financial statements?
   a. balance sheet only
   b. income statement only
   c. both the balance sheet and the income statement
   d. neither the balance sheet nor the income statement

© Cengage Learning 2013

The Conceptual Framework: Foundation for Financial Statements

OVERVIEW: Financial statements are prepared based on an underlying set of assumptions. Among the most important of these are the economic entity concept, the cost principle, the going concern assumption, and the time period assumption.

Many people perceive the work of an accountant as being routine. In reality, accounting is anything but routine and requires a great deal of judgment on the part of the accountant. The record-keeping aspect of accounting—what we normally think of as bookkeeping—is the routine part of the accountant's work and is only a small part of it. Most of the job deals with communicating relevant information to financial statement users.

Conceptual Framework for Accounting

The accounting profession has developed a *conceptual framework for accounting* that aids accountants in their role as interpreters and communicators of relevant information. The purpose of the framework is to act as a foundation for the specific principles and standards needed by the profession. An important part of the conceptual framework is a set of assumptions accountants make in preparing financial statements. We will briefly consider these assumptions, returning to a more detailed discussion of them in later chapters.

Economic Entity Concept

The *economic entity concept* was discussed earlier in this chapter when we explored the different types of business entities. **This assumption requires that an identifiable,**

Name: Susan Koch Renner

Education: B.S., University of Connecticut

College Major: Accounting

Occupation: CFO and Controller

Age: 50

Position: CFO and Treasurer

Company Name: American Cruise Lines, Inc.

See Susan Renner's interview clip in CNOW.

SPOTLIGHT
This Woman's Accounting Background Helps Her in Personal and Professional Ways

Susan Renner is a successful accountant living in Guilford, CT. Over the years Susan has worked in public accounting with large national firms and has also owned her own successful practice. Currently she is the CFO and treasurer for American Cruise Lines, a privately held company specializing in small ship cruises along the inland waterways and rivers of the United States. Studying accounting has provided Susan with a rewarding and flexible career that has enhanced all aspects of her life.

As a teenager, Susan was interested in law. A family friend who was an attorney suggested she start in the accounting field in order to learn about a variety of different businesses from the inside. She became hooked on what she calls the "orderliness" of accounting—the idea that a business situation can be translated into a financial statement that all users could read to gain an understanding of the business.

In her current position at American Cruise Lines, Susan must prepare what she calls "solid, complete GAAP financial statements" on a quarterly basis. This is required by lenders and is also the appropriate frequency for monitoring the business. Even though technology has allowed American Cruise Lines to gather and analyze both financial data and nonfinancial data in forms other than traditional financial statements, she still needs to prepare the traditional GAAP financial statements to provide outsiders with information in a format that can be easily understood.

Accounting also promotes a very organized approach to most aspects of her life. Susan is on the finance committee of the local board of education, and she's held the treasurer role for school PTA. She says her accounting background even helps her household run more smoothly!

❝ **Financial accounting is a common language that businesspeople speak, and you need to be comfortable with the language in order to be able to communicate.** ❞

specific entity be the subject of a set of financial statements. For example, even though some of Kellogg's employees are stockholders and therefore own part of Kellogg's, their personal affairs must be kept separate from the business affairs. When we look at a balance sheet for the company, we need assurance that it shows the financial position of that entity only and does not intermingle the personal assets and liabilities of the employees or any of the other stockholders.

Asset Valuation: Cost or Fair Value?

According to the **cost principle**, all assets are initially recorded at the cost to acquire them. For example, Kellogg's would record in its Inventories account the amount paid to acquire grain used to make cereal. Similarly, if Kellogg's buys a parcel of land, the cost of this asset would be included in its Property account on the balance sheet.

    Once assets have been recorded at their cost, an important accounting question still remains: how should these assets be *valued on* subsequent balance sheets? One approach is to continue to report assets at their original cost. Accountants use the term *historical cost* to refer to the original cost of an asset. Under current accounting standards, certain assets are valued at historical cost on all balance sheets until the company disposes of them. For example, the amount Kellogg's paid to acquire land is verifiable by an independent observer and is considered more objective than some measure of what the asset *might be* worth today.

    But what if the value of an asset could be objectively determined? Would it be more useful to the reader of a balance sheet to know what the asset is worth today rather than what the company paid for it sometime in the past? As you will learn in later chapters, certain assets are valued on subsequent balance sheets at market value rather than historical cost. For example, assume that Kellogg's buys stock in another company. Kellogg's would initially record as an asset the amount it paid to buy the stock, but on subsequent balance sheets, it would value its investment at the current market price. Specifically, it would use the amount for which it could *sell* the shares of stock on the date of the balance sheet. An accounting rule requires a company to determine the amount an asset could be *sold for,* rather than the amount it could be bought for, when market prices are used to value assets on the balance sheet.[3]

Going Concern

Accountants assume that the entity being accounted for is a **going concern**. That is, they assume that Kellogg's is **not in the process of liquidation and that it will continue indefinitely into the future.** Another important reason for using historical cost rather than market value to report assets is the going concern assumption. When we assume that a business is *not* a going concern, we assume that it is in the process of liquidation. If this is the case, market value might be more relevant than cost as a basis for recognizing the assets. But if we are able to assume that a business will continue indefinitely, cost can be more easily justified as a basis for valuation. The **monetary unit** used in preparing Kellogg's statements is the dollar. The dollar is used as the monetary unit because it is the recognized medium of exchange in the United States. It provides a convenient yardstick to measure the business's position and earnings. However, the dollar, like the currencies of all other countries, is subject to instability. A dollar will not buy as much today as it did ten years ago.

    Inflation is evidenced by a general rise in the level of prices in an economy. Its effect on the measuring unit used in preparing financial statements is an important concern to the accounting profession. Although accountants have experimented with financial statements adjusted for the changing value of the measuring unit, the financial statements of corporations are prepared under the assumption that the monetary unit is relatively stable. At various times in the past, this has been a reasonable assumption and at other times not so reasonable.

Cost principle
Assets are recorded at the cost to acquire them.

Alternate term: Original cost or historical cost.

Going concern
The assumption that an entity is not in the process of liquidation and that it will continue indefinitely.

Monetary unit
The yardstick used to measure amounts in financial statements; the dollar in the United States.

---

[3] The FASB has created a new system of classification using topic numbers to identify all accounting pronouncements. In this text, the codification topic and number are noted first followed by the reference to each original pronouncement. For example, *Fair Value Measurements and Disclosures*, ASC Topic 820 (formerly *Fair Value Measurements*, Statement of Financial Accounting Standards No. 157).

Time period
An artificial segment on the calendar used as the basis for preparing financial statements.

Time Period Assumption

Under the **time period** assumption, **accountants assume that it is possible to prepare an income statement that accurately reflects net income or earnings for a specific time period.** In the case of Kellogg's, this time period is one year. It is somewhat artificial to measure the earnings of a business for a period of time indicated on a calendar, whether it be a month, a quarter, or a year. Of course, the most accurate point in time to measure the earnings of a business is at the end of its life. Accountants prepare periodic statements, however, because the users of the statements demand information about the entity on a regular basis.

Generally Accepted Accounting Principles

Generally accepted accounting principles (GAAP)
The various methods, rules, practices, and other procedures that have evolved over time in response to the need to regulate the preparation of financial statements.

Financial statements prepared by accountants must conform to **generally accepted accounting principles (GAAP)**. This term refers to the various methods, rules, practices, and other procedures that have evolved over time in response to the need for some form of regulation over the preparation of financial statements. As changes have taken place in the business environment over time, GAAP have developed in response to these changes. As we will see later in this chapter, there is currently no one authoritative global source for GAAP. Attempts are being made to eliminate the differences in the standards followed by companies located in different parts of the world.

Accounting as a Social Science

Accounting is a service activity. As we have seen, its purpose is to provide financial information to decision makers. Thus, accounting is a *social* science. Accounting principles are much different from the rules that govern the *physical* sciences. The principles that govern financial reporting are not governed by nature; instead, they develop in response to changing business conditions. For example, consider the lease of an office building. Leasing has developed in response to the need to have access to valuable assets such as office space without spending the large sum necessary to buy the asset. As leasing has increased in popularity, the accounting profession has been left to develop guidelines in accounting for leases. Those guidelines are now part of GAAP.

LO6 Identify and explain the primary assumptions made in preparing financial statements.

- The usefulness of accounting information is enhanced through the various assumptions set forth in the conceptual framework developed by the accounting profession. This conceptual framework is the foundation for the methods, rules, and practices that make up generally accepted accounting principles (GAAP).
- Important assumptions in the conceptual framework are as follows:
  - Economic entity concept
  - Cost principle
  - Going concern
  - Monetary unit
  - Time period

POD REVIEW 1.6

QUESTIONS   **Answers to these questions are on the last page of the chapter.**

1. You decide to form a partnership with a friend. Which accounting concept requires that you separate your personal affairs from those of the partnership?

   a. cost principle
   b. going concern
   c. time period
   d. economic entity

2. How do accountants justify reporting assets on a balance sheet at their historical cost?

   a. Cost is more objective than market value.
   b. Cost is more subjective than market value.
   c. Cost is an indication of what assets are worth.
   d. Cost is never used to report assets on a balance sheet.

Setting Accounting Standards

OVERVIEW: Various groups are involved in determining the rules companies must follow in preparing their financial statements. In the United States, the Securities and Exchange Commission (SEC) has ultimate authority for companies whose securities are sold to the general public. However, the SEC has relegated much of the standard setting to the private sector in the form of the Financial Accounting Standards Board (FASB).

LO7 Identify the various groups involved in setting accounting standards and the role of auditors in determining whether the standards are followed.

Management of a company is responsible for preparation of the financial statements. So how can a stockholder be assured that the statements are an accurate picture of the company's financial health? This section looks at who determines the rules that must be followed in preparing financial statements and what the role of auditors is in making sure the rules are followed.

Who Determines the Rules of the Game?

No one group is totally responsible for setting the standards or principles to be followed in preparing financial statements. The process is a joint effort among the following groups.

- The federal government, through the **Securities and Exchange Commission (SEC)**, has the ultimate authority to determine the rules for preparing financial statements by companies whose securities are sold to the general public. However, for the most part, the SEC has allowed the accounting profession to establish its own rules.

- The **Financial Accounting Standards Board (FASB)** sets these accounting standards in the United States. A small, independent group with a large staff, the board has issued standards on a variety of topics as well as statements of financial accounting concepts since its creation in the early 1970s. The standards deal with a variety of financial reporting issues, such as the proper accounting for lease arrangements and pension plans, and the concepts are used to guide the board in setting accounting standards.

- The **American Institute of Certified Public Accountants (AICPA)** is the professional organization of **Certified Public Accountants (CPAs)**. The CPA is the designation for an individual who has passed a uniform exam administered by the AICPA and met other requirements as determined by individual states. AICPA advises the FASB and in the past was involved in setting the auditing standards to be followed by public accounting firms. However, the **Public Company Accounting Oversight Board (PCAOB)** was created by an act of Congress in 2002, and this five-member body now has the authority to set the standards for conducting audits.

- Finally, if you are considering buying stock in **Porsche**, the German-based car manufacturer, you'll want to be sure that the rules Porsche follows in preparing its statements are similar to those the FASB requires for U.S. companies. Unfortunately, accounting standards can differ considerably from one country to another. The **International Accounting Standards Board (IASB)** is the group responsible for developing worldwide accounting standards. Organizations from many different countries, including the FASB in this country, participate in the IASB's efforts to develop international reporting standards. In fact, the FASB currently has a project on its agenda to work with the IASB toward convergence of accounting standards. Appendix A at the end of the book describes in more detail the joint efforts of the two groups as well as some of the major differences in U.S. and international standards.

Earlier in this chapter, we saw that the cost principle requires that assets such as property and equipment be reported on the balance sheet at their historical cost, that is, at the amount paid to acquire them. However, under international accounting standards, it is permissible to report certain types of assets on the balance sheet at their market value. With significant differences such as this between U.S. and international standards, it may be some time before all differences are eliminated.

Securities and Exchange Commission (SEC)
The federal agency with ultimate authority to determine the rules for preparing statements for companies whose stock is sold to the public.

Financial Accounting Standards Board (FASB)
The group in the private sector with authority to set accounting standards.

American Institute of Certified Public Accountants (AICPA)
The professional organization of certified public accountants.

Certified Public Accountant (CPA)
The designation for an individual who has passed a uniform exam administered by the AICPA and has met other requirements as determined by individual states.

Public Company Accounting Oversight Board (PCAOB)
A five-member body created by an act of Congress in 2002 to set auditing standards.

International Accounting Standards Board (IASB)
The organization formed to develop worldwide accounting standards.

In the meantime, U.S. standard setters continue to work closely with those in the international community. At one time, foreign companies that filed their financial statements with the SEC were required to adjust those statements to conform to U.S. accounting standards. As long as foreign companies follow IASB standards, they are no longer required to make these adjustments.

The Audit of Financial Statements

Auditing
The process of examining the financial statements and the underlying records of a company to render an opinion as to whether the statements are fairly presented.

Financial statements are prepared by a company's accountants and are the responsibility of the company's management. Because most stockholders are not actively involved in the daily affairs of the business, they must rely on someone else to ensure that management is fairly presenting the financial statements. The primary objective of an audit is to assure stockholders and other users that the statements are fairly presented. In this respect, **auditing** is the process of examining the financial statements and underlying records of a company to render an opinion as to whether they are fairly presented.

The external auditor performs various tests and procedures to be able to render an opinion. The next chapter will examine the auditors' report, which is essentially the auditors' opinion concerning the fairness of the presentation of the financial statements. Note that the auditors' report is an *opinion*, not a statement of fact. The firms that provide external audits for their clients are called public accounting firms. These firms range in size from those with a single owner to others with thousands of partners.

LO7 Identify the various groups involved in setting accounting standards and the role of auditors in determining whether the standards are followed.

- Financial statements are the responsibility of management. Various groups are involved in setting the standards that are used in preparing the statements. Although the SEC has the ultimate authority to determine the rules, the FASB currently sets the standards in the United States.

- The role of the external auditor is to perform various tests and procedures to render an opinion as to whether the financial statements of a company are fairly presented.

POD REVIEW 1.7

QUESTIONS   **Answers to these questions are on the last page of the chapter.**

1. Which of the following groups currently sets U.S. accounting standards?

   a. American Institute of Certified Public Accountants
   b. Financial Accounting Standards Board
   c. Public Company Accounting Oversight Board
   d. International Accounting Standards Board

2. Who ultimately has responsibility for a company's financial statements?

   a. stockholders
   b. management
   c. external auditors
   d. Securities and Exchange Commission

Introduction to Ethics in Accounting

LO8 Explain the critical role that ethics plays in providing useful financial information.

OVERVIEW: Ethics plays a critical role in providing useful financial information. Investors and other users must have confidence in a company, its accountants, and its outside auditors that the information presented in financial statements is relevant, complete, neutral, and free from error.

Why Should Accountants Be Concerned with Ethics?

In the modern business world, rapidly changing markets, technological improvements, and business innovation all affect financial decisions. Decision makers consider information received from many sources, such as other investors in the marketplace, analysts' forecasts, and companies whose corporate officers and executives may be encouraging "aggressive" accounting and reporting practices.

Business Ethics Takes a Hit In recent years, the news has been filled with reports of questionable accounting practices by some companies.

- **As a decision maker outside a company, you should be aware of the potential for ethical conflicts that arise within organizations. Ask questions, do research, and don't just accept everything as fact.**
- **If you are a decision maker inside a company, you should stay alert for potential pressures on you or others to make choices that are not in the best interest of the company, its owners, and its employees as a whole.**

Companies may use aggressive accounting practices to misrepresent their earnings; executives may misuse their companies' funds. You may encounter a corporate board of directors that undermines the goals of its own company or a public accounting firm that fails its auditing duty to watch for and disclose wrongdoing.

As a decision maker, you may analyze business information to project capital expansion, to open markets for new products, or to anticipate tax liabilities. You may be responsible for making financial reporting decisions that will affect others inside or outside the organization. Knowledge of the professional standards of accounting procedures will be critical for your decision-making process. It will also help you recognize when information is not consistent with the standards and needs to be questioned.

Applying Different Rules for Different Circumstances: Ethical Dilemmas in Accounting

You may encounter circumstances when it appears as if GAAP may not have been used to resolve particular accounting issues because there are several conflicting rules, because no specific GAAP rules seem applicable, or because of fraud. In such situations, an ethical dilemma is likely to exist. Resolving the dilemma may involve one or more decision makers. In most instances, an accountant plays a significant role in the process.

As accountants analyze and attempt to solve the ethical dilemmas posed by certain financial transactions and complex business reporting decisions, they can turn to their profession's conceptual framework. (You will learn more about this framework in Chapter 2.) According to the profession, the purpose of financial reporting is to provide information about a company that investors, lenders, and other creditors can use when deciding whether to provide resources to the entity.[4]

Is the Information Relevant and a Faithful Representation?

When the accountant asks if the quality of the information that is disclosed is good or if it needs to be improved, the answer (which shapes all accounting decisions that follow) is this: **If the information is both relevant and a faithful representation, its quality is good.**[5]

Relevant information is information that is useful to the decision-making process. Relevant information may provide clear information about past financial events that is helpful for predicting the future. To be relevant, the information must also be timely; that is, it must be available at the time the decision is being made.

Accounting information should also be a faithful representation. This means that the information is complete, neutral, and free from error. *Neutrality* means the presentation of information is free from bias toward a particular result. Neutral information can be used by anyone, and it does not try to influence the decision in one direction.

Normally, the uncertainties of business transactions and reporting decisions must be resolved in accordance with GAAP, following the FASB statements. However, the appropriate application of accounting principles may not be easy to determine. You must be alert to pressures on the decision-making process that may be due to the self-interests of one or more of the decision makers. Bias, deception, and even fraud may distort the

---

[4] *Statement of Financial Accounting Concepts [SFAC] No. 8, Conceptual Framework for Financial Reporting,* Chapter 1, "The Objective of General Purpose Financial Reporting." (Norwalk, Conn.: Financial Accounting Standards Board, October 2010).

[5] *Statement of Financial Accounting Concepts [SFAC] No. 8, Conceptual Framework for Financial Reporting,* Chapter 3, "Qualitative Characteristics of Useful Financial Information" (Norwalk, Conn.: Financial Accounting Standards Board, October 2010).

disclosed information. Whatever the circumstances, the dilemmas should be resolved by questioning and analyzing the situation.

Moral and Social Context of Ethical Behavior All decision makers should consider the moral and social implications of their decisions. How will the decisions affect others, such as shareholders, creditors, employees, suppliers, customers, and the local community? The process of determining the most ethical choice involves identifying the most significant facts of the situation. For financial reporting, this includes identifying who may be affected and how, the relevant GAAP principles, and a realistic appraisal of the possible consequences of the decision. To assist your decision making for the cases and assignments, we offer an ethical decision model, shown in Exhibit 1-9 and explained here.

Identification

1. Recognize the ethical dilemma. A dilemma occurs when this awareness is combined with the inability to clearly apply accounting principles to represent the situation accurately.

EXHIBIT 1-9 Ethics and Accounting: A Decision-Making Model

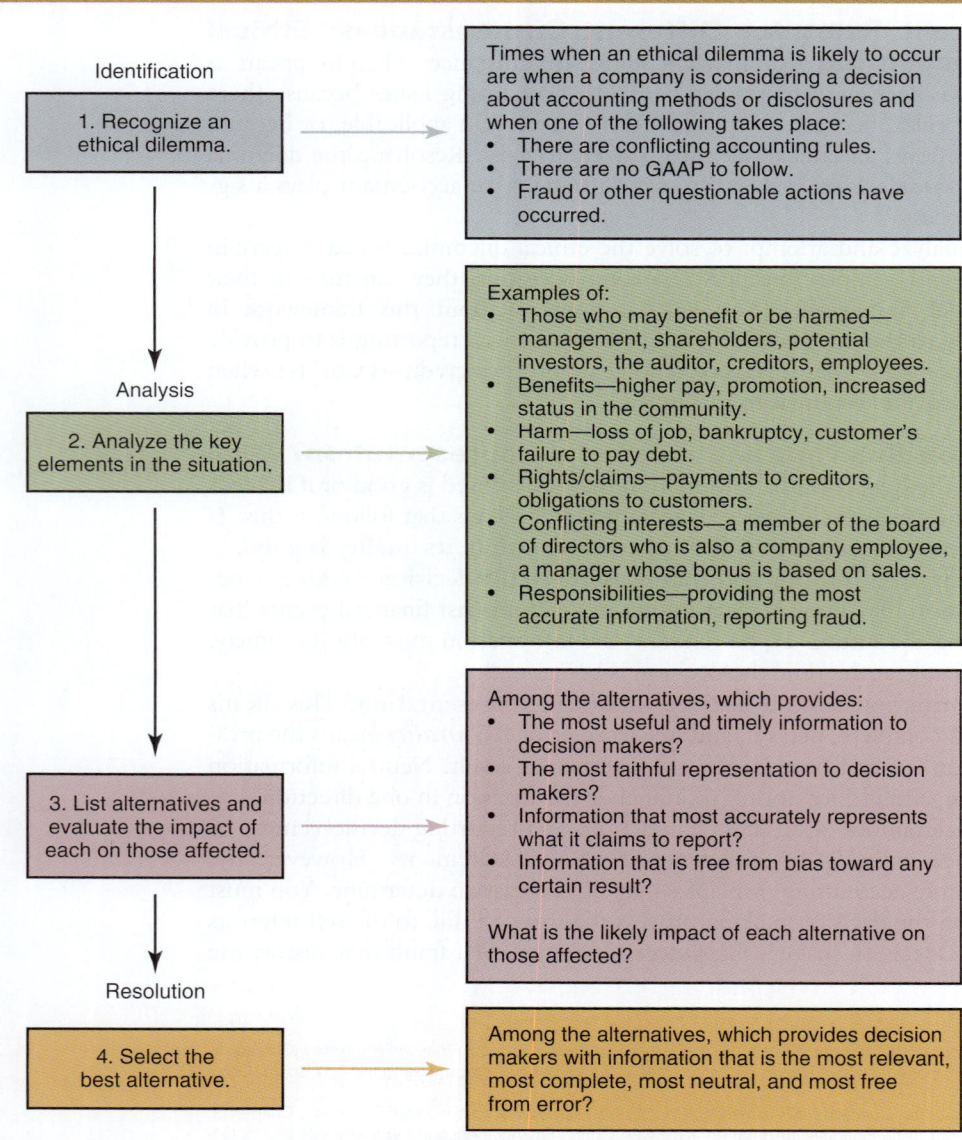

HOT TOPICS
Kellogg's—One of the World's Most Ethical Companies

Edouard H.R. Gluck/Bloomberg/Getty Images

Ethisphere magazine placed Kellogg's on its 2009 list of most ethical companies. Given the inherent judgments necessary in making ethical decisions, you can imagine the challenge presented in trying to determine the World's Most Ethical Companies™. However, this is just what *Ethisphere* magazine does. For its 2009 list, *Ethisphere* looked at companies in over 100 countries, across 35 separate industries and eventually came up with 99 companies for this honor. *Ethisphere* compares companies in the same industry, and Kellogg's was chosen in the Food and Beverage category. In 2008,

Kellogg's issued its first global Corporate Responsibility Report. Today, Kellogg's uses 100% recycled fiber packaging for almost all of its cereal cartons, and more than 100 years ago, the company introduced boxes that could be recycled.

Other well-known companies that made this prestigious list in 2009 included **American Express**; **PepsiCo**; **Mattel**; **Patagonia**; and one of Kellogg's main competitors, **General Mills**. Undoubtedly, the firms named as one of the World's Most Ethical Companies™ are proud of this designation. Whether they make the list in future years, the challenge is to seek continuous improvement in their ethical business practices, including ways in which they present accounting information to external users.

Source: http://www.kelloggs.com and http://ethisphere.com.

Analysis

2. Analyze the key elements in the situation by answering these questions in sequence:
   a. Who may benefit or be harmed?
   b. How are they likely to benefit or be harmed?
   c. What rights or claims may be violated?
   d. What specific interests are in conflict?
   e. What are my responsibilities and obligations?
3. Determine what alternative methods are available to report the transaction, situation, or event. Answer the following questions:
   a. Which of the alternatives is most relevant and a faithful representation? Timeliness should be considered; potential bias must be identified.
   b. Does the report accurately represent the situation it claims to describe?
   c. Is the information free from bias?

Resolution

4. Select the best or most ethical alternative, considering all of the circumstances and consequences.

Accountants and Ethical Judgments

Remember the primary goal of accounting: to provide useful information to aid in the decision-making process. As discussed, the work of the accountant in providing useful information is anything but routine and requires the accountant to make subjective judgments about what information to present and how to present it. The latitude given accountants in this respect is one of the major reasons accounting is a profession and its members are considered professionals. Along with this designation as a professional, however, comes a serious responsibility. As we noted, financial statements are prepared for external parties who must rely on these statements to provide information on which to base important decisions.

At the end of each chapter are cases titled "Ethical Decision Making." The cases require you to evaluate difficult issues and make a decision. Judgment is needed in deciding which accounting method to select or how to report a certain item in the statements. As you are faced with these decisions, keep in mind the trust that various financial statement users place in the accountant.

The Changing Face of the Accounting Profession

Probably no time in the history of the accounting profession in the United States has seen more turmoil and change than the period since the start of the new millennium. Corporate scandals have led to some of the largest bankruptcies in the history of business. The involvement of the auditors in one of these scandals resulted in the demise of one of the oldest and most respected public accounting firms in the world. Many have referred to the "financial reporting crisis" that grew out of this time period.

Although the issues involved in the financial reporting crisis are complex, the accounting questions in these cases were often very basic. For example, the most fundamental accounting issue involved in the **Enron** case revolved around the entity concept that was explained earlier in this chapter. Specifically, should various entities under the control of Enron have been included in the company's financial statements? Similarly, the major question in the **WorldCom** case was whether certain costs should have been treated as expenses when incurred rather than accounted for as assets.

The scandals of the last few years have resulted in a major focus on the nonaudit services provided by public accounting firms and the issue of auditor independence. For example, is it possible for an accounting firm to remain independent in rendering an opinion on a company's financial statements while simultaneously advising the company on other matters?

Sarbanes-Oxley Act
An act of Congress in 2002 intended to bring reform to corporate accountability and stewardship in the wake of a number of major corporate scandals.

In 2002, Congress passed the **Sarbanes-Oxley Act**. The act was a direct response to the corporate scandals mentioned earlier and was an attempt to bring about major reforms in corporate accountability and stewardship, given the vast numbers of stockholders, creditors, employees, and others affected in one way or another by these scandals. Among the most important provisions in the act are the following:

1. The establishment of a new Public Company Accounting Oversight Board
2. A requirement that the external auditors report directly to the company's audit committee
3. A clause to prohibit public accounting firms that audit a company from providing any other services that could impair their ability to act independently in the course of their audit

In addition to corporate scandals, the ongoing global economic crisis continues to present challenges for accountants.

Events of the last few years have placed accountants and the work they do in the spotlight more than ever before. More than ever, accountants realize the burden of responsibility they have to communicate openly and honestly with the public concerning the financial well-being of businesses. Whether you will someday be an accountant or simply a user of the information an accountant provides, it is important to appreciate the critical role accounting plays in the smooth functioning of the free enterprise system.

LOOKING AHEAD

It is rare today to find a U.S company that doesn't have an international presence. As pointed out in the chapter opener, Kellogg Company makes its products in 18 countries and sells them in over 180 countries. Increasingly, companies turn to investors and creditors from outside the United States for capital to grow their businesses. In turn, providers of capital in this country look to foreign companies for profitable investments. What does all of this mean for the future of accounting standards? It means continuing pressure for a single set of accounting principles worldwide, regardless of where a company happens to have its home base. And this is why the standard setting body in the United States, the Financial Accounting Standards Board, continues to work closely with the international group, the International Accounting Standards Board, on a convergence project. No date has been set for a unified set of accounting standards, but it is likely that sometime in the near future companies around the world will prepare their financial statements using the same underlying principles.

LO8 Explain the critical role that ethics plays in providing useful financial information.

- All decision makers must consider the moral and social implications of their decisions.
- Recent news of questionable accounting practices has placed increased scrutiny on the accounting profession. Professional judgment is often needed to arrive at appropriate decisions when some question arises about the application of GAAP.

QUESTIONS   **Answers to these questions are on the last page of the chapter.**

1. For accounting information to be useful in making informed decisions, it must be

   a. relevant.
   b. a faithful representation.
   c. both relevant and a faithful representation.
   d. Neither of these qualities is important.

2. The first step in the ethical decision-making model presented in this section is to

   a. list the alternatives and evaluate the impact of each on those who may be affected.
   b. recognize an ethical dilemma.
   c. analyze the key elements in the situation.
   d. select the best alternative.

KEY TERMS QUIZ

Note to the student: We conclude each chapter with a quiz on the key terms, which are shown in color in the chapter. Because of the large number of terms introduced in this chapter, there are two quizzes on key terms.

Read each definition below and write the number of the definition in the blank beside the appropriate term. The first one has been done for you. The quiz solutions appear at the end of the chapter. When reviewing terminology, come back to your completed key terms quiz. *Study tip:* Also check the glossary in the margin or at the end of the book.

Quiz 1: Introduction to Business

_____	Business	_____	Nonbusiness entity
_____	Business entity	_____	Liability
_____	Sole proprietorship	_____	Capital stock
_____	Economic entity concept	_____	Stockholder
_____	Partnership	_____	Creditor
_____	Corporation	__1__	Asset
_____	Share of stock	_____	Revenue
_____	Bond	_____	Expense

1. A future economic benefit.
2. A business owned by two or more individuals; the organization form often used by accounting firms and law firms.
3. An inflow of assets resulting from the sale of goods and services.
4. A form of entity organized under the laws of a particular state; ownership evidenced by shares of stock.
5. An organization operated for some purpose other than to earn a profit.
6. An outflow of assets resulting from the sale of goods and services.
7. An obligation of a business.
8. A certificate that acts as evidence of ownership in a corporation.
9. A certificate that represents a corporation's promise to repay a certain amount of money and interest in the future.
10. One of the owners of a corporation.
11. Someone to whom a company or person has a debt.
12. The assumption that a single, identifiable unit must be accounted for in all situations.
13. A form of organization with a single owner.

(Continued)

14. Indicates the owners' contributions to a corporation.
15. All of the activities necessary to provide the members of an economic system with goods and services.
16. An organization operated to earn a profit.

Quiz 2: Introduction to Accounting

_____ Accounting	_____ Generally accepted accounting
_____ Management accounting	principles (GAAP)
_____ Financial accounting	_____ Securities and Exchange
_____ Owners' equity	Commission (SEC)
_____ Stockholders' equity	_____ Financial Accounting Standards
_____ Retained earnings	Board (FASB)
_____ Balance sheet	_____ American Institute of Certified
_____ Income statement	Public Accountants (AICPA)
_____ Net income	_____ Certified Public Accountant (CPA)
_____ Dividends	_____ Public Company Accounting
_____ Statement of retained earnings	Oversight Board (PCAOB)
_____ Statement of cash flows	_____ International Accounting Standards
_____ Cost principle	Board (IASB)
_____ Going concern	_____ Auditing
_____ Monetary unit	_____ Sarbanes-Oxley Act
_____ Time period	

1. A statement that summarizes revenues and expenses for a period of time.
2. The statement that summarizes the income earned and dividends paid over the life of a business.
3. The owners' equity of a corporation.
4. The process of identifying, measuring, and communicating economic information to various users.
5. The branch of accounting involving communication with outsiders through financial statements.
6. The owners' claims to the assets of an entity.
7. The financial statement that summarizes the assets, liabilities, and owners' equity at a specific point in time.
8. The part of owners' equity that represents the income earned less dividends paid over the life of an entity.
9. The branch of accounting concerned with providing management with information to facilitate the planning and control functions.
10. A distribution of the net income of a business to its stockholders.
11. The various methods, rules, practices, and other procedures that have evolved over time in response to the need to regulate the preparation of financial statements.
12. Assets are recorded and reported at the cost paid to acquire them.
13. The federal agency with ultimate authority to determine the rules for preparing statements for companies whose stock is sold to the public.
14. The assumption that an entity is not in the process of liquidation and that it will continue indefinitely.
15. The group in the private sector with authority to set accounting standards.
16. The yardstick used to measure amounts in financial statements; the dollar in the United States.
17. The professional organization for certified public accountants.
18. A length of time on the calendar used as the basis for preparing financial statements.
19. The process of examining the financial statements and the underlying records of a company to render an opinion as to whether the statements are fairly presented.
20. The organization formed to develop worldwide accounting standards.
21. An act of Congress in 2002 intended to bring reform to corporate accountability and stewardship in the wake of a number of major corporate scandals.
22. The excess of revenues over expenses.

23. The designation for an individual who has passed a uniform exam administered by the AICPA and has met other requirements as determined by individual states.
24. A five-member body created by an act of Congress in 2002 to set auditing standards.
25. The financial statement that summarizes a company's cash receipts and cash payments during the period from operating, investing, and financing activities.

ALTERNATE TERMS

balance sheet statement of financial position
cost principle original cost or historical cost
creditor lender
income statement statement of income or statement of operations

net income profits or earnings
stockholder shareholder
stockholders' equity shareholders' equity

WARMUP EXERCISES & SOLUTIONS

Warmup Exercise 1-1 Your Assets and Liabilities

Consider your own situation in terms of assets and liabilities.

Required

1. Name three of your financial assets.
2. Name three of your financial liabilities.

KEY TO THE SOLUTION Refer to Exhibit 1-4 for examples of assets and liabilities.

Warmup Exercise 1-2 Kellogg's Assets and Liabilities   LO2

Think about **Kellogg's** business in balance sheet terms.

Required

1. Name three of Kellogg's assets.
2. Name three of Kellogg's liabilities.

KEY TO THE SOLUTION Refer to Exhibit 1-7 if you need to see Kellogg's balance sheet.

Warmup Exercise 1-3 Kellogg's and the Accounting Equation   LO2

Place **Kellogg's** total assets, total liabilities, and total stockholders' equity in the form of the accounting equation. (Use the 2010 year-end amounts.)

KEY TO THE SOLUTION Refer to Exhibit 1-7.

Solutions to Warmup Exercises

Warmup Exercise 1-1

1. Possible personal financial assets might include checking accounts, savings accounts, certificates of deposit, money market accounts, stocks, bonds, and mutual funds.
2. Possible personal financial liabilities might include student loans, car loans, home mortgages, and amounts borrowed from relatives.

Warmup Exercise 1-2

1. Kellogg's assets are Cash and cash equivalents, Accounts receivable, Inventories, Other current assets, Property, Goodwill, Other intangibles, and Other assets.
2. Kellogg's liabilities are Current maturities of long-term debt, Notes payable, Accounts payable, Other current liabilities, Long-term debt, Other liabilities, Deferred income taxes, and Pension liability.

STUDY TIP

Use these exercises to become accustomed to the assignments that follow.

LO2

Warmup Exercise 1-3

Assets = Liabilities + Stockholders' Equity

$11,847,000,000 = $9,693,000,000 + $2,154,000,000

REVIEW PROBLEM & SOLUTION

Greenway Corporation is organized on June 1, 2012. The company will provide lawn-care and tree-trimming services on a contract basis. Following is an alphabetical list of the items that should appear on its income statement for the first month and on its balance sheet at the end of the first month. (You will need to determine on which statement each should appear.)

Accounts payable	$ 800	Lawn-care revenue	$1,500
Accounts receivable	500	Notes payable	6,000
Building	2,000	Retained earnings (beginning balance)	0
Capital stock	5,000	Salaries and wages expense	900
Cash	3,300	Tools	800
Gas, utilities, and other expenses	300	Tree-trimming revenue	500
Land	4,000	Truck	2,000

Required

1. Prepare an income statement for the month of June.
2. Prepare a balance sheet at June 30, 2012. *Note:* You will need to determine the balance in Retained Earnings at the end of the month.
3. The financial statements you have prepared are helpful, but in many ways, they are just a starting point. Assuming that this is your business, what additional questions do the financial statements raise that you need to consider?

Solutions to Review Problem

1.
Greenway Corporation
Income Statement
For the Month Ended June 30, 2012

Revenues:		
Lawn care	$1,500	
Tree trimming	500	$2,000
Expenses:		
Salaries and wages	$ 900	
Gas, utilities, and other expenses	300	1,200
Net income		$ 800

2.
Greenway Corporation
Balance Sheet
June 30, 2012

Assets		**Liabilities and Stockholders' Equity**	
Cash	$ 3,300	Accounts payable	$ 800
Accounts receivable	500	Notes payable	6,000
Truck	2,000	Capital stock	5,000
Tools	800	Retained earnings	800
Building	2,000		
Land	4,000	Total liabilities and	
Total assets	$12,600	stockholders' equity	$12,600

3. Following are examples of questions that the financial statements raise:

- During June, 75% of the revenue was from lawn care and the other 25% was from tree trimming. Will this relationship hold in future months?
- Are the expenses representative of those that will be incurred in the future? Will any other expenses arise, such as advertising and income taxes?
- When can we expect to collect the accounts receivable? Is there a chance that not all will be collected?
- How soon will the accounts payable need to be paid?
- What is the interest rate on the note payable? When is interest paid? When is the note itself due?

QUESTIONS

1. What is business about? What do all businesses have in common?
2. What is an asset? Give three examples.
3. What is a liability? How does the definition of *liability* relate to the definition of *asset*?
4. Business entities are organized as one of three distinct forms. What are these three forms?
5. What are the three distinct types of business activity in which companies engage? Assume that you start your own company to rent bicycles in the summer and skis in the winter. Give an example of at least one of each of the three types of business activities in which you would engage.
6. What is accounting? Define it in terms understandable to someone without a business background.
7. How do financial accounting and management accounting differ?
8. What are five different groups of users of accounting information? Briefly describe the types of decisions each group must make.
9. How does owners' equity fit into the accounting equation?
10. What are the two distinct elements of owners' equity in a corporation? Define each element.
11. What is the purpose of a balance sheet?
12. How should a balance sheet be dated: as of a particular day or for a particular period of time? Explain your answer.
13. What does the term *cost principle* mean?

14. What is the purpose of an income statement?
15. How should an income statement be dated: as of a particular day or for a particular period of time? Explain your answer.
16. Rogers Corporation starts the year with a Retained Earnings balance of $55,000. Net income for the year is $27,000. The ending balance in Retained Earnings is $70,000. What was the amount of dividends for the year?
17. ⒾⒻⓇⓈ Evaluate the following statement: Companies based in the United States can choose whether to follow the standards of the FASB or those of the IASB since the rules of the two groups have converged.
18. What are some of the most important provisions in the Sarbanes-Oxley Act?
19. Evaluate the following statement: The auditors are in the best position to evaluate a company because they have prepared the financial statements.
20. What is the relationship between the cost principle and the going concern assumption?
21. Why does inflation present a challenge to the accountant? Relate your answer to the monetary unit assumption.
22. What is meant by the term *generally accepted accounting principles*?
23. What role has the Securities and Exchange Commission played in setting accounting standards? Contrast its role with that played by the Financial Accounting Standards Board.

BRIEF EXERCISES

Brief Exercise 1-1 Types of Businesses

List the names of three companies with which you are familiar that are manufacturers or producers. Also list the names of three companies that are retailers. Finally, provide the names of three service providers.

LO1

EXAMPLE 1-1

LO2   **Brief Exercise 1-2 Forms of Organization**

EXAMPLE 1-2   What does it mean when you own a share of stock in a company rather than one of its bonds?

LO3   **Brief Exercise 1-3 Business Activities**

Assume that you are starting a new business. In which type of business activity will you engage first? Identify the order in which the remaining two activities will occur.

LO4   **Brief Exercise 1-4 Users of Accounting Information**

List three examples of external users of accounting information.

LO5   **Brief Exercise 1-5 Accounting Equation and the Balance Sheet**

EXAMPLE 1-4   State the accounting equation. What two distinct parts make up stockholders' equity?

LO6   **Brief Exercise 1-6 Monetary Unit**

What monetary unit is used to prepare financial statements for companies in the United States? for companies in Japan?

LO7   **Brief Exercise 1-7 The Role of Auditors**

Do a company's external auditors prepare the company's financial statements? Explain.

LO8   **Brief Exercise 1-8 Making Ethical Decisions**

List the four steps that can help a person make ethical decisions.

EXERCISES

LO3   **Exercise 1-1 Types of Business Activities**

Braxton Corp. was organized on January 1, 2012, to operate a limousines service to and from the airport. For each of the following business activities, indicate whether it is a financing (F), investing (I), or operating (O) activity.

_____   1. Issued shares of stock to each of the four owners.
_____   2. Purchased two limousines.
_____   3. Paid first month's rent for use of garage.
_____   4. Obtained loan from local bank.
_____   5. Received cash from customer for trip to the airport.
_____   6. Paid driver first week's wages.
_____   7. Purchased 500-gallon fuel tank.

LO4   **Exercise 1-2 Users of Accounting Information and Their Needs**

Listed below are a number of the important users of accounting information. Following the list are descriptions of a major need of each of these various users. Fill in each blank with the one user group that is most likely to have the need described.

Company management   Banker
Stockholder   Supplier
Securities and Exchange Commission   Labor union
Internal Revenue Service

User Group   **Needs Information About**

_____   1. The profitability of each division in the company

_____   2. The prospects for future dividend payments

_____   3. The profitability of the company since the last contract with the workforce was signed

_____   4. The financial status of a company issuing securities to the public for the first time

User Group	Needs Information About
_____	5. The prospects that a company will be able to meet its interest payments on time
_____	6. The prospects that a company will be able to pay for its purchases on time
_____	7. The company's profitability based on the tax code

Exercise 1-3 Classification of Financial Statement Items

LO5

EXAMPLE 1-3, 1-4, 1-5

Classify each of the following items according to (1) whether it belongs on the income statement (IS) or balance sheet (BS) and (2) whether it is a revenue (R), expense (E), asset (A), liability (L), or stockholders' equity (SE) item.

Item	Appears on the	Classified as
Example: Cash	BS	A
1. Salaries expense	_____	_____
2. Equipment	_____	_____
3. Accounts payable	_____	_____
4. Membership fees earned	_____	_____
5. Capital stock	_____	_____
6. Accounts receivable	_____	_____
7. Buildings	_____	_____
8. Advertising expense	_____	_____
9. Retained earnings	_____	_____

Exercise 1-4 The Accounting Equation

LO5

EXAMPLE 1-4

For each of the following independent cases, fill in the blank with the appropriate dollar amount.

	Assets	=	Liabilities	+	Owners' Equity
Case 1	$ 125,000		$ 75,000		$_____
Case 2	400,000		_____		100,000
Case 3	_____		320,000		95,000

Exercise 1-5 The Accounting Equation

LO5

EXAMPLE 1-4

Ginger Enterprises began the year with total assets of $500,000 and total liabilities of $250,000. Using this information and the accounting equation, answer each of the following independent questions.
1. What was the amount of Ginger's owners' equity at the beginning of the year?
2. If Ginger's total assets increased by $100,000 and its total liabilities increased by $77,000 during the year, what was the amount of Ginger's owners' equity at the end of the year?
3. If Ginger's total liabilities increased by $33,000 and its owners' equity decreased by $58,000 during the year, what was the amount of its total assets at the end of the year?
4. If Ginger's total assets doubled to $1,000,000 and its owners' equity remained the same during the year, what was the amount of its total liabilities at the end of the year?

Exercise 1-6 The Accounting Equation

LO5

EXAMPLE 1-4

Using the accounting equation, answer each of the following independent questions.
1. Burlin Company starts the year with $100,000 in assets and $80,000 in liabilities. Net income for the year is $25,000, and no dividends are paid. How much is owners' equity at the end of the year?
2. Chapman Inc. doubles the amount of its assets from the beginning to the end of the year. Liabilities at the end of the year amount to $40,000, and owners' equity is $20,000. What is the amount of Chapman's assets at the beginning of the year?
3. During the year, the liabilities of Dixon Enterprises triple in amount. Assets at the beginning of the year amount to $30,000, and owners' equity is $10,000. What is the amount of liabilities at the end of the year?

LO5

Exercise 1-7 The Accounting Equation

For each of the following cases, fill in the blank with the appropriate dollar amount.

	Case 1	Case 2	Case 3	Case 4
Total assets, end of period	$ 40,000	$_____	$ 75,000	$ 50,000
Total liabilities, end of period	_____	15,000	25,000	10,000
Capital stock, end of period	10,000	5,000	20,000	15,000
Retained earnings, beginning of period	15,000	8,000	10,000	20,000
Net income for the period	8,000	7,000	_____	9,000
Dividends for the period	2,000	1,000	3,000	_____

LO5

EXAMPLE 1-4

Exercise 1-8 Changes in Owners' Equity

The following amounts are available from the records of Coaches and Carriages Inc. at the end of the years indicated:

December 31	Total Assets	Total Liabilities
2010	$ 25,000	$ 12,000
2011	79,000	67,000
2012	184,000	137,000

Required

1. Compute the changes in Coaches and Carriages owners' equity during 2011 and 2012.
2. Compute the amount of Coaches and Carriages' net income (or loss) for 2011 assuming that no dividends were paid and the owners made no additional contributions during the year.
3. Compute the amount of Coaches and Carriages' net income (or loss) for 2012 assuming that dividends paid during the year amounted to $10,000 and no additional contributions were made by the owners.

LO5

EXAMPLE 1-7

Exercise 1-9 Classification of Items on the Statement of Cash Flows

Classify each of the following items according to the section on the statement of cash flows in which it should appear: operating (O), investing (I), or financing (F):

Item	Section
Example: Cash paid for insurance	O
1. Cash paid for land	_____
2. Cash received from issuance of note	_____
3. Cash paid for dividends	_____
4. Cash received from issuance of capital stock	_____
5. Cash collected from customers	_____
6. Cash paid for income taxes	_____

LO5

EXAMPLE 1-4, 1-5, 1-6

Exercise 1-10 Net Income (or Loss) and Retained Earnings

The following information is available from the records of Prestige Landscape Design Inc. at the end of the year:

Accounts payable	$ 5,000	Landscaping revenues	$25,000
Accounts receivable	4,500	Office equipment	7,500
Capital stock	8,000	Rent expense	6,500
Cash	13,000	Retained earnings, beginning of year	8,500
Dividends paid during the year	3,000	Salary and wage expense	12,000

Required

Use the previous information to answer the following questions.

1. What is Prestige's net income for the year?
2. What is Prestige's Retained Earnings balance at the end of the year?
3. What is the total amount of Prestige's assets at the end of the year?
4. What is the total amount of Prestige's liabilities at the end of the year?
5. How much owners' equity does Prestige have at the end of the year?
6. What is Prestige's accounting equation at the end of the year?

Exercise 1-11 Classification of Financial Statement Items

LO5
EXAMPLE 1-5

Carnival Corporation & plc is one of the largest cruise companies in the world with such well-known brands as Carnival Cruise Lines, Holland America Line, and Princess Cruises. Classify each of the following items found in the company's 2010 annual report according to (1) whether it belongs on the income statement (IS) or balance sheet (BS) and (2) whether it is a revenue (R), expense (E), asset (A), liability (L), or stockholders' equity (SE) item.

Item	Appears on the	Classified as
Example: Cash and cash equivalents	BS	A
1. Trade and other receivables, net		
2. Common stock of Carnival Corporation		
3. Short-term borrowings		
4. Passenger tickets		
5. Selling and administrative		
6. Property and equipment, net		
7. Accounts payable		
8. Retained earnings		
9. Income tax expense		
10. Long-term debt		

Exercise 1-12 Accounting Principles and Assumptions

LO6

The following basic accounting principles and assumptions were discussed in the chapter:

Economic entity
Monetary unit
Cost principle
Going concern
Time period

Fill in each of the blanks with the accounting principle or assumption that is relevant to the situation described.

_____ 1. Genesis Corporation is now in its 30th year of business. The founder of the company is planning to retire at the end of the year and turn the business over to his daughter.

_____ 2. Nordic Company purchased a 20-acre parcel of property on which to build a new factory. The company recorded the property on the records at the amount of cash given to acquire it.

_____ 3. Jim Bailey enters into an agreement to operate a new law firm in partnership with a friend. Each partner will make an initial cash investment of $10,000. Jim opens a checking account in the name of the partnership and transfers $10,000 from his personal account into the new account.

_____ 4. Multinational Corp. has a division in Japan. Prior to preparing the financial statements for the company and all of its foreign divisions, Multinational translates the financial statements of its Japanese division from yen to U.S. dollars.

_____ 5. Camden Company has always prepared financial statements annually, with a year-end of June 30. Because the company is going to sell its stock to the public for the first time, quarterly financial reports will also be required by the SEC.

LO7   **Exercise 1-13 Organizations and Accounting**

Match each of the organizations listed below with the statement that most adequately describes the role of the group.

Securities and Exchange Commission
International Accounting Standards Board
Financial Accounting Standards Board
American Institute of Certified Public Accountants

_____   1. The federal agency with ultimate authority to determine rules used for preparing financial statements for companies whose stock is sold to the public

_____   2. The group in the private sector with authority to set accounting standards

_____   3. The professional organization for certified public accountants

_____   4. The organization formed to develop worldwide accounting standards

LO5   **Exercise 1-14 Statement of Retained Earnings**

EXAMPLE 1-6   Ace Corporation has been in business for many years. Retained earnings on January 1, 2012, is $235,800. The following information is available for the first two months of 2012:

	January	February
Revenues	$83,000	$96,000
Expenses	89,000	82,000
Dividends paid	0	5,000

Required

Prepare a statement of retained earnings for the month ended February 29, 2012.

MULTI-CONCEPT EXERCISES

LO4 • 5   **Exercise 1-15 Users of Accounting Information and the Financial Statements**

Following are a number of users of accounting information and examples of questions they need answered before making decisions. Fill in each blank to indicate whether the user is most likely to find the answer by looking at the income statement (IS), the balance sheet (BS), the statement of retained earnings (RE), or the statement of cash flows (SCF).

User	Question	Financial Statement
Stockholder	How did this year's sales compare to last year's?	_____
Banker	How much debt does the company already have on its books?	_____
Supplier	How much does the company currently owe to its suppliers?	_____
Stockholder	How much did the company pay in dividends this past year?	_____
Advertising account manager	How much did the company spend this past year to generate sales?	_____
Banker	What collateral or security can the company provide to ensure that any loan I make will be repaid?	_____

LO5 • 6   **Exercise 1-16 Kellogg's Land**

Refer to **Kellogg's** balance sheet reproduced in the chapter.

Required

In which of the assets would you expect Kellogg's land to be included? What does this amount represent (i.e., cost, market value)? Why does Kellogg's carry its land at one or the other values?

PROBLEMS

Problem 1-1 Information Needs and Setting Accounting Standards

LO4

The Financial Accounting Standards Board requires companies to supplement their consolidated financial statements with disclosures about segments of their businesses. To comply with this standard, **Time Warner Inc.**'s 2010 annual report provides various disclosures for the three segments in which it operates: Filmed Entertainment, Networks, and Publishing.

Required

Which users of accounting information do you think the FASB had in mind when it set this standard? What types of disclosures do you think these users would find helpful?

Problem 1-2 You Won the Lottery

LO4

You have won a lottery! You will receive $200,000, after taxes, each year for the next five years.

Required

Describe the process you will go through in determining how to invest your winnings. Consider at least two options and make a choice. You may consider the stock of a certain company, bonds, real estate investments, bank deposits, and so on. Be specific. What information do you need to make a final decision? How will your decision be affected by the fact that you will receive the winnings over a five-year period rather than in one lump sum? Would you prefer one payment? Explain.

Problem 1-3 Balance Sheet

LO5

The following items are available from records of Freescia Corporation at the end of the 2012 calendar year:

Accounts payable	$12,550	Notes payable	$50,000
Accounts receivable	23,920	Office equipment	12,000
Advertising expense	2,100	Retained earnings, end of year	37,590
Buildings	85,000	Salary and wage expense	8,230
Capital stock	25,000	Sales revenue	14,220
Cash	4,220		

Required

Prepare a balance sheet. *Hint:* Not all of the items listed should appear on a balance sheet. For each non-balance-sheet item, indicate where it should appear.

Problem 1-4 Corrected Financial Statements

LO5

Hometown Cleaners Inc. operates a small dry-cleaning business. The company has always maintained a complete and accurate set of records. Unfortunately, the company's accountant left in a dispute with the president and took the 2012 financial statements with him. The following income statement and balance sheet were prepared by the company's president:

Hometown Cleaners Inc.
Income Statement
For the Year Ended December 31, 2012

Revenues:		
Accounts receivable	$15,200	
Cleaning revenue—cash sales	32,500	$47,700
Expenses:		
Dividends	$ 4,000	
Accounts payable	4,500	
Utilities	12,200	
Salaries and wages	17,100	37,800
Net income		$ 9,900

Hometown Cleaners Inc.
Balance Sheet
December 31, 2012

Assets		Liabilities and Stockholders' Equity	
Cash	$ 7,400	Cleaning revenue—	
Building and equipment	80,000	credit sales	$26,200
Less: Notes payable	(50,000)	Capital stock	20,000
Land	40,000	Net income	9,900
		Retained earnings	21,300
		Total liabilities and	
Total assets	$ 77,400	stockholders' equity	$77,400

The president is very disappointed with the net income for the year because it has averaged $25,000 over the last ten years. She has asked for your help in determining whether the reported net income accurately reflects the profitability of the company and whether the balance sheet is prepared correctly.

Required

1. Prepare a corrected income statement for the year ended December 31, 2012.
2. Prepare a statement of retained earnings for the year ended December 31, 2012. (The actual balance of Retained Earnings on January 1, 2012, was $42,700. Note that the December 31, 2012, Retained Earnings balance shown is incorrect. The president simply "plugged in" this amount to make the balance sheet balance.)
3. Prepare a corrected balance sheet at December 31, 2012.
4. Draft a memo to the president explaining the major differences between the income statement she prepared and the one you prepared.

LO5   **Problem 1-5 Income Statement, Statement of Retained Earnings, and Balance Sheet**

The following list, in alphabetical order, shows the various items that regularly appear on the financial statements of Maple Park Theatres Corp. The amounts shown for balance sheet items are balances as of September 30, 2012 (with the exception of retained earnings, which is the balance on September 1, 2012), and the amounts shown for income statement items are balances for the month ended September 30, 2012.

Accounts payable	$17,600	Furniture and fixtures	$34,000
Accounts receivable	6,410	Land	26,000
Advertising expense	14,500	Notes payable	20,000
Buildings	60,000	Projection equipment	25,000
Capital stock	50,000	Rent expense—movies	50,600
Cash	15,230	Retained earnings	73,780
Concessions revenue	60,300	Salaries and wages expense	46,490
Cost of concessions sold	23,450	Ticket sales	95,100
Dividends paid during the month	8,400	Water, gas, and electricity	6,700

Required

1. Prepare an income statement for the month ended September 30, 2012.
2. Prepare a statement of retained earnings for the month ended September 30, 2012.
3. Prepare a balance sheet at September 30, 2012.
4. You have $1,000 to invest. On the basis of the statements you prepared, would you use it to buy stock in Maple Park? Explain. What other information would you want before making a final decision?

LO5   **Problem 1-6 Corrected Balance Sheet**

Dave is the president of Avon Consulting Inc. Avon began business on January 1, 2012. The company's controller is out of the country on business. Dave needs a copy of the company's balance sheet for a meeting tomorrow and asks his assistant to obtain the required information from the company's records. She presents Dave with the following balance sheet. He asks you to review it for accuracy.

Avon Consulting Inc.
Balance Sheet
For the Year Ended December 31, 2012

Assets		Liabilities and Stockholders' Equity	
Accounts payable	$13,000	Accounts receivable	$16,000
Cash	21,000	Capital stock	20,000
Cash dividends paid	16,000	Net income for 2012	72,000
Furniture and equipment	43,000	Supplies	9,000

Required

1. Prepare a corrected balance sheet.
2. Draft a memo explaining the major differences between the balance sheet Dave's assistant prepared and the one you prepared.

Problem 1-7 Statement of Retained Earnings for The Coca-Cola Company LO5

The Coca-Cola Company and Subsidiaries reported the following amounts in various statements included in its 2010 annual report. (All amounts are stated in millions of dollars.)

Net income for 2010	$11,809
Cash dividends declared in 2010	4,068
Reinvested earnings, December 31, 2009	41,537
Reinvested earnings, December 31, 2010	49,278

Required

1. Prepare a statement of retained earnings for The Coca-Cola Company for the year ended December 31, 2010.
2. The Coca-Cola Company does not actually present a statement of retained earnings in its annual report. Instead, it presents a broader statement of shareholders' equity. Describe the information that would be included on this statement that is not included on a statement of retained earnings.

Problem 1-8 Income Statement and Balance Sheet LO5

Green Bay Corporation began business in July 2012 as a commercial fishing operation and a passenger service between islands. Shares of stock were issued to the owners in exchange for cash. Boats were purchased by making a down payment in cash and signing a note payable for the balance. Fish are sold to local restaurants on open account, and customers are given 15 days to pay their account. Cash fares are collected for all passenger traffic. Rent for the dock facilities is paid at the beginning of each month. Salaries and wages are paid at the end of the month. The following amounts are from the records of Green Bay Corporation at the end of its first month of operations:

Accounts receivable	$18,500	Notes payable	$60,000
Boats	80,000	Passenger service revenue	12,560
Capital stock	40,000	Rent expense	4,000
Cash	7,730	Retained earnings	?
Dividends	5,400	Salary and wage expense	18,230
Fishing revenue	21,300		

Required

1. Prepare an income statement for the month ended July 31, 2012.
2. Prepare a balance sheet at July 31, 2012.
3. What information would you need about Notes Payable to fully assess Green Bay's long-term viability? Explain your answer.

LO4   ## Problem 1-9 Users of Accounting Information and Their Needs

Havre Company would like to buy a building and equipment to produce a new product line. Information about Havre is more useful to some people involved in the project than to others.

Required

Complete the following chart by identifying the information listed on the left with the user's need to know the information. Identify the information as one of the following:

a. *Need* to know
b. *Helpful* to know
c. *Not necessary* to know

	User of the Information		
Information	**Management**	**Stockholders**	**Banker**
1. Amount of current debt, repayment schedule, and interest rate	_____	_____	_____
2. Fair market value of the building	_____	_____	_____
3. Condition of the roof and heating and cooling, electrical, and plumbing systems	_____	_____	_____
4. Total cost of the building, improvements, and equipment to set up production	_____	_____	_____
5. Expected sales from the new product, variable production costs, and related selling costs	_____	_____	_____

MULTI-CONCEPT PROBLEM

LO5 • 6   ## Problem 1-10 Primary Assumptions Made in Preparing Financial Statements

Joe Hale opened a machine repair business in leased retail space, paying the first month's rent of $300 and a $1,000 security deposit with a check on his personal account. He took the tools, worth about $7,500, from his garage to the shop. He also bought some equipment to get started. The new equipment had a list price of $5,000, but Joe was able to purchase it on sale at **Sears** for only $4,200. He charged the new equipment on his personal Sears charge card. Joe's first customer paid $400 for services rendered, so Joe opened a checking account for the company. He completed a second job, but the customer has not paid Joe the $2,500 for his work. At the end of the first month, Joe prepared the following balance sheet and income statement:

Joe's Machine Repair Shop
Balance Sheet
July 31, 2012

Cash	$ 400		
Equipment	5,000	Equity	$5,400
Total	$5,400	Total	$5,400

Joe's Machine Repair Shop
Income Statement
For the Month Ended July 31, 2012

Sales		$ 2,900
Rent	$ 300	
Tools	4,200	4,500
Net loss		$(1,600)

Joe believes that he should show a greater profit next month because he won't have large expenses for items such as tools.

Required

Identify the assumptions that Joe has violated and explain how each event should have been handled. Prepare a corrected balance sheet and income statement.

ALTERNATE PROBLEMS

Problem 1-1A Users of Accounting Information and Their Needs   LO4

Billings Inc. would like to buy a franchise to provide a specialized service. Information about Billings is more useful to some people involved in the project than to others.

Required

Complete the following chart by identifying the information listed on the left with the user's need to know the information. Identify the information as one of the following:

a. *Need* to know
b. *Helpful* to know
c. *Not necessary* to know

Information	User of the Information		
	Manager	Stockholders	Franchisor
1. Expected revenue from the new service	_____	_____	_____
2. Cost of the franchise fee and recurring fees to be paid to the franchisor	_____	_____	_____
3. Cash available to Billings, the franchisee, to operate the business after the franchise is purchased	_____	_____	_____
4. Expected overhead costs of the service outlet	_____	_____	_____
5. Billings' required return on its investment	_____	_____	_____

Problem 1-2A What to Do with a Million Dollars?   LO4

You have inherited $1 million!

Required

Describe the process you will go through in determining how to invest your inheritance. Consider at least two options and choose one. You may consider the stock of a certain company, bonds, real estate investments, bank deposits, and so on. Be specific. What information do you need to make a final decision? Where will you find the information you need? What additional information will you need to consider if you want to make a change in your investment?

Problem 1-3A Information Needs and Setting Accounting Standards   LO4

The Financial Accounting Standards Board requires companies to supplement their consolidated financial statements with disclosures about segments of their businesses. To comply with this standard, **Marriott International**'s 2010 annual report provides various disclosures for the five segments in which it operates: North American Full-Service Lodging, North American Limited-Service Lodging, International Lodging, Luxury Lodging, and Timeshare.

Required

Which users of accounting information do you think the FASB had in mind when it set this standard? What types of disclosures do you think these users would find helpful?

Problem 1-4A Statement of Retained Earnings for Brunswick Corporation   LO5

Brunswick Corporation reported the following amounts in various statements included in its 2010 annual report. (All amounts are stated in millions of dollars.)

Net loss for 2010	$110.6
Cash dividends declared and paid in 2010	4.4
Retained earnings, December 31, 2009	505.3
Retained earnings, December 31, 2010	390.3

Required

1. Prepare a statement of retained earnings for Brunswick Corporation for the year ended December 31, 2010.
2. Brunswick does not actually present a statement of retained earnings in its annual report. Instead, it presents a broader statement of shareholders' equity. Describe the information that would be included on this statement that is not included on a statement of retained earnings.

LO5 Problem 1-5A Income Statement, Statement of Retained Earnings, and Balance Sheet

The following list, in alphabetical order, shows the various items that regularly appear on the financial statements of Sterns Audio Book Rental Corp. The amounts shown for balance sheet items are balances as of December 31, 2012 (with the exception of retained earnings, which is the balance on January 1, 2012), and the amounts shown for income statement items are balances for the year ended December 31, 2012.

Accounts payable	$ 4,500	Notes payable	$ 10,000
Accounts receivable	300	Rental revenue	125,900
Advertising expense	14,500	Rent expense	60,000
Capital stock	50,000	Retained earnings	35,390
Cash	2,490	Salaries and wages expense	17,900
Display fixtures	45,000	Supplies inventory	70,000
Dividends paid during the year	12,000	Water, gas, and electricity	3,600

Required

1. Prepare an income statement for the year ended December 31, 2012.
2. Prepare a statement of retained earnings for the year ended December 31, 2012.
3. Prepare a balance sheet at December 31, 2012.
4. You have $1,000 to invest. On the basis of the statements you prepared, would you use it to buy stock in this company? Explain. What other information would you want before deciding?

LO5 Problem 1-6A Balance Sheet

The following items are available from the records of Victor Corporation at the end of its fiscal year, July 31, 2012:

Accounts payable	$16,900	Delivery expense	$ 4,600
Accounts receivable	5,700	Notes payable	50,000
Buildings	35,000	Office equipment	12,000
Butter and cheese inventory	12,100	Retained earnings, end of year	26,300
Capital stock	25,000	Salary and wage expense	8,230
Cash	21,800	Sales revenue	14,220
Computerized mixers	25,800	Tools	5,800

Required

Prepare a balance sheet. *Hint:* Not all of the items listed should appear on a balance sheet. For each non-balance-sheet item, indicate where it should appear.

LO5 Problem 1-7A Corrected Balance Sheet

Pete is the president of Island Enterprises. Island Enterprises began business on January 1, 2012. The company's controller is out of the country on business. Pete needs a copy of the company's balance sheet for a meeting tomorrow and asks his assistant to obtain the required information from the company's records. She presents Pete with the following balance sheet. He asks you to review it for accuracy.

Island Enterprises
Balance Sheet
For the Year Ended December 31, 2012

Assets		Liabilities and Stockholders' Equity	
Accounts payable	$ 29 600	Accounts receivable	$ 23 200
Building and equipment	177,300	Supplies	12,200
Cash	14,750	Capital stock	100,000
Cash dividends paid	16,000	Net income for 2012	113,850

Required

1. Prepare a corrected balance sheet.
2. Draft a memo explaining the major differences between the balance sheet Pete's assistant prepared and the one you prepared.

Problem 1-8A Corrected Financial Statements   LO5

Heidi's Bakery Inc. operates a small pastry business. The company has always maintained a complete and accurate set of records. Unfortunately, the company's accountant left in a dispute with the president and took the 2012 financial statements with her. The following balance sheet and income statement were prepared by the company's president:

Heidi's Bakery Inc.
Income Statement
For the Year Ended December 31, 2012

Revenues:		
Accounts receivable	$15,500	
Pastry revenue—cash sales	23,700	$39,200
Expenses:		
Dividends	$ 5,600	
Accounts payable	6,800	
Utilities	9,500	
Salaries and wages	18,200	40,100
Net loss		$ (900)

Heidi's Bakery Inc.
Balance Sheet
December 31, 2012

Assets		Liabilities and Stockholders' Equity	
Cash	$ 3,700	Pastry revenue—	
Building and equipment	60,000	credit sales	$22,100
Less: Notes payable	(40,000)	Capital stock	30,000
Land	50,000	Net loss	(900)
		Retained earnings	22,500
Total assets	$ 73,700	Total liabilities and stockholders' equity	$73,700

The president is very disappointed with the net loss for the year because net income has averaged $21,000 over the last ten years. He has asked for your help in determining whether the reported net loss accurately reflects the profitability of the company and whether the balance sheet is prepared correctly.

Required

1. Prepare a corrected income statement for the year ended December 31, 2012.
2. Prepare a statement of retained earnings for the year ended December 31, 2012. (The actual amount of retained earnings on January 1, 2012, was $39,900. The December 31, 2012,

Retained Earnings balance shown is incorrect. The president simply "plugged in" this amount to make the balance sheet balance.)

3. Prepare a corrected balance sheet at December 31, 2012.
4. Draft a memo to the president explaining the major differences between the income statement he prepared and the one you prepared.

LO5   Problem 1-9A   Income Statement and Balance Sheet

Fort Worth Corporation began business in January 2012 as a commercial carpet-cleaning and drying service. Shares of stock were issued to the owners in exchange for cash. Equipment was purchased by making a down payment in cash and signing a note payable for the balance. Services are performed for local restaurants and office buildings on open account, and customers are given 15 days to pay their accounts. Rent for office and storage facilities is paid at the beginning of each month. Salaries and wages are paid at the end of the month. The following amounts are from the records of Fort Worth Corporation at the end of its first month of operations:

Accounts receivable	$24,750	Equipment	$62,000
Capital stock	80,000	Notes payable	30,000
Cash	51,650	Rent expense	3,600
Cleaning revenue	45,900	Retained earnings	?
Dividends	5,500	Salary and wage expense	8,400

Required

1. Prepare an income statement for the month ended January 31, 2012.
2. Prepare a balance sheet at January 31, 2012.
3. What information would you need about Notes Payable to fully assess Fort Worth's long-term viability? Explain your answer.

ALTERNATE MULTI-CONCEPT PROBLEM

LO5 · 6   Problem 1-10A   Primary Assumptions Made in Preparing Financial Statements

Millie Abrams opened a ceramic studio in leased retail space, paying the first month's rent of $300 and a $1,000 security deposit with a check on her personal account. She took molds and paint, worth about $7,500, from her home to the studio. She also bought a new firing kiln to start the business. The new kiln had a list price of $5,000, but Millie was able to trade in her old kiln, worth $500 at the time of trade, on the new kiln. Therefore, she paid only $4,500 cash. She wrote a check on her personal account. Millie's first customers paid a total of $1,400 to attend classes for the next two months. Millie opened a checking account in the company's name with the $1,400. She has conducted classes for one month and has sold $3,000 of unfinished ceramic pieces called *greenware*. All greenware sales are cash. Millie incurred $1,000 of personal cost in making the greenware. At the end of the first month, Millie prepared the following balance sheet and income statement:

Millie's Ceramic Studio
Balance Sheet
July 31, 2012

Cash	$1,400		
Kiln	5,000	Equity	$6,400
Total	$6,400	Total	$6,400

Millie's Ceramic Studio
Income Statement
For the Month Ended July 31, 2012

Sales		$4,400
Rent	$300	
Supplies	600	900
Net income		$3,500

Millie needs to earn at least $3,000 each month for the business to be worth her time. She is pleased with the results.

Required

Identify the assumptions that Millie has violated and explain how each event should have been handled. Prepare a corrected balance sheet and income statement.

DECISION CASES

Reading and Interpreting Financial Statements

Decision Case 1-1 An Annual Report as Ready Reference

LO4 • 5

Refer to the excerpts from **Kellogg's** annual report reprinted at the back of the book and identify where each of the following users of accounting information would first look to answer their respective questions about Kellogg's.
1. *Investors:* How much did the company earn for each share of stock that I own? Were any dividends paid, and how much was reinvested in the company?
2. *Potential investors:* What amount of earnings can I expect to see from Kellogg's in the near future?
3. *Suppliers:* Should I extend credit to Kellogg's? Does it have sufficient cash or cashlike assets to repay accounts payable?
4. *IRS:* How much does Kellogg's owe for taxes?
5. *Bankers:* What is Kellogg's long-term debt? Should I make a new loan to the company?

Decision Case 1-2 Reading and Interpreting Kellogg's Financial Statements

LO5

Refer to the financial statements for **Kellogg's** reproduced in the chapter and answer the following questions.

1. What was the company's net income for 2010?
2. State Kellogg's financial position on January 1, 2011 (the end of its 2010 fiscal year), in terms of the accounting equation.
3. By what amount did Property, net, increase during 2010? Explain what would cause an increase in this item.

Decision Case 1-3 Comparing Two Companies in the Same Industry: Kellogg's and General Mills

LO5

Refer to the financial information for **Kellogg's** and **General Mills** reproduced at the end of the book and answer the following questions.

1. What was the net sales amount for each company for the most recent year? Did each company's net sales increase or decrease from its total amount in the prior year?
2. What was each company's net income for the most recent year? Did each company's net income increase or decrease from its net income for the prior year?
3. What was the total asset balance for each company at the end of its most recent year? Among its assets, what was the largest asset each company reported on its year-end balance sheet?
4. Did either company pay its stockholders any dividends during the most recent year? Explain how you can tell.

Making Financial Decisions

Decision Case 1-4 An Investment Opportunity

LO4

You have saved enough money to pay for your college tuition for the next three years when a high-school friend comes to you with a deal. He is an artist who has spent most of the past two years drawing on the walls of old buildings. The buildings are about to be demolished, and your friend thinks you should buy the walls before the buildings are demolished and open a gallery featuring his work. Of course, you are levelheaded and would normally say no. Recently, however, your friend has been featured on several local radio and television shows and is talking to some national networks about doing a feature on a well-known news show. To set up the gallery would take all of your savings, but your friend thinks that you will be able to sell his artwork for ten times the cost of your investment. What information about the business do you need before deciding to invest your savings? What kind of profit split would you suggest to your friend?

LO5 ## Decision Case 1-5 Preparation of Projected Statements for a New Business

Upon graduation from MegaState University, you and your roommate decide to start your respective careers in accounting and salmon fishing in Remote, Alaska. Your career as a CPA in Remote is going well, as is your roommate's job as a commercial fisherman. After one year in Remote, he approaches you with a business opportunity.

As we are well aware, the DVD rental business has yet to reach Remote and the nearest rental facility is 250 miles away. We each put up our first year's savings of $5,000 and file for articles of incorporation with the state of Alaska to do business as Remote DVD World. In return for our investment of $5,000, we will each receive equal shares of capital stock in the corporation. Then we go to Corner National Bank and apply for a $10,000 loan. We take the total cash of $20,000 we have now raised and buy 2,000 DVDs at $10 each from a mail-order supplier. We rent the movies for $3 per title and sell monthly memberships for $25, allowing a member to check out an unlimited number of movies during the month. Individual rentals would be a cash-and-carry business, but we would give customers until the 10th of the following month to pay for a monthly membership. My most conservative estimate is that during the first month alone, we will rent 800 movies and sell 200 memberships. As I see it, we will have only two expenses. First, we will hire two high-school students to run the store for 15 hours each per week and pay them $10 per hour. Second, the landlord of a vacant store in town will rent us space in the building for $1,000 per month.

Required

1. Prepare a projected income statement for the first month of operations.
2. Prepare a balance sheet as it would appear at the end of the first month of operations.
3. Assume that the bank is willing to make the $10,000 loan. Would you be willing to join your roommate in this business? Explain your response. Also indicate any information other than what he has provided that you would like to have before making a final decision.

Ethical Decision Making

LO4 • 5 • 8 ## Decision Case 1-6 Identification of Errors in Financial Statements and Preparation of Revised Statements

Lakeside Slammers Inc. is a minor league baseball organization that has just completed its first season. You and three other investors organized the corporation; each put up $10,000 in cash for shares of capital stock. Because you live out of state, you have not been actively involved in the daily affairs of the club. However, you are thrilled to receive a dividend check for $10,000 at the end of the season—an amount equal to your original investment. Included with the check are the following financial statements, along with supporting explanations:

Lakeside Slammers Inc.
Income Statement
For the Year Ended December 31, 2012

Revenues:		
Single-game ticket revenue	$420,000	
Season ticket revenue	140,000	
Concessions revenue	280,000	
Advertising revenue	100,000	$940,000

Expenses:

Cost of concessions sold	$110,000	
Salary expense—players	225,000	
Salary and wage expense—staff	150,000	
Rent expense	210,000	695,000
Net income		$245,000

Lakeside Slammers Inc.
Statement of Retained Earnings
For the Year Ended December 31, 2012

Beginning balance, January 1, 2012	$ 0
Add: Net income for 2012	245,000
Deduct: Cash dividends paid in 2012	(40,000)
Ending balance, December 31, 2012	$205,000

Lakeside Slammers Inc.
Balance Sheet
December 31, 2012

Assets		Liabilities and Stockholders' Equity	
Cash	$ 5,000	Notes payable	$ 50,000
Accounts receivable:		Capital stock	40,000
Season tickets	140,000	Additional owners' capital	80,000
Advertisers	100,000	Parent club's equity	125,000
Auxiliary assets	80,000	Retained earnings	205,000
Equipment	50,000		
Player contracts	125,000	Total liabilities and	
Total assets	$500,000	stockholders' equity	$500,000

Additional information:

a. Single-game tickets sold for $4 per game. The team averaged 1,500 fans per game. With 70 home games × $4 per game × 1,500 fans, single-game ticket revenue amounted to $420,000.

b. No season tickets were sold during the first season. During the last three months of 2012, however, an aggressive sales campaign resulted in the sale of 500 season tickets for the 2013 season. Therefore, the controller (who is also one of the owners) chose to record an Account Receivable—Season Tickets and corresponding revenue for 500 tickets × $4 per game × 70 games, or $140,000.

c. Advertising revenue of $100,000 resulted from the sale of the 40 signs on the outfield wall at $2,500 each for the season. However, none of the advertisers have paid their bills yet (thus, an account receivable of $100,000 on the balance sheet) because the contract with Lakeside required payment only if the team averaged 2,000 fans per game during the 2012 season. The controller believes that the advertisers will be sympathetic to the difficulties of starting a new franchise and will be willing to overlook the slight deficiency in the attendance requirement.

d. Lakeside has a working agreement with one of the major league franchises. The minor league team is required to pay $5,000 *every year* to the major league team for each of the 25 players on its roster. The controller believes that each of the players is an asset to the organization and has therefore recorded $5,000 × 25, or $125,000, as an asset called Player Contracts. The item on the right side of the balance sheet entitled Parent Club's Equity is the amount owed to the major league team by February 1, 2013, as payment for the players for the 2012 season.

e. In addition to the cost described in item (d), Lakeside directly pays each of its 25 players a $9,000 salary for the season. This amount—$225,000—has already been paid for the 2012 season and is reported on the income statement.

(Continued)

f. The items on the balance sheet entitled Auxiliary Assets on the left side and Additional Owners' Capital on the right side represent the value of the controller's personal residence. She has a mortgage with the bank for the full value of the house.

g. The $50,000 note payable resulted from a loan that was taken out at the beginning of the year to finance the purchase of bats, balls, uniforms, lawn mowers, and other miscellaneous supplies needed to operate the team. (Equipment is reported as an asset for the same amount.) The loan, with interest, is due on April 15, 2013. Even though the team had a very successful first year, Lakeside is a little short of cash at the end of 2012 and has asked the bank for a three-month extension of the loan. The controller reasons, "By the due date of April 15, 2013, the cash due from the new season ticket holders will be available, things will be cleared up with the advertisers, and the loan can be easily repaid."

Required

1. Identify any errors you think the controller has made in preparing the financial statements.
2. On the basis of your answer in part (1), prepare a revised income statement, statement of retained earnings, and balance sheet.
3. On the basis of your revised financial statements, identify any ethical dilemma you now face. Does the information regarding the season ticket revenue provide reliable information to an outsider? Does the $100,000 advertising revenue on the income statement represent the underlying economic reality of the transaction? Do you have a responsibility to share these revisions with the other three owners? What is your responsibility to the bank?
4. Using Exhibit 1-9 and the related text as your guide, analyze the key elements in the situation and answer the following questions. Support your answers by explaining your reasoning.

   a. Who may benefit or be harmed?
   b. How are they likely to benefit or be harmed?
   c. What rights or claims may be violated?
   d. What specific interests are in conflict?
   e. What are your responsibilities and obligations?
   f. Do you believe the information provided by the organization is relevant and is a faithful representation?

LO8 Decision Case 1-7 Responsibility for Financial Statements and the Role of the Auditor

Financial statements are the means by which accountants communicate to external users. Recent financial reporting scandals have focused attention on the accounting profession and its role in the preparation of these statements and the audits performed on the statements.

Required

1. Who is responsible for the preparation of the financial statements that are included in a company's annual report?
2. Who performs an audit of the financial statements referred to in part (1)?
3. Why is it important for those who are responsible for an audit of the financial statements to be independent of those who prepare the statements? Explain your answer.

SOLUTIONS TO KEY TERMS QUIZ

Quiz 1: Introduction to Business

15	Business	5	Nonbusiness entity
16	Business entity	7	Liability
13	Sole proprietorship	14	Capital stock
12	Economic entity concept	10	Stockholder
2	Partnership	11	Creditor
4	Corporation	1	Asset
8	Share of stock	3	Revenue
9	Bond	6	Expense

Quiz 2: Introduction to Accounting

4	Accounting	11	Generally accepted accounting principles (GAAP)
9	Management accounting		
5	Financial accounting	13	Securities and Exchange Commission (SEC)
6	Owners' equity		
3	Stockholders' equity	15	Financial Accounting Standards Board (FASB)
8	Retained earnings		
7	Balance sheet	17	American Institute of Certified Public Accountants (AICPA)
1	Income statement		
22	Net income	23	Certified Public Accountant (CPA)
10	Dividends	24	Public Company Accounting Oversight Board (PCAOB)
2	Statement of retained earnings		
25	Statement of cash flows	20	International Accounting Standards Board (IASB)
12	Cost principle		
14	Going concern	19	Auditing
16	Monetary unit	21	Sarbanes-Oxley Act
18	Time period		

ANSWERS TO POD REVIEW

LO1	1. c	2. a		**LO5**	1. b	2. a	3. b
LO2	1. c	2. d		**LO6**	1. d	2. a	
LO3	1. b	2. a	3. c	**LO7**	1. b	2. b	
LO4	1. c	2. b		**LO8**	1. c	2. b	

Financial Statements and the Annual Report

2

AFTER STUDYING THIS CHAPTER, YOU SHOULD BE ABLE TO:

LO1 Describe the objectives of financial reporting.

LO2 Describe the qualitative characteristics of accounting information.

LO3 Explain the concept and purpose of a classified balance sheet and prepare the statement.

LO4 Use a classified balance sheet to analyze a company's financial position.

LO5 Explain the difference between a single-step and a multiple-step income statement and prepare each type of income statement.

LO6 Use a multiple-step income statement to analyze a company's operations.

LO7 Identify the components of the statement of retained earnings and prepare the statement.

LO8 Identify the components of the statement of cash flows and prepare the statement.

LO9 Read and use the financial statements and other elements in the annual report of a publicly held company.

STUDY LINKS

A Look at the Previous Chapter Chapter 1 introduced how investors, creditors, and others use accounting and how the outputs of the accounting system—financial statements—are used in making business decisions. Chapter 1 introduced the Financial Decision Model and the Ethical Decision Framework—two of the three key decision tools needed for informed and ethical decision making.

A Look at This Chapter Chapter 2 takes a closer look at the financial statements as well as other elements that make up an annual report. It also introduces the third decision model needed for making financial decisions, the

Ratio Decision Model. Here you'll learn how to use financial statement numbers to develop ratios that reflect the financial trends of a business.

A Look at the Upcoming Chapter Chapter 3 steps back from a firm's financial statements to discuss how business transactions and the resulting accounting information are handled. The chapter begins by looking at transactions—what they are; how they are analyzed; and how accounting procedures facilitate turning them into journal entries, ledger accounts, and trial balances on which financial statements are based.

boysenberry

70% less sugar®
thick & creamy

strawberry

MAKING BUSINESS DECISIONS
GENERAL MILLS

If you were investing in a company, what would be more important to you—a brand name or financials that are in great shape? No question, brand names are the lifeblood of any consumer product company. **General Mills** boasts some of the most recognizable names in the world. Who cannot identify with Cheerios® and Wheaties® in General Mills's Big G division? Or is there anyone who is not familiar with the name Betty Crocker®? Finally, Yoplait® is a leader among U.S. yogurt brands.

But having great financials is essential to attracting investors and managing a business for growth. General Mills and **Kellogg's**, which was introduced in Chapter 1, compete in many of the same markets and have also reported similar financial results in recent years. Compare the Financial Highlights for General Mills shown on the next page with those for Kellogg's in Chapter 1. General Mills reported net sales for the 2010 fiscal year of $14.8 billion, compared to Kellogg's net sales of $12.4 billion. The similarities extend to the bottom line as well: General Mills reported net income of $1.5 billion, while Kellogg's net income was $1.2 billion.

The steady climb in earnings for both companies in recent years is commendable, especially in the face of a challenging economic environment. But with limited resources:

- How could you decide in which company to invest?

- What else can an income statement tell you that would help in making this decision?

- Does a balance sheet provide useful information about the company's future prospects?

- What does a statement of cash flows reveal about a company's performance that an income statement does not?

As you continue your study of accounting, you should look for answers to these questions as well as to a number of others:

- What makes a set of financial statements understandable to you? (See p. 58.)

- How can you distinguish a current asset from a long-term asset? a current liability from a long-term liability? (See pp. 63–65.)

- How can you use the numbers on a classified balance sheet to measure a company's liquidity? (See p. 78.)

- How can you use the numbers on an income statement to measure a company's profitability? (See pp. 79–80.)

- What useful nonfinancial information can be found in a company's annual report? (See pp. 81–83.)

Without understanding a company's financial statements, selecting a brand name to invest in can be a recipe for losing money.

	Our Fiscal 2010 Financial Highlights		
In Millions, Except per Share and Return on Capital Data	52 weeks ended May 30, 2010	53 weeks ended May 31, 2009	Change
Net Sales	$14,796	$14,691	+1%
Segment Operating Profit*	2,861	2,643	+8
Net Earnings Attributable to General Mills	1,530	1,304	+17
Diluted Earnings per Share (EPS)	2.24	1.90	+18
Adjusted Diluted EPS, Excluding Items Affecting Comparability[a]	2.30	1.99	+16
Return on Average Total Capital*	13.8%	12.3%	+150 basis pts.
Average Diluted Shares Outstanding	683	687	−1%
Dividends per Share	$ 0.96	$ 0.86	+12

*See page 87 for discussion of non-GAAP measures.

Data throughout this report reflects our two-for-one stock split with a record date of May 28, 2010.

Source: General Mills 2010 annual report.

Objectives of Financial Reporting

LO1 Describe the objectives of financial reporting.

OVERVIEW: Financial reporting has one overriding objective: to provide useful information to those who must make financial decisions.

A variety of external users need information to make sound business decisions, including stockholders, bondholders, bankers, and other types of creditors such as suppliers. These users must make an initial decision about investing in a company, regardless of whether it is in the form of a stock, a bond, or a note. The balance sheet, the income statement, and the statement of cash flows, along with the supporting notes and other information found in an annual report, are the key sources of information needed to make sound decisions. These statements are not intended to tell the reader the value of a company, but they should provide information that will allow the users to make their own estimates.

- The *balance sheet* tells what obligations will be due in the near future and what assets will be available to satisfy them.
- The *income statement* tells the revenues and expenses for a period of time.
- The *statement of cash flows* tells where cash came from and how it was used during the period.
- The *notes* provide essential details about the company's accounting policies and other key factors that affect its financial condition and performance.

Decision makers must understand the underlying accounting principles that have been applied to create the reported information in the statements. In preparing financial statements, accountants consider:

- The objectives of financial reporting.
- The characteristics that make accounting information useful.
- The most useful way to display the information found in the balance sheet, the income statement, and the statement of cash flows.

Financial information users are the main reason financial statements are prepared. After all, it is the investors, creditors, and other groups and individuals outside and inside the company who must make economic decisions based on these statements. Therefore, as you learned in Chapter 1, financial statements must be based on agreed-upon assumptions such as time period, going concern, and other GAAP.

Moreover, when the accountants for companies such as **General Mills** prepare their financial statements, they must keep in mind financial reporting objectives that are focused on providing the most understandable and useful information possible. **Financial reporting has one overall objective and a set of related objectives, all of them concerned with how the information may be most useful to the readers.**

The Objective of General-Purpose Financial Reporting

The objective of financial reporting is to provide financial information to permit external users of the information to make informed decisions. Users include both the management of a company (internal users) and others not involved in the daily operations of the business (external users). External users, such as investors and creditors, usually do not have access to the detailed records of the business or the benefit of daily involvement in the company's affairs. They make decisions based on *general-purpose financial statements* prepared by management. According to the FASB, the objective of financial reporting is to provide these external users with information about a company that will be useful in making decisions on whether to provide resources to the company.[1]

You can now see how closely the objective of financial reporting is tied to decision making. **The purpose of financial reporting is to help the users reach their decisions in an informed manner.** What types of information do these users need? How does the information they need relate to what is reported on financial statements? To answer these questions, consider the following:

- **Investors and Creditors Need Information about Prospective Cash Receipts**
  INVESTOR: If I buy stock in this company, how much cash will I receive:
  - In dividends?
  - From the sale of the stock?

  BANKER: If I lend money to this company, how much cash will I receive:
  - In interest on the loan?
  - When and if the loan is repaid?
- **The Company Needs Information about Its Own Prospective Cash Flows**
  Investors, bankers, and other users ultimately care about their cash receipts, but this depends to some extent on the company's skills in managing its *own* cash flows.
- **The Company Also Needs Information about Its Resources and Claims to Those Resources**
  A company's cash flows are inherently tied to the information on the:
  - Balance sheet (assets, liabilities, and owners' equity).
  - Income statement (revenues and expenses).
  - Statement of cash flows (operating, investing, and financing activities).

Example 2-1 Using Financial Reporting Objectives to Make Investment Decisions

---

Assume that you are trying to decide whether to buy stock in General Mills. Even though the financial reporting objectives may seem abstract, think about how they can be used to help make a decision.

Financial Reporting Objectives	Potential Investor's Questions
1. Provide information for decision making.	Based on the financial information, should I buy shares of stock in General Mills?
2. Reflect prospective cash receipts to investors and creditors.	How much cash, if any, will I receive in dividends each year and how much from the sale of the stock of General Mills in the future?
3. Reflect prospective cash flows to an enterprise.	After paying its suppliers and employees and meeting all of its obligations, how much cash will General Mills take in during the time I own the stock?
4. Reflect resources and claims to resources.	How much has General Mills invested in new buildings and equipment?

© Cengage Learning 2013

---

[1] *Statement of Financial Accounting Concepts [SFAC] No. 8, Conceptual Framework for Financial Reporting*, Chapter 1, "The Objective of General Purpose Financial Reporting" (Norwalk, Conn.: Financial Accounting Standards Board, October 2010).

LO1 Describe the objectives of financial reporting.

- The objective of financial reporting is to convey useful and timely information to parties for making economic decisions.
  - Decision makers include investors, creditors, and other individuals or groups inside and outside the firm.
- These decision makers need information to evaluate cash flows, resources of the company, and claims to those resources.

POD REVIEW 2.1

QUESTIONS   **Answers to these questions are on the last page of the chapter.**

1. The primary purpose of financial reporting is
   a. to help users reach decisions in an informed manner.
   b. to provide the information necessary to prepare a tax return.
   c. to provide a historical record of a company's performance.
   d. none of the above.

2. All of the following are important to decision makers except
   a. prospective cash receipts to investors and creditors.
   b. prospective cash flows to the company.
   c. the company's resources and claims to its resources.
   d. All of the above are important to decision makers.

What Makes Accounting Information Useful? Qualitative Characteristics

LO2 Describe the qualitative characteristics of accounting information.

OVERVIEW: To be useful, accounting information must be understandable and relevant to the decision being made. It must also be a faithful representation. Comparability and consistency are also important if statements are to be useful.

Since accounting information must be useful for decision making, what makes it useful? This section focuses on the qualities that accountants strive for in their financial reporting and on some challenges they face in making reporting judgments. It also reveals what users of financial information expect from financial statements.

Quantitative considerations such as tuition costs certainly were a concern when you chose your current school. In addition, you made subjective judgments about your college's *qualitative* characteristics. Similarly, certain qualities make accounting information useful.

Understandability

For anything to be useful, it must be understandable.

Understandability
The quality of accounting information that makes it comprehensible to those willing to spend the necessary time.

Usefulness and understandability go hand in hand. However, **understandability** of financial information varies considerably depending on the user's background. For example, should financial statements be prepared so that they are understandable by anyone with a college education? Or should it be assumed that all users have completed at least one accounting course? Is a background in business necessary for a good understanding of financial reports, regardless of one's formal training? There are no simple answers to these questions. However, **financial information should be comprehensible to** *those who are willing to spend the time to understand it.*

Understandability alone is certainly not enough to render information useful. According to the FASB, two fundamental characteristics make accounting information useful. The information must be **relevant**, and it must be a **faithful representation**.[2]

Relevance

To be useful, information must be relevant.

Relevance
The capacity of information to make a difference in a decision.

Relevance is the capacity of information to make a difference in a decision. Sometimes, information may have **predictive value**. For example, assume that you are a banker

---

[2] *Statement of Financial Accounting Concepts [SFAC] No. 8, Conceptual Framework for Financial Reporting*, Chapter 3, "Qualitative Characteristics of Useful Accounting Information" (Norwalk, Conn.: Financial Accounting Standards Board, October 2010).

evaluating the financial statements of a company seeking a loan. The financial statements point to a strong, profitable company. However, today's news revealed that the company has been named in a multimillion-dollar lawsuit. This information would be relevant to your talks with the company. Disclosure of the lawsuit in the financial statements would help you *predict* whether it would be wise to make a loan to the company.

In other cases, information may have **confirming value**. For example, assume you invest in a company because you think it may enter new Asian markets in the near future. Disclosure in the statements that the company acquired a Chinese subsidiary would *confirm* you made the right decision to invest in the company.

Faithful Representation

According to the FASB, information is a **faithful representation** when it is **complete**, **neutral**, and **free from error**. Information is neutral when it is not slanted to make a company's position look any better or worse than the actual circumstances would dictate—such as when the probable losses from a major lawsuit are disclosed accurately in the notes to the financial statements, with all potential effects on the company, rather than minimized as a very remote possible loss.

Faithful representation
The quality of information that makes it complete, neutral, and free from error.

Comparability and Consistency

Comparability allows comparisons to be made *between or among companies.*

GAAP allow a certain amount of freedom in choosing among alternative treatments for certain transactions.

For example, under GAAP, companies may choose from several methods of accounting for the depreciation of certain long-term assets. **Depreciation** is the *process of allocating* the cost of a long-term tangible asset, such as a building or equipment, over its useful life. Each method may affect the value of the assets differently. How does this freedom of choice affect investors' ability to compare companies?

Comparability
For accounting information, the quality that allows a user to analyze two or more companies and look for similarities and differences.

Depreciation
The process of allocating the cost of a long-term tangible asset over its useful life.

SPOTLIGHT
Reading Financial Statements Key to Successful Commercial Lending

Paul C. Stumb, Jr. is an Assistant Vice President at SunTrust Bank in Nashville, TN. According to Paul, the most important statements to review as a commercial lender are a company's balance sheet and income statement. Not only do these give an accurate picture of the current condition of a company (that is, year-to-date performance), but they provide the bank with an idea of how well the company is positioned to fare in future conditions. "If someone is seeking financing, we like to review at least three years of financial statement history. For existing clients, we generally receive monthly or quarterly financials to stay on top of what is going on in their company."

According to Paul, underwriting and credit analysis is an art, not a science. There are many factors that go into making an informed credit decision. For example, it is extremely important to have a complete understanding of a firm's operating cycle in order to make an informed lending decision. Financial analysis and accounting measures make up a large portion of what he does on a day-to-day basis.

For a bank to be comfortable lending money to a business or individual, it has to be comfortable with the quality and figures in the financial statements. You can't be successful in lending if you can't read the financial statements.

❝I have yet to meet a successful banker (in any field) that lacks a solid foundation in accounting. Accounting (especially financial accounting) is the root of lending.❞

Name: Paul C. Stumb, Jr.
Education: BS, Business Administration, Auburn University; MBA, Mississippi State University
College Major: Finance
Occupation: Commercial Banker
Age: 26
Position: Assistant Vice President, Commercial Banking Relationship Manager
Company Name: SunTrust Bank
See Paul Stumb's interview clip in CNOW.

© Cengage Learning 2013

Assume that you are considering buying stock in one of three companies. Their annual reports indicate that one company uses the "accelerated" depreciation method and the other two companies use the "straight-line" depreciation method. (We'll learn about these methods in Chapter 8.) Does this lack of a common depreciation method make it impossible to compare the performance of the three companies?

Obviously, comparing these companies would be easier and more meaningful if all three used the same depreciation method. However, comparisons are not impossible just because companies use different methods. Certainly, the more uniform statements are in terms of the principles used to prepare them, the more comparable they will be. However, the profession allows a certain freedom of choice in selecting from alternative GAAP.

To render statements of companies using different methods more meaningful, *disclosure* assumes a very important role. For example, as we will see later in this chapter, the first note in the annual report of a publicly traded company is the disclosure of its accounting policies. The reader of this note is made aware that the companies do not use the same depreciation method. Disclosure of accounting policies allows the reader to make a subjective adjustment to the statements of one or more of the companies and thus to compensate for the different depreciation method being used.

Consistency means that financial statements can be compared *within a single company from one accounting period to the next.* Consistency is closely related to comparability. Both involve the relationship between two numbers—comparability between numbers of different companies (usually for the same period) and comparability between the numbers of a single company for different periods. However, whereas financial statements are comparable when they can be compared between one company and another, statements are consistent when they can be compared within a single company from one accounting period to the next.

Occasionally, companies decide to change their accounting method. Will it be possible to compare a company's earnings in a period in which it switches methods with its earnings in prior years? Changes in accounting methods from one period to the next do not make comparisons impossible, only more difficult. When a company makes an accounting change, accounting standards require various disclosures to help the reader evaluate the impact of the change.

Materiality

For accounting information to be useful, it must be relevant to a decision.

Materiality is closely related to relevance and deals with the size of an error in accounting information. The issue is whether the error is large enough to affect the judgment of someone relying on the information. Suppose a company pays cash for two separate purchases: a $5 pencil sharpener and a $50,000 computer. Each expenditure results in the acquisition of an asset that should be depreciated over its useful life. However, what if the company decides to account for the $5 paid for the pencil sharpener as an expense of the period rather than treat it in the theoretically correct manner by depreciating it over the life of the pencil sharpener? *Will this error in any way affect the judgment of someone relying on the financial statements?* Because such a slight error will *not* affect any decisions, minor expenditures of this nature are considered *immaterial* and are accounted for as an expense of the period.

The *threshold* for determining materiality varies from one company to the next depending largely on the company's size. Many companies establish policies that *any* expenditure under a certain dollar amount should be accounted for as an expense of the period. The threshold might be $50 for the corner grocery store but $1,000 for a large corporation. Finally, the amount of a transaction may be immaterial by company standards but still be considered significant by financial statement users. For example, a transaction involving illegal or unethical behavior by a company officer would be of concern, regardless of the dollar amounts involved.

Conservatism

Conservatism is the practice of using the least optimistic estimate when two estimates of amounts are about equally likely. It is a holdover from earlier days when the

---

Consistency
For accounting information, the quality that allows a user to compare two or more accounting periods for a single company.

Materiality
The magnitude of an accounting information omission or misstatement that will affect the judgment of someone relying on the information.

Conservatism
The practice of using the least optimistic estimate when two estimates of amounts are about equally likely.

primary financial statement was the balance sheet and the primary user of this statement was the banker. It was customary to deliberately understate assets on the balance sheet because this resulted in an even larger margin of safety that the assets being provided as collateral for a loan were sufficient. Today, the balance sheet is not the only financial statement, and deliberate understatement of assets is no longer considered desirable. The practice of conservatism is reserved for those situations in which there is *uncertainty* about how to account for a particular item or transaction.

Various accounting rules are based on the concept of conservatism. For example, inventory held for resale is reported on the balance sheet at *the lower-of-cost-or-market value*. This rule requires a company to compare the cost of its inventory with the market price, or current cost to replace that inventory, and to report the lower of the two amounts on the balance sheet at year-end. Chapter 5 will more fully explore the lower-of-cost-or-market rule as it pertains to inventory.

Example 2-2 Summarizing the Characteristics That Make Information Useful

The various qualities that make information useful in making decisions can be summarized by asking a series of questions as follows:

Characteristic	Why Important?
Understandability	Must understand information to use it
Relevance	Must be information that could affect a decision
Faithful representation	Must be information that is complete, neutral, and free from error
Comparability	Must be able to compare with other companies
Consistency	Must be able to compare with prior years
Materiality	Must be an amount large enough to affect a decision
Conservatism	If any doubt, use the least optimistic estimate

© Cengage Learning 2013

An International Perspective on Qualitative Characteristics

Chapter 1 introduced the IASB and its efforts to improve the development of accounting standards around the world. Recently, this group completed a joint project with the FASB in this country on the conceptual framework of accounting. Now the objectives and qualitative characteristics of financial reporting as described in this chapter are the same for both groups.

© Kasia Biel/istockphoto.com

LO2 Describe the qualitative characteristics of accounting information.

- Qualitative characteristics make accounting information useful to financial statements users and include:
  - Understandability—pertains to those willing to spend time to understand the information.
  - Relevance—the capacity of information to make a difference in a decision.
  - Faithful representation—information that investors can depend on must be complete, neutral, and free from error.
  - Comparability and consistency—GAAP provide guidelines that standardize accounting practices and make information comparable from one company to another or from one period to the next for the same company.
  - Conservatism—where uncertainty about how to account for economic activity exists, accounting choices that result in the least optimistic amount should be employed.

POD REVIEW 2.2

QUESTIONS   Answers to these questions are on the last page of the chapter.

1. The accounting characteristic that allows for comparisons to be made within a single company from one period to the next is
   a. comparability.
   b. consistency.
   c. neutrality.
   d. materiality.

2. All of the following characteristics make accounting information useful except
   a. relevance.
   b. understandability.
   c. faithful representation.
   d. All of the above are characteristics of useful accounting information.

© Cengage Learning 2013

The Classified Balance Sheet

LO3 Explain the concept and purpose of a classified balance sheet and prepare the statement.

OVERVIEW: A classified balance sheet separates both assets and liabilities into current and noncurrent. Current assets will be realized in cash, sold, or consumed during the operating cycle or within one year if the cycle is shorter than one year. Current liabilities will be satisfied within the next cycle or within one year if the cycle is shorter than one year.

Now that we have learned about the conceptual framework of accounting, we turn to the outputs of the system: the financial statements. First, we will use a hypothetical company, Dixon Sporting Goods, to consider the significance of a *classified balance sheet*. We will then examine the *income statement*, the *statement of retained earnings*, and the *statement of cash flows* for this company. The chapter concludes with a brief look at the financial statements of General Mills and at the other elements in an annual report.[3]

Understanding the Operating Cycle

The first part of this chapter stressed the importance of *cash flow*. For a company that sells a product, the **operating cycle** begins when cash is invested in inventory and ends when cash is collected by the enterprise from its customers. Determining the operating cycle is a key skill in understanding any business.

Operating cycle
The period of time between the purchase of inventory and the collection of any receivable from the sale of the inventory.

Example 2-3 Determining the Operating Cycle

Consider the typical operating cycle for a bike shop. On August 1, the shop buys a bike from the manufacturer for $400. At this point, the shop has merely substituted one asset, cash, for another, inventory. On August 20, the shop sells it to a customer for $500. If the customer pays cash for the bike, the bike shop will have completed its cash-to-cash operating cycle in a total of 20 days, as shown below.

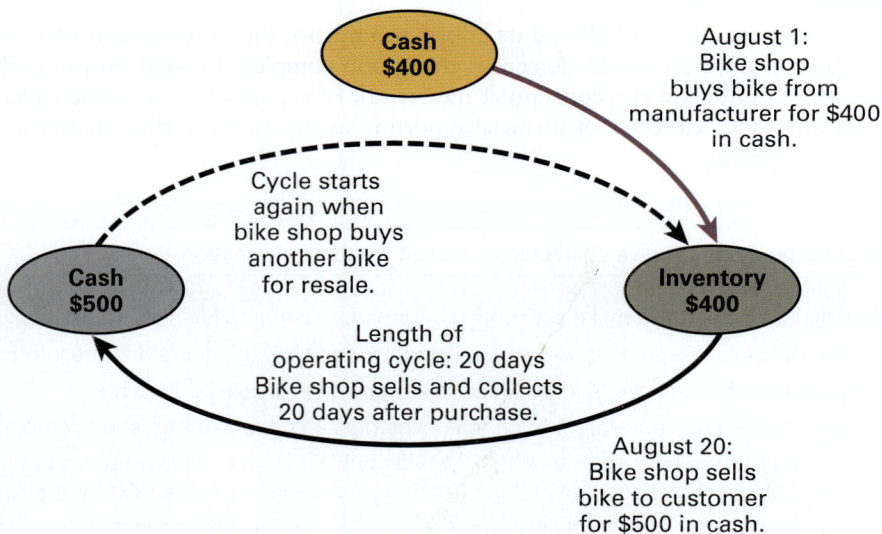

Consider how the shop's operating cycle is extended if it sells the same bike to a customer on August 20 and allows the customer to pay for it in 30 days. Instead of an operating cycle of 20 days, a total of 50 days has passed between the use of cash to buy the bike from the manufacturer and the collection of cash from the customer, as shown on the next page.

(Continued)

---

[3] The FASB is currently considering a number of changes in the format and presentation of the financial statements. Any changes in the financial statements have yet to be finalized.

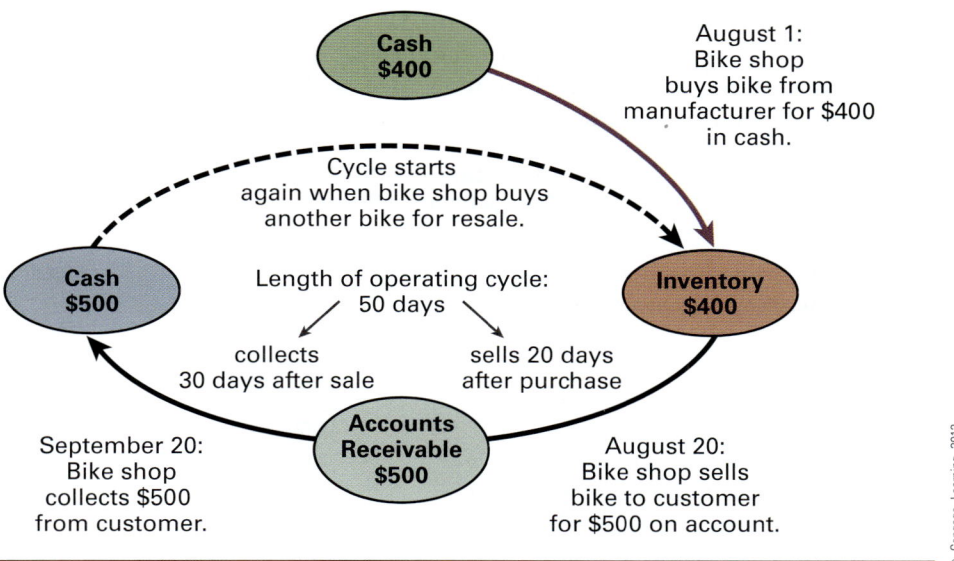

© Cengage Learning 2013

Current Assets

The basic distinction on a classified balance sheet is between current and noncurrent items. **Current assets** are "cash and other assets that are reasonably expected to be realized in cash or sold or consumed during the normal operating cycle of a business or within one year if the operating cycle is shorter than one year."[4]

The Current Assets section of Dixon Sporting Goods' balance sheet appears as follows:

Current asset
An asset that is expected to be realized in cash or sold or consumed during the operating cycle or within one year if the cycle is shorter than one year.

Dixon Sporting Goods Partial Balance Sheet	
Current assets	
Cash	$ 5,000
Marketable securities	11,000
Accounts receivable	23,000
Merchandise inventory	73,500
Prepaid insurance	4,800
Store supplies	700
Total current assets	$118,000

Most businesses have an operating cycle shorter than one year. For example, the bike shop's cycle in the second half of Example 2-3 was assumed to be 50 days. Therefore, for most companies, the cutoff for current classification is one year. We will use the one-year cutoff for current classification in the remainder of this chapter. Thus, on Dixon's balance sheet, cash, accounts receivable, and inventory are classified as current assets because they *are* cash or will be *realized* in (converted to) cash (accounts receivable) or will be *sold* (inventory) within one year.

In addition to cash, accounts receivable, and inventory, the two other most common types of current assets are marketable securities and prepaid expenses. Excess cash is often invested in the stocks and bonds of other companies as well as in various government instruments. If the investments are made for the short term, they are classified as current and are typically called *short-term investments* or *marketable securities*. (Alternatively, some investments are made for the purpose of exercising influence over another company and thus are made for the long term. These investments are classified as noncurrent assets.) Various prepayments, such as office supplies, rent, and insurance, are classified as *prepaid expenses* and thus are current assets. These assets qualify as current because they are usually *consumed* within one year.

---

[4] Accounting Principles Board, *Statement of the Accounting Principles Board, No. 4*, "Basic Concepts and Accounting Principles Underlying Financial Statements of Business Enterprises" (New York: American Institute of Certified Public Accountants, 1970), par. 198.

Noncurrent Assets

Any asset not meeting the definition of a current asset is classified as *long term* or *noncurrent*. Three common categories of long-term assets are investments; property, plant, and equipment; and intangibles. For Dixon, these are as follows:

Dixon Sporting Goods **Partial Balance Sheet**			
Investments			
Land held for future office site			$150,000
Property, plant, and equipment			
Land		$100,000	
Buildings	$150,000		
Less: Accumulated depreciation	60,000	90,000	
Store furniture and fixtures	$ 42,000		
Less: Accumulated depreciation	12,600	29,400	
Total property, plant, and equipment			219,400
Intangible assets			
Franchise agreement			55,000

Investments Recall from the discussion of current assets that stocks and bonds expected to be sold within the next year are classified as current assets. Securities not expected to be sold within the next year are classified as *investments*. In many cases, the investment is in the common stock of another company. Sometimes, companies invest in another company to exercise some influence over it or to control its operations. Other assets classified as investments are land held for future use and buildings and equipment not currently used in operations. Dixon classifies as an investment some land it holds for a future office site. A special fund held for the retirement of debt or for the construction of new facilities is also an investment.

Property, Plant, and Equipment This category consists of the various *tangible, productive assets* used in the operation of a business. Land, buildings, equipment, machinery, furniture and fixtures, trucks, and tools are all examples of assets held for use in the *operation* of a business rather than for *resale*. The distinction between inventory and equipment, for instance, depends on the company's *intent* in acquiring the asset. For example, **IBM** classifies a computer system as inventory because IBM's intent in manufacturing the asset is to offer it for resale. This same computer in the hands of a law firm would be classified as equipment because the firm's intent in buying the asset is to use it in the long-term operation of the business.

The relative size of property, plant, and equipment depends largely on a company's business. Consider **Carnival Cruise Corporation**, a cruise company with over $37 billion in total assets at the end of 2010. Carnival's property and equipment, including its ships, make up a very large portion of the company's total assets. In fact, this category accounted for nearly 83% of total assets. On the other hand, property and equipment represented only 8% of the total assets of **Microsoft** on March 31, 2011. Regardless of the relative size of property, plant, and equipment, all assets in this category are subject to depreciation except land. A separate accumulated depreciation account is used to account for the depreciation recorded on each of these assets over its life.

Intangibles Intangible assets are similar to property, plant, and equipment in that they provide benefits to the firm over the long term. The distinction, however, is in the *form* of the asset. *Intangible assets lack physical substance.* Trademarks, copyrights, franchise rights, patents, and goodwill are examples of intangible assets. The cost principle governs the accounting for intangibles, just as it does for tangible assets. For example, the amount paid to an inventor for the patent rights to a new project is recorded as an intangible asset. Similarly, the amount paid to purchase a franchise for a fast-food restaurant for the exclusive right to operate in a certain geographic area is recorded as an intangible asset. With a few exceptions, intangibles are written off to expense over their useful lives. *Depreciation* is the name given to the process of writing off tangible assets; the same process for intangible assets is called *amortization*. Depreciation and amortization are explained more fully in Chapter 8.

Current Liabilities

The definition of a current liability is closely tied to that of a current asset. A **current liability** is an obligation that will be satisfied within the next operating cycle or within one year if the cycle (as is normally the case) is shorter than one year. The classification of a note payable on the balance sheet depends on its maturity date. If the note will be paid within the next year, it is classified as current; otherwise, it is classified as a long-term liability. Accounts payable, wages payable, and income taxes payable are all short-term or current liabilities, as on Dixon's balance sheet:

Dixon Sporting Goods
Partial Balance Sheet

Current liabilities		
Accounts payable	$15,700	
Salaries and wages payable	9,500	
Income taxes payable	7,200	
Interest payable	2,500	
Bank loan payable	25,000	
Total current liabilities		$59,900

Most liabilities are satisfied by the payment of cash. However, certain liabilities are eliminated from the balance sheet when the company performs services. The liability Subscriptions Received in Advance, which would appear on the balance sheet of a magazine publisher, is satisfied not by the payment of any cash, but by delivery of the magazine to the customers. Finally, it is possible to satisfy one liability by substituting another in its place. A supplier might ask a customer to sign a written promissory note to replace an existing account payable if the customer is unable to pay at the present time.

Long-Term Liabilities

Any obligation that will not be paid or otherwise satisfied within the next year or the operating cycle, whichever is longer, is classified as a long-term liability, or long-term debt. Notes payable and bonds payable, both promises to pay money in the future, are two common forms of long-term debt. Some bonds have a life as long as 25 or 30 years. Dixon's notes payable for $120,000 is classified as a long-term liability because it is not due in the next year:

Dixon Sporting Goods
Partial Balance Sheet

Long-term debt	
Notes payable, due December 31, 2022	$120,000

Stockholders' Equity

Recall that stockholders' equity represents the owners' claims on the assets of the business that arise from two sources: *contributed capital* and *earned capital*. The Stockholders' Equity section of Dixon's balance sheet reports the following:

Dixon Sporting Goods
Partial Balance Sheet

Contributed capital		
Capital stock, $10 par, 5,000 shares issued and outstanding	$ 50,000	
Paid-in capital in excess of par value	25,000	
Total contributed capital	$ 75,000	
Retained earnings	287,500	
Total stockholders' equity		$362,500

Contributed capital appears on the balance sheet in the form of capital stock, and earned capital takes the form of retained earnings. *Capital stock* indicates the owners' investment in the business. *Retained earnings* represents the accumulated earnings, or net income, of the business since its inception less all dividends paid during that time.

Most companies have a single class of capital stock called *common stock*. This is the most basic form of ownership in a business. All other claims against the company, such as those of *creditors* and *preferred stockholders,* take priority. *Preferred stock* is a form of capital stock that carries with it certain preferences. For example, the company must pay dividends on preferred stock before it makes any distribution of dividends on common stock. In the event of liquidation, preferred stockholders have priority over common stockholders in the distribution of the entity's assets.

Capital stock may appear as two separate items on the balance sheet: *Par Value* and *Paid-In Capital in Excess of Par Value.* The total of these two items tells us the amount that has been paid by the owners for the stock. We will take a closer look at these items in Chapter 11.

Example 2-4 Preparing a Classified Balance Sheet

A classified balance sheet can be prepared using each of the categories presented in the previous section:

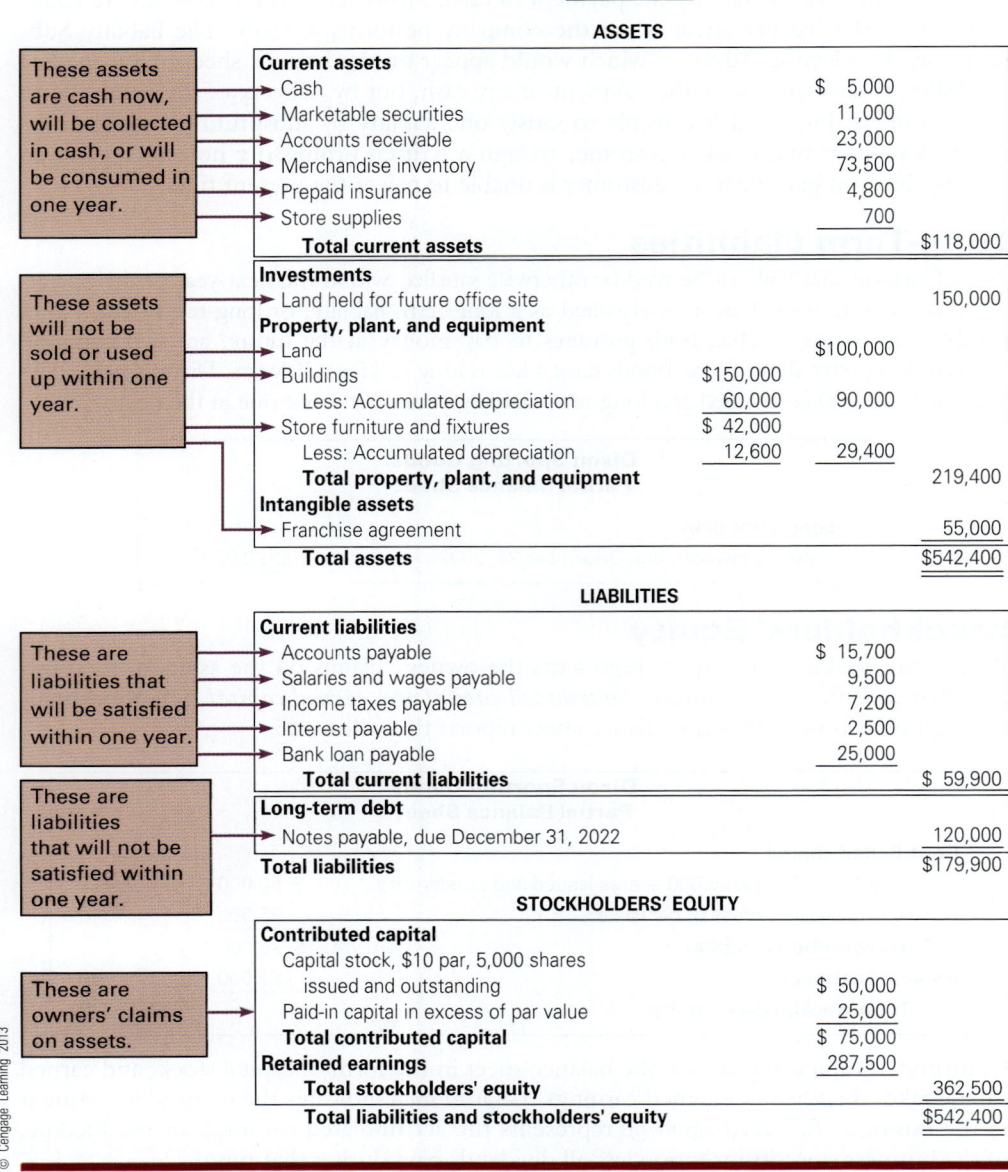

Dixon Sporting Goods
Balance Sheet
at December 31, 2012

ASSETS

These assets are cash now, will be collected in cash, or will be consumed in one year.

Current assets		
Cash		$ 5,000
Marketable securities		11,000
Accounts receivable		23,000
Merchandise inventory		73,500
Prepaid insurance		4,800
Store supplies		700
Total current assets		**$118,000**

These assets will not be sold or used up within one year.

Investments			
Land held for future office site			150,000
Property, plant, and equipment			
Land		$100,000	
Buildings	$150,000		
Less: Accumulated depreciation	60,000	90,000	
Store furniture and fixtures	$ 42,000		
Less: Accumulated depreciation	12,600	29,400	
Total property, plant, and equipment			219,400
Intangible assets			
Franchise agreement			55,000
Total assets			**$542,400**

LIABILITIES

These are liabilities that will be satisfied within one year.

Current liabilities		
Accounts payable		$ 15,700
Salaries and wages payable		9,500
Income taxes payable		7,200
Interest payable		2,500
Bank loan payable		25,000
Total current liabilities		**$ 59,900**

These are liabilities that will not be satisfied within one year.

Long-term debt		
Notes payable, due December 31, 2022		120,000
Total liabilities		**$179,900**

STOCKHOLDERS' EQUITY

These are owners' claims on assets.

Contributed capital		
Capital stock, $10 par, 5,000 shares		
issued and outstanding		$ 50,000
Paid-in capital in excess of par value		25,000
Total contributed capital		**$ 75,000**
Retained earnings		287,500
Total stockholders' equity		362,500
Total liabilities and stockholders' equity		**$542,400**

© Cengage Learning 2013

LO3 Explain the concept and purpose of a classified balance sheet and prepare the statement.

- The classified balance sheet classifies items of assets, liabilities, and stockholders' equity in a way that makes them useful to users of this financial statement.

- Assets and liabilities are classified according to the length of time they will serve the company or require its resources.

- Current assets or liabilities are those whose expected lives are one year or one operating cycle, whichever is longer. Noncurrent assets or liabilities are expected to last beyond this period of time.

- Assets and liabilities are further subclassified into categories that describe the nature of these assets and liabilities; for example, "Property, Plant, and Equipment."

POD REVIEW 2.3

QUESTIONS   **Answers to these questions are on the last page of the chapter.**

1. All of the following are examples of current assets except
   a. cash.
   b. prepaid insurance.
   c. land.
   d. accounts receivable.

2. A company has an obligation due in 2016. On a balance sheet prepared at the end of 2012, the obligation should be classified as
   a. a current asset.
   b. a current liability.
   c. a long-term debt.
   d. none of the above.

Using a Classified Balance Sheet: Introduction to Ratios

OVERVIEW: **A company's ability to pay its debts as they come due can be judged by computing the amount of working capital and the current ratio.**

LO4 Use a classified balance sheet to analyze a company's financial position.

A classified balance sheet separates assets and liabilities into those that are current and those that are noncurrent.

Working Capital

Investors, bankers, and other interested readers use the balance sheet to evaluate liquidity. **Liquidity** is a relative term and deals with the ability of a company to pay its debts as they come due. Bankers and other creditors are particularly interested in the liquidity of businesses to which they have lent money. A comparison of current assets and current liabilities is a starting point in evaluating a company's ability to meet its obligations. **Working capital** is the difference between current assets and current liabilities at a point in time. As Example 2-4 shows, Dixon Sporting Goods' working capital on December 31, 2012, is as follows:

Liquidity
The ability of a company to pay its debts as they come due.

Working capital
Current assets minus current liabilities.

Working Capital	
Formula	For Dixon Sporting Goods
Current Assets − Current Liabilities	$118,000 − $59,900 = $58,100

A company must continually strive for a *balance* in managing its working capital. Too little working capital—or in the extreme, negative working capital—may signal the inability to pay creditors on a timely basis. However, a large amount of working capital could indicate that the company is not investing enough of its available funds in productive resources such as new machinery and equipment.

Current Ratio

Because it is an absolute dollar amount, working capital is limited in its informational value. For example, $1 million may be an inadequate amount of working capital for a large corporation but far too much for a smaller company. In addition, a certain dollar amount of working capital may have been adequate for a company earlier in its life but is inadequate now. However, a related measure of liquidity, the **current ratio**, allows us

Current ratio
Current assets divided by current liabilities.

to *compare* the liquidity of companies of different sizes and of a single company over time. The ratio is computed by dividing current assets by current liabilities.

Example 2-5 Computing the Current Ratio

The following formula shows that Dixon Sporting Goods has a current ratio of just under 2 to 1:

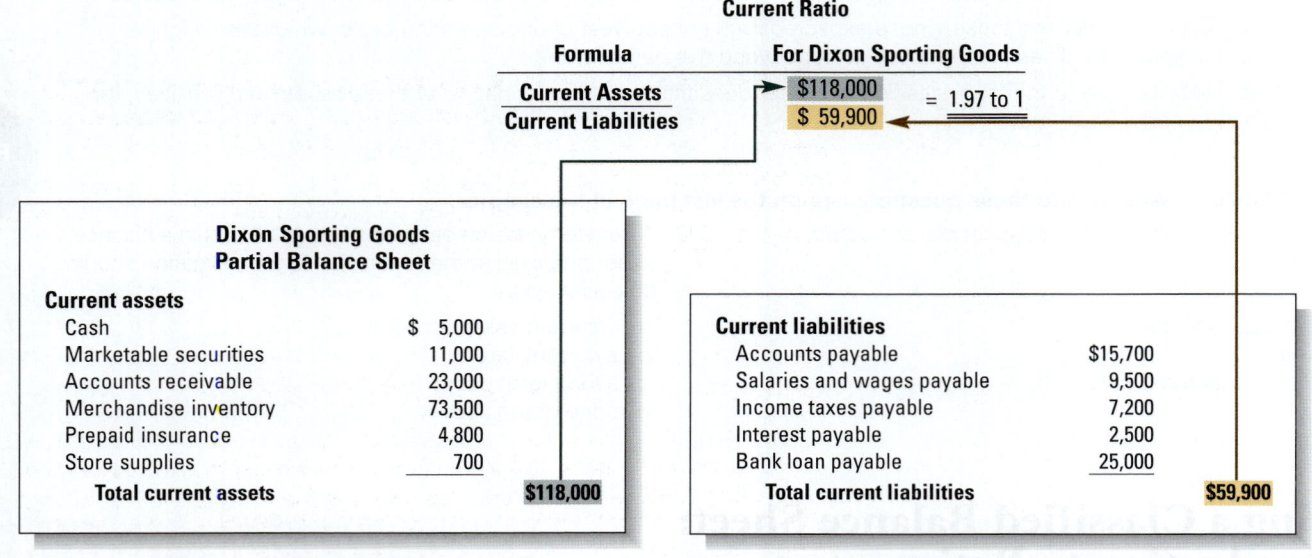

Current Ratio

Formula	For Dixon Sporting Goods
$\dfrac{\text{Current Assets}}{\text{Current Liabilities}}$	$\dfrac{\$118,000}{\$\ 59,900} = 1.97 \text{ to } 1$

Dixon Sporting Goods
Partial Balance Sheet

Current assets	
Cash	$ 5,000
Marketable securities	11,000
Accounts receivable	23,000
Merchandise inventory	73,500
Prepaid insurance	4,800
Store supplies	700
Total current assets	**$118,000**

Current liabilities	
Accounts payable	$15,700
Salaries and wages payable	9,500
Income taxes payable	7,200
Interest payable	2,500
Bank loan payable	25,000
Total current liabilities	**$59,900**

In general, the higher the current ratio, the more liquid the company. Some analysts use a rule of thumb of 2 to 1 for the current ratio as a sign of short-term financial health. However, rules of thumb can be dangerous. Historically, companies in certain industries have operated quite efficiently with a current ratio of less than 2 to 1, whereas a ratio much higher than that is necessary to survive in other industries. Consider **American Eagle Outfitters**. On January 29, 2011, it had a current ratio of 3.03. On the other hand, companies in the telephone communication business routinely have current ratios from well under 1 to 1. **AT&T**'s current ratio at the end of 2010 was only 0.59 to 1.

Unfortunately, neither the amount of working capital nor the current ratio tells us anything about the *composition* of current assets and current liabilities. For example, assume that two companies have total current assets equal to $100,000. Company A has cash of $10,000, accounts receivable of $50,000, and inventory of $40,000. Company B also has cash of $10,000 but accounts receivable of $20,000 and inventory of $70,000.

All other things being equal, Company A is more liquid than Company B because more of its total current assets are in receivables than inventory. Receivables are only one step away from being cash, whereas inventory must be sold and then the receivable collected. Note that Dixon's inventory of $73,500 makes up a large portion of its total current assets of $118,000. An examination of the *relative* size of the various current assets for a company may reveal certain strengths and weaknesses not evident in the current ratio.

In addition to the composition of the current assets, the *frequency* with which they are "turned over" is important. For instance, how long does it take to sell an item of inventory? How long is required to collect an account receivable? Many companies could not exist with the current ratio of 0.64 reported by **Delta Air Lines** at the end of 2010. However, think about the nature of the airline business. Without large amounts in inventories or accounts receivable, compared to a manufacturing company, an airline can operate with a lower current ratio.

LO4 Use a classified balance sheet to analyze a company's financial position.

- Balance sheet classifications allow users to analyze a company's financial position.
- Liquidity relates to the ability of a company to pay its obligations as they come due.
- Working capital and the current ratio are two measures of liquidity.

POD REVIEW 2.4

QUESTIONS   **Answers to these questions are on the last page of the chapter.**

1. Working capital is computed by

   a. dividing current assets by current liabilities.
   b. dividing current liabilities by current assets.
   c. deducting current liabilities from current assets.
   d. deducting current assets from current liabilities.

2. A company reports current assets of $50,000 and current liabilities of $20,000. Its current ratio is

   a. 0.40.
   b. 2.50.
   c. 1.00.
   d. none of the above.

The Income Statement

OVERVIEW: Gross profit, income from operations, and income before income taxes are all important subtotals on a multiple-step income statement.

LO5 Explain the difference between a single-step and a multiple-step income statement and prepare each type of income statement.

The income statement summarizes the results of operations of an entity for a *period of time*. At a minimum, all companies prepare income statements at least once a year. Companies that must report to the SEC prepare financial statements, including an income statement, every three months. Monthly income statements are usually prepared for internal use by management.

What Appears on the Income Statement?

It is important to understand what transactions of an entity should appear on the income statement. In general, the income statement reports the excess of revenue over expense—that is, the *net income* (or in the event of an excess of expense over revenue, the net loss of the period). It is common to use the term *profits* or *earnings* as a synonym for *net income*.

As discussed in Chapter 1, *revenue* is the inflow of assets resulting from the sale of products and services. Revenue is the dollar amount of sales of products and services for a period of time. An *expense* is the outflow of assets resulting from the sale of goods and services for a period of time. Wages and salaries, utilities, and taxes are examples of expenses.

Certain special types of revenues, *called gains*, are sometimes reported on the income statement, as are certain special types of expenses, called *losses*. For example, assume that Sanders Company holds a parcel of land for a future building site. It paid $50,000 for the land ten years ago. The state pays Sanders $60,000 for the property to use in a new highway project. Sanders has a special type of revenue from the condemnation of its property. It will recognize a *gain* of $10,000: the excess of the cash received from the state, $60,000, over the cost of the land, $50,000.

Format of the Income Statement

Corporations use one of two formats to prepare the income statement: single-step or multiple-step form. Both forms are generally accepted, although more companies use the multiple-step form. Next, we'll explain the differences between the two forms.

Single-Step Format for the Income Statement In a **single-step income statement**, all expenses and losses are added together and then deducted *in a single step* from all revenues and gains to arrive at net income.

Single-step income statement An income statement in which all expenses are added together and subtracted from all revenues.

Example 2-6 Preparing a Single-Step Income Statement

A single-step format for the income statement of Dixon Sporting Goods is presented below. The primary advantage of the single-step form is its simplicity. No attempt is made to classify revenues or expenses or to associate any of the expenses with any of the revenues.

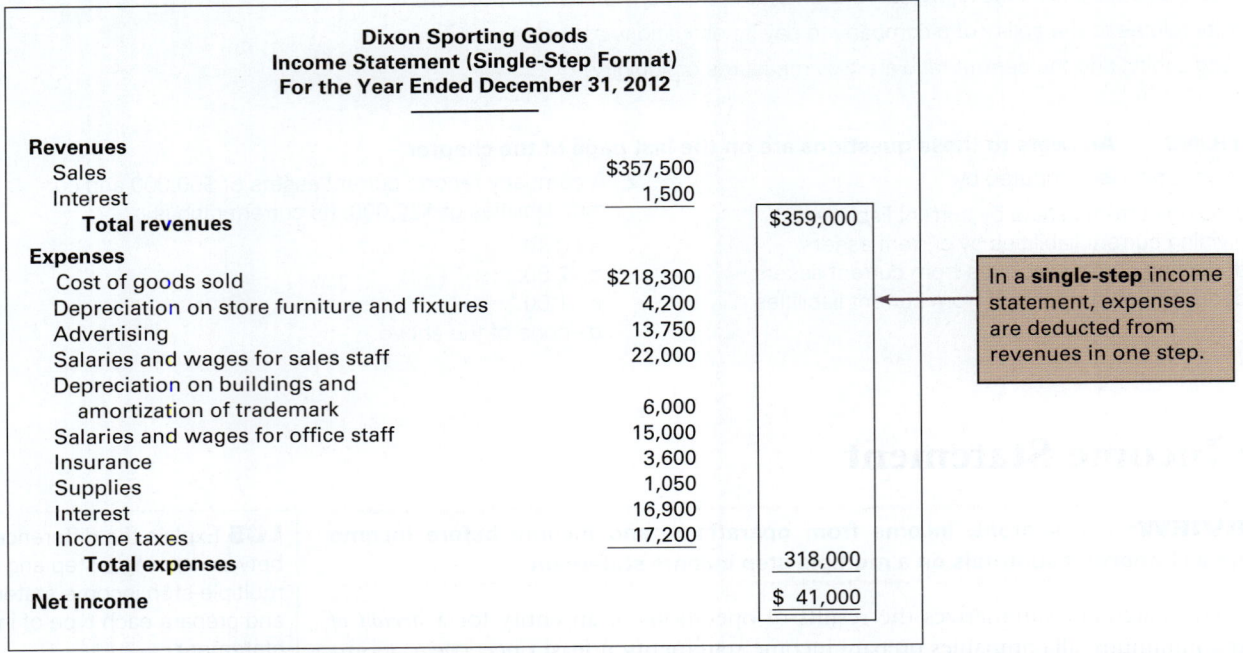

Dixon Sporting Goods
Income Statement (Single-Step Format)
For the Year Ended December 31, 2012

Revenues		
Sales	$357,500	
Interest	1,500	
Total revenues		$359,000
Expenses		
Cost of goods sold	$218,300	
Depreciation on store furniture and fixtures	4,200	
Advertising	13,750	
Salaries and wages for sales staff	22,000	
Depreciation on buildings and amortization of trademark	6,000	
Salaries and wages for office staff	15,000	
Insurance	3,600	
Supplies	1,050	
Interest	16,900	
Income taxes	17,200	
Total expenses		318,000
Net income		$ 41,000

> In a **single-step** income statement, expenses are deducted from revenues in one step.

Multiple-step income statement
An income statement that shows classifications of revenues and expenses as well as important subtotals.

Gross profit
Sales less cost of goods sold.

Multiple-Step Format for the Income Statement

The purpose of the **multiple-step income statement** is to subdivide the income statement into specific sections and provide the reader with important subtotals.

Example 2-7 Preparing a Multiple-Step Income Statement

The multiple-step format is illustrated for Dixon Sporting Goods below. The multiple-step income statement for Dixon (shown on the next page) indicates three important subtotals.

First, ❶ cost of goods sold is deducted from sales to arrive at **gross profit**:

Gross Profit = Sales − Cost of Goods Sold	
Sales	$357,500
Cost of goods sold	218,300
Gross profit	$139,200

Cost of goods sold is the cost of the units of inventory sold during the year. It is logical to associate cost of goods sold with the sales revenue for the year because the latter represents the *selling price* of the inventory sold during the period.

The second important subtotal on Dixon's income statement is ❷ *income from operations* of $73,600. This is found by subtracting *total operating expenses* of $65,600 from the gross profit of $139,200. Operating expenses are further subdivided between *selling expenses* and *general and administrative expenses*. Note that two depreciation amounts are included in operating expenses. Depreciation on store furniture and fixtures is classified as a selling expense because the store is where sales take place. On the other hand, assume that the buildings are offices for the administrative staff; thus, depreciation on the buildings is classified as a general and administrative expense.

The third important subtotal on the income statement is ❸ *income before income taxes* of $58,200. Interest revenue and interest expense, neither of which is an operating item, are

(Continued)

included in *other revenues and expenses.* The excess of interest expense of $16,900 over interest revenue of $1,500, which equals $15,400, is subtracted from income from operations to arrive at income before income taxes. Finally, ❹ *income tax expense* of $17,200 is deducted to arrive at *net income* of $41,000.

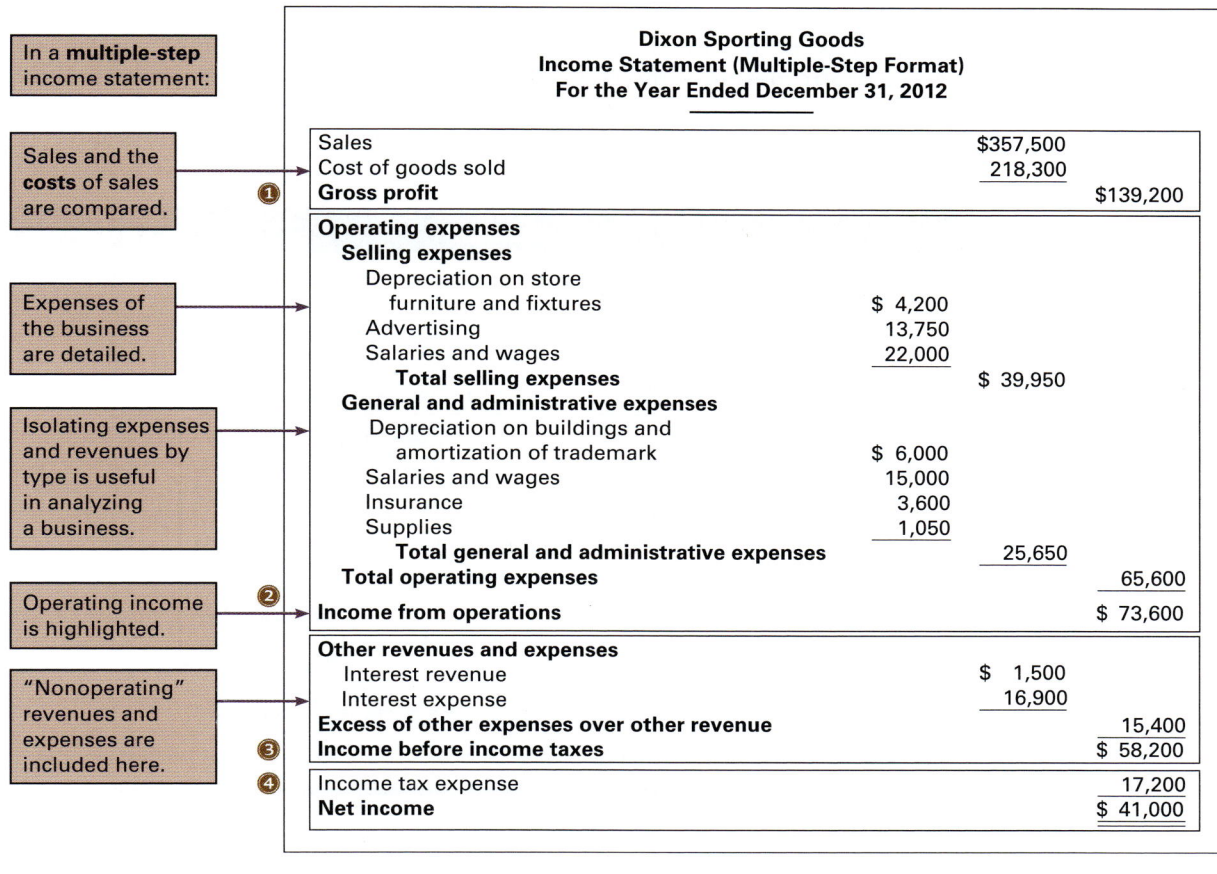

In a **multiple-step** income statement:

Sales and the **costs** of sales are compared.

Expenses of the business are detailed.

Isolating expenses and revenues by type is useful in analyzing a business.

Operating income is highlighted.

"Nonoperating" revenues and expenses are included here.

Dixon Sporting Goods
Income Statement (Multiple-Step Format)
For the Year Ended December 31, 2012

Sales			$357,500
Cost of goods sold			218,300
Gross profit			**$139,200**
Operating expenses			
Selling expenses			
Depreciation on store			
furniture and fixtures		$ 4,200	
Advertising		13,750	
Salaries and wages		22,000	
Total selling expenses		$ 39,950	
General and administrative expenses			
Depreciation on buildings and			
amortization of trademark		$ 6,000	
Salaries and wages		15,000	
Insurance		3,600	
Supplies		1,050	
Total general and administrative expenses		25,650	
Total operating expenses			65,600
Income from operations			**$ 73,600**
Other revenues and expenses			
Interest revenue		$ 1,500	
Interest expense		16,900	
Excess of other expenses over other revenue			15,400
Income before income taxes			**$ 58,200**
Income tax expense			17,200
Net income			**$ 41,000**

LO5 Explain the difference between a single-step and a multiple-step income statement and prepare each type of income statement.

- The multiple-step income statement classifies revenues and expenses in a manner that makes the statement more useful than the simple single-step income statement. Important subtotals are presented in the multiple-step income statement, including the following:
- Gross profit
- Income from operations
- Income before income taxes

POD REVIEW 2.5

QUESTIONS   **Answers to these questions are on the last page of the chapter.**

1. The income statement summarizes the results of operations
   a. at a given point in time.
   b. for a period of time.
   c. since a company began its business.
   d. none of the above.

2. Which of the following would appear on a multiple-step income statement but not on a single-step income statement?
   a. total revenues
   b. total expenses
   c. income before income taxes
   d. net income

Using an Income Statement

LO6 Use a multiple-step income statement to analyze a company's operations.

Profit margin
Net income divided by sales.

Alternate term: Return on sales.

OVERVIEW: A company's profit margin, computed by dividing net income by sales, is a good indicator of its profitability.

An important use of the income statement is to evaluate the *profitability* of a business. A company's **profit margin** is the ratio of its net income to its sales or revenues. Some analysts refer to a company's profit margin as its *return on sales*. If the profit margin is high, this generally means that the company is generating revenue but that it is also controlling its costs.

Example 2-8 Computing the Profit Margin

Dixon Sporting Goods would compute its profit margin by dividing its net income by its total sales as follows:

Profit Margin

Formula	For Dixon Sporting Goods
$\dfrac{\text{Net Income}}{\text{Sales}}$	$\dfrac{\$41,000}{\$357,500} = 11\%$

Dixon Sporting Goods
Partial Income Statement

Sales	$357,500
Net income	$41,000

© Cengage Learning 2013

A profit margin of 11% tells you that for every dollar of sales, Dixon has $0.11 in net income.

Keep two key factors in mind when evaluating any financial statement ratio.

- **How does this year's ratio differ from ratios of prior years?** A decrease in the profit margin may indicate that the company is having trouble controlling certain costs.
- **How does the ratio compare with industry norms?** In some industries, the profit margin is considerably lower than in others, such as in mass merchandising. (Although **Wal-Mart's** profit margin was only 3.9% for the year ended January 31, 2011, net income reached a record level of $16.4 billion.) It is helpful to compare key ratios such as the profit margin with an industry average or with the same ratio for a close competitor of the company.

POD REVIEW 2.6

LO6 Use a multiple-step income statement to analyze a company's operations.

- The multiple-step income statement can be used to evaluate different aspects of a company's profitability.
- Profit margin is one useful ratio used to evaluate the relative profitability.

QUESTIONS   Answers to these questions are on the last page of the chapter.

1. Profit margin is computed by
   a. dividing net income by operating revenues.
   b. dividing operating revenues by net income.
   c. deducting net income from operating revenues.
   d. none of the above.

2. In evaluating a company's profit margin, it is important to compare it with
   a. prior years.
   b. industry norms.
   c. both prior years and industry norms.
   d. neither prior years nor industry norms.

© Cengage Learning 2013

The Statement of Retained Earnings

OVERVIEW: The statement of retained earnings reports the net income and any dividends declared during the period. It is an important link between the income statement and the balance sheet.

LO7 Identify the components of the statement of retained earnings and prepare the statement.

The purpose of a statement of stockholders' equity is to explain the changes in the components of owners' equity during the period. Retained earnings and capital stock are the two primary components of stockholders' equity. If during the period no changes occur in a company's capital stock, the company may choose to present a statement of retained earnings instead of a statement of stockholders' equity.

Example 2-9 Preparing a Statement of Retained Earnings

A statement of retained earnings for Dixon Sporting Goods is shown below.

Dixon Sporting Goods
Statement of Retained Earnings
For the Year Ended December 31, 2012

Retained earnings, January 1, 2012	$271,500
Add: Net income for 2012	41,000
	$312,500
Less: Dividends declared and paid in 2012	(25,000)
Retained earnings, December 31, 2012	$287,500

The statement of retained earnings provides an important link between the income statement and the balance sheet. Dixon's net income of $41,000, as detailed on the income statement, is an *addition* to retained earnings. Note that the dividends declared and paid of $25,000 do not appear on the income statement because they are a payout, or *distribution,* of net income to stockholders rather than one of the expenses deducted to arrive at net income. Accordingly, they appear as a direct deduction on the statement of retained earnings. The beginning balance in retained earnings is carried forward from last year's statement of retained earnings.

© Cengage Learning 2013

LO7 Identify the components of the statement of retained earnings and prepare the statement.

- The statement of retained earnings provides a link between the income statement and the balance sheet.
- It explains the changes in retained earnings during the period, of which net income (loss) is an important component.

POD REVIEW 2.7

QUESTIONS   Answers to these questions are on the last page of the chapter.

1. Which of the following indicates the proper treatment of net income and dividends on a statement of retained earnings?
   a. Net income is added and dividends are deducted.
   b. Net income is deducted and dividends are added.
   c. Net income is added and dividends are added.
   d. Net income is deducted and dividends are deducted.

2. Dividends are reported on
   a. the income statement and the statement of retained earnings.
   b. the income statement but not the statement of retained earnings.
   c. the statement of retained earnings but not the income statement.
   d. neither the income statement nor the statement of retained earnings.

© Cengage Learning 2013

The Statement of Cash Flows

LO8 Identify the components of the statement of cash flows and prepare the statement.

OVERVIEW: The statement of cash flows summarizes a company's operating, investing, and financing activities for the period.

All publicly held corporations are required to present a statement of cash flows in their annual reports. **The purpose of the statement is to summarize the cash flow effects of a company's operating, investing, and financing activities for the period.** Each of these categories can result in a net inflow or a net outflow of cash.

- Dixon's **operating activities** generated $56,100 of cash during the period, as shown below. Operating activities concern the purchase and sale of a product—in this case, the acquisition of sporting goods from distributors and the subsequent sale of those goods. Dixon had one major source of cash, the collection from its customers of $362,500. Dixon's largest use of cash was the $217,200 it paid for inventory. Chapter 12 discusses the statement of cash flows in detail and the preparation of this section of the statement.

Dixon Sporting Goods Partial Statement of Cash Flows		
CASH FLOWS FROM OPERATING ACTIVITIES		
Cash collected from customers	$362,500	
Cash collected in interest	1,500	
Total cash collections		$364,000
Cash payments for:		
Inventory	$217,200	
Salaries and wages	38,500	
Interest	16,900	
Store supplies	850	
Insurance	4,800	
Advertising	13,750	
Income taxes	15,900	
Total cash payments		307,900
Net cash provided by operating activities		$ 56,100

Investing and financing activities were described in Chapter 1.

- **Investing activities** involve the acquisition and sale of long-term or noncurrent assets such as long-term investments; property, plant, and equipment; and intangible assets.

Dixon Sporting Goods Partial Statement of Cash Flows	
CASH FLOWS FROM INVESTING ACTIVITIES	
Purchase of land for future office site	$(150,000)

Dixon spent $150,000 for land for a future office site. This is an investing activity.

- **Financing activities** result from the issuance and repayment, or retirement, of long-term liabilities and capital stock and the payment of dividends.

Dixon Sporting Goods Partial Statement of Cash Flows		
CASH FLOWS FROM FINANCING ACTIVITIES		
Dividends declared and paid	$ (25,000)	
Proceeds from issuance of long-term note	120,000	
Net cash provided by financing activities		$95,000

Dixon had two financing activities: dividends of $25,000 required the use of cash, and the issuance of a long-term note generated cash of $120,000.

Example 2-10 Preparing a Statement of Cash Flows

The complete cash flow statement for Dixon Sporting Goods is given below. The balance of cash on the bottom of the statement of $5,000 must agree with the balance for cash shown on the balance sheet in Example 2-4.

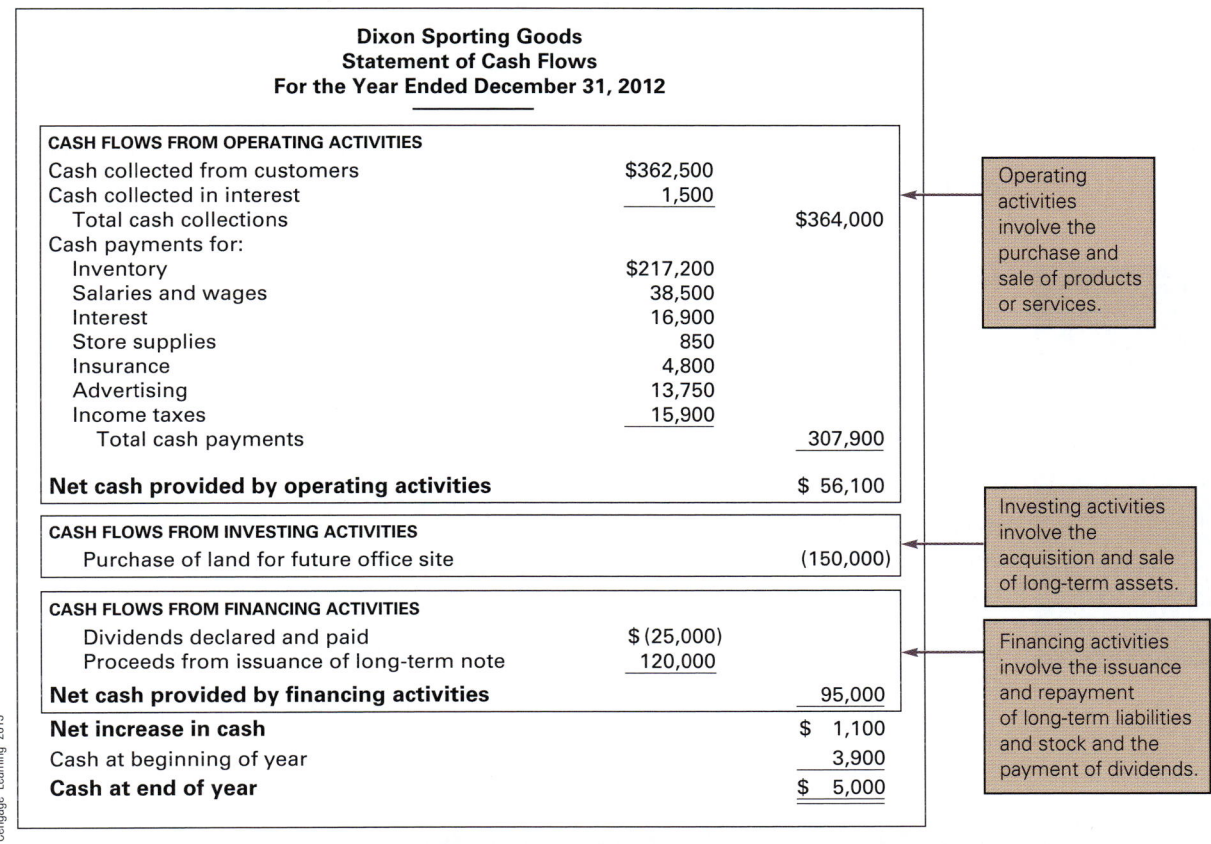

Dixon Sporting Goods
Statement of Cash Flows
For the Year Ended December 31, 2012

CASH FLOWS FROM OPERATING ACTIVITIES		
Cash collected from customers	$362,500	
Cash collected in interest	1,500	
Total cash collections		$364,000
Cash payments for:		
Inventory	$217,200	
Salaries and wages	38,500	
Interest	16,900	
Store supplies	850	
Insurance	4,800	
Advertising	13,750	
Income taxes	15,900	
Total cash payments		307,900
Net cash provided by operating activities		**$ 56,100**
CASH FLOWS FROM INVESTING ACTIVITIES		
Purchase of land for future office site		(150,000)
CASH FLOWS FROM FINANCING ACTIVITIES		
Dividends declared and paid	$ (25,000)	
Proceeds from issuance of long-term note	120,000	
Net cash provided by financing activities		95,000
Net increase in cash		$ 1,100
Cash at beginning of year		3,900
Cash at end of year		**$ 5,000**

Operating activities involve the purchase and sale of products or services.

Investing activities involve the acquisition and sale of long-term assets.

Financing activities involve the issuance and repayment of long-term liabilities and stock and the payment of dividends.

© Cengage Learning 2013

LO8 Identify the components of the statement of cash flows and prepare the statement.

- The statement of cash flows classifies cash inflows and outflows as originating from three activities: operating, investing, and financing.
- Operating activities are related to the primary purpose of a business.
- Investing activities are those generally involved with the acquisition and sale of noncurrent assets.
- Financing activities are related to the acquisition and repayment of capital that ultimately funds the operations of a business; for example, issuing stock or borrowing.

POD REVIEW 2.8

QUESTIONS Answers to these questions are on the last page of the chapter.

1. The three categories of activities reported on a statement of cash flows are
   a. operating, investing, and producing.
   b. operating, investing, and financing.
   c. investing, financing, and selling.
   d. none of the above.

2. The purchase of new equipment would be reported on a statement of cash flows as
   a. an operating activity.
   b. a financing activity.
   c. an investing activity.
   d. none of the above.

© Cengage Learning 2013

Looking at Financial Statements for a Real Company: General Mills, Inc.

OVERVIEW: The financial statements of real companies are similar to those we have just seen, although more complex. In addition to the financial statements, other elements are included in a company's annual report, including the auditors' report, management's discussion and analysis, and the notes to the financial statements.

Dixon's financial statements introduced the major categories on each of the statements. We now turn to these categories on the financial statements of an actual company, General Mills. The statements for a real company are more complex and require additional analysis and a better understanding of accounting to fully appreciate them. Therefore, we will concentrate on certain elements of the statements.

General Mills's Balance Sheet

Balance sheets for General Mills are shown in Exhibit 2-1. General Mills releases what are called *consolidated financial statements*, which reflect the position and results of all operations that are controlled by a single entity. Like most other large corporations, General Mills owns other companies. Often, these companies are legally separate and are called *subsidiaries*. How a company accounts for its investment in a subsidiary is covered in advanced accounting courses.

General Mills presents comparative balance sheets to indicate its financial position at the end of each of the last two years. As a minimum standard, the SEC requires that the annual report include balance sheets as of the two most recent year-ends and income statements for each of the three most recent years. Note that all amounts on the balance sheet are stated in millions of dollars. This type of rounding is common and is justified under the materiality concept. Knowing the exact dollar amount of each asset would not change an investor's decision.

The current ratio was introduced earlier in the chapter. We will use the information on General Mills's balance sheet to analyze its current ratio. (See page 78.)

General Mills's Income Statement

We have already examined the single- and multiple-step formats for the income statement. In practice, numerous variations on these two basic formats exist, depending to a large extent on the nature of a company's business.

Multiple-step income statements for General Mills for a three-year period are presented in Exhibit 2-2, on page 79. The inclusion of three years allows the reader to note certain general trends during this period. For example, note the steady increase in net sales during this period. In fact, the increase in net sales from the first year, 2008, to the third year, 2010, can be calculated as:

Increase in net sales from 2008 to 2010:
Net sales in 2008

$$\frac{\$14{,}796.5 - \$13{,}652.1}{\$13{,}652.1} = \frac{\$1{,}144.4}{\$13{,}652.1} = 8.4\%$$

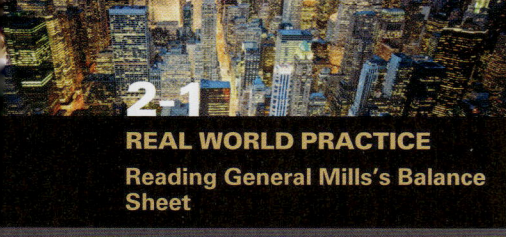

2-1

REAL WORLD PRACTICE

Reading General Mills's Balance Sheet

What was the amount of working capital at May 30, 2010? at May 31, 2009? Did the company's total assets increase or decrease during the year?

2-2

REAL WORLD PRACTICE

Reading General Mills's Income Statements

Compute the percentage increase in General Mills's net income over the three years. That is, by what percent did it increase from 2008 to 2010? Compare the percentage increase in net income to the percentage increase in net sales. What does a comparison of the two tell you?

© Nikada/istockphoto.com

EXHIBIT 2-1 Comparative Balance Sheets for General Mills, Inc.

Consolidated Balance Sheets General Mills, Inc. and Subsidiaries (In Millions, Except Par Value)		
Assets	**May 30, 2010**	**May 31, 2009**
Current assets:		
Cash and cash equivalents	$ 673.2	$ 749.8
Receivables	1,041.6	953.4
Inventories	1,344.0	1,346.8
Deferred income taxes	42.7	15.6
Prepaid expenses and other current assets	378.5	469.3
Total current assets	3,480.0	3,534.9
Land, buildings, and equipment	3,127.7	3,304.9
Goodwill	6,592.8	6,663.0
Other intangible assets	3,715.0	3,747.0
Other assets	763.4	895.0
Total assets	$17,678.9	$17,874.8
Liabilities and Equity		
Current liabilities:		
Accounts payable	$ 849.5	$ 803.4
Current portion of long-term debt	107.3	508.5
Notes payable	1,050.1	812.2
Other current liabilities	1,762.2	1,481.9
Total current liabilities	3,769.1	3,606.0
Long-term debt	5,268.5	5,754.8
Deferred income taxes	874.6	1,165.3
Other liabilities	2,118.7	1,932.2
Total liabilities	12,030.9	12,458.3
Stockholders' equity:		
Common stock, 754.6 shares issued, $0.10 par value	75.5	75.5
Additional paid-in capital	1,307.1	1,212.1
Retained earnings	8,122.4	7,235.6
Common stock in treasury, at cost, shares of 98.1 and 98.6	(2,615.2)	(2,473.1)
Accumulated other comprehensive loss	(1,486.9)	(877.8)
Total stockholders' equity	5,402.9	5,172.3
Noncontrolling interests	245.1	244.2
Total equity	5,648.0	5,416.5
Total liabilities and equity	$17,678.9	$17,874.8
See accompanying notes to consolidated financial statements.		

> Look at the headings on comparative balance sheets to see whether the most recent year-end is placed before or after the prior year's year-end. General Mills places the latest year on the left, which is the most common technique.

Source: General Mills 2010 annual report

USING THE RATIO DECISION MODEL

Analyzing the Current Ratio

Use the following Ratio Decision Model to evaluate the current ratio for General Mills or any other public company.

1. Formulate the Question

Managers, investors, and creditors are all interested in a company's liquidity. They must be able to answer the following question:

Is the company liquid enough to pay its obligations as they come due?

2. Gather the Information from the Financial Statements

The current ratio measures liquidity. To calculate the ratio, it is essential to know a company's current assets and liabilities. Current assets are the most liquid of all assets. Current liabilities are the debts that will be paid the soonest.

- Current assets: From the balance sheet
- Current liabilities: From the balance sheet

3. Calculate the Ratio

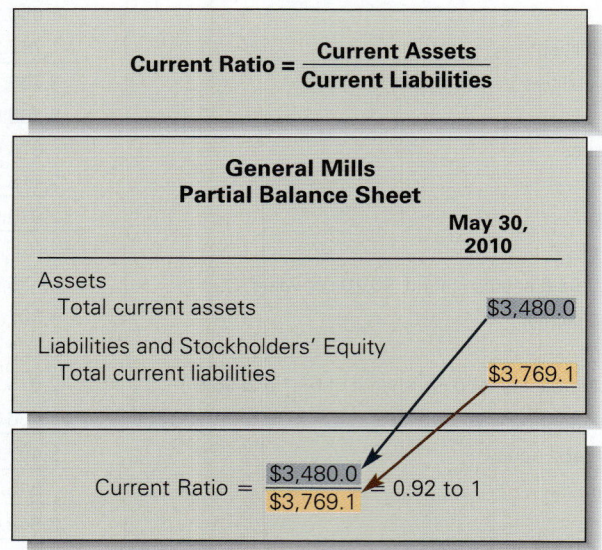

4. Compare the Ratio with Others

Ratios are of no use in a vacuum. It is necessary to compare them with prior years and with competitors.

General Mills		Kellogg's	
May 30, 2010	**May 31, 2009**	**January 1, 2011**	**January 2, 2010**
0.92 to 1	0.98 to 1	0.92 to 1	1.12 to 1

5. Interpret the Results

In general, the higher the current ratio, the more liquid the company. However, the rules of thumb do not always apply. It is necessary to take into account the nature of a company's business when evaluating ratios and other measures of performance. Also, ratios should be compared with those of prior years and with the same ratios of competitors. However, the year-end is different for General Mills (end of May) and Kellogg's (end of December). Both companies operate with a relatively low current ratio compared to companies in other industries. ∎

EXHIBIT 2-2 Comparative Income Statements for General Mills, Inc.

Consolidated Statements of Earnings General Mills, Inc. and Subsidiaries (In Millions, Except per Share Data)	Fiscal Year		
	2010	2009	2008
Net sales	$14,796.5	$14,691.3	$13,652.1
Cost of sales	8,922.9	9,457.8	8,778.3
Selling, general, and administrative expenses	3,236.1	2,951.8	2,623.6
Divestitures (gain), net	—	(84.9)	—
Restructuring, impairment, and other exit costs	31.4	41.6	21.0
Operating profit	2,606.1	2,325.0	2,229.2
Interest, net	401.6	382.8	399.7
Earnings before income taxes and after-tax earnings from joint ventures	2,204.5	1,942.2	1,829.5
Income taxes	771.2	720.4	622.2
After-tax earnings from joint ventures	101.7	91.9	110.8
Net earnings, including earnings attributable to noncontrolling interests	$ 1,535.0	$ 1,313.7	$ 1,318.1
Net earnings attributable to noncontrolling interests	4.5	9.3	23.4
Net earnings attributable to General Mills	$ 1,530.5	$ 1,304.4	$ 1,294.7
Earnings per share—basic	$ 2.32	$ 1.96	$ 1.93
Earnings per share—diluted	$ 2.24	$ 1.90	$ 1.85
Dividends per share	$ 0.96	$ 0.86	$ 0.78

See accompanying notes to consolidated financial statements.

Source: General Mills 2010 annual report

We now turn to how to calculate General Mills's profit margin and what it can tell us about the company's profitability.

USING THE RATIO DECISION MODEL

Analyzing the Profit Margin

Use the following Ratio Decision Model to evaluate the profit margin for General Mills or any other public company.

1. Formulate the Question

Managers, investors, and creditors are all interested in a company's profitability. They must be able to answer the following question:

How profitable has the company been in recent years?

2. Gather the Information from the Financial Statements

The profit margin is a measure of a company's profitability. To calculate the ratio, it is essential to know a company's sales and expenses and the difference between the two, net income.

- Net income—from the income statement
- Net sales—from the income statement

3. Calculate the Ratio

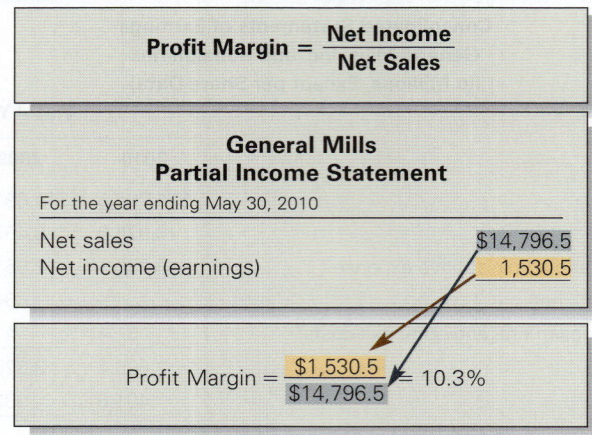

$$\text{Profit Margin} = \frac{\text{Net Income}}{\text{Net Sales}}$$

General Mills
Partial Income Statement

For the year ending May 30, 2010

Net sales	$14,796.5
Net income (earnings)	1,530.5

$$\text{Profit Margin} = \frac{\$1,530.5}{\$14,796.5} = 10.3\%$$

4. Compare the Ratio with Others

A comparison with prior performance helps determine whether profitability is increasing or decreasing.

General Mills		Kellogg's	
Year Ended May 30, 2010	**Year Ended May 31, 2009**	**Year Ended January 1, 2011**	**Year Ended January 2, 2010**
10.3	8.9	10.1	9.6

5. Interpret the Results

A high profit margin indicates that the company is controlling its expenses. This is because sales minus expenses equals net income; if the ratio of net income to sales is high, the company is not only generating revenue but also minimizing expenses. Also, ratios should be compared with those of prior years and with the same ratios for competitors. Both companies' profit margins indicate that the companies are able to control their expenses while increasing their sales.

Note that both companies increased their profit margins over the two-year period, General Mills's ratio rising from 8.9% to 10.3% and the profit margin for Kellogg's increasing from 9.6% to 10.1%. ■

HOT TOPICS

Paying Dividends in Challenging Economic Times

Jack Atley/Bloomberg via Getty Images

Today's economy presents challenges for all businesses. All companies have had to tighten their belts and look for ways to cut costs and save cash. Cutting costs can improve a company's bottom line and at the same time conserve cash and reduce a company's dependence on outside money in the form of borrowings. But what can a company do beyond the bottom line to improve its cash flow? One way would be to either reduce or eliminate quarterly dividend payments to stockholders.

General Mills decided to look for other ways than cutting dividends to conserve cash. In fact, its board of directors voted to not only continue paying the regular quarterly dividend but to increase it to $0.28 per share, resulting in an annualized rate that is a 17% increase over dividends paid in the prior fiscal year. This means that the company and its predecessor firm have paid dividends without interruption or reduction for 111 years. Whether the home of Cheerios® and Yoplait® is able to maintain this enviable record will depend on its ability to compete in an increasingly competitive market and keep a lid on the costs of doing business.

Source: General Mills's press release, June 28, 2010.

Other Elements of an Annual Report

No two annual reports look the same. The appearance of an annual report depends not only on the size of a company but also on the budget devoted to the report. Some companies publish bare-bones annual reports, whereas others issue a glossy report complete with pictures of company products and employees. In recent years, many companies, as a cost-cutting measure, have scaled back the amount spent on the annual report.

Privately held companies tend to distribute only financial statements, without the additional information normally included in the annual reports of public companies. For the annual reports of public companies, however, certain basic elements are considered standard:

- A letter to the stockholders from either the president or the chair of the board of directors appears in the first few pages of most annual reports.
- A section describing the company's products and markets is usually included.
- The financial report or review, which consists of the financial statements accompanied by notes to explain various items on the statements, is included.

Report of Independent Accountants (Auditors' Report) As Exhibit 2-3 shows, General Mills is audited by **KPMG LLP**, one of the largest international accounting firms in the world. Two key phrases should be noted in the first sentence of the fifth paragraph of the independent accountants' report (also called the **auditors' report**): *in our opinion* and *present fairly*. The report indicates that responsibility for the statements rests with General Mills and that the auditors' job is to *express an opinion* on the statements based on certain tests. It would be impossible for an auditing firm to spend the time or money to retrace and verify every single transaction that General Mills entered into during the year. Instead, the auditing firm performs various tests of the accounting records to be able to assure itself that the statements are free of *material misstatement*. Auditors do not "certify" the total accuracy of a set of financial statements, but render an opinion as to the reasonableness of those statements.

Auditors' report
The opinion rendered by a public accounting firm concerning the fairness of the presentation of the financial statements.

Alternate term: Report of independent accountants.

The Ethical Responsibility of Management and the Auditors A company's management and its auditors must protect the interests of stockholders. In large corporations, the stockholders are normally removed from the daily affairs of the business. A professional management team must run the business, and a periodic independent audit must be performed on the company's records. Stockholders cannot run the business themselves, so they need assurances that the business is being operated effectively and efficiently and that the financial statements are a fair representation of the company's operations and financial position. The management and the auditors have a very important ethical responsibility to stockholders.

Management Discussion and Analysis Preceding the financial statements is a section of General Mills's annual report titled "Management's Discussion and Analysis of Financial Condition and Results of Operations." This report gives management the opportunity to discuss the financial statements and provide the stockholders with explanations for certain amounts reported in the statements. For example, management explains the change in its selling, general, and administrative expenses as follows:

> *Selling, general and administrative (SG&A) expenses were up $284 million in fiscal 2010 versus fiscal 2009. SG&A expenses as a percent of net sales in fiscal 2010 increased by 2 percentage points compared to fiscal 2009. The increase in SG&A expenses was primarily driven by a 24 percent increase in advertising and media expense.[5]*

---

[5] General Mills 2010 annual report.

Notes to Consolidated Financial Statements The sentence *See accompanying notes to consolidated financial statements* appears at the bottom of each of General Mills's four financial statements. These comments, or *notes*, are necessary to satisfy the need for *full disclosure* of all facts relevant to a company's results and financial position. Note 2 is a summary of *significant accounting policies*. General Mills describes its policy for depreciating buildings and equipment as follows:

EXHIBIT 2-3 Report of Independent Accountants for General Mills, Inc.

Report of Independent Registered Public Accounting Firm

The Board of Directors and Stockholders
General Mills, Inc.:

We have audited the accompanying consolidated balance sheets of General Mills, Inc. and subsidiaries as of May 30, 2010, and May 31, 2009, and the related consolidated statements of earnings, total equity and comprehensive income, and cash flows for each of the fiscal years in the three-year period ended May 30, 2010. In connection with our audits of the consolidated financial statements, we have audited the accompanying financial statement schedule. We also have audited General Mills Inc.'s internal control over financial reporting as of May 30, 2010, based on criteria established in *Internal Control—Integrated Framework* issued by the Committee of Sponsoring Organizations of the Treadway Commission (COSO). General Mills, Inc.'s management is responsible for these consolidated financial statements and financial statement schedule, for maintaining effective internal control over financial reporting, and for its assessment of the effectiveness of internal control over financial reporting, included in Management's Report on Internal Control over Financial Reporting. Our responsibility is to express an opinion on these consolidated financial statements and financial statement schedule and an opinion on the Company's internal control over financial reporting based on our audits.

We conducted our audits in accordance with the standards of the Public Company Accounting Oversight Board (United States). Those standards require that we plan and perform the audits to obtain reasonable assurance about whether the financial statements are free of material misstatement and whether effective internal control over financial reporting was maintained in all material respects. Our audits of the consolidated financial statements included examining, on a test basis, evidence supporting the amounts and disclosures in the financial statements, assessing the accounting principles used and significant estimates made by management, and evaluating the overall financial statement presentation. Our audit of internal control over financial reporting included obtaining an understanding of internal control over financial reporting, assessing the risk that a material weakness exists, and testing and evaluating the design and operating effectiveness of internal control based on the assessed risk. Our audits also included performing such other procedures as we considered necessary in the circumstances. We believe that our audits provide a reasonable basis for our opinions.

A company's internal control over financial reporting is a process designed to provide reasonable assurance regarding the reliability of financial reporting and the preparation of financial statements for external purposes in accordance with generally accepted accounting principles. A company's internal control over financial reporting includes those policies and procedures that (1) pertain to the maintenance of records that, in reasonable detail, accurately and fairly reflect the transactions and dispositions of the assets of the company; (2) provide reasonable assurance that transactions are recorded as necessary to permit preparation of financial statements in accordance with generally accepted accounting principles, and that receipts and expenditures of the company are being made only in accordance with authorizations of management and directors of the company; and (3) provide reasonable assurance regarding prevention or timely detection of unauthorized acquisition, use, or disposition of the company's assets that could have a material effect on the financial statements.

Because of its inherent limitations, internal control over financial reporting may not prevent or detect misstatements. Also, projections of any evaluation of effectiveness to future periods are subject to the risk that controls may become inadequate because of changes in conditions, or that the degree of compliance with the policies or procedures may deteriorate.

In our opinion, the consolidated financial statements referred to above present fairly, in all material respects, the financial position of General Mills, Inc. and subsidiaries as of May 30, 2010, and May 31, 2009, and the results of their operations and their cash flows for each of the fiscal years in the three-year period ended May 30, 2010, in conformity with U.S. generally accepted accounting principles. Also in our opinion, the accompanying financial statement schedule, when considered in relation to the basic consolidated financial statements taken as a whole, presents fairly, in all material respects, the information set forth therein. Also in our opinion, General Mills, Inc. maintained, in all material respects, effective internal control over financial reporting as of May 30, 2010, based on criteria established in *Internal Control—Integrated Framework* issued by the Committee of Sponsoring Organizations of the Treadway Commission.

As disclosed in Note 1 to the Consolidated Financial Statements, the Company changed its method of accounting for noncontrolling interests in fiscal year 2010.

Minneapolis, Minnesota   /s/KPMG LLP
July 9, 2010

Source: General Mills, Inc., 10-K, July 13, 2009, pp. 45–46.

Land is recorded at historical cost. Buildings and equipment, including capitalized interest and internal engineering costs, are recorded at cost and depreciated over estimated useful lives, primarily using the straight-line method. Ordinary maintenance and repairs are charged to cost of sales. Buildings are usually depreciated over 40 to 50 years, and equipment, furniture and software are usually depreciated over 3 to 10 years.[6]

Other notes discuss such topics as income taxes and stock option plans.

This completes discussion of the makeup of the annual report. By now, you should appreciate the flexibility that companies have in assembling the report, aside from the need to follow GAAP. The accounting standards followed in preparing the statements, as well as the appearance of the annual report itself, differ in other countries. As has been noted elsewhere, although many corporations operate internationally, accounting principles are far from being standardized.

LO9 Read and use the financial statements and other elements in the annual report of a publicly held company.

- The classified balance sheet and multiple-step income statement are more complex than simpler versions of these financial statements and yield more useful information to decision makers.

- Annual reports contain more information than just the financial statements. This information can be used alone or in conjunction with the financial statements to gain a more complete financial picture of a company.

  - Management's Discussion and Analysis provides explanatory comments about certain results reflected in the financial statements and sometimes forward-looking commentary.

  - The Report of Independent Accountants is provided by the company's auditor, whose job is to express an opinion on whether the financial statements fairly represent the accounting treatment of a company's economic activity for the year.

  - Notes to the Consolidated Financial Statements are generally supplementary disclosures required by GAAP that help explain detail behind the accounting treatment of certain items in the financial statements.

POD REVIEW 2.9

QUESTIONS　**Answers to these questions are on the last page of the chapter.**

1. The SEC requires that the annual report include

   a. balance sheets for the two most recent year-ends and income statements for each of the three most recent years.
   b. balance sheets for the three most recent year-ends and income statements for each of the three most recent years.
   c. balance sheets for the two most recent year-ends and income statements for each of the two most recent years.
   d. balance sheets for the three most recent year-ends and income statements for each of the two most recent years.

2. Which of the following is usually *not* included in a company's annual report?

   a. Management Discussion and Analysis
   b. Notes to the Consolidated Financial Statements
   c. Report of Independent Accountants
   d. All of the above are included in an annual report.

Among the joint projects of the IASB and the FASB is one that could significantly alter the appearance of the financial statements presented in this chapter. It is possible that in the future both the format and presentation of financial statements will be different. These two groups consider this project a critical step as they look to improve the usefulness of general-purpose financial statements.

LOOKING AHEAD

Tetra Images/Getty Images

---

[6] General Mills, Inc., 2010 10-K, p. 52.

RATIO REVIEW

$$\text{Current Ratio} = \frac{\text{Current Assets(balance sheet)}}{\text{Current Liabilities (balance sheet)}}$$

$$\text{Profit Margin} = \frac{\text{Net Income(income statement)}}{\text{Sales or Revenues (income statement)}}$$

KEY TERMS QUIZ

Read each definition below and write the number of the definition in the blank beside the appropriate term. The quiz solutions appear at the end of the chapter.

_____ Understandability	_____ Current liability
_____ Relevance	_____ Liquidity
_____ Faithful representation	_____ Working capital
_____ Comparability	_____ Current ratio
_____ Depreciation	_____ Single-step income statement
_____ Consistency	_____ Multiple-step income statement
_____ Materiality	_____ Gross profit
_____ Conservatism	_____ Profit margin
_____ Operating cycle	_____ Auditors' report
_____ Current asset	

1. An income statement in which all expenses are added together and subtracted from all revenues.
2. The magnitude of an omission or a misstatement in accounting information that will affect the judgment of someone relying on the information.
3. The capacity of information to make a difference in a decision.
4. An income statement that provides the reader with classifications of revenues and expenses as well as with important subtotals.
5. The practice of using the least optimistic estimate when two estimates of amounts are about equally likely.
6. The quality of accounting information that makes it comprehensible to those willing to spend the necessary time.
7. Current assets divided by current liabilities.
8. The quality of accounting information that makes it complete, neutral, and free from error.
9. An obligation that will be satisfied within the next operating cycle or within one year if the cycle is shorter than one year.
10. Current assets minus current liabilities.
11. Net income divided by sales.
12. The quality of accounting information that allows a user to analyze two or more companies and look for similarities and differences.
13. An asset that is expected to be realized in cash or sold or consumed during the operating cycle or within one year if the cycle is shorter than one year.
14. The ability of a company to pay its debts as they come due.
15. The quality of accounting information that allows a user to compare two or more accounting periods for a single company.
16. The allocation of the cost of a long-term tangible asset over its useful life.
17. The period of time between the purchase of inventory and the collection of any receivable from the sale of the inventory.
18. Sales less cost of goods sold.
19. The opinion rendered by a public accounting firm concerning the fairness of the presentation of the financial statements.

ALTERNATE TERMS

auditor's report report of independent accountants

long-term assets noncurrent assets

long-term liability long-term debt

net income profits or earnings

profit margin return on sales

WARMUP EXERCISES & SOLUTIONS

Warmup Exercise 2-1 Identifying Ratios

LO4 • 6

State the equation for each of the following:
1. Working capital
2. Current ratio
3. Profit margin

KEY TO THE SOLUTION Review the various ratios discussed in the chapter.

Warmup Exercise 2-2 Calculating Ratios

LO4 • 6

Bridger reported net income of $150,000 and sales of $1,000,000 for the year. Its current assets were $300,000 and its current liabilities were $200,000 at year-end.

Required

Compute each of the following ratios for Bridger:
1. Current ratio
2. Profit margin

KEY TO THE SOLUTION Recall the equation for each of these ratios as presented in the chapter.

Warmup Exercise 2-3 Determining Liquidity

LO4

Big has current assets of $500,000 and current liabilities of $400,000. Small reports current assets of $80,000 and current liabilities of $20,000.

Required

Which company is more liquid? Why?

KEY TO THE SOLUTION Calculate the current ratio for each company and compare them.

Solutions to Warmup Exercises

Warmup Exercise 2-1

1. Working Capital = Current Assets − Current Liabilities

2. $\text{Current Ratio} = \dfrac{\text{Current Assets}}{\text{Current Liabilities}}$

3. $\text{Profit Margin} = \dfrac{\text{Net Income}}{\text{Sales or Revenues}}$

Warmup Exercise 2-2

1. $\dfrac{\$300,000}{\$200,000} = \underline{\underline{1.5 \text{ to } 1}}$

2. $\dfrac{\$150,000}{\$1,000,000} = \underline{\underline{15\%}}$

Warmup Exercise 2-3

On the surface, Small appears to be more liquid. Its current ratio of $80,000/$20,000, or 4 to 1, is significantly higher than Big's current ratio of $500,000/$400,000, or 1.25 to 1.

REVIEW PROBLEM & SOLUTION

The following review problem will give you the opportunity to apply what you have learned by preparing both an income statement and a balance sheet.

The following items, listed in alphabetical order, are taken from the records of Grizzly Inc., a chain of outdoor recreational stores in the Northwest. Use the items to prepare two statements. First, prepare an income statement for the year ended December 31, 2012. The income statement should be in multiple-step form. Second, prepare a classified balance sheet at December 31, 2012. All amounts are in thousands of dollars.

Accounts payable	$ 6,500	Income tax expense	$ 13,000
Accounts receivable	8,200	Insurance expense	2,000
Accumulated depreciation—buildings	25,000	Interest expense	12,000
Accumulated depreciation—furniture		Interest payable	1,000
and fixtures	15,000	Interest revenue	2,000
Advertising expense	3,100	Land	100,000
Buildings	80,000	Long-term notes payable, due	
Capital stock, $1 par, 10,000 shares		December 31, 2020	120,000
issued and outstanding	10,000	Merchandise inventories	6,000
Cash	2,400	Office supplies	900
Commissions expense	8,600	Paid-in capital in excess of par value	40,000
Cost of goods sold	110,000	Prepaid rent	3,000
Depreciation on buildings	2,500	Rent expense for salespeople's autos	9,000
Depreciation on furniture and fixtures	1,200	Retained earnings	48,800
Furniture and fixtures	68,000	Salaries and wages for office staff	11,000
Income taxes payable	2,200	Sales revenue	190,000

Solution to Review Problem

1.   Multiple-step income statement:

Grizzly Inc.
Income Statement
For the Year Ended December 31, 2012
(In thousands of dollars)

Sales revenue		$190,000	
Cost of goods sold		110,000	
Gross profit			$80,000
Operating expenses:			
Selling expenses:			
Advertising expense	$ 3,100		
Depreciation on furniture and fixtures	1,200		
Rent expense for salespeople's autos	9,000		
Commissions expense	8,600		
Total selling expenses		$ 21,900	
General and administrative expenses:			
Depreciation on buildings	$ 2,500		
Insurance expense	2,000		
Salaries and wages for office staff	11,000		
Total general and administrative expenses		15,500	
Total operating expenses			37,400
Income from operations			$42,600
Other revenues and expenses:			
Interest revenue		$ 2,000	
Interest expense		12,000	
Excess of other expense over other revenue			10,000
Income before income taxes			$32,600
Income tax expense			13,000
Net income			$19,600

2. Classified balance sheet:

Grizzly Inc.
Balance Sheet
At December 31, 2012
(In thousands of dollars)

Assets

Current assets:			
Cash		$ 2,400	
Accounts receivable		8,200	
Merchandise inventories		6,000	
Office supplies		900	
Prepaid rent		3,000	
Total current assets			$ 20,500
Property, plant, and equipment:			
Land		$100,000	
Buildings	$80,000		
Less: Accumulated depreciation	25,000	55,000	
Furniture and fixtures	$68,000		
Less: Accumulated depreciation	15,000	53,000	
Total property, plant, and equipment			208,000
Total assets			$228,500

Liabilities

Current liabilities:			
Accounts payable		$ 6,500	
Income taxes payable		2,200	
Interest payable		1,000	
Total current liabilities			$ 9,700
Long-term notes payable, due December 31, 2020			120,000
Total liabilities			$129,700

Stockholders' Equity

Contributed capital:			
Capital stock, $1 par, 10,000 shares issued and outstanding		$ 10,000	
Paid-in capital in excess of par value		40,000	
Total contributed capital		$ 50,000	
Retained earnings		48,800	
Total stockholders' equity			98,800
Total liabilities and stockholders' equity			$228,500

QUESTIONS

1. How would you evaluate the following statement: The cash flows to a company are irrelevant to an investor; all the investor cares about is the potential for receiving dividends on the investment.

2. A key characteristic of useful financial information is understandability. How does this qualitative characteristic relate to the background of the user of the information?

3. What does *relevance* mean with regard to the use of accounting information?

4. What is the qualitative characteristic of comparability? Why is it important in preparing financial statements?

5. What is the difference between comparability and consistency as they relate to the use of accounting information?

6. How does the concept of materiality relate to the size of a company?

7. Does the IASB recognize similar qualitative characteristics of useful financial information to those recognized by the FASB? Explain your answer.

8. How does the concept of the operating cycle relate to the definition of a current asset?

9. How would you evaluate the following statement: A note payable with an original maturity of five years will be classified on the balance sheet as a long-term liability until it matures.

10. How do the two basic forms of owners' equity items for a corporation—capital stock and retained earnings—differ?

11. What are the limitations of working capital as a measure of the liquidity of a business as opposed to the current ratio?

12. What is meant by a company's capital structure?

13. What is the major weakness of the single-step form for the income statement?

14. How does a statement of retained earnings act as a link between an income statement and a balance sheet?

15. In auditing the financial statements of a company, does the auditor *certify* that the statements are totally accurate without errors of any size or variety? Explain.

16. What is the first note in the annual report of all publicly held companies? What is its purpose?

BRIEF EXERCISES

LO1
EXAMPLE 2-1

Brief Exercise 2-1 Objectives of Financial Reporting

State the overriding objective of financial reporting. Are financial statements intended to report the value of the reporting entity? Explain your answer.

LO2
EXAMPLE 2-2

Brief Exercise 2-2 Qualitative Characteristics of Accounting Information

What two fundamental characteristics make accounting information useful? What other qualities enhance the usefulness of financial information?

LO3
EXAMPLE 2-3, 2-4

Brief Exercise 2-3 Classification of Assets

Indicate whether each of the following assets is a current asset (CA) or a noncurrent asset (NCA).

_____ Accounts receivable
_____ Land
_____ Inventories
_____ Cash
_____ Furniture and fixtures
_____ Office supplies
_____ Buildings

LO4
EXAMPLE 2-5

Brief Exercise 2-4 Working Capital and Current Ratio

A company reported current assets of $80,000 and current liabilities of $60,000. Compute the amount of working capital and the current ratio.

LO5
EXAMPLE 2-6, 2-7

Brief Exercise 2-5 Multiple- versus Single-Step Income Statement

A retailer is considering whether to prepare a multiple- or single-step income statement. Provide three lines that appear on a multiple-step statement that do not appear on a single-step statement.

LO6
EXAMPLE 2-8

Brief Exercise 2-6 Profit Margin

A company reported sales of $100,000; cost of goods sold of $60,000; selling, general, and administrative expenses of $15,000; and income tax expense of $10,000. Compute the company's profit margin.

LO7
EXAMPLE 2-9

Brief Exercise 2-7 Retained Earnings

A company started the year with retained earnings of $200,000. During the year, it reported net income of $80,000 and paid dividends of $50,000. Compute the company's ending retained earnings.

Brief Exercise 2-8   Investing and Financing Activities

LO8
EXAMPLE 2-10

A company borrowed $100,000 from its bank and the next day used $80,000 of the cash from the loan to buy a new piece of equipment for its plant. Explain how each of those activities is reported on a statement of cash flows.

Brief Exercise 2-9   Elements of an Annual Report

LO9

List three examples of the types of information that normally appear in a company's annual report.

EXERCISES

Exercise 2-1   Characteristics of Useful Accounting Information

LO2
EXAMPLE 2-2

Fill in the blank with the qualitative characteristic for each of the following descriptions.

_____ 1. The information to include in reports should take into account whether an omission or misstatement could influence a user's decision.

_____ 2. Information that has the capacity to make a difference in a decision

_____ 3. Information that is complete, neutral, and free from error

_____ 4. Information that allows for comparisons to be made for two or more accounting periods for a single company

_____ 5. Information that is meaningful to those who are willing to learn to use it properly

_____ 6. Information that allows for comparisons to be made between or among companies

Exercise 2-2   Classification of Assets and Liabilities

LO3
EXAMPLE 2-3, 2-4

Indicate the appropriate classification of each of the following as a current asset (CA), noncurrent asset (NCA), current liability (CL), or long-term liability (LTL).

_____ 1. Inventory
_____ 2. Accounts payable
_____ 3. Cash
_____ 4. Patents
_____ 5. Notes payable, due in six months
_____ 6. Taxes payable
_____ 7. Prepaid rent (for the next nine months)
_____ 8. Bonds payable, due in ten years
_____ 9. Machinery

Exercise 2-3   The Operating Cycle

LO3
EXAMPLE 2-3

Two Wheeler Cycle Shop buys all of its bikes from one manufacturer, Baxter Bikes. On average, bikes are on hand for 45 days before Two Wheeler sells them. The company sells some bikes for cash but also extends credit to its customers for 30 days.

Required

1. On average, what is the minimum length of Two Wheeler's operating cycle? the maximum length?
2. Explain why the operating cycle for Baxter, the manufacturer of the bikes, would normally be longer than that of Two Wheeler, the retailer.

Exercise 2-4   Current Ratio

LO4
EXAMPLE 2-5

Baldwin Corp. reported the following current accounts at the end of two recent years:

	December 31, 2012	December 31, 2011
Cash	$ 3,000	$ 6,000
Accounts receivable	15,000	10,000
Inventory	12,000	8,000
Accounts payable	12,000	7,000
Wages payable	2,000	1,000
Notes payable	6,000	4,000

Required

1. Compute Baldwin's current ratio at the end of each of the two years.
2. How has Baldwin's liquidity changed at the end of 2012 compared to the end of 2011?
3. Comment on the relative composition of Baldwin's current assets at the end of 2012 compared to the end of 2011.

LO3
EXAMPLE 2-4

Exercise 2-5 Classification of Financial Statement Items

Carnival Corporation & plc is one of the largest cruise companies in the world with such well-known brands as Carnival Cruise Lines, Holland America Line, and Princess Cruises. Classify each of the following items found on the company's November 30, 2010, balance sheet as a current asset (CA), noncurrent asset (NCA), current liability (CL), long-term liability (LTL), or stockholders' equity (SE) item.

_____ 1. Trade and other receivables, net
_____ 2. Common stock of Carnival Corporation
_____ 3. Short-term borrowings
_____ 4. Inventories
_____ 5. Property and equipment, net
_____ 6. Prepaid expenses and other
_____ 7. Accounts payable
_____ 8. Goodwill
_____ 9. Retained earnings
_____ 10. Long-term debt

LO5
EXAMPLE 2-7

Exercise 2-6 Missing Income Statement Amounts

For each of the following cases, fill in the blank with the appropriate dollar amount.

	Sara's Coffee Shop	Amy's Deli	Jane's Bagels
Net sales	$ 35,000	$_____	$ 78,000
Cost of goods sold	_____	45,000	_____
Gross profit	7,000	18,000	_____
Selling expenses	3,000	_____	9,000
General and administrative expenses	1,500	2,800	_____
Total operating expenses	_____	8,800	13,600
Net income	$ 2,500	$ 9,200	$ 25,400

LO5
EXAMPLE 2-7

Exercise 2-7 Selling Expenses and General and Administrative Expenses

Operating expenses are subdivided between selling expenses and general and administrative expenses when a multiple-step income statement is prepared. Identify each of the following items as a selling expense (S) or general and administrative expense (G&A).

_____ 1. Advertising expense
_____ 2. Depreciation expense—store furniture and fixtures
_____ 3. Office rent expense
_____ 4. Office salaries expense
_____ 5. Store rent expense
_____ 6. Store salaries expense
_____ 7. Insurance expense
_____ 8. Supplies expense
_____ 9. Utilities expense

Exercise 2-8 Income Statement Ratio

The income statement of Holly Enterprises shows operating revenues of $134,800, selling expenses of $38,310, general and administrative expenses of $36,990, interest expense of $580, and income tax expense of $13,920. Holly's stockholders' equity was $280,000 at the beginning of the year and $320,000 at the end of the year. The company has 20,000 shares of stock outstanding at the end of the year.

LO6
EXAMPLE 2-8

Required

Compute Holly's profit margin. What other information would you need in order to comment on whether this ratio is favorable?

Exercise 2-9 Statement of Retained Earnings

Landon Corporation was organized on January 2, 2010, with the investment of $100,000 by each of its two stockholders. Net income for its first year of business was $85,200. Net income increased during 2011 to $125,320 and to $145,480 during 2012. Landon paid $20,000 in dividends to each of the two stockholders in each of the three years.

LO7
EXAMPLE 2-9

Required

Prepare a statement of retained earnings for the year ended December 31, 2012.

Exercise 2-10 Components of the Statement of Cash Flows

Identify each of the following items as operating (O), investing (I), financing (F), or not on the statement of cash flows (N).

LO8
EXAMPLE 2-10

_____ 1. Paid for supplies
_____ 2. Collected cash from customers
_____ 3. Purchased land (held for resale)
_____ 4. Purchased land (for construction of new building)
_____ 5. Paid dividend
_____ 6. Issued stock
_____ 7. Purchased computers (for use in the business)
_____ 8. Sold old equipment

Exercise 2-11 Basic Elements of Financial Reports

Most financial reports contain the following list of basic elements. For each element, identify the person(s) who prepared the element and describe the information a user would expect to find in each element. Some information is verifiable; other information is subjectively chosen by management. Comment on the verifiability of information in each element.

LO9

1.   Management discussion and analysis
2.   Product/markets of company
3.   Financial statements
4.   Notes to financial statements
5.   Independent accountants' report

MULTI-CONCEPT EXERCISES

Exercise 2-12 Financial Statement Classification

Potential stockholders and lenders are interested in a company's financial statements. Identify the statement—balance sheet (BS), income statement (IS), or retained earnings statement (RE)—on which each of the following items would appear.

LO3 • 5 • 7
EXAMPLE 2-4, 2-7, 2-9

_____ 1. Accounts payable
_____ 2. Accounts receivable
_____ 3. Advertising expense
_____ 4. Bad debt expense

_____ 5. Bonds payable
_____ 6. Buildings
_____ 7. Cash
_____ 8. Common stock

(Continued)

_____ 9. Depreciation expense
_____ 10. Dividends
_____ 11. Land held for future expansion
_____ 12. Loan payable
_____ 13. Office supplies
_____ 14. Patent
_____ 15. Patent amortization expense

_____ 16. Prepaid insurance
_____ 17. Retained earnings
_____ 18. Sales
_____ 19. Utilities expense
_____ 20. Wages payable

LO5 • 6
EXAMPLE 2-7, 2-8

Exercise 2-13 Multiple-Step Income Statement

Gaynor Corporation's partial income statement is as follows:

Sales	$1,200,000
Cost of sales	450,000
Selling expenses	60,800
General and administrative expenses	75,000

Required

Determine the profit margin. Would you invest in Gaynor Corporation? Explain your answer.

LO5 • 6
EXAMPLE 2-6, 2-7

Exercise 2-14 Single- and Multiple-Step Income Statement

Some headings and/or items are used on either the single- or multiple-step income statement. Some are used on both. Identify each of the following items as single-step (S), multiple-step (M), both formats (B), or not used on either income statement (N).

_____ 1. Sales
_____ 2. Cost of goods sold
_____ 3. Selling expenses
_____ 4. Total revenues
_____ 5. Utilities expense
_____ 6. Administrative expense

_____ 7. Net income
_____ 8. Supplies on hand
_____ 9. Accumulated depreciation
_____ 10. Income before income taxes
_____ 11. Gross profit

PROBLEMS

LO2

Problem 2-1 Costs and Expenses

The following costs are incurred by a retailer:
1. Display fixtures in a retail store
2. Advertising
3. Merchandise for sale
4. Incorporation (i.e., legal costs, stock issue costs)
5. Cost of a franchise
6. Office supplies
7. Wages and salaries
8. Computer software
9. Computer hardware

Required

For each cost, explain whether all of the cost or only a portion of the cost would appear as an expense on the income statement for the period in which the cost was incurred. If not all of the cost would appear on the income statement for that period, explain why not.

LO2

Problem 2-2 Materiality

Joseph Knapp, a newly hired accountant wanting to impress his boss, stayed late one night to analyze the office supplies expense. He determined the cost by month for the previous 12 months of each of the following: computer paper, copy paper, fax paper, pencils and pens, notepads, postage, stationery, and miscellaneous items.

Required

1. What did Joseph think his boss would learn from this information? What action might be taken as a result of knowing it?
2. Would this information be more relevant if Joseph worked for a hardware store or for a real estate company? Discuss.

Problem 2-3 Classified Balance Sheet   LO3

The following balance sheet items, listed in alphabetical order, are available from the records of Ruth Corporation at December 31, 2012:

Accounts payable	$ 18,255	Income taxes payable	$ 6,200
Accounts receivable	23,450	Interest payable	1,500
Accumulated depreciation—		Inventory	45,730
automobiles	22,500	Land	250,000
Accumulated depreciation—		Long-term investments	85,000
buildings	40,000	Notes payable, due June 30, 2013	10,000
Automobiles	112,500	Office supplies	2,340
Bonds payable, due December 31,		Paid-in capital in excess of par value	50,000
2016	160,000	Patents	40,000
Buildings	200,000	Prepaid rent	1,500
Capital stock, $10 par value	150,000	Retained earnings	311,095
Cash	13,230	Salaries and wages payable	4,200

Required

1. Prepare in good form a classified balance sheet as of December 31, 2012.
2. Compute Ruth's current ratio.
3. On the basis of your answer to (2), does Ruth appear to be liquid? What other information do you need to fully answer that question?

Problem 2-4 Working Capital and Current Ratio   LO4

The balance sheet of Stevenson Inc. includes the following items:

Cash	$23,000	Accounts payable	$ 54,900
Accounts receivable	13,000	Salaries payable	1,200
Inventory	45,000	Capital stock	100,000
Prepaid insurance	800	Retained earnings	5,700
Land	80,000		

Required

1. Determine the current ratio and working capital.
2. Beyond the information provided in your answers to (1), what does the composition of the current assets tell you about Stevenson's liquidity?
3. What other information do you need to fully assess Stevenson's liquidity?

Problem 2-5 Financial Statement Ratios   LO4

The following items, in alphabetical order, are available from the records of Walker Corporation as of December 31, 2012 and 2011:

	December 31, 2012	December 31, 2011
Accounts payable	$ 8,400	$ 5,200
Accounts receivable	27,830	35,770
Cash	20,200	19,450
Cleaning supplies	450	700
Interest payable	0	1,200
Inventory	24,600	26,200
Marketable securities	6,250	5,020
Note payable, due in six months	0	12,000

(Continued)

	December 31, 2012	December 31, 2011
Prepaid rent	3,600	4,800
Taxes payable	1,450	1,230
Wages payable	1,200	1,600

Required

1. Calculate the following as of December 31, 2012, and December 31, 2011:
   a. Working capital
   b. Current ratio
2. On the basis of your answers to (1), comment on the company's relative liquidity at the beginning and end of the year. Explain the change in the company's liquidity from the beginning to the end of 2012.

LO5 Problem 2-6 Single-Step Income Statement

The following income statement items, arranged in alphabetical order, are taken from the records of Shaw Corporation for the year ended December 31, 2012:

Advertising expense	$ 1,500	Interest expense	$ 1,400
Commissions expense	2,415	Interest revenue	1,340
Cost of goods sold	29,200	Rent revenue	6,700
Depreciation expense—office		Salaries and wages	
building	2,900	expense—office	12,560
Income tax expense	1,540	Sales revenue	48,300
Insurance expense—		Supplies expense—office	890
salesperson's auto	2,250		

Required

1. Prepare a single-step income statement for the year ended December 31, 2012.
2. What weaknesses do you see in this form for the income statement?

LO5 Problem 2-7 Multiple-Step Income Statement and Profit Margin

Refer to the list of income statement items in Problem 2-6. Assume that Shaw Corporation classifies all operating expenses into two categories: (1) selling and (2) general and administrative.

Required

1. Prepare a multiple-step income statement for the year ended December 31, 2012.
2. What advantages do you see in this form for the income statement?
3. Compute Shaw's profit margin.
4. Comment on Shaw's profitability. What other factors need to be taken into account to assess Shaw's profitability?

LO8 Problem 2-8 Statement of Cash Flows

Colorado Corporation was organized on January 1, 2012, with the investment of $250,000 in cash by its stockholders. The company immediately purchased an office building for $300,000, paying $210,000 in cash and signing a three-year promissory note for the balance. Colorado signed a five-year, $60,000 promissory note at a local bank during 2012 and received cash in the same amount. During its first year, Colorado collected $93,970 from its customers. It paid $65,600 for inventory, $20,400 in salaries and wages, and another $3,100 in taxes. Colorado paid $5,600 in cash dividends.

Required

1. Prepare a statement of cash flows for the year ended December 31, 2012.
2. What does this statement tell you that an income statement does not?

Problem 2-9 Basic Elements of Financial Reports

LO9

Comparative income statements for Grammar Inc. are as follows:

	2012	2011
Sales	$1,000,000	$500,000
Cost of sales	500,000	300,000
Gross profit	$ 500,000	$200,000
Operating expenses	120,000	100,000
Operating income	$ 380,000	$100,000
Loss on sale of subsidiary	(400,000)	—
Net income (loss)	$ (20,000)	$100,000

Required

The president and management believe that the company performed better in 2012 than it did in 2011. Write the president's letter to be included in the 2012 annual report. Explain why the company is financially sound and why shareholders should not be alarmed by the $20,000 loss in a year when operating revenues increased significantly.

MULTI-CONCEPT PROBLEMS

Problem 2-10 Comparing The Coca-Cola Company and PepsiCo

LO2 • 4

The current items, listed in alphabetical order, are taken from the consolidated balance sheets of **The Coca-Cola Company** as of December 31, 2010, and **PepsiCo** as of December 25, 2010. (All amounts are in millions of dollars.)

The Coca-Cola Company

Accounts payable and accrued expenses	$ 8,859
Accrued income taxes	273
Cash and cash equivalents	8,517
Current maturities of long-term debt	1,276
Inventories	2,650
Loans and notes payable	8,100
Marketable securities	138
Prepaid expenses and other assets	3,162
Short-term investments	2,682
Trade accounts receivable, less allowance of $48	4,430

PepsiCo

Accounts and notes receivable, net	$ 6,323
Accounts payable and other current liabilities	10,923
Cash and cash equivalents	5,943
Income taxes payable	71
Inventories	3,372
Prepaid expenses and other current assets	1,505
Short-term investments	426
Short-term obligations	4,898

Required

1. Compute working capital and the current ratio for both companies.
2. On the basis of your answers to (1), which company appears to be more liquid?
3. Other factors affect a company's liquidity besides working capital and current ratio. Comment on the *composition* of each company's current assets and ways this composition affects liquidity.

LO2 • 5   **Problem 2-11 Comparability and Consistency in Income Statements**

The following income statements were provided by Gleeson Company, a retailer:

2012 Income Statement		2011 Income Statement	
Sales	$1,700,000	Sales	$1,500,000
Cost of sales	520,000	Cost of sales	$ 450,000
Gross profit	$1,180,000	Sales salaries	398,000
Selling expense	$ 702,000	Advertising	175,000
Administrative expense	95,000	Office supplies	54,000
Total selling and		Depreciation—building	40,000
administrative expense	$ 797,000	Delivery expense	20,000
		Total expenses	$1,137,000
Net income	$ 383,000	Net income	$ 363,000

Required

1. Identify each income statement as either single- or multiple-step format.
2. Convert the 2011 income statement to the same format as the 2012 income statement.

LO1 • 4 • 8   **Problem 2-12 Cash Flow**

Franklin Co., a specialty retailer, has a history of paying quarterly dividends of $0.50 per share. Management is trying to determine whether the company will have adequate cash on December 31, 2013, to pay a dividend if one is declared by the board of directors. The following additional information is available:

- All sales are on account, and accounts receivable are collected one month after the sale. Sales volume has been increasing 5% each month.
- All purchases of merchandise are on account, and accounts payable are paid one month after the purchase. Cost of sales is 40% of the sales price. Inventory levels are maintained at $75,000.
- Operating expenses in addition to the mortgage are paid in cash. They amount to $3,000 per month and are paid as they are incurred.

Franklin Co.
Balance Sheet
September 30, 2013

Cash	$ 5,000	Accounts payable	$ 5,000
Accounts receivable	12,500	Mortgage note**	150,000
Inventory	75,000	Common stock—$1 par	50,000
Note receivable*	10,000	Retained earnings	66,500
Building/Land	169,000	Total liabilities and	
Total assets	$271,500	stockholders' equity	$271,500

*Note receivable represents a one-year, 5% interest-bearing note due November 1, 2013.
**Mortgage note is a 30-year, 7% note due in monthly installments of $1,200.

Required

Determine the cash that Franklin will have available to pay a dividend on December 31, 2013. Round all amounts to the nearest dollar. What can Franklin's management do to increase the cash available? Should management recommend that the board of directors declare a dividend? Explain.

ALTERNATE PROBLEMS

Problem 2-1A Costs and Expenses

LO2

The following costs are incurred by a retailer:
1. Point-of-sale systems in a retail store
2. An ad in the yellow pages
3. An inventory-control computer software system
4. Shipping merchandise for resale to chain outlets

Required

For each cost, explain whether all of the cost or only a portion of the cost would appear as an expense on the income statement for the period in which the cost was incurred. If not all of the cost would appear on the income statement for that period, explain why not.

Problem 2-2A Materiality

LO2

Jane Erving, a newly hired accountant wanting to impress her boss, stayed late one night to analyze the long-distance calls by area code and time of day placed. She determined the monthly cost for the previous 12 months by hour and area code called.

Required

1. What did Jane think her boss would learn from this information? What action might be taken as a result of knowing it?
2. Would this information be more relevant if Jane worked for a hardware store or for a real estate company? Discuss.

Problem 2-3A Classified Balance Sheet

LO3

The following balance sheet items, listed in alphabetical order, are available from the records of Singer Company at December 31, 2012:

Accounts payable	$ 34,280	Interest payable	$ 2,200
Accounts receivable	26,700	Land	250,000
Accumulated depreciation—		Marketable securities	15,000
buildings	40,000	Merchandise inventory	112,900
Accumulated depreciation—		Notes payable, due April 15, 2013	6,500
equipment	12,500	Office supplies	400
Bonds payable, due December 31,		Paid-in capital in excess of	
2018	250,000	par value	75,000
Buildings	150,000	Patents	45,000
Capital stock, $1 par value	200,000	Prepaid rent	3,600
Cash	60,790	Retained earnings	113,510
Equipment	84,500	Salaries payable	7,400
Income taxes payable	7,500		

Required

1. Prepare a classified balance sheet as of December 31, 2012.
2. Compute Singer's current ratio.
3. On the basis of your answer to (2), does Singer appear to be liquid? What other information do you need to fully answer that question?

Problem 2-4A Working Capital and Current Ratio

LO4

The balance sheet of Kapinski Inc. includes the following items:

Cash	$23,000	Accounts payable	$ 84,900
Accounts receivable	43,000	Salaries payable	3,200
Inventory	75,000	Capital stock	100,000
Prepaid insurance	2,800	Retained earnings	35,700
Land	80,000		

Required

1. Determine the current ratio and working capital.
2. Kapinski appears to have a positive current ratio and a large net working capital. Why would it have trouble paying bills as they come due?
3. Suggest three things that Kapinski can do to help pay its bills on time.

LO4   Problem 2-5A Financial Statement Ratios

The following items, in alphabetical order, are available from the records of Quinn Corporation as of December 31, 2012 and 2011:

	December 31, 2012	December 31, 2011
Accounts payable	$10,500	$ 6,500
Accounts receivable	16,500	26,000
Cash	12,750	11,800
Interest receivable	200	0
Note receivable, due 12/31/2014	12,000	12,000
Office supplies	900	1,100
Prepaid insurance	400	250
Salaries payable	1,800	800
Taxes payable	10,000	5,800

Required

1. Calculate the following as of December 31, 2012, and December 31, 2011:

    a. Working capital
    b. Current ratio

2. On the basis of your answers to (1), comment on the company's relative liquidity at the beginning and end of the year. Explain the change in the company's liquidity from the beginning to the end of 2012.

LO5   Problem 2-6A Single-Step Income Statement

The following income statement items, arranged in alphabetical order, are taken from the records of Corbin Enterprises for the year ended December 31, 2012:

Advertising expense	$ 9,000	Rent expense—office	$ 26,400
Cost of goods sold	150,000	Rent expense—salesperson's car	18,000
Depreciation expense—computer	4,500	Sales revenue	350,000
Dividend revenue	2,700	Supplies expense—office	1,300
Income tax expense	30,700	Utilities expense	6,750
Interest expense	1,900	Wages expense—office	45,600

Required

1. Prepare a single-step income statement for the year ended December 31, 2012.
2. What weaknesses do you see in this form for the income statement?

LO5   Problem 2-7A Multiple-Step Income Statement and Profit Margin

Refer to the list of income statement items in Problem 2-6A. Assume that Corbin Enterprises classifies all operating expenses into two categories: (1) selling and (2) general and administrative.

Required

1. Prepare a multiple-step income statement for the year ended December 31, 2012.
2. What advantages do you see in this form for the income statement?
3. Compute Corbin's profit margin.
4. Comment on Corbin's profitability. What other factors need to be taken into account to assess Corbin's profitability?

Problem 2-8A Statement of Cash Flows

LO8

Wisconsin Corporation was organized on January 1, 2012, with the investment of $400,000 in cash by its stockholders. The company immediately purchased a manufacturing facility for $300,000, paying $150,000 in cash and signing a five-year promissory note for the balance. Wisconsin signed another five-year note at the bank for $50,000 during 2012 and received cash in the same amount. During its first year, Wisconsin collected $310,000 from its customers. It paid $185,000 for inventory, $30,100 in salaries and wages, and another $40,000 in taxes. Wisconsin paid $4,000 in cash dividends.

Required

1. Prepare a statement of cash flows for the year ended December 31, 2012.
2. What does this statement tell you that an income statement does not?

Problem 2-9A Basic Elements of Financial Reports

LO9

Comparative income statements for Thesaurus Inc. are as follows:

	2012	2011
Operating revenues	$500,000	$200,000
Operating expenses	120,000	100,000
Operating income	$380,000	$100,000
Gain on the sale of subsidiary	—	400,000
Net income	$380,000	$500,000

Required

The president and management believe that the company performed better in 2012 than it did in 2011. Write the president's letter to be included in the 2012 annual report. Explain why the company is financially sound and why shareholders should not be alarmed by the reduction in income in a year when operating revenues increased significantly.

ALTERNATE MULTI-CONCEPT PROBLEMS

Problem 2-10A Comparing Starwood Hotels & Resorts and Hyatt Hotels Corporation and Subsidiaries

LO2 • 4

The following current items, listed in alphabetical order, are taken from the consolidated balance sheets of **Starwood Hotels & Resorts Worldwide, Inc**. as of December 31, 2010, and **Hyatt Hotels Corporation and Subsidiaries** as of December 31, 2010. (All amounts are in millions of dollars.)

Starwood Hotels & Resorts Worldwide, Inc.

Accounts payable	$ 138
Accounts receivable, net of allowance for doubtful accounts of $45	513
Accrued expenses	1,104
Accrued salaries, wages and benefits	410
Accrued taxes and other	373
Cash and cash equivalents	753
Inventories	802
Current maturities of long-term securitized vacation ownership debt	127
Prepaid expenses and other	126
Restricted cash	53
Securitized vacation ownership notes receivable, net of allowance for doubtful accounts of $10	59
Short-term borrowings and current maturities of long-term debt	9

Hyatt Hotels Corporation and Subsidiaries

Accounts payable	$ 145
Accrued compensation and benefits	108
Accrued expenses and other current liabilities	286
Assets held for sale	18
Cash and cash equivalents	1,110
Current maturities of long-term debt	57
Deferred tax assets	29
Inventories	100
Prepaids and other assets	73
Prepaid income taxes	6
Receivables, net of allowances of $15	199
Restricted cash	106
Short-term investments	524

Required

1. Compute working capital and the current ratio for both companies.
2. On the basis of your answers to (1), which company appears to be more liquid?
3. Other factors affect a company's liquidity besides working capital and current ratio. Comment on the *composition* of each company's current assets and ways this composition affects liquidity.

LO2 • 5   Problem 2-11A Comparability and Consistency in Income Statements

The following income statements were provided by Chisholm Company, a wholesale food distributor:

	2012	2011
Sales	$1,700,000	$1,500,000
Cost of sales	$ 612,000	$ 450,000
Sales salaries	427,000	398,000
Delivery expense	180,000	175,000
Office supplies	55,000	54,000
Depreciation—truck	40,000	40,000
Total expenses	23,000	20,000
Net income	$ 1,337,00	$1,137,000
	$ 363,000	$ 363,000

Required

1. Identify each income statement as either single- or multiple-step format.
2. Restate each item in the income statements as a percentage of sales. Why did net income remain unchanged when sales increased in 2012?

LO1 • 4 • 8   Problem 2-12A Cash Flow

Roosevelt Inc., a consulting service, has a history of paying annual dividends of $1 per share. Management is trying to determine whether the company will have adequate cash on December 31, 2013, to pay a dividend if one is declared by the board of directors. The following additional information is available:

- All sales are on account, and accounts receivable are collected one month after the sale. Sales volume has been decreasing 5% each month.
- Operating expenses are paid in cash in the month incurred. Average monthly expenses are $10,000 (excluding the biweekly payroll).
- Biweekly payroll is $4,500, and it will be paid December 15 and December 31.
- Unearned revenue is expected to be earned in December. This amount was taken into consideration in the expected sales volume.

Roosevelt Inc.
Balance Sheet
December 1, 2013

Cash	$ 15,000	Unearned revenue	$ 2,000
Accounts receivable	40,000	Note payable*	30,000
Computer equipment	120,000	Common stock—$2 par	50,000
		Retained earnings	93,000
		Total liabilities and	
Total assets	$175,000	stockholders' equity	$175,000

*The note payable plus 3% interest for six months is due January 15, 2014.

Required

Determine the cash that Roosevelt will have available to pay a dividend on December 31, 2013. Round all amounts to the nearest dollar. Should management recommend that the board of directors declare a dividend? Explain.

DECISION CASES

Reading and Interpreting Financial Statements

Decision Case 2-1 Comparing Two Companies in the Same Industry: General Mills and Kellogg's

LO4

Refer to the financial information for **General Mills** and **Kellogg's** reproduced at the back of the book for the information needed to answer the following questions.

Required

1. Compute each company's working capital at the end of the two most recent years. Also, for each company, compute the change in working capital during the most recent year.
2. Compute each company's current ratio at the end of the two most recent years. Compute the percentage change in the ratio during the most recent year.
3. How do the two companies differ in terms of the accounts that made up their current assets at the end of the most recent year? What is the largest current asset each company reports on the balance sheet at the end of the most recent year?
4. On the basis of your answers to (2) and (3), comment on each company's liquidity.

Decision Case 2-2 Reading General Mills's Balance Sheet

LO4

Refer to **General Mills's** balance sheet reproduced at the back of the book to answer the following questions.

Required

1. Which is the largest of General Mills's current assets on May 30, 2010? What percentage of total current assets does it represent? Explain what this asset represents and why it is such a significant asset for a company such as General Mills.
2. Which is the second largest of General Mills's current assets on May 30, 2010? What percentage of total current assets does it represent? Is it favorable or unfavorable that this is such a significant asset? Explain your answer.
3. Explain what events would cause each of those accounts to both increase and decrease during the year.

Making Financial Decisions

Decision Case 2-3 Analysis of Cash Flow for a Small Business

LO8

Charles, a financial consultant, has been self-employed for two years. His list of clients has grown, and he is earning a reputation as a shrewd investor. Charles rents a small office, uses the pool secretarial services, and has purchased a car that he is depreciating over three years. The following income statements cover Charles's first two years of business:

	Year1	Year 2
Commissions revenue	$ 25,000	$65,000
Rent	$ 12,000	$12,000
Secretarial services	3,000	9,000
Car expenses, gas, insurance	6,000	6,500
Depreciation	15,000	15,000
Net income	$(11,000)	$22,500

Charles believes that he should earn more than $11,500 for working very hard for two years. He is thinking about going to work for an investment firm where he can earn $40,000 per year. What would you advise Charles to do?

LO9 Decision Case 2-4 Factors Involved in an Investment Decision

As an investor, you are considering purchasing stock in a chain of theaters. The annual reports of several companies are available for comparison.

Required

Prepare an outline of the steps you would follow to make your comparison. Start by listing the first section that you would read in the financial reports. What would you expect to find there? Why did you choose that section to read first? Continue with the other sections of the financial report.

Ethical Decision Making

LO2 Decision Case 2-5 The Expenditure Approval Process

Roberto is the plant superintendent of a small manufacturing company that is owned by a large corporation. The corporation has a policy that any expenditure over $1,000 must be approved by the chief financial officer in the corporate headquarters. The approval process takes a minimum of three weeks. Roberto would like to order a new labeling machine that is expected to reduce costs and pay for itself in six months. The machine costs $2,200, but Roberto can buy the sales rep's demo for $1,800. Roberto has asked the sales rep to send two separate bills for $900 each.

What would you do if you were the sales rep? Do you agree or disagree with Roberto's actions? What do you think about the corporate policy?

LO4 • 6 Decision Case 2-6 Susan Applies for a Loan

Susan Spiffy, owner of Spiffy Cleaners, a drive-through dry cleaners, would like to expand her business from its current location to a chain of cleaners. Revenues at the one location have been increasing an average of 8% each quarter. Profits have been increasing accordingly. Susan is conservative in spending and is a very hard worker. She has an appointment with a banker to apply for a loan to expand the business. To prepare for the appointment, she instructs you, as chief financial officer and payroll clerk, to copy the quarterly income statements for the past two years but not to include a balance sheet. Susan already has a substantial loan from another bank. In fact, she has very little of her own money invested in the business.

Required

Before answering the following questions, you may want to refer to Exhibit 1-9 and the related text on pages 28 and 29. Support each answer with your reasoning.
1. What is the ethical dilemma in this case? Who would be affected and how would they be affected if you follow Susan's instructions? (Would they benefit? Would they be harmed?) What responsibility do you have in this situation?
2. If the banker does not receive the balance sheet, will he have all of the relevant information needed for his decision-making process? Why or why not? Will the information provided by Susan be neutral?
3. What should you do? Might someone be harmed by Susan's accounting decision? Explain.

SOLUTIONS TO KEY TERMS QUIZ

6	Understandability		16	Liquidity
3	Relevance		10	Working capital
8	Faithful representation		7	Current ratio
12	Comparability		1	Single-step income statement
16	Depreciation		4	Multiple-step income statement
15	Consistency		18	Gross profit
2	Materiality		11	Profit margin
5	Conservatism		19	Auditors' report
17	Operating cycle			
13	Current asset			
9	Current liability			

ANSWERS TO POD REVIEW

LO1	1. a	2. d		**LO6**	1. a	2. c
LO2	1. b	2. d		**LO7**	1. a	2. c
LO3	1. c	2. c		**LO8**	1. b	2. c
LO4	1. c	2. b		**LO9**	1. a	2. d
LO5	1. b	2. c				

Processing Accounting Information

3

AFTER STUDYING THIS CHAPTER, YOU SHOULD BE ABLE TO:

LO1 Explain the difference between external and internal events.

LO2 Explain the role of source documents in an accounting system.

LO3 Analyze the effects of transactions on the accounting equation and understand how these transactions affect the balance sheet and the income statement.

LO4 Describe the use of the account and the general ledger to accumulate amounts of financial statement items.

LO5 Explain the rules of debits and credits [Appendix].

LO6 Explain the purposes of a journal and the posting process [Appendix].

LO7 Explain the purpose of a trial balance [Appendix].

STUDY LINKS

A Look at Previous Chapters Up to this point, we have focused on the role of accounting in decision making and the way accountants use financial statements to communicate useful information to various users of the statements.

A Look at This Chapter This chapter considers how accounting information is processed. We begin by considering the *inputs* to an accounting system, that is, the transactions entered into by a business. We look at how transactions are analyzed, and then we turn to a number of accounting tools and procedures designed to facilitate the preparation of the *outputs* of the system, the financial statements. Ledger accounts, journal entries, and trial balances are tools that allow a company to process vast amounts of data efficiently.

A Look at the Upcoming Chapter Chapter 4 concludes our overview of the accounting model. We examine the accrual basis of accounting and its effect on the measurement of income. Adjustments, which are the focus of the accrual basis, are discussed in detail in Chapter 4, along with the other steps in the accounting cycle.

MAKING BUSINESS DECISIONS
CARNIVAL CORPORATION & PLC

In these difficult economic times, all companies face challenges in generating revenues. This is certainly true of those that rely on consumer discretionary spending. The vacation and cruise business is a prime example. How do companies convince families to take cruises and spend money on board and, at the same time, hold down their own costs in this tough economy?

As the largest cruise company and one of the largest vacation companies in the world, **Carnival Corporation & PLC** (hereinafter referred to as "Carnival") presides over a vast fleet of ships operating under a number of recognizable brand names. Carnival Cruise Lines™, Princess™, Costa™, Holland America Line™, and Cunard™ are among the names on the company's fleet of 100 ships sailing around the world. As shown on the accompanying comparative income statements, revenues rose by over $1 billion in 2010 to $14.469 billion in total. Passenger tickets made up the vast majority of this revenue, increasing by nearly 8% in 2010 from the prior year.

As you know by now in your study of accounting, revenues are only one side of the equation in determining a company's profitability. Profit, or net income, is the result of deducting expenses from revenues. What do you suppose are some of the major expenses in running a cruise company? As the income statement reports, the largest of these is "Commissions, transportation and other," which includes commissions paid to travel agents and other transportation-related costs. This expense increased by only about 2%.

With 85,000 employees worldwide, you can imagine that the company's payroll is one of its largest expenses, amounting to over $1.6 billion in 2010. However, Carnival was able to limit the increase in this critical cost to about 7.5% in 2010.

Another major cost in running a cruise business is the fuel needed to power a fleet of ships. Note the $1.6 billion spent on fuel in 2010, a 40% increase from the prior year! Even with the $466 million increase in the cost of fuel, Carnival was able to report a bottom line of nearly $2 billion, over 10% more than in 2009. The company's ability to remain profitable in the future will certainly be impacted by the amount it has to pay for fuel.

In our study of accounting, we have not yet given any thought to how the numbers on an income statement (or on any of the other statements) got where they did. After all, before the information on the statements can be used for decision making, someone must decide how to record the various transactions that underlie the amounts reported. As a user of financial information, you will need to answer the following questions:

- What source documents are used as the necessary evidence to record transactions? (See p. 108.)
- What is the double-entry system of accounting? What is its role in the recording process? (See pp. 117–121.)
- What are some of the tools that accountants use to effectively and efficiently process the information that appears on financial statements? (See pp. 117–127.)

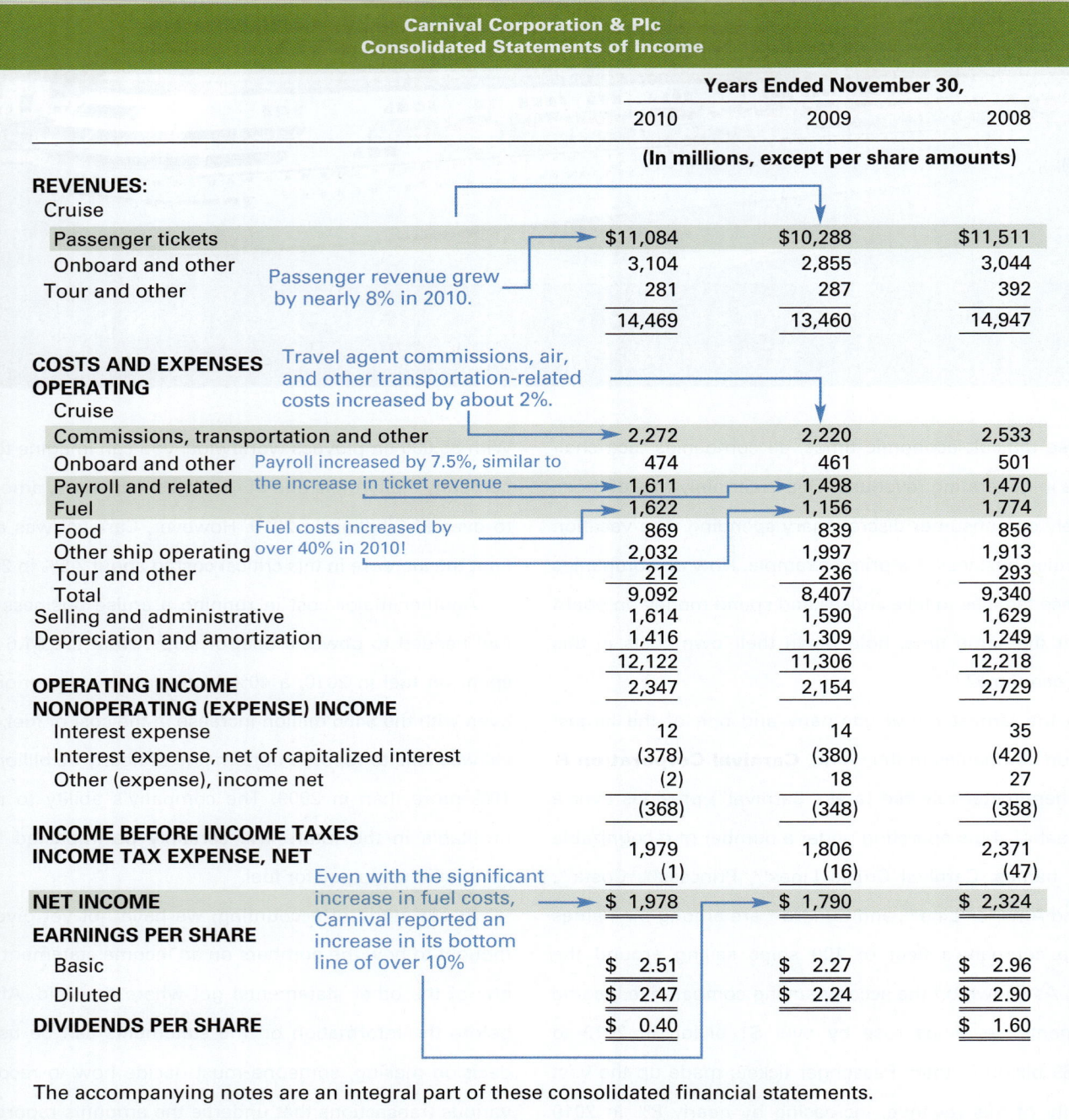

Carnival Corporation & Plc
Consolidated Statements of Income

	Years Ended November 30,		
	2010	**2009**	**2008**
	(In millions, except per share amounts)		
REVENUES:			
Cruise			
Passenger tickets	$11,084	$10,288	$11,511
Onboard and other	3,104	2,855	3,044
Tour and other	281	287	392
	14,469	13,460	14,947
COSTS AND EXPENSES			
OPERATING			
Cruise			
Commissions, transportation and other	2,272	2,220	2,533
Onboard and other	474	461	501
Payroll and related	1,611	1,498	1,470
Fuel	1,622	1,156	1,774
Food	869	839	856
Other ship operating	2,032	1,997	1,913
Tour and other	212	236	293
Total	9,092	8,407	9,340
Selling and administrative	1,614	1,590	1,629
Depreciation and amortization	1,416	1,309	1,249
	12,122	11,306	12,218
OPERATING INCOME	2,347	2,154	2,729
NONOPERATING (EXPENSE) INCOME			
Interest expense	12	14	35
Interest expense, net of capitalized interest	(378)	(380)	(420)
Other (expense), income net	(2)	18	27
	(368)	(348)	(358)
INCOME BEFORE INCOME TAXES	1,979	1,806	2,371
INCOME TAX EXPENSE, NET	(1)	(16)	(47)
NET INCOME	$ 1,978	$ 1,790	$ 2,324
EARNINGS PER SHARE			
Basic	$ 2.51	$ 2.27	$ 2.96
Diluted	$ 2.47	$ 2.24	$ 2.90
DIVIDENDS PER SHARE	$ 0.40		$ 1.60

Annotations on chart:
Passenger revenue grew by nearly 8% in 2010.

Travel agent commissions, air, and other transportation-related costs increased by about 2%.

Payroll increased by 7.5%, similar to the increase in ticket revenue

Fuel costs increased by over 40% in 2010!

Even with the significant increase in fuel costs, Carnival reported an increase in its bottom line of over 10%

The accompanying notes are an integral part of these consolidated financial statements.

Source: Carnival Corporation & PLC web site and 2010 annual report.

Economic Events: The Basis for Recording Transactions

LO1 Explain the difference between external and internal events.

OVERVIEW: External events involve interaction between a company and its environment, while internal events occur entirely within an entity. Transactions are those events that are recognized in the financial statements.

Many different types of economic events affect an entity during the year. A sale is made to a customer. Supplies are purchased from a vendor. A loan is taken out at a bank. A fire destroys a warehouse. A new contract is signed with a union. In short, "An **event** is a happening of consequence to an entity."[1]

External and Internal Events

Two types of events affect an entity: internal and external.

- An **external event** "involves interaction between the entity and its environment."[2] For example, the *payment* of wages to an employee is an external event, as is a *sale* to a customer.
- An **internal event** occurs entirely within the entity. The use of a piece of equipment is an internal event.

We will use the term **transaction** to refer to any event, external or internal, that is recognized in a set of financial statements.[3]

What is necessary to recognize an event in the records? Are all economic events recognized as transactions by the accountant? The answers to those questions involve the concept of *measurement*. An event must be measured to be recognized. Certain events are relatively easy to measure: the payroll for the week, the amount of equipment destroyed by an earthquake, or the sales for the day. Not all events that affect an entity can be measured *reliably*, however. For example, how does a manufacturer of breakfast cereal measure the effect of a drought on the price of wheat? A company hires a new chief executive. How can it reliably measure the value of the new officer to the company? There is no definitive answer to the measurement problem in accounting. It is a continuing challenge to the accounting profession and something we will return to throughout the text.

Event
A happening of consequence to an entity.

External event
An event involving interaction between an entity and its environment.

Internal event
An event occurring entirely within an entity.

Transaction
Any event that is recognized in a set of financial statements.

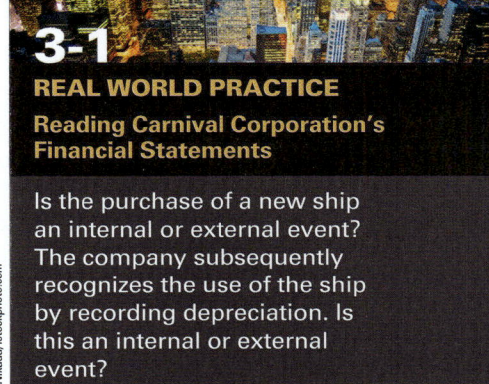

3-1

REAL WORLD PRACTICE
Reading Carnival Corporation's Financial Statements

Is the purchase of a new ship an internal or external event? The company subsequently recognizes the use of the ship by recording depreciation. Is this an internal or external event?

© Nikada/istockphoto.com

LO1 Explain the difference between external and internal events.

- Both of these different types of events affect an entity and are usually recorded in the accounting system as a transaction.
  - External events are interactions between an entity and its environment.
  - Internal events are interactions entirely within an entity.

POD REVIEW 3.1

QUESTIONS   **Answers to these questions are on the last page of the chapter.**

1. Which of the following events is not an external event?

   a. a sale to a customer
   b. a purchase of inventory from a supplier
   c. payment to the newspaper for advertising
   d. recognition of the use of equipment by the recording of depreciation

2. Which of the following is necessary to recognize an event as a transaction?

   a. It must be subject to measurement.
   b. It must be an external event.
   c. It must be an internal event.
   d. It must be an event that recurs regularly.

© Cengage Learning 2013

---

[1] *Statement of Financial Accounting Concepts (SFAC) No. 3*, "Elements of Financial Statements of Business Enterprises" (Stamford, Conn.: Financial Accounting Standards Board, 1982), par. 65.

[2] *SFAC No. 3*.

[3] Technically, a *transaction* is defined by the FASB as a special kind of external event in which the entity exchanges something of value with an outsider. Because the term *transaction* is used in practice to refer to any event that is recognized in the statements, we will use this broader definition.

The Role of Source Documents in Recording Transactions

LO2 Explain the role of source documents in an accounting system.

Source document
A piece of paper that is used as evidence to record a transaction.

OVERVIEW: Source documents are the basis for recording transactions. They take many different forms, such as invoices, cash register tapes, and time cards.

The first step in the recording process is *identification.* A business needs a systematic method for recognizing events as transactions. A **source document** provides the evidence needed in an accounting system to record a transaction. Source documents take many different forms. An invoice received from a supplier is the source document for a purchase of inventory on credit. A cash register tape is the source document used by a retailer to recognize a cash sale. The payroll department sends the accountant the time cards for the week as the necessary documentation to record wages.

Not all recognizable events are supported by a standard source document. For certain events, some form of documentation must be generated. For example, no standard source document exists to recognize the financial consequences from a fire or the settlement of a lawsuit. Documentation is just as important for those types of events as it is for standard, recurring transactions.

POD REVIEW 3.2

LO2 Explain the role of source documents in an accounting system.

- Source documents provide the evidence needed to begin the procedures for recording and processing a transaction.
- These documents need not be in hard copy form and can come from parties that are either internal or external to the company.

QUESTIONS   Answers to these questions are on the last page of the chapter.

1. A source document is
   a. the same form for all transactions.
   b. the evidence needed to record a transaction.
   c. not used in a computerized accounting system.
   d. none of the above.

2. Which of the following is an example of a source document?
   a. a cash register tape
   b. an invoice from a customer's purchase
   c. an employee's time card
   d. All of the above are examples of source documents.

Analyzing the Effects of Transactions on the Accounting Equation

LO3 Analyze the effects of transactions on the accounting equation and understand how these transactions affect the balance sheet and the income statement.

OVERVIEW: Some transactions affect just the balance sheet, and others affect both the balance sheet and the income statement. Regardless, as transactions are recorded, the accounting equation must remain in balance:

Assets = Liabilities + Stockholders' Equity

Economic events are the basis for recording transactions in an accounting system. For every transaction, it is essential to analyze its effect on the accounting equation:

Assets = Liabilities + Stockholders' Equity

We will now consider a series of events and their recognition as transactions for a hypothetical corporation, Glengarry Health Club. The transactions are for the month of January 2012, the first month of operations for the new business.

Example 3-1 Analyzing the Effects of Transactions on the Accounting Equation

(1) Issuance of capital stock. The company is started when Karen Bradley and Kathy Drake file articles of incorporation with the state to obtain a charter. Each invests $50,000 in the business. In return, each receives 5,000 shares of capital stock. Thus, at this point, each of them owns 50% of the outstanding stock of the company and has a claim to 50% of its assets. The effect of this transaction on the accounting equation is to increase both assets and stockholders' equity:

Transaction Number	**Assets**					=	**Liabilities**		+	**Stockholders' Equity**	
	Cash	Accounts Receivable	Equipment	Building	Land		Accounts Payable	Notes Payable		Capital Stock	Retained Earnings
1	$100,000									$100,000	
Totals			$100,000							$100,000	

As you can see, each side of the accounting equation increases by $100,000. Cash is increased, and because the owners contributed this amount, their claim to the assets is increased in the form of Capital Stock.

(2) Acquisition of property in exchange for a note. The company buys a piece of property for $200,000. The seller agrees to accept a five-year promissory note. The note is given by the health club to the seller and is a written promise to repay the principal amount of the loan at the end of five years. To the company, the promissory note is a liability. The property consists of land valued at $50,000 and a newly constructed building valued at $150,000. The effect of this transaction on the accounting equation is to increase both assets and liabilities by $200,000:

Transaction Number	**Assets**					=	**Liabilities**		+	**Stockholders' Equity**	
	Cash	Accounts Receivable	Equipment	Building	Land		Accounts Payable	Notes Payable		Capital Stock	Retained Earnings
Bal.	$100,000									$100,000	
2				$150,000	$50,000			$200,000			
Bal.	$100,000			$150,000	$50,000			$200,000		$100,000	
Totals			$300,000							$300,000	

(3) Acquisition of equipment on an open account. Karen and Kathy contact an equipment supplier and buy $20,000 of exercise equipment: treadmills, barbells, and stationary bicycles. The supplier agrees to accept payment in full in 30 days. The health club has acquired an asset and, at the same time, incurred a liability:

Transaction Number	**Assets**					=	**Liabilities**		+	**Stockholders' Equity**	
	Cash	Accounts Receivable	Equipment	Building	Land		Accounts Payable	Notes Payable		Capital Stock	Retained Earnings
Bal.	$100,000			$150,000	$50,000			$200,000		$100,000	
3			$20,000				$20,000				
Bal.	$100,000		$20,000	$150,000	$50,000		$20,000	$200,000		$100,000	
Totals			$320,000							$320,000	

(4) Sale of monthly memberships on account. The owners open their doors for business. During January, they sell 300 monthly club memberships for $50 each, or a total of $15,000. The members have until the 10th of the following month to pay. Glengarry does not have cash from the new members; instead, it has a promise from each member to pay cash in the future. The promise from a customer to pay an amount owed is an asset called an *account receivable.* The other side of this transaction is an increase in the stockholders' equity (specifically, Retained Earnings) in the business. In other words, the assets have increased by $15,000 without any increase in a liability or any decrease in another asset. The increase in stockholders' equity indicates that the owners' residual interest in the assets of the business has increased by this amount. More specifically, an inflow of assets resulting from the sale of goods and services by a business is called *revenue.* The change in the accounting equation is as follows:

Transaction Number	**Assets**					=	**Liabilities**		+	**Stockholders' Equity**	
	Cash	Accounts Receivable	Equipment	Building	Land		Accounts Payable	Notes Payable		Capital Stock	Retained Earnings
Bal.	$100,000		$20,000	$150,000	$50,000		$20,000	$200,000		$100,000	
4		$15,000									$15,000
Bal.	$100,000	$15,000	$20,000	$150,000	$50,000		$20,000	$200,000		$100,000	$15,000
Totals			$335,000							$335,000	

(Continued)

(5) Sale of court time for cash. In addition to memberships, Glengarry sells court time. Court fees are paid at the time of use and amount to $5,000 for the first month:

Transaction Number	Cash	Accounts Receivable	Equipment	Building	Land	=	Accounts Payable	Notes Payable	+	Capital Stock	Retained Earnings
			Assets			=	**Liabilities**		+	**Stockholders' Equity**	
Bal.	$100,000	$15,000	$20,000	$150,000	$50,000		$20,000	$200,000		$100,000	$15,000
5	5,000										5,000
Bal.	$105,000	$15,000	$20,000	$150,000	$50,000		$20,000	$200,000		$100,000	$20,000
Totals			$340,000							$340,000	

The only difference between this transaction and that of (4) is that cash is received rather than a promise being made to pay at a later date. Both transactions result in an increase in an asset and an increase in the owners' claim to the assets. In both cases, there is an inflow of assets in the form of Accounts Receivable or Cash. Thus, in both cases, the company has earned revenue.

(6) Payment of wages and salaries. The wages and salaries for the first month amount to $10,000. The payment of this amount results in a decrease in Cash and a decrease in the owners' claim on the assets, that is, a decrease in Retained Earnings. More specifically, an outflow of assets resulting from the sale of goods or services is called an *expense.* The effect of this transaction is to decrease both sides of the accounting equation:

Transaction Number	Cash	Accounts Receivable	Equipment	Building	Land	=	Accounts Payable	Notes Payable	+	Capital Stock	Retained Earnings
			Assets			=	**Liabilities**		+	**Stockholders' Equity**	
Bal.	$105,000	$15,000	$20,000	$150,000	$50,000		$20,000	$200,000		$100,000	$20,000
6	−10,000										−10,000
Bal.	$ 95,000	$15,000	$20,000	$150,000	$50,000		$20,000	$200,000		$100,000	$10,000
Totals			$330,000							$330,000	

(7) Payment of utilities. The cost of utilities for the first month is $3,000. Glengarry pays this amount in cash. Both the utilities and the salaries and wages are expenses, and they have the same effect on the accounting equation. Cash is decreased, accompanied by a corresponding decrease in the owners' claim on the assets of the business:

Transaction Number	Cash	Accounts Receivable	Equipment	Building	Land	=	Accounts Payable	Notes Payable	+	Capital Stock	Retained Earnings
			Assets			=	**Liabilities**		+	**Stockholders' Equity**	
Bal.	$95,000	$15,000	$20,000	$150,000	$50,000		$20,000	$200,000		$100,000	$10,000
7	−3,000										−3,000
Bal.	$92,000	$15,000	$20,000	$150,000	$50,000		$20,000	$200,000		$100,000	$ 7,000
Totals			$327,000							$327,000	

(8) Collection of accounts receivable. Even though the January monthly memberships are not due until the 10th of the following month, some of the members pay their bills by the end of January. The amount received from members in payment of their accounts is $4,000. The effect of the collection of an open account is to increase Cash and decrease Accounts Receivable:

Transaction Number	Cash	Accounts Receivable	Equipment	Building	Land	=	Accounts Payable	Notes Payable	+	Capital Stock	Retained Earnings
			Assets			=	**Liabilities**		+	**Stockholders' Equity**	
Bal.	$92,000	$15,000	$20,000	$150,000	$50,000		$20,000	$200,000		$100,000	$7,000
8	4,000	−4,000									
Bal.	$96,000	$11,000	$20,000	$150,000	$50,000		$20,000	$200,000		$100,000	$7,000
Totals			$327,000							$327,000	

This is the first transaction we have seen that affects only one side of the accounting equation. In fact, the company simply traded assets: Accounts Receivable for Cash. Thus, note that the totals for the accounting equation remain at $327,000. Also, note that Retained Earnings is not affected by this transaction because revenue was recognized earlier, in **(4)**, when Accounts Receivable was increased.

(Continued)

(9) Payment of dividends. At the end of the month, Karen and Kathy, acting on behalf of Glengarry Health Club, decide to pay a dividend of $1,000 on the shares of stock that each of them owns, or $2,000 in total. The effect of this dividend is to decrease both Cash and Retained Earnings. That is, the company is returning cash to the owners based on the profitable operations of the business for the first month. The transaction not only reduces Cash but also decreases the owners' claims on the assets of the company. Dividends are not an expense, but rather a direct reduction of Retained Earnings. The effect on the accounting equation is as follows:

	Assets					=	**Liabilities**		+	**Stockholders' Equity**	
Transaction Number	Cash	Accounts Receivable	Equipment	Building	Land		Accounts Payable	Notes Payable		Capital Stock	Retained Earnings
Bal.	$96,000	$11,000	$20,000	$150,000	$50,000		$20,000	$200,000		$100,000	$7,000
9	−2,000										−2,000
Bal.	$94,000	$11,000	$20,000	$150,000	$50,000		$20,000	$200,000		$100,000	$5,000
Totals			$325,000						$325,000		

© Cengage Learning 2013

The Cost Principle

An important principle governs the accounting for both the exercise equipment in (3) and the building and land in (2). The *cost principle* **requires that we record an asset at the cost to acquire it and continue to show this amount on all balance sheets until we dispose of the asset.** With a few exceptions, an asset is not carried at its market value, but at its original cost. *Why not show the land on future balance sheets at its market value?* Although this might seem more appropriate in certain instances, the subjectivity inherent in determining market values is a major reason behind the practice of carrying assets at their historical cost. The cost of an asset can be verified by an independent observer and is more *objective* than market value.

Exhibit 3-1 summarizes the effect of each transaction on the accounting equation, specifically the individual items increased or decreased by each transaction. Note the *dual* effect of each transaction. At least two items were involved in each transaction. For example, the initial investment by the owners resulted in an increase in an asset and an increase in Capital Stock. The payment of the utility bill caused a decrease in an asset and a decrease in Retained Earnings.

You can now see the central idea behind the accounting equation:

- **Even though individual transactions may change the amount and composition of the assets and liabilities, the *equation* must always balance *for* each transaction and the *balance sheet* must balance *after* each transaction.**

Balance Sheet and Income Statement for Glengarry Health Club

A balance sheet for Glengarry Health Club appears in Exhibit 3-2. All of the information needed to prepare this statement is available in Exhibit 3-1. The balances at the bottom of this exhibit are entered on the balance sheet, with assets on the left side and liabilities and stockholders' equity on the right side.

An income statement for Glengarry is shown in Exhibit 3-3. An income statement summarizes the revenues and expenses of a company for a period of time. In the example, the statement is for the month of January, as indicated on the third line of the heading of the statement. Glengarry earned revenues from two sources: (1) memberships and (2) court fees. Two types of expenses were incurred: (1) salaries and wages and (2) utilities. The difference between the total revenues of $20,000 and the total expenses of $13,000 is the net income for the month of $7,000. **Finally, remember that dividends appear on a statement of retained earnings rather than on the income statement. They are a *distribution* of net income of the period, not a *determinant* of net income as are expenses.**

EXHIBIT 3-1 Glengarry Health Club Transactions for the Month of January

Trans. No.	Assets					=	Liabilities		+	Stockholders' Equity	
	Cash	Accounts Receivable	Equipment	Building	Land		Accounts Payable	Notes Payable		Capital Stock	Retained Earnings
1	$100,000									$100,000	
2				$150,000	$50,000			$200,000			
Bal.	$100,000			$150,000	$50,000			$200,000		$100,000	
3			$20,000				$20,000				
Bal.	$100,000		$20,000	$150,000	$50,000		$20,000	$200,000		$100,000	
4		$15,000									$15,000
Bal.	$100,000	$15,000	$20,000	$150,000	$50,000		$20,000	$200,000		$100,000	$15,000
5	5,000										5,000
Bal.	$105,000	$15,000	$20,000	$150,000	$50,000		$20,000	$200,000		$100,000	$20,000
6	–10,000										–10,000
Bal.	$ 95,000	$15,000	$20,000	$150,000	$50,000		$20,000	$200,000		$100,000	$10,000
7	–3,000										–3,000
Bal.	$ 92,000	$15,000	$20,000	$150,000	$50,000		$20,000	$200,000		$100,000	$ 7,000
8	4,000	–4,000									
Bal.	$ 96,000	$11,000	$20,000	$150,000	$50,000		$20,000	$200,000		$100,000	$ 7,000
9	–2,000										–2,000
	$ 94,000	$11,000	$20,000	$150,000	$50,000		$20,000	$200,000		$100,000	$ 5,000

Total assets: $325,000   Total liabilities and stockholders' equity: $325,000

EXHIBIT 3-2 Balance Sheet for Glengarry Health Club

Glengarry Health Club
Balance Sheet
January 31, 2012

Assets		Liabilities and Stockholders' Equity	
Cash	$ 94,000	Accounts payable	$ 20,000
Accounts receivable	11,000	Notes payable	200,000
Equipment	20,000	Capital stock	100,000
Building	150,000	Retained earnings	5,000
Land	50,000	Total liabilities and	
Total assets	$325,000	stockholders' equity	$325,000

EXHIBIT 3-3 Income Statement for Glengarry Health Club

Glengarry Health Club
Income Statement
For the Month Ended January 31, 2012

Revenues:		
Memberships	$15,000	
Court fees	5,000	$20,000
Expenses:		
Wages and salaries	$10,000	
Utilities	3,000	13,000
Net income		$ 7,000

We have seen how transactions are analyzed and how they affect the accounting equation and ultimately the financial statements. While the approach we took in analyzing the nine transactions of the Glengarry Health Club was manageable, can you imagine using this type of analysis for a company with *thousands* of transactions in any one month? We now turn to various *tools* that the accountant uses to process a large volume of transactions effectively and efficiently.

LO3 Analyze the effects of transactions on the accounting equation and understand how these transactions affect the balance sheet and the income statement.

- The accounting equation illustrates the relationship between assets, liabilities, and stockholders' equity accounts. Understanding these relationships helps to see the logic behind the double-entry system in recording transactions.
  - The accounting equation: Assets = Liabilities + Stockholders' Equity
  - This equality must always be maintained. The equation can be expanded to show the linkage between the balance sheet and the income statement through the Retained Earnings account:

$$\text{Assets} = \text{Liabilities} + \text{Capital Stock} + \text{Retained Earnings}$$

POD REVIEW 3.3

QUESTIONS   **Answers to these questions are on the last page of the chapter.**

1. A company borrows $5,000 at a local bank. This transaction would result in
   a. an increase in Cash and a decrease in Retained Earnings.
   b. an increase in Cash and an increase in Accounts Payable.
   c. an increase in Cash and an increase in Notes Payable.
   d. none of the above.

2. The collection of the amount owed by a customer on account would result in
   a. an increase in Cash and an increase in Accounts Receivable.
   b. an increase in Cash and a decrease in Accounts Receivable.
   c. an increase in Cash and an increase in Retained Earnings.
   d. none of the above.

What Is an Account?

OVERVIEW: An account is used to record changes in individual items in the financial statements. The general ledger contains all the accounts and is the basis for preparation of the statements.

LO4 Describe the use of the account and the general ledger to accumulate amounts of financial statement items.

An **account** is the basic unit for recording transactions. It is the record used to accumulate monetary amounts for each asset, liability, and component of stockholders' equity, such as Capital Stock, Retained Earnings, and Dividends. It is the basic recording unit for each element in the financial statements. Each revenue and expense has its own account. In the Glengarry Health Club example, nine accounts were used: Cash, Accounts Receivable, Equipment, Building, Land, Accounts Payable, Notes Payable, Capital Stock, and Retained Earnings. (Recall that revenues, expenses, and dividends were recorded directly in the Retained Earnings account. The appendix illustrates the use of separate accounts for each revenue and expense.) In the real world, a company might have hundreds, even thousands, of individual accounts.

No two entities have exactly the same set of accounts. To a certain extent, the accounts used by a company depend on its business. For example, a manufacturer normally has three inventory accounts: Raw Materials, Work in Process, and Finished Goods. A retailer uses just one account for inventory, a Merchandise Inventory account. A service business has no need for an inventory account.

Account
A record used to accumulate amounts for each individual asset, liability, revenue, expense, and component of stockholders' equity.

Chart of Accounts

Chart of accounts
A numerical list of all accounts used by a company.

Companies need a way to organize the large number of accounts they use to record transactions. A **chart of accounts** is a numerical list of all of the accounts an entity uses. The numbering system is a convenient way to identify accounts. For example, all asset accounts might be numbered from 100 to 199; liability accounts, from 200 to 299; equity accounts, from 300 to 399; revenues, from 400 to 499; and expenses, from 500 to 599. A chart of accounts for a hypothetical company, Widescreen Theaters Corporation, is shown in Exhibit 3-4. Note the division of account numbers within each of the financial statement categories. Within the asset category, the various cash accounts are numbered from 100 to 109; receivables, from 110 to 119; etc. Not all of the numbers are assigned. For example, only three of the available nine numbers are currently utilized for cash accounts. This allows the company to add accounts as needed.

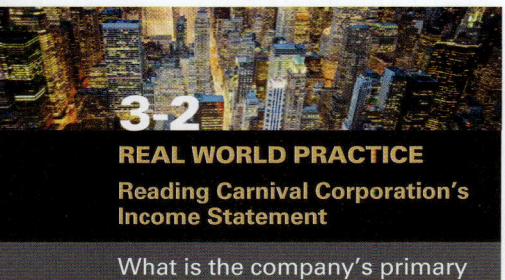

3-2

REAL WORLD PRACTICE

Reading Carnival Corporation's Income Statement

What is the company's primary source of revenue? How many operating expenses does the company report? What is the dollar amount of the largest of these?

© Nikada/istockphoto.com

EXHIBIT 3-4 Chart of Accounts for a Theater

100–199:	ASSETS		300–399:		STOCKHOLDERS' EQUITY
100–109:	Cash		301:		Preferred Stock
101:	Cash, Checking, Second National Bank		302:		Common Stock
102:	Cash, Savings, Third State Bank		303:		Retained Earnings
103:	Cash, Change, or Petty Cash Fund (coin and currency)		400–499:		REVENUES
			401:		Tickets
110–119:	Receivables		402:		Video Rentals
111:	Accounts Receivable		403:		Concessions
112:	Due from Employees		404:		Interest
113:	Notes Receivable		500–599:		EXPENSES
120–129:	Prepaid Assets		500–509:		Rentals
121:	Cleaning Supplies		501:		Films
122:	Prepaid Insurance		502:		Videos
130–139:	Property, Plant, and Equipment		510–519:		Concessions
131:	Land		511:		Candy
132:	Theater Buildings		512:		Soda
133:	Projection Equipment		513:		Popcorn
134:	Furniture and Fixtures		520–529:		Wages and Salaries
200–299:	LIABILITIES		521:		Hourly Employees
200–209:	Short-Term Liabilities		522:		Salaries
201:	Accounts Payable		530–539:		Utilities
202:	Wages and Salaries Payable		531:		Heat
203:	Taxes Payable		532:		Electric
203.1:	Income Taxes Payable		533:		Water
203.2:	Sales Taxes Payable		540–549:		Advertising
203.3:	Unemployment Taxes Payable		541:		Newspaper
204:	Short-Term Notes Payable		542:		Radio
204.1:	Six-Month Note Payable to First State Bank		550–559:		Taxes
			551:		Income Taxes
210–219:	Long-Term Liabilities		552:		Unemployment Taxes
211:	Bonds Payable, due in 2017				

© Cengage Learning 2013

The General Ledger

Companies store their accounts in different ways depending on their accounting system. In a manual system, a separate card or sheet is used to record the activity in each account. A **general ledger** is simply the file or book that contains the accounts.[4] For example, the general ledger for Widescreen Theaters Corporation might consist of a file of cards in a cabinet, with a card for each of the accounts listed in the chart of accounts.

In today's business world, most companies have an automated accounting system. The computer is ideally suited for the job of processing vast amounts of data rapidly. **All of the tools discussed in this chapter are as applicable to computerized systems as they are to manual systems. It is merely the appearance of the tools that differs between manual and computerized systems.** For example, the ledger in an automated system might be contained on a computer file server rather than stored in a file cabinet. Throughout the book, a manual system will be used to explain the various tools, such as ledger accounts. The reason is that it is easier to illustrate and visualize the tools in a manual system. However, all of the ideas apply just as well to a computerized system of accounting.

General ledger

A book, a file, a hard drive, or another device containing all of the accounts.

Alternate term: Set of accounts.

Identify & Analyze

In this chapter, we analyzed the effects of the transactions of Glengarry Health Club on the accounting equation. Because the accounting equation is the basis for financial statements, the ability to analyze transactions in terms of their effect on the equation is an essential skill to master. In the appendix to this chapter, tools used by the accountant to effectively and efficiently process large volumes of transactions during the period are examined. One of the key tools used by the accountant is a system of debits and credits.

The emphasis throughout this book is on the use of financial statements to make decisions, as opposed to the tools used by accountants to process information. Therefore, in future chapters, our emphasis will not be on the accountant's various tools, such as debits and credits, but on the effects of the transactions on the accounting equation and financial statements.

For every transaction three questions must be answered:

1. What type of **activity** did the transaction reflect? All transactions are the result of an operating, financing, or investing activity of the company.
2. What **accounts** are affected by the transaction and are they increased or decreased? Every transaction involves at least two accounts.
3. Which **financial statements** are affected by the transaction? All transactions affect either just the balance sheet or both the balance sheet and the income statement.

Recall transaction 4, Glengarry Health Club's sale of monthly memberships on account, discussed on page 109 and summarized in Exhibit 3-1:

		Assets				=	Liabilities		+	Stockholder's Equity	
Transaction Number	Cash	Accounts Receivable	Equipment	Building	Land		Accounts Payable	Notes Payable		Capital Stock	Retained Earnings
4		$15,000									$15,000

Each of the three questions would be answered for this transaction as follows:

1. The sale of memberships on account is an **operating** activity.
2. Two accounts are affected by this transaction: Both **Accounts Receivable** and revenue, specifically **Membership Revenue** are increased.
3. The sale of memberships affects both the **balance sheet** (Accounts Receivable) and the **income statement** (specifically, Membership Revenue).

---

[4] In addition to a general ledger, many companies maintain subsidiary ledgers. For example, an accounts receivable subsidiary ledger contains a separate account for each customer. The use of a subsidiary ledger for Accounts Receivable is discussed further in Chapter 7.

In future chapters, we will start by answering each of these questions for all transactions and then we will use a variation of the format in Exhibit 3-1:

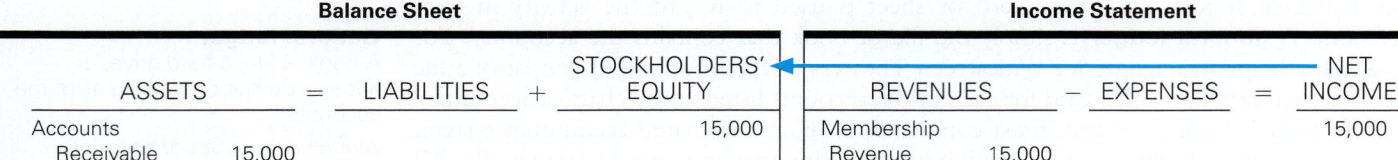

Balance Sheet				Income Statement		
ASSETS	=	LIABILITIES	+	STOCKHOLDERS' EQUITY	REVENUES – EXPENSES =	NET INCOME
				15,000		15,000
Accounts Receivable 15,000					Membership Revenue 15,000	

Note two important changes in this version of the equation. First, rather than having a separate column for each individual financial statement item (Cash, Accounts Receivable, and so on), the items are simply listed under the appropriate categories. For example, transaction 4 results in an increase in Accounts Receivable, which is shown in the assets category. Second, in this **expanded version** of the accounting equation, the income statement is viewed as an extension of the balance sheet. Membership Revenue is recorded in the Revenues column and then extended to the final column as an increase in net income. Because net income increases Retained Earnings, and Retained Earnings is part of Stockholders' Equity, an arrow is drawn to illustrate the flow of net income into stockholders' equity.

To illustrate how this new element will appear in future chapters, recall transaction 6 for Glengarry in which $10,000 was paid in wages and salaries:

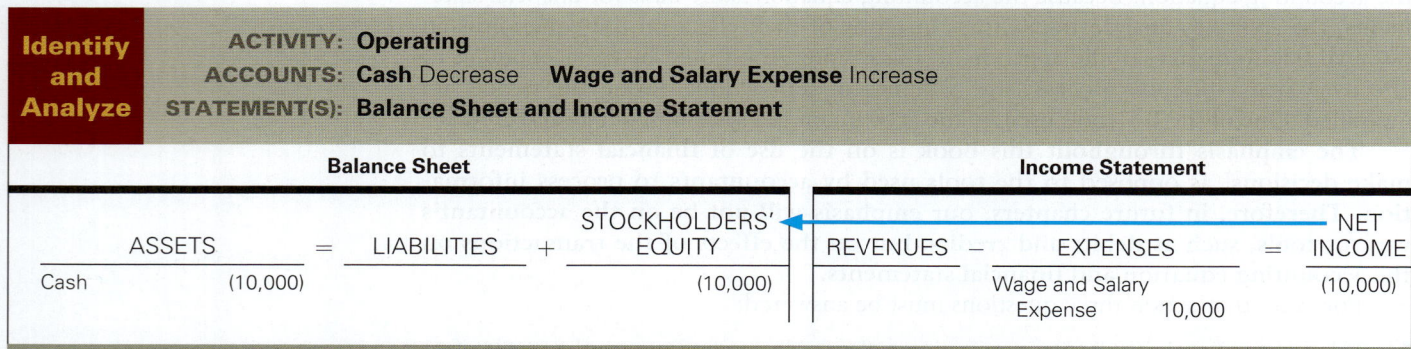

Identify and Analyze

ACTIVITY: Operating
ACCOUNTS: Cash Decrease   Wage and Salary Expense Increase
STATEMENT(S): Balance Sheet and Income Statement

Balance Sheet				Income Statement		
ASSETS	=	LIABILITIES	+	STOCKHOLDERS' EQUITY	REVENUES –	EXPENSES =	NET INCOME
Cash (10,000)				(10,000)		Wage and Salary Expense 10,000	(10,000)

Because the asset account Cash decreased, the amount of decrease is in brackets. The increase in Wage and Salary Expense is shown without brackets in the Expenses column. But because an expense reduces net income on the income statement, the amount is bracketed in the Net Income column. Finally, because a decrease in net income reduces Retained Earnings and thus stockholders' equity, the amount is bracketed in the Stockholders' Equity column to indicate a decrease.

Exhibit 3-5, on page 117, summarizes how the new element "Identify and Analyze" will be used in Chapters 4–13.

LO4 Describe the use of the account and the general ledger to accumulate amounts of financial statement items.

- An account is the basic unit for recording transactions.
- The general ledger is a crucial part of the accounting system that lists all accounts and their balances. Financial statements may be prepared from current account balances in the general ledger.

POD REVIEW 3.4

QUESTIONS   Answers to these questions are on the last page of the chapter.

1. As an accounting convention, the left side of an asset account is used to record
   a. increases.
   b. decreases.
   c. both increases and decreases.
   d. none of the above.

2. The file or book that contains all of a company's accounts is called
   a. a journal.
   b. a general ledger.
   c. a balance sheet.
   d. none of the above.

EXHIBIT 3-5 Introducing the Identify and Analyze Transaction Format

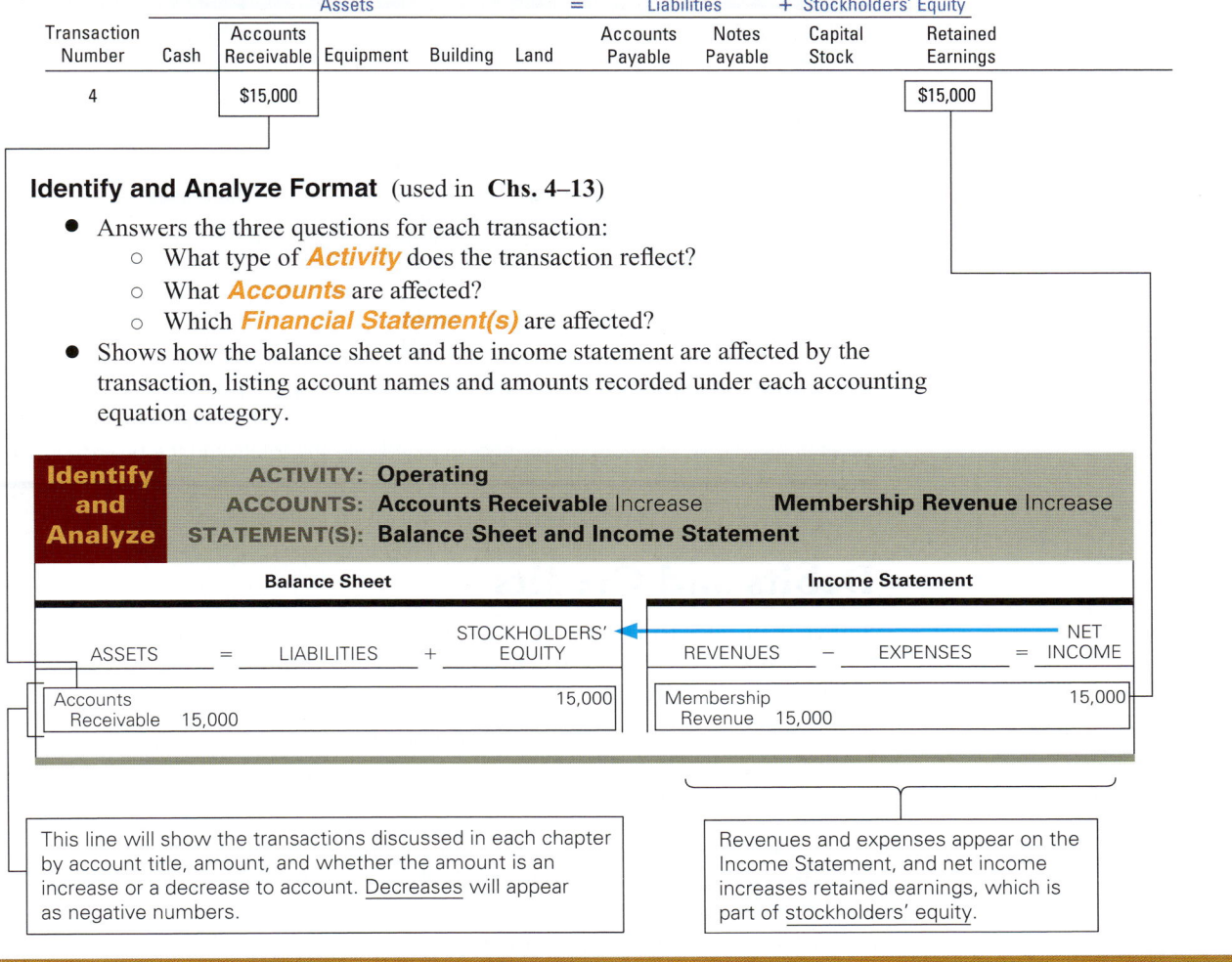

Example: Transaction 4, p.109 : Sale of monthly memberships on account:

Transaction Analysis Format (used in **Ch. 3**)

- Shows how transactions are analyzed in account names (**Cash, Accounts Receivable**, etc., as shown below) and accounting equation categories (**Assets, Liabilities, Stockholders' Equity**). (Amounts are eventually reflected in the financial statements.)

Transaction Number	Cash	Accounts Receivable	Equipment	Building	Land	Accounts Payable	Notes Payable	Capital Stock	Retained Earnings
		Assets				=	**Liabilities**	+	**Stockholders' Equity**
4		$15,000							$15,000

Identify and Analyze Format (used in **Chs. 4–13**)

- Answers the three questions for each transaction:
  - What type of *Activity* does the transaction reflect?
  - What *Accounts* are affected?
  - Which *Financial Statement(s)* are affected?
- Shows how the balance sheet and the income statement are affected by the transaction, listing account names and amounts recorded under each accounting equation category.

Identify and Analyze

ACTIVITY: Operating
ACCOUNTS: Accounts Receivable Increase   **Membership Revenue** Increase
STATEMENT(S): Balance Sheet and Income Statement

Balance Sheet			Income Statement		
ASSETS	= LIABILITIES	+ STOCKHOLDERS' EQUITY	REVENUES	− EXPENSES	= NET INCOME
Accounts Receivable 15,000		15,000	Membership Revenue 15,000		15,000

This line will show the transactions discussed in each chapter by account title, amount, and whether the amount is an increase or a decrease to account. <u>Decreases</u> will appear as negative numbers.

Revenues and expenses appear on the Income Statement, and net income increases retained earnings, which is part of <u>stockholders' equity</u>.

© Cengage Learning 2013

Appendix Accounting Tools: The Double-Entry System

OVERVIEW: Debits and credits are tools to record increases and decreases in accounts. Debits increase asset accounts, and credits increase liability and stockholders' equity accounts. Additionally, debits increase expense accounts, and credits increase revenue accounts.

LO5 Explain the rules of debits and credits [Appendix].

The origin of the double-entry system of accounting can be traced to Venice, Italy, in 1494. In that year, Fra Luca Pacioli, a Franciscan monk, wrote a mathematical treatise. Included in his book was the concept of debits and credits that is still used almost universally today.

The T Account

The form for a general ledger account will be illustrated later in the chapter. However, the form of account often used to analyze transactions is called the *T account*, so named because it resembles the capital letter T. The name of the account appears across the horizontal line. One side is used to record increases; the other side, decreases. But as you will see, the same side is not used for increases for every account. As a matter of convention, the *left* side of an *asset* account is used to record *increases*; the *right* side, to record *decreases*.

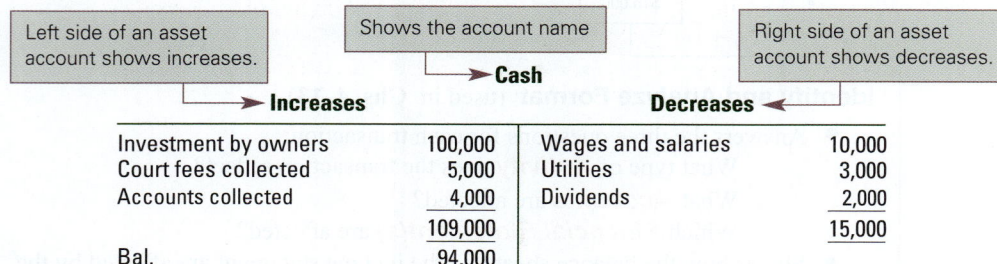

Example 3-2 Using a T Account

To illustrate a T account, we will look at the Cash account for Glengarry Health Club. The transactions recorded in the account can be traced to Exhibit 3-1.

| Left side of an asset account shows increases. | | Shows the account name | | Right side of an asset account shows decreases. |

Cash

Increases		Decreases
Investment by owners	100,000	Wages and salaries	10,000
Court fees collected	5,000	Utilities	3,000
Accounts collected	4,000	Dividends	2,000
	109,000		15,000
Bal.	94,000		

The amounts $109,000 and $15,000 are called *footings.* They represent the totals of the amounts on each side of the account. Neither these amounts nor the balance of $94,000 represents transactions. They are simply shown to indicate the totals and the balance in the account.

© Cengage Learning 2013

Debits and Credits

Rather than refer to the left or right side of an account, accountants use specific labels for each side. The *left* side of any account is the **debit** side, and the *right* side of any account is the **credit** side.

Debit
An entry on the left side of an account.

Credit
An entry on the right side of an account.

Account Name

Left Side	Right Side
Debits	Credits

We will also use the terms *debit* and *credit* as verbs. If we *debit the* Cash account, we enter an amount on the left side. Similarly, if we want to enter an amount on the right side of an account, we *credit the* account. To *charge* an account has the same meaning as to *debit* it. No such synonym exists for the act of crediting an account.

Debit and *credit* are *locational* terms. They simply refer to the left or right side of a T account. They do *not* represent increases or decreases. **When one type of account is increased (for example, the Cash account), the increase is on the left, or *debit*, side. When certain other types of accounts are increased, however, the entry will be on the right, or *credit*, side.**

As you would expect from your understanding of the accounting equation, the conventions for using T accounts for assets and liabilities are opposite. Assets are future economic benefits, and liabilities are obligations to transfer economic benefits in the future. If an asset is *increased* with a *debit,* how do you think a liability would be increased? **Because assets and liabilities are opposites, if an asset is increased with a debit, a liability is increased with a credit.** Thus, the right side, or credit side, of a liability account is used to record an increase. Like liabilities, stockholders' equity accounts are on the opposite side of the accounting equation from assets. **Thus, like a liability, a stockholders' equity account is increased with a credit.** We can summarize the logic of debits and credits, increases and decreases, and the accounting equation in the following way:

Assets		=	Liabilities		+	Stockholders' Equity	
Debits	Credits		Debits	Credits		Debits	Credits
Increases	Decreases		Decreases	Increases		Decreases	Increases
+	−		−	+		−	+

Note again that debits and credits are location-oriented. Debits are always on the left side of an account; credits, always on the right side.

Debits and Credits for Revenues, Expenses, and Dividends

Revenues In the Glengarry Health Club example, revenues recognized in (4) and (5) were an increase in Retained Earnings. The sale of memberships was not only an increase in the asset Accounts Receivable but also an increase in the stockholders' equity account, Retained Earnings. The transaction resulted in an increase in the owners' claim on the assets of the business. Rather than being recorded directly in Retained Earnings, however, each revenue item is maintained in a separate account. The following logic is used to arrive at the rules for increasing and decreasing revenues:[5]

Retained Earnings

−	+
Debit	Credit

Revenues

−	+
Debit	Credit

1. Retained Earnings is increased with a credit.
2. Revenue is an increase in Retained Earnings.
3. Revenue is increased with a credit.
4. Because revenue is increased with a credit, it is decreased with a debit.

Expenses The same logic is applied to the expenses recognized in (6) and (7). The rules for increasing and decreasing expense accounts are as follows:

Retained Earnings

−	+
Debit	Credit

Expenses

+	−
Debit	Credit

1. Retained Earnings is decreased with a debit.
2. Expense is a decrease in Retained Earnings.
3. Expense is increased with a debit.
4. Because expense is increased with a debit, it is decreased with a credit.

Dividends Recall that the dividend in (9) reduced cash. But dividends also reduce the owners' claim on the assets of the business. Earlier, we recognized this decrease in the owners' claim as a reduction of Retained Earnings. As we do for revenue and expense accounts, we will use a separate Dividends account.

Retained Earnings

−	+
Debit	Credit

Dividends

+	−
Debit	Credit

1. Retained Earnings is decreased with a debit.
2. Dividends are a decrease in Retained Earnings.
3. Dividends are increased with a debit.
4. Because dividends are increased with a debit, they are decreased with a credit.

Summary of the Rules for Increasing and Decreasing Accounts

Using the accounting equation, the rules for increasing and decreasing the various types of accounts can be summarized as follows:

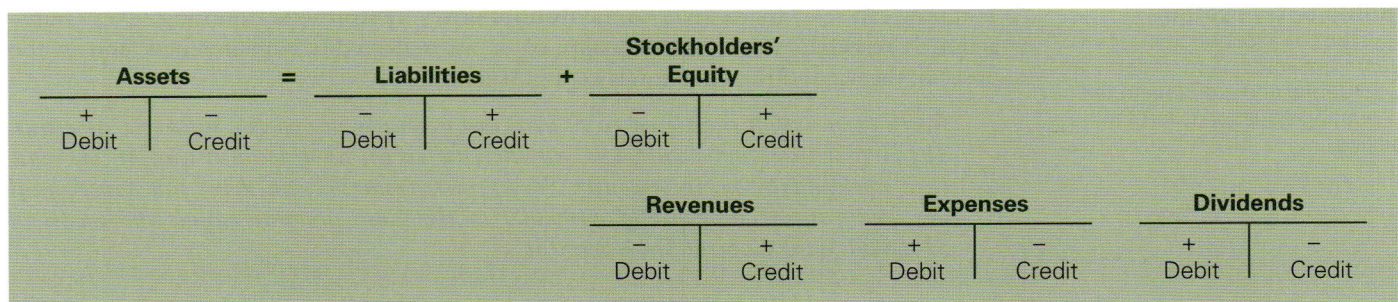

Normal Account Balances

Each account has a "normal" balance. For example, assets normally have debit balances. Would it be possible for an asset such as Cash to have a credit balance? Assume that a company has a checking account with a bank. A credit balance in the account would indicate that the decreases in the account, from checks written and other bank charges, were more than the deposits into the account. If this were the case, however, the company would no longer have an asset, Cash, but instead would have a liability to the bank.

Example 3-3 Determining Normal Account Balances

The normal balances for the accounts we have looked at are as follows:

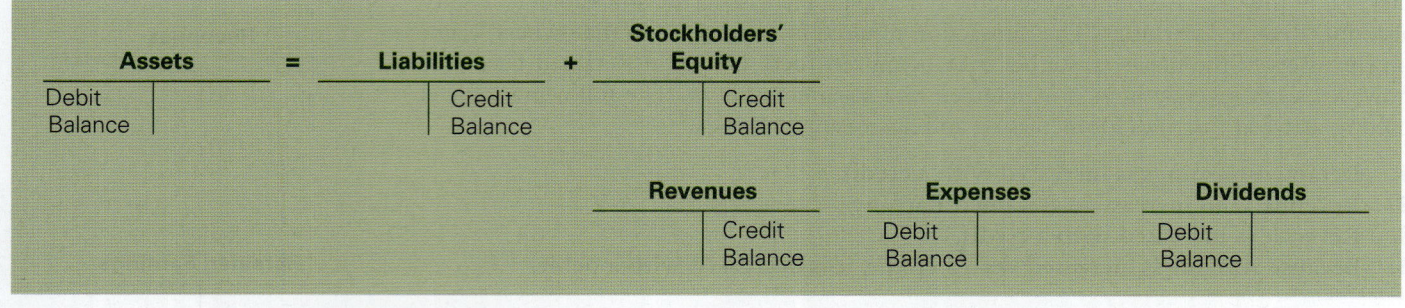

Debits Aren't Bad, and Credits Aren't Good

Students often approach their first encounter with debits and credits with preconceived notions. The use of the terms *debit* and *credit* in everyday language leads to many of these notions: Joe is a real credit to his team. Nancy should be credited with saving Mary's career. They both appear to be positive statements. You must resist the temptation to associate the term *credit* with something good or positive and the term *debit* with something bad or negative. **In accounting, debit means one thing: an entry made on the left side of an account. A credit means an entry made on the right side of an account.**

Debits and Credits Applied to Transactions

Recall the first transaction recorded by Glengarry Health Club earlier in the chapter: the owners invested $100,000 cash in the business. The transaction resulted in an increase in the Cash account and an increase in the Capital Stock account. Applying the rules of debits and credits, we would *debit* the Cash account for $100,000 and *credit* the Capital Stock account for the same amount.[6]

Cash		Capital Stock	
100,000			100,000

Double-entry system
A system of accounting in which every transaction is recorded with equal debits and credits and the accounting equation is kept in balance.

You now can see why we refer to the **double-entry system** of accounting. Every transaction is recorded so that the equality of debits and credits is maintained, and in the process, the accounting equation is kept in balance.

Every transaction is entered in at least two accounts on opposite sides of T accounts. The first transaction resulted in an increase in an asset account and an increase in a stockholders' equity account. For every transaction, the debit side must equal the credit side. The debit of $100,000 to the Cash account equals the credit of $100,000 to the Capital Stock account.

---

[6] We will use the number of each transaction as it was labeled earlier in the chapter to identify the transaction. In practice, a formal ledger account is used and transactions are entered according to their date.

It naturally follows that if the debit side must equal the credit side for every transaction, at any time, the total of all debits recorded must equal the total of all credits recorded. Thus, the fundamental accounting equation remains in balance.

Transactions for Glengarry Health Club

Three distinct steps are involved in recording a transaction in the accounts:

1. *Analyze* **the transaction.** That is, decide what accounts are increased or decreased and by how much.
2. *Recall* **the rules of debits and credits** as they apply to the transaction being analyzed.
3. *Record* **the transaction** using the rules of debits and credits.

As we will see later in the chapter, transactions are first recorded in journal entries and then transferred to accounts. However, for purposes of analysis, we will show transactions recorded in T accounts in this section.

In the section just above, we explained the logic for the debit to the Cash account and the credit to the Capital Stock account for the initial investment by the health club owners. We now analyze the remaining eight transactions for the month. Refer to Exhibit 3-1 for a summary of the transactions.

Example 3-4 Analyzing and Recording Transactions Using Debits and Credits

(2) ***Acquisition of property in exchange for a note.*** A building and land are exchanged for a promissory note.

Analyze: Two asset accounts are increased: Building and Land. The liability account Notes Payable is also increased.

Recall: An asset is increased with a debit, and a liability is increased with a credit.

Record:

Building		Notes Payable	
(2) 150,000			200,000 (2)

Land	
(2) 50,000	

(3) ***Acquisition of equipment on an open account.*** Exercise equipment is purchased from a supplier on open account. The purchase price is $20,000.

Analyze: An asset account, Equipment, is increased. A liability account, Accounts Payable, is also increased. Thus, the transaction is identical to the last transaction in that an asset or assets are increased and a liability is increased.

Recall: An asset is increased with a debit, and a liability is increased with a credit.

Record:

Equipment		Accounts Payable	
(3) 20,000			20,000 (3)

(4) ***Sale of monthly memberships on account.*** Three hundred club memberships are sold for $50 each. The members have until the 10th of the following month to pay.

Analyze: The asset account Accounts Receivable is increased by $15,000. This amount is an asset because the company has the right to collect it in the future. The owners' claim to the assets is increased by the same amount. Recall, however, that we do not record these claims—revenues—directly in a stockholders' equity account, but instead use a separate revenue account. We will call the account Membership Revenue.

Recall: An asset is increased with a debit. Stockholders' equity is increased with a credit. Because revenue is an increase in stockholders' equity, it is increased with a credit.

Record:

Accounts Receivable		Membership Revenue	
(4) 15,000			15,000 (4)

(Continued)

(5) **Sale of court time for cash.** Court fees are paid at the time of use and amount to $5,000 for the first month.

Analyze: The asset account Cash is increased by $5,000. The stockholders' claim to the assets is increased by the same amount. The account used to record the increase in the stockholders' claim is Court Fee Revenue.

Recall: An asset is increased with a debit. Stockholders' equity is increased with a credit. Because revenue is an increase in stockholders' equity, it is increased with a credit.

Record:

Cash			Court Fee Revenue	
(1) 100,000				5,000 (5)
(5) 5,000				

(6) **Payment of wages and salaries.** Wages and salaries amount to $10,000, and they are paid in cash.

Analyze: The asset account Cash is decreased by $10,000. At the same time, the owners' claim to the assets is decreased by this amount. However, rather than record a decrease directly to Retained Earnings, we set up an expense account, Wage and Salary Expense.

Recall: An asset is decreased with a credit. Stockholders' equity is decreased with a debit. Because expense is a decrease in stockholders' equity, it is increased with a debit.

Record:

Cash		Wage and Salary Expense	
(1) 100,000	10,000 (6)	(6) 10,000	
(5) 5,000			

(7) **Payment of utilities.** The utility bill of $3,000 for the first month is paid in cash.

Analyze: The asset account Cash is decreased by $3,000. At the same time, the owners' claim to the assets is decreased by this amount. However, rather than record a decrease directly to Retained Earnings, we set up an expense account, Utilities Expense.

Recall: An asset is decreased with a credit. Stockholders' equity is decreased with a debit. Because expense is a decrease in stockholders' equity, it is increased with a debit.

Record:

Cash		Utilities Expense	
(1) 100,000	10,000 (6)	(7) 3,000	
(5) 5,000	3,000 (7)		

(8) **Collection of accounts receivable.** Cash of $4,000 is collected from members for their January dues.

Analyze: Cash is increased by the amount collected from the members. Another asset, Accounts Receivable, is decreased by the same amount. Glengarry has simply traded one asset for another.

Recall: An asset is increased with a debit and decreased with a credit. Thus, one asset is debited, and another is credited.

Record:

Cash		Accounts Receivable	
(1) 100,000	10,000 (6)	(4) 15,000	4,000 (8)
(5) 5,000	3,000 (7)		
(8) 4,000			

(9) **Payment of dividends.** Dividends of $2,000 are distributed to the owners.

Analyze: The asset account Cash is decreased by $2,000. At the same time, the owners' claim to the assets is decreased by this amount. Earlier in the chapter, we decreased Retained Earnings for dividends paid to the owners. Now we will use a separate account, Dividends, to record these distributions.

Recall: An asset is decreased with a credit. Retained earnings is decreased with a debit. Because dividends are a decrease in retained earnings, they are increased with a debit.

Record:

Cash		Dividends	
(1) 100,000	10,000 (6)	(9) 2,000	
(5) 5,000	3,000 (7)		
(8) 4,000	2,000 (9)		

LO5 Explain the rules of debits and credits.

- Debits and credits represent the left and right sides of a T account, respectively. They take on meaning only when associated with the recording of transactions involving asset, liability, and equity accounts.
  - In general, debits increase asset accounts and credits increase liability and equity accounts.
  - The double-entry system requires that total debits equal total credits for any transaction recorded in the accounting system.

POD REVIEW 3.5

QUESTIONS   **Answers to these questions are on the last page of the chapter.**

1. The payment of the amount owed to a supplier on account would be recorded as
   a. a debit to Cash and a credit to Accounts Payable.
   b. a debit to Accounts Payable and a credit to Cash.
   c. a debit to Accounts Receivable and a credit to Cash.
   d. none of the above.

2. A theater sells a movie ticket for cash. This would be recorded as
   a. a debit to Sales Revenue and a credit to Cash.
   b. a debit to Cash and a credit to Accounts Receivable.
   c. a debit to Cash and a credit to Sales Revenue.
   d. none of the above.

© Cengage Learning 2013

The Journal: The Firm's Chronological Record of Transactions

OVERVIEW: A journal is a chronological record of a company's transactions. Transactions are periodically posted from the journal to ledger accounts.

LO6 Explain the purposes of a journal and the posting process [Appendix].

To focus attention on analysis, each of Glengarry Health Club's nine transactions was entered directly in the ledger accounts in the previous section. By looking at the Cash account, we see that it increased by $5,000 in (5). But what was the other side of this transaction? That is, what account was credited? To have a record of *each entry,* transactions are recorded first in a journal. A **journal** is a chronological record of transactions entered into by a business. Because a journal lists transactions in the order in which they took place, it is called the *book of original entry.* Transactions are recorded first in a journal and then are posted to the ledger accounts. **Posting** is the process of transferring a journal entry to the ledger accounts:

Journal
A chronological record of transactions.
Alternate term: Book of original entry.

Transactions are entered in

| The Journal | and then posted to → | Ledger Accounts: Cash Land Other accounts |

Posting
The process of transferring amounts from a journal to the ledger accounts.

Note that posting does not result in any change in the amounts recorded. It is simply a process of re-sorting the transactions from a chronological order to a topical arrangement.

A journal entry is recorded for each transaction. **Journalizing** is the process of recording entries in a journal. A standard format is normally used for recording journal entries.

Journalizing
The act of recording journal entries.

Example 3-5 Recording Transactions in Journal Entry Form

Consider the original investment [see (1), Issuance of capital stock, on page 109] by the owners of Glengarry Health Club. The format of the journal entry is as follows:

		Debit	Credit
Jan. xx	Cash	100,000	
	Capital Stock		100,000
	To record the issuance of 10,000 shares of stock for cash.		

(Continued)

Each journal entry contains a date with columns for the amounts debited and credited. Accounts credited are indented to distinguish them from accounts debited. A brief explanation normally appears on the line below the entry.

The remaining eight transactions for Glengarry Health Club would appear in journal entry form as follows:

		Debit	Credit
Jan. xx	Building	150,000	
	Land	50,000	
	Notes Payable		200,000
	To record acquisition of property in exchange for note.		
Jan. xx	Equipment	20,000	
	Accounts Payable		20,000
	To record acquisition of equipment on open account.		
Jan. xx	Accounts Receivable	15,000	
	Membership Revenue		15,000
	To record sale of monthly memberships on account.		
Jan. xx	Cash	5,000	
	Court Fee Revenue		5,000
	To record sale of court time for cash.		
Jan. xx	Wage and Salary Expense	10,000	
	Cash		10,000
	To record payment of wages and salaries.		
Jan. xx	Utilities Expense	3,000	
	Cash		3,000
	To record payment of utilities.		
Jan. xx	Cash	4,000	
	Accounts Receivable		4,000
	To record collection of accounts receivable.		
Jan. xx	Dividends	2,000	
	Cash		2,000
	To record payment of dividends.		

© Cengage Learning 2013

General journal
The journal used in place of a specialized journal.

Transactions are normally recorded in a **general journal**. Specialized journals may be used to record repetitive transactions. For example, a cash receipts journal may be used to record all transactions in which cash is received. Special journals accomplish the same purpose as a general journal, but they save time in recording similar transactions. This chapter will use a general journal to record all transactions.

An excerpt from Glengarry Health Club's general journal appears in the top portion of Example 3-6. One column needs further explanation. *Post. Ref.* is an abbreviation for *Posting Reference*. As part of the posting process, which is explained later in this section, the debit and credit amounts are posted to the appropriate accounts and this column is filled in with the number assigned to the account.

Journal entries and ledger accounts are *tools* used by the accountant. The end result, a set of financial statements, is the most important part of the process. Journalizing provides a chronological record of each transaction. So why not just prepare financial statements directly from the journal entries? Isn't it extra work to *post* the entries to the ledger accounts? In the simple example of Glengarry Health Club, it would be possible to prepare the statements directly from the journal entries. In real-world situations, however, the number of transactions in any given period is so large that it would be virtually impossible, if not very inefficient, to bypass the accounts. Accounts provide a convenient summary of the activity as well as the balance for a specific financial statement item.

Example 3-6 Posting from the Journal to the Ledger

The posting process for Glengarry Health Club is illustrated below for the health club's fifth transaction, in which cash is collected for court fees. Rather than a T-account format for the general ledger accounts, the *running balance form* is illustrated. A separate column indicates the balance in the ledger account after each transaction. The use of the explanation column in a ledger account is optional. Because an explanation of the entry in the account can be found by referring to the journal, this column is often left blank.

General Journal   **Page No. 1**

Date			Account Titles and Explanation		Post. Ref.	Debit	Credit
2012							
Jan.	xx		Accounts Receivable		5	15,000	
			Membership Revenue		40		15,000
			Sold 300 memberships at $50 each.				
	xx		Cash		1	5,000	
			Court Fee Revenue		44		5,000
			Collected court fees.				

General Ledger
Cash   **Account No. 1**

Date		Explanation	Post. Ref.	Debit	Credit	Balance
2012						
Jan.	xx		GJ1	100,000		100,000
	xx		GJ1	5,000		105,000

Court Fee Revenue   **Account No. 44**

Date		Explanation	Post. Ref.	Debit	Credit	Balance
2012						
Jan.	xx		GJ1		5,000	5,000

Note the cross-referencing between the journal and the ledger. As amounts are entered in the ledger accounts, the Posting Reference column is filled in with the page number of the journal. For example, GJ1 indicates page 1 from the general journal. At the same time, the Posting Reference column of the journal is filled in with the appropriate account number.

The frequency of posting differs among companies, partly based on the degree to which their accounting system is automated. For example, in some computerized systems, amounts are posted to the ledger accounts at the time an entry is recorded in the journal. In a manual system, posting is normally done periodically; for example, daily, weekly, or monthly. Regardless of when it is performed, the posting process changes nothing. It simply reorganizes the transactions by account.

HOT TOPICS
Conserving Cash to Invest in the Future

As you can imagine, the life blood of a cruise company's operations is its fleet of ships. By the end of April 2011, Carnival Corporation & PLC had 100 ships sailing the seas. Of Carnival's total assets at the end of 2010 of 37.5 billion, over 80% of this was invested in the company's Property & Equipment. The 2010 statement of cash flows reported nearly $3.6 billion spent on additions to this asset. Obviously, the nature of the cruise business requires that the company continually have available large amounts of cash needed to add to its fleet of ships.

Operations can only generate so much of the cash needed to pay for new ships. Where else can a company turn to find the sizeable amounts needed for additions to the fleet? One potential source is the financial markets, where a company can borrow on either a short- or long-term basis. However, given the highly volatile state of the financial markets, Carnival made a decision to go a different route.

Carnival weighed the options available and made the difficult decision in October 2008 to suspend its regular quarterly dividend beginning in 2009. In doing so, the company had to weigh competing interests. Surely, it would be in the short-term interests of stockholders to continue to receive their dividends. However, Carnival took a longer-term view and estimated that suspension of dividends would result in annualized cash savings of $1.3 billion. This would allow the world's largest cruise company to pay for the ships on order for 2009 without borrowing money in the relatively expensive capital markets.

Weighing options and making strategic decisions are always crucial to a company's future, but even more so in these challenging economic times. Interestingly, Carnival made another strategic decision in 2010 when it reinstated quarterly dividends, beginning with one paid in March of that year.

Source: Carnival Cruise Corporation & PLC press releases, October 31, 2008 and January 21, 2010; http://www.carnival.com.

POD REVIEW 3.6

LO6 Explain the purposes of a journal and the posting process.

- A journal documents the details of transactions by date. Entries are made to a journal every time a transaction occurs.
  - Similar transactions that occur regularly may be recorded in special journals.
- Ultimately, information is posted from the journal to the ledger for each individual account.

QUESTIONS   **Answers to these questions are on the last page of the chapter.**

1. The Posting Reference column in a general journal is used
   a. to indicate the page number of the journal.
   b. to indicate the account number for the account being debited or credited.
   c. to indicate the date of the transaction.
   d. This column is normally left blank.

2. Entries are posted from
   a. the journal to the ledger.
   b. the ledger to the journal.
   c. the journal directly to the financial statements.
   d. The order of posting differs depending on the type of company.

The Trial Balance

LO7 Explain the purpose of a trial balance [Appendix].

OVERVIEW: A trial balance is used to prove the equality of debits and credits. It is normally prepared at the end of the accounting period and is the basis for preparation of financial statements.

Trial balance
A list of each account and its balance; used to prove equality of debits and credits.

Accountants use one other tool to facilitate the preparation of a set of financial statements. A **trial balance** is a list of each account and its balance at a specific point in time. The trial balance is *not* a financial statement but merely a convenient device to prove the equality of the debit and credit balances in the accounts. It can be as informal as an adding machine tape with the account titles penciled in next to the debit and credit amounts.

Example 3-7 Preparing a Trial Balance

A trial balance for Glengarry Health Club as of January 31, 2012, is shown below. The balance in each account was determined by adding the increases and subtracting the decreases for the account for the transactions detailed earlier.

Glengarry Health Club
Trial Balance
January 31, 2012

Account Titles	Debits	Credits
Cash	$ 94,000	
Accounts Receivable	11,000	
Equipment	20,000	
Building	150,000	
Land	50,000	
Accounts Payable		$ 20,000
Notes Payable		200,000
Capital Stock		100,000
Membership Revenue		15,000
Court Fee Revenue		5,000
Wage and Salary Expense	10,000	
Utilities Expense	3,000	
Dividends	2,000	
Totals	$340,000	$340,000

© Cengage Learning 2013

Certain types of errors are detectable from a trial balance. For example, if the balance of an account is incorrectly computed, the total of the debits and credits in the trial balance will not equal. If a debit is posted to an account as a credit, or vice versa, the trial balance will be out of balance. The omission of part of a journal entry in the posting process will also be detected by the preparation of a trial balance.

Do not attribute more significance to a trial balance, however, than is warranted. It does provide a convenient summary of account balances for preparing financial statements. It also assures us that the balances of all of the debit accounts equal the balances of all of the credit accounts. But an equality of debits and credits does not necessarily mean that the *correct* accounts were debited and credited in an entry. For example, the entry to record the purchase of land by signing a promissory note *should* result in a debit to Land and a credit to Notes Payable. If the accountant incorrectly debited Cash instead of Land, the trial balance would still show an equality of debits and credits. A trial balance can be prepared at any time; it is usually prepared before the release of a set of financial statements.

LO7 Explain the purpose of a trial balance.

- At the end of a period, a trial balance may be prepared that lists all of the accounts in the general ledger along with their debit or credit balances.
- The purpose of the trial balance is to see whether total debits equal total credits. This provides some assurance that the accounting equation was adhered to in the processing of transactions but is no guarantee that transactions have been recorded properly.

POD REVIEW 3.7

QUESTIONS   Answers to these questions are on the last page of the chapter.

1. A trial balance
   a. is one of the primary financial statements.
   b. will not balance if the wrong account is debited.
   c. is a list of each account and its balance.
   d. None of the above applies.

2. Which of the following errors would not be detected by the preparation of a trial balance?

   a. Cash was debited when the debit should have been to Accounts Receivable.
   b. An entry was recorded with a debit to Cash for $500 and a credit to Accounts Receivable for $5,000.
   c. The balance in one of the accounts was computed incorrectly.
   d. All of the above errors would be detected by the preparation of a trial balance.

KEY TERMS QUIZ

Note: A separate quiz is available for the terms in the appendix to this chapter.

Read each definition below and write the number of the definition in the blank beside the appropriate term. The quiz solutions appear at the end of the chapter.

Quiz 1: Processing Accounting Information

_____ Event	_____ Source document
_____ External event	_____ Account
_____ Internal event	_____ Chart of accounts
_____ Transaction	_____ General ledger

1. A numerical list of all the accounts used by a company.
2. A happening of consequence to an entity.
3. An event occurring entirely within an entity.
4. A piece of paper, such as a sales invoice, that is used as the evidence to record a transaction.
5. An event involving interaction between an entity and its environment.
6. The record used to accumulate monetary amounts for each individual asset, liability, revenue, expense, and component of owners' equity.
7. A book, file, hard drive, or other device containing all of a company's accounts.
8. Any event, external or internal, that is recognized in a set of financial statements.

Quiz 2: Appendix

_____ Debit	_____ Posting
_____ Credit	_____ Journalizing
_____ Double-entry system	_____ General journal
_____ Journal	_____ Trial balance

1. A list of each account and its balance at a specific point in time; used to prove the equality of debits and credits.
2. An entry on the right side of an account.
3. The act of recording journal entries.
4. An entry on the left side of an account.
5. The process of transferring amounts from a journal to the appropriate ledger accounts.
6. A chronological record of transactions, also known as the *book of original entry*.
7. The journal used in place of a specialized journal.
8. A system of accounting in which every transaction is recorded with equal debits and credits and the accounting equation is kept in balance.

ALTERNATE TERMS

credit side of an account right side of an account

debit an account charge an account

debit side of an account left side of an account

general ledger set of accounts

journal book of original entry

journalizing an entry recording an entry

posting an account transferring an amount from the journal to the ledger

WARMUP EXERCISES & SOLUTIONS

Warmup Exercise 3-1 Your Personal Accounting Equation   **LO3**

Assume that you borrow $1,000 from your roommate by signing an agreement to repay the amount borrowed in six months.

Required

What is the effect of this transaction on your own accounting equation?

KEY TO THE SOLUTION Refer to Exhibit 3-1 for the effects of transactions on the accounting equation.

Warmup Exercise 3-2 A Bank's Accounting Equation   **LO3**

Third State Bank loans a customer $5,000 in exchange for a promissory note.

Required

What is the effect of this transaction on the bank's accounting equation?

KEY TO THE SOLUTION Refer to Exhibit 3-1 for the effects of the transaction on the accounting equation.

Warmup Exercise 3-3 Carnival Corporation's Accounting Equation   **LO3**

Assume that **Carnival Corporation** borrows $250 million by signing a promissory note. The next day the company uses the money to buy a new ship.

Required

What is the effect of each of these transactions on Carnival Corporation's accounting equation?

KEY TO THE SOLUTION Refer to Exhibit 3-1 for the effects of transactions on the accounting equation.

Solutions to Warmup Exercises

Warmup Exercise 3-1

If you borrow $1,000 from your roommate, assets in the form of cash increase $1,000 and liabilities in the form of a note payable increase $1,000.

Warmup Exercise 3-2

If a bank loans a customer $5,000, the bank's assets in the form of a note receivable increase $5,000 and its assets in the form of cash decrease $5,000.

Warmup Exercise 3-3

If Carnival Corporation borrows $250 million, assets in the form of cash increase $250 million and liabilities in the form of a note payable increase $250 million. If the company uses the money to buy a ship, assets in the form of ships increase $250 million and assets in the form of cash decrease $250 million.

REVIEW PROBLEM & SOLUTION

The following transactions are entered into by Sparkle Car Wash during its first month of operations:

a. Articles of incorporation are filed with the state, and 20,000 shares of capital stock are issued. Cash of $40,000 is received from the new owners for the shares.

(Continued)

b. A five-year promissory note is signed at the local bank. The cash received from the loan is $120,000.

c. An existing car wash is purchased for $150,000 in cash. The values assigned to the land, building, and equipment are $25,000, $75,000, and $50,000, respectively.

d. Cleaning supplies are purchased on account for $2,500 from a distributor. None of the supplies are used in the first month.

e. During the first month, $1,500 is paid to the distributor for the cleaning supplies. The remaining $1,000 will be paid next month.

f. Gross receipts from car washes during the first month of operations amount to $7,000.

g. Wages and salaries paid in the first month amount to $2,000.

h. The utility bill of $800 for the month is paid.

i. A total of $1,000 in dividends is paid to the owners.

Required

1. Prepare a table to summarize the preceding transactions as they affect the accounting equation. Use the format in Exhibit 3-1. Identify each transaction by letter.
2. Prepare an income statement for the month.
3. Prepare a balance sheet at the end of the month.

Solutions to Review Problem

1.
Sparkle Car Wash
Transactions for the Month

	Assets					=	Liabilities		+	Stockholders' Equity	
Trans No.	Cash	Cleaning Supplies	Land	Building	Equipment		Accounts Payable	Note Payables		Capital Stock	Retained Earnings
a.	$ 40,000									$40,000	
b.	120,000							$120,000			
Bal.	$160,000							$120,000		$40,000	
c.	−150,000		$25,000	$75,000	$50,000						
Bal.	$ 10,000		$25,000	$75,000	$50,000			$120,000		$40,000	
d.		$2,500					$2,500				
Bal.	$ 10,000	$2,500	$25,000	$75,000	$50,000		$2,500	$120,000		$40,000	
e.	−1,500						−1,500				
Bal.	$ 8,500	$2,500	$25,000	$75,000	$50,000		$1,000	$120,000		$40,000	
f.	7,000										$7,000
Bal.	$ 15,500	$2,500	$25,000	$75,000	$50,000		$1,000	$120,000		$40,000	$7,000
g.	−2,000										−2,000
Bal.	$ 13,500	$2,500	$25,000	$75,000	$50,000		$1,000	$120,000		$40,000	$5,000
h.	−800										−800
Bal.	$ 12,700	$2,500	$25,000	$75,000	$50,000		$1,000	$120,000		$40,000	$4,200
i.	−1,000										−1,000
Bal.	$ 11,700	$2,500	$25,000	$75,000	$50,000		$1,000	$120,000		$40,000	$3,200

Total assets: $164,200

Total liablities and stockholders' equity: $164,200

2.

Sparkle Car Wash
Income Statement
For the Month Ended XX/XX/XX

Car wash revenue		$7,000
Expenses:		
Wages and salaries	$2,000	
Utilities	800	2,800
Net income		$4,200

3.

Sparkle Car Wash
Balance Sheet
XX/XX/XX

Assets		Liabilities and Stockholders' Equity	
Cash	$ 11,700	Accounts payable	$ 1,000
Cleaning supplies	2,500	Notes payable	120,000
Land	25,000	Capital stock	40,000
Building	75,000	Retained earnings	3,200
Equipment	50,000	Total liabilities and	
Total assets	$164,200	stockholders' equity	$164,200

QUESTIONS

1. What are the two types of events that affect an entity? Describe each.
2. What is the significance of source documents to the recording process? Give two examples of source documents.
3. What are four different forms of cash?
4. How does an account receivable differ from a note receivable?
5. Explain what is meant by this statement: One company's account receivable is another company's account payable.
6. What do accountants mean when they refer to the double-entry system of accounting? (Appendix)
7. Stockholders' equity represents the claim of the owners on the assets of the business. What is the distinction relative to the owners' claim between the Capital Stock account and the Retained Earnings account?
8. If an asset account is increased with a debit, what is the logic for increasing a liability account with a credit? (Appendix)
9. A friend comes to you with the following plight: "I'm confused. An asset is something positive, and it is increased with a debit. However, an expense is something negative, and it is also increased with a

debit. I don't get it." How can you "straighten out" your friend? (Appendix)
10. The payment of dividends reduces cash. If the Cash account is reduced with a credit, why is the Dividends account debited when dividends are paid? (Appendix)
11. If Cash is increased with a debit, why does the bank credit your account when you make a deposit? (Appendix)
12. Your friend presents the following criticism of the accounting system: "Accounting involves so much duplication of effort. First, entries are recorded in a journal; then the same information is recorded in a ledger. No wonder accountants work such long hours!" Do you agree with this criticism? Explain. (Appendix)
13. How does the T account differ from the running balance form for an account? How are they similar? (Appendix)
14. What is the benefit of using a cross-referencing system between a ledger and a journal? (Appendix)
15. How often should a company post entries from the journal to the ledger? (Appendix)
16. What is the purpose of a trial balance? (Appendix)

BRIEF EXERCISES

LO1 **Brief Exercise 3-1 External and Internal Events**

Explain how an external event differs from an internal event.

LO2 **Brief Exercise 3-2 Source Documents**

Provide three examples of source documents and the event for which each would provide the evidence to record.

LO3 **Brief Exercise 3-3 Effects of Transactions on the Accounting Equation**

EXAMPLE 3-1   List the three elements in the accounting equation. How is the third element expanded to show the linkage between the balance sheet and the income statement?

LO4 **Brief Exercise 3-4 Types of Accounts**

For each of the following accounts, indicate whether it is a balance sheet (BS) account or an income statement (IS) account.

_____ Prepaid Insurance	_____ Utilities Expense
_____ Sales Revenue	_____ Furniture and Fixtures
_____ Income Taxes Payable	_____ Retained Earnings
_____ Accounts Receivable	

LO5 **Brief Exercise 3-5 Debits and Credits (Appendix)**

EXAMPLE 3-3   For each of the following accounts, indicate whether it would be increased with a debit or a credit.

_____ Accounts Payable	_____ Income Tax Payable
_____ Office Supplies	_____ Cash
_____ Interest Revenue	_____ Common Stock
_____ Income Tax Expense	_____ Land

LO6 **Brief Exercise 3-6 Journalizing Transactions (Appendix)**

EXAMPLE 3-4, 3-5   Prepare in good form the journal entry to record each of the following transactions on the books of ABC.

January 10:   ABC is incorporated by issuing $50,000 of common stock to each of the three owners.

January 12:   ABC borrows $100,000 at the local bank.

January 15:   ABC pays $200,000 cash to buy ten acres of land.

LO7 **Brief Exercise 3-7 Trial Balance (Appendix)**

For each of the following errors, indicate with a *Y* for yes or an *N* for no whether it would be detected by preparation of a trial balance.

_____ a. Cash is debited instead of Accounts Receivable for a sale on account.

_____ b. A sale on account for $500 is recorded with a debit to Accounts Receivable for $500 and a credit to Sales for $5,000.

_____ c. A cash sale is recorded by debiting Cash and Sales for the same amount.

EXERCISES

Exercise 3-1 Types of Events

LO1

For each of the following events, identify whether it is an external event that would be recorded as a transaction (E), an internal event that would be recorded as a transaction (I), or not recorded (NR).

_____ 1. A vendor for a company's supplies is paid an amount owed on account.
_____ 2. A customer pays its open account.
_____ 3. A new chief executive officer is hired.
_____ 4. The biweekly payroll is paid.
_____ 5. Depreciation on equipment is recognized.
_____ 6. A new advertising agency is hired to develop a series of newspaper ads for the company.
_____ 7. The advertising bill for the first month is paid.
_____ 8. The accountant determines the federal income taxes owed based on the income earned during the period.

Exercise 3-2 Source Documents Matched with Transactions

LO2

Following are a list of source documents and a list of transactions. Indicate by letter next to each transaction the source document that would serve as evidence for the recording of the transaction.

Source Documents

a. Purchase invoice
b. Sales invoice
c. Cash register tape
d. Time cards
e. Promissory note

f. Stock certificates
g. Monthly statement from utility company
h. No standard source document would normally be available.

Transactions

_____ 1. Utilities expense for the month is recorded.
_____ 2. A cash settlement is received from a pending lawsuit.
_____ 3. Owners contribute cash to start a new corporation.
_____ 4. The biweekly payroll is paid.
_____ 5. Services are provided in exchange for cash.
_____ 6. Equipment is acquired on a 30-day open account.
_____ 7. Service is provided to a customer.
_____ 8. A building is acquired by signing an agreement to repay a stated amount plus interest in six months.

Exercise 3-3 Analyzing Transactions

LO3
EXAMPLE 3-1

Prepare a table to summarize the following transactions as they affect the accounting equation. Use the format in Exhibit 3-1.

1. Services provided on account of $1,530
2. Purchases of supplies on account for $1,365
3. Services provided for cash of $750
4. Purchase of equipment for cash of $4,240
5. Issuance of a promissory note for $2,500
6. Collections on account for $890
7. Sale of capital stock in exchange for a parcel of land; the land is appraised at $50,000
8. Payment of $4,000 in salaries and wages
9. Payment of open account in the amount of $500

Exercise 3-4 The Effect of Transactions on the Accounting Equation

LO3
EXAMPLE 3-1

For each of the following transactions, indicate whether it increases (I), decreases (D), or has no effect (NE) on the total dollar amount of each of the elements of the accounting equation.

(Continued)

Transactions	Assets =	Liabilities +	Stockholders' Equity
Example: Common stock is issued in exchange for cash.	I	NE	I

1. Equipment is purchased for cash.
2. Services are provided to customers on account.
3. Services are provided to customers in exchange for cash.
4. An account payable is paid off.
5. Cash is collected on an account receivable.
6. Buildings are purchased in exchange for a three-year note payable.
7. Advertising bill for the month is paid.
8. Dividends are paid to stockholders.
9. Land is acquired by issuing shares of stock to the owner of the land.

LO3
EXAMPLE 3-1

Exercise 3-5 Types of Transactions

There are three elements to the accounting equation: assets, liabilities, and stockholders' equity. Although other possibilities exist, five types of transactions are described here. For *each* of these five types, write descriptions of two transactions that illustrate the type of transaction.

Type of Transaction	Assets =	Liabilities +	Stockholders' Equity
1.	Increase	Increase	
2.	Increase		Increase
3.	Decrease	Decrease	
4.	Decrease		Decrease
5.	Increase Decrease		

LO4

Exercise 3-6 Balance Sheet Accounts and Their Use

Choose from the following list of account titles the one that most accurately fits the description of that account or is an example of that account. An account title may be used more than once or not at all.

Cash	Accounts Receivable	Notes Receivable
Prepaid Asset	Land	Buildings
Investments	Accounts Payable	Notes Payable
Taxes Payable	Retained Earnings	Common Stock
Preferred Stock		

_____ 1. A written obligation to repay a fixed amount, with interest, at some time in the future

_____ 2. Twenty acres of land held for speculation

_____ 3. An amount owed by a customer

_____ 4. Corporate income taxes owed to the federal government

_____ 5. Ownership in a company that allows the owner to receive dividends before common shareholders receive any distributions

_____ 6. Five acres of land used as the site for a factory

_____ 7. Amounts owed on an open account to a vendor, due in 90 days

_____ 8. A checking account at a bank

_____ 9. A warehouse used to store equipment

_____ 10. Claims by the owners on the undistributed net income of a business

_____ 11. Rent paid on an office building in advance of use of the facility

Exercise 3-7 Normal Account Balances (Appendix)

LO5
EXAMPLE 3-3

Each account has a normal balance. For the following list of accounts, indicate whether the normal balance of each is a debit or a credit.

Account	Normal Balance
1. Cash	_____
2. Prepaid Insurance	_____
3. Retained Earnings	_____
4. Bonds Payable	_____
5. Investments	_____
6. Capital Stock	_____
7. Advertising Fees Earned	_____
8. Wages and Salaries Expense	_____
9. Wages and Salaries Payable	_____
10. Office Supplies	_____
11. Dividends	_____

Exercise 3-8 Debits and Credits (Appendix)

LO5
EXAMPLE 3-4, 3-5

The new bookkeeper for Darby Corporation is getting ready to mail the daily cash receipts to the bank for deposit. Because his previous job was at a bank, he is aware that the bank "credits" an account for all deposits and "debits" an account for all checks written. Therefore, he makes the following entry before sending the daily receipts to the bank:

June 5	Accounts Receivable	10,000	
	Sales Revenue	2,450	
	Cash		12,450
	To record cash received on June 5: $10,000 collections on account and $2,450 in cash sales.		

Required

Explain why that entry is wrong and prepare the correct journal entry. Why does the bank refer to cash received from a customer as a *credit* to that customer's account?

Exercise 3-9 Normal Account Balances for Carnival Corporation (Appendix)

LO5
EXAMPLE 3-3

Each account has a normal balance. Classify each of the following items found in **Carnival Corporation's** 2010 annual report according to (1) whether it is a revenue (R), expense (E), asset (A), liability (L), or stockholders' equity (SE) item and (2) whether it has a normal balance of a debit (D) or a credit (C).

Item	Classified as	Normal Balance
Example: Cash and cash equivalents	A	D
1. Trade and other receivables, net	_____	_____
2. Fuel*	_____	_____
3. Common stock of Carnival Corporation	_____	_____
4. Short-term borrowings	_____	_____
5. Passenger tickets	_____	_____
6. Selling and administrative	_____	_____
7. Property and equipment, net	_____	_____
8. Payroll and related*	_____	_____
9. Accounts payable	_____	_____
10. Retained earnings	_____	_____
11. Income tax expense	_____	_____
12. Long-term debt	_____	_____

*Income statement account

LO7

EXAMPLE 3-7

Exercise 3-10 Trial Balance (Appendix)

The following list of accounts was taken from the general ledger of Spencer Corporation on December 31. The bookkeeper thought it would be helpful if the accounts were arranged in alphabetical order. Each account contains the balance that is normal for that type of account; for example, Cash normally has a debit balance. Prepare a trial balance as of this date with the accounts arranged in the following order: (1) assets, (2) liabilities, (3) stockholders' equity, (4) revenues, (5) expenses, and (6) dividends.

Account	Balance	Account	Balance
Accounts Payable	$ 7,650	Heat, Light, and Water Expense	$ 1,400
Accounts Receivable	5,325	Income Tax Expense	1,700
Automobiles	9,200	Income Taxes Payable	2,500
Buildings	150,000	Interest Revenue	1,300
Capital Stock	100,000	Land	50,000
Cash	10,500	Notes Payable	90,000
Commissions Expense	2,600	Office Salaries Expense	6,000
Commissions Revenue	12,750	Office Supplies	500
Dividends	2,000	Retained Earnings	110,025
Equipment	85,000		

MULTI-CONCEPT EXERCISES

LO3 • 4 • 5

EXAMPLE 3-2, 3-4

Exercise 3-11 Reconstructing a Beginning Account Balance (Appendix)

During the month, services performed for customers on account amounted to $7,500 and collections from customers in payment of their accounts totaled $6,000. At the end of the month, the Accounts Receivable account had a balance of $2,500. What was the Accounts Receivable balance at the beginning of the month?

LO3 • 4 • 5

EXAMPLE 3-2, 3-4, 3-5

Exercise 3-12 Journal Entries Recorded Directly in T Accounts (Appendix)

Record each of the following transactions for We-Go Delivery Service directly in T accounts using the numbers preceding the transactions to identify them in the accounts. Each account needs a separate T account.
1. Received contribution of $6,500 from each of the three principal owners of We-Go Delivery Service in exchange for shares of stock.
2. Purchased office supplies for cash of $130.
3. Purchased a van for $15,000 on an open account. The company has 25 days to pay for the van.
4. Provided delivery services to residential customers for cash of $125.
5. Billed a local business $200 for delivery services. The customer is to pay the bill within 15 days.
6. Paid the amount due on the van.
7. Received the amount due from the local business billed in (5).

LO3 • 4 • 5

EXAMPLE 3-2, 3-4

Exercise 3-13 Determining an Ending Account Balance (Appendix)

Jessie's Accounting Services was organized on June 1. The company received a contribution of $1,000 from each of the two principal owners. During the month, Jessie's Accounting Services provided services for cash of $1,400 and services on account for $450, received $250 from customers in payment of their accounts, purchased supplies on account for $600 and equipment on account for $1,350, received a utility bill for $250 that will not be paid until July, and paid the full amount due on the equipment. Use a T account to determine the company's Cash balance on June 30.

LO4 • 7

EXAMPLE 3-7

Exercise 3-14 Trial Balance (Appendix)

Refer to the transactions recorded directly in T accounts for We-Go Delivery Service in Exercise 3-12. Assume that all of the transactions took place during December. Prepare a trial balance at December 31.

Exercise 3-15 Journal Entries for Carnival Corporation (Appendix)

LO3 • 5 • 6
EXAMPLE 3-4, 3-5

Refer to the income statement for **Carnival Corporation** shown in the chapter opener. Using the account titles reported there, prepare the journal entry for each of the following hypothetical transactions. Assume that all transactions include either a debit or a credit to Cash.
1. Fuel is purchased for $10,000.
2. A passenger purchases a ticket for $2,000.
3. Salaries and wages of $4,000 are paid.
4. A passenger pays $50 for pictures in the photo gallery.
5. A travel agent is paid $700 in commissions.

Exercise 3-16 Journal Entries (Appendix)

LO3 • 5 • 6
EXAMPLE 3-4, 3-5

Prepare the journal entry to record each of the following independent transactions. (Use the number of the transaction in lieu of a date for identification purposes.)
1. Services provided on account of $1,530
2. Purchases of supplies on account for $1,365
3. Services provided for cash of $750
4. Purchase of equipment for cash of $4,240
5. Issuance of a promissory note for $2,500
6. Collections on account for $890
7. Sale of capital stock in exchange for a parcel of land; the land is appraised at $50,000
8. Payment of $4,000 in salaries and wages
9. Payment of open account in the amount of $500

Exercise 3-17 Journal Entries (Appendix)

LO3 • 5 • 6
EXAMPLE 3-4, 3-5

Following is a list of transactions entered into during the first month of operations of Gardener Corporation, a new landscape service. Prepare in journal form the entry to record each transaction.

April 1:   Articles of incorporation are filed with the state, and 100,000 shares of common stock are issued for $100,000 in cash.

April 4:   A six-month promissory note is signed at the bank. Interest at 9% per annum will be repaid in six months along with the principal amount of the loan of $50,000.

April 8:   Land and a storage shed are acquired for a lump sum of $80,000. On the basis of an appraisal, 25% of the value is assigned to the land and the remainder to the building.

April 10:   Mowing equipment is purchased from a supplier at a total cost of $25,000. A down payment of $10,000 is made, with the remainder due by the end of the month.

April 18:   Customers are billed for services provided during the first half of the month. The total amount billed of $5,500 is due within ten days.

April 27:   The remaining balance due on the mowing equipment is paid to the supplier.

April 28:   The total amount of $5,500 due from customers is received.

April 30:   Customers are billed for services provided during the second half of the month. The total amount billed is $9,850.

April 30:   Salaries and wages of $4,650 for the month of April are paid.

Exercise 3-18 The Process of Posting Journal Entries to General Ledger Accounts (Appendix)

LO5 • 6
EXAMPLE 3-6

On June 1, Campbell Corporation purchased ten acres of land in exchange for a promissory note in the amount of $50,000. Using the formats shown in Example 3-6, prepare the journal entry to record this transaction in a general journal and post it to the appropriate general ledger accounts. The entry will be recorded on page 7 of the general journal. Use whatever account numbers you like in the general ledger. Assume that none of the accounts to be debited or credited currently contain a balance.

    If at a later date you wanted to review this transaction, would you examine the general ledger or the general journal? Explain your answer.

PROBLEMS

LO1 ## Problem 3-1 Events to Be Recorded in Accounts

The following events take place at Dillon's Delivery Service:
1. Supplies are ordered from vendors who will deliver the supplies within the week.
2. Vendors deliver supplies on account, payment due in 30 days.
3. Customers' deliveries are made, and the customers are billed.
4. Trash is taken to dumpsters, and the floors are cleaned.
5. Cash is received from customers billed in (3).
6. Cash is deposited in the bank night depository.
7. Employees are paid weekly paychecks.
8. Vendors noted in (2) are paid for the supplies delivered.

Required

Identify each event as internal (I) or external (E) and indicate whether each event would or would not be recorded in the *accounts* of the company. For each event that is to be recorded, identify the names of at least two accounts that would be affected.

LO3 ## Problem 3-2 Transactions Reconstructed from Financial Statements

The following financial statements are available for Elm Corporation for its first month of operations:

Elm Corporation
Income Statement
For the Month Ended June 30, 2012

Service revenue		$93,600
Expenses:		
Rent	$ 9,000	
Salaries and wages	27,900	
Utilities	13,800	50,700
Net income		$42,900

Elm Corporation
Balance Sheet
June 30, 2012

Assets		Liabilities and Stockholders' Equity	
Cash	$ 22,800	Accounts payable	$ 18,000
Accounts receivable	21,600	Notes payable	90,000
Equipment	18,000	Capital stock	30,000
Building	90,000	Retained earnings	38,400
Land	24,000	Total liabilities and	
Total assets	$176,400	stockholders' equity	$176,400

Required

Using the format illustrated in Exhibit 3-1, prepare a table to summarize the transactions entered into by Elm Corporation during its first month of business. State any assumptions you believe are necessary in reconstructing the transactions.

LO3 ## Problem 3-3 Transaction Analysis and Financial Statements

Expert Consulting Services Inc. was organized on March 1, 2012, by two former college roommates. The corporation provides computer consulting services to small businesses. The following transactions occurred during the first month of operations:

March 2:   Received contributions of $20,000 from each of the two principal owners of the new business in exchange for shares of stock.

March 7:   Signed a two-year promissory note at the bank and received cash of $15,000. Interest, along with the $15,000, will be repaid at the end of the two years.

March 12:   Purchased $700 in miscellaneous supplies on account. The company has 30 days to pay for the supplies.

March 19:   Billed a client $4,000 for services rendered by Expert in helping to install a new computer system. The client is to pay 25% of the bill upon its receipt and the remaining balance within 30 days.

March 20:   Paid $1,300 bill from the local newspaper for advertising for the month of March.

March 22:   Received 25% of the amount billed to the client on March 19.

March 26:   Received cash of $2,800 for services provided in assisting a client in selecting software for its computer.

March 29:   Purchased a computer system for $8,000 in cash.

March 30:   Paid $3,300 of salaries and wages for March.

March 31:   Received and paid $1,400 in gas, electric, and water bills.

Required

1. Prepare a table to summarize the preceding transactions as they affect the accounting equation. Use the format in Exhibit 3-1. Identify each transaction with the date.
2. Prepare an income statement for the month ended March 31, 2012.
3. Prepare a classified balance sheet at March 31, 2012.
4. From reading the balance sheet you prepared in part (3), what events would you expect to take place in April? Explain your answer.

Problem 3-4 Transaction Analysis and Financial Statements   LO3

Just Rolling Along Inc. was organized on May 1, 2012, by two college students who recognized an opportunity to make money while spending their days at a beach along Lake Michigan. The two entrepreneurs plan to rent bicycles and in-line skates to weekend visitors to the lakefront. The following transactions occurred during the first month of operations:

May 1:   Received contribution of $9,000 from each of the two principal owners of the new business in exchange for shares of stock.

May 1:   Purchased ten bicycles for $300 each on an open account. The company has 30 days to pay for the bicycles.

May 5:   Registered as a vendor with the city and paid the $15 monthly fee.

May 9:   Purchased 20 pairs of in-line skates at $125 per pair, 20 helmets at $50 each, and 20 sets of protective gear (knee and elbow pads and wrist guards) at $45 per set for cash.

May 10:   Purchased $100 in miscellaneous supplies on account. The company has 30 days to pay for the supplies.

May 15:   Paid $125 bill from local radio station for advertising for the last two weeks of May.

May 17:   Customers rented in-line skates and bicycles for cash of $1,800.

May 24:   Billed the local park district $1,200 for in-line skating lessons provided to neighborhood children. The park district is to pay one-half of the bill within five working days and the rest within 30 days.

May 29:   Received 50% of the amount billed to the park district.

May 30:   Customers rented in-line skates and bicycles for cash of $3,000.

May 30:   Paid wages of $160 to a friend who helped over the weekend.

May 31:   Paid the balance due on the bicycles.

Required

1. Prepare a table to summarize the preceding transactions as they affect the accounting equation. Use the format in Exhibit 3-1. Identify each transaction with the date.
2. Prepare an income statement for the month ended May 31, 2012.
3. Prepare a classified balance sheet at May 31, 2012.
4. Why do you think the two college students decided to incorporate their business rather than operate it as a partnership?

MULTI-CONCEPT PROBLEMS

LO1 • 2   Problem 3-5 Identification of Events with Source Documents

Many events are linked to a source document. The following is a list of events that occurred in an entity:

a. Paid a one-year insurance policy.
b. Paid employee payroll.
c. Provided services to a customer on account.
d. Identified supplies in the storeroom destroyed by fire.
e. Received payment of bills from customers.
f. Purchased land for future expansion.
g. Calculated taxes due.
h. Entered into a car lease agreement and paid the tax, title, and license.

Required

For each item (a) through (h), indicate whether the event should or should not be recorded in the entity's accounts. For each item that should be recorded in the entity's books:

1. Identify one or more source documents that are generated from the event.
2. Identify which source document would be used to record an event when it produces more than one source document.
3. For each document, identify the information that is most useful in recording the event in the accounts.

LO1 • 3   Problem 3-6 Transaction Analysis and Financial Statements

Blue Jay Delivery Service is incorporated on January 2, 2012, and enters into the following transactions during its first month of operations:

January 2:   Filed articles of incorporation with the state and issued 100,000 shares of capital stock. Cash of $100,000 is received from the new owners for the shares.

January 3:   Purchased a warehouse and land for $80,000 in cash. An appraiser values the land at $20,000 and the warehouse at $60,000.

January 4:   Signed a three-year promissory note at Third State Bank in the amount of $50,000.

January 6:   Purchased five new delivery trucks for a total of $45,000 in cash.

January 31:   Performed services on account that amounted to $15,900 during the month. Cash amounting to $7,490 was received from customers on account during the month.

January 31:   Established an open account at a local service station at the beginning of the month. Purchases of gas and oil during January amounted to $3,230. Blue Jay has until the 10th of the following month to pay its bill.

Required

1. Prepare a table to summarize the preceding transactions as they affect the accounting equation. Ignore depreciation expense and interest expense. Use the format in Exhibit 3-1.
2. Prepare an income statement for the month ended January 31, 2012.
3. Prepare a classified balance sheet at January 31, 2012.
4. Assume that you are considering buying stock in this company. Beginning with the transaction to record the purchase of the property on January 3, list any additional information you would like to have about each of the transactions during the remainder of the month.

LO3 • 4 • 5   Problem 3-7 Transaction Analysis and Journal Entries Recorded Directly in T Accounts (Appendix)

Four brothers organized Beverly Entertainment Enterprises on October 1, 2012. The following transactions occurred during the first month of operations:

October 1:	Received contributions of $10,000 from each of the four principal owners of the new business in exchange for shares of stock.
October 2:	Purchased the Ace Theater for $125,000. The seller agreed to accept a down payment of $12,500 and a seven-year promissory note for the balance. The Ace property consists of land valued at $35,000 and a building valued at $90,000.
October 3:	Purchased new seats for the theater at a cost of $5,000, paying $2,500 down and agreeing to pay the remainder in 60 days.
October 12:	Purchased candy, popcorn, cups, and napkins for $3,700 on an open account. The company has 30 days to pay for the concession supplies.
October 13:	Sold tickets for the opening-night movie for cash of $1,800 and took in $2,400 at the concession stand.
October 17:	Rented out the theater to a local community group for $1,500. The community group is to pay one-half of the bill within five working day sand has 30 days to pay the remainder.
October 23:	Received 50% of the amount billed to the community group.
October 24:	Sold movie tickets for cash of $2,000 and took in $2,800 at the concession stand.
October 26:	The four brothers, acting on behalf of Beverly Entertainment, paid a dividend of $750 on the shares of stock owned by each of them, or $3,000 in total.
October 27:	Paid $500 for utilities.
October 30:	Paid wages and salaries of $2,400 total to the ushers, projectionist, concession stand workers, and maintenance crew.
October 31:	Sold movie tickets for cash of $1,800 and took in $2,500 at the concession stand.

Required

1. Prepare a table to summarize the preceding transactions as they affect the accounting equation. Use the format in Exhibit 3-1. Identify each transaction with a date.
2. Record each transaction directly in T accounts using the dates preceding the transactions to identify them in the accounts. Each account involved in the problem needs a separate T account.

Problem 3-8 Transaction Analysis and Financial Statements   LO1 • 3

Neveranerror Inc. was organized on June 2, 2012, by a group of accountants to provide accounting and tax services to small businesses. The following transactions occurred during the first month of business:

June 2:	Received contributions of $10,000 from each of the three owners of the business in exchange for shares of stock.
June 5:	Purchased a computer system for $12,000. The agreement with the vendor requires a down payment of $2,500 with the balance due in 60 days.
June 8:	Signed a two-year promissory note at the bank and received cash of $20,000.
June 15:	Billed $12,350 to clients for the first half of June. Clients are billed twice a month for services performed during the month, and the bills are payable within ten days.
June 17:	Paid a $900 bill from the local newspaper for advertising for the month of June.
June 23:	Received the amounts billed to clients for services performed during the first half of the month.
June 28:	Received and paid gas, electric, and water bills. The total amount is $2,700.
June 29:	Received the landlord's bill for $2,200 for rent on the office space that Neveranerror leases. The bill is payable by the 10th of the following month.
June 30:	Paid salaries and wages for June. The total amount is $5,670.
June 30:	Billed $18,400 to clients for the second half of June.
June 30:	Declared and paid dividends in the amount of $6,000.

Required

1. Prepare a table to summarize the preceding transactions as they affect the accounting equation. Ignore depreciation expense and interest expense. Use the format in Exhibit 3-1.

(Continued)

2. Prepare the following financial statements:
   a. Income statement for the month ended June 30, 2012
   b. Statement of retained earnings for the month ended June 30, 2012
   c. Classified balance sheet at June 30, 2012

3. Assume that you have just graduated from college and have been approached to join this company as an accountant. From your reading of the financial statements for the first month, would you consider joining the company? Explain your answer. Limit your answer to financial considerations only.

LO3 • 5   Problem 3-9 Accounts Used to Record Transactions (Appendix)

A list of accounts, with an identifying number for each, is provided. Following the list of accounts is a series of transactions entered into by a company during its first year of operations.

Required

For each transaction, indicate the account or accounts that should be debited and credited.

1. Cash	7. Accounts Payable	13. Wage and Salaries
2. Accounts Receivable	8. Income Taxes Payable	Expense
3. Office Supplies	9. Notes Payable	14. Selling Expense
4. Buildings	10. Capital Stock	15. Utilities Expense
5. Automobiles	11. Retained Earnings	16. Income Tax Expense
6. Land	12. Service Revenue	

	Accounts	
Transactions	**Debited**	**Credited**
Example: Purchased land and building in exchange for a three-year promissory note.	4,6	9
a. Issued capital stock for cash.	_____	_____
b. Purchased ten automobiles; paid part in cash and signed a 60-day note for the balance.	_____	_____
c. Purchased land in exchange for a note due in six months.	_____	_____
d. Purchased office supplies; agreed to pay total bill by the 10th of the following month.	_____	_____
e. Billed clients for services performed during the month and gave them until the 15th of the following month to pay.	_____	_____
f. Received cash on account from clients for services rendered to them in past months.	_____	_____
g. Paid employees salaries and wages earned during the month.	_____	_____
h. Paid newspaper for company ads appearing during the month.	_____	_____
i. Received monthly gas and electric bill from the utility company; payment is due anytime within the first ten days of the following month.	_____	_____
j. Computed amount of taxes due based on the income of the period; amount will be paid in the following month.	_____	_____

LO4 • 7   Problem 3-10 Trial Balance and Financial Statements (Appendix)

Refer to the table for Beverly Entertainment Enterprises in part (1) of Problem 3-7.

Required

1. Prepare a trial balance at October 31, 2012.
2. Prepare an income statement for the month ended October 31, 2012.
3. Prepare a statement of retained earnings for the month ended October 31, 2012.
4. Prepare a classified balance sheet at October 31, 2012.

Problem 3-11 Journal Entries (Appendix)

LO3 • 5 • 6

Atkins Advertising Agency began business on January 2, 2012. The transactions entered into by Atkins during its first month of operations are as follows:

a. Acquired its articles of incorporation from the state and issued 100,000 shares of capital stock in exchange for $200,000 in cash.
b. Purchased an office building for $150,000 in cash. The building is valued at $110,000, and the remainder of the value is assigned to the land.
c. Signed a three-year promissory note at the bank for $125,000.
d. Purchased office equipment at a cost of $50,000, paying $10,000 down and agreeing to pay the remainder in ten days.
e. Paid wages and salaries of $13,000 for the first half of the month. Office employees are paid twice a month.
f. Paid the balance due on the office equipment.
g. Sold $24,000 of advertising during the first month. Customers have until the 15th of the following month to pay their bills.
h. Paid wages and salaries of $15,000 for the second half of the month.
i. Recorded $3,500 in commissions earned by the salespeople during the month. They will be paid on the fifth of the following month.

Required

Prepare in journal form the entry to record each transaction.

Problem 3-12 Journal Entries Recorded Directly in T Accounts (Appendix)

LO3 • 4 • 5

Refer to the transactions for Atkins Advertising Agency in Problem 3-11.

Required

1. Record each transaction directly in T accounts using the letters preceding the transactions to identify them in the accounts. Each account involved in the problem needs a separate T account.
2. Prepare a trial balance at January 31, 2012.

Problem 3-13 Journal Entries, Trial Balance, and Financial Statements (Appendix)

LO3 • 5 • 6 • 7

Refer to the transactions for Neveranerror Inc. in Problem 3-8.

Required

1. Prepare journal entries on the books of Neveranerror Inc. to record the transactions entered into during the month. Ignore depreciation expense and interest expense.
2. Prepare a trial balance at June 30, 2012.
3. Prepare the following financial statements:
    a. Income statement for the month ended June 30, 2012
    b. Statement of retained earnings for the month ended June 30, 2012
    c. Classified balance sheet at June 30, 2012
4. Assume that you have just graduated from college and have been approached to join this company as an accountant. From your reading of the financial statements for the first month, would you consider joining the company? Explain your answer. Limit your answer to financial considerations only.

Problem 3-14 Journal Entries, Trial Balance, and Financial Statements (Appendix)

LO3 • 5 • 6 • 7

Refer to the transactions for Blue Jay Delivery Service in Problem 3-6.

Required

1. Prepare journal entries on the books of Blue Jay to record the transactions entered into during the month.

(Continued)

2. Prepare a trial balance at January 31, 2012.
3. Prepare an income statement for the month ended January 31, 2012.
4. Prepare a classified balance sheet at January 31, 2012.
5. Assume that you are considering buying stock in this company. Beginning with the transaction to record the purchase of the property on January 3, list any additional information you would like to have about each of the transactions during the remainder of the month.

LO3 • 5 • 7   Problem 3-15   The Detection of Errors in a Trial Balance and Preparation of a Corrected Trial Balance (Appendix)

Malcolm Inc. was incorporated on January 1, 2012, with the issuance of capital stock in return for $90,000 of cash contributed by the owners. The only other transaction entered into prior to beginning operations was the issuance of a $75,300 note payable in exchange for building and equipment. The following trial balance was prepared at the end of the first month by the bookkeeper for Malcolm Inc:

Malcolm Inc.
Trial Balance
January 31, 2012

Account Titles	Debits	Credits
Cash	$ 9,980	
Accounts Receivable	8,640	
Land	80,000	
Building	50,000	
Equipment	23,500	
Notes Payable		$ 75,300
Capital Stock		90,000
Service Revenue		50,340
Wage and Salary Expense	23,700	
Advertising Expense	4,600	
Utilities Expense	8,420	
Dividends		5,000
Totals	$208,840	$220,640

Required

1. Identify the *two* errors in the trial balance. Ignore depreciation expense and interest expense.
2. Prepare a corrected trial balance.

ALTERNATE PROBLEMS

LO1   Problem 3-1A   Events to Be Recorded in Accounts

The following events take place at Anaconda Accountants Inc.:
1. Supplies are ordered from vendors, who will deliver the supplies within the week.
2. Vendors deliver supplies on account, payment due in 30 days.
3. New computer system is ordered.
4. Old computer system is sold for cash.
5. Services are rendered to customers on account. The invoices are mailed and due in 30 days.
6. Cash received from customer payments is deposited in the bank night depository.
7. Employees are paid weekly paychecks.
8. Vendors noted in (2) are paid for the supplies delivered.

Required

Identify each event as internal (I) or external (E) and indicate whether each event would or would not be recorded in the *accounts* of the company. For each event that is to be recorded, identify the names of at least two accounts that would be affected.

Problem 3-2A Transactions Reconstructed from Financial Statements **LO3**

The following financial statements are available for Oak Corporation for its first month of operations:

Oak Corporation
Income Statement
For the Month Ended July 31, 2012

Service revenue		$75,400
Expenses:		
Rent	$ 6,000	
Salaries and wages	24,600	
Utilities	12,700	43,300
Net income		$32,100

Oak Corporation
Balance Sheet
July 31, 2012

Assets		Liabilities and Stockholders' Equity	
Cash	$ 13,700	Wages payable	$ 6,000
Accounts receivable	25,700	Notes payable	50,000
Equipment	32,000	Unearned service revenue	4,500
Furniture	14,700	Capital stock	30,000
Land	24,000	Retained earnings	19,600
		Total liabilities and	
Total assets	$110,100	stockholders' equity	$110,100

Required

Describe as many transactions as you can that were entered into by Oak Corporation during the first month of business.

Problem 3-3A Transaction Analysis and Financial Statements **LO3**

Dynamic Services Inc. was organized on March 1, 2012, by two former college roommates. The corporation will provide computer tax services to small businesses. The following transactions occurred during the first month of operations:

March 2: Received contributions of $10,000 from each of the two principal owners in exchange for shares of stock.

March 7: Signed a two-year promissory note at the bank and received cash of $7,500. Interest, along with the $7,500, will be repaid at the end of the two years.

March 12: Purchased miscellaneous supplies on account for $350, payment due in 30 days.

March 19: Billed a client $2,000 for tax preparation services. According to an agreement between the two companies, the client is to pay 25% of the bill upon its receipt and the remaining balance within 30 days.

March 20: Paid a $650 bill from the local newspaper for advertising for the month of March.

March 22: Received 25% of the amount billed the client on March 19.

March 26: Received cash of $1,400 for services provided in assisting a client in preparing its tax return.

March 29: Purchased a computer system for $4,000 in cash.

March 30: Paid $1,650 in salaries and wages for March.

March 31: Received and paid $700 of gas, electric, and water bills.

Required

1. Prepare a table to summarize the preceding transactions as they affect the accounting equation. Use the format in Exhibit 3-1. Identify each transaction with the date.
2. Prepare an income statement for the month ended March 31, 2012.
3. Prepare a classified balance sheet at March 31, 2012.
4. From reading the balance sheet you prepared in part (3), what events would you expect to take place in April? Explain your answer.

LO3   **Problem 3-4A Transaction Analysis and Financial Statements**

Beachway Enterprises was organized on June 1, 2012, by two college students who recognized an opportunity to make money while spending their days at a beach in Florida. The two entrepreneurs plan to rent beach umbrellas. The following transactions occurred during the first month of operations:

June 1:   Received contributions of $2,000 from each of the two principal owners of the new business in exchange for shares of stock.

June 1:   Purchased 25 beach umbrellas for $250 each on account. The company has 30 days to pay for the beach umbrellas.

June 5:   Registered as a vendor with the city and paid the $35 monthly fee.

June 10:   Purchased $50 in miscellaneous supplies on an open account. The company has 30 days to pay for the supplies.

June 15:   Paid $70 bill from a local radio station for advertising for the last two weeks of June.

June 17:   Customers rented beach umbrellas for cash of $1,000.

June 24:   Billed a local hotel $2,000 for beach umbrellas provided for use during a convention being held at the hotel. The hotel is to pay one-half of the bill in five days and the rest within 30 days.

June 29:   Received 50% of the amount billed to the hotel.

June 30:   Customers rented beach umbrellas for cash of $1,500.

June 30:   Paid wages of $90 to a friend who helped over the weekend.

June 30:   Paid the balance due on the beach umbrellas.

Required

1. Prepare a table to summarize the preceding transactions as they affect the accounting equation. Use the format in Exhibit 3-1. Identify each transaction with a date.
2. Prepare an income statement for the month ended June 30, 2012.
3. Prepare a classified balance sheet at June 30, 2012.

ALTERNATE MULTI-CONCEPT PROBLEMS

LO1 • 2   **Problem 3-5A Identification of Events with Source Documents**

Many events are linked to a source document. The following is a list of events that occurred in an entity:

a. Paid a security deposit and six months' rent on a building.
b. Hired three employees and agreed to pay them $400 per week.
c. Provided services to a customer for cash.
d. Reported a fire that destroyed a billboard that is on the entity's property and that is owned and maintained by another entity.
e. Received payment of bills from customers.
f. Purchased stock in another entity to gain some control over it.
g. Signed a note at the bank and received cash.
h. Contracted with a cleaning service to maintain the interior of the building in good repair. No money is paid at this time.

Required

For each item (a) through (h), indicate whether the event should or should not be recorded in the entity's accounts. For each item that should be recorded in the entity's books:

1. Identify one or more source documents that are generated from the event.
2. Identify which source document would be used to record an event when it produces more than one source document.
3. For each document, identify the information that is most useful in recording the event in the accounts.

Problem 3-6A Transaction Analysis

LO1 • 3

Overnight Delivery Inc. is incorporated on February 1, 2012, and enters into the following transactions during its first month of operations:

February 15:   Received $8,000 cash from customer accounts.
February 26:   Provided $16,800 of services on account during the month.
February 27:   Received a $3,400 bill from the local service station for gas and oil used during
               February.
February 28:   Paid $400 for wages earned by employees for the month.
February 28:   Paid $3,230 for February advertising.
February 28:   Declared and paid $2,000 cash dividends to stockholders.

Required

1. Prepare a table to summarize the preceding transactions as they affect the accounting equation. Use the format in Exhibit 3-1.
2. Explain why you agree or disagree with the following: The transactions on February 28 all represent expenses for the month of February because cash was paid. The transaction on February 27 does not represent an expense in February because cash has not yet been paid.

Problem 3-7A Accounts Used to Record Transactions (Appendix)

LO3 • 5

A list of accounts, with an identifying number for each, is provided. Following the list of accounts is a series of transactions entered into by a company during its first year of operations.

Required

For each transaction, indicate the account or accounts that should be debited and credited.

1. Cash	6. Land	11. Retained Earnings
2. Accounts Receivable	7. Accounts Payable	12. Service Revenue
3. Prepaid Insurance	8. Income Taxes Payable	13. Wage and Salary Expense
4. Office Supplies	9. Notes Payable	14. Utilities Expense
5. Automobiles	10. Capital Stock	15. Income Tax Expense

	Accounts	
Transactions	Debited	Credited
Example: Purchased office supplies for cash.	4	1
a. Issued capital stock for cash.		
b. Purchased an automobile and signed a 60-day note for the total amount.		
c. Acquired land in exchange for capital stock.		
d. Received cash from clients for services performed during the month.		
e. Paid employees salaries and wages earned during the month.		
f. Purchased flyers and signs from a printer, payment due in ten days.		
g. Paid for the flyers and signs purchased in (f).		
h. Received monthly telephone bill; payment is due within ten days of receipt.		
i. Paid for a six-month liability insurance policy.		
j. Paid monthly telephone bill.		
k. Computed amount of taxes due based on the income of the period and paid the amount.		

Problem 3-8A Transaction Analysis and a Balance Sheet

LO1 • 3

Krittersbegone Inc. was organized on July 1, 2012, by a group of technicians to provide termite inspections and treatment to homeowners and small businesses. The following transactions occurred during the first month of business:

(Continued)

July 2:   Received contributions of $3,000 from each of the six owners in exchange for shares of stock.

July 3:   Paid $1,000 rent for the month of July.

July 5:   Purchased flashlights, tools, spray equipment, and ladders for $18,000, with a down payment of $5,000 and the balance due in 30 days.

July 17:   Paid a $200 bill for the distribution of door-to-door advertising.

July 28:   Paid August rent and July utilities to the landlord in the amounts of $1,000 and $450, respectively.

July 30:   Received $8,000 in cash from homeowners for services performed during the month. In addition, billed $7,500 to other customers for services performed during the month. Billings are due in 30 days.

July 30:   Paid commissions of $9,500 to the technicians for July.

Required

1. Prepare a table to summarize the preceding transactions as they affect the accounting equation. Ignore depreciation expense. Use the format in Exhibit 3-1.
2. Prepare a classified balance sheet dated July 31, 2012. From the balance sheet, what cash inflow and what cash outflow can you predict in the month of August? Who would be interested in the cash flow information? Why?

LO3 • 4 • 5   ### Problem 3-9A Transaction Analysis and Journal Entries Recorded Directly in T Accounts (Appendix)

Three friends organized Rapid City Roller Rink on October 1, 2012. The following transactions occurred during the first month of operations:

October 1:   Received contribution of $22,000 from each of the three principal owners of the new business in exchange for shares of stock.

October 2:   Purchased land valued at $15,000 and a building valued at $75,000. The seller agreed to accept a down payment of $9,000 and a five-year promissory note for the balance.

October 3:   Purchased new tables and chairs for the lounge at the roller rink at a cost of $25,000, paying $5,000 down and agreeing to pay for the remainder in 60 days.

October 9:   Purchased 100 pairs of roller skates for cash at $35 per pair.

October 12:   Purchased food and drinks for $2,500 on an open account. The company has 30 days to pay for the concession supplies.

October 13:   Sold tickets for cash of $400 and took in $750 at the concession stand.

October 17:   Rented out the roller rink to a local community group for $750. The community group is to pay one-half of the bill within five working days and has 30 days to pay the remainder.

October 23:   Received 50% of the amount billed to the community group.

October 24:   Sold tickets for cash of $500 and took in $1,200 at the concession stand.

October 26:   The three friends, acting on behalf of Rapid City Roller Rink, paid a dividend of $250 on the shares of stock owned by each of them, or $750 in total.

October 27:   Paid $1,275 for utilities.

October 30:   Paid wages and salaries of $2,250.

October 31:   Sold tickets for cash of $700 and took in $1,300 at the concession stand.

Required

1. Prepare a table to summarize the preceding transactions as they affect the accounting equation. Use the format in Exhibit 3-1. Identify each transaction with a date.
2. Record each transaction directly in T accounts using the dates preceding the transactions to identify them in the accounts. Each account involved in the problem needs a separate T account.

Problem 3-10A Journal Entries (Appendix)

LO3 • 5 • 6

Castle Consulting Agency began business in February 2012. The transactions entered into by Castle during its first month of operations are as follows:

a. Acquired articles of incorporation from the state and issued 10,000 shares of capital stock in exchange for $150,000 in cash.
b. Paid monthly rent of $400.
c. Signed a five-year promissory note for $100,000 at the bank.
d. Purchased software to be used on future jobs. The software costs $950 and is expected to be used on five to eight jobs over the next two years.
e. Billed customers $12,500 for work performed during the month.
f. Paid office personnel $3,000 for the month of February.
g. Received a utility bill of $100. The total amount is due in 30 days.

Required

Prepare in journal form the entry to record each transaction.

Problem 3-11A Journal Entries Recorded Directly in T Accounts (Appendix)

LO3 • 4 • 5 • 7

Refer to the transactions for Castle Consulting Agency in Problem 3-10A.

Required

1. Record each transaction directly in T accounts using the letters preceding the transactions to identify them in the accounts. Each account involved in the problem needs a separate T account.
2. Prepare a trial balance at February 29, 2012.

Problem 3-12A Entries Prepared from a Trial Balance and Proof of the Cash Balance (Appendix)

LO3 • 4 • 5 • 7

Russell Company was incorporated on January 1, 2012, with the issuance of capital stock in return for $120,000 of cash contributed by the owners. The only other transaction entered into prior to beginning operations was the issuance of a $50,000 note payable in exchange for equipment and fixtures. The following trial balance was prepared at the end of the first month by the bookkeeper for Russell Company:

Russell Company
Trial Balance
January 31, 2012

Account Titles	Debits	Credits
Cash	$?	
Accounts Receivable	30,500	
Equipment and Fixtures	50,000	
Wages Payable		$ 10,000
Notes Payable		50,000
Capital Stock		120,000
Service Revenue		60,500
Wage and Salary Expense	24,600	
Advertising Expense	12,500	
Rent Expense	5,200	

Required

1. Determine the balance in the Cash account.
2. Identify all of the transactions that affected the Cash account during the month. Use a T account to prove what the balance in Cash will be after all transactions are recorded.

LO3 • 5 • 6   **Problem 3-13A Journal Entries and a Balance Sheet (Appendix)**

Refer to the transactions for Krittersbegone Inc. in Problem 3-8A.

Required

1. Prepare journal entries on the books of Krittersbegone to record the transactions entered into during the month. Ignore depreciation expense.
2. Prepare a classified balance sheet dated July 31, 2012. From the balance sheet, what cash inflow and what cash outflow can you predict in the month of August? Who would be interested in the cash flow information? Why?

LO3 • 5 • 6   **Problem 3-14A Journal Entries (Appendix)**

Refer to the transactions for Overnight Delivery Inc. in Problem 3-6A.

Required

1. Prepare journal entries on the books of Overnight to record the transactions entered into during February.
2. Explain why you agree or disagree with the following: The transactions on February 29 all represent expenses for the month of February because cash was paid. The transaction on February 27 does not represent an expense in February because cash has not yet been paid.

LO4 • 7   **Problem 3-15A Trial Balance and Financial Statements**

Refer to the table for Rapid City Roller Rink in part (1) of Problem 3-9A.

Required

1. Prepare a trial balance at October 31, 2012.
2. Prepare an income statement for the month ended October 31, 2012.
3. Prepare a statement of retained earnings for the month ended October 31, 2012.
4. Prepare a classified balance sheet at October 31, 2012.

DECISION CASES

Reading and Interpreting Financial Statements

LO4   **Decision Case 3-1 Comparing Two Companies in the Same Industry: Kellogg's and General Mills**

Refer to the income statements for **Kellogg's** and **General Mills** reproduced at the end of the book.

Required

1. Which is the largest expense for each company in the most recent year? What is its dollar amount? Is it logical that this would be the largest expense given the nature of each company's business? Explain your answer.
2. One of the accounts on each company's income statement is "Selling, general and administrative expense." For each of the two most recent years, compute the ratio of this expense to net sales for each company. Did this ratio increase or decrease from one year to the next? Which company has the lower ratio in each of the two years?
3. Compute the ratio of income taxes to income (earnings) before taxes (use "Earnings before Income Taxes and After-Tax Earnings from Joint Ventures" for General Mills) for the two most recent years for each company. Is the ratio the same for Kellogg's for both years? Is the ratio the same for General Mills for both years? Which company has the higher ratio for each of the two years?

Decision Case 3-2 Reading and Interpreting General Mills's Statement of Cash Flows LO3

Refer to **General Mills**'s statement of cash flows for the year ended May 30, 2010, as reproduced at the end of the book.

Required

1. What amount did the company spend on purchases of land, buildings, and equipment during the year? Determine the effect on the accounting equation from these purchases.
2. What amount did the company pay to retire long-term debt during the year? Determine the effect on the accounting equation from the retirement of debt.

Decision Case 3-3 Reading and Interpreting Carnival Corporation's Balance Sheet LO1 • 3

The following item appears in the current liabilities section of **Carnival Corporation**'s balance sheet at November 30, 2010:

Customer deposits $2,805 million

In addition, Note 2 to the financial statements includes the following:

Revenue and Expense Recognition

Guest cruise deposits represent unearned revenues and are initially recorded as customer deposit liabilities generally when received. Customer deposits are subsequently recognized as cruise revenues, together with revenues from onboard and other activities, and all associated direct costs and expenses of a voyage are recognized as cruise costs and expenses, upon completion of voyages with durations of ten nights or less and on a pro rata basis for voyages in excess of ten nights.

Required

1. What economic event caused Carnival to incur this liability? Was it an external or internal event?
2. Describe the effect on the accounting equation from the transaction to record the customer deposits.
3. Assume that one customer makes a deposit of $1,000 on a future cruise. Determine the effect on the accounting equation from this transaction.
4. What economic event will cause Carnival to reduce its customer deposits liability? Is this an external or internal event?

Making Financial Decisions

Decision Case 3-4 Cash Flow versus Net Income LO2 • 3

Shelia Young started a real estate business at the beginning of January. After approval by the state for a charter to incorporate, she issued 1,000 shares of stock to herself and deposited $20,000 in a bank account under the name Young Properties. Because business was booming, she spent all of her time during the first month selling properties rather than keeping financial records.

At the end of January, Shelia comes to you with the following plight:

I put $20,000 in to start this business at the beginning of the month. My January 31 bank statement shows a balance of $17,000. After all of my efforts, it appears as if I'm "in the hole" already! On the other hand, that seems impossible—we sold five properties for clients during the month. The total sales value of these properties was $600,000, and I received a commission of 5% on each sale. Granted, one of the five sellers still owes me an $8,000 commission, but the other four have been collected in full. Three of the sales, totaling $400,000, were actually made by my assistants. I pay them 4% of the sales value of a property. Sure, I have a few office expenses for my car, utilities, and a secretary, but that's about it. How can I have possibly lost $3,000 this month?

(Continued)

You agree to help Shelia figure out how she did this month. The bank statement is helpful. The total deposits during the month amount to $22,000. Shelia explains that this amount represents the commissions on the four sales collected so far. The canceled checks reveal the following expenditures:

Check No.	Payee—Memo at Bottom of Check	Amount
101	Stevens Office Supply	$ 2,000
102	Why Walk, Let's Talk Motor Co.—new car	3,000
103	City of Westbrook—heat and lights	500
104	Alice Hill—secretary	2,200
105	Ace Property Management—office rent for month	1,200
106	Jerry Hayes (sales assistant)	10,000
107	Joan Harper (sales assistant)	6,000
108	Don's Fillitup—gas and oil for car	100

According to Shelia, the $2,000 check to Stevens Office Supply represents the down payment on a word processor and a copier for the office. The remaining balance is $3,000 that must be paid to Stevens by February 15. Similarly, the $3,000 check is the down payment on a car for the business. A $12,000 note was given to the car dealer and is due along with interest in one year.

Required

1. Prepare an income statement for the month of January for Young Properties.
2. Prepare a statement of cash flows for the month of January for Young Properties.
3. Draft a memo to Shelia Young explaining as simply and clearly as possible why she *did* in fact have a profitable first month in business but experienced a decrease in her Cash account. Support your explanation with any necessary figures.
4. The down payments on the car and the office equipment are reflected on the statement of cash flows. They are assets that will benefit the business for a number of years. Do you think that any of the cost associated with the acquisition of these assets should be recognized in some way on the income statement? Explain your answer.

LO3 • 5 • 7   **Decision Case 3-5 Loan Request (Appendix)**

Simon Fraser started a landscaping and lawn-care business in April 2012 by investing $20,000 cash in the business in exchange for capital stock. Because his business is in the Midwest, the season begins in April and concludes in September. He prepared the following trial balance (with accounts in alphabetical order) at the end of the first season in business:

Fraser Landscaping
Trial Balance
September 30, 2012

	Debits	Credits
Accounts Payable	—	$13,000
Accounts Receivable	$23,000	
Capital Stock		20,000
Cash	1,200	
Gas and Oil Expense	15,700	
Insurance Expense	2,500	
Landscaping Revenue		33,400
Lawn Care Revenue		24,000
Mowing Equipment	5,000	
Rent Expense	6,000	
Salaries Expense	22,000	
Truck	15,000	
Totals	$90,400	$90,400

Simon is pleased with his first year in business. "I paid myself a salary of $22,000 during the year and still have $1,200 in the bank. Sure, I have a few bills outstanding, but my accounts receivable will more than cover those." In fact, Simon is so happy with the first year that he has come to you in your role as a lending officer at the local bank to ask for a $20,000 loan to allow him to add another truck and mowing equipment for the second season.

Required

1. From your reading of the trial balance, what do you believe Simon did with the $20,000 in cash he originally contributed to the business? Determine the effect on the accounting equation from the transaction that you think took place.
2. Prepare an income statement for the six months ended September 30, 2012.
3. The mowing equipment and truck are assets that will benefit the business for a number of years. Do you think that any of the costs associated with the purchase of these assets should have been recognized as expenses in the first year? How would this have affected the income statement?
4. Prepare a classified balance sheet as of September 30, 2012. As a banker, what two items on the balance sheet concern you the most? Explain your answer.
5. As a banker, would you loan Simon $20,000 to expand his business during the second year? Draft a memo to respond to Simon's request for the loan, indicating whether you will make the loan.

Ethical Decision Making

Decision Case 3-6 Revenue Recognition

LO1 • 3

You are controller for an architectural firm whose accounting year ends on December 31. As part of the management team, you receive a year-end bonus directly related to the firm's earnings for the year. One of your duties is to review the transactions recorded by the bookkeepers. A new bookkeeper recorded the receipt of $10,000 in cash as an increase in cash and an increase in service revenue. The $10,000 is a deposit, and the bookkeeper explains to you that the firm plans to provide the services to the client in March of the following year.

Required

1. Did the bookkeeper correctly record the client's deposit? Explain your answer.
2. What would you do as controller for the firm? Do you have a responsibility to do anything to correct the books? Explain your answer.

Decision Case 3-7 Delay in the Posting of a Journal Entry (Appendix)

LO3 • 5 • 6

As assistant controller for a small consulting firm, you are responsible for recording and posting the daily cash receipts and disbursements to the ledger accounts. After you have posted the entries, your boss, the controller, prepares a trial balance and the financial statements. You make the following entries on June 30, 2012:

2012			
June 30	Cash	1,430	
	Accounts Receivable	1,950	
	Service Revenue		3,380
	To record daily cash sales and sales on account.		
June 30	Advertising Expense	12,500	
	Utilities Expense	22,600	
	Rent Expense	24,000	
	Salary and Wage Expense	17,400	
	Cash		76,500
	To record daily cash disbursements.		

The daily cash disbursements are much larger on June 30 than on any other day because many of the company's major bills are paid on the last day of the month. After you have recorded these two transactions and *before* you have posted them to the ledger accounts, your boss comes to you with the following request:

(Continued)

As you are aware, the first half of the year has been a tough one for the consulting industry and for our business in particular. With first-half bonuses based on net income, I am wondering whether you or I will get a bonus this time around. However, I have a suggestion that should allow us to receive something for our hard work and at the same time not hurt anyone. Go ahead and post the June 30 cash receipts to the ledger, but don't bother to post that day's cash disbursements. Even though the treasurer writes the checks on the last day of the month and you normally journalize the transaction on the same day, it is silly to bother posting the entry to the ledger since it takes at least a week for the checks to clear the bank.

Required

1. Explain why the controller's request will result in an increase in net income.
2. Do you agree with the controller that the omission of the entry on June 30 "will not hurt anyone"? Whom could it hurt? Does omitting the entry provide information that is free from bias? Explain your answer.
3. What would you do if the controller told you to do this? To whom should you talk about this issue? Is this situation an ethical issue? Why or why not?

SOLUTIONS TO KEY TERMS QUIZ

Quiz 1: Processing Accounting Information

2	Event		4	Source document
5	External event		6	Account
3	Internal event		1	Chart of accounts
8	Transaction		7	General ledger

Quiz 2: Appendix

4	Debit		5	Posting
2	Credit		3	Journalizing
8	Double-entry system		7	General journal
6	Journal		1	Trial balance

ANSWERS TO POD REVIEW

LO1	1. d	2. a		**LO5**	1. b	2. c
LO2	1. b	2. d		**LO6**	1. b	2. a
LO3	1. c	2. b		**LO7**	1. c	2. a
LO4	1. a	2. b				

Income Measurement and Accrual Accounting

4

AFTER STUDYING THIS CHAPTER, YOU SHOULD BE ABLE TO:

LO1 Explain the significance of recognition and measurement in the preparation and use of financial statements.

LO2 Explain the differences between the cash and accrual bases of accounting.

LO3 Describe the revenue recognition principle and explain its application in various situations.

LO4 Describe the matching principle and the various methods for recognizing expenses.

LO5 Identify the four major types of adjustments and analyze their effects on the financial statements.

LO6 Explain the steps in the accounting cycle and the significance of each step.

STUDY LINKS

A Look at the Previous Chapter Chapter 3 looked at how information is processed. Various tools were introduced as convenient aids in the preparation of periodic financial statements.

A Look at This Chapter This chapter begins by considering the roles of recognition and measurement in the process of preparing financial statements. The accrual basis of accounting is examined, and we see how this basis affects the measurement of income. We look at how revenues and expenses are recognized in an accrual system and at what role adjustments have in this process.

A Look at the Upcoming Chapter Chapter 4 completes our overview of the accounting model. In the next section, we examine accounting for the various assets of a business. Chapter 5 begins by looking at how companies that sell products account for their inventory.

From a single shoe store in Seattle, Washington, in 1901, **Nordstrom, Inc.**, has grown to become one of the most highly respected fashion retailers in the country. With its reputation for superior customer service, the company has seen its sales climb to a record of over $9.3 billion in its fiscal year 2010.

Because Nordstrom uses the accrual basis of accounting, certain accounts appear on its balance sheet that would not appear if it used the simpler cash basis. These accounts are important not just to ensure that debits equal credits in an accounting system but also to provide information to stockholders, bankers, and other users of the statements. Consider the four accounts highlighted in the Current Assets and Current Liabilities sections of Nordstrom's partial balance sheet shown on the next page.

Accounts receivable come about when a company sells a product or service and gives the customer a certain period of time to pay the amount due. For Nordstrom, these receivables arise when its customers use the company's private label card or two cobranded Nordstrom VISA® credit cards. As shown in the Current Assets section of the partial balance sheets, accounts receivable is the largest of these assets at the end of the most recent year.

Prepaid expenses represent amounts Nordstrom has paid in advance for items such as supplies and other operating costs. For example, when the company buys supplies, an asset is created. Over time, the asset expires and is replaced by an expense. Users of the statements understand that prepaid expenses are different from accounts receivable in that prepayments will not be converted into cash as will receivables.

Accrued salaries, wages and related benefits appear on the liabilities side of Nordstrom's balance sheet. For a retailer such as Nordstrom, payroll is one of its largest costs. This account represents amounts owed to employees that have not yet been paid at the balance sheet date. Accrued salaries and wages are examples of **accrued expenses**. They represent amounts owed to employees in wages and salaries, to the government in taxes, and to a variety of other short-term creditors. The amount of outstanding accrued expenses provides important information to users of the balance sheet. For example, a banker knows that within the next year, the amount of accrued expenses will need to be satisfied, usually by the payment of cash.

Finally, note the line for Other current liabilities on the partial balance sheet. A note to the financial statements explains that this account includes the company's gift card liabilities. These liabilities arise when the company receives cash from someone who purchases a gift card to be used at a later date. Up until the time the card is used, Nordstrom has a liability. As you will see later in the chapter, gift card liabilities are one example of what accountants call **deferred revenue**. This term is used for situations in which a company receives cash in advance of providing products or services to its customers.

Why do you need to study this chapter?

Simply put, you cannot read and interpret financial statements without understanding the basis for their preparation, which is the accrual system of accounting.

- You need to know what information the accrual basis of accounting provides to users of the statements that a cash basis does not. (See pp. 162–163.)

- You need to know what the revenue recognition principle is and why it is important. (See pp. 165–166.)

- You need to know what is meant by the matching principle and how it is applied. (See pp. 166–168.)

- You need to know the various types of adjustments companies make and how they are recorded in an accounting system. (See pp. 168–178.)

Nordstrom, Inc. Consolidated Balance Sheets (Partial)		
	January 29, 2011	January 30, 2010
Assets	(In millions)	
Current assets:		
Cash and cash equivalents	$1,506	$ 795
Accounts receivable, net	2,026	2,035
Merchandise inventories	977	898
Current deferred tax assets, net	236	238
Prepaid expenses and other	79	88
Total current assets	4,824	4,054
Liabilities and Shareholders' Equity		
Current liabilities:		
Accounts payable	$ 846	$ 726
Accrued salaries, wages and related benefits	375	336
Other current liabilities	652	596
Current portion of long-term debt	6	356
Total current liabilities	1,879	2,014

The accompanying Notes to Consolidated Financial Statements are an integral part of these financial statements.

Recognition and Measurement in Financial Statements

LO1 Explain the significance of recognition and measurement in the preparation and use of financial statements.

OVERVIEW: Recognition is the process of recording items in the financial statements. Measurement of an item in the statements requires the choice of an attribute to be measured, such as historical cost. A unit of measure must also be selected, such as the dollar in the United States.

Accounting is a communication process. To successfully communicate information to the users of financial statements, accountants and managers must answer two questions:

1. **What economic events should be communicated, or *recognized*, in the statements?**
2. **How should the effects of these events be *measured* in the statements?**

The dual concepts of recognition and measurement are crucial to the success of accounting as a form of communication.

Recognition
The process of recording an item in the financial statements as an asset, a liability, a revenue, an expense, or the like.

Recognition

"**Recognition** is the process of formally recording or incorporating an item into the financial statements of an entity as an asset, a liability, a revenue, an expense, or the like. Recognition includes depiction of an item in both words and numbers, with the amount included in the totals of the financial statements."[1] We see in this definition the central idea behind general-purpose financial statements. They are a form of communication between the entity and external users. Stockholders, bankers, and other creditors have limited access to relevant information about a company. They depend on the periodic financial statements that management issues to provide the necessary information to make decisions. Acting on behalf of management, accountants have a moral and ethical responsibility to provide users with financial information that will be useful in making their decisions. The process by which the accountant depicts, or describes, the effects of economic events on the entity is called *recognition*.

Items such as assets, liabilities, revenues, and expenses depicted in financial statements are *representations*. Simply stated, the accountant cannot show a stockholder or another user the company's assets, such as cash and buildings. What the user sees in a set of financial statements is a depiction of the real thing. That is, the accountant describes, with words and numbers, the various items in a set of financial statements. The system is imperfect at best and, for that reason, is always in the process of change. As society and the business environment have become more complex, the accounting profession has searched for ways to improve financial statements as a means of communicating with statement users.

© Cengage Learning 2013

SPOTLIGHT
Income Measurement, Accrual Accounting, and Ethics

In the construction industry, income measurement and accrual accounting are very important to the success of a company. Showing an accurate account balance and managing cash flow is critical when applying for credit, which is necessary within this very competitive industry. **James H. Kennedy**, CPA, specializes in providing accounting services to construction companies. A classically trained chef, he made a career change at 34 to return to accounting and become a CPA.

According to James, it is critical to get a balance between receivables and payables in this ever-changing industry. With the recent changes in the economy, construction customers are slower paying, with the average receivables taking close to 50 days to be paid. At the same time, payables are due within 30 days. Taking longer than 30 days to pay can negatively affect a company's ability to receive orders. Because of this, many companies are forced to make difficult decisions regarding pricing and payables.

When applying for a loan, James recommends that construction firms make sure that all receivables are classified as current or noncurrent assets and not understated; that current portions of long-term debt are properly recorded; and that accrued expenses are not overstated. These are all very important because they can greatly affect the ratios that many banks review before they lend money. He says that applying for a loan is like a first date. You only have one opportunity to make a good first impression.

While there can be pressure to adjust the financials to reflect a "better" picture, James makes clear that an accountant must accurately reflect a firm's income. Protect your integrity and your CPA license at all times, he says. James is a third-generation CPA, and his grandfather told him, "All you ever really have is your reputation. You only get one CPA license and it's how you feed your family. It makes all the difference in the world."

❝Learn to communicate well. . . . Develop an excellent style of writing. It will differentiate you from your colleagues immediately. . . . Know your debits and credits cold, automatically, by heart, inside out, upside down, day or night. ❞

Name: James H. Kennedy, CPA

Education: B.S., Business Administration, Rowan University

College Major: Accounting

Occupation: CPA

Age: 53

Position: Founding partner of peer reviewed CPA firm that works closely with construction firms

Company Name: Kennedy & Associates, LLC CPA Services

See James Kennedy's interview clip in CNOW.

---

[1] *Statement of Financial Accounting Concepts No. 5,* "Recognition and Measurement in Financial Statements of Business Enterprises" (Stamford, Conn.: Financial Accounting Standards Board, December 1984), par. 6.

Measurement

Accountants depict a financial statement item in both words and *numbers*. The accountant must *quantify* the effects of economic events on the entity. It is not enough to decide that an event is important and thus warrants recognition in the financial statements. To be able to recognize an event, the statement preparer must measure the event's financial effects on the company.

Measurement of an item in financial statements requires that two choices be made:

1. The accountant must decide on the *attribute* to be measured.
2. A scale of measurement, or *unit of measure*, must be chosen.

Choice 1: The Attribute to Be Measured Assume that a company holds a parcel of real estate as an investment. What attribute—that is, *characteristic*—of the property should be used to measure and thus recognize it as an asset on the balance sheet? The cost of the asset at the time it is acquired is the most logical choice. *Cost* is the amount of cash or its equivalent paid to acquire the asset. But how do we report the property on a balance sheet a year from now?

Historical cost
The amount paid for an asset and used as a basis for recognizing it on the balance sheet and carrying it on later balance sheets.

Current value
The amount of cash or its equivalent that could be received by selling an asset currently.

- The simplest approach is to show the property on the balance sheet at its original cost, thus the designation **historical cost**. The use of historical cost is not only simple but also an amount that can be agreed upon. Assume that two accountants are asked to independently measure the cost of the asset. After examining the sales contract for the land, they should arrive at the same amount.
- An alternative to historical cost as the attribute to be measured is **current value**. Current value is the amount of cash or its equivalent that could be received currently from the sale of the asset. For the company's piece of property, current value is the *estimated* selling price of the land, reduced by any commissions or other fees involved in making the sale. But the amount is only an estimate, not an actual amount. If the company has not yet sold the property, how can we know for certain its selling price? We have to compare it to similar properties that have sold recently.

The choice between current value and historical cost as the attribute to be measured is a good example of the trade-offs that must sometimes be made. As indicated earlier, historical cost is an amount that can be agreed upon. But is it as relevant to the needs of the decision makers as current value? Put yourself in the position of a banker trying to decide whether to lend money to the company. In evaluating the company's assets as collateral for the loan, is it more relevant to your decision to know what the firm paid for a piece of land 20 years ago or what it could be sold for today? But what *could* the property be sold for today? Two accountants might not arrive at the same current value for the land. Whereas value or selling price may be more relevant to your decision on the loan, differing opinions on an asset's current value make use of this attribute more difficult.

Because of its objective nature, historical cost is the attribute used to measure many of the assets recognized on the balance sheet. However, certain other attributes, such as current value, have increased in popularity in recent years. Other chapters of the book will discuss some of the alternatives to historical cost.

Choice 2: The Unit of Measure Regardless of the attribute of an item to be measured, it is still necessary to choose a yardstick, or unit of measure. The yardstick currently used is units of money. *Money* is something accepted as a medium of exchange or as a means of payment. The unit of money in the United States is the dollar. In Japan, the medium of exchange is the yen, and in Great Britain, it is the pound.

The use of the dollar as a unit of measure for financial transactions is widely accepted. The *stability* of the dollar as a yardstick is subject to considerable debate, however. Assume that you are thinking about buying a certain parcel of land. As part of your decision process, you measure the dimensions of the property and determine that the lot is 80 feet wide and 120 feet deep. Thus, the unit of measure used to determine the lot's size is the square foot. The company that owns the land offers to sell it for $10,000. Although the offer sounds attractive, you decide against the purchase today.

You return in one year to take a second look at the lot. You measure the lot again and, not surprisingly, find the width still to be 80 feet and the depth 120 feet. The owner is still willing to sell the lot for $10,000. This may appear to be the same price as last year. But the *purchasing power* of the unit of measure, the dollar, may very possibly have changed since last year. Even though the foot is a stable measuring unit, the dollar often is not. A *decline* in the purchasing power of the dollar is evidenced by a continuing *rise* in the general level of prices in an economy. For example, rather than paying $10,000 last year to buy the lot, you could have spent the $10,000 on other goods or services. However, a year later the same $10,000 may very well not buy the same amount of goods and services.

Inflation, or a rise in the general level of prices in the economy, results in a decrease in purchasing power. In the past, the accounting profession has experimented with financial statements adjusted for the changing value of the dollar. As inflation has declined in recent years in the United States, the debate over the use of the dollar as a stable measuring unit has somewhat subsided.[2] It is still important to recognize the inherent weakness in the use of a measuring unit that is subject to change, however.

Summary of Recognition and Measurement in Financial Statements

The purpose of financial statements is to communicate various types of economic information about a company. The job of the accountant is to decide which information should be recognized in the financial statements and how the effects of that information on the entity should be measured. Exhibit 4-1 summarizes the role of recognition and measurement in the preparation of financial statements.

EXHIBIT 4-1 Recognition and Measurement in Financial Statements

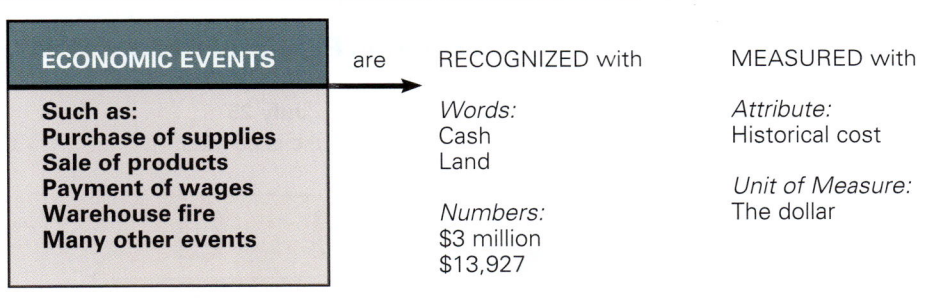

LO1 Explain the significance of recognition and measurement in the preparation and use of financial statements.

- Determining which economic events should be recognized and how they should be measured is critical for accounting information to be useful.
  - Recognition drives how and when the effects of economic events are described in the financial statements.
  - Measurement involves deciding on the attribute of an economic event that must be measured and the appropriate unit of measure.

POD REVIEW 4.1

QUESTIONS Answers to these questions are on the last page of the chapter.

1. The process of recording an item in the financial statements is called
   a. measurement.
   b. recognition.
   c. posting.
   d. none of the above.

2. The amount of cash that could be received by selling an asset currently is called
   a. current value.
   b. historical cost.
   c. depreciated cost.
   d. none of the above.

---

[2] The rate of inflation in some countries, most noticeably those in South America, has far exceeded the rate in the United States. Companies operating in some of these countries with hyperinflationary economies are required to make adjustments to their statements.

The Accrual Basis of Accounting

LO2 Explain the differences between the cash and accrual bases of accounting.

OVERVIEW: Throughout this book, we assume the use of an accrual basis. This means that revenues are recognized when earned and expenses when incurred.

The accrual basis of accounting is the foundation for the measurement of income in our modern system of accounting. The best way to understand the accrual basis is to compare it with the simpler cash approach.

Comparing the Cash and Accrual Bases of Accounting

The cash and accrual bases of accounting differ with respect to the *timing* of the recognition of revenues and expenses.

Example 4-1 Comparing the Cash and Accrual Bases of Accounting

Assume that on July 24, Barbara White, a salesperson for Spiffy House Painters, contracts with a homeowner to repaint a house for $1,000. A large crew comes in and paints the house the next day, July 25. The customer has 30 days from the day of completion of the job to pay and does, in fact, pay Spiffy on August 25. When should Spiffy recognize the $1,000 as revenue—as soon as the contract is signed on July 24; on July 25, when the work is done; or on August 25, when the customer pays the bill?

When Is Revenue Recognized?

July 24	**July 25**	**August 25**
Contract is signed.	House is painted.	Customer pays for job.

No Revenue Yet	**Accrual Basis:**	**Cash Basis:**
	When house is painted	When cash is received

Cash basis
A system of accounting in which revenues are recognized when cash is received and expenses are recognized when cash is paid.

Accrual basis
A system of accounting in which revenues are recognized when earned and expenses are recognized when incurred.

- In an income statement prepared on a **cash basis**, revenues are recognized when cash is *received*. Thus, on a cash basis, the $1,000 would not be recognized as revenue until the cash is collected, on August 25.
- In an income statement prepared on an **accrual basis**, revenue is recognized when it is *earned*. On this basis, the $1,000 would be recognized as revenue on July 25, when the house is painted. This is the point at which the revenue is earned.

© Cengage Learning 2013

Under the accrual basis, cash has not yet been received on July 25, but another account, Accounts Receivable, is recognized as an asset. This asset represents the right to receive cash in the future. The effect of the transaction can be identified and analyzed as follows:

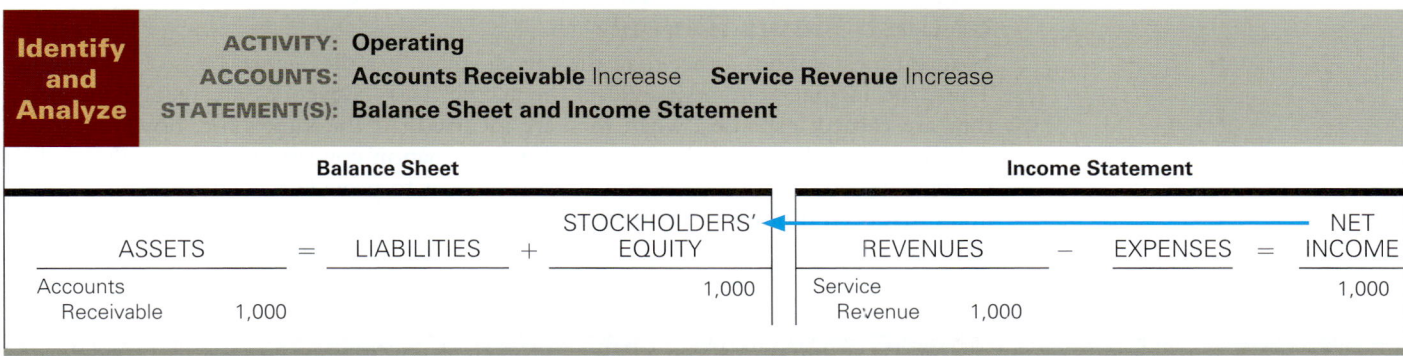

At the time cash is collected, accounts receivable is reduced and cash is increased. The effect of the transaction can be identified and analyzed as follows:

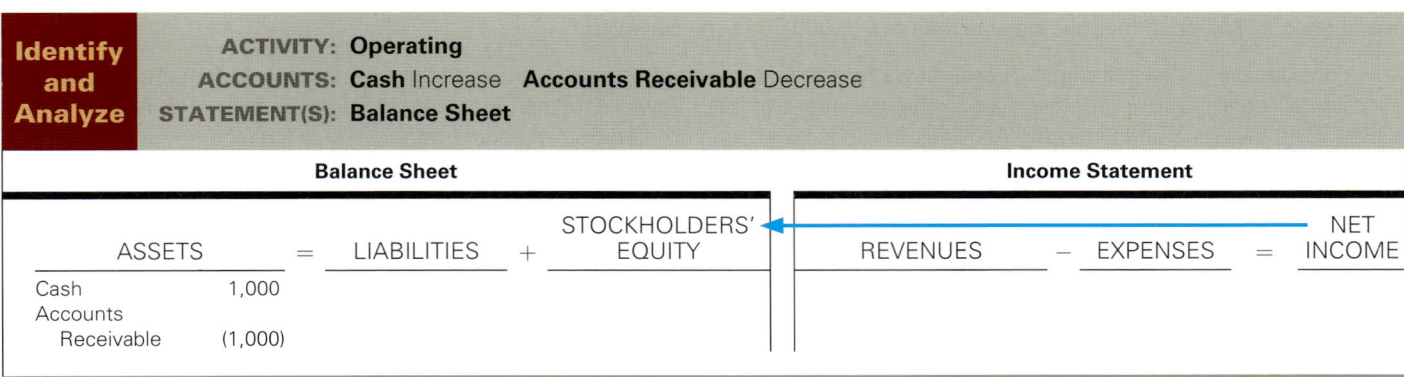

Assume that Barbara White is paid a 10% commission for all contracts and is paid on the 15th of the month following the month a house is painted. Thus, for this job, she will receive a $100 commission check on August 15. When should Spiffy recognize her commission of $100 as an expense? On July 24, when White gets the homeowner to sign a contract? When the work is completed, on July 25? Or on August 15, when she receives the commission check? Again, on a cash basis, commission expense would be recognized on August 15, when cash is *paid* to the salesperson. But on an accrual basis, expenses are recognized when they are *incurred*. In Example 4-1 the commission expense is incurred when the house is painted, on July 25.

Exhibit 4-2 summarizes the essential differences between recognition of revenues and expenses on a cash basis and recognition on an accrual basis.

EXHIBIT 4-2 Comparing the Cash and Accrual Bases of Accounting

	Cash Basis	Accrual Basis
Revenue is recognized	**When Received**	**When Earned**
Expense is recognized	**When Paid**	**When Incurred**

What the Income Statement and the Statement of Cash Flows Reveal

Most business entities, other than the very smallest, use the accrual basis of accounting. Thus, the income statement reflects the accrual basis. Revenues are recognized when they are earned; expenses, when they are incurred. At the same time, however, stockholders and creditors are also interested in information concerning the cash flows of an entity. The purpose of a statement of cash flows is to provide this information. Keep in mind that even though a statement of cash flows is presented in a complete set of financial statements, the accrual basis is used for recording transactions and for preparing a balance sheet and an income statement.

Example 4-2   Comparing the Income Statement and the Statement of Cash Flows

Recall the example of Glengarry Health Club in Chapter 3. The club earned revenue from two sources—memberships and court fees. Both forms of revenue were recognized on the income statement presented in that chapter and are reproduced in the top portion of the income statement shown below. Recall, however, that members have 30 days to pay and that at the end of the first month of operation, only $4,000 of the membership fees of $15,000 had been collected.

Now consider the partial statement of cash flows for the first month of operation, shown below the income statement. Because we want to compare the income statement to the statement of cash flows, only the Operating Activities section of the statement is shown. (The Investing and Financing Activities sections have been omitted from the statement.) Why is net income for the month a *positive* $7,000 but cash from operating activities is a *negative* $4,000? Of the membership revenue of $15,000 reflected on the income statement, only $4,000 was collected in cash. Glengarry has accounts receivable for the other $11,000. Thus, cash from operating activities, as reflected on a statement of cash flows, is $11,000 *less* than net income of $7,000, or a negative $4,000.

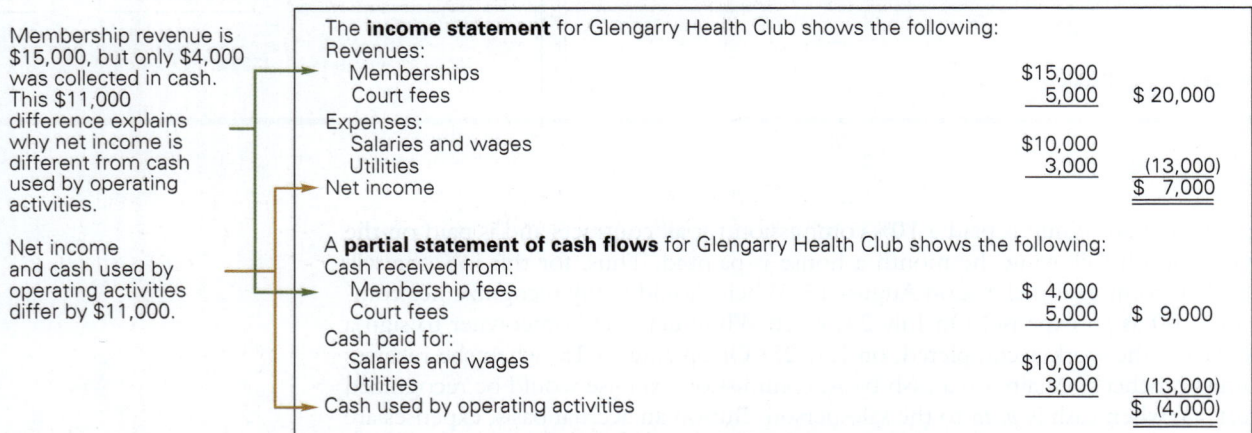

Membership revenue is $15,000, but only $4,000 was collected in cash. This $11,000 difference explains why net income is different from cash used by operating activities.

Net income and cash used by operating activities differ by $11,000.

The **income statement** for Glengarry Health Club shows the following:

Revenues:		
Memberships	$15,000	
Court fees	5,000	$ 20,000
Expenses:		
Salaries and wages	$10,000	
Utilities	3,000	(13,000)
Net income		$ 7,000

A **partial statement of cash flows** for Glengarry Health Club shows the following:

Cash received from:		
Membership fees	$ 4,000	
Court fees	5,000	$ 9,000
Cash paid for:		
Salaries and wages	$10,000	
Utilities	3,000	(13,000)
Cash used by operating activities		$ (4,000)

Each of these two financial statements serves a useful purpose:

- The income statement reflects the revenues actually earned by the business, regardless of whether cash has been collected.
- The statement of cash flows tells the reader about the actual cash inflows during a period of time.

Accrual Accounting and Time Periods

The *time period assumption* was introduced in Chapter 1. We assume that it is possible to prepare an income statement that fairly reflects the earnings of a business for a specific period of time, such as a month or a year. It is somewhat artificial to divide the operations of a business into periods of time as indicated on a calendar. The conflict arises because earning income is a *process* that takes place over a period of time rather than at any one point in time.

Consider an alternative to our present system of reporting the operations of a business on a periodic basis. A new business begins operations with an investment of $50,000. The business operates for ten years, during which time no records are kept other than a checkbook for the cash on deposit at the bank. At the end of the ten years, the owners decide to go their separate ways and convert all of their assets to cash. They divide among them the balance of $80,000 in the bank account. What is the profit of the business for the ten-year period? The answer is $30,000, the difference between the original cash of $50,000 contributed and the cash of $80,000 available at liquidation.

The point of this simple scenario is that we could be very precise and accurate in measuring the income of a business if it were not necessary to artificially divide operations according to a calendar. Stockholders, bankers, and other interested parties cannot wait until a business liquidates to make decisions, however. They need information on a periodic basis. Thus, the justification for the accrual basis of accounting lies in the needs of financial statement users for periodic information on the financial position and the profitability of the entity.

LO2 Explain the differences between the cash and accrual bases of accounting.

- Cash and accrual bases are two alternatives used to account for transactions or economic events. They differ in the timing of when revenues and expenses are recognized.
  - Under the accrual method, which is the focus of this text, revenues are recognized when earned and expenses are recognized when incurred.
  - By contrast, under the cash method, revenues are recognized when cash is received and expenses are recognized when cash is paid.

POD REVIEW 4.2

QUESTIONS   Answers to these questions are on the last page of the chapter.

1. Under the accrual method, expenses are recognized
   a. when cash is paid.
   b. at the end of the accounting period.
   c. when they are incurred.
   d. when revenue is earned.

2. A landscaping business signs a contract with a new customer on April 1. New trees are planted for the customer on May 1, and the bill for the services is paid on June 1. Under the accrual basis, the business should recognize revenue on
   a. April 1.
   b. May 1.
   c. June 1.
   d. December 31.

The Revenue Recognition Principle

OVERVIEW: Revenues are inflows of assets or reductions of liabilities from providing goods or services to customers. They must be realized and earned to be recognized on the income statement.

LO3 Describe the revenue recognition principle and explain its application in various situations.

"**Revenues** are inflows or other enhancements of assets of an entity or settlements of its liabilities (or a combination of both) from delivering or producing goods, rendering services, or other activities that constitute the entity's ongoing major or central operations."[3] Two points should be noted about this formal definition of revenues.

First, an asset is not always involved when revenue is recognized. The recognition of revenue may result from the settlement of a liability rather than from the acquisition of an asset. Second, entities generate revenue in different ways: some companies produce goods, others distribute or deliver the goods to users, and still others provide some type of service.

On the accrual basis, revenues are recognized when earned. However, the **revenue recognition principle** involves two factors. Revenues are recognized in the income

Revenues
Inflows of assets or settlements of liabilities from delivering or producing goods, rendering services, or conducting other activities.

Revenue recognition principle
Revenues are recognized in the income statement when they are realized, or realizable, and earned.

---

[3] *Statement of Financial Accounting Concepts No. 6*, "Elements of Financial Statements" (Stamford, Conn.: Financial Accounting Standards Board, December 1985), par. 78.

statement when they are both *realized* and *earned*. Revenues are realized when goods or services are exchanged for cash or claims to cash, usually at the time of sale. This is normally interpreted to mean at the time the product or service is delivered to the customer. However, in certain situations, it may be necessary to modify or interpret the meaning of the revenue recognition principle. The application of the principle to long-term contracts, franchises, commodities, and installment sales is covered in intermediate accounting courses.

In some cases, revenue is earned continuously over time. In these cases, a product or service is not delivered at a specific point in time; instead, the earnings process takes place with the passage of time. Rent and interest are two examples. Interest is the cost associated with the use of someone else's money. When should a bank recognize the interest earned from granting a 90-day loan? Even though the interest may not be received until the loan is repaid, interest is earned every day the loan is outstanding. Later in the chapter, we will look at the process for recognizing interest earned but not yet received. The same procedure is used to recognize revenue from rent that is earned but uncollected.

LO3 Describe the revenue recognition principle and explain its application in various situations.

- Revenues are inflows of assets (or reductions of liabilities), generally from providing goods or services to customers.
  - Revenues must be realized and earned to be recognized on the income statement.

POD REVIEW 4.3

QUESTIONS   **Answers to these questions are on the last page of the chapter.**

1. Under the revenue recognition principle, revenues are recognized
   a. when they are realized, or realizable, and earned.
   b. when cash is received.
   c. when expenses are incurred.
   d. at the end of the accounting period.

2. Which of the following would result in the recognition of revenue?
   a. A manufacturer delivers a component to a supplier.
   b. A retailer sells a product to a consumer.
   c. A bank provides a service to a customer.
   d. All of the above would result in the recognition of revenue.

Expense Recognition and the Matching Principle

LO4 Describe the matching principle and the various methods for recognizing expenses.

OVERVIEW: To determine the net income in a period, revenues must be matched with the costs necessary to generate the revenue. Some costs can be directly matched with revenue, while others are indirectly matched with the periods in which they will provide benefits. Still other costs expire immediately and are recognized as an expense in the period incurred.

Companies incur a variety of costs.

- A new office building is constructed.
- Supplies are purchased.
- Employees perform services.
- The electric meter is read.

In each of those situations, the company incurs a cost regardless of when it pays cash. Conceptually, **anytime a cost is incurred, an asset is acquired.** However, according to the definition in Chapter 1, an asset represents a future economic benefit. An asset ceases being an asset and becomes an expense when the economic benefits from having incurred the cost have expired. Assets are unexpired costs, and expenses are expired costs.

At what point do costs expire and become expenses? The expense recognition principle requires that expenses be recognized in different ways depending on the nature of the cost. The ideal approach to recognizing expenses is to match them with revenues. Under the **matching principle**, the accountant attempts to associate revenues of a period with the costs necessary to generate those revenues. For certain types of expenses, a direct form of matching is possible; for others, it is necessary to associate costs with a particular period. The classic example of direct matching is cost of goods sold expense with sales revenue. Cost of goods sold is the cost of the inventory associated with a particular sale. A cost is incurred and an asset is recorded when the inventory is purchased. The asset, inventory, becomes an expense when it is sold. Another example of a cost that can be matched directly with revenue is commissions. The commission paid to a salesperson can be matched directly with the sale.

An indirect form of matching is used to recognize the benefits associated with certain types of costs, most noticeably long-term assets such as buildings and equipment. These costs benefit many periods, but it is not usually possible to match them directly with a specific sale of a product. Instead, they are matched with the periods during which they will provide benefits. For example, an office building may be useful to a company for 30 years. *Depreciation* is the process of allocating the cost of a tangible long-term asset to its useful life. Depreciation Expense is the account used to recognize this type of expense.

The benefits associated with the incurrence of certain other costs are treated in accounting as expiring simultaneously with the acquisition of the costs. The justification for this treatment is that no future benefits from the incurrence of the cost are discernible. This is true of most selling and administrative costs. For example, the costs of heat and light in a building benefit only the current period and therefore are recognized as expenses as soon as the costs are incurred. Likewise, income taxes incurred during the period do not benefit any period other than the current period; thus, they are written off as an expense in the period incurred.

Matching principle
The association of revenue of a period with all of the costs necessary to generate that revenue.

Example 4-3 Comparing Three Methods for Matching Costs with Revenue

The relationships among costs, assets, and expenses are depicted below.

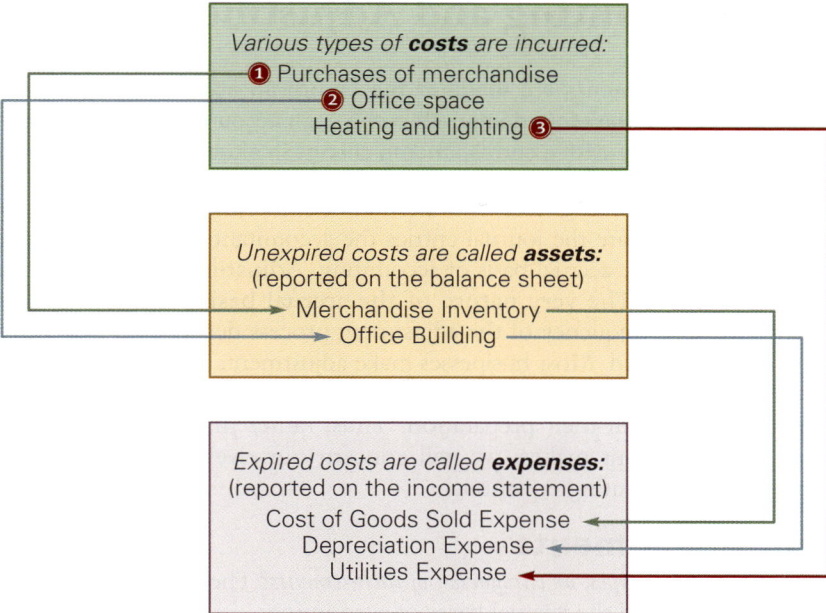

❶ Costs incurred for purchases of merchandise result in an asset, Merchandise Inventory, and are eventually matched with revenue at the time the product is sold.

❷ Costs incurred for office space result in an asset, Office Building, which is recognized as Depreciation Expense over the useful life of the building.

❸ The cost of heating and lighting benefits only the current period and thus is recognized immediately as Utilities Expense.

(Continued)

Expenses
Outflows of assets or incurrences of liabilities resulting from delivering goods, rendering services, or carrying out other activities.

According to the FASB, **expenses** are "outflows or other using up of assets or incurrences of liabilities (or a combination of both) from delivering or producing goods, rendering services, or carrying out other activities that constitute the entity's ongoing major or central operations."[4] The key point to note about expenses is that they come about in two different ways:

- From the use of an asset
- From the recognition of a liability

For instance, when a retailer sells a product, the asset sacrificed is Inventory. Cost of Goods Sold is the expense account that is increased when the Inventory account is decreased. As you will see in the next section, the incurrence of an expense also may result in a liability.

LO4 Describe the matching principle and the various methods for recognizing expenses.

- The matching principle attempts to associate expenses with the time periods in which the expenditures help generate revenues.
- This principle is particularly important with expenditures for items that last for more than one accounting period. An example is the depreciation of a building.

POD REVIEW 4.4

QUESTIONS   Answers to these questions are on the last page of the chapter.

1. The association of revenue of a period with all of the costs necessary to generate that revenue is called
   a. the revenue recognition principle.
   b. the matching principle.
   c. the income recognition principle.
   d. none of the above.

2. The matching principle requires that the cost of a new piece of equipment be recognized as an expense
   a. in the period the equipment is purchased.
   b. in the period cash is paid for the equipment.
   c. over the estimated useful life of the equipment.
   d. Never; the cost of equipment is not recognized as an expense.

Accrual Accounting and Adjustments

LO5 Identify the four major types of adjustments and analyze their effects on the financial statements.

OVERVIEW: Adjustments are made at the end of an accounting period. They are internal transactions and therefore do not affect the Cash account. Each adjustment affects either an asset or a liability with a corresponding change in either revenue or expense.

Adjusting entries
Journal entries made at the end of a period by a company using the accrual basis of accounting.

The accrual basis of accounting necessitates a number of adjustments at the end of a period. **Adjusting entries** are the journal entries the accountant makes at the end of a period for a company on the accrual basis of accounting. **Adjusting entries are not needed if a cash basis is used. The very nature of the accrual basis results in the need for adjusting entries.** The frequency of the adjustment process depends on how often financial statements are prepared. Most businesses make adjustments at month-end.

Recall from Chapter 3 that the emphasis throughout this book is on the *use* of financial statements rather than their preparation. Thus, rather than focus on the adjusting *entries* that the accountant makes, we will concern ourselves with the effect of these adjustments on the accounting equation.

Types of Adjustments
Why are there four basic types, or categories, of adjustments? The answer lies in the distinction between the cash and the accrual bases of accounting:

- On a cash basis, no differences exist in the timing of revenue and the receipt of cash. The same holds true for expenses.
- On an accrual basis, *revenue* can be earned before or after cash is received. *Expenses* can be incurred before or after cash is paid. Each of these four distinct situations requires a different type of adjustment at the end of the period.

---
[4] SFAC No. 6, par. 80.

© Cengage Learning 2013

We will consider each of the four categories and look at some examples of each.

(1) Cash Paid Before Expense Is Incurred (Deferred Expense) Assets
are often acquired before their actual use in the business. Insurance policies typically are
prepaid, as is rent. Office supplies are purchased in advance of their use, as are all types of
property and equipment. Recall that unexpired costs are assets. As the costs expire and the
benefits are used up, the asset must be written off and replaced with an expense.

Example 4-4 Adjusting a Deferred Expense Account

Assume that on September 1, **Nordstrom** prepays $2,400 for an insurance policy for the
next 12 months. The effect of the transaction can be identified and analyzed as follows:

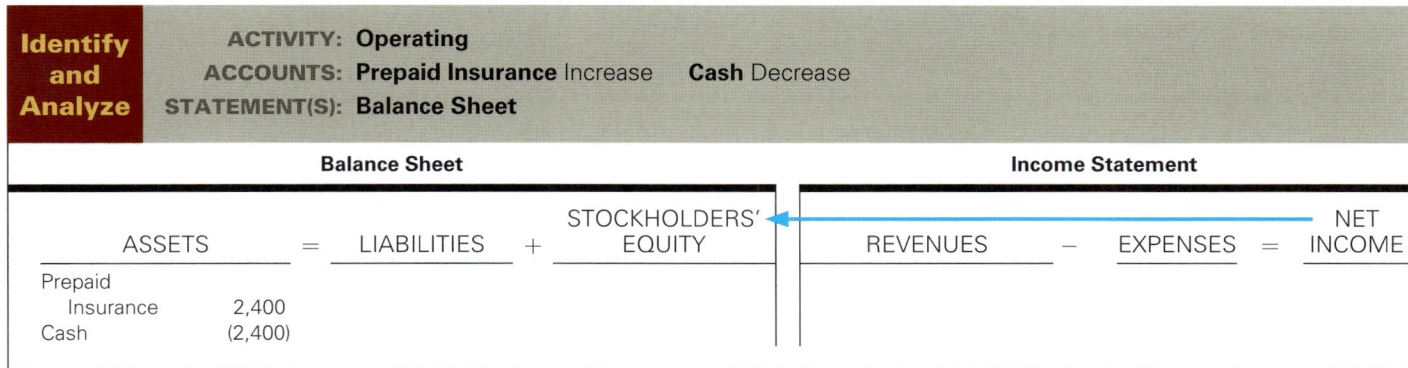

An asset account, Prepaid Insurance, is recorded because the company will receive benefits over the
next 12 months. Because the insurance is for a 12-month period, $200 of benefits from the asset
expires at the end of each month. The adjustment at the end of September to record this expiration
accomplishes two purposes: (1) it recognizes the reduction in the asset Prepaid Insurance, and (2) it recognizes the expense associated with using up the benefits for one month. On September 30, the
accountant makes an adjustment to recognize the expense and reduce the asset. The effect of the
adjustment can be identified and analyzed as follows:

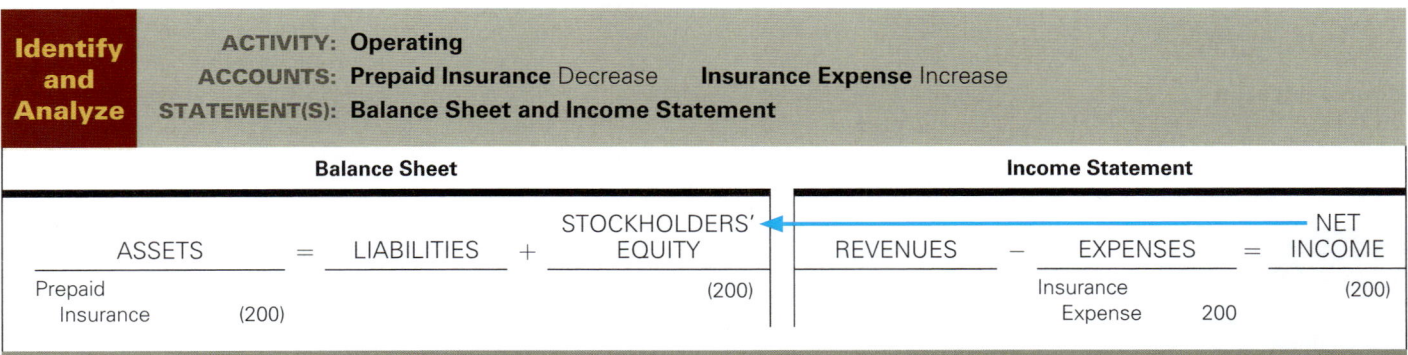

The balance in Prepaid Insurance represents the unexpired benefits from the prepayment of
insurance for the remaining 11 months: $200 × 11 = $2,200. The Insurance Expense account
reflects the expiration of benefits during the month of September.

Recall that depreciation is the process of allocating the cost of a long-term tangible
asset over its estimated useful life. The accountant does not attempt to measure the
decline in *value* of the asset, but tries to allocate the cost of the asset over its useful life.
Thus, the deferred expense adjustment for depreciation (shown in Example 4-5 below)
is similar to the one made for insurance expense in Example 4-4 above.

Example 4-5 Recording Depreciation

Assume that on January 1, Nordstrom buys new store fixtures, for which it pays $5,000. The effect of the transaction can be identified and analyzed as follows:

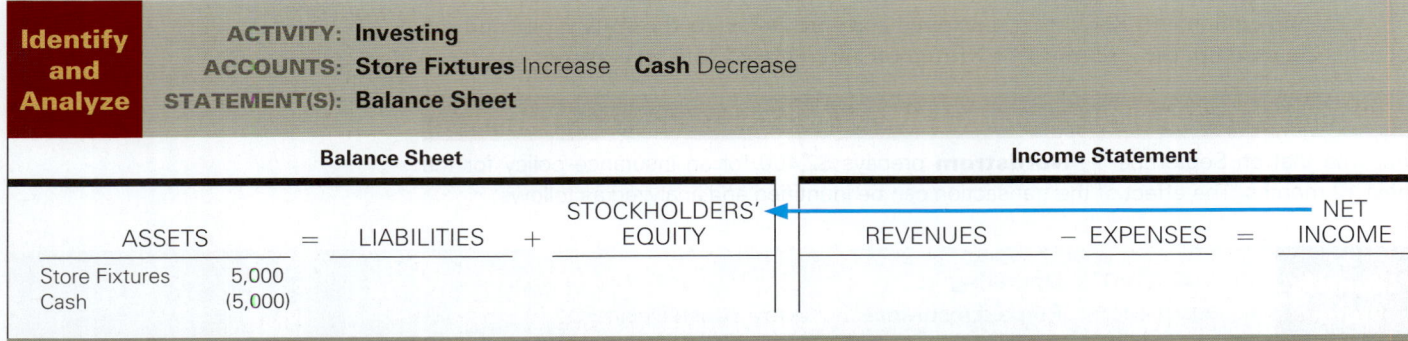

Identify and Analyze	**ACTIVITY:** Investing
	ACCOUNTS: Store Fixtures Increase Cash Decrease
	STATEMENT(S): Balance Sheet

Balance Sheet					Income Statement			
ASSETS	=	LIABILITIES	+	STOCKHOLDERS' EQUITY	REVENUES	− EXPENSES	=	NET INCOME
Store Fixtures	5,000							
Cash	(5,000)							

Two estimates must be made in depreciating the fixtures:

1. The useful life of the asset

2. The salvage value of the fixtures at the end of their useful lives. *Estimated salvage value* is the amount a company expects to receive when it sells an asset at the end of its estimated useful life.

According to a note on page 46 of Nordstrom's 2010 10K, the company uses an estimated useful life for its store fixtures and equipment of 3 to 15 years. Although it is not stated, assume that Nordstrom uses an estimated useful life of five years and an estimated salvage value of $500 at the end of that time for these particular fixtures. Thus, the *depreciable cost* of the fixtures is $5,000 − $500, or $4,500. A later chapter will consider alternative methods for allocating the depreciable cost over the useful life of an asset. For now, we will use the simplest approach (and the one that Nordstrom uses) called the **straight-line method**, which assigns an equal amount of depreciation to each period. The monthly depreciation is found by dividing the depreciable cost of $4,500 over the estimated useful life of 60 months (5 years = 60 months), which equals $75 per month.

Straight-line method
The assignment of an equal amount of depreciation to each period.

The adjustment to recognize depreciation is conceptually the same as the adjustment to write off Prepaid Insurance. That is, the asset account is reduced and an expense is recognized. However, accountants normally use a contra account to reduce the total amount of long-term tangible assets by the amount of depreciation. A **contra account** has a balance that is opposite the balance in its related account. For example, Accumulated Depreciation is used to record the decrease in a long-term asset for depreciation. The effect of the adjustment can be identified and analyzed as follows:

Contra account
An account with a balance that is opposite that of a related account.

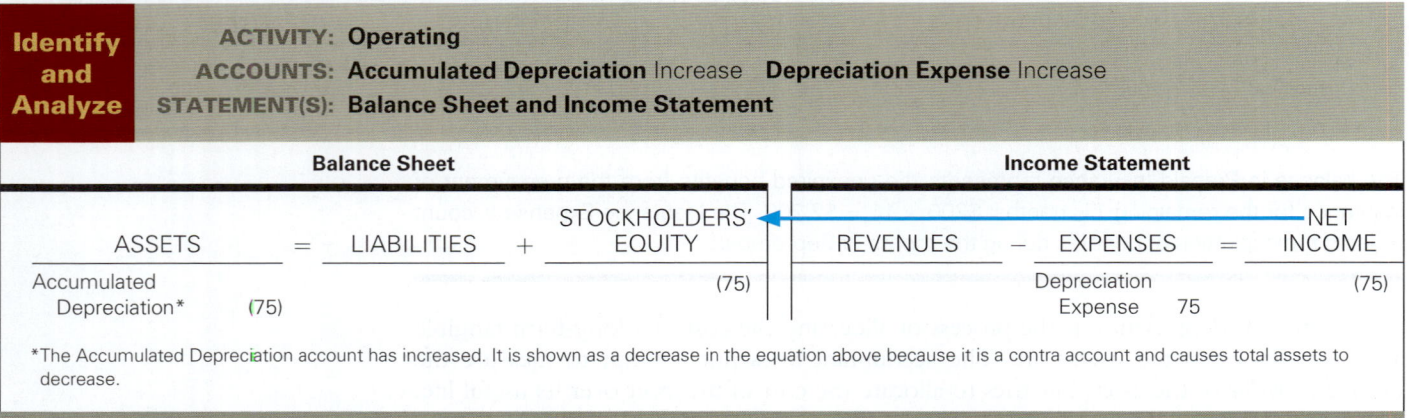

Identify and Analyze	**ACTIVITY:** Operating
	ACCOUNTS: Accumulated Depreciation Increase Depreciation Expense Increase
	STATEMENT(S): Balance Sheet and Income Statement

Balance Sheet					Income Statement			
ASSETS	=	LIABILITIES	+	STOCKHOLDERS' EQUITY	REVENUES	− EXPENSES	=	NET INCOME
Accumulated Depreciation*	(75)			(75)		Depreciation Expense 75		(75)

*The Accumulated Depreciation account has increased. It is shown as a decrease in the equation above because it is a contra account and causes total assets to decrease.

(Continued)

Why do companies use a contra account for depreciation rather than simply reduce the long-term asset directly? If the asset account were reduced each time depreciation was recorded, its original cost would not be readily determinable from the accounting records. For various reasons, businesses need to know the original cost of each asset. One of the most important reasons is the need to know historical cost for computation of depreciation for tax purposes.

On a balance sheet prepared on January 31, the contra account is shown as a reduction in the carrying value of the store fixtures:

Store Fixtures	$5,000	
Less: Accumulated Depreciation	75	4,925

> **STUDY TIP**
>
> Think of the Accumulated Depreciation account as an extension of the related asset account, in this case, the Store Fixtures account. Therefore, although the Store Fixtures account is not directly reduced for depreciation, an increase in its companion account, Accumulated Depreciation, has the effect of reducing the asset.

(2) Cash Received Before Revenue Is Earned (Deferred Revenue)

Recognizing accounting's symmetry will be a great help in your studies. Example 4-6 below shows that one company's asset is another company's liability.

Example 4-6 Adjusting a Deferred Revenue Account

In Example 4-4 involving the purchase of an insurance policy, a second company, the insurance company, received the cash paid by the first company, Nordstrom. At the time cash is received, the insurance company has a liability because it has taken cash from Nordstrom but has not yet performed the service to earn the revenue. The revenue will be earned with the passage of time. The effect of the transaction to the insurance company can be identified and analyzed as follows:

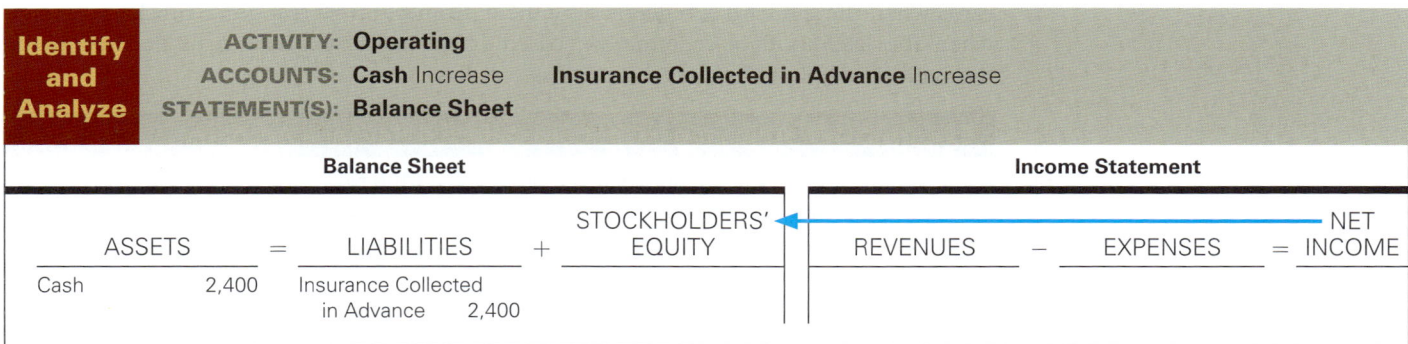

The account Insurance Collected in Advance is a liability. The insurance company is obligated to provide Nordstrom protection for the next 12 months. With the passage of time, the liability is satisfied. The adjustment at the end of each month accomplishes two purposes: it recognizes (1) the reduction in the liability and (2) the revenue earned each month. The effect of the adjustment can be identified and analyzed as follows:

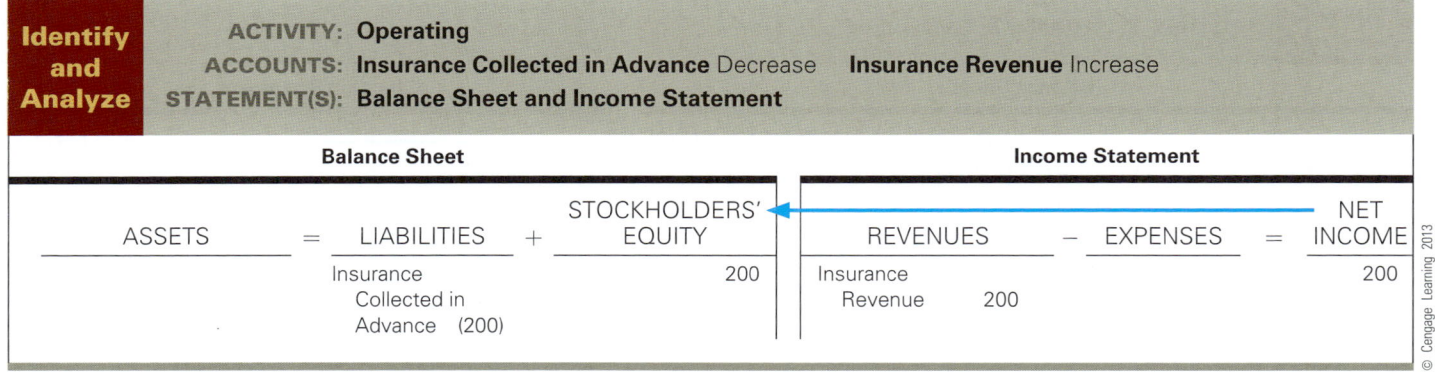

(Continued)

After the adjustment is made, the insurance company's remaining liability is $2,400 − $200, or $2,200, which represents 11 months of insurance collected in advance at $200 per month.

HOT TOPICS
Keeping a Watchful Eye on Sales

All companies must pay close attention to their sales figures. Still, it is hard to imagine any segment of the economy more revenue conscious than retailers. Nordstrom is no exception. Like its competition, the company reports monthly to the financial press, as it did recently in announcing its May 2011 sales. Retailers report both total sales as well as what they call "same-store sales," numbers that only include stores that operated in both the current and prior reporting periods. Analysts can more easily discern trends when sales at new stores are excluded.

Nordstom's investors should be encouraged by the recent announcement. Same-store sales for May 2011 were $796 million, an increase of 13% over the same period in 2010. With the economic downturn, even more encouraging were the results for Nordstrom's "full line stores" as compared to its discount "rack stores." Same-store sales for May 2011 increased by nearly 6% for the full line stores, while rack store sales increased by only 2.3% from the prior period. This is just the sort of information that is crucial in planning for the future as Nordstrom decides where to invest its valuable resources.

Source: Nordstrom news release, June 2, 2011; http://www.nordstrom.com.

As another example of deferred revenue, consider the following sentence from a note in Nordstrom's 2010 10K (page 45): "We recognize revenue from the sale of gift cards when the gift card is redeemed by the customer, or we recognize breakage income when the likelihood of redemption, based on historical experience, is deemed to be remote." Example 4-7 shows this process.

Example 4-7 Adjusting a Gift Card Deferred Revenue Account

Assume that on March 1, a generous friend gives you a $100 Nordstrom gift card. At the time the friend buys the card, Nordstrom has an increase in cash of $100 but has yet to earn any revenue. As the above note explains, Nordstrom does not recognize any revenue until you redeem the card. This will be the point at which Nordstrom gives you merchandise and earns revenue. Until the card is redeemed, Nordstrom has a liability; that is, it is obligated to deliver merchandise in the future. That liability is mentioned in the same note on page 45 of Nordstrom's annual report (amounts are in millions of dollars): "We had outstanding gift card liabilities of $188 and $174 at the end of 2010 and 2009, which are included in other current liabilities."

The effect of Nordstrom's receipt of $100 from your friend can be identified and analyzed as follows:

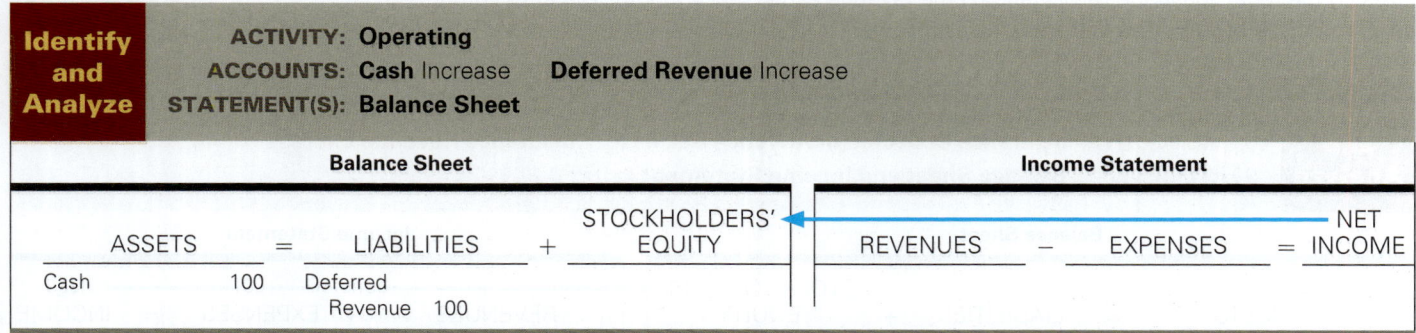

Like Insurance Collected in Advance in Example 4-6, Deferred Revenue is a liability. Assume that you redeem your card at a Nordstrom store on March 31. The effect of the adjustment on Nordstrom's books on this date can be identified and analyzed as follows:

(Continued)

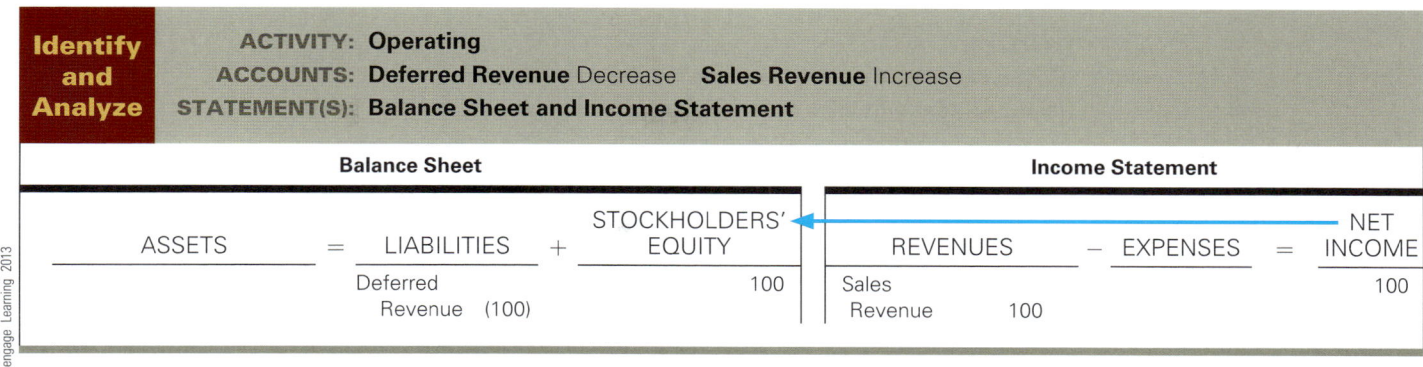

	Balance Sheet				Income Statement			
Identify and Analyze	ACTIVITY: **Operating** ACCOUNTS: **Deferred Revenue** Decrease **Sales Revenue** Increase STATEMENT(S): **Balance Sheet and Income Statement**							

	Balance Sheet					Income Statement		
ASSETS	=	LIABILITIES	+	STOCKHOLDERS' EQUITY	REVENUES	−	EXPENSES	= NET INCOME
		Deferred Revenue (100)		100	Sales Revenue 100			100

(3) Expense Incurred Before Cash Is Paid (Accrued Liability)

This situation is the opposite of (1). That is, cash is paid after an expense is actually incurred rather than before its incurrence, as was the case in (1). Many normal operating costs, such as payroll, various types of taxes, and utilities, fit this situation. Refer to Nordstrom's partial balance sheet in the chapter opener. The second line under current liabilities represents the company's accrued liabilities for salaries, wages, and related benefits, amounting to $375 million on January 29, 2011.

Example 4-8 Recording an Accrued Liability for Wages

Assume that at one of its stores, Nordstrom pays a total of $280,000 in wages on every other Friday. Assume that the last payday was Friday, May 31. The next two paydays will be Friday, June 14, and Friday, June 28. The effect of the transaction on each of these paydays can be identified and analyzed as follows:

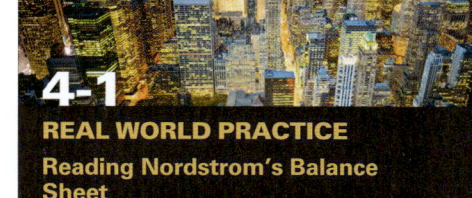

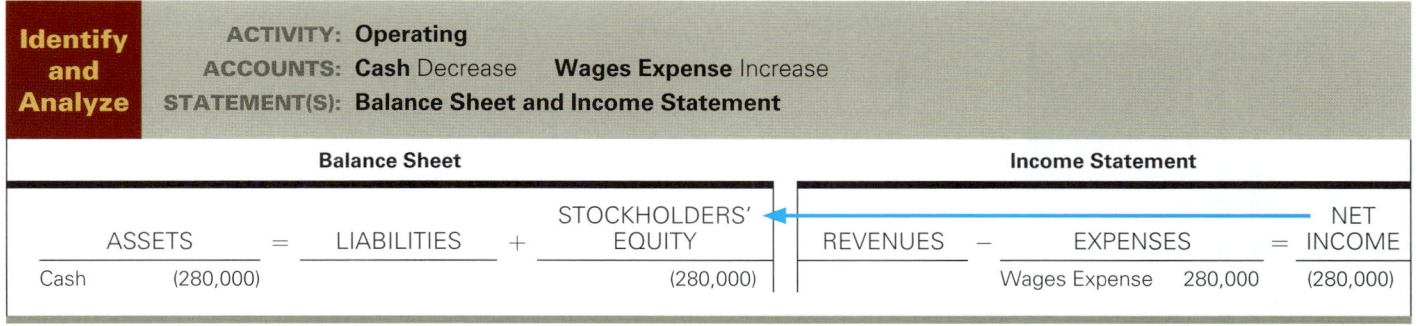

	Balance Sheet				Income Statement			
Identify and Analyze	ACTIVITY: **Operating** ACCOUNTS: **Cash** Decrease **Wages Expense** Increase STATEMENT(S): **Balance Sheet and Income Statement**							

	Balance Sheet					Income Statement		
ASSETS	=	LIABILITIES	+	STOCKHOLDERS' EQUITY	REVENUES	−	EXPENSES	= NET INCOME
Cash (280,000)				(280,000)			Wages Expense 280,000	(280,000)

On a balance sheet prepared as of June 30, a liability must be recognized. Even though the next payment is not until July 12, Nordstrom owes employees wages for the last two days of June and must recognize an expense for the wages earned by employees for those two days. We will assume that the store is open seven days a week and that the daily cost is 1/14th of the biweekly amount of $280,000, or $20,000. In addition to recognizing a liability on June 30, Nordstrom must adjust the records to reflect an expense associated with the cost of wages for the last two days of the month. The effect of the adjustment can be identified and analyzed as follows:

(Continued)

© Cengage Learning 2013

© Nikada/istockphoto.com

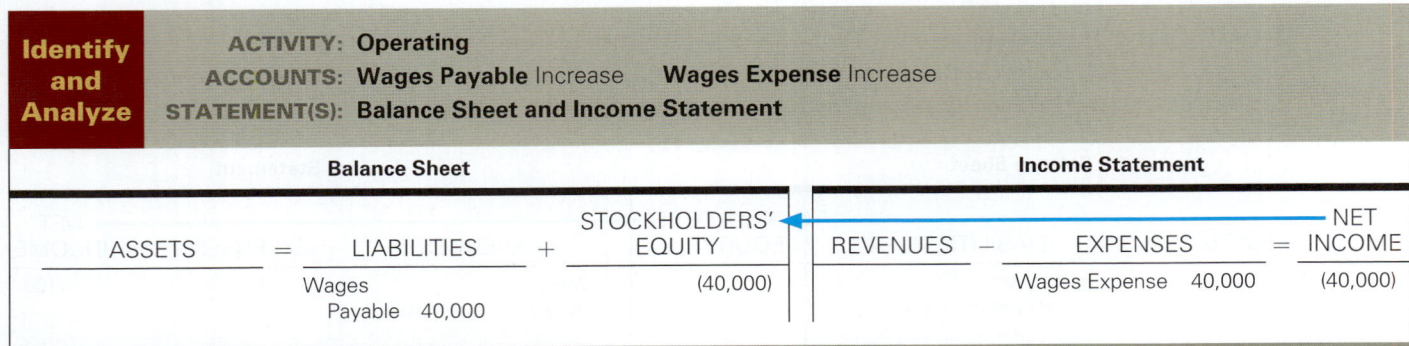

What adjustment will be made on the next payday, July 12? Nordstrom will need to eliminate the liability of $40,000 for the last two days of wages recorded on June 30 because the amount has now been paid. An additional $240,000 of expense has been incurred for the $20,000 cost per day associated with the first 12 days in July. Finally, cash is reduced by $280,000, which represents the biweekly payroll. The effect of the transaction can be identified and analzyed as follows:

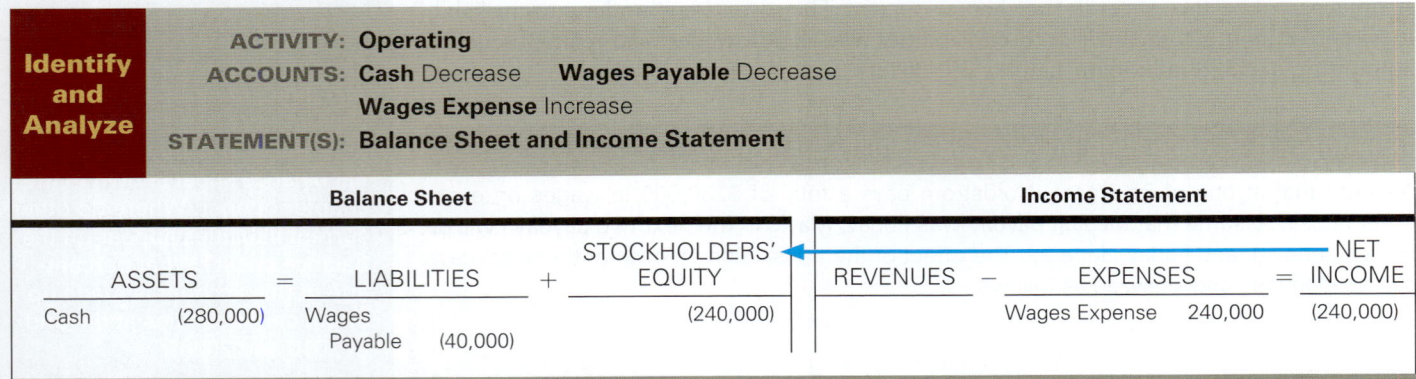

The following time line illustrates the amount of expense incurred in each of the two months, June and July, for the biweekly payroll:

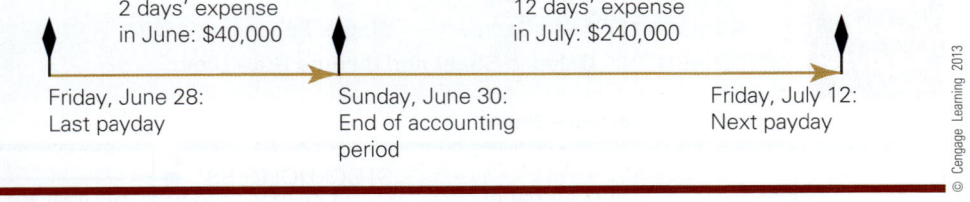

Another typical expense incurred before the payment of cash is interest. In many cases, the interest on a short-term loan is repaid with the amount of the loan, called the *principal* (see Example 4-9).

Example 4-9 Recording an Accrued Liability for Interest

Assume that Granger Company takes out a 9%, 90-day, $20,000 loan with its bank on March 1. Granger will repay the principal and interest on May 30. On March 1, both an asset and a liability, Notes Payable, are increased. The effect of the transaction can be identified and analyzed as follows:

(Continued)

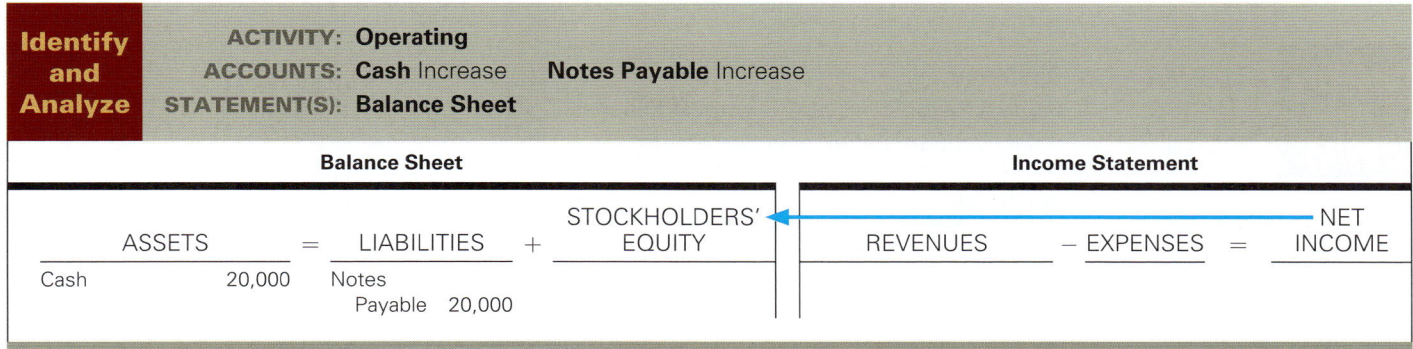

The basic formula for computing interest follows:

$$I = P \times R \times T$$

where I = the dollar amount of interest

P = the principal amount of the loan

R = the annual rate of interest as a percentage

T = time in years (often stated as a fraction of a year)

The total interest on Granger's loan is as follows:

$$\$20,000 \times 0.09 \times 3/12 = \underline{\$450}$$

Therefore, the amount of interest that must be recognized as expense at the end of March is one-third of $450 because one month of a total of three has passed. Alternatively, the formula for finding the total interest on the loan can be modified to compute the interest for one month.[5]

$$\$20,000 \times 0.09 \times 1/12 = \underline{\$150}$$

On March 31 and April 30, the accountant records adjustments to recognize interest both as an expense and an obligation. The effect of the adjustment on March 31 can be identified and analyzed as follows:

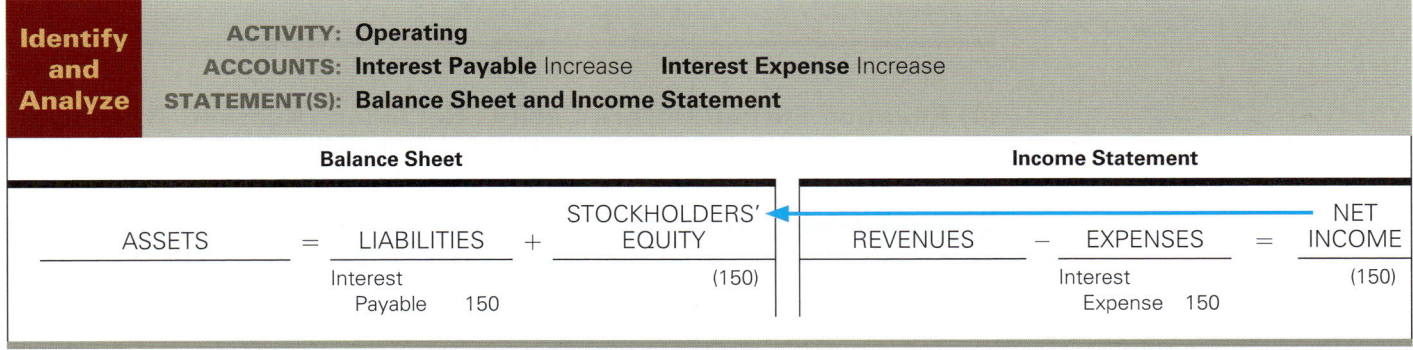

(Continued)

---

[5] In practice, interest is calculated on the basis of days rather than months. For example, the interest for March would be $20,000 × 0.09 × 30/365, or $147.95, to reflect 30 days in the month out of a total of 365 days in the year. The reason the number of days in March is 30 rather than 31 is because in computing interest, **businesses normally count the day a note matures but not the day it is signed.** To simplify the calculations, we will use months, even though the result is slightly inaccurate.

The effect of the adjustment at the end of April is the same as the one at the end of March:

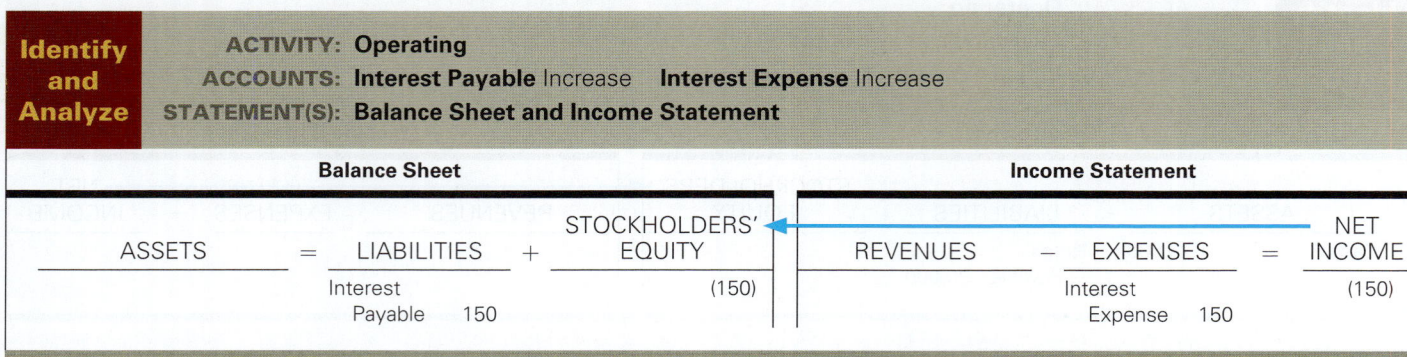

The adjustment on Granger's books on May 30 when it repays the principal and interest can be identified and analyzed as follows:

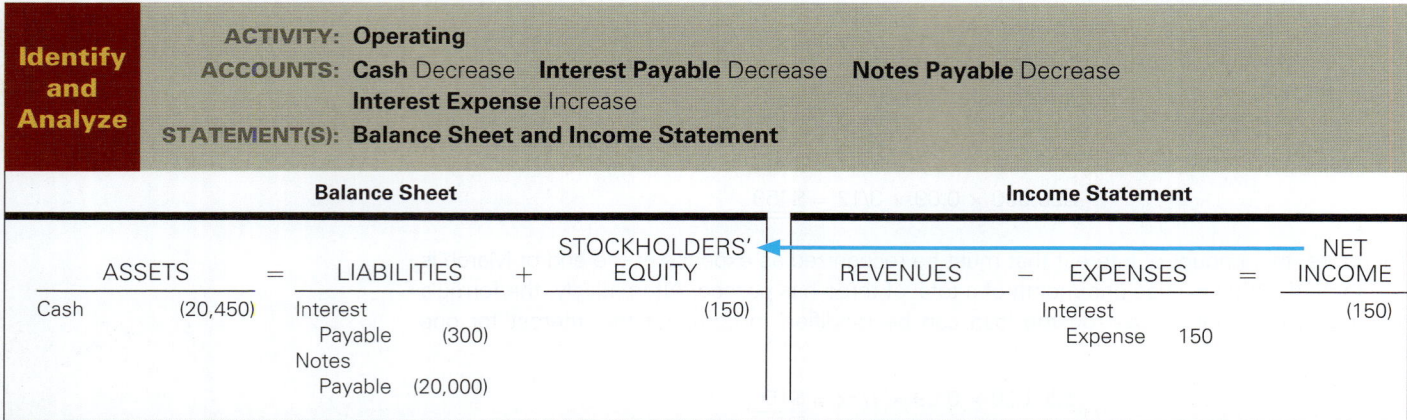

The reduction in Interest Payable eliminates the liability recorded at the end of March and April. The recognition of $150 in Interest Expense is the cost associated with the month of May.[6] The reduction in Cash represents the $20,000 of principal and the total interest of $450 for three months.

(4) Revenue Earned Before Cash Is Received (Accrued Asset)
Revenue is sometimes earned before the receipt of cash. Rent and interest are earned with the passage of time and require an adjustment if cash has not yet been received.

Example 4-10 Recording an Accrued Asset

Assume that Grand Management Company rents warehouse space to a number of tenants. Most of its contracts call for prepayment of rent for six months at a time. Its agreement with one tenant, however, allows the tenant to pay Grand $2,500 in monthly rent anytime within the first ten days of the following month. The effect of the adjustment on April 30, the end of the first month of the agreement, can be identified and analyzed as follows:

(Continued)

---

[6] This assumes that Granger did not make an adjustment prior to this to recognize interest expense for the month of May. If a separate adjustment had been made, Interest Payable would be reduced by $450.

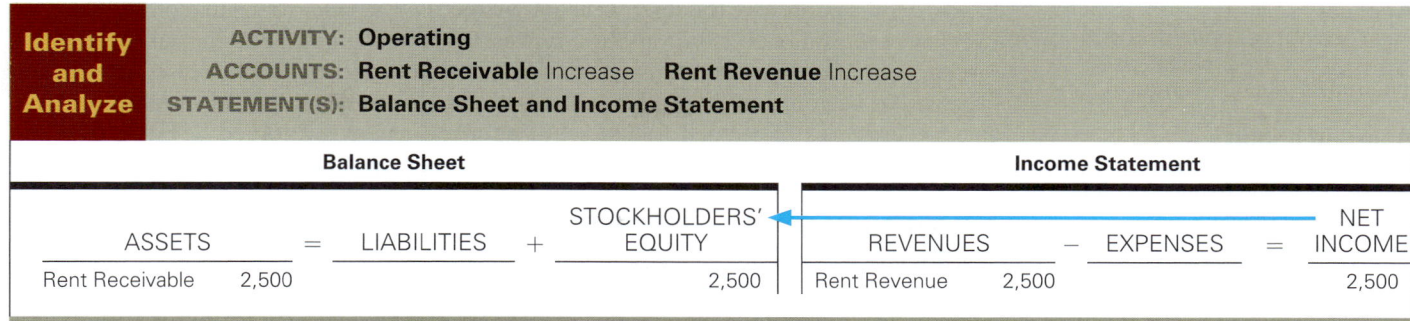

The effect of the transaction when the tenant pays its rent on May 7 can be identified and analyzed as follows:

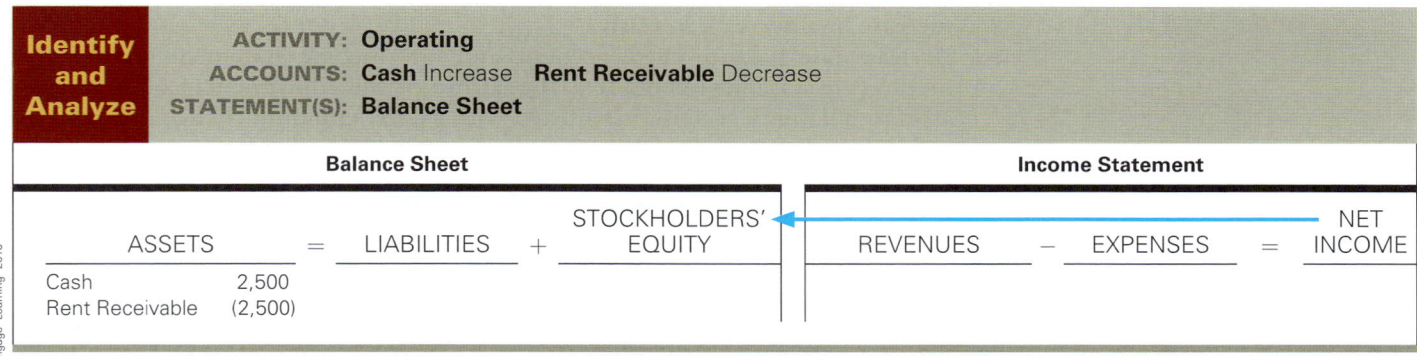

Although the example of rent was used to illustrate this category, the membership revenue of Glengarry Health Club in Chapter 3 also could be used as an example. **Whenever a company records revenue before cash is received, some type of receivable is increased and revenue is also increased.** In Chapter 3, Glengarry earned membership revenue even though members had until the following month to pay their dues.

The same principle would apply to any amounts that customers owed to Nordstrom at the end of a period. As shown in the chapter opener, Nordstrom reported Accounts Receivable, net of $2,026 million on January 29, 2011. A note to the financial statements explains that these receivables arise from two forms of credit that the company offers customers. First, Nordstrom has its own private label card. Second, the company offers two VISA® credit cards.

Accruals and Deferrals

One of the challenges in learning accounting concepts is to gain an understanding of the terminology. Part of the difficulty stems from the alternative terms used by different accountants to mean the same thing. For example, the asset created when insurance is paid for in advance is termed a *prepaid asset* by some and a *prepaid expense* by others. Someone else might refer to it as a *deferred expense*.

The term **deferral** will be used here to refer to a situation in which cash has been paid or received but the expense or revenue has been deferred to a later time. A **deferred expense** indicates that cash has been paid but the recognition of expense has been deferred. Because a deferred expense represents a *future benefit* to a company, it is an asset. An alternative name for deferred expense is *prepaid expense*. Prepaid insurance and office supplies are deferred expenses. An adjustment is made periodically to record the portion of the deferred expense that has expired. A **deferred revenue** means that cash has been received but the recognition of any revenue has been deferred until a later time. Because a deferred revenue represents an *obligation* to a company, it is a liability. An alternative name for deferred revenue is *unearned revenue*. Rent collected in advance is deferred revenue. The periodic adjustment recognizes the portion of the deferred revenue that is earned in that period.

This chapter has discussed in detail the accrual basis of accounting, which involves recognizing changes in resources and obligations as they occur, not simply when cash changes

---

STUDY TIP

Now that you have seen examples of all four types of adjustments, think about a key difference between deferrals (the first two categories) and accruals (the last two categories). When you make adjustments involving deferrals, you must consider any existing balance in a deferred balance sheet account. Conversely, there is no existing account when an accrual is made.

Deferral
Cash has been paid or received but expense or revenue has not yet been recognized.

Deferred expense
An asset resulting from the payment of cash before the incurrence of expense.

Deferred revenue
A liability resulting from the receipt of cash before the recognition of revenue.

Accrual
Cash has not yet been paid or received but expense has been incurred or revenue earned.

Accrued liability
A liability resulting from the recognition of an expense before the payment of cash.

Accrued asset
An asset resulting from the recognition of a revenue before the receipt of cash.

hands. More specifically, the term **accrual** will be used to refer to a situation in which no cash has been paid or received yet but it is necessary to recognize, or accrue, an expense or a revenue. An **accrued liability** is recognized at the end of the period in cases in which an expense has been incurred but cash has not yet been paid. Wages payable and interest payable are examples of accrued liabilities. An **accrued asset** is recorded when revenue has been earned but cash has not yet been collected. Rent receivable is an accrued asset.

Summary of Adjustments

The four types of adjustments are summarized in Exhibit 4-3. Common examples of each are shown, along with the structure of the adjustments associated with the four categories. Finally, the following generalizations should help you gain a better understanding of adjustments and how they are used:

1. An adjustment is an internal transaction. It does not involve another entity.
2. Because it is an internal transaction, an adjustment does not involve an increase or a decrease in Cash.
3. At least one balance sheet account and one income statement account are involved in an adjustment. It is the nature of the adjustment process that an asset or a liability account is adjusted with a corresponding change in a revenue or an expense account.

Comprehensive Example of Adjustments

We will now consider a comprehensive example involving the transactions for the first month of operations and the end-of-period adjustments for a hypothetical business, Duffy Transit Company. A list of accounts and their balances is shown for Duffy Transit at January 31, the end of the first month of business (prior to making any adjustments):

Assets	
Cash	$ 50,000
Prepaid Insurance	48,000
Land	20,000
Buildings—Garage	160,000
Equipment—Buses	300,000
Liabilities	
Discount Tickets Sold in Advance	25,000
Notes Payable	150,000

EXHIBIT 4-3 Accruals and Deferrals

Type	Situation	Examples	Transaction during Period	Adjustment at End of Period
Deferred expense	Cash paid before expense is incurred	Insurance policy	Increase Asset	Increase Expense
		Supplies	Decrease Cash	Decrease Asset
		Rent		
		Buildings, equipment		
Deferred revenue	Cash received before revenue is earned	Deposits, rent	Increase Cash	Decrease Liability
		Subscriptions	Increase Liability	Increase Revenue
		Gift certificates		
Accrued liability	Expense incurred before cash is paid	Salaries, wages	No Transaction	Increase Expense
		Interest		Increase Liability
		Taxes		
		Rent		
Accrued asset	Revenue earned before cash is received	Interest	No Transaction	Increase Asset
		Rent		Increase Revenue

Stockholders' Equity	
Capital Stock	400,000
Revenues	
Daily Ticket Revenue	30,000
Expenses	
Gas, Oil, and Maintenance Expense	12,000
Wage and Salary Expense	10,000
Dividends	5,000

Duffy wants to prepare a balance sheet at the end of January and an income statement for its first month of operations. Use of the accrual basis necessitates a number of adjustments to update certain asset and liability accounts and to recognize the correct amounts for the various revenues and expenses.

Example 4-11 Using a List of Accounts to Prepare Adjustments

1. At the beginning of January, Duffy issued an 18-month, 12%, $150,000 promissory note for cash. Although interest will not be repaid until the loan's maturity date, Duffy must accrue interest for the first month. The calculation of interest for one month is $150,000 \times 0.12 \times 1/12$. The effect of the adjustment can be identified and analyzed as follows:

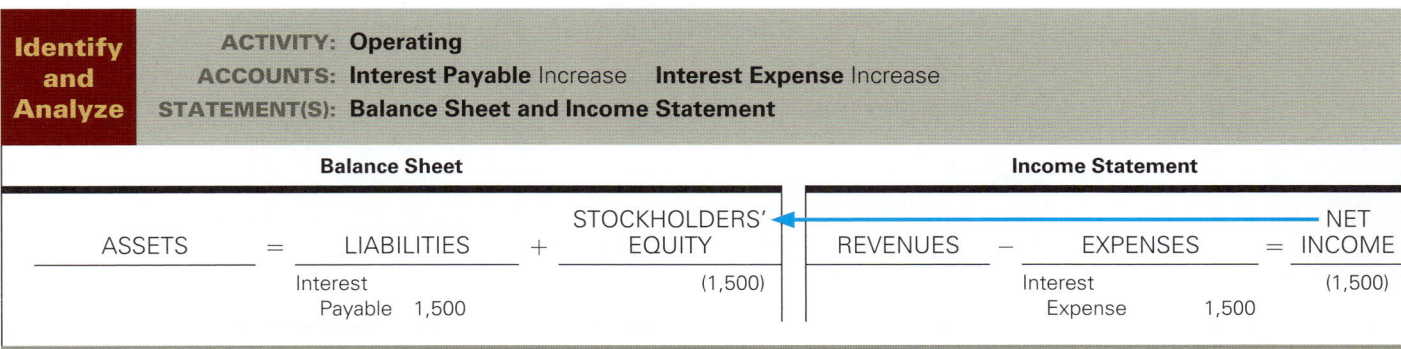

Identify and Analyze

ACTIVITY: **Operating**
ACCOUNTS: **Interest Payable** Increase **Interest Expense** Increase
STATEMENT(S): **Balance Sheet and Income Statement**

Balance Sheet			Income Statement		
ASSETS =	LIABILITIES +	STOCKHOLDERS' EQUITY	REVENUES −	EXPENSES =	NET INCOME
	Interest Payable 1,500	(1,500)		Interest Expense 1,500	(1,500)

2. Wage and salary expense of $10,000 reflects the amount paid to employees during January. At the end of the month, Duffy owes employees an additional $2,800 in salaries and wages. The effect of the adjustment can be identified and analyzed as follows:

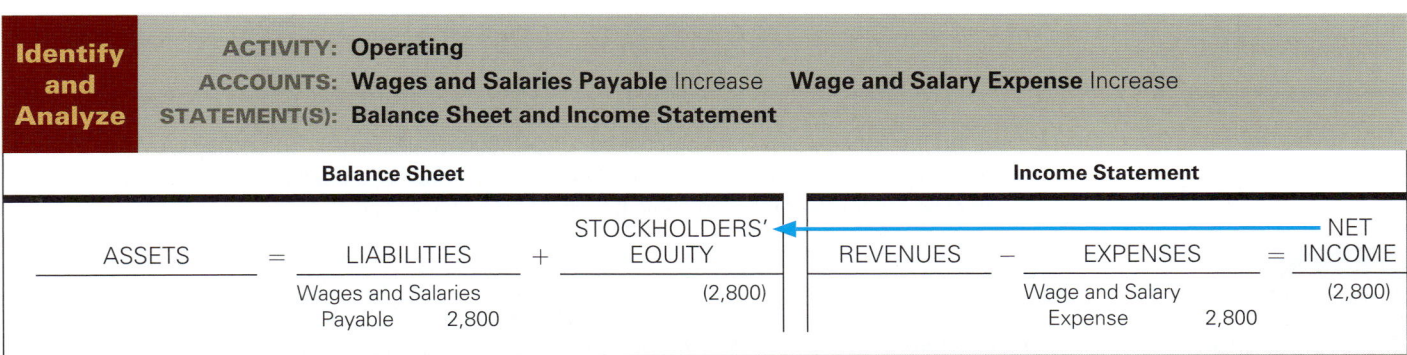

Identify and Analyze

ACTIVITY: **Operating**
ACCOUNTS: **Wages and Salaries Payable** Increase **Wage and Salary Expense** Increase
STATEMENT(S): **Balance Sheet and Income Statement**

Balance Sheet			Income Statement		
ASSETS =	LIABILITIES +	STOCKHOLDERS' EQUITY	REVENUES −	EXPENSES =	NET INCOME
	Wages and Salaries Payable 2,800	(2,800)		Wage and Salary Expense 2,800	(2,800)

3. At the beginning of January, Duffy acquired a garage to house the buses at a cost of $160,000. Land is not subject to depreciation. The cost of the land acquired in connection with the purchase of the building will remain on the books until the property is sold. The garage has an estimated useful life of 20 years and an estimated salvage value of $16,000 at the end of its life. The monthly depreciation is found by dividing the depreciable cost of $144,000 by the useful life of 240 months:

$$\frac{\$160,000 - \$16,000}{20 \text{ Years} \times 12 \text{ months}} = \frac{\$144,000}{240 \text{ months}} = \underline{\$600} \text{ per month}$$

The effect of the adjustment to record the depreciation on the garage for January for a full month can be identified and analyzed as follows:

(Continued)

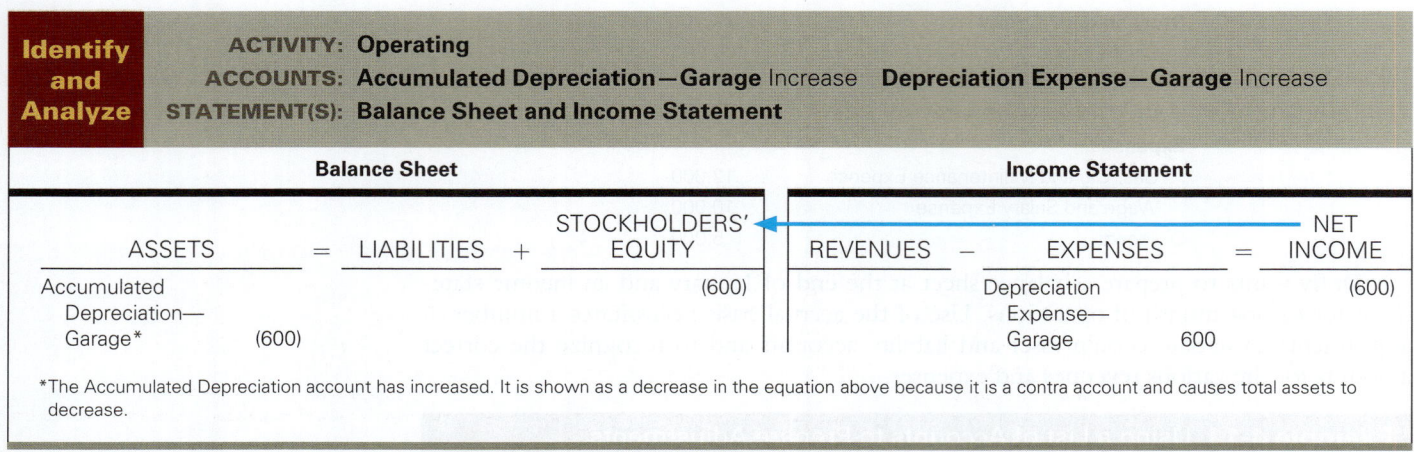

4. Duffy purchased ten buses for $30,000 each at the beginning of January. The buses have an estimated useful life of five years, at which time the company plans to sell them for $6,000 each. The monthly depreciation on the ten buses is as follows:

$$10 \times \frac{\$30,000 - \$6,000}{5 \text{ Years} \times 12 \text{ months}} = 10 \times \frac{\$24,000}{60 \text{ months}} = \underline{\$4,000} \text{ per month}$$

The effect of the adjustment to record the depreciation on the buses for the first month can be identified and analyzed as follows:

Identify and Analyze

ACTIVITY: Operating
ACCOUNTS: Accumulated Depreciation—Buses Increase   **Depreciation Expense—Buses** Increase
STATEMENT(S): Balance Sheet and Income Statement

Balance Sheet				Income Statement			
ASSETS	= LIABILITIES	+	STOCKHOLDERS' EQUITY	REVENUES	–	EXPENSES	= NET INCOME
Accumulated Depreciation— Buses* (4,000)			(4,000)			Depreciation Expense— Buses 4,000	(4,000)

*The Accumulated Depreciation account has increased. It is shown as a decrease in the equation above because it is a contra account and causes total assets to decrease.

5. An insurance policy was purchased for $48,000 on January 1. The policy provides property and liability protection for a 24-month period. The effect of the adjustment to allocate the cost to expense for the first month can be identified and analyzed as follows:

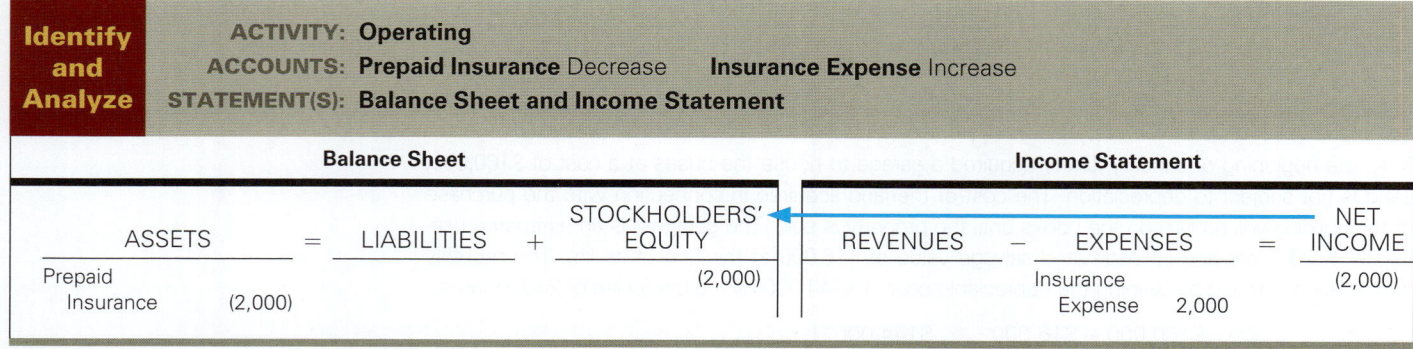

6. In addition to selling tickets on the bus, Duffy sells discount tickets at the terminal. The tickets are good for a ride anytime within 12 months of purchase. Thus, as these tickets are sold, Duffy increases Cash as well as a liability account, Discount Tickets Sold in Advance. The sale of $25,000 worth of these tickets was recorded during January. At the end of the first month, Duffy counts the number of tickets that has been redeemed. Because $20,400 worth of tickets has been turned in, this is the amount by which the company reduces its liability and recognizes revenue for the month. The effect of the adjustment can be identified and analyzed as follows:

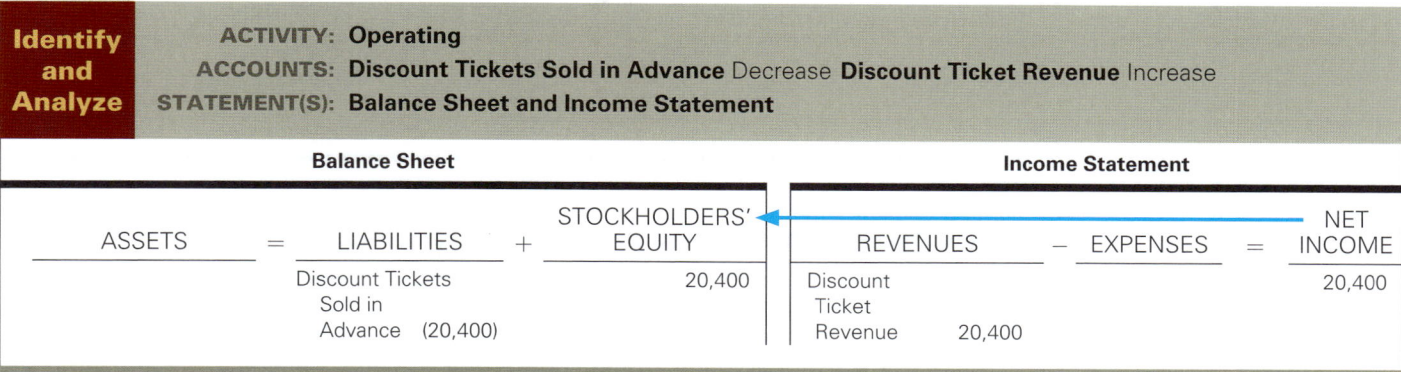

7. Duffy does not need all of the space in its garage and rents a section of it to another company for $2,500 per month. The tenant has until the 10th day of the following month to pay its rent. The effect of the adjustment on Duffy's books on the last day of the month can be identified and analyzed as follows:

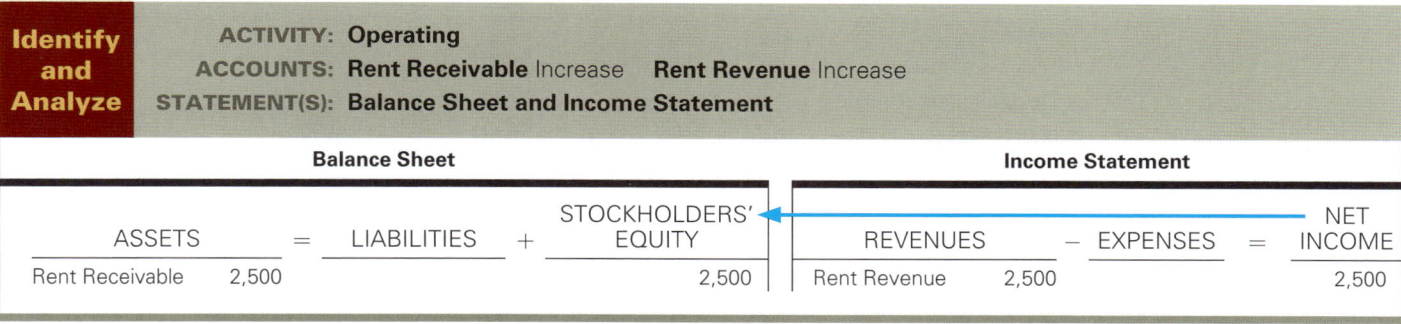

8. Corporations pay estimated taxes on a quarterly basis. Because Duffy is preparing an income statement for the month of January, it must estimate its taxes for the month. We will assume a corporate tax rate of 34% on income before tax. The computation of income tax expense is as follows. (The amounts shown for the revenues and expenses reflect the effect of the adjustments.)

Revenues:		
Daily ticket revenue	$30,000	
Discount ticket revenue	20,400	
Rent revenue	2,500	$ 52,900
Expenses:		
Gas, oil, and maintenance expense	$12,000	
Wage and salary expense	12,800	
Depreciation expense	4,600	
Insurance expense	2,000	
Interest expense	1,500	32,900
Net income before tax		$ 20 000
Times the corporate tax rate		× 0.34
Income tax expense		$ 6,800

Based on this estimate of taxes, the effect of the final adjustment Duffy makes can be identified and analyzed as follows:

(Continued)

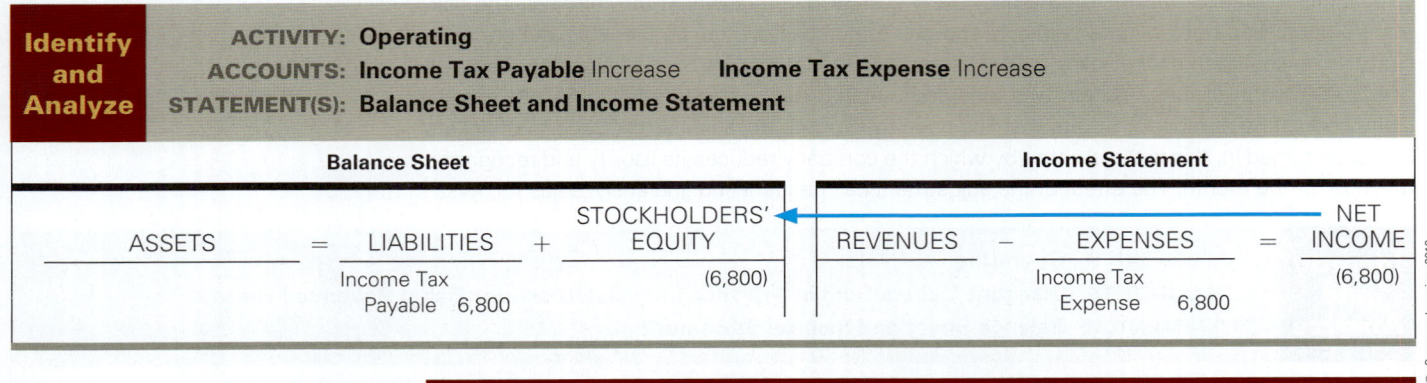

Income Statement and Balance Sheet for Duffy Transit

Now that the adjustments have been made, financial statements can be prepared. An income statement for January and a balance sheet as of January 31 are shown in Exhibit 4-4. Each of the account balances on the statements was determined by taking the balances in the list of accounts on pp. 178–179 and adding or subtracting as appropriate

EXHIBIT 4-4 Financial Statements for Duffy Transit Company

Duffy Transit Company
Balance Sheet
January 31

Revenues:		
Daily ticket revenue	$30,000	
Discount ticket revenue	20,400	
Rent revenue	2,500	$52,900
Expenses:		
Gas, oil, and maintenance	$12,000	
Wages and salaries	12,800	
Depreciation—garage	600	
Depreciation—buses	4,000	
Insurance	2,000	
Interest	1,500	
Income taxes	6,800	39,700
Net income		$13,200

Assets			Liabilities and Stockholders' Equity	
Cash		$ 50,000	Discount tickets sold in advance	$ 4,600
Rent receivable		2,500	Notes payable	150,000
Prepaid insurance		46,000	Interest payable	1,500
Land		20,000	Wages and salaries payable	2,800
Buildings—garage	$160,000		Income tax payable	6,800
Accumulated depreciation	600	159,400	Capital stock	400,000
Equipment—buses	$300,000		Retained earnings	8,200
Accumulated depreciation	4,000	296,000		
Total assets		$573,900	Total liabilities and stockholders' equity	$573,900

the necessary adjustments. Note the balance in Retained Earnings of $8,200. This amount was found by taking the net income of $13,200 and deducting the dividends of $5,000.

Ethical Considerations for a Company on the Accrual Basis

The accrual basis requires the recognition of revenues when earned and expenses when incurred regardless of when cash is received or paid. Adjustments are *internal* transactions in that they do not involve an exchange with an outside entity. Because adjustments do not involve another company, accountants may at times feel pressure from others within the organization either to speed or delay the recognition of certain adjustments.

Consider the following two examples for a landscaping company that is concerned about its bottom line—that is, its net income. A number of jobs are in progress, but because of inclement weather, none of them are very far along.

1. Management asks the accountant to recognize all of the revenue from a job in progress even though no significant work has been done on the job.
2. The accountant has been asked to delay the recognition of various short-term accrued liabilities (and, of course, the accompanying expenses) until the beginning of the new year.

The "correct" response of the accountant to each of those requests may seem obvious: no revenue on the one job should be recognized, and all accrued liabilities should be expensed at year-end. The pressures of the daily work environment make these decisions difficult for the accountant, however. **The accountant must remember that his or her primary responsibility in preparing financial statements is to portray the affairs of the company accurately to the various outside users.** Bankers, stockholders, and others rely on the accountant to serve their best interests.

LO5 Identify the four major types of adjustments and analyze their effects on the financial statements.

- Adjustments are made at the end of an accounting period to update revenue or expense accounts in accordance with the revenue recognition and matching principles.
- There are four basic categories of adjustments:
  - Adjustments where cash is paid before expenses are incurred—deferred expenses.
  - Adjustments where cash is received before revenues are earned—deferred revenues.
  - Adjustments where expenses are incurred before cash is paid—accrued liabilities.
  - Adjustments where revenues are recognized before cash is received—accrued assets.

POD REVIEW 4.5

QUESTIONS   **Answers to these questions are on the last page of the chapter.**

1. A company owes its employees wages not yet paid at the end of an accounting period. The adjustment needed at the end of the period will include
   a. an increase in an expense and an increase in a liability.
   b. an increase in an expense and a decrease in an asset.
   c. an increase in an expense and a decrease in cash.
   d. a decrease in a liability and a decrease in an expense.

2. A magazine publisher makes the appropriate entry when it receives cash in advance of providing magazines to its subscribers. When the magazines are delivered, the publisher will make an adjustment that includes
   a. an increase in cash and an increase in revenue.
   b. an increase in Accounts Receivable and an increase in revenue.
   c. a decrease in a liability and an increase in revenue.
   d. none of the above.

The Accounting Cycle

LO6 Explain the steps in the accounting cycle and the significance of each step.

OVERVIEW: The accounting cycle consists of all of the steps performed each period in order to prepare a set of financial statements. Some of the steps, such as journalizing transactions, are performed continuously, while others, such as preparing adjusting entries, are performed only at the end of the period.

Accounting cycle
A series of steps performed each period and culminating with the preparation of a set of financial statements.

This chapter has focused on accrual accounting and the adjustments it necessitates. Adjustments are one key component in the **accounting cycle**. The accountant for a business follows a series of steps each period. The objective is always the same: **collect the necessary information to prepare a set of financial statements**. Together these steps make up the **accounting cycle**. The name comes from the fact that the steps are repeated each period.

The steps in the accounting cycle are shown in Exhibit 4-5. Note that Step 1 involves not only *collecting* information but also *analyzing* it. Transaction analysis is probably the most challenging of all of the steps in the accounting cycle. It requires the ability to think logically about an event and its effect on the financial position of the entity. Once the transaction is analyzed, it is recorded in the journal, as indicated by the second step in the exhibit. The first two steps in the cycle take place continuously.

Transactions are posted to the accounts on a periodic basis. The frequency of posting to the accounts depends on two factors: the type of accounting system used by a company and the volume of transactions. In a manual system, entries might be posted daily, weekly, or even monthly depending on the amount of activity. The larger the

EXHIBIT 4-5 Steps in the Accounting Cycle

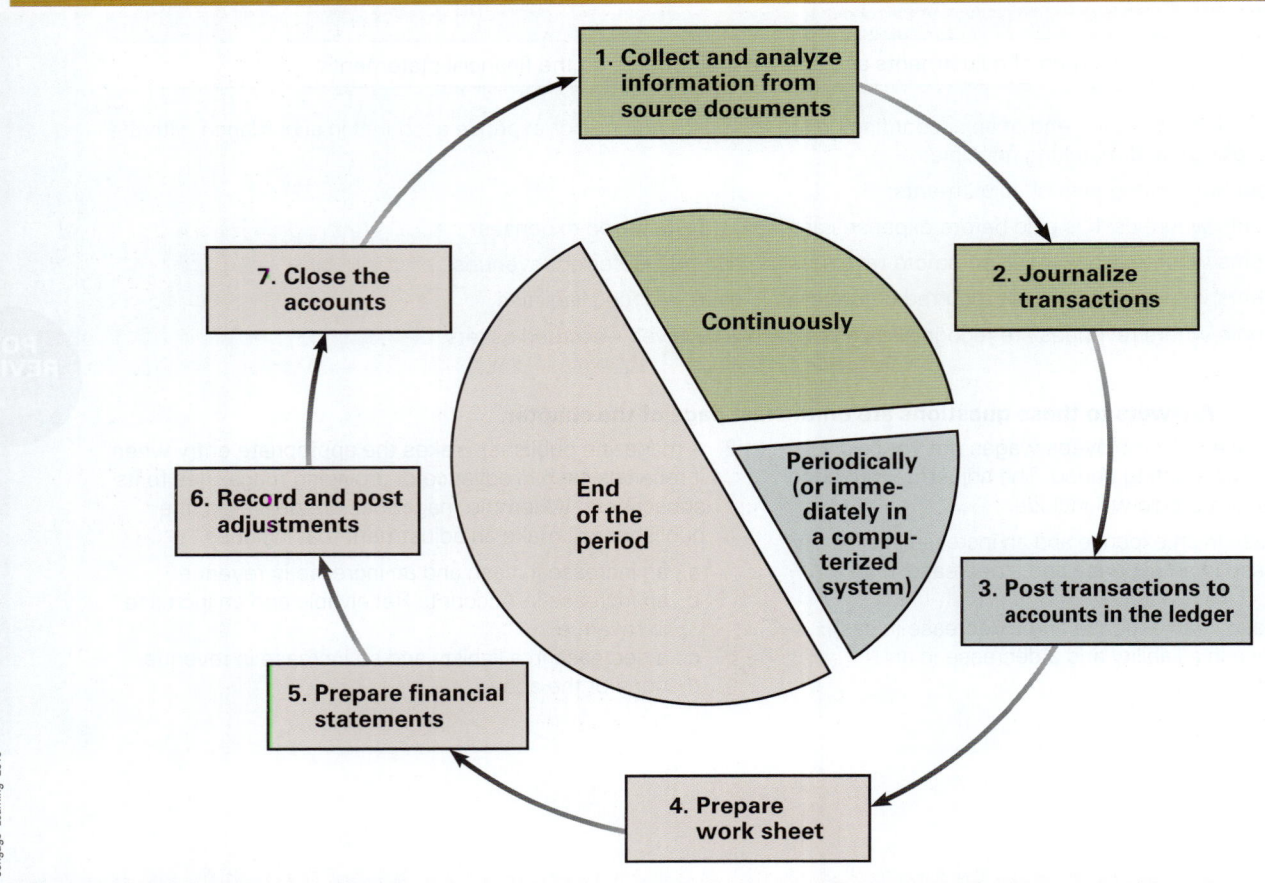

1. Collect and analyze information from source documents
2. Journalize transactions
3. Post transactions to accounts in the ledger
4. Prepare work sheet
5. Prepare financial statements
6. Record and post adjustments
7. Close the accounts

Continuously

Periodically (or immediately in a computerized system)

End of the period

number of transactions a company records, the more often it posts. In an automated accounting system, posting is likely done automatically by the computer each time a transaction is recorded.

The Use of a Work Sheet

Step 4 in Exhibit 4-5 calls for the preparation of a work sheet. The end of an accounting period is a busy time. In addition to recording daily recurring transactions, the accountant must record adjustments as the basis for preparing financial statements. The time available to prepare the statements is usually very limited. The use of a **work sheet** allows the accountant to gather and organize the information required to adjust the accounts without actually recording and posting the adjustments to the accounts. Recording adjustments and posting them to the accounts can be done after the financial statements are prepared. **The work sheet itself is not a financial statement.** Instead, it is a useful device to organize the information needed to prepare the financial statements at the end of the period.

It is not essential that a work sheet be used before financial statements are prepared. If it is not used, Step 6, recording and posting adjustments, comes before Step 5, preparing the financial statements.

The Closing Process

Step 7 in Exhibit 4-5 is the closing process. For purposes of closing the books, accountants categorize accounts into two types.

1. Balance sheet accounts are called **real accounts** because they are permanent in nature. For this reason, they are never closed. The balance in each of these accounts is carried over from one period to the next.
2. Revenue, expense, and dividend accounts are *temporary* or **nominal accounts**. The balances in the income statement accounts and the Dividends account are *not* carried forward from one accounting period to the next. For this reason, these accounts are closed at the end of the period.

Closing entries serve two important purposes: (1) to return the balances in all temporary or nominal accounts to zero to start the next accounting period and (2) to transfer the net income (or net loss) and the dividends of the period to the Retained Earnings account.

Interim Financial Statements

Recall that certain steps in the accounting cycle are sometimes carried out only once a year rather than each month, as in the Duffy Transit Company example. For ease of illustration, we assumed a monthly accounting cycle. Many companies adjust and close the accounts only once a year, however. They use a work sheet more frequently than that as the basis for preparing interim statements. Statements prepared monthly, quarterly, or at other intervals less than a year in duration are called **interim statements**. Many companies prepare monthly financial statements for their own internal use. Similarly, corporations whose shares are publicly traded on one of the stock exchanges are required to file quarterly financial statements with the SEC.

Suppose a company prepares monthly financial statements for internal use and completes the accounting cycle in its entirety only once a year. In this case, a work sheet is prepared each month as the basis for interim financial statements. Formal adjusting and closing of the books is done only at the end of each year. The adjustments that appear on the monthly work sheet are not posted to the accounts. They are entered on the work sheet simply as a basis for preparing the monthly financial statements.

Work sheet
A device used at the end of the period to gather the information needed to prepare financial statements without actually recording and posting adjustments.

Real accounts
The name given to balance sheet accounts because they are permanent and are not closed at the end of the period.

Nominal accounts
The name given to revenue, expense, and dividend accounts because they are temporary and are closed at the end of the period.

Closing entries
Journal entries made at the end of the period to return the balance in all nominal accounts to zero and transfer the net income or loss and the dividends to Retained Earnings.

Interim statements
Financial statements prepared monthly, quarterly, or at other intervals less than a year in duration.

LO6 Explain the steps in the accounting cycle and the significance of each step.

- The accounting cycle involves seven steps that are repeated each period. (See Exhibit 4-5.)
  - Collecting and analyzing data and journalizing transactions occur on a continuous basis.
  - Periodically, transactions are posted to accounts in the ledger.
  - At the end of the period, a work sheet is prepared, financial statements are prepared, adjustments are recorded and posted, and accounts are closed.

POD REVIEW 4.6

QUESTIONS   Answers to these questions are on the last page of the chapter.

1. Which of the following steps in the accounting cycle is *not* in the correct order?
   a. Journalize transactions and post them to accounts in the ledger.
   b. Prepare a work sheet and prepare financial statements.
   c. Close the accounts and record and post adjustments.
   d. All of the above are in the correct order.

2. Which of the following steps in the accounting cycle is not performed at the end of the accounting period?
   a. Collect and analyze information from source documents.
   b. Prepare a work sheet.
   c. Record and post adjustments.
   d. Close the accounts.

© Cengage Learning 2013

ACCOUNTS HIGHLIGHTED

Account Titles	Where It Appears	In What Section	Page Number
Prepaid Insurance	Balance Sheet	Current Assets	169
Accumulated Depreciation	Balance Sheet	Noncurrent Assets (contra)	170
Deferred Revenue	Balance Sheet	Current Liabilities*	172
Wages Payable	Balance Sheet	Current Liabilities	174
Interest Payable	Balance Sheet	Current Liabilities	175
Rent Receivable	Balance Sheet	Current Assets	177

*If any part of deferred revenue will not be earned within the next year, it should be classified as a noncurrent liability.

KEY TERMS QUIZ

Read each definition below and write the number of the definition in the blank beside the appropriate term. The quiz solutions appear at the end of the chapter.

_____ Recognition
_____ Historical cost
_____ Current value
_____ Cash basis
_____ Accrual basis
_____ Revenues
_____ Revenue recognition principle
_____ Matching principle
_____ Expenses
_____ Adjusting entries
_____ Straight-line method
_____ Contra account

_____ Deferral
_____ Deferred expense
_____ Deferred revenue
_____ Accrual
_____ Accrued liability
_____ Accrued asset
_____ Accounting cycle
_____ Work sheet
_____ Real accounts
_____ Nominal accounts
_____ Closing entries
_____ Interim statements

1. A device used at the end of the period to gather the information needed to prepare financial statements without actually recording and posting adjustments.

2. Inflows or other enhancements of assets or settlements of liabilities from delivering or producing goods, rendering services, or conducting other activities.
3. Journal entries made at the end of a period by a company using the accrual basis of accounting.
4. Journal entries made at the end of the period to return the balance in all nominal accounts to zero and transfer the net income or loss and the dividends of the period to Retained Earnings.
5. A liability resulting from the receipt of cash before the recognition of revenue.
6. The name given to balance sheet accounts because they are permanent and are not closed at the end of the period.
7. An asset resulting from the recognition of a revenue before the receipt of cash.
8. The amount of cash or its equivalent that could be received by selling an asset currently.
9. The assignment of an equal amount of depreciation to each period.
10. Cash has been paid or received but expense or revenue has not yet been recognized.
11. A system of accounting in which revenues are recognized when earned and expenses are recognized when incurred.
12. Cash has not yet been paid or received but expense has been incurred or revenue earned.
13. Financial statements prepared monthly, quarterly, or at other intervals less than a year in duration.
14. Revenues are recognized in the income statement when they are realized, or realizable, and earned.
15. The process of recording an item in the financial statements as an asset, a liability, a revenue, an expense, or the like.
16. An asset resulting from the payment of cash before the incurrence of expense.
17. The name given to revenue, expense, and dividend accounts because they are temporary and are closed at the end of the period.
18. A system of accounting in which revenues are recognized when cash is received and expenses are recognized when cash is paid.
19. A liability resulting from the recognition of an expense before the payment of cash.
20. The association of revenue of a period with all of the costs necessary to generate that revenue.
21. An account with a balance that is opposite that of a related account.
22. The amount that is paid for an asset and that is used as a basis for recognizing it on the balance sheet and carrying it on later balance sheets.
23. Outflows or other using up of assets or incurrences of liabilities resulting from delivering goods, rendering services, or carrying out other activities.
24. A series of steps performed each period and culminating with the preparation of a set of financial statements.

ALTERNATE TERMS

historical cost original cost
asset unexpired cost
deferred expense prepaid expense, prepaid asset

deferred revenue unearned revenue
expense expired cost
nominal account temporary account
real account permanent account

WARMUP EXERCISES & SOLUTIONS

Warmup Exercise 4-1 Prepaid Insurance   LO5

ABC Corp. purchases a 24-month fire insurance policy on January 1, for $5,400.

Required

Identify and analyze the effect of the adjustment on January 31.

(Continued)

Key to the Solution Determine what proportion and therefore what dollar amount of the policy has expired after one month.

LO5   Warmup Exercise 4-2 Depreciation

DEF Corp. purchased a new car for one of its salespeople on March 1, for $25,000. The estimated useful life of the car is four years with an estimated salvage value of $1,000.

Required

Identify and analyze the effect of the adjustment on March 31.

Key to the Solution Determine what dollar amount of the cost of the car should be depreciated and what amount should be depreciated each month.

LO5   Warmup Exercise 4-3 Interest on a Note

On April 1, GHI Corp. took out a 12%, 120-day, $10,000 loan at its bank.

Required

Identify and analyze the effect of the adjustment on April 30.

Key to the Solution Determine the monthly interest cost on a loan that accrues interest at the rate of 12% per year.

Solutions to Warmup Exercises

Warmup Exercise 4-1

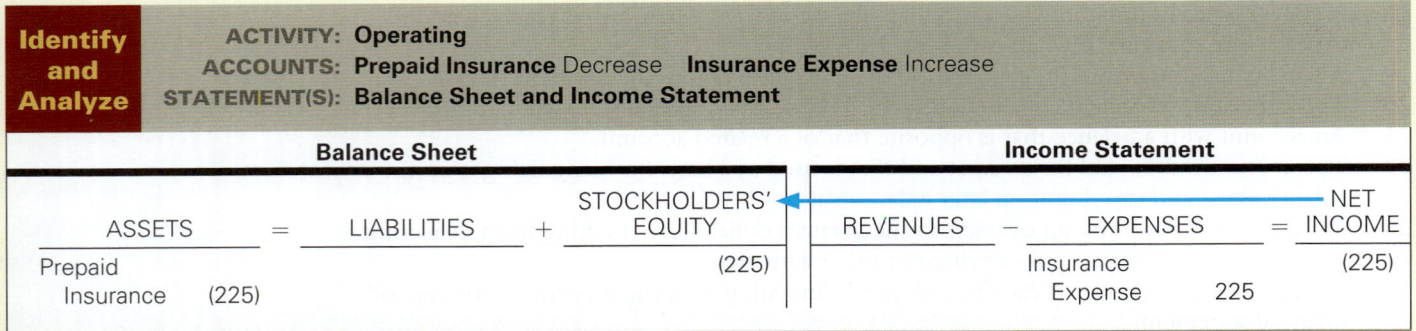

Warmup Exercise 4-2

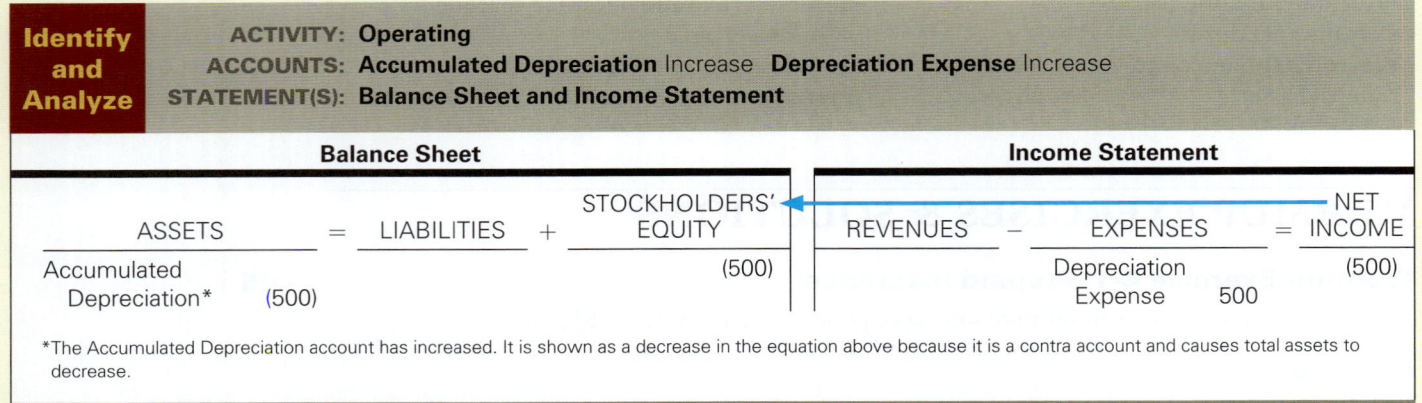

*The Accumulated Depreciation account has increased. It is shown as a decrease in the equation above because it is a contra account and causes total assets to decrease.

Warmup Exercise 4-3

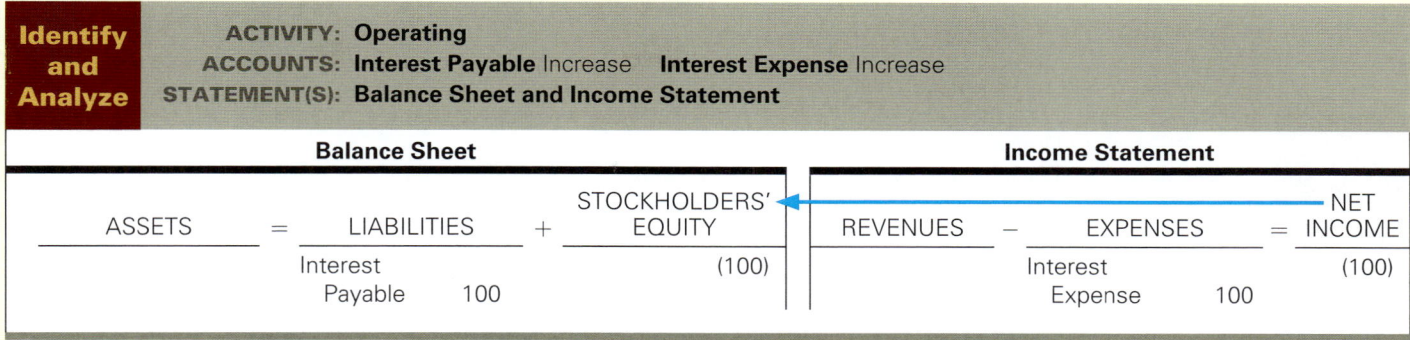

REVIEW PROBLEM

A list of accounts for Northern Airlines at January 31 is shown. It reflects the recurring transactions for the month of January, but it does not reflect any month-end adjustments.

Cash	$ 75,000
Parts Inventory	45,000
Land	80,000
Buildings—Hangars	250,000
Accumulated Depreciation—Hangars	24,000
Equipment—Aircraft	650,000
Accumulated Depreciation—Aircraft	120,000
Tickets Sold in Advance	85,000
Capital Stock	500,000
Retained Earnings	368,000
Ticket Revenue	52,000
Maintenance Expense	19,000
Wage and Salary Expense	30,000

The following additional information is available:

a. Airplane parts needed for repairs and maintenance are purchased regularly, and the amounts paid are added to the asset account Parts Inventory. At the end of each month, the inventory is counted. At the end of January, the amount of parts on hand is $36,100. *Hint:* What adjustment is needed to reduce the asset account to its proper carrying value? Any expense involved should be included in Maintenance Expense.

b. The estimated useful life of the hangar is 20 years with an estimated salvage value of $10,000 at the end of its life. The original cost of the hangar was $250,000.

c. The estimated useful life of the aircraft is ten years with an estimated salvage value of $50,000. The original cost of the aircraft was $650,000.

d. As tickets are sold in advance, the amounts are added to Cash and to the liability account Tickets Sold in Advance. A count of the redeemed tickets reveals that $47,000 worth of tickets were used during January.

e. Wages and salaries owed but unpaid to employees at the end of January total $7,600.

f. Northern rents excess hangar space to other companies. The amount owed but unpaid to Northern at the end of January is $2,500.

g. Assume a corporate income tax rate of 34%.

Required

1. For each of the preceding items of additional information, identify and analyze the effect of the adjustment.

2. Prepare an income statement for January and a balance sheet at January 31.

Solution to Review Problem

1.

a.

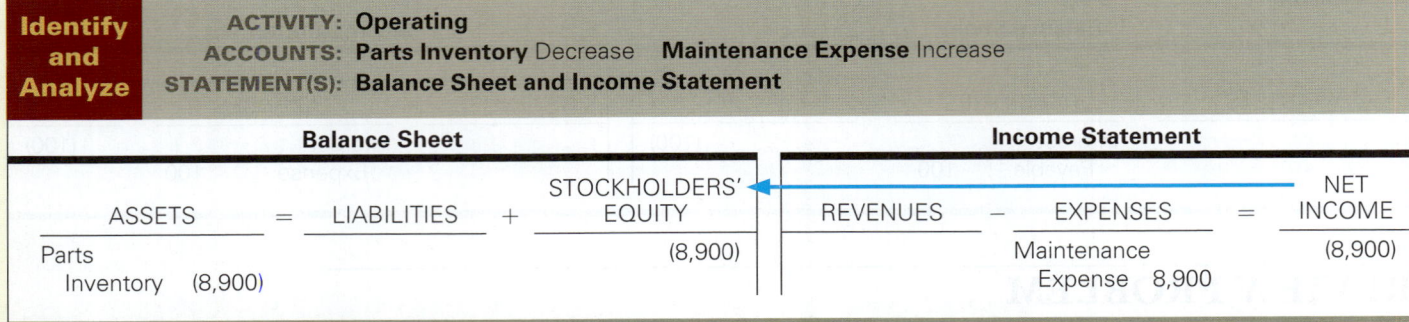

Identify and Analyze

ACTIVITY: **Operating**
ACCOUNTS: **Parts Inventory** Decrease   **Maintenance Expense** Increase
STATEMENT(S): **Balance Sheet and Income Statement**

Balance Sheet				Income Statement				
ASSETS	=	LIABILITIES	+	STOCKHOLDERS' EQUITY	REVENUES	−	EXPENSES	= NET INCOME
Parts Inventory (8,900)				(8,900)			Maintenance Expense 8,900	(8,900)

b.

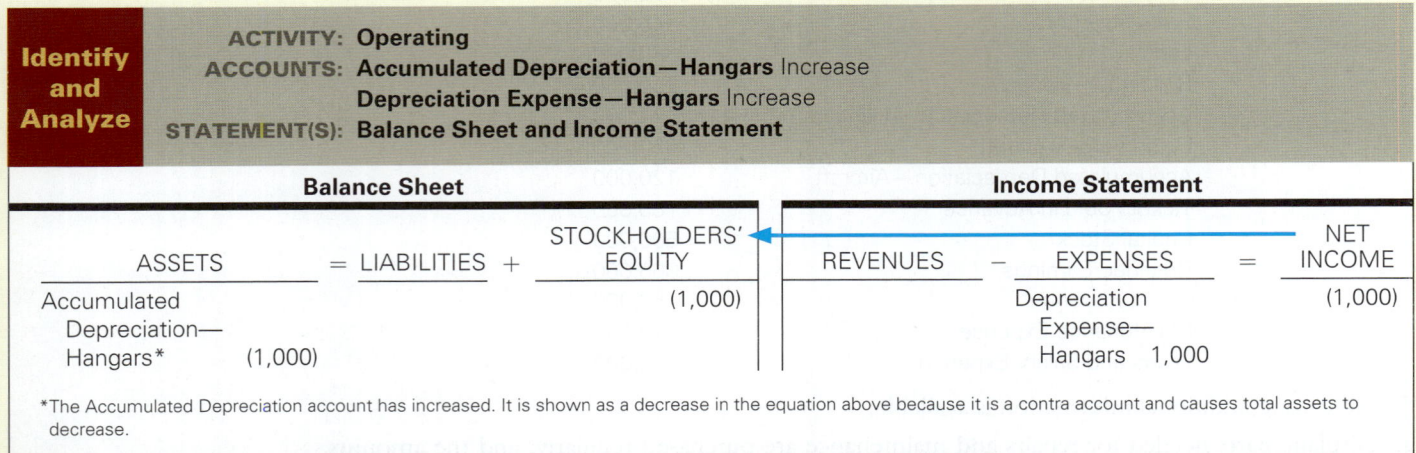

Identify and Analyze

ACTIVITY: **Operating**
ACCOUNTS: **Accumulated Depreciation—Hangars** Increase
Depreciation Expense—Hangars Increase
STATEMENT(S): **Balance Sheet and Income Statement**

Balance Sheet				Income Statement				
ASSETS	=	LIABILITIES	+	STOCKHOLDERS' EQUITY	REVENUES	−	EXPENSES	= NET INCOME
Accumulated Depreciation— Hangars* (1,000)				(1,000)			Depreciation Expense— Hangars 1,000	(1,000)

*The Accumulated Depreciation account has increased. It is shown as a decrease in the equation above because it is a contra account and causes total assets to decrease.

c.

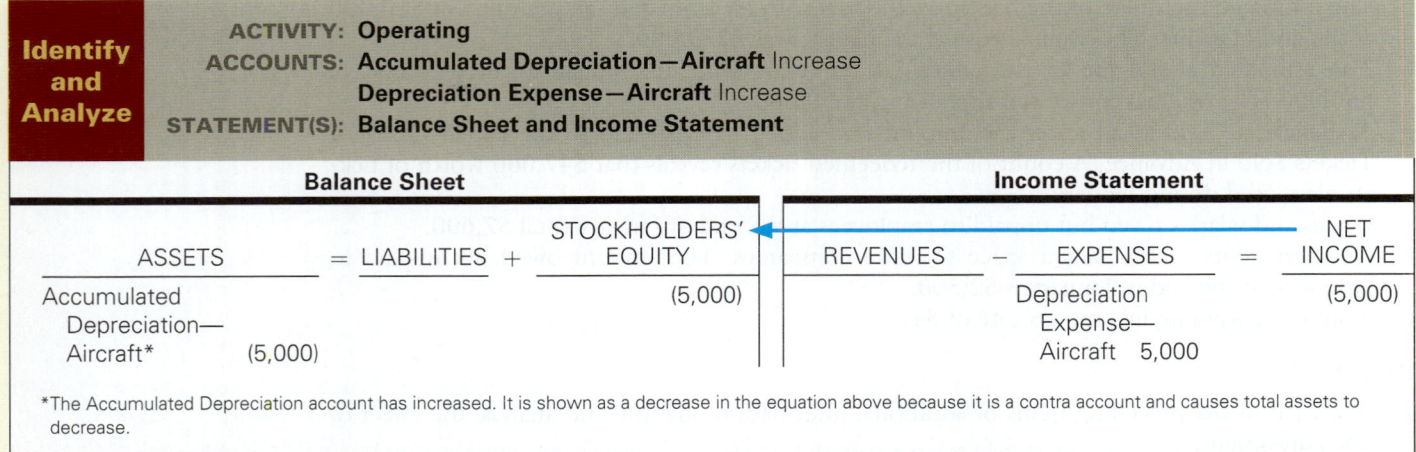

Identify and Analyze

ACTIVITY: **Operating**
ACCOUNTS: **Accumulated Depreciation—Aircraft** Increase
Depreciation Expense—Aircraft Increase
STATEMENT(S): **Balance Sheet and Income Statement**

Balance Sheet				Income Statement				
ASSETS	=	LIABILITIES	+	STOCKHOLDERS' EQUITY	REVENUES	−	EXPENSES	= NET INCOME
Accumulated Depreciation— Aircraft* (5,000)				(5,000)			Depreciation Expense— Aircraft 5,000	(5,000)

*The Accumulated Depreciation account has increased. It is shown as a decrease in the equation above because it is a contra account and causes total assets to decrease.

d.

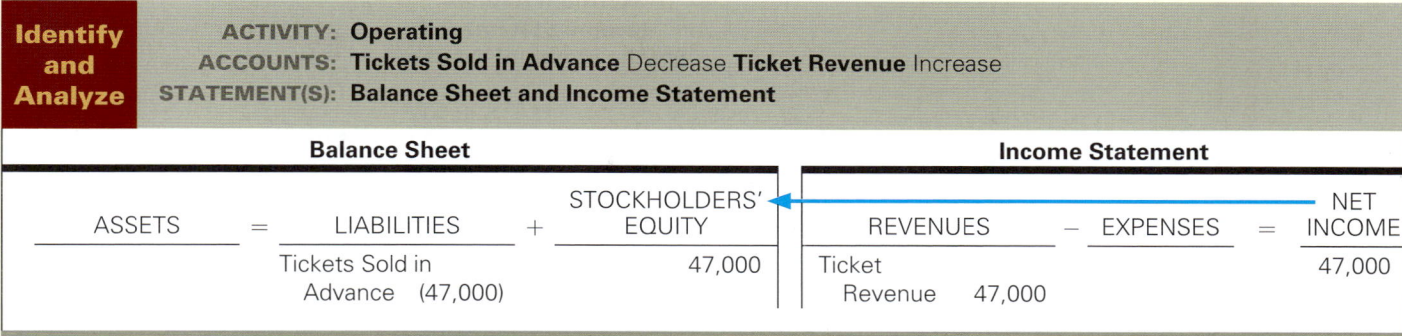

Identify and Analyze	**ACTIVITY: Operating** **ACCOUNTS: Tickets Sold in Advance** Decrease **Ticket Revenue** Increase **STATEMENT(S): Balance Sheet and Income Statement**

Balance Sheet				Income Statement			
ASSETS	=	LIABILITIES	+	STOCKHOLDERS' EQUITY	REVENUES	− EXPENSES	= NET INCOME
		Tickets Sold in Advance (47,000)		47,000	Ticket Revenue 47,000		47,000

e.

Identify and Analyze	**ACTIVITY: Operating** **ACCOUNTS: Wages and Salaries Payable** Increase **Wage and Salary Expense** Increase **STATEMENT(S): Balance Sheet and Income Statement**

Balance Sheet				Income Statement			
ASSETS	=	LIABILITIES	+	STOCKHOLDERS' EQUITY	REVENUES	− EXPENSES	= NET INCOME
		Wages and Salaries Payable 7,600		(7,600)		Wage and Salary Expense 7,600	(7,600)

f.

Identify and Analyze	**ACTIVITY: Operating** **ACCOUNTS: Rent Receivable** Increase **Rent Revenue** Increase **STATEMENT(S): Balance Sheet and Income Statement**

Balance Sheet				Income Statement			
ASSETS	=	LIABILITIES	+	STOCKHOLDERS' EQUITY	REVENUES	− EXPENSES	= NET INCOME
Rent Receivable 2,500				2,500	Rent Revenue 2,500		2,500

g.

Identify and Analyze	**ACTIVITY: Operating** **ACCOUNTS: Income Tax Payable** Increase **Income Tax Expense** Increase **STATEMENT(S): Balance Sheet and Income Statement**

Balance Sheet				Income Statement			
ASSETS	=	LIABILITIES	+	STOCKHOLDERS' EQUITY	REVENUES	− EXPENSES	= NET INCOME
		Income Tax Payable 10,200		(10,200)		Income Tax Expense 10,200	(10,200)

(Continued)

2.   Financial Statements:

Northern Airlines
Income Statement
For the Month of January

Revenues:		
Ticket revenue	$99,000	
Rent revenue	2,500	$101,500
Expenses:		
Maintenance	$27,900	
Wages and salaries	37,600	
Depreciation—hangars	1,000	
Depreciation—aircraft	5,000	
Income taxes	10,200	81,700
Net income		$ 19,800

Northern Airlines
Balance Sheet
January 31

Assets			Liabilities and Stockholders' Equity	
Cash		$ 75,000	Tickets sold in advance	$ 38,000
Rent receivable		2,500	Wages and salaries payable	7,600
Parts inventory		36,100	Income tax payable	10,200
Land		80,000	Capital stock	500,000
Buildings—Hangars	$250,000		Retained earnings	387,800
Accumulated		225,000		
depreciation	25,000			
Aircraft	$650,000			
Accumulated				
depreciation	125,000	525,000	Total liabilities and	
Total assets		$943,600	stockholders' equity	$943,600

QUESTIONS

1. What is meant by the following statement? The items depicted in financial statements are merely *representations* of the real thing.
2. What is the meaning of the following statement? The choice between historical cost and current value is a good example of the trade-offs in accounting that must sometimes be made.
3. A realtor earns a 10% commission on the sale of a $150,000 home. The realtor lists the home on June 5, the sale occurs on June 12, and the seller pays the realtor the $15,000 commission on July 8. When should the realtor recognize revenue from the sale assuming (a) the cash basis of accounting and (b) the accrual basis of accounting?
4. What does the following statement mean? If I want to assess the cash flow prospects for a company "down the road," I look at the company's most recent statement of cash flows. An income statement prepared under the accrual basis of accounting is useless for this purpose.

5. What is the relationship between the time period assumption and accrual accounting?
6. Is it necessary for an asset to be acquired when revenue is recognized? Explain your answer.
7. A friend says to you: "I just don't get it. Assets cost money. Expenses reduce income. There must be some relationship among assets, costs, and expenses—I'm just not sure what it is!" What is the relationship? Can you give an example of it?
8. What is the meaning of *depreciation* to the accountant?
9. What are the four basic types of adjustments? Give an example of each.
10. What is the difference between a real account and a nominal account?
11. What two purposes are served in making closing entries?

BRIEF EXERCISES

Brief Exercise 4-1 Measurement in Financial Statements   LO1

What are two possible attributes to be measured when an item is to be included in financial statements? What unit of money is used to measure items in the United States?

Brief Exercise 4-2 Accrual Basis of Accounting   LO2

EXAMPLE 4-1, 4-2

For the following situations, indicate the date on which revenue would be recognized, assuming the accrual basis of accounting.

_____ a. On June 10, a customer orders a product over the phone. The product is shipped to the customer on June 14, and the customer pays the amount owed on July 10.

_____ b. On March 15, a law firm agrees to draft a legal document for a client. The document is completed and delivered to the client on April 5, and the client pays the amount owed on May 2.

_____ c. A homeowner signs a contract on August 6 to have a company install a central air conditioning system. The work is completed on August 30, and the homeowner pays the amount owed on September 25.

Brief Exercise 4-3 Revenue Recognition   LO3

Explain whether a company must have an inflow of an asset to be able to recognize revenue. Also, give two examples of situations in which revenue is earned continuously over a period of time.

Brief Exercise 4-4 Matching Principle   LO4

EXAMPLE 4-3

Assume that a company purchases merchandise for resale on December 20, 2012. The merchandise is still on hand on December 31, the company's year-end. On January 12, 2013, the merchandise is sold to a customer. Explain how the merchandise will be treated on any of the financial statements at year-end. In which year will revenue from the sale be recorded? In which year will cost of goods sold expense be recorded?

Brief Exercise 4-5 Adjustments   LO5

EXAMPLE 4-4, 4-7, 4-8, 4-10

For the following situations, indicate the types of accounts affected in a year-end adjustment. Use the following legend: IA = Increase in Asset; DA = Decrease in Asset; IL = Increase in Liability; DL= Decrease in Liability; IR = Increase in Revenue; IE = Increase in Expense.

Accounts Affected		Situation
_____	_____	1. A company owes employees for wages earned but not yet paid.
_____	_____	2. Rent is earned for the month, and the tenant is given until the 10th of the following month to pay.
_____	_____	3. A portion of an insurance policy paid for in advance has expired.
_____	_____	4. A gift card is redeemed by its recipient.

Brief Exercise 4-6 Steps in the Accounting Cycle   LO6

Recall the steps in the accounting cycle shown in Exhibit 4-5. Assume that a company does not prepare a work sheet. Which of the two remaining steps in the accounting cycle are performed in a different order than they would be if a work sheet were prepared? Explain your answer.

EXERCISES

Exercise 4-1 Comparing the Income Statement and the Statement of Cash Flows   LO2

EXAMPLE 4-1, 4-2

On January 1, Campus Internet Connection opened for business across the street from Upper Eastern University. The company charges students a monthly fee of $20 and $1 for each hour

(Continued)

they are online. During January, 500 students signed up for the service, and each will have until the fifth of the following month to pay the monthly fee. By the end of January, 200 students had paid the monthly fee. Student usage, payable at the time connected, was 3,000 hours during January. Assume that Campus uses the accrual basis of accounting.

Required

1. Prepare the Revenues section of Campus's income statement for the month of January.
2. Prepare the Cash Receipts section of Campus's statement of cash flows for the month of January.
3. In addition to the Cash account, what other account will appear on Campus's balance sheet at the end of January? What amount will be in this account?

LO3   **Exercise 4-2 Revenue Recognition**

The highway department contracted with a private company to collect tolls and maintain facilities on a turnpike. Users of the turnpike can pay cash as they approach the toll booth, or they can purchase a pass. The pass is equipped with an electronic sensor that subtracts the toll fee from the pass balance as the motorist slowly approaches a special toll booth. The passes are issued in $10 increments. Refunds are available to motorists who do not use the pass balance, but they are issued very infrequently. Last year, $3,000,000 was collected at the traditional toll booths, $2,000,000 of passes were issued, and $1,700,000 of passes were used at the special toll booth. How much should the company recognize as revenue for the year? Explain how the revenue recognition rule should be applied in this case.

LO4   **Exercise 4-3 The Matching Principle**

EXAMPLE 4-3

Three methods of matching costs with revenue were described in the chapter: (a) directly match a specific form of revenue with a cost incurred in generating that revenue, (b) indirectly match a cost with the periods during which it will provide benefits or revenue, and (c) immediately recognize a cost incurred as an expense because no future benefits are expected. For each of the following costs, indicate how it is normally recognized as expense by indicating either (a), (b), or (c). If you think that more than one answer is possible for any of the situations, explain why.

1. New office copier
2. Monthly bill from the utility company for electricity
3. Office supplies
4. Biweekly payroll for office employees
5. Commissions earned by salespeople
6. Interest incurred on a six-month loan from the bank
7. Cost of inventory sold during the current period
8. Taxes owed on income earned during current period
9. Cost of three-year insurance policy

LO5   **Exercise 4-4 Customer Deposits**

EXAMPLE 4-6

Wolfe & Wolfe collected $9,000 from a customer on April 1 and agreed to provide legal services during the next three months. Wolfe & Wolfe expects to provide an equal amount of services each month.

Required

1. Identify and analyze the transaction for the receipt of the customer deposit on April 1.
2. Identify and analyze the adjustment on April 30.
3. What will be the effect on net income for April if the adjustment in (2) is not recorded?

LO5   **Exercise 4-5 The Effect of Ignoring Adjustments on Net Income**

EXAMPLE 4-4, 4-5, 4-6, 4-8, 4-9, 4-10

For each of the following independent situations, determine whether the effect of ignoring the required adjustment will result in an understatement (U), will result in an overstatement (O), or will have no effect (NE) on net income for the period.

Situation	Effect on Net Income
Example: Taxes owed but not yet paid are ignored.	O
1. A company fails to record depreciation on equipment.	____
2. Sales made during the last week of the period are not recorded.	____
3. A company neglects to record the expired portion of a prepaid insurance policy. (Its cost was originally recorded in an asset account.)	____
4. Interest due but not yet paid on a long-term note payable is ignored.	____
5. Commissions earned by salespeople but not payable until the 10th of the following month are ignored.	____
6. A landlord receives cash on the date a lease is signed for the rent for the first six months and records Unearned Rent Revenue. The landlord fails to make any adjustment at the end of the first month.	____

Exercise 4-6 The Accounting Cycle

LO6

The steps in the accounting cycle are listed in random order. Fill in the blank next to each step to indicate its order in the cycle. The first step in the cycle is filled in as an example.

Order	Procedure
____	Prepare a work sheet.
____	Close the accounts.
1	Collect and analyze information from source documents.
____	Prepare financial statements.
____	Post transactions to accounts in the ledger.
____	Record and post adjustments.
____	Journalize daily transactions.

Exercise 4-7 Accruals and Deferrals

LO5
EXAMPLE 4-4, 4-5, 4-7, 4-8, 4-10

For the following situations, indicate whether each involves a deferred expense (DE), a deferred revenue (DR), an accrued liability (AL), or an accrued asset (AA).

Example: <u>DE</u> Office supplies purchased in advance of their use

____ 1. Wages earned by employees but not yet paid
____ 2. Cash collected from subscriptions in advance of publishing a magazine
____ 3. Interest earned on a customer loan for which principal and interest have not yet been collected
____ 4. One year's premium on life insurance policy paid in advance
____ 5. Office building purchased for cash
____ 6. Rent collected in advance from a tenant
____ 7. State income taxes owed at the end of the year
____ 8. Rent owed by a tenant but not yet collected

Exercise 4-8 Property Taxes Payable—Annual Adjustments

LO5
EXAMPLE 4-8

Lexington Builders owns property in Kaneland County. Lexington's 2011 property taxes amounted to $50,000. Kaneland County will send out the 2012 property tax bills to property owners during April 2013. Taxes must be paid by June 1, 2013. Assume that Lexington prepares adjustments only once a year, on December 31, and that property taxes for 2012 are expected to increase by 5% over those for 2011.

Required

1. Identify and analyze the adjustment to record the property taxes payable on December 31, 2012.
2. Identify and analyze the transaction to record the payment of the 2012 property taxes on June 1, 2013.

LO5
EXAMPLE 4-5

Exercise 4-9 Working Backward: Depreciation

Polk Corp. purchased new store fixtures for $55,000 on January 31, 2010. Polk depreciates assets using the straight-line method and estimated a salvage value for the machine of $5,000. On its December 31, 2012, balance sheet, Polk reported the following:

Property, plant, and equipment:		
Store fixtures	$55,000	
Less: Accumulated depreciation	15,000	$40,000

Required

1. What is the yearly amount of depreciation expense for the store fixtures?
2. What is the estimated useful life in years for the store fixtures? Explain your answer.

LO5
EXAMPLE 4-10

Exercise 4-10 Interest Receivable

On June 1, 2012, Micro Tel Enterprises lends $60,000 to MaxiDriver Inc. The loan will be repaid in 60 days with interest at 10%.

Required

1. Identify and analyze the transaction on MicroTel's books on June 1, 2012.
2. Identify and analyze the adjustment on MicroTel's books on June 30, 2012.
3. Identify and analyze the transaction on MicroTel's books on July 31, 2012, when Maxi-Driver repays the principal and interest.

LO5
EXAMPLE 4-10

Exercise 4-11 Rent Receivable

Hudson Corp. has extra space in its warehouse and agrees to rent it out to Stillwater Company at the rate of $2,000 per month. The space was made available to Stillwater beginning on September 1. Under the terms of the agreement, Stillwater pays the month's rent on the fifth day after the end of the month. Assume that Hudson prepares adjustments at the end of each month.

Required

1. How much revenue should Hudson record in September? How much revenue should Hudson record in October?
2. Identify and analyze the transactions, including any adjustments, on Hudson's books during the month of October.

LO5
EXAMPLE 4-10

Exercise 4-12 Working Backward: Rent Receivable

Randy's Rentals reported the following on its year-end balance sheets:

	December 31, 2012	December 31, 2011
Current Assets:		
Rent receivable	$55,000	$35,800

Randy's rents space to a number of tenants, all of whom pay their monthly rent on the tenth of the following month. Randy's reported rent revenue for 2012 of $64,200.

Required

How much cash did Randy's collect from its tenants during 2012? Explain your answer.

LO5
EXAMPLE 4-7

Exercise 4-13 Working Backward: Gift Card Liability

Dexter Department Stores reported the following on its year-end balance sheets:

	December 31, 2012	December 31, 2011
Current Liabilities:		
Gift card liability	$25,750	$22,640

During 2012, gift cards redeemed at the stores amounted to $33,750.

Required

How much did Dexter receive during 2012 from the sale of gift cards? Explain your answer.

Exercise 4-14 Working Backward: Interest Payable

LO5
EXAMPLE 4-9

On July 1, 2012, Rogers Corp. took out a 60-day, $100,000 loan at the bank. On July 31, 2012, Rogers made the following adjustment:

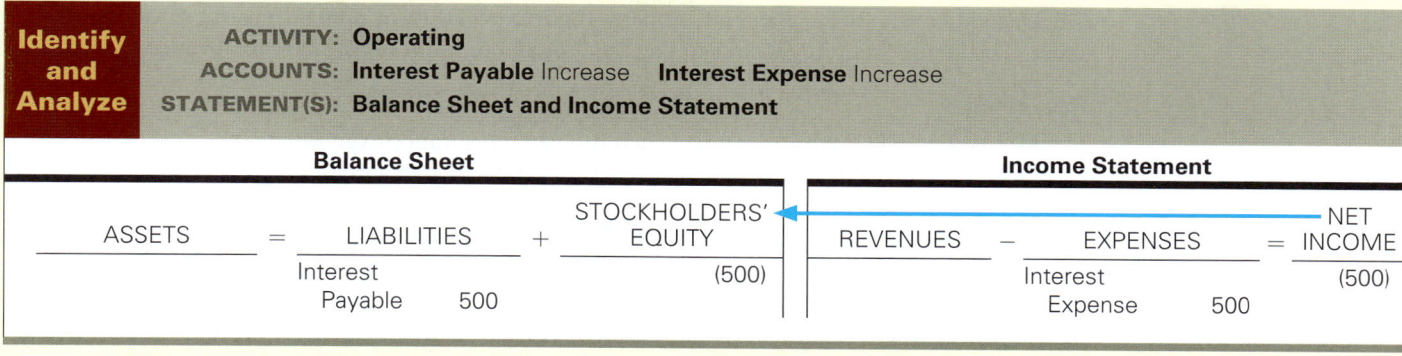

Required

1. What is the interest rate on the loan? Explain your answer.
2. Identify and analyze the adjustment on Rogers Corp.'s books on August 31, 2012, when the company repays the principal and interest on the loan.

Exercise 4-15 Interest Payable

LO5
EXAMPLE 4-9, 4-11

Billings Company takes out a 12%, 90-day, $100,000 loan with First National Bank on March 1, 2012.

Required

1. Identify and analyze the transaction to take out the loan on March 1, 2012.
2. Identify and analyze the adjustments for the months of March and April 2012.
3. Identify and analyze the transaction on May 30, 2012, when Billings repays the principal and interest to First National.

Exercise 4-16 Wages Payable

LO5
EXAMPLE 4-8, 4-11

Denton Corporation employs 50 workers in its plant. Each employee is paid $10 per hour and works seven hours per day, Monday through Friday. Employees are paid every Friday. The last payday was Friday, October 20.

Required

1. Compute the dollar amount of the weekly payroll.
2. Identify and analyze the transaction on Friday, October 27, for the payment of the weekly payroll.
3. Denton prepares monthly financial statements. Identify and analyze the adjustment on Tuesday, October 31, the last day of the month.
4. Identify and analyze the transaction on Friday, November 3, for the payment of the weekly payroll.
5. Will net income for the month of October be understated or overstated if Denton doesn't bother with an adjustment on October 31? Explain your answer.

Exercise 4-17 Interest Payable—Quarterly Adjustments

LO5
EXAMPLE 4-9

Glendive takes out a 12%, 90-day, $100,000 loan with Second State Bank on March 1, 2012. Assume that Glendive prepares adjustments only four times a year: on March 31, June 30, September 30, and December 31.

(Continued)

Required

1. Identify and analyze the transaction to take out the loan on March 1, 2012.
2. Identify and analyze the adjustment on March 31, 2012.
3. Identify and analyze the adjustment on May 30, 2012, when Glendive repays the principal and interest to Second State Bank.

LO5
EXAMPLE 4-4

Exercise 4-18 Working Backward: Prepaid Insurance

On December 31, 2012, Baxter Company reported $8,000 in prepaid insurance on its balance sheet. The insurer requires Baxter to pay the annual premium of $24,000 in advance.

Required

1. How much will Baxter recognize each month in insurance expense?
2. On what date does Baxter renew its insurance policy? Explain your answer.

LO5
EXAMPLE 4-7

Exercise 4-19 Concert Tickets Sold in Advance

Rock N Roll produces an outdoor concert festival that runs from June 28, 2012, through July 1, 2012. Concertgoers pay $80 for a four-day pass to the festival, and all 10,000 tickets are sold out by the May 1, 2012, deadline to buy tickets. Assume that Rock N Roll prepares adjustments at the end of each month.

Required

1. Identify and analyze the transaction on May 1, 2012, assuming that all 10,000 tickets are sold on this date.
2. Identify and analyze the adjustment on June 30, 2012.
3. Identify and analyze the adjustment on July 31, 2012.

LO5
EXAMPLE 4-5, 4-11

Exercise 4-20 Depreciation

On July 1, 2012, Dexter Corp. buys a computer system for $260,000 in cash. Assume that the computer is expected to have a four-year life and an estimated salvage value of $20,000 at the end of that time.

Required

1. Identify and analyze the transaction for the purchase of the computer on July 1, 2012.
2. Compute the depreciable cost of the computer.
3. Using the straight-line method, compute the monthly depreciation.
4. Identify and analyze the adjustment to record depreciation at the end of July 2012.
5. Compute the computer's carrying value that will be shown on Dexter's balance sheet prepared on December 31, 2012.

LO5
EXAMPLE 4-4

Exercise 4-21 Prepaid Insurance—Annual Adjustments

On April 1, 2012, Briggs Corp. purchases a 24-month property insurance policy for $72,000. The policy is effective immediately. Assume that Briggs prepares adjustments only once a year, on December 31.

Required

1. Compute the monthly cost of the insurance policy.
2. Identify and analyze the transaction to record the purchase of the policy on April 1, 2012.
3. Identify and analyze the adjustment on December 31, 2012.
4. Assume that the accountant forgets to record an adjustment on December 31, 2012. Will net income for the year ended December 31, 2012, be understated or overstated? Explain your answer.

LO5
EXAMPLE 4-7

Exercise 4-22 Subscriptions

Horse Country Living publishes a monthly magazine for which a 12-month subscription costs $30. All subscriptions require payment of the full $30 in advance. On August 1, the balance in the Subscriptions Received in Advance account was $40,500. During the month of August, the company sold 900 yearly subscriptions. After the adjustment at the end of August, the balance in the Subscriptions Received in Advance account is $60,000.

Required

1. Identify and analyze the transaction to record the sale of the 900 yearly subscriptions during the month of August.
2. Identify and analyze the adjustment on August 31.
3. Assume that the accountant made the correct entry during August to record the sale of the 900 subscriptions but forgot to make the adjustment on August 31. Would net income for August be overstated or understated? Explain your answer.

Exercise 4-23 Office Supplies

LO5
EXAMPLE 4-4

Somerville Corp. purchases office supplies once a month and prepares monthly financial statements. The asset account Office Supplies on Hand has a balance of $1,450 on May 1. Purchases of supplies during May amount to $1,100. Supplies on hand at May 31 amount to $920. Identify and analyze the effect of the adjustment on May 31. What will be the effect on net income for May if this adjustment is *not* recorded?

Exercise 4-24 Prepaid Rent—Quarterly Adjustments

LO5
EXAMPLE 4-4

On September 1, Northhampton Industries signed a six-month lease for office space, which is effective September 1. Northhampton agreed to prepay the rent and mailed a check for $12,000 to the landlord on September 1. Assume that Northhampton prepares adjustments only four times a year: on March 31, June 30, September 30, and December 31.

Required

1. Compute the rental cost for each full month.
2. Identify and analyze the effect of the transaction for the payment of rent on September 1.
3. Identify and analyze the effect of the adjustment on September 30.
4. Assume that the accountant prepares the adjustment on September 30 but forgets to record an adjustment on December 31. Will net income for the year be understated or overstated? by what amount?

Exercise 4-25 The Effect of Adjustments on the Accounting Equation

LO5
EXAMPLE 4-4, 4-5, 4-6, 4-8, 4-9, 4-10

Determine whether recording each of the following adjustments will increase (I), decrease (D), or have no effect (NE) on each of the three elements of the accounting equation.

	Assets =	Liabilities +	Stock. Equity
Example: Wages earned during the period but not yet paid are accrued.	NE	I	D
1. Prepaid insurance is reduced for the portion of the policy that has expired during the period.	___	___	___
2. Interest incurred during the period but not yet paid is accrued.	___	___	___
3. Depreciation for the period is recorded.	___	___	___
4. Revenue is recorded for the earned portion of a liability for amounts collected in advance from customers.	___	___	___
5. Rent revenue is recorded for amounts owed by a tenant but not yet received.	___	___	___
6. Income taxes owed but not yet paid are accrued.	___	___	___

MULTI-CONCEPT EXERCISES

Exercise 4-26 Accrual of Interest on a Loan

LO4 • 5
EXAMPLE 4-9

On July 1, Paxson Corporation takes out a 12%, two-month, $50,000 loan at Friendly National Bank. Principal and interest are to be repaid on August 31.

(Continued)

Required

1. Identify and analyze the transactions or adjustments for July 1 to record the borrowing, for July 31 to record the accrual of interest, and for August 31 to record repayment of the principal and interest.
2. Evaluate the following statement: It would be much easier not to bother with an adjustment on July 31 and simply record interest expense on August 31 when the loan is repaid.

LO1 • 2 • 3

EXAMPLE 4-1, 4-2

Exercise 4-27 Revenue Recognition, Cash and Accrual Bases

Hathaway Health Club sold three-year memberships at a reduced rate during its opening promotion. It sold 1,000 three-year nonrefundable memberships for $366 each. The club expects to sell 100 additional three-year memberships for $900 each over each of the next two years. Membership fees are paid when clients sign up. The club's bookkeeper has prepared the following income statement for the first year of business and projected income statements for Years 2 and 3.

Cash-basis income statements:

	Year 1	Year 2	Year 3
Sales	$366,000	$90,000	$90,000
Equipment*	$100,000	$ 0	$ 0
Salaries and wages	50,000	50,000	50,000
Advertising	5,000	5,000	5,000
Rent and utilities	36,000	36,000	36,000
Net income (loss)	$175,000	$ (1,000)	$ (1,000)

*Equipment was purchased at the beginning of Year 1 for $100,000 and is expected to last for three years and then to be worth $1,000.

Required

1. Convert the income statements for each of the three years to the accrual basis.
2. Describe how the revenue recognition principle applies. Do you believe that the cash-basis or the accrual-basis income statements are more useful to management? to investors? Why?

LO4 • 5

EXAMPLE 4-5

Exercise 4-28 Depreciation Expense

During 2012, Carter Company acquired three assets with the following costs, estimated useful lives, and estimated salvage values:

Date	Asset	Cost	Estimated Useful Life	Estimated Salvage Value
March 28	Truck	$ 18,000	5 years	$ 3,000
June 22	Computer	55,000	10 years	5,000
October 3	Building	250,000	30 years	10,000

The company uses the straight-line method to depreciate all assets and computes depreciation to the nearest month. For example, the computer system will be depreciated for six months in 2012.

Required

1. Compute the depreciation expense that Carter will record on each of the three assets for 2012.
2. Comment on the following statement: Accountants could save time and money by simply expensing the cost of long-term assets when they are purchased. In addition, this would be more accurate because depreciation requires estimates of useful life and salvage value.

PROBLEMS

Problem 4-1 Reconstruction of Adjustments from Account Balances   LO5

Taggart Corp. records adjustments each month before preparing monthly financial statements. The following selected account balances on May 31, 2012 and June 30, 2012, reflect month-end adjustments:

	May 31, 2012	June 30, 2012
Prepaid Insurance	$3,600	$3,450
Equipment	9,600	9,600
Accumulated Depreciation	1,280	1,360
Notes Payable	9,600	9,600
Interest Payable	2,304	2,448

Required

1. The company purchased a 36-month insurance policy on June 1, 2011. Identify and analyze the adjustment necessary for insurance on June 30, 2012.
2. What was the original cost of the insurance policy? Explain your answer.
3. The equipment was purchased on February 1, 2011, for $9,600. Taggart uses straight-line depreciation and estimates that the equipment will have no salvage value. Identify and analyze the adjustment necessary for depreciation on June 30, 2012.
4. What is the equipment's estimated useful life in months? Explain your answer.
5. Taggart signed a two-year note payable on February 1, 2011, for the purchase of the equipment. Interest on the note accrues on a monthly basis and will be paid at maturity along with the principal amount of $9,600. Identify and analyze the adjustment necessary for interest on June 30, 2012.
6. What is the monthly interest rate on the loan? Explain your answer.

Problem 4-2 Use of Account Balances as a Basis for Adjustments   LO5

Four Star Video has been in the video rental business for five years. The following is a list of accounts for Four Star Video at May 31, 2012. It reflects the recurring transactions for the month of May but does not reflect any month-end adjustments.

Cash	$ 4,000
Prepaid Rent	6,600
Video Inventory	25,600
Display Stands	8,900
Accumulated Depreciation	5,180
Accounts Payable	3,260
Customer Subscriptions	4,450
Capital Stock	5,000
Retained Earnings	22,170
Rental Revenue	9,200
Wage and Salary Expense	2,320
Utilities Expense	1,240
Advertising Expense	600

The following additional information is available:

a. Four Star rents a store in a shopping mall and prepays the annual rent of $7,200 on April 1 of each year.
b. The asset account Video Inventory represents the cost of videos purchased from suppliers. When a new title is purchased from a supplier, its cost is added to this account. When a title has served its useful life and can no longer be rented (even at a reduced price), it is removed from the inventory in the store. Based on the monthly count, the cost of titles on hand at the end of May is $23,140.

(Continued)

c. The display stands have an estimated useful life of five years and an estimated salvage value of $500.

d. Wages and salaries owed but unpaid to employees at the end of May amount to $1,450.

e. In addition to individual rentals, Four Star operates a popular discount subscription program. Customers pay an annual fee of $120 for an unlimited number of rentals. Based on the $10 per month earned on each of these subscriptions, the amount earned for the month of May is $2,440.

f. Four Star accrues income taxes using an estimated tax rate equal to 30% of the income for the month.

Required

1. For each of the items of additional information, (a) through (f), identify and analyze the necessary adjustment on May 31, 2012.

2. On the basis of the information you have, does Four Star appear to be a profitable business? Explain your answer.

LO5   Problem 4-3 Use of Account Balances as a Basis for Adjustments

Bob Reynolds operates a real estate business. A list of accounts on April 30, 2012, *before* any adjustments are recorded, appears as follows:

Cash	$15,700
Prepaid Insurance	450
Office Supplies	250
Office Equipment	50,000
Accumulated Depreciation—Office Equipment	5,000
Automobile	12,000
Accumulated Depreciation—Auto	1,400
Accounts Payable	6,500
Unearned Commissions	9,500
Notes Payable	2,000
Capital Stock	10,000
Retained Earnings	40,000
Dividends	2,500
Commissions Earned	17,650
Utilities Expense	2,300
Salaries Expense	7,400
Advertising Expense	1,450

Other Data

a. The monthly insurance cost is $50.

b. Office supplies on hand on April 30, 2012, amount to $180.

c. The office equipment was purchased on April 1, 2011. On that date, it had an estimated useful life of ten years.

d. On September 1, 2011, the automobile was purchased; it had an estimated useful life of five years.

e. A deposit is received in advance of providing any services for first-time customers. Amounts received in advance are recorded initially in the account Unearned Commissions. Based on services provided to these first-time customers, the balance in this account at the end of April should be $5,000.

f. Repeat customers are allowed to pay for services one month after the date of the sale of their property. Services rendered during the month but not yet collected or billed to these customers amount to $1,500.

g. Interest owed on the note payable but not yet paid amounts to $20.

h. Salaries owed but unpaid to employees at the end of the month amount to $2,500.

Required

1. For each of the items of other data (a) through (h), identify and analyze the adjustment necessary on April 30, 2012.

2. Compute the net increase or decrease in net income for the month from the recognition of the adjustments in (1). (Ignore income taxes.)

3. Note the balance in Accumulated Depreciation—Office Equipment of $5,000. Explain why the account contains a balance of $5,000 on April 30, 2012.

Problem 4-4 Recurring Transactions and Adjustments   **LO5**

Following are Butler Realty Corporation's accounts, identified by number. The company has been in the real estate business for ten years and prepares financial statements monthly. Following the list of accounts is a series of transactions entered into by Butler. For each transaction, enter the number(s) of the account(s) affected.

Accounts

1. Cash	11. Notes Payable
2. Accounts Receivable	12. Capital Stock, $10 par
3. Prepaid Rent	13. Paid-In Capital in Excess of Par
4. Office Supplies	14. Commissions Revenue
5. Automobiles	15. Office Supply Expense
6. Accumulated Depreciation	16. Rent Expense
7. Land	17. Salaries and Wages Expense
8. Accounts Payable	18. Depreciation Expense
9. Salaries and Wages Payable	19. Interest Expense
10. Income Tax Payable	20. Income Tax Expense

Transaction

a. Example: Issued additional shares of stock to owners at amount in excess of par.   <u>1, 12, 13</u>

b. Purchased automobiles for cash.   _____

c. Purchased land; made cash down payment and signed a promissory note for the balance.   _____

d. Paid cash to landlord for rent for next 12 months.   _____

e. Purchased office supplies on account.   _____

f. Collected cash for commissions from clients for properties sold during the month.   _____

g. Collected cash for commissions from clients for properties sold the prior month.   _____

h. During the month, sold properties for which cash for commissions will be collected from clients next month.   _____

i. Paid for office supplies purchased on account in an earlier month.   _____

j. Recorded an adjustment to recognize wages and salaries incurred but not yet paid.   _____

k. Recorded an adjustment for office supplies used during the month.   _____

l. Recorded an adjusting entry for the portion of prepaid rent that expired during the month.   _____

m. Made required month-end payment on note taken out in (c); payment is part principal and part interest.   _____

n. Recorded adjustment for monthly depreciation on the autos.   _____

o. Recorded adjustment for income taxes.   _____

Problem 4-5 Use of Account Balances as a Basis for Annual Adjustments   **LO5**

The following account balances are taken from the records of Chauncey Company at December 31, 2012. The Prepaid Insurance account represents the cost of a three-year policy purchased on August 1, 2012. The Rent Collected in Advance account represents the cash received from a tenant on June 1, 2012, for 12 months' rent beginning on that date. The Note Receivable represents a nine-month promissory note received from a customer on September 1, 2012. Principal and interest at an annual rate of 9% will be received on June 1, 2013.

(Continued)

Prepaid Insurance	$ 7,200
Rent Collected in Advance	6,000
Note Receivable	50,000

Required

1. Identify and analyze the three necessary adjustments on the books of Chauncey on December 31, 2012. Assume that Chauncey prepares adjustments only once a year, on December 31.
2. Assume that adjustments are made at the end of each month rather than only at the end of the year. What would be the balance in Prepaid Insurance *before* the December adjustment was made? Explain your answer.

LO5 Problem 4-6 Adjustments

Kretz Corporation prepares monthly financial statements and therefore adjusts its accounts at the end of every month. The following information is available for March 2012:

a. Kretz Corporation takes out a 90-day, 8%, $15,000 note on March 1, 2012, with interest and principal to be paid at maturity.
b. The asset account Office Supplies on Hand has a balance of $1,280 on March 1, 2012. During March, Kretz adds $750 to the account for purchases during the period. A count of the supplies on hand at the end of March indicates a balance of $1,370.
c. The company purchased office equipment last year for $62,600. The equipment has an estimated useful life of six years and an estimated salvage value of $5,000.
d. The company's plant operates seven days per week with a daily payroll of $950. Wage earners are paid every Sunday. The last day of the month is Saturday, March 31.
e. The company rented an idle warehouse to a neighboring business on February 1, 2012, at a rate of $2,500 per month. On this date, Kretz Corporation recorded Rent Collected in Advance for six months' rent received in advance.
f. On March 1, 2012, Kretz Corporation recorded a liability account, Customer Deposits, for $4,800. This sum represents an amount that a customer paid in advance and that Kretz will earn evenly over a four-month period.
g. Based on its income for the month, Kretz Corporation estimates that federal income taxes for March amount to $3,900.

Required

1. For each of the preceding situations, identify and analyze the adjustments to be recorded on March 31, 2012.
2. Assume that Kretz reports income of $23,000 before any of the adjustments. What net income will Kretz report for March?

LO5 Problem 4-7 Annual Adjustments

Palmer Industries prepares annual financial statements and adjusts its accounts only at the end of the year. The following information is available for the year ended December 31, 2012:

a. Palmer purchased computer equipment two years ago for $15,000. The equipment has an estimated useful life of five years and an estimated salvage value of $250.
b. The Office Supplies account had a balance of $3,600 on January 1, 2012. During 2012, Palmer added $17,600 to the account for purchases of office supplies during the year. A count of the supplies on hand at the end of December 2012 indicates a balance of $1,850.
c. On August 1, 2012, Palmer created a liability account, Customer Deposits, for $24,000. This sum represents an amount that a customer paid in advance and that will be earned evenly by Palmer over a six-month period.
d. Palmer rented some office space on November 1, 2012, at a rate of $2,700 per month. On that date, Palmer recorded Prepaid Rent for three months' rent paid in advance.
e. Palmer took out a 120-day, 9%, $200,000 note on November 1, 2012, with interest and principal to be paid at maturity.
f. Palmer operates five days per week with an average daily payroll of $500. Palmer pays its employees every Thursday. December 31, 2012, is a Monday.

Required

1. For each of the preceding situations, identify and analyze the adjustment to be recorded on December 31, 2012.
2. Assume that Palmer's accountant forgets to record the adjustments on December 31, 2012. Will net income for the year be understated or overstated? by what amount? (Ignore the effect of income taxes.)

MULTI-CONCEPT PROBLEMS

Problem 4-8 Revenue and Expense Recognition

LO3 • 4

Two years ago, Darlene Darby opened a delivery service. Darby reports the following accounts on her income statement:

Sales	$69,000
Advertising Expense	3,500
Salaries Expense	39,000
Rent Expense	10,000

These amounts represent two years of revenue and expenses. Darby asks you how she can tell how much of the income is from the first year of business and how much is from the second year. She provides the following additional data:

a. Sales in the second year are double those of the first year.
b. Advertising expense is for a $500 opening promotion and weekly ads in the newspaper.
c. Salaries represent one employee for the first nine months and two employees for the remainder of the time. Each is paid the same salary. No raises have been granted.
d. Rent has not changed since the business opened.

Required

Prepare income statements for Years 1 and 2.

Problem 4-9 Monthly Transactions, Adjustments, and Financial Statements

LO5 • 6

Moonlight Bay Inn is incorporated on January 2, 2012, by its three owners, each of whom contributes $20,000 in cash in exchange for shares of stock in the business. In addition to the sale of stock, the following transactions are entered into during the month of January:

January 2: A Victorian inn is purchased for $50,000 in cash. An appraisal performed on this date indicates that the land is worth $15,000, and the remaining balance of the purchase price is attributable to the house. The owners estimate that the house will have an estimated useful life of 25 years and an estimated salvage value of $5,000.

January 3: A two-year, 12%, $30,000 promissory note was signed at Second State Bank. Interest and principal will be repaid on the maturity date of January 3, 2014.

January 4: New furniture for the inn is purchased at a cost of $15,000 in cash. The furniture has an estimated useful life of ten years and no salvage value.

January 5: A 24-month property insurance policy is purchased for $6,000 in cash.

January 6: An advertisement for the inn is placed in the local newspaper. Moonlight Bay pays $450 cash for the ad, which will run in the paper throughout January.

January 7: Cleaning supplies are purchased on account for $950. The bill is payable within 30 days.

January 15: Wages of $4,230 for the first half of the month are paid in cash.

January 16: A guest mails the business $980 in cash as a deposit for a room to be rented for two weeks. The guest plans to stay at the inn during the last week of January and the first week of February.

January 31: Cash receipts from rentals of rooms for the month amount to $8,300.

(Continued)

January 31:   Cash receipts from operation of the restaurant for the month amount to $6,600.

January 31:   Each stockholder is paid $200 in cash dividends.

Required

1. Identify and analyze each of the preceding transactions.
2. Prepare a list of accounts and their balances for Moonlight Bay at January 31, 2012. Reflect the recurring transactions for the month of January but not the necessary month-end adjustments.
3. Identify and analyze the necessary adjustments for each of the following:

   a. Depreciation of the house
   b. Depreciation of the furniture
   c. Interest on the promissory note
   d. Recognition of the expired portion of the insurance
   e. Recognition of the earned portion of the guest's deposit
   f. Wages earned during the second half of January amount to $5,120 and will be paid on February 3.
   g. Cleaning supplies on hand on January 31 amount to $230.
   h. A gas and electric bill that is received from the city amounts to $740 and is payable by February 5.
   i. Income taxes are to be accrued at a rate of 30% of income before taxes.

4. Prepare in good form the following financial statements:

   a. Income statement for the month ended January 31, 2012
   b. Statement of retained earnings for the month ended January 31, 2012
   c. Balance sheet at January 31, 2012

5. Assume that you are the loan officer at Second State Bank. (Refer to the transaction on January 3.) What are your reactions to Moonlight's first month of operations? Are you comfortable with the loan you made? Explain your answer.

ALTERNATE PROBLEMS

LO5   **Problem 4-1A Recurring Transactions and Adjustments**

Following are the accounts of Dominique Inc., an interior decorator. The company has been in the decorating business for ten years and prepares quarterly financial statements. Following the list of accounts is a series of transactions entered into by Dominique. For each transaction, enter the number(s) of the account(s) affected.

Accounts

1. Cash	11. Capital Stock, $1 par
2. Accounts Receivable	12. Paid-In Capital in Excess of Par
3. Prepaid Rent	13. Consulting Revenue
4. Office Supplies	14. Office Supply Expense
5. Office Equipment	15. Rent Expense
6. Accumulated Depreciation	16. Salaries and Wages Expense
7. Accounts Payable	17. Depreciation Expense
8. Salaries and Wages Payable	18. Interest Expense
9. Income Tax Payable	19. Income Tax Expense
10. Interim Financing Notes Payable	

Transaction	
a. Example: Issued additional shares of stock to owners; shares issued at greater than par.	1,11,12
b. Purchased office equipment for cash.	_____
c. Collected open accounts receivable from customer.	_____
d. Purchased office supplies on account.	_____

Transaction

e. Paid office rent for the next six months.	_____
f. Paid interest on an interim financing note.	_____
g. Paid salaries and wages.	_____
h. Purchased office equipment; made a down payment in cash and signed an interim financing note.	_____
i. Provided services on account.	_____
j. Recorded depreciation on equipment.	_____
k. Recorded income taxes due next month.	_____
l. Recorded the used office supplies.	_____
m. Recorded the used portion of prepaid rent.	_____

Problem 4-2A Use of Account Balances as a Basis for Annual Adjustments

LO5

The following account balances are taken from the records of Laugherty Inc. at December 31, 2012. The Supplies account represents the cost of supplies on hand at the beginning of the year plus all purchases. A physical count on December 31, 2012, shows only $1,520 of supplies on hand. The Unearned Revenue account represents the cash received from a customer on May 1, 2012, for 12 months of service beginning on that date. The Note Payable represents a six-month promissory note signed with a supplier on September 1, 2012. Principal and interest at an annual rate of 10% will be paid on March 1, 2013.

Supplies	$ 5,790
Unearned Revenue	1,800
Note Payable	60,000

Required

1. Identify and analyze the adjustments necessary on the books of Laugherty on December 31, 2012. Assume that Laugherty prepares adjustments only once a year, on December 31.
2. Assume that adjustments are made at the end of each month rather than only at the end of the year. What would be the balance in Unearned Revenue *before* the December adjustment was made? Explain your answer.

Problem 4-3A Reconstruction of Adjustments from Account Balances

LO5

Zola Corporation records adjustments each month before preparing monthly financial statements. The following selected account balances on May 31, 2012, and June 30, 2012, reflect month-end adjustments:

Account Title	May 31, 2012	June 30, 2012
Prepaid Rent	$4,000	$3,000
Equipment	9,600	9,600
Accumulated Depreciation	800	900
Notes Payable	9,600	9,600
Interest Payable	768	864

Required

1. The company paid for a six-month lease on April 1, 2012. Identify and analyze the adjustment for rent on June 30, 2012.
2. What amount was prepaid on April 1, 2012? Explain your answer.
3. The equipment was purchased on September 30, 2011, for $9,600. Zola uses straight-line depreciation and estimates that the equipment will have no salvage value. Identify and analyze the adjustment for depreciation on June 30, 2012.
4. What is the equipment's estimated useful life in months? Explain your answer.
5. Zola signed a two-year note on September 30, 2011, for the purchase of the equipment. Interest on the note accrues on a monthly basis and will be paid at maturity along with the principal amount of $9,600. Identify and analyze the adjustment for interest expense on June 30, 2012.
6. What is the monthly interest rate on the loan? Explain your answer.

LO5 Problem 4-4A Adjustments

Flood Relief Inc. prepares monthly financial statements and therefore adjusts its accounts at the end of every month. The following information is available for June 2012:

a. Flood received a $10,000, 4%, two-year note receivable from a customer for services rendered. The principal and interest are due on June 1, 2014. Flood expects to be able to collect the note and interest in full at that time.

b. Office supplies totaling $5,600 were purchased during the month. The asset account Supplies is increased whenever a purchase is made. A count in the storeroom on June 30, 2012, indicates that supplies on hand amount to $507. The supplies on hand at the beginning of the month total $475.

c. The company purchased machines last year for $170,000. The machines are expected to be used for four years and have an estimated salvage value of $2,000.

d. On June 1, the company paid $4,650 for rent for June, July, and August, and increased the asset Prepaid Rent. It did not have a balance on June 1.

e. The company operates seven days per week with a weekly payroll of $7,000. Wage earners are paid every Sunday. The last day of the month is Saturday, June 30.

f. Based on its income for the month, Flood estimates that federal income taxes for June amount to $2,900.

Required

1. For each of the preceding situations, identify and analyze the adjustment necessary on June 30, 2012.

2. Assume that Flood Relief reports income of $35,000 before any of the adjustments. What net income will Flood Relief report for June?

LO5 Problem 4-5A Annual Adjustments

Ogonquit Enterprises prepares annual financial statements and adjusts its accounts only at the end of the year. The following information is available for the year ended December 31, 2012:

a. Ogonquit purchased office furniture last year for $25,000. The furniture has an estimated useful life of seven years and an estimated salvage value of $4,000.

b. The Supplies account had a balance of $1,200 on January 1, 2012. During 2012, Ogonquit added $12,900 to the account for purchases of supplies during the year. A count of the supplies on hand at the end of December 2012 indicates a balance of $900.

c. On July 1, 2012, Ogonquit created a liability account, Customer Deposits, for $8,800. This sum represents an amount that a customer paid in advance and that will be earned evenly by Ogonquit over an eight-month period.

d. Ogonquit rented some warehouse space on September 1, 2012, at a rate of $4,000 per month. On that date, Ogonquit recorded Prepaid Rent for six months' rent paid in advance.

e. Ogonquit took out a 90-day, 6%, $30,000 note on November 1, 2012, with interest and principal to be paid at maturity.

f. Ogonquit operates five days per week with an average weekly payroll of $4,150. Ogonquit pays its employees every Thursday. December 31, 2012, is a Monday.

Required

1. For each of the preceding situations, identify and analyze the adjustment necessary on December 31, 2012.

2. Assume that Ogonquit's accountant forgets to record the adjustments on December 31, 2012. Will net income for the year be understated or overstated? by what amount? (Ignore the effect of income taxes.)

LO5 Problem 4-6A Use of Account Balances as a Basis for Adjustments

Lori Matlock operates a graphic arts business. A trial balance on June 30, 2012, *before* recording any adjustments, appears as follows:

Cash	$ 7,000
Prepaid Rent	18,000
Supplies	15,210
Office Equipment	46,120

Accumulated Depreciation—Equipment	$ 4,000
Accounts Payable	1,800
Notes Payable	2,000
Capital Stock	50,000
Retained Earnings	24,350
Dividends	8,400
Revenue	46,850
Utilities Expense	2,850
Salaries Expense	19,420
Advertising Expense	12,000

Other Data

a. The monthly rent is $600.

b. Supplies on hand on June 30, 2012, amount to $1,290.

c. The office equipment was purchased on June 1, 2011. On that date, it had an estimated useful life of ten years and a salvage value of $6,120.

d. Interest owed on the note payable but not yet paid amounts to $50.

e. Salaries of $620 are owed but unpaid to employees at the end of the month.

Required

1. For each of the items of other data, (a) through (e), identify and analyze the necessary adjustments at June 30, 2012.

2. Note the balance in Accumulated Depreciation—Equipment of $4,000. Explain why the account contains a balance of $4,000 on June 30, 2012.

Problem 4-7A Use of Account Balances as a Basis for Adjustments   LO5

Lewis and Associates has been in the termite inspection and treatment business for five years. The following is a list of accounts for Lewis on June 30, 2012. It reflects the recurring transactions for the month of June but does not reflect any month-end adjustments.

Cash	$ 6,200
Accounts Receivable	10,400
Prepaid Rent	4,400
Chemical Inventory	9,400
Equipment	18,200
Accumulated Depreciation	1,050
Accounts Payable	1,180
Capital Stock	5,000
Retained Earnings	25,370
Treatment Revenue	40,600
Wages and Salary Expense	22,500
Utilities Expense	1,240
Advertising Expense	860

The following additional information is available:

a. Lewis rents a warehouse with office space and prepays the annual rent of $4,800 on May 1 of each year.

b. The asset account Equipment represents the cost of treatment equipment, which has an estimated useful life of ten years and an estimated salvage value of $200.

c. Chemical inventory on hand equals $1,300.

d. Wages and salaries owed but unpaid to employees at the end of the month amount to $1,080.

e. Lewis accrues income taxes using an estimated tax rate equal to 30% of the income for the month.

(Continued)

Required

1. For each of the items of additional information, (a) through (e), identify and analyze the necessary adjustment on June 30, 2012.
2. On the basis of the information you have, does Lewis appear to be a profitable business? Explain your answer.

ALTERNATE MULTI-CONCEPT PROBLEMS

LO3 • 4   Problem 4-8A Revenue and Expense Recognition

Two years ago, Sue Stern opened an audio book rental shop. Sue reports the following accounts on her income statement:

Sales	$84,000
Advertising Expense	10,500
Salaries Expense	12,000
Depreciation on CDs	5,000
Rent Expense	18,000

These amounts represent two years of revenue and expenses. Sue asks you how she can tell how much of the income is from the first year and how much is from the second year of business. She provides the following additional data:

a. Sales in the second year are triple those of the first year.
b. Advertising expense is for a $1,500 opening promotion and weekly ads in the newspaper.
c. Salaries represent one employee who was hired eight months ago. No raises have been granted.
d. Rent has not changed since the shop opened.

Required

Prepare income statements for Years 1 and 2.

LO5 • 6   Problem 4-9A Adjustments and Financial Statements

The following account balances are available for Tenfour Trucking Company on January 31, 2012:

Cash	$ 27,340
Accounts Receivable	41,500
Prepaid Insurance	18,000
Warehouse	40,000
Accumulated Depreciation—Warehouse	21,600
Truck Fleet	240,000
Accumulated Depreciation—Truck Fleet	112,500
Land	20,000
Accounts Payable	32,880
Notes Payable	50,000
Interest Payable	4,500
Customer Deposits	6,000
Capital Stock	100,000
Retained Earnings	40,470
Freight Revenue	165,670
Gas and Oil Expense	57,330
Maintenance Expense	26,400
Wage and Salary Expense	43,050
Dividends	20,000

Required

1. Identify and analyze the necessary adjustments at January 31, 2012, for each of the following:

    a. Prepaid insurance represents the cost of a 24-month policy purchased on January 1, 2012.

b. The warehouse has an estimated useful life of 20 years and an estimated salvage value of $4,000.

c. The truck fleet has an estimated useful life of six years and an estimated salvage value of $15,000.

d. The promissory note was signed on January 1, 2011. Interest at an annual rate of 9% and the principal of $50,000 are due on December 31, 2012.

e. The customer deposits represent amounts paid in advance by new customers. A total of $4,500 of the balance in Customer Deposits was earned during January 2012.

f. Wages and salaries earned by employees at the end of January but not yet paid amount to $8,200.

g. Income taxes are accrued at a rate of 30% at the end of each month.

2. Prepare in good form the following financial statements:

   a. Income statement for the month ended January 31, 2012
   b. Statement of retained earnings for the month ended January 31, 2012
   c. Balance sheet at January 31, 2012

3. Compute Tenfour's current ratio. What does this ratio tell you about the company's liquidity?

4. Compute Tenfour's profit margin. What does this ratio tell you about the company's profitability?

DECISION CASES

Reading and Interpreting Financial Statements

Decision Case 4-1 Comparing Two Companies in the Same Industry: Kellogg's and General Mills   LO3

Refer to the financial information for **Kellogg's** and **General Mills** reproduced at the end of the book for the information needed to answer the following questions.

Required

1. Locate the note in each company's annual report in which it discusses revenue recognition. How does each company describe the point at which it recognizes revenue from customers? Are there any significant differences in the organizations' revenue recognition policies?

2. What dollar amount does Kellogg's report for accounts receivable on its most recent balance sheet? What percent of the company's total current assets are comprised of accounts receivable? What is the dollar amount of General Mills's receivables on its most recent balance sheet? What percent of total current assets is comprised of receivables? For which company does its receivables constitute a higher percentage of its total current assets?

Decision Case 4-2 Reading and Interpreting Nordstrom's Notes— Revenue Recognition   LO3

The following excerpt is taken from Note 1 on page 43 of **Nordstrom** 's 2010 10K (amounts are in millions of dollars):

Net Sales

We recognize revenue from sales at our retail stores at the point of sale, net of estimated returns and excluding sales taxes. Revenue from our sales to customers shipped directly from our stores and our online and catalog sales includes shipping revenue, when applicable, and is recognized upon estimated receipt by the customer. We estimate customer merchandise returns based on historical return patterns and reduce sales and cost of sales accordingly.

The following excerpt on page 45 is from the same note:

Gift Cards

We recognize revenue from the sale of gift cards when the gift card is redeemed by the customer, or we recognize breakage income when the likelihood of redemption, based on historical experience, is deemed to be remote.

(Continued)

Required

1. According to the note, when does Nordstrom recognize revenue from sales in its retail stores? How does this differ from the way the company recognizes revenue from sales to customers shipped directly from its stores, its catalog, and online sales? Why would the way in which revenue is recognized from these three types of sales differ?
2. According to the note, how does Nordstrom recognize revenue associated with its gift cards? Assume that you buy a gift card for a friend. Identify and analyze the transaction Nordstrom records at the time you buy the card? Identify and analyze the adjustment Nordstrom records when your friend redeems the card?

LO3 Decision Case 4-3 Reading and Interpreting Sears Holdings Corporation's Notes—Revenue Recognition

The following excerpt is taken from page 59 of the **Sears Holdings Corporation** (parent company of Kmart and Sears) 2010 annual report: "Revenues from the sale of service contracts and the related direct acquisition costs are deferred and amortized over the lives of the associated contracts, while the associated service costs are expensed as incurred."

Required

1. Assume that you buy a wide-screen television from Sears for $2,500, including a $180 service contract that will cover three years. Why does Sears recognize the revenue associated with the service contract over its life even though cash is received at the time of the sale?
2. How much revenue will Sears recognize from your purchase of the television and the service contract in Years 1, 2, and 3? (Assume a straight-line approach.) What corresponding account can you look for in the financial statements to determine the amount of service contract revenue that will be recognized in the future?

Making Financial Decisions

LO2 • 3 • 4 Decision Case 4-4 The Use of Net Income and Cash Flow to Evaluate a Company

After you have gained five years of experience with a large CPA firm, one of your clients, Duke Inc., asks you to take over as chief financial officer for the business. Duke advises its clients on the purchase of software products and assists them in installing the programs on their computer systems. Because the business is relatively new (it began servicing clients in January 2012), its accounting records are somewhat limited. In fact, the only statement available is the following income statement for the first year:

Duke Inc.
Statement of Income
For the Year Ended December 31, 2012

Revenues		$1,250,000
Expenses:		
Salaries and wages	$480,000	
Supplies	65,000	
Utilities	30,000	
Rent	120,000	
Depreciation	345,000	
Interest	138,000	
Total expenses		1,178,000
Net income		$ 72,000

Based on its relatively modest profit margin of 5.76% (net income of $72,000 divided by revenues of $1,250,000), you are concerned about joining the new business. To alleviate your concerns, the president of the company is able to give you the following additional information:

a. Clients are given 90 days to pay their bills for consulting services provided by Duke. On December 31, 2012, $230,000 of the revenues is yet to be collected in cash.

b. Employees are paid on a monthly basis. Salaries and wages of $480,000 include the December payroll of $40,000, which will be paid on January 5, 2013.

c. The company purchased $100,000 of operating supplies when it began operations in January. The balance of supplies on hand at December 31 amounts to $35,000.

d. Office space is rented in a downtown high-rise building at a monthly cost of $10,000. When the company moved into the office in January, it prepaid its rent for the next 18 months beginning January 1, 2012.

e. On January 1, 2012, Duke purchased a computer system and related accessories at a cost of $1,725,000. The estimated useful life of the system is five years.

f. The computer system was purchased by signing a three-year, 8% note payable for $1,725,000 on the date of purchase. The principal amount of the note and interest for the three years are due on January 1, 2015.

Required

1. Based on the income statement and the additional information given, prepare a statement of cash flows for Duke for 2012. (*Hint:* Simply list all of the cash inflows and outflows that relate to operations.)

2. On the basis of the income statement given and the statement of cash flows prepared in part (1), do you think it would be a wise decision to join the company as its chief financial officer? Include in your response any additional questions that you believe are appropriate to ask before joining the company.

Decision Case 4-5 Depreciation

LO4

Jenner Inc., a graphic arts studio, is considering the purchase of computer equipment and software for a total cost of $18,000. Jenner can pay for the equipment and software over three years at the rate of $6,000 per year. The equipment is expected to last 10 to 20 years, but because of changing technology, Jenner believes it may need to replace the system in as soon as three to five years. A three-year lease of similar equipment and software is available for $6,000 per year. Jenner's accountant has asked you to recommend whether the company should purchase or lease the equipment and software and to suggest the length of time over which to depreciate the software and equipment if the company makes the purchase.

Required

Ignoring the effect of taxes, would you recommend the purchase or the lease? Why or why not? Referring to the definition of *depreciation,* what appropriate useful life should be used for the equipment and software?

Ethical Decision Making

Decision Case 4-6 Revenue Recognition and the Matching Principle

LO2 • 3 • 4 • 5

Listum & Sellum Inc. is a medium-sized midwestern real estate company. It was founded five years ago by its two principal stockholders, Willie Listum and Dewey Sellum. Willie is president of the company, and Dewey is vice president of sales. Listum & Sellum has enjoyed tremendous growth since its inception by aggressively seeking out listings for residential real estate and paying a generous commission to the selling agent.

The company receives a 6% commission for selling a client's property and gives two-thirds of this, or 4% of the selling price, to the selling agent. For example, if a house sells for $100,000, Listum & Sellum receives $6,000 and pays $4,000 of this to the selling agent. At the time of the sale, the company records increases in Accounts Receivable and Sales Revenue of $6,000 each. The accounts receivable is normally collected within 30 days. Also at the time of sale, the company records increases in Commissions Expense and Commissions Payable of $4,000 each. Sales agents are paid by the 15th of the month following the month of the sale. In addition to the commissions expense, Listum & Sellum's other two major expenses are advertising of listings in local newspapers and depreciation of the company's fleet of Cadillacs. (Dewey believes that all of

(Continued)

the sales agents should drive Cadillacs.) The newspaper ads will run for one month, and the company has until the 10th of the following month to pay that month's bill. The automobiles are depreciated over four years. (Dewey doesn't believe that any salesperson should drive a car that is more than four years old.)

Due to a downturn in the economy in the Midwest, sales have been sluggish for the first 11 months of the current year, which ends on June 30. Willie is very disturbed by the slow sales this particular year because a large note payable to the local bank is due in July and the company plans to ask the bank to renew the note for another three years. Dewey seems less concerned by the unfortunate timing of the recession and has some suggestions as to how he and Willie can "paint the rosiest possible picture for the banker" when they go for the loan extension in July. In fact, Dewey has some very specific recommendations for you as to how to account for transactions during June, the last month in the fiscal year.

You are the controller for Listum & Sellum and have been treated very well by Willie and Dewey since joining the company two years ago. In fact, Dewey insists that you drive the top-of-the-line Cadillac. Following are his suggestions:

First, for any sales made in June, we can record the 6% commission revenue immediately but delay recording the 4% commission expense until July, when the sales agent is paid. We record the sales at the same time we always have, the sales agents get paid when they always have, the bank sees how profitable we have been, we get our loan, and everybody is happy!

Second, since we won't be paying our advertising bills for the month of June until July 10, we can wait until then to record the expense. The timing seems perfect since we are meeting with the bank for the loan extension on July 8.

Third, since we will be depreciating the fleet of "Caddys" for the year ending June 30, how about changing the estimated useful life on them to eight years instead of four years? We won't say anything to the sales agents; no need to rile them up about having to drive their cars for eight years. Anyhow, the change to eight years would just be for accounting purposes. In fact, we could even switch back to four years for accounting purposes next year. Likewise, the changes in recognizing commission expense and advertising expense don't need to be permanent either; these are just slight bookkeeping changes to help us get over the hump!

Required

1. Explain why each of the three proposed changes in accounting will result in an increase in net income for the year ending June 30.
2. Identify any concerns you have with each of the three proposed changes in accounting from the perspective of GAAP. If these changes are made, do the financial statements faithfully represent what they claim to represent? Are these changes merely bookkeeping changes? Explain your answer.
3. From an ethical perspective, identify any concerns you have with each of the three proposed changes in accounting. Do the proposed changes provide information that is free from bias? Explain your answer.
4. Does the controller benefit by making the proposed changes? Are outsiders harmed? Explain your answers in the form of a memo written to the two owners.

LO4   Decision Case 4-7   Advice to a Potential Investor

Century Company was organized 15 months ago as a management consulting firm. At that time, the owners invested a total of $50,000 cash in exchange for stock. Century purchased equipment for $35,000 cash and supplies to be used in the business. The equipment is expected to last seven years with no salvage value. Supplies are purchased on account and paid for in the month after the purchase. Century normally has about $1,000 of supplies on hand. Its client base has increased so dramatically that the president and chief financial officer have approached an investor to provide additional cash for expansion. The balance sheet and income statement for the first year of business are as follows:

Century Company
Balance Sheet
December 31, 2012

Assets		Liabilities and Stockholders' Equity	
Cash	$10,100	Accounts payable	$ 2,300
Accounts receivable	1,200	Common stock	50,000
Supplies	16,500	Retained earnings	10,500
Equipment	35,000		
Total	$62,800	Total	$62,800

Century Company
Income Statement
For the Year Ended December 31, 2012

Revenues		$82,500
Wages and salaries	$60,000	
Utilities	12,000	72,000
Net income		$10,500

Required

The investor has asked you to look at these financial statements and give an opinion about Century's future profitability. Are the statements prepared in accordance with GAAP? Why or why not? Based on these two statements, what would you advise? What additional information would you need to give an educated opinion?

SOLUTIONS TO KEY TERMS QUIZ

15	Recognition	10	Deferral
22	Historical cost	16	Deferred expense
8	Current value	5	Deferred revenue
18	Cash basis	12	Accrual
11	Accrual basis	19	Accrued liability
2	Revenues	7	Accrued asset
14	Revenue recognition principle	24	Accounting cycle
20	Matching principle	1	Work sheet
23	Expenses	6	Real accounts
3	Adjusting entries	17	Nominal accounts
2	Straight-line method	4	Closing entries
21	Contra account	13	Interim statements

INTEGRATIVE PROBLEM

Completing Financial Statements, Computing Ratios, Comparing Accrual versus Cash Income, and Evaluating the Company's Cash Needs

Mountain Home Health Inc. provides home nursing services in the Great Smoky Mountains of Tennessee. When contacted by a client or referred by a physician, nurses visit the patient and discuss needed services with the physician.

Mountain Home Health earns revenue from patient services. Most of the revenue comes from billing insurance companies, the state of Tennessee, or the Medicare program. Amounts billed are recorded in the Billings Receivable account. Insurance companies, the state

(Continued)

government, and the federal government do not fully fund all procedures. For example, the state of Tennessee pays an average 78% of billed amounts. Mountain Home Health has already removed the uncollectible amounts from the Billings Receivable account and reports it and Medical Services Revenue at the net amount. Services provided but not yet recorded totaled $16,000, net of allowances for uncollectible amounts. The firm earns a minor portion of its total revenue directly from patients in the form of cash.

Employee salaries, medical supplies, depreciation, and gasoline are the major expenses. Employees are paid every Friday for work performed during the Saturday-to-Friday pay period. Salaries amount to $800 per day. In 2012, December 31 falls on a Monday. Medical supplies (average use of $1,500 per week) are purchased periodically to support healthcare coverage. The inventory of supplies on hand on December 31 amounted to $8,653.

The firm owns five automobiles (all purchased at the same time) that average 50,000 miles per year and are replaced every three years. They typically have no residual value. The building has an expected life of 20 years with no residual value. Straight-line depreciation is used on all of the firm's assets. Gasoline costs, which are a cash expenditure, average $375 per day. The firm purchases a three-year extended warranty contract to cover maintenance costs. The contract costs $9,000. (Assume equal use each year.)

On December 29, 2012, Mountain Home Health declared a dividend of $10,000, payable on January 15, 2013. The firm makes annual mortgage payments of principal and interest each June 30. The interest rate on the mortgage is 6%.

The following account balances are available for Mountain Home Health on December 31, 2012:

Cash	$ 77,400
Billings Receivable (net)	151,000
Medical Supplies	73,000
Extended Warranty	3,000
Automobiles	90,000
Accumulated Depreciation—Automobiles	60,000
Building	200,000
Accumulated Depreciation—Building	50,000
Accounts Payable	22,000
Dividend Payable	10,000
Mortgage Payable	100,000
Capital Stock	100,000
Additional Paid-In Capital	50,000
Retained Earnings	99,900
Medical Services Revenue	550,000
Salary and Wages Expense	288,000
Gasoline Expense	137,500
Utilities Expense	12,000
Dividends	10,000

Required

1. Identify and analyze the necessary adjustments on December 31, 2012.
2. Prepare a statement of income and a statement of retained earnings for Mountain Home Health for the year ended December 31, 2012.
3. Prepare a balance sheet for Mountain Home Health as of December 31, 2012.
4. Compute the following as of December 31, 2012: (a) working capital and (b) current ratio.
5. Which of the adjustments could cause a difference between cash- and accrual-based income?
6. Mary Francis, controller of Mountain Home, became concerned about the company's cash flow after talking to a local bank loan officer. The firm tries to maintain a seven-week supply of cash to meet the demands of payroll, medical supply purchases, and gasoline. Determine the amount of cash Mountain Home needs to meet the seven-week supply.

ANSWERS TO POD REVIEW

LO1	1. b	2. a		**LO4**	1. b	2. c
LO2	1. c	2. b		**LO5**	1. a	2. c
LO3	1. a	2. d		**LO6**	1. c	2. a

Inventories and Cost of Goods Sold

5

AFTER STUDYING THIS CHAPTER, YOU SHOULD BE ABLE TO:

LO1 Identify the forms of inventory held by different types of businesses and the types of costs incurred.

LO2 Show that you understand how wholesalers and retailers account for sales of merchandise.

LO3 Show that you understand how wholesalers and retailers account for cost of goods sold.

LO4 Use the gross profit ratio to analyze a company's ability to cover its operating expenses and earn a profit.

LO5 Explain the relationship between the valuation of inventory and the measurement of income.

LO6 Apply the inventory costing methods of specific identification, weighted average, FIFO, and LIFO by using a periodic system.

LO7 Analyze the effects of the different costing methods on inventory, net income, income taxes, and cash flow.

LO8 Analyze the effects of an inventory error on various financial statement items.

LO9 Apply the lower-of-cost-or-market rule to the valuation of inventory.

LO10 Analyze the management of inventory.

LO11 Explain the effects that inventory transactions have on the statement of cash flows.

LO12 Explain the differences in the accounting for periodic and perpetual inventory systems and apply the inventory costing methods using a perpetual system (Appendix).

STUDY LINKS

A Look at the Previous Chapter Chapter 4 completed our introduction to the accounting model. That chapter examined the role of adjustments in an accrual accounting system.

A Look at This Chapter Starting in this chapter, we move beyond the basic accounting model to consider the accounting for the various elements in the financial statements. We start by looking at how companies that sell a product account for their inventories and the eventual sale of them.

A Look at the Upcoming Chapter Each of the remaining chapters in this section of the book examines other assets of a company. Chapter 6 considers the most liquid of all assets, cash, and looks at the ways in which companies maintain control over it and other valuable assets.

MAKING BUSINESS DECISIONS
GAP INC.

Billing itself as one of the world's largest specialty retailers, **Gap Inc.** had its humble beginning when Doris and Don Fisher opened their first store in San Francisco in 1969. From that single store, the company has grown to operate over 3,200 stores worldwide and to generate revenue that exceeded $14.6 billion in fiscal 2010. It counts among its brands some of the most recognizable in the world of apparel: Gap®, Banana Republic®, Old Navy®, Athleta®, and Piperlime®.

As a retailer, Gap Inc. measures success in terms of what it earns from buying and selling jeans and other clothing apparel. The statements of income shown on the next page provide an accounting of the company's success in this regard. Net sales have ranged from a high of $14.7 billion in 2010 to a low of $14.2 billion in 2009. As is evident from the income statements, the cost that a retailer pays for the merchandise that it sells is the most important factor in determining whether the company is profitable. For Gap Inc., "Cost of goods sold and occupancy expenses" amounted to $9.1 billion in 2008, but even with an increase in sales in 2010, this major cost dropped to $8.8 billion. One of the biggest challenges a retailer faces is controlling the cost of its inventory while at the same time ensuring the quality of its merchandise.

Besides being important for retailers to control the cost of what they sell, it is also imperative that they minimize the amount of stock they carry at any one time. The cost of carrying inventory, including storage and insurance, can be significant. Gap Inc. must minimize the amount of inventory on hand, but at the same time make sure it has enough merchandise to meet customers' demands. The significance of inventory as an asset to Gap Inc. is indicated by the partial balance sheet shown on the next page.

Why do you need to study this chapter?

Inventory is the lifeblood of any company that sells a product, including Gap Inc.

- You need to know how a company keeps track of the cost of its inventory. (See pp. 227–229.)
- You need to know how the relationship between the company's sales and the cost of those sales can be used to help assess the company's performance. (See pp. 233–235.)
- You need to know how inventory methods assign costs to the products sold. (See pp. 237–242.)
- You need to know how the relationship between sales on the income statement and inventory on the balance sheet can be used to assess how well a company is managing its inventory. (See pp. 253–255.)

The Gap, Inc.
Consolidated Statements of Income

($ and shares in millions except per share amounts)	Fiscal Year		
	2010	2009	2008
Net sales	$14,664	$14,197	$14,526
Cost of goods sold and occupancy expenses	8,775	8,473	9,079
Gross profit	5,889	5,724	5,447
Operating expenses	3,921	3,909	3,889
Operating income	1,968	1,815	1,548
Interest expense (reversal)	(8)	6	1
Interest income	(6)	(7)	(37)
Interest before income taxes	1,982	1,816	1,584
Income taxes	778	714	617
Net income	$ 1,204	$ 1,102	$ 967
Weighted-average number of shares—basic	636	694	716
Weighted-average number of shares—diluted	641	699	719
Earnings per share—basic	$ 1.89	$ 1.59	$ 1.35
Earnings per share—diluted	$ 1.88	$ 1.58	$ 1.34
Cash dividends declared and paid per share	$ 0.40	$ 0.34	$ 0.34

> Net Sales increased by 3.3% in 2010.

> And the cost of the products sold increased proportionately, by 3.6%

See Accompanying Notes to Consolidated Financial Statements

The Gap, Inc.
Consolidated Balance Sheets (Partial)

($ and shares in millions except par value)	January 29, 2011	January 30, 2010
Assets		
Current assets:		
Cash and cash equivalents	$1,561	$2,348
Short-term investments	100	255
Merchandise inventory	1,620	1,477
Other current assets	645	614
Total current assets	3,926	4,664

> The company's inventory on hand increased during the year and represents over 40% of the current assets.

See Accompanying Notes to Consolidated Financial Statements

Source: Gap Inc. Form 10-K for 2010.

The Nature of Inventory

LO1 Identify the forms of inventory held by different types of businesses and the types of costs incurred.

OVERVIEW:

1. There are two types of inventory held by businesses: finished inventory, held by retailers and wholesalers, and materials inventory, held by manufacturers.
2. There are three types of inventory costs borne by manufacturers: direct materials, direct labor, and manufacturing overhead.
3. There are three distinct forms of inventory for a manufacturer: raw materials, work in process, and finished goods.

SPOTLIGHT
Inventories and Cost of Goods Sold

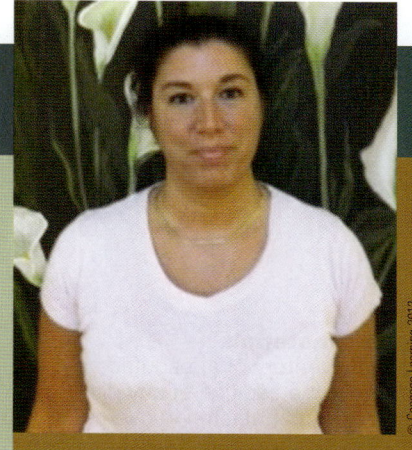

In the retail automotive industry, inventory control is very important to the success of a company. **Wendy Rosasco** is a margin control specialist for the very successful Pep Boys. Pep Boys is a multi-billion dollar nationwide retail and service chain with over 700 stores across the United States and Puerto Rico. With a company this size, inventory valuation standards are critical to success.

According to Wendy, there are several levels of inventory control for each store in the chain. Each week a store must conduct an out-of-stock audit. When a shelf or merchandise hook is empty, an associate, using an inventory hand-held unit, will scan the price label and verify the item is out of stock. In addition, once a week the store manager will run an audit variance detail report for all items that have a +/− $100 variance. This allows each store to identify possible inventory mistakes from audits completed during the prior week.

And finally, each fiscal year, through a rotating corporate schedule, every store is inventoried by an outside company that works with the store team to complete a full inventory of all merchandise assets.

Wendy explains that accounting adjustments are made when a particular category is no longer being purchased from the same vendor, since this may present a change in cost. For example, if Pep Boys changes the vendor who supplies the company with batteries, there may be a change in cost, based on the new purchase agreement.

Wendy stresses that timely inventory information is important for Pep Boys' category managers, analysts, and buyers who work closely with vendors and warehouses to ensure they have enough merchandise to fill store needs.

> ❝ **The value of inventory is important when assessing a category line change when using a different vendor.** ❞

Name: Wendy Rosasco

Education: B.S., concentration in Business Marketing, Goldey-Beacom College

College Major: Business Administration

Occupation: Automotive Retail Asset Protection

Age: 36

Position: Margin Control Specialist

Company Name: Pep Boys

See Wendy Rosasco's interview clip in CNOW.

This chapter discusses accounting by companies that sell products, or what accountants call inventory. Companies that sell inventory can be broadly categorized into two types:

- **Retailers and wholesalers purchase inventory in finished form and hold it for resale.** For example, as a retailer, **Gap Inc.** buys clothes directly from other companies and then offers them for sale to consumers.
- **Manufacturers transform raw materials into a finished product prior to sale.** A good example of a manufacturing company is **IBM**. It buys all of the various materials that are needed to make computers and then sells the finished product to its customers.

Whether a company is a wholesaler, retailer, or manufacturer, its inventory is an asset that is held for *resale* in the normal course of business. The distinction between inventory and an operating asset is the *intent* of the owner. For example, some of the computers that IBM owns are operating assets because they are used in various activities of the business, such as the payroll and accounting functions. Many more of the computers IBM owns are inventory, however, because the company makes them and intends to sell them. This chapter is concerned with the proper valuation of inventory and the related effect on cost of goods sold.

Types of Inventory Cost and Forms of Inventory

It is important to distinguish between the *types* of inventory costs incurred and the *form* the inventory takes. Wholesalers and retailers incur a single type of cost, the *purchase price*, of the inventory they sell. On the balance sheet, they use a single account for inventory, titled **Merchandise Inventory**. Wholesalers and retailers buy merchandise in finished form and offer it for resale without transforming the product in any way.

Merchandise Inventory
The account wholesalers and retailers use to report inventory held for resale.

Merchandise companies typically have a relatively large dollar amount in inventory. For example, on its January 29, 2011, balance sheet, Gap Inc. reported merchandise inventory of $1,620 million and total assets of $7,065 million. It is not unusual for inventories to account for half the total assets of a merchandise company.

Three Types of Manufacturing Costs The cost of inventory to a *merchandiser* is limited to the product's purchase price, which may include other costs mentioned soon. Conversely, three distinct *types* of costs are incurred by a *manufacturer*—direct materials, direct labor, and manufacturing overhead. Each is explained here.

Raw materials
The inventory of a manufacturer before the addition of any direct labor or manufacturing overhead.

Alternate term: Direct materials.

1. *Direct materials*, also called **raw materials**, are the ingredients used in making a product. The costs of direct materials used in making a pair of shoes include the *costs* of fabric, plastic, and rubber.
2. *Direct labor* consists of the amounts paid to workers to manufacture the product. The hourly wage paid to an assembly line worker is a primary ingredient in the cost to make the shoes.
3. *Manufacturing overhead* includes all other costs that are related to the manufacturing process but cannot be directly matched to specific units of output. Depreciation of a factory building and the salary of a supervisor are two examples of overhead costs. Accountants have developed various techniques to assign, or allocate, these manufacturing overhead costs to specific products.

Three Forms of Inventory for a Manufacturer In addition to the three types of costs incurred in a production process, the inventory of a manufacturer takes three distinct *forms*.

1. Direct materials or raw materials enter a production process in which they are transformed into a finished product by the addition of direct labor and manufacturing overhead.
2. At any time, including the end of an accounting period, some of the materials have entered the process and some labor costs have been incurred but the product is not finished. The cost of unfinished products is appropriately called **work in process** or *work in progress*.

Work in process
The cost of unfinished products in a manufacturing company.

Alternate term: Work in progress.

3. Inventory that has completed the production process and is available for sale is called **finished goods**. Finished goods are the equivalent of merchandise inventory for a retailer or wholesaler in that both represent the inventory of goods held for sale.

Finished goods
A manufacturer's inventory that is complete and ready for sale.

Many manufacturers disclose the dollar amounts of the various forms of inventory in their annual report. For example, IBM disclosed on page 90 of its 2010 annual report the following amounts, stated in millions of dollars:

Inventories: at December 31	Millions
Finished goods	$ 432
Work in process and raw materials	2,018
Total	$2,450

As you can see, finished goods make up less than 18% of IBM's total inventories. However, this may not be the case for other types of businesses, where finished goods are more significant. For example, consider the following excerpt from Note 7 of **Caterpillar Inc.**'s 2010 annual report:

December 31	(In millions)
Raw materials	$2,766
Work-in-process	1,483
Finished goods	5,098
Supplies	240
Total inventories	$9,587

As a company that makes construction machinery and other related products, Caterpillar has over one-half of its inventory in finished products.

Exhibit 5-1 summarizes the relationships between the types of costs incurred and the forms of inventory for different types of businesses.

EXHIBIT 5-1 Relationships between Types of Businesses and Inventory Costs

Type of Company	Activities	Assets on Balance Sheet	Income Statement When Inventory Is Sold
Retailer/ Wholesaler	Buys finished products →	Merchandise inventory →	Cost of goods sold
Manufacturer	Buys raw materials and then adds: → Direct labor Overhead	Raw materials Work in process Finished goods →	Cost of goods sold

© Cengage Learning 2013

LO1 Identify the forms of inventory held by different types of businesses and the types of costs incurred.

- Inventory is a current asset held for resale in the normal course of business. The nature of inventory held depends on whether a business is a reseller of goods (wholesaler or retailer) or a manufacturer.
  - Resellers incur a single cost to purchase inventory held for sale.
  - Manufacturers incur costs that can be classified as raw materials, direct labor, and manufacturing overhead.

POD REVIEW 5.1

QUESTIONS   Answers to these questions are on the last page of the chapter.

1. The inventory of a retailer is limited to a single type of cost, the purchase price of the inventory it sells. The three distinct types of cost to a manufacturer are
   a. direct materials, direct labor, and work in process.
   b. direct materials, direct labor, and manufacturing overhead.
   c. direct labor, manufacturing overhead, and finished goods.
   d. none of the above.

2. The three forms or states in the development of inventory for a manufacturer are
   a. direct materials, direct labor, and finished goods.
   b. direct materials, direct labor, and manufacturing overhead.
   c. direct materials, work in process, and finished goods.
   d. none of the above.

© Cengage Learning 2013

Net Sales of Merchandise

OVERVIEW: Net sales represents sales less deductions for discounts and merchandise returned (returns and allowances) and is a key figure on the income statement.

LO2 Show that you understand how wholesalers and retailers account for sales of merchandise.

A *condensed* multiple-step income statement for Daisy's Running Depot is presented in Exhibit 5-2. First, note the period covered by the statement: for the year ended December 31, 2012. Daisy's ends its fiscal year on December 31; however, many merchandisers end their fiscal year on a date other than December 31. Retailers often choose a date toward the end of January because the busy holiday shopping season is over and time can be devoted to closing the records and preparing financial statements. For example, Gap Inc. ends its fiscal year on the Saturday closest to the end of January.

We will concentrate on the first two items on Daisy's statement: net sales and cost of goods sold. The major difference between this income statement and one for a service company is the inclusion of cost of goods sold. Because a service company does not sell a product, it does not report cost of goods sold. On the income statement of a merchandising company, cost of goods sold is deducted from net sales to arrive at **gross profit**, or gross margin.

Gross profit
Net sales less cost of goods sold.
Alternate term: Gross margin.

EXHIBIT 5-2 Condensed Income Statement for a Merchandiser

Daisy's Running Depot Income Statement For the Year Ended December 31, 2012	
Net sales	$100,000
Cost of goods sold	60,000
Gross profit	$ 40,000
Selling and administrative expenses	29,300
Net income before tax	$ 10,700
Income tax expense	4,280
Net income	$ 6,420

© Cengage Learning 2013

Net sales
Sales revenue less sales returns and allowances and sales discounts.

Sales revenue
A representation of the inflow of assets.
Alternate term: Sales.

Sales Returns and Allowances
Contra-revenue account used to record refunds to customers and reductions of their accounts.

STUDY TIP

Recall Accumulated Depreciation, a contra account introduced in Chapter 4. It reduces a long-term asset. In other cases, such as this one involving sales, a contra account reduces an income statement account.

© Cengage Learning 2013

The first section of Daisy's income statement is presented in Exhibit 5-3. Two deductions—for sales returns and allowances and sales discounts—are made from sales revenue to arrive at **net sales**. **Sales revenue**, or sales, is a *representation of the inflow of assets,* either cash or accounts receivable, from the sale of a product during the period.

Sales Returns and Allowances

The cornerstone of marketing is to satisfy the customer. Most companies have standard policies that allow the customer to return merchandise within a stipulated period of time. **Nordstrom**, the Seattle-based retailer, has a very liberal policy regarding returns. That policy has, in large measure, fueled its growth. A company's policy might be that a customer who is not completely satisfied can return the merchandise anytime within 30 days of purchase for a full refund. Alternatively, the customer may be given an *allowance* for spoiled or damaged merchandise—that is, the customer keeps the merchandise but receives a credit for a certain amount in the account balance. Typically, a single account, **Sales Returns and Allowances**, is used to account for both returns and allowances. If the customer has already paid for the merchandise, either a cash refund is given or the credit amount is applied to future purchases.

Credit Terms and Sales Discounts

Most companies have a standard credit policy. Special notation is normally used to indicate a particular firm's policy for granting credit. For example, credit terms of n/30 mean that the net amount of the selling price (i.e., the amount determined after deducting any returns or allowances) is due within 30 days of the date of the invoice. Net, 10 EOM means that the net amount is due anytime within ten days after the end of the month in which the sale took place.

Another common element of the credit terms offered to customers is sales discounts, a reduction from the selling price given for early payment. Assume that Daisy's offers a customer credit terms of 1/10, n/30. This means that the customer can deduct 1% from the selling price if the bill is paid within ten days of the date of the invoice. Normally, the discount period begins the day *after* the invoice date. If the customer does not pay within the first ten days, the full invoice amount is due within 30 days. Finally, note that the use of *n* for *net* in this notation is a misnomer. Although the amount due is net of

EXHIBIT 5-3 Net Sales Section of the Income Statement

Daisy's Running Depot Partial Income Statement For the Year Ended December 31, 2012		
Sales revenue	$103,500	
Less: Sales returns and allowances	2,000	
Sales discounts	1,500	
Net sales		$100,000

© Cengage Learning 2013

any returns and allowances, it is the *gross* amount that is due within 30 days. That is, no discount is given if the customer does not pay early.

Example 5-1 Determining Whether to Take a Discount

Assume a $1,000 sale with a 1% discount for payment within the first ten days with the full amount due within 30 days. Should a customer take advantage of this discount?

If customer pays at end of ten days: $1,000 − 0.01($1,000) = $990

So, $1,000 − $990, or $10, was saved by paying 20 days early.

Number of periods of 20 days in a year: 360/20 = 18

Equivalent savings in a year: 18 × $10 = $180

Rate of return: $180/$990 = 18.2%

Conclusion: The customer should pay in the first ten days unless another investment can be found offering a return in excess of 18.2%.

The **Sales Discounts** account is a contra-revenue account and thus reduces sales as shown on the partial income statement in Exhibit 5-3.

© Cengage Learning 2013

Sales Discounts
A contra-revenue account used to record discounts given to customers for early payment of their accounts.

HOT TOPICS
Looking Outside the United States for Opportunities

Richard Levine/Alamy

With the downturn in the economy, where does a U.S. retailer turn to boost its sales? In late 2010, Gap Inc. opened its first Gap and Banana Republic stores in Italy, as well as four stores in China, the most populous country in the world. The popular retailer's theme for the opening of two stores in Shanghai and another two in Beijing was "Let's Gap Together." Each store offers the full line of Gap collections, including Gap®, GapKids®, babyGap®, and GapBody®. At the same time, the San Francisco-based retailer launched an online retail store in China, www.gap.cn.

It will be years before Gap can fully assess its decisions to expand into Italy and China. However, the early results are encouraging. In April 2011, the company announced that since their openings, the new stores in these two countries have been among the company's top 10% performing stores in the world. In fact, the retailer planned to open ten new stores in China and Italy in the year ahead. Stockholders, analysts, and competitors in the retail sector will be watching closely over the next few years to see if Gap's strategy to look outside the United States for growth opportunities will pay off.

Source: Gap Inc. news releases: November 11, 2010, November 19, 2010, and April 19, 2011.

LO2 Show that you understand how wholesalers and retailers account for sales of merchandise.

- Net sales represents sales less deductions for discounts and merchandise returned (returns and allowances) and is a key figure on the income statement.
  - Sales discounts are given to customers who pay their bills promptly.
  - Returns and allowances have the same effect on sales that sales discounts do; that is, they reduce sales.

POD REVIEW 5.2

QUESTIONS Answers to these questions are on the last page of the chapter.

1. Net sales is equal to
   a. sales revenue less sales returns and allowances and sales discounts.
   b. sales revenue less cost of goods sold.
   c. sales revenue less selling and administrative expenses.
   d. none of the above.

2. What type of account is Sales Discounts?
   a. contra-asset
   b. revenue
   c. contra-revenue
   d. expense

© Cengage Learning 2013

Cost of Goods Sold

LO3 Show that you understand how wholesalers and retailers account for cost of goods sold.

OVERVIEW: Cost of goods sold is deducted from sales to determine the gross profit for the period. Cost of goods sold is found by adding the purchases of the period to the beginning inventory and then deducting the ending inventory.

The Cost of Goods Sold section of the income statement for Daisy's is shown in Exhibit 5-4. Let's take a look at the basic model for cost of goods sold.

The Cost of Goods Sold Model

The recognition of cost of goods sold as an expense is an excellent example of the *matching principle*. Sales revenue represents the *inflow* of assets, in the form of cash and accounts receivable, from the sale of products during the period. Likewise, cost of goods sold represents the *outflow* of an asset, inventory, from the sale of those same products. The company needs to match the revenue of the period with one of the most important costs necessary to generate the revenue, the cost of the merchandise sold.

It may be helpful in understanding cost of goods sold to realize what it is not. *Cost of goods sold is not necessarily equal to the cost of purchases of merchandise during the period*. Except in the case of a new business, a merchandiser starts the year with a certain stock of inventory on hand, called *beginning inventory*. For Daisy's, beginning inventory is the dollar cost of merchandise on hand on January 1, 2012. During the year, Daisy's purchases merchandise. When the cost of goods purchased is added to beginning inventory, the result is **cost of goods available for sale**. Just as the merchandiser starts the period with an inventory of merchandise on hand, a certain amount of ending inventory is usually on hand at the end of the year. For Daisy's, this is its inventory on December 31, 2012.

Cost of goods available for sale
Beginning inventory plus cost of goods purchased.

As shown in Exhibit 5-5, think of cost of goods available for sale as a "pool" of costs to be distributed between what was sold and what was not sold. If we subtract from the pool the cost of what did not sell, the *ending inventory*, we will have the amount that did sell, the **cost of goods sold**. Cost of goods sold is simply the difference between the cost of goods available for sale and the ending inventory.

Cost of goods sold
Cost of goods available for sale minus ending inventory.

Beginning inventory	What is on hand to start the period
+ Cost of goods purchased	What was acquired for resale during the period
= Cost of goods available for sale	The "pool" of costs to be distributed
− Ending inventory	What was not sold during the period and therefore is on hand to start the next period
= Cost of goods sold	What was sold during the period

EXHIBIT 5-4 Cost of Goods Sold Section of the Income Statement

Daisy's Running Depot Partial Income Statement For the Year Ended December 31, 2012		
Cost of goods sold:		
Inventory, January 1, 2012		$15,000
Purchases	$65,000	
Less: Purchase returns and allowances	1,800	
Purchase discounts	3,700	
Net purchases	$59,500	
Add: Transportation-in	3,500	
Cost of goods purchased		63,000
Cost of goods available for sale		$78,000
Less: Inventory, December 31, 2012		18,000
Cost of goods sold		$60,000

EXHIBIT 5-5 The Cost of Goods Sold Model

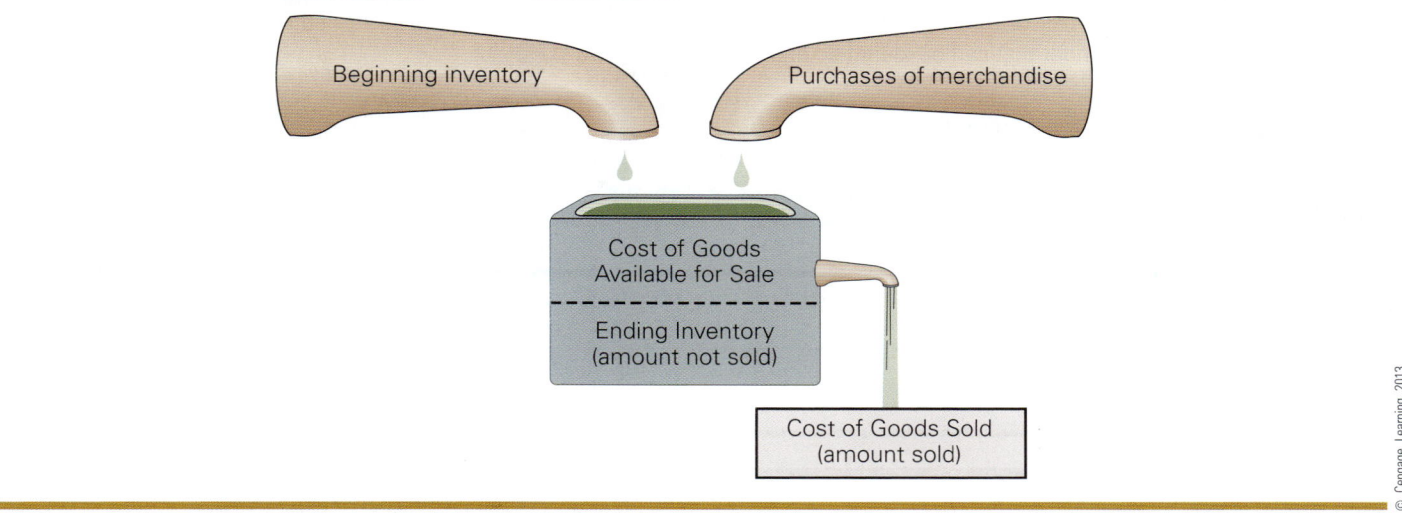

© Cengage Learning 2013

Example 5-2 Calculating Cost of Goods Sold

The amounts shown below are taken from the Cost of Goods Sold section of Daisy's income statement as shown in Exhibit 5-4.

Description	Item	Amount
Merchandise on hand to start the period	Beginning inventory	$ 15,000
Acquisitions of merchandise during the period	+ Cost of goods purchased	63,000
Pool of merchandise available for sale during the period	= Cost of goods available for sale	$ 78,000
Merchandise on hand at end of period	− Ending inventory	(18,000)
Expense recognized on the income statement	= Cost of goods sold	$ 60,000

A $3,000 excess of ending inventory over beginning inventory means that the company bought $3,000 more than it sold ($63,000 bought versus $60,000 sold).

Notice that ending inventory exceeds beginning inventory by $3,000. That means that the cost of goods purchased exceeds cost of goods sold by that same amount. Indeed, a key point for stockholders, bankers, and other users is whether inventory is building up, that is, whether a company is not selling as much inventory during the period as it is buying. A buildup may indicate that the company's products are becoming less desirable or that prices are becoming uncompetitive.

© Cengage Learning 2013

Inventory Systems: Perpetual and Periodic

Before looking more closely at the accounting for cost of goods sold, you need to understand the difference between the periodic and the perpetual inventory systems. All businesses use one of these two distinct approaches to account for inventory. With the **perpetual system**, the Inventory account is updated perpetually after each sale or purchase of merchandise. Conversely, with the **periodic system**, the Inventory account is updated only at the end of the period.

In a perpetual system, every time goods are purchased, the Inventory account is increased. When that inventory is sold, the accountant records an entry to recognize the cost of the goods sold and the decrease in the cost of inventory on hand.

Perpetual system
A system in which the Inventory account is increased at the time of each purchase and decreased at the time of each sale.

Periodic system
A system in which the Inventory account is updated only at the end of the period.

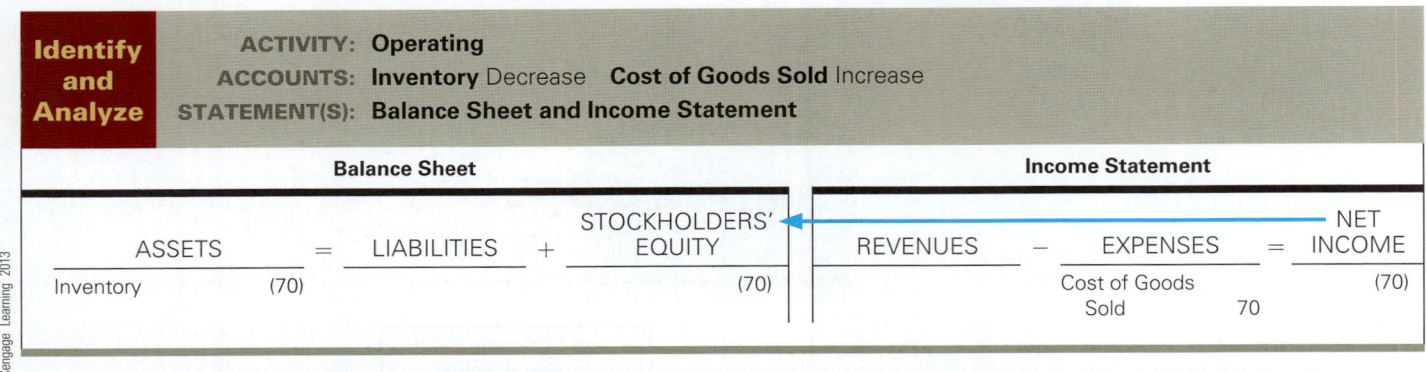

Example 5-3 Recording Cost of Goods Sold in a Perpetual System

Assume that Daisy's sells a pair of running shoes that costs the company $70. In addition to the entry to record the sale, Daisy's would also record an adjustment that can be identified and analyzed as follows:

Identify and Analyze

ACTIVITY: **Operating**
ACCOUNTS: **Inventory** Decrease   **Cost of Goods Sold** Increase
STATEMENT(S): **Balance Sheet and Income Statement**

Balance Sheet			Income Statement		
ASSETS	= LIABILITIES +	STOCKHOLDERS' EQUITY	REVENUES –	EXPENSES	= NET INCOME
Inventory (70)		(70)		Cost of Goods Sold 70	(70)

© Cengage Learning 2013

Thus, at any point during the period, the Inventory account is up to date. It has been increased for the cost of purchases during the period and reduced for the cost of the sales.

Why don't all companies use the perpetual system? Depending on the volume of inventory transactions (i.e., purchases and sales of merchandise), a perpetual system can be extremely costly to maintain. Historically, businesses with a relatively small volume of sales at a high unit price have used perpetual systems. For example, dealers in automobiles, furniture, appliances, and jewelry normally use a perpetual system. Each purchase of a unit of merchandise, such as an automobile, can be easily identified and an increase recorded in the Inventory account. For instance, when an auto is sold, the dealer can determine the cost of the particular car sold by looking at a perpetual inventory record.

To a certain extent, the ability of mass merchandisers to maintain perpetual inventory records has improved with the advent of point-of-sale terminals. When a cashier runs a can of corn over the sensing glass at the checkout stand and the bar code is read, the company's computer receives a message that a can of corn has been sold. In some companies, however, an update of the inventory record is in units only and is used as a means to determine when a product needs to be reordered. The company still relies on a periodic system to maintain the *dollar* amount of inventory. The remainder of this chapter limits its discussion to the periodic system. The perpetual system is discussed in more detail in the appendix to this chapter.

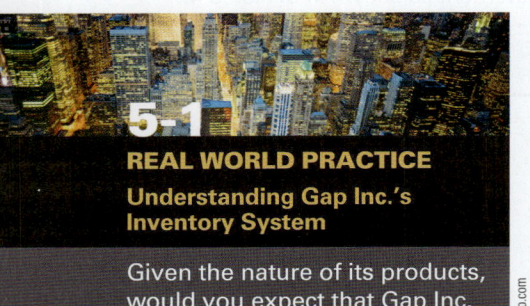

5-1

REAL WORLD PRACTICE

Understanding Gap Inc.'s Inventory System

Given the nature of its products, would you expect that Gap Inc. uses a perpetual or a periodic inventory system? Explain your answer.

© Nikada/istockphoto.com

Beginning and Ending Inventories in a Periodic System

In a periodic system, the Inventory account is *not* updated each time a sale or purchase is made. Throughout the year, the Inventory account contains the amount of merchandise on hand at the beginning of the year. The account is adjusted only at the end of the year. A company using the periodic system must physically count the units of inventory on hand at the end of the period. The number of units of each product is then multiplied by the cost per unit to determine the dollar amount of ending inventory. Refer to Exhibit 5-4 for Daisy's Running Depot. The procedure just described was used to determine its ending inventory of $18,000. Because one period's ending inventory is the next period's beginning inventory, the beginning inventory of $15,000 was based on the count at the end of the prior year.

In summary, the ending inventory in a periodic system is determined by counting the merchandise, not by looking at the Inventory account at the end of the period. The periodic system results in a trade-off. Use of the periodic system reduces record keeping, but at the expense of a certain degree of control. Losses of merchandise due to theft, breakage, spoilage, or other reasons may go undetected in a periodic system because management may assume that all merchandise not on hand at the end of the year was sold. In a retail store, some of the merchandise may have been shoplifted rather than sold. In contrast, with a perpetual inventory system, a count of inventory at the end of the period serves as a control device. For example, if the Inventory account shows a balance of $45,000 at the end of the year but only $42,000 of merchandise is counted, management is able to investigate the discrepancy. No such control feature exists in a periodic system.

In addition to the loss of control, the use of a periodic system presents a dilemma when a company wants to prepare *interim* financial statements. Because most companies that use a periodic system find it cost prohibitive to count the entire inventory more than once a year, they use estimation techniques to determine inventory for monthly or quarterly statements. These techniques are discussed later in this chapter.

Cost of Goods Purchased

The cost of goods purchased section of Daisy's income statement is shown in Exhibit 5-6. The company purchased $65,000 of merchandise during the period. Two amounts are deducted from purchases to arrive at net purchases: purchase returns and allowances of $1,800 and purchase discounts of $3,700. The cost of $3,500 incurred by Daisy's to ship the goods to its place of business is called **transportation-in** and is added to net purchases of $59,500 to arrive at the cost of goods purchased of $63,000. Another name for transportation-in is *freight-in*.

Purchases Purchases is the temporary account used in a periodic inventory system to record acquisitions of merchandise.

Transportation-In
An adjunct account used to record freight costs paid by the buyer.
Alternate term: Freight-In.

Purchases
An account used in a periodic inventory system to record acquisitions of merchandise.

Example 5-4 Recording Purchases in a Periodic System

Assume that Daisy's buys shoes on account from Nike at a cost of $4,000. The effect of this transaction is to increase liabilities and increase cost of goods sold, which is an expense. The effect of the transaction can be identified and analyzed as follows:

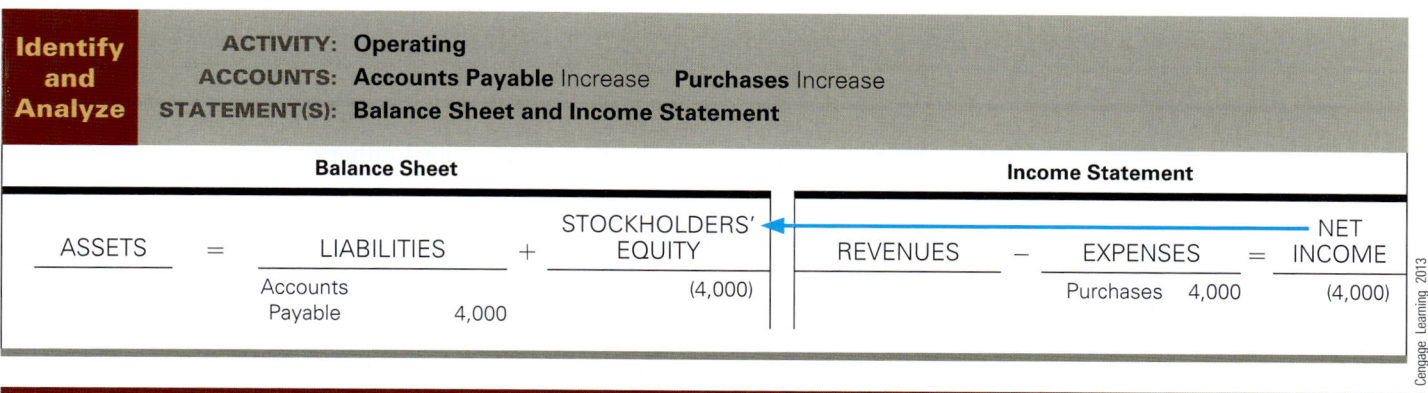

Identify and Analyze	ACTIVITY: **Operating**
	ACCOUNTS: **Accounts Payable** Increase **Purchases** Increase
	STATEMENT(S): **Balance Sheet and Income Statement**

Balance Sheet				Income Statement		
ASSETS	=	LIABILITIES	+	STOCKHOLDERS' EQUITY		
		Accounts Payable 4,000		(4,000)		

REVENUES	−	EXPENSES	=	NET INCOME
		Purchases 4,000		(4,000)

© Cengage Learning 2013

It is important to understand that Purchases is *not* an asset account. It is included in the income statement as an integral part of the calculation of cost of goods sold and is therefore shown as an increase in expenses and thus a reduction in net income and stockholders' equity in the accounting equation.

EXHIBIT 5-6 Cost of Goods Purchased

Daisy's Running Depot Partial Income Statement For the Year Ended December 31, 2012	
Purchases	$65,000
Less: Purchase returns and allowances	1,800
Purchase discounts	3,700
Net purchases	$59,500
Add: Transportation-in	3,500
Cost of goods purchased	$63,000

© Cengage Learning 2013

Purchase Returns and Allowances

A contra-purchases account used in a periodic inventory system when a refund is received from a supplier or a reduction is given in the balance owed to a supplier.

Purchase Returns and Allowances Returns and allowances were discussed earlier in the chapter from the seller's point of view. From the buyer's standpoint, purchase returns and allowances are reductions in the cost to purchase merchandise. Rather than record these reductions directly in the Purchases account, the accountant uses a separate account. The account **Purchase Returns and Allowances** is a contra account to Purchases. The use of a contra account allows management to monitor the amount of returns and allowances. For example, a large number of returns during the period relative to the amount purchased may signal that the purchasing department is not buying from reputable sources.

Example 5-5 Recording Purchase Returns in a Periodic System

Suppose that Daisy's returns $850 of merchandise to **Nike** for credit on Daisy's account. The return decreases both liabilities and purchases. Note that because a return reduces purchases, it has the effect of reducing expenses and increasing net income and stockholders' equity. The effect of the transaction can be identified and analyzed as follows:

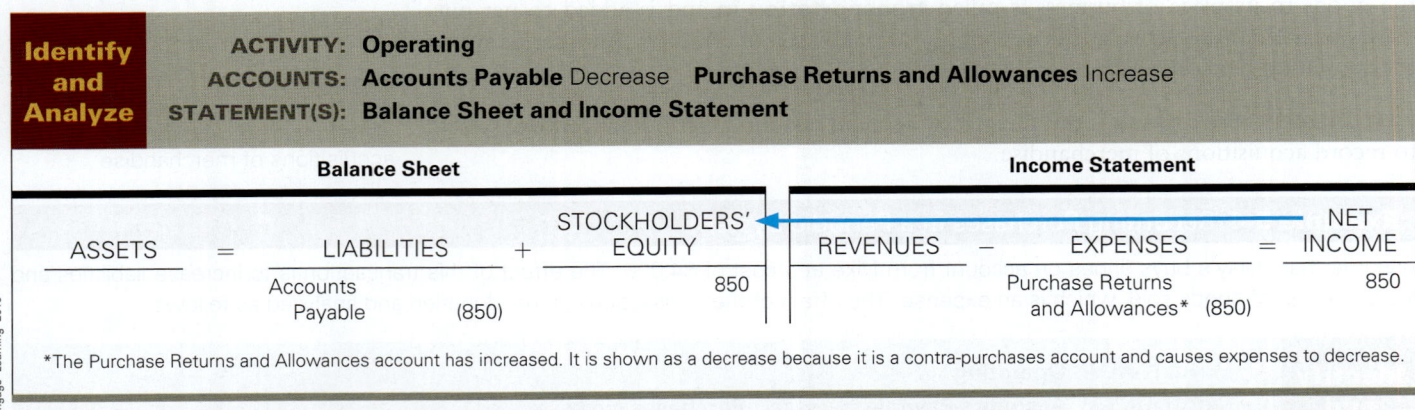

Identify and Analyze

ACTIVITY: **Operating**
ACCOUNTS: **Accounts Payable** Decrease **Purchase Returns and Allowances** Increase
STATEMENT(S): **Balance Sheet and Income Statement**

Balance Sheet					Income Statement			
ASSETS	=	LIABILITIES	+	STOCKHOLDERS' EQUITY	REVENUES	−	EXPENSES	= NET INCOME
		Accounts Payable (850)		850			Purchase Returns and Allowances* (850)	850

*The Purchase Returns and Allowances account has increased. It is shown as a decrease because it is a contra-purchases account and causes expenses to decrease.

The effect of an allowance for merchandise retained rather than returned is the same as the effect of a return.

Purchase Discounts Discounts were discussed earlier in the chapter from the seller's viewpoint. Merchandising companies often purchase inventory on terms that allow for a cash discount for early payment, such as 2/10, n/30. To the buyer, a cash discount is called a *purchase discount* and results in a reduction of the cost to purchase merchandise. Management must monitor the amount of purchase discounts taken as well as those opportunities missed by not taking advantage of the discounts for early payment.

Example 5-6 Recording Purchase Discounts in a Periodic System

Assume a purchase of merchandise on March 13 for $500, with credit terms of 1/10, n/30. The effect of the transaction can be identified and analyzed as follows:

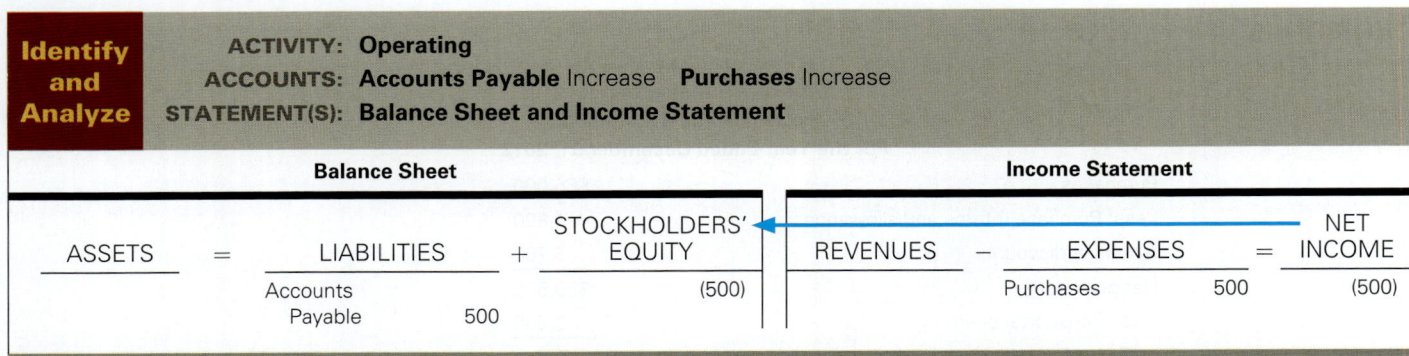

Identify and Analyze

ACTIVITY: **Operating**
ACCOUNTS: **Accounts Payable** Increase **Purchases** Increase
STATEMENT(S): **Balance Sheet and Income Statement**

Balance Sheet					Income Statement			
ASSETS	=	LIABILITIES	+	STOCKHOLDERS' EQUITY	REVENUES	−	EXPENSES	= NET INCOME
		Accounts Payable 500		(500)			Purchases 500	(500)

(Continued)

© Cengage Learning 2013

If the company does not pay within the discount period, the accountant simply records the payment of $500 cash and the reduction of accounts payable. However, if the company does pay within the discount period, the discount is recorded in the Purchases Discount account and deducted from purchases on the income statement. Assume the customer pays its bill on March 23. The effect of the transaction can be identified and analyzed as follows:

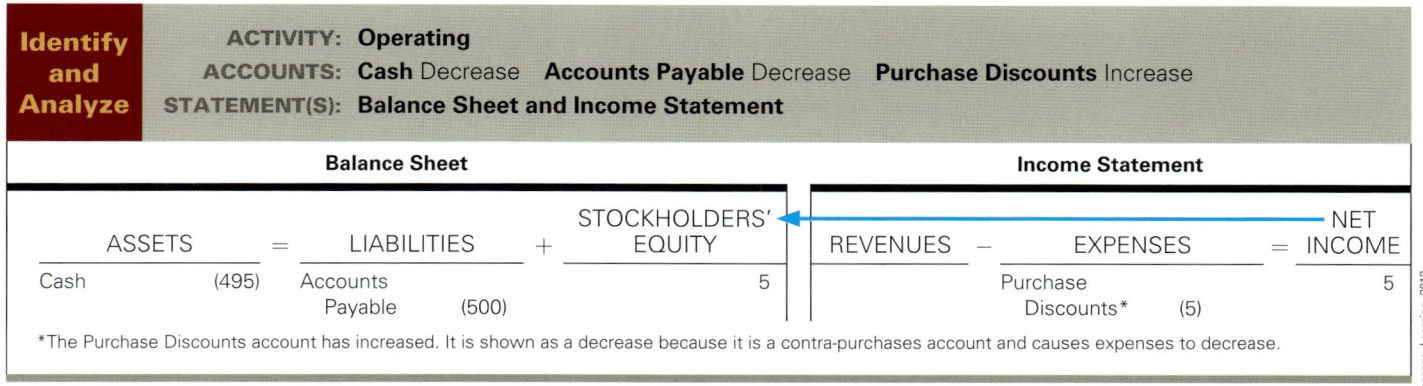

Identify and Analyze	**ACTIVITY: Operating**
	ACCOUNTS: Cash Decrease **Accounts Payable** Decrease **Purchase Discounts** Increase
	STATEMENT(S): Balance Sheet and Income Statement

Balance Sheet						Income Statement			
ASSETS	=	LIABILITIES	+	STOCKHOLDERS' EQUITY		REVENUES	−	EXPENSES	= NET INCOME
Cash	(495)	Accounts Payable	(500)		5			Purchase Discounts*	(5)	5

*The Purchase Discounts account has increased. It is shown as a decrease because it is a contra-purchases account and causes expenses to decrease.

The **Purchase Discounts** account is contra to the Purchases account and thus increases net income and stockholders' equity, as shown in the previous accounting equation. Also, note in Exhibit 5-6 that purchase discounts are deducted from purchases on the income statement. Finally, note that the effect on the income statement is the same as illustrated earlier for a purchase return: because purchases are reduced, net income is increased.

Purchase Discounts
A contra-purchases account used to record reductions in purchase price for early payment to a supplier.

Shipping Terms and Transportation Costs

The *cost principle* governs the recording of all assets. All costs necessary to prepare an asset for its intended use should be included in its cost. The cost of an item to a merchandising company is not necessarily limited to its invoice price. For example, any sales tax paid should be included in computing total cost. Any transportation costs incurred by the buyer should likewise be included in the cost of the merchandise.

The buyer does not always pay to ship the merchandise. This depends on the terms of shipment. Goods are normally shipped either **FOB destination point** or **FOB shipping point**; *FOB* stands for "free on board." When merchandise is shipped FOB destination point, it is the responsibility of the seller to deliver the products to the buyer. Thus, the seller either delivers the product to the customer or pays a trucking firm, the railroad, or another carrier to transport it. Alternatively, the agreement between the buyer and the seller may provide for the goods to be shipped FOB shipping point. In this case, the merchandise is the responsibility of the buyer as soon as it leaves the seller's premises. When the terms of shipment are FOB shipping point, the buyer incurs transportation costs.

FOB destination point
Terms that require the seller to pay for the cost of shipping the merchandise to the buyer.

FOB shipping point
Terms that require the buyer to pay for the shipping costs.

Example 5-7 Recording Transportation-In in a Periodic System

Assume that on delivery of a shipment of goods, Daisy's pays an invoice for $300 from Rocky Mountain Railroad. The terms of shipment are FOB shipping point. The effect of the transaction can be identified and analyzed as follows:

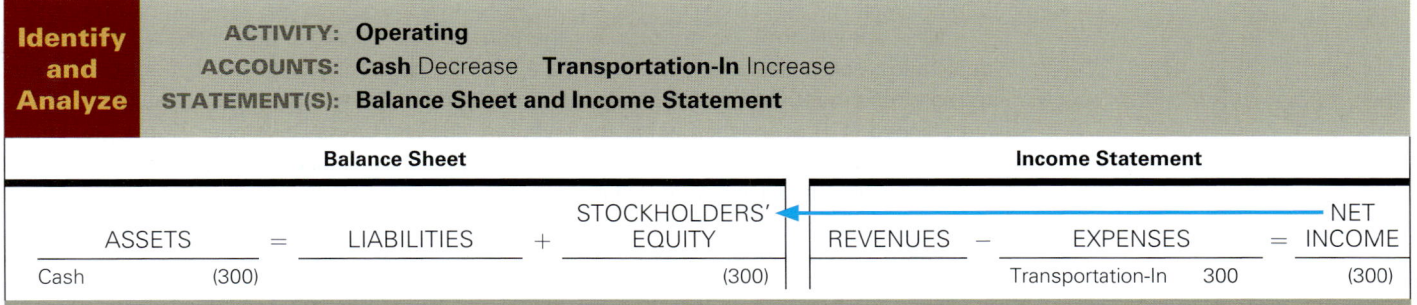

Identify and Analyze	**ACTIVITY: Operating**
	ACCOUNTS: Cash Decrease **Transportation-In** Increase
	STATEMENT(S): Balance Sheet and Income Statement

Balance Sheet						Income Statement			
ASSETS	=	LIABILITIES	+	STOCKHOLDERS' EQUITY		REVENUES	−	EXPENSES	= NET INCOME
Cash	(300)				(300)			Transportation-In	300	(300)

Transportation-in represents the freight costs Daisy's paid for in-bound merchandise. As seen in Exhibit 5-6, these costs are added to net purchases, which increases the cost of goods purchased, and are therefore added in the Expenses column of the equation here.

© Cengage Learning 2013

The total of net purchases and transportation-in is called the *cost of goods purchased*. Transportation-In will be closed at the end of the period. In summary, cost of goods purchased consists of the following:

> Purchases
> Less: Purchase returns and allowances
>   Purchase discounts
> Equals: Net purchases
> Add: Transportation-in
> Equals: Cost of goods purchased

How should the seller account for the freight costs it pays when the goods are shipped FOB destination point? This cost, sometimes called *transportation-out*, is not an addition to the cost of purchases of the seller; instead, it is one of the costs necessary to *sell* the merchandise. Transportation-out is classified as a *selling expense* on the income statement.

Shipping Terms and Transfer of Title to Inventory
Terms of shipment take on additional significance at the end of an accounting period. It is essential that a company establish a proper cutoff at year-end. For example, what if Daisy's purchases merchandise that is in transit at the end of the year? To whom does the inventory belong, Daisy's or the seller? The answer depends on the terms of shipment. If goods are shipped FOB destination point, they remain the legal property of the seller until they reach their destination. Alternatively, legal title to goods shipped FOB shipping point passes to the buyer as soon as the seller turns the goods over to the carrier.

Example 5-8 Determining the Effect of Shipping Terms on Purchases and Sales

Assume that on December 28, 2012, Nike ships running shoes to Daisy's Running Depot. The trucking company delivers the merchandise to Daisy's on January 2, 2013. Daisy's fiscal year-end is December 31. The effect of shipping terms on purchases and sales can be summarized as follows:

Company		If Merchandise Is Shipped FOB	
		Destination Point	Shipping Point
Nike	Pay freight costs?	Yes	No
(seller)	Record sale in 2012?	No	Yes
	Include inventory on balance sheet at December 31, 2012?	Yes	No
Daisy's	Pay freight costs?	No	Yes
(buyer)	Record purchase in 2012?	No	Yes
	Include inventory on balance sheet at December 31, 2012?	No	Yes

Nike, the seller of the goods, pays the transportation charges only if the terms are FOB destination point. However, Nike records a sale for goods in transit at year-end only if the terms of shipment are FOB shipping point. If Nike does not record a sale because the goods are shipped FOB destination point, the inventory appears on its December 31 balance sheet. Daisy's, the buyer, pays freight costs only if the goods are shipped FOB shipping point. Only in this situation does Daisy's record a purchase of the merchandise and include it as an asset on its December 31 balance sheet.

LO3 Show that you understand how wholesalers and retailers account for cost of goods sold.

- The cost of goods sold represents goods sold, as opposed to the inventory purchased during the year. Cost of goods sold is matched with the sales of the period.
  - The cost of goods sold in any one period is equal to: Beginning inventory + Purchases − Ending inventory.
  - Under the perpetual method, the Inventory account is updated after each sale or purchase of merchandise.
  - In contrast, under the periodic method, the Inventory account is updated only at the end of the period.
- The cost of goods purchased includes any costs necessary to acquire the goods less any purchase discounts, returns, and allowances.
  - Transportation-in is the cost to ship goods to a company and is typically classified as part of cost of goods purchased.

POD REVIEW 5.3

QUESTIONS   **Answers to these questions are on the last page of the chapter.**

1. Cost of goods available for sale is equal to
   a. cost of goods sold less beginning inventory.
   b. beginning inventory less ending inventory.
   c. beginning inventory less cost of goods sold.
   d. none of the above.

2. The type of inventory system in which the Inventory account is updated at the time of each sale is called
   a. a periodic system.
   b. a perpetual system.
   c. an accrual system.
   d. none of the above.

© Cengage Learning 2013

The Gross Profit Ratio

OVERVIEW: The gross profit ratio, found by dividing gross profit by net sales, is an important measure of profitability. It indicates a company's ability to cover operating expenses and earn a profit.

LO4 Use the gross profit ratio to analyze a company's ability to cover its operating expenses and earn a profit.

The first three lines on Daisy's income statement in Exhibit 5-2 are as follows:

Net sales	$100,000
Cost of goods sold	60,000
Gross profit	$ 40,000

The relationship between gross profit and net sales—as measured by the **gross profit ratio**—is one of the most important measures used by managers, investors, and creditors to assess the performance of a company.

Gross profit ratio
Gross profit divided by net sales.

Gross Profit Ratio

Formula	For Daisy's Running Depot
$\dfrac{\text{Gross Profit}}{\text{Net Sales}}$	$\dfrac{\$40,000}{\$100,000} = 40\%$

A 40% gross profit ratio says that for every dollar of sales, Daisy's has a gross profit of 40 cents. In other words, after deducting 60 cents for the cost of the product, the company has 40 cents on the dollar to cover its operating costs and to earn a profit. We will now apply the Ratio Decision Model to analyze this ratio for Gap Inc.

USING THE RATIO DECISION MODEL

Analyzing the Gross Profit Ratio

Use the following Ratio Decision Model to evaluate the gross profit ratio for Gap Inc. or any other public company.

1. Formulate the Question

The gross profit ratio tells us how many cents on every dollar are available to cover expenses other than cost of goods sold and to earn a profit.

How much of the sales revenue is used for the cost of the products? Thus, how much is left to cover other expenses and to earn net income?

2. Gather the Information from the Financial Statements

Both gross profit and net sales are reported on Gap Inc.'s income statement for its 2010 fiscal year:

- Net sales: From the income statement for the year
- Gross profit: From the income statement for the year

3. Calculate the Ratio

$$\text{Gross Profit Ratio} = \frac{\text{Gross Profit}}{\text{Net Sales}}$$

Gap Inc.
Partial Consolidated Statements of Income (in millions)

| | Fiscal Year | | |
	2010	2009	2008
Net sales	$14,664	$14,197	$14,526
Cost of goods sold and occupancy expenses	8,775	8,473	9,079
Gross profit	5,889	5,724	5,447

$$\text{Gross Profit Ratio} = \frac{\$\,5,889}{\$14,664} = 40.2\%$$

4. Compare the Ratio with Others

Management and other users compare the gross profit ratio with that of prior years to see if it has increased, decreased, or remained relatively steady. It is also important to compare the ratio with those of other companies in the same industry.

Gap Inc.		American Eagle Outfitters, Inc.	
Year Ended January 29, 2011	Year Ended January 30, 2010	Year Ended January 29, 2011	Year Ended January 30, 2010
40.2%	40.3%	39.5%	39.9%

5. Interpret the Results

For every dollar of sales, Gap Inc. has 40.2 cents available after deducting the cost of its products. The ratio was almost the same in the prior year. The ratios for the two years for one of Gap's competitors, American Eagle Outfitters, are very similar. Of course, the gross profit ratio alone is not enough to determine a company's profitability. Only if all of the expenses other than cost of goods sold are less than a company's gross profit will it report net income on the bottom line of the income statement. ■

LO4 Use the gross profit ratio to analyze a company's ability to cover its operating expenses and earn a profit.

- The gross profit ratio is the relationship between gross profit and net sales. Managers, investors, and creditors use this important ratio to measure one aspect of profitability.
  - The ratio is calculated as follows: $\dfrac{\text{Gross Profit}}{\text{Net Sales}}$

POD
REVIEW
5.4

QUESTIONS   Answers to these questions are on the last page of the chapter.

1. The gross profit ratio is computed by
   a. dividing gross profit by net sales.
   b. dividing net sales by gross profit.
   c. dividing gross profit by cost of goods sold.
   d. none of the above.

2. To evaluate a company's gross profit ratio,
   a. the ratio should be compared with those of prior years.

   b. the ratio should be compared with those of competitors.
   c. the ratio should be compared with those of both prior years and competitors.
   d. the ratio should be evaluated without any comparisons made to those of prior years or competitors.

Inventory Valuation and the Measurement of Income

OVERVIEW: Determining the correct amount to assign to inventory when it is purchased will ultimately affect cost of goods sold and thus net income during the period in which the inventory is sold.

LO5 Explain the relationship between the valuation of inventory and the measurement of income.

One of the most fundamental concepts in accounting is the relationship between *asset valuation* and the *measurement of income*. Recall a point made in Chapter 4:

Assets are unexpired costs, and expenses are expired costs.

Thus, **the value assigned to an asset such as inventory on the balance sheet determines the amount eventually recognized as an expense on the income statement.** An error in assigning the proper amount to inventory on the balance sheet will affect the amount recognized as cost of goods sold on the income statement. You can understand the relationship between inventory as an asset and cost of goods sold by recalling the Cost of Goods Sold section of the income statement. Assume the following amounts:

Beginning inventory	$ 500
Add: Purchases	1,200
Cost of goods available for sale	$1,700
Less: Ending inventory	(600)
Cost of goods sold	$1,100

The amount assigned to ending inventory is deducted from cost of goods available for sale to determine cost of goods sold. **If the ending inventory amount is incorrect, cost of goods sold will be wrong; thus, the net income of the period will be in error as well.** (Inventory errors will be discussed later in the chapter.)

Inventory Costs: What Should Be Included?

All assets, including inventory, are initially recorded at cost. Cost is defined as "the price paid or consideration given to acquire an asset. As applied to inventories, cost means in principle the sum of the applicable expenditures and charges directly or indirectly incurred in bringing an article to its existing condition and location."[1]

Note the reference to the existing *condition* and *location*. This means that certain costs may also be included in the "price paid." Here are examples:

- Any **freight costs** incurred by the buyer in shipping inventory to its place of business should be included in the cost of the inventory.
- The **cost of insurance** taken out during the time that inventory is in transit should be added to the cost of the inventory.
- The **cost of storing inventory** before it is ready to be sold should be included in the cost of the inventory.
- Various types of **taxes paid,** such as excise and sales taxes, are other examples of costs necessary to put the inventory into a position to be able to sell it.

However, it is often difficult to allocate many of these incidental costs among the various items of inventory purchased. For example, consider a $500 freight bill that a supermarket paid on a merchandise shipment that included 100 different items of inventory. To address the practical difficulty in assigning this type of cost to the different products, many companies have a policy by which transportation costs are charged to expense of the period when they are immaterial in amount. Thus, shipments of merchandise are recorded at the net invoice price, that is, after taking any cash discounts for early payment. It is a practical solution to a difficult allocation problem. Once again, the company must apply the cost/benefit test to accounting information.

LO5 Explain the relationship between the valuation of inventory and the measurement of income.

- Inventory costs ultimately become the cost of goods sold reflected in the income statement.
  - Since inventory is not expensed as the cost of goods sold until merchandise is sold, determining which costs belong in inventory affects the timing of when these expenses are reflected in net income.

POD REVIEW 5.5

QUESTIONS   **Answers to these questions are on the last page of the chapter.**

1. Why is it important that the proper amount be assigned to inventory?

   a. Because the amount assigned to inventory will affect the amount eventually recorded as cost of goods sold.
   b. Because the amount assigned to inventory will affect the amount eventually recorded as selling and administrative expenses.
   c. Because the amount assigned to inventory will affect the amount eventually recorded as net sales.
   d. None of the above applies.

2. Which of the following should not be included in the cost of inventory?

   a. freight cost incurred to buy inventory
   b. cost of insurance taken out during the time inventory is in transit
   c. cost to store inventory before it is ready to be sold
   d. freight cost incurred to ship inventory to a customer

---

[1] *Inventory,* ASC Topic 330 (formerly *Inventory Pricing,* Accounting Research Bulletin No. 43).

Inventory Costing Methods with a Periodic System

OVERVIEW: A company must use one of a number of methods available in assigning costs to ending inventory and to cost of goods sold. Unless a company can specifically identify the units sold, it will need to choose among the weighted average, FIFO, and LIFO methods.

LO6 Apply the inventory costing methods of specific identification, weighted average, FIFO, and LIFO by using a periodic system.

To this point, we have assumed that the cost to purchase an item of inventory is constant. For most merchandisers, however, the unit cost of inventory changes frequently.

Example 5-9 Assigning Costs to Units Sold and Units on Hand

Everett Company purchases merchandise twice during the first year of business. The dates, number of units purchased, and costs are as follows:

| February 4 | 200 units purchased at $1.00 per unit = $200 |
| October 13 | 200 units purchased at $1.50 per unit = $300 |

Everett sells 200 units during the first year. Individual sales of the units take place relatively evenly throughout the year. The question is, *which* 200 units did the company sell—the $1.00 units, the $1.50 units, or some combination of each? Recall the earlier discussion of the relationship between asset valuation and income measurement. The question is important because the answer determines not only the value assigned to the 200 units of ending inventory but also the amount allocated to cost of goods sold for the 200 units sold.

One possible method of assigning amounts to ending inventory and cost of goods sold is to specifically identify which 200 units were sold and which 200 units are on hand. This method is feasible for a few types of businesses in which units can be identified by serial numbers, but it is totally impractical in most situations. As an alternative to specific identification, we could make an assumption as to which units were sold and which are on hand. Three different answers are possible, as follows:

1. 200 units sold at $1.00 each   = $200 cost of goods sold
   and 200 units on hand at $1.50 each   = $300 ending inventory
   or
2. 200 units sold at $1.50 each   = $300 cost of goods sold
   and 200 units on hand at $1.00 each   = $200 ending inventory
   or
3. 200 units sold at $1.25 each   = $250 cost of goods sold
   and 200 units on hand at $1.25 each   = $250 ending inventory

The third alternative assumes an *average cost* for the 200 units on hand and the 200 units sold. The average cost is the cost of the two purchases of $200 and $300, or $500, divided by the 400 units available to sell, or $1.25 per unit.

© Cengage Learning 2013

If we are concerned with the actual physical flow of the units of inventory, all three methods illustrated may be incorrect. The only approach that will yield a "correct" answer in terms of the actual flow of *units* of inventory is the specific identification method. In the absence of a specific identification approach, it is impossible to say which particular units were actually sold. In fact, there may have been sales from each of the two purchases; that is, some of the $1.00 units may have been sold and some of the $1.50 units may have been sold. To solve the problem of assigning costs to identical units, accountants have developed inventory costing assumptions or methods. Each of these methods makes a specific assumption about the flow of costs rather than the physical flow of units. The only approach that uses the actual flow of the units in assigning costs is the specific identification method.

To take a closer look at specific identification as well as three alternative approaches to valuing inventory, assume the following set of data for Examples 5-10, 5-11, 5-12, 5-13, and 5-14.

	Units	Unit Cost	Total Cost
Beginning inventory			
January 1	500	$10	$ 5,000*
Purchases			
January 20	300	11	$ 3,300
April 8	400	12	4,800
September 5	200	13	2,600
December 12	100	14	1,400
Total purchases	1,000		$12,100
Available for sale	1,500		$17,100
Units sold	900		?
Units in ending inventory	600		?

*Beginning inventory of $5,000 is carried over as the ending inventory from the prior period. It is highly unlikely that each of the four methods we will illustrate would result in the same dollar amount of inventory at any point in time. It is helpful when first learning the methods, however, to assume the same amount of beginning inventory.

The question marks indicate the dilemma. What portion of the cost of goods available for sale of $17,100 should be assigned to the 900 units sold? What portion should be assigned to the 600 units remaining in ending inventory? The purpose of an inventory costing method is to provide a reasonable answer to those two questions.

Specific Identification Method

It is not always necessary to make an assumption about the flow of costs. In certain situations, it may be possible to specifically identify which units are sold and which units are on hand. As shown in the illustration on the next page, the unique characteristics of each automobile allow a dealer to specifically identify which one has been sold. Similarly, an appliance dealer with 15 refrigerators on hand at the end of the year can identify the unit cost of each by matching a tag number with the purchase records.

Specific identification method
An inventory costing method that relies on matching unit costs with the actual units sold.

Example 5-10 Determining Ending Inventory and Cost of Goods Sold Using Specific Identification

To illustrate the **specific identification method**, assume that a merchandiser is able to identify the specific units in the inventory at the end of the year and their costs as follows:

Units on Hand

Date Purchased	Units	Cost	Total Cost
January 20	100	$11	$1,100
April 8	300	12	3,600
September 5	200	13	2,600
Ending inventory	600		$7,300

One of two techniques can be used to find cost of goods sold. Ending inventory can be deducted from the cost of goods available for sale as follows:

Cost of goods available for sale	$17,100
Less: Ending inventory	7,300
Equals: Cost of goods sold	$ 9,800

(Continued)

Or cost of goods sold can be calculated independently by matching the units sold with their respective unit costs. By eliminating the units in ending inventory from the original acquisition schedule, the units sold and their costs are determined as follows:

Units Sold

Date Purchased	Units	Cost	Total Cost
Beginning inventory	500	$10	$5,000
January 20	200	11	2,200
April 8	100	12	1,200
December 12	100	14	1,400
Cost of goods sold	900		$9,800

The practical difficulty of keeping track of individual items of inventory sold is not the only problem with the use of this method. It also allows management to manipulate income. For example, assume that a company is not having a particularly good year. Management may be tempted to do whatever it can to boost net income. It can do this by selectively selling units with the lowest possible unit cost to keep cost of goods sold down and net income up. Because of the potential for manipulation with the specific identification method, coupled with the practical difficulty of applying it in most situations, it is not widely used.

Specific Identification

Cars on the Lot:

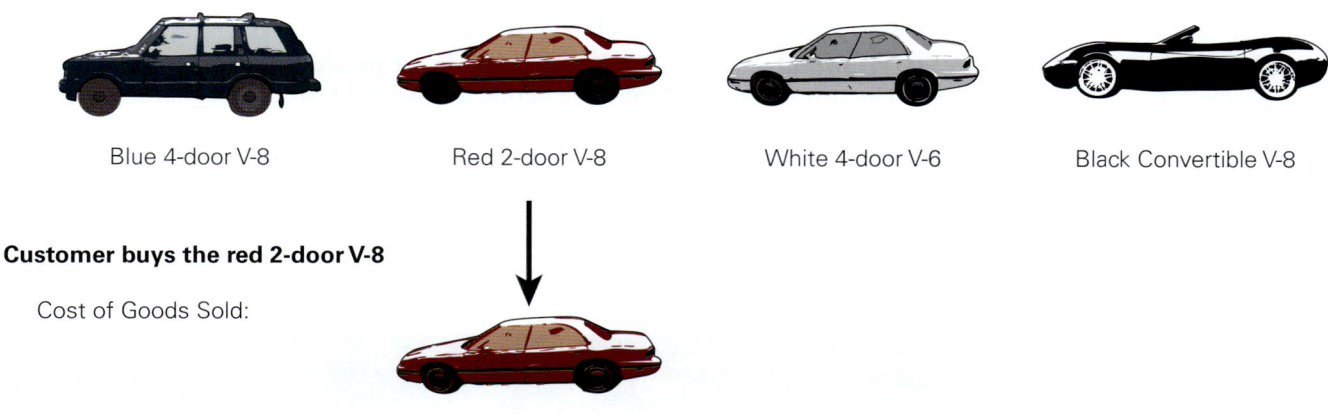

Blue 4-door V-8   Red 2-door V-8   White 4-door V-6   Black Convertible V-8

Customer buys the red 2-door V-8

Cost of Goods Sold:

Red 2-door V-8

Weighted Average Cost Method

The **weighted average cost method** is a relatively easy approach to costing inventory. It assigns the same unit cost to all units available for sale during the period.

Weighted average cost method
An inventory costing method that assigns the same unit cost to all units available for sale during the period.

> **Example 5-11** Determining Ending Inventory and Cost of Goods Sold Using Weighted Average

The weighted average cost is calculated as follows for the data given:

$$\frac{\text{Cost of Goods Available for Sale}}{\text{Units Available for Sale}} = \text{Weighted Average Cost}$$

$$\frac{\$17,100}{1,500} = \$11.40$$

(Continued)

Ending inventory is found by multiplying the weighted average unit cost by the number of units on hand.

Weighted Average Cost		Number of Units in Ending Inventory		Ending Inventory
$11.40	×	600	=	$6,840

Cost of goods sold can be calculated in one of two ways.

Cost of goods available for sale	$17,100
Less: Ending inventory	6,840
Equals: Cost of goods sold	$10,260

or

Weighted Average Cost		Number of Units Sold		Cost of Goods Sold
$11.40	×	900	=	$10,260

Note that the computation of the weighted average cost is based on the cost of all units available for sale during the period, not just the beginning inventory or purchases. Also, note that the method is called the weighted average cost method. As the name indicates, each of the individual unit costs is multiplied by the number of units acquired at each price. The simple arithmetic average of the unit costs for the beginning inventory and the four purchases is ($10 + $11 + $12 + $13 + $14)/5 = $12. The weighted average cost is slightly less than $12 ($11.40), however, because more units were acquired at the lower prices than at the higher prices.

First-In, First-Out Method (FIFO)

FIFO method

An inventory costing method that assigns the most recent costs to ending inventory.

The **FIFO method** assumes that the first units in, or purchased, are the first units out, or sold. The first units sold during the period are assumed to come from the beginning inventory. After the beginning inventory is sold, the next units sold are assumed to come from the first purchase during the period, and so on. Thus, ending inventory consists of the most recent purchases of the period. In many businesses, this cost-flow assumption is a fairly accurate reflection of the physical flow of products. For example, to maintain a fresh stock of products, the physical flow in a grocery store is first-in, first-out.

Example 5-12 Determining Ending Inventory and Cost of Goods Sold Using FIFO

To calculate ending inventory using FIFO, we start with the most recent inventory acquired and work backward as follows:

Units on Hand

Date Purchased	Units	Cost	Total Cost
December 12	100	$14	$1,400
September 5	200	13	2,600
April 8	300	12	3,600
Ending inventory	600		$7,600

Cost of goods sold can then be found as follows:

Cost of goods available for sale	$17,100
Less: Ending inventory	7,600
Equals: Cost of goods sold	$ 9,500

(Continued)

Or because the FIFO method assumes that the first units purchased are the first ones sold, cost of goods sold can be calculated by starting with the beginning inventory and working forward as follows:

Units Sold

Date Purchased	Units	Cost	Total Cost
Beginning inventory	500	$10	$5,000
January 20	300	11	3,300
April 8	100	12	1,200
Units sold	900	Cost of goods sold	$9,500

Last-In, First-Out Method (LIFO)

The **LIFO method** assumes that the last units in, or purchased, are the first units out, or sold. The first units sold during the period are assumed to come from the latest purchase made during the period, and so on. Can you think of any businesses where the physical flow of products is last-in, first-out? Although this situation is not as common as a FIFO physical flow, a stockpiling operation, such as in a rock quarry, operates on this basis.

LIFO method
An inventory method that assigns the most recent costs to cost of goods sold.

Example 5-13 Determining Ending Inventory and Cost of Goods Sold Using LIFO

To calculate ending inventory using LIFO, we start with the beginning inventory and work forward.

Units on Hand

Date Purchased	Units	Cost	Total Cost
Beginning inventory	500	$10	$5,000
January 20	100	11	1,100
Ending inventory	600		$6,100

Cost of goods sold can then be found as follows:

Cost of goods available for sale	$17,100
Less: Ending inventory	6,100
Equals: Cost of goods sold	$11,000

STUDY TIP

There may be cases, such as this illustration of LIFO, in which it is easier to determine ending inventory and then deduct it from cost of goods available for sale to find cost of goods sold. This approach is easier in this example because there are fewer layers in ending inventory than in cost of goods sold. In other cases, it may be quicker to determine cost of goods sold first and then plug in ending inventory.

Or because the LIFO method assumes that the last units purchased are the first ones sold, cost of goods sold can be calculated by starting with the most recent inventory acquired and working backward.

Units Sold

Date Purchased	Units	Cost	Total Cost
December 12	100	$14	$ 1,400
September 5	200	13	2,600
April 8	400	12	4,800
January 20	200	11	2,200
Units sold	900	Cost of goods sold	$11,000

LO6 Apply the inventory costing methods of specific identification, weighted average, FIFO, and LIFO by using a periodic system.

- The purchase price of inventory items may change frequently, and several alternatives are available to assign costs to the goods sold and those that remain in ending inventory.
  - Specific identification assigns the actual costs of acquisition to items of inventory. In some circumstances, it is not practical to do this.
  - Three other methods involve making assumptions about the cost of inventory.
    - Weighted average assigns the same unit cost to all units available for sale during the period.
    - The FIFO method assumes that the first units purchased are the first units sold.
    - The LIFO method assumes that the last units purchased are the first units sold.

POD REVIEW 5.6

QUESTIONS   Answers to these questions are on the last page of the chapter.

1. For which of the following products is a company most likely to use the specific identification method?
   a. boxes of soap in a grocery store
   b. automobiles at a car dealer
   c. car batteries at an auto parts store
   d. Specific identification cannot be used by any companies.

2. Which inventory method assigns the most recent costs to ending inventory?
   a. FIFO
   b. LIFO
   c. weighted average
   d. specific identification

Selecting an Inventory Costing Method

LO7 Analyze the effects of the different costing methods on inventory, net income, income taxes, and cash flow.

OVERVIEW: The choice of an inventory method will impact cost of goods sold and thus net income. A company should choose the method that results in the most accurate measure of net income for the period.

The mechanics of each of the inventory costing methods are straightforward. But how does a company decide on the best method to use to value its inventory? According to the accounting profession, **the primary determinant in selecting an inventory costing method should be the ability of the method to accurately reflect the net income of the period.** But how and why does a particular costing method accurately reflect the net income of the period? Because there is no easy answer to this question, accountants have raised a number of arguments to justify the use of one method over the others. We turn now to some of those arguments.

Costing Methods and Cash Flow

Comparative income statements for the three methods used in Examples 5-11, 5-12, and 5-13 are presented in Exhibit 5-7. Note that with the use of the weighted average method, net income is between the amounts for FIFO and LIFO. Because the weighted average method normally yields results between the other two methods, we concentrate on the two extremes, LIFO and FIFO. The major advantage of using the weighted average method is its simplicity.

The original data on page 239 involved a situation in which prices were rising throughout the period: beginning inventory cost $10 per unit, and the last purchase during the year was at $14. With LIFO, the most recent costs are assigned to cost of goods sold; with FIFO, the older costs are assigned to expense. Thus, in a period of rising prices, the assignment of the higher prices to cost of goods sold under LIFO results in a lower gross profit under LIFO than under FIFO ($7,000 for LIFO and $8,500 for FIFO).

EXHIBIT 5-7 Income Statements for the Inventory Costing Methods

	Weighted Average	FIFO	LIFO
Sales revenue—$20 each	$18,000	$18,000	$18,000
Beginning inventory	$ 5,000	$ 5,000	$ 5,000
Purchases	12,100	12,100	12,100
Cost of goods available for sale	$17,100	$17,100	$17,100
Ending inventory	**6,840**	**7,600**	**6,100**
Cost of goods sold	**$10,260**	**$ 9,500**	**$11,000**
Gross profit	**$ 7,740**	**$ 8,500**	**$ 7,000**
Operating expenses	2,000	2,000	2,000
Net income before tax	**$ 5,740**	**$ 6,500**	**$ 5,000**
Income tax expense (40%)	**2,296**	**2,600**	**2,000**
Net income	**$ 3,444**	**$ 3,900**	**$ 3,000**

NOTE: Figures that differ among the three methods are in bold.

© Cengage Learning 2013

Example 5-14 Computing Taxes Saved by Using LIFO Instead of FIFO

Because operating expenses are not affected by the choice of inventory method, the lower gross profit under LIFO results in lower income before tax, which in turn leads to lower taxes. If we assume a 40% tax rate, income tax expense under LIFO is only $2,000, compared with $2,600 under FIFO, a savings of $600 in taxes. Another way to look at the taxes saved by using LIFO is to focus on the difference in the expense under each method, as follows:

LIFO cost of goods sold	$11,000
− FIFO cost of goods sold	9,500
Additional expense from use of LIFO	$ 1,500
× Tax rate	0.40
Tax savings from the use of LIFO	$ 600

© Cengage Learning 2013

To summarize, during a period of rising prices, the two methods result in the following:

Item	LIFO	Relative to	FIFO
Cost of goods sold	Higher		Lower
Gross profit	Lower		Higher
Income before taxes	Lower		Higher
Taxes	Lower		Higher

In conclusion, lower taxes with the use of LIFO result in cash savings.

The tax savings available from the use of LIFO during a period of rising prices is largely responsible for its popularity. Keep in mind, however, that the cash saved from a lower tax bill with LIFO is only a temporary savings, or what is normally called a *tax deferral*. At some point in the life of the business, the inventory that is carried at the older, lower-priced amounts will be sold. This will result in a tax bill higher than that under FIFO. Yet even a tax deferral is beneficial; given the opportunity, it is better to pay less tax today and more in the future because today's tax savings can be invested.

LIFO Liquidation

Recall the assumption made about which costs remain in inventory when LIFO is used. The costs of the oldest units remain in inventory, and if prices are rising, the costs of these units will be lower than the costs of more recent purchases. Now assume that the company sells more units than it buys during the period. When a company using LIFO experiences a liquidation, some of the units assumed to be sold come from the older

LIFO liquidation
The result of selling more units than are purchased during the period, which can have negative tax consequences if a company is using LIFO.

layers, with a relatively low unit cost. This situation, called a **LIFO liquidation**, presents a dilemma for the company.

A partial or complete liquidation of the older, lower-priced units will result in a low cost of goods sold figure and a correspondingly high gross profit for the period. In turn, the company faces a large tax bill because of the relatively high gross profit. In fact, a liquidation causes the tax advantages of using LIFO to reverse on the company, which is faced with paying off some of the taxes that were deferred in earlier periods. Should a company facing this situation buy inventory at the end of the year to avoid the consequences of a liquidation? That is a difficult question to answer and depends on many factors, including the company's cash position. The accountant must at least be aware of the potential for a large tax bill if a liquidation occurs.

Of course, a LIFO liquidation also benefits—and may even distort—reported earnings if the liquidation is large enough. For this reason and the tax problem, many companies are reluctant to liquidate their LIFO inventory. The problem often festers, and companies find themselves with inventory costed at decade-old price levels.

The LIFO Conformity Rule

LIFO conformity rule
The IRS requirement that when LIFO is used on a tax return, it must also be used in reporting income to stockholders.

Would it be possible for a company to have the best of both worlds? That is, could it use FIFO to report its income to stockholders, thus maximizing the amount of net income reported to this group, and use LIFO to report to the IRS, minimizing its taxable income and the amount paid to the government? Unfortunately, the IRS says that if a company chooses LIFO for reporting cost of goods sold on its tax return, it must also use LIFO on its books, that is, in preparing its income statement. This is called the **LIFO conformity rule**. Note that the rule applies only to the use of LIFO on the tax return. A company is free to use different methods in preparing its tax return and its income statement as long as the method used for the tax return is *not* LIFO.

The LIFO Reserve: Estimating LIFO's Effect on Income and on Taxes Paid for Winnebago Industries

If a company decides to use LIFO, an investor can still determine how much more income the company would have reported had it used FIFO. In addition, he or she can approximate the tax savings to the company from the use of LIFO.

Example 5-15 Computing Taxes Saved by Using LIFO Instead of FIFO for Winnebago Industries

Consider Note 4 from the 2008 annual report for Winnebago Industries, the RV maker.
Note 4: Inventories

Inventories consist of the following: (in thousands)	August 30, 2008	August 25, 2007
Finished goods	$ 41,716	$ 45,489
Work-in-process	31,187	41,417
Raw materials	75,010	47,007
	147,913	133,913
LIFO reserve	(37,317)	(32,705)
Total inventories	$110,596	$101,208

The above value of inventories, before reduction for the LIFO reserve, approximates replacement cost at the respective dates.

The following steps explain the logic for using the information in the inventory note to estimate LIFO's effect on income and on taxes:

LIFO reserve
The excess of the value of a company's inventory stated at FIFO over the value stated at LIFO.

1. The excess of the value of a company's inventory stated at FIFO over the value stated at LIFO is called the **LIFO reserve**. The cumulative excess of the value of Winnebago Industries' inventory on a FIFO basis over the value on a LIFO basis is $37,317,000 at the end of 2008.
2. Because Winnebago Industries reports inventory at a lower value on its balance sheet using LIFO, it will report a higher cost of goods sold amount on the income statement.

(Continued)

Thus, the LIFO reserve not only represents the excess of the inventory balance on a FIFO basis over that on a LIFO basis but also represents the cumulative amount by which cost of goods sold on a LIFO basis exceeds cost of goods sold on a FIFO basis.

3. The increase in Winnebago Industries' LIFO reserve in 2008 was $4,612,000 ($37,317,000 – $32,705,000). This means that the increase in cost of goods sold for 2008 from using LIFO instead of FIFO was also this amount. Thus, income before tax for 2008 was $4,612,000 lower because the company used LIFO.

4. If we assume a corporate tax rate of 35%, the tax savings from using LIFO amounted to $4,612,000 × 0.35, or $1,614,200.

© Cengage Learning 2013

Costing Methods and Inventory Profits

FIFO, LIFO, and weighted average are all cost-based methods to value inventory. They vary in terms of which costs are assigned to inventory and which are assigned to cost of goods sold, but all three assign *historical costs* to inventory. In the set of data given on page 239, the unit cost for inventory purchases gradually increased during the year from $10 for the beginning inventory to a high of $14 on the date of the last purchase.

An alternative to assigning any of the historical costs incurred during the year to ending inventory and cost of goods sold is to use **replacement cost** to value each of these. Assume that the cost to replace a unit of inventory at the end of the year is $15. Use of a replacement cost system results in the following:

Replacement cost
The current cost of a unit of inventory.

$$\text{Ending inventory} = 600 \text{ units} \times \$15 \text{ per unit} = \$\ 9{,}000$$
$$\text{Cost of goods sold} = 900 \text{ units} \times \$15 \text{ per unit} = \$13{,}500$$

A replacement cost approach is not acceptable under the profession's current standards, but many believe that it provides more relevant information to users. Inventory must be replaced if a company is to remain in business. Many accountants argue that the use of historical cost in valuing inventory leads to what is called **inventory profit**, particularly when FIFO is used in a period of rising prices. For example, cost of goods sold in Example 5-12 was only $9,500 on a FIFO basis, compared with $13,500 when the replacement cost of $15 per unit was used. The $4,000 difference between the two cost of goods sold figures is a profit from holding the inventory during a period of rising prices and is called *inventory profit*.

Inventory profit
The portion of the gross profit that results from holding inventory during a period of rising prices.

Example 5-16 Reconciling the Difference Between Gross Profit on a FIFO Basis and on a Replacement Cost Basis

Assume that the units are sold for $20 each. The following analysis reconciles the difference between gross profit on a FIFO basis and on a replacement cost basis:

Sales revenue (900 units × $20)		$18,000
Cost of goods sold—FIFO basis		9,500
Gross profit—FIFO basis		$ 8,500
Cost of goods sold—replacement cost basis	$13,500	
Cost of goods sold—FIFO basis	9,500	
Profit from holding inventory during a period of inflation		4,000
Gross profit on a replacement cost basis		$ 4,500

© Cengage Learning 2013

Those who argue in favor of a replacement cost approach would report only $4,500 of gross profit. They believe that the additional $4,000 of profit reported on a FIFO basis is simply due to holding the inventory during a period of rising prices. According to this viewpoint, if the 900 units sold during the period are to be replaced, a necessity if the company is to continue operating, the use of replacement cost in calculating cost of goods sold results in a better measure of gross profit than if it is calculated using FIFO.

Given that our current standards require the use of historical costs rather than replacement costs, does any one of the costing methods result in a better approximation of replacement cost of goods sold than the others? Because LIFO assigns the cost of the most recent purchases to cost of goods sold, it most nearly approximates the results with a replacement cost system. The other side of the argument, however, is that whereas LIFO results in the best approximation of replacement cost of goods sold on the income statement, FIFO most nearly approximates replacement cost of the inventory on the balance sheet. A comparison of the amounts from the running example verifies this:

	Ending Inventory	Cost of Goods Sold
Weighted average	$6,840	$10,260
FIFO	7,600	9,500
LIFO	6,100	11,000
Replacement cost	9,000	13,500

Changing Inventory Methods

The purpose of each of the inventory costing methods is to match costs with revenues. If a company believes that a different method will result in a better matching than that being provided by the method currently being used, the company should change methods. A company must be able to justify a change in methods, however. Taking advantage of the tax breaks offered by LIFO is *not* a valid justification for a change in methods.

Inventory Valuation in Other Countries

The acceptable methods of valuing inventory differ considerably around the world. Although FIFO is the most popular method in the United States, LIFO continues to be widely used, as is the average cost method. Many countries prohibit the use of LIFO for tax or financial reporting purposes. Additionally, the IASB strictly prohibits the use of LIFO by companies that follow its standards. As GAAP in the United States comes closer to converging with the international standards, it is still uncertain whether LIFO will survive as an acceptable inventory valuation method.

LOOKING AHEAD   Whether LIFO survives in the United States is not only a matter of convergence with international standards. Because the method allows companies with rising inventory costs to report lower income, the White House and its supporters in Congress see the repeal of LIFO as one avenue for raising tax revenues and thus cutting into the ever-increasing federal deficit. Naturally, companies currently using the method are adamantly opposed to its elimination and are lobbying for its continuation. In addition to the budgetary implications, those in Congress who would like to see LIFO eliminated point to its prohibition under IFRS. This issue is a prime example of how accounting choices affect much more than a company's bottom line and can sometimes be at the center of national policy debates. Stay tuned.

L07 Analyze the effects of the different costing methods on inventory, net income, income taxes, and cash flow.

- The ability to measure net income accurately for a period should be the driving force behind selecting an inventory costing method.
  - Inventory costing methods impact the cost of goods sold and, therefore, net income.
  - When a company uses LIFO for tax purposes, it must use it for financial reporting purposes as well.

POD REVIEW 5.7

QUESTIONS   **Answers to these questions are on the last page of the chapter.**

1. Which inventory method results in the least amount of income before taxes, assuming a period of rising prices?
   a. FIFO
   b. LIFO
   c. weighted average cost
   d. none of the above

2. The LIFO conformity rule requires that if a company
   a. uses LIFO in reporting income to stockholders, it also must use LIFO on its tax return.
   b. uses LIFO on its tax return, it also must use LIFO in reporting income to stockholders.
   c. uses LIFO on its tax return, it must use FIFO in reporting income to stockholders.
   d. none of the above.

© Cengage Learning 2013

Inventory Errors

OVERVIEW: Inventory errors arise for a variety of reasons. If ending inventory is overstated, cost of goods sold will be understated and thus net income for the period overstated. The opposite effects will occur when ending inventory is understated.

> **LO8** Analyze the effects of an inventory error on various financial statement items.

Earlier in the chapter, we considered the inherent tie between the valuation of assets, such as inventory, and the measurement of income, such as cost of goods sold. The importance of inventory valuation to the measurement of income can be illustrated by considering inventory errors. Many different types of inventory errors exist. Some errors are mathematical; for example, a bookkeeper may incorrectly add a column total. Other errors relate specifically to the physical count of inventory at year-end. For example, the count might inadvertently omit one section of a warehouse. Other errors arise from cut-off problems at year-end.

Assume that merchandise in transit at the end of the year is shipped FOB shipping point. Under these shipment terms, the inventory belongs to the buyer at the time it is shipped. Because the shipment has not arrived at the end of the year, however, it cannot be included in the physical count. Unless some type of control is in place, the amount in transit may be erroneously omitted from the valuation of inventory at year-end.

To demonstrate the effect of an inventory error on the income statement, consider the following situation. Through a scheduling error, two different inventory teams were assigned to count the inventory in the same warehouse on December 31, 2012. The correct amount of ending inventory is $250,000 but because two different teams counted the same inventory in one warehouse, the amount recorded is $300,000. First, we consider the effect of the error on net income.

Example 5-17 Analyzing the Effect of an Inventory Error on Net Income

The overstatement of ending inventory in 2012 leads to an understatement of the 2012 cost of goods sold expense. Because cost of goods sold is understated, gross profit for the year is overstated. Operating expenses are unaffected by an inventory error. Thus, net income in 2012 is overstated by the same amount of overstatement of gross profit,[2] as shown in the following analysis:

	2012		Effect of	2013		Effect of
	Reported	Corrected	Error	Reported	Corrected	Error
Sales	$1,000*	$1,000		$1,500	$1,500	
Cost of goods sold:						
Beginning inventory	$ 200	$ 200		$ 300	$ 250	$50 OS
Add: Purchases	700	700		1,100	1,100	
Cost of goods available for sale	$ 900	$ 900		$1,400	$1,350	50 OS
Less: Ending inventory	300	250	$50 OS†	350	350	
Cost of goods sold	$ 600	$ 650	50 US‡	$1,050	$1,000	50 OS
Gross profit	$ 400	$ 350	50 OS	$ 450	$ 500	50 US
Operating expenses	100	100		120	120	
Net income	$ 300	$ 250	50 OS	$ 330	$ 380	50 US

NOTE: Figures that differ as a result of the error are in bold.

*All amounts are in thousands of dollars.

†OS = Overstatement

‡US = Understatement

© Cengage Learning 2013

The most important conclusion from the analysis is that an overstatement of ending inventory leads to a corresponding overstatement of net income.

Unfortunately, the effect of a misstatement of the year-end inventory is not limited to the net income for that year. The error also affects the income statement for the

---

[2] An overstatement of gross profit also results in an overstatement of income tax expense. Thus, because tax expense is overstated, the overstatement of net income is not as large as the overstatement of gross profit. For now, we will ignore the effect of taxes.

following year, as indicated in the two "2013" columns. This happens simply because the ending inventory of one period is the beginning inventory of the following period. The overstatement of the 2013 beginning inventory leads to an overstatement of cost of goods available for sale. Because cost of goods available for sale is overstated, cost of goods sold is also overstated. The overstatement of cost of goods sold expense results in an understatement of gross profit and thus an understatement of net income.

Example 5-17 illustrates the nature of a *counterbalancing error*. The effect of the overstatement of net income in the first year, 2012, is offset, or counterbalanced, by the understatement of net income by the same dollar amount in the following year. If the net incomes of two successive years are misstated in the opposite direction by the same amount, what is the effect on retained earnings?

Example 5-18 Analyzing the Effect of an Inventory Error on Retained Earnings

Assume that retained earnings at the beginning of 2012 is correctly stated at $300,000. The counterbalancing nature of the error is seen by analyzing retained earnings. For 2012, the analysis would indicate the following (OS = overstated and US = understated):

	2012 Reported	2012 Corrected	Effect of Error
Beginning retained earnings	$300,000	$300,000	Correct
Add: Net income	300,000	250,000	$50,000 OS
Ending retained earnings	$600,000	$550,000	$50,000 OS

An analysis for 2013 would show the following:

	2013 Reported	2013 Corrected	Effect of Error
Beginning retained earnings	$600,000	$550,000	$50,000 OS
Add: Net income	330,000	380,000	$50,000 US
Ending retained earnings	$930,000	$930,000	Correct

Thus, even though retained earnings is overstated at the end of the first year, it is correctly stated at the end of the second year. This is the nature of a counterbalancing error.

Example 5-19 Analyzing the Effect of an Inventory Error on the Balance Sheet

The only accounts on the balance sheet affected by the error are Inventory and Retained Earnings. The overstatement of the 2012 ending inventory results in an overstatement of total assets at the end of the first year. Similarly, as the earlier analysis indicates, the overstatement of 2012 net income leads to an overstatement of retained earnings by the same amount. Because the error is counterbalancing, the 2013 year-end balance sheet is correct. That is, ending inventory is not affected by the error; thus, the amount for total assets at the end of 2013 is also correct. The effect of the error on retained earnings is limited to the first year because of the counterbalancing nature of the error.

	2012		2013	
	Reported	Corrected	Reported	Corrected
Inventory	$ 300*	$ 250	$ 350	$ 350
All other assets	1,700	1,700	2,080	2,080
Total assets	$2,000	$1,950	$ 2,430	$ 2,430
Total liabilities	$ 400	$ 400	$ 500	$ 500
Capital stock	1,000	1,000	1,000	1,000
Retained earnings	600	550	930	930
Total liabilities and stockholders' equity	$2,000	$1,950	$ 2,430	$ 2,430

NOTE: Figures that differ as a result of the error are in bold.
*All amounts are in thousands of dollars.

© Cengage Learning 2013

The effects of inventory errors on various financial statement items are summarized in Exhibit 5-8. The analysis focused on the effects of an overstatement of inventory. The effects of an understatement are just the opposite and are summarized in the bottom portion of the exhibit.

Not all errors are counterbalancing. For example, if a section of a warehouse continues to be omitted from the physical count every year, both beginning and ending inventories will be incorrect each year and the error will not counterbalance.

Part of the auditor's job is to perform the necessary tests to obtain reasonable assurance that inventory has not been overstated or understated. If there is an error and inventory is wrong, however, both the balance sheet and the income statement will be distorted. For example, if ending inventory is overstated, inflating total assets, cost of goods sold will be understated, boosting profits. Thus, such an error overstates the financial health of the organization in two ways. A lender or an investor must make a decision based on the current year's statement and cannot wait until the next accounting cycle, when this error is reversed. This is one reason that investors and creditors insist on audited financial statements.

> **STUDY TIP**
>
> Note the logic behind the notion that an overstatement of ending inventory leads to overstatements of total assets and retained earnings at the end of the year. This is logical because a balance sheet must balance; that is, the left side must equal the right side. If the left side (inventory) is overstated, the right side (retained earnings) will also be overstated.

EXHIBIT 5-8 Summary of the Effects of Inventory Errors

	Effect of Overstatement of Ending Inventory on	
	Current Year	Following Year
Cost of goods sold	Understated	Overstated
Gross profit	Overstated	Understated
Net income	Overstated	Understated
Retained earnings, end of year	Overstated	Correctly stated
Total assets, end of year	Overstated	Correctly stated

	Effect of Understatement of Ending Inventory on	
	Current Year	Following Year
Cost of goods sold	Overstated	Understated
Gross profit	Understated	Overstated
Net income	Understated	Overstated
Retained earnings, end of year	Understated	Correctly stated
Total assets, end of year	Understated	Correctly stated

© Cengage Learning 2013

LO8 Analyze the effects of an inventory error on various financial statement items.

- The link between the balance sheet and the income statement can be seen through the effect of errors in inventory valuation.
  - Overstatement of ending inventory results in an understatement of the cost of goods sold and therefore an overstatement of net income.
- The effects of errors in inventory may offset themselves over time. These are known as counterbalancing errors.

POD REVIEW 5.8

QUESTIONS   Answers to these questions are on the last page of the chapter.

1. A company erroneously omits one section of its warehouse in the year-end inventory. The error will result in
   a. an overstatement of cost of goods sold for the current year.
   b. an understatement of cost of goods sold for the current year.
   c. an overstatement of inventory on the year-end balance sheet.
   d. none of the above.

2. A company erroneously counts the same section of its warehouse twice in the year-end inventory. Assuming that no error is made in the year-end count the following year, the error will result in
   a. an overstatement of cost of goods sold in the following year.
   b. an understatement of cost of goods sold in the following year.
   c. an overstatement of ending inventory on the year-end balance sheet of the following year.
   d. none of the above.

Valuing Inventory at Lower of Cost or Market

LO9 Apply the lower-of-cost-or-market rule to the valuation of inventory.

OVERVIEW: The lower-of-cost-or-market rule is a departure from the historical cost principle. Accounting standards require that inventory be written down at the end of the period if the market value of the inventory is less than its cost.

Lower-of-cost-or-market (LCM) rule
A conservative inventory valuation approach that is an attempt to anticipate declines in the value of inventory before its actual sale.

One of the components sold by an electronics firm has become economically obsolete. A particular style of suit sold by a retailer is outdated and can no longer be sold at the regular price. In both instances, it is likely that the retailer will have to sell the merchandise for less than the normal selling price. In these situations, a departure from the cost basis of accounting may be necessary because the market value of the inventory may be less than its cost to the company. The departure is called the **lower-of-cost-or-market (LCM) rule**.

At the end of each accounting period, the original cost, as determined using one of the costing methods such as FIFO, is compared with the market price of the inventory. If market is less than cost, the inventory is written down to the lower amount.

For example, if cost is $100,000 and market value is $85,000, the accountant makes an adjustment that can be identified and analyzed as follows:

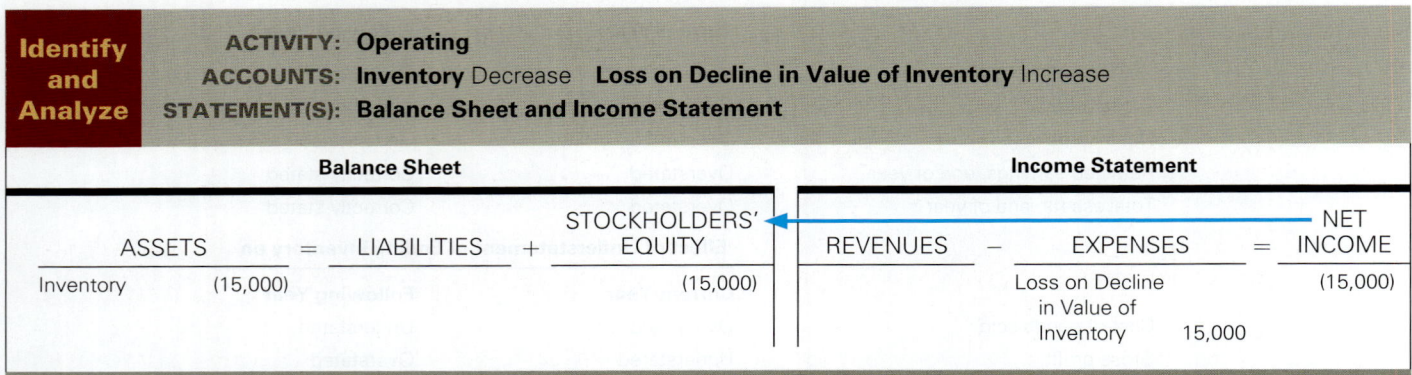

Note that the adjustment reduces assets in the form of inventory and net income. The reduction in net income is the result of reporting the Loss on Decline in Value of Inventory on the income statement as an item of Other Expense.

Why Replacement Cost Is Used as a Measure of Market

A better name for the lower-of-cost-or-market rule would be the lower-of-cost-or-replacement-cost rule because accountants define *market* as "replacement cost."[3] To understand why replacement cost is used as a basis to compare with original cost, consider the following situation. Assume that Daisy's Running Depot pays $75 for a pair of running shoes and normally sells them for $100. Thus, the normal markup on selling price is $25/$100, or 25%, as indicated in the column Before Price Change in Exhibit 5-9. Now assume that this style of running shoes becomes less popular. The retailer checks with Nike and finds that because of the style change, the cost to the retailer to replace the pair of running shoes is now only $60. The retailer realizes that if the shoes are to be sold at all, they will have to be offered at a reduced price. The selling price is dropped from $100 to $80. If the retailer now buys a pair of shoes for $60 and sells them for $80, the gross profit will be $20 and the gross profit percentage will be maintained at 25%, as indicated in the right-hand column of Exhibit 5-9.

---

[3] Technically, the use of replacement cost as a measure of market value is subject to two constraints. First, market cannot be more than the net realizable value of the inventory. Second, inventory should not be recorded at less than net realizable value less a normal profit margin. The rationale for these two constraints is covered in intermediate accounting texts. For our purposes, we assume that replacement cost falls between the two constraints.

EXHIBIT 5-9 Gross Profit Percentage Before and After Price Change

	Before Price Change	After Price Change
Selling price	$100	$80
Cost	75	60
Gross profit	$ 25	$20
Gross profit percentage	25%	25%

© Cengage Learning 2013

To compare the results with and without the use of the LCM rule, assume that the facts are the same as before and that the retailer has ten pairs of those shoes in inventory on December 31, 2012. In addition, assume that all ten pair are sold at a clearance sale in January 2013 at the reduced price of $80 each. If the lower-of-cost-or-market rule is not used, the results for the years will be as follows:

LCM Rule Not Used	2012	2013	Total
Sales revenue ($80 per unit)	$0	$ 800	$ 800
Cost of goods sold (original cost of $75 per unit)	0	(750)	(750)
Gross profit	$0	$ 50	$ 50

If the LCM rule is not applied, the gross profit is distorted. Instead of the normal 25%, a gross profit percentage of $50/$800, or 6.25%, is reported in 2013 when the ten pairs of shoes are sold. If the LCM rule is applied, however, the results for the two years are as follows:

LCM Rule Used	2012	2013	Total
Sales revenue ($80 per unit)	$ 0	$ 800	$ 800
Cost of goods sold			
(replacement cost of $60 per unit)	0	(600)	(600)
Loss on decline in value of inventory:			
10 units × ($75 – $60)	(150)	0	(150)
Gross profit	$(150)	$ 200	$ 50

The use of the LCM rule serves two important functions: (1) to report the loss in value of the inventory, $15 per pair of running shoes, or $150 total, in the year the loss occurs; and (2) to report in the year the shoes are actually sold the normal gross profit of $200/ $800, or 25%, which is not affected by a change in the selling price.

Conservatism Is the Basis for the Lower-of-Cost-or-Market Rule

The departure from the cost basis is normally justified on the basis of conservatism. This concept is invoked by accountants when there is uncertainty. For example, in the preceding scenario, the future selling price of a pair of shoes is uncertain because of style changes. The use of the LCM rule serves two purposes. First, the inventory of shoes is written down from $75 to $60 for each pair. Second, the decline in value of the inventory is recognized at the time it is first observed rather than after the shoes are sold. An investor in a company with deteriorating inventory has good reason to be alarmed. Merchandisers who do not make the proper adjustments to their product lines go out of business as they compete with the lower prices of warehouse clubs and the lower overhead of e-business and home shopping networks.

You should realize that the write-down of the shoes violates the historical cost principle, which says that assets should be carried on the balance sheet at their original cost. But the LCM rule is considered a valid exception to the principle because it is a prudent reaction to the uncertainty involved and thus an application of conservatism in accounting.

5-2

REAL WORLD PRACTICE

Reading Kellogg's Financial Statements

A note to Kellogg's financial statements states that "[i]nventories are valued at the lower of cost or market. Cost is determined on an average cost basis." Why do you think the application of the lower-of-cost-or-market rule would be important to a business such as Kellogg's? In applying the rule, how does the company define "cost"?

© Nikada/istockphoto.com

Application of the LCM Rule

We have yet to consider how the LCM rule is applied to the entire inventory of a company. Three different interpretations of the rule are possible.

1. The lower of total cost or total market value for the **entire inventory** could be reported.
2. The lower of cost or market value for **each individual product or item** could be reported.
3. The lower of cost or market value for **groups of items** could be reported.

A company is free to choose any one of these approaches in applying the lower-of-cost-or-market rule. Three different answers are possible depending on the approach selected. The item-by-item approach (Number 2) is the most popular of the three approaches for two reasons. First, it produces the most conservative result. The reason is that with either a group-by-group or a total approach, increases in the values of some items of inventory offset declines in the values of other items. The item-by-item approach, however, ignores increases in value and recognizes all declines in value. Second, the item-by-item approach is the method required for tax purposes, although unlike LIFO, it is not required for book purposes merely because it is used for tax computations.

Consistency is important in deciding which approach to use in applying the LCM rule. As is the case with the selection of one of the inventory costing methods discussed earlier in the chapter, the approach chosen to apply the rule should be used consistently from one period to the next.

Lower-of-Cost-or-Market under International Standards

Both U.S. GAAP and international financial reporting standards (IFRS) require the use of the lower-of-cost-or-market rule to value inventories. However, these sets of standards differ in two respects. The first difference is the result of how market value is defined. U.S. GAAP defines market value as *replacement cost,* subject to a maximum and a minimum amount. In contract, IFRS uses *net realizable value* with no upper or lower limits imposed. The second difference relates to what happens in future periods after inventory has been written down to a lower market value. Under U.S. standards, this new amount becomes the basis for any future adjustments. However, under IFRS, write-downs of inventory can be reversed in later periods. This means that a gain is recognized when the value of the inventory goes back up.

LO9 Apply the lower-of-cost-or-market rule to the valuation of inventory.

- The principle of conservatism in accounting may warrant a departure from historical cost. This departure is known as the lower-of-cost-or-market rule (LCM).
  - Under LCM, the historical cost of inventory is compared with its replacement cost. If the replacement cost is lower, the Inventory account is reduced and a loss is recognized.

POD REVIEW 5.9

QUESTIONS　　**Answers to these questions are on the last page of the chapter.**

1. The use of the lower-of-cost-or-market rule to value inventory is justified on the basis of what principle?

   a. cost
   b. materiality
   c. conservatism
   d. revenue recognition

2. The adjustment to write down inventory to its market value results in a(n)

   a. gain on the income statement.
   b. loss on the income statement.
   c. increase in Retained Earnings.
   d. increase in a liability.

Analyzing the Management of Inventory

OVERVIEW: A company's ability to sell its inventory quickly can be measured by computing the inventory turnover ratio. How often a company sells its inventory during a period is found by dividing cost of goods sold by average inventory.

LO10 Analyze the management of inventory.

Inventory is the lifeblood of a company that sells a product. Gap Inc. must strike a balance between maintaining a sufficient variety of products to meet customers' needs and incurring the high cost of carrying inventory. The cost of storage and the lost income from the money tied up in inventory make inventory very expensive to keep on hand. Thus, the more quickly a company can sell—that is, turn over—its inventory, the better. Using data from Exhibit 5-4, the **inventory turnover ratio** for Daisy's Running Depot is calculated as follows:

Inventory turnover ratio
A measure of the number of times inventory is sold during the period.

$$\frac{\text{Cost of Goods Sold}}{\text{Average inventory}} = \frac{60{,}000}{(15{,}000 + 18{,}000)/2} = \frac{60{,}000}{16{,}500} = 3.6 \text{ times}$$

It is a measure of the number of times inventory is sold during the period.

Use the Ratio Decision Model below and on the following page to compute and analyze the inventory turnover ratio for Gap Inc.

USING THE RATIO DECISION MODEL

Analyzing the Management of Inventory

Use the following Ratio Decision Model to analyze the inventory of Gap Inc. or any other public company.

1. Formulate the Question

Managers, investors, and creditors are all interested in how well a company manages its inventory. The quicker inventory can be sold, the sooner the money will be available to invest in more inventory or to use for other purposes. Those interested must be able to answer the following question:

How many times a year does a company turn over its inventory?

2. Gather the Information from the Financial Statements

Cost of goods sold is reported on the income statement, representing a flow for a period of time. On the other hand, inventory is an asset, representing a balance at a point in time. Thus, a comparison of the two requires the cost of goods sold for the year and an average of the balance in inventory:

- Cost of goods sold: From the income statement for the year
- Average inventory: From the balance sheets at the end of the two most recent years

3. Calculate the Ratio

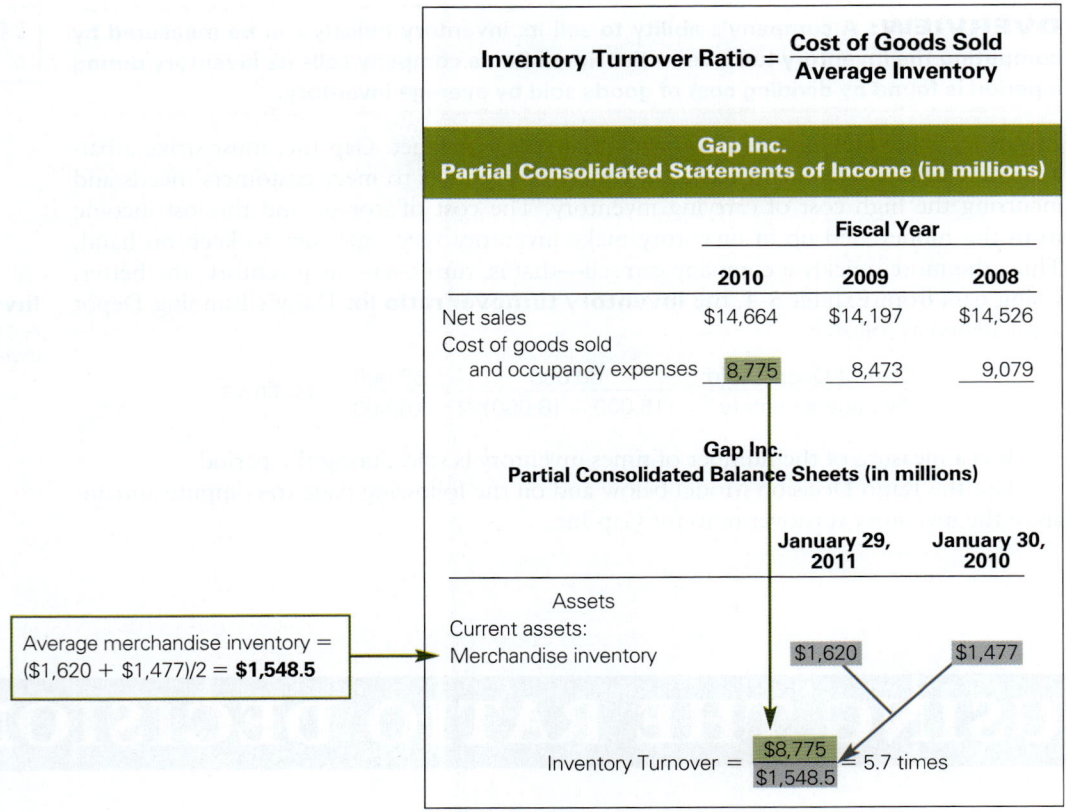

$$\text{Inventory Turnover Ratio} = \frac{\text{Cost of Goods Sold}}{\text{Average Inventory}}$$

Gap Inc.
Partial Consolidated Statements of Income (in millions)

| | Fiscal Year | | |
	2010	2009	2008
Net sales	$14,664	$14,197	$14,526
Cost of goods sold and occupancy expenses	8,775	8,473	9,079

Gap Inc.
Partial Consolidated Balance Sheets (in millions)

	January 29, 2011	January 30, 2010
Assets		
Current assets:		
Merchandise inventory	$1,620	$1,477

Average merchandise inventory = ($1,620 + $1,477)/2 = **$1,548.5**

$$\text{Inventory Turnover} = \frac{\$8,775}{\$1,548.5} = 5.7 \text{ times}$$

4. Compare the Ratio with Others

Management compares the current year's turnover rate with prior years to see if the company is experiencing slower or faster turns of its inventory. It is also important to compare the rate with that of other companies in the same industry.

Gap Inc.		American Eagle Outfitters Inc.	
Year Ended January 29, 2011	Year Ended January 30, 2010	Year Ended January 29, 2011	Year Ended January 30, 2010
5.7 times	5.7 times	5.7 times	5.6 times

5. Interpret the Results

This ratio tells us that in fiscal year 2010, Gap Inc. turned over its inventory an average of 5.7 times. This is the same as the turnover in the prior year and comparable to the turnover rates for Gap's competitor, American Eagle Outfitters, Inc. An alternative way to look at a company's efficiency in managing its inventory is to calculate the number of days, on average, that inventory is on hand before it is sold. This measure is called the **number of days' sales in inventory** and is calculated as follows for Gap Inc. in 2010, assuming 360 days in a year:

Number of days' sales in inventory
A measure of how long it takes to sell inventory.

$$\text{Number of Day's Sales in Inventory} = \frac{\text{Number of Days in the Period}}{\text{Inventory Turnover Ratio}}$$

$$= \frac{360}{5.7}$$

$$= 63 \text{ days}$$

This measure tells us that it took Gap Inc. 63 days, or two months, on average to sell its inventory. ∎

LO10 Analyze the management of inventory.

- Inventory turnover is a measure of how efficiently inventory is managed. The ratio measures how quickly inventory is sold and is calculated as follows:

$$\frac{\text{Cost of Goods Sold}}{\text{Average Inventory}}$$

The higher the ratio, the less time inventory resides in storage (i.e., the more quickly it turns over).

- The average length of time that it takes to sell inventory can be derived from the inventory turnover ratio:

$$\text{Number of Days' Sales in Inventory} = \frac{\text{Number of Days in the Period}}{\text{Inventory Turnover Ratio}}$$

POD REVIEW 5.10

QUESTIONS   **Answers to these questions are on the last page of the chapter.**

1. Which of the following strategies should a company pursue concerning its inventory?

   a. Maintain an inventory stock much higher than anticipated demand so that there is virtually no risk of running out of inventory.
   b. Maintain an inventory stock lower than anticipated demand so as to avoid the high costs of carrying it.
   c. Attempt to strike a balance between maintaining a sufficient amount of inventory to meet demand and incurring the high cost of carrying it.
   d. None of the above applies.

2. A company began the year with $50,000 in inventory and ended the year with $70,000 in inventory. Cost of goods sold for the year amounted to $720,000. Assuming 360 days in a year, how long, on average, does it take the company to sell its inventory?

   a. 12 days
   b. 30 days
   c. 60 days
   d. none of the above

How Inventories Affect the Cash Flows Statement

OVERVIEW: Changes in both inventory and accounts payable are reported on a statement of cash flows prepared using the indirect method. An increase in inventory is deducted, and a decrease is added back. An increase in accounts payable is deducted, and a decrease is added back.

LO11 Explain the effects that inventory transactions have on the statement of cash flows.

The effects on the income statement and the statement of cash flows from inventory-related transactions differ significantly. This chapter has focused on how the purchase and sale of inventory are reported on the income statement. We found that the cost of the inventory sold during the period is deducted on the income statement as cost of goods sold.

The appropriate reporting on a statement of cash flows for inventory transactions depends on whether the direct or indirect method is used. If the direct method is used to prepare the Operating Activities category of the statement, the amount of cash paid to suppliers of inventory is shown as a deduction in this section of the statement.

If the more popular indirect method is used, it is necessary to make adjustments to net income for the changes in two accounts: Inventory and Accounts Payable. These adjustments are summarized in Exhibit 5-10. An increase in inventory is deducted because it indicates that the company is building up its stock of inventory and thus expending cash. A decrease in inventory is added to net income. An increase in accounts payable is added because it indicates that during the period, the company increased the amount it owes suppliers and therefore conserved its cash. A decrease in accounts payable is deducted because the company actually reduced the amount owed suppliers during the period.

EXHIBIT 5-10 Inventories and the Statement of Cash Flows

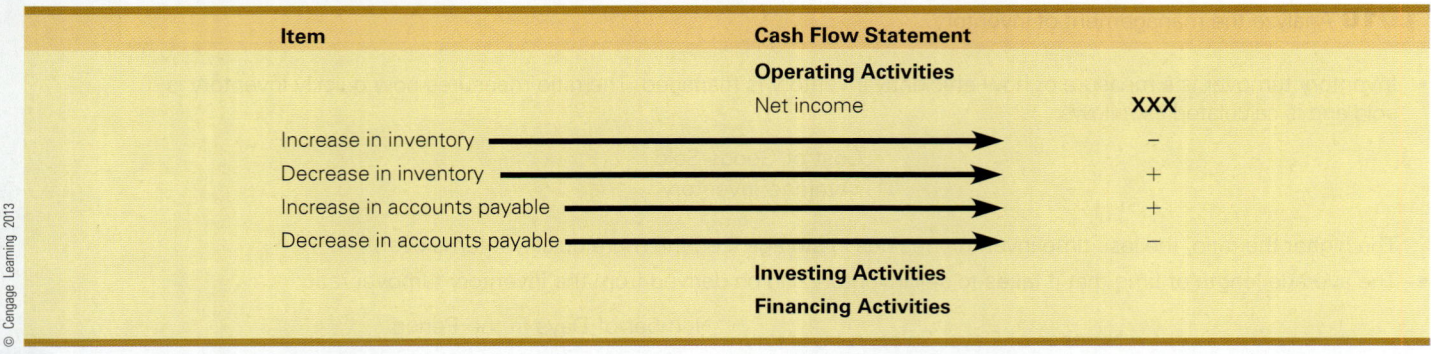

Item	Cash Flow Statement
	Operating Activities
	Net income
Increase in inventory	–
Decrease in inventory	+
Increase in accounts payable	+
Decrease in accounts payable	–
	Investing Activities
	Financing Activities

The Operating Activities category of the statement of cash flows for **Kellogg Company** is presented in Exhibit 5-11. The increase in inventory is deducted because the increase in this asset uses the company's cash. An increase in accounts payable conserves Kellogg's cash. Thus, the increase in this item in 2010 is added to net income.

EXHIBIT 5-11 Partial Consolidated Statement of Cash Flows for Kellogg's

Kellogg Company and Subsidiaries
Consolidated Statements of Cash Flows

(millions)	Fiscal Year		
	2010	**2009**	**2008**
Operating activities			
Net income	$1,240	$1,208	$1,146
Adjustments to reconcile net income to operating cash flows:			
Depreciation and amortization	392	384	375
Deferred income taxes	266	(40)	157
Other	97	13	121
Pension and other postretirement benefit contributions	(643)	(100)	(451)
Change in operating assets and liabilities:			
Trade receivables	59	(75)	48
Inventories	(146)	(13)	41
Accounts payable	72	(59)	32
Accured income taxes	(192)	112	(85)
Accounts interest expense	9	(5)	3
Accrued and prepaid advertising, promotion and trade allowances	(12)	91	(10)
Accured salaries and wages	(169)	42	(47)
All other current assets and liabilities	35	85	(63)
Net cash provided by operating activities	$1,008	$1,643	$1,267

> Increase here uses cash and thus is deducted.

> Increase here conserves cash and thus is added.

Refer to Notes to Consolidated Financial Statements

Source: Kellogg Company Form 10-K for 2010.

© Cengage Learning 2013

LO11 Explain the effects that inventory transactions have on the statement of cash flows.

- Under the indirect method of calculating cash flows from operating activities, both the changes in the Inventory account and the Accounts Payable account must be taken into consideration.

POD REVIEW 5.11

QUESTIONS   Answers to these questions are on the last page of the chapter.

1. On a statement of cash flows prepared using the indirect method, a decrease in inventory is

   a. deducted from net income.
   b. added to net income.
   c. ignored.
   d. deducted from net income or added to net income depending on the size of the decrease.

2. A company's change in accounts payable was added back to net income on the statement of cash flows prepared using the indirect method. This is an indication that the amount owed to suppliers during the period

   a. increased.
   b. decreased.
   c. was unchanged.
   d. none of the above.

© Cengage Learning 2013

APPENDIX

Accounting Tools: Inventory Costing Methods with the Use of a Perpetual Inventory System

OVERVIEW: The results from using the LIFO method differ if a company uses a perpetual system rather than a periodic system. The same is true of the weighted average method.

LO12 Explain the differences in the accounting for periodic and perpetual inventory systems and apply the inventory costing methods using a perpetual system (Appendix).

The illustrations of the inventory costing methods in the chapter assumed the use of a periodic inventory system. This appendix will show how the methods are applied when a company maintains a perpetual inventory system. It is important to understand the difference between inventory *costing systems* and inventory *methods*. The two inventory systems differ in terms of how often the Inventory account is updated: periodically or perpetually. However, when a company sells identical units of product and the cost to purchase each unit is subject to change, the company also must choose an inventory costing method such as FIFO, LIFO, or weighted average.

Earlier, the chapter provided illustrations of the various costing methods with a periodic system. The same data are now used to illustrate how the methods differ when a perpetual system is used. Keep in mind that if a company uses specific identification, the results will be the same regardless of whether it uses the periodic or perpetual system. To compare the periodic and perpetual systems for the other methods, we must add one important piece of information: the date of each of the sales. The original data as well as number of units sold on the various dates are summarized as follows:

Date	Purchases	Sales	Balance
Beginning inventory			500 units @ $10
January 20	300 units @ $11		800 units
February 18		450 units	350 units
April 8	400 units @ $12		750 units
June 19		300 units	450 units
September 5	200 units @ $13		650 units
October 20		150 units	500 units
December 12	100 units @ $14		600 units

FIFO Costing with a Perpetual System

Example 5-20, shown below, illustrates the FIFO method on a perpetual basis. The basic premise of FIFO applies whether a periodic or a perpetual system is used: the first units purchased are assumed to be the first units sold. With a perpetual system, however, this concept is applied at the time of each sale. For example, note in Example 5-20 which 450 units are assumed to be sold on February 18. The 450 units sold are taken from the beginning inventory of 500 units with a unit cost of $10. Thus, the inventory or balance after this sale as shown in the last three columns is 50 units at $10 and 300 units at $11, for a total of $3,800. The purchase on April 8 of 400 units at $12 is added to the running balance. On a FIFO basis, the sale of 300 units on June 19 comes from the remainder of the beginning inventory of 50 units and another 250 units from the first purchase at $11 on January 20. The balance after this sale is 50 units at $11 and 400 units at $12. You should follow through the last three transactions in Example 5-20 to make sure you understand the application of FIFO on a perpetual basis. An important point to note about the ending inventory of $7,600 is that it is the same amount calculated for FIFO periodic earlier in the chapter:

FIFO periodic (Example 5-12)	$7,600
FIFO perpetual (Example 5-20)	$7,600

Whether the method is applied each time a sale is made or only at the end of the period, the earliest units in are the first units out and the two systems will yield the same ending inventory under FIFO.

Example 5-20 Determining Ending Inventory Using FIFO with a Perpetual System

Date	Purchases			Sales			Balance		
	Units	Unit Cost	Total Cost	Units	Unit Cost	Total Cost	Units	Unit Cost	Balance
1/1							500	$10	$5,000
1/20	300	$11	$3,300				500	10	
							300	11	8 300
2/18				450	$10	$4,500	50	10	
							300	11	3,800
4/8	400	12	4,800				50	10	
							300	11	
							400	12	8,600
6/19				50	10	500	50	11	
				250	11	2,750	400	12	5,350
9/5	200	13	2,600				50	11	
							400	12	
							200	13	7,950
10/20				50	11	550	300	12	
				100	12	1,200	200	13	6,200
12/12	100	14	1,400				300	12	
							200	13	
							100	14	7,600

LIFO Costing with a Perpetual System

A LIFO cost flow with the use of a perpetual system is illustrated in Example 5-21. First, note which 450 units are assumed to be sold on February 18. The sale consists of the most recent units acquired, 300 units at $11, and then 150 units from the beginning inventory at $10. Thus, the balance after this sale is simply the remaining 350 units from the beginning inventory priced at $10. The purchase on April 8 results in a balance of 350 units at $10 and 400 units at $12.

Note what happens with LIFO when it is applied on a perpetual basis. In essence, a gap is created. Units acquired at the earliest price of $10 and units acquired at the most recent price of $12 are on hand, but none of those at the middle price of $11 remain. This situation arises because LIFO is applied every time a sale is made rather than only at the end of the year. Because of this difference, the amount of ending inventory differs depending on which system is used:

LIFO periodic (Example 5-13)	$6,100
LIFO perpetual (Example 5-21)	$6,750

Example 5-21 Determining Ending Inventory Using LIFO with a Perpetual System

	Purchases			Sales			Balance		
Date	Units	Unit Cost	Total Cost	Units	Unit Cost	Total Cost	Units	Unit Cost	Balance
1/1							500	$10	$5,000
1/20	300	$11	$3,300				500	10	
							300	11	8,300
2/18				300	$11	$3,300			
				150	10	1,500	350	10	3,500
4/8	400	12	4,800				350	10	
							400	12	8,300
6/19				300	12	3,600	350	10	
							100	12	4,700
9/5	200	13	2,600				350	10	
							100	12	
							200	13	7,300
10/20				150	13	1,950	350	10	
							100	12	
							50	13	5,350
12/12	100	14	1,400				350	10	
							100	12	
							50	13	
							100	14	6,750

© Cengage Learning 2013

Moving Average with a Perpetual System

When a weighted average cost assumption is applied with a perpetual system, it is sometimes called a **moving average**. As indicated in Example 5-22, each time a purchase is made, a new weighted average cost must be computed, thus the name *moving average*. For example, the goods available for sale after the January 20 purchase consist of 500 units at $10 and 300 units at $11, which results in an average cost of $10.38. This is the unit cost applied to the 450 units sold on February 18. The 400 units purchased on

Moving average
The name given to an average cost method when a weighted average cost assumption is used with a perpetual inventory system.

April 8 require the computation of a new unit cost, as indicated in the second footnote in Example 5-22. As you might have suspected, the ending inventory with an average cost flow differs depending on whether a periodic or a perpetual system is used:

Weighted average periodic (Example 5-11)	$6,840
Moving average perpetual (Example 5-22)	$7,290

Example 5-22 Determining Ending Inventory Using Moving Average with a Perpetual System

	Purchases			Sales			Balance		
Date	Units	Unit Cost	Total Cost	Units	Unit Cost	Total Cost	Units	Unit Cost	Balance
1/1							500	$10.00	$5,000
1/20	300	$11	$3,300				800	10.38*	8,304
2/18				450	$10.38	$4,671	350	10.38	3,633
4/8	400	12	4,800				750	11.24†	8,430
6/19				300	11.24	3,372	450	11.24	5,058
9/5	200	13	2,600				650	11.78‡	7,657
10/20				150	11.78	1,767	500	11.78	5,890
12/12	100	14	1,400				600	12.15§	7,290

The moving average prices per unit are calculated as follows:

*($5,000 + $3,300)/800 units = $10.38 (rounded to nearest cent)
†($3,633 + $4,800)/750 units = $11.24
‡($5,058 + $2,600)/650 units = $11.78
§($5,890 + $1,400)/600 units = $12.15

© Cengage Learning 2013

LO12 Explain the differences in the accounting for periodic and perpetual inventory systems and apply the inventory costing methods using a perpetual system.

- The three inventory costing methods—FIFO, LIFO, and weighted average—may be used in combination with a perpetual inventory system.
  - The inventory costing method is applied after each sale of merchandise to update the Inventory account.
  - The results from using LIFO differ depending on whether a periodic or perpetual system is used. The same is true with weighted average, which is called moving average in a perpetual system.

POD REVIEW

5.12

QUESTIONS   Answers to these questions are on the last page of the chapter.

1. For which inventory method does the dollar amount of inventory on hand at the end of the period not differ regardless of whether a company uses a periodic or a perpetual inventory system?
   a. weighted average cost
   b. FIFO
   c. LIFO
   d. The results always differ depending on the system used.

2. Moving average is the name given to the use of
   a. the specific identification method used with a perpetual inventory system.
   b. an average cost method used with a periodic inventory system.
   c. an average cost method used with a perpetual inventory system.
   d. none of the above.

RATIO REVIEW

$$\text{Gross Profit Ratio} = \frac{\text{Gross Profit (Income Statement)}}{\text{Net Sales (Income Statement)}}$$

$$\text{Inventory Turnover Ratio} = \frac{\text{Cost of Goods Sold (Income Statement)}}{\text{Average Inventory}^*\text{(Balance Sheet)}}$$

*Average inventory can be estimated using the following calculation:

$$\frac{\text{Beginning Inventory} + \text{Ending Inventory}}{2}$$

$$\text{Number of Days Sales in Inventory} = \frac{\text{Number of Days in the Period}^{**}}{\text{Inventory Turnover Ratio}}$$

**Usually assume 360 days unless some other number is a better estimate of the number of days in the period.

ACCOUNTS HIGHLIGHTED

Account Titles	Where It Appears	In What Section	Page Number
Merchandise Inventory	Balance Sheet	Current Assets	221
Sales Revenue	Income Statement	Sales	224
Sales Returns and Allowances	Income Statement	Contra to Sales Revenue	224
Sales Discounts	Income Statement	Contra to Sales Revenue	225
Cost of Goods Sold	Income Statement	Expenses	226
Purchases	Income Statement	Cost of Goods Sold	229
Purchase Returns and Allowances	Income Statement	Contra to Purchases	230
Transportation-In	Income Statement	Added to Purchases	229
Purchase Discounts	Income Statement	Contra to Purchases	231
Transportation-Out	Income Statement	Selling Expense	232
Loss on Decline in Value of Inventory	Income Statement	Other Expenses	250

KEY TERMS QUIZ

Because of the large number of terms introduced in this chapter, there are two quizzes on key terms. Read each definition below and write the number of the definition in the blank beside the appropriate term. The quiz solutions appear at the end of the chapter.

Quiz 1: Merchandise Accounting

_____ Merchandise Inventory		_____ Cost of goods sold	
_____ Raw materials		_____ Perpetual system	
_____ Work in process		_____ Periodic system	
_____ Finished goods		_____ Transportation-In	
_____ Gross profit		_____ Purchases	
_____ Net sales		_____ Purchase Returns and Allowances	
_____ Sales revenue		_____ Purchase Discounts	
_____ Sales Returns and Allowances		_____ FOB destination point	
_____ Sales Discounts		_____ FOB shipping point	
_____ Cost of goods available for sale		_____ Gross profit ratio	

(Continued)

1. The contra-revenue account used to record refunds to customers and reductions of their accounts.
2. The adjunct account used to record freight costs paid by the buyer.
3. The system in which the Inventory account is increased at the time of each purchase of merchandise and decreased at the time of each sale.
4. The contra-purchases account used in a periodic inventory system when a refund is received from a supplier or a reduction is given in the balance owed to the supplier.
5. The contra-revenue account used to record discounts given to customers for early payment of their accounts.
6. Terms that require the seller to pay for the cost of shipping the merchandise to the buyer.
7. Terms that require the buyer to pay the shipping costs.
8. The system in which the Inventory account is updated only at the end of the period.
9. Beginning inventory plus cost of goods purchased.
10. The contra-purchases account used to record reductions in purchase price for early payment to the supplier.
11. The account used in a periodic inventory system to record acquisitions of merchandise.
12. Sales revenue less sales returns and allowances and sales discounts.
13. Cost of goods available for sale minus ending inventory.
14. Gross profit divided by net sales.
15. Sales less cost of goods sold.
16. The cost of unfinished products in a manufacturing company.
17. The account that wholesalers and retailers use to report inventory held for sale.
18. The inventory of a manufacturer before the addition of any direct labor or manufacturing overhead.
19. A manufacturer's inventory that is complete and ready for sale.
20. A representation of the inflow of assets from the sale of a product.

Quiz 2: Inventory Valuation

_____ Specific identification method	_____ Replacement cost
_____ Weighted average cost method	_____ Inventory profit
_____ FIFO method	_____ Lower-of-cost-or-market (LCM)
_____ LIFO method	— rule
_____ LIFO liquidation	_____ Inventory turnover ratio
_____ LIFO conformity rule	_____ Number of days' sales in inventory
_____ LIFO reserve	_____ Moving average (Appendix)

1. The name given to an average cost method when a weighted average cost assumption is used with a perpetual inventory system.
2. An inventory costing method that assigns the same unit cost to all units available for sale during the period.
3. A conservative inventory valuation approach that is an attempt to anticipate declines in the value of inventory before its actual sale.
4. An inventory costing method that assigns the most recent costs to ending inventory.
5. The current cost of a unit of inventory.
6. An inventory costing method that assigns the most recent costs to cost of goods sold.
7. A measure of how long it takes to sell inventory.
8. The IRS requirement that when LIFO is used on a tax return, it must also be used in reporting income to stockholders.
9. An inventory costing method that relies on matching unit costs with the actual units sold.
10. The portion of the gross profit that results from holding inventory during a period of rising prices.
11. The result of selling more units than are purchased during the period, which can have negative tax consequences if a company is using LIFO.
12. The excess of the value of a company's inventory stated at FIFO over the value stated at LIFO.
13. A measure of the number of times inventory is sold during a period.

ALTERNATE TERMS

gross profit gross margin
merchandiser wholesaler, retailer
raw materials direct materials

sales revenue sales
transportation-in freight-in
work in process work in progress

WARMUP EXERCISES & SOLUTIONS

Warmup Exercise 5-1 Net Sales

LO2

McDowell Merchandising reported sales revenue, sales returns and allowances, and sales discounts of $57,000, $1,500, and $900, respectively, in 2012.

Required

Prepare the Net Sales section of McDowell's 2012 income statement.

Key to the Solution Refer to Exhibit 5-3.

Warmup Exercise 5-2 Cost of Goods Sold

LO3

The following amounts are taken from White Wholesalers' records. (All amounts are for 2012.)

Inventory, January 1	$14,200
Inventory, December 31	10,300
Purchases	87,500
Purchase discounts	4,200
Purchase returns and allowances	1,800
Transportation-in	4,500

Required

Prepare the Cost of Goods Sold section of White's 2012 income statement.

Key to the Solution Refer to Exhibit 5-4.

Warmup Exercise 5-3 Inventory Valuation

LO6

Busby Corp. began the year with 75 units of inventory that it paid $2 each to acquire. During the year, it purchased an additional 100 units for $3 each. Busby sold 150 units during the year.

Required

1. Compute cost of goods sold and ending inventory assuming Busby uses FIFO.
2. Compute cost of goods sold and ending inventory assuming Busby uses LIFO.

Key to the Solution Refer to the mechanics of the methods beginning on page 239.

Warmup Exercise 5-4 Lower of Cost or Market

LO9

Glendive reports its inventory on a FIFO basis and has inventory with a cost of $78,000 on December 31. The cost to replace the inventory on this date would be only $71,000.

Required

Identify and analyze the necessary adjustment on December 31.

Key to the Solution Recall the need to write down inventory when market is less than cost.

LO10   Warmup Exercise 5-5 Inventory Turnover

Sidney began the year with $130,000 in merchandise inventory and ended the year with $190,000. Sales and cost of goods sold for the year were $900,000 and $640,000, respectively.

Required

1. Compute Sidney's inventory turnover ratio.
2. Compute the number of days' sales in inventory.

Key to the Solution Review how these two statistics are computed on pages 253–255.

Solutions to Warmup Exercises

Warmup Exercise 5-1

McDowell Merchandising
Partial Income Statement
For the Year Ended December 31, 2012

Sales revenue	$57,000	
Less: Sales returns and allowances	1,500	
Sales discounts	900	
Net sales		$54,600

Warmup Exercise 5-2

White Wholesalers
Partial Income Statement
For the Year Ended December 31, 2012

Inventory, January 1, 2012		$ 14,200	
Purchases	$87,500		
Less: Purchase returns and allowances	1,800		
Purchase discounts	4,200		
Net purchases	$81,500		
Add: Transportation-in	4,500		
Cost of goods purchased		86,000	
Cost of goods available for sale		$100,200	
Less: Inventory, December 31, 2012		10,300	
Cost of goods sold			$89,900

Warmup Exercise 5-3

1. Cost of goods sold: $(75 \times \$2) + (75 \times \$3)$ = $375
   Ending inventory: $25 \times \$3$ = $ 75

2. Cost of goods sold: $(100 \times \$3) + (50 \times \$2)$ = $400
   Ending inventory: $25 \times \$2$ = $ 50

Warmup Exercise 5-4

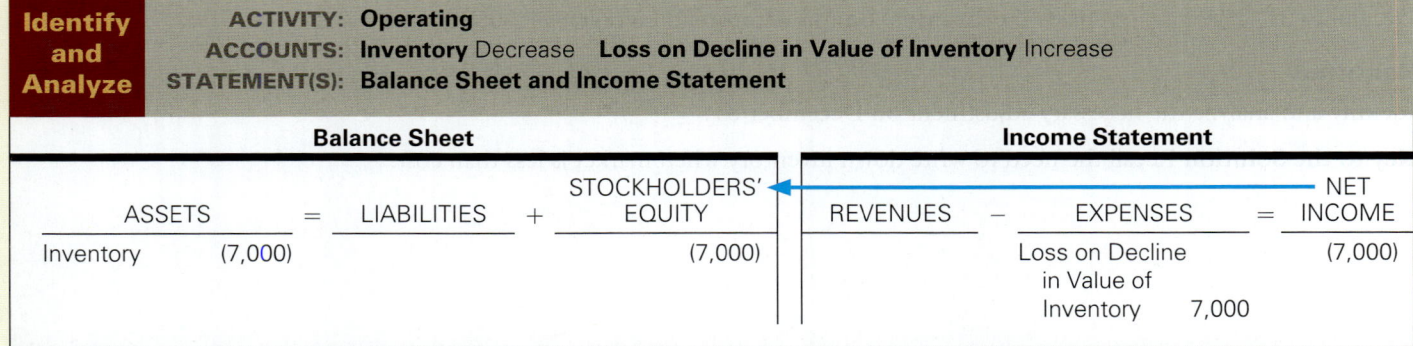

Identify and Analyze	ACTIVITY: **Operating**
	ACCOUNTS: **Inventory** Decrease **Loss on Decline in Value of Inventory** Increase
	STATEMENT(S): **Balance Sheet and Income Statement**

Balance Sheet				**Income Statement**		
ASSETS	=	LIABILITIES	+	STOCKHOLDERS' EQUITY	REVENUES	− EXPENSES = NET INCOME
Inventory (7,000)				(7,000)		Loss on Decline in Value of Inventory 7,000 (7,000)

Warmup Exercise 5-5

1. Inventory Turnover Ratio $= \dfrac{\text{Cost of Goods Sold}}{\text{Average Inventory}}$

$$= \dfrac{\$640,000}{(\$130,000 + \$190,000)/2}$$

$$= \dfrac{\$640,000}{\$160,000} = 4 \text{ times}$$

2. Number of Days' Sales in Inventory $= \dfrac{\text{Number of Days in the Period}}{\text{Inventory Turnover Ratio}}$

$$= \dfrac{360}{4} = 90 \text{ days}$$

REVIEW PROBLEM & SOLUTION

Stewart Distributing Company sells a single product for $2 per unit and uses a periodic inventory system. The following data are available for the year:

Date	Transaction	Number of Units	Unit Cost	Total
1/1	Beginning inventory	500	$1.00	$500.00
2/5	Purchase	350	1.10	385.00
4/12	Sale	(550)		
7/17	Sale	(200)		
9/23	Purchase	400	1.30	520.00
11/5	Sale	(300)		

Required

1. Compute cost of goods sold assuming the use of the weighted average costing method.
2. Compute the dollar amount of ending inventory assuming the FIFO costing method.
3. Compute gross profit assuming the LIFO costing method.
4. Assume a 40% tax rate. Compute the amount of taxes saved if Stewart uses the LIFO method rather than the FIFO method.

Solution to Review Problem

1. Cost of goods sold, weighted average cost method:

Cost of goods available for sale	
$500 + $385 + $520 =	$ 1,405
Divided by:	
Units available for sale:	
500 + 350 + 400 =	÷ 1,250 units
Weighted average cost	$ 1.124 per unit
× Number of units sold:	
550 + 200 + 300 =	× 1,050 units
Cost of goods sold	$ 1,180.20

2. Ending inventory, FIFO cost method:

Units available for sale	1,250
– Units sold	– 1,050
= Units in ending inventory	200
× Most recent purchase price of	× $ 1.30
= Ending inventory	$ 260

(Continued)

3. Gross profit, LIFO cost method:

Sales revenue: 1,050 units × $2 each		$ 2,100
Cost of goods sold		
400 units × $1.30 = $520		
350 units × $1.10 = 385		
300 units × $1.00 = 300		−1,205
Gross profit		$ 895

4. Taxes saved from using LIFO instead of FIFO:

LIFO Cost of goods sold		$1,205
− FIFO Cost of goods sold:		
Cost of goods available for sale	$1,405	
Ending inventory from part (2)	260	
Cost of goods sold		− 1,145
Additional expense from use of LIFO		$ 60
× Tax rate		× 0.40
Tax savings from the use of LIFO		$ 24

QUESTIONS

1. What are three distinct types of costs that manufacturers incur? Describe each of them.
2. When a company gives a cash refund on returned merchandise, why doesn't it just reduce Sales Revenue instead of using a contra-revenue account?
3. What do credit terms 3/20, n/60 mean? How valuable to the customer is the discount offered in these terms?
4. What is the difference between a periodic inventory system and a perpetual inventory system?
5. How have point-of-sale terminals improved the ability of mass merchandisers to use a perpetual inventory system?
6. In a periodic inventory system, what kind of account is Purchases? Is it an asset, an expense, or neither?
7. Why are shipping terms such as FOB shipping point or FOB destination point important in deciding ownership of inventory at the end of the year?
8. How and why are transportation-in and transportation-out recorded differently?
9. How is a company's gross profit determined? What does the gross profit ratio tell you about a company's performance during the year?
10. What is the relationship between the valuation of inventory as an asset on the balance sheet and the measurement of income?
11. What is the justification for including freight costs incurred in acquiring incoming goods in the cost of the inventory rather than simply treating the cost as an expense of the period? What is the significance of this decision for accounting purposes?
12. What are the inventory characteristics that would allow a company to use the specific identification method? Give at least two examples of inventory for which the method is appropriate.
13. How can the specific identification method allow management to manipulate income?
14. What is the significance of the adjective *weighted* in the weighted average cost method? Use an example to illustrate your answer.
15. Which inventory method, FIFO or LIFO, more nearly approximates the physical flow of products in most businesses? Explain your answer.
16. York Inc. manufactures notebook computers and has experienced noticeable declines in the purchase price of many of the components it uses, including computer chips. Which inventory costing method should York use if it wants to maximize net income? Explain your answer.
17. Which inventory costing method should a company use when it wants to minimize taxes? Does your response depend on whether prices are rising or falling? Explain your answers.
18. The president of Ace Retail commented on the company's new controller: "The woman is brilliant! She has shown us how

we can maximize our income and at the same time minimize the amount of taxes we have to pay the government. Because the cost to purchase our inventory constantly goes up, we will use FIFO to calculate cost of goods sold on the income statement to minimize the amount charged to cost of goods sold and thus maximize net income. For tax purposes, however, we will use LIFO because this will minimize taxable income and thus minimize the amount we have to pay in taxes." Should the president be enthralled with the new controller? Explain your answer.

19. What does the term *LIFO liquidation* mean? How can it lead to poor buying habits?

20. Historical-based costing methods are sometimes criticized for leading to inventory profits. In a period of rising prices, which inventory costing method will lead to the most "inventory profit"? Explain your answer.

21. Is it acceptable for a company to disclose in its annual report that it is switching from some other inventory costing method to LIFO to save on taxes? Explain.

22. Delevan Corp. uses a periodic inventory system and is counting its year-end inventory. Due to a lack of communication, two different teams count the same section of the warehouse. What effect will this error have on net income?

23. What is the rationale for valuing inventory at the lower of cost or market?

24. Why is it likely that the result from applying the lower-of-cost-or-market rule using a total approach (i.e., by comparing total cost to total market value) and the result from applying the rule on an item-by-item basis will differ?

25. Ralston Corp.'s cost of sales has remained steady over the last two years. During this same time period, however, its inventory has increased considerably. What does this information tell you about the company's inventory turnover? Explain your answer.

26. Why is the weighted average cost method called a moving average when a company uses a perpetual inventory system? (Appendix)

BRIEF EXERCISES

Brief Exercise 5-1   Types and Forms of Inventory Costs for a Manufacturer   LO1

What are the three types of costs incurred by a manufacturer? What are the three forms that inventory can take for a manufacturer?

Brief Exercise 5-2   Net Sales   LO2

During the current period, Boston Corp. sold products to customers for a total of $85,000. Due to defective products, customers were given $2,000 in refunds for products that were returned and another $4,500 in reductions to their account balances. Discounts in the amount of $6,500 were given for early payment of account balances. Prepare the Net Sales section of Boston's income statement.

Brief Exercise 5-3   Cost of Goods Sold   LO3

For each of the following items, indicate whether it increases (I) or decreases (D) cost of goods sold.

_____ Purchases		_____ Transportation-in
_____ Beginning inventory		_____ Ending inventory
_____ Purchase discounts		_____ Purchase returns and allowances

Brief Exercise 5-4   Gross Profit Ratio   LO4

Dexter Inc. recorded net sales of $50,000 during the period, and its cost of goods sold amounted to $30,000. Compute the company's gross profit ratio.

LO5 **Brief Exercise 5-5 Valuation of Inventory and Measurement of Income**

Baxter operates a chain of electronics stores and buys its products from a number of different manufacturers around the world. Give at least three examples of costs that Baxter might incur that should be added to the purchase price of its inventory.

LO6 **Brief Exercise 5-6 Inventory Costing Methods**

EXAMPLE 5-12, 5-13

Belden started the year with 1,000 units of inventory with a unit cost of $5. During the year, it bought 3,000 units at a cost of $6 per unit. A year-end count revealed 500 units on hand. Compute ending inventory assuming both FIFO and LIFO.

LO7 **Brief Exercise 5-7 Selecting an Inventory Costing Method**

A company currently uses the LIFO method to value its inventory. For each of the following items, indicate whether it would be higher (H) or lower (L) if the company changed to the FIFO method. Assume a period of rising prices.

_____	Cost of goods sold	_____	Income taxes
_____	Gross profit	_____	Cash outflow
_____	Income before taxes		

LO8 **Brief Exercise 5-8 Inventory Error**

EXAMPLE 5-17, 5-18, 5-19

Due to a clerical error, a company overstated by $50,000 the amount of inventory on hand at the end of the year. Will net income for the year be overstated or understated? Identify the two accounts on the year-end balance sheet that will be in error and indicate whether they will be understated or overstated.

LO9 **Brief Exercise 5-9 Lower-of-Cost-or-Market Rule**

The cost of Wright Corp.'s inventory at the end of the year was $75,000; however, due to obsolescence, the cost to replace the inventory was only $55,000. Identify and analyze the adjustment needed at the end of the year.

LO10 **Brief Exercise 5-10 Inventory Turnover**

Two companies each recorded $10 million in cost of goods sold for the year. Company A had average inventory of $100,000 on hand during the year. Company B's average inventory was $1 million. One company is a car dealer, and the other is a wholesaler of fresh fruits and vegetables. Which company sells cars, and which company sells fruits and vegetables? Explain your answer.

LO11 **Brief Exercise 5-11 Cash Flow Effects**

Grogan's inventory increased by $50,000 during the year, and its accounts payable increased by $35,000. Indicate how each of those changes would be reflected on a statement of cash flows prepared using the indirect method.

LO12 **Brief Exercise 5-12 Inventory Methods Using a Perpetual System (Appendix)**

EXAMPLE 5-11, 5-22

Will the dollar amount assigned to inventory differ when a company uses the weighted average cost method depending on whether a periodic or perpetual inventory system is used? Explain your answer.

EXERCISES

LO1 **Exercise 5-1 Inventoriable Costs**

During the first month of operations, ABC Company incurred the following costs in ordering and receiving merchandise for resale. No inventory was sold.

List price, $100, 200 units purchased
Volume discount, 10% off list price
Paid freight costs, $56
Insurance cost while goods were in transit, $32
Long-distance phone charge to place orders,
$4.35

Purchasing department salary, $1,000
Supplies used to label goods at retail price,
$9.75
Interest paid to supplier, $46

Required

What amount do you recommend the company record as merchandise inventory on its balance sheet? Explain your answer. For any items not to be included in inventory, indicate their appropriate treatment in the financial statements.

Exercise 5-2 Classification of Inventory Costs

LO1

Put an *X* in the appropriate column next to the inventory item to indicate its most likely classification on the books of a company that manufactures furniture and then sells it in retail company stores.

	Classification			
Inventory Item	**Raw Material**	**Work in Process**	**Finished Goods**	**Merchandise Inventory**
Fabric				
Lumber				
Unvarnished tables				
Chairs on the showroom floor				
Cushions				
Decorative knobs				
Drawers				
Sofa frames				
Chairs in the plant warehouse				
Chairs in the retail storeroom				

Exercise 5-3 Perpetual and Periodic Inventory Systems

LO2

From the following list, identify whether the merchandisers described would most likely use a perpetual or a periodic inventory system.

_____	Appliance store	_____	Grocery store
_____	Car dealership	_____	Hardware store
_____	Drugstore	_____	Jewelry store
_____	Furniture store		

How might changes in technology affect the ability of merchandisers to use perpetual inventory systems?

Exercise 5-4 Perpetual and Periodic Inventory Systems

LO2
EXAMPLE 5-3

Following is a partial list of account balances for two different merchandising companies. The amounts in the accounts represent the balances at the end of the year *before* any adjustments are made or the books are closed.

Company A		Company B	
Sales Revenue	$50,000	Sales Revenue	$85,000
Sales Discounts	3,000	Sales Discounts	2,000
Merchandise Inventory	12,000	Merchandise Inventory	9,000
Cost of Goods Sold	38,000	Purchases	41,000
		Purchase Discounts	4,000
		Purchase Returns and Allowances	1,000

(Continued)

Required

1. Identify which inventory system, perpetual or periodic, each of the two companies uses. Explain how you know which system each company uses by looking at the types of accounts on its books.
2. How much inventory should Company A have on hand at the end of the year? What is its cost of goods sold for the year?
3. Explain why you cannot determine Company B's cost of goods sold for the year from the information available.

LO3
EXAMPLE 5-8

Exercise 5-5   Transfer of Title to Inventory

For each of the following transactions, indicate which company should include the inventory on its December 31, 2012, balance sheet:
1. Michelson Supplies Inc. shipped merchandise to PJ Sales on December 28, 2012, terms FOB destination. The merchandise arrives at PJ's on January 4, 2013.
2. Quarton Inc. shipped merchandise to Filbrandt on December 25, 2012, FOB destination. Filbrandt received the merchandise on December 31, 2012.
3. James Bros. Inc. shipped merchandise to Randall Company on December 27, 2012, FOB shipping point. Randall Company received the merchandise on January 3, 2013.
4. Hinz Company shipped merchandise to Barner Inc. on December 24, 2012, FOB shipping point. The merchandise arrived at Barner's on December 29, 2012.

LO3
EXAMPLE 5-1, 5-4, 5-6

Exercise 5-6   Purchase Discounts

Identify and analyze each of the following transactions of Buckeye Corporation. (All purchases on credit are made with terms of 1/10, n/30, and Buckeye uses the periodic system of inventory.)

July	3:	Purchased merchandise on credit from Wildcat Corp. for $3,500.
July	6:	Purchased merchandise on credit from Cyclone Company for $7,000.
July	12:	Paid amount owed to Wildcat Corp.
August	5:	Paid amount owed to Cyclone Company.

LO3
EXAMPLE 5-8

Exercise 5-7   Shipping Terms and Transfer of Title

On December 23, 2012, Miller Wholesalers ships merchandise to Michael Retailers with terms of FOB destination point. The merchandise arrives at Michael's warehouse on January 3, 2013.

Required

1. Identify who pays to ship the merchandise.
2. Determine whether the inventory should be included as an asset on Michael's December 31, 2012, balance sheet. Should the sale be included on Miller's 2012 income statement? Explain.
3. Explain how your answers to part (2) would have been different if the terms of shipment had been FOB shipping point.

LO3
EXAMPLE 5-1, 5-4, 5-5, 5-6, 5-7

Exercise 5-8   Purchases—Periodic System

Identify and analyze each of the following transactions of Wolverine Corporation. The company uses the periodic system.

March	3:	Purchased merchandise from Spartan Corp. for $2,500 with terms of 2/10, n/30. Shipping costs of $250 were paid to Neverlate Transit Company.
March	7:	Purchased merchandise from Boilermaker Company for $1,400 with terms of n/30.
March	12:	Paid amount owed to Spartan Corp.
March	15:	Received a credit of $500 on defective merchandise purchased from Boilermaker Company. The merchandise was kept.
March	18:	Purchased merchandise from Gopher Corp. for $1,600 with terms of 2/10, n/30.
March	22:	Received a credit of $400 from Gopher Corp. for spoiled merchandise returned to Gopher. This is the amount of credit exclusive of any discount.
April	6:	Paid amount owed to Boilermaker Company.
April	18:	Paid amount owed to Gopher Corp.

Exercise 5-9 Missing Amounts in Cost of Goods Sold Model

LO3

For each of the following independent cases, fill in the missing amounts.

	Case 1	Case 2	Case 3
Beginning inventory	$ (a)	$2,350	$1,890
Purchases (gross)	6,230	5,720	(e)
Purchase returns and allowances	470	800	550
Purchase discounts	200	(c)	310
Transportation-in	150	500	420
Cost of goods available for sale	7,110	(d)	8,790
Ending inventory	(b)	1,750	1,200
Cost of goods sold	5,220	5,570	(f)

Exercise 5-10 Working Backward: Gross Profit Ratio

LO4

Acme's gross profit ratio increased by 20% over the prior year. Net sales and cost of goods sold for the prior year were $120,000 and $90,000, respectively. Cost of goods sold for the current year is $140,000.

Required

Determine the amount of Acme's sales for the current year.

Exercise 5-11 Inventory and Income Manipulation

LO5

The president of SOS Inc. is concerned that the net income at year-end will not reach the expected figure. When the sales manager receives a large order on the last day of the fiscal year, the president tells the accountant to record the sale but to ignore any inventory adjustment because the physical inventory has already been taken. How will this affect the current year's net income? next year's income? What would you do if you were the accountant? Would your answer differ if your company followed IFRS rather than U.S. GAAP? Assume that SOS uses a periodic inventory system.

© Kasia Biel/istockphoto.com

IFRS

Exercise 5-12 Inventory Costing Methods

LO6

EXAMPLE 5-10, 5-11, 5-12, 5-13

VanderMeer Inc. reported the following information for the month of February:

Inventory, February 1	65 units @ $20
Purchases:	
February 7	50 units @ $22
February 18	60 units @ $23
February 27	45 units @ $24

During February, VanderMeer sold 140 units. The company uses a periodic inventory system.

Required

What is the value of ending inventory and cost of goods sold for February under the following assumptions:
1. Of the 140 units sold, 55 cost $20, 35 cost $22, 45 cost $23, and 5 cost $24.
2. FIFO
3. LIFO
4. Weighted average

Exercise 5-13 Evaluation of Inventory Costing Methods

LO7

EXAMPLE 5-16

Write the letter of the method that is most applicable to each statement.

a. Specific identification
b. Average cost
c. First-in, first-out (FIFO)
d. Last-in, first-out (LIFO)

_____ 1. Is the most realistic ending inventory
_____ 2. Results in cost of goods sold being closest to current product costs

(Continued)

_____ 3. Results in highest income during periods of inflation
_____ 4. Results in highest ending inventory during periods of inflation
_____ 5. Smooths out costs during periods of inflation
_____ 6. Is not practical for most businesses
_____ 7. Puts more weight on the cost of the larger number of units purchased
_____ 8. Is an assumption that most closely reflects the physical flow of goods for most businesses
_____ 9. Is not an acceptable method under IFRS

LO8
EXAMPLE 5-17, 5-18, 5-19

Exercise 5-14 Inventory Errors

For each of the following independent situations, fill in the blanks to indicate the effect of the error on each of the various financial statement items. Indicate an understatement (U), an overstatement (O), or no effect (NE). Assume that each of the companies uses a periodic inventory system.

| | Balance Sheet | | Income Statement | |
Error	Inventory	Retained Earnings	Cost of Goods Sold	Net Income
1. Goods in transit at year-end are not included in the physical count; they were shipped FOB shipping point.	_____	_____	_____	_____
2. One section of a warehouse is counted twice during the year-end count of inventory.	_____	_____	_____	_____
3. During the count at year-end, the inventory sheets for one of the stores of a discount retailer are lost.	_____	_____	_____	_____

LO3
EXAMPLE 5-8

Exercise 5-15 Transfer of Title to Inventory

Identify whether the transactions described should be recorded by Cameron Companies during December 2012 (fill in the blank with a D) or January 2013 (fill in the blank with a J).

Purchases of merchandise that are in transit from vendors to Cameron Companies on December 31, 2012.

_____ Shipped FOB shipping point
_____ Shipped FOB destination point

Sales of merchandise that are in transit to customers of Cameron Companies on December 31, 2012.

_____ Shipped FOB shipping point
_____ Shipped FOB destination point

LO10

Exercise 5-16 Working Backward: Inventory Turnover

It takes Bradley Retailers 90 days on average to sell its inventory. The company began the year with $17,000 in inventory. Sales and cost of goods sold for the year amounted to $95,000 and $60,000, respectively.

Required

Assuming 360 days in a year, determine the amount of Bradley's ending inventory.

LO10

Exercise 5-17 Inventory Turnover for Nordstrom

The following amounts are available from the 2010 annual report of **Nordstrom, Inc.**, the fashion retailer. (All amounts are in millions of dollars and January 29, 2011, is the end of the company's 2010 fiscal year.)

Cost of sales and related buying and occupancy costs	$5,897
Merchandise inventories, January 29, 2011	977
Merchandise inventories, January 30, 2010	898

Required

1. Compute Nordstrom's inventory turnover ratio for 2010.
2. What is the average length of time it takes to sell an item of inventory? Explain your answer.
3. Do you think the average length of time it took Nordstrom to sell inventory in 2010 is reasonable? What other information do you need to fully answer that question?

Exercise 5-18 Effects of Transactions Involving Inventories on the Statement of Cash Flows—Direct Method

LO11

Masthead Company's comparative balance sheets included inventory of $180,400 at December 31, 2011, and $241,200 at December 31, 2012. Masthead's comparative balance sheets also included accounts payable of $85,400 at December 31, 2011, and $78,400 at December 31, 2012. Masthead's accounts payable balances are composed solely of amounts due to suppliers for purchases of inventory on account. Cost of goods sold, as reported by Masthead on its 2012 income statement, amounted to $1,200,000.

Required

What is the amount of cash payments for inventory that Masthead will report in the Operating Activities category of its 2012 statement of cash flows assuming that the direct method is used?

Exercise 5-19 Effects of Transactions Involving Inventories on the Statement of Cash Flows—Indirect Method

LO11

Refer to all of the facts in Exercise 5-18.

Required

Assume instead that Masthead uses the indirect method to prepare its statement of cash flows. Indicate how each item will be reflected as an adjustment to net income in the Operating Activities category of the statement of cash flows.

Exercise 5-20 Impact of Transactions Involving Inventories on Statement of Cash Flows

LO11

From the following list, identify whether the change in the account balance during the year is added to (A) or deducted from (D) net income when the indirect method is used to determine cash flows from operating activities.

	Increase in accounts payable		Increase in inventories
	Decrease in accounts payable		Decrease in inventories

MULTI-CONCEPT EXERCISES

Exercise 5-21 Income Statement for a Merchandiser

LO2 • 3

EXAMPLE 5-2

Fill in the missing amounts in the following income statement for Carpenters Department Store Inc.

Sales revenue		$125,600	
Less: Sales returns and allowances		(a)	
Net sales			$122,040
Cost of goods sold:			
Beginning inventory		$ 23,400	

(Continued)

Purchases	$ (b)	
Less: Purchase discounts	1,300	
Net purchases	$ (c)	
Add: Transportation-in	6,550	
Cost of goods purchased	81,150	
Cost of goods available for sale	$104,550	
Less: Ending inventory	(e)	
Cost of goods sold		(d)
Gross profit		$ 38,600
Operating expenses		(f)
Income before tax		$ 26,300
Income tax expense		10,300
Net income		$ (g)

LO2 • 3   ## Exercise 5-22 Partial Income Statement—Periodic System

LaPine Company has the following account balances as of December 31, 2012:

Purchase returns and allowances	$ 400
Inventory, January 1	4,000
Sales	80,000
Transportation-in	1,000
Sales returns and allowances	500
Purchase discounts	800
Inventory, December 31	3,800
Purchases	30,000
Sales discounts	1,200

Required

Prepare a partial income statement for LaPine Company for 2012 through gross profit. Calculate LaPine's gross profit ratio for 2012.

LO3 • 11
EXAMPLE 5-2   ## Exercise 5-23 Working Backward: Cost of Goods Sold and the Statement of Cash Flows

Texas Corp.'s statement of cash flows reported an addition of $6,000 for the change in the Inventory account during the year. Cost of goods sold expense on the income statement amounted to $50,000.

Required

Determine the amount of purchases during the year.

LO3 • 6
EXAMPLE 5-2, 5-12, 5-13   ## Exercise 5-24 Cost of Goods Sold, FIFO, and LIFO

Kramer began operations early in 2012 and made the following purchases:

February 5	200	$5
June 10	500	6
October 4	300	7

Kramer used the FIFO method to value its inventory and reported cost of goods sold expense for the year of $4,000.

Required

Determine the cost of goods sold expense assuming Kramer had used the LIFO method instead of the FIFO method.

Exercise 5-25 Inventory Costing Methods—Periodic System

LO6 • 7
EXAMPLE 5-11, 5-12, 5-13, 5-14, 5-15

The following information is available concerning the inventory of Carter Inc.:

	Units	Unit Cost
Beginning inventory	200	$10
Purchases:		
March 5	300	11
June 12	400	12
August 23	250	13
October 2	150	15

During the year, Carter sold 1,000 units. It uses a periodic inventory system.

Required

1. Calculate ending inventory and cost of goods sold for each of the following three methods:
   a. Weighted average
   b. FIFO
   c. LIFO
2. Assume an estimated tax rate of 30%. How much more or less (indicate which) will Carter pay in taxes by using FIFO instead of LIFO? Explain your answer.
3. Assume that Carter prepares its financial statements in accordance with IFRS. Which costing method should it use to pay the least amount of taxes? Explain your answer.

© Kasia Biel/istockphoto.com

Exercise 5-26 Lower-of-Cost-or-Market Rule

LO5 • 9

Awards Etc. carries an inventory of trophies and ribbons for local sports teams and school clubs. The cost of trophies has dropped in the past year, which pleases the company except for the fact that it has on hand considerable inventory that was purchased at the higher prices. The president is not pleased with the lower profit margin the company is earning. "The lower profit margin will continue until we sell all of this old inventory," he grumbled to the new staff accountant. "Not really," replied the accountant. "Let's write down the inventory to the replacement cost this year, and then next year our profit margin will be in line with the competition."

Required

Explain why the inventory can be carried at an amount less than its cost. Which accounts will be affected by the write-down? What will be the effect on income in the current year and future years?

Exercise 5-27 Weighted Average Cost Method and Gross Profit Ratio

LO4 • 6
EXAMPLE 5-11

Martin Corp. began the year with 2,000 units of inventory that had been purchased for $6 per unit. During the year, 5,000 units were purchased for $8 each and 8,000 units for $10 each. Martin sold 9,000 units during the year for $15 each. The company uses the weighted average cost method.

Required

1. Compute cost of goods sold expense.
2. Compute the gross profit ratio.

Exercise 5-28 Inventory Costing Methods—Perpetual System (Appendix)

LO7 • 12
EXAMPLE 5-20, 5-21, 5-22

The following information is available concerning Stillwater Inc.:

	Units	Unit Cost
Beginning inventory	200	$10
Purchases:		
March 5	300	11
June 12	400	12
August 23	250	13
October 2	150	15

(Continued)

Stillwater, which uses a perpetual system, sold 1,000 units for $22 each during the year. Sales occurred on the following dates:

	Units
February 12	150
April 30	200
July 7	200
September 6	300
December 3	150

Required

1. Calculate ending inventory and cost of goods sold for each of the following three methods:
   a. Moving average
   b. FIFO
   c. LIFO
2. For each of the three methods, compare the results with those of Carter in Exercise 5-25. Which method gives a different answer depending on whether a company uses a periodic or a perpetual inventory system?
3. Assume the use of the perpetual system and an estimated tax rate of 30%. How much more or less (indicate which) will Stillwater pay in taxes by using LIFO instead of FIFO? Explain your answer.

PROBLEMS

LO1   **Problem 5-1 Inventory Costs in Various Businesses**

Businesses incur various costs in selling goods and services. Each business must decide which costs are expenses of the period and which should be included in the cost of the inventory. The following table lists various types of businesses along with certain types of costs they incur:

Business	Types of Costs	Accounting Treatment		
		Expense of the Period	Inventory Cost	Other Treatment
Retail shoe store	Shoes for sale			
	Shoe boxes			
	Advertising signs			
Grocery store	Canned goods on the shelves			
	Produce			
	Cleaning supplies			
	Cash registers			
Frame shop	Wooden frame supplies			
	Nails			
	Glass			
Walk-in print shop	Paper			
	Copy machines			
	Toner cartridges			
Restaurant	Frozen food			
	China and silverware			
	Prepared food			
	Spices			

Required

Fill in the table to indicate the correct accounting for each type of cost by placing an X in the appropriate column. For any costs that receive other treatment, explain what the appropriate treatment is for accounting purposes.

Problem 5-2 Calculation of Gross Profit Ratio for Wal-Mart and Target LO4

The following information was summarized from the consolidated statements of income of **Wal-Mart Stores, Inc. and Subsidiaries** for the years ended January 31, 2011 and 2010, and the consolidated statements of operations of **Target Corporation** for the years ended January 29, 2011, and January 30, 2010. (For each company, years are labeled as 2010 and 2009, respectively, although Wal-Mart labels these as the 2011 and 2010 fiscal years.)

(in Millions)	2010		2009	
	Sales*	Cost of Sales	Sales*	Cost of Sales
Wal-Mart	$418,952	$315,287	$405,132	$304,444
Target	65,786	45,725	63,435	44,062

*Described as net sales by Wal-Mart.

Required

1. Calculate the gross profit ratios for Wal-Mart and Target for 2010 and 2009.
2. Which company appears to be performing better? What factors might cause the difference in the gross profit ratios of the two companies? What other information should you consider to determine how these companies are performing in this regard?

Problem 5-3 Evaluation of Inventory Costing Methods LO7

Users of financial statements rely on the information available to them to decide whether to invest in a company or lend it money. As an investor, you are comparing three companies in the same industry. The cost to purchase inventory is rising in the industry. Assume that all expenses incurred by the three companies are the same except for cost of goods sold. The companies use the following methods to value ending inventory:

Company A—weighted average cost
Company B—first-in, first-out (FIFO)
Company C—last-in, first-out (LIFO)

Required

1. Which of the three companies will report the highest net income? Explain your answer.
2. Which of the three companies will pay the least in income taxes? Explain your answer.
3. Which method of inventory costing do you believe is superior to the others in providing information to potential investors? Explain.
4. Explain how your answers to parts (1), (2), and (3) would change if the costs to purchase inventory had been falling instead of rising.

Problem 5-4 Inventory Error LO8

The following highly condensed income statements and balance sheets are available for Budget Stores for a two-year period. (All amounts are stated in thousands of dollars.)

Income Statements	2012	2011
Revenues	$20,000	$15,000
Cost of goods sold	13,000	10,000
Gross profit	$ 7,000	$ 5,000
Operating expenses	3,000	2,000
Net income	$ 4,000	$ 3,000

Balance Sheets	December 31, 2012	December 31, 2011
Cash	$ 1,700	$ 1,500
Inventory	4,200	3,500
Other current assets	2,500	2,000
Long-term assets	15,000	14,000
Total assets	$23,400	$21,000

(Continued)

Balance Sheets	December 31, 2012	December 31, 2011
Liabilities	$ 8,500	$ 7,000
Capital stock	5,000	5,000
Retained earnings	9,900	9,000
Total liabilities and stockholders' equity	$23,400	$21,000

Before releasing the 2012 annual report, Budget's controller learns that the inventory of one of the stores (amounting to $600,000) was inadvertently omitted from the count on December 31, 2011. The inventory of the store was correctly included in the December 31, 2012, count.

Required

1. Prepare revised income statements and balance sheets for Budget Stores for each of the two years. Ignore the effect of income taxes.
2. If Budget did not prepare revised statements before releasing the 2012 annual report, what would be the amount of overstatement or understatement of net income for the two-year period? What would be the overstatement or understatement of retained earnings at December 31, 2012, if revised statements were not prepared?
3. Given your answers in part (2), does it matter if Budget bothers to restate the financial statements of the two years to rectify the error? Explain your answer.

LO10 Problem 5-5 Inventory Turnover for Apple Computer and Hewlett-Packard

The following information was summarized from the fiscal year 2010 annual report of **Apple Computer, Inc.**:

	(in millions)
Cost of sales for the year ended:	
September 25, 2010	$39,541
September 26, 2009	25,683
Inventories:	
September 25, 2010	1,051
September 26, 2009	455
Net sales for the year ended:	
September 25, 2010	65,225
September 26, 2009	42,905

The following information was summarized from the fiscal year 2010 annual report of **Hewlett-Packard Company**:

	(in millions)
Cost of sales* for the year ended:	
October 31, 2010	$65,064
October 31, 2009	56,503
Inventory:	
October 31, 2010	6,466
October 31, 2009	6,128
Net revenue (products) for the year ended:	
October 31, 2010	84,799
October 31, 2009	74,051

*Described as "cost of products" by Hewlett-Packard.

Required

1. Calculate the gross profit ratios for Apple Computer and Hewlett-Packard for each of the two years presented.
2. Calculate the inventory turnover ratios for both companies for the most recent year.
3. Which company appears to be performing better? What other information should you consider to determine how these companies are performing in this regard?

Problem 5-6 Effects of Changes in Inventory and Accounts Payable Balances on Statement of Cash Flows

LO11

Copeland Antiques reported a net loss of $33,200 for the year ended December 31, 2012. The following items were included on Copeland's balance sheets at December 31, 2012 and 2011:

	12/31/12	12/31/11
Cash	$ 65,300	$ 46,100
Trade accounts payable	123,900	93,700
Inventories	192,600	214,800

Copeland uses the indirect method to prepare its statement of cash flows. Copeland does not have any other current assets or current liabilities and did not enter into any investing or financing activities during 2012.

Required

1. Prepare Copeland's 2012 statement of cash flows.
2. Draft a brief memo to the president explaining why cash increased during such an unprofitable year.

MULTI-CONCEPT PROBLEMS

Problem 5-7 Interpreting Gannett Co.'s Inventory Accounting Policy

LO1 • 7 • 9

The 2010 annual report of **Gannett Co., Inc.** (publisher of *USA Today* and many other newspapers) includes the following in the note that summarizes its accounting policies:

Inventories Inventories, consisting principally of newsprint, printing ink and plate material for the company's publishing operations, are valued primarily at the lower of cost (first-in, first-out) or market. At certain U.S. publishing operations however, newsprint inventory is carried on a last-in, first-out basis.

Required

1. What *types* of inventory cost does Gannett carry? What about newspapers? Are newspapers considered inventory?
2. Why would the company choose two different methods to value its inventory?

Problem 5-8 Purchases and Sales of Merchandise, Cash Flows

LO2 • 3 • 11

Two Wheeler, a bike shop, opened for business on April 1. It uses a periodic inventory system. The following transactions occurred during the first month of business:

April 1: Purchased five units from Duhan Co. for $500 total, with terms 3/10, n/30, FOB destination.

April 10: Paid for the April 1 purchase.

April 15: Sold one unit for $200 cash.

April 18: Purchased ten units from Clinton Inc. for $900 total, with terms 3/10, n/30, FOB destination.

April 25: Sold three units for $200 each, cash.

April 28: Paid for the April 18 purchase.

Required

1. Identify and analyze each of the preceding transactions of Two Wheeler.
2. Determine net income for the month of April. Two Wheeler incurred and paid $100 for rent and $50 for miscellaneous expenses during April. Ending inventory is $967. (Ignore income taxes.)
3. Assuming that these are the only transactions during April (including rent and miscellaneous expenses), compute net cash flow from operating activities.
4. Explain why cash outflow is so much larger than expenses on the income statement.

LO2 • 3   **Problem 5-9 Financial Statements**

A list of accounts for Maple Inc. at December 31, 2012, follows:

Accounts Receivable	$ 2,359	Land	$20,000
Advertising Expense	4,510	Purchase Discounts	800
Buildings and Equipment, Net	55,550	Purchases	40,200
Capital Stock	50,000	Retained Earnings, January 1, 2012	32,550
Cash	590	Salaries Expense	25,600
Depreciation Expense	2,300	Salaries Payable	650
Dividends	6,000	Sales	84,364
Income Tax Expense	3,200	Sales Returns	780
Income Tax Payable	3,200	Transportation-In	375
Interest Receivable	100	Utilities Expense	3,600
Inventory:			
January 1, 2012	6,400		
December 31, 2012	7,500		

Required

1. Determine cost of goods sold for 2012.
2. Determine net income for 2012.
3. Prepare a balance sheet dated December 31, 2012.

LO2 • 3 • 4   **Problem 5-10 Gap Inc.'s Sales, Cost of Goods Sold, and Gross Profit**

The consolidated balance sheets of **Gap Inc.** included merchandise inventory in the amount of $1,620,000,000 as of January 29, 2011 (the end of fiscal year 2010) and $1,477,000,000 as of January 30, 2010 (the end of fiscal year 2009). Net sales were $14,664,000,000 and $14,197,000,000 at the end of fiscal years 2010 and 2009, respectively. Cost of goods sold and occupancy expenses were $8,775,000,000 and $8,473,000,000 at the end of fiscal years 2010 and 2009, respectively.

Required

1. Unlike most other merchandisers, Gap Inc. doesn't include accounts receivable on its balance sheet. Why doesn't Gap Inc.'s balance sheet include this account?
2. Identify and analyze the transaction to record sales during the year ended January 29, 2011.
3. Gap Inc. sets forth net sales but not gross sales on its income statement. What type(s) of deduction(s) would be made from gross sales to arrive at the amount of net sales reported? Why might the company decide not to report the amount(s) of the deduction(s) separately?
4. Reconstruct the Cost of Goods Sold section of Gap Inc.'s 2010 income statement.
5. Calculate the gross profit ratios for Gap Inc. for 2010 and 2009 and comment on any change noted. Is the company's performance improving? Explain. What factors might have caused the change in the gross profit ratio?

LO5 • 6 • 7   **Problem 5-11 Comparison of Inventory Costing Methods—Periodic System**

Bitten Company's inventory records show 600 units on hand on October 1 with a unit cost of $5 each. The following transactions occurred during the month of October:

Date	Unit Purchases	Unit Sales
October 4		500 @ $10.00
8	800 @ $5.40	
9		700 @ $10.00
18	700 @ $5.76	
20		800 @ $11.00
29	800 @ $5.90	

All expenses other than cost of goods sold amount to $3,000 for the month. The company uses an estimated tax rate of 30% to accrue monthly income taxes.

Required

1. Prepare a chart comparing cost of goods sold and ending inventory using the periodic system and the following costing methods:

	Cost of Goods Sold	Ending Inventory	Total
Weighted average			
FIFO			
LIFO			

2. What does the Total column represent?
3. Prepare income statements for each of the three methods.
4. Will the company pay more or less tax if it uses FIFO rather than LIFO? How much more or less?

Problem 5-12 Inventory Costing Methods—Periodic System   LO5 • 6 • 7

Oxendine Company's inventory records for the month of November reveal the following:

Inventory, November 1	200 units @ $18.00
November 4, purchase	250 units @ $18.50
November 7, sale	300 units @ $42.00
November 13, purchase	220 units @ $18.90
November 18, purchase	150 units @ $19.00
November 22, sale	380 units @ $42.50
November 24, purchase	200 units @ $19.20
November 28, sale	110 units @ $43.00

Selling and administrative expenses for the month were $10,800. Depreciation expense was $4,000. Oxendine's tax rate is 35%.

Required

1. Calculate the cost of goods sold and ending inventory under each of the following three methods assuming a periodic inventory system: (a) FIFO, (b) LIFO, and (c) weighted average.
2. Calculate the gross profit and net income under each costing assumption.
3. Under which costing method will Oxendine pay the least taxes? Explain your answer.
4. Assume that Oxendine prepares its financial statements in accordance with IFRS. Which costing method should the company use to pay the least amount of taxes? Explain your answer.

© Kasia Biel/istockphoto.com IFRS

Problem 5-13 Comparison of Inventory Costing Methods—Perpetual   LO5 • 7 • 12
System (Appendix)

Repeat Problem 5-11 using the perpetual system.

Problem 5-14 Inventory Costing Methods—Periodic System   LO5 • 6 • 7

Following is an inventory acquisition schedule for Weaver Corp. for 2012:

	Units	Unit Cost
Beginning inventory	5,000	$10
Purchase:		
February 4	3,000	9
April 12	4,000	8
September 10	2,000	7
December 5	1,000	6

(Continued)

During the year, Weaver sold 12,500 units at $12 each. All expenses except cost of goods sold and taxes amounted to $20,000. The tax rate is 30%.

Required

1. Compute cost of goods sold and ending inventory under each of the following three methods assuming a periodic inventory system: (a) weighted average, (b) FIFO, and (c) LIFO.
2. Prepare income statements under each of the three methods.
3. Which method do you recommend so that Weaver pays the least amount of taxes during 2012? Explain your answer.
4. Weaver anticipates that unit costs for inventory will increase throughout 2013. Will Weaver be able to switch from the method you recommended that it use in 2012 to another method to take advantage of the increase in prices for tax purposes? Explain your answer.

ALTERNATE PROBLEMS

LO1   **Problem 5-1A Inventory Costs in Various Businesses**

Sound Traxs Inc. sells and rents DVDs to retail customers. The accountant is aware that at the end of the year, she must account for inventory, but is unsure what DVDs are considered inventory and how to value them. DVDs purchased by the company are placed on the shelf for rental. Every three weeks, the company performs a detailed analysis of the rental income from each DVD and decides whether to keep it as a rental or to offer it for sale in the resale section of the store. Resale DVDs sell for $10 each regardless of the price Sound Traxs paid for the DVD.

Required

1. How should Sound Traxs account for each of the two types of DVDs—rentals and resales—on its balance sheet?
2. How would you suggest Sound Traxs account for the DVDs as they are transferred from one department to another?

LO4   **Problem 5-2A Calculation of Gross Profit Ratio for Coca-Cola and PepsiCo**

The following information was summarized from the 2010 and 2009 consolidated statements of income of **The Coca-Cola Company and Subsidiaries** (for years ended December 31 each year) and **PepsiCo, Inc. and Subsidiaries** (for years ended December 25, 2010, and December 26, 2009).

	2010		2009	
(in Millions)	**Sales***	**Cost of Goods Sold****	**Sales***	**Cost of Goods Sold****
Coca-Cola	$35,119	$12,693	$30,990	$11,088
PepsiCo	57,838	26,575	43,232	20,099

**Described as "Net operating revenues" by Coca-Cola and as "Net revenue" by PepsiCo.*
***Described as "Cost of Sales" by PepsiCo.*

Required

1. Calculate the gross profit ratios for Coca-Cola and PepsiCo for 2010 and 2009.
2. Which company appears to be performing better? What factors might cause the difference in the gross profit ratios of the two companies? What other information should you consider to determine how these companies are performing in this regard?

LO7   **Problem 5-3A Evaluation of Inventory Costing Methods**

Three large mass merchandisers use the following methods to value ending inventory:

Company X—weighted average cost
Company Y—first-in, first-out (FIFO)
Company Z—last-in, first-out (LIFO)

The cost of inventory has steadily increased over the past ten years of the product life. Recently, however, prices have started to decline slightly due to foreign competition.

Required

1. Will the effect on net income of the decline in cost of goods sold be the same for all three companies? Explain your answer.
2. Company Z would like to change its inventory costing method from LIFO to FIFO. Write an acceptable note for its annual report to justify the change.

Problem 5-4A Inventory Error

LO8

The following condensed income statements and balance sheets are available for Planter Stores for a two-year period. (All amounts are stated in thousands of dollars.)

Income Statements	2012	2011
Revenues	$35,982	$26,890
Cost of goods sold	12,594	9,912
Gross profit	$23,388	$16,978
Operating expenses	13,488	10,578
Net income	$ 9,900	$ 6,400

Balance Sheets	December 31, 2012	December 31, 2011
Cash	$ 9,400	$ 4,100
Inventory	4,500	5,400
Other current assets	1,600	1,250
Long-term assets, net	24,500	24,600
Total assets	$40,000	$35,350
Current liabilities	$ 9,380	$10,600
Capital stock	18,000	18,000
Retained earnings	12,620	6,750
Total liabilities and stockholders' equity	$40,000	$35,350

Before releasing the 2012 annual report, Planter's controller learns that the inventory of one of the stores (amounting to $500,000) was counted twice in the December 31, 2011, inventory. The inventory was correctly counted in the December 31, 2012, inventory.

Required

1. Prepare revised income statements and balance sheets for Planter Stores for each of the two years. Ignore the effect of income taxes.
2. Compute the current ratio at December 31, 2011, before the statements are revised and compute the current ratio at the same date after the statements are revised. If Planter applied for a loan in early 2012 and the lender required a current ratio of at least 1 to 1, would the error have affected the loan? Explain your answer.
3. If Planter did not prepare revised statements before releasing the 2012 annual report, what would be the amount of overstatement or understatement of net income for the two-year period? What would be the overstatement or understatement of retained earnings at December 31, 2012, if revised statements were not prepared?
4. Given your answers to parts (2) and (3), does it matter if Planter bothers to restate the financial statements of the two years to correct the error? Explain your answer.

Problem 5-5A Inventory Turnover for Wal-Mart and Target

LO10

The following information was summarized from the 2011 annual report of **Wal-Mart Stores, Inc. and Subsidiaries**:

(Continued)

	(in millions)
Cost of sales for the year ended January 31:	
2011	$315,287
2010	304,444
Inventories, January 31:	
2011	36,318
2010	32,713

The following information was summarized from the 2010 annual report of **Target Corporation**:

	(in millions)
Cost of sales for the year ended:	
January 29, 2011	$45,725
January 30, 2010	44,062
Inventory:	
January 29, 2011	7,596
January 30, 2010	7,179

Required

1. Calculate the inventory turnover ratios for Wal-Mart and Target for the years ending January 31, 2011 and January 29, 2011, respectively.
2. Which company appears to be performing better? What other information should you consider to determine how these companies are performing in this regard?

LO11   **Problem 5-6A Effects of Changes in Inventory and Accounts Payable Balances on Statement of Cash Flows**

Carpetland City reported net income of $78,500 for the year ended December 31, 2012. The following items were included on Carpetland's balance sheet at December 31, 2012 and 2011:

	12/31/12	12/31/11
Cash	$ 14,400	$26,300
Trade accounts payable	23,900	93,700
Inventories	105,500	84,900

Carpetland uses the indirect method to prepare its statement of cash flows. Carpetland does not have any other current assets or current liabilities, and did not enter into any investing or financing activities during 2012.

Required

1. Prepare Carpetland's 2012 statement of cash flows.
2. Draft a brief memo to the president to explain why cash decreased during a profitable year.

ALTERNATE MULTI-CONCEPT PROBLEMS

LO1 • 7 • 8   **Problem 5-7A Interpreting The New York Times Company's Financial Statements**

The 2010 annual report of **The New York Times Company** includes the following note:

4. Inventories

Inventories as shown in the accompanying Consolidated Balance Sheets were as follows:

(In thousands)	December 26, 2010	December 27, 2009
Newsprint and magazine paper	$12,596	$12,013
Other inventory	3,536	4,290
Total	$16,132	$16,303

Inventories are stated at the lower of cost or current market value. Cost was determined utilizing the LIFO method for 66% of inventory in 2010 and 70% of inventory in 2009. The excess of replacement or current cost over stated LIFO value was approximately $5 million as of December 26, 2010 and $3 million as of December 27, 2009. The remaining portion of inventory is accounted for under the FIFO method.

Required

1. What *types* of inventory costs does The New York Times Company carry? What about newspapers? Are newspapers considered inventory?
2. Why would the company choose more than one method to value its inventory?

Problem 5-8A Walgreen's Sales, Cost of Goods Sold, and Gross Profit   LO2 • 3 • 4

The following information was summarized from the consolidated balance sheets of **Walgreen Co. and Subsidiaries** as of August 31, 2010 and 2009 and the consolidated statements of earnings for the years ended August 31, 2010 and 2009.

(in millions)	2010	2009
Accounts receivable, net	$ 2,450	$ 2,496
Cost of sales	48,444	45,722
Inventories	7,378	6,789
Net sales	67,420	63,335

Required

1. Identify and analyze the transactions related to the collection of accounts receivable and sales during 2010. Assume that all of Walgreen's sales are on account.
2. Walgreen Co. sets forth net sales but not gross sales on its income statement. What type(s) of deduction(s) would be made from gross sales to arrive at the amount of net sales reported? Why might the company decide not to report the amount(s) of the deduction(s) separately?
3. Reconstruct the Cost of Goods Sold section of Walgreen's 2010 income statement.
4. Calculate the gross profit ratios for Walgreen Co. for 2010 and 2009 and comment on the change noted, if any. Is the company's performance improving? What factors might have caused the change in the gross profit ratio?

Problem 5-9A Financial Statements   LO2 • 3

A list of accounts for Lloyd Inc. at December 31, 2012, follows:

Accounts Receivable	$56,359	Purchase Discounts	$ 1,237
Advertising Expense	12,900	Purchases	62,845
Capital Stock	50,000	Retained Earnings, January 1, 2012	28,252
Cash	22,340	Salaries Payable	650
Dividends	6,000	Sales	112,768
Income Tax Expense	1,450	Sales Returns	1,008
Income Tax Payable	1,450	Transportation-In	375
Inventory:		Utilities Expense	1,800
January 1, 2012	6,400	Wages and Salaries Expense	23,000
December 31, 2012	5,900	Wages Payable	120

Required

1. Determine cost of goods sold for 2012.
2. Determine net income for 2012.
3. Prepare a balance sheet dated December 31, 2012.

Problem 5-10A Purchases and Sales of Merchandise, Cash Flows   LO2 • 3 • 11

Chestnut Corp., a ski shop, opened for business on October 1. It uses a periodic inventory system. The following transactions occurred during the first month of business:

October 1: Purchased three units from Elm Inc. for $249 total, terms 2/10, n/30, FOB destination.

October 10: Paid for the October 1 purchase.

October 15: Sold one unit for $200 cash.

(Continued)

October 18:   Purchased ten units from Wausau Company for $800 total, with terms 2/10, n/30, FOB destination.

October 25:   Sold three units for $200 each, cash.

October 30:   Paid for the October 18 purchase.

Required

1. Identify and analyze each of the preceding transactions of Chestnut.
2. Determine the number of units on hand on October 31.
3. If Chestnut started the month with $2,000, determine its balance in cash at the end of the month assuming that these are the only transactions that occurred during October. Why has the cash balance decreased when the company reported net income?

LO5 • 6 • 7   Problem 5-11A Comparison of Inventory Costing Methods—Periodic System

Stellar Inc.'s inventory records show 300 units on hand on November 1 with a unit cost of $4 each. The following transactions occurred during the month of November:

Date	Unit Purchases	Unit Sales
November 4		200 @ $9.00
8	500 @ $4.50	
9		500 @ $9.00
18	700 @ $4.75	
20		400 @ $9.50
29	600 @ $5.00	

All expenses other than cost of goods sold amount to $2,000 for the month. The company uses an estimated tax rate of 25% to accrue monthly income taxes.

Required

1. Prepare a chart comparing cost of goods sold and ending inventory using the periodic system and the following costing methods:

	Cost of Goods Sold	Ending Inventory	Total
Weighted average			
FIFO			
LIFO			

2. What does the Total column represent?
3. Prepare income statements for each of the three methods.
4. Will the company pay more or less tax if it uses FIFO rather than LIFO? How much more or less?

LO5 • 6 • 7   Problem 5-12A Inventory Costing Methods—Periodic System

Story Company's inventory records for the month of November reveal the following:

Inventory, November 1	300 units @ $27.00
November 4, purchase	375 units @ $26.50
November 7, sale	450 units @ $63.00
November 13, purchase	330 units @ $26.00
November 18, purchase	225 units @ $25.40
November 22, sale	570 units @ $63.75
November 24, purchase	300 units @ $25.00
November 28, sale	165 units @ $64.50

Selling and administrative expenses for the month were $16,200. Depreciation expense was $6,000. Story's tax rate is 35%.

Required

1. Calculate the cost of goods sold and ending inventory under each of the following three methods assuming a periodic inventory system: (a) FIFO, (b) LIFO, and (c) weighted average.
2. Calculate the gross profit and net income under each costing assumption.
3. Under which costing method will Story pay the least taxes? Explain your answer.

Problem 5-13A Comparison of Inventory Costing Methods—Perpetual System (Appendix)

LO5 • 7 • 12

Repeat Problem 5-11A using the perpetual system.

Problem 5-14A Inventory Costing Methods—Periodic System

LO5 • 6 • 7

Following is an inventory acquisition schedule for Fees Corp. for 2012:

	Units	Unit Cost
Beginning inventory	4,000	$20
Purchases:		
February 4	2,000	18
April 12	3,000	16
September 10	1,000	14
December 5	2,500	12

During the year, Fees sold 11,000 units at $30 each. All expenses except cost of goods sold and taxes amounted to $60,000. The tax rate is 30%.

Required

1. Compute cost of goods sold and ending inventory under each of the following three methods assuming a periodic inventory system: (a) weighted average, (b) FIFO, and (c) LIFO.
2. Prepare income statements under each of the three methods.
3. Which method do you recommend so that Fees pays the least amount of taxes during 2012? Explain your answer.
4. Fees anticipates that unit costs for inventory will increase throughout 2013. Will Fees be able to switch from the method you recommended that it use in 2012 to another method to take advantage of the increase in prices for tax purposes? Explain your answer.

DECISION CASES

Reading and Interpreting Financial Statements

Decision Case 5-1 Comparing Two Companies in the Same Industry: Kellogg's and General Mills

LO1 • 3

Refer to the financial information for **Kellogg's** and **General Mills** reproduced at the end of this book and answer the following questions:

Required

1. Are Kellogg's and General Mills merchandisers, manufacturers, or service providers?
2. What is the dollar amount of inventories that each company reports on its balance sheet at the end of the most recent year? What percentage of total assets do inventories represent for each company?
3. Refer to Note 1 in Kellogg's annual report. What inventory valuation method does the company use? What is the advantage to the company of using this method?
4. Refer to Note 1 in General Mills's annual report. What inventory valuation method(s) does the company use? Does the fact that Kellogg's and General Mills use different methods make it difficult to compare the two companies?
5. Given the nature of their businesses, which inventory system, periodic or perpetual, would you expect both Kellogg's and General Mills to use? Explain your answer.

LO6 • 7   Decision Case 5-2 Reading and Interpreting Walgreen Co.'s Inventory Note

Walgreen Co.'s 2010 annual report includes the following in the note that summarizes its accounting policies:

Inventories

Inventories are valued on a lower of last-in, first-out (LIFO) cost or market basis. At August 31, 2010 and 2009, inventories would have been greater by $1,379 million and $1,239 million, respectively, if they had been valued on a lower of first-in, first-out (FIFO) cost or market basis. Inventory includes product costs, inbound freight, warehousing costs and vendor allowances.

Required

1. What inventory costing method does Walgreen Co. use?
2. What is the amount of the LIFO reserve at the end of each of the two years?
3. Explain the meaning of the increase or decrease in the LIFO reserve during 2010. What does this tell you about inventory costs for the company? Are they rising or falling? Explain your answer.

LO6 • 9   Decision Case 5-3 Reading and Interpreting Gap Inc.'s Inventory Note

The 2010 annual report for **Gap Inc.** includes the following information in the note that summarizes its accounting policies:

Merchandise Inventory

We value inventory at the lower of cost or market, with cost determined using the weighted-average cost method. We record an adjustment when future estimated selling price is less than cost. We review our inventory levels in order to identify slow-moving merchandise and broken assortments (items no longer in stock in a sufficient range of sizes) and use markdowns to clear merchandise. In addition, we estimate and accrue shortage for the period between the last physical count and the balance sheet date.

Required

1. What inventory costing method does Gap Inc. use? Explain why you think Gap uses this method.
2. Gap Inc. values its inventory at the lower of cost or market. How does the company define *market*? What factors does it take into account in deciding whether to write down its inventory?

Making Financial Decisions

LO2 • 3 • 4   Decision Case 5-4 Gross Profit for a Merchandiser

Emblems For You sells specialty sweatshirts. The purchase price is $10 per unit plus 10% tax and a shipping cost of 50¢ per unit. When the units arrive, they must be labeled, at an additional cost of 75¢ per unit. Emblems purchased, received, and labeled 1,500 units, of which 750 units were sold during the month for $20 each. The controller has prepared the following income statement:

Sales	$15,000
Cost of sales ($11 × 750)	8,250
Gross profit	$ 6,750
Shipping expense	750
Labeling expense	1,125
Net income	$ 4,875

Emblems is aware that a gross profit of 40% is standard for the industry. The marketing manager believes that Emblems should lower the price because the gross profit is higher than the industry average.

Required

1. Calculate Emblems' gross profit ratio.
2. Explain why Emblems should or should not lower its selling price.

Decision Case 5-5 Pricing Decision

LO2 • 3 • 4

Caroline's Candy Corner sells gourmet chocolates. The company buys chocolates in bulk for $5 per pound plus 5% sales tax. Credit terms are 2/10, n/25, and the company always pays promptly to take advantage of the discount. The chocolates are shipped to Caroline FOB shipping point. Shipping costs are $0.05 per pound. When the chocolates arrive at the shop, Caroline's Candy repackages them into one-pound boxes labeled with the store name. Boxes cost $0.70 each. The company pays its employees an hourly wage of $5.25 plus a commission of $0.10 per pound.

Required

1. What is the cost per one-pound box of chocolates?
2. What price must Caroline's Candy charge in order to have a 40% gross profit?
3. Do you believe this is a sufficient gross profit for this kind of business? Explain. What other costs might the company still incur?

Decision Case 5-6 Use of a Perpetual Inventory System

LO3

Darrell Keith is starting a new business. He plans to keep a tight control over it. Therefore, he wants to know *exactly* how much gross profit he earns on each unit that he sells. Darrell sets up an elaborate numbering system to identify each item as it is purchased and to match the item with a sales price. Each unit is assigned a number as follows:

0000-000-00-000

a. The first four numbers represent the month and day an item was received.
b. The second set of numbers is the last three numbers of the purchase order that authorized the purchase of the item.
c. The third set of numbers is the two-number department code assigned to different types of products.
d. The last three numbers are a chronological code assigned to units as they are received during a given day.

Required

1. Write a short memo to Darrell explaining the benefits and costs involved in a perpetual inventory system in conjunction with his quest to know exactly how much he will earn on each unit.
2. Comment on Darrell's inventory system assuming that he is selling (a) automobiles or (b) trees, shrubs, and plants.

Decision Case 5-7 Inventory Costing Methods

LO6 • 7

You are the controller for Georgetown Company. At the end of its first year of operations, the company is experiencing cash flow problems. The following information has been accumulated during the year:

Purchases	
January	1,000 units @ $8
March	1,200 units @ 8
October	1,500 units @ 9

During the year, Georgetown sold 3,000 units at $15 each. The expected tax rate is 35%. The president doesn't understand how to report inventory in the financial statements because no record of the cost of the units sold was kept as each sale was made.

(Continued)

Required

1. What inventory system must Georgetown use?
2. Determine the number of units on hand at the end of the year.
3. Explain cost-flow assumptions to the president and the method you recommend. Prepare income statements to justify your position, comparing your recommended method with at least one other method.

LO8   Decision Case 5-8   Inventory Errors

You are the controller of a rapidly growing mass merchandiser. The company uses a periodic inventory system. As the company has grown and accounting systems have developed, errors have occurred in both the physical count of inventory and the valuation of inventory on the balance sheet. You have been able to identify the following errors as of December 2012:

- In 2010, one of the retail sections was omitted from the physical count of inventory. The error resulted in inventory being understated on December 31, 2010, by approximately $28,700.
- In 2010, one section of the warehouse was counted twice. The error resulted in inventory being overstated on December 31, 2010, by approximately $45,600.
- In 2011, the replacement cost of some inventory was less than the FIFO value used on the balance sheet. The inventory would have been $6,000 less on the balance sheet dated December 31, 2011.

Required

What, if anything, should you do to correct each of these errors? Explain your answers.

Ethical Decision Making

LO2   Decision Case 5-9   Sales Returns and Allowances

You are the controller for a large chain of discount merchandise stores. You receive a memo from the sales manager for the midwestern region. He raises an issue regarding the proper treatment of sales returns. The manager urges you to discontinue the "silly practice" of recording Sales Returns and Allowances each time a customer returns a product. In the manager's mind, this is a waste of time and unduly complicates the financial statements. The manager recommends, "Things could be kept a lot simpler by just reducing Sales Revenue when a product is returned."

Required

1. What might the sales manager's motivation have been for writing the memo? Might he believe that the present practice is a waste of time that unduly complicates the financial statements? Explain.
2. Do you agree with the sales manager's recommendation? Explain why you agree or disagree.
3. Write a brief memo to the sales manager outlining your position on this matter.

LO7   Decision Case 5-10   Selection of an Inventory Method

As controller of a widely held public company, you are concerned with making the best decisions for the stockholders. At the end of its first year of operations, you are faced with the choice of method to value inventory. Specific identification is out of the question because the company sells a large quantity of diversified products. You are trying to decide between FIFO and LIFO. Inventory costs have increased 33% over the year. The chief executive officer has instructed you to do whatever it takes in all areas to report the highest income possible.

Required

1. Which method will satisfy the chief executive officer?
2. Which method is in the best interest of the stockholders? Explain your answer.
3. Write a brief memo to the chief executive officer to convince him that reporting the highest income is not always the best approach for the shareholders.

Decision Case 5-11 Write-Down of Obsolete Inventory **LO9**

As a newly hired staff accountant, you are assigned the responsibility of physically counting inventory at the end of the year. The inventory count proceeds in a timely fashion. The inventory is outdated, however. You suggest that the inventory cannot be sold for the cost at which it is carried and that the inventory should be written down to a much lower level. The controller replies that experience has taught her how the market changes and she knows that the units in the warehouse will be more marketable again. The company plans to keep the goods until they are back in style.

Required

1. What effect will writing off the inventory have on the current year's income?
2. What effect does not writing off the inventory have on the year-end balance sheet?
3. What factors should you consider in deciding whether to persist in your argument that the inventory should be written down?
4. If you fail to write down the inventory, do outside readers of the statements have information that is a faithful representation? Explain your answer.
5. Assume that the company prepares its financial statements in accordance with IFRS. Is it necessary that the inventory be written down?

SOLUTIONS TO KEY TERMS QUIZ

Quiz 1: Merchandise Accounting

17	Merchandise Inventory	13	Cost of goods sold
18	Raw materials	3	Perpetual system
16	Work in process	8	Periodic system
19	Finished goods	2	Transportation-In
15	Gross profit	11	Purchases
12	Net sales	4	Purchase Returns and Allowances
20	Sales revenue	10	Purchase Discounts
1	Sales Returns and Allowances	6	FOB destination point
5	Sales Discounts	7	FOB shipping point
9	Cost of goods available for sale	14	Gross profit ratio

Quiz 2: Inventory Valuation

9	Specific identification method	5	Replacement cost
2	Weighted average cost method	10	Inventory profit
4	FIFO method	3	Lower-of-cost-or-market (LCM) rule
6	LIFO method	13	Inventory turnover ratio
11	LIFO liquidation	7	Number of days' sales in inventory
8	LIFO conformity rule	1	Moving average (Appendix)
12	LIFO reserve		

ANSWERS TO POD REVIEW

LO1	1. b	2. c		**LO7**	1. b	2. b
LO2	1. a	2. c		**LO8**	1. a	2. a
LO3	1. d	2. b		**LO9**	1. c.	2. b
LO4	1. a	2. c		**LO10**	1. c	2. b
LO5	1. a	2. d		**LO11**	1. b	2. a
LO6	1. b	2. a		**LO12**	1. b	2. c

Cash and Internal Control

6

LO1 Identify and describe the various forms of cash reported on a balance sheet.

LO2 Show that you understand various techniques that companies use to control cash.

LO3 Explain the importance of internal control to a business and the significance of the Sarbanes-Oxley Act of 2002.

LO4 Describe the basic internal control procedures.

LO5 Describe the various documents used in recording purchases and their role in controlling cash disbursements.

STUDY LINKS

A Look at the Previous Chapter Chapter 5 introduced companies that sell products and examined how they account for purchases and sales of merchandise. It also considered how companies track product costs and value inventory according to one of the cost flow methods.

A Look at This Chapter Sale of merchandise results in the collection of cash at some point from the customer. Chapter 6 considers this most liquid of all assets and the ways in which companies try to maintain control over cash as well as other valuable assets.

A Look at the Upcoming Chapter Two other liquid assets appear toward the top of a balance sheet. Chapter 7 considers how companies account for receivables that result from credit sales and for investments made with available cash.

MAKING BUSINESS DECISIONS
SEARS HOLDINGS CORPORATION

AP Photo/Gene J. Puskar

Sears Holdings Corporation is the parent company of Kmart and Sears, Roebuck and Co. As its name implies, the parent's purpose is to "hold" two of the oldest and most recognizable retailers in the country. The Kmart and Sears merger in 2005 resulted in what is now the fourth-largest broad line U.S. retailer, with total revenues in the 2010 fiscal year of over $43 billion. Between its Kmart and Sears U.S. locations and its Sears Canada outlets, the company operates over 4,000 full-line and specialty retail stores.

Sears Holding Corporation, like all businesses, relies on a steady flow of cash to run smoothly. Cash is needed to continually supply Kmart and Sears stores with merchandise that they stock—from home appliances to clothing apparel. As the most liquid of all assets, cash is needed for many other uses, including acquisition of other businesses, purchase of property and equipment, and repayment of long-term debt. The accompanying balance sheet shows that cash and cash equivalents actually decreased during the 2010 fiscal year but still amounted to $1.375 billion at year-end and still accounted for nearly 12% of total current assets.

Because cash is such a liquid asset, control over cash is crucial to a company's long-term success. And with so many locations, retailers such as Sears Holdings must pay particular attention to the flow of cash and merchandise into and out of all of its stores. This chapter will look closely at the accounting for cash and cash equivalents and at the ways companies maintain effective control over all valuable assets, including cash.

Why do you need to study this chapter?

- You need to know what is included in cash and cash equivalents. (See pp. 294–295.)
- You need to know the techniques that companies use to control cash. (See pp. 297–301.)
- You need to know why a company must maintain an effective internal control system and what basic procedures help make a system effective. (See pp. 305–310.)
- You need to know how the use of business documents can add to the effectiveness of an internal control system. (See pp. 310–316.)

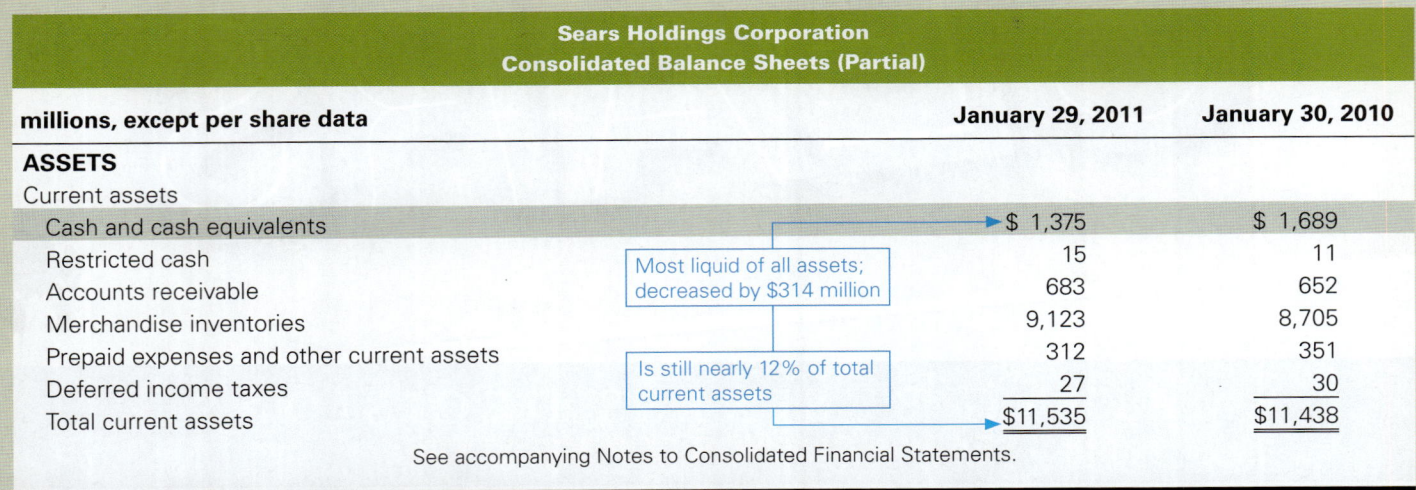

Sears Holdings Corporation
Consolidated Balance Sheets (Partial)

millions, except per share data	January 29, 2011	January 30, 2010
ASSETS		
Current assets		
Cash and cash equivalents	$ 1,375	$ 1,689
Restricted cash	15	11
Accounts receivable	683	652
Merchandise inventories	9,123	8,705
Prepaid expenses and other current assets	312	351
Deferred income taxes	27	30
Total current assets	$11,535	$11,438

Most liquid of all assets; decreased by $314 million

Is still nearly 12% of total current assets

See accompanying Notes to Consolidated Financial Statements.

Source: Sears Holdings Corporation 2010 annual report.

What Constitutes Cash?

LO1 Identify and describe the various forms of cash reported on a balance sheet.

OVERVIEW: Regardless of the form it takes, cash reported on a balance sheet must be readily available to pay debts. Cash equivalents are those investments readily convertible to a known amount of cash.

Cash takes many forms. Coin and currency on hand and cash on deposit in the form of checking, savings, and money market accounts are the most obvious forms of cash. Also included in cash are checks, including undeposited checks from customers, cashier's checks, and certified checks. The current proliferation of different types of financial instruments makes it very difficult to decide on the appropriate classification of these various items. The key to the classification of an amount as cash is that it be *readily available to pay debts.* Technically, a bank has the legal right to demand that a customer notify it before making withdrawals from savings accounts, or time deposits, as they are often called. Because this right is rarely exercised, however, savings accounts are normally classified as cash. In contrast, a certificate of deposit has a specific maturity date and carries a penalty for early withdrawal and therefore is not included in cash.

Cash Equivalents and the Statement of Cash Flows

The first item on **Sears Holdings'** balance sheet in the chapter opener is Cash and cash equivalents. Examples of items normally classified as cash equivalents are commercial paper issued by corporations, Treasury bills issued by the federal government, and money market funds offered by financial institutions. According to U.S. GAAP, classification as a **cash equivalent** is limited to those investments that are readily convertible to known amounts of cash and that have an original maturity to the investor of three months or less. According to that definition, a six-month bank certificate of deposit would *not* be classified as a cash equivalent. The IFRS definition of cash equivalents is very similar to that used by U.S. GAAP.

The statement of cash flows that accompanies Sears Holdings' balance sheet is shown in Exhibit 6-1. Note the direct tie between this statement and the balance sheet.

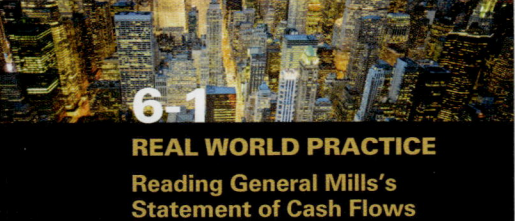

6-1

REAL WORLD PRACTICE

Reading General Mills's Statement of Cash Flows

According to the company's statement of cash flows, did its cash and cash equivalents increase or decrease during the most recent year? Summarize the changes in cash and cash equivalents for the year using the framework shown at the top of the next page.

IFRS

Cash equivalent
An investment that is readily convertible to a known amount of cash and has an original maturity to the investor of three months or less.

© Nikada/istockphoto.com

© Kasia Biel/istockphoto.com

EXHIBIT 6-1 Sears Holdings' Statement of Cash Flows

Sears Holdings Corporation
Consolidated Statements of Cash Flows

millions	2010	2009	2008
CASH FLOWS FROM OPERATING ACTIVITIES			
Net income	$ 150	$ 297	$ 99
Adjustments to reconcile net income to net cash provided by operating activities:			
Depreciation and amortization	900	926	981
Impairment charges	—	—	360
Gain on sales of assets	(67)	(74)	(51)
Pension and post-retirement plan contributions	(316)	(209)	(286)
Settlement of Canadian dollar hedges	(3)	—	(64)
Change in operating assets and liabilities (net of acquisitions and dispositions):			
Deferred income taxes	(20)	90	(385)
Merchandise inventories	(366)	188	1,003
Merchandise payables	(264)	272	(389)
Income and other taxes	(35)	101	(173)
Mark-to-market asset on Sears Canada U.S. dollar collar contracts	7	65	(74)
Other operating assets	4	48	207
Other operating liabilities	140	(197)	(236)
Net cash provided by operating activities	130	1,507	992
CASH FLOWS FROM INVESTING ACTIVITIES			
Acquisitions of businesses, net of cash acquired	—	—	(37)
Proceeds from sales of property and investments	35	23	86
Net decrease (increase) in investments and restricted cash	—	166	(189)
Purchases of property and equipment	(441)	(361)	(497)
Net cash used in investing activities	(406)	(172)	(637)
CASH FLOWS FROM FINANCING ACTIVITIES			
Stock issued under executive compensation plans	—	13	—
Proceeds from debt issuances	1,452	—	17
Repayments of long-term debt	(486)	(335)	(262)
Increase (decrease) in short-term borrowings, primarily 90 days or less	35	(117)	280
Debt issuance costs	(30)	(81)	—
Purchase of Sears Canada shares	(603)	(7)	—
Sears Canada dividends paid to minority shareholders	(69)	—	—
Purchase of treasury stock	(394)	(424)	(678)
Net cash used in financing activities	(95)	(951)	(643)
Effect of exchange rate changes on cash and cash equivalents	57	132	(161)
NET INCREASE (DECREASE) IN CASH AND CASH EQUIVALENTS	(314)	516	(449)
CASH AND CASH EQUIVALENTS, BEGINNING OF YEAR	1,689	1,173	1,622
CASH AND CASH EQUIVALENTS, END OF YEAR	$1,375	$1,689	$1,173
SUPPLEMENTAL DISCLOSURE ABOUT NON-CASH INVESTING AND FINANCING ACTIVITIES:			
Bankruptcy related settlements resulting in the receipt of treasury stock	$ —	$ —	$ 12
Capital lease obligation incurred	17	7	12
Supplemental Cash Flow Data:			
Income taxes paid (refunds received)	59	(70)	107
Cash interest paid	180	185	207

See accompanying Notes to Consolidated Financial Statements.

(Refer to the Current Assets section of the company's balance sheet shown in the chapter opener.)

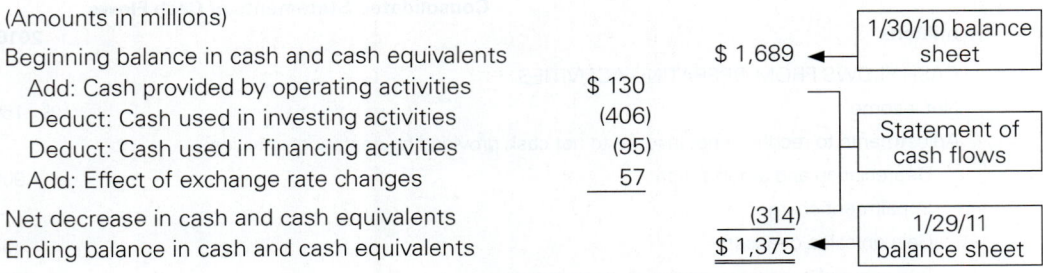

(Amounts in millions)

Beginning balance in cash and cash equivalents		$ 1,689 ← 1/30/10 balance sheet
Add: Cash provided by operating activities	$ 130	
Deduct: Cash used in investing activities	(406)	
Deduct: Cash used in financing activities	(95)	Statement of cash flows
Add: Effect of exchange rate changes	57	
Net decrease in cash and cash equivalents		(314)
Ending balance in cash and cash equivalents		$ 1,375 ← 1/29/11 balance sheet

---

Example 6-1 Determining the Amount of Cash and Cash Equivalents

Given the following items, what amount should be reported on the balance sheet as Cash and cash equivalents?

Cashier's check	$ 2,000
Certificate of deposit due in nine months	10,000
Checking account	4,500
Coin and currency on hand	1,500
Employee IOU	3,000
Money market account	12,000
Postage stamps	500
Savings account	8,000
Undeposited customer checks	850

Cash and cash equivalents would be reported as $28,850 ($2,000 + $4,500 + $1,500 + $12,000 + $8,000 + $850).

© Cengage Learning 2013

LO1 Identify and describe the various forms of cash reported on a balance sheet.

- Cash can take many forms; however, the key attribute is that the asset is readily available to pay debts.
- Cash equivalents are investments that are readily convertible to a known amount of cash. *Readily* means three months or less.

POD REVIEW 6.1

QUESTIONS   Answers to these questions are on the last page of the chapter.

1. Which of the following items should not be included in cash on the balance sheet?

   a. coin and currency on hand
   b. customer's undeposited check
   c. money market account
   d. All of the above should be included in cash on the balance sheet.

2. A cash equivalent is

   a. an investment in the stock of another company that can be sold on demand.
   b. an investment that is readily convertible to a known amount of cash and has an original maturity to the investor of three months or less.
   c. coin and currency on hand, checking and savings accounts, and money market accounts.
   d. none of the above.

© Cengage Learning 2013

"Cash is king," and nowhere is this more true than in the retail sector. Sears Holdings, with its over 4,000 Sears and Kmart stores in the United States and Canada, can attest to the truth in this statement. While Sears reported cash and cash equivalents of $952 million at the end of the first quarter of its 2011 fiscal year, current liabilities—those due within the next year—amounted to nearly ten times this number, $9,438 million.

Some of the cash needed to satisfy these debts will be generated by Sears' operations, that is by selling its merchandise at a profit. But where else does a retailing giant turn for the funds it needs to pay suppliers, meet its payroll, and address other cash needs? On April 8, 2011, the company announced the extension of its existing revolving credit facility until April 2016. Agreements of this sort are critical to the day-to-day viability of companies such as Sears. Sears' credit arrangement will allow the company to borrow $3.275 billion on an as-needed basis and reassure its investors of its ability to withstand the challenges in the current economic environment.

Sources: http://www.searsholdings.com/invest; April 8, 2011 press release and 10Q for first quarter, 2011.

Control Over Cash

OVERVIEW: Companies use a variety of devices to control cash. Among them are bank reconciliations and petty cash funds.

> **LO2** Show that you understand various techniques that companies use to control cash.

Because cash is universally accepted as a medium of exchange, control over it is critical to the smooth functioning of any business, no matter how large or small.

Cash Management

In addition to the need to guard against theft and other abuses related to the physical custody of cash, management of this asset is also important. Sears Holdings must constantly be sure that it has neither too little nor too much cash on hand. The need to have enough cash on hand is obvious: suppliers, employees, taxing agencies, banks, and all other creditors must be paid on time. It is equally important that a company not maintain cash on hand and on deposit in checking accounts beyond the minimal amount necessary to support ongoing operations since cash is essentially a nonearning asset. Granted, some checking accounts pay a very meager rate of interest. However, the potential superior return from investing idle cash in various forms of marketable securities dictates that companies carefully monitor cash on hand at all times.

An important tool in cash management, the cash flows statement, is discussed in detail in Chapter 12. Cash budgets, which are also critical to cash management, are discussed in management accounting and business finance texts. Companies often use two other cash control features: bank reconciliations and petty cash funds. Before turning to those control devices, we need to review the basic features of a bank statement.

Reading a Bank Statement

Two fundamental principles of internal control are applicable to cash:

1. All cash receipts should be deposited intact daily.
2. All cash payments should be made by check.

Checking accounts at banks are critical in this regard. These accounts allow a company to carefully monitor and control cash receipts and cash payments. Control is aided

Bank statement
A detailed list, provided by the bank, of all activity for a particular account during the month.

further by the monthly **bank statement**. The statement provides a detailed list of all activity for a particular account during the month. An example of a typical bank statement is shown in Exhibit 6-2. The bank statement indicates the activity in one of the cash accounts maintained by Mickey's Marathon Sports at Mt. Etna State Bank.

It is important to understand the route a check takes after it is written. Assume that Mickey's writes a check on its account at Mt. Etna State Bank. Mickey's mails the check to one of its suppliers, Keese Corp., which deposits the check in its account at Second City Bank. At this point, Second City presents the check to Mt. Etna for payment, and Mt. Etna reduces the balance in Mickey's account accordingly. The canceled check has now "cleared" the banking system.

The following types of items appear on Mickey's bank statement:

Canceled checks—Mickey's checks that cleared the bank during the month of June are listed with the corresponding check number and the date paid. Some of these checks may have been written by Mickey's in a previous month but were not presented for payment to the bank until June. Also, during June Mickey's may have written some checks that do not yet appear on the bank statement because they have not been presented for payment. A check written by a company but not yet presented to the bank for payment is called an **outstanding check**.

Outstanding check
A check written by a company but not yet presented to the bank for payment.

Deposits—Most companies deposit all checks, coin, and currency on a daily basis; this is in keeping with an internal control principle that all cash receipts should be deposited in their entirety. For the sake of brevity, we have limited to four the number of deposits that Mickey's made during the month. Mickey's also may have

EXHIBIT 6-2 Bank Statement

Mt. Etna State Bank
Chicago, Illinois
Statement of Account

Mickey's Marathon Sports
502 Dodge St.
Chicago, IL 66666

For the Month Ending Account   June 30, 2012
Account   0371-22-514

Date	Description	Subtractions	Additions	Balance
6-01	Previous balance			3,236.41
6-01	Check 497	723.40		2,513.01
6-02	Check 495	125.60		2,387.41
6-06	Check 491	500.00		1,887.41
6-07	Deposit		1,423.16	3,310.57
6-10	Check 494	185.16		3,125.41
6-13	NSF check	245.72		2,879.69
6-15	Deposit		755.50	3,635.19
6-18	Check 499	623.17		3,012.02
6-20	Check 492	125.00		2,887.02
6-22	Deposit		1,875.62	4,762.64
6-23	Service charge	20.00		4,742.64
6-24	Check 493	875.75		3,866.89
6-24	Check 503	402.10		3,464.79
6-26	Customer note, interest		550.00	4,014.79
6-26	Service fee on note	16.50		3,998.29
6-27	Check 500	1,235.40		2,762.89
6-28	Deposit		947.50	3,710.39
6-30	Check 498	417.25		3,293.14
6-30	Interest earned		15.45	3,308.59
6-30	Statement Totals	5,495.05	5,567.23	

sit on the last day or two of the month, and this deposit may not yet be made the bank statement. This type of deposit is called a **deposit in transit**.

eck—NSF stands for "not sufficient funds." The NSF check listed on the ment on June 13 is a customer's check that Mickey's recorded on its posited, and thus included in its Cash account. When Mt. Etna State Bank hat the customer did not have sufficient funds on hand in its bank account the check, the bank deducted the amount from Mickey's account. Mickey's to contact its customer to collect the amount due; ideally, the customer will a new check once it has sufficient funds in its account.

service charge—Banks charge for various services. The most common bank serv-charges are monthly activity fees and fees charged for new checks, for the rental lockbox at the bank in which to store valuable company documents, and for the llection of customer notes by the bank.

Customer note and interest—It is often convenient to have customers pay amounts owed to a company directly to that company's bank. The bank simply acts as a collection agency for the company.

Interest earned—Most checking accounts pay interest on the average daily balance in the account. Rates paid on checking accounts are usually significantly less than could be earned on most other forms of investment.

The Bank Reconciliation

With over 4,000 retail stores, you can imagine the large number of bank accounts that Sears maintains. A **bank reconciliation** should be prepared for each individual bank account as soon as the bank statement is received. Ideally, the reconciliation should be performed or, at a minimum, thoroughly reviewed by someone independent of custody, record-keeping, and authorization responsibilities relating to cash. As the name implies, the purpose of a bank reconciliation is to *reconcile,* or resolve, any differences between the bank's recorded balance and the balance that appears on the company's books. Differences between the two amounts are investigated, and necessary adjustments are made. The following steps are used in preparing a bank reconciliation:

1. Trace deposits listed on the bank statement to the books. Any deposits recorded on the books but not yet shown on the bank statement are deposits in transit. **Prepare a list of the deposits in transit.**

2. Arrange the canceled checks in numerical order and trace each of them to the books. Any checks recorded on the books but not yet listed on the bank statement are outstanding. **Prepare a list of the outstanding checks.**

3. List all items, other than deposits, shown as additions on the bank statement, such as interest paid by the bank for the month and amounts collected by the bank from one of the company's customers. When the bank pays interest or collects an amount owed to a company by one of the company's customers, the bank increases its liability to the company on its own books. These items are called **credit memoranda**. **Prepare a list of credit memoranda.**

4. List all amounts, other than canceled checks, shown as subtractions on the bank statement, such as any NSF checks and the various service charges mentioned earlier. When a company deposits money in a bank, a liability is created on the books of the bank. This liability is reduced for items such as NSF checks and service charges. These items are called **debit memoranda**. **Prepare a list of debit memoranda.**

5. **Identify any errors** made by the bank or by the company in recording the various cash transactions.

6. Use the information collected in Steps 1 through 5 to **prepare a bank reconciliation.**

Companies use a number of different formats in preparing bank reconciliations. For example, some companies take the balance shown on the bank statement and reconcile this amount to the balance shown on the books. Another approach, which will be illustrated for Mickey's, involves reconciling the bank balance and the book balance to an adjusted balance, rather than one to the other. The advantage of this second approach is

Deposit in transit
A deposit recorded on the books but not yet reflected on the bank statement.

STUDY TIP

Review your own bank statement to see the similarities and differences between it and the one illustrated here. Also look on the reverse side of your statement for the form of a reconciliation the bank provides. It may or may not be the same format illustrated in Example 6-2.

Bank reconciliation
A form used by the accountant to reconcile or resolve any differences between the balance shown on the bank statement for a particular account with the balance shown in the accounting records.

Credit memoranda
Additions on a bank statement for such items as interest paid on the account and notes collected by the bank for the customer.

Debit memoranda
Deductions on a bank statement for items such as NSF checks and various service charges.

that it yields the correct balance and makes it easy for the company to m̶ necessary adjustments to its books.

Example 6-2 Preparing a Bank Reconciliation

A bank reconciliation for Mickey's Marathon Sports is shown below.

Mickey's Marathon Sports
Bank Reconciliation
June 30, 2012

Balance per bank statement, June 30			$3,308.59
Add:	Deposit in transit		642.30
Deduct:	Outstanding checks:		
	No. 496	$ 79.89	
	No. 501	213.20	
	No. 502	424.75	(717.84)
Adjusted balance, June 30			$3,233.05
Balance per books, June 30			$2,895.82
Add:	Customer note collected	$500.00	
	Interest on customer note	50.00	
	Interest earned during June	15.45	
	Error in recording check 498	54.00	619.45
Deduct:	NSF check	$245.72	
	Collection fee on note	16.50	
	Service charge for lockbox	20.00	(282.22)
Adjusted balance, June 30			$3,233.05

The following are explanations for the various items on the reconciliation.

1. The balance per bank statement of $3,308.59 is taken from the June statement as shown in Exhibit 6-2.

2. Mickey's records showed a deposit for $642.30 made on June 30 that is not reflected on the bank statement. The deposit in transit is listed as an addition to the bank statement balance.

3. The accounting records indicate three checks written but not yet reflected on the bank statement. The three outstanding checks are as follows:

496	$ 79.89
501	$213.20
502	$424.75

Outstanding checks are the opposite of deposits in transit and therefore are deducted from the bank statement balance.

4. The adjusted balance of $3,233.05 is found by adding the deposit in transit and deducting the outstanding checks from the bank statement balance.

5. The $2,895.82 book balance on June 30 is taken from the company's records as of that date.

6. According to the bank statement, $550 was added to the account on June 26 for the collection of a note with interest. We assume that the repayment of the note accounted for $500 of this amount and that the other $50 was for interest. The bank statement notifies Mickey's that the note with interest has been collected. Therefore, Mickey's must add $550 to the book balance.

7. An entry on June 30 on the bank statement shows an increase of $15.45 for interest earned on the bank account during June. This amount is added to the book balance.

8. A review of the canceled checks returned with the bank statement detected an error that Mickey's made. The company records indicated that check 498 was recorded incorrectly as $471.25; the check was actually written for $417.25 and reflected as such on the bank statement. This error, referred to as a *transposition error*, resulted from transposing the 7 and the 1 in recording the check in the books. The error is the difference between the amount of $471.25 recorded and the amount of $417.25 that should have been recorded, or $54.00. Because Mickey's recorded the cash payment at too large an amount, $54.00 must be added back to the book balance.

(Continued)

9. In addition to canceled checks, three other deductions appear on the bank statement. Each of these must be deducted from the book balance:

    a. A customer's NSF check for $245.72 (see June 13 entry on bank statement)

    b. A $16.50 fee charged by the bank to collect the customer's note discussed in (6) (see June 26 entry on bank statement)

    c. A service fee of $20.00 charged by the bank for rental of a lockbox (see June 23 entry on bank statement)

10. The additions of $619.45 and deductions of $282.22 resulted in an adjusted cash balance of $3,233.05. Note that this adjusted balance agrees with the adjusted bank statement balance on the bank reconciliation [see (4)]. Thus, all differences between the two balances have been explained.

The Need for Adjustments to the Records

After it completes the bank reconciliation, Mickey's must prepare a number of adjustments to its records. In fact, all of the information for these adjustments will be from one section of the bank reconciliation. Are the additions and deductions made to the bank balance or the ones made to the book balance the basis for the adjustments? The additions and deductions to the Cash account *on the books* should be the basis for the adjustments because these are items that Mickey's was unaware of before receiving the bank statement. Conversely, the additions and deductions to the bank's balance (i.e., the deposits in transit and the outstanding checks) are items that Mickey's has already recorded on its books.

Establishing a Petty Cash Fund

Recall one of the fundamental rules in controlling cash: all disbursements should be made by check. Most businesses make an exception to this rule in the case of minor expenditures, for which they use a **petty cash fund**. This fund consists of coin and currency kept on hand to make minor disbursements. The necessary steps in setting up and maintaining a petty cash fund are as follows:

Petty cash fund
Money kept on hand for making minor disbursements in coin and currency rather than by writing checks.

1. A check is written for a lump-sum amount, such as $100 or $500. The check is cashed, and the coin and currency are entrusted to a petty cash custodian.
2. A journal entry is made to record the establishment of the fund.
3. Upon presentation of the necessary documentation, employees receive minor disbursements from the fund. In essence, cash is traded from the fund in exchange for a receipt.
4. Periodically, the fund is replenished by writing and cashing a check in the amount necessary to bring the fund back to its original balance.
5. At the time the fund is replenished, an adjustment is made to record its replenishment and to recognize the various expenses incurred.

The use of this fund is normally warranted on the basis of cost versus benefits. That is, the benefits in time saved in making minor disbursements from cash are thought to outweigh the cost associated with the risk of loss from decreased control over cash disbursements. The fund also serves a practical purpose for certain expenditures, such as taxi fares and postage, that often must be paid in cash.

LO2 Show that you understand various techniques that companies use to control cash.

- The liquidity of cash makes controls over it very important to have in place.
  - Cash management means managing the need to have enough cash on hand to ensure cash flow needs but not so much that excess funds earn little return and may be vulnerable to misappropriation.
  - Bank reconciliations use third-party documents (bank statements) to reconcile differences between the amount in the bank and on the books. Done by an independent party, bank reconciliations are effective control procedures.
  - Petty cash funds are an effective way to minimize access to large cash accounts to pay for relatively small expenditures.

POD REVIEW 6.2

QUESTIONS Answers to these questions are on the last page of the chapter.

1. Which of the following is not an addition to the balance per the books on a bank reconciliation that adjusts both the bank statement and balance per the books to the adjusted balance?
   a. interest earned on the bank account
   b. deposits in transit
   c. collection by the bank on a customer's note
   d. All of the above are additions.

2. Which of the following is a deduction to the balance per bank statement on a bank reconciliation that adjusts both the bank statement and balance per books to the adjusted balance?
   a. NSF checks
   b. outstanding checks
   c. bank service charges
   d. All of the above are deductions to the balance per the bank statement.

An Introduction to Internal Control

LO3 Explain the importance of internal control to a business and the significance of the Sarbanes-Oxley Act of 2002.

OVERVIEW: An internal control system includes the policies and procedures necessary to safeguard assets and the reliability of the records. Improvement in internal control was a major focus of the Sarbanes-Oxley Act of 2002.

An employee of a large auto parts warehouse routinely takes spare parts home for personal use. A payroll clerk writes and signs two checks for an employee and then splits the amount of the second check with the worker. Through human error, an invoice is paid for merchandise never received from the supplier. These cases share one important characteristic. They all point to a deficiency in a company's internal control system. An **internal control system** consists of the policies and procedures necessary to ensure the safeguarding of an entity's assets, the reliability of its accounting records, and the accomplishment of its overall objectives.

Three assets are especially critical to the operation of a merchandising company such as Sears Holdings: cash, accounts receivable, and inventory. Activities related to those three assets compose the operating cycle of a business. Cash is used to buy inventory; the inventory is eventually sold; and assuming a sale on credit, the account receivable from the customer is collected. After looking at the government's response to huge lapses in internal control by major U.S. companies, we turn to the ways in which a company attempts to *control* the assets at its disposal.

Internal control system
Policies and procedures necessary to ensure the safeguarding of an entity's assets, the reliability of its accounting records, and the accomplishment of overall company objectives.

The Sarbanes-Oxley Act of 2002

Sarbanes-Oxley Act
An act of Congress in 2002 intended to bring reform to corporate accountability and stewardship in the wake of a number of major corporate scandals.

As briefly described in Chapter 1, the **Sarbanes-Oxley Act** of 2002 (or SOX) was a direct response by Congress to the numerous corporate scandals that surfaced in the first few years of the new millennium. High-profile cases involving questionable accounting practices by companies such as **Enron** and **WorldCom** caused the federal government to step in and attempt to restore the public's confidence in the financial reporting system. SOX's various provisions are far-reaching, including provisions designed to ensure the independence of a company's auditors. For example, external auditors can no longer provide bookkeeping, human resource, information system design, and brokerage services for clients that they audit.

Another major part of SOX, Section 404, deals with a company's internal control system. Section 404 requires the annual report to include an **internal control report** in which management is required to:

1. State its responsibility to establish and maintain an adequate internal control structure and procedures for financial reporting.
2. Assess the effectiveness of its internal control structure and procedures for financial reporting.

Sears Holdings' Report on Internal Control over Financial Reporting is shown in Exhibit 6-3. The first paragraph states management's responsibility for its system of internal control, and the fourth paragraph indicates that management believes internal control over financial reporting is effective.

Another important provision in SOX is that a company's outside auditors must issue a report on their assessment of the company's internal control. The statement in the last paragraph in Exhibit 6-3 calls attention to this report. **Deloitte & Touche** is Sears Holdings' independent auditor, and its report is shown in Exhibit 6-4. Note the

Internal control report
A report required by Section 404 of the Sarbanes-Oxley Act to be included in a company's annual report in which management assesses the effectiveness of the internal control structure.

EXHIBIT 6-3 Management Report on Internal Control—Sears Holdings

Management's Annual Report on Internal Control over Financial Reporting

The management of Sears Holdings Corporation is responsible for establishing and maintaining adequate internal control over financial reporting. Internal control over financial reporting is a process designed by, or under the supervision of, the Company's principal executive and principal financial officers and effected by the Company's board of directors, management and other personnel to provide reasonable assurance regarding the reliability of financial reporting and the preparation of financial statements for external purposes in accordance with generally accepted accounting principles and includes those policies and procedures that:

[**Management states its responsibility for the internal control system.**]

- pertain to the maintenance of records that in reasonable detail accurately and fairly reflect the transactions and dispositions of the assets of the Company;
- provide reasonable assurance that transactions are recorded as necessary to permit preparation of financial statements in accordance with generally accepted accounting principles, and that receipts and expenditures of the Company are being made only in accordance with authorizations of management and directors of the Company; and
- provide reasonable assurance regarding prevention or timely detection of unauthorized acquisition, use or disposition of the Company's assets that could have a material effect on the financial statements.

Because of inherent limitations, internal control over financial reporting may not prevent or detect misstatements. Projections of any evaluation of effectiveness to future periods are subject to the risks that controls may become inadequate because of changes in conditions, or that the degree of compliance with the policies or procedures may deteriorate.

Management assessed the effectiveness of the Company's internal control over financial reporting at January 29, 2011. In making its assessment, management used the criteria set forth in the *Internal Control—Integrated Framework* issued by the Committee of Sponsoring Organizations of the Treadway Commission ("COSO"). The assessment included the documentation and understanding of the Company's internal control over financial reporting. Management evaluated the design effectiveness and tested the operating effectiveness of internal controls over financial reporting to form its conclusion.

[**Management assesses the effectiveness of the internal control system.**]

Based on this evaluation, management concluded that, at January 29, 2011, the Company's internal control over financial reporting is effective to provide reasonable assurance that the Company's financial statements are fairly presented in conformity with generally accepted accounting principles.

Deloitte & Touche LLP, independent registered public accounting fi rm, has reported on the effectiveness of the Company's internal control over financial reporting at January 29, 2011, as stated in their report included herein.

[**Auditors have issued a report on management's assessment.**]

Source: Sears Holdings Corporation 2010 annual report.

EXHIBIT 6-4 Auditor's Report—Sears Holdings

Report of Independent Registered Public Accounting Firm

To the Board of Directors and Shareholders of Sears Holdings Corporation

We have audited the accompanying consolidated balance sheets of Sears Holdings Corporation and subsidiaries (the "Company") as of January 29, 2011 and January 30, 2010, and the related consolidated statements of income, equity, and cash flows for each of the three years in the period ended January 29, 2011. Our audits also included the financial statement schedule listed in the Index at Item 8. We also have audited the Company's internal control over financial reporting as of January 29, 2011, based on criteria established in *Internal Control—Integrated Framework* issued by the Committee of Sponsoring Organizations of the Treadway Commission. The Company's management is responsible for these financial statements and financial statement schedule, for maintaining effective internal control over financial reporting, and for its assessment of the effectiveness of internal control over financial reporting, included in the accompanying Management's Annual Report on Internal Control Over Financial Reporting. Our responsibility is to express an opinion on these financial statements and financial statement schedule and an opinion on the Company's internal control over financial reporting based on our audits.

> **Audit followed the standards of the Public Company Accounting Oversight Board.**

We conducted our audits in accordance with the standards of the Public Company Accounting Oversight Board (United States). Those standards require that we plan and perform the audit to obtain reasonable assurance about whether the financial statements are free of material misstatement and whether effective internal control over financial reporting was maintained in all material respects. Our audits of the financial statements included examining, on a test basis, evidence supporting the amounts and disclosures in the financial statements, assessing the accounting principles used and significant estimates made by management, and evaluating the overall financial statement presentation. Our audit of internal control over financial reporting included obtaining an understanding of internal control over financial reporting, assessing the risk that a material weakness exists, testing and evaluating the design and operating effectiveness of internal control based on the assessed risk. Our audits also included performing such other procedures as we considered necessary in the circumstances. We believe that our audits provide a reasonable basis for our opinions.

A company's internal control over financial reporting is a process designed by, or under the supervision of, the company's principal executive and principal financial officers, or persons performing similar functions, and effected by the company's board of directors, management, and other personnel to provide reasonable assurance regarding the reliability of financial reporting and the preparation of financial statements for external purposes in accordance with generally accepted accounting principles. A company's internal control over financial reporting includes those policies and procedures that (1) pertain to the maintenance of records that, in reasonable detail, accurately and fairly reflect the transactions and dispositions of the assets of the company; (2) provide reasonable assurance that transactions are recorded as necessary to permit preparation of financial statements in accordance with generally accepted accounting principles and that receipts and expenditures of the company are being made only in accordance with authorizations of management and directors of the company; and (3) provide reasonable assurance regarding prevention or timely detection of unauthorized acquisition, use, or disposition of the company's assets that could have a material effect on the financial statements.

Because of the inherent limitations of internal control over financial reporting, including the possibility of collusion or improper management override of controls, material misstatements due to error or fraud may not be prevented or detected on a timely basis. Also, projections of any evaluation of the effectiveness of the internal control over financial reporting to future periods are subject to the risk that the controls may become inadequate because of changes in conditions, or that the degree of compliance with the policies or procedures may deteriorate.

> **Auditors' opinion**

In our opinion, the consolidated financial statements referred to above present fairly, in all material respects, the financial position of the Sears Holdings Corporation and subsidiaries as of January 29, 2011 and January 30, 2010, and the results of their operations and their cash flows for each of the three years in the period ended January 29, 2011, in conformity with accounting principles generally accepted in the United States of America. Also, in our opinion, such financial statement schedule, when considered in relation to the basic consolidated financial statements taken as a whole, presents fairly, in all material respects, the information set forth therein. Also, in our opinion, the Company maintained, in all material respects, effective internal control over financial reporting as of January 29, 2011, based on the criteria established in *Internal Control—Integrated Framework* issued by the Committee of Sponsoring Organizations of the Treadway Commission.

/s/ DELOITTE & TOUCHE LLP
Deloitte & Touche LLP
Chicago, Illinois
March 11, 2011

Source: Sears Holdings Corporation 2010 annual report.

reference in the second paragraph to the **Public Company Accounting Oversight Board (PCAOB)**. The PCAOB is the five-member body created by SOX that was given authority to set auditing standards in the United States. The last sentence in Deloitte & Touche's report also contains the important statement, namely, that in their opinion, Sears Holdings has maintained effective internal control over financial reporting.

The top of the independent auditors' report in Exhibit 6-4 states that it is directed to the board of directors and shareholders of Sears Holdings. The **board of directors** usually consists of key officers of the corporation as well as a number of directors whom it does not directly employ. Another key provision in SOX required that the audit committee be made up entirely of outside directors. The **audit committee** is a subset of the board of directors that provides direct contact between stockholders and the independent accounting firm.

One of the most frequently debated issues in many of the high-profile financial reporting scandals was the behavior of the companies' key officers. Stockholders and others affected by these scandals thought that top management should have taken more responsibility for the accuracy of the information presented in the financial statements. SOX directly addresses this issue. For the first time ever, a company's chief executive officer (CEO) and chief financial officer (CFO) must sign a statement certifying that the information in the financial statements fairly presents the financial condition and results of operations of the company. This provision places the responsibility for the information in the financial statements directly in the hands of the company's CEO and CFO.

The Control Environment

The success of an internal control system begins with the competence of the people in charge of it. Management's operating style will have a major impact on the effectiveness of various policies. An *autocratic* style, in which a few key officers tightly control operations, will result in an environment different from that of a *decentralized* organization, in which departments have more freedom to make decisions. Personnel policies and practices form another factor in the internal control of a business. An appropriate system for hiring competent employees and firing incompetent ones is crucial to an efficient operation. After all, no internal control system will work very well if employees who are dishonest or poorly trained are on the payroll. On the other hand, too few people doing too many tasks defeats the purpose of an internal control system. Finally, the effectiveness of internal control in a business is influenced by the board of directors, particularly its audit committee.

The Accounting System

An **accounting system** consists of all of the methods and records used to report an entity's transactions accurately and to maintain accountability for its assets and liabilities. Regardless of the degree of computer automation, the use of a journal to record transactions is an integral part of all accounting systems. Refinements may be made to the basic components of the system depending on the company's needs. For example, most companies use specialized journals to record recurring transactions, such as sales of merchandise on credit.

An accounting system can be completely manual, fully computerized, or as is often the case, a mixture of the two. Internal controls are important to all businesses regardless of the degree of automation of the accounting system. The system must be capable of handling the volume and complexity of transactions entered into by a business. Businesses use computers because they are ideally suited to the task of processing large numbers of repetitive transactions efficiently and quickly.

Public Company Accounting Oversight Board (PCAOB)
The five-member body created by the Sarbanes-Oxley Act that was given the authority to set auditing standards in the United States.

Board of directors
A group composed of key officers of a corporation and outside members responsible for general oversight of the affairs of the entity.

Audit committee
A board of directors subset that acts as a direct contact between the stockholders and the independent accounting firm.

Accounting system
Methods and records used to accurately report an entity's transactions and to maintain accountability for its assets and liabilities.

LO3 Explain the importance of internal control to a business and the significance of the Sarbanes-Oxley Act of 2002.

- The Sarbanes-Oxley Act of 2002 required publicly traded companies to improve the documentation and functioning of their internal controls.
  - Management must now render an opinion on the efficiency of the company's internal control system. A strong control environment is a must for companies.
  - Auditors also must increase their documentation and understanding of the internal controls of their clients.
  - Significant amounts of resources have been devoted to comply with the provisions of Sarbanes-Oxley.

POD REVIEW 6.3

QUESTIONS   Answers to these questions are on the last page of the chapter.

1. What five-member body created by the Sarbanes-Oxley Act was given authority to set U.S. auditing standards?
   a. Securities and Exchange Commission
   b. Financial Accounting Standards Board
   c. International Accounting Standards Board
   d. none of the above

2. A company's audit committee
   a. must consist of a majority of directors who are key officers of the company.
   b. must consist of a majority of directors who are outsiders.
   c. must consist entirely of directors who are outsiders.
   d. is none of the above.

Internal Control Procedures

LO4 Describe the basic internal control procedures.

OVERVIEW: Internal control procedures can be either administrative or accounting in nature. The former are concerned with efficient operation of a business and the latter with safeguarding assets and reliability of the financial statements.

Management establishes policies and procedures on a number of different levels to ensure that corporate objectives will be met. Some procedures are formalized in writing. Others may not be written but are just as important. Certain **administrative controls** within a company are more concerned with the efficient operation of the business and adherence to managerial policies than with the accurate reporting of financial information. For example, a company policy that requires all prospective employees to be interviewed by the personnel department is an administrative control. Other **accounting controls** primarily concern safeguarding assets and ensuring the reliability of the financial statements. Some of the most important internal control procedures are as follows:

Administrative controls
Procedures concerned with efficient operation of the business and adherence to managerial policies.

Accounting controls
Procedures concerned with safeguarding the assets or the reliability of the financial statements.

- Proper authorizations
- Segregation of duties
- Independent verification

- Safeguarding of assets and records
- Independent review and appraisal
- Design and use of business documents

Proper Authorizations Management grants specific departments the authority to perform various activities. Along with the *authority* comes *responsibility*. Most large organizations give the authority to hire new employees to the personnel department. Management authorizes the purchasing department to order goods and services for the company and the credit department to establish specific policies for granting credit to customers. By specifically authorizing certain individuals to carry out specific tasks for the business, management is able to hold those same people accountable for the outcome of their actions.

The authorizations for some transactions are general in nature; others are specific. For example, a cashier authorizes the sale of a book in a bookstore by ringing up the transaction (a general authorization). However, the bookstore manager's approval may be required before a book can be returned (a specific authorization).

Segregation of Duties *What might happen if one employee is given the authority to prepare checks and to sign them? What might happen if a single employee is allowed to order inventory and receive it from the shipper? Or what if the cashier at a checkout stand records the daily receipts in the journal?* If the employee in each of these situations is honest and never makes mistakes, nothing bad will happen. However, if the employee is dishonest or makes errors, the company can experience losses. All of these situations point to the need for the segregation of duties, which is one of the most fundamental of all internal control procedures. Without segregation of duties, an employee is able not only to perpetrate a fraud but also to conceal it. A good system of internal control requires that the *physical custody* of assets be separated from the *accounting* for those same assets.

Like most internal control principles, the concept of segregation of duties is an ideal that is not always attainable. Many smaller businesses do not have adequate personnel to achieve complete segregation of key functions. In certain instances, these businesses need to rely on the direct involvement of the owners and on independent verification.

Independent Verification Independent verification means the work of one department should act as a check on the work of another. For example, the physical count of the inventory in a perpetual inventory system provides such a check. The accounting department maintains the general ledger card for inventory and updates it as sales and purchases are made. The physical count of the inventory by an independent department acts as the check on the work of the accounting department.

As another example, consider the bank reconciliation shown earlier in the chapter as a control device. The reconciliation of a company's bank account with the bank statement by someone not responsible for either the physical custody of cash or the cash records acts as an independent check on the work of these parties.

Safeguarding of Assets and Records Adequate safeguards must be in place to protect assets and the accounting records from losses of various kinds. Cash registers, safes, and lockboxes are important safeguards for cash. Secured storage areas with limited access are essential for the safekeeping of inventory. Protection of the accounting records against misuse is equally important. Access to a computerized accounting record should be limited to those employees authorized to prepare journal entries. This can be done with the use of a personal identification number and a password to access the system.

Independent Review and Appraisal A well-designed system of internal control provides for periodic review and appraisal of the accounting system as well as the people operating it. The group primarily responsible for review and appraisal of the system is the **internal audit staff**. Most large corporations have a full-time staff of internal auditors. They provide management with periodic reports on the effectiveness of the control system and the efficiency of operations.

Internal audit staff
The department responsible for monitoring and evaluating the internal control system.

The primary concern of the independent public accountants (or external auditors) is whether the financial statements have been presented fairly. Internal auditors focus more on the efficiency with which the organization is run. They are responsible for periodically reviewing both accounting and administrative controls. The internal audit staff also helps to ensure that the company's policies and procedures are followed.

Design and Use of Business Documents *Business documents* are the crucial link between economic transactions entered into by an entity and the accounting record of those events. They are often called *source documents* and may be generated by computer or completed manually. The source document for the recognition of the expense of an employee's wages is the time card. The source documents for a sale include the sales order, the sales invoice, and the related shipping document. Business documents must be designed to capture all relevant information about an economic event and to ensure that related transactions are properly classified.

Business documents must be properly controlled. For example, a key feature for documents is a *sequential numbering system* just like you have for your personal checks. This system results in a complete accounting for all documents in the series and negates the opportunity for an employee to misdirect one. Another key feature of well-designed business documents is the use of *multiple copies*. The various departments involved in a particular activity, such as sales or purchasing, are kept informed of the status of outstanding orders through the use of copies of documents.

Limitations on Internal Control

Internal control is a relative term. No system of internal control is totally foolproof. An entity's size affects the degree of control that it can obtain. In general, large organizations are able to devote a substantial amount of resources to safeguarding assets and records. Because the installation and maintenance of controls can be costly, an internal audit staff is a luxury that many small businesses cannot afford. The mere segregation of duties can result in added costs if two employees must be involved in a task previously performed by only one.

Segregation of duties can be effective in preventing collusion, but no system of internal control can ensure that it will not happen. It does no good to have one employee count the cash at the end of the day and another to record it if the two act in concert to steal from the company. Rotation of duties can help lessen the likelihood of such problems. An employee is less likely to collude with someone to steal if the assignment is a temporary one. Another control feature, a system of authorizations, is meaningless if management continually overrides or fails to support it.

Intentional acts to misappropriate company assets are not the only control problem. Human errors can weaken a system of internal control. Misunderstood instructions, carelessness, fatigue, and distraction can all lead to errors. A well-designed internal control system should result in the best possible people being hired to perform the various tasks, but no one is perfect.

© Nikada/istockphoto.com

6-2

REAL WORLD PRACTICE

Reading Sears' Holdings Management's Report

Refer to Exhibit 6-3 for Management's Annual Report on Internal Control over Financial Reporting for Sears Holdings. Where does management discuss limitations on internal control? Why are there risks in making any projections about the effectiveness of controls in the future?

LO4 Describe the basic internal control procedures.

- Control procedures are actions that company personnel take to make sure that policies set forth by management are followed.
- Important accounting controls are concerned with safeguarding assets and producing accurate and timely financial statements. They include:
  - Proper authorizations—only certain personnel may authorize transactions.
  - Segregation of duties—physical custody of assets must not be combined with the ability to account for those assets.
  - Independent verification—for example, an inventory count.
  - Safeguarding of assets and records—both must be adequately protected.
  - Independent review and appraisal—done primarily by internal audit.
  - Design and use of business documents—source document control.

POD REVIEW

6.4

QUESTIONS   **Answers to these questions are on the last page of the chapter.**

1. Controls that a company establishes to safeguard assets and ensure the reliability of the financial statements are called
   a. administrative controls.
   b. accounting controls.
   c. fiscal controls.
   d. none of the above.

2. The group within an organization that is responsible for monitoring and evaluating the internal control system is called the
   a. internal audit staff.
   b. accounting staff.
   c. board of directors.
   d. audit committee.

© Cengage Learning 2013

Computerized Business Documents and Internal Control

OVERVIEW: Companies use a variety of documents to record purchases that are instrumental in controlling both cash and inventory.

LO5 Describe the various documents used in recording purchases and their role in controlling cash disbursements.

Specific internal controls are necessary to control cash receipts and cash disbursements for all of the stores owned by Sears Holdings. In addition to separating the custodianship of cash from its recording in the accounts, two other fundamental principles apply to its control. **First, all cash receipts should be deposited intact in the bank on a daily basis.** *Intact* means that no disbursements should be made from the cash received from customers. Second, **all cash disbursements should be made by check.** Using sequentially numbered checks results in a clear record of all disbursements. The only exception to this rule is the use of a petty cash fund to make cash disbursements for minor expenditures such as postage stamps and repairs.

Control Over Cash Receipts

Most merchandisers receive checks and currency from customers in two ways: (1) cash received over the counter from cash sales and (2) cash received in the mail from credit sales. Each type of cash receipt poses its own control problems.

Cash Received Over the Counter Several control mechanisms are used to handle these cash payments. First, cash registers allow the customer to see the display, which deters the salesclerk from ringing up a sale for less than the amount received from the customer and pocketing the difference. A locked-in cash register tape is another control feature. At various times during the day, an employee other than the clerk unlocks the register, removes the tape, and forwards it to the accounting department. At the end of the shift, the salesclerk remits the coin and currency from the register to a central cashier. Any difference between the amount of cash remitted to the cashier and the amount on the tape submitted to the accounting department is investigated.

Finally, prenumbered customer receipts, prepared in duplicate, are a useful control mechanism. The customer is given a copy, and the salesclerk retains another. The salesclerk is accountable for all numbers in a specific series of receipts and must be able to explain any differences between the amount of cash remitted to the cashier and the amount collected per the receipts.

Cash Received in the Mail Most customers send checks rather than currency through the mail. Any form of cash received in the mail from customers should be applied to their account balances. The customer wants assurance that the account is appropriately reduced for the amount of the payment. The company must be assured that all cash received is deposited in the bank and that the account receivable is reduced accordingly.

To achieve a reasonable degree of control, two employees should be present when the mail is opened.[1] The first employee opens the mail in the presence of the second employee, counts the money received, and prepares a control list of the amount received on that particular day. The list, often called a *prelist*, is prepared in triplicate. The second employee takes the original to the cashier along with the total cash received on that day. The cashier is the person who makes the bank deposit. One copy of the prelist is forwarded to the accounting department to be used as the basis for recording the increase in Cash and the decrease in Accounts Receivable. The other copy is retained by one of the two people who opens the mail. A comparison of the prelist to the bank deposit slip is a timely way to detect receipts that do not make it to the bank. Because the two employees acting in concert could circumvent the control process, rotation of duties is important.

---

[1] In some companies, this control procedure may be omitted because of the cost of having two employees present when the mail is opened.

Monthly customer statements act as an additional control device for customer payments received in the mail. Assume that the two employees responsible for opening the mail and remitting checks to the cashier decide to pocket a check received from a customer. Checks made payable to a company can be stolen and cashed. The customer provides the control element. Because the check is not remitted to the cashier, the accounting department will not be notified to reduce the customer's account for the payment. The monthly statement, however, should alert the customer to the problem. The amount the customer thought was owed will be smaller than the balance due on the statement. At this point, the customer should ask the company to investigate the discrepancy. As evidence of its payment on account, the customer will be able to point to a canceled check—which was cashed by the unscrupulous employees.

Finally, the use of customer statements as a control device will be effective only if the employees responsible for the custody of cash received through the mail, for record keeping, and for authorization of adjustments to customers' accounts are not allowed to prepare and mail statements to customers. Employees allowed to do so are in a position to alter customers' statements.

Cash Discrepancies Discrepancies occur occasionally due to theft by dishonest employees and to human error. For example, if a salesclerk intentionally or unintentionally gives the wrong amount of change, the amount remitted to the cashier will not agree with the cash register tape. Any material differences should be investigated.

Of particular significance are *recurring* differences between the amount remitted by any one cashier and the amount on the cash register tape.

The Role of Computerized Business Documents in Controlling Cash Disbursements

A company makes cash payments to purchase merchandise, supplies, plants, and equipment; to pay operating expenditures; and to cover payroll expenses. We will concentrate on the disbursement of cash to purchase goods for resale, focusing particularly on the role of business documents in the process. Merchandising companies rely on a smooth and orderly inflow of quality goods for resale to customers. Suppliers must be paid on time so that the companies can continue to make goods available.

Business documents play a vital role in the purchasing function. The following example begins with a requisition for merchandise by Mickey's Marathon Sports, continues through the receipt of the goods, and concludes with the eventual payment to the supplier. The entire process is summarized in Exhibit 6-5. You will want to refer to this exhibit throughout the remainder of this section.

Purchase requisition form
A form a department uses to initiate a request to order merchandise.

Purchase Requisition The shoe department at Mickey's Marathon Sports reviews its stock weekly to determine if any items need replenishing. On the basis of its needs, the supervisor of the shoe department fills out the **purchase requisition form** shown in Exhibit 6-6 on page 312. The form indicates the supplier or vendor, Fleet Foot.

The purchasing department makes the final decision on a vendor. The purchasing department is thus held accountable for acquiring the goods at the lowest price, given certain standards for merchandise quality. Mickey's assigns a separate item number to each of the thousands of individual items of merchandise it stocks. Note that the requisition also indicates the vendor's number for each item. The unit of measure for each item is indicated in the quantity column. For example, "24 PR" means 24 pairs of shoes. The original and a copy of the purchase requisition are sent to the purchasing department. The shoe department keeps one copy for its records.

Purchase Order Most companies have purchased software or have developed software internally to perform such functions as purchasing, sales, and payroll. The software is capable not only of increasing the speed and accuracy of the process but also of generating the necessary documents.

EXHIBIT 6-5 Document Flow for the Purchasing Function

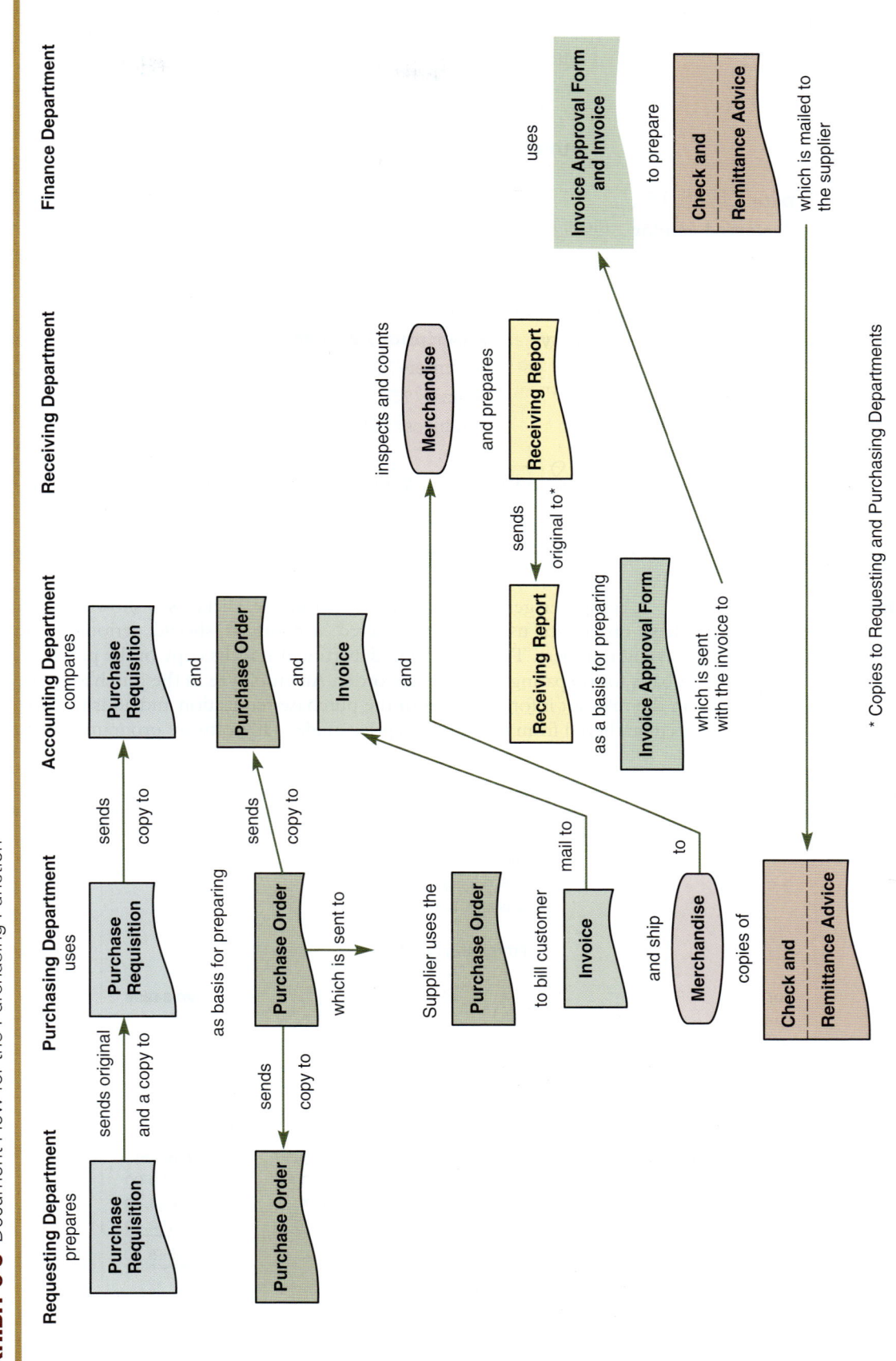

EXHIBIT 6-6 Purchase Requisition

Mickey's Marathon Sports
502 Dodge St.
Chicago, IL 66666

PURCHASE REQUISITION

Date 5/28/12   **PR 75638**

Preferred vendor Fleet Foot

Date needed by 6/5/12

The following items are requested for   weekly dept. order

Item No.	Quantity	Description/Vendor No.
314627	24 PR	Sprinter/5265
323515	12 PR	Blazer/7512
323682	6 PR	Enduros/1580

Requested by *Joe Smith*   **Department** Shoe department

Purchase order
A form sent by the purchasing department to the supplier.

A computer-generated **purchase order** for Mickey's is shown in Exhibit 6-7. Purchase orders are usually prenumbered; a company should periodically investigate any missing numbers. The purchasing department uses its copy of the purchase requisition as a basis for preparing the purchase order. An employee in the purchasing department keys in the relevant information from the purchase requisition and adds the unit cost for each item gathered from the vendor's price guide. The software program generates a purchase

EXHIBIT 6-7 Computer-Generated Purchase Order

Mickey's Marathon Sports
502 Dodge St.
Chicago, IL 66666

PURCHASE ORDER

TO: **PO 54296**

Fleet Foot
590 West St.
Milwaukee, WI 77777

Date 5/30/12   Ship by   Best Express   Instructions   FOB destination point
Terms 2/10, net 30   Date required 6/5/12

Item No.	Quantity	Description/Vendor No.	Unit price	Amount
314627	24 PR	Sprinter/5265	$60.50	$1,452.00
323515	12 PR	Blazer/7512	53.70	644.40
323682	6 PR	Enduros/1580	75.40	452.40
				$2,548.80

Approved by *Mary Jones*

order, as shown in Exhibit 6-7. You should trace all of the information for at least one of the three items ordered from the purchase requisition to the purchase order.

The system generates the original purchase order and three copies. As indicated in Exhibit 6-5, the original is sent to the supplier after a supervisor in the purchasing department approves it. One copy is sent to the accounting department, where it will be matched with the original requisition. A second copy is sent to the shoe department as confirmation that its request for the items has been attended to by the purchasing department. The purchasing department keeps the third copy for its records.

A purchase order is not the basis for recording a purchase and a liability. Legally, the order is merely an offer by the company to purchase goods from the supplier. Technically, the receipt of goods from the supplier is the basis for the purchaser's recognition of a liability. However, most companies record the payable upon receipt of the invoice.

Invoice When Fleet Foot ships the merchandise, it also mails an invoice to Mickey's, requesting payment according to the agreed-upon terms, in this case 2/10, net 30. Recall from Chapter 5 that this means that the customer (Mickey's) receives a 2% discount by paying within 10 days of purchase; if not, the full amount is due within 30 days of purchase. The **invoice** may be mailed separately or included with the shipment of merchandise. Fleet Foot, the seller, calls this document a *sales invoice;* it is the basis for recording a sale and an account receivable. Mickey's, the buyer, calls the same document a *purchase invoice,* which is the basis for recording a purchase and an account payable. The invoice that Fleet Foot sent to Mickey's accounting department is shown in Exhibit 6-8.

Invoice
A form sent by the seller to the buyer as evidence of a sale.

Receiving Report The accounting department receives the invoice for the three items ordered. Within a few days before or after the receipt of the invoice, the merchandise arrives at Mickey's warehouse. As soon as the items are unpacked, the receiving department inspects and counts them. The same software used to generate the purchase order also generates a receiving report, as shown in Exhibit 6-9.

EXHIBIT 6-8 Invoice

NO. 427953

Fleet Foot
590 West St.
Milwaukee, WI 77777

INVOICE

Sold to Mickey's Marathon Sports		**Date** 6/2/12	
502 Dodge St.		**Order No.** 54296	
Chicago, IL 66666		**Shipped via** Best Express	
Ship to Same		**Date shipped** 6/2/12	
Terms 2/10, net 30		**Ship terms** FOB destination	

Quantity	Description/No.	Price	Amount
24 PR	Sprinter/5265	$60.50	$1,452.00
12 PR	Blazer/7512	53.70	644.40
6 PR	Enduros/1580	75.40	452.40
			$2,548.80

© Cengage Learning 2013

EXHIBIT 6-9 Computer-Generated Receiving Report

Mickey's Marathon Sports
502 Dodge St.
Chicago, IL 66666

Receiving Report

RR 23637

Purchase Order No. 54296

Vendor Fleet Foot

Ship via Best Express

Terms 2/10, net 30

Date ordered 5/30/12

Date required 6/5/12

Quantity Received	Our Item No.	Description/ Item No.	Remarks
24 PR	314627	Sprinter/5265	Box damaged but merchandise ok
12 PR	323515	Blazer/7512	
6 PR	323682	Enduros/1580	

Received by _Bob Reed_   **Date** _6/4/12_

Blind receiving report
A form used by the receiving department to account for the quantity and condition of merchandise received from a supplier.

Mickey's uses a **blind receiving report**. The column for the quantity received is left blank and is filled in by the receiving department. Rather than simply being able to indicate that the number ordered was received, an employee must count the pairs of shoes to determine that the number ordered is actually received. You should trace all of the relevant information for one of the three items ordered from the purchase order to the receiving report. The accounting system generates an original receiving report and three copies. The receiving department keeps one copy for its records and sends the original to the accounting department. One copy is sent to the purchasing department to be matched with the purchase order, and the other copy is sent to the shoe department as verification that the items it originally requested have been received.

Invoice approval form
A form the accounting department uses before making payment to document the accuracy of all information about a purchase.
Alternate term: Voucher.

Invoice Approval Form At this point, Mickey's accounting department has copies of the purchase requisition from the shoe department, the purchase order from the purchasing department, the invoice from the supplier, and the receiving report from the warehouse. The accounting department uses an **invoice approval form** to document the accuracy of the information on each of these other forms. The invoice approval form for Mickey's Marathon Sports is shown in Exhibit 6-10.

The invoice is compared to the purchase requisition to ensure that the company is billed for goods that it requested. A comparison of the invoice with the purchase order ensures that the goods were in fact ordered. Finally, the receiving report is compared with the invoice to verify that all goods for which the company is being billed were received. An accounting department employee must also verify the mathematical accuracy of the amounts that appear on the invoice. The date the invoice must be paid to take advantage of the discount is noted so that the finance department will be sure to send the check by this date. At this point, the accounting department prepares the journal entry to increase the inventory and accounts payable accounts. The invoice approval form and the invoice are then sent to the finance department. Some businesses call the invoice approval form a *voucher;* it is used for all

EXHIBIT 6-10 Invoice Approval Form

```
                    Mickey's Marathon Sports
                          502 Dodge St.
                        Chicago, IL 66666

                      Invoice Approval Form

                                      No.              Check
    Purchase Requisition         PR 75638              ✓
    Purchase Order               PO 54296              ✓
    Receiving Report             RR 23637              ✓
    Invoice:
        No.       427953
        Date      6/2/12
        Price            ✓
        Extensions       ✓
        Footings         ✓

    Last Day to Pay for Discount     6/12/12
    Approved for Payment by      Alice Johnson
```

© Cengage Learning 2013

expenditures, not just for purchases of merchandise. Finally, it is worth noting that some businesses do not use a separate invoice approval form; they simply note approval directly on the invoice.

Check with Remittance Advice Mickey's finance department is responsible for issuing checks. This results from the need to segregate custody of cash (the signed check) from record keeping (the updating of the ledger). Upon receipt of the invoice approval form from the accounting department, a clerk in the finance department processes a check with a remittance advice attached, as shown in Exhibit 6-11.[2]

Before the check is signed, the documents referred to on the invoice approval form are reviewed and canceled to prevent reuse. The clerk then forwards the check to one of the company officers authorized to sign checks. According to one of Mickey's internal control policies, only the treasurer and the assistant treasurer are authorized to sign checks. Both officers must sign check amounts above a specified dollar limit. To maintain separation of duties, the finance department should mail the check. The remittance advice informs the supplier as to the nature of the payment and is torn off by the supplier before cashing the check.

---

[2] In some companies, an employee in the accounting department prepares checks and sends them to the finance department for review and signature. Most companies use computer-generated checks rather than manually typed ones.

EXHIBIT 6-11 Check with Remittance Advice

```
                                                              3690
        Mickey's Marathon Sports
        502 Dodge St.
        Chicago, IL 66666                        June 12  2012


        PAY TO THE
        ORDER OF _____Fleet Foot_____    $2,497.82
        Two thousand four hundred ninety seven and 82/100    DOLLARS

           Second National Bank
           Chicago, IL
        3690 035932 9321                        John B. Martin
```

Purchase Order No.	Invoice No.	Invoice Date	Description	Amount
PO 54296	427953	6/2/12	24 PR Sprinter	$1,452.00
			12 PR Blazer	644.40
			6 PR Enduros	452.40
			Total	$2,548.80
			Less: 2% discount	50.98
			Net remitted	$2,497.82

© Cengage Learning 2013

LO5 Describe the various documents used in recording purchase and their role in controlling cash disbursements.

- The documents used to record purchase transactions are instrumental in controlling both cash and inventory.
- The document flow diagram in Exhibit 6-5 provides an excellent summary of documents in the purchasing process. Some of the key documents are as follows:
  - Purchase
  - Receiving report
  - Vendor invoice
  - Check

POD REVIEW 6.5

QUESTIONS   Answers to these questions are on the last page of the chapter.

1. The form sent by the seller to the buyer as evidence of a sale is called a(n)
   a. purchase requisition form.
   b. purchase order.
   c. invoice.
   d. invoice approval form.

2. Which of the following departments in an organization is responsible for preparing the invoice approval form to document all the information about a particular purchase?
   a. the department making a purchase request
   b. the purchasing department
   c. the accounting department
   d. the receiving department

© Cengage Learning 2013

ACCOUNTS HIGHLIGHTED

Account Titles	Where It Appears	In What Section	Page Number
Cash and Cash Equivalents	Balance Sheet	Current Assets	294
Petty Cash Fund	Balance Sheet	Current Assets	301

KEY TERMS QUIZ

Read each definition below and write the number of the definition in the blank beside the appropriate term. The quiz solutions appear at the end of the chapter.

_____ Cash equivalent
_____ Bank statement
_____ Outstanding check
_____ Deposit in transit
_____ Bank reconciliation
_____ Credit memoranda
_____ Debit memoranda
_____ Petty cash fund
_____ Internal control system
_____ Sarbanes-Oxley Act
_____ Internal control report
_____ Public Company Accounting Oversight Board

_____ Board of directors
_____ Audit committee
_____ Accounting system
_____ Administrative controls
_____ Accounting controls
_____ Internal audit staff
_____ Purchase requisition form
_____ Purchase order
_____ Invoice
_____ Blind receiving report
_____ Invoice approval form

1. The form sent by the seller to the buyer as evidence of a sale.
2. The group composed of key officers of a corporation and outside members responsible for the general oversight of the affairs of the entity.
3. Policies and procedures necessary to ensure the safeguarding of an entity's assets, the reliability of its accounting records, and the accomplishment of overall company objectives.
4. Procedures concerned with safeguarding the assets or the reliability of the financial statements.
5. The form a department uses to initiate a request to order merchandise.
6. A form the accounting department uses before making payment to document the accuracy of all information about a purchase.
7. A form used by the accountant to reconcile or resolve any differences between the balance shown on the bank statement for a particular account with the balance shown in the accounting records.
8. An investment that is readily convertible to a known amount of cash and has an original maturity to the investor of three months or less.
9. Deductions on a bank statement for items such as NSF checks and various service charges.
10. A check written by a company but not yet presented to the bank for payment.
11. A detailed list, prepared by the bank, of all activity for a particular account during the month.
12. A report required by Section 404 of SOX to be included in a company's annual report in which management assesses the effectiveness of the internal control structure.
13. A deposit recorded on the books but not yet reflected on the bank statement.
14. The methods and records used to accurately report an entity's transactions and to maintain accountability for its assets and liabilities.
15. Additions on a bank statement for such items as interest paid on the account and notes collected by the bank.
16. The board of directors subset that acts as a direct contact between the stockholders and the independent accounting firm.
17. Money kept on hand for making minor disbursements in coin and currency rather than by writing checks.

(Continued)

18. The five-member body created by the Sarbanes-Oxley Act that was given the authority to set auditing standards in the United States.
19. A form used by the receiving department to account for the quantity and condition of merchandise received from a supplier.
20. Procedures concerned with efficient operation of the business and adherence to managerial policies.
21. The form sent by the purchasing department to the supplier.
22. An act of Congress in 2002 intended to bring reform to corporate accountability and stewardship in the wake of a number of major corporate scandals.
23. The department responsible for monitoring and evaluating the internal control system.

ALTERNATE TERMS

invoice purchase invoice, sales invoice   **invoice approval form** voucher

WARMUP EXERCISES

LO1 **Warmup Exercise 6-1 Composition of Cash**

For the following items, indicate whether each should be included (I) or excluded (E) from the line item titled Cash and cash equivalents on the balance sheet.

_____ 1. Certificate of deposit maturing in 60 days
_____ 2. Checking account
_____ 3. Certificate of deposit maturing in six months
_____ 4. Savings account
_____ 5. Shares of GM stock
_____ 6. Petty cash
_____ 7. Corporate bonds maturing in 30 days
_____ 8. Certified check

KEY TO THE SOLUTION Recall the key to classification as part of cash: the amount must be readily available to pay debts, and cash equivalents must have an original maturity to the investor of three months or less.

LO4 **Warmup Exercise 6-2 Internal Control**

List the internal control procedures discussed in the text.

KEY TO THE SOLUTION Refer to the section in the chapter that discusses internal control procedures.

Solutions to Warmup Exercises

Warmup Exercise 6-1

1. I 2. I 3. E 4. I 5. E 6. I 7. E 8. I

Warmup Exercise 6-2

1. Proper authorizations
2. Segregation of duties
3. Independent verification
4. Safeguarding of assets and records
5. Independent review and appraisal
6. Design and use of business documents

REVIEW PROBLEM

The following information is available for McCarthy Corp. on June 30, 2012:

a. The balance in cash as reported on the June 30, 2012, bank statement is $5,654.98.
b. McCarthy made a deposit of $865 on June 30 that is not included on the bank statement.
c. A comparison between the canceled checks returned with the bank statement and McCarthy's records indicated that two checks had not yet been returned to the bank for payment. The amounts of the two checks were $236.77 and $116.80.
d. The Cash account on the company's books reported a balance on June 30 of $4,165.66.
e. McCarthy rents some excess storage space in one of its warehouses, and the tenant pays its monthly rent directly to the bank for deposit in McCarthy's account. The bank statement indicates that a deposit of $1,500 was made during the month of June.
f. Interest earned on the checking account and added to McCarthy's account during June was $11.75.
g. Bank service charges were $15 for the month of June as reported on the bank statement.
h. A comparison between the checks returned with the bank statement and the company's records revealed that a check written by the company in the amount of $56 was recorded by the company erroneously as a check for $560.

Required

Prepare a bank reconciliation for the month of June in good form.

Solution to Review Problem

McCarthy Corp.
Bank Reconciliation
June 30, 2012

Balance per bank statement, June 30		$5,654.98
Add: Deposit in transit		865.00
Deduct: Outstanding checks:	$ 236.77	
	116.80	(353.57)
Adjusted balance, June 30		$6,166.41
Balance per books, June 30		$4,165.66
Add: Tenant's rent collected by bank	$1,500.00	
Interest earned on checking account	11.75	
Error in recording check	504.00	2,015.75
Deduct: Bank service charges		(15.00)
Adjusted balance, June 30		$6,166.41

QUESTIONS

1. What is a cash equivalent? Why is it included with cash on the balance sheet?
2. Why does the purchase of an item classified as a cash equivalent *not* appear on the statement of cash flows as an investing activity?
3. A friend says to you: "I understand why it is important to deposit all receipts intact and not keep coin and currency sitting around the business. Beyond this control feature, however, I believe that a company should strive to keep the maximum amount possible in checking accounts to be able to pay bills on time." How would you evaluate your friend's statement?

(Continued)

4. Different formats for bank reconciliations are possible. What is the format for a bank reconciliation in which a service charge for a lockbox is *added* to the balance per the bank statement? Explain your answer.
5. What circumstances led to the passage of the Sarbanes-Oxley Act in 2002?
6. What is the typical composition of a board of directors of a publicly held corporation?
7. An order clerk fills out a purchase requisition for an expensive item of inventory and the receiving report when the merchandise arrives. The clerk takes the inventory home, then sends the invoice to the accounting department so that the supplier will be paid. What basic internal control procedure could have prevented this misuse of company assets?
8. What are some of the limitations on a company's effective system of internal control?

9. What two basic procedures are essential to an effective system of internal control over cash?
10. How would you evaluate the following statement? The only reason a company positions its cash register so that customers can see the display is so customers feel comfortable knowing they are being charged the correct amount for the purchase.
11. Which document, a purchase order or an invoice, is the basis for recording a purchase and a corresponding liability? Explain your answer.
12. What is a blind receiving report? How does it act as a control device?
13. What is the purpose of comparing a purchase invoice with a purchase order? of comparing a receiving report with a purchase invoice?

BRIEF EXERCISES

LO1
EXAMPLE 6-1

Brief Exercise 6-1 Composition of Cash

Using Y for yes and N for no, indicate whether each of the following items should or should not be included with cash and cash equivalents on the balance sheet.

_____ Cash in a checking account
_____ Coin and currency in a cash register drawer
_____ A six-month certificate of deposit
_____ Postage stamps
_____ An amount owed by an employee for a travel advance
_____ A three-month Treasury bill
_____ Cash in a money market account

LO2
EXAMPLE 6-2

Brief Exercise 6-2 Bank Reconciliation

Indicate whether each of the following items is an adjustment to the balance per books (BK) or to the balance per bank statement (BS) on a reconciliation that adjusts the bank balance and the bank statement to the correct balance.

_____ Customer's NSF check
_____ Service charge for a lockbox
_____ Outstanding checks
_____ Interest earned on an account for the month
_____ Check written on the account but recorded on the books at the wrong amount
_____ Deposits in transit

LO3

Brief Exercise 6-3 Sarbanes-Oxley Act

Provide answers to each of the following questions.
1. Who is responsible for establishing and maintaining an adequate internal control structure for a company?
2. Who provides an independent opinion as to whether management has maintained effective internal control over financial reporting?

3. To whom should the independent auditors' report be directed?

4. Which committee of the board of directors provides direct contact between stockholders and the independent accounting firm?

Brief Exercise 6-4 Internal Control Procedures   LO4

List the names of at least four important internal control procedures.

Brief Exercise 6-5 Business Documents   LO5

Number each of the following documents to indicate the order in which each document would be used.

_____	Purchase order	_____ Purchase requisition
_____	Invoice approval form	_____ Invoice
_____	Check and remittance advice	_____ Receiving report

EXERCISES

Exercise 6-1 Cash Equivalents   LO1

EXAMPLE 6-1

Systematic Enterprises invested its excess cash in the following instruments during December 2012:

Certificate of deposit, due January 31, 2015	$ 75,000
Certificate of deposit, due March 30, 2013	150,000
Commercial paper, original maturity date	
February 28, 2013	125,000
Deposit into a money market fund	25,000
Investment in stock	65,000
90-day Treasury bills	100,000
Treasury note, due December 1, 2042	500,000

Required

Determine the amount of cash equivalents that should be combined with cash on the company's balance sheet at December 31, 2012, and for purposes of preparing a statement of cash flows for the year ended December 31, 2012.

Exercise 6-2 Cash and Cash Equivalents and the Statement of Cash Flows   LO1

Bedford Corp. began the year with $15,000 in cash and another $8,500 in cash equivalents. During the year, operations generated $140,000 in cash. Net cash used in investing activities during the year was $210,000, and the company raised a net amount of $180,000 from financing activities.

Required

Determine the year-end balance in cash and cash equivalents.

Exercise 6-3 Working Backward: Bank Reconciliation   LO2

EXAMPLE 6-2

Dexter Company's bank reconciliation shows an adjusted cash balance of $3,254.33. The following items also appear on the reconciliation:

NSF check	$110.50
Deposit in transit	332.10
Interest earned	65.42
Outstanding checks	560.55
Bank service charges	30.00

(Continued)

Required

1. Determine the balance on the bank statement prior to adjustment.
2. Determine the balance on the books prior to adjustment.

LO2   Exercise 6-4 Items on a Bank Reconciliation

EXAMPLE 6-2

Assume that a company is preparing a bank reconciliation for the month of June. It reconciles the bank balance and the book balance to the correct balance. For each of the following items, indicate whether the item is an addition to the bank balance (A-Bank), an addition to the book balance (A-Book), a deduction from the bank balance (D-Bank), a deduction from the book balance (D-Book), or would not appear on the June reconciliation (NA). Also, place an ADJ next to your answer for any items that will require an adjustment on the company's books.

_____   1. Check written in June but not yet returned to the bank for payment
_____   2. Customer's NSF check
_____   3. Customer's check written in the amount of $54 but recorded on the books in the amount of $45*
_____   4. Service charge for new checks
_____   5. Principal and interest on a customer's note collected for the company by the bank
_____   6. Customer's check deposited on June 30 but not reflected on the bank statement
_____   7. Check written on the company's account, paid by the bank, and returned with the bank statement
_____   8. Check written on the company's account for $123 but recorded on the books as $132*
_____   9. Interest on the checking account for the month of June

*Answer in terms of the adjustment needed to correct for the error.

LO4   Exercise 6-5 Segregation of Duties

The following tasks are performed by three employees, each of whom is capable of performing all of the tasks. Do not be concerned with the time required to perform the tasks, but with the need to provide for segregation of duties. Assign the duties by using a check mark to indicate which employee should perform each task. You can assign any one of the tasks to any of the employees.

Task	Employee		
	Mary	Sue	John
Prepare invoices			
Mail invoices			
Pick up mail from post office			
Open mail, separate checks			
List checks on deposit slip in triplicate			
Post payment to customer's account			
Deposit checks			
Prepare monthly schedule of accounts receivable			
Reconcile bank statements			

LO4   Exercise 6-6 Internal Control

The university drama club is planning a raffle. The president overheard you talking about internal control to another accounting student, so she asked you to set up some guidelines to "make sure" that all money collected for the raffle is accounted for by the club.

Required

1. Describe guidelines that the club should follow to achieve an acceptable level of internal control.
2. Comment on the president's request that she "be sure" all money is collected and recorded.

MULTI-CONCEPT EXERCISE

Exercise 6-7 Composition of Cash

LO1 • 2
EXAMPLE 6-1, 6-2

Using Y for yes and N for no, indicate whether each of the following items should be included in cash and cash equivalents on the balance sheet. If an item should not be included in cash and cash equivalents, indicate where it should appear on the balance sheet.

_____ 1. Checking account at Third County Bank
_____ 2. Petty cash fund
_____ 3. Coin and currency
_____ 4. Postage stamps
_____ 5. An IOU from an employee
_____ 6. Savings account at Ft. Worth Savings & Loan

_____ 7. A six-month CD
_____ 8. Undeposited customer checks
_____ 9. A customer's check returned by the bank and marked NSF
_____ 10. Sixty-day U.S. Treasury bills
_____ 11. A cashier's check.

PROBLEMS

Problem 6-1 Bank Reconciliation

LO2

The following information is available to assist you in preparing a bank reconciliation for Calico Corners on May 31, 2012:

a. The balance on the May 31, 2012, bank statement is $8,432.11.
b. Not included on the bank statement is a $1,250 deposit made by Calico Corners late on May 31.
c. A comparison between the canceled checks returned with the bank statement and the company records indicated that the following checks are outstanding at May 31:

No. 123	$ 23.40
No. 127	145.00
No. 128	210.80
No. 130	67.32

d. The Cash account on the company's books shows a balance of $9,965.34.
e. The bank acts as a collection agency for interest earned on some municipal bonds held by Calico Corners. The May bank statement indicates interest of $465.00 earned during the month.
f. Interest earned on the checking account and added to Calico Corners' account during May was $54.60. Miscellaneous bank service charges amounted to $50.00.
g. A customer's NSF check in the amount of $166.00 was returned with the May bank statement.
h. A comparison between the deposits listed on the bank statement and the company's books revealed that a customer's check in the amount of $123.45 was recorded on the books during May but was never added to the company's account. The bank erroneously added the check to the account of Calico Closet, which has an account at the same bank.
i. The comparison of deposits per the bank statement with those per the books revealed that another customer's check in the amount of $101.10 was correctly added to the company's account. In recording the check on the company's books, however, the accountant erroneously increased the Cash account by $1,011.00.

Required

1. Prepare a bank reconciliation in good form.
2. A friend says to you: "I don't know why companies bother to prepare bank reconciliations—it seems a waste of time. Why don't they just do like I do and adjust the Cash account for any difference between what the bank shows as a balance and what shows up in the books?" Explain to your friend why a bank reconciliation should be prepared as soon as a bank statement is received.

LO4   ## Problem 6-2 Internal Control Procedures

You are opening a summer business, a chain of three drive-through snow-cone stands. You have hired other college students to work and have purchased a cash register with locked-in tapes. You retain one key, and the other is available to the lead person on each shift.

Required

1. Write a list of the procedures for all employees to follow when ringing up sales and giving change.
2. Write a list of the procedures for the lead person to follow in closing out at the end of the day. Be specific so that employees will have few if any questions.
3. What is your main concern in the design of internal control for the snow-cone stands? How did you address that concern? Be specific.

LO5   ## Problem 6-3 The Design of Internal Control Documents

Motel $49.99 has purchased a large warehouse to store all supplies used by housekeeping departments in the company's expanding chain of motels. In the past, each motel bought supplies from local distributors and paid for the supplies from cash receipts.

Required

1. Name some potential problems with the old system.
2. Design a purchase requisition form and a receiving report to be used by the housekeeping departments and the warehouse. Indicate how many copies of each form should be used and who should receive each copy.

MULTI-CONCEPT PROBLEMS

LO1 • 2   ## Problem 6-4 Cash and Liquid Assets on the Balance Sheet

The following accounts are listed in a company's general ledger. The accountant wants to place the items in order of liquidity on the balance sheet.

Accounts Receivable
Certificates of Deposit (six months)
Investment in Stock
Prepaid Rent
Money Market Fund
Petty Cash Fund

Required

Rank the accounts in terms of liquidity. Identify items to be included in the total of cash and explain why the items not included in cash on the balance sheet are not as liquid as cash. Explain how these items should be classified.

LO3 • 4   ## Problem 6-5 Internal Control

At Morris Mart Inc., all sales are on account. Mary Morris-Manning is responsible for mailing invoices to customers, recording the amount billed, opening mail, and recording the payment. Mary is very devoted to the family business and never takes off more than one or two days for a long weekend. The customers know Mary and sometimes send personal notes with their payments. Another clerk handles all aspects of accounts payable. Mary's brother, who is president of Morris Mart, has hired an accountant to help with expansion.

Required

1. List some problems with the current accounts receivable system.
2. What suggestions would you make to improve internal control?
3. How would you explain to Mary that she personally is not the problem?

ALTERNATE PROBLEMS

Problem 6-1A Bank Reconciliation

The following information is available to assist you in preparing a bank reconciliation for Karen's Catering on March 31, 2012:

a. The balance on the March 31, 2012, bank statement is $6,506.10.

b. Not included on the bank statement is a $423 deposit made by Karen's late on March 31.

c. A comparison between the canceled checks listed on the bank statement and the company records indicated that the following checks are outstanding at March 31:

No. 112	$ 42.92
No. 117	307.00
No. 120	10.58
No. 122	75.67

d. The bank acts as a collection agency for checks returned for insufficient funds. The March bank statement indicates that one such check in the amount of $45.00 was collected and deposited and a collection fee of $4.50 was charged.

e. Interest earned on the checking account and added to Karen's account during March was $4.30. Miscellaneous bank service charges amounted to $22.

f. A comparison between the deposits listed on the bank statement and the company's books revealed that a customer's check in the amount of $1,250 appears on the bank statement in March but was never added to the customer's account on the company's books.

g. The comparison of checks cleared per the bank statement with those per the books revealed that the wrong amount was charged to the company's account for a check. The amount of the check was $990. The proof machine encoded the check in the amount of $909, the amount charged against the company's account.

Required

1. Determine the balance on the books before any adjustments as well as the corrected balance to be reported on the balance sheet.

2. What would you recommend Karen's do as a result of the bank error in (g)? Why?

Problem 6-2A Internal Control Procedures

The loan department in a bank is subject to regulation. Internal auditors work for the bank to ensure that the loan department complies with requirements. The internal auditors must verify that each car loan file has a note signed by the maker, verification of insurance, and a title issued by the state that names the bank as co-owner.

Required

1. Explain why the bank and the regulatory agency are concerned with these documents.

2. Describe the internal control procedures that should be in place to ensure that these documents are obtained and safeguarded.

Problem 6-3A The Design of Internal Control Documents

Tiger's Group is a newly formed company that produces and sells children's movies about an imaginary character. The movies are in such great demand that they are shipped to retail outlets as soon as they are produced. The company must pay a royalty to several actors for each movie that it sells to retail outlets.

Required

1. Describe some internal control features that should be in place to ensure that all royalties are paid to the actors.

2. Design the shipping form that Tiger's Group should use for the movies. Make sure you include authorizations and indicate the number of copies and the routing of the copies.

ALTERNATE MULTI-CONCEPT PROBLEMS

LO1 • 2   Problem 6-4A Cash and Liquid Assets on the Balance Sheet

The following accounts are listed in a company's general ledger:

	December 31, 2012	December 31, 2011
Accounts Receivable	$12,300	$10,000
Certificates of Deposit (three months)	10,000	10,000
Marketable Securities	4,500	4,000
Petty Cash Fund	1,200	1,500
Money Market Fund	25,800	28,000
Cash in Checking Account	6,000	6,000

Required

1. Which items are cash equivalents?
2. Explain where items that are not cash equivalents should be classified on the balance sheet.
3. What are the amount and the direction of change in cash and cash equivalents for 2012? Is the company as liquid at the end of 2012 as it was at the end of 2011? Explain your answer.

LO3 • 4   Problem 6-5A Internal Control

Abbott Inc. is expanding and needs to hire more personnel in the accounting office. Barbara Barker, the chief accounting clerk, knew that her cousin Cheryl was looking for a job. Barbara and Cheryl are also roommates. Barbara offered Cheryl a job as her assistant. Barbara will be responsible for Cheryl's performance reviews and training.

Required

1. List some problems with the proposed personnel situations in the accounting department.
2. Explain why accountants are concerned with the hiring of personnel. What suggestions would you make to improve internal control at Abbott?
3. How would you explain to Barbara and Cheryl that they personally are not the problem?

DECISION CASES

LO1   ## Reading and Interpreting Financial Statements

Decision Case 6-1 Comparing Two Companies in the Same Industry: Kellogg's and General Mills

Refer to the financial information for **Kellogg's** and **General Mills** reproduced at the end of this book.

Required

1. What is the balance in Cash and cash equivalents on the balance sheet of each company at the end of the most recent year? What is the amount of increase or decrease in this balance from the end of the prior year?
2. On what other statement in each company's annual report does the increase or decrease in Cash and cash equivalents appear? Explain why it appears on this statement.
3. According to the notes to their financial statements, how does each company define "Cash and cash equivalents"? Are there any differences in their definitions?

LO3   ### Decision Case 6-2 Reading and Interpreting IBM's Report of Management

IBM's 2010 annual report includes the following selected paragraphs from its Report of Management found on page 60:

IBM maintains an effective internal control structure. It consists, in part, of organizational arrangements with clearly defined lines of responsibility and delegation of authority, and comprehensive systems and control procedures. An important element of the control environment is an ongoing internal audit program. Our system also contains self-monitoring mechanisms, and actions are taken to correct deficiencies as they are identified. . . .

PricewaterhouseCoopers LLP, an independent registered public accounting firm, is retained to audit IBM's Consolidated Financial Statements and the effectiveness of the internal control over financial reporting. Its accompanying report is based on audits conducted in accordance with the standards of the Public Company Accounting Oversight Board (United States). . . .

The Audit Committee of the Board of Directors is composed solely of independent, non-management directors, and is responsible for recommending to the Board the independent registered public accounting firm to be retained for the coming year, subject to stockholder ratification. The Audit Committee meets periodically and privately with the independent registered public accounting firm, with the company's internal auditors, as well as with IBM management, to review accounting, auditing, internal control structure and financial reporting matters.

Required

1. Describe the main components of IBM's internal control structure.
2. Who is IBM's external auditor? In addition to auditing IBM's financial statements, what else does this firm audit? What body's standards does the firm follow in conducting its audit?
3. What is the composition of IBM's Audit Committee? Describe its role.

Making Financial Decisions

Decision Case 6-3 Liquidity

LO1

R Montague and J Capulet distribute films to movie theaters. Following are the current assets for each distributor at the end of the year. (All amounts are in millions of dollars.)

	R Montague	J Capulet
Cash	$10	$ 5
Six-month certificates of deposit	9	0
Short-term investments in stock	0	6
Accounts receivable	15	23
Allowance for doubtful accounts	(1)	(1)
Total current assets	$33	$33

Required

As a loan officer for First National Bank of Verona Heights, assume that both companies have come to you asking for a $10 million six-month loan. If you could lend money to only one of the two, which one would it be? Justify your answer by writing a brief memo to the president of the bank.

Ethical Decision Making

Decision Case 6-4 Using a Bank Reconciliation to Determine Cash Balance

LO1 • 2

You have just forwarded to your boss the monthly bank reconciliation you prepared for the company. One of the reconciling items is a customer's NSF check in the amount of $10,000. As part of your responsibility, you have drafted an adjustment to reduce Cash and increase Accounts Receivable for the amount of the check. Your boss comes to you and indicates that based on his personal relationship with the customer, he knows "they are good for the money" and that you should revise the reconciliation to treat the NSF check as an outstanding check and also remove the adjustment you prepared.

(Continued)

Required

1. Explain how the treatment of the check as an outstanding check rather than an NSF check would affect the company's liquidity.
2. Why might your boss be motivated to instruct you to treat the check as an outstanding check rather than an NSF check?
3. If your boss insists that you follow his instructions, what should you do?

LO3 • 4　Decision Case 6-5　Cash Receipts in a Bookstore

You were recently hired by a large retail bookstore chain. Your training involved spending a week at the largest and most profitable store in the district. The store manager assigned the head cashier to train you on the cash register and closing procedures required by the company's home office. In the process, the head cashier instructed you to keep an envelope for cash over and short that would include cash or IOUs equal to the net amount of overages or shortages in the cash drawer. "It is impossible to balance exactly, so just put extra cash in this envelope and use the cash when you are short." You studied accounting for one semester in college and remembered your professor saying that "all deposits should be made intact daily."

Required

Draft a memo to the store manager detailing any problems you see with the current system. This memo should address the issue of the accuracy of the cash receipts number. It should also answer the following question: Does this method provide information to the company that would enable someone to detect whether theft has occurred during the particular day in question? Your memo should suggest an alternative method of internal control for cash receipts.

SOLUTIONS TO KEY TERMS QUIZ

8	Cash equivalent	2	Board of directors
11	Bank statement	16	Audit committee
10	Outstanding check	14	Accounting system
13	Deposit in transit	20	Administrative controls
7	Bank reconciliation	4	Accounting controls
15	Credit memoranda	23	Internal audit staff
9	Debit memoranda	5	Purchase requisition form
17	Petty cash fund	21	Purchase order
3	Internal control system	1	Invoice
22	Sarbanes-Oxley Act	19	Blind receiving report
12	Internal control report	6	Invoice approval form
18	Public Company Accounting Oversight Board		

ANSWERS TO POD REVIEW

LO1　1. d　2. b　　　**LO4**　1. b　2. a
LO2　1. b　2. b　　　**LO5**　1. c　2. c
LO3　1. d　2. c

Receivables and Investments

7

LO1 Show that you understand how to account for accounts receivable, including bad debts.

LO2 Explain how information about sales and receivables can be combined to evaluate how efficient a company is in collecting its receivables.

LO3 Show that you understand how to account for interest-bearing notes receivable.

LO4 Explain various techniques that companies use to accelerate the inflow of cash from sales.

LO5 Show that you understand the accounting for and disclosure of various types of investments that companies make.

LO6 Explain the effects of transactions involving liquid assets on the statement of cash flows.

STUDY LINKS

A Look at the Previous Chapter Chapter 6 looked at the various forms that cash can take and the importance of cash control to a business.

A Look at This Chapter As you learned in earlier chapters, receivables result from the sale of products and services on account. This chapter examines the accounting for accounts and notes receivable, including how to account for bad debts. Many companies invest the cash they collect from customers in various types of financial instruments as well as in the stocks and bonds of other companies. This chapter also illustrates the accounting and reporting for these investments.

A Look at Upcoming Chapters This chapter concludes our look at a company's most liquid assets, that is, its current assets. Chapter 8 focuses on the long-term operational assets, such as property, plant, and equipment and intangibles, necessary to run a business. Chapters 9 and 10 explore the use of liabilities to finance the purchase of assets.

MAKING BUSINESS DECISIONS
APPLE INC.

For years, the names **Apple Inc.** and Macintosh have been synonymous. Incorporated in the state of California in 1977, the company made a name for itself by carving out a niche in the personal computer (PC) market and developing its own operating system to run its desktops and laptops.

A few years ago, however, Apple broadened its horizons and in the process revolutionized the music business by introducing the iPod. To provide synergies between its Mac PCs and the new iPods, Apple developed its iTunes Music Store, from which customers can download songs on either a Mac or Windows® PC.

Apple's innovations did not stop with the iPod. In early 2007, looking to capitalize on the success of the iPod, the company announced its new iPhone. In 2010, the iPad became an overnight success, followed a year later with the sleeker, faster iPad 2.

Have Apple's key product innovations paid off for it and its stockholders? The tools you learned how to use in previous chapters, as well as those presented in this chapter, will help you answer that question. Recall that a company's comparative income statements show the reader whether sales have increased and, if so, whether that increase has translated to an improved bottom line, that is, an increase in net income. As reported in its 2010 annual report, Apple's sales increased dramatically from about $43 billion in 2009 to over $65 billion in 2010. The bottom line increased by 70%, from $8.235 billion in 2009 to $14.013 billion in 2010.

What company wouldn't be envious of Apple's steady sales climb over recent years? Keep in mind, though, that sales and cash are not the same. As with most companies, Apple makes many of its sales on credit, and it must collect the resulting accounts receivable to add cash to its balance sheet. As you know from personal experience, idle cash does not earn a very good return. Investments on Apple's balance sheet (Apple calls these marketable securities) indicate what it does with idle cash, cash that is not immediately needed to buy more inventory or plant and equipment or to repay loans.

The partial balance sheet shown on the next page gives you an idea of the importance of Apple's three most liquid assets: cash and cash equivalents, short-term marketable securities (investments), and accounts receivable.

Why do you need to study this chapter?

- You need to know how a company reports accounts receivable on its balance sheet. (See pp. 332–335.)
- You need to know the purpose of subtracting an allowance from the balance of accounts receivable. (See pp. 336–337.)

- You need to know how you can use the relationship between sales on the income statement and accounts receivable on the balance sheet to assess a company's performance. (See pp. 341–343.)

- You need to know what types of investments companies make. (See pp. 351–352.)

- You need to know how they report short-term investments on their balance sheets. (See p. 355.)

- You need to know how they earn income from these investments. (See pp. 352–355.)

Knowing these things can help you decide whether Apple's string of rapid-fire innovations were wise business decisions.

Consolidated Balance Sheets (Partial) (In millions, except share amounts)		
Assets	**September 25, 2010**	**September 26, 2009**
Current assets:		
Cash and cash equivalents	$ 11,261	$ 5,263
Short-term investments	14,359	18,201
Accounts receivable, less allowances of $55 and $52, respectively	5,510	3,361
Inventories	1,051	455
Deferred tax assets	1,636	1,135
Vendor non-trade receivables	4,414	1,696
Other current assets	3,447	1,444
Total current assets	$ 41,678	$ 31,555
See accompanying Notes to Consolidated Financial Statements.		

Apple's three most important liquid assets

Source: Apple Computer Company's 2010 annual report.

Accounts Receivable

L01 Show that you understand how to account for accounts receivable, including bad debts.

OVERVIEW: Accounts receivable are stated on the balance sheet at net realizable, which takes into account an estimate of the uncollectible amount. Two methods are possible in estimating bad debts: (1) a percentage of sales approach and (2) a percentage of receivables approach.

Account receivable
A receivable arising from the sale of goods or services with a verbal promise to pay.

Receivables can result from a variety of transactions. The most common type of receivable is the one that arises from the sale of goods or services to customers with a verbal promise to pay within a specified period of time. This type of receivable is called an **accounts receivable**. Accounts receivable do not bear interest. **Apple** or any other company would rather not sell on credit, preferring to make all sales for cash. Selling on credit causes two problems: it slows down the inflow of cash to the company, and it raises the possibility that the customer may not pay its bill on time or possibly ever. To remain competitive, however, Apple and most other businesses must sell their products and services on credit.

SPOTLIGHT
The Importance of Understanding Credit

In the manufacturing industry, working with credit is very important to the success of a company. **Brad Solberg** is the chief financial officer of Lytle Signs, Inc., a medium-sized manufacturing concern in Meridian, Idaho. Brad was an accounting major in college, and he uses financial accounting practices daily in his position as CFO.

There are many factors that go into credit decisions. According to Brad, his company grants credit on a case-by-case basis. Management considers the size of the job, the company's workload, and the financial stability of the company. If manufacturing is slowing down, Lytle may be more likely to offer credit terms to a customer.

Generally, Lytle Signs collects financial statements from its customers when determining whether to offer credit terms. The balance sheet and statement of cash flows are the two most common financial statements the company requests. Using these two statements, Brad can determine the customer's current debt/asset and liquidity ratios.

Since determining creditworthiness is a complex decision, Brad has developed a formula for offering credit. He reviews the percent collected in the deposit; the profitability of the job; and his own company's level of cash on hand, its accounts payable, and its accounts receivable. "We may determine that even though the customer is creditworthy, the particular manufacturing job has low profitability, and we will refuse credit to future customers based on our experience," Brad says.

With the recent downturn in the economy, Lytle has tightened its credit policy. It is offering fewer customers credit because receivables are growing quickly and cash is shrinking rapidly. Customers are slower to pay, so Lytle Signs is effectively "financing" more work than it would like simply through work-in-process and late-paying customers. Because losses from bad debts are difficult to predict and relatively small, Lytle uses the direct write-off method.

Brad believes financial accounting has significantly helped his career. Of all his past experience, he believes his financial accounting education was given the most credence by his employer.

Name: Brad Solberg

Education: B.S., Business, University of Phoenix

College Major: Accounting

Occupation: National Sign Manufacturing Company

Age: 32

Position: Chief Financial Officer

Company Name: Lytle Signs, Inc.

See Brad Solberg's interview clip in CNOW.

> **In essence, my knowledge of financial accounting is solely responsible for my career success. My financial accounting education was given more credence by my employer than 10 years of officer and ownership positions in the insurance and banking industries.**

The Use of a Subsidiary Ledger

Accounts receivable is the asset that arises from a sale on credit. Assume that Apple sells $25,000 of hardware to a school. The sale results in the recognition of an asset and revenue. The transaction can be identified and analyzed as follows:

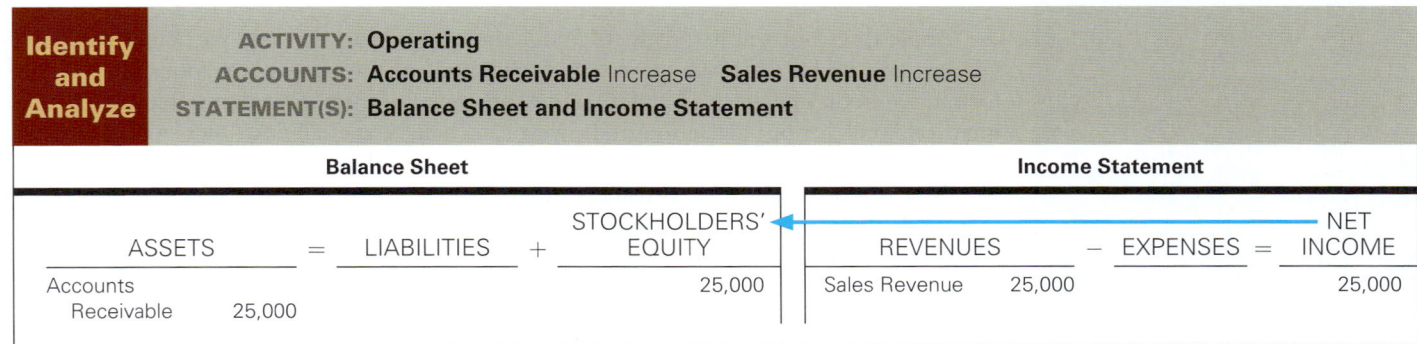

Identify and Analyze

ACTIVITY: Operating
ACCOUNTS: Accounts Receivable Increase Sales Revenue Increase
STATEMENT(S): Balance Sheet and Income Statement

Balance Sheet					Income Statement			
ASSETS	=	LIABILITIES	+	STOCKHOLDERS' EQUITY	REVENUES	−	EXPENSES =	NET INCOME
Accounts Receivable 25,000				25,000	Sales Revenue 25,000			25,000

It is important for control purposes that Apple keep a record of to whom the sale was made and include that amount on a periodic statement or bill sent to the customer (in this case, a school). What if a company has a hundred or a thousand different customers? Some mechanism is needed to track the balance owed by each of these customers. The mechanism that companies use is called a **subsidiary ledger**.

A subsidiary ledger contains the necessary detail on each of a number of items that collectively make up a single general ledger account, called the **control account**. This detail is shown in the following example for accounts receivable:

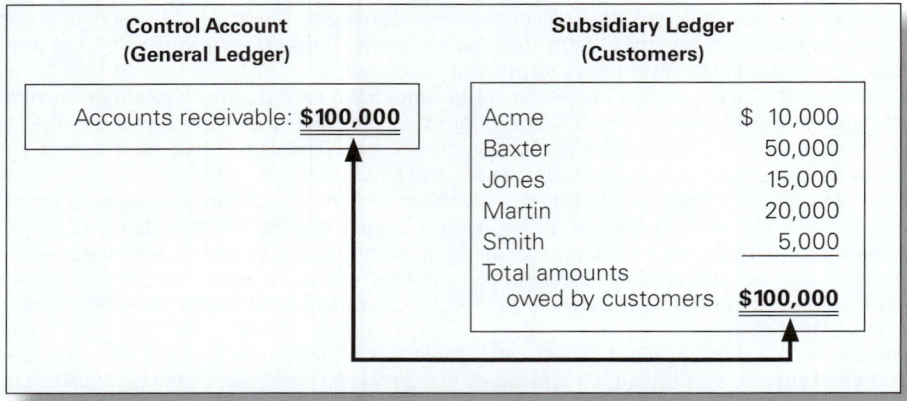

Subsidiary ledger
The detail for a number of individual items that collectively make up a single general ledger account.

Control account
The general ledger account that is supported by a subsidiary ledger.

In theory, any one of the accounts in the general ledger could be supported by a subsidiary ledger. In addition to Accounts Receivable, two other common accounts supported by subsidiary ledgers are Plant and Equipment and Accounts Payable. An accounts payable subsidiary ledger contains a separate account for each of the suppliers or vendors from which a company purchases inventory. A plant and equipment subsidiary ledger consists of individual accounts, along with their balances, for each of the various long-term tangible assets the company owns.

It is important to understand that a subsidiary ledger does not take the place of the control account in the general ledger. Instead, at any point in time, the balances of the accounts that make up the subsidiary ledger should total to the single balance in the related control account. The remainder of this chapter will illustrate the use of only the control account. However, whenever a specific customer's account is increased or decreased, the name of the customer will be noted next to the control account.

The Valuation of Accounts Receivable

Apple's 2010 annual report revealed the following receivables on the balance sheet

(amounts in millions)	September 25, 2010	September 26, 2009
Accounts receivable, less allowances of $55 and $52, respectively	$5,510	$3,361

Apple does not sell its products under the assumption that any particular customer will not pay its bill. In fact, the credit department of a business is responsible for performing a credit check on all potential customers before granting them credit. Management of Apple is not naive enough, however, to believe that all customers will be able to pay their accounts when due. This would be the case only if (1) all customers were completely trustworthy and (2) customers never experienced unforeseen financial difficulties that made it impossible to pay on time.

The reduction in Apple's receivables for an allowance is how most companies deal with bad debts in their accounting records. Bad debts are unpaid customer accounts that a company gives up trying to collect. Some companies describe the allowance more fully as the allowance for doubtful accounts or the allowance for uncollectible accounts. Using the end of 2010 as an example, Apple believes that the net recoverable amount of its receivables is $5,510 million even though the gross amount of receivables is $55 million higher

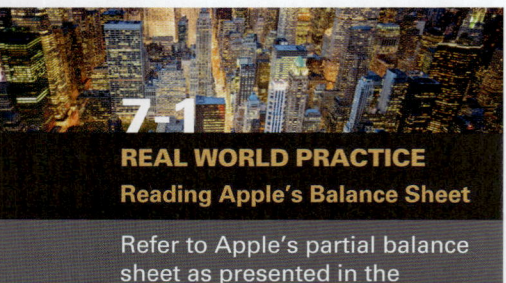

7-1
REAL WORLD PRACTICE
Reading Apple's Balance Sheet

Refer to Apple's partial balance sheet as presented in the chapter opener. By what amount did accounts receivable increase or decrease during 2010? How significant are accounts receivable to the amount of total current assets at the end of 2010?

than this amount. The company has reduced the gross receivables for an amount it believes is necessary to reflect the asset on the books at the net recoverable amount or **net realizable value**. We now take a closer look at how a company accounts for bad debts.

Two Methods to Account for Bad Debts

Example 7-1 Using the Direct Write-Off Method for Bad Debts

Assume that Roberts Corp. makes a $500 sale to Dexter Inc. on November 10, 2012, with credit terms of 2/10, n/60. (Credit terms were explained in Chapter 5.) The effect of the transaction can be identified and analyzed as follows:

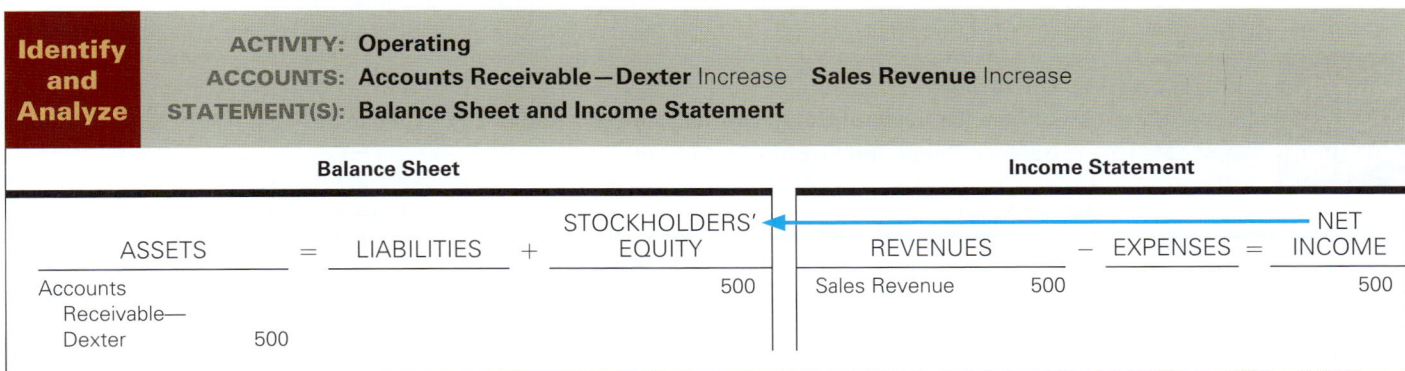

Assume further that Dexter not only misses taking advantage of the discount for early payment but also is unable to pay within 60 days. After pursuing the account for four months into 2013, the credit department of Roberts informs the accounting department that it has given up on collecting the $500 from Dexter and advises that the account be written off. To do so, the accounting department makes an adjustment. The effect of the adjustment can be identified and analyzed as follows:

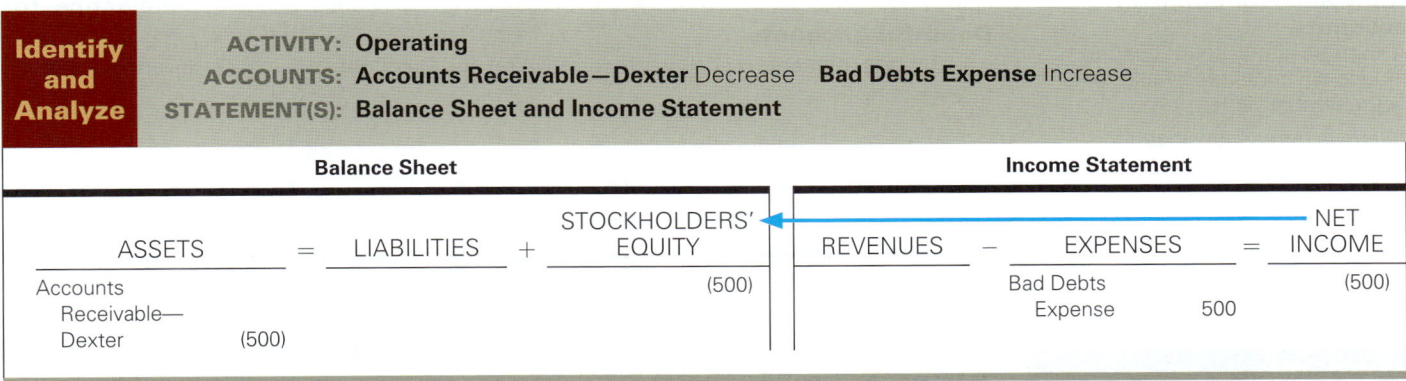

This approach to accounting for bad debts is called the **direct write-off method**. Do you see any problems with its use?

- *What about Roberts' balance sheet at the end of 2012?* By ignoring the possibility that not all of its outstanding accounts receivable will be collected, Roberts is overstating the value of this asset at December 31, 2012.
- *What about the income statement for 2012?* By ignoring the possibility of bad debts on sales made during 2012, Roberts has violated the matching principle. This principle requires that all costs associated with making sales in a period be matched with the sales of that period. Roberts has overstated net income for 2012 by ignoring bad debts as expense. The problem is one of timing: even though any one particular account may not prove to be uncollectible until a later period (e.g., the Dexter account), the cost associated with making sales on credit (bad debts) should be recognized in the period of sale.

Direct write-off method
The recognition of bad debts expense at the point an account is written off as uncollectible.

Allowance method
A method of estimating bad debts on the basis of either the net credit sales of the period or the accounts receivable at the end of the period.

Accountants use the **allowance method** to overcome the deficiencies of the direct write off method. They estimate the amount of bad debts before these debts actually occur.

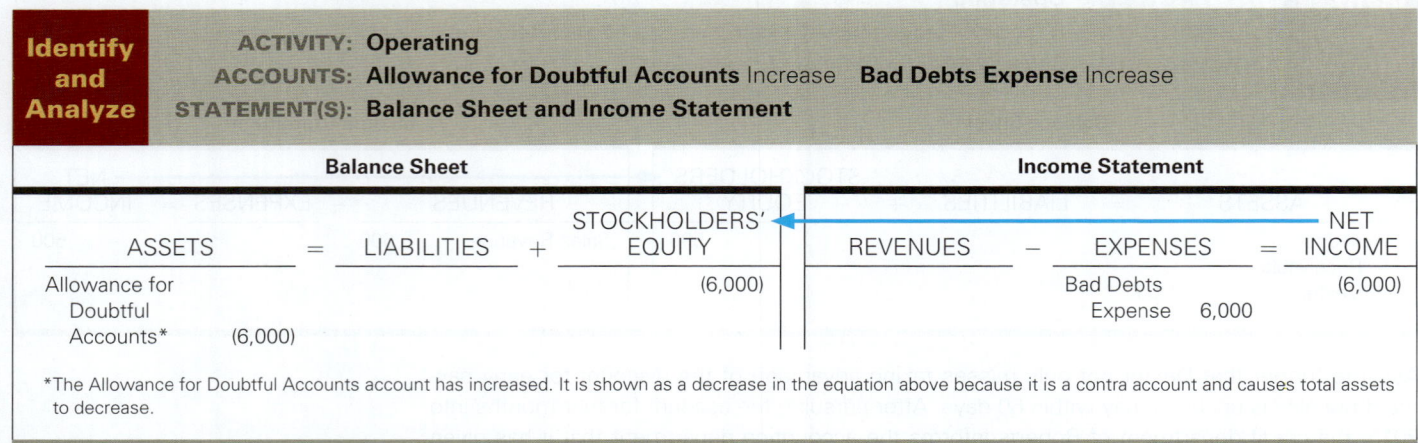

Example 7-2 Using the Allowance Method for Bad Debts

Assume that Roberts' total sales during 2012 amount to $600,000 and that at the end of the year, the outstanding accounts receivable total $250,000. Also, assume that Roberts estimates from past experience that 1% of the sales of the period, or $6,000, will prove to be uncollectible. Under the allowance method, Roberts makes an adjustment at the end of 2012. The effect of the adjustment can be identified and analyzed as follows:

Identify and Analyze

ACTIVITY: Operating
ACCOUNTS: Allowance for Doubtful Accounts Increase   **Bad Debts Expense** Increase
STATEMENT(S): Balance Sheet and Income Statement

Balance Sheet					Income Statement			
ASSETS	=	LIABILITIES	+	STOCKHOLDERS' EQUITY	REVENUES	−	EXPENSES	= NET INCOME
Allowance for Doubtful Accounts* (6,000)				(6,000)			Bad Debts Expense 6,000	(6,000)

*The Allowance for Doubtful Accounts account has increased. It is shown as a decrease in the equation above because it is a contra account and causes total assets to decrease.

Allowance for doubtful accounts
A contra-asset account used to reduce accounts receivable to its net realizable value.

Alternate term: Allowance for uncollectible accounts.

Bad Debts Expense recognizes the cost associated with the reduction in value of the asset Accounts Receivable. A contra-asset account is used to reduce the asset to its net realizable value. This is accomplished by creating an allowance account, **Allowance for Doubtful Accounts**.

Roberts presents accounts receivable on its December 31, 2012, balance sheet as follows:

Accounts receivable	$250,000
Less: Allowance for doubtful accounts	(6,000)
Net accounts receivable	$244,000

© Cengage Learning 2013

Write-Offs of Uncollectible Accounts with the Allowance Method

Like the direct write-off method, the allowance method reduces Accounts Receivable to write off a specific customer's account. If the account receivable no longer exists, there is no need for the related allowance account; thus, this account is reduced as well.

Example 7-3 Writing Off Accounts Using the Allowance Method

Assume, as we did earlier, that Dexter's $500 account is written off on May 1, 2013. Under the allowance method, the effect can be identified and analyzed as follows:

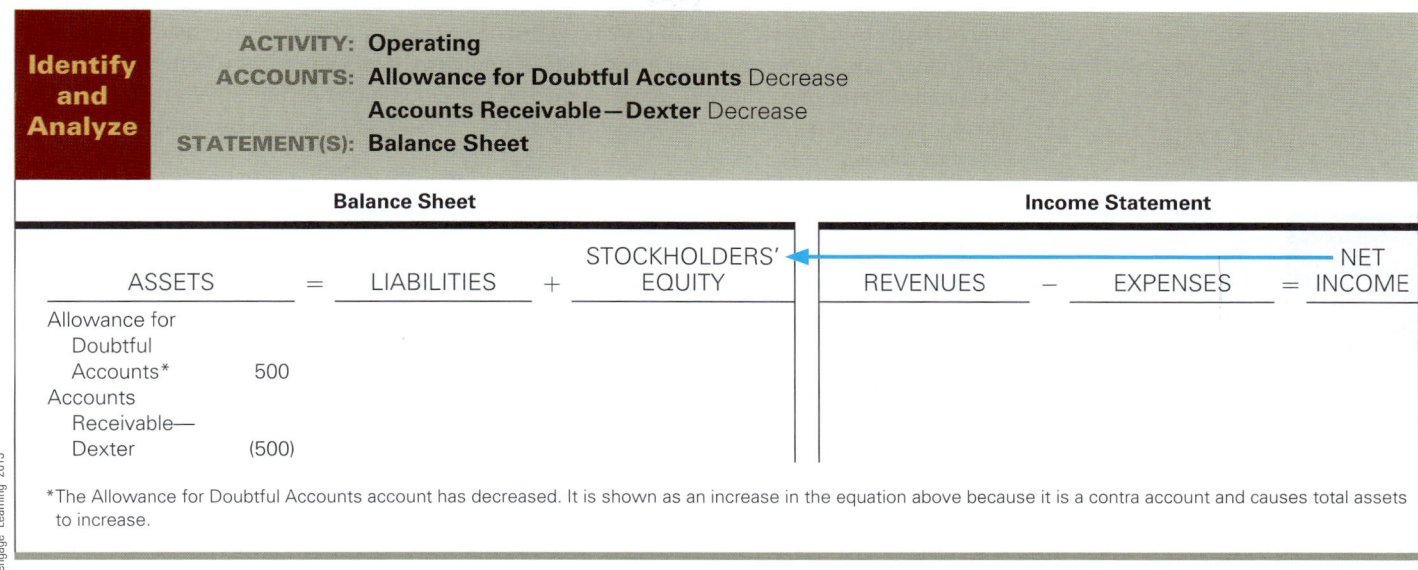

Identify and Analyze

ACTIVITY: **Operating**
ACCOUNTS: **Allowance for Doubtful Accounts** Decrease
                  Accounts Receivable—Dexter Decrease
STATEMENT(S): **Balance Sheet**

Balance Sheet								Income Statement					
ASSETS	=	LIABILITIES	+	STOCKHOLDERS' EQUITY				REVENUES	−	EXPENSES	=	NET INCOME
Allowance for Doubtful Accounts*	500											
Accounts Receivable— Dexter	(500)											

*The Allowance for Doubtful Accounts account has decreased. It is shown as an increase in the equation above because it is a contra account and causes total assets to increase.

To summarize, whether the direct write-off method or the allowance method is used, the adjustment to write off a specific customer's account reduces Accounts Receivable. It is the other side of the adjustment that differs between the two methods:

- Under the direct write-off method, an *expense* is increased.
- Under the allowance method, the *allowance* account is reduced.

Two Approaches to the Allowance Method of Accounting for Bad Debts

Because the allowance method results in a better matching, accounting standards require the use of it rather than the direct write-off method unless bad debts are immaterial in amount. Accountants use one of two different variations of the allowance method to estimate bad debts. One approach emphasizes matching bad debts expense with revenue on the income statement and bases bad debts on a percentage of the sales of the period. This was the method illustrated earlier for Roberts Corp. The other approach emphasizes the net realizable amount (value) of accounts receivable on the balance sheet and bases bad debts on a percentage of the accounts receivable balance at the end of the period.

Percentage of Net Credit Sales Approach If a company has been in business for enough years, it may be able to use the past relationship between bad debts and net credit sales to predict bad debt amounts. *Net* means that credit sales have been adjusted for sales discounts and returns and allowances.

Example 7-4 Using the Percentage of Net Credit Sales Approach

Assume that the accounting records for Bosco Corp. reveal the following:

Year	Net Credit Sales	Bad Debts
2007	$1,250,000	$ 26,400
2008	1,340,000	29,350
2009	1,200,000	23,100
2010	1,650,000	32,150
2011	2,120,000	42,700
	$7,560,000	$153,700

(Continued)

© Cengage Learning 2013

Although the exact percentage varied slightly over the five-year period, the average percentage of bad debts to net credit sales is very close to 2% ($153,700/$7,560,000 = 0.02033). Bosco needs to determine whether this estimate is realistic for the current period. For example, are current economic conditions considerably different from those in prior years? Has the company made sales to any new customers with significantly different credit terms? If the answers to these types of questions are yes, Bosco should consider adjusting the 2% experience rate to estimate future bad debts. Otherwise, it should proceed with this estimate. Assuming that it uses the 2% rate and that its net credit sales during 2012 are $2,340,000, Bosco makes an adjustment of 0.02 × $2,340,000, or $46,800 that can be identified and analyzed as follows:

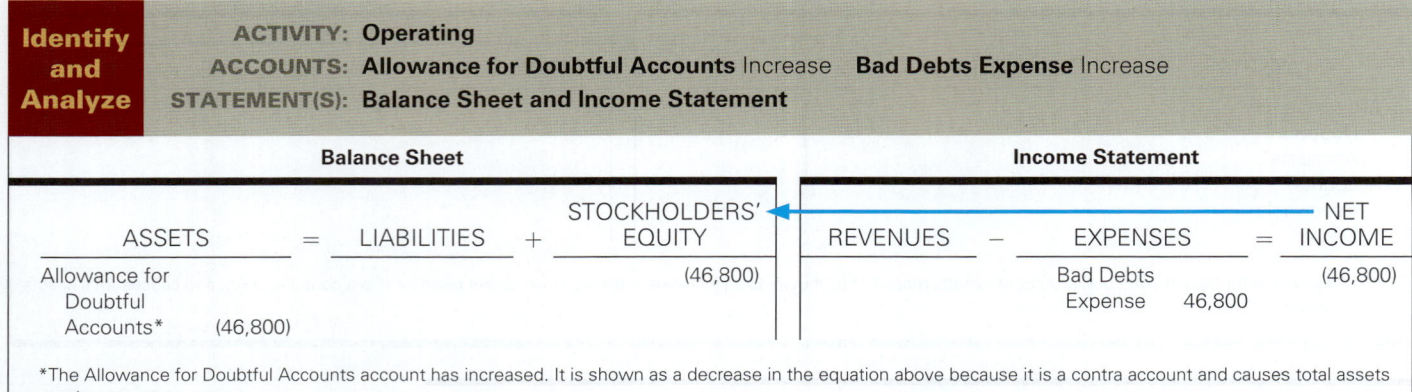

Identify and Analyze

ACTIVITY: Operating
ACCOUNTS: Allowance for Doubtful Accounts Increase   Bad Debts Expense Increase
STATEMENT(S): Balance Sheet and Income Statement

Balance Sheet					Income Statement			
ASSETS	=	LIABILITIES	+	STOCKHOLDERS' EQUITY	REVENUES	−	EXPENSES	=	NET INCOME
Allowance for Doubtful Accounts* (46,800)				(46,800)			Bad Debts Expense 46,800		(46,800)

*The Allowance for Doubtful Accounts account has increased. It is shown as a decrease in the equation above because it is a contra account and causes total assets to decrease.

Thus, Bosco matches bad debts expense of $46,800 with sales revenue of $2,340,000.

© Cengage Learning 2013

Percentage of Accounts Receivable Approach

Some companies believe that they can more accurately estimate bad debts by relating them to the balance in the Accounts Receivable account at the end of the period rather than to the sales of the period. The objective with both approaches is the same, however: to use past experience with bad debts to predict future amounts.

Example 7-5 Using the Percentage of Accounts Receivable Approach

Assume that the records for Cougar Corp. reveal the following:

Year	Balance in Accounts Receivable, December 31	Bad Debts
2007	$ 650,000	$ 5,250
2008	785,000	6,230
2009	854,000	6,950
2010	824,000	6,450
2011	925,000	7,450
	$4,038,000	$32,330

The ratio of bad debts to the ending balance in Accounts Receivable over the past five years is $32,330/$4,038,000, or approximately 0.008 (0.8%). Assuming balances in Accounts Receivable and Allowance for Doubtful Accounts on December 31, 2012, of $865,000 and $2,100, respectively, Cougar makes an adjustment that can be identified and analyzed as follows:

(Continued)

Identify and Analyze	ACTIVITY: Operating
	ACCOUNTS: Allowance for Doubtful Accounts Increase Bad Debts Expense Increase
	STATEMENT(S): Balance Sheet and Income Statement

Balance Sheet				Income Statement			
ASSETS	=	LIABILITIES	+	STOCKHOLDERS' EQUITY	REVENUES	−	EXPENSES	=	NET INCOME

Balance Sheet	Income Statement
ASSETS = **LIABILITIES** + **STOCKHOLDERS' EQUITY**	**REVENUES** − **EXPENSES** = **NET INCOME**
	(4,820)		(4,820)
Allowance for Doubtful Accounts* (4,820)		Bad Debts Expense 4,820**	

*The Allowance for Doubtful Accounts account has increased. It is shown as a decrease in the equation above because it is a contra account and causes total assets to decrease.

**Balance required in allowance account after adjustment ($865,000 × 0.8%) $6,920

Less: Balance in allowance account before adjustment   2,100

Amount of adjustment $4,820

Note the one major difference between this approach and the percentage of sales approach:

- Under the percentage of net credit sales approach, the balance in the allowance account is ignored, and the bad debts expense is simply a percentage of the sales of the period.
- Under the percentage of accounts receivable approach, however, the balance in the allowance account must be considered.

The net realizable value of Accounts Receivable is determined as follows:

Accounts receivable	$865,000
Less: Allowance for doubtful accounts	(6,920)
Net realizable value	$858,080

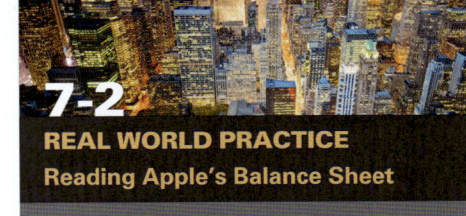

7-2

REAL WORLD PRACTICE

Reading Apple's Balance Sheet

Refer to the excerpt from Apple's balance sheet in the chapter opener. Compute for each of the two year-ends the amount of accounts receivable before deducting the balance in the allowance account. Did this amount increase or decrease during 2010? Did the allowance account increase or decrease during 2010? What would cause the allowance account to increase or decrease in any one year?

Aging of Accounts Receivable Some companies use a variation of the percentage of accounts receivable approach to estimate bad debts. This variation is actually a refinement of the approach because it considers the length of time that the receivables have been outstanding. The older an account receivable is, the less likely it is to be collected. An **aging schedule** categorizes the various accounts by length of time outstanding. An example of an aging schedule is shown in Exhibit 7-1. We assume that the company's policy is to allow 30 days for payment of an outstanding account. After that time, the account is past due. An alphabetical list of customers appears in the first column, with the balance in each account shown in the appropriate column to the right. The dotted lines after A. Matt's account indicate that many more accounts appear in the records; only a few have been included to show the format of the schedule.

Aging schedule

A form used to categorize the various individual accounts receivable according to the length of time each has been outstanding.

Example 7-6 Using an Aging Schedule to Estimate Bad Debts

The totals on the aging schedule are used as the basis for estimating bad debts, as shown below.

Category	Amount	Estimated Percent Uncollectible	Estimated Amount Uncollectible
Current	$ 85,600	1%	$ 856
Past due:			
1–30 days	31,200	4%	1,248
31–60 days	24,500	10%	2,450
61–60 days	18,000	30%	5,400
Over 90 days	9,200	50%	4,600
Totals	$168,500		$14,554

(Continued)

EXHIBIT 7-1 Aging Schedule

Customer	Current	Number of Days Past Due			
		1–30	31–60	61–90	Over 90
L. Ash	$ 4,400				
B. Budd	3,200				
C Cox		$ 6,500			
E. Fudd					$6,300
G. Hoff			$ 900		
A. Matt	5,500				
....					
....					
....					
T. West		3,100			
M. Young				$ 4,200	
Totals*	$85,600	$31,200	$24,500	$18,000	$9,200

*Only a few of the customer accounts are illustrated; thus, the column totals are higher than the amounts for the accounts illustrated.

Note that the estimated percentage of uncollectibles increases as the period of time the accounts have been outstanding lengthens. If we assume that Allowance for Doubtful Accounts has a balance of $1,230 before adjustment, an adjustment is made that can be identified and analyzed as follows:

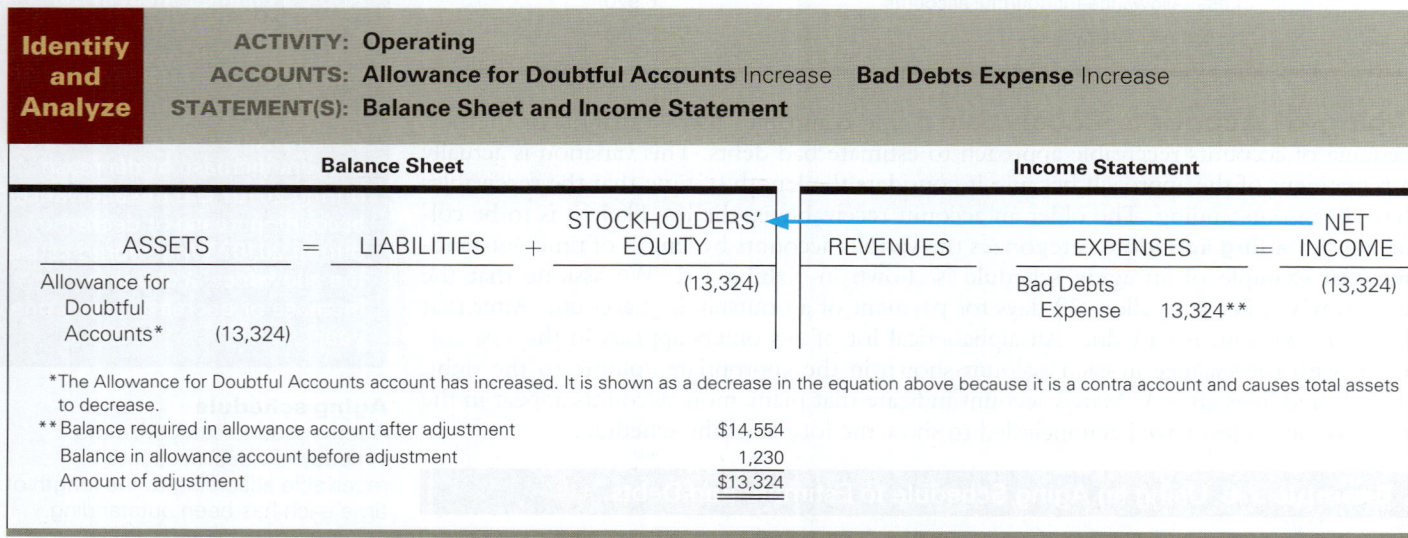

Identify and Analyze

ACTIVITY: Operating
ACCOUNTS: Allowance for Doubtful Accounts Increase   **Bad Debts Expense** Increase
STATEMENT(S): Balance Sheet and Income Statement

Balance Sheet				Income Statement		
ASSETS	=	LIABILITIES	+	STOCKHOLDERS' EQUITY	REVENUES − EXPENSES	= NET INCOME
Allowance for Doubtful Accounts* (13,324)				(13,324)	Bad Debts Expense 13,324**	(13,324)

*The Allowance for Doubtful Accounts account has increased. It is shown as a decrease in the equation above because it is a contra account and causes total assets to decrease.

** Balance required in allowance account after adjustment $14,554
Balance in allowance account before adjustment 1,230
Amount of adjustment $13,324

The net realizable value of accounts receivable would be determined as follows:

Accounts receivable	$168,500
Less: Allowance for doubtful accounts	14,554
Net realizable value	$153,946

LO1 Show that you understand how to account for accounts receivable, including bad debts.

- Accounts receivable arise from sales on credit. Companies with many customers may keep detailed records of accounts receivable in a separate subsidiary ledger.

- Because not all customers pay their accounts receivable, an estimate of the accounts receivable less any doubtful accounts must be presented on the balance sheet.

- Bad debts are estimated under the allowance method by one of two approaches:
  - Percentage of net credit sales
  - Percentage of accounts receivable

POD REVIEW 7.1

QUESTIONS   **Answers to these questions are on the last page of the chapter.**

1. Why is the allowance method of recognizing bad debts used?

   a. It results in recognizing the expense of granting credit in the period in which the account is written off.

   b. It results in matching expense with the revenue of the period in which the sale took place.

   c. It results in recognizing the maximum amount of write-off in each period.

   d. The allowance method cannot be justified and therefore is not allowed.

2. What accounts are adjusted at the end of the period to recognize bad debts under the allowance method?

   a. Bad Debts expense is increased, and Accounts Receivable is decreased.

   b. Allowance for Doubtful Accounts is decreased, and Bad Debts Expense is decreased.

   c. Bad Debts Expense is increased, and Allowance for Doubtful Accounts is increased.

   d. None of the above is correct.

3. Which of the two approaches to recognizing bad debts considers any existing balance in Allowance for Doubtful Accounts?

   a. percentage of net credit sales approach

   b. percentage of accounts receivable approach

   c. both the percentage of net credit sales approach and the percentage of accounts receivable approach

   d. Neither method takes into account any existing balance in Allowance for Doubtful Accounts.

© Cengage Learning 2013

The Accounts Receivable Turnover Ratio

OVERVIEW: The accounts receivable turnover ratio is a measure of how well a company manages its receivables. It is the ratio of net credit sales to average accounts receivable.

LO2 Explain how information about sales and receivables can be combined to evaluate how efficient a company is in collecting its receivables.

Managers, investors, and creditors are keenly interested in how well a company manages its accounts receivable. One simple measure is to compare a company's sales to its accounts receivable. The result is the accounts receivable turnover ratio:

$$\text{Accounts Receivable Turnover} = \frac{\text{Net Credit Sales}}{\text{Average Accounts Receivable}}$$

Example 7-7 Computing the Accounts Receivable Turnover Ratio

Assume that a company has sales of $10 million and an average accounts receivable of $1 million. This means it turns over its accounts receivable $10 million/$1 million, or ten times per year. If we assume 360 days in a year, that is once every 360/10, or 36 days. An observer would compare that figure with historical figures to see if the company is experiencing slower or faster collections. A comparison also could be made to other companies in the same industry. If receivables are turning over too slowly, the company's credit department may not be operating effectively; therefore, the company is missing opportunities with the cash that isn't available. On the other hand, a turnover rate that is too fast might mean that the company's credit policies are too stringent and that sales are being lost as a result.

© Cengage Learning 2013

USING THE RATIO DECISION MODEL

Analyzing the Accounts Receivable Rate of Collection

Use the following Ratio Decision Model to evaluate the accounts receivable rate of collection of Apple or any public company:

1. Formulate the Question
Managers, investors, and creditors are interested in how well a company manages its accounts receivable. Each dollar of sales on credit produces a dollar of accounts receivable. And the quicker each dollar of accounts receivable can be collected, the sooner the money will be available for other purposes. *So how quickly is a company such as Apple able to collect its accounts receivable?*

2. Gather the Information from the Financial Statements
Recall from earlier chapters that sales are recorded on an income statement, representing a *flow* for a period of time. Accounts receivable, an asset, represents a *balance* at a point in time. Thus, a comparison of the two requires the amount of net credit sales for the year and an average of the balance in accounts receivable:

- Net credit sales: From the income statement for the year
- Average accounts receivable: From the beginning and ending balance sheets

3. Calculate the Ratio

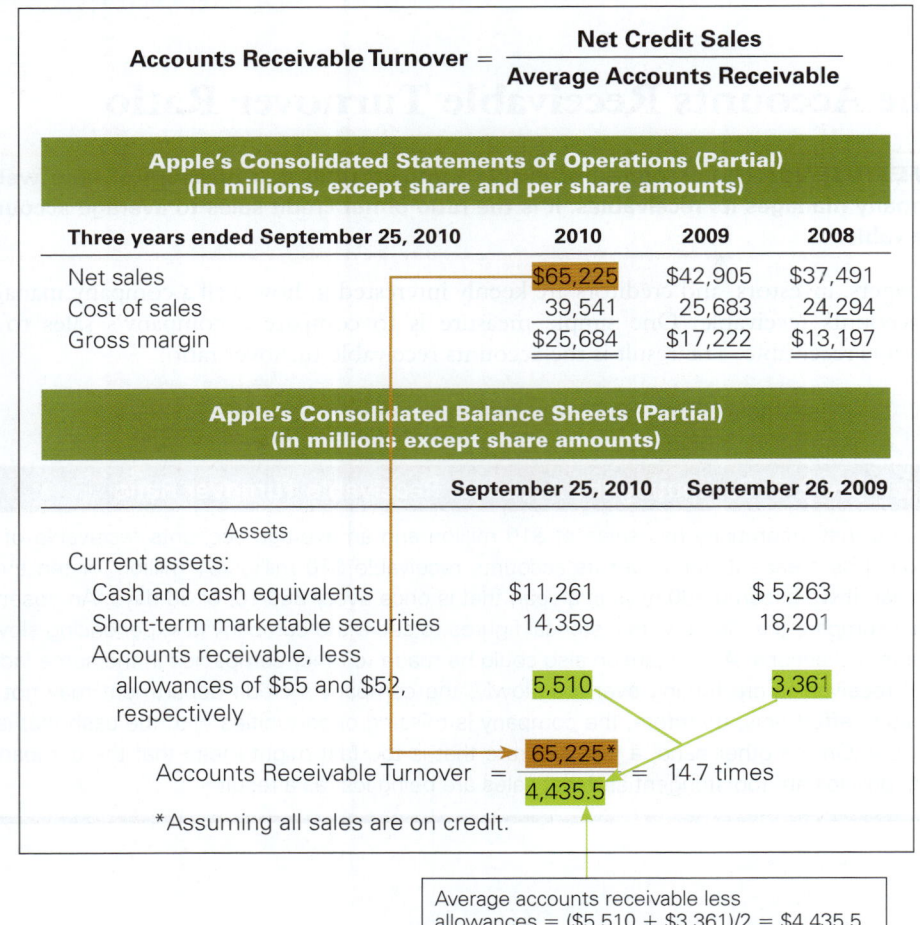

$$\text{Accounts Receivable Turnover} = \frac{\text{Net Credit Sales}}{\text{Average Accounts Receivable}}$$

Apple's Consolidated Statements of Operations (Partial)
(In millions, except share and per share amounts)

Three years ended September 25, 2010	2010	2009	2008
Net sales	$65,225	$42,905	$37,491
Cost of sales	39,541	25,683	24,294
Gross margin	$25,684	$17,222	$13,197

Apple's Consolidated Balance Sheets (Partial)
(in millions except share amounts)

	September 25, 2010	September 26, 2009
Assets		
Current assets:		
Cash and cash equivalents	$11,261	$ 5,263
Short-term marketable securities	14,359	18,201
Accounts receivable, less allowances of $55 and $52, respectively	5,510	3,361

$$\text{Accounts Receivable Turnover} = \frac{65,225^*}{4,435.5} = 14.7 \text{ times}$$

*Assuming all sales are on credit.

Average accounts receivable less allowances = ($5,510 + $3,361)/2 = $4,435.5

4. Compare the Ratio with Others

Management compares the current year's turnover rate with that of prior years to see if the company is experiencing slower or faster collections. It is also important to compare the rate with that of other companies in the same industry:

Apple Computer		Hewlett-Packard	
Year Ended September 25, 2010	Year Ended September 26, 2009	Year Ended October 31, 2010	Year Ended October 31, 2009
14.7 times	14.8 times	7.2 times	6.8 times

5. Interpret the Results

Typically, the more times a company turns over its receivables each year, the better. Apple's turnover decreased slightly, from 14.8 times in 2009 to 14.7 times in 2010. If we assume 360 days in a year, a turnover of 14.7 times means receivables are collected on average every 24.5 days (360/14.7). Apple's turnover is faster than Hewlett-Packard's, resulting in fewer days to collect receivables. ■

LO2 Explain how information about sales and receivables can be combined to evaluate how efficient a company is in collecting its receivables.

- Information about net credit sales and the average accounts receivable balance may be combined to calculate the accounts receivables turnover to see how well a company is managing its collections on account.

POD REVIEW 7.2

QUESTIONS   Answers to these questions are on the last page of the chapter.

1. The amounts needed to compute the accounts receivable turnover ratio can be found on

   a. the balance sheet only.
   b. the income statement only.
   c. both the balance sheet and the income statement.
   d. the statement of cash flows.

2. Oak Corp. had sales during the year of $10,000,000 and an average accounts receivable of $2,000,000. Its accounts receivable turnover ratio is

   a. 5 times.
   b. 0.2 time.
   c. 10 times.
   d. none of the above.

© Cengage Learning 2013

HOT TOPICS
Keeping Investors Informed

Financial information can only be of use if it is presented in a timely manner. This is why the SEC requires companies to file not only an annual report, but also a quarterly report, Form 10Q. Companies usually issue a press release concurrent with the filing of the quarterly report as a way to announce the most recent results to the investment community. When the results are as favorable as those reported recently by Apple, it is a cause for celebration. In an April 2011 press release, Apple reported its financial results for the second quarter of its 2011 fiscal year. Both revenue and net profits set second quarter records. In fact, revenue rose by 83% and net profit by 95% from what they were in the same quarter of the prior year.

Companies often use the quarterly report to tout other favorable trends in their operations. As a signal to the investment community that its reach extends far beyond the United States, Apple announced in this same report that international sales accounted for 59% of the second quarter's record-setting revenue. The California-based technology superstar also reported on the sheer volume of its popular products sold in the quarter: 18.65 million iPhones, 9.02 million iPods, and 4.69 million iPads. Finally, the press release surrounding an earnings announcement can be used to set expectations for the upcoming quarter. With its record-setting second quarter, Apple sees little leveling off, expecting revenue of about $23 billion in the third quarter of its 2011 fiscal year.

Source: Apple Inc., April 20, 2011, press release.

SKD/Alamy

Notes Receivable

LO3 Show that you understand how to account for interest-bearing notes receivable.

OVERVIEW: A note receivable is an asset resulting from accepting a promissory note from another entity. The holder of the note earns interest revenue during the time the note is outstanding.

A **promissory note** is a written promise to repay a definite sum of money on demand or at a fixed or determinable date in the future. Promissory notes normally require the payment of interest for the use of someone else's money. The party that agrees to repay money is the **maker** of the note, and the party that receives money in the future is the **payee**. A company that holds a promissory note received from another company has an asset, called a **note receivable**; the company that makes or gives a promissory note to another company has a liability, a **note payable**. Over the life of the note, the maker incurs interest expense on its note payable and the payee earns interest revenue on its note receivable. The following summarizes this relationship:

Promissory note
A written promise to repay a definite sum of money on demand or at a fixed or determinable date in the future.

Maker
The party that agrees to repay the money for a promissory note at some future date.

Payee
The party that will receive the money from a promissory note at some future date.

Note receivable
An asset resulting from the acceptance of a promissory note from another company.

Note payable
A liability resulting from the signing of a promissory note.

Party	Recognizes on Balances Sheet	Recognizes on Income Statement
Maker	Note payable	Interest expense
Payee	Note receivable	Interest revenue

Maker	**Gives a Note to**	**Payee**
Smith, Inc. Has a Liability (Note Payable) and Incurs an Expense (Interest Expense)	"I promise to pay you."	Jones, Inc. Has an Asset (Note Receivable) and Earns Revenue (Interest Revenue)

Promissory notes are used for a variety of purposes. Banks normally require a company to sign a promissory note to borrow money. Promissory notes are often used in the sale of consumer durables with relatively high purchase prices, such as appliances and automobiles. At times, a promissory note is issued to replace an existing overdue account receivable.

Important Terms Connected with Promissory Notes

It is important to understand the following terms when dealing with promissory notes:

Principal—the amount of cash received, or the fair value of the products or services received, by the maker when a promissory note is issued.

Key terms for promissory notes
These terms, with their definitions in the text, are important for your understanding.

Maturity date—the date the promissory note is due.

Term—the length of time a note is outstanding, that is, the period of time between the date it is issued and the date it matures.

Maturity value—the amount of cash the maker is to pay the payee on the maturity date of the note.

Interest—the difference between the principal amount of the note and its maturity value.

Example 7-8 Accounting for a Note Receivable

Assume that on December 13, 2012, High Tec sells a computer to Baker Corp. at an invoice price of $15,000. Because Baker is short of cash, it gives High Tec a 90-day, 12% promissory note. The total amount of interest due on the maturity date is determined as follows:

$$\$15,0000 \times 0.12 \times 90/360 = \underline{\$450}$$

(Continued)

The effect of the receipt of the note by High Tec can be identified and analyzed as follows:

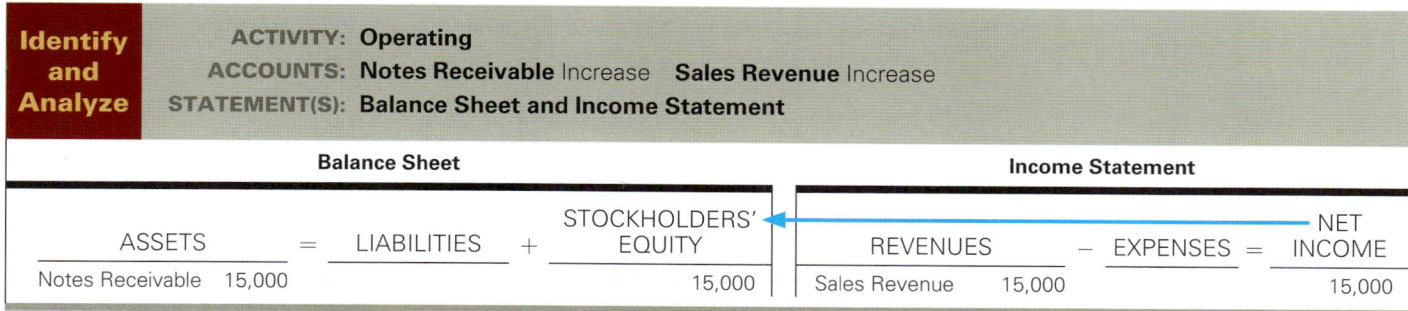

Identify and Analyze

ACTIVITY: Operating
ACCOUNTS: Notes Receivable Increase   Sales Revenue Increase
STATEMENT(S): Balance Sheet and Income Statement

Balance Sheet				Income Statement			
ASSETS	=	LIABILITIES	+	STOCKHOLDERS' EQUITY	REVENUES	− EXPENSES =	NET INCOME
Notes Receivable 15,000				15,000	Sales Revenue 15,000		15,000

If we assume that December 31 is the end of High Tec's accounting year, an adjustment is needed to recognize interest earned but not yet received. It is required when a company uses the accrual basis of accounting. The question is, how many days of interest have been earned during December? It is normal practice to count the day a note matures but not the day it is signed in computing interest. Thus, in the example, interest would be earned for 18 days (December 14 to December 31) during 2012 and for 72 days in 2013:

Month	Number of Days Outstanding
December 2012	18 days
January 2013	31 days
February 2013	28 days
March 2013	13 days (matures on March 13, 2013)
Total days	90 days

The amount of interest earned during 2012 is $15,000 × 0.12 × 18/360, or $90. An adjustment is made on December 31 to record interest earned during 2012. The effect of the adjustment can be identified and analyzed as follows:

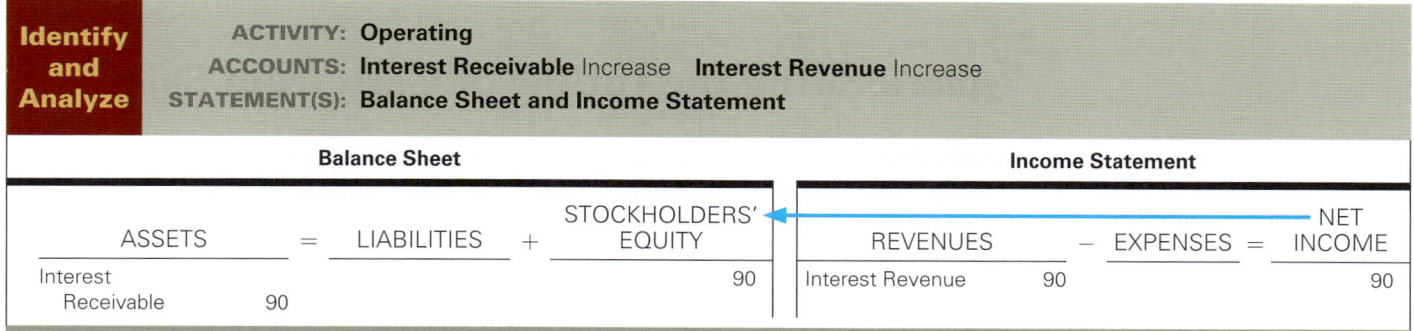

Identify and Analyze

ACTIVITY: Operating
ACCOUNTS: Interest Receivable Increase   Interest Revenue Increase
STATEMENT(S): Balance Sheet and Income Statement

Balance Sheet				Income Statement			
ASSETS	=	LIABILITIES	+	STOCKHOLDERS' EQUITY	REVENUES	− EXPENSES =	NET INCOME
Interest Receivable 90				90	Interest Revenue 90		90

On March 13, 2013, High Tec collects the principal amount of the note and interest from Baker. The effect of the transaction can be identified and analyzed as follows:

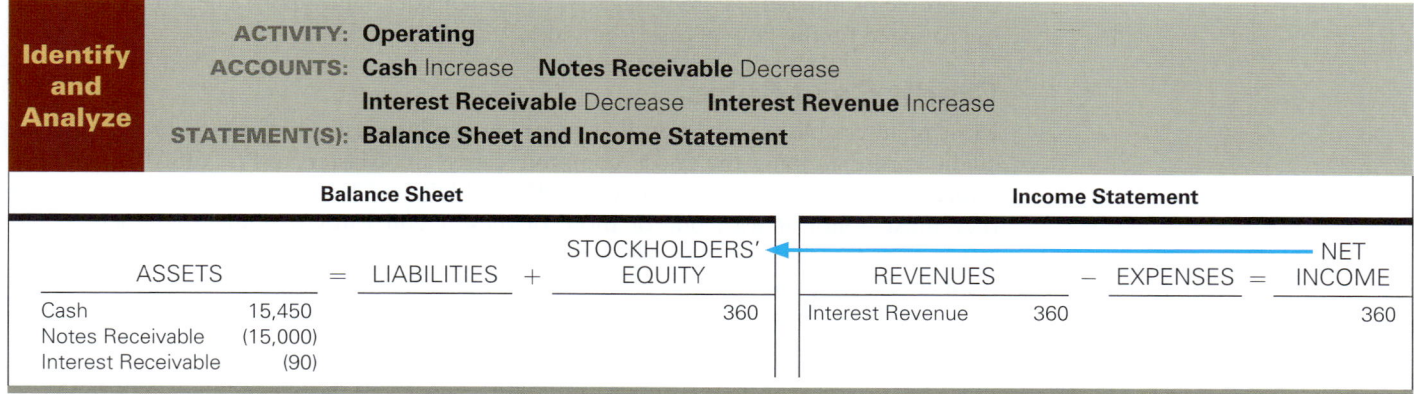

Identify and Analyze

ACTIVITY: Operating
ACCOUNTS: Cash Increase   Notes Receivable Decrease
Interest Receivable Decrease   Interest Revenue Increase
STATEMENT(S): Balance Sheet and Income Statement

Balance Sheet				Income Statement			
ASSETS	=	LIABILITIES	+	STOCKHOLDERS' EQUITY	REVENUES	− EXPENSES =	NET INCOME
Cash 15,450				360	Interest Revenue 360		360
Notes Receivable (15,000)							
Interest Receivable (90)							

(Continued)

This adjustment accomplishes a number of purposes. First, it removes the amount of $15,000 originally recorded in the Notes Receivable account. Second, it increases Interest Revenue for the interest earned during the 72 days in 2013 that the note was outstanding. The calculation of interest earned during 2013 is as follows:

$$\$15,000 \times 0.12 \times 72/360 = \$360$$

Third, Interest Receivable for $90 is removed from the records now that the note has been collected. Finally, Cash of $15,450 is collected, which represents the principal amount of the note, $15,000, plus interest of $450 for 90 days.

© Cengage Learning 2013

LO3 Show that you understand how to account for interest-bearing notes receivable.

- Notes receivable ultimately result in the receipt of both interest and principal to the holder of the notes.
- Because interest receipts may not coincide with the end of the period, adjustments may need to be made to accrue interest receivable and interest revenue.

POD REVIEW 7.3

QUESTIONS   **Answers to these questions are on the last page of the chapter.**

1. Maple Corp. borrows $10,000 at a local bank. Maple will recognize the following accounts:
   a. Notes Payable and Interest Revenue
   b. Notes Receivable and Interest Revenue
   c. Notes Payable and Interest Expense
   d. Notes Receivable and Interest Expense

2. Elm Inc. borrows $50,000 on a 120-day, 12% promissory note. The total interest that Elm will repay at maturity is
   a. $500.
   b. $2,000.
   c. $6,000.
   d. none of the above.

© Cengage Learning 2013

Accelerating the Inflow of Cash from Sales

LO4 Explain various techniques that companies use to accelerate the inflow of cash from sales.

OVERVIEW: Credit card sales accelerate the collection of cash from a customer and pass the risk of nonpayment to the credit card company. Similarly, discounting a note receivable allows a company to accelerate the inflow of cash.

Earlier in the chapter, we pointed out why cash sales are preferable to credit sales: credit sales slow down the inflow of cash to the company and create the potential for bad debts. To remain competitive, most businesses find it necessary to grant credit to customers. If one company won't grant credit to a customer, the customer may find another company that will. Companies have found it possible, however, to circumvent the problems inherent in credit sales. We now consider some approaches that companies use to speed up the flow of cash from sales.

Credit Card Sales

Most retail establishments as well as many service businesses accept one or more major credit cards. Among the most common cards are MasterCard®, VISA®, American Express®, Carte Blanche®, Discover Card®, and Diners Club®. Most merchants find that they must honor at least one or more of these credit cards to remain competitive. In return for a fee, the merchant passes the responsibility for collection on to the credit card company. Thus, the credit card issuer assumes the risk of nonpayment. The basic relationships among the three parties—the customer, the merchant, and the credit company—are illustrated in Exhibit 7-2.

EXHIBIT 7-2 Basic Relationships among Parties with Credit Card Sales

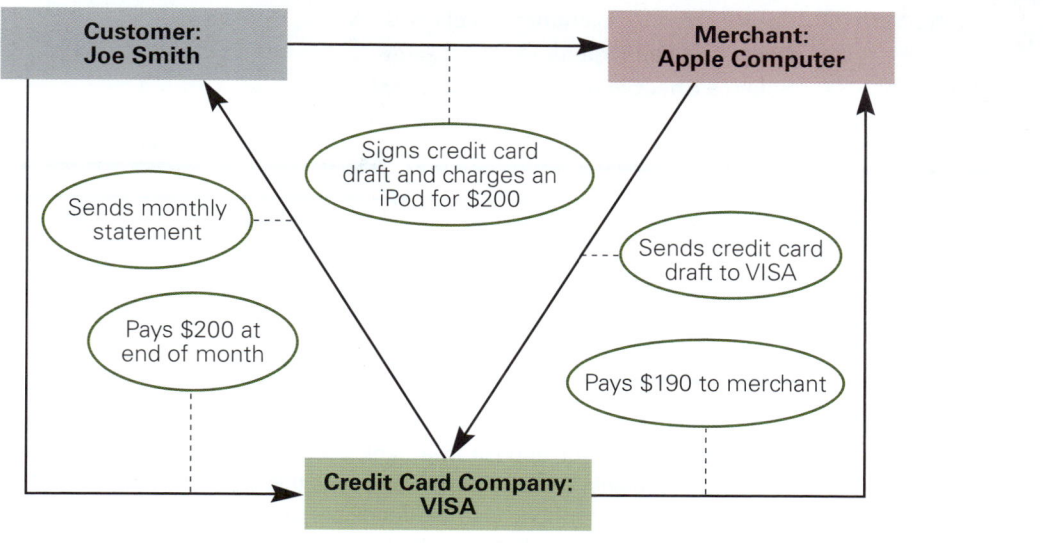

Example 7-9 Accounting for Credit Card Sales

Assume that Joe Smith buys an iPod in an Apple store and charges the $200 cost to his VISA credit card. When Joe is presented with his bill, he is asked to sign a multiple-copy **credit card draft**, or invoice. Joe keeps one copy of the draft and leaves the other two copies at the Apple store. The store keeps one copy as the basis for recording its sales of the day and sends the other copy to VISA for payment. VISA uses the copy of the draft it gets for two purposes: to reimburse Apple $190 (keeping $10, or 5% of the original sale, as a collection fee) and to include Joe Smith's $200 purchase on the monthly bill it mails him.

Credit card draft
A multiple-copy document used by a company that accepts a credit card for a sale.

Alternate term: Invoice.

Assume that total credit card sales on June 5 amount to $8,000. The effect of the transaction can be identified and analyzed as follows:

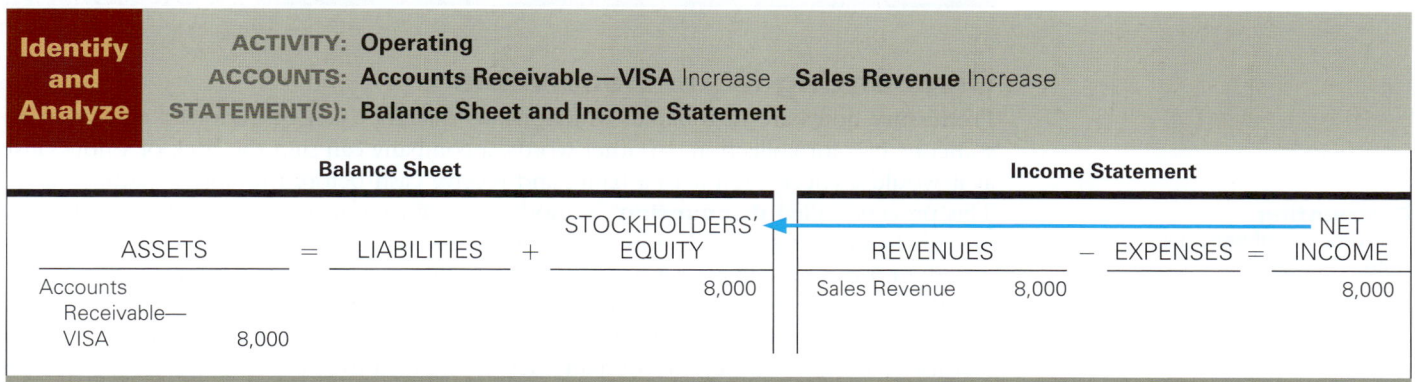

Assume that Apple remits the credit card drafts to VISA once a week and that the total sales for the week ending June 11 amount to $50,000. Further assume that on June 13, VISA pays the amount due to Apple after deducting a 5% collection fee. The effect of the collection can be identified and analyzed as follows:

(Continued)

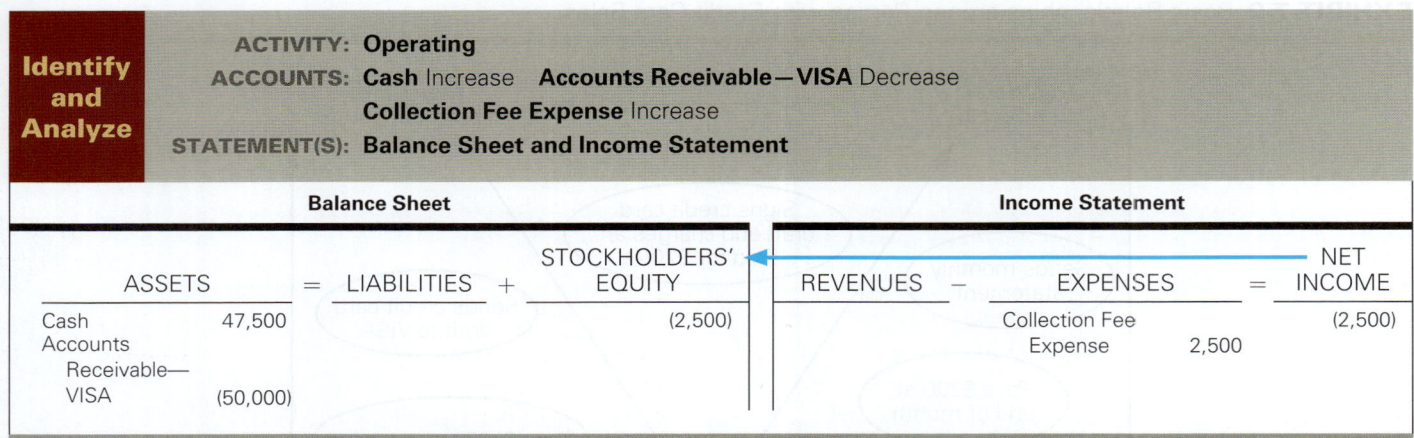

Some credit cards, such as MasterCard and VISA, allow a merchant to present a credit card draft directly for deposit in a bank account, in much the same way the merchant deposits checks, coins, and currency. Obviously, this type of arrangement is even more advantageous for the merchant because the funds are available as soon as the drafts are added to the bank account. Assume that on July 9, Apple presents VISA credit card drafts to its bank for payment in the amount of $20,000 and that the collection charge is 4%. The effect of the collection can be identified and analyzed as follows:

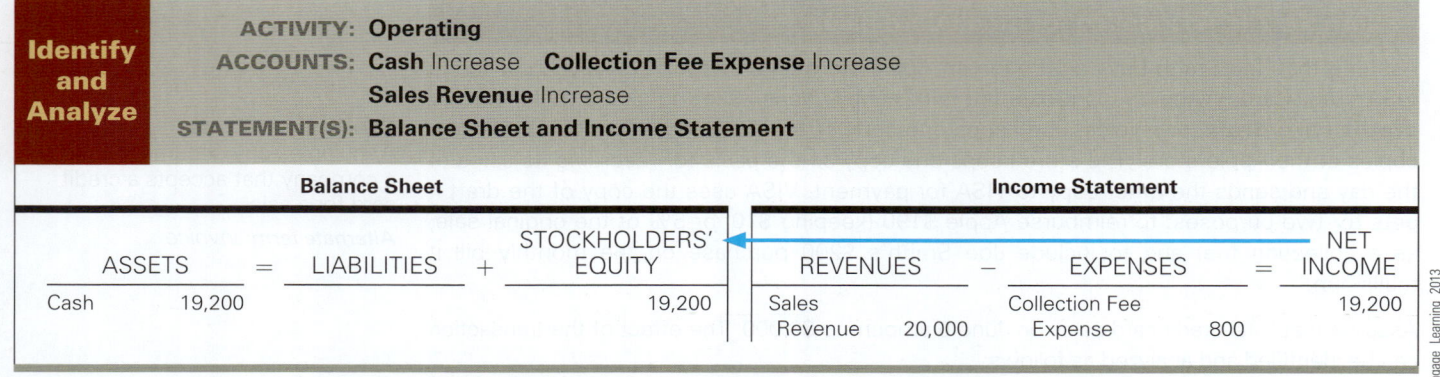

Discounting Notes Receivable

Promissory notes are negotiable, which means that they can be endorsed and given to someone else for collection. In other words, a company can sign the back of a note (just as it would a check), sell it to a bank, and receive cash before the note's maturity date. This process, called **discounting**, is another way for companies to speed the collection of cash from receivables. A note can be sold immediately to a bank on the date it is issued, or it can be sold after it has been outstanding but before the due date.

Discounting
The process of selling a promissory note.

When a note is discounted at a bank, it is normally done "with recourse." This means that if the original customer fails to pay the bank the total amount due on the maturity date of the note, the company that transferred the note to the bank is liable for the full amount. Because there is uncertainty as to whether the company will have to make good on any particular note that it discounts at the bank, a contingent liability exists from the time the note is discounted until its maturity date. The accounting profession has adopted guidelines to decide whether a particular uncertainty requires that the company record a contingent liability on its balance sheet. Under these guidelines, the contingency created by the discounting of a note with recourse is not recorded as a liability. However, a note in the financial statements is used to inform the reader of the existing uncertainty.

© Cengage Learning 2013

LO4 Explain various techniques that companies use to accelerate the inflow of cash from sales.

- To be competitive, companies must make sales on credit to customers.
- One way to avoid bad debts associated with extending credit directly to the customer and to accelerate cash collections from sales is to accept credit cards for payment of goods and services.

POD REVIEW 7.4

QUESTIONS **Answers to these questions are on the last page of the chapter.**

1. Boston makes $20,000 of credit card sales during the week and is charged 5% by the credit card company. Boston will record sales revenue of

   a. $10,000.
   b. $19,000.
   c. $20,000.
   d. none of the above.

2. When a company discounts a promissory note at the bank,

   a. it receives cash later than it would if it held the note to maturity.
   b. it receives cash sooner than it would if it held the note to maturity.
   c. it receives cash at the same time it would if it held the note to maturity.
   d. Discounting is not allowed as a standard practice.

Accounting for Investments

OVERVIEW: Companies invest idle cash in a variety of financial instruments, including CDs, debt securities (bonds), and equity securities (stock). Interest revenue is earned on the first two, and dividend income is earned on equity securities that pay dividends.

LO5 Show that you understand the accounting for and disclosure of various types of investments that companies make.

Companies' investments take a variety of forms and are made for various reasons. Some corporations find themselves with excess cash during certain times of the year and invest this idle cash in various highly liquid financial instruments such as certificates of deposit and money market funds. Chapter 6 pointed out that these investments are included with cash and are called cash equivalents when they have an original maturity to the investor of three months or less. Otherwise, they are accounted for as short-term investments.

In addition to investments in highly liquid financial instruments, some companies invest in the stocks and bonds of other corporations as well as bonds issued by various government agencies. Securities issued by corporations as a form of ownership in the business, such as common stock and preferred stock, are called **equity securities**. Because these securities are a form of ownership, they do not have a maturity date. As we will see later, investments in equity securities can be classified as either current or long term depending on the company's intent. Alternatively, securities issued by corporations and governmental bodies as a form of borrowing are called **debt securities** and often take the form of bonds. The term of a bond can be relatively short, such as five years, or much longer, such as 20 or 30 years. Regardless of the term, classification as a current or noncurrent asset by the investor depends on whether it plans to sell or redeem the debt securities within the next year.

Equity securities
Securities issued by corporations as a form of ownership in the business
Alternate term: Stocks.

Debt securities
Securities issued by corporations and governmental bodies as a form of borrowing.
Alternate term: Bonds.

Investments in Highly Liquid Financial Instruments

We now turn to the appropriate accounting for these various types of investments. We begin by considering the accounting for highly liquid financial instruments such as certificates of deposit and then turn to the accounting for investments in the stocks and bonds of other companies.

Investing Idle Cash The seasonal nature of most businesses leads to a potential cash shortage during certain times of the year and an excess of cash during other times. Companies typically deal with cash shortages by borrowing on a short-term basis either from a bank in the form of notes or from other entities in the form of commercial paper. The maturities of the bank notes or the commercial paper generally range anywhere from 30 days to six months. These same companies use various financial instruments as a way to invest excess cash during other times of the year. We will present the accounting for the most common type of highly liquid financial instrument, a certificate of deposit (CD).

Example 7-10   Accounting for an Investment in a Certificate of Deposit

Assume that on October 2, 2012, Creston Corp. invests $100,000 of excess cash in a 120-day CD. The CD matures on January 30, 2013, at which time Creston receives the $100,000 invested and interest at an annual rate of 6%. The effect of the transaction to record the purchase of the CD can be identified and analyzed as follows:

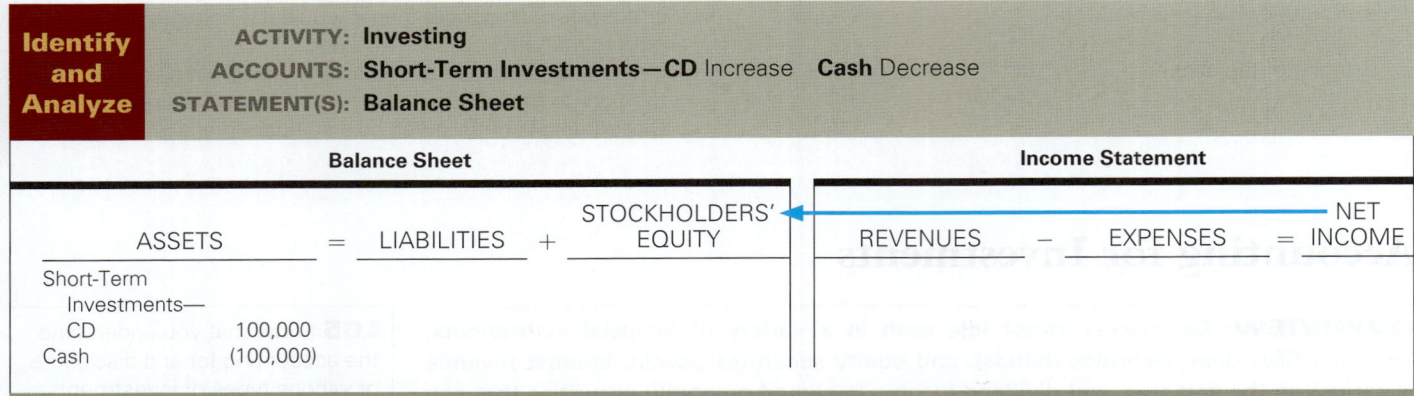

Assuming December 31 is the end of Creston's fiscal year, an adjustment is needed on this date to record interest earned during 2012 even though no cash will be received until the CD matures in 2013. The effect of the adjustment can be identified and analyzed as follows:

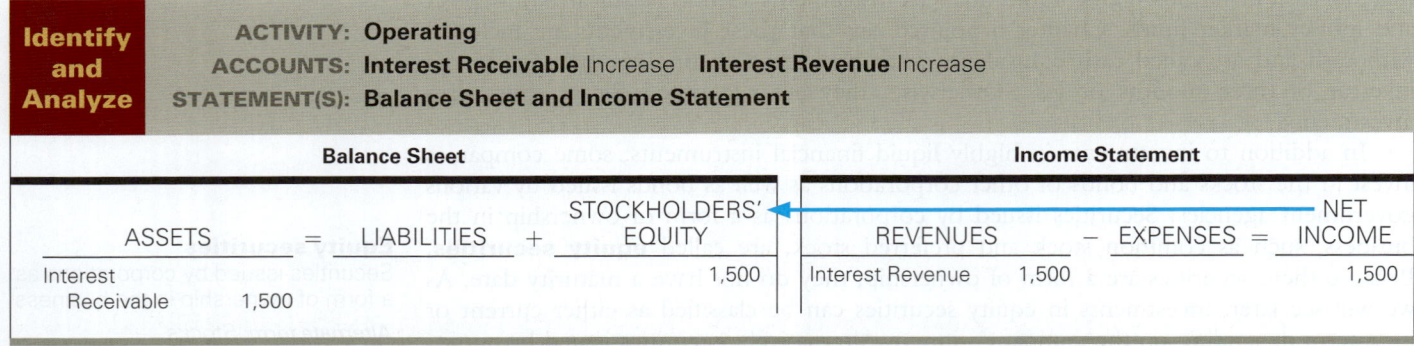

The basic formula to compute interest is as follows:

$$\text{Interest (I)} = \text{Principal (P)} \times \text{Interest Rate (R)} \times \text{Time (T)}$$

Because interest rates are normally stated on an annual basis, time is interpreted to mean the fraction of a year that the investment is outstanding. The amount of interest is based on the principal or amount invested ($100,000) times the rate of interest (6%) times the fraction of a year the CD was outstanding in 2012 (29 days in October + 30 days in November + 31 days in December = 90 days). To simplify interest calculations, it is easiest to assume 360 days in a year. With the availability of computers to do the work, however, most businesses now use 365 days in a year to calculate interest. Throughout this book, we assume 360 days in a year to allow us to focus on concepts rather than detailed calculations. Thus, in this example, the fraction of a year that the CD is outstanding during 2012 is 90/360.

(Continued)

The effect of the receipt of the principal amount of the CD of $100,000 and interest for 120 days can be identified and analyzed as follows:

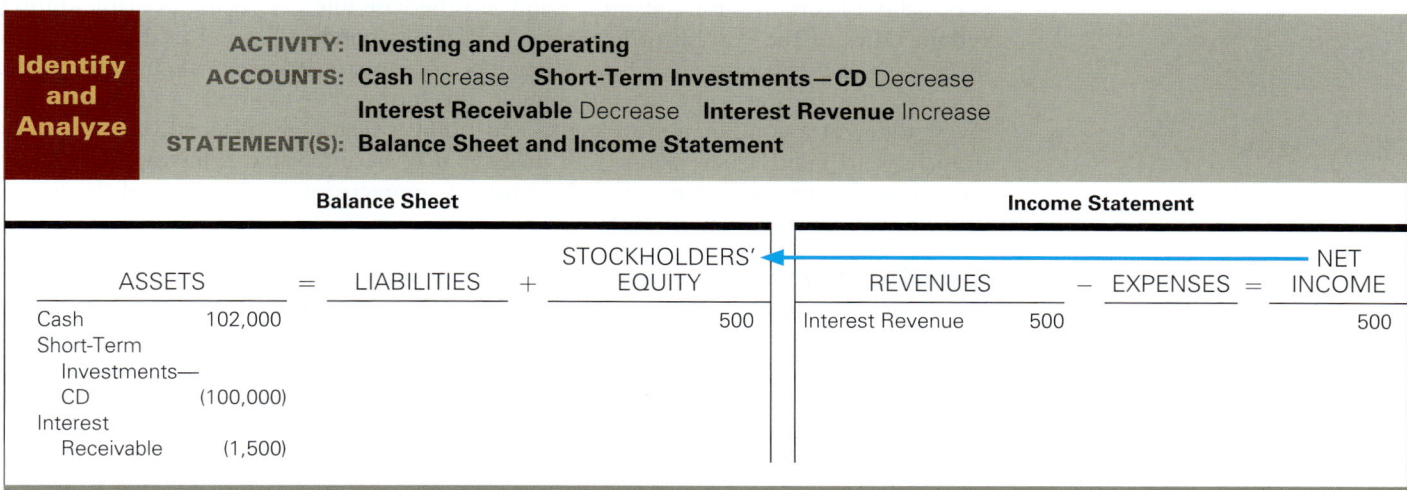

Identify and Analyze	ACTIVITY: **Investing and Operating**
	ACCOUNTS: **Cash** Increase **Short-Term Investments—CD** Decrease
	Interest Receivable Decrease **Interest Revenue** Increase
	STATEMENT(S): **Balance Sheet and Income Statement**

Balance Sheet						Income Statement			
ASSETS	=	LIABILITIES	+	STOCKHOLDERS' EQUITY		REVENUES	−	EXPENSES =	NET INCOME
Cash 102,000				500		Interest Revenue 500			500
Short-Term Investments— CD (100,000)									
Interest Receivable (1,500)									

This results in the removal of both the CD and the interest receivable from the records and recognizes $500 in interest earned during the first 30 days of 2013: $100,000 × 0.06 × 30/360 = $500. Exhibit 7-3 summarizes the calculation of interest in each of the two accounting periods.

Investments in Stocks and Bonds

Corporations frequently invest in the securities of other businesses. As mentioned earlier, these investments take two forms: debt securities (bonds) and equity securities (stocks).

No Significant Influence Corporations have varying motivations for investing. The company that invests is the *investor*, and the company whose stocks or bonds are

EXHIBIT 7-3 Interest Calculation

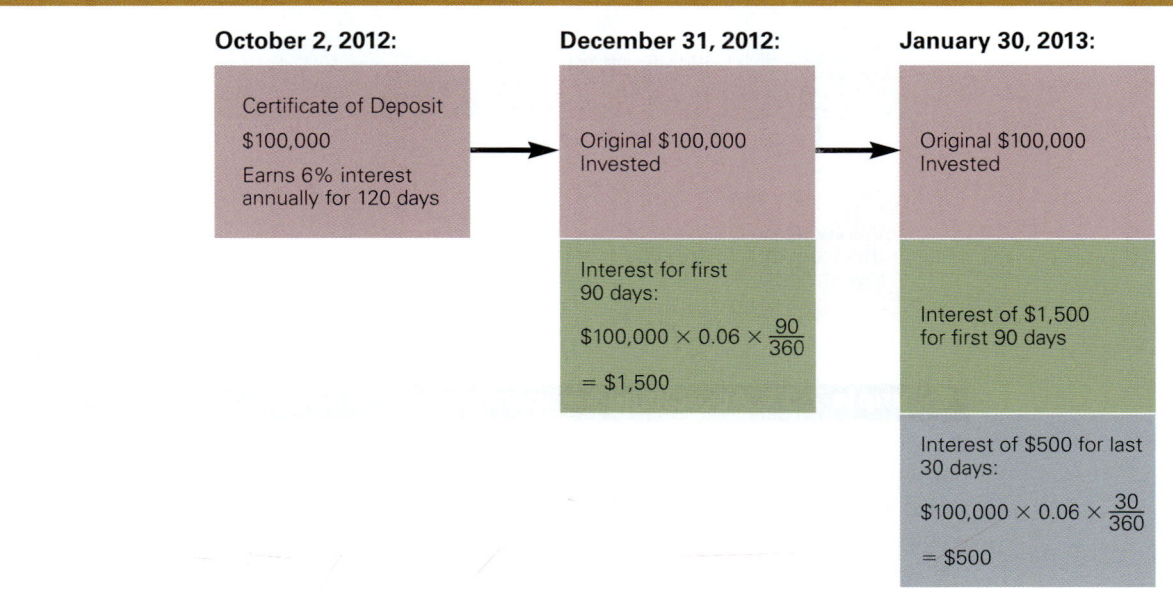

purchased is the *investee*. In addition to buying certificates of deposit and other financial instruments, companies invest excess funds in stocks and bonds over the short run. The seasonality of certain businesses may result in otherwise idle cash being available during certain times of the year. In other cases, stocks and bonds are purchased as a way to invest cash over the long run. Often, these types of investments are made in anticipation of a need for cash at some distant point in the future. For example, a company may invest today in a combination of stocks and bonds because it will need cash ten years from now to build a new plant. The investor may be interested primarily in periodic income in the form of interest and dividends, in appreciation in the value of the securities, or in some combination of the two.

Significant Influence Sometimes shares of stock in another company are bought for a different purpose. If a company buys a relatively large percentage of the common stock of the investee, it may be able to secure significant influence over this company's policies. For example, a company might buy 30% of the common stock of a supplier of its raw materials to ensure a steady source of inventory. When an investor is able to secure influence over the investee, the equity method of accounting is used. According to current accounting standards, this method is appropriate when an investor owns at least 20% of the common stock of the investee.

Control Finally, a corporation may buy stock in another company with the purpose of obtaining control over that other entity. Normally, this requires an investment in excess of 50% of the common stock of the investee. When an investor owns more than half the stock of another company, accountants normally prepare a set of consolidated financial statements. This involves combining the financial statements of the individual entities into a single set of statements. An investor with an interest of more than 50% in another company is called the *parent*, and the investee in these situations is called the *subsidiary*.

The remainder of this section will discuss how companies account for investments that do not give them any significant influence over the other company. (Accounting for investments in which there is either significant influence or control is covered in advanced accounting textbooks.) The following chart summarizes the accounting by an investor for investments in the common stock of another company:

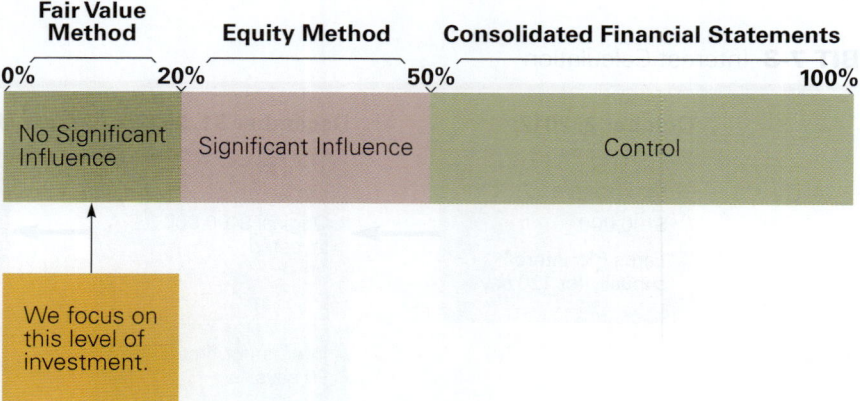

Example 7-11 Accounting for an Investment in Bonds

On January 1, 2012, ABC issues $10,000,000 of bonds that will mature in ten years. Assume that Atlantic buys $100,000 of these bonds at face value, which is the amount that will be repaid to the investor when the bonds mature. In many instances, bonds are purchased at an amount more or less than face value. However, the discussion here will be limited to the simpler case in which bonds are purchased for face value. The bonds pay 10% interest

(Continued)

semiannually on June 30 and December 31. Atlantic will receive 5% of $100,000, or $5,000, on each of those dates. The transaction on Atlantic's books to record the purchase can be identified and analyzed as follows:

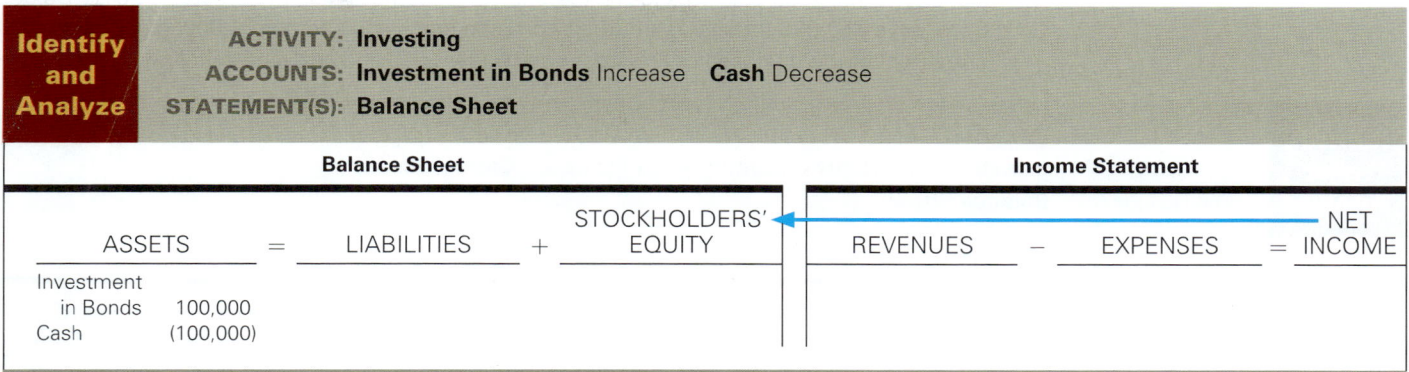

On June 30, Atlantic must record the receipt of semiannual interest. The transaction on this date can be identified and analyzed follows:

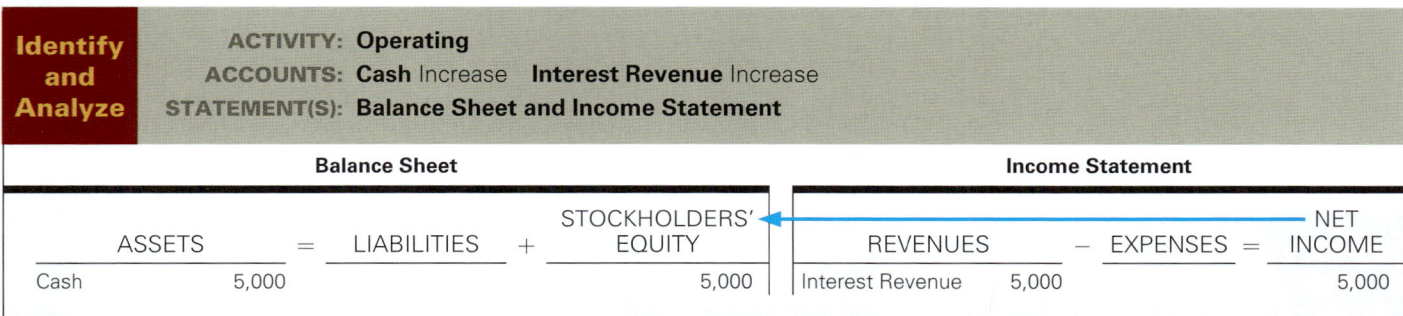

Note that income was recognized when interest was received. If interest is not received at the end of an accounting period, a company should accrue interest earned but not yet received.

Assume that before the maturity date, Atlantic needs cash and decides to sell the bonds. Any difference between the proceeds received from the sale of the bonds and the amount paid for the bonds is recognized as either a gain or a loss. On July 1, 2012, Atlantic sells all of its ABC bonds at 99. The amount of cash received is 0.99 × $100,000, or $99,000. The effect of the sale of the bonds can be identified and analyzed as follows:

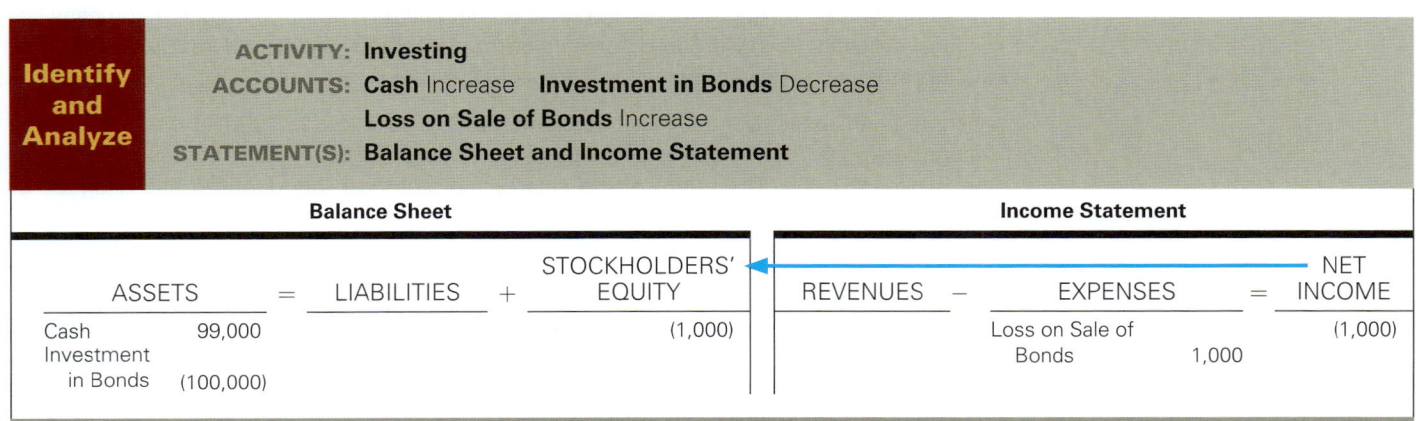

The $1,000 loss on the sale of the bonds is the excess of the amount paid for the purchase of the bonds of $100,000 over the cash proceeds from the sale of $99,000. The loss is reported in the Other Income and Expenses section on the 2012 income statement.

Example 7-12 Accounting for an Investment in Stock

All investments in stock are recorded initially at cost, including any brokerage fees, commissions, or other fees paid to acquire the shares. Assume that on February 1, 2012, Dexter Corp. pays $50,000 for shares of Stuart common stock and another $1,000 in commissions. The effect of the purchase of the stock can be identified and analyzed as follows:

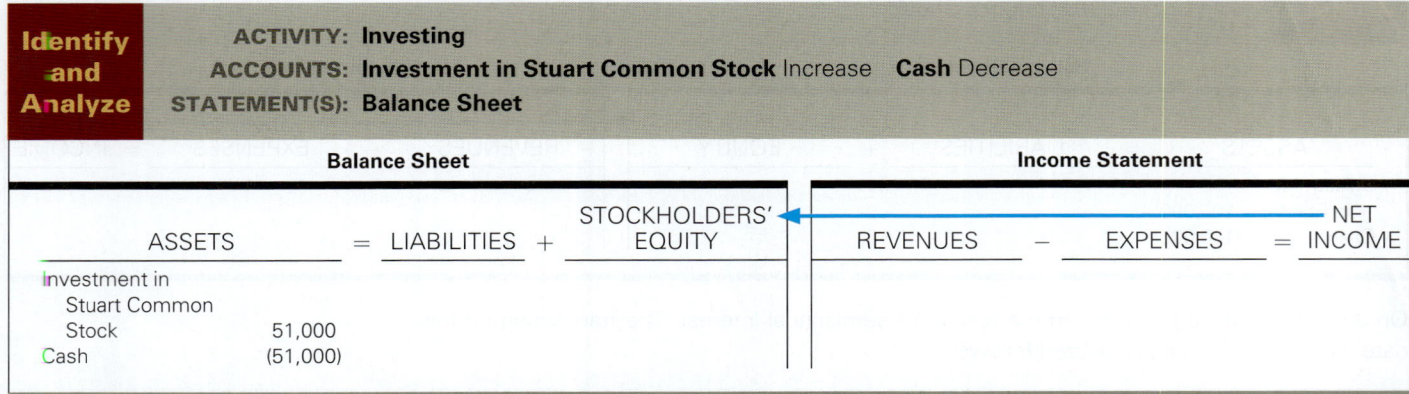

Identify and Analyze

ACTIVITY: **Investing**
ACCOUNTS: **Investment in Stuart Common Stock** Increase **Cash** Decrease
STATEMENT(S): **Balance Sheet**

Balance Sheet				Income Statement			
ASSETS	=	LIABILITIES +	STOCKHOLDERS' EQUITY	REVENUES	−	EXPENSES	= NET INCOME
Investment in Stuart Common Stock 51,000							
Cash (51,000)							

Many companies attempt to pay dividends every year as a signal of overall financial strength and profitability.[1] Assume that on March 31, 2012, Dexter received dividends of $500 from Stuart. The dividends received are recognized as income in a transaction that can be identified and analyzed as follows:

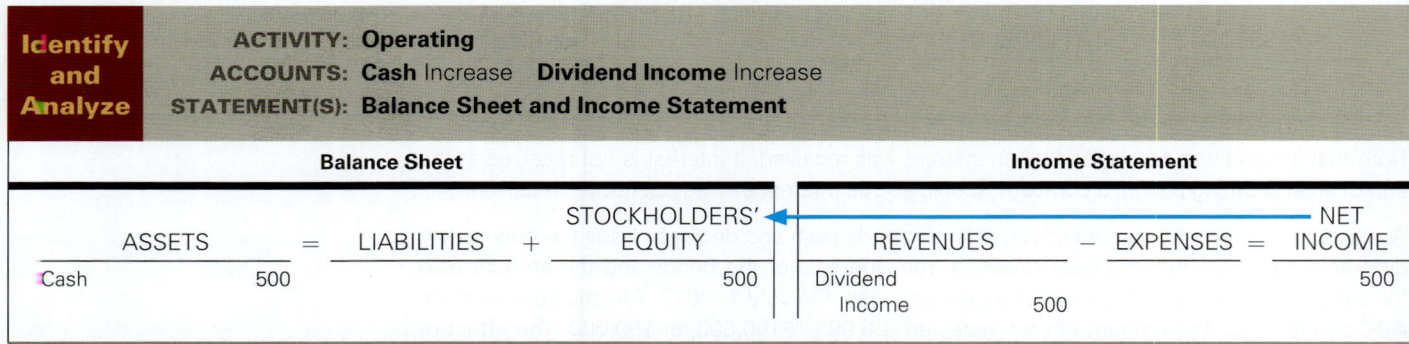

Identify and Analyze

ACTIVITY: **Operating**
ACCOUNTS: **Cash** Increase **Dividend Income** Increase
STATEMENT(S): **Balance Sheet and Income Statement**

Balance Sheet				Income Statement			
ASSETS	=	LIABILITIES +	STOCKHOLDERS' EQUITY	REVENUES	−	EXPENSES =	NET INCOME
Cash 500			500	Dividend Income 500			500

Unlike interest on a bond or note, dividends do not accrue over time. In fact, a company has no legal obligation to pay dividends until its board of directors declares them. Up to that point, the investor has no guarantee that dividends will ever be paid.

Assume that Dexter sells the Stuart stock on May 20, 2012, for $53,000. In this case, Dexter recognizes a gain for the excess of the cash proceeds, $53,000, over the amount recorded on the books, $51,000. The effect of the sale of the stock can be identified and analyzed as follows:

(Continued)

---

[1] IBM's September 2011 dividend continued a string of consecutive quarterly dividends that started in 1916.

Identify and Analyze	**ACTIVITY:** Investing
	ACCOUNTS: **Cash** Increase **Investment in Stuart Common Stock** Decrease
	Gain on Sale of Stock Increase
	STATEMENT(S): Balance Sheet and Income Statement

Balance Sheet			Income Statement		
ASSETS	= LIABILITIES +	STOCKHOLDERS' EQUITY	REVENUES	− EXPENSES =	NET INCOME
Cash 53,000		2,000	Gain on Sale of Stock 2,000		2,000
Investment in Stuart Common Stock (51,000)					

The gain is classified on the income statement as other income.

Valuation and Reporting for Investments on the Financial Statements

Investments in other companies' bonds and stocks are reported on a company's balance sheet as assets. Whether the investments are reported as current assets or noncurrent assets depends on the company's intent. If the company intends to sell the investments within the next year, they are normally classified as current assets. All other investments are classified on the balance sheet as noncurrent.

In addition to the question of where investments are reported at the end of the period, another issue is their valuation. For example, you know that accounts receivable are reported at net realizable value. How should an investment in the bonds or stock of another company be reported on a year-end balance sheet? Investments could be reported at their cost, or because most investments in other companies' bonds and stocks are actively traded, they could be reported at their market, or fair, value. Investments are generally reported on the balance sheet at their fair value. However, the question still remains as to when any gains or losses from recognizing the changes in the fair value of investments should be recorded on the income statement. The accounting rules in this area are somewhat complex and thus are usually covered in advanced accounting courses.

LO5 Show that you understand the accounting for and disclosure of various types of investments that companies make.

- Typically, excess cash expected to last for short periods of time is invested in highly liquid financial instruments such as CDs.
- Sometimes cash is invested in securities of other corporations:
  - Equity securities—securities issued by corporations as a form of ownership in the business.
  - Debt securities—securities issued by corporations as a form of borrowing.
- At times, a company may want to purchase a relatively large portion of another firm's stock to acquire influence over that firm.

POD REVIEW 7.5

QUESTIONS **Answers to these questions are on the last page of the chapter.**

1. A company invests excess cash in a certificate of deposit. At the end of an accounting period before the CD matures, the company will recognize

   a. interest expense.
   b. interest revenue.
   c. the receipt of cash.
   d. none of the above.

2. Baxter pays $15,000 to buy stock in another company and an additional $400 in commissions. Three months later, Baxter sells the stock for $16,000. At the time of sale, Baxter will recognize a

   a. gain of $1,000.
   b. loss of $1,000.
   c. gain of $600.
   d. loss of $600.

How Liquid Assets Affect the Statement of Cash Flows

LO6 Explain the effects of transactions involving liquid assets on the statement of cash flows.

OVERVIEW: Changes in accounts and notes receivable are reported in the Operating Activities section of a statement of cash flows prepared using the indirect method. An increase in either is deducted, and a decrease is added back. Purchases of investments are cash outflows and sales and maturities are cash inflows in the Investing Activities section of the statement.

As was discussed in Chapter 6, cash equivalents are combined with cash on the balance sheet. These items are very near maturity and do not present any significant risk of collectibility. Because of this, any purchases or redemptions of cash equivalents are not considered significant activities to be reported on a statement of cash flows.

The purchase and sale of investments are considered significant activities and therefore are reported on the statement of cash flows. Cash flows from purchases, sales, and maturities of investments are usually classified as investing activities. The following excerpt from Apple's 2010 statement of cash flows illustrates the reporting for these activities (all amounts in millions of dollars):

Investing Activities	2010	2009	2008
Purchases of marketable securities	$(57,793)	$(46,724)	$(22,965)
Proceeds from maturities of marketable securities	24,930	19,790	11,804
Proceeds from sales of marketable securities	21,788	10,888	4,439
Purchases of other long-term investments	(18)	(101)	(38)

The collection of either accounts receivable or notes receivable generates cash for a business and affects the Operating Activities section of the statement of cash flows. Most companies use the indirect method of reporting cash flows and begin the statement of cash flows with the net income of the period. Net income includes the sales revenue for the period. Therefore, a decrease in accounts receivable or notes receivable during the period indicates that the company collected more cash than it recorded in sales revenue. Thus, a decrease in accounts receivable or notes receivable must be added back to net income because more cash was collected than is reflected in the sales revenue number. Alternatively, an increase in accounts receivable or notes receivable indicates that the company recorded more sales revenue than cash collected during the period. Therefore, an increase in accounts receivable or notes receivable requires deduction from the net income of the period to arrive at cash flow from operating activities. The following excerpt from Apple's 2010 statement of cash flows illustrates how it reports the change in accounts receivable on its statement of cash flows (all amounts in millions of dollars):

Operating Activities	2010	2009	2008
Changes in operating assets and liabilities:			
Accounts receivable, net	$(2,142)	$(939)	$(785)

These adjustments as well as the cash flows from buying and selling investments are summarized in Exhibit 7-4. A complete discussion of the statement of cash flows, including the reporting of investments, will be presented in Chapter 12.

EXHIBIT 7-4 How Investments and Receivables Affect the Statement of Cash Flows

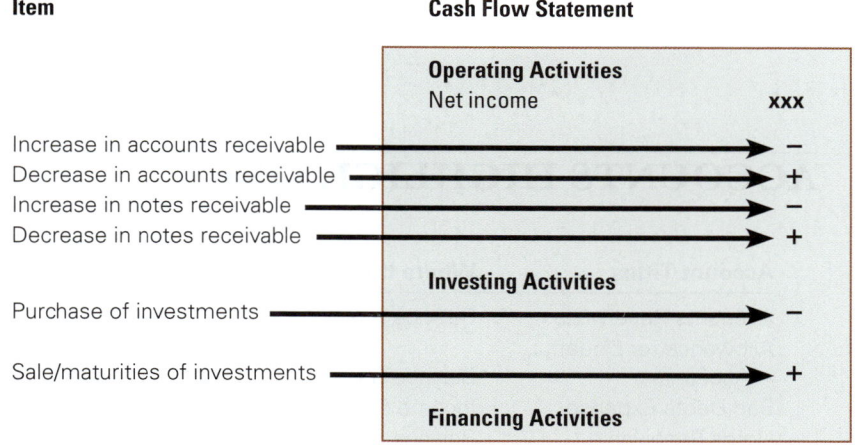

The FASB and the IASB have a joint project underway to consider how financial statements could be constructed to be more useful. The project focuses specifically on the organization and presentation of information in the financial statements. As one of the primary financial statements, the statement of cash flows could look significantly different in the future. Most importantly, companies would be required to use the direct method in the Operating Activities section of the statement of cash flows. Under this approach, the cash receipts from customers during the period would be reported in the Operating Activities section of the statement. A vast majority of companies now use the indirect method. As illustrated in the preceding section, the indirect method requires adjustments to be made to net income for the changes in accounts and notes receivable during the period.

The joint project of the two standard-setting bodies is still in development. At present, no date has been set for when a new layout of the financial statements would take effect. Until then, most companies will likely continue to use the indirect method to present cash flows from operating activities.

LOOKING AHEAD

Tetra Images/Getty Images

LO6 Explain the effects of transactions involving liquid assets on the statement of cash flows.

- Changes in cash equivalents are not shown on the statement.
- Cash flows related to the purchase and sale of investments are classified as Investing Activities in the statement of cash flows.
- Under the indirect method, increases in accounts and notes receivable are deducted and decreases in these accounts are added back in the Operating Activities section of the statement.

POD REVIEW 7.6

QUESTIONS   Answers to these questions are on the last page of the chapter.

1. How should an increase in accounts receivable be reported on the statement of cash flows using the indirect method?
   a. as an addition
   b. as a deduction
   c. It depends on the amount of the increase.
   d. Changes in accounts receivable balances are not reported on the statement of cash flows.

2. How should a decrease in notes receivable be reported on the statement of cash flows using the indirect method?
   a. as an addition
   b. as a deduction
   c. It depends on the amount of the increase.
   d. Changes in notes receivable balances are not reported on the statement of cash flows.

RATIO REVIEW

$$\text{Accounts Receivable Turnover} = \frac{\text{Net Credit Sales (Income Statement)}}{\text{Average Accounts Receivable (Balance Sheet)}}$$

ACCOUNTS HIGHLIGHTED

Account Titles	Where It Appears	In What Section	Page Number
Accounts Receivable	Balance Sheet	Current Assets	332
Allowance for Doubtful Accounts	Balance Sheet	Current Assets	336
Bad Debts Expense	Income Statement	Operating Expenses	336
Notes Receivable	Balance Sheet	Current or Noncurrent Assets	344
Interest Receivable	Balance Sheet	Current Assets	345
Interest Revenue	Income Statement	Other Income	345
Short-Term Investments	Balance Sheet	Current Assets	350

KEY TERMS QUIZ

Read each definition below and write the number of the definition in the blank beside the appropriate term. The quiz solutions appear at the end of the chapter.

_____ Account receivable	_____ Note payable
_____ Subsidiary ledger	_____ Principal
_____ Control account	_____ Maturity date
_____ Direct write-off method	_____ Term
_____ Allowance method	_____ Maturity value
_____ Allowance for doubtful accounts	_____ Interest
_____ Aging schedule	_____ Credit card draft
_____ Promissory note	_____ Discounting
_____ Maker	_____ Equity securities
_____ Payee	_____ Debt securities
_____ Note receivable	

1. Securities issued by corporations as a form of ownership in the business.
2. Securities issued by corporations and governmental bodies as a form of borrowing.
3. A method of estimating bad debts on the basis of either the net credit sales of the period or the accounts receivable at the end of the period.
4. The party that will receive the money from a promissory note at some future date.
5. A written promise to repay a definite sum of money on demand or at a fixed or determinable date in the future.
6. A liability resulting from the signing of a promissory note.
7. A multiple-copy document used by a company that accepts a credit card for a sale.
8. An asset resulting from the acceptance of a promissory note from another company.
9. The process of selling a promissory note.
10. The party that agrees to repay the money for a promissory note at some future date.
11. A form used to categorize the various individual accounts receivable according to the length of time each has been outstanding.

12. The detail for a number of individual items that collectively make up a single general ledger account.
13. The recognition of bad debts expense at the point an account is written off as uncollectible.
14. The general ledger account that is supported by a subsidiary ledger.
15. The difference between the principal amount of the note and its maturity value.
16. The amount of cash received, or the fair value of the products or services received, by the maker when a promissory note is issued.
17. The amount of cash the maker is to pay the payee on the maturity date of the note.
18. The length of time a note is outstanding, that is, the period of time between the date it is issued and the date it matures.
19. The date the promissory note is due.
20. A contra-asset account used to reduce accounts receivable to its net realizable value.
21. A receivable arising from the sale of goods or services with a verbal promise to pay.

ALTERNATE TERMS

allowance for doubtful accounts allowance for uncollectible accounts

credit card draft invoice

debt securities bonds

equity securities stocks

net realizable value net recoverable amount

WARMUP EXERCISES & SOLUTIONS

Warmup Exercise 7-1 Accounting for Bad Debts   LO1

Brown Corp. ended the year with balances in Accounts Receivable of $60,000 and in Allowance for Doubtful Accounts of $800 (balance before adjustment). Net sales for the year amounted to $200,000. Identify and analyze the effect of the adjustment at the end of the year assuming the following:

1. Estimated percentage of net sales uncollectible is 1%.
2. Estimated percentage of year-end accounts receivable uncollectible is 4%.

Key to the Solution Recall that the percentage of net credit sales approach does not take into account any existing balance in the allowance account, but the percentage of accounts receivables approach does.

Warmup Exercise 7-2 Investments   LO5

Indicate whether each of the following events will result in an increase (I), will result in a decrease (D), or will have no effect (NE) on net income for the period.

1. Stock held as an investment is sold for more than its carrying value.
2. An interest check is received for bonds held as an investment.
3. Stock held as an investment is sold for less than its carrying value.
4. Bonds held as an investment are redeemed on their maturity date at face value.
5. Stock is purchased and a commission is paid to a broker.

Key to the Solution Recall from earlier in the chapter the accounting for the various types of investments.

Solutions to Warmup Exercises

Warmup Exercise 7-1

1.

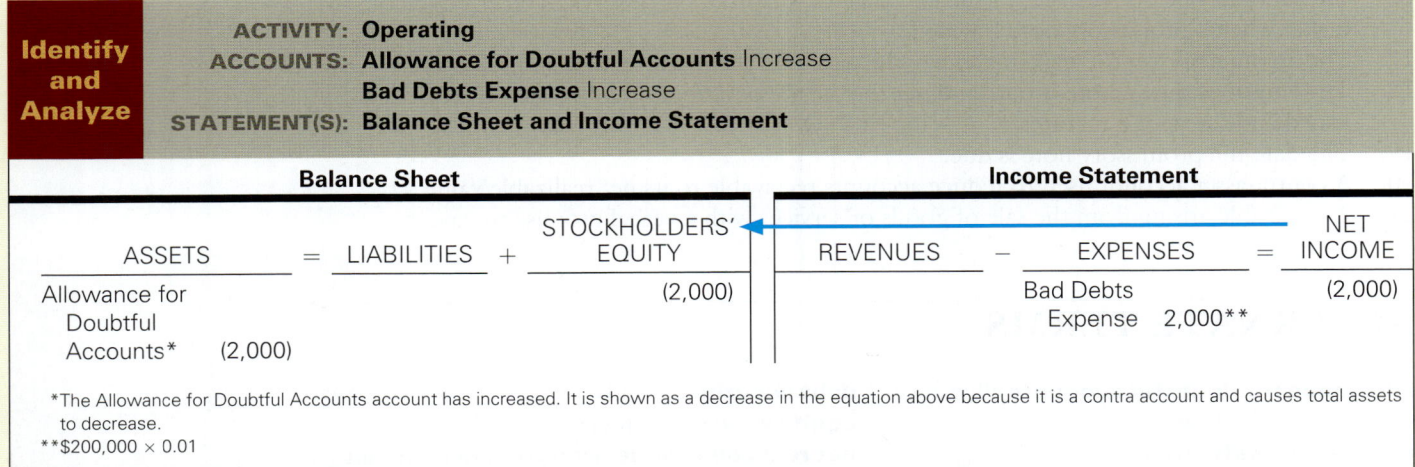

2.

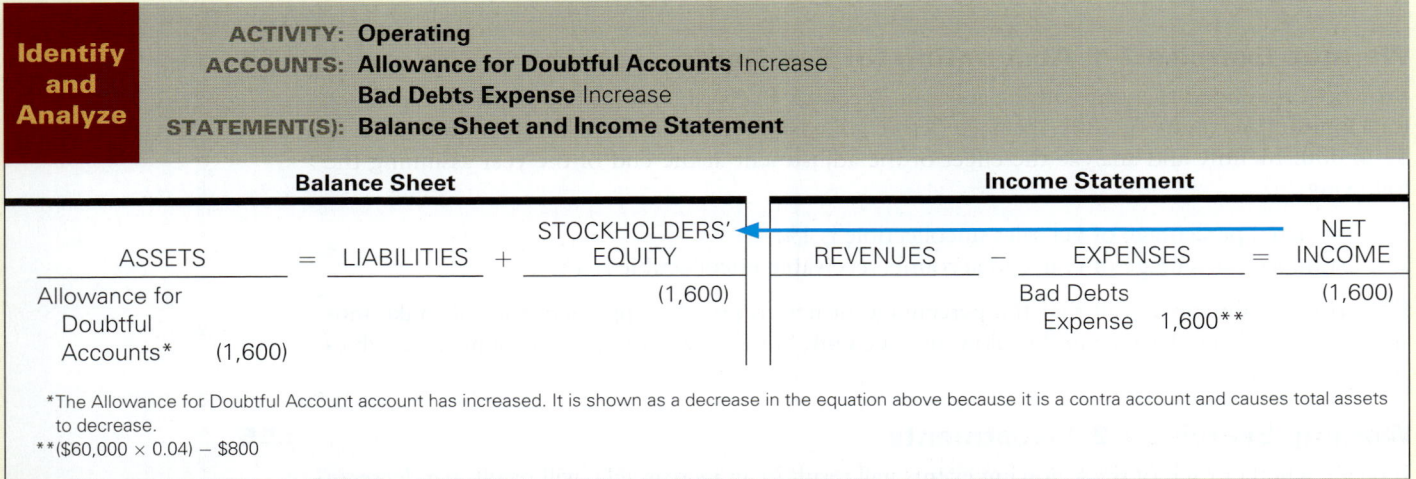

Warmup Exercise 7-2

1. I   2. I   3. D   4. NE   5. NE

REVIEW PROBLEM & SOLUTION

The following items pertain to the Current Assets section of the balance sheet for Jackson Corp. at the end of its accounting year, December 31, 2012. Each item must be considered and any necessary adjustment recognized. Additionally, the accountant for Jackson wants to develop the Current Assets section of the balance sheet as of the end of 2012.

a. Cash and cash equivalents amount to $19,375.

b. A 9%, 120-day certificate of deposit was purchased on December 1, 2012, for $10,000.

c. Gross accounts receivable at December 31, 2012, amount to $44,000. Before adjustment, the balance in Allowance for Doubtful Accounts is $340. Based on past experience, the accountant estimates that 3% of the gross accounts receivable outstanding at December 31, 2012, will prove to be uncollectible.

d. A customer's 12%, 90-day promissory note in the amount of $6,000 is held at the end of the year. The note has been held for 45 days during 2012.

Required

1. Identify and analyze the adjustments needed in (b), (c), and (d).
2. Prepare the Current Assets section of Jackson's balance sheet as of December 31, 2012. In addition to the information in the preceding items, the balances in Inventory and Prepaid Insurance on this date are $65,000 and $4,800, respectively.

Solution to Review Problem

1. The following adjustments are needed at December 31, 2012:

   b. Jackson needs an adjustment to record interest earned on the certificate of deposit at Second State Bank. The CD has been outstanding for 30 days during 2012; therefore, the amount of interest earned is calculated as follows:

   $$\$10,000 \times 0.09 \times 30/360 = \$75$$

   The adjustment can be identified and analyzed as follows:

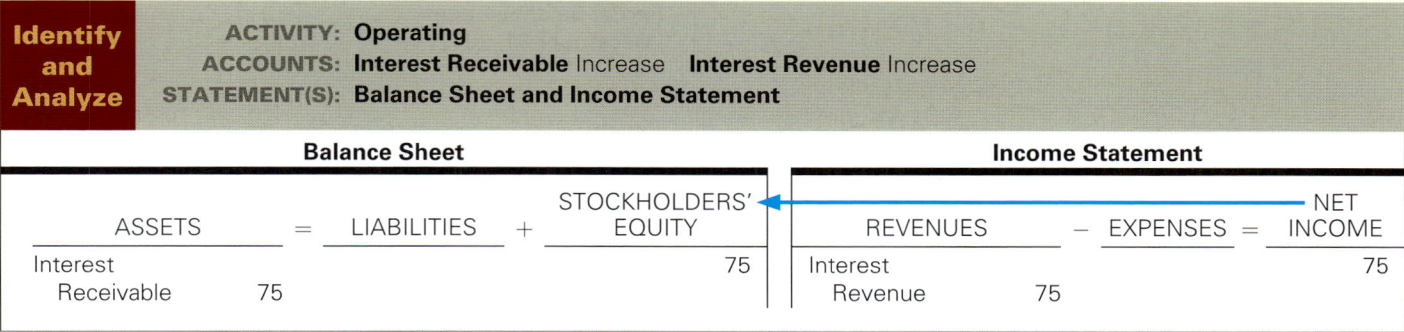

Identify and Analyze	**ACTIVITY: Operating**
	ACCOUNTS: Interest Receivable Increase **Interest Revenue** Increase
	STATEMENT(S): Balance Sheet and Income Statement

Balance Sheet				**Income Statement**			
ASSETS	=	LIABILITIES	+	STOCKHOLDERS' EQUITY	REVENUES	− EXPENSES =	NET INCOME
Interest Receivable 75				75	Interest Revenue 75		75

   c. Based on gross accounts receivable of $44,000 at year-end and an estimate that 3% of this amount will be uncollectible, the balance in Allowance for Doubtful Accounts should be $1,320 ($44,000 × 3%). Given a current balance of $340, an adjustment for $980 ($1,320 − $340) is needed to bring the balance to the desired amount of $1,320. The adjustment can be identified and analyzed as follows:

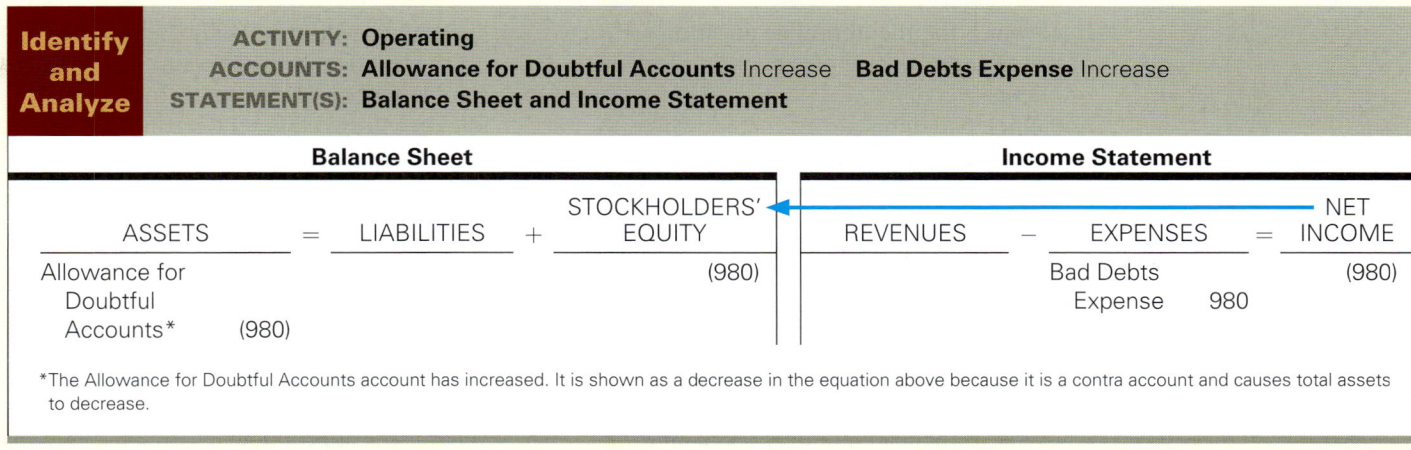

Identify and Analyze	**ACTIVITY: Operating**
	ACCOUNTS: Allowance for Doubtful Accounts Increase **Bad Debts Expense** Increase
	STATEMENT(S): Balance Sheet and Income Statement

Balance Sheet				**Income Statement**			
ASSETS	=	LIABILITIES	+	STOCKHOLDERS' EQUITY	REVENUES	− EXPENSES =	NET INCOME
Allowance for Doubtful Accounts* (980)				(980)		Bad Debts Expense 980	(980)

*The Allowance for Doubtful Accounts account has increased. It is shown as a decrease in the equation above because it is a contra account and causes total assets to decrease.

(Continued)

d. An adjustment is needed to accrue interest on the promissory note ($6,000 × 0.12 × 45/360 = $90). The effect of the adjustment can be identified and analyzed as follows:

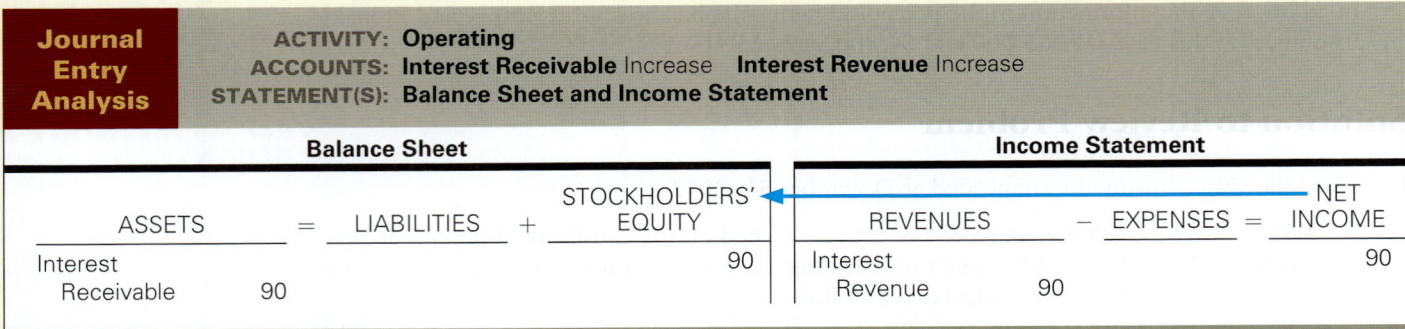

Journal Entry Analysis	ACTIVITY: **Operating**
	ACCOUNTS: **Interest Receivable** Increase **Interest Revenue** Increase
	STATEMENT(S): **Balance Sheet and Income Statement**

Balance Sheet

ASSETS	=	LIABILITIES	+	STOCKHOLDERS' EQUITY
Interest Receivable 90				90

Income Statement

REVENUES	−	EXPENSES	=	NET INCOME
Interest Revenue 90				90

2. The Current Assets section of Jackson's balance sheet appears as follows:

Jackson Corp.
Partial Balance Sheet
December 31, 2012

Current assets:		
Cash and cash equivalents		$ 19,375
Certificate of deposit		10,000
Accounts receivable	$44,000	
Less: Allowance for doubtful accounts	1,320	42,680
Notes receivable		6,000
Interest receivable		165*
Inventory		65,000
Prepaid insurance		4,800
Total current assets		$148,020

*$75 from CD and $90 from promissory note.

QUESTIONS

1. What is the theoretical justification for the allowance method of accounting for bad debts?

2. When bad debts are estimated, why is the balance in Allowance for Doubtful Accounts considered when the percentage of accounts receivable approach is used but not when the percentage of net credit sales approach is used?

3. When estimating bad debts on the basis of a percentage of accounts receivable, what is the advantage of using an aging schedule?

4. What is the distinction between an account receivable and a note receivable?

5. Why does the discounting of a note receivable with recourse result in a contingent

liability? Should the liability be reported on the balance sheet? Explain.

6. On December 31, Stockton Inc. invests idle cash in two different certificates of deposit. The first is an 8%, 90-day CD, and the second has an interest rate of 9% and matures in 120 days. How is each of these CDs classified on the December 31 balance sheet?

7. Stanzel Corp. purchased 1,000 shares of **IBM** common stock. What will determine whether the shares are classified as current assets or noncurrent assets?

8. What is the appropriate treatment of any fees or commissions paid to purchase stock in another company?

BRIEF EXERCISES

Brief Exercise 7-1 Accounting for Bad Debts

Badger recorded $500,000 of net sales for the year of which 2% is estimated to be uncollectible. Identify and analyze the adjustment required at the end of the year to record bad debts.

LO1
EXAMPLE 7-2

Brief Exercise 7-2 Accounts Receivable Turnover

Hawkeye recorded sales of $240,000 for the year. Accounts receivable amounted to $40,000 at the beginning of the year and $20,000 at the end of the year. Compute the company's accounts receivable turnover for the year.

LO2
EXAMPLE 7-7

Brief Exercise 7-3 Accounting for Notes Receivable

On November 1, 2012, Gopher received a $50,000, 6%, 90-day promissory note. Identify and analyze the adjustment required on December 31, the end of the company's fiscal year.

LO3
EXAMPLE 7-8

Brief Exercise 7-4 Accounting for Credit Card Sales

On July 20, Wolverine presents credit card drafts to its bank in the amount of $10,000; the collection charge is 4%. Identify and analyze the transaction on Wolverine's books on July 20, the date of deposit.

LO4
EXAMPLE 7-9

Brief Exercise 7-5 Accounting for Sale of Stock

On March 5, Spartan sold stock in another company for $12,300. Spartan bought the stock on February 14 for $10,100. Identify and analyze the transaction on Spartan's books on March 5.

LO5
EXAMPLE 7-12

Brief Exercise 7-6 Accounts Receivable on the Statement of Cash Flows

Wildcat started the year with $25,000 in accounts receivable and ended the year with $40,000 in the account. Describe how information regarding the company's accounts receivable should be reflected on its statement of cash flows, assuming use of the indirect method.

LO6

EXERCISES

Exercise 7-1 Using an Aging Schedule to Account for Bad Debts

Carter Company sells on credit with terms of n/30. For the $500,000 of accounts at the end of the year that are not overdue, there is a 90% probability of collection. For the $200,000 of accounts that are less than a month past due, Carter estimates the likelihood of collection going down to 70%. The probability of collecting the $100,000 of accounts more than a month past due is estimated to be 25%.

LO1
EXAMPLE 7-6

Required

1. Prepare an aging schedule to estimate the amount of uncollectible accounts.
2. On the basis of the schedule in part (1), identify and analyze the adjustment needed to estimate bad debts. Assume that the balance in Allowance for Doubtful Accounts is $20,000.

Exercise 7-2 Working Backward: Allowance for Doubtful Accounts

Olson Corp. reported the following in the Current Assets section of its December 31, 2012, balance sheet:

LO1
EXAMPLE 7-2, 7-3

	12/31/12	12/31/11
Accounts receivable, net of allowances of $5,000 and $3,000, respectively	$54,000	$48,000

During 2012, Olson recorded $80,000 of sales on credit and wrote off $4,000 of uncollectible accounts.

(Continued)

Required

1. Determine the amount of cash collected during 2012 from sales on credit.
2. Determine the amount of bad debts expense for 2012.

LO1
EXAMPLE 7-2, 7-4, 7-5

Exercise 7-3 Allowance Method of Accounting for Bad Debts—Comparison of the Two Approaches

Kandel Company had the following data available for 2012 (before making any adjustments):

Accounts receivable, 12/31/12	$320,100
Allowance for doubtful accounts	2,600
Net credit sales, 2012	834,000

Required

1. Identify and analyze the adjustment to recognize bad debts under the following assumptions: (a) bad debts expense is expected to be 2% of net credit sales for the year and (b) Kandel expects it will not be able to collect 6% of the balance in accounts receivable at year-end.
2. Assume instead that the balance in the allowance account is a negative $2,600. How will this affect your answers to part (1)?

LO1
EXAMPLE 7-1, 7-3, 7-4

Exercise 7-4 Comparison of the Direct Write-Off and Allowance Methods of Accounting for Bad Debts

In its first year of business, Rideaway Bikes has net income of $145,000, exclusive of any adjustment for bad debts expense. The president of the company has asked you to calculate net income under each of two alternatives of accounting for bad debts: the direct write-off method and the allowance method. The president would like to use the method that will result in the higher net income. So far, no adjustments have been made to write off uncollectible accounts or to estimate bad debts. The relevant data are as follows:

Write-offs of uncollectible accounts during the year	$ 10,500
Net credit sales	$650,000
Estimated percentage of net credit sales that will be uncollectible	2%

Required

Compute net income under each of the two alternatives. Does Rideaway have a choice as to which method to use? If so, should it base its choice on which method will result in the higher net income? (Ignore income taxes.) Explain.

LO2
EXAMPLE 7-7

Exercise 7-5 Working Backward: Accounts Receivable Turnover

It takes Carlson Corp. 30 days on average to collect its accounts receivable. The company began the year with $10,500 in accounts receivable. Sales on credit for the year amounted to $150,000.

Required

Assuming 360 days in a year, determine the amount of Carlson's accounts receivable at the end of the year.

LO2
EXAMPLE 7-7

Exercise 7-6 Accounts Receivable Turnover for General Mills

The 2010 annual report of **General Mills** (the maker of Cheerios® and Wheaties®) reported the following amounts (in millions of dollars):

Net sales, for the year ended May 30, 2010	$14,796.5
Receivables, May 30, 2010	1,041.6
Receivables, May 31, 2009	953.4

Required

1. Compute General Mills's accounts receivable turnover ratio for the year ended May 30, 2010. (Assume that all sales are on credit.)
2. What is the average collection period in days for an account receivable? Explain your answer.

3. Give some examples of the types of customers you would expect General Mills to have. Do you think the average collection period for sales to these customers is reasonable? What other information do you need to fully answer that question?

Exercise 7-7 Working Backward: Notes Receivable

LO3
EXAMPLE 7-8

On December 1, 2012, Roper Corp. accepted a two-month, $24,000 interest-bearing note from a customer in payment of an accounts receivable. On December 31, 2012, Roper made an adjustment with the following effect on the accounting equation:

Identify and Analyze	ACTIVITY: **Operating**
	ACCOUNTS: **Interest Receivable** Increase **Interest Revenue** Increase
	STATEMENT(S): **Balance Sheet and Income Statement**

Balance Sheet						Income Statement			
ASSETS	=	LIABILITIES	+	STOCKHOLDERS' EQUITY		REVENUES	−	EXPENSES =	NET INCOME
Interest Receivable	200				200	Interest Revenue	200		200

Required

1. What is the interest rate on the note? Explain your answer.
2. Identify and analyze the transaction recorded on January 31, 2013, when the company collects the principal and interest on the note.

Exercise 7-8 Notes Receivable

LO3
EXAMPLE 7-8

On September 1, 2012, Dougherty Corp. accepted a six-month, 7%, $45,000 interest-bearing note from Rozelle Company in payment of an accounts receivable. Dougherty's year-end is December 31. Rozelle paid the note and interest on the due date.

Required

1. Who is the maker and who is the payee of the note?
2. What is the maturity date of the note?
3. Identify and analyze the effect of the transactions or adjustments to be recorded on each of the following dates:
    a. September 1, 2012
    b. December 31, 2012
    c. March 1, 2013

Exercise 7-9 Credit Card Sales

LO4
EXAMPLE 7-9

Darlene's Diner accepts American Express® credit cards from its customers. Darlene's is closed on Sundays and on that day records the weekly sales and remits the credit card drafts to American Express. For the week ending on Sunday, June 12, cash sales totaled $2,430 and credit card sales amounted to $3,500. On June 15, Darlene's received $3,360 from American Express as payment for the credit card drafts. Identify and analyze the transactions on June 12 and June 15. As a percentage, what collection fee is American Express charging Darlene?

Exercise 7-10 Working Backward: Investment in Stock

LO5
EXAMPLE 7-12

On its December 31, 2012, income statement, Durango reported a loss on sale of stock of $4,500. The loss resulted from the sale of 2,000 shares of ABC Corp. stock that Durango purchased during 2012 at $25 per share, excluding $500 in commissions to buy the shares.

Required

Determine the amount of cash Durango received from the sale of the ABC stock.

LO5
EXAMPLE 7-12

Exercise 7-11 Investment in Stock

On August 15, 2012, Cubs Corp. purchases 5,000 shares of common stock in Sox Inc. at a market price of $15 per share. In addition, Cubs pays brokerage fees of $1,000. On October 20, 2012, Cubs sells the Sox stock for $10 per share.

Required

Identify and analyze all transactions on Cubs's books in connection with the investment beginning with the purchase of the common stock on August 15, 2012, and the sale on October 20, 2012.

LO5
EXAMPLE 7-12

Exercise 7-12 Investment in Stock

On October 1, 2012, Chicago Corp. purchases 1,000 shares of the preferred stock of Denver Corp. for $40 per share. Chicago pays another $1,000 in commissions. On October 20, 2012, Denver declares and pays a dividend of $1 per share. Chicago sells the stock on November 5, 2012, at a price of $45 per share.

Required

Identify and analyze all transactions on Chicago's books in connection with its investment, beginning with the purchase of the preferred stock on October 1, 2012; the dividend received on October 20, 2012; and the sale on November 5, 2012.

LO5
EXAMPLE 7-11

Exercise 7-13 Purchase and Sale of Bonds

Starship Enterprises enters into the following transactions during 2012 and 2013:

2012

Jan. 1:   Purchased $100,000 face value of Northern Lights Inc. bonds at face value.
             The newly issued bonds have an interest rate of 8% paid semiannually on June 30 and December 31. The bonds mature in five years.

June 30:   Received interest on the Northern Lights Inc. bonds.

Dec. 31:   Received interest on the Northern Lights Inc. bonds.

2013

Jan. 1:   Sold the Northern Lights Inc. bonds for $102,000.

Required

1. Identify and analyze all transactions on Starship's records to account for its investment in the Northern Lights bonds.
2. Why was Starship able to sell its Northern Lights bonds for $102,000?

LO5

Exercise 7-14 Classification of Cash Equivalents and Investments on a Balance Sheet

Classify each of the following items as a cash equivalent (CE), a short-term investment (STI), or a long-term investment (LTI).

1. A 120-day certificate of deposit.
2. Three hundred shares of GM common stock. The company plans on selling the stock in six months.
3. A six-month U.S Treasury bill.
4. A 60-day certificate of deposit.
5. Ford Motor Co. bonds maturing in 15 years. The company intends to hold the bonds until maturity.
6. Commercial paper issued by ABC Corp., maturing in four months.
7. Five hundred shares of Chrysler common stock. The company plans to sell the stock in 60 days to help pay for a note due at that time at the bank.

8. Two hundred shares of GE preferred stock. The company intends to hold the stock for ten years and then sell it to help finance construction of a new factory.
9. Ten-year U.S. Treasury bonds. The company plans to sell the bonds on the open market in six months.
10. A 90-day U.S. Treasury bill.

Exercise 7-15 Certificate of Deposit

LO5

EXAMPLE 7-10

On May 31, 2012, Elmer Corp. purchased a 120-day, 9% certificate of deposit for $50,000. The CD was redeemed on September 28, 2012. Identify and analyze the adjustments on Elmer's books to account for:

a. The purchase of the CD.
b. The accrual of interest adjustment for interest earned through June 30, the end of the company's fiscal year.
c. The redemption of the CD.

Assume 360 days in a year.

Exercise 7-16 Working Backward: Accounts Receivable and the Statement of Cash Flows

LO6

Troy Corp.'s statement of cash flows reported an addition of $2,000 for the change in the Accounts Receivable account during the year. Sales on account for the year amounted to $24,500.

Required

Determine the cash collected on accounts receivable for the year.

Exercise 7-17 Cash Collections—Direct Method

LO6

Emily Enterprises' comparative balance sheets included accounts receivable of $224,600 at December 31, 2011, and $205,700 at December 31, 2012. Sales reported on Emily's 2012 income statement amounted to $2,250,000. What is the amount of cash collections that Emily will report in the Operating Activities category of its 2012 statement of cash flows assuming that the direct method is used?

Exercise 7-18 Impact of Transactions Involving Receivables on Statement of Cash Flows

LO6

From the following list, identify whether the change in the account balance during the year would be added to or deducted from net income when the indirect method is used to determine cash flows from operating activities:

Increase in accounts receivable
Decrease in accounts receivable
Increase in notes receivable
Decrease in notes receivable

MULTI-CONCEPT EXERCISE

Exercise 7-19 Impact of Transactions Involving Cash, Investments, and Receivables on Statement of Cash Flows

LO1 • 5 • 6

From the following list, identify each item as operating (O), investing (I), financing (F), or not separately reported on the statement of cash flows (N). Assume that the indirect method is used to determine the cash flows from operating activities.

Purchase of cash equivalents
Redemption of cash equivalents
Purchase of investments
Sale of investments
Write-off of customer account (under the allowance method)

PROBLEMS

LO1   Problem 7-1 Allowance Method for Accounting for Bad Debts

At the beginning of 2012, EZ Tech Company's Accounts Receivable balance was $140,000, and the balance in Allowance for Doubtful Accounts was $2,350. EZ Tech's sales in 2012 were $1,050,000, 80% of which were on credit. Collections on account during the year were $670,000. The company wrote off $4,000 of uncollectible accounts during the year.

Required

1. Identify and analyze the transactions related to the sale, collections, and write-offs of accounts receivable during 2012.
2. Identify and analyze the adjustments to recognize bad debts assuming that (a) bad debts expense is 3% of credit sales and (b) amounts expected to be uncollectible are 6% of the year-end accounts receivable.
3. What is the net realizable value of accounts receivable on December 31, 2012, under each assumption in part (2)?
4. What effect does the recognition of bad debts expense have on the net realizable value? What effect does the write-off of accounts have on the net realizable value?

LO1   Problem 7-2 Using an Aging Schedule to Account for Bad Debts

Sparkle Jewels distributes fine stones. It sells on credit to retail jewelry stores and extends terms that require the stores to pay in 60 days. For accounts that are not overdue, Sparkle has found that there is a 95% probability of collection. For accounts up to one month past due, the likelihood of collection decreases to 80%. If accounts are between one and two months past due, the probability of collection is 60%, and if an account is over two months past due, Sparkle Jewels estimates only a 40% chance of collecting the receivable.

On December 31, 2012, the credit balance in Allowance for Doubtful Accounts is $12,300. The amounts of gross receivables by age on this date are as follows:

Category	Amount
Current	$200,000
Past due:	
Less than one month	45,000
One to two months	25,000
Over two months	1,000

Required

1. Prepare a schedule to estimate the amount of uncollectible accounts at December 31, 2012.
2. On the basis of the schedule in part (1), identify and analyze the adjustment on December 31, 2012, to estimate bad debts.
3. Show how accounts receivable would be presented on the December 31, 2012, balance sheet.

LO2   Problem 7-3 Accounts Receivable Turnover for The Coca-Cola Company and PepsiCo

The following information was summarized from the 2010 annual report of **The Coca-Cola Company**:

	(In millions)
Trade accounts receivable, less allowances	
of $48 and $55, respectively	
December 31, 2010	$ 4,430
December 31, 2009	3,758
Net operating revenues for the year ended	
December 31:	
2010	35,119
2009	30,990

The following information was summarized from the 2010 annual report of **PepsiCo**:

	(In millions)
Accounts and notes receivable, net	
December 25, 2010	$ 6,323
December 26, 2009	4,624
Net revenue for the year ended:	
December 25, 2010	57,838
December 26, 2009	43,232

Required

1. Calculate the accounts receivable turnover ratios for The Coca-Cola Company and PepsiCo for 2010.
2. Calculate the average collection period, in days, for both companies for 2010. Comment on the reasonableness of the collection periods for these companies considering the nature of their business.
3. Which company appears to be performing better? What other information should you consider in determining how these companies are performing?

Problem 7-4 Credit Card Sales LO4

Gas stations sometimes sell gasoline at a lower price to customers who pay cash than to customers who use a credit card. A local gas station owner pays 2% of the sales price to the credit card company when customers pay with a credit card. The owner pays $0.75 per gallon of gasoline and must earn at least $0.25 per gallon of gross margin to stay competitive.

Required

1. Determine the price the owner must charge credit card customers to maintain the station's gross margin.
2. How much discount could the owner offer to cash customers and still maintain the same gross margin?

Problem 7-5 Investments in Bonds and Stock LO5

Swartz Inc. enters into the following transactions during 2012:

July 1: Paid $10,000 to acquire on the open market $10,000 face value of Gallatin bonds. The bonds have a stated annual interest rate of 6% with interest paid semiannually on June 30 and December 31. The bonds mature in 5½ years.

Oct. 23: Purchased 600 shares of Eagle Rock common stock at $20 per share.

Nov. 21: Purchased 200 shares of Montana preferred stock at $30 per share.

Dec. 10: Received dividends of $1.50 per share on the Eagle Rock stock and $2.00 per share on the Montana stock.

Dec. 28: Sold 400 shares of Eagle Rock common stock at $25 per share.

Dec. 31: Received interest from the Gallatin bonds.

Required

Identify and analyze all transactions on Swartz's records to account for its investments during 2012.

Problem 7-6 Effects of Changes in Receivable Balances on Statement of Cash Flows LO6

Stegner Inc. reported net income of $130,000 for the year ended December 31, 2012. The following items were included on Stegner's balance sheets at December 31, 2012 and 2011:

	12/31/12	12/31/11
Cash	$105,000	$110,000
Accounts receivable	223,000	83,000
Notes receivable	95,000	100,000

(Continued)

Stegner uses the indirect method to prepare its statement of cash flows. Stegner does not have any other current assets or current liabilities and did not enter into any investing or financing activities during 2012.

Required

1. Prepare Stegner's 2012 statement of cash flows.
2. Draft a brief memo to the owner to explain why cash decreased during a profitable year.

LO5   Problem 7-7 Investments in Stock

Atlas Superstores occasionally finds itself with excess cash to invest and consequently entered into the following transactions during 2012:

Jan. 15:   Purchased 200 shares of Bassett common stock at $50 per share, plus $500 in commissions.

May 23:   Received dividends of $2 per share on the Bassett stock.

June 1:   Purchased 100 shares of Boxer stock at $74 per share, plus $300 in commissions.

Oct. 20:   Sold all of the Bassett stock at $42 per share, less commissions of $400.

Dec. 15:   Received notification from Boxer that a $1.50-per-share dividend had been declared. The checks will be mailed to stockholders on January 10, 2013.

Required

Identify and analyze all transactions on the books of Atlas Superstores during 2012, including any necessary adjustment on December 15 when the dividend was declared.

MULTI-CONCEPT PROBLEM

LO1 • 3   Problem 7-8 Accounts and Notes Receivable

Lenox Corp. sold merchandise for $5,000 to M. Baxter on May 15, 2012, with payment due in 30 days. Subsequent to this, Baxter experienced cash flow problems and was unable to pay its debt. On August 10, 2012, Lenox stopped trying to collect the outstanding receivable from Baxter and wrote off the account as uncollectible. On December 1, 2012, Baxter sent Lenox a check for $1,000 and offered to sign a two-month, 9%, $4,000 promissory note to satisfy the remaining obligation. Baxter paid the entire amount due Lenox, with interest, on January 31, 2013. Lenox ends its accounting year on December 31 each year and uses the allowance method to account for bad debts.

Required

1. Identify and analyze all transactions on the books of Lenox Corp. from May 15, 2012 to January 31, 2013.
2. Why would Baxter bother to send Lenox a check for $1,000 on December 1 and agree to sign a note for the balance, given that such a long period of time had passed since the original purchase?

ALTERNATE PROBLEMS

LO1   Problem 7-1A Allowance Method for Accounting for Bad Debts

At the beginning of 2012, Miyazaki Company's Accounts Receivable balance was $105,000, and the balance in Allowance for Doubtful Accounts was $1,950. Miyazaki's sales in 2012 were $787,500, 80% of which were on credit. Collections on account during the year were $502,500. The company wrote off $3,000 of uncollectible accounts during the year.

Required

1. Identify and analyze the transactions related to the sales, collections, and write-offs of accounts receivable during 2012.

2. Identify and analyze the adjustments to recognize bad debts assuming that (a) bad debts expense is 3% of credit sales and (b) amounts expected to be uncollectible are 6% of the year-end accounts receivable.
3. What is the net realizable value of accounts receivable on December 31, 2012, under each assumption in part (2)?
4. What effect does the recognition of bad debts expense have on the net realizable value? What effect does the write-off of accounts have on the net realizable value?

Problem 7-2A Using an Aging Schedule to Account for Bad Debts   LO1

Rough Stuff is a distributor of large rocks. It sells on credit to commercial landscaping companies and extends terms that require customers to pay in 60 days. For accounts that are not overdue, Rough Stuff has found that there is a 90% probability of collection. For accounts up to one month past due, the likelihood of collection decreases to 75%. If accounts are between one and two months past due, the probability of collection is 65%, and if an account is over two months past due, Rough Stuff estimates only a 25% chance of collecting the receivable.

On December 31, 2012, the balance in Allowance for Doubtful Accounts is $34,590. The amounts of gross receivables, by age, on this date are as follows:

Category	Amount
Current	$200,000
Past due:	
Less than one month	60,300
One to two months	35,000
Over two months	45,000

Required

1. Prepare a schedule to estimate the amount of uncollectible accounts at December 31, 2012.
2. Rough Stuff knows that $40,000 of the $45,000 amount that is more than two months overdue is due from one customer that is in severe financial trouble. It is rumored that the customer will be filing for bankruptcy in the near future. As controller for Rough Stuff, how would you handle this situation?
3. Show how accounts receivable would be presented on the December 31, 2012, balance sheet.

Problem 7-3A Accounts Receivable Turnover for The Hershey   LO2
Company and Kraft Foods, Inc.

The following information was summarized from a recent annual report of **The Hershey Company**:

	(In thousands)
Accounts receivable—trade:	
December 31, 2010	$ 390,061
December 31, 2009	410,390
Net sales for the year ended:	
December 31, 2010	5,671,009
December 31, 2009	5,298,668

The following information was summarized from a recent annual report of **Kraft Foods, Inc.**:

	(In millions)
Receivables, net of allowances of $246 and	
$121, respectively	
December 31, 2010	$ 6,539
December 31, 2009	5,197
Net revenues for the year ended:	
December 31, 2010	49,207
December 31, 2009	40,386

(Continued)

Required

1. Calculate the accounts receivable turnover ratios for The Hershey Company and Kraft Foods, Inc., for the most recent year.
2. Calculate the average collection period, in days, for both companies for the most recent year. Comment on the reasonableness of the collection periods for these companies considering the nature of their business.
3. Which company appears to be performing better? What other information should you consider in determining how these companies are performing?

LO4 Problem 7-4A Credit Card Sales

A local fast-food store is considering accepting major credit cards in its outlets. Current annual sales are $800,000 per outlet. The company can purchase the equipment needed to handle credit cards and have an additional phone line installed in each outlet for approximately $800 per outlet. The equipment will be an expense in the year it is installed. The employee training time is minimal. The credit card company will charge a fee equal to 1.5% of sales for the use of credit cards. The company is unable to determine by how much, if any, sales will increase and whether cash customers will use a credit card rather than cash. No other fast-food stores in the local area accept credit cards for sales payment.

Required

1. Assuming that only 5% of existing cash customers will use a credit card, what increase in sales is necessary to pay for the credit card equipment in the first year?
2. What other factors might the company consider in addition to an increase in sales dollars?

LO5 Problem 7-5A Investments in Stock

Trendy Supercenter occasionally finds itself with excess cash to invest and consequently entered into the following transactions during 2012:

Jan. 15:	Purchased 100 shares of BMI common stock at $130 per share, plus $250 in commissions.
May 23:	Received dividends of $1 per share on the BMI stock.
June 1:	Purchased 200 shares of MG stock at $60 per share, plus $300 in commissions.
Oct. 20:	Sold all of the BMI stock at $140 per share, less commissions of $400.
Dec. 15:	Received notification from MG that a $0.75-per-share dividend had been declared. The checks will be mailed to stockholders on January 10, 2013.

Required

Identify and analyze all transactions on the books of Trendy Supercenter during 2012, including any necessary adjustment on December 15 when the dividend was declared.

LO5 Problem 7-6A Investments in Bonds and Stock

Vermont Corp. enters into the following transactions during 2012:

July 1:	Paid $10,000 to acquire on the open market $10,000 face value of Maine bonds. The bonds have a stated annual interest rate of 8% with interest paid semiannually on June 30 and December 31. The remaining life of the bonds on the date of purchase is 3½ years.
Oct. 23:	Purchased 1,000 shares of Virginia common stock at $15 per share.
Nov. 21:	Purchased 600 shares of Carolina preferred stock at $8 per share.
Dec. 10:	Received dividends of $0.50 per share on the Virginia stock and $1.00 per share on the Carolina stock.
Dec. 28:	Sold 700 shares of Virginia common stock at $19 per share.
Dec. 31:	Received interest from the Maine bonds.

Required

Identify and analyze all transactions on Vermont's records to account for its investments during 2012.

Problem 7-7A Effects of Changes in Receivable Balances on Statement of Cash Flows

LO6

St. Charles Antique Market reported a net loss of $6,000 for the year ended December 31, 2012. The following items were included on St. Charles Antique Market's balance sheets at December 31, 2012 and 2011:

	12/31/12	12/31/11
Cash	$ 36,300	$ 3,100
Accounts receivable	79,000	126,000
Notes receivable	112,600	104,800

St. Charles Antique Market uses the indirect method to prepare its statement of cash flows. It does not have any other current assets or current liabilities and did not enter into any investing or financing activities during 2012.

Required

1. Prepare St. Charles Antique Market's 2012 statement of cash flows.
2. Draft a brief memo to the owner to explain why cash increased during such an unprofitable year.

ALTERNATE MULTI-CONCEPT PROBLEM

Problem 7-8A Accounts and Notes Receivable

LO1 • 3

Tuscon Inc. sold merchandise for $6,000 to P. Paxton on July 31, 2012, with payment due in 30 days. Subsequent to this, Paxton experienced cash flow problems and was unable to pay its debt. On December 24, 2012, Tuscon stopped trying to collect the outstanding receivable from Paxton and wrote off the account as uncollectible. On January 15, 2013, Paxton sent Tuscon a check for $1,500 and offered to sign a two-month, 8%, $4,500 promissory note to satisfy the remaining obligation. Paxton paid the entire amount due Tuscon, with interest, on March 15, 2013. Tuscon ends its accounting year on December 31 each year.

Required

1. Identify and analyze all transactions on the books of Tuscon Inc. from July 31, 2012, to March 15, 2013.
2. Why would Paxton bother to send Tuscon a check for $1,500 on January 15 and agree to sign a note for the balance, given that such a long period of time had passed since the original purchase?

DECISION CASES

Reading and Interpreting Financial Statements

Decision Case 7-1 Reading Kraft Foods, Inc.'s Balance Sheet: Receivables

LO1

The following current asset appears on the balance sheet in **Kraft Foods, Inc.'s** 2010 annual report (amounts in millions of dollars):

	12/31/10	12/31/09
Receivables (net of allowances of $246 in 2010 and $121 in 2009)	$6,539	$5,197

Required

1. What is the balance in Kraft Foods, Inc.'s Allowance for Doubtful Accounts at the end of 2010 and 2009?
2. What is the net realizable value of Kraft Foods, Inc.'s receivables at the end of each of these two years?
3. What caused increases in the allowance account during 2010? What caused decreases? Explain what a net increase in the account for the year means.

LO1 • 6 **Decision Case 7-2 Reading Apple Computer's Statement of Cash Flows**

The following items appeared in the Investing Activities section of **Apple Computer's** 2010 statement of cash flows. (All amounts are in millions of dollars.)

	2010	2009	2008
Purchases of marketable securities	$(57,793)	$(46,724)	$(22,965)
Proceeds from maturities of marketable securities	24,930	19,790	11,804
Proceeds from sales of marketable securities	21,788	10,888	4,439
Purchases of other long-term investments	(18)	(101)	(38)

Required

1. What amount did Apple spend in 2010 to purchase marketable securities? How does this amount compare to the amounts spent in the two prior years?
2. What amount did Apple receive from marketable securities that matured in 2010? How does this amount compare to the amounts received in the two prior years?
3. The third line in the preceding excerpt reports proceeds from sales, rather than maturities, of marketable securities. Why would certain types of marketable securities mature while others would be sold?

LO2 **Decision Case 7-3 Comparing Two Companies in the Same Industry: Kellogg's and General Mills**

Refer to the financial statement information of **Kellogg's** and **General Mills** reproduced at the end of this book.

Required

1. Calculate the accounts receivable turnover ratios for both companies for the most recent year.
2. Calculate the average length of time it takes each company to collect its accounts receivable.
3. Compare the two companies on the basis of your calculations in parts (1) and (2).

Making Financial Decisions

LO1 • 5 **Decision Case 7-4 Liquidity**

Oak and Maple both provide computer consulting services to their clients. The following are the current assets for each company at the end of the year. (All amounts are in millions of dollars.)

	Oak	Maple
Cash	$10	$ 5
Six-month certificates of deposit	9	0
Short-term investments in stock	0	6
Accounts receivable	15	23
Allowance for doubtful accounts	(1)	(1)
Total current assets	$33	$33

Required

As a loan officer for First National Bank of Verona Heights, assume that both companies have come to you asking for a $10 million, six-month loan. If you could lend money to only one of the two, which one would it be? Justify your answer by writing a brief memo to the president of the bank.

Ethical Decision Making

Decision Case 7-5 Notes Receivable LO3

Patterson Company is a large diversified business with a unit that sells commercial real estate. As a company, Patterson has been profitable in recent years with the exception of the real estate business, where economic conditions have resulted in weak sales. The vice president of the real estate division is aware of the poor performance of his group and needs to find ways to "show a profit."

During the current year, the division is successful in selling a 100-acre tract of land for a new shopping center. The original cost of the property to Patterson was $4 million. The buyer has agreed to sign a $10 million note with payments of $2 million due at the end of each of the next five years. The property was appraised late last year at a market value of $7.5 million. The vice president has come to you, the controller, asking that you record a sale for $10 million with a corresponding increase in Notes Receivable for $10 million.

Required

1. Does the suggestion by the vice president as to how to record the sale violate any accounting principle? If so, explain the principle it violates.
2. What would you do? Write a brief memo to the vice president explaining the proper accounting for the sale.

SOLUTIONS TO KEY TERMS QUIZ

21	Account receivable		6	Note payable
12	Subsidiary ledger		16	Principal
14	Control account		19	Maturity date
13	Direct write-off method		18	Term
3	Allowance method		17	Maturity value
20	Allowance for doubtful accounts		15	Interest
11	Aging schedule		7	Credit card draft
5	Promissory note		9	Discounting
10	Maker		1	Equity securities
4	Payee		2	Debt securities
8	Note receivable			

ANSWERS TO POD REVIEW

LO1	1. b	2. c	3. b	**LO4**	1. c	2. b	
LO2	1. c	2. a		**LO5**	1. b	2. c	
LO3	1. c	2. b		**LO6**	1. b	2. a	

Operating Assets: Property, Plant, and Equipment, and Intangibles

8

AFTER STUDYING THIS CHAPTER, YOU SHOULD BE ABLE TO:

LO1 Understand balance sheet disclosures for operating assets.

LO2 Determine the acquisition cost of an operating asset.

LO3 Explain how to calculate the acquisition cost of assets purchased for a lump sum.

LO4 Describe the impact of capitalizing interest as part of the acquisition cost of an asset.

LO5 Compare depreciation methods and understand the factors affecting the choice of method.

LO6 Understand the impact of a change in the estimate of the asset life or residual value.

LO7 Determine which expenditures should be capitalized as asset costs and which should be treated as expenses.

LO8 Analyze the effect of the disposal of an asset at a gain or loss.

LO9 Understand the balance sheet presentation of intangible assets.

LO10 Understand the proper amortization of intangible assets.

LO11 Explain the impact that long-term assets have on the statement of cash flows.

LO12 Understand how investors can analyze a company's operating assets.

STUDY LINKS

A Look at Previous Chapters Chapter 7 presented the accounting for a company's current assets of accounts receivable, notes receivable, and investments. These assets are important aspects of short-term liquidity.

A Look at This Chapter This chapter examines a company's operating assets of property, plant, and equipment as well as intangibles. These assets are an important indicator of a company's ability to produce revenue in the long term.

A Look at Upcoming Chapters Later chapters discuss the financing of long-term assets. Chapter 10 presents long-term liabilities as a source of financing. Chapter 11 describes the use of stock as a source of funds for financing long-term assets.

MAKING BUSINESS DECISIONS
NIKE

© Hugh Threlfall/Alamy

Nike is the largest seller of athletic footwear, apparel, equipment, and accessories in the world. Reaching this position of dominance requires a large investment in property, plant, and equipment. The Nike World Campus, owned by Nike and located in Beaverton, Oregon, is a 176-acre facility of 16 buildings that functions as the world headquarters and is occupied by almost 6,000 employees. The company has distribution and customer service facilities in Tennessee, Oregon, and New Hampshire as well as in Japan and Europe. At May 31, 2010, the company's balance sheet indicates more than $1.9 billion of property, plant, and equipment. The company's decisions to continually invest in new plant and equipment are vital to its future. Investors and others who read Nike's financial statements must analyze its tangible assets to gauge its ability to generate future profits.

But Nike's intangible assets are equally important. The Nike brand name and company logo are some of the most recognizable in the world. In fact, Nike believes its NIKE® and Swoosh Design® trademarks are among its most valuable assets and has registered them in over 100 countries. In addition, the company owns many other trademarks, including the Converse®, Chuck Taylor®, All Star®, and One Star® line of athletic footwear and the Cole Haan® and Bragano® brands of apparel and accessories. Nike also has valuable licenses and patents on its revolutionary footwear production method known as "Air" technology. A portion of Nike's growth has come from acquiring other sports-related companies. A large portion of the purchase in such Nike acquisitions represents the intangible asset of goodwill. These acquisitions have strengthened Nike's already dominant position in the athletic footwear, apparel, and equipment industry.

Accountants have had to consider carefully the accounting for all long-lived assets, but especially for intangible assets. Investors must be able to read Nike's financial statements and understand how these assets influence the value of the company. The stock price should accurately reflect the value of those assets and the company's ability to use the assets wisely.

The accompanying partial balance sheet presents Nike's property, plant, and equipment and its intangible assets.

Why is the chapter important?

- You need to know what financial statement information is available on the balance sheet for a company's operating assets. (See pp. 378–379.)

- You need to know how a company calculates the cost of its operating assets and how a company should depreciate or amortize those assets. (See pp. 379–382.)

- You need to know how to analyze the operating assets portion of the balance sheet when evaluating a company. (See pp. 402–406.)

This chapter, and the accompanying financial statements of Nike and other companies, will help you as you study the accounting for operating assets.

Nike, Inc. Consolidated Balance Sheets		
	May 31,	
	2010	**2009**
Assets	**(In millions)**	
Current assets:		
Cash and equivalents	$ 3,079.1	$ 2,291.1
Short-term investments	2,066.8	1,164.0
Accounts receivable, net	2,649.8	2,883.9
Inventories	2,040.8	2,357.0
Deferred income taxes	248.8	272.4
Prepaid expenses and other current assets	873.9	765.6
Total current assets	10,959.2	9,734.0
Property, plant and equipment, net	1,931.9	1,957.7
Identifiable intangible assets, net	467.0	467.4
Goodwill	187.6	193.5
Deferred income taxes and other assets	873.6	897.0
Total assets	$14,419.3	$13,249.6

Operating Assets: Property, Plant, and Equipment

LO1 Understand balance sheet disclosures for operating assets.

OVERVIEW: Operating assets are generally presented in two categories on the balance sheet: (1) Property, Plant and Equipment and (2) Intangible Assets. They are presented at their acquisition cost (or *historical cost*) that includes all normal and necessary costs to acquire an asset and prepare it for its intended use. When more than one asset is purchased for a lump-sum price, the acquisition cost of each individual asset must be determined using the proportionate fair market value of each asset. Interest is not a part of the cost of the related asset. An exception is made if the company constructs an asset. A portion of the interest during the construction period is considered part of the acquisition cost of the asset.

Balance Sheet Presentation

Operating assets constitute the major productive assets of many companies. Current assets are important to a company's short-term liquidity, but operating assets are absolutely essential to its long-term future. These assets must be used to produce the goods or services the company sells to customers. The dollar amount invested in operating assets may be very large, as is the case with most manufacturing companies. On the other hand, operating assets on the balance sheet may be insignificant to a company's value, as is the case with a computer software firm and many of the so-called Internet firms. Users of financial statements must assess the operating assets to make important decisions. For example, lenders are interested in the value of the operating assets as collateral when they make lending decisions. Investors must evaluate whether the operating assets indicate long-term potential and can provide a return to the stockholders.

The terms used to describe the operating assets and the balance sheet presentation of those assets vary somewhat by company. Some firms refer to this category of assets as *fixed* or *plant assets*. Other firms present operating assets in two categories: *tangible assets* and *intangible assets*. **Nike, Inc.'s** balance sheet uses one line item for *property, plant, and equipment* and presents the details in the notes. Because the latter term can encompass a variety of items, we will use the more descriptive term *intangible assets* for the second category. We begin by examining the accounting issues concerned with the first category: property, plant, and equipment.

The May 31, 2010, notes of Nike, Inc., present property, plant, and equipment shown below (in millions). Note that the acquisition costs of the land, buildings, machinery and equipment, leasehold improvements, and construction in process are stated and that the amount of accumulated depreciation is deducted to determine the net amount. The accumulated depreciation is related to the last four assets since land is not depreciable.

Note 3 — Property, Plant and Equipment

Property, plant and equipment included the following:

	As of May 31,	
	2010	2009
	(In millions)	
Land	$ 222.8	$ 221.6
Buildings	951.9	974.0
Machinery and equipment	2,217.5	2,094.3
Leasehold improvements	820.6	802.0
Construction in process	177.0	163.8
	4,389.8	4,255.7
Less accumulated depreciation	2,457.9	2,298.0
	$1,931.9	$1,957.7

LO1 Understand balance sheet disclosures for operating assets.

- Operating assets are the major productive assets of many companies, and investors must be able to evaluate the long-term potential of these assets for a return on their investments.

- Operating assets may be classified as being either tangible or intangible assets.

- Tangible assets are referred to as property, plant, and equipment (or fixed assets).

- Intangible assets include goodwill, patents, copyrights, and various types of intellectual property.

POD REVIEW 8.1

QUESTIONS Answers to these questions are on the last page of the chapter.

1. The Property, Plant, and Equipment category should include all of the following except
   a. land.
   b. buildings.
   c. equipment.
   d. long-term investments.

2. What is the effect of accumulated depreciation in the Property, Plant, and Equipment category?
   a. It decreases some accounts.
   b. It increases some accounts.
   c. There is no effect since accumulated depreciation is not part of the category.
   d. Accumulated depreciation is deducted from all accounts in the category.

Acquisition of Property, Plant, and Equipment

Assets classified as property, plant, and equipment are initially recorded at acquisition cost (also referred to as *historical cost*). As indicated in Nike's notes, these assets are normally presented on the balance sheet at original acquisition cost minus accumulated depreciation. It is important, however, to define the term *acquisition cost* (also known as

LO2 Determine the acquisition cost of an operating asset.

Acquisition cost
The amount that includes all of the cost normally necessary to acquire an asset and prepare it for its intended use.

Alternate term: Historical cost and original cost.

original cost) in a more exact manner. What items should be included as part of the original acquisition? **Acquisition cost** should include all of the costs that are normal and necessary to acquire the asset and prepare it for its intended use, such as

- Purchase price
- Taxes paid at time of purchase (for example, sales tax)
- Transportation charges
- Installation costs

An accountant must exercise careful judgment to determine which costs are "normal" and "necessary" and should be included in calculating the acquisition cost of operating assets. Acquisition cost should not include expenditures unrelated to the acquisition (e.g., repair costs if an asset is damaged during installation) or costs incurred after the asset was installed and use begun.

LO2 Determine the acquisition cost of an operating asset.

- Assets classified as property, plant, and equipment (or fixed assets) are initially recorded at the cost to acquire the assets, also referred to as historical cost.
- Acquisition costs include those costs that are normal and necessary to acquire the asset and prepare it for its intended use. Generally, acquisition costs include purchase price, taxes paid at time of purchase, transportation charges, and installation costs.

POD REVIEW 8.2

QUESTIONS   Answers to these questions are on the last page of the chapter.

1. Which of the following should not be included in the acquisition cost of property, plant, and equipment?

   a. installation costs
   b. repair costs if an asset is damaged after purchase
   c. taxes paid at time of purchase
   d. transportation costs

2. Another term for acquisition cost is

   a. fair market value.
   b. replacement cost.
   c. historical cost.
   d. net realizable value.

LO3 Explain how to calculate the acquisition cost of assets purchased for a lump sum.

Group Purchase Quite often, a firm purchases several assets as a group and pays a lump-sum amount. This is most common when a company purchases land and a building situated on it and pays a lump-sum amount for both. It is important to measure the acquisition cost of the land and the building separately. Land is not a depreciable asset, but the amount allocated to the building is subject to depreciation. In cases such as this, the purchase price should be allocated between land and building on the basis of the proportion of the *fair market value* of each.

Example 8-1 Determining Cost When a Group of Assets Is Purchased

Assume that on January 1, ExerCo purchased a building and the land on which it is situated for $100,000. The accountant established the assets' fair market value on January 1 as follows:

Land	$ 30,000
Building	90,000
Total	$120,000

Based on the estimated market values, the purchase price should be allocated as follows:

To land	$100,000 × $30,000/$120,000 = $25,000
To building	$100,000 × $90,000/$120,000 = $75,000

© Cengage Learning 2013

The effect of the transaction can be identified and analyzed as follows:

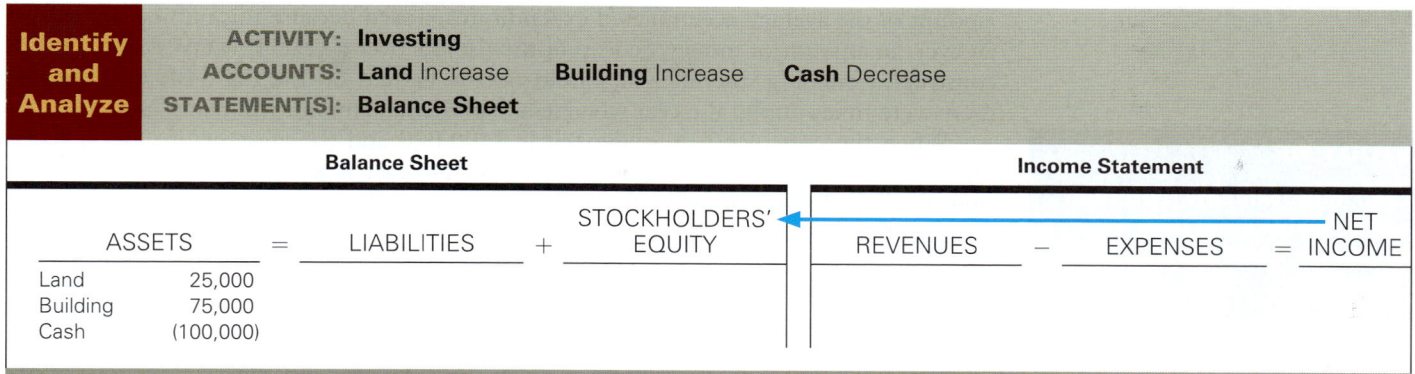

Identify and Analyze	ACTIVITY: **Investing**
	ACCOUNTS: **Land** Increase **Building** Increase **Cash** Decrease
	STATEMENT[S]: **Balance Sheet**

Balance Sheet						Income Statement			
ASSETS	=	LIABILITIES	+	STOCKHOLDERS' EQUITY		REVENUES	−	EXPENSES	= NET INCOME
Land 25,000									
Building 75,000									
Cash (100,000)									

Market value is best established by an independent appraisal of the property. If such appraisal is not possible, the accountant must rely on the market value of other similar assets, on the value of the assets in tax records, or on other available evidence.

LO3 Explain how to calculate the acquisition cost of assets purchased for a lump sum.

- If more than one asset is purchased for a single sum of money, the acquisition costs must be allocated between the assets.
- In these cases, the purchase price should be allocated between the assets acquired based on the proportion of the fair market value each asset represents of the total purchase price.

POD REVIEW 8.3

QUESTIONS **Answers to these questions are on the last page of the chapter.**

1. When land and building are acquired for a lump sum,
   a. the entire amount should be considered cost of the land.
   b. the entire amount should be considered cost of the building.
   c. the purchase amount should be allocated on the basis of the historical cost of the two assets.
   d. the purchase amount should be allocated on the basis of the market values of the two assets.

2. It is important to allocate the lump-sum purchase price between land and building because
   a. land is not depreciable.
   b. building is not depreciable.
   c. neither land nor building is depreciable.
   d. both land and building are depreciable.

Capitalization of Interest We have seen that acquisition cost may include several items. But should the acquisition cost of an asset include the interest cost necessary to finance the asset? That is, should interest be treated as an asset, or should it be treated as an expense of the period?

LO4 Describe the impact of capitalizing interest as part of the acquisition cost of an asset.

Generally, **the interest on borrowed money should be treated as an expense of the period.** If a company buys an asset and borrows money to finance the purchase, the interest on the borrowed money is not considered part of the asset's cost. Financial statements generally treat investing and financing as separate decisions. Purchase of an asset, an investing activity, is treated as a business decision that is separate from the decision concerning the financing of the asset. Therefore, interest is treated as a period cost and should appear on the income statement as interest expense in the period incurred.

There is one exception to this general guideline, however. If a company constructs an asset over a period of time and borrows money to finance the construction, the interest incurred during the construction period is not treated as interest expense. Instead, the interest must be included as part of the acquisition cost of

Capitalization of interest
Interest on constructed assets is added to the asset account.

the asset. This is referred to as **capitalization of interest**. The amount of interest that is capitalized (treated as an asset) is based on the *average accumulated expenditures*. The amount of the average accumulated expenditures is used because this number represents an average amount of money tied up in the project over a year. If it takes $400,000 to construct a building, the interest should not be figured on the full $400,000 because there were times during the year when less than the full amount was being used.

When the cost of building an asset is $400,000 and the amount of interest to be capitalized is $10,000, the acquisition cost of the asset is $410,000. The asset should appear on the balance sheet at that amount. Depreciation of the asset should be based on $410,000 less any residual value.

STUDY TIP

Land improvements represent a depreciable asset with a limited life. Land itself is not depreciable.

Land Improvements It is important to distinguish between land and other costs associated with it. The acquisition cost of land should be kept in a separate account because land has an unlimited life and is not subject to depreciation. Other costs associated with land should be recorded in an account such as Land Improvements. For example, the costs of paving a parking lot are properly treated as **land improvements**, which have a limited life. Some landscaping costs also have a limited life. Therefore, the acquisition costs of land improvements should be depreciated over their useful lives.

Land improvements
Costs that are related to land but that have a limited life.

LO4 Describe the impact of capitalizing interest as a part of the acquisition cost of an asset.

- Generally, the interest on borrowed money used to acquire assets should not be capitalized; instead, it should be treated as an expense of the period.

POD REVIEW 8.4

- One important exception to this general guideline exists for interest incurred from money borrowed to construct assets. This interest must be capitalized as part of the acquisition cost of the asset.

QUESTIONS   **Answers to these questions are on the last page of the chapter.**

1. Interest should be capitalized on which of the following?
   a. all assets
   b. all purchased assets
   c. all assets constructed by the company
   d. assets that have a cost exceeding $1 million

2. The amount of interest capitalized should be based on
   a. expenditures existing at the period's end.
   b. expenditures existing at the period's beginning.
   c. the average accumulated expenditures.
   d. an amount specified by the company's auditors.

Use and Depreciation of Property, Plant, and Equipment

LO5 Compare depreciation methods and understand the factors affecting the choice of method.

OVERVIEW: All property, plant, and equipment, except land, have a limited life and are depreciated. Several depreciation methods are available, including the straight-line method, the units-of-production method, and the double-declining-balance method. The method chosen should be one that best matches the expense to the revenue generated by the asset. Sometimes an estimate of the useful life or residual value of an asset must be altered. A change in estimate should be recorded prospectively, with no adjustments to previous periods. When a company repairs an asset, it must determine if the costs are a capital expenditure and thus added to the cost of the asset or if they are a revenue expenditure and treated as an expense of the period.

Depreciation
The allocation of the original cost of an asset to the periods benefited by its use.

All property, plant, and equipment, except land, have a limited life and decline in usefulness over time. The accrual accounting process requires a proper *matching* of expenses and revenue to measure income accurately. Therefore, the accountant must estimate the decline in usefulness of operating assets and allocate the acquisition cost in a manner consistent with the decline in usefulness. This allocation is the process generally referred to as **depreciation**.

© Cengage Learning 2013

Unfortunately, proper matching for operating assets is not easy because of the many factors involved. An asset's decline in usefulness is related to:

- Physical deterioration from usage or from the passage of time
- Obsolescence factors such as changes in technology
- The company's repair and maintenance policies

Because the decline in an asset's usefulness is related to a variety of factors, several depreciation methods have been developed. A company should use a depreciation method that allocates the original cost of the asset to the periods benefited and that allows the company to accurately match the expense to the revenue generated by the asset. We will present three methods of depreciation: *straight line, units of production,* and *double declining balance.*

All depreciation methods are based on the asset's original acquisition cost. In addition, all methods require an estimate of two additional factors: the asset's *life* and its *residual value.* The residual value (also referred to as *salvage value*) should represent the amount that could be obtained from selling or disposing of the asset at the end of its useful life. Often, this amount may be small or even zero.

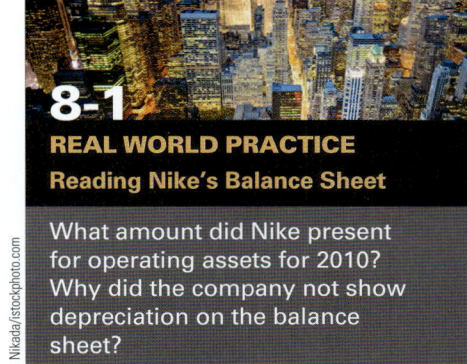

8-1

REAL WORLD PRACTICE
Reading Nike's Balance Sheet

What amount did Nike present for operating assets for 2010? Why did the company not show depreciation on the balance sheet?

Straight-Line Method

The **straight-line method** of depreciation allocates the cost of the asset evenly over time. This method calculates the annual depreciation as follows:

$$\text{Depreciation} = \frac{\text{Acquisition Cost} - \text{Residual Value}}{\text{Life}}$$

Straight-line method
A method by which the same dollar amount of depreciation is recorded in each year of asset use.

Example 8-2 Computing Depreciation Using the Straight-Line Method

Assume that on January 1, 2012, ExerCo, a manufacturer of exercise equipment, purchased a machine for $20,000. The machine's estimated life would be five years, and its residual value at the end of 2016 would be $2,000. The annual depreciation should be calculated as follows:

$$\begin{aligned} \text{Depreciation} &= \frac{\text{Acquisition Cost} - \text{Residual Value}}{\text{Life}} \\ &= (\$20,000 - \$2,000)/5 \\ &= \$3,600 \end{aligned}$$

An asset's **book value** is defined as its acquisition cost minus its total amount of accumulated depreciation. Thus, the book value of the machine in this example is $16,400 at the end of 2012.

$$\begin{aligned} \text{Book Value} &= \text{Acquisition Cost} - \text{Accumulated Depreciation} \\ &= \$20,000 - \$3,600 \\ &= \$16,400 \end{aligned}$$

Book value
The original cost of an asset minus the amount of accumulated depreciation.

The book value at the end of 2013 is $12,800.

$$\begin{aligned} \text{Book Value} &= \text{Acquisition Cost} - \text{Accumulated Depreciation} \\ &= \$20,000 - (2 \times \$3,600) \\ &= \$12,800 \end{aligned}$$

The most attractive features of the straight-line method are its ease and its simplicity. It is the most popular method for presenting depreciation in the annual report to stockholders.

Units-of-Production Method

In some cases, the decline in an asset's usefulness is directly related to wear and tear as a result of the number of units it produces. In those cases, depreciation should be calculated by the **units-of-production method**. With this

Units-of-production method
Depreciation is determined as a function of the number of units the asset produces.

method, the asset's life is expressed in terms of the number of units that the asset can produce. The depreciation *per unit* can be calculated as follows:

$$\text{Depreciation per Unit} = \frac{\text{Acquisition Cost} - \text{Residual Value}}{\text{Total Number of Units in Asset's Life}}$$

The annual depreciation for a given year can be calculated based on the number of units produced during that year, as follows:

$$\text{Annual Depreciation} = \text{Depreciation per Unit} \times \text{Units Produced in Current Year}$$

Example 8-3 Computing Depreciation Using the Units-of-Production Method

Assume that ExerCo in Example 8-2 wanted to use the units-of-production method for 2012. ExerCo has estimated that the total number of units that will be produced during the asset's five-year life is 18,000. During 2012, ExerCo produced 4,000 units. The depreciation per unit for ExerCo's machine can be calculated as follows:

$$\text{Depreciation per Unit} = (\text{Acquisition Cost} - \text{Residual Value})/\text{Life in Units}$$
$$= (\$20,000 - \$2,000)/18,000$$
$$= \$1 \text{ per Unit}$$

The amount of depreciation that should be recorded as an expense for 2012 is $4,000.

$$\text{Annual Depreciation} = \text{Depreciation per Unit} \times \text{Units Produced in 2012}$$
$$= \$1 \text{ per Unit} \times 4,000 \text{ Units}$$
$$= \$4,000$$

In Example 8-2, depreciation will be recorded until the asset produces 18,000 units. The machine cannot be depreciated below its residual value of $2,000.

The units-of-production method is most appropriate when the accountant is able to estimate the total number of units that will be produced over the asset's life. For example, if a factory machine is used to produce a particular item, the life of the asset may be expressed in terms of the number of units produced. Further, the units produced must be related to particular time periods so that depreciation expense can be matched accurately with the related revenue. A variation of the units-of-production method can be used when the life of the asset is expensed in other factors, such as miles driven or hours of use.

Accelerated Depreciation Methods

Accelerated depreciation
A higher amount of depreciation is recorded in the early years and a lower amount in the later years.

Double-declining-balance method
Depreciation is recorded at twice the straight-line rate, but the balance is reduced each period.

In some cases, more cost should be allocated to the early years of an asset's use and less to the later years. For those assets, an accelerated method of depreciation is appropriate. The term **accelerated depreciation** refers to several depreciation methods by which a higher amount of depreciation is recorded in the early years than in later years.

One form of accelerated depreciation is the **double-declining-balance method**. Under this method, depreciation is calculated at double the straight-line rate but on a declining amount.

Example 8-4 Computing Depreciation Using the Double-Declining-Balance Method

Assume that ExerCo wants to depreciate its asset using the double-declining-balance method. The first step is to calculate the straight-line rate as a percentage. The straight-line rate for the ExerCo asset with a five-year life is as follows:

$$100\% / 5 \text{ Years} = 20\%$$

The second step is to double the straight-line rate, as follows:

$$2 \times 20\% = 40\%$$

(Continued)

This rate will be applied in all years to the asset's book value at the beginning of each year. As depreciation is recorded, the book value declines. Thus, a constant rate is applied to a declining amount. This constant rate is applied to the full cost or initial book value, not to cost minus residual value as in the other methods. However, the machine cannot be depreciated below its residual value.

The amount of depreciation for 2012 would be calculated as follows:

$$\textbf{Depreciation} = \textbf{Beginning Book Value} \times \textbf{Rate}$$
$$= \$20{,}000 \times 40\%$$
$$= \$8{,}000$$

The amount of depreciation for 2013 would be calculated as follows:

$$\text{Depreciation} = \text{Beginning Book Value} \times \text{Rate}$$
$$= (\$20{,}000 - \$8{,}000) \times 40\%$$
$$= \$4{,}800$$

The complete depreciation schedule for ExerCo for all five years of the machine's life would be as follows:

Year	Rate	Book Value at Beginning of Year	Depreciation	Book Value at End of Year
2012	40%	$20,000	$ 8,000	$12,000
2013	40	12,000	4,800	7,200
2014	40	7,200	2,880	4,320
2015	40	4,320	1,728	2,592
2016	40	2,592	592	2,000
Total			$18,000	

In Example 8-4, the depreciation for 2016 cannot be calculated as $2,592 × 40% because this would result in an accumulated depreciation amount of more than $18,000. The total amount of depreciation recorded in Years 1 through 4 is $17,408. The accountant should record only $592 depreciation ($18,000 − $17,408) in 2016 so that the remaining value of the machine is $2,000 at the end of 2016.

The double-declining-balance method of depreciation results in an accelerated depreciation pattern. It is most appropriate for assets subject to a rapid decline in usefulness as a result of technical or obsolescence factors. Double-declining-balance depreciation is not widely used for financial statement purposes but may be appropriate for certain assets. As discussed earlier, most companies use straight-line depreciation for financial statement purposes because it generally produces the highest net income, especially in growing companies that have a stable or expanding base of assets.

Comparison of Depreciation Methods In this section, you have learned about several methods of depreciating operating assets. Exhibit 8-1 presents a comparison of the depreciation and book values of the ExerCo asset for 2012–2016 using the straight-line and double-declining-balance methods. (We have excluded the units-of-production method.) Note that both methods result in a depreciation total of $18,000 over the five-year period. The amount of depreciation per year depends, however, on the method of depreciation chosen.

Nonaccountants often misunderstand the accountant's concept of depreciation. Accountants do not consider depreciation to be a process of *valuing* the asset. That is, depreciation does not describe the increase or decrease in the market value of the asset. Accountants consider depreciation to be a process of *cost allocation*. The purpose is to allocate the original acquisition cost to the periods benefited by the asset. The depreciation method chosen should be based on the decline in the asset's usefulness. A company can choose a different depreciation method for each individual fixed asset or for each class or category of fixed assets.

EXHIBIT 8-1 Comparison of Depreciation and Book Values of Straight-Line and Double-Declining-Balance Methods

Year	Straight-Line		Double-Declining-Balance	
	Depreciation	Book Value	Depreciation	Book Value
2012	$ 3,600	$16,400	$ 8,000	$12,000
2013	3,600	12,800	4,800	7,200
2014	3,600	9,200	2,880	4,320
2015	3,600	5,600	1,728	2,592
2016	3,600	2,000	592	2,000
Totals	$18,000		$18,000	

© Cengage Learning 2013

The choice of depreciation method can have a significant impact on the bottom line. If two companies are essentially identical in every other respect, a different depreciation method for fixed assets can make one company look more profitable than the other. Or a company that uses accelerated depreciation for one year can find that its otherwise declining earnings are no longer declining if it switches to straight-line depreciation. Investors should pay some attention to depreciation methods when comparing companies. Statement users must be aware of the different depreciation methods to understand the calculation of income and to compare companies that may not use the same methods.

Depreciation and Income Taxes Financial accounting involves the presentation of financial statements to external users of accounting information, users such as investors and creditors. When depreciating an asset for financial accounting purposes, the accountant should choose a depreciation method that is consistent with the asset's decline in usefulness and that properly allocates its cost to the periods that benefit from its use.

Depreciation is also deducted for income tax purposes. Sometimes depreciation is referred to as a *tax shield* because it reduces (as do other expenses) the amount of income tax that would otherwise have to be paid. When depreciating an asset for tax purposes, a company should generally choose a depreciation method that reduces the present value of its tax burden to the lowest possible amount over the life of the asset. Normally, this is best accomplished with an accelerated depreciation method, which allows a company to save more income tax in the early years of the asset. This happens because the higher depreciation charges reduce taxable income more than the straight-line method does. The method allowed for tax purposes is referred to as the Modified Accelerated Cost Recovery System (MACRS). As a form of accelerated depreciation, it results in a larger amount of depreciation in the asset's early years and a smaller amount in later years.

Choice of Depreciation Method As stated, in theory, a company should choose the depreciation method that best allocates the asset's original cost to the periods benefited by its use. Theory aside, the other factors that affect a company's choice of a depreciation method(s) should be examined. Exhibit 8-2 presents the factors that affect this decision and the likely choice that arises from each factor. Usually, the most important factor is whether depreciation is calculated for presentation on the financial statements to stockholders or whether it is calculated for income tax purposes.

When depreciation is calculated for financial statement purposes, a company generally wants to present the most favorable impression (the highest income) possible. More than 90% of large companies use the straight-line method for financial statement purposes.

If management's objective is to minimize the company's income tax liability, the company will generally not choose the straight-line method for tax purposes. As discussed in the preceding section, accelerated depreciation allows the company to save more on income taxes because depreciation is a tax shield.

EXHIBIT 8-2 Management's Choice of Depreciation Method

Factor	Likely Choice
Simplicity	The straight-line method is easiest to compute and record.
Reporting to stockholders	Usually, firms want to maximize net income in reporting to stockholders and will use the straight-line method.
Comparability	Usually, firms use the same depreciation method as other firms in the same industry or line of business.
Management bonus plans	If management is paid a bonus based on net income, it will likely use the straight-line method.
Technological competitiveness	If technology is changing rapidly, a firm should consider an accelerated method of depreciation.
Reporting to the Internal Revenue Service	Firms usually use an accelerated method of depreciation to minimize taxable income in reporting to the IRS.

© Cengage Learning 2013

Therefore, it is not unusual for a company to use *two* depreciation methods for the same asset, one for financial reporting purposes and another for tax purposes. This may seem somewhat confusing, but it is the direct result of the differing goals of financial and tax accounting. See Chapter 10 for more about this issue.

LO5 Compare depreciation methods and understand the factors affecting the choice of method.

- All property, plant, and equipment (except land) have a limited life, and a proper matching of expenses through depreciation is required. Several depreciation methods are available, including straight-line, units-of-production, and accelerated depreciation methods.
- In theory, the depreciation method that best allocates the original cost of the asset to the periods benefited by the use of the asset should be chosen. However, depreciation method choices are often influenced by tax and shareholder perceptions.

POD REVIEW
8.5

QUESTIONS   Answers to these questions are on the last page of the chapter.

1. Which of the following assets is not depreciated, depleted, or amortized over its life?

   a. land
   b. natural resources
   c. buildings
   d. equipment

2. Which of the following statements about the Accumulated Depreciation account is true?

   a. It is a long-term liability.

   b. It provides a contra account to intangible assets.
   c. It provides a contra account to tangible assets so that their net book value approximates their market value.
   d. It represents the total depreciation charged over the life of the asset to which it relates and reduces the book value of the asset.

© Cengage Learning 2013

LO6 Understand the impact of a change in the estimate of the asset life or residual value.

Change in estimate
A change in the life of the asset or in its residual value.

Change in Depreciation Estimate An asset's acquisition cost is known at the time it is purchased, but its life and residual value must be estimated. These estimates are then used as the basis for depreciating it. Occasionally, an estimate of the asset's life or residual value must be altered after the depreciation process has begun. This type of accounting change is referred to as a **change in estimate**.

A change in estimate should be recorded *prospectively*, meaning that the depreciation recorded in prior years is not corrected or restated. Instead, the new estimate should affect the current year and future years.

Example 8-5 Calculating a Change in Depreciation Estimate

ExerCo purchased a machine on January 1, 2012, for $20,000. ExerCo estimated that the machine's life would be five years and its residual value at the end of five years would be $2,000. ExerCo has depreciated the machine using the straight-line method for two years. At the beginning of 2014, ExerCo believes that the total machine life will be seven years, or another five years beyond the two years the machine has been used. Thus, depreciation must be adjusted to reflect the new estimate of the asset's life.

ExerCo should depreciate the remaining depreciable amount during 2014 through 2018. The amount to be depreciated over that time period should be calculated as follows:

Acquisition cost, January 1, 2012	$20,000
Less: Accumulated depreciation (2 years at $3,600 per year)	7,200
Book value, January 1, 2014	$12,800
Less: Residual value	2,000
Remaining depreciable amount	$10,800

The remaining depreciable amount should be recorded as depreciation over the remaining life of the machine. The depreciation amount for 2014 and the following four years would be $2,160:

$$\text{Depreciation} = \textbf{Remaining Depreciable Amount/Remaining Life}$$
$$= \$10,800/5 \text{ Years}$$
$$= \$2,160$$

© Cengage Learning 2013

In Example 8-5, the effect of the transaction can be identified and analyzed as follows:

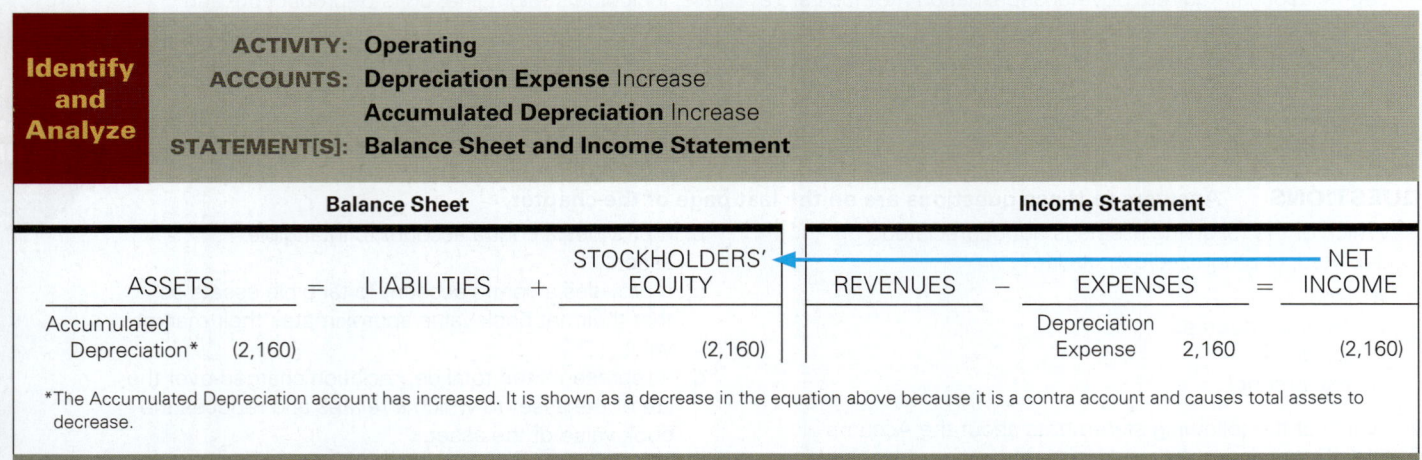

Identify and Analyze

ACTIVITY: Operating
ACCOUNTS: Depreciation Expense Increase
Accumulated Depreciation Increase
STATEMENT[S]: Balance Sheet and Income Statement

Balance Sheet				Income Statement			
ASSETS	=	LIABILITIES	+	STOCKHOLDERS' EQUITY	REVENUES	−	EXPENSES = NET INCOME
Accumulated Depreciation* (2,160)				(2,160)			Depreciation Expense 2,160 (2,160)

*The Accumulated Depreciation account has increased. It is shown as a decrease in the equation above because it is a contra account and causes total assets to decrease.

If the change in estimate is a material amount, the company should disclose in the footnotes to the 2014 financial statements that depreciation has changed as a result of a change in estimate. The company's auditors have to be very careful that management's decision to change its estimate of the depreciable life of the asset is not an attempt to manipulate earnings. Particularly in capital-intensive manufacturing concerns, lengthening the useful life of equipment can have a material impact on earnings.

A change in estimate of an asset's residual value is treated in a manner that is similar to a change in an asset's life. There should be no attempt to correct or restate the income statements of past periods that were based on the original estimate. Instead, the accountant should use the new estimate of residual value to calculate depreciation for the current and future years.

LO6 Understand the impact of a change in the estimate of the asset life or residual value.

- Occasionally, an estimate of the asset's life or residual value must be modified after the depreciation process has begun. This is an example of an accounting change that is referred to as a change in estimate.

POD REVIEW 8.6

QUESTIONS   Answers to these questions are on the last page of the chapter.

1. An example of a change in estimate is
   a. a change in the estimated life of a depreciable asset.
   b. a change in the salvage value of an asset.
   c. Both (a) and (b) are changes in estimate.
   d. Neither (a) nor (b) is a change in estimate.

2. When a change in estimate occurs,
   a. the company should restate the statements of past periods because of the change.
   b. the company should show a line on its income statement titled Change in Estimate.
   c. the change should not be recorded by the company.
   d. the change should affect the current period and future periods.

Capital versus Revenue Expenditures

Accountants often must decide whether certain expenditures related to operating assets should be treated as an addition to the cost of the asset or as an expense. One of the most common examples involving this decision concerns repairs to an asset. Should the repairs constitute capital expenditures or revenue expenditures?

- A **capital expenditure** is a cost that is added to the acquisition cost of an asset.
- A **revenue expenditure** is not treated as part of the cost of the asset, but as an expense on the income statement.

Thus, the company must decide whether to treat an item as an asset (balance sheet) and depreciate its cost over its life or to treat it as an expense (income statement) of a single period.

The distinction between capital and revenue expenditures is a matter of judgment. Generally, the following guidelines should be followed:

- When an expenditure *increases the life of the asset or its productivity*, it should be treated as a capital expenditure and added to the asset account.
- When an expenditure *simply maintains an asset in its normal operating condition*, however, it should be treated as an expense.

The *materiality* of the expenditure must also be considered. Most companies establish a policy of treating an expenditure that is smaller than a specified amount as a revenue expenditure (an expense on the income statement).

A company must not improperly capitalize a material expenditure that should have been written off right away. Wall Street analysts trying to assess the value of a company closely monitor its capitalization policies. When a company is capitalizing rather than expensing certain items to artificially boost earnings, that revelation can be very damaging to the stock price.

LO7 Determine which expenditures should be capitalized as asset costs and which should be treated as expenses.

Capital expenditure
A cost that improves the asset and is added to the asset account.
Alternate term: Item treated as asset.

Revenue expenditure
A cost that keeps an asset in its normal operating condition and is treated as an expense.
Alternate term: Item treated as an expense of the period.

Expenditures related to operating assets may be classified in several categories. For each type of expenditure, its treatment as capital or revenue should be as follows:

Category	Example	Asset or Expense
Normal maintenance	Repaint	Expense
Minor repair	Replace spark plugs	Expense
Major repair	Replace a vehicle's engine	Asset if life or productivity is enhanced
Addition	Add a wing to a building	Asset

An item treated as a capital expenditure affects the amount of depreciation that should be recorded over the asset's remaining life. We will use an example involving ExerCo to illustrate. Assume again that ExerCo purchased a machine on January 1, 2012, for $20,000. ExerCo estimated that its residual value at the end of five years would be $2,000 and has depreciated the machine using the straight-line method for 2012 and 2013.

For the years 2012 and 2013, ExerCo recorded depreciation of $3,600 per year.

$$\text{Depreciation} = (\text{Acquisition Cost} - \text{Residual Value})/\text{Life}$$
$$= (\$20{,}000 - \$2{,}000)/5$$
$$= \$3{,}600$$

Example 8-6 Capitalizing Costs of a Major Repair

At the beginning of 2014, ExerCo made a $3,000 overhaul to the machine, extending its life by three years. Because the expenditure qualifies as a capital expenditure, the cost of overhauling the machine should be added to the asset account.

Beginning in 2014, the company should record depreciation of $2,300 per year, computed as follows:

Original cost, January 1, 2012	$20,000
Less: Accumulated depreciation (2 years × $3,600)	7,200
Book value, January 1, 2014	$12,800
Plus: Major overhaul	3,000
Less: Residual value	(2,000)
Remaining depreciable amount	$13,800

$$\text{Depreciation} = \text{Remaining Depreciable Amount}/\text{Remaining Life}$$
$$= \$13{,}800/6 \text{ Years}$$
$$= \$2{,}300$$

© Cengage Learning 2013

The effect of the transaction for the overhaul is as follows:

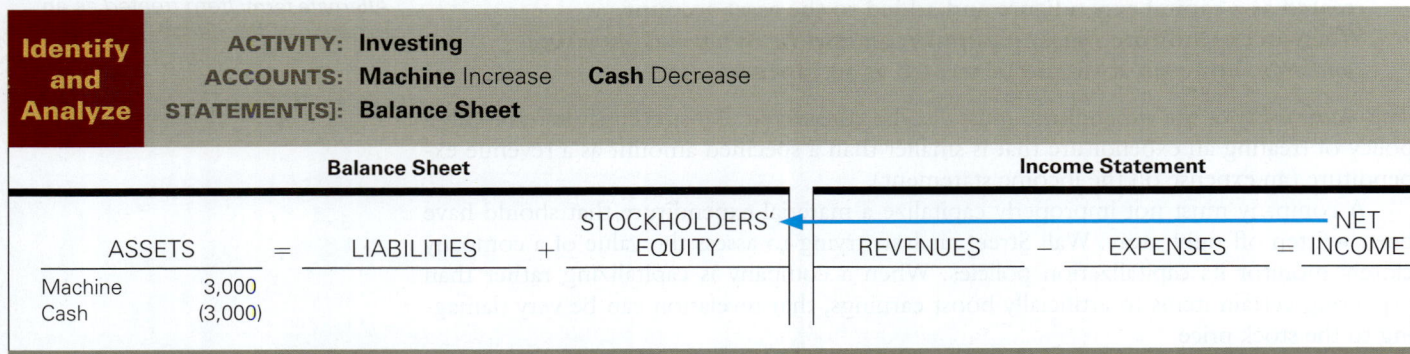

Identify and Analyze	ACTIVITY: **Investing**
	ACCOUNTS: **Machine** Increase **Cash** Decrease
	STATEMENT[S]: **Balance Sheet**

Balance Sheet						Income Statement			
ASSETS		=	LIABILITIES	+	STOCKHOLDERS' EQUITY	REVENUES	−	EXPENSES	= NET INCOME
Machine	3,000								
Cash	(3,000)								

The effect of the transaction to record depreciation for 2014 can be identified and analyzed as follows:

Identify and Analyze	
ACTIVITY:	**Operating**
ACCOUNTS:	**Depreciation Expense** Increase
	Accumulated Depreciation—Asset Increase
STATEMENT[S]:	**Balance Sheet and Income Statement**

Balance Sheet					Income Statement				
ASSETS	=	LIABILITIES	+	STOCKHOLDERS' EQUITY	REVENUES	−	EXPENSES	=	NET INCOME
Accumulated Depreciation— Asset* (2,300)				(2,300)			Depreciation Expense 2,300		(2,300)

*The Accumulated Depreciation account has increased. It is shown as a decrease in the equation above because it is a contra account and causes total assets to decrease.

Environmental Aspects of Operating Assets

As the government's environmental regulations have increased, businesses have been required to expend more money complying with them. A common example involves costs to comply with federal requirements to clean up contaminated soil surrounding plant facilities. In some cases, the costs are high and may exceed the value of the property. Should such costs be considered an expense and recorded entirely in one accounting period, or should they be treated as a capital expenditure and added to the cost of the asset? If there is a legal obligation to clean up the property or restore it to its original condition, companies are required to record the cost of asset retirement obligations as part of the asset's cost. For example, if a company owns a factory and has made a binding promise to restore to its original condition the property used by the factory, the costs of restoring the property must be added to the asset account. Of course, it is sometimes difficult to determine whether a legal obligation exists. However, companies should at least conduct a thorough investigation to determine the potential environmental considerations that may affect the value of operating assets and to ponder carefully the accounting implications of new environmental regulations.

LO7 Determine which expenditures should be capitalized as asset costs and which should be treated as expenses.

- The nature of some expenditures related to a capital asset, such as repairs and replacement parts, must be determined for the proper financial accounting treatment.
- Expenditures are added to the acquisition cost of an asset and are depreciated over time.
- Revenue expenditures are not treated as part of the cost of the asset, but as an expense on the income statement in the period incurred.

POD REVIEW 8.7

QUESTIONS **Answers to these questions are on the last page of the chapter.**

1. A capital expenditure is
   a. added to the cost of the asset.
   b. treated as an expense of the period.
   c. an expenditure that maintains the asset in its normal operating condition.
   d. deducted from the cost of the asset.

2. A revenue expenditure is
   a. added to the cost of the asset.
   b. treated as an expense of the period.
   c. an expenditure that improves the asset.
   d. deducted from the cost of the asset.

Disposal of Property, Plant, and Equipment

LO8 Analyze the effect of the disposal of an asset at a gain or loss.

OVERVIEW: Disposal of an asset occurs when the asset is sold, traded, or discarded. At that time, the company must update depreciation to the date of sale and must calculate a gain or loss on the disposal. A gain occurs when the selling price of the asset exceeds its book value. A loss occurs when the selling price of the asset is less than its book value.

An asset may be disposed of in several different ways. One common method is to sell the asset for cash. Sale of an asset involves two important considerations. First, depreciation must be recorded up to the date of sale. If the sale does not occur at the fiscal year-end, usually December 31, depreciation must be recorded for a partial period from the beginning of the year to the date of sale. Second, the company selling the asset must calculate and record the gain or loss on its sale.

Gain on Sale of Assets Refer again to the ExerCo example. Assume that ExerCo purchased a machine on January 1, 2012, for $20,000, estimating its life to be five years and the residual value to be $2,000. ExerCo used the straight-line method of depreciation. Assume that ExerCo sold the machine on July 1, 2014. Depreciation for the six-month time period from January 1 to July 1, 2014, is $1,800 ($3,600 per year × 1/2 year = $1,800). The effect of the transaction for depreciation can be identified and analyzed as follows:

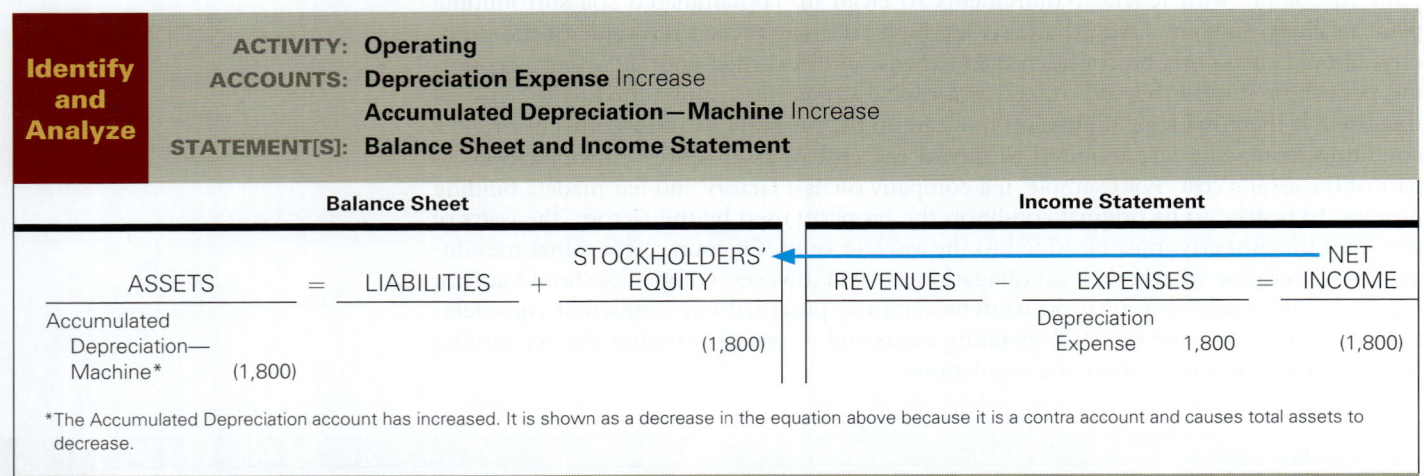

Identify and Analyze	ACTIVITY:	**Operating**				
	ACCOUNTS:	**Depreciation Expense** Increase				
		Accumulated Depreciation—Machine Increase				
	STATEMENT[S]:	**Balance Sheet and Income Statement**				

Balance Sheet					Income Statement			
ASSETS	=	LIABILITIES	+	STOCKHOLDERS' EQUITY	REVENUES	−	EXPENSES	= NET INCOME
Accumulated Depreciation—Machine* (1,800)				(1,800)			Depreciation Expense 1,800	(1,800)

*The Accumulated Depreciation account has increased. It is shown as a decrease in the equation above because it is a contra account and causes total assets to decrease.

Example 8-7 Calculating the Gain on Sale of an Asset

Assume that ExerCo sold the asset on July 1, 2014, for $12,400. The gain can be calculated as follows:

Asset cost	$20,000
Less: Accumulated depreciation	9,000
Book value	$11,000
Sales price	12,400
Gain on sale of asset	$ 1,400

© Cengage Learning 2013

After the July 1 entry, the balance of the Accumulated Depreciation—Machine account is $9,000, which reflects depreciation for the 2½ years from the date of purchase to the date of sale. The effect of the transaction for the sale can be identified and analyzed as follows:

Identify and Analyze

ACTIVITY: Investing

ACCOUNTS: Accumulated Depreciation—Machine Decrease   Cash Increase
Machine Decrease   Gain on Sale of Asset Increase

STATEMENT[S]: Balance Sheet and Income Statement

Balance Sheet					
ASSETS	=	LIABILITIES	+	STOCKHOLDERS' EQUITY	
Accumulated Depreciation— Machine*	9,000			1,400	
Cash	12,400				
Machine	(20,000)				

Income Statement				
REVENUES	−	EXPENSES	=	NET INCOME
Gain on Sale of Asset 1,400				1,400

*The Accumulated Depreciation account has decreased. It is shown as an increase in the equation above because it is a contra account and causes total assets to increase.

When an asset is sold, all accounts related to it must be removed. In the preceding entry, the Machine account is reduced to eliminate the account and the Accumulated Depreciation—Machine account is reduced to eliminate it. The **Gain on Sale of Asset** indicates the amount by which the sales price of the machine *exceeds* the book value. The account **is an income statement account** and should appear in the Other Income/ Expense category of the statement. The Gain on Sale of Asset account is not treated as revenue because it does not constitute the company's ongoing or central activity. Instead, it appears as income, but in a separate category to denote its incidental nature.

Gain on Sale of Asset
The excess of the selling price over the asset's book value.

Loss on Sale of Assets The calculation of a loss on the sale of an asset is similar to that of a gain. As in the example, depreciation must be recorded to the date of sale, July1.

Example 8-8 Calculating the Loss on Sale of an Asset

Assume that ExerCo sold the asset on July 1, 2014, for $10,000. Thus, the loss could be calculated as follows:

Asset cost	$20,000
Less: Accumulated depreciation	9,000
Book value	$11,000
Sales price	10,000
Loss on sale of asset	$ 1,000

© Cengage Learning 2013

The effect of the transaction for the sale can be identified and analyzed as follows:

Identify and Analyze

ACTIVITY: Investing

ACCOUNTS: Accumulated Depreciation—Machine Decrease   Cash Increase
Loss on Sale of Asset Increase   Machine Decrease

STATEMENT[S]: Balance Sheet and Income Statement

Balance Sheet					
ASSETS	=	LIABILITIES	+	STOCKHOLDERS' EQUITY	
Accumulated Depreciation— Machine*	9,000			(1,000)	
Cash	10,000				
Machine	(20,000)				

Income Statement				
REVENUES	−	EXPENSES	=	NET INCOME
		Loss on Sale of Asset 1,000		(1,000)

*The Accumulated Depreciation account has decreased. It is shown as an increase in the equation above because it is a contra account and causes total assets to increase.

Loss on Sale of Asset
The amount by which selling price is less than book value.

The **Loss on Sale of Asset** indicates the amount by which the asset's sales price is less than its book value.

The **Loss on Sale of Asset** account is an income statement account and should appear in the Other Income/Expense category of the income statement.

POD REVIEW 8.8

LO8 Analyze the effect of the disposal of an asset at a gain or loss.

- Assets are usually disposed of through sales, which are exchange transactions that result in a gain or loss.
  - The gain or loss on an asset is the difference between the sales (or exchange) price and the book value of the asset, where book value is the acquisition cost less any accumulated depreciation on the asset.

QUESTIONS   **Answers to these questions are on the last page of the chapter.**

1. A gain on sale of asset occurs when the sales price of the asset is
   a. less than its book value.
   b. less than accumulated depreciation.
   c. more than its book value.
   d. more than accumulated depreciation.

2. A loss on sale of asset occurs when the sales price of the asset is
   a. less than its book value.
   b. less than accumulated depreciation.
   c. more than its book value.
   d. more than accumulated depreciation.

IFRS and Property, Plant, and Equipment

Generally, the Financial Accounting Standards Board's (FASB) standards concerning property, plant, and equipment are similar to the international accounting standards, and conversion to those standards should not impose great difficulties for U.S. companies. There are important differences, however. First, when depreciation is calculated, the international standards require that estimates of residual value and the life of the asset be reviewed at least annually and revised if necessary. If the estimate is revised, it should be treated as a change in estimate as we have described in this chapter. The FASB standards do not have a specific rule that requires residual value and asset life to be reviewed annually, so this is an instance where the international standards are more explicit than U.S. standards. The international standards also indicate that companies should determine the components of an asset and depreciate each component separately. For example, if a company buys a building, some parts of the building may be depreciated using one estimate of useful life and other parts may use a different estimate of useful life.

Another difference involves the valuation of property, plant, and equipment. The FASB generally requires operating assets to be recorded at acquisition cost, less depreciation, and the assets' values are not changed to reflect their fair market values, or selling prices. International accounting standards allow but do not require companies to revalue their property, plant, and equipment to reflect fair market values. This gives firms additional flexibility in portraying their assets, but may also cause difficulties in comparing one company with another.

Operating Assets: Intangible Assets

LO9 Understand the balance sheet presentation of intangible assets.

OVERVIEW: Intangible assets are long-lived, have no physical properties, but provide rights or privileges. Intangible assets are recorded at their acquisition cost. An intangible asset with a limited life should be amortized over the shorter of its legal life or useful life. Intangibles with an indefinite life should not be amortized. Research and development costs are not considered to be an intangible asset and are treated as an expense instead. Goodwill is an intangible asset. It is not amortized, but must be evaluated every year to determine any impairment in value.

Intangible assets are long-term assets with no physical properties. Because one cannot see or touch most intangible assets, it is easy to overlook their importance. Intangibles are recorded as assets, however, because they provide future economic benefits to the company. In fact, an intangible asset may be the most important asset a company owns or controls. For example, a pharmaceutical company may own some property, plant, and equipment, but its most important asset may be its patent for a particular drug or process. Likewise, the company that publishes this textbook may consider the copyrights to textbooks to be among its most important revenue-producing assets.

The balance sheet includes the intangible assets that meet the accounting definition of assets. Patents, copyrights, and brand names are included because they are owned by the company and will produce a future benefit that can be identified and measured. The balance sheet, however, would indicate only the acquisition cost of those assets, not the value of the assets to the company or the sales value of the assets.

Of course, the balance sheet does not include all of the items that may produce future benefit to the company. A company's employees, its management team, its location, or the intellectual capital of a few key researchers may well provide important future benefits and value. They are not recorded on the balance sheet, however, because they do not meet the accountant's definition of *assets* and cannot be easily identified or measured.

Balance Sheet Presentation

Intangible assets are long-term assets and should be shown separately from property, plant, and equipment. Exhibit 8-3 lists the most common intangible assets. Some companies develop a separate category, Intangible Assets, for the various types of intangibles. Nike presents only two lines for intangible assets: Identifiable Intangible Assets and Goodwill. Exhibit 8-4 presents the note that indicates that the company's intangible assets consist of patents, trademarks, and goodwill. The presentation of intangible assets varies widely, however.

The nature of many intangibles is fairly evident, but goodwill is not so easily understood. **Goodwill** represents the amount of the purchase price paid in excess of the market value of the individual net assets when a business is purchased. Goodwill is recorded only when a business is purchased. It is not recorded when a company engages in activities that do not involve the purchase of another business entity. For example, customer loyalty or a good management team may represent goodwill, but neither meets the accountants' criteria to be recorded as an asset on a firm's financial statements.

Acquisition Cost of Intangible Assets

As was the case with property, plant, and equipment, the acquisition cost of an intangible asset includes all of the costs to acquire the asset and prepare it for its intended use. This should include all necessary costs, such as legal costs incurred at the time of acquisition. Acquisition cost also should include those costs that are incurred after acquisition and

Intangible assets
Assets with no physical properties.

Goodwill
The excess of the purchase price to acquire a business over the value of the individual net assets acquired.

Alternate term: Purchase price in excess of the market value of the assets.

HOT TOPICS
The Nike Brand: Intangible? Yes. Valuable? Absolutely!

Nike's brand name and company logo are among the most recognizable in the world. They may be intangible assets, but they are some of the company's most valuable assets. How does Nike use these assets to create sales? By having great-looking and great-performing products that sport the brand name using recognizable athletes and effective marketing and advertising campaigns. In April 2011, Nike debuted a Jordan Fly Wade shoe, basketball star Dwayne Wade's first shoe with the company. It was inspired by his aggressive style on the court and features both the Nike Zoom and Max Air designs. The ad campaign features print, broadcast, and digital advertising and public relations applications. But all of it is based on the brand name and identity that Nike has established for many years.

EXHIBIT 8-3 Most Common Intangible Assets

Intangible Asset	Description
Patent	Right to use, manufacture, or sell a product; granted by the U.S. Patent Office. Patents have a legal life of 20 years.
Copyright	Right to reproduce or sell a published work. Copyrights are granted for the life of the creator plus 70 years.
Trademark	A symbol or name that allows a product or service to be identified; provides legal protection for 20 years in addition to an indefinite number of renewal periods.
Goodwill	The excess of the purchase price to acquire a business over the value of the individual net assets acquired.

that are necessary to the existence of the asset. For example, if a firm must pay legal fees to protect a patent from infringement, the costs should be considered part of the acquisition cost and should be included in the Patent account.

Research and Development Costs You should also be aware of one item that is similar to intangible assets but is *not* on the balance sheet. **Research and development costs** are expenditures incurred in the discovery of new knowledge and the translation of research into a design or plan for a new product or service or in a significant improvement to an existing product or service. Firms that engage in research and development do so because they believe such activities provide future benefit to the company. In fact, many firms have become leaders in an industry by engaging in research and development and the discovery of new products or technology. It is often very difficult, however, to identify the amount of future benefits of research and development and to associate those benefits with specific time periods. Because of the difficulty in predicting future benefits, the FASB has ruled that firms are not allowed to treat research and development costs as assets; all such expenditures must be treated as expenses in the period incurred. Many firms, especially high-technology ones, argue that this accounting rule results in seriously understated balance sheets. In their view, an important "asset" is

Research and development costs
Costs incurred in the discovery of new knowledge.

EXHIBIT 8-4 The Nike, Inc., Consolidated Assets Section and Intangibles Notes

The following table summarizes the Company's identifiable intangible assets balances as of May 31, 2010:

(In millions)	Gross Carrying Amount	Accumulated Amortization	Net Carrying Amount
	May 31, 2010		
Amortized intangible assets:			
Patents	$ 68.5	$(20.8)	$ 47.7
Trademarks	40.2	(17.8)	22.4
Other	32.7	(18.8)	13.9
Total	$141.4	$(57.4)	$ 84.0
Unamortized intangible assets—			
Trademarks			$383.0
Identifiable intangible assets, net			$467.0

Goodwill

	Goodwill	Accumulated Impairment	Goodwill, net
May 31, 2009	$392.8	$(199.3)	$193.5
Other[1]	(5.9)	—	(5.9)
May 31, 2010	$386.9	$(199.3)	$187.6

[1] Other consists of foreign currency translation adjustments in Umbro goodwill.

© Cengage Learning 2013

not portrayed on their balance sheet. They also argue that they are at a competitive dis-advantage when compared with foreign companies that are allowed to treat at least a portion of research and development as an asset. Financial statement users need to be aware of those "hidden assets" when analyzing the balance sheets of companies that must expense research and development costs.

It is important to distinguish between patent costs and research and development costs. Patent costs include legal and filing fees necessary to acquire a patent. Such costs are capitalized as an intangible asset, Patent. However, the Patent account should not include the costs of research and development of a new product. Those costs are not capitalized, but are treated as an expense, Research and Development.

LO9 Understand the balance sheet presentation of intangible assets.

- Intangible assets are long-term assets that should be shown separately from property, plant, and equipment on the balance sheet.

POD REVIEW 8.9

QUESTIONS   **Answers to these questions are on the last page of the chapter.**

1. Which of the following is not an intangible asset?

   a. patents
   b. improvements to a building that the company already owns
   c. trademarks
   d. goodwill arising as a result of an acquisition

2. Research and development costs should be

   a. presented as an intangible asset.
   b. presented as property, plant, and equipment.
   c. presented as an intangible asset if the research was conducted internally.
   d. treated as an expense.

Amortization of Intangibles

There has been considerable discussion over the past few years about whether intangible assets should be amortized and, if so, over what period of time. The term *amortization* is very similar to depreciation of property, plant, and equipment. Amortization involves allocating the acquisition cost of an intangible asset to the periods benefited by the use of the asset. When an intangible asset is amortized, most companies use the straight-line method of amortization. We will use that method for illustration purposes. Occasionally, however, you may see instances of an accelerated form of amortization if the decline in usefulness of the intangible asset does not occur evenly over time.

LO10 Understand the proper amortization of intangible assets.

Intangibles with Finite Life If an intangible asset has a finite life, amortization must be recognized. A finite life exists when an intangible asset is legally valid for only a certain length of time. For example, a patent is granted for a time period of 20 years and gives the patent holder the legal right to exclusive use of the patented design or invention. A copyright is likewise granted for a specified legal life. A finite life also exists when there is no legal life but company management knows for certain that it will be able to use the intangible asset for only a specified period of time. For example, a company may have purchased the right to use a list of names and addresses of customers for a two-year time period. In that case, the intangible asset can be used for only two years and has a finite life.

When an intangible asset with a finite life is amortized, the time period over which amortization should be recorded must be considered carefully. The general guideline that should be followed is this: **amortization should be recorded over the legal life or the useful life, whichever is shorter.** For example, patents may have a legal life of 20 years, but many are not useful for that long because new products and technology make the patent obsolete. The patent should be amortized over the number of years in which the firm receives benefits, which may be a period shorter than the legal life.

Example 8-9 Calculating the Amortization of Intangibles

Assume that Nike developed a patent for a new shoe product on January 1, 2012. The costs involved with patent approval were $10,000, and the company wants to record amortization on the straight-line basis over a five-year life with no residual value. In this case, the useful life of the patent is less than the legal life. Nike should record amortization over the useful life as $10,000/5 years = $2,000.

The effect of the amortization for 2012 is as follows:

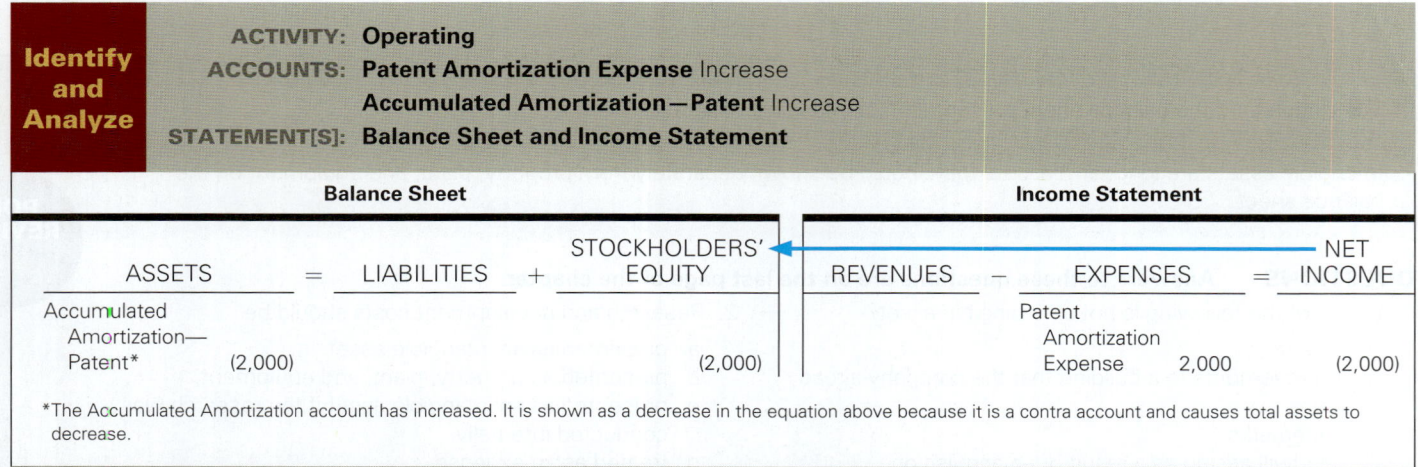

Identify and Analyze

ACTIVITY: **Operating**
ACCOUNTS: **Patent Amortization Expense** Increase
Accumulated Amortization—Patent Increase
STATEMENT[S]: **Balance Sheet and Income Statement**

Balance Sheet				Income Statement			
ASSETS	=	LIABILITIES	+	STOCKHOLDERS' EQUITY	REVENUES	−	EXPENSES	=	NET INCOME
Accumulated Amortization— Patent* (2,000)				(2,000)		Patent Amortization Expense 2,000	(2,000)

*The Accumulated Amortization account has increased. It is shown as a decrease in the equation above because it is a contra account and causes total assets to decrease.

Rather than use an accumulated amortization account, some companies decrease (credit) the intangible asset account directly. In that case, the effect of the amortization can be identified and analyzed as follows:

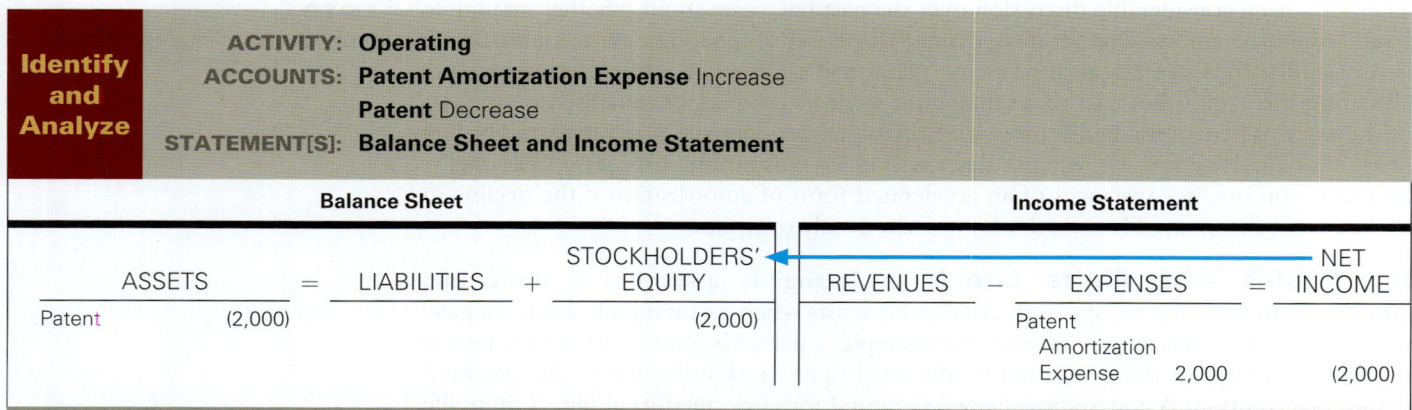

Identify and Analyze

ACTIVITY: **Operating**
ACCOUNTS: **Patent Amortization Expense** Increase
Patent Decrease
STATEMENT[S]: **Balance Sheet and Income Statement**

Balance Sheet				Income Statement			
ASSETS	=	LIABILITIES	+	STOCKHOLDERS' EQUITY	REVENUES	−	EXPENSES	=	NET INCOME
Patent (2,000)				(2,000)		Patent Amortization Expense 2,000	(2,000)

No matter which of the two preceding methods is used, the asset should be reported on the balance sheet at acquisition cost ($10,000) less accumulated amortization ($2,000), or $8,000, as of December 31, 2012.

Intangibles with Indefinite Life While intangibles such as patents and copyrights have a finite life, many others do not. **If an intangible asset has an indefinite life, amortization should not be recognized.** For example, a television or radio station may have paid to acquire a broadcast license. A broadcast license is usually for a certain time period but can be renewed at the end of that time period. In that case, the life of the asset is indefinite and amortization of the intangible asset representing the broadcast rights should not be recognized. A second example would be a trademark. For many companies, such as Nike and **The Coca-Cola Company**, a trademark is a valuable asset that provides name recognition and enhances sales. A trademark is granted for a certain

SPOTLIGHT
The Importance of Operating Assets for a Lender

In the investment banking industry, credit risk analysis is critical when evaluating companies in which to invest. **John Davenport** is an assistant vice president in charge of investment banking credit risk analysis. He uses financial accounting tools to be successful in this position.

Why should students learn about a company's operating assets? John says that it's important because it dictates how the company operates and where it is likely to spend money. For example, the operating assets of a manufacturing company will consist predominantly of PP&E and require a certain level of regular capital expenditures to ensure that equipment is properly maintained and at a profitable (and competitive) point in the cost curve. Therefore, these businesses are considered to be highly "capital intensive." Alternatively, a pharmaceutical company's operating assets have a large component that consists of intangible assets such as patents, which will require a certain level of R&D expenditures.

The valuation of operating assets is often a key component to John's analysis. Oftentimes valuing operating assets such as property, plant, and equipment (or PP&E) can create difficulties as book value of such assets are rarely representative of fair (or market) value. To facilitate lending against such assets, John often uses third-party valuations.

John also evaluates goodwill as part of his analysis of a company. Goodwill is a unique intangible asset that arises out of a business acquisition. It reflects the excess of the fair value of an acquired entity over the net of the amount assigned to assets acquired and liabilities assumed. Such excess may be paid because of the acquired company's outstanding management, earnings record, or other similar features. From a lender's perspective, a company's goodwill balance can be quite telling for a number of reasons. A large balance can hint a company's history of overpaying for acquisitions or being highly acquisitive in general. Additionally, a large amount of goodwill can also be an indication that a company may later have to declare that some of these assets are impaired.

> **"It's important to gain an understanding of the composition (and condition) of a company's operating assets, as it dictates how the company operates and where it is likely to spend money."**

Name: John Davenport

Education: B.S.B.A., Cameron School of Business, University of North Carolina Wilmington

College Major: Finance/ Economics

Occupation: Investment Banking Credit Risk Analyst

Age: 25

Position: Assistant Vice President

Company Name: Barclays Capital

See John Davenport's interview clip in CNOW.

time period but can be renewed at the end of that period, so the life may be quite indefinite. The value of some trademarks may continue for a long time. If the life of an intangible asset represented by trademarks is indefinite, amortization should not be recorded. Note in Exhibit 8-4 that Nike has considered some trademarks to have an indefinite life and has not amortized them. Others have been amortized because they have a limited life.

Goodwill and Impairments Goodwill is an important intangible asset on the balance sheet of many companies. At one time, accounting rules had required companies to record amortization of goodwill over a time period not to exceed 40 years. However, the current stance of the FASB is that goodwill should be treated as an intangible asset with an *indefinite* life and that companies should no longer record amortization expense related to goodwill. Companies have generally favored the new accounting stance. The hope is that it will allow companies to more accurately inform statement users of their true value.

While companies should not record amortization of intangible assets with an indefinite life, they are required each year to determine whether the asset has been *impaired*. A discussion of asset impairment is beyond the scope of this text, but generally, it means that a loss should be recorded when the value of the asset has declined. For example, some trademarks, such as **Xerox** and **Polaroid**, that were quite powerful in the past have declined in value over time. When an impairment of the asset is recognized, the loss is recorded in the time period that the value declines rather than the date the asset is sold. It requires a great deal of judgment to determine when intangible assets have been impaired because the true value of an intangible asset is often difficult to determine. A rather drastic example of impairment occurs when a company realizes that an intangible asset has become completely worthless and should be written off.

Assume that Nike learns on January 1, 2013, when accumulated amortization is $2,000 (or the book value of the patent is $8,000), that a competing company has developed a new product that renders Nike's patent worthless. Nike has a loss of $8,000 and should record an entry to write off the asset. The effect of the transaction can be identified and analyzed as follows:

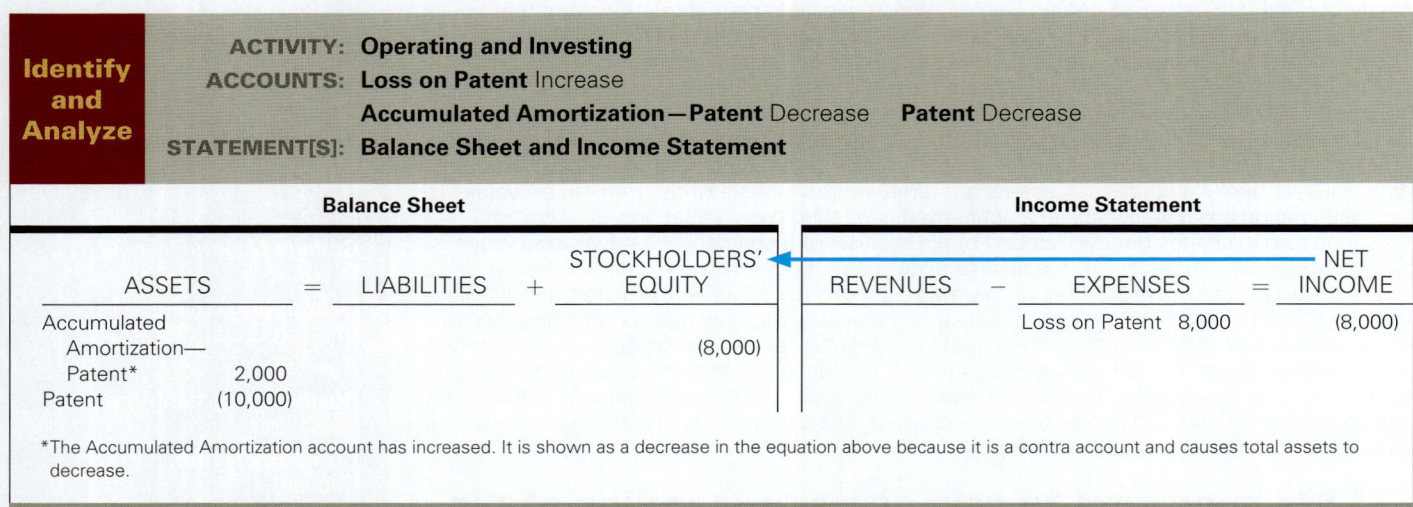

Identify and Analyze

ACTIVITY: Operating and Investing
ACCOUNTS: Loss on Patent Increase
Accumulated Amortization—Patent Decrease   Patent Decrease
STATEMENT[S]: Balance Sheet and Income Statement

Balance Sheet						Income Statement		
ASSETS	=	LIABILITIES	+	STOCKHOLDERS' EQUITY		REVENUES −	EXPENSES	= NET INCOME
Accumulated Amortization—Patent*	2,000			(8,000)			Loss on Patent 8,000	(8,000)
Patent	(10,000)							

*The Accumulated Amortization account has increased. It is shown as a decrease in the equation above because it is a contra account and causes total assets to decrease.

LO10 Understand the proper amortization of intangible assets.

- The amortization of intangibles is a process similar to that of depreciating capital assets.
- If an intangible asset has a finite useful life, amortization expense must be taken on the asset over the legal life or useful life, whichever is shorter.

POD REVIEW 8.10

QUESTIONS   **Answers to these questions are on the last page of the chapter.**

1. Regarding amortization of intangible assets,
   a. all intangible assets should be amortized.
   b. no intangible assets should be amortized.
   c. intangible assets with an infinite life should be amortized.
   d. intangible assets with a finite life should be amortized.

2. Intangibles that have a finite life
   a. should not be amortized.
   b. should be treated in the same manner as those that have an infinite life.
   c. should be amortized over the legal life or useful life, whichever is shorter.
   d. should be amortized over the legal life or useful life, whichever is longer.

IFRS

IFRS and Intangible Assets

Over time, many of the differences between FASB and international standards have been eliminated, but some important distinctions remain. The international standards are more flexible in allowing the use of fair market values for intangible assets. However, such values can only be used for those assets where an "active market" exists and it is possible to determine fair value.

The treatment of research and development costs also differs. FASB standards require all research and development costs to be treated as an expense. The international standards make a distinction between research costs and development costs. All research costs must be treated as an expense, but development costs can be capitalized as an asset if certain criteria are met.

These differences between U.S. and international standards will likely be addressed and eliminated as U.S. companies move to adopt the international standards.

How Long-Term Assets Affect the Statement of Cash Flows

OVERVIEW: The acquisition of operating assets is presented as an investing activity, a cash outflow. The depreciation or amortization of an operating asset is presented in the Operating Activities section (indirect method). It is a noncash item because it neither provides nor uses cash. The disposal of an operating asset is presented in the Investing Activities section as a cash outflow. If a gain or loss occurs, it must be eliminated from the Operating section of the statement.

LO11 Explain the impact that long-term assets have on the statement of cash flows.

Determining the impact that acquisition, depreciation, and sale of long-term assets have on the statement of cash flows is important. Each of these business activities influences the statement of cash flows. Exhibit 8-5 illustrates the items discussed in this chapter and their effect on the statement of cash flows.

The acquisition of a long-term asset is an investing activity and should be reflected in the Investing Activities category of the statement of cash flows. The acquisition should appear as a deduction, or negative item, in that section because it requires the use of cash to purchase the asset. This applies whether the long-term asset is property, plant, and equipment or an intangible asset.

The depreciation or amortization of a long-term asset is not a cash item. It was referred to earlier as a noncash charge to earnings. Nevertheless, it must be presented on the statement of cash flows (if the indirect method is used for the statement). The reason is that it was deducted from earnings in calculating the net income figure. Therefore, it must be eliminated or "added back" if the net income amount is used to indicate the amount of cash generated from operations. **Thus, depreciation and amortization should be presented in the Operating Activities category of the statement of cash flows as an addition to net income.**

The sale or disposition of long-term assets is an investing activity. When an asset is sold, the amount of cash received should be reflected as an addition or plus

EXHIBIT 8-5 Long-Term Assets and the Statement of Cash Flows

Item	Cash Flow Statement	
	Operating Activities	
	Net Income	**xxx**
Depreciation and amortization ——————————————▶		+
Gain on sale of asset ————————————————————▶		−
Loss on sale of asset ————————————————————▶		+
	Investing Activities	
Purchase of asset ————————————————————▶		−
Sale of asset ——————————————————————————▶		+
	Financing Activities	

© Cengage Learning 2013

amount in the Investing Activities category of the statement of cash flows. If the asset was sold at a gain or loss, however, one additional aspect should be reflected. Because the gain or loss was reflected on the income statement, it should be eliminated from the net income amount presented in the Operating Activities category (if the indirect method is used). A sale of an asset is not an activity related to normal ongoing operations, and all amounts involved with the sale should be removed from the Operating Activities category. Exhibit 8-6 indicates the Operating and Investing categories of the 2010 statement of cash flows of Nike, Inc. The company had a net income of $1,906.7 million during 2010. Nike's performance is an excellent example of the difference between net income and actual cash flow. Note that the company generated a positive cash flow from operating activities of $3,164.2 million. One of the primary reasons was that depreciation of $323.7 million and amortization of $71.8 million affected the income statement but did not involve a cash outflow and therefore are added back on the statement of cash flows. Also note that the Investing Activities category indicates major outlays of cash for new property, plant, and equipment of $335.1 million. These cash outflows are indications of Nike's need for cash that must be generated from its operating activities.

EXHIBIT 8-6 Nike, Inc.'s Consolidated Partial Statement of Cash Flows

Year Ended May 31, (In millions)	2010
Cash provided by operations:	
Net income	$1,906.70
Income charges (credits) not affecting cash:	
Depreciation	323.7
Deferred income taxes	8.3
Stock-based compensation	159.0
Impairment of goodwill, intangibles and other assets	—
Gain on divestitures	—
Amortization and other	71.8
Changes in certain working capital components and other assets and liabilities excluding the impact of acquisition and divestitures:	
Decrease (increase) in accounts receivable	181.7
Decrease (increase) in inventories	284.6
(Increase) decrease in prepaid expenses and other current assets	(69.6)
Increase (decrease) in accounts payable, accrued liabilities and income taxes payable	298.0
Cash provided by operations	$ 3,164.2
Cash used by investing activities:	
Purchases of short-term investments	(3,724.4)
Maturities and sales of short-term investments	2,787.6
Additions to property, plant and equipment	(335.1)
Disposals of property, plant and equipment	10.1
Increase in other assets, net of other liabilities	(11.2)
Settlement of net investment hedges	5.5
Acquisition of subsidiary, net of cash acquired	—
Proceeds from divestitures	—
Cash used by investing activities	$ (1,267.5)

LO11 Explain the impact that long-term assets have on the statement of cash flows.

- Long-term assets impact the statement of cash flows when they are acquired, depreciated, and sold.
- Cash used to acquire long-term assets or cash received on the sale of long-term assets is reflected in the Investing Activities section of the statement of cash flows.
- Depreciation and amortization are noncash expenses recorded on the accrual income statement. Accordingly, net income on a cash basis must be arrived at by adding depreciation and amortization back to accrual net income.

POD REVIEW 8.11

QUESTIONS **Answers to these questions are on the last page of the chapter.**

1. On the statement of cash flows (indirect method), the amount for depreciation should be presented in which category?

   a. Operating
   b. Investing
   c. Financing
   d. The amount should not be presented.

2. When a company purchases property, plant, and equipment, an amount should appear in which category of the statement of cash flows?

   a. Operating
   b. Investing
   c. Financing
   d. The amount should not be presented.

© Cengage Learning 2013

Analyzing Long-Term Assets for Average Life and Asset Turnover

OVERVIEW: Ratios are used to determine the age, composition, and quality of the operating assets. The average life is determined by dividing the amount of property, plant, and equipment by depreciation expense. The average age can be determined by dividing accumulated depreciation by depreciation expense. The asset turnover ratio is a measure of how productive the assets are in producing revenue and can be determined by dividing net sales by average total assets.

LO12 Understand how investors can analyze a company's operating assets.

Because long-term assets constitute the major productive assets of most companies, the age and composition of these assets should be analyzed. Analysis of the age of the assets can be accomplished fairly easily for those companies that use the straight-line method of depreciation. A rough measure of the average life of the assets can be calculated as follows:

$$\text{Average Life} = \frac{\text{Property, Plant, and Equipment}}{\text{Depreciation Expense}}$$

The average age of the assets can be calculated as follows:

$$\text{Average Age} = \frac{\text{Accumulated Depreciation}}{\text{Depreciation Expense}}$$

The Assets category of the balance sheet is also important in analyzing a company's profitability. The asset turnover is a measure of the assets' productivity and is measured as follows:

$$\text{Asset Turnover} = \frac{\text{Net Sales}}{\text{Average Total Assets}}$$

This ratio is a measure of how many dollars of assets are necessary for every dollar of sales. That is, the ratio is a measure of how productive the assets are in generating sales. If a company is using its assets efficiently, each dollar of assets will create a high amount of sales. A company with less productive assets will generate fewer sales from its dollar of assets. Technically, a ratio is based on average total assets, but long-term assets often constitute the largest portion of a company's total assets.

For more on these measures of the age, life, and performance of the assets of Nike, Inc., and the way they are used, see the Ratio Decision Model on pages 404–406.

LO12 Understand how investors can analyze a company's operating assets.

- Investors are interested in how productive a company's operating assets are.
- The Ratio Decision Model is a valuable tool that can be used to examine the productivity of operating assets with the asset turnover ratio.

POD REVIEW 8.12

QUESTIONS   Answers to these questions are on the last page of the chapter.

1. Which of the following sets of ratios can be used to gain insight into a company's management of its fixed assets?
   a. current ratio, quick ratio
   b. inventory turnover ratio, accounts receivable turnover
   c. debt-to-equity ratio times interest earned
   d. average age, asset turnover

2. What does it mean when the asset turnover ratio increases for a company?
   a. It is a favorable indication.
   b. It is an unfavorable indication.
   c. It means that less sales were created for each dollar of assets.
   d. It means that the average life of the assets has increased.

USING THE RATIO DECISION MODEL

Analyzing Average Life and Asset Turnover

Use the following Ratio Decision Model to evaluate the average life and asset turnover for Nike or any other public company.

1. Formulate the Question

Long-term assets constitute the major productive assets of most companies. Investors and others who read financial statements must determine the age and composition of the operating assets. Two important questions are:

What is the average *life* of the assets?
What is the average *age* of the assets?

The Operating Assets category is also important in analyzing whether the operating assets will allow the company to be profitable in future periods. Therefore, a third question is:

How *productive* are the operating assets?

The productivity of assets can be calculated using the asset turnover ratio.

2. Gather the Information from the Financial Statements
Average Life and Average Age
For companies that use the straight-line method of depreciation:

- Total property, plant, and equipment: From the balance sheet (see Nike's Note 3)
- Total accumulated depreciation: From the balance sheet (see Nike's Note 3)
- Annual depreciation expense: From the statement of cash flows

Asset Turnover

- Average total assets: From the income statement

3. Calculate the Ratio

$$\text{Average Life} = \frac{\text{Property, Plant, and Equipment}}{\text{Depreciation Expense}}$$

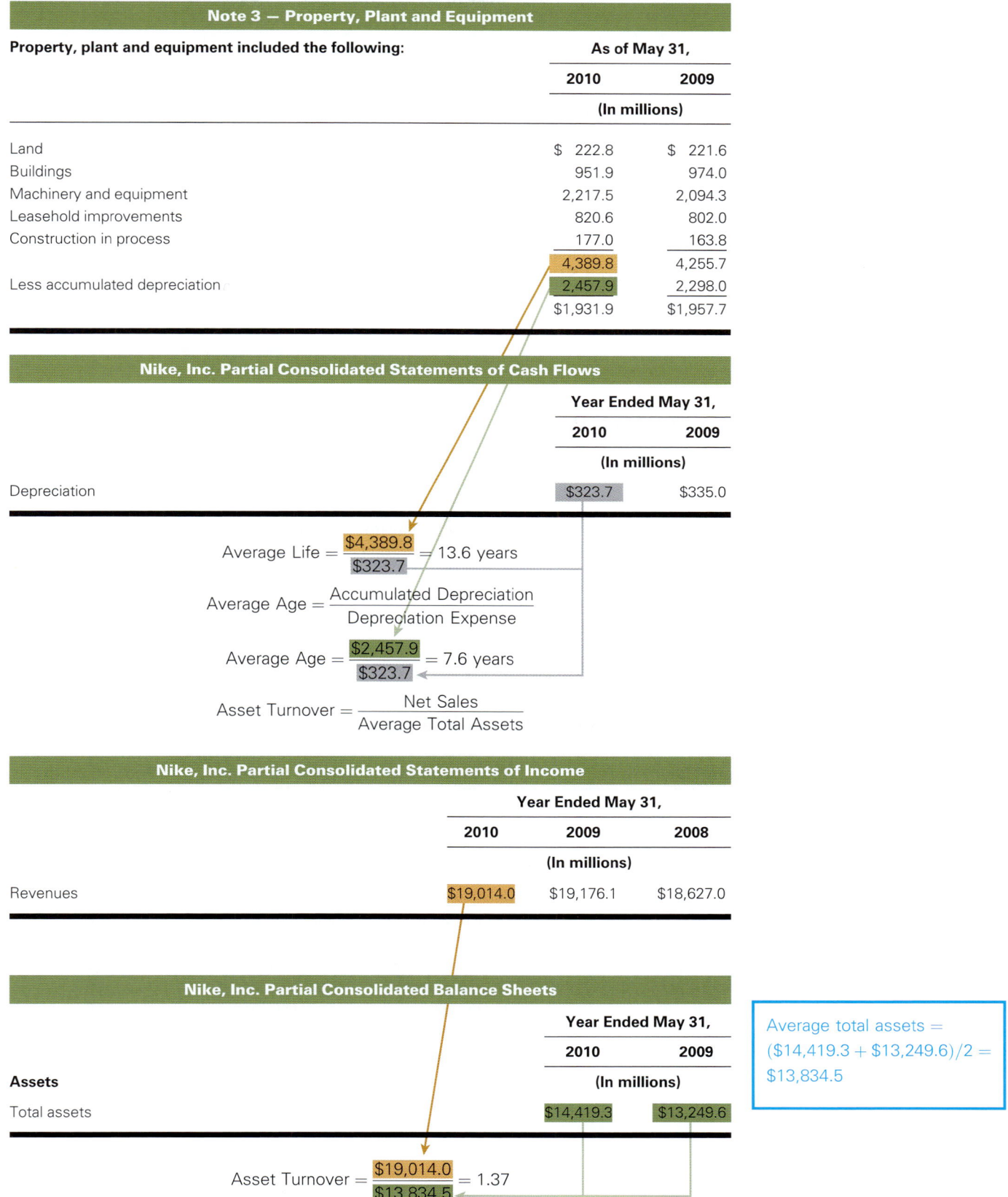

Note 3 — Property, Plant and Equipment

Property, plant and equipment included the following:

	As of May 31,	
	2010	**2009**
	(In millions)	
Land	$ 222.8	$ 221.6
Buildings	951.9	974.0
Machinery and equipment	2,217.5	2,094.3
Leasehold improvements	820.6	802.0
Construction in process	177.0	163.8
	4,389.8	4,255.7
Less accumulated depreciation	2,457.9	2,298.0
	$1,931.9	$1,957.7

Nike, Inc. Partial Consolidated Statements of Cash Flows

	Year Ended May 31,	
	2010	**2009**
	(In millions)	
Depreciation	$323.7	$335.0

$$\text{Average Life} = \frac{\$4,389.8}{\$323.7} = 13.6 \text{ years}$$

$$\text{Average Age} = \frac{\text{Accumulated Depreciation}}{\text{Depreciation Expense}}$$

$$\text{Average Age} = \frac{\$2,457.9}{\$323.7} = 7.6 \text{ years}$$

$$\text{Asset Turnover} = \frac{\text{Net Sales}}{\text{Average Total Assets}}$$

Nike, Inc. Partial Consolidated Statements of Income

	Year Ended May 31,		
	2010	**2009**	**2008**
	(In millions)		
Revenues	$19,014.0	$19,176.1	$18,627.0

Nike, Inc. Partial Consolidated Balance Sheets

	Year Ended May 31,	
	2010	**2009**
Assets	**(In millions)**	
Total assets	$14,419.3	$13,249.6

Average total assets =
($14,419.3 + $13,249.6)/2 =
$13,834.5

$$\text{Asset Turnover} = \frac{\$19,014.0}{\$13,834.5} = 1.37$$

4. Compare the Ratio with Others

Nike's age, composition, and productivity of operating assets should be compared to those of prior years and to those of companies in the same industry.

	Nike 2010	Nike 2009	Foot Locker 10	Foot Locker 09
Average life of assets	13.6	12.7	7.66	7.38
Average age of assets	7.6	6.86	5.89	5.72
Asset turnover	1.37	1.45	1.77	1.72

5. Interpret the Results

The average life and age of Nike's assets have been consistent from year to year and are in line with other companies in the industry. The asset turnover ratio is a measure of how many dollars of assets are necessary for every dollar of sales. If a company uses its assets efficiently, each dollar of asset will create a high amount of sales. Technically, this ratio is based on average total assets, but operating assets constitute the largest portion of a company's total assets. Nike's asset turnover ratio indicates that each dollar of assets in 2010 produced $1.37 of sales. It is an indication that the assets are currently productive and will be able to provide a profit in future periods. ■

RATIO REVIEW

$$\text{Average Life} = \frac{\text{Property, Plant, and Equipment}}{\text{Depreciation Expense}}$$

$$\text{Average Age} = \frac{\text{Accumulated Depreciation}}{\text{Depreciation Expenses}}$$

$$\text{Asset Turnover} = \frac{\text{Net Sales}}{\text{Average Total Assets}}$$

ACCOUNTS HIGHLIGHTED

Account Title	Appears on the	In the Section of	Page Number
Land	Balance Sheet	Operating Assets	379
Buildings	Balance Sheet	Operating Assets	379
Machinery	Balance Sheet	Operating Assets	389
Accumulated Depreciation (a contra account)	Balance Sheet	Operating Assets	388
Depreciation Expense	Income Statement	Operating Expenses	388
Gain on Sale of Asset	Income Statement	Other Income	392
Loss on Sale of Asset	Income Statement	Other Expense	393
Copyright	Balance Sheet	Intangible Assets	396
Trademark	Balance Sheet	Intangible Assets	396
Goodwill	Balance Sheet	Intangible Assets	396
Amortization Expense	Income Statement	Operating Expenses	398
Accumulated Amortization (a contra account)	Balance Sheet	Intangible Assets	400

KEY TERMS QUIZ

Read each definition below and write the number of the definition in the blank beside the appropriate term. The quiz solutions appear at the end of the chapter.

_____ Acquisition cost
_____ Capitalization of interest
_____ Land improvements
_____ Depreciation
_____ Straight-line method
_____ Book value
_____ Units-of-production method
_____ Accelerated depreciation
_____ Double-declining-balance method

_____ Change in estimate
_____ Capital expenditure
_____ Revenue expenditure
_____ Gain on Sale of Asset
_____ Loss on Sale of Asset
_____ Intangible assets
_____ Goodwill
_____ Research and development costs

1. This amount includes all of the costs normally necessary to acquire an asset and prepare it for its intended use.
2. Additions made to a piece of property, such as paving or landscaping a parking lot. The costs are treated separately from land for purposes of recording depreciation.
3. A method by which the same dollar amount of depreciation is recorded in each year of asset use.
4. A method by which depreciation is determined as a function of the number of units the asset produces.
5. The process of treating the cost of interest on constructed assets as a part of the asset cost rather than an expense.
6. A change in the life of an asset or in its expected residual value.
7. The allocation of the original acquisition cost of an asset to the periods benefited by its use.
8. A cost that improves an operating asset and is added to the asset account.
9. The original acquisition cost of an asset minus the amount of accumulated depreciation.
10. A cost that keeps an operating asset in its normal operating condition and is treated as an expense of the period.
11. An account whose amount indicates that the selling price received on an asset's disposal exceeds its book value.
12. An account whose amount indicates that the book value of an asset exceeds the selling price received on its disposal.
13. A term that refers to several methods by which a higher amount of depreciation is recorded in the early years of an asset's life and a lower amount is recorded in the later years.
14. Long-term assets that have no physical properties; for example, patents, copyrights, and goodwill.
15. A method by which depreciation is recorded at twice the straight-line rate, but the depreciable balance is reduced in each period.
16. The amount indicating that the purchase price of a business exceeded the total fair market value of the identifiable net assets at the time the business was acquired.
17. Expenditures incurred in the discovery of new knowledge and the translation of research into a design or plan for a new product.

ALTERNATE TERMS

accumulated depreciation allowance for depreciation

acquisition cost historical cost and original cost

capitalize expenditure item treated as asset

construction in progress construction in process

goodwill purchase price in excess of the market value of the assets

hidden assets unrecorded or off–balance-sheet assets

property, plant, and equipment fixed assets

prospective current and future years

residual value salvage value

revenue expenditure item treated as an expense of the period

WARMUP EXERCISES & SOLUTIONS

LO5   **Warmup Exercise 8-1**   **Depreciation Methods**

Assume that a company purchases a depreciable asset on January 1 for $10,000. The asset has a four-year life and will have zero residual value at the end of the fourth year.

Required

Calculate depreciation expense for each of the four years using the straight-line method and the double-declining-balance method.

LO5   **Warmup Exercise 8-2**   **Depreciation and Cash Flow**

Use the information from Exercise 8-1. Assume that the double-declining-balance method will be used for tax purposes and the straight-line method will be used for the financial statement to be given to the stockholders. Also assume that the tax rate is 40%.

Required

How much will the tax savings be in the first year as a result of using the accelerated method of depreciation?

Solutions to Warmup Exercises

Warmup Exercise 8-1

Year	Straight-Line	Double-Declining-Balance	
1	$2,500*	$10,000 × 0.50**	= $5,000
2	2,500	($10,000 − $5,000) × 0.50	= $2,500
3	2,500	($10,000 − $7,500) × 0.50	= $1,250
4	2,500	($10,000 − $8,750) × 0.50	= $ 625

*$10,000/4 years

**Straight-line rate as a percentage is 1 year/4 years, or 25%. Double the rate is 25% × 2, or 50%.

Warmup Exercise 8-2

The tax savings is equal to the difference in depreciation between the two methods times the tax rate. Therefore, the tax savings is ($5,000 − $2,500) × 0.40 = $1,000.

REVIEW PROBLEM & SOLUTION

The accountant for Becker Company wants to develop a balance sheet as of December 31, 2012. A review of the asset records has revealed the following information:

a. Asset A was purchased on July 1, 2010, for $40,000 and has been depreciated on the straight-line basis using an estimated life of six years and a residual value of $4,000.

b. Asset B was purchased on January 1, 2011, for $66,000. The straight-line method has been used for depreciation purposes. Originally, the estimated life of the asset was projected to be six years with a residual value of $6,000; however, at the beginning of 2012, the accountant learned that the remaining life of the asset was only three years with a residual value of $2,000.

c. Asset C was purchased on January 1, 2011, for $50,000. The double-declining-balance method has been used for depreciation purposes, with a four-year life and a residual value estimate of $5,000.

Required

1. Assume that these assets represent pieces of equipment. Calculate the acquisition cost, accumulated depreciation, and book value of each asset as of December 31, 2012.
2. How would the assets appear on the balance sheet on December 31, 2012?
3. Assume that Becker Company sold Asset B on January 2, 2013, for $25,000. Calculate the amount of the resulting gain or loss and identify and analyze the effect of the sale. Where would the gain or loss appear on the income statement?

Solutions to Review Problem Part A

1.

Asset A

2010	Depreciation	($40,000 − $4,000)/6 × 1/2 Year	=	$ 3,000
2011		($40,000 − $4,000)/6	=	6,000
2012		($40,000 − $4,000)/6	=	6,000
	Accumulated Depreciation			$15,000

Asset B

2011	Depreciation	($66,000 − $6,000)/6	=	$10,000
2012		($66,000 − $10,000 − $2,000)/3	=	18,000
	Accumulated Depreciation			$28,000

Note the impact of the change in estimate on 2011 depreciation.

Asset C

2011	Depreciation	$50,000 × 25% × 2	=	$25,000
2012		($50,000 − $25,000) × (25% × 2)	=	12,500
	Accumulated Depreciation			$37,500

Becker Company
Summary of Asset Cost and Accumulated Depreciation
As of December 31, 2012

Asset	Acquisition Cost	Accumulated Depreciation	Book Value
A	$ 40,000	$15,000	$25,000
B	66,000	28,000	38,000
C	50,000	37,500	12,500
Totals	$156,000	$80,500	$75,500

2. The assets would appear in the Long-Term Assets category of the balance sheet as follows:

Equipment	$156,000
Less: Accumulated depreciation	80,500
Equipment (net)	$ 75,500

3.

Asset B book value	$38,000
Selling price	25,000
Loss on sale of asset	$13,000

(Continued)

The effect of the transaction for the sale can be identified and analyzed as follows:

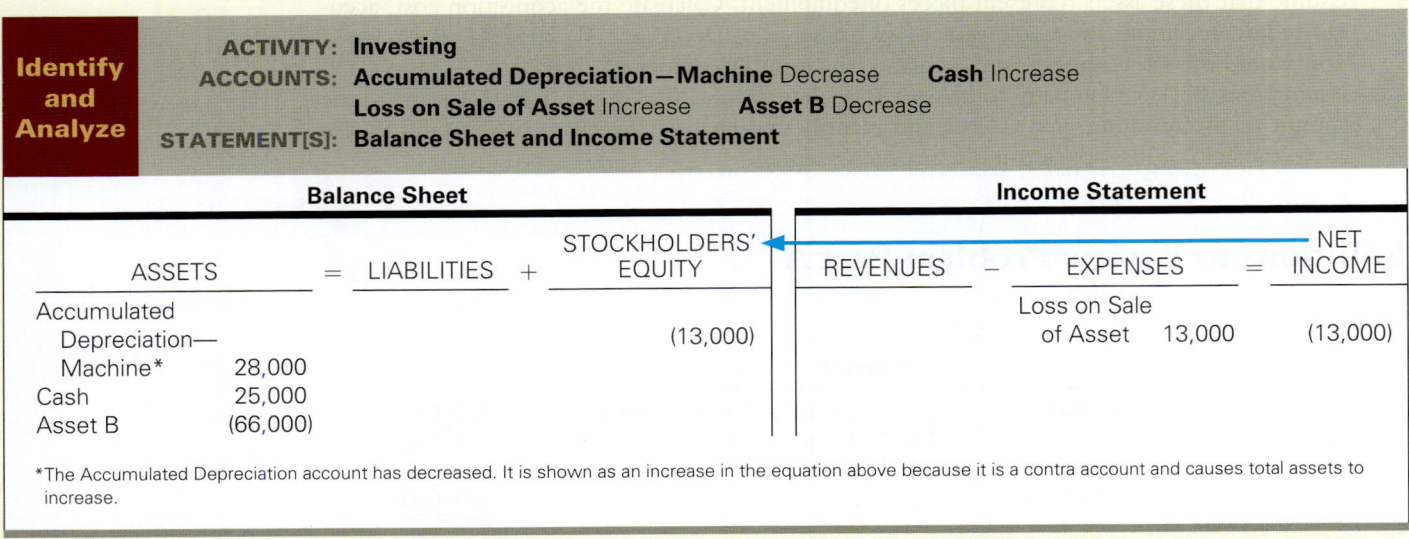

The Loss on Sale of Asset account should appear in the Other Income/Other Expense category of the income statement. It is similar to an expense but is not the company's major activity.

QUESTIONS

1. What are several examples of operating assets? Why are operating assets essential to a company's long-term future?

2. What is the meaning of the term *acquisition cost of operating assets*? Give some examples of costs that should be included in the acquisition cost.

3. When assets are purchased as a group, how should the acquisition cost of the individual assets be determined?

4. Why is it important to account separately for the cost of land and building even when the two assets are purchased together?

5. Under what circumstances should interest be capitalized as part of the cost of an asset?

6. What factors may contribute to the decline in usefulness of operating assets? Should the choice of depreciation method be related to these factors? Must a company choose just one method of depreciation for all assets?

7. Why do most companies use the straight-line depreciation method?

8. How should the residual value of an operating asset be treated when the straight-line method is used? How should it be treated when the double-declining-balance method is used?

9. Why do many companies use one method to calculate depreciation for the income statement developed for stockholders and another method for income tax purposes?

10. What should a company do if it finds that the original estimate of the life of an asset or the residual value of the asset must be changed?

11. Define the terms *capital expenditures* and *revenue expenditures*. What determines whether an item is a capital or revenue expenditure?

12. How is the gain or loss on the sale of an operating asset calculated? Where would the Gain on Sale of Asset account appear on the financial statements?

13. Give several examples of intangible assets. In what balance sheet category should intangible assets appear?

14. Define the term *goodwill*. Give an example of a transaction that would result in the recording of goodwill on the balance sheet.

15. Do you agree with the FASB's ruling that all research and development costs should be treated as an expense on the income statement? Explain.

16. Do you agree with some accountants who argue that intangible assets have an indefinite life and therefore should not be subject to amortization? Explain.

17. When an intangible asset is amortized, should the asset's amortization occur over its legal life or its useful life? Give an example in which the legal life exceeds the useful life.
18. Suppose that an intangible asset is being amortized over a ten-year time period but a competitor has just introduced a new product that will have a serious negative impact on the asset's value. Should the company continue to amortize the intangible asset over the ten-year life?

BRIEF EXERCISES

Brief Exercise 8-1 Property, Plant, and Equipment Classification   LO1

Which of the following would be in the Property, Plant, and Equipment balance sheet category?

Land
Buildings
Accumulated depreciation
Patent
Leasehold improvements
Construction in process

Brief Exercise 8-2 Determine Acquisition Cost   LO2

Which of the following would be considered part of the acquisition cost of an asset?

Transportation costs
Installation costs
Repair costs incurred at time of purchase
Repair costs incurred after the asset has been installed and used
Interest on loan to purchase the asset

Brief Exercise 8-3 Lump-Sum Purchase   LO3
EXAMPLE 8-1

On December 1, 2012, Company X bought from Company Y land and an accompanying warehouse for $800,000. The fair market values of the land and the building at the time of purchase were $700,000 and $300,000, respectively. How much of the purchase price should Company X allocate to land? How much to the building?

Brief Exercise 8-4 Capitalization of Interest   LO4

A company begins construction of an asset on January 1, 2012, and completes construction on December 31, 2012. The company pays the following amounts related to construction:

$1,000,000	January 1
$2,000,000	July 1
$1,000,000	December 1

Calculate the average accumulated expenditures for the purpose of capitalizing interest.

Brief Exercise 8-5 Depreciation Methods   LO5
EXAMPLE 8-4

A company uses the double-declining-balance method of depreciation. The company purchases an asset for $40,000, which is expected to have a ten-year life and a $4,000 residual value.

What depreciation rate will be applied each year?
What amount will be charged for depreciation in the first and second years?
What amount will be treated as depreciation over the ten-year life?

Brief Exercise 8-6 Change in Depreciation Estimate   LO6
EXAMPLE 8-5

A company purchased an asset on January 1, 2010, for $10,000. The asset was expected to have a ten-year life and a $1,000 salvage value. The company uses the straight-line method of depreciation. On January 1, 2012, the company determines that the asset will last only five more years.
Calculate the amount of depreciation for 2012.

LO7
EXAMPLE 8-6

Brief Exercise 8-7 Capital Expenditure

A company purchased an asset on January 1, 2010, for $10,000. The asset was expected to have a ten-year life and a $1,000 salvage value. The company uses the straight-line method of depreciation. On January 1, 2012, the company made a major repair to the asset of $5,000, extending its life. The asset is expected to last ten years from January 1, 2012.

Calculate the amount of depreciation for 2012.

LO8
EXAMPLE 8-8

Brief Exercise 8-8 Sale of Asset

A machine with a cost of $100,000 and accumulated depreciation of $80,000 was sold at a loss of $6,000. What amount of cash was received from the sale?

LO9
EXAMPLE 8-9

Brief Exercise 8-9 Classification of Intangible Assets

Which of the following would be considered intangible assets on the balance sheet? Which intangibles should be amortized?

Patents
Copyrights
Research and development
Goodwill
The company's advantageous location
Broadcast rights

LO10

Brief Exercise 8-10 Amortization of Intangible

A company develops a patent on January 1, 2010, and the costs involved with patent approval are $12,000. The legal life of the patent is 20 years, but the company projects that it will provide useful benefits for only 12 years. At January 1, 2012, the company discovers that a competitor will introduce a new product, making this patent useless in five years. How much amortization should be recorded in 2010, 2011, and 2012?

LO11

Brief Exercise 8-11 Operating Assets and Cash Flows

In which category of the statement of cash flows (indirect method) should the following items appear?

Depreciation of an operating asset
Gain on the sale of an asset
Amortization of an intangible
Loss on the sale of an asset
Amount paid to purchase an asset
Amount received upon sale of an asset

LO12

Brief Exercise 8-12 Analysis of Operating Assets

At December 31, 2012, a company has the following amounts on its financial statements:

Property, plant, and equipment	$10,000
Accumulated depreciation	5,000
Total assets at January 1, 2012	30,000
Total assets at December 31, 2012	40,000
Net sales	62,000
Depreciation expense	1,000

Calculate the following ratios:

Average life of the assets
Average age of the assets
Asset turnover

EXERCISES

Exercise 8-1 Acquisition Cost

LO2

On January 1, 2012, Ruby Company purchased a piece of equipment with a list price of $60,000. The following amounts were related to the equipment purchase:

- Terms of the purchase were 2/10, net 30. Ruby paid for the purchase on January 8.
- Freight costs of $1,000 were incurred.
- A state agency required that a pollution control device be installed on the equipment at a cost of $2,500.
- During installation, the equipment was damaged and repair costs of $4,000 were incurred.
- Architect's fees of $6,000 were paid to redesign the work space to accommodate the new equipment.
- Ruby purchased liability insurance to cover possible damage to the asset. The three-year policy cost $8,000.
- Ruby financed the purchase with a bank loan. Interest of $3,000 was paid on the loan during 2012.

Required

Determine the acquisition cost of the equipment.

Exercise 8-2 Lump-Sum Purchase

LO3
EXAMPLE 8-1

To add to his growing chain of grocery stores, on January 1, 2012, Danny Marks bought a grocery store of a small competitor for $520,000. An appraiser, hired to assess the acquired assets' value, determined that the land, building, and equipment had market values of $200,000, $150,000, and $250,000, respectively.

Required

1. What is the acquisition cost of each asset? Identify and analyze the effect of the acquisition.
2. Danny plans to depreciate the operating assets on a straight-line basis for 20 years. Determine the amount of depreciation expense for 2012 on these newly acquired assets. You can assume zero residual value for all assets.
3. How would the assets appear on the balance sheet as of December 31, 2012?

Exercise 8-3 Accelerated Depreciation

LO5
EXAMPLE 8-4

Koffman's Warehouse purchased a forklift on January 1, 2012, for $6,000. The forklift is expected to last for five years and have a residual value of $600. Koffman's uses the double-declining-balance method for depreciation.

Required

1. Calculate the depreciation expense, accumulated depreciation, and book value for each year of the forklift's life.
2. Identify and analyze the effect of the transaction for depreciation for 2012.
3. Refer to Exhibit 8-2. What factors may have influenced Koffman to use the double-declining-balance method?

Exercise 8-4 Straight-Line and Units-of-Production Methods

LO5
EXAMPLE 8-2, 8-3

Assume that Sample Company purchased factory equipment on January 1, 2012, for $60,000. The equipment has an estimated life of five years and an estimated residual value of $6,000. Sample's accountant is considering whether to use the straight-line or the units-of-production method to depreciate the asset. Because the company is beginning a new production process, the equipment will be used to produce 10,000 units in 2012, but production subsequent to 2012 will increase by 10,000 units each year.

Required

Calculate the depreciation expense, accumulated depreciation, and book value of the equipment under both methods for each of the five years of its life. Would the units-of-production method yield reasonable results in this situation? Explain.

LO6
EXAMPLE 8-5

Exercise 8-5 Change in Estimate

Assume that Bloomer Company purchased a new machine on January 1, 2012, for $80,000. The machine has an estimated useful life of nine years and a residual value of $8,000. Bloomer has chosen to use the straight-line method of depreciation. On January 1, 2014, Bloomer discovered that the machine would not be useful beyond December 31, 2017, and estimated its value at that time to be $2,000.

Required

1. Calculate the depreciation expense, accumulated depreciation, and book value of the asset for each year 2012 to 2017.
2. Was the depreciation recorded wrong in 2012 and 2013? If so, why was it not corrected?

LO8

Exercise 8-6 Asset Disposal

Assume that Gonzalez Company purchased an asset on January 1, 2010, for $60,000. The asset had an estimated life of six years and an estimated residual value of $6,000. The company used the straight-line method to depreciate the asset. On July 1, 2012, the asset was sold for $40,000.

Required

1. Identify and analyze the effect of the transaction for depreciation for 2012. Identify and analyze the effect of the sale of the asset.
2. How should the gain or loss on the sale of the asset be presented on the income statement?

LO8
EXAMPLE 8-7, 8-8

Exercise 8-7 Asset Disposal

Refer to Exercise 8-6. Assume that Gonzalez Company sold the asset on July 1, 2012, and received $15,000 cash and a note for an additional $15,000.

Required

1. Identify and analyze the effect of the transaction for depreciation for 2012. Identify and analyze the effect of the sale of the asset.
2. How should the gain or loss on the sale of the asset be presented on the income statement?

LO10
EXAMPLE 8-9

Exercise 8-8 Amortization of Intangibles

For each of the following intangible assets, indicate the amount of amortization expense that should be recorded for the year 2012 and the amount of accumulated amortization on the balance sheet as of December 31, 2012.

	Trademark	Patent	Copyright
Cost	$40,000	$50,000	$80,000
Date of purchase	1/1/05	1/1/07	1/1/10
Useful life	indefinite	10 yrs.	20 yrs.
Legal life	undefined	20 yrs.	50 yrs.
Method	SL*	SL	SL

*Represents the straight-line method.

LO11

Exercise 8-9 Impact of Transactions Involving Intangible Assets on Statement of Cash Flows

From the following list, identify each item as operating (O), investing (I), financing (F), or not separately reported on the statement of cash flows (N).

_____ Cost incurred to acquire copyright
_____ Proceeds from sale of patent

_____ Gain on sale of patent
_____ Research and development costs
_____ Amortization of patent

Exercise 8-10 Impact of Transactions Involving Operating Assets on Statement of Cash Flows

LO11

From the following list, identify each item as operating (O), investing (I), financing (F), or not separately reported on the statement of cash flows (N).

_____ Purchase of land
_____ Proceeds from sale of land
_____ Gain on sale of land
_____ Purchase of equipment
_____ Depreciation expense
_____ Proceeds from sale of equipment
_____ Loss on sale of equipment

MULTI-CONCEPT EXERCISES

Exercise 8-11 Capital versus Revenue Expenditures

LO1 • 7
EXAMPLE 8-6

On January 1, 2010, Jose Company purchased a building for $200,000 and a delivery truck for $20,000. The following expenditures have been incurred during 2012:

- The building was painted at a cost of $5,000.
- To prevent leaking, new windows were installed in the building at a cost of $10,000.
- To improve production, a new conveyor system was installed at a cost of $40,000.
- The delivery truck was repainted with a new company logo at a cost of $1,000.
- To allow better handling of large loads, a hydraulic lift system was installed on the truck at a cost of $5,000.
- The truck's engine was overhauled at a cost of $4,000.

Required

1. Determine which of those costs should be capitalized. Also, identify and analyze the effect of the capitalized costs. Assume that all costs were incurred on January 1, 2012.
2. Determine the amount of depreciation for the year 2012. The company uses the straight-line method and depreciates the building over 25 years and the truck over six years. Assume zero residual value for all assets.
3. How would the assets appear on the balance sheet of December 31, 2012?

Exercise 8-12 Capitalization of Interest and Depreciation

LO4 • 5
EXAMPLE 8-2

During 2012, Mercator Company borrowed $80,000 from a local bank. In addition, Mercator used $120,000 of cash to construct a new corporate office building. Based on average accumulated expenditures, the amount of interest capitalized during 2012 was $8,000. Construction was completed, and the building was occupied on January 1, 2013.

Required

1. Determine the acquisition cost of the new building.
2. The building has an estimated useful life of 20 years and a $5,000 salvage value. Assuming that Mercator uses the straight-line basis to depreciate its operating assets, determine the amount of depreciation expense for 2012 and 2013.

Exercise 8-13 Research and Development and Patents

LO9 • 10

Erin Company incurred the following costs during 2012 and 2013:

a. Research and development costing $20,000 was conducted on a new product to sell in future years. A product was successfully developed, and a patent for it was granted during 2012. Erin

(Continued)

is unsure of the period benefited by the research, but believes the product will result in increased sales over the next five years.

b. Legal costs and application fees of $10,000 for the 20-year patent were incurred on January 1, 2012.

c. A patent infringement suit was successfully defended at a cost of $8,000. Assume that all costs were incurred on January 1, 2013.

Required

Determine how the costs in (a) and (b) should be presented on Erin's financial statements as of December 31, 2012. Also determine the amount of amortization of intangible assets that Erin should record in 2012 and 2013.

PROBLEMS

LO3   **Problem 8-1 Lump-Sum Purchase of Assets and Subsequent Events**

Carter Development Company purchased, for cash, a large tract of land that was immediately platted and deeded into the following smaller sections:

Section 1, retail development with highway frontage
Section 2, multifamily apartment development
Section 3, single-family homes in the largest section

Based on recent sales of similar property, the fair market values of the three sections are as follows:

Section 1, $630,000
Section 2, $378,000
Section 3, $252,000

Required

1. What value is assigned to each section of land if the tract was purchased for (a) $1,260,000, (b) $1,560,000, and (c) $1,000,000?
2. How does the purchase of the tract affect the balance sheet?
3. Why would Carter be concerned with the value assigned to each section? Would Carter be more concerned with the values assigned if instead of purchasing three sections of land, it purchased land with buildings? Explain.

LO5   **Problem 8-2 Depreciation as a Tax Shield**

The term *tax shield* refers to the amount of income tax saved by deducting depreciation for income tax purposes. Assume that Supreme Company is considering the purchase of an asset as of January 1, 2012. The cost of the asset with a five-year life and zero residual value is $100,000. The company will use the straight-line method of depreciation.

Supreme's income for tax purposes before recording depreciation on the asset will be $50,000 per year for the next five years. The corporation is currently in the 35% tax bracket.

Required

Calculate the amount of income tax that Supreme must pay each year if the asset is not purchased. Calculate the amount of income tax that Supreme must pay each year if the asset is purchased. What is the amount of the depreciation tax shield?

LO5   **Problem 8-3 Book versus Tax Depreciation**

Griffith Delivery Service purchased a delivery truck for $33,600. The truck has an estimated useful life of six years and no salvage value. For purposes of preparing financial statements, Griffith is planning to use straight-line depreciation. For tax purposes, Griffith follows MACRS. Depreciation expense using MACRS is $6,720 in Year 1, $10,750 in Year 2, $6,450 in Year 3, $3,870 in each of Years 4 and 5, and $1,940 in Year 6.

Required

1. What is the difference between straight-line and MACRS depreciation expense for each of the six years?
2. Griffith's president has asked why you use one method for the books and another for tax calculations. "Can you do this? Is it legal? Don't we take the same total depreciation either way?" he asked. Write a brief memo answering his questions and explaining the benefits of using two methods for depreciation.

Problem 8-4 Reconstruct Net Book Values Using Statement of Cash Flows

Centralia Stores Inc. had property, plant, and equipment, net of accumulated depreciation, of $4,459,000 and intangible assets, net of accumulated amortization, of $673,000 at December 31, 2012. The company's 2012 statement of cash flows, prepared using the indirect method, included the following items:

a. The Cash Flows from Operating Activities section included three additions to net income:
   (1) Depreciation expense of $672,000
   (2) Amortization expense of $33,000
   (3) Loss on the sale of equipment of $35,000
b. The Cash Flows from Operating Activities section also included a subtraction from net income for the gain on the sale of a copyright of $55,000.
c. The Cash Flows from Investing Activities section included outflows for the purchase of a building of $292,000 and $15,000 for the payment of legal fees to protect a patent from infringement.
d. The Cash Flows from Investing Activities section also included inflows from the sale of equipment of $315,000 and the sale of a copyright of $75,000.

Required

1. Determine the book values of the assets that were sold during 2012.
2. Reconstruct the amount of property, plant, and equipment, net of accumulated depreciation, that was reported on the company's balance sheet at December 31, 2011.
3. Reconstruct the amount of intangibles, net of accumulated amortization, that was reported on the company's balance sheet at December 31, 2011.

Problem 8-5 Depreciation and Cash Flow

O'hare Company's only asset as of January 1, 2012, was a limousine. During 2012, only the following three transactions occurred:

   Services of $100,000 were provided on account.
   All accounts receivable were collected.
   Depreciation on the limousine was $15,000.

Required

1. Develop an income statement for O'hare for 2012.
2. Determine the amount of the net cash inflow for O'hare for 2012.
3. Explain why O'hare's net income does not equal net cash inflow.
4. If O'hare developed a cash flow statement for 2012 using the indirect method, what amount would appear in the category titled Cash Flow from Operating Activities?

MULTI-CONCEPT PROBLEMS

Problem 8-6 Cost of Assets, Subsequent Book Values, and Balance Sheet Presentation

The following events took place at Pete's Painting Company during 2012:

a. On January 1, Pete bought a used truck for $14,000. He added a tool chest and side racks for ladders for $4,800. The truck is expected to last four years and then be sold for $800. Pete uses straight-line depreciation.

(Continued)

b. On January 1, he purchased several items at an auction for $2,400. These items had fair market values as follows:

10 cases of paint trays and roller covers	$ 200
Storage cabinets	600
Ladders and scaffolding	2,400

Pete will use all of the paint trays and roller covers this year. The storage cabinets are expected to last nine years; the ladders and scaffolding, four years.

c. On February 1, Pete paid the city $1,500 for a three-year license to operate the business.

d. On September 1, Pete sold an old truck for $4,800 that had cost $12,000 when it was purchased on September 1, 2007. It was expected to last eight years and have a salvage value of $800.

Required

1. For each situation, explain the value assigned to the asset when it is purchased [or for (d), the book value when sold].
2. Determine the amount of depreciation or other expense to be recorded for each asset for 2012.
3. How would these assets appear on the balance sheet as of December 31, 2012?

LO2 • 5   Problem 8-7 Cost of Assets and the Effect on Depreciation

Early in its first year of business, Toner Company, a fitness and training center, purchased new workout equipment. The acquisition included the following costs:

Purchase price	$150,000
Tax	15,000
Transportation	4,000
Setup*	25,000
Painting*	3,000

*The equipment was adjusted to Toner's specific needs
 and painted to match the other equipment in the gym.

The bookkeeper recorded an asset, Equipment, $165,000 (purchase price and tax). The remaining costs were expensed for the year. Toner used straight-line depreciation. The equipment was expected to last ten years with zero salvage value.

Required

1. How much depreciation did Toner report on its income statement related to this equipment in Year 1? What is the correct amount of depreciation to report in Year 1?
2. Income is $100,000 before costs related to the equipment are reported. How much income will Toner report in Year 1? What amount of income should it report? You can ignore income tax.
3. Using the equipment as an example, explain the difference between a cost and an expense.

LO5 • 7 • 8   Problem 8-8 Capital Expenditures, Depreciation, and Disposal

Merton Company purchased a building on January 1, 2011, at a cost of $364,000. Merton estimated that its life would be 25 years and its residual value would be $14,000.

On January 1, 2012, the company made several expenditures related to the building. The entire building was painted and floors were refinished at a cost of $21,000. A federal agency required Merton to install additional pollution control devices in the building at a cost of $42,000. With the new devices, Merton believed it was possible to extend the life of the building by six years.

In 2013, Merton altered its corporate strategy dramatically. The company sold the building on April 1, 2013, for $392,000 in cash and relocated all operations to another state.

Required

1. Determine the depreciation that should be on the income statement for 2011 and 2012.
2. Explain why the cost of the pollution control equipment was not expensed in 2012. What conditions would have allowed Merton to expense the equipment? If Merton has a choice, would it prefer to expense or capitalize the equipment?
3. What amount of gain or loss did Merton record when it sold the building? What amount of gain or loss would have been reported if the pollution control equipment had been expensed in 2012?

Problem 8-9 Amortization of Intangible, Revision of Rate

LO6 • 10

During 2007, Reynosa Inc.'s research and development department developed a new manufacturing process. Research and development costs were $85,000. The process was patented on October 1, 2007. Legal costs to acquire the patent were $11,900. Reynosa decided to expense the patent over a 20-year time period. Reynosa's fiscal year ends on September 30.

On October 1, 2012, Reynosa's competition announced that it had obtained a patent on a new process that would make Reynosa's patent completely worthless.

Required

1. How should Reynosa record the $85,000 and $11,900 costs?
2. How much amortization expense should Reynosa report in each year through the year ended September 30, 2012?
3. What amount of loss should Reynosa report in the year ended September 30, 2013?

Problem 8-10 Purchase and Disposal of Operating Asset and Effects on Statement of Cash Flows

LO8 • 11

On January 1, 2012, Castlewood Company purchased machinery for its production line for $104,000. Using an estimated useful life of eight years and a residual value of $8,000, the annual straight-line depreciation of the machinery was calculated to be $12,000. Castlewood used the machinery during 2012 and 2013, but then decided to automate its production process. On December 31, 2013, Castlewood sold the machinery at a loss of $5,000 and purchased new, fully automated machinery for $205,000.

Required

1. How would the previous transactions be presented on Castlewood's statements of cash flows for the years ended December 31, 2012 and 2013?
2. Why would Castlewood sell at a loss machinery that had a remaining useful life of six years and purchase new machinery with a cost almost twice that of the old?

Problem 8-11 Amortization of Intangibles and Effects on Statement of Cash Flows

LO9 • 10 • 11

Tableleaf Inc. purchased a patent a number of years ago. The patent is being amortized on a straight-line basis over its estimated useful life. The company's comparative balance sheets as of December 31, 2012 and 2011, included the following line item:

	12/31/12	12/31/11
Patent, less accumulated amortization of $119,000 (2012) and $102,000 (2011)	$170,000	$187,000

Required

1. How much amortization expense was recorded during 2012?
2. What was the patent's acquisition cost? When was it acquired? What is its estimated useful life? How was the acquisition of the patent reported on that year's statement of cash flows?
3. Assume that Tableleaf uses the indirect method to prepare its statement of cash flows. How is the amortization of the patent reported annually on the statement of cash flows?
4. How would the sale of the patent on January 1, 2013, for $200,000 be reported on the 2013 statement of cash flows?

ALTERNATE PROBLEMS

LO3 **Problem 8-1A** **Lump-Sum Purchase of Assets and Subsequent Events**

Dixon Manufacturing purchased, for cash, three large pieces of equipment. Based on recent sales of similar equipment, the fair market values are as follows:

Piece 1	$200,000
Piece 2	$200,000
Piece 3	$440,000

Required

1. What value is assigned to each piece of equipment if the equipment was purchased for (a) $480,000, (b) $680,000, and (c) $800,000?
2. How does the purchase of the equipment affect total assets?

LO5 **Problem 8-2A** **Depreciation as a Tax Shield**

The term *tax shield* refers to the amount of income tax saved by deducting depreciation for income tax purposes. Assume that Rummy Company is considering the purchase of an asset as of January 1, 2012. The cost of the asset with a five-year life and zero residual value is $60,000. The company will use the double-declining-balance method of depreciation.

Rummy's income for tax purposes before recording depreciation on the asset will be $62,000 per year for the next five years. The corporation is currently in the 30% tax bracket.

Required

Calculate the amount of income tax that Rummy must pay each year if (a) the asset is not purchased and (b) the asset is purchased. What is the amount of tax shield over the life of the asset? What is the amount of tax shield for Rummy if it uses the straight-line method over the life of the asset? Why would Rummy choose to use the accelerated method?

LO5 **Problem 8-3A** **Book versus Tax Depreciation**

Payton Delivery Service purchased a delivery truck for $28,200. The truck will have a useful life of six years and zero salvage value. For the purposes of preparing financial statements, Payton is planning to use straight-line depreciation. For tax purposes, Payton follows MACRS. Depreciation expense using MACRS is $5,650 in Year 1, $9,025 in Year 2, $5,400 in Year 3, $3,250 in each of Years 4 and 5, and $1,625 in Year 6.

Required

1. What is the difference between straight-line and MACRS depreciation expense for each of the six years?
2. Payton's president has asked why you use one method for the books and another for tax calculations. "Can you do this? Is it legal? Don't we take the same total depreciation either way?" he asked. Write a brief memo answering his questions and explaining the benefits of using two methods for depreciation.

LO11 **Problem 8-4A** **Reconstruct Net Book Values Using Statement of Cash Flows**

E-Gen Enterprises Inc. had property, plant, and equipment, net of accumulated depreciation, of $1,555,000 and intangible assets, net of accumulated amortization, of $34,000 at December 31, 2012. The company's 2012 statement of cash flows, prepared using the indirect method, included the following items:

a. The Cash Flows from Operating Activities section included three additions to net income:
   (1) Depreciation expense of $205,000
   (2) Amortization expense of $3,000
   (3) Loss on the sale of land of $17,000

b. The Cash Flows from Operating Activities section also included a subtraction from net income for the gain on the sale of a trademark of $7,000.

c. The Cash Flows from Investing Activities section included outflows for the purchase of equipment of $277,000 and $6,000 for the payment of legal fees to protect a copyright from infringement.

d. The Cash Flows from Investing Activities section also included inflows from the sale of land of $187,000 and the sale of a trademark of $121,000.

Required

1. Determine the book values of the assets that were sold during 2012.
2. Reconstruct the amount of property, plant, and equipment, net of accumulated depreciation, that was reported on the company's balance sheet at December 31, 2011.
3. Reconstruct the amount of intangibles, net of accumulated amortization, that was reported on the company's balance sheet at December 31, 2011.

Problem 8-5A Amortization and Cash Flow

LO11

Book Company's only asset as of January 1, 2012, was a copyright. During 2012, only the following three transactions occurred:

Royalties earned from copyright use, $500,000 in cash
Cash paid for advertising and salaries, $62,500
Amortization, $50,000

Required

1. What amount of income will Book report in 2012?
2. What is the amount of cash on hand at December 31, 2012?
3. Explain how the cash balance increased from zero at the beginning of the year to its year-end balance. Why does the increase in cash not equal the income?

ALTERNATE MULTI-CONCEPT PROBLEMS

Problem 8-6A Cost of Assets, Subsequent Book Values, and Balance Sheet Presentation

LO1 • 5 • 8 • 9 • 10

The following events took place at Tasty-Toppins Inc., a pizza shop that specializes in home delivery, during 2012:

a. January 1, purchased a truck for $16,000 and added a cab and an oven at a cost of $10,900. The truck is expected to last five years and be sold for $300 at the end of that time. The company uses straight-line depreciation for its trucks.

b. January 1, purchased equipment for $2,700 from a competitor who was retiring. The equipment is expected to last three years with zero salvage value. The company uses the double-declining-balance method to depreciate its equipment.

c. April 1, sold a truck for $1,500. The truck had been purchased for $8,000 exactly five years earlier, had an expected salvage value of $1,000, and was depreciated over an eight-year life using the straight-line method.

d. July 1, purchased a $14,000 patent for a unique baking process to produce a new product. The patent is valid for 15 more years; however, the company expects to produce and market the product for only four years. The patent's value at the end of the four years will be zero.

Required

For each situation, explain the amount of depreciation or amortization recorded for each asset in the current year and the book value of each asset at the end of the year. For (c), indicate the accumulated depreciation and book value at the time of sale.

LO2 • 5   Problem 8-7A Cost of Assets and the Effect on Depreciation

Early in its first year of business, Key Inc., a locksmith and security consultant, purchased new equipment. The acquisition included the following costs:

Purchase price	$168,000
Tax	16,500
Transportation	4,400
Setup*	1,100
Operating cost for first year	26,400

*The equipment was adjusted to Key's specific needs.

The bookkeeper recorded the asset Equipment at $216,400. Key used straight-line depreciation. The equipment was expected to last ten years with zero residual value.

Required

1. Was $216,400 the proper amount to record for the acquisition cost? If not, explain how each expenditure should be recorded.
2. How much depreciation did Key report on its income statement related to this equipment in Year 1? How much should have been reported?
3. If Key's income before the costs associated with the equipment is $55,000, what amount of income did Key report? What amount should it have reported? You can ignore income tax.
4. Explain how Key should determine the amount to capitalize when recording an asset. What is the effect of Key's error on the income statement and balance sheet?

LO7 • 8   Problem 8-8A Capital Expenditures, Depreciation, and Disposal

Wagner Company purchased a retail shopping center on January 1, 2011, at a cost of $612,000. Wagner estimated that its life would be 25 years and its residual value would be $12,000.

On January 1, 2012, the company made several expenditures related to the building. The entire building was painted and floors were refinished at a cost of $115,200. A local zoning agency required Wagner to install additional fire protection equipment, including sprinklers and built-in alarms, at a cost of $87,600. With the new protection, Wagner believed it was possible to increase the residual value of the building to $30,000.

In 2013, Wagner altered its corporate strategy dramatically. The company sold the retail shopping center on January 1, 2013, for $360,000 cash.

Required

1. Determine the depreciation that should be on the income statement for 2011 and 2012.
2. Explain why the cost of the fire protection equipment was not expensed in 2012. What conditions would have allowed Wagner to expense it? If Wagner has a choice, would it prefer to expense or capitalize the equipment?
3. What amount of gain or loss did Wagner record when it sold the building? What amount of gain or loss would have been reported if the fire protection equipment had been expensed in 2012?

LO6 • 10   Problem 8-9A Amortization of Intangible, Revision of Rate

During 2007, Maciel Inc.'s research and development department developed a new manufacturing process. Research and development costs were $350,000. The process was patented on October 1, 2007. Legal costs to acquire the patent were $23,800. Maciel decided to expense the patent over a 20-year time period using the straight-line method. Maciel's fiscal year ends on September 30.

On October 1, 2012, Maciel's competition announced that it had obtained a patent on a new process that would make Maciel's patent completely worthless.

Required

1. How should Maciel record the $350,000 and $23,800 costs?
2. How much amortization expense should Maciel report in each year through the year ended September 30, 2012?
3. What amount of loss should Maciel report in the year ended September 30, 2013?

Problem 8-10A Purchase and Disposal of Operating Asset and Effects on Statement of Cash Flows

LO8 • 11

On January 1, 2012, Mansfield Inc. purchased a medium-sized delivery truck for $45,000. Using an estimated useful life of five years and a residual value of $5,000, the annual straight-line depreciation of the trucks was calculated to be $8,000. Mansfield used the truck during 2012 and 2013, but then decided to purchase a larger delivery truck. On December 31, 2013, Mansfield sold the delivery truck at a loss of $12,000 and purchased a new, larger delivery truck for $80,000.

Required

1. How would the previous transactions be presented on Mansfield's statements of cash flows for the years ended December 31, 2012 and 2013?
2. Why would Mansfield sell at a loss a truck that had a remaining useful life of three years and purchase a new truck with a cost almost twice that of the old?

Problem 8-11A Amortization of Intangibles and Effects on Statement of Cash Flows

LO9 • 10 • 11

Quickster Inc. acquired a patent a number of years ago. The patent is being amortized on a straight-line basis over its estimated useful life. The company's comparative balance sheets as of December 31, 2012 and 2011, included the following line item:

	12/31/12	12/31/11
Patent, less accumulated amortization of $1,661,000 (2012) and $1,510,000 (2011)	$1,357,000	$1,508,000

Required

1. How much amortization expense was recorded during 2012?
2. What was the patent's acquisition cost? When was it acquired? What is its estimated useful life? How was the acquisition of the patent reported on that year's statement of cash flows?
3. Assume that Quickster uses the indirect method to prepare its statement of cash flows. How is the amortization of the patent reported annually on the statement of cash flows?
4. How would the sale of the patent on January 1, 2013, for $1,700,000 be reported on the 2013 statement of cash flows?

DECISION CASES

Reading and Interpreting Financial Statements

Decision Case 8-1 General Mills

LO1 • 9

Refer to the financial statements and notes for **General Mills** included at the back of the book.

Required

1. What items does the company list in the Property and Equipment category?
2. What method is used to depreciate the operating assets?
3. What is the estimated useful life of the operating assets?
4. What are the accumulated depreciation and book values of property and equipment for the most recent fiscal year?
5. Were any assets purchased or sold during the most recent fiscal year? Explain.

Decision Case 8-2 Comparing Two Companies in the Same Industry: General Mills and Kellogg's

LO1 • 9

Refer to the financial information for **General Mills** and **Kellogg's** included at the back of the book.

(Continued)

Required

1. Compare the list of property, plant, and equipment for General Mills to the list on the Kellogg's balance sheet. How are the lists similar? Note the differences between the lists and provide a logical reason for the differences.
2. What method is used by each company to depreciate the assets? Why do you think each company has chosen the method it uses?
3. What are the accumulated depreciation and book values of the property and equipment for each company? What does this information tell you about these competitors?
4. What is the estimated life of General Mills's assets? How does this compare to the estimated life of Kellogg's assets?
5. Refer to the Investing Activities portion of the cash flow statements of the two companies. Were any assets purchased or sold by either company during the year? This section of the statements does not tell whether there was a gain or loss on the sale of long-term assets. Where would you find that information?

Making Financial Decisions

LO1 • 5   Decision Case 8-3 Comparing Companies

Assume that you are a financial analyst attempting to compare the financial results of two companies. The 2012 income statement of Straight Company is as follows:

Sales		$720,000
Cost of goods sold		360,000
Gross profit		$360,000
Administrative costs	$ 96,000	
Depreciation expense	120,000	216,000
Income before tax		$144,000
Tax expense (40%)		57,600
Net income		$ 86,400

Straight Company depreciates all operating assets using the straight-line method for tax purposes and for the annual report provided to stockholders. All operating assets were purchased on the same date, and all assets had an estimated life of five years when purchased. Straight Company's balance sheet reveals that on December 31, 2012, the balance of the Accumulated Depreciation account was $240,000.

You want to compare the annual report of Straight Company to that of Accelerated Company. Both companies are in the same industry, and both have the same assets, sales, and expenses except that Accelerated uses the double-declining-balance method for depreciation for income tax purposes and for the annual report provided to stockholders.

Required

Develop Accelerated Company's 2012 income statement. As a financial analyst interested in investing in one of the companies, do you find Straight or Accelerated to be more attractive? Because depreciation is a "noncash" expense, should you be indifferent in deciding between the two companies? Explain your answer.

LO5   Decision Case 8-4 Depreciation Alternatives

Medsupply Inc. produces supplies used in hospitals and nursing homes. Its sales, production, and costs to produce are expected to remain constant over the next five years. The corporate income tax rate is expected to increase over the next three years. The current rate, 15%, is expected to increase to 20% next year, then to 25%, continuing at that rate indefinitely.

Medsupply is considering the purchase of new equipment that is expected to last five years and to cost $150,000 with zero salvage value. As the controller, you are aware that the company can use one method of depreciation for accounting purposes and another method for tax purposes. You are trying to decide between the straight-line and the double-declining-balance methods.

Required

Recommend which method to use for accounting purposes and which to use for tax purposes. Be able to justify your answer on both a numerical and a theoretical basis. How does a noncash adjustment to income, such as depreciation, affect cash flow?

Ethical Decision Making

Decision Case 8-5 Valuing Assets   LO3

Denver Company recently hired Terry Davis as an accountant. He was given responsibility for all accounting functions related to fixed asset accounting. Tammy Sharp, Terry's boss, asked him to review all transactions involving the current year's acquisition of fixed assets and to take necessary action to ensure that acquired assets were recorded at proper values. Terry is satisfied that all transactions are proper except for an April 15 purchase of an office building and the land on which it is situated. The purchase price of the acquisition was $200,000. However, Denver Company has not reported the land and building separately. Terry hired an appraiser to determine the market values of the land and the building. The appraiser reported that his best estimates of the values were $150,000 for the building and $70,000 for the land. When Terry proposed that these values be used to determine the acquisition cost of the assets, Tammy disagreed. She told Terry to request another appraisal of the property and asked him to stress to the appraiser that the land component of the acquisition could not be depreciated for tax purposes. The second appraiser estimated that the values were $180,000 for the building and $40,000 for the land. Terry and Tammy agreed that the second appraisal should be used to determine the acquisition cost of the assets.

Required

Did Terry and Tammy act ethically in this situation? Explain your answer.

Decision Case 8-6 Depreciation Estimates   LO5

Langsom's Mfg. is planning for a new project. Usually, Langsom's depreciates long-term equipment for ten years. The equipment for this project is specialized and will have no further use at the end of the project in three years. The manager of the project wants to depreciate the equipment over the usual ten years and plans on writing off the remaining book value at the end of Year 3 as a loss. You believe that the equipment should be depreciated over the three-year life.

Required

Which method do you think is conceptually better? What should you do if the manager insists on depreciating the equipment over ten years?

SOLUTIONS TO KEY TERMS QUIZ

1	Acquisition cost	6	Change in estimate
5	Capitalization of interest	8	Capital expenditure
2	Land improvements	10	Revenue expenditure
7	Depreciation	11	Gain on Sale of Asset
3	Straight-line method	12	Loss on Sale of Asset
9	Book value	14	Intangible assets
4	Units-of-production method	16	Goodwill
13	Accelerated depreciation	17	Research and development costs
15	Double-declining-balance method		

INTEGRATIVE PROBLEM

Correct an income statement and statement of cash flows and assess the impact of a change in inventory method; compute the effect of a bad debt recognition.

The following income statement, statement of cash flows, and additional information are available for PEK Company:

PEK Company
Income Statement
For the Year Ended December 31, 2012

Sales revenue		$1,250,000
Cost of goods sold		636,500
Gross profit		$ 613,500
Depreciation on plant equipment	$58,400	
Depreciation on buildings	12,000	
Interest expense	33,800	
Other expenses	83,800	188,000
Income before taxes		$ 425,500
Income tax expense (30% rate)		127,650
Net income		$ 297,850

PEK Company
Statement of Cash Flows
For the Year Ended December 31, 2012

Cash flows from operating activities:	
Net income	$297,850
Adjustments to reconcile net income to net cash provided by operating activities (includes depreciation expense)	83,200
Net cash provided by operating activities	$381,050
Cash flows from financing activities:	
Dividends	(35,000)
Net increase in cash	$346,050

Additional information:

a. Beginning inventory and purchases for the one product the company sells are as follows:

	Units	Unit Cost
Beginning inventory	50,000	$2.00
Purchases:		
February 5	25,000	2.10
March 10	30,000	2.20
April 15	40,000	2.50
June 16	75,000	3.00
September 5	60,000	3.10
October 3	40,000	3.25

b. During the year, the company sold 250,000 units at $5 each.

c. PEK uses the periodic FIFO method to value its inventory and the straight-line method to depreciate all of its long-term assets.

d. During the year-end audit, it was discovered that a January 3, 2012, transaction for the lump-sum purchase of a mixing machine and a boiler was not recorded. The fair market values of the mixing machine and the boiler were $200,000 and $100,000, respectively. Each asset has an estimated useful life often years with no residual value expected. The purchase of the assets was financed by issuing a $270,000 five-year promissory note directly to the seller. Interest of 8% is paid annually on December 31.

Required

1. Prepare a revised income statement and a revised statement of cash flows to take into account the omission of the entry to record the purchase of the two assets. (*Hint:* You will need to take into account any change in income taxes as a result of changes in any income statement items. Assume that income taxes are paid on December 31 of each year.)
2. Assume the same facts as in part (1), except that the company is considering the use of an accelerated method rather than the straight-line method for the assets purchased on January 3, 2012. All other assets would continue to be depreciated on a straight-line basis. Prepare a revised income statement and a revised statement of cash flows assuming that the company decides to use the accelerated method for these two assets rather than the straight-line method, resulting in depreciation of $49,091 for 2012.

Treat the answers in parts (3) and (4) as independent of the other parts.

3. Assume that PEK decides to use the LIFO method rather than the FIFO method to value its inventory and recognize cost of goods sold for 2012. Compute the effect (amount of increase or decrease) this would have on cost of goods sold, income tax expense, and net income.
4. Assume that PEK failed to record an estimate of bad debts for 2012. (Bad debt expense is normally included in "other expenses.") Before any adjustment, the balance in Allowance for Doubtful Accounts is $8,200. The credit manager estimates that 3% of the $800,000 of sales on account will prove to be uncollectible. Based on this information, compute the effect (amount of increase or decrease) of recognition of the bad debt estimate on other expenses, income tax expense, and net income.

ANSWERS TO POD REVIEW

LO1	1. d	2. a		**LO7**	1. a	2. b
LO2	1. b	2. c		**LO8**	1. c	2. a
LO3	1. d	2. a		**LO9**	1. b	2. d
LO4	1. c	2. c		**LO10**	1. d	2. c
LO5	1. a	2. d		**LO11**	1. a	2. b
LO6	1. c	2. d		**LO12**	1. d	2. a

Current Liabilities, Contingencies, and the Time Value of Money

9

AFTER STUDYING THIS CHAPTER, YOU SHOULD BE ABLE TO:

LO1 Identify the components of the Current Liability category of the balance sheet.

LO2 Examine how accruals affect the Current Liability category.

LO3 Explain how changes in current liabilities affect the statement of cash flows.

LO4 Determine when contingent liabilities should be presented on the balance sheet

or disclosed in notes and how to calculate their amounts.

LO5 Explain the difference between simple and compound interest.

LO6 Calculate amounts using the future value and present value concepts.

LO7 Apply the compound interest concepts to some common accounting situations.

STUDY LINKS

A Look at Previous Chapters The previous chapters were concerned with the asset portion of the balance sheet. We examined the accounting for current assets, such as inventory, as well as long-term assets such as property, plant, and equipment.

A Look at This Chapter This chapter examines the accounting for current liabilities that are an important aspect of a company's liquidity. Chapter 9 also discusses

how contingent liabilities should be treated on the financial statement. Finally, the chapter introduces the concept of the time value of money. This important concept will be used extensively in future chapters.

A Look at the Upcoming Chapter Chapter 10 presents the accounting for long-term liabilities. The time value of money concept developed in Chapter 9 is applied to several long-term liability issues in Chapter 10.

MAKING BUSINESS DECISIONS
STARBUCKS CORPORATION

When you think of coffee, **Starbucks Corporation** may come to mind. The company's objective is to establish itself as one of the most recognized and respected brands in the world. It took only a few years for the company to be well on its way to achieving that goal. The company offers brewed coffees, espresso beverages, cold blended beverages, various complementary food items, coffee-related accessories and equipment, a selection of premium teas, and a line of compact discs through its retail stores. For several years, the company experienced a very high growth rate, and its stock skyrocketed. But beginning in 2006, the growth began to slow, and the company faced increased competition from other outlets such as Caribou Coffee and Green Mountain Coffee. The company even closed some outlets during the tough economic conditions of 2008. By 2010, business had increased dramatically, and the company reported earnings of over $948 million for the year.

Starbucks' balance sheet reveals that it must monitor liquidity carefully. A significant portion of the company's assets are current assets because most of its sales involve cash, credit card, and debit card. Starbucks also has a significant amount of current liabilities. The company realizes the importance of maintaining its current liabilities at a level that will allow them to be paid when they are due. In short, the company's long-term profitability goals are directly linked to its ability to effectively manage its current liabilities and liquidity.

The accompanying partial balance sheet presents Starbucks Corporation's current assets and liabilities. Why is this chapter important to you?

- You need to know what accounts are presented in the Current Liabilities section of the balance sheet. (See pp. 430–437).
- You need to know how changes in the current liabilities affect a company's liquidity and ability to pay its bills. (See pp. 438–439.)
- You need to know how lawsuits and other contingent liabilities affect a company's balance sheet. (See pp. 440–443.)
- You need to know how to do interest rate calculations using the time value of money concept. (See pp. 444–455.)

The financial statements of Starbucks, and other companies, will aid in your understanding of the important concepts related to current and contingent liabilities.

Starbucks Corporation Consolidated Balance Sheets

	Oct. 3, 2010	Sept. 27, 2009
	(In millions, except per share data)	
Assets		
Current assets:		
Cash and cash equivalents	$1,164.0	$ 599.8
Short-term investments—available-for-sale securities	236.5	21.5
Short-term investments—trading securities	49.2	44.8
Accounts receivable, net	302.7	271.0
Inventories	543.3	664.9
Prepaid expenses and other current assets	156.5	147.2
Deferred income taxes, net	304.2	286.6
Total current assets	2,756.4	2,035.8
Long-term investments—available-for-sale securities	191.8	71.2
Equity and cost investments	341.5	352.3
Property, plant and equipment, net	2,416.5	2,536.4
Other assets	346.5	253.8
Other intangible assets	70.8	68.2
Goodwill	262.4	259.1
Total assets	$6,385.9	$5,576.8
Liabilities and Equity		
Current liabilities:		
Accounts payable	282.6	267.1
Accrued compensation and related costs	400.0	307.5
Accrued occupancy costs	173.2	188.1
Accrued taxes	100.2	127.8
Insurance reserves	146.2	154.3
Other accrued liabilities	262.8	147.5
Deferred revenue	414.1	388.7
Total current liabilities	$1,779.1	$1,581.0

Current Liabilities

LO1 Identify the components of the Current Liability category of the balance sheet.

OVERVIEW: Current liabilities are obligations that will be satisfied within one year. They are normally recorded at face value and are important because they are indications of a company's liquidity. Specific examples of current liabilities include accounts payable, notes payable due within one year, the current portion of long-term debt, taxes payable, and other accrued liabilities.

A classified balance sheet presents financial statement items by category to provide more information to financial statement users. The balance sheet generally presents two categories of liabilities: current and long term.

Current liabilities finance the working capital of the company. At any given time during the year, current liabilities may fluctuate substantially. The company must generate sufficient cash flow to retire these debts as they come due. As long as the company's ratio of current assets to current liabilities stays fairly constant from quarter to quarter or year to year, financial statement users will not be too concerned.

The current liability portion of the 2010 balance sheet of **Starbucks Corporation** is presented in the chapter opener. Some companies list the accounts in the Current Liability category in the order of payment due date. That is, the account that requires payment first is listed first, the account requiring payment next is listed second, etc. This allows users of the statement to assess the cash flow implications of each account. Starbucks presents the Accounts Payable account as the first current liability and that account likely requires payment first, but it is difficult to tell if the other current liabilities are presented in the order that they will require payment.

Current liabilities were first introduced in Chapter 2. In general, a **current liability** is an obligation that will be satisfied within one year. Although current liabilities are not due immediately, they are still recorded at face value, that is, the time until payment is not taken into account. If it were taken into account, current liabilities would be recorded at a slight discount to reflect interest earned between now and the due date. The face value amount is generally used for all current liabilities because the time period involved is short enough that it is not necessary to record or calculate an interest factor. In addition, when interest rates are low, there is no need to worry about the interest that could be earned in this short period of time. Chapter 10 shows that many long-term liabilities must be stated at their present value on the balance sheet.

The current liability classification is important because it is closely tied to the concept of *liquidity*. Management of a firm must be prepared to pay current liabilities within a short time period. Therefore, management must have access to liquid assets, cash, or other assets that can be converted to cash in amounts sufficient to pay the current liabilities. Firms that do not have sufficient resources to pay their current liabilities are often said to have a liquidity problem.

A handy ratio to help creditors or potential creditors determine a company's liquidity is the current ratio. (See Chapter 2 for an introduction to the current ratio.) A current ratio of current assets to current liabilities of 2 to 1 is usually a comfortable margin. If the firm has a large amount of inventory, it is sometimes useful to exclude inventory (prepayments are also excluded) when computing the ratio. That provides the "quick" ratio. Usually, a quick ratio of at least 1.5 to 1 would be preferred so that the company could pay its bills on time. Of course, the guidelines given for the current ratio 2 to 1 and the quick ratio 1.5 to 1 are only rules of thumb. The actual current and quick ratios of companies vary widely and depend on the company, the management policies, and the type of industry. Exhibit 9-1 presents the current and quick ratios for Starbucks and two of its competitors. The ratios vary from company to company, yet all are solid companies without liquidity problems. Note especially that the current ratio for Starbucks is less than 2 to 1 because of the nature of its business and because of the efficient use of its current assets.

Accounting for current liabilities is an area in which U.S. accounting standards are similar to those of most other countries. Nearly all countries encourage firms to provide a breakdown of liabilities into current and long term to allow users to evaluate liquidity.

Current liability
Accounts that will be satisfied within one year or the current operating cycle.
Alternate term: Short-term liability.

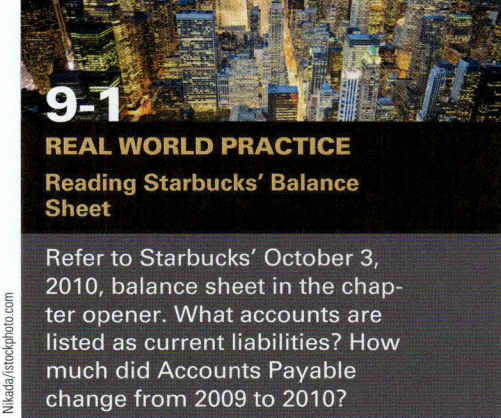

9-1
REAL WORLD PRACTICE
Reading Starbucks' Balance Sheet
Refer to Starbucks' October 3, 2010, balance sheet in the chapter opener. What accounts are listed as current liabilities? How much did Accounts Payable change from 2009 to 2010?

Accounts Payable

Accounts payable represent amounts owed for the purchase of inventory, goods, or services acquired in the normal course of business. Often, Accounts Payable is the first account listed in the Current Liability category because it requires the payment of cash before other current liabilities.

Accounts payable
Amounts owed for inventory, goods, or services acquired in the normal course of business.

EXHIBIT 9-1 Current and Quick Ratios of Selected Companies for 2010

Company	Industry	Current Ratio	Quick Ratio
Starbucks	Food	1.55	0.98
Caribou Coffee	Food	2.00	1.13
Green Mountain	Food	2.08	0.88

© Cengage Learning 2013

Name: Karen Stephens

Education: Bachelor of Science

College Major: Fashion Merchandising

Occupation: Broker/Owner of Real Estate Company

Age: 57

Position: President

Company Name: Page Taft Real Estate

See Karen Stephens's interview clip in CNOW.

SPOTLIGHT
Knowledge of Accounting Has Helped This Business Owner

The use of accounting information systems is significant to the success of any small business. **Karen Stephens**, the owner of Page Taft Real Estate in Guilford, Connecticut, believes her college accounting courses, along with the tools offered through a robust accounting information system, have helped her remain successful during somewhat difficult times in the real estate industry.

According to Karen, it is very important to maintain control over a company's current liabilities. This is especially true in the real estate business with its seasonal fluctuations. When her company needs to apply for a loan, the bank wants to make sure that the owner has a proven record of using financial information to make well-thought-out decisions. It is of paramount importance that Karen is aware of her cash flow position at all times.

From an expense perspective, she has used financial information to make informed decisions on utility usage and office location among other things. When the real estate market started to slow, she was able to use the accounting information on salaries by office location to figure out how to modify hours to retain each paid employee. Evaluation of agent production and their commission structure is vital to planning for future growth.

It is no secret that the real estate market has suffered a downturn in recent years. Karen has been able to remain profitable in a declining marketplace due to her use of accounting information.

> **"It is very important for the real estate business to maintain control over current liabilities, as there are definite fluctuations in sales seasonally."**

Normally, a firm has an established relationship with several suppliers, and formal contractual arrangements with those suppliers are unnecessary. Accounts payable usually do not require the payment of interest, but terms may be given to encourage early payment. For example, terms may be stated as 2/10, n/30, which means that a 2% discount is available if payment occurs within the first ten days and that if payment is not made within ten days, the full amount must be paid within 30 days.

Timely payment of accounts payable is an important aspect of cash flow management. Generally, it is to the company's benefit to take advantage of available discounts. After all, if your supplier is going to give you a 2% discount for paying on Day 10 instead of Day 30, that means you are earning 2% on your money over 20/360 of a year. If you took the 2% discount throughout the year, you would be getting a 36% annual return on your money, since there are 18 periods of 20 days each in a year. Therefore, the accounts payable system must be established in a manner that alerts management to take advantage of discounts offered.

Notes Payable

Many companies have an account in the Current Liability category designated as Notes Payable. *How is a note payable different from an account payable?* The most important difference is that an account payable is not a formal contractual arrangement, whereas a **note payable** is represented by a formal agreement or note signed by the parties to the transaction. Notes payable may arise from dealing with a supplier or from acquiring a cash loan from a bank or creditor. Those notes that are expected to be paid within one year of the balance sheet date should be classified as current liabilities.

The accounting for notes payable depends on whether the interest is paid on the note's due date or is deducted before the borrower receives the loan proceeds. With the first type of note, the terms stipulate that the borrower receives a short-term loan and agrees to repay the principal and interest at the note's due date.

Notes payable
Amounts owed that are represented by a formal contract.

Example 9-1 Recording the Interest on Notes Payable

Assume that Hot Coffee Inc. receives a one-year loan from First National Bank on January 1. The face amount of the note of $1,000 must be repaid on December 31 along with interest at the rate of 12%. Hot Coffee could identify and analyze the effect of the loan as follows:

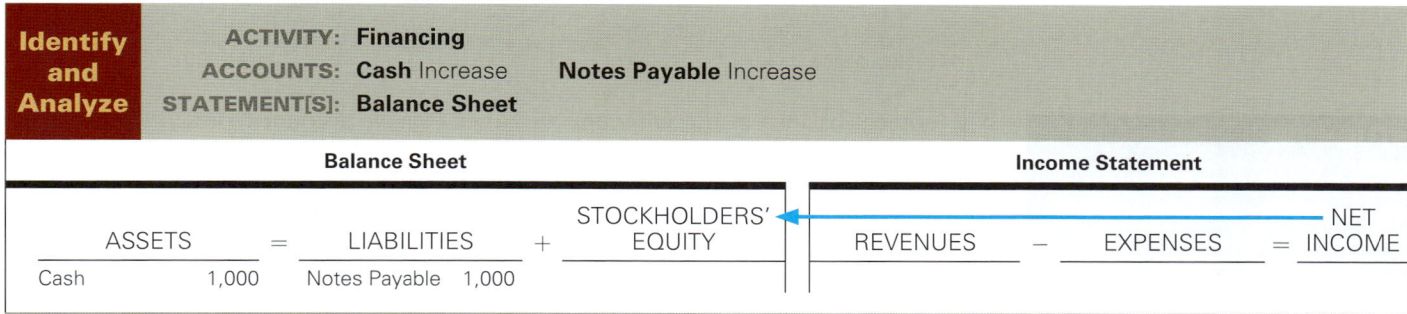

Identify and Analyze	ACTIVITY: **Financing**
	ACCOUNTS: **Cash** Increase **Notes Payable** Increase
	STATEMENT[S]: **Balance Sheet**

Balance Sheet

ASSETS	=	LIABILITIES	+	STOCKHOLDERS' EQUITY
Cash 1,000		Notes Payable 1,000		

Income Statement

REVENUES	−	EXPENSES	=	NET INCOME

The company could identify and analyze the effect of the repayment as follows:

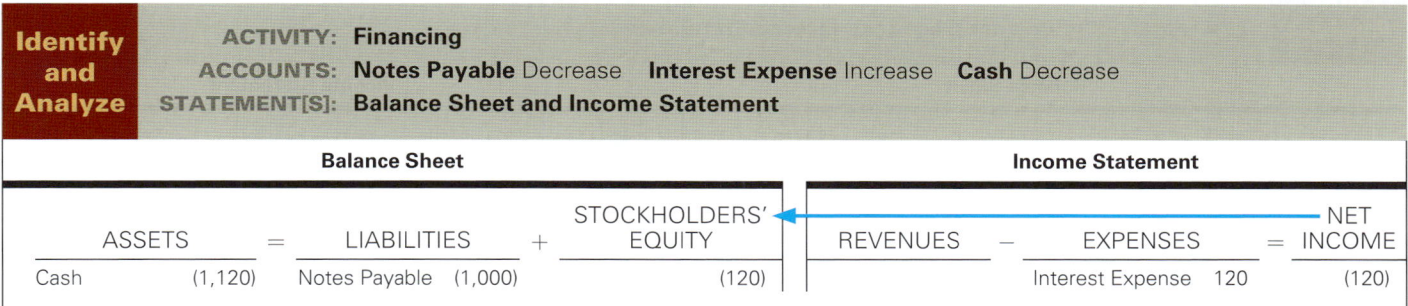

Identify and Analyze	ACTIVITY: **Financing**
	ACCOUNTS: **Notes Payable** Decrease **Interest Expense** Increase **Cash** Decrease
	STATEMENT[S]: **Balance Sheet and Income Statement**

Balance Sheet

ASSETS	=	LIABILITIES	+	STOCKHOLDERS' EQUITY
Cash (1,120)		Notes Payable (1,000)		(120)

Income Statement

REVENUES	−	EXPENSES	=	NET INCOME
		Interest Expense 120		(120)

© Cengage Learning 2013

Banks also use another form of note, one in which the interest is deducted in advance. This is sometimes referred to as *discounting a note* because a Discount on Notes Payable account is established when the loan is recorded.

Example 9-2 Discounting a Note

Suppose that on January 1, 2012, First National Bank granted to Hot Coffee a $1,000 loan, due on December 31, 2012, but deducted the interest in advance and gave Hot Coffee the remaining amount of $880 ($1,000 face amount of the note less interest of $120). Hot Coffee could identify and analyze the effect of the loan on January 1 as follows:

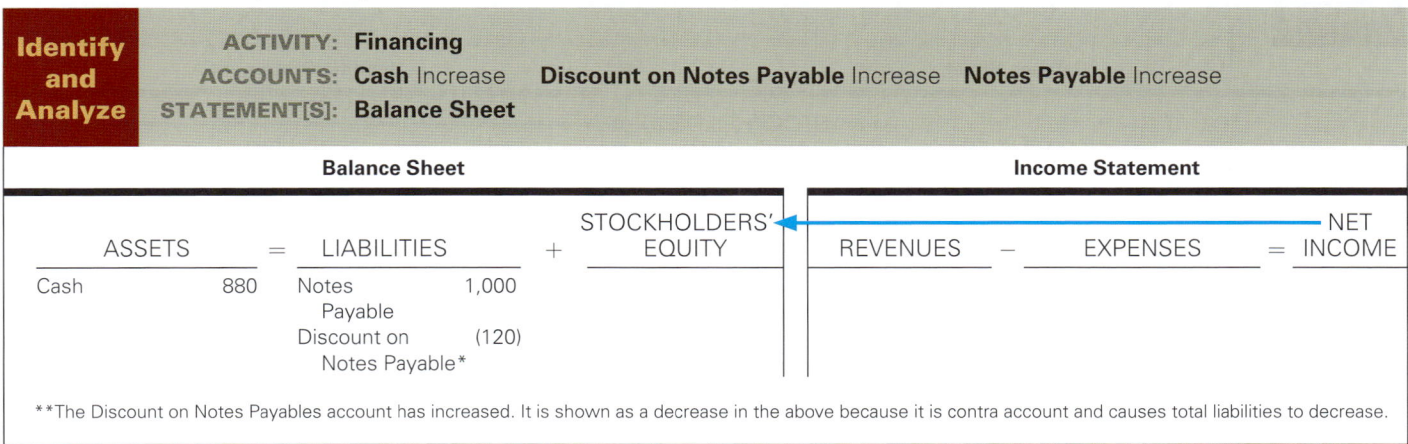

Identify and Analyze	ACTIVITY: **Financing**
	ACCOUNTS: **Cash** Increase **Discount on Notes Payable** Increase **Notes Payable** Increase
	STATEMENT[S]: **Balance Sheet**

Balance Sheet

ASSETS	=	LIABILITIES	+	STOCKHOLDERS' EQUITY
Cash 880		Notes Payable 1,000		
		Discount on Notes Payable* (120)		

Income Statement

REVENUES	−	EXPENSES	=	NET INCOME

**The Discount on Notes Payables account has increased. It is shown as a decrease in the above because it is contra account and causes total liabilities to decrease.

© Cengage Learning 2013

Discount on notes payable
A contra liability that represents interest deducted from a loan in advance.

The **Discount on Notes Payable** account should be treated as a reduction of Notes Payable. If a balance sheet was developed immediately after the January 1 loan, the note would appear in the Current Liability category as follows:

Notes payable	$1,000
Less: Discount on notes payable	120
Net liability	$ 880

STUDY TIP

Discount on Notes Payable is a contra-liability account and will have a debit balance.

The original balance in the Discount on Notes Payable account represents interest that must be transferred to interest expense over the life of the note. Refer to Example 9-2. Before Hot Coffee presents its year-end financial statements, it must make an adjustment to transfer the discount to interest expense. The effect of the adjustment on December 31 is as follows:

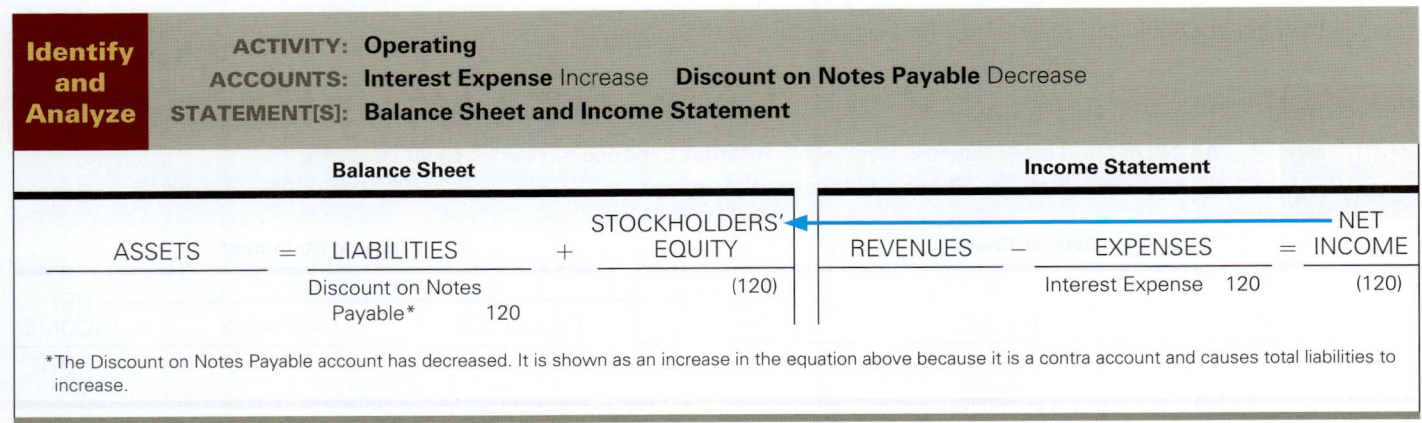

Thus, the balance of the Discount on Notes Payable account is zero, and $120 has been transferred to interest expense. When the note is repaid on December 31, 2012, Hot Coffee must repay the full amount of the note. The effect could be identified and analyzed as follows:

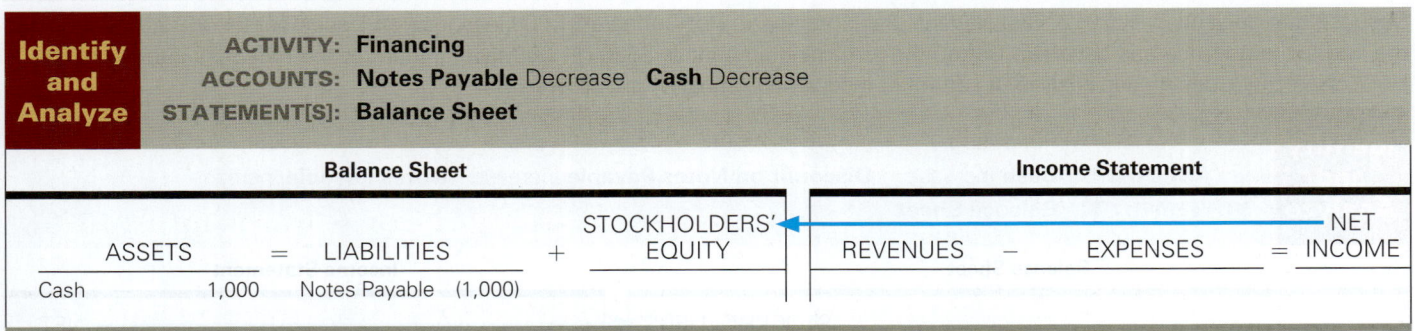

It is important to compare the two types of notes payable. In the previous two examples, the stated interest rate on each note was 12%. The dollar amount of interest incurred in each case was $120. However, the interest *rate* on a discounted note, the second example, is always higher than it appears. Hot Coffee received the use of only $880, yet it was required to repay $1,000. Therefore, the interest rate incurred on the note was actually $120/$880, or approximately 13.6%.

Current Maturities of Long-Term Debt

Another account that appears in the Current Liability category of Starbucks' balance sheet is Current Portion of Long-Term Debt. On other companies' balance sheets, this item may appear as **Current Maturities of Long-Term Debt**. This account should appear when a firm has a liability and must make periodic payments.

Current maturities of long-term debt
The portion of a long-term liability that will be paid within one year.

Alternate term: Long-term debt, current portion.

Example 9-3 Recording Current Maturities of Long-Term Debt

Assume that on January 1, 2012, your firm obtained a $10,000 loan from the bank. The terms of the loan require you to make payments in the amount of $1,000 per year for ten years payable each January 1 beginning January 1, 2013. On December 31, 2012, an entry should be made to classify a portion of the balance as a current liability. The effect could be identified and analyzed as follows:

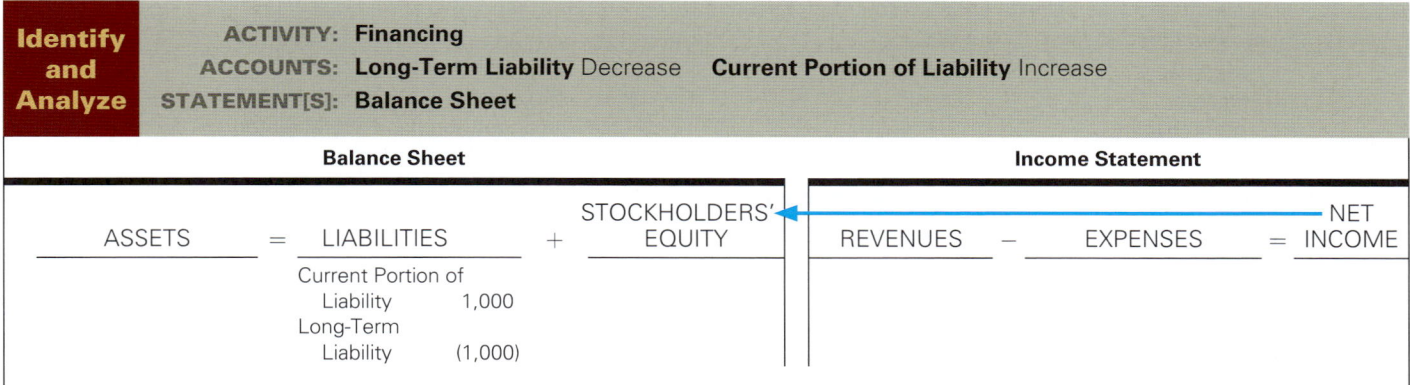

The December 31, 2012, balance sheet should indicate that the liability for the note payable is classified into two portions: a $1,000 current liability that must be repaid within one year and a $9,000 long-term liability.

Refer to the information in Example 9-3. On January 1, 2013, the company must pay $1,000. The effect could be identified and analyzed as follows:

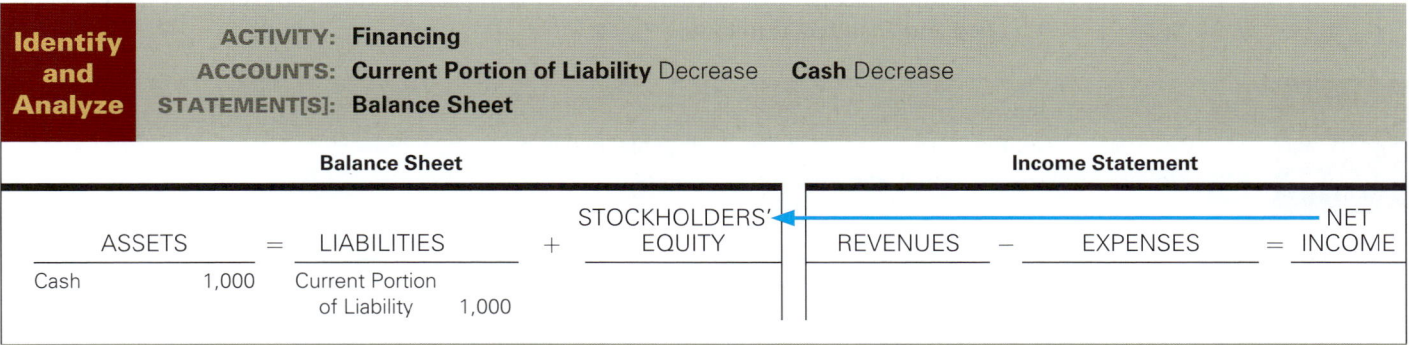

On December 31, 2013, the company should again record the current portion of the liability. Therefore, the 2013 year-end balance sheet should indicate that the liability is classified into two portions: a $1,000 current liability and an $8,000 long-term liability. The process should be repeated each year until the bank loan has been fully paid. When an investor or a creditor reads a balance sheet, he or she wants to distinguish between debt that is long term and debt that is short term. Therefore, it is important to segregate the portion of the debt that becomes due within one year.

The balance sheet account labeled Current Portion of Long-Term Debt should include only the amount of principal to be paid. The amount of interest that has been incurred but is unpaid should be listed separately in an account such as Interest Payable.

POD REVIEW 9.1

LO1 Identify the components of the Current Liability category of the balance sheet.

- Current liabilities are obligations of a company that generally must be satisfied within one year. Some companies list them in the balance sheet in order of the account that requires payment first.
- Current liability accounts include Accounts Payable, Notes Payable, Current Portion of Long-Term Debt, Taxes Payable, and Accrued Liabilities.

QUESTIONS   **Answers to these questions are on the last page of the chapter.**

1. For users of financial statements, the current liability classification in the balance sheet is important because it is closely tied to the concept of

   a. materiality.
   b. liquidity.
   c. profitability.
   d. leverage.

2. Alpha Company has current assets of $100,000 and current liabilities of $40,000. How much inventory could it

   purchase on account and achieve its minimum desired current ratio of 2 to 1?

   a. $10,000
   b. $20,000
   c. $40,000
   d. It cannot purchase any inventory on account and achieve its minimum desired current ratio.

Taxes Payable

LO2 Examine how accruals affect the Current Liability category.

Starbucks has an amount of $100.2 million in the Current Liability category designated as Accrued Taxes. Other companies may label the account as Taxes Payable. Corporations pay a variety of taxes, including federal and state income taxes, property taxes, and other taxes. Usually, the largest dollar amount is incurred for state and federal income taxes. Taxes are an expense of the business and should be accrued in the same manner as any other business expense. A company that ends its accounting year on December 31 is not required to calculate the amount of tax owed to the government until the following March 15 or April 15, depending on the type of business. Therefore, the business must make an accounting entry, usually as one of the year-end adjusting entries, to record the amount of tax that has been incurred but is unpaid. Normally, the effect could be identified and analyzed as follows:

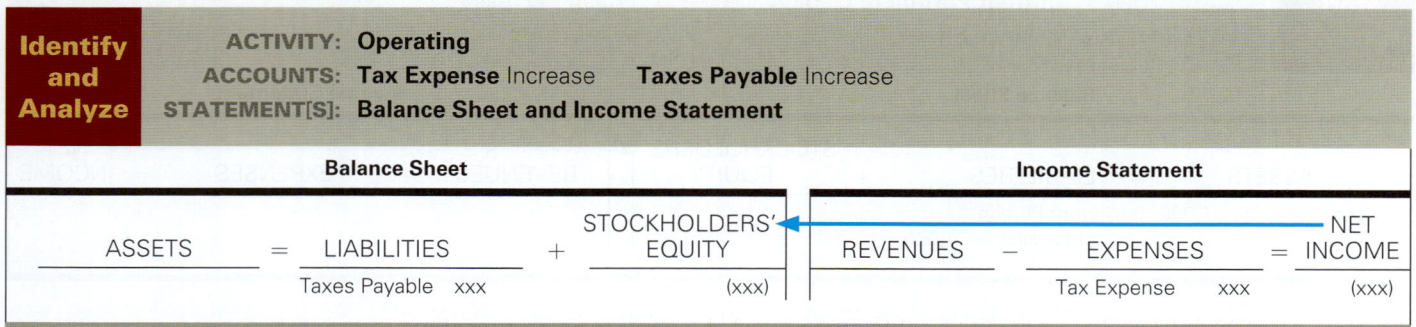

Identify and Analyze

ACTIVITY: **Operating**
ACCOUNTS: **Tax Expense** Increase   **Taxes Payable** Increase
STATEMENT[S]: **Balance Sheet and Income Statement**

Balance Sheet			Income Statement		
ASSETS	= LIABILITIES	+ STOCKHOLDERS' EQUITY	REVENUES	− EXPENSES	= NET INCOME
	Taxes Payable xxx	(xxx)		Tax Expense xxx	(xxx)

The calculation of the amount of tax a business owes is very complex. For now, the important point is that taxes are an expense when incurred (not when paid) and must be recorded as a liability as incurred.

Other Accrued Liabilities

Starbucks' 2010 balance sheet listed an amount of $262.8 million as current liability under the category of Other Accrued Liabilities. What items might be included in this category?

Previous chapters, especially Chapter 4, provided many examples of accrued liabilities. **Accrued liabilities** include any amount that has been incurred due to the passage of time but has not been paid as of the balance sheet date. A common example is salary or wages payable.

Accrued liability
A liability that has been incurred but has not yet been paid.

Example 9-4 Recording Accrued Liabilities

Suppose that your firm has a payroll of $1,000 per day Monday through Friday and that employees are paid at the close of work each Friday. Also, suppose that December 31 is the end of your accounting year and that it falls on a Tuesday. The effect of the adjusting entry for salaries could be identified and analyzed as follows:

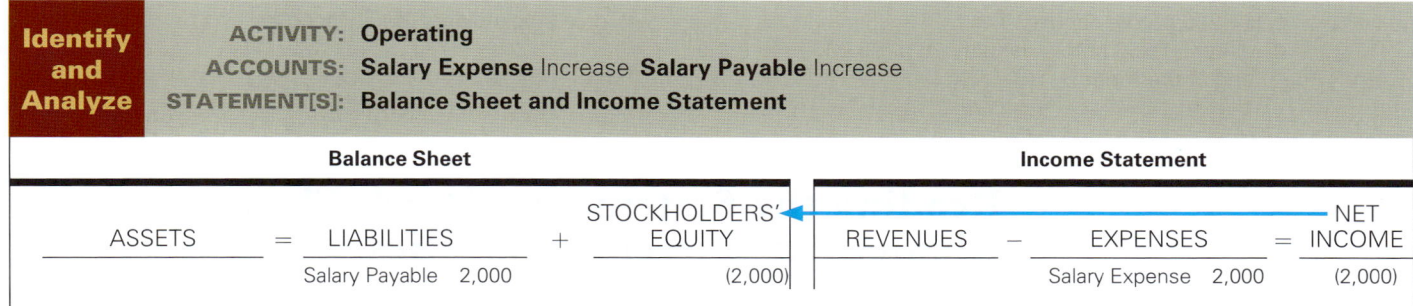

Identify and Analyze	ACTIVITY: **Operating**
	ACCOUNTS: **Salary Expense** Increase **Salary Payable** Increase
	STATEMENT[S]: **Balance Sheet and Income Statement**

Balance Sheet				Income Statement		
ASSETS	=	LIABILITIES	+	STOCKHOLDERS' EQUITY		
		Salary Payable 2,000		(2,000)		

REVENUES	−	EXPENSES	=	NET INCOME
		Salary Expense 2,000		(2,000)

The amount of the salary payable would be classified as a current liability and could appear in a category such as Other Accrued Expenses.

Interest is another item that often must be accrued at year-end. Assume that you received a one-year loan of $10,000 on December 1. The loan carries a 12% interest rate. On December 31, an accounting entry must be made to record interest even though the money may not actually be due. The effect could be identified and analyzed as follows:

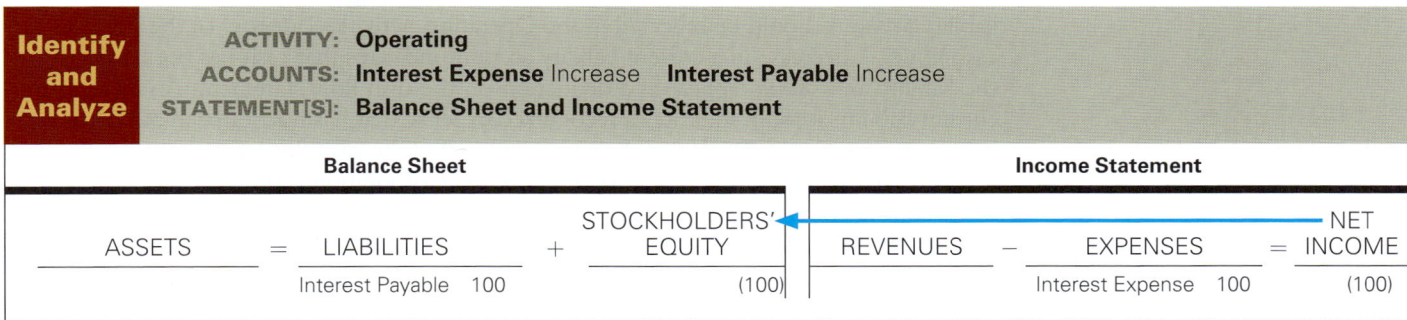

Identify and Analyze	ACTIVITY: **Operating**
	ACCOUNTS: **Interest Expense** Increase **Interest Payable** Increase
	STATEMENT[S]: **Balance Sheet and Income Statement**

Balance Sheet				Income Statement		
ASSETS	=	LIABILITIES	+	STOCKHOLDERS' EQUITY		
		Interest Payable 100		(100)		

REVENUES	−	EXPENSES	=	NET INCOME
		Interest Expense 100		(100)

The Interest Payable account should be classified as a current liability, assuming that it is to be paid within one year of the December 31 date.

IFRS and Current Liabilities

The accounting for current liabilities in U.S. and international standards is generally similar, but there are a few important differences. In this chapter, we have presented classified balance sheets with liabilities classified as either current or long term. Interestingly, U.S. standards do not require a classified balance sheet, and financial statements of some U.S. companies may list liabilities in order by size or by order of liquidity.

International accounting standards require companies to present classified balance sheets with liabilities classified as either current or long term. An unclassified balance sheet based on the order of liquidity is acceptable only when it provides more reliable information.

© Cengage Learning 2013

© Kasia Biel/istockphoto.com

LO2 Examine how accruals affect the Current Liability category.

- Accrued liabilities result from expenses that are incurred but have not yet been paid.
- Common accrued liabilities include taxes payable, salaries payable, and interest payable.

POD REVIEW 9.2

QUESTIONS   **Answers to these questions are on the last page of the chapter.**

1. An invoice received from a supplier for $5,000 on January 1 with terms 3/15, n/30 means that the company should pay
   a. $5,000 between January 4 and January 16.
   b. $4,850 before the end of January.
   c. $4,250 before January 4.
   d. either $4,850 before January 16 or $5,000 before the end of the month.

2. When a liability is accrued, the account debited in the transaction is
   a. an asset.
   b. an expense.
   c. another liability account.
   d. a stockholders' equity account.

Reading the Statement of Cash Flows for Changes in Current Liabilities

LO3 Explain how changes in current liabilities affect the statement of cash flows.

OVERVIEW: Most current liabilities are reflected in the Operating Activities section of the statement of cash flows. If a current liability increased during the period, the amount of the change should appear as a positive amount. If it decreased, the change should appear as a negative amount. An exception may occur for some types of notes payable which may appear in the Financing section if not directly related to operating activities.

It is important to understand the impact that current liabilities have on a company's cash flows. Exhibit 9-2 illustrates the placement of current liabilities on the statement of cash flows (using the indirect method) and their effect. Most current liabilities are directly related to a firm's ongoing operations. Therefore, the change in the balance of each current liability account should be reflected in the Operating Activities category of the statement of cash flows. A decrease in a current liability account indicates that cash has been used to pay the liability and should appear as a deduction on the cash flow statement. An increase in a current liability account indicates a recognized expense that has not yet been paid. Look for it as an increase in the Operating Activities category of the cash flow statement.

A partial statement of cash flows of Starbucks Corporation is presented in Exhibit 9-3. In 2010, the company has a negative amount on the statement of cash flows of $3.6 million for Accounts Payable and a negative amount of $12.9 million for Accrued Taxes. This is an indication that Accounts Payable and Accrued Taxes decreased, resulting in a decrease in cash.

EXHIBIT 9-2 Current Liabilities on the Statement of Cash Flows

Item	Cash Flow Statement
	Operating Activities
Net Income	XXX
Increase in current liability ➝	+
Decrease in current liability ➝	−
	Investing Activities
	Financing Activities
Increase in notes payable ➝	+
Decrease in notes payable ➝	−

EXHIBIT 9-3 Starbucks Corporation Partial Consolidated Statement of Cash Flows (In millions)

Fiscal Year Ended	Oct. 3, 2010	Sept. 27, 2009
OPERATING ACTIVITIES:		
Net earnings including noncontrolling interests	$ 948.3	$ 391.5
Adjustments to reconcile net earnings to net cash provided by operating activities:		
Depreciation and amortization	540.8	563.3
Provision for impairments and asset disposals	67.7	224.4
Deferred income taxes, net	(42.0)	(69.6)
Equity in income of investees	(108.6)	(78.4)
Distributions of income from equity investees	91.4	53.0
Stock-based compensation	113.6	83.2
Tax benefit from exercise of stock options	13.5	2.0
Excess tax benefit from exercise of stock options	(36.9)	(15.9)
Other	(15.3)	5.4
Cash provided/(used) by changes in operating assets and liabilities:		
Inventories	123.2	28.5
Accounts payable	(3.6)	(53.0)
Accrued taxes	(12.9)	57.2
Deferred revenue	24.2	16.3
Other operating assets	(16.1)	120.5
Other operating liabilities	17.6	60.6
Net cash provided by operating activities	1,704.9	1,389.0

© Cengage Learning 2013

Almost all current liabilities appear in the Operating Activities category of the statement of cash flows, but there are exceptions. If a current liability is not directly related to operating activities, it should not appear in that category. For example, if Starbucks uses some notes payable as a means of financing, distinct from operating activities, those borrowings and repayments are reflected in the Financing Activities rather than the Operating Activities category. Perhaps that is the reason the rather large increase in short-term borrowings does not appear in the Operating Activities portion of the statement of cash flows.

LO3 Explain how changes in current liabilities affect the statement of cash flows.

- Most current liabilities are directly related to the ongoing operations of a company.
- Decreases in current liabilities indicate that cash has been used to satisfy obligations and are cash outflows not represented by some expenses in the income statement.
- Increases in current liabilities indicate that some expenses in the income statement have not been paid in cash and are not cash outflows represented by some expenses on the income statement.

POD REVIEW 9.3

QUESTIONS   Answers to these questions are on the last page of the chapter.

1. In the statement of cash flows, a decrease in accounts payable would be shown as a(n)

   a. increase in the Operating Activities category.
   b. decrease in the Operating Activities category.
   c. increase in the Financing category.
   d. decrease in the Financing category.

2. In the statement of cash flows, an increase in a current liability will appear as a(n)

   a. increase in the Operating Activities category.
   b. decrease in the Operating Activities category.
   c. increase in the Financing category.
   d. decrease in the Financing category.

© Cengage Learning 2013

Contingent Liabilities

OVERVIEW: A contingent liability is an existing item whose outcome is unknown because it is dependent on some future event. Contingent liabilities should be recorded if the liability is probable and the amount can be reasonably estimated. Contingent liabilities should be disclosed if they do not meet probable criterion but are *"reasonably possible."* These are generally disclosed in the notes to the statement but are not accrued and reported on the balance sheet. Contingent amounts that are considered "remote" are not required to be disclosed.

Accountants must exercise a great deal of expertise and judgment in deciding what to record and in determining the amount to record. This is certainly true regarding contingent liabilities. A **contingent liability** is an obligation that involves an existing condition for which the outcome is not known with certainty and depends on some event that will occur in the future. The actual amount of the liability must be estimated because we cannot clearly predict the future. **The important accounting issues are whether contingent liabilities should be recorded and, if so, in what amounts.**

Contingent liability
An existing condition for which the outcome is not known but depends on some future event.

Alternate term: Contingent loss.

This judgment call is normally resolved through discussions between a company's management and its outside auditors. Management would rather not disclose contingent liabilities until they come due because investors and creditors judge management based on the company's earnings, and the recording of a contingent liability must be accompanied by a charge to (reduction in) earnings. Auditors, on the other hand, want to see as much information as possible because they essentially represent the interests of investors and creditors who want to know as much as possible.

Contingent Liabilities That Are Recorded

A contingent liability should be accrued and presented on the balance sheet if it is probable and if the amount can be reasonably estimated. But when is an event *probable*, and what does *reasonably estimated* mean? The terms must be defined based on the facts of each situation. A financial statement user would want the company to err on the side of full disclosure. On the other hand, the company should not be required to disclose every remote possibility.

Product Warranties and Guarantees: Common Contingent Liabilities That Are Recorded
A common contingent liability that firms must present as a liability involves product warranties and guarantees. Many firms sell products for which they provide the customer a warranty against potential defects. If a product becomes defective within the warranty period, the selling firm ensures that it will repair or replace the item. This is an example of a contingent liability because the expense of fixing a product depends on some of the products becoming defective—an uncertain, although likely, event.

Estimated liability
A contingent liability that is accrued and reflected on the balance sheet.

At the end of each period, the selling firm must estimate how many of the products sold in the current year will become defective in the future and the cost of repair or replacement. This type of contingent liability is often referred to as an **estimated liability** to emphasize that the costs are not known at year-end and must be estimated.

© Cengage Learning 2013

Example 9-5 Recording a Liability for Warranties

Assume that Quickkey Computer sells a computer product for $5,000 with a one-year warranty in case the product must be repaired. Assume that in 2012, Quickkey sold 100 computers for a total sales revenue of $500,000. At the end of 2012, Quickkey must record an estimate of the warranty costs that will occur on 2012 sales. Using an analysis of past warranty records, Quickkey estimates that repairs will average 2% of total sales. The effect of the recording of warranty costs at the end of 2012 could be identified and analyzed as follows:

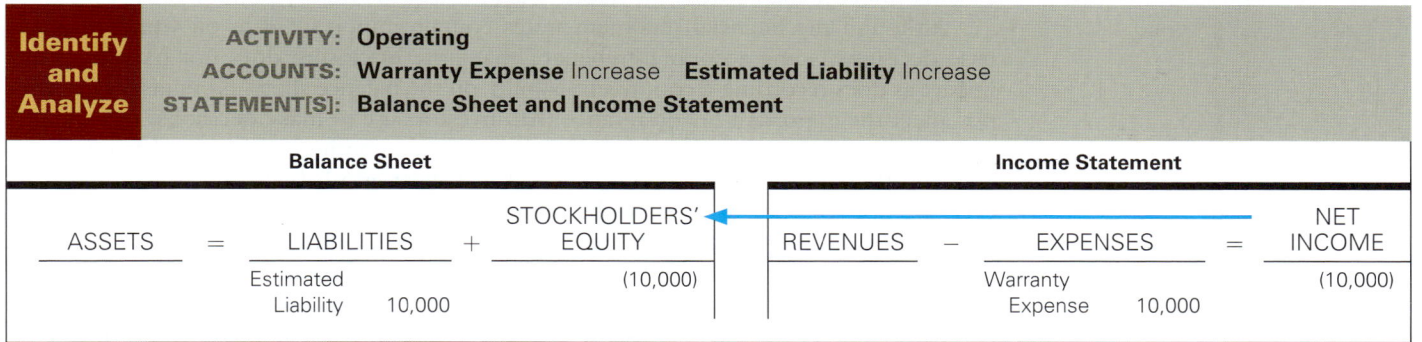

Identify and Analyze

ACTIVITY: Operating
ACCOUNTS: Warranty Expense Increase   **Estimated Liability** Increase
STATEMENT[S]: Balance Sheet and Income Statement

Balance Sheet			Income Statement		
ASSETS =	LIABILITIES +	STOCKHOLDERS' EQUITY	REVENUES −	EXPENSES =	NET INCOME
	Estimated Liability 10,000	(10,000)		Warranty Expense 10,000	(10,000)

© Cengage Learning 2013

The amount of warranty costs that a company presents as an expense is of interest to investors and potential creditors. If the expense as a percentage of sales begins to rise, a logical conclusion is that the product is becoming less reliable.

Warranties are an excellent example of the matching principle. In Example 9-5, the warranty costs related to 2012 sales were estimated and recorded in 2012. This was done to match the 2012 sales with the expenses related to those sales. When actual repairs of the computers occur in 2013, they do not result in an expense. The repair costs incurred in 2013 should be treated as a reduction in the liability that had been estimated previously.

Because items such as warranties involve estimation, you may wonder what happens if the amount estimated is not accurate. The company must analyze past warranty records carefully and incorporate any changes in customer buying habits, usage, technological changes, and other changes. Still, even with careful analysis, the actual amount of the expense is not likely to equal the estimated amount. Generally, firms do not change the amount of the expense recorded in past periods for such differences. They may adjust the amount recorded in future periods, however.

Premiums or Coupons: Other Contingent Liabilities That Are Recorded
Warranties provide an example of a contingent liability that must be estimated and recorded. Another example is premium or coupon offers that accompany many products. Cereal boxes are an everyday example of premium offers. The boxes often allow customers to purchase a toy or game at a reduced price if the purchase is accompanied by cereal box tops or proof of purchase. The offer given to cereal customers represents a contingent liability. At the end of each year, the cereal company must estimate the number of premium offers that will be redeemed and the cost involved and must report a contingent liability for that amount.

Some Lawsuits and Legal Claims Are Contingent Liabilities That Must Be Recorded
Legal claims that have been filed against a firm are also examples of contingent liabilities. In today's business environment, lawsuits and legal claims are a fact of life. They represent a contingent liability because an event has occurred but the outcome of that event, the resolution of the lawsuit, is not known. The defendant must make a judgment about the lawsuit's outcome to decide whether the item should be recorded on the balance sheet or disclosed in the notes. When the legal claim's outcome is likely to be unfavorable, a contingent liability should be recorded on the balance sheet.

As you might imagine, firms are not very eager to record contingent lawsuits as liabilities because the amount of loss is often difficult to estimate. Also, some may view the accountant's decision as an admission of guilt when a lawsuit is recorded as a liability before the courts have finalized a decision. Accountants often must consult with lawyers or other legal experts to determine the probability of the loss of a lawsuit. In cases involving contingencies, the accountant must make an independent judgment based on the facts and not be swayed by the desires of other parties.

Contingent Liabilities That Are Disclosed

Any contingent liability that is probable and that can be reasonably estimated must be reported as a liability. We now must consider contingent liabilities that do not meet the probable criterion or cannot be reasonably estimated. In either case, **a contingent liability must be disclosed in the financial statement notes but not reported on the balance sheet if the contingent liability is at least reasonably possible.**

Although the financial statement notes contain important data on which investors base decisions, some accountants believe that note disclosure does not have the same impact as does recording a contingent liability on the balance sheet. Note disclosure does not affect the important financial ratios that investors use to make decisions.

The previous section discussed the treatment of a contingent liability that was probable and therefore was recorded on the balance sheet as a liability. Most lawsuits, however, are not recorded as liabilities because the risk of loss is not considered probable or the amount of the loss cannot be reasonably estimated. If a company does not record a lawsuit as a liability, it still must consider whether the lawsuit should be disclosed in the notes to the financial statements. When the risk of loss is at least *reasonably possible,* the company should provide note disclosure. This is the course of action taken for most contingent liabilities involving lawsuits.

Exhibit 9-4 contains excerpts from the notes to the 2010 financial statements of **Burger King Corporation**. The note indicates that Burger King is subject to a variety of lawsuits. The excerpt in Exhibit 9-4 is an example of contingent liabilities that have been disclosed in the notes to the financial statements *but have not been recorded as liabilities on the balance sheet.* In fact, Burger King has chosen not to record a liability even though these legal issues have been in the courts for several years. Readers of the financial statements and analysts must read the notes carefully to determine the impact of such contingent liabilities.

The amount and the timing of the cash outlays associated with contingent liabilities are especially difficult to determine. Lawsuits, for example, may extend several years into the future, and the dollar amount of possible loss may be subject to great uncertainty.

EXHIBIT 9-4 Note Disclosure of Contingencies for Burger King Corporation

Litigation

On July 30, 2008, the Company was sued by four Florida franchisees over its decision to mandate extended operating hours in the United States. The plaintiffs seek damages, declaratory relief and injunctive relief. The court dismissed the plaintiffs' original complaint in November 2008. In December 2008, the plaintiffs filed an amended complaint. In August 2010, the court entered an order reaffirming the legal bases for dismissal of the original complaint, again holding that BKC had the authority under its franchise agreements to mandate extended operating hours. However, BKC's motion to dismiss the plaintiff's amended complaint is still before the court.

On September 10, 2008, a class action lawsuit was filed against the Company in the United States District Court for the Northern District of California. The complaint alleged that all 96 Burger King restaurants in California leased by the Company and operated by franchisees violate accessibility requirements under federal and state law.

In September 2009, the court issued a decision on the plaintiffs' motion for class certification. In its decision, the court limited the class action to the 10 restaurants visited by the named plaintiffs, with a separate class of plaintiffs for each of the 10 restaurants and 10 separate trials. In March 2010, the Company agreed to settle the lawsuit with respect to the 10 restaurants and, in July 2010, the court gave final approval to the settlement. In April 2010, the Company received a demand from the law firm representing the plaintiffs in the class action lawsuit, notifying the Company that the firm was prepared to bring a class action covering the other restaurants. If a lawsuit is filed, the Company intends to vigorously defend against all claims in the lawsuit, but the Company is unable to predict the ultimate outcome of this litigation.

Starbucks' annual report of 2010 lists several "risk factors." Included among the risk factors is the fact that some of its products contain caffeine, dairy products, sugar, and other active compounds. This has led to the criticism that some of its products could lead to adverse health effects. In the United States, there is increasing awareness of health risks, including obesity, due to increased publicity from health organizations. There has also been increased consumer litigation based on alleged adverse health impacts of consumption of various products. While Starbucks has not had a lawsuit concerning the health effects of its products, it must consider such possible liabilities. Does Starbucks have a contingent liability? If so, how should it be recorded or disclosed on the financial statements?

Contingent Liabilities versus Contingent Assets

Contingent liabilities that are probable and can be reasonably estimated must be presented on the balance sheet before the outcome of the future events is known. This accounting rule applies only to contingent losses or liabilities. It does not apply to contingencies by which the firm may gain. Generally, contingent gains or **contingent assets** are not reported until the gain actually occurs. **That is, contingent liabilities may be accrued but contingent assets are not accrued.** This may seem inconsistent— it is. Remember that accounting is a discipline based on a conservative set of principles. It is prudent and conservative to delay the recording of a gain until an asset is actually received but to record contingent liabilities in advance.

Of course, even though the contingent assets are not reported, the information still may be important to investors. Wall Street analysts make their living trying to place a value on contingent assets that they believe will result in future benefits. By buying stock of a company that has unrecorded assets (or advising their clients to do so), investment analysts hope to make money when those assets become a reality.

Contingent asset
An existing condition for which the outcome is not known but by which the company stands to gain.
Alternate term: Contingent gain.

IFRS and Contingencies

There are very important differences between U.S. and international standards regarding contingencies. Even the terms used to refer to situations with unknown outcomes differ. In this chapter, we have presented the U.S. standards under which a contingent liability must be recorded on the balance sheet, if the loss or outflow is "probable" and can be "reasonably estimated." The meaning of *probable* is subject to the accountant's judgment, but the standards indicate it should mean an event is "likely to occur." If a contingency does not meet the probable and reasonably estimated criteria, it still must be disclosed in the notes, if the loss or outflow is "reasonably possible."

International standards use the term *provision* for those items that must be recorded on the balance sheet. As in U.S. standards, an item should be recorded if the loss or outflow is probable and can be reasonably estimated. But the meaning of the term *probable* is somewhat different. In international standards, *probable* means the loss or outflow is "more likely than not" to occur. This is a lower threshold than in U.S. standards and may cause more items to be recorded as liabilities. Also, international standards require the amount recorded as a liability to be "discounted" or recorded as a present value amount, while U.S. standards do not have a similar requirement.

In international standards, the term *contingent liability* is used only for those items that are not recorded on the balance sheet but are disclosed in the notes that accompany the statements.

Tetra Images/Getty Images

LOOKING AHEAD

The differences between U.S. and international accounting standards regarding contingencies are very significant. Two important issues are involved: (1) In what cases should future possible liabilities be recorded on the balance sheet and (2) at what amount should the liabilities be recorded? Over time the U.S. and international accounting standard setters will work to eliminate the differences in accounting treatment. But the differences in the accounting for contingent liabilities will be some of the most difficult to resolve.

LO4 Determine when contingent liabilities should be presented on the balance sheet or disclosed in notes and how to calculate their amounts.

- Contingent liabilities should be accrued and disclosed only when the event they depend on is probable and the amount can be reasonably estimated.
- The amount of a contingent liability is often an estimate made by experts both inside the firm (managers for amounts of warranty expenses) and outside the firm (e.g., attorneys for amounts in a lawsuit).

POD REVIEW 9.4

QUESTIONS   **Answers to these questions are on the last page of the chapter.**

1. Omega Company is involved in two unrelated lawsuits, one as the plaintiff and one as the defendant. As a result, the company has a contingent asset and a contingent liability. How should Omega record these on its balance sheet?

   a. Omega should record the contingent liability and the contingent asset separately on the balance sheet.
   b. Omega should record the contingent liability and the contingent asset on the balance sheet by offsetting the liability against the asset.
   c. Omega must record the contingent asset if the realization of the asset is probable and the amount can be reasonably estimated, but Omega must not record the contingent liability on the balance sheet.

   d. Omega must not record the contingent asset, but Omega must record the contingent liability on the balance sheet if the liability is probable and the amount can be reasonably estimated.

2. A contingent liability that is probable and where the amount can reasonably be estimated should

   a. be recorded as a liability.
   b. not be recorded as a liability but disclosed in the notes.
   c. be neither recorded as a liability nor disclosed in the notes.
   d. be recorded in the same manner as a contingent asset.

Time Value of Money Concepts: Compounding of Interest

LO5 Explain the difference between simple and compound interest.

OVERVIEW: The time value of money means that people prefer a payment at the present time rather than in the future because of the interest factor. The amount can be invested, and the resulting accumulation will be larger than the amount received in the future. Simple interest is the amount of interest earned on the principal amount alone. Compound interest means that the interest is calculated on the principal plus previous amounts of accumulated interest.

Time value of money
An immediate amount should be preferred over an amount in the future.

This section will discuss the impact that interest has on decision making because of the time value of money. The **time value of money** concept means that people prefer a payment at the present time rather than in the future because of the interest factor. If an amount is received at the present time, it can be invested and the resulting accumulation will be larger than if the same amount is received in the future. Thus, there is a *time value* to cash receipts and payments. This time value concept is important to you for two reasons: it affects your personal financial decisions, and it affects accounting valuation decisions.

Exhibit 9-5 indicates some of the personal and accounting decisions affected by the time value of money concept. In your personal life, you make decisions based on the time value of money concept nearly every day. When you invest money, you are interested in how much will be accumulated and you must determine the *future value* based on the amount of interest that will be compounded. When you borrow money, you must determine the amount of the loan payments. You may not always realize it, but the amount of the loan payment is based on the *present value* of the loan, another time value of money concept.

Time value of money is also important because of its implications for accounting valuations. Chapter 10 explains that the issue price of a bond is based on the present value of the cash flows that the bond will produce. The valuation of the bond and the recording of the bond on the balance sheet are based on this concept. Further, the amount that is considered interest expense on the financial statements is also based on time value of money concepts. The bottom portion of Exhibit 9-5 indicates that the valuations of many other accounts, including Notes Receivable and Leases, are based on compound interest calculations.

Almost every advanced business course, such as investment, marketing, and many other business courses, uses the time value of money concept. **In fact, it is probably the most important decision-making tool to master in preparation for the business world.** This section of the text begins with an explanation of how simple interest and compound interest differ and proceeds to the concepts of present values and future values.

Simple Interest

Simple interest is interest earned on the principal amount. If the amount of principal is unchanged from year to year, the interest per year will remain the same. Interest can be calculated using the following formula:

$$I = P \times R \times T$$

Simple interest
Interest is calculated on the principal amount only.

EXHIBIT 9-5 Importance of the Time Value of Money

Personal Financial Decision	Action
• How much money will accumulate if you invest in a CD or money market account?	Calculate the future value based on compound interest.
• If you take out an auto loan, what will be the monthly loan payments?	Calculate the payments based on the present value of the loan.
• If you invest in the bond market, what should You pay for a bond?	Calculate the present value of the bond based on compound interest.
• If you win the lottery, should you take an immediate payment or payment over time?	Calculate the present value of the alternatives based on compound interest.

Valuation Decisions on the Financial Statements	Valuation
• Long-term assets	Historical cost, but not higher than present value of the cash flows
• Notes receivable	Present value of the cash flows
• Loan payments	Based on the present value of the loan
• Bond issue price	Present value of the cash flows
• Leases	Present value of the cash flows

© Cengage Learning 2013

where

I = Dollar amount of interest per year
P = Principal
R = Interest rate as a percentage
T = Time in years

For example, assume that a firm has signed a two-year note payable for $3,000. Interest and principal are to be paid at the due date with simple interest at the rate of 10% per year. The amount of interest on the note would be $600, calculated as $3,000 × 0.10 × 2. The firm would be required to pay $3,600 on the due date: $3,000 principal and $600 interest.

Compound Interest

Compound interest
Interest calculated on the principal plus previous amounts of interest.

Alternate term: Interest on interest.

Compound interest means that interest is calculated on the principal plus previous amounts of accumulated interest. Thus, interest is compounded, or there is interest on interest.

Example 9-6 Calculating Compound Interest

Assume a $3,000 note payable for which interest and principal are due in two years with interest compounded annually at 10% per year. Interest would be calculated as follows:

Year	Principal Amount at Beginning of Year	Interest at 10%	Accumulated at Year-End
1	$3,000	$300	$3,300
2	3,300	330	3,630

We would be required to pay $3,630 at the end of two years, $3,000 principal and $630 interest.

© Cengage Learning 2013

A comparison of the note payable with 10% simple interest with the note payable with 10% compound interest in Example 9-6 clearly indicates that the amount accumulated with compound interest is a higher amount because of the interest-on-interest feature.

POD REVIEW 9.5

LO5 Explain the difference between simple and compound interest.

• Simple interest is earned only on the principal amount, whereas compound interest is earned on the principal plus previous amounts of accumulated interest.

QUESTIONS   Answers to these questions are on the last page of the chapter.

1. If you invest money for five years, which will be larger?
   a. an investment that earns simple interest
   b. an investment that earns compound interest
   c. The investments will be the same.
   d. It depends on how frequently compounding occurs.

2. If you invest money for five years, which will be larger?
   a. an investment where interest is compounded annually
   b. an investment where interest is compounded semiannually
   c. an investment where interest is compounded daily
   d. The investments will be the same.

© Cengage Learning 2013

LO6 Calculate amounts using the future value and present value concepts.

Interest Compounding

For most accounting problems, we will assume that compound interest is compounded annually. In actual business practice, compounding usually occurs over much shorter intervals. This can be confusing because the interest rate is often stated as an annual rate even though it is compounded over a shorter period. If compounding is not done annually, you must adjust the interest rate by dividing the annual rate by the number of compounding periods per year.

Example 9-7 Compounding Interest Semiannually

Assume that the note payable from the previous example carried a 10% interest rate compounded semiannually for two years. The 10% annual rate should be converted to 5% per period for four semiannual periods. The amount of interest would be compounded, as in the previous example, but for four periods instead of two. The compounding process is as follows:

Period	Principal Amount at Beginning of Year	Interest at 5% per Period	Accumulated at End of Period
1	$3,000	$150	$3,150
2	3,150	158	3,308
3	3,308	165	3,473
4	3,473	174	3,647

© Cengage Learning 2013

Example 9-7 illustrates that compounding more frequently results in a larger amount accumulated. In fact, many banks and financial institutions now compound interest on savings accounts on a daily basis.

In the remainder of this section, we will assume that compound interest is applicable. The following four compound interest calculations must be understood:

Future value of a single amount
Present value of a single amount
Future value of an annuity
Present value of an annuity

Present Value and Future Value: Single Amounts

OVERVIEW: A future value of a single amount is calculated if we want to calculate how much a known amount at the present time will accumulate in the future, given the rate of interest it will earn, and the number of periods over which it will earn that interest. The present value of a single amount is the opposite. It represents the value today of a single amount to be received or paid at a time in the future earning interest at a given rate.

Future Value of a Single Amount

We are often interested in the amount of interest plus principal that will be accumulated at a future time. This is called a *future amount* or *future value*. The future amount is always larger than the principal amount (payment) because of the interest that accumulates. In some cases, we will use time diagrams to illustrate the relationships. A time diagram to illustrate a future value would be of the following form:

Payment ————————— Interest ——————————— FV

Known Amount of Payment (Present Value)   Future Value = ?

The formula to calculate the **future value of a single amount** is as follows:

$$FV = p(1 + i)^n$$

where

FV = Future value to be calculated
p = Present value or principal amount
i = Interest rate
n = Number of periods of compounding

Future value of a single amount
Amount accumulated at a future time from a single payment or investment.

Example 9-8 Calculating Future Values with Formula

Your three-year-old son Robert inherits $50,000 in cash and securities from his grandfather. If the funds are left in the bank and in the stock market and receive an annual return of 10%, how much will be available in 15 years when Robert starts college?

Solution:

$$FV = \$50,000(1 + 0.10)^{15}$$
$$= \$50,000(4.17725)$$
$$= \$208,863 \text{ (rounded to the nearest dollar)}$$

Consider a $2,000 note payable that carries interest at the rate of 10% compounded annually. The note is due in two years, and the principal and interest must be paid at that time. The amount that must be paid in two years is the future value. The future value can be calculated in the manner used in the previous examples:

Year	Principal Amount at Beginning of Year	Interest at 10%	Accumulated at Year-End
1	$2,000	$200	$2,200
2	2,200	220	2,420

The future value can also be calculated by using the following formula:

$$FV = \$2,000(1 + 0.10)^{2}$$
$$= \$2,000(1.21000)$$
$$= \$2,420$$

Instead of a formula, other methods can be used to calculate future value. Tables can be constructed to assist in the calculations. Table 9-1 on page 454 indicates the future value of $1 at various interest rates for various time periods. To find the future value of a two-year note at 10% compounded annually, you read across the line for two periods and down the 10% column, which gives you an interest rate factor of 1.21000. Because the table has been constructed for future values of $1, we would determine the future value of $2,000 as follows:

$$FV = \$2,000 \times 1.21000$$
$$= \$2,420$$

A second method is to use the built-in functions of a computerized spreadsheet. The appendix to this chapter will illustrate how to use a common spreadsheet, Microsoft® Excel®, to perform the same calculations. **The numbers produced by each method may differ by a few dollars because of rounding differences. Ignore those small differences and concentrate on the methods used to perform the interest rate calculations.**

Remember that compounding does not always occur annually. How does this affect the calculation of future value amounts?

Example 9-9 Calculating Future Values with Quarterly Compounding

Suppose we want to find the future value of a $2,000 note payable due in two years. The note payable requires interest to be compounded quarterly at the rate of 12% per year. To calculate the future value, we must adjust the interest rate to a quarterly basis by dividing the 12% rate by the number of compounding periods per year, which in the case of quarterly compounding is four:

12%/4 quarters = 3% per quarter

Also, the number of compounding periods is eight—four per year times two years.

(Continued)

The future value of the note can be found in two ways. First, we can insert the proper values into the future value formula:

$$FV = \$2,000(1 + 0.03)^8$$
$$= \$2,000(1.26677)$$
$$= \$2,534 \text{ (rounded to the nearest dollar)}$$

We can arrive at the same future value amount with the use of Table 9-1. Refer to the interest factor in the table indicated for eight periods and 3%. The future value would be calculated as follows:

$$FV = \$2,000 \text{ (interest factor)}$$
$$= \$2,000(1.26677)$$
$$= \$2,534$$

Present Value of a Single Amount

In many situations, we do not want to calculate how much will be accumulated at a future time. Rather, we want to determine the present amount that is equivalent to an amount at a future time. This is the present value concept. The **present value of a single amount** represents the value today of a single amount to be received or paid at a future time. This can be portrayed in a time diagram as follows:

Present value of a single amount
The amount at a present time that is equivalent to a payment or an investment at a future time.

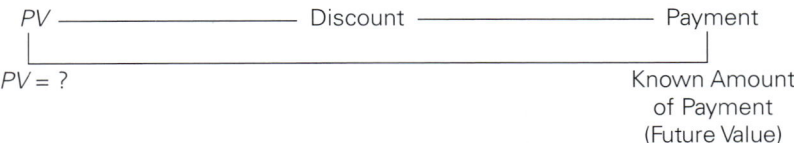

The time diagram portrays discount rather than interest because we often speak of "discounting" the future payment back to the present time.

Example 9-10 Calculating Present Value of a Single Amount

Suppose you know that you will receive $2,000 in two years. If you had the money now, you could invest it at 10% compounded annually. What is the present value of the $2,000? In other words, what amount must be invested today at 10% compounded annually to have $2,000 accumulated in two years?

The formula used to calculate present value is as follows:

$$PV = \text{Future Value} \times (1 + i)^{-n}$$

where

$$PV = \text{Present value amount in dollars}$$
$$\text{Future value} = \text{Amount to be received in the future}$$
$$i = \text{Interest rate or discount rate}$$
$$n = \text{Number of periods}$$

We can use the present value formula to solve for the present value of the $2,000 note as follows:

$$PV = \$2,000 \times (1 + 0.10)^{-2}$$
$$= \$2,000 \times (0.82645)$$
$$= \$1,653 \text{ (rounded to the nearest dollar)}$$

STUDY TIP

When interest rates *increase*, present values *decrease*. This is called an *inverse relationship*.

Tables have also been developed to determine the present value of $1 at various interest rates and number of periods. Table 9-2 on page 455 presents the present value or discount factors for an amount of $1 to be received at a future time. To use the table for Example 9-10, you must read across the line for two periods and down the 10% column to the discount factor of 0.82645. The present value of $2,000 would be calculated as follows:

$$PV = \$2,000 \,(\text{discount factor})$$
$$= \$2,000(0.82645)$$
$$= \$1,653 \,(\text{rounded to the nearest dollar})$$

Two other points are important. First, the example illustrates that the present value amount is always less than the future payment. This happens because of the discount factor. In other words, if we had a smaller amount at the present (the present value), we could invest it and earn interest that would accumulate to an amount equal to the larger amount (the future payment). Second, study of the present value and future value formulas indicates that each is the reciprocal of the other. When we want to calculate a present value amount, we normally use Table 9-2 and multiply a discount factor times the payment. However, we could also use Table 9-1 and divide by the interest factor. Thus, the present value of the $2,000 to be received in the future could also be calculated as follows:

$$PV = \$2,000/1.21000$$
$$= \$1,653 \,(\text{rounded to the nearest dollar})$$

Present Value and Future Value of an Annuity

OVERVIEW: An annuity is a series of equal payments with all payments occurring at equal time intervals. A future value of an annuity is calculated if we want to calculate how much a series of payments will accumulate in the future, at a given rate of interest, and over a certain number of payments. A present value of an annuity is calculated if we must determine a single amount today that is equivalent to the series of payments that will occur at future time intervals and at a given rate of interest.

Future Value of an Annuity

The present value and future value amounts are useful when a single amount is involved. Many accounting situations involve an annuity, however. **Annuity** means a series of payments of equal amounts. Consider the calculation of the future value when a series of payments is involved.

Annuity
A series of payments of equal amounts.

Suppose you are to receive $3,000 per year at the end of each of the next four years. Also, assume that each payment could be invested at an interest rate of 10% compounded annually. How much would be accumulated in principal and interest by the end of the fourth year? This is an example of an annuity of payments of equal amounts. A time diagram would portray the payments as follows:

$3,000		$3,000		$3,000		$3,000
	Interest		Interest		Interest	

$$FV = ?$$

Because we are interested in calculating the future value, we could use the future value of $1 concept and calculate the future value of each $3,000 payment using Table 9-1 as follows:

$3,000 × 1.33100 Interest for 3 Periods	$ 3,993
3,000 × 1.21000 Interest for 2 Periods	3,630
3,000 × 1.10000 Interest for 1 Period	3,300
3,000 × 1.00000 Interest for 0 Periods	3,000
Total Future Value	$13,923

Future value of an annuity
The amount accumulated in the future when a series of payments is invested and accrues interest.

Alternate term: Amount of an annuity.

Note that four payments would be received but that only three of them would draw interest because the payments are received at the end of each period.

Fortunately, there is an easier method to calculate the **future value of an annuity**. Table 9-3 on page 456 has been constructed to indicate the future value of a series of payments of $1 per period at various interest rates and number of periods. The table can be used for the previous example by reading across the four-period line and down the 10% column to a table factor of 4.64100. The future value of an annuity of $3,000 per year can be calculated as follows:

$$FV = \$3,000(\text{table factor})$$
$$= \$3,000(4.64100)$$
$$= \$13,923$$

Example 9-11 Calculating Future Value of an Annuity

Your cousin had a baby girl two weeks ago and is already thinking about sending her to college. When the girl is 15, how much money would be in her college account if your cousin deposited $2,000 into it on each of her 15 birthdays? The interest rate is 10%. The future value could be calculated as follows.

$$FV = \$2,000(\text{table factor})$$
$$= \$2,000(31.77248)$$
$$= \$63,545 \text{ (rounded to the nearest dollar)}$$

When compounding occurs more frequently than annually, adjustments must be made to the interest rate and number of periods.

What if the scenario was modified so that $1,000 was deposited semiannually and the interest rate was 10% compounded semiannually (or 5% per period) for 15 years? Table 9-3 could be used by reading across the line for 30 periods and down the column for 5% to obtain a table factor of 66.43885. The future value would be calculated as follows:

$$FV = \$1,000(\text{table factor})$$
$$= \$1,000(66.43885)$$
$$= \$66,439 \text{ (rounded to the nearest dollar)}$$

Comparing the two scenarios illustrates once again that more frequent compounding results in larger accumulated amounts.

Present Value of an Annuity

Many accounting applications of the time value of money concept concern situations for which we want to know the present value of a series of payments that will occur in the future. This involves calculating the present value of an annuity. An annuity is a series of payments of equal amounts.

Suppose you will receive an annuity of $4,000 per year for four years, with the first received one year from today. The amounts received can be invested at a rate of 10% compounded annually. What amount would you need at the present time to have an amount equivalent to the series of payments and interest in the future? To answer that question, you must calculate the **present value of an annuity**. A time diagram of the series of payments would appear as follows:

Present value of an annuity
The amount at a present time that is equivalent to a series of payments and interest in the future.

$4,000		$4,000		$4,000		$4,000
Discount		Discount		Discount		Discount

PV = ?

Because you are interested in calculating the present value, you could refer to the present value of $1 concept and discount each of the $4,000 payments individually using table factors from Table 9-2 as follows:

$4,000 × 0.68301 Factor for 4 Periods	$ 2,732
4,000 × 0.75131 Factor for 3 Periods	3,005
4,000 × 0.82645 Factor for 2 Periods	3,306
4,000 × 0.90909 Factor for 1 Period	3,636
Total Present Value	$12,679

For a problem of any size, it is very cumbersome to calculate the present value of each payment individually. Therefore, tables have been constructed to ease the computational burden. Table 9-4 on page 457 provides table factors to calculate the present value of an annuity of $1 per year at various interest rates and number of periods. The previous example can be solved by reading across the four-year line and down the 10% column to obtain a table factor of 3.16987. The present value would then be calculated as follows:

$$PV = \$4,000(\text{table factor})$$
$$= \$4,000(3.16987)$$
$$= \$12,679 \text{ (rounded to the nearest dollar)}$$

Example 9-12 Calculating Present Value of an Annuity

You just won the lottery. You can take your $1 million in a lump sum today, or you can receive $100,000 per year over the next 12 years. Assuming a 5% interest rate, which would you prefer, ignoring tax considerations? The present value of the series of payments can be calculated as follows:

$$PV = \$100,000(\text{table factor})$$
$$= \$100,000(8.86325)$$
$$= \$886,325$$

Because the present value of the payments over 12 years is less than the $1 million immediate payment, you should take the immediate payment.

© Cengage Learning 2013

LO6 Calculate amounts using the future value and present value concepts.

- Present and future value calculations are made for four different scenarios:
  - Future value of a single amount
  - Present value of a single amount
  - Future value of an annuity
  - Present value of an annuity

POD REVIEW 9.6

QUESTIONS   **Answers to these questions are on the last page of the chapter.**

1. You plan to invest $1,000 and want to determine how much will be accumulated in five years if you earn interest at 8% per year. This is an example of
   a. future value of a single amount.
   b. future value of an annuity.
   c. present value of a single amount.
   d. present value of an annuity.

2. You plan to invest $1,000 per year and want to determine how much will be accumulated in five years if you earn interest at 8% per year compounded annually. This is an example of
   a. future value of a single amount.
   b. future value of an annuity.
   c. present value of a single amount.
   d. present value of an annuity.

© Cengage Learning 2013

LO7 Apply the compound interest concepts to some common accounting situations.

Solving for Unknowns

In some cases, the present value or future value amounts will be known but the interest rate or the number of payments must be calculated. The formulas presented thus far can be used for such calculations, but you must be careful to analyze each problem to make sure you have chosen the correct relationship.

Example 9-13 Solving for an Interest Rate

Assume that you have just purchased an automobile for $14,419 and must decide how to pay for it. Your local bank has graciously granted you a five-year loan. Because you are a good credit risk, the bank will allow you to make annual payments on the loan at the end of each year. The amount of the loan payments, which include principal and interest, is $4,000 per year. You are concerned that your total payments will be $20,000 ($4,000 per year for five years) and want to calculate the interest rate that is being charged on the loan.

Because the market or present value of the car, as well as the loan, is $14,419, a time diagram of the example would appear as follows:

$4,000	$4,000	$4,000	$4,000	$4,000
Discount	Discount	Discount	Discount	Discount

$PV = \$14,419$

The interest rate we must solve for represents the discount rate that was applied to the $4,000 payments to result in a present value of $14,419. Therefore, the applicable formula is the following:

$$PV = \$4,000(\text{table factor})$$

In this case, PV is known, so the formula can be rearranged as follows:

$$\begin{aligned}\text{Table factor} &= PV/\$4,000 \\ &= \$14,419/\$4,000 \\ &= 3.605\end{aligned}$$

You need to use Table 9-4 to find the interest rate. You must read across the five-year line until you find a table factor that is near the value of 3.605. In this case, that table factor of 3.60478 is found in the 12% column. Therefore, the rate of interest being paid on the auto loan is approximately 12%.

© Cengage Learning 2013

Example 9-14 Solving for the Number of Years

Assume that you want to accumulate $12,000 as a down payment on a home. You believe that you can save $1,000 per semiannual period, and your bank will pay interest of 8% per year, or 4% per semiannual period. How long will it take you to accumulate the desired amount?

The accumulated amount of $12,000 represents the future value of an annuity of $1,000 per semiannual period. Therefore, we can use the interest factors of Table 9-3 to assist in the solution. The applicable formula in this case is the following:

$$FV = \$1,000(\text{table factor})$$

The future value is known to be $12,000, and we must solve for the interest factor or table factor. Therefore, we can rearrange the formula as follows:

$$\begin{aligned}\text{Table factor} &= FV/\$1,000 \\ &= \$12,000/\$1,000 \\ &= 12.00\end{aligned}$$

You need to use Table 9-3 and the 4% column to find a table value that is near 12.00. The closest table value you find is 12.00611. That table value corresponds to ten periods. Therefore, if $1,000 is deposited per semiannual period and the money is invested at 4% per semiannual period, it will take ten semiannual periods (five years) to accumulate $12,000.

© Cengage Learning 2013

LO7 Apply the compound interest concepts to some common accounting situations.

- Often, all of the variables necessary to calculate amounts related to present and future value concepts will be available except for one unknown amount that can be solved for.
- Financial calculators allow for these situations and easily solve for unknown values such as present or future value, payments, and interest rate.

POD REVIEW 9.7

QUESTIONS   **Answers to these questions are on the last page of the chapter.**

1. You want to buy a car costing $20,000 and make loan payments over five years at 10% interest per year. You must solve for the amount of the payments. In doing so, the amount of $20,000 represents

   a. an annuity.
   b. a future value.
   c. a present value.
   d. the payment amount.

2. You want to accumulate $20,000 by your 25th birthday and will invest money each year where it will earn interest at 10% compounded annually. In solving for the amount to invest each year, the $20,000 amount represents

   a. an annuity.
   b. a future value.
   c. a present value.
   d. the amount to invest.

TABLE 9-1 Future Value of $1

(N) Periods	2%	3%	4%	5%	6%	7%	8%	10%	12%	15%
1	1.02000	1.03000	1.04000	1.05000	1.06000	1.07000	1.08000	1.10000	1.12000	1.15000
2	1.04040	1.06090	1.08160	1.10250	1.12360	1.14490	1.16640	1.21000	1.25440	1.32250
3	1.06121	1.09273	1.12486	1.15763	1.19102	1.22504	1.25971	1.33100	1.40493	1.52088
4	1.08243	1.12551	1.16986	1.21551	1.26248	1.31080	1.36049	1.46410	1.57352	1.74901
5	1.10408	1.15927	1.21665	1.27628	1.33823	1.40255	1.46933	1.61051	1.76234	2.01136
6	1.12616	1.19405	1.26532	1.34010	1.41852	1.50073	1.58687	1.77156	1.97382	2.31306
7	1.14869	1.22987	1.31593	1.40710	1.50363	1.60578	1.71382	1.94872	2.21068	2.66002
8	1.17166	1.26677	1.36857	1.47746	1.59385	1.71819	1.85093	2.14359	2.47596	3.05902
9	1.19509	1.30477	1.42331	1.55133	1.68948	1.83846	1.99900	2.35795	2.77308	3.51788
10	1.21899	1.34392	1.48024	1.62889	1.79085	1.96715	2.15892	2.59374	3.10585	4.04556
11	1.24337	1.38423	1.53945	1.71034	1.89830	2.10485	2.33164	2.85312	3.47855	4.65239
12	1.26824	1.42576	1.60103	1.79586	2.01220	2.25219	2.51817	3.13843	3.89598	5.35025
13	1.29361	1.46853	1.66507	1.88565	2.13293	2.40985	2.71962	3.45227	4.36349	6.15279
14	1.31948	1.51259	1.73168	1.97993	2.26090	2.57853	2.93719	3.79750	4.88711	7.07571
15	1.34587	1.55797	1.80094	2.07893	2.39656	2.75903	3.17217	4.17725	5.47357	8.13706
16	1.37279	1.60471	1.87298	2.18287	2.54035	2.95216	3.42594	4.59497	6.13039	9.35762
17	1.40024	1.65285	1.94790	2.29202	2.69277	3.15882	3.70002	5.05447	6.86604	10.76126
18	1.42825	1.70243	2.02582	2.40662	2.85434	3.37993	3.99602	5.55992	7.68997	12.37545
19	1.45681	1.75351	2.10685	2.52695	3.02560	3.61653	4.31570	6.11591	8.61276	14.23177
20	1.48595	1.80611	2.19112	2.65330	3.20714	3.86968	4.66096	6.72750	9.64629	16.36654
22	1.54598	1.91610	2.36992	2.92526	3.60354	4.43040	5.43654	8.14027	12.10031	21.64475
24	1.60844	2.03279	2.56330	3.22510	4.04893	5.07237	6.34118	9.84973	15.17863	28.62518
26	1.67342	2.15659	2.77247	3.55567	4.54938	5.80735	7.39635	11.91818	19.04007	37.85680
28	1.74102	2.28793	2.99870	3.92013	5.11169	6.64884	8.62711	14.42099	23.88387	50.06561
30	1.81136	2.42726	3.24340	4.32194	5.74349	7.61226	10.06266	17.44940	29.95992	66.21177

TABLE 9-2 Present Value of $1

(N) Periods	2%	3%	4%	5%	6%	7%	8%	10%	12%	15%
1	.98039	.97087	.96154	.95238	.94340	.93458	.92593	.90909	.89286	.86957
2	.96117	.94260	.92456	.90703	.89000	.87344	.85734	.82645	.79719	.75614
3	.94232	.91514	.88900	.86384	.83962	.81630	.79383	.75131	.71178	.65752
4	.92385	.88849	.85480	.82270	.79209	.76290	.73503	.68301	.63552	.57175
5	.90573	.86261	.82193	.78353	.74726	.71299	.68058	.62092	.56743	.49718
6	.88797	.83748	.79031	.74622	.70496	.66634	.63017	.56447	.50663	.43233
7	.87056	.81309	.75992	.71068	.66506	.62275	.58349	.51316	.45235	.37594
8	.85349	.78941	.73069	.67684	.62741	.58201	.54027	.46651	.40388	.32690
9	.83676	.76642	.70259	.64461	.59190	.54393	.50025	.42410	.36061	.28426
10	.82035	.74409	.67556	.61391	.55839	.50835	.46319	.38554	.32197	.24718
11	.80426	.72242	.64958	.58468	.52679	.47509	.42888	.35049	.28748	.21494
12	.78849	.70138	.62480	.55684	.49697	.44401	.39711	.31863	.25668	.18691
13	.77303	.68095	.60057	.53032	.46884	.41496	.36770	.28966	.22917	.16253
14	.75788	.66112	.57748	.50507	.44230	.38782	.34046	.26333	.20462	.14133
15	.74301	.64186	.55526	.48102	.41727	.36245	.31524	.23939	.18270	.12289
16	.72845	.62317	.53391	.45811	.39365	.33873	.29189	.21763	.16312	.10686
17	.71416	.60502	.51337	.43630	.37136	.31657	.27027	.19784	.14564	.09293
18	.70016	.58739	.49363	.41552	.35034	.29586	.25025	.17986	.13004	.08081
19	.68643	.57029	.47464	.39573	.33051	.27651	.23171	.16351	.11611	.07027
20	.67297	.55368	.45639	.37689	.31180	.25842	.21455	.14864	.10367	.06110
22	.64684	.52189	.42196	.34185	.27751	.22571	.18394	.12285	.08264	.04620
24	.62172	.49193	.39012	.31007	.24698	.19715	.15770	.10153	.06588	.03493
26	.59758	.46369	.36069	.28124	.21981	.17220	.13520	.08391	.05252	.02642
28	.57437	.43708	.33348	.25509	.19583	.15040	.11591	.06934	.04187	.01997
30	.55207	.41199	.30832	.23138	.17411	.13137	.09938	.05731	.03338	.01510

Source: From STICKNEY/WEIL/SCHIPPER/FRANCIS. Financial Accounting, 13E. © 2010 South-Western, a part of Cengage Learning, Inc. Reproduced by permission. www.cengage.com/permissions

TABLE 9-3 Future Value of Annuity of $1

(N) Periods	2%	3%	4%	5%	6%	7%	8%	10%	12%	15%
1	1.00000	1.00000	1.00000	1.00000	1.00000	1.00000	1.00000	1.00000	1.00000	1.00000
2	2.02000	2.03000	2.04000	2.05000	2.06000	2.07000	2.08000	2.10000	2.12000	2.15000
3	3.06040	3.09090	3.12160	3.15250	3.18360	3.21490	3.24640	3.31000	3.37440	3.47250
4	4.12161	4.18363	4.24646	4.31013	4.37462	4.43994	4.50611	4.64100	4.77933	4.99338
5	5.20404	5.30914	5.41632	5.52563	5.63709	5.75074	5.86660	6.10510	6.35285	6.74238
6	6.30812	6.46841	6.63298	6.80191	6.97532	7.15329	7.33593	7.71561	8.11519	8.75374
7	7.43428	7.66246	7.89829	8.14201	8.39384	8.65402	8.92280	9.48717	10.08901	11.06680
8	8.58297	8.89234	9.21423	9.54911	9.89747	10.25980	10.63663	11.43589	12.29969	13.72682
9	9.75463	10.15911	10.58280	11.02656	11.49132	11.97799	12.48756	13.57948	14.77566	16.78584
10	10.94972	11.46388	12.00611	12.57789	13.18079	13.81645	14.48656	15.93742	17.54874	20.30372
11	12.16872	12.80780	13.48635	14.20679	14.97164	15.78360	16.64549	18.53117	20.65458	24.34928
12	13.41209	14.19203	15.02581	15.91713	16.86994	17.88845	18.97713	21.38428	24.13313	29.00167
13	14.68033	15.61779	16.62684	17.71298	18.88214	20.14064	21.49530	24.52271	28.02911	34.35192
14	15.97394	17.08632	18.29191	19.59863	21.01507	22.55049	24.21492	27.97498	32.39260	40.50471
15	17.29342	18.59891	20.02359	21.57856	23.27597	25.12902	27.15211	31.77248	37.27971	47.58041
16	18.63929	20.15688	21.82453	23.65749	25.67253	27.88805	30.32428	35.94973	42.75328	55.71747
17	20.01207	21.76159	23.69751	25.84037	28.21288	30.84022	33.75023	40.54470	48.88367	65.07509
18	21.41231	23.41444	25.64541	28.13238	30.90565	33.99903	37.45024	45.59917	55.74971	75.83636
19	22.84056	25.11687	27.67123	30.53900	33.75999	37.37896	41.44626	51.15909	63.43968	88.21181
20	24.29737	26.87037	29.77808	33.06595	36.78559	40.99549	45.76196	57.27500	72.05244	102.44358
22	27.29898	30.53678	34.24797	38.50521	43.39229	49.00574	55.45676	71.40275	92.50258	137.63164
24	30.42186	34.42647	39.08260	44.50200	50.81558	58.17667	66.76476	88.49733	118.15524	184.16784
26	33.67091	38.55304	44.31174	51.11345	59.15638	68.67647	79.95442	109.18177	150.33393	245.71197
28	37.05121	42.93092	49.96758	58.40258	68.52811	80.69769	95.33883	134.20994	190.69889	327.10408
30	40.56808	47.57542	56.08494	66.43885	79.05819	94.46079	113.28321	164.49402	241.33268	434.74515

TABLE 9-4 Present Value of Annuity of $1

(N) Periods	2%	3%	4%	5%	6%	7%	8%	10%	12%	15%
1	.98039	.97087	.96154	.95238	.94340	.93458	.92593	.90909	.89286	.86957
2	1.94156	1.91347	1.88609	1.85941	1.83339	1.80802	1.78326	1.73554	1.69005	1.62571
3	2.88388	2.82861	2.77509	2.72325	2.67301	2.62432	2.57710	2.48685	2.40183	2.28323
4	3.80773	3.71710	3.62990	3.54595	3.46511	3.38721	3.31213	3.16987	3.03735	2.85498
5	4.71346	4.57971	4.45182	4.32948	4.21236	4.10020	3.99271	3.79076	3.60478	3.35216
6	5.60143	5.41719	5.24214	5.07569	4.91732	4.76654	4.62288	4.35526	4.11141	3.78448
7	6.47199	6.23028	6.00205	5.78637	5.58238	5.38929	5.20637	4.86842	4.56376	4.16042
8	7.32548	7.01969	6.73274	6.46321	6.20979	5.97130	5.74664	5.33493	4.96764	4.48732
9	8.16224	7.78611	7.43533	7.10782	6.80169	6.51523	6.24689	5.75902	5.32825	4.77158
10	8.98259	8.53020	8.11090	7.72173	7.36009	7.02358	6.71008	6.14457	5.65022	5.01877
11	9.78685	9.25262	8.76048	8.30641	7.88687	7.49867	7.13896	6.49506	5.93770	5.23371
12	10.57534	9.95400	9.38507	8.86325	8.38384	7.94269	7.53608	6.81369	6.19437	5.42062
13	11.34837	10.63496	9.98565	9.39357	8.85268	8.35765	7.90378	7.10336	6.42355	5.58315
14	12.10625	11.29607	10.56312	9.89864	9.29498	8.74547	8.24424	7.36669	6.62817	5.72448
15	12.84926	11.93794	11.11839	10.37966	9.71225	9.10791	8.55948	7.60608	6.81086	5.84737
16	13.57771	12.56110	11.65230	10.83777	10.10590	9.44665	8.85137	7.82371	6.97399	5.95423
17	14.29187	13.16612	12.16567	11.27407	10.47726	9.76322	9.12164	8.02155	7.11963	6.04716
18	14.99203	13.75351	12.65930	11.68959	10.82760	10.05909	9.37189	8.20141	7.24967	6.12797
19	15.67846	14.32380	13.13394	12.08532	11.15812	10.33560	9.60360	8.36492	7.36578	6.19823
20	16.35143	14.87747	13.59033	12.46221	11.46992	10.59401	9.81815	8.51356	7.46944	6.25933
22	17.65805	15.93692	14.45112	13.16300	12.04158	11.06124	10.20074	8.77154	7.64465	6.35866
24	18.91393	16.93554	15.24696	13.79864	12.55036	11.46933	10.52876	8.98474	7.78432	6.43377
26	20.12104	17.87684	15.98277	14.37519	13.00317	11.82578	10.80998	9.16095	7.89566	6.49056
28	21.28127	18.76411	16.66306	14.89813	13.40616	12.13711	11.05108	9.30657	7.98442	6.53351
30	22.39646	19.60044	17.29203	15.37245	13.76483	12.40904	11.25778	9.42691	8.05518	6.56598

Source: From STICKNEY/WEIL/SCHIPPER/FRANCIS. Financial Accounting, 13E. © 2010 South-Western, a part of Cengage Learning, Inc. Reproduced by permission. www.cengage.com/permissions

APPENDIX

Accounting Tools: Using Excel® for Problems Involving Interest Calculations

The purpose of this appendix is to illustrate how the functions built in to the Excel® spreadsheet can be used to calculate future value and present value amounts. The use of Excel® will be illustrated with the same examples that are used in this chapter.

To view the Excel® functions, click on the PASTE function of the Excel® toolbar (the paste function is on the top of the Excel® toolbar and is noted by the symbol *fx*); then choose the FINANCIAL option. Several different calculations are available. We will illustrate two of them: FV and PV.

Example 9-15 Using Excel® for Future Values

Your three-year-old son Robert inherits $50,000 in cash and securities from his grandfather. If the funds are left in the bank and in the stock market and receive an annual return of 10%, how much will be available in 15 years when Robert starts college?

Solution: In Excel®, use the FV function and enter the values as follows:

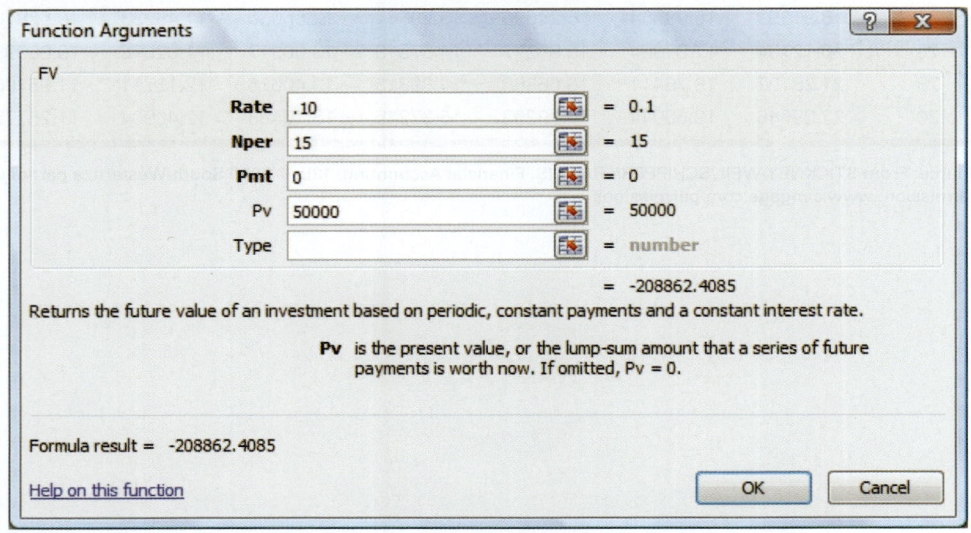

Note that the future value of $208,862 is slightly different from that given in the body of the text because of rounding when using the table factors.

Example 9-16 Using Excel® for Annual Compounding

Consider a $2,000 note payable that carries interest at the rate of 10% compounded annually. The note is due in two years, and the principal and interest must be paid at that time. What amount must be paid in two years?

Solution: In Excel®, use the FV function and enter the values as follows:

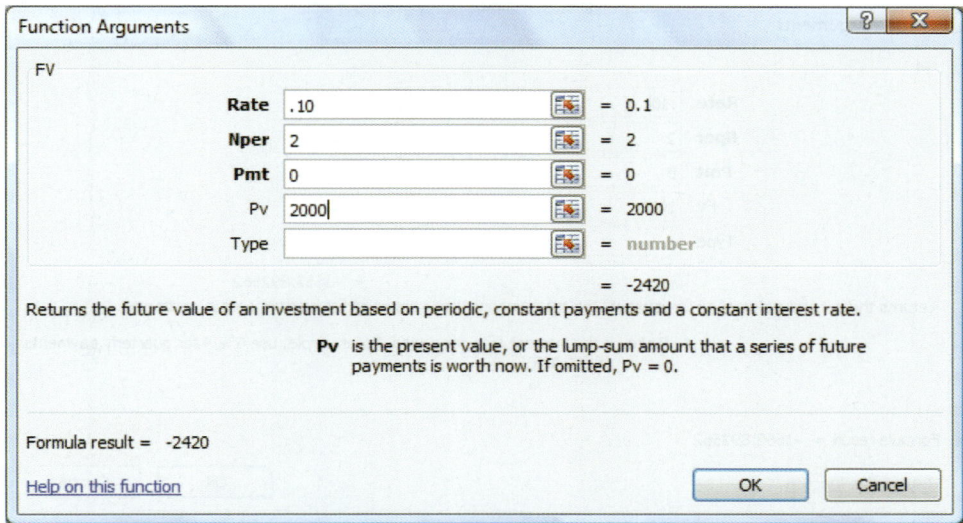

The future value is $2,420.

Example 9-17 Using Excel® for Quarterly Compounding

Suppose we want to find the future value of a $2,000 note payable due in two years. The note payable requires interest to be compounded quarterly at the rate of 12% per year. What future amount must be paid in two years?

Solution: In Excel®, use the FV function and enter the values as follows:

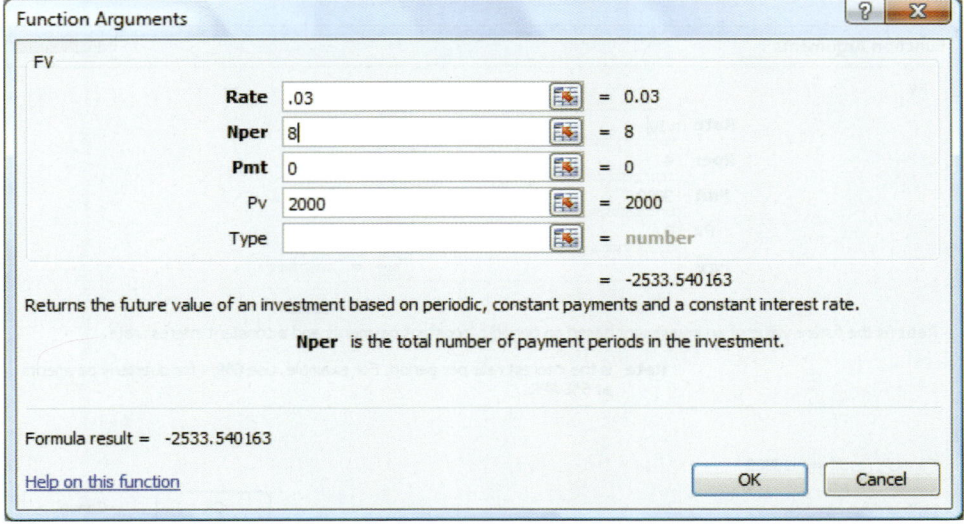

The future value is $2,534 (rounded to the nearest dollar).

Example 9-18 Using Excel® for Present Values

Suppose you know that you will receive $2,000 in two years. If you had the money now, you could invest it at 10% compounded annually. What is the present value of the $2,000?

Solution: Since this problem requires the calculation of a present value, the PV function of Excel® should be chosen and used as follows:

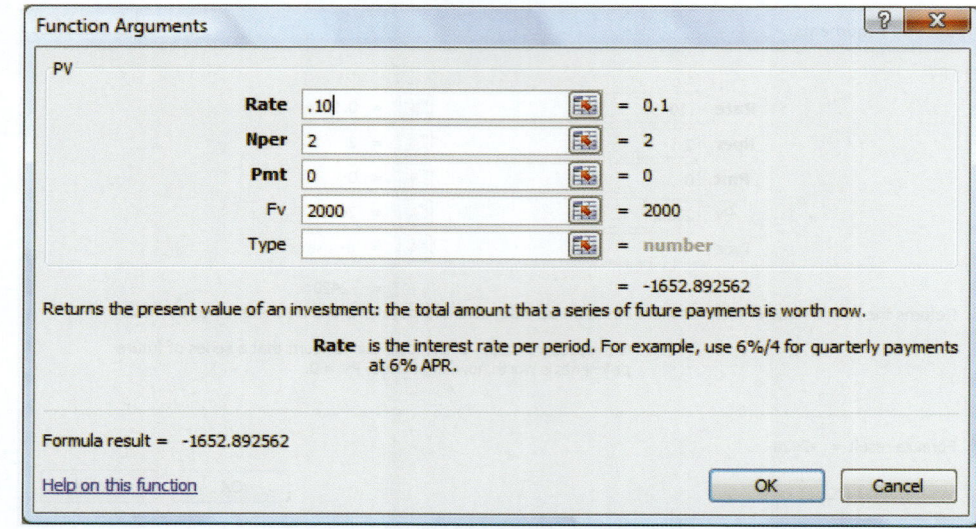

The present value is $1,653 (rounded to the nearest dollar).

Example 9-19 Using Excel® for Future Value of an Annuity

Suppose you are to receive $3,000 per year at the end of each of the next four years. Also, assume that each payment could be invested at an interest rate of 10% compounded annually. How much would be accumulated in principal and interest by the end of the fourth year?

Solution: This problem involves the calculation of the future value of an annuity; you should use the FV function of Excel® as follows:

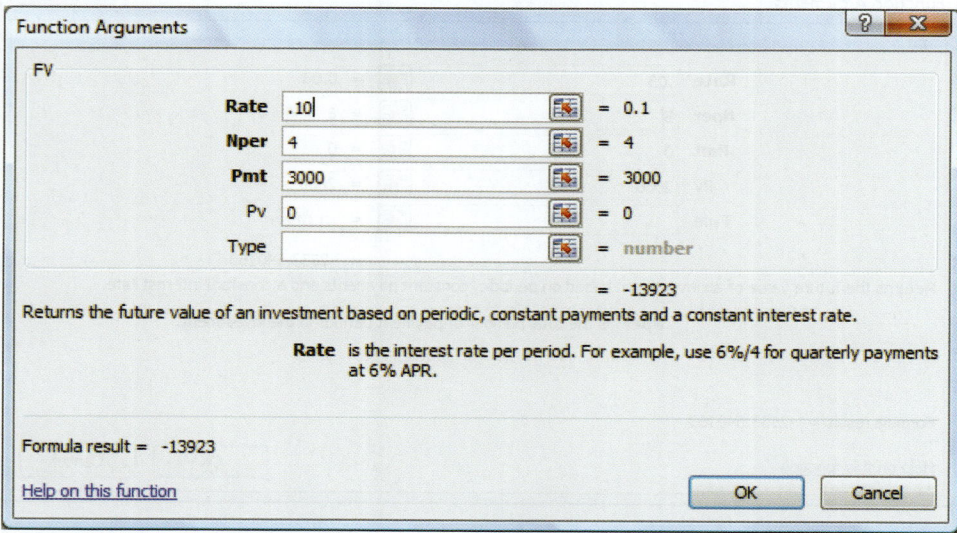

The future value of the series of payments is $13,923. Note that the payments are simply entered as the Pmt variable in the spreadsheet.

Example 9-20 Using Excel® for Semiannual Compounding Annuities

Your cousin had a baby girl two weeks ago and is already thinking about sending her to college. When the girl is 15, how much money would be in her college account if your cousin deposited $2,000 into it on each of her 15 birthdays? The interest rate is 10%.

Solution: Use the Excel® FV function as follows:

```
Function Arguments                                              ?  X

FV
              Rate   .10                              = 0.1
              Nper   15                               = 15
              Pmt    2000                             = 2000
              Pv     0                                = 0
              Type                                    = number

                                                      = -63544.96339
Returns the future value of an investment based on periodic, constant payments and a constant interest rate.

              Rate   is the interest rate per period. For example, use 6%/4 for quarterly payments
                     at 6% APR.


Formula result =  -63544.96339

Help on this function                                    OK        Cancel
```

The future value amount is $63,545 (rounded to the nearest dollar).

What if the scenario was modified so that $1,000 was deposited semiannually and the interest rate was 10% compounded semiannually (or 5% per period) for 15 years?

Solution Because the compounding is semiannual, use the FV function of Excel® as follows:

```
Function Arguments                                              ?  X

FV
              Rate   .05                              = 0.05
              Nper   30                               = 30
              Pmt    1000                             = 1000
              Pv     0                                = 0
              Type                                    = number

                                                      = -66438.8475
Returns the future value of an investment based on periodic, constant payments and a constant interest rate.

              Pmt    is the payment made each period; it cannot change over the life of the
                     investment.


Formula result =  -66438.8475

Help on this function                                    OK        Cancel
```

The future value is $66,439 (rounded to the nearest dollar).

Example 9-21 Using Excel® for Present Value of an Annuity

You just won the lottery. You can take your $1 million in a lump sum today, or you can receive $100,000 per year over the next 12 years. Assuming a 5% interest rate, which would you prefer, ignoring tax considerations?

Solution: Use the PV function of Excel® as follows:

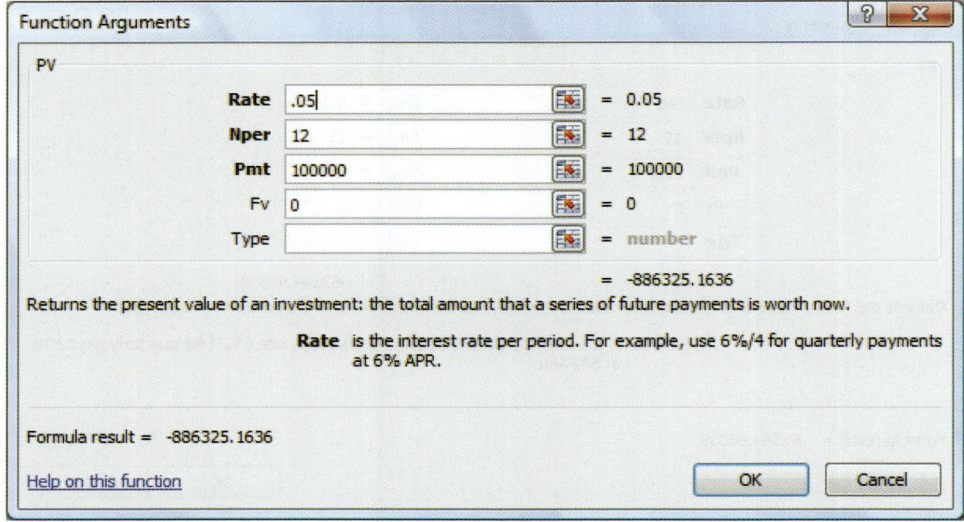

Because the present value of the payments over 12 years is $886,325 (rounded to the nearest dollar) and is less than the $1 million available immediately, you should choose the immediate payment.

© Cengage Learning 2013

RATIO REVIEW

Working Capital* = Current Assets − Current Liabilities
Current Ratio = Current Assets/Current Liabilities
Quick Ratio = Quick Assets**/Current Liabilities

 *Working capital is defined and discussed in Chapter 2.
**Quick assets are those assets that can be converted into cash quickly. They may be measured
  differently by different companies but generally are measured as Total Current Assets −
  Inventory − Prepaid Expenses.

ACCOUNTS HIGHLIGHTED

Account Titles	Where It Appears	In What Section	Page Number
Accounts Payable	Balance Sheet	Current Liabilities	431
Notes Payable	Balance Sheet	Current Liabilities	432
Current Maturities of Long-Term Debt	Balance Sheet	Current Liabilities	435
Taxes Payable	Balance Sheet	Current Liabilities	436
Accrued Liabilities	Balance Sheet	Current Liabilities	437
Contingent Liabilities	Balance Sheet	Current Liabilities or Long-Term (depending upon when it will be paid)	440

KEY TERMS QUIZ

Read each definition below and write the number of the definition in the blank beside the appropriate term. The quiz solutions appear at the end of the chapter.

_____ Current liability	_____ Time value of money
_____ Accounts payable	_____ Simple interest
_____ Notes payable	_____ Compound interest
_____ Discount on notes payable	_____ Future value of a single amount
_____ Current maturities of long-term debt	_____ Present value of a single amount
_____ Accrued liability	_____ Annuity
_____ Contingent liability	_____ Future value of an annuity
_____ Estimated liability	_____ Present value of an annuity
_____ Contingent asset	

1. Accounts that will be satisfied within one year or the next operating cycle.
2. The amount needed at the present time to be equivalent to a series of payments and interest in the future.
3. Amounts owed for the purchase of inventory, goods, or services acquired in the normal course of business.
4. A contra-liability account that represents interest deducted from a loan or note in advance.
5. A series of payments of equal amount.
6. The portion of a long-term liability that will be paid within one year of the balance sheet date.
7. A liability that has been incurred but has not been paid as of the balance sheet date.
8. Amounts owed that are represented by a formal contractual agreement. These amounts usually require the payment of interest.
9. A liability that involves an existing condition for which the outcome is not known with certainty and depends on some future event.
10. Interest that is earned or paid on the principal amount only.
11. A contingent liability that is accrued and is reflected on the balance sheet. Common examples are warranties, guarantees, and premium offers.
12. An amount that involves an existing condition dependent upon some future event by which the company stands to gain. These amounts are not normally reported.
13. Interest calculated on the principal plus previous amounts of interest accumulated.
14. The concept that indicates that people should prefer to receive an immediate amount at the present time over an equal amount in the future.
15. The amount that will be accumulated in the future when one amount is invested at the present time and accrues interest until the future time.
16. The amount that will be accumulated in the future when a series of payments is invested and accrues interest until the future time.
17. The present amount that is equivalent to an amount at a future time.

ALTERNATE TERMS

accrued interest interest payable
compound interest interest on interest
contingent asset contingent gain
contingent liability contingent loss
current liability short-term liability
current maturities of long-term debt long-term debt, current portion

discounting a note interest in advance
future value of an annuity amount of an annuity
income tax liability income tax payable
warranties guarantees

WARMUP EXERCISES & SOLUTIONS

LO1   **Warmup Exercise 9-1**

A company has the following current assets: Cash, $10,000; Accounts Receivable, $70,000; and Inventory, $20,000. The company also has current liabilities of $40,000. Calculate the company's current ratio and quick ratio.

LO3   **Warmup Exercise 9-2**

A company has the following current liabilities at the beginning of the period: Accounts Payable, $30,000; Taxes Payable, $10,000. At the end of the period, the balances of the account are as follows: Accounts Payable, $20,000; Taxes Payable, $15,000. What amounts will appear in the cash flow statement? In what category of the statement will they appear?

LO6   **Warmup Exercise 9-3**

1. You invest $1,000 at the beginning of the year. How much will be accumulated in five years if you earn 10% interest compounded annually?
2. You invest $1,000 *per year* at the end of each year for five years. How much will be accumulated in five years if you earn 10% interest compounded annually?
3. You will receive $1,000 in five years. What is the present value of that amount if you earn 10% interest compounded annually?
4. You will receive $1,000 *per year* at the end of each year for five years. What is the present value of that amount if you earn 10% interest compounded annually?

Solutions to Warmup Exercises

Warmup Exercise 9-1

Current Ratio: Current Assets/Current Liabilities
Cash ($10,000) + Accounts Receivable ($70,000) + Inventory ($20,000) = $100,000
$$\$100,000/\$40,000 = 2.5 \text{ Current Ratio}$$

Quick Ratio: Quick Assets/Current Liabilities
Cash ($10,000) + Accounts Receivable ($70,000) = $80,000
$$\$80,000/\$40,000 = 2.0 \text{ Quick Ratio}$$

Warmup Exercise 9-2

The amounts appearing in the cash flow statement should be in the Operating Activities category of the statement. The amounts shown should be the *changes* in the balances of the accounts.

Accounts Payable decreased by $10,000 and should appear as a decrease in the cash flow statement.

Taxes Payable increased by $5,000 and should appear as an increase in the cash flow statement.

Warmup Exercise 9-3

1. $FV = \$1,000$(table factor)   using Table 9-1
   $= \$1,000(1.61051)$ where $i = 10\%$, $n = 5$
   $= \$1,611$ (rounded to the nearest dollar)

2. $FV = \$1,000$(table factor)   using Table 9-3
   $= \$1,000(6.10510)$ where $i = 10\%$, $n = 5$
   $= \$6,105$ (rounded to the nearest dollar)

3. $PV = \$1,000$(table factor)   using Table 9-2
   $= \$1,000(0.62092)$ where $i = 10\%$, $n = 5$
   $= \$621$ (rounded to the nearest dollar)

4. $PV = \$1,000$(table factor)   using Table 9-4
   $= \$1,000(3.79079)$ where $i = 10\%$, $n = 5$
   $= \$3,791$ (rounded to the nearest dollar)

REVIEW PROBLEM & SOLUTION

Part A

The accountant for Lunn Express wants to develop a balance sheet as of December 31, 2012. The following items pertain to the Liability category and must be considered to determine the items that should be reported in the Current Liabilities section of the balance sheet. You may assume that Lunn began business on January 1, 2012; therefore, the beginning balance of all accounts was zero.

a. During 2012, Lunn purchased $100,000 of inventory on account from suppliers. By year-end, $40,000 of the balance had been eliminated as a result of payments. All items were purchased on terms of 2/10, n/30. Lunn uses the gross method of recording payables.

b. On April 1, 2012, Lunn borrowed $10,000 on a one-year note payable from Philips Bank. Terms of the loan indicate that Lunn must repay the principal and 12% interest at the due date of the note.

c. On October 1, 2012, Lunn also borrowed $8,000 from Dove Bank on a one-year note payable. Dove Bank deducted 10% interest in advance and gave to Lunn the net amount. At the due date, Lunn must repay the principal of $8,000.

d. On January 1, 2012, Lunn borrowed $20,000 from Owens Bank by signing a ten-year note payable. Terms of the note indicate that Lunn must make annual payments of principal each January 1 beginning in 2013 and must pay interest each January 1 in the amount of 8% of the outstanding balance of the loan.

e. The accountant for Lunn has completed an income statement for 2012 that indicates that income before taxes was $10,000. Lunn must pay tax at the rate of 40% and must remit the tax to the Internal Revenue Service by April 15, 2013.

f. As of December 31, 2012, Lunn owes its employees salaries of $3,000 for work performed in 2012. The employees will be paid on the first payday of 2013.

g. During 2012, two lawsuits were filed against Lunn. In the first lawsuit, a customer sued for damages because of an injury that occurred on Lunn's premises. Lunn's legal counsel advised that it is probable that the lawsuit will be settled in 2013 at an amount of $7,000. The second lawsuit involves a patent infringement suit of $14,000 filed against Lunn by a competitor. The legal counsel has advised that Lunn may be at fault but that a loss does not appear probable at this time.

Part B

a. What amount will be accumulated by January 1, 2016, if $5,000 is invested on January 1, 2012, at 10% interest compounded semiannually?

b. Assume that $5,000 is to be received on January 1, 2016. What amount at January 1, 2012, is equivalent to the $5,000 that is to be received in 2016? Assume that interest is compounded annually at 10%.

c. What amount will be accumulated by January 1, 2016, if $5,000 is invested each semiannual period for eight periods beginning June 30, 2012, and ending December 31, 2015? Interest will accumulate at 10% compounded semiannually.

d. Assume that $5,000 is to be received each semiannual period for eight periods beginning on June 30, 2012. What amount at January 1, 2016, is equivalent to the future series of payments? Assume that interest will accrue at 10% compounded semiannually.

e. Assume that a new bank has begun a promotional campaign to attract savings accounts. The bank advertisement indicates that customers who invest $1,000 will double their money in ten years. Assuming annual compounding of interest, what rate of interest is the bank offering?

Required

1. Consider all items in Part A. Develop the Current Liabilities section of Lunn's balance sheet as of December 31, 2012. To make investment decisions about this company, what additional data would you need? You do not need to consider the notes that accompany the balance sheet.

2. Answer the five questions in Part B.

Solutions to Review Problem Part A

1. The accountant's decisions for items (a) through (g) of Part A should be as follows:

   a. The balance of the Accounts Payable account should be $60,000. The payables should be reported at the gross amount, and discounts would not be reported until the time of payment.
   b. The note payable to Philips Bank of $10,000 should be included as a current liability. Also, interest payable of $900 ($10,000 × 12% × 9/12) should be considered a current liability.
   c. The note payable to Dove Bank should be considered a current liability and listed at $8,000 minus the contra account Discount on Notes Payable of $600 ($8,000 × 10% × 9/12 remaining).
   d. The debt to Owens Bank should be split between current liability and long-term liability with the current portion shown as $2,000. Also, interest payable of $1,600 ($20,000 × 8% × 1 year) should be considered a current liability.
   e. Income taxes payable of $4,000 ($10,000 × 40%) is a current liability.
   f. Salaries payable of $3,000 represent a current liability.
   g. The lawsuit involving the customer must be reported as a current liability of $7,000 because the possibility of loss is probable. The second lawsuit should not be reported but should be disclosed as a note to the balance sheet.

Lunn Express
Partial Balance Sheet
As of December 31, 2012

Current Liabilities		
Accounts payable		$60,000
Interest payable ($900 + $1,600)		2,500
Salaries payable		3,000
Taxes payable		4,000
Note payable to Philips Bank		10,000
Note payable to Dove Bank	$8,000	
Less: Discount on notes payable	(600)	7,400
Current maturity of long-term debt		2,000
Contingent liability for pending lawsuit		7,000
Total Current Liabilities		$95,900

Other data necessary to make an investment decision might include current assets and total assets as of December 31, 2012. If current assets are significantly larger than current liabilities, you can be assured that the company is capable of paying its short-term debt. The dollar amount of current assets and liabilities must be evaluated with regard to the size of the company. The larger the company, the less significant $95,900 in current liabilities would be.

Solutions to Review Problem Part B

a. $FV = \$5,000$(table factor)   using Table 9-1
   $= \$5,000(1.47746)$ where $i = 5\%$, $n = 8$
   $= \$7,387$ (rounded to the nearest dollar)

b. $PV = \$5,000$(table factor)   using Table 9-2
   $= \$5,000(0.68301)$ where $i = 10\%$, $n = 4$
   $= \$3,415$ (rounded to the nearest dollar)

c. FV annuity $= \$5,000$(table factor)   using Table 9-3
   $= \$5,000(9.54911)$ where $i = 5\%$, $n = 8$
   $= \$47,746$ (rounded to the nearest dollar)

d. PV annuity $= \$5,000$(table factor)   using Table 9-4
   $= \$5,000(6.46321)$ where $i = 5\%$, $n = 8$
   $= \$32,316$ (rounded to the nearest dollar)

e. $FV = \$1,000$(table factor)   using Table 9-1

Because the future value is known to be $2,000,
the formula can be written as

$\$2,000 = \$1,000$(table factor)

and rearranged as

Table factor = $2,000/$1,000 = 2.0.

In Table 9-1, the table factor of 2.0 and ten years corresponds with an interest rate
of between 7% and 8%.

QUESTIONS

1. What is the definition of *current liabilities*? Why is it important to distinguish between current and long-term liabilities?
2. Most firms attempt to pay their accounts payable within the discount period to take advantage of the discount. Why is that normally a sound financial move?
3. Assume that your local bank gives you a $1,000 loan at 10% per year but deducts the interest in advance. Is 10% the "real" rate of interest that you will pay? How can the true interest rate be calculated?
4. Is the account Discount on Notes Payable an income statement or a balance sheet account? Does it have a debit or credit balance?
5. A firm's year ends on December 31. Its tax is computed and submitted to the U.S. Treasury on March 15 of the following year. When should the taxes be reported as a liability?
6. What is a contingent liability? Why are contingent liabilities accounted for differently than contingent assets?
7. Many firms believe that it is very difficult to estimate the amount of a possible future contingency. Should a contingent liability be reported even when the dollar amount of the loss is not known? Should it be disclosed in the notes to financial statements?

8. Assume that a lawsuit has been filed against your firm. Your legal counsel has assured you that a loss is not probable. How should the lawsuit be disclosed on the financial statements?
9. What is the difference between simple interest and compound interest? Is the amount of interest higher or lower when the interest is simple rather than compound?
10. What is the effect when interest is compounded quarterly versus annually?
11. What is the meaning of the terms *present value* and *future value*? How can you determine whether to calculate the present value or the future value of an amount?
12. What is the meaning of the word *annuity*? Can the present value of an annuity be calculated as a series of single amounts? If so, how?
13. Assume that you know the total dollar amount of a loan and the amount of the monthly payments. How can you determine the interest rate as a percentage of the loan?
14. The present value and future value concepts are applied to measure the amount of several accounts common in accounting. What are some accounts that are valued in this manner?

BRIEF EXERCISES

Brief Exercise 9-1 Liquidity   LO1

Beta Company has current assets of $80,000 and current liabilities of $60,000. How much of its short-term notes payable could it pay in cash and achieve its minimum desired current ratio of 2 to 1?

Brief Exercise 9-2 Credit Terms   LO2

You receive an invoice from a supplier for $5,000 on January 1 with terms 3/15, n/30. If you pay between January 1 and January 16, how much must you pay? If you pay after January 16, how much must you pay?

LO3   Brief Exercise 9-3 Current Liabilities and Cash Flows

In the statement of cash flows, how should the following appear?

A decrease in a current liability account
An increase in a current liability account

Should changes in current liability accounts always appear in the Operating Activities category? Give an example of a current liability account that may not appear in the Operating Activities category.

LO4   Brief Exercise 9-4 Contingent Liabilities

Omega Company is involved in two unrelated lawsuits, one as the plaintiff and one as the defendant. As a result of these two lawsuits, the company has a contingent asset and a contingent liability. How should Omega record these on its balance sheet?

LO5   Brief Exercise 9-5 Simple and Compound Interest

EXAMPLE 9-6   You invest $1,000 for five years at 5% simple interest at Bank 1. You invest $1,000 for five years at Bank 2 where interest at 5% is compounded annually. Compute the amounts that will be accumulated.

LO6   Brief Exercise 9-6 Present Value and Future Value

EXAMPLE 9-12   You are required to pay $5,000 for college fees for each of the next four years, and a generous uncle has offered to give you enough money now to cover these future payments. How much must he give you now if you can invest at 10% per year compounded annually?

LO7   Brief Exercise 9-7 Solving for an Interest Rate

EXAMPLE 9-13   You are required to pay $5,000 for college fees for each of the next four years, and a not-quite-as-generous uncle offers to give you $15,187 toward your college fees. What annual interest rate do you need to earn to allow you to invest the money and meet the four payments?

EXERCISES

LO1   Exercise 9-1 Current Liabilities

The following items represent liabilities on a firm's balance sheet:

a. An amount of money owed to a supplier based on the terms 2/20, n/40, for which no note was executed.
b. An amount of money owed to a creditor on a note due April 30, 2013.
c. An amount of money owed to a creditor on a note due August 15, 2014.
d. An amount of money owed to employees for work performed during the last week in December.
e. An amount of money owed to a bank for the use of borrowed funds due on March 1, 2013.
f. An amount of money owed to a creditor as an annual installment payment on a ten-year note.
g. An amount of money owed to the federal government based on the company's annual income.

Required

1. For each item, state whether it should be classified as a current liability on the December 31, 2012, balance sheet. Assume that the operating cycle is shorter than one year. If the item should not be classified as a current liability, indicate where on the balance sheet it should be presented.

2. For each item identified as a current liability in part (1), state the account title that is normally used to report the item on the balance sheet.
3. Why would an investor or a creditor be interested in whether an item is a current or a long-term liability?

Exercise 9-2 Current Liabilities Section   LO1

Jackie Company had the following accounts and balances on December 31, 2012:

Income Taxes Payable	$61,250	Notes Payable, 10%, due June 2, 2013	$ 1,000
Allowance for Doubtful Accounts	17,800	Accounts Receivable	67,500
Accounts Payable	24,400	Discount on Notes Payable	150
Interest Receivable	5,000	Current Maturities of Long-Term Debt	6,900
Unearned Revenue	4,320	Interest Payable	3,010
Wages Payable	6,000		

Required

Prepare the Current Liabilities section of Jackie Company's balance sheet as of December 31, 2012.

Exercise 9-3 Current Liabilities   LO1

The following items are accounts on Smith's balance sheet of December 31, 2012:

Taxes Payable
Accounts Receivable
Notes Payable, 9%, due in 90 days
Investment in Bonds
Capital Stock
Accounts Payable
Estimated Warranty Payable in 2013
Retained Earnings
Trademark
Mortgage Payable ($10,000 due every year until 2030)

Required

Identify which of the accounts should be classified as a current liability on Smith's balance sheet. For each item that is not a current liability, indicate the category of the balance sheet in which it would be classified. Assume the company has the following balance sheet categories: current asset; property, plant, and equipment; long-term investment; intangible; current liability; long-term liability; and stockholders' equity.

Exercise 9-4 Discounts   LO2

Each of the following situations involves the use of discounts:
1. How much discount may Seals Inc. take in each of the following transactions? What was the annualized interest rate?
   a. Seals purchases inventory costing $450, terms 2/10, n/40.
   b. Seals purchases new office furniture costing $1,500, terms 1/10, n/30.
2. Calculate the discount rate that Croft Co. received in each of these transactions.
   a. Croft purchased office supplies costing $200 and paid within the discount period with a check for $196.
   b. Croft purchased merchandise for $2,800. It paid within the discount period with a check for $2,674.

LO2 **Exercise 9-5 Current Liabilities and Ratios**

Several accounts that appeared on Kruse's 2012 balance sheet are as follows:

Accounts Payable	$ 55,000	Equipment	$950,000
Marketable Securities	40,000	Taxes Payable	15,000
Accounts Receivable	180,000	Retained Earnings	250,000
Notes Payable, 12%, due in 60 days	20,000	Inventory	85,000
Capital Stock	1,150,000	Allowance for Doubtful Accounts	20,000
Salaries Payable	10,000	Land	600,000
Cash	15,000		

Required

1. Prepare the Current Liabilities section of Kruse's 2012 balance sheet.
2. Compute Kruse's working capital.
3. Compute Kruse's current ratio. What does this ratio indicate about Kruse's condition?

LO2
EXAMPLE 9-1, 9-4

Exercise 9-6 Notes Payable and Interest

On July 1, 2012, Jo's Flower Shop borrowed $25,000 from the bank. Jo signed a ten-month, 8% promissory note for the entire amount. Jo's uses a calendar year-end.

Required

1. Identify and analyze the effect of the promissory note.
2. Identify and analyze the effect of any adjustments necessary at year-end.
3. Identify and analyze the effect of the repayment of the principal and interest.

LO2
EXAMPLE 9-2

Exercise 9-7 Non-Interest-Bearing Notes Payable

On October 1, 2012, Ratkowski Inc. borrowed $18,000 from Second National Bank by issuing a 12-month note. The bank discounted the note at 9%.

Required

1. Identify and analyze the effect of the issuance of the note.
2. Identify and analyze the effect of the accrual of interest on December 31, 2012.
3. Identify and analyze the effect of the payment of the note on October 1, 2013.
4. What effective rate of interest did Ratkowski pay?

LO2
EXAMPLE 9-1, 9-4

Exercise 9-8 Transaction Analysis

Polly's Cards & Gifts Shop had the following transactions during the year:

a. Polly's purchased inventory on account from a supplier for $8,000. Assume that Polly's uses a periodic inventory system.
b. On May 1, land was purchased for $44,500. A 20% down payment was made, and an 18-month, 8% note was signed for the remainder.
c. Polly's returned $450 worth of inventory purchased in (a), which was found broken when the inventory was received.
d. Polly's paid the balance due on the purchase of inventory.
e. On June 1, Polly signed a one-year, $15,000 note to First State Bank and received $13,800.
f. Polly's sold 200 gift certificates for $25 each for cash. Sales of gift certificates are recorded as a liability. At year-end, 35% of the gift certificates had been redeemed.
g. Sales for the year were $120,000, of which 90% were for cash. State sales tax of 6% applied to all sales must be remitted to the state by January 31.

Required

1. Identify and analyze the effect of transactions a–g.
2. Assume that Polly's accounting year ends on December 31. Identify and analyze the effect of any necessary adjusting journal entries.
3. What is the total of the current liabilities at the end of the year?

Exercise 9-9 Impact of Transactions Involving Contingent Liabilities on Statement of Cash Flows

LO3

From the following list, identify whether the change in the account balance during the year would be reported as an operating (O), an investing (I), or a financing (F) activity or not separately reported on the statement of cash flows (N). Assume that the indirect method is used to determine the cash flows from operating activities.

_____ Estimated liability for warranties
_____ Estimated liability for product premiums
_____ Estimated liability for probable loss relating to litigation

Exercise 9-10 Impact of Transactions Involving Current Liabilities on Statement of Cash Flows

LO3

From the following list, identify whether the change in the account balance during the year would be reported as an operating (O), an investing (I), or a financing (F) activity or not separately reported on the statement of cash flows (N). Assume that the indirect method is used to determine the cash flows from operating activities.

_____ Accounts payable
_____ Current maturities of long-term debt
_____ Notes payable

_____ Other accrued liabilities
_____ Salaries and wages payable
_____ Taxes payable

Exercise 9-11 Warranties

LO4

EXAMPLE 9-5

Clean Corporation manufactures and sells dishwashers. Clean provides all customers with a two-year warranty guaranteeing to repair, free of charge, any defects reported during this time period. During the year, it sold 100,000 dishwashers for $325 each. Analysis of past warranty records indicates that 12% of all sales will be returned for repair within the warranty period. Clean expects to incur expenditures of $14 to repair each dishwasher. The account Estimated Liability for Warranties had a balance of $120,000 on January 1. Clean incurred $150,000 in actual expenditures during the year.

Required

Identify and analyze the effect of the events related to the warranty transactions during the year. Determine the adjusted ending balance in the Estimated Liability for Warranties account.

Exercise 9-12 Simple versus Compound Interest

LO5

EXAMPLE 9-6, 9-7

For each of the following notes, calculate the simple interest due at the end of the term.

Note	Face Value (Principal)	Rate	Term
1	$20,000	4%	6 years
2	20,000	6%	4 years
3	20,000	8%	3 years

Now assume that the interest on the notes is compounded annually. Calculate the amount of interest due at the end of the term for each note.

Finally, assume that the interest on the notes is compounded semiannually. Calculate the amount of interest due at the end of the term for each note.

What conclusion can you draw from a comparison of your results of each of the three scenarios?

Exercise 9-13 Present Value and Future Value

LO6

EXAMPLE 9-9, 9-10

The following situations involve time value of money calculations:
1. A deposit of $7,000 is made on January 1, 2012. The deposit will earn interest at a rate of 8%. How much will be accumulated on January 1, 2017, assuming that interest is compounded (a) annually, (b) semiannually, and (c) quarterly?
2. A deposit is made on January 1, 2012, to earn interest at an annual rate of 8%. The deposit will accumulate to $15,000 by January 1, 2017. How much money was originally deposited assuming that interest is compounded (a) annually, (b) semiannually, and (c) quarterly?

LO6

EXAMPLE 9-9, 9-10

Exercise 9-14   Present Value and Future Value

The following situations require the application of the time value of money:

1. On January 1, 2012, $16,000 is deposited. Assuming an 8% interest rate, calculate the amount accumulated on January 1, 2017, if interest is compounded (a) annually, (b) semiannually, and (c) quarterly.
2. Assume that a deposit made on January 1, 2012, earns 8% interest. The deposit plus interest accumulated to $20,000 on January 1, 2017. How much was invested on January 1, 2012, if interest was compounded (a) annually, (b) semiannually, and (c) quarterly?

LO6

EXAMPLE 9-11

Exercise 9-15   Annuity

Steve Jones has decided to start saving for his son's college education by depositing $2,000 at the end of every year for 15 years. A bank has agreed to pay interest at the rate of 4% compounded annually. How much will Steve have in the bank immediately after his 15th deposit?

LO6

EXAMPLE 9-9

Exercise 9-16   Effect of Compounding Period

Kern Company deposited $1,000 in the bank on January 1, 2012, earning 8% interest. Kern Company withdraws the deposit plus accumulated interest on January 1, 2014. Compute the amount of money Kern withdraws from the bank assuming that interest is compounded (a) annually, (b) semiannually, and (c) quarterly.

LO6

EXAMPLE 9-10

Exercise 9-17   Present Value and Future Value

Brian Inc. estimates that it will need $150,000 in ten years to expand its manufacturing facilities. A bank has agreed to pay Brian 5% interest compounded annually if the company deposits the entire amount now needed to accumulate $150,000 in ten years. How much money does Brian need to deposit?

LO7

EXAMPLE 9-8

Exercise 9-18   Value of Payments

Upon graduation from college, Susana Lopez signed an agreement to buy a used car. Her annual payments, which are due at the end of each year for two years, are $1,480. The car dealer used a 12% rate compounded annually to determine the amount of the payments.

Required

1. What should Susana consider the value of the car to be?
2. If she had wanted to make quarterly payments, what would her payments have been based on the value of the car as determined in part (1)? How much less interest would she have paid if she had been making quarterly payments instead of annual payments? What would have happened to the payment amount and the interest if she had asked for monthly payments?

LO7

EXAMPLE 9-13

Exercise 9-19   Calculation of Years

Kelly Seaver has decided to start saving for her daughter's college education. Kelly wants to accumulate $32,000. The bank will pay interest at the rate of 4% compounded annually. If Kelly plans to make payments of $1,600 at the end of each year, how long will it take her to accumulate $32,000?

MULTI-CONCEPT EXERCISES

LO6 • 7

EXAMPLE 9-13

Exercise 9-20   Two Situations

The following situations involve the application of the time value of money concepts:

1. Sampson Company just purchased a piece of equipment with a value of $53,300. Sampson financed this purchase with a loan from the bank and must make annual loan payments of $13,000 at the end of each year for the next five years. Interest is compounded annually on the loan. What is the interest rate on the bank loan?

2. Simon Company needs to accumulate $200,000 to repay bonds due in six years. Simon estimates it can save $13,300 at the end of each semiannual period at a local bank offering an annual interest rate of 8% compounded semiannually. Will Simon have enough money saved at the end of six years to repay the bonds?

Exercise 9-21 Comparison of Alternatives

Jane Bauer has won the lottery and has the following four options for receiving her winnings:
1. Receive $100,000 at the beginning of the current year
2. Receive $108,000 at the end of the year
3. Receive $20,000 at the end of each year for eight years
4. Receive $10,000 at the end of each year for 30 years

Jane can invest her winnings at an interest rate of 8% compounded annually at a major bank. Which of the payment options should Jane choose?

LO6 • 7

EXAMPLE 9-10, 9-12

PROBLEMS

Problem 9-1 Notes and Interest

Glencoe Inc. operates with a June 30 year-end. During 2012, the following transactions occurred:

a. January 1: Signed a one-year, 10% loan for $25,000. Interest and principal are to be paid at maturity.
b. January 10: Signed a line of credit with Little Local Bank to establish a $400,000 line of credit. Interest of 9% will be charged on all borrowed funds.
c. February 1: Issued a $20,000 non-interest-bearing, six-month note to pay for a new machine. Interest on the note, at 12%, was deducted in advance.
d. March 1: Borrowed $150,000 on the line of credit.
e. June 1: Repaid $100,000 on the line of credit plus accrued interest.
f. June 30: Made all necessary adjusting entries.
g. August 1: Repaid the non-interest-bearing note.
h. September 1: Borrowed $200,000 on the line of credit.
i. November 1: Issued a three-month, 8%, $12,000 note in payment of an overdue open account,
j. December 31: Repaid the one-year loan [from transaction (a)] plus accrued interest.

Required

1. Identify and analyze the effect of these transactions.
2. As of December 31, which notes are outstanding? How much interest is due on each?

LO2

Problem 9-2 Effects of Brinker International's Current Liabilities on Its Statement of Cash Flows

LO3

Brinker International operates Chili's, Macaroni Grill, and other restaurant chains. The following items are classified as current liabilities on Brinker International's balance sheets as of June 30, 2010, and June 24, 2009:

	2010	2009
	(In thousands)	
Current Liabilities:		
Current installments of long-term debt	$ 16,866	$ 1,815
Accounts payable	112,824	121,483
Accrued liabilities	300,540	285,406
Income taxes payable	19,647	—
Liabilities associated with assets held for sale	—	9,798
Total current liabilities	$449,877	$418,502

(Continued)

Required

1. Brinker uses the indirect method to prepare its statement of cash flows. Prepare the Operating Activities section of the cash flow statement, which indicates how each item will be reflected as an adjustment to net income.
2. Explain why a decrease in a current liability account such as Accounts Payable appears as a negative amount on the statement of cash flows.

LO3 Problem 9-3 Effects of Burger King's Current Liabilities on Its Statement of Cash Flows

The following items are classified as current liabilities on **Burger King Holdings, Inc.**'s balance sheets as of June 30, 2010, and June 30, 2009:

	As of June 30,	
	2010	2009
	(In millions)	
Current liabilities:		
Accounts and drafts payable	$ 106.9	$ 127.0
Accrued advertising	71.9	67.8
Other accrued liabilities	200.9	220.0
Current portion of long-term debt and capital leases	93.3	67.5
Total current liabilities	473.0	482.3
Term debt, net of current portion	667.7	755.6
Capital leases, net of current portion	65.3	65.8
Other liabilities, net	344.6	354.5
Deferred income taxes, net	68.2	74.1
Total liabilities	$1,618.8	$1,732.3

Required

1. Burger King uses the indirect method to prepare its statement of cash flows. Prepare the Operating Activities section of the cash flow statement, which indicate show each item will be reflected as an adjustment to net income. If you did not include any of the preceding items, explain why.
2. How would you decide if Burger King has the ability to pay these liabilities as they become due?

LO4 Problem 9-4 Warranties

Bombeck Company sells a product for $1,500. When the customer buys it, Bombeck provides a one-year warranty. Bombeck sold 120 products during 2012. Based on analysis of past warranty records, Bombeck estimates that repairs will average 3% of total sales.

Required

1. Identify and analyze the effect of recording the estimated liability.
2. Assume that during 2012 products under warranty must be repaired using repair parts from inventory costing $4,950. Identify and analyze the effect of recording the repair of products.

LO4 Problem 9-5 Warranties

Clearview Company manufactures and sells high-quality television sets. The most popular line sells for $1,000 each and is accompanied by a three-year warranty to repair, free of charge, any defective unit. Average costs to repair each defective unit will be $90 for replacement parts and $60 for labor. Clearview estimates that warranty costs of $12,600 will be incurred during 2012. The company actually sold 600 television sets and incurred replacement part costs of $3,600 and labor costs of $5,400 during the year. The adjusted 2012 ending balance in the Estimated Liability for Warranties account is $10,200.

Required

1. How many defective units from this year's sales does Clearview Company estimate will be returned for repair?
2. What percentage of sales does Clearview Company estimate will be returned for repair?
3. What steps should Clearview take if actual warranty costs incurred during 2013 are significantly higher than the estimated liability recorded at the end of 2012?

Problem 9-6 Comparison of Simple and Compound Interest LO5

On June 30, 2012, Rolf Inc. borrowed $25,000 from its bank, signing an 8%, two-year note.

Required

1. Assuming that the bank charges simple interest on the note, prepare the journal entry Rolf will record on each of the following dates:

   December 31, 2012
   December 31, 2013
   June 30, 2014

2. Assume instead that the bank charges 8% on the note, which is compounded semiannually. Identify and analyze the effects on the dates in part (1).
3. How much additional interest expense will Rolf have in part (2) than in part (1)?

Problem 9-7 Comparison of Alternatives LO6

On January 1, 2012, Chen Yu's Office Supply Store plans to remodel the store and install new display cases. Chen has the following options of payment. Chen's interest rate is 8%.

a. Pay $180,000 on January 1, 2012.
b. Pay $196,200 on January 1, 2013.
c. Pay $220,500 on January 1, 2014.
d. Make four annual payments of $55,000 beginning on December 31, 2012.

Required

Which option should he choose? (*Hint:* Calculate the present value of each option as of January 1, 2012.)

Problem 9-8 Investment with Varying Interest Rate LO6

Shari Thompson invested $1,000 in a financial institution on January 1, 2012. She leaves her investment in the institution until December 31, 2016. How much money does Shari accumulate if she earns interest, compounded annually, at the following rates?

2012	4%
2013	5
2014	6
2015	7
2016	8

MULTI-CONCEPT PROBLEMS

Problem 9-9 Interest in Advance versus Interest Paid When Loan Is Due LO2 • 5

On July 1, 2012, Leach Company needs exactly $103,200 in cash to pay an existing obligation. Leach has decided to borrow from State Bank, which charges 14% interest on loans. The loan will be due in one year. Leach is unsure, however, whether to ask the bank for (a) an interest-bearing loan with interest and principal payable at the end of the year or (b) a loan due in one year but with interest deducted in advance.

(Continued)

Required

1. What will be the face value of the note assuming that:
   a. Interest is paid when the loan is due?
   b. Interest is deducted in advance?

2. Calculate the effective interest rate on the note assuming that:
   a. Interest is paid when the loan is due.
   b. Interest is deducted in advance.

3. Assume that Leach negotiates and signs the one-year note with the bank on July 1, 2012. Also, assume that Leach's accounting year ends December 31. Identify and analyze the effect of the issuance of the note and the interest on the note assuming that:
   a. Interest is paid when the loan is due.
   b. Interest is deducted in advance.

4. Prepare the appropriate balance sheet presentation for July 1, 2012, immediately after the note has been issued assuming that:
   a. Interest is paid when the loan is due.
   b. Interest is deducted in advance.

LO1•4   Problem 9-10 Contingent Liabilities

Several independent items are listed for which the outcome of events is unknown at year-end.

   a. A company offers a two-year warranty on sales of new computers. It believes that 4% of the computers will require repairs.
   b. A company is involved in a trademark infringement suit. The company's legal experts believe that an award of $500,000 in the company's favor will be made.
   c. A company is involved in an environmental cleanup lawsuit. The company's legal counsel believes that the outcome may be unfavorable but has not been able to estimate the costs of the possible loss.
   d. A soap manufacturer has included a coupon offer in the Sunday newspaper supplements. The manufacturer estimates that 25% of the 50¢ coupons will be redeemed.
   e. A company has been sued by the federal government for price fixing. The company's legal counsel believes that there will be an unfavorable verdict and has made an estimate of the probable loss.

Required

1. Identify which of the items (a) through (e) should be recorded at year-end.
2. Identify which of the items (a) through (e) should not be recorded but should be disclosed in the year-end financial statements.

LO6•7   Problem 9-11 Comparison of Alternatives

Brian Imhoff's grandparents want to give him some money when he graduates from high school. They have offered Brian three choices as follows:

   a. Receive $15,000 immediately. Assume that interest is compounded annually.
   b. Receive $2,250 at the end of each six months for four years. Brian will receive the first check in six months.
   c. Receive $4,350 at the end of each year for four years. Assume that interest is compounded annually.

Required

Brian wants to have money for a new car when he graduates from college in four years. Assuming an interest rate of 8%, what option should he choose to have the most money in four years?

LO6•7   Problem 9-12 Time Value of Money Concept

The following situations involve the application of the time value of money concept:

1. Janelle Carter deposited $9,750 in the bank on January 1, 1995, at an interest rate of 12% compounded annually. How much has accumulated in the account by January 1, 2012?

2. Mike Smith deposited $21,600 in the bank on January 1, 2002. On January 2, 2012, this deposit has accumulated to $42,486. Interest is compounded annually on the account. What rate of interest did Mike earn on the deposit?

3. Lee Spony made a deposit in the bank on January 1, 2005. The bank pays interest at the rate of 8% compounded annually. On January 1, 2012, the deposit has accumulated to $15,000. How much money did Lee originally deposit on January 1, 2005?

4. Nancy Holmes deposited $5,800 in the bank on January 1 a few years ago. The bank pays an interest rate of 10% compounded annually, and the deposit is now worth $15,026. How many years has the deposit been invested?

ALTERNATE PROBLEMS

Problem 9-1A Notes and Interest

LO2

McLaughlin Inc. operates with a June 30 year-end. During 2012, the following transactions occurred:

a. January 1: Signed a one-year, 10% loan for $35,000. Interest and principal are to be paid at maturity.

b. January 10: Signed a line of credit with Little Local Bank to establish a $560,000 line of credit. Interest of 9% will be charged on all borrowed funds.

c. February 1: Issued a $28,000 non-interest-bearing, six-month note to pay for a new machine. Interest on the note, at 12%, was deducted in advance.

d. March 1: Borrowed $210,000 on the line of credit.

e. June 1: Repaid $140,000 on the line of credit plus accrued interest.

f. June 30: Made all necessary adjusting entries.

g. August 1: Repaid the non-interest-bearing note.

h. September 1: Borrowed $280,000 on the line of credit.

i. November 1: Issued a three-month, 8%, $16,800 note in payment of an overdue open account

j. December 31: Repaid the one-year loan [from transaction (a)] plus accrued interest.

Required

1. Identify and analyze the effect of these transactions.

2. As of December 31, which notes are outstanding? How much interest is due on each?

Problem 9-2A Effects of Darden Restaurants' Changes in Current Assets and Liabilities on Its Statement of Cash Flows

LO3

The following items are included in the Current Liabilities category on the consolidated balance sheet of **Darden Restaurants** at May 30, 2010, and May 31, 2009:

(in millions)	May 30, 2010	May 31, 2009
Current liabilities:		
Accounts payable	$ 246.4	$ 237.0
Short-term debt	—	150.0
Accrued payroll	161.8	138.3
Accrued income taxes	1.0	—
Other accrued taxes	62.0	60.2
Unearned revenues	167.2	138.3
Current portion long-term debt	225.0	—
Other current liabilities	391.2	372.3
Total current liabilities	$1,254.6	$1,096.1

Required

1. Darden Restaurants uses the indirect method to prepare its statement of cash flows. Prepare the Operating Activities section of the cash flow statement, which indicates how each item will be reflected as an adjustment to net income.
2. If you did not include any of the preceding items in your answer to part (1), explain how these items would be reported on the statement of cash flows.

LO3   Problem 9-3A Effects of McDonald's Current Liabilities on Its Statement of Cash Flows

The following items are classified as current liabilities on **McDonald's** consolidated statements of financial condition (or balance sheet) at December 31 (in millions):

	December 31,	
	2010	**2009**
Current liabilities		
Accounts payable	$ 943.9	$ 636.0
Income taxes	111.3	202.4
Other taxes	275.6	277.4
Accrued interest	200.7	195.8
Accrued payroll and other liabilities	1,384.9	1,659.0
Current maturities of long-term debt	8.3	18.1
Total current liabilities	$2,924.7	$2,988.7

Required

1. McDonald's uses the indirect method to prepare its statement of cash flows. Prepare the Operating Activities section of the cash flow statement, which indicates how each item will be reflected as an adjustment to net income. If you did not include any of the preceding items, explain why.
2. How would you decide if McDonald's has the ability to pay these liabilities as they become due?

LO4   Problem 9-4A Warranties

Sound Company manufactures and sells high-quality stereos. The most popular line sells for $2,000 each and is accompanied by a three-year warranty to repair, free of charge, any defective unit. Average costs to repair each defective unit will be $180 for replacement parts and $120 for labor. Sound estimates that warranty costs of $25,200 will be incurred during 2012. The company actually sold 600 sets and incurred replacement part costs of $7,200 and labor costs of $10,800 during the year. The adjusted 2012 ending balance in the Estimated Liability for Warranties account is $20,400.

Required

1. How many defective units from this year's sales does Sound Company estimate will be returned for repair?
2. What percentage of sales does Sound Company estimate will be returned for repair?

LO4   Problem 9-5A Warranties

Beck Company sells a product for $3,200. When the customer buys it, Beck provides a one-year warranty. Beck sold 120 products during 2012. Based on analysis of past warranty records, Beck estimates that repairs will average 4% of total sales.

Required

1. Identify and analyze the effect of recording the estimated liability.
2. Assume that during 2012, products under warranty must be repaired using repair parts from inventory costing $10,200. Identify and analyze the effect of the repair of the products.
3. Assume that the balance of the Estimated Liability for Warranties account as of the beginning of 2012 was $1,100. Calculate the balance of the account as of the end of 2012.

Problem 9-6A Comparison of Simple and Compound Interest   LO5

On June 30, 2012, Rolloff Inc. borrowed $25,000 from its bank, signing a 6% note. Principal and interest are due at the end of two years.

Required

1. Assuming that the note earns simple interest for the bank, calculate the amount of interest accrued on each of the following dates:

    December 31, 2012
    December 31, 2013
    June 30, 2014

2. Assume instead that the note earns 6% for the bank but is compounded semiannually. Calculate the amount of interest accrued on the same dates as in part (1).
3. How much additional interest expense will Rolloff have to pay with semiannual interest?

Problem 9-7A Comparison of Alternatives   LO6

On January 1, 2012, Chen Yu's Office Supply Store plans to remodel the store and install new display cases. Chen has the following options of payment. Chen's interest rate is 8%.

a. Pay $270,000 on January 1, 2012.
b. Pay $294,300 on January 1, 2013.
c. Pay $334,750 on January 1, 2014.
d. Make four annual payments of $82,500 beginning on December 31, 2012.

Required

Which option should he choose? (*Hint:* Calculate the present value of each option as of January 1, 2012.)

Problem 9-8A Investment with Varying Interest Rate   LO6

Trena Thompson invested $2,000 in a financial institution on January 1, 2012. She leaves her investment in the institution until December 31, 2016. How much money does Trena accumulate if she earns interest, compounded annually, at the following rates?

2012	4%
2013	5
2014	6
2015	7
2016	8

ALTERNATE MULTI-CONCEPT PROBLEMS

Problem 9-9A Interest in Advance versus Interest Paid When Loan Is Due   LO2 • 5

On July 1, 2012, Moton Company needs exactly $206,400 in cash to pay an existing obligation. Moton has decided to borrow from State Bank, which charges 14% interest on loans. The loan will be due in one year. Moton is unsure, however, whether to ask the bank for (a) an interest-bearing loan with interest and principal payable at the end of the year or (b) a non-interest-bearing loan due in one year but with interest deducted in advance.

Required

1. What will be the face value of the note assuming that:
    a. Interest is paid when the loan is due?
    b. Interest is deducted in advance?

(Continued)

2. Calculate the effective interest rate on the note assuming that:
   a. Interest is paid when the loan is due.
   b. Interest is deducted in advance.

3. Assume that Moton negotiates and signs the one-year note with the bank on July 1, 2012. Also, assume that Moton's accounting year ends December 31. Identify and analyze the effect of the issuance of the note and the interest on the note assuming that:
   a. Interest is paid when the loan is due.
   b. Interest is deducted in advance.

4. Prepare the appropriate balance sheet presentation for July 1, 2012, immediately after the note has been issued assuming that:
   a. Interest is paid when the loan is due.
   b. Interest is deducted in advance.

LO1 • 4 **Problem 9-10A Contingent Liabilities**

Several independent items are listed for which the outcome of events is unknown at year-end.

a. A company has been sued by the federal government for price fixing. The company's legal counsel believes that there will be an unfavorable verdict and has made an estimate of the probable loss.

b. A company is involved in an environmental cleanup lawsuit. The company's legal counsel believes that the outcome may be unfavorable but has not been able to estimate the costs of the possible loss.

c. A company is involved in a trademark infringement suit. The company's legal experts believe that an award of $750,000 in the company's favor will be made.

d. A company offers a three-year warranty on sales of new computers. It believes that 6% of the computers will require repairs.

e. A snack food manufacturer has included a coupon offer in the Sunday newspaper supplements. The manufacturer estimates that 30% of the 40¢ coupons will be redeemed.

Required

1. Identify which of the items (a) through (e) should be recorded at year-end.
2. Identify which of the items (a) through (e) should not be recorded but should be disclosed in the year-end financial statements.

LO6 • 7 **Problem 9-11A Time Value of Money Concept**

The following situations involve the application of the time value of money concept:

1. Jan Cain deposited $19,500 in the bank on January 1, 1995, at an interest rate of 12% compounded annually. How much has accumulated in the account by January 1, 2012?

2. Mark Schultz deposited $43,200 in the bank on January 1, 2002. On January 2, 2012, this deposit has accumulated to $84,974. Interest is compounded annually on the account. What rate of interest did Mark earn on the deposit?

3. Les Hinckle made a deposit in the bank on January 1, 2005. The bank pays interest at the rate of 8% compounded annually. On January 1, 2012, the deposit has accumulated to $30,000. How much money did Les originally deposit on January 1, 2005?

4. Val Hooper deposited $11,600 in the bank on January 1 a few years ago. The bank pays an interest rate of 10% compounded annually, and the deposit is now worth $30,052. For how many years has the deposit been invested?

LO6 • 7 **Problem 9-12A Comparison of Alternatives**

Darlene Page's grandparents want to give her some money when she graduates from high school. They have offered Darlene the following three choices:

a. Receive $16,000 immediately. Assume that interest is compounded annually.

b. Receive $2,400 at the end of each six months for four years. Darlene will receive the first check in six months.

c. Receive $4,640 at the end of each year for four years. Assume that interest is compounded annually.

Required

Darlene wants to have money for a new car when she graduates from college in four years. Assuming an interest rate of 8%, what option should she choose to have the most money in four years?

DECISION CASES

Reading and Interpreting Financial Statements

Decision Case 9-1 Comparing Two Companies: General Mills's and Kellogg's Current Liabilities   LO1 • 2

Refer to **General Mills**'s and **Kellogg's** annual reports reprinted at the back of the book. Using the companies' balance sheets and accompanying notes, write a response to the following questions:

Required

1. Determine General Mills's current ratio for fiscal years 2010 and 2009. What do the ratios indicate about the liquidity of the company?
2. How do the current liabilities of Kellogg's and General Mills compare?
3. Refer to the companies' notes. Do the companies have any contingent liabilities for lawsuits or litigation? If so, how were these contingent liabilities treated on the financial statements?

Decision Case 9-2 Caribou Coffee's Cash Flow Statement   LO4

Following is the current assets and current liabilities portion of the balance sheet of **Caribou Coffee** for the years ended January 2, 2011, and January 3, 2010:

	January 2, 2011	January 3, 2010
	In thousands except per share data	
Current assets:		
Cash and cash equivalents	$23,092	$23,578
Accounts receivable, net	8,096	5,887
Other receivables, net	1,227	1,461
Inventories	25,931	13,278
Prepaid expenses and other current assets	1,122	1,546
Total current assets	$59,468	$45,750
Current liabilities:		
Accounts payable	$ 8,080	$ 9,042
Accrued compensation	5,954	6,296
Accrued expenses	6,916	7,563
Deferred revenue	8,726	8,747
Total current liabilities	$29,676	$31,648

Required

1. Determine the company's current ratio for each fiscal year. What do the ratios indicate about the liquidity of the company? What were the major causes for any changes in liquidity?
2. Explain why deferred revenue is considered a current liability on the company's balance sheet.

Decision Case 9-3 Walmart's Contingent Liabilities   LO3 • 4

The following excerpts are from **Walmart**'s annual report of January 31, 2011.

<u>Wage-and-Hour Class Action</u>: The Company is a defendant in Braun/Hummel v. Wal-Mart Stores, Inc., a class action lawsuit commenced in March 2002 in the Court of Common Pleas in Philadelphia, Pennsylvania. The plaintiffs allege that the Company failed to pay class members for

all hours worked and prevented class members from taking their full meal and rest breaks. On October 13, 2006, a jury awarded back-pay damages to the plaintiffs of approximately $78 million on their claims for off-the-clock work and missed rest breaks. The jury found in favor of the Company on the plaintiffs' meal-period claims. On November 14, 2007, the trial judge entered a final judgment in the approximate amount of $188 million, which included the jury's back-pay award plus statutory penalties, prejudgment interest and attorneys' fees. The Company believes it has substantial factual and legal defenses to the claims at issue, and on December 7, 2007, the Company filed its Notice of Appeal.

Hazardous Materials Investigations: On November 8, 2005, the Company received a grand jury subpoena from the United States Attorney's Office for the Central District of California, seeking documents and information relating to the Company's receipt, transportation, handling, identification, recycling, treatment, storage and disposal of certain merchandise that constitutes hazardous materials or hazardous waste. The Company has been informed by the U.S. Attorney's Office for the Central District of California that it is a target of a criminal investigation into potential violations of the Resource Conservation and Recovery Act ("RCRA"), the Clean Water Act and the Hazardous Materials Transportation Statute. This U.S. Attorney's Office contends, among other things, that the use of Company trucks to transport certain returned merchandise from the Company's stores to its return centers is prohibited by RCRA because those materials may be considered hazardous waste. The government alleges that, to comply with RCRA, the Company must ship from the store certain materials as "hazardous waste" directly to a certified disposal facility using a certified hazardous waste carrier. The U.S. Attorney's Office in the Northern District of California subsequently joined in this investigation. The Company contends that the practice of transporting returned merchandise to its return centers for subsequent disposition, including disposal by certified facilities, is compliant with applicable laws and regulations. While management cannot predict the ultimate outcome of this matter, management does not believe the outcome will have a material effect on the Company's financial condition or results of operations.

Required

1. Regarding the first paragraph of the contingency note, at what point should an accrual of a contingent liability occur? What is the effect on the financial statements of an accrual?
2. Regarding the second paragraph, is disclosure of an environmental issue in the notes that accompany the financial statements all that is required by the company, or is accrual required?

LO4   Decision Case 9-4 Hewlett-Packard's Contingent Liability

Following are excerpts from the notes that accompanied the financial statements of **Hewlett-Packard** for the year ended October 31, 2010.

Copyright Levies: As described below, proceedings are ongoing or have been concluded involving HP in certain European Union ("EU") member countries, including litigation in Germany and Belgium, seeking to impose or modify levies upon equipment [such as multifunction devices ("MFDs"), personal computers ("PCs") and printers] and alleging that these devices enable producing private copies of copyrighted materials. The levies are generally based upon the number of products sold and the per-product amounts of the levies, which vary. Some EU member countries that do not yet have levies on digital devices are expected to implement similar legislation to enable them to extend existing levy schemes, while some other EU member countries are expected to limit the scope of levy schemes and applicability in the digital hardware environment. HP, other companies and various industry associations have opposed the extension of levies to the digital environment and have advocated alternative models of compensation to rights holders.

Based on industry opposition to the extension of levies to digital products, HP's assessments of the merits of various proceedings and HP's estimates of the units impacted and levies, HP has accrued amounts that it believes are adequate to address the matters described above. However, the ultimate resolution of these matters and the associated financial impact on HP, including the number of units impacted, the amount of levies imposed and the ability of HP to recover such amounts through increased prices, remains uncertain.

Environmental: HP is subject to various federal, state, local and foreign laws and regulations concerning environmental protection, including laws addressing the discharge of pollutants into the air and water, the management and disposal of hazardous substances and wastes, the cleanup of contaminated sites, the materials used in its products, and the recycling, treatment and disposal of its products including batteries. In particular, HP faces increasing complexity in its product design and procurement operations as it adjusts to new and future requirements relating to the chemical and materials composition of its products, their safe use, and the energy consumption associated with those products, including requirements relating to climate change. HP products are also subject to product take-back legislation in an increasing number of jurisdictions. HP could incur substantial costs, its products could be restricted from entering certain jurisdictions, and it could face other sanctions, if it were to violate or become liable under environmental laws or if its products become non-compliant with environmental laws. HP's potential exposure includes fines and civil or criminal sanctions, third-party property damage or personal injury claims and clean up costs. The amount and timing of costs under environmental laws are difficult to predict.

HP is party to, or otherwise involved in, proceedings brought by U.S. or state environmental agencies under the Comprehensive Environmental Response, Compensation and Liability Act ("CERCLA"), known as "Superfund," or state laws similar to CERCLA. HP is also conducting environmental investigations or remediations at several current or former operating sites pursuant to administrative orders or consent agreements with state environmental agencies.

Required

1. Based on the excerpt, how did the company treat the contingency on its financial statements for the year ended October 31, 2010? What criteria were likely used to lead to that treatment?
2. What was the effect on the financial statements of the company's treatment of the contingency?

Making Financial Decisions

Decision Case 9-5 Current Ratio Loan Provision   LO1 • 2

Assume that you are the controller of a small, growing sporting-goods company. The prospects for your firm in the future are quite good, but like many other firms, it has been experiencing some cash flow difficulties because all available funds have been used to purchase inventory and to finance start-up costs associated with a new business. At the beginning of the current year, your local bank advanced a loan to your company. Included in the loan is the following provision:

> The company is obligated to pay interest payments each month for the next five years. Principal is due and must be paid at the end of Year 5. The company is further obligated to maintain a current assets to current liabilities ratio of 2 to 1 as indicated on quarterly statements to be submitted to the bank. If the company fails to meet any loan provisions, all amounts of interest and principal are due immediately upon notification by the bank.

You, as controller, have just gathered the following information as of the end of the first month of the current quarter:

Current liabilities:	
Accounts payable	$400,000
Taxes payable	100,000
Accrued expenses	50,000
Total current liabilities	$550,000

You are concerned about the loan provision that requires a 2 to 1 ratio of current assets to current liabilities.

Required

1. Indicate what actions could be taken during the next two months to meet the loan provision. Which of the available actions should be recommended?
2. Could management take short-term actions to make the company's liquidity appear to be better? What are the long-run implications of such actions?

LO7   Decision Case 9-6 Alternative Payment Options

Kathy Clark owns a small company that makes ice machines for restaurants and food-service facilities. Kathy knows a great deal about producing ice machines but is less familiar with the best terms to extend to her customers. One customer is opening a new business and has asked Kathy to consider one of the following options that he can use to pay for his new $20,000 ice machine.

a. Term 1: 10% down, the remainder paid at the end of the year plus 8% simple interest
b. Term 2: 10% down, and $1,800 each quarter for 3 years
c. Term 3: $0 down, but $21,600 due at the end of the year

Required

Make a recommendation to Kathy. She believes that 8% is a fair return on her money at this time. Should she accept option (a), (b), or (c) or take the $20,000 cash at the time of the sale? Justify your recommendation with calculations. What factors other than the actual amount of cash received from the sale should you consider?

Ethical Decision Making

LO4   Decision Case 9-7 Warranty Cost Estimate

John Walton is an accountant for ABC Auto Dealers, a large auto dealership in a metropolitan area. ABC sells both new and used cars. New cars are sold with a five-year warranty, the cost of which is carried by the manufacturer. For several years, however, ABC has offered a two-year warranty on used cars. The cost of the warranty is an expense to ABC, and John has been asked by his boss, Mr. Sawyer, to review warranty costs and recommend the amount to accrue on the year-end financial statements.

For the past several years, ABC has recorded as warranty expense 5% of used car sales. John analyzed past repair records and found that repairs, although fluctuating somewhat from year to year, have averaged near the 5% level. John is convinced, however, that 5% is inadequate for the coming year. He bases his judgment on industry reports of increased repair costs and on the fact that several cars that were recently sold on warranty have experienced very high repair costs. John believes that the current year repair accrual will be at least 10%. He discussed the higher expense amount with Mr. Sawyer, who is the controller of ABC.

Mr. Sawyer was not happy with John's decision concerning warranty expense. He reminded John of the need to control expenses during the recent sales downturn. He also reminded John that ABC was seeking a large loan from the bank and that its loan officers might not be happy with recent operating results, especially if ABC began to accrue larger amounts for future estimated amounts such as warranties. Finally, Mr. Sawyer reminded John that most of the employees of ABC, including Mr. Sawyer, were members of the company's profit-sharing plan and would not be happy with the reduced share of profits. Mr. Sawyer thanked John for his judgment concerning warranty cost but told him that the accrual for the current year would remain at 5%.

John left the meeting with Mr. Sawyer feeling somewhat frustrated. He was convinced that his judgment concerning the warranty costs was correct. He knew that the owner of ABC would be visiting the office next week and wondered whether he should discuss the matter with him at that time. John also had met one of the loan officers from the bank several times and considered calling her to discuss his concern about the warranty expense amount on the year-end statements.

Required

Discuss the courses of action available to John. What should John do concerning his judgment of warranty costs?

Decision Case 9-8 Retainer Fees as Sales   **LO4**

Bunch o' Balloons markets balloon arrangements to companies that want to thank clients and employees. Bunch o' Balloons has a unique style that has put it in high demand. Consequently, Bunch o' Balloons has asked clients to establish an account. Clients are asked to pay a retainer fee equal to about three months of purchases. The fee will be used to cover the cost of arrangements delivered and will be reevaluated at the end of each month. At the end of the current month, Bunch o' Balloons has $43,900 of retainer fees in its possession. The controller is eager to show this amount as sales because "it represents certain sales for the company."

Required

Do you agree with the controller? When should the sales be reported? Why would the controller be eager to report the cash receipts as sales?

SOLUTIONS TO KEY TERMS QUIZ

1	Current liability	14	Time value of money
3	Accounts payable	10	Simple interest
8	Notes payable	13	Compound interest
4	Discount on notes payable	15	Future value of a single amount
6	Current maturities of long-term debt	17	Present value of a single amount
7	Accrued liability	5	Annuity
9	Contingent liability	16	Future value of an annuity
11	Estimated liability	2	Present value of an annuity
12	Contingent asset		

ANSWERS TO POD REVIEW

LO1	1. b	2. b		**LO5**	1. b	2. c
LO2	1. d	2. b		**LO6**	1. a	2. b
LO3	1. b	2. a		**LO7**	1. c	2. b
LO4	1. d	2. a				

Long-Term Liabilities

10

AFTER STUDYING THIS CHAPTER, YOU SHOULD BE ABLE TO:

LO1 Identify the components of the Long-Term Liability category of the balance sheet.

LO2 Define the important characteristics of bonds payable.

LO3 Determine the issue price of a bond using compound interest techniques.

LO4 Show that you understand the effect on the balance sheet of the issuance of bonds.

LO5 Find the amortization of premium or discount using the effective interest method.

LO6 Find the gain or loss on retirement of bonds.

LO7 Determine whether a lease agreement must be reported as a liability on the balance sheet.

LO8 Explain how investors use ratios to evaluate long-term liabilities.

LO9 Explain the effects that transactions involving long-term liabilities have on the statement of cash flows.

LO10 Explain deferred taxes and calculate the deferred tax liability. (Appendix)

STUDY LINKS

A Look at Previous Chapters Chapter 9 was concerned with current liabilities and short-term liquidity. It also introduced the concept of the time value of money.

A Look at This Chapter This chapter examines the use of long–term liabilities as an important source of financing a company's needs. Chapter 10 will utilize the time value of money concept because it is the basis for the valuation of all long-term liabilities.

A Look at Upcoming Chapters Chapter 11 examines the presentation of stockholders' equity, the other major category on the right-hand side of the balance sheet.

MAKING BUSINESS DECISIONS
COCA-COLA

Coca-Cola® is one of the world's foremost brands with worldwide sales of nearly $35 billion in 2010. The company is truly a global corporation with nearly 300 brands in almost 200 countries. While it began many years ago in the United States, now more than 70% of **The Coca-Cola Company**'s income comes from business outside the United States. Recently, the growth in company sales has slowed to nearly zero in the United States, and the company has faced new challenges in the beverage industry. Despite continued turbulence in worldwide markets and challenges from competitors, the firm maintains its focus on growth.

To meet long-term growth objectives, Coca-Cola must make significant investments to support its products. The process also involves investment to develop new global brands and to acquire local or global brands when appropriate. In addition, the company makes significant marketing investments to encourage consumer loyalty. Coca-Cola has developed relationships with many sports organizations, including the **NBA** and **NASCAR**, to enhance consumer awareness and promote sales of its products. Outside the United States, there is a strong push to sell in many other markets, including India, Brazil, Africa, and Europe.

To expand profitably, Coca-Cola requires more money than it generates in profits. Therefore, it uses a common financing tool: *long-term debt*. In fact, the balance sheet of December 31, 2010, indicates the company has over $23 billion of long-term debt, other liabilities, and deferred income taxes. The company monitors interest rate conditions carefully and in 2010 retired over $1 billion in long-term debt and in some cases replaced it with other debt. Because it is a global company, Coca-Cola has access to key financial markets around the world, which allows it to borrow at the lowest possible rates. While most of its loans are in U.S. dollars, management continually adjusts the composition of the debt to accommodate shifting interest rates and currency exchange rates to minimize the overall cost.

The accompanying balance sheet presents the Liabilities and Shareowners' Equity portion of the balance sheet for The Coca-Cola Company and its subsidiaries.

Why do you need to study this chapter?

- You need to know the components of the Long-Term Liabilities section of the balance sheet. (See pp. 488–489.)
- You need to know the proper accounting and reporting for bonds payable. (See pp. 490–503.)
- You need to understand the importance of financial arrangements such as leases as a means of financing a company. (See pp. 504–509.)
- You need to know how investors use ratios to evaluate long-term liabilities. (See pp. 510–511.)

Coca-Cola's 2010 Annual Report Consolidated Partial Balance Sheets		
December 31,	**2010**	**2009**
	(In millions except par value)	
LIABILITIES AND EQUITY		
CURRENT LIABILITIES		
Accounts payable and accrued expenses	$ 8,859	$ 6,657
Loans and notes payable	8,100	6,749
Current maturities of long-term debt	1,276	51
Accrued income taxes	273	264
TOTAL CURRENT LIABILITIES	18,508	13,721
LONG-TERM DEBT	14,041	5,059
OTHER LIABILITIES	4,794	2,965
DEFERRED INCOME TAXES	4,261	1,580
THE COCA-COLA COMPANY SHAREOWNERS' EQUITY		
Common stock, $0.25 par value; Authorized — 5,600 shares; Issued — 3,520 and 3,520 shares, respectively	880	880
Capital surplus	10,057	8,537
Reinvested earnings	49,278	41,537
Accumulated other comprehensive income (loss)	(1,450)	(757)
Treasury stock, at cost—1,228 and 1,217 shares, respectively	(27,762)	(25,398)
EQUITY ATTRIBUTABLE TO SHAREOWNERS OF THE COCA-COLA COMPANY	31,003	24,799
EQUITY ATTRIBUTABLE TO NONCONTROLLING INTERESTS	314	547
TOTAL EQUITY	$ 31,317	$ 25,346

© Cengage Learning 2013

Balance Sheet Presentation of Long-Term Liabilities

LO1 Identify the components of the Long-Term Liability category of the balance sheet.

OVERVIEW: Long-term liabilities are obligations that will not be satisfied within one year. They usually represent the primary source of financing for a company. Long-term liabilities include bonds or notes payable, leases, and deferred taxes.

In general, **long-term liabilities** are obligations that will not be satisfied within one year. Essentially, all liabilities that are not classified as current liabilities are classified as long term. We will concentrate on the long-term liabilities of bonds or notes, leases, and deferred taxes. On the balance sheet, the items are listed after current liabilities. For example, the Noncurrent Liabilities section of **PepsiCo, Inc.**'s balance sheet is highlighted in Exhibit 10-1. PepsiCo has acquired financing through a combination of long-term debt, stock issuance, and internal growth or retained earnings. Exhibit 10-1 indicates that long-term debt is one portion of the **Long-Term Liability** category of the balance sheet. But the balance sheet also reveals two other items that must be considered part of the Long-Term Liability category: deferred income taxes and other liabilities. We begin by looking at a particular type of long-term debt: bonds payable. We will concentrate on these long-term liabilities:

Long-term liability
An obligation that will not be satisfied within one year or the current operating cycle.

- Bonds or notes
- Leases
- Deferred taxes

EXHIBIT 10-1 PepsiCo's Balance Sheet

Consolidated Balance Sheet PepsiCo, Inc. and Subsidiaries December 25, 2010 and December 26, 2009		
(in millions except per share amounts)	2010	2009
LIABILITIES AND EQUITY		
Current Liabilities		
Short-term obligations	$ 4,898	$ 464
Accounts payable and other current liabilities	10,923	8,127
Income taxes payable	71	165
Total Current Liabilities	15,892	8,756
Long-Term Debt Obligations	19,999	7,400
Other Liabilities	6,729	5,591
Deferred Income Taxes	4,057	659
Total Liabilities	46,677	22,406
Commitments and Contingencies		
Preferred Stock, no par value	41	41
Repurchased Preferred Stock	(150)	(145)
PepsiCo Common Shareholders' Equity		
Common stock, par value 1⅔ per share (authorized 3,600 shares, issued 1,865 and 1,782 shares, respectively)	31	30
Capital in excess of par value	4,527	250
Retained earnings	37,090	33,805
Accumulated other comprehensive loss	(3,630)	(3,794)
Repurchased common stock, at cost (284 and 217 shares, respectively)	(16,745)	(13,383)
Total PepsiCo Common Shareholders' Equity	21,273	16,908
Noncontrolling interests	312	638
Total Equity	21,476	17,442
Total Liabilities and Equity	$ 68,153	$ 39,848

© Cengage Learning 2013

HOT TOPICS
Coca-Cola versus PepsiCo

Barisican Celik/iStockphoto.com

Hoping to capitalize on a growing interest in Eastern healing traditions, Coca-Cola Co. has quietly begun selling in the United States an unsweetened, blended tea originally developed for health-and-beauty conscious young Japanese women. The beverage giant plucked Sokenbicha from its line-up in Japan in 2009 and launched sales in the United States. The company hasn't said when or if it might expand U.S. distribution of Sokenbicha, but it says sales have exceeded expectations. Sokenbicha in Japan is a slightly bitter-tasting brew, a mix of 15 ingredients such as loquat leaves and azuki beans. Coca-Cola reformulated the drink for its U.S. market by eliminating exotic ingredients that troubled regulators, such as an herb called lizard's tail.

Coca-Cola and rival PepsiCo Inc. have been working for more than a decade to diversify their U.S. beverage portfolios as sales of their flagship soda brands stagnate.

POD REVIEW 10.1

LO1 Identify the components of the Long-Term Liability category of the balance sheet.

- Generally, long-term liabilities are obligations of a company that will not be satisfied within one year. On the balance sheet, they are listed after current liabilities.

QUESTIONS   **Answers to these questions are on the last page of the chapter.**

1. Which of the following is likely to appear in the Long-Term Liability category of the balance sheet?
   a. accounts payable
   b. bonds payable
   c. unearned revenue
   d. warranty liability

2. The account Discount on Bonds Payable should be considered what type of account?
   a. current liability
   b. asset
   c. deferred revenue
   d. contra-liability

Bonds Payable: Characteristics

LO2 Define the important characteristics of bonds payable.

OVERVIEW: A bond is a security or financial instrument that allows firms to borrow large sums of money and repay the loan over a long period of time. The borrower (issuing company) agrees to pay interest on specific dates, usually semiannually or annually. The borrower also agrees to repay the principal at the maturity, or due date, of the bond. Bonds are usually in denominations of $1,000, called face value or par value. Bond contracts can have other features concerning the collateral or due date and features that make the bonds convertible to stock or callable by the issuer.

SPOTLIGHT
Bond Fund Manager Offers Career Advice

Bond fund managers analyze many factors affecting bond investing—such as creditworthiness, maturity, price, face value, coupon rate, and yield. According to **William Matthes**, CEO of Compass Asset Management in Guilford, Conn., a successful bond fund manager uses his or her accounting or finance degree daily to serve clients.

The most successful asset managers determine risk on a continual basis using their accounting and finance expertise. The relative value of individual securities also must be assessed. And the risk versus yield must be compared between companies and across industry groups. While research about stocks tends to concentrate on earnings growth, research about bonds tends to center on the balance sheet. William obtains this information from brokerage research reports, company filings, and sources such as from Value Line, Inc. and Standard & Poor's. His accounting and finance expertise allows him to evaluate a tremendous amount of financial information and determine what funds are best suited for his clients. His firm reviews several debt level ratios when evaluating corporate bonds, most often reviewing debt to total assets and times interest earned.

According to William, risk analysis is an art, not a science subject to rigid formulas. The risk of default that the rating agencies assign to an entity is generally a measure of balance sheet stability—but it doesn't begin to address other issues such as potential industry disruptions or changes in market share.

William states that a successful career for graduates with degrees in accounting or finance "will most likely be a series of positions in multiple industries. Try to build a resume of skills that have multiple applications and allow for mobility and growth."

Name: William L. Matthes

Education: University of Virginia/ Northeastern University/ University of Bridgeport

College Major: Masters of Sociology/MBA

Occupation: Financial Advisor

Age: 64

Position: Owner and Chief Executive Officer

Company Name: Compass Asset Management LLC

See William Matthes's interview clip in CNOW.

❝Graduates with degrees in accounting or finance should realize that their education is a potential foot in the door to a career that will most likely diverge to many paths.❞

A bond is a security or financial instrument that allows firms to borrow money and repay the loan over a long period of time. The bonds are sold, or *issued,* to investors who have amounts to invest and want a return on their investment. The *borrower* (issuing firm) promises to pay interest on specified dates, usually annually or semiannually. The borrower also promises to repay the principal on a specified date, the *due date* or maturity date.

A bond certificate, illustrated in Exhibit 10-2, is issued at the time of purchase and indicates the terms of the bond. Unlike the bond in the exhibit, generally, bonds are issued in denominations of $1,000. The denomination of the bond is usually referred to as the **face value** or par value. This is the amount that the firm must pay at the maturity date of the bond.

Face value
The principal amount of the bond as stated on the bond certificate.

Alternate term: Par value

Firms issue bonds in very large amounts, often in millions in a single issue. After bonds are issued, they may be traded on a bond exchange in the same way that stocks are sold on the stock exchanges. Therefore, bonds are not always held until maturity by the initial investor, but may change hands several times before their eventual due date. Because bond maturities are as long as 30 years, the "secondary" market in bonds—the market for bonds already issued—is a critical factor in a company's ability to raise money. Investors in bonds may want to sell them if interest rates paid by competing investments become more attractive or if the issuer becomes less creditworthy. Buyers of these bonds may be betting that interest rates will reverse course or that the company will get back on its feet. Trading in the secondary market does not affect the financial statements of the issuing company.

We have described the general nature of bonds, but all bonds do not have the same terms and features. Following are some important features that often appear in the bond certificate.

EXHIBIT 10-2 Bond Certificate

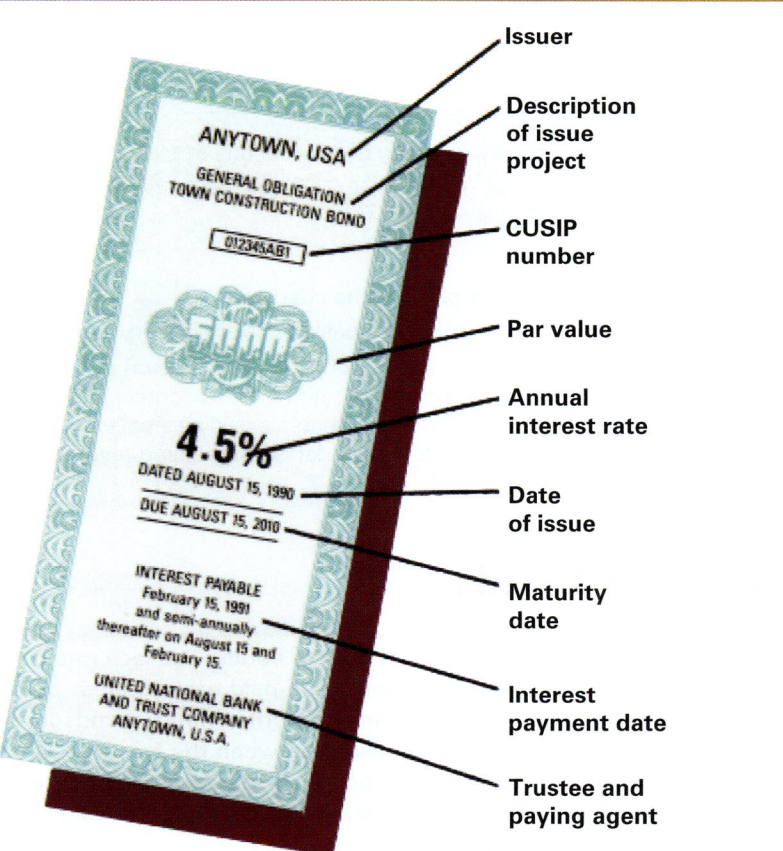

© Cengage Learning 2013

Debenture bonds
Bonds that are not backed by specific collateral.

Collateral The bond certificate should indicate the *collateral* of the loan. Collateral represents the assets that back the bonds in case the issuer cannot make the interest and principal payments and must default on the loan. **Debenture bonds** are not backed by specific collateral of the issuing company. Rather, the investor must examine the general creditworthiness of the issuer. If a bond is a *secured bond*, the certificate indicates specific assets that serve as collateral in case of default.

Due Date The bond certificate specifies the date that the bond principal must be repaid. Normally, bonds are *term bonds*, meaning that the entire principal amount is due on a single date. Alternatively, bonds may be issued as **serial bonds**, meaning that not all of the principal is due on the same date. For example, a firm may issue serial bonds that have a portion of the principal due each year for the next ten years. Issuing firms may prefer serial bonds because a firm does not need to accumulate the entire amount for principal repayment at one time.

Serial bonds
Bonds that do not all have the same due date; a portion of the bonds comes due each time period.

Other Features Some bonds are issued as convertible or callable bonds. *Convertible bonds* can be converted into common stock at a future time. This feature allows the investor to buy a security that pays a fixed interest rate but that can be converted at a future date into an equity security (stock) if the issuing firm is growing and profitable. The conversion feature is also advantageous to the issuing firm because convertible bonds normally carry a lower rate of interest.

Callable bonds
Bonds that may be redeemed or retired before their specified due date.

Callable bonds may be retired before their specified due date. *Callable* generally refers to the issuer's right to retire the bonds. If the buyer or investor has the right to retire the bonds, they are referred to as *redeemable bonds*. Usually, callable bonds stipulate the price to be paid at redemption; this price is referred to as the *redemption price* or the *reacquisition price*.

As you can see, bonds have various terms and features. Each firm seeks to structure the bond agreement in the manner that best meets the firm's financial needs and will attract investors at the most favorable rates.

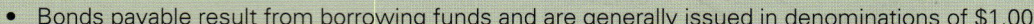

LO2 Define the important characteristics of bonds payable.

- Bonds payable result from borrowing funds and are generally issued in denominations of $1,000.
- Important characteristics of bonds payable include par value, due date, interest rate, an indication of whether the bonds are convertible or callable, and any property collateralizing the bonds.

POD REVIEW 10.2

QUESTIONS   Answers to these questions are on the last page of the chapter.

1. Bonds usually pay interest
   a. only at the due date of the bond.
   b. monthly.
   c. either annually or semiannually.
   d. at the time of issuance.

2. When serial bonds are issued,
   a. the bonds all come due on the same date.
   b. not all of the bonds come due on the same date.
   c. the interest is paid as a series of monthly payments.
   d. the lender is not required to repay the bond principal.

Issuance of Bonds

LO3 Determine the issue price of a bond using compound interest techniques.

OVERVIEW: Two rates of interest apply to bonds. The face rate is specified on the bond certificate and determines the cash to be paid each interest period. The market rate is the rate bondholders could obtain from other similar bonds in the market. The issue price is determined by the relationship between the face rate and market rate of interest and by the market's perception of risk. It represents the present value of interest payments (annuity) discounted at market rate plus present value of maturity value (single sum) discounted at market rate.

Factors Affecting Bond Price

With bonds payable, two interest rates are always involved: the face rate and the market rate.

1. The **face rate of interest** (also called the *stated rate, nominal rate, contract rate, or coupon rate)* is the rate specified on the bond certificate. It is the amount of interest that will be paid each interest period.

- For example, if $10,000 worth of bonds was issued with an 8% *annual* face rate of interest, interest of $800 ($10,000 × 8% × 1 year) would be paid at the end of each annual period.
- Alternatively, bonds often require the payment of interest semiannually. If the bonds in the example required the 8% annual face rate to be paid *semiannually* (at 4%), interest of $400 ($10,000 × 8% × 1/2 year) would be paid each semiannual period.

2. The **market rate of interest** (also called the effective rate or bond yield) is the rate that bondholders could obtain by investing in other bonds that are similar to the issuing firm's bonds.

- The issuing firm does not set the market rate of interest. That rate is determined by the bond market on the basis of many transactions for similar bonds. The market rate incorporates all of the "market's" knowledge about economic conditions and all of its expectations about future conditions. Normally, issuing firms try to set a face rate that is equal to the market rate. However, because the market rate changes daily, small differences usually occur between the face rate and the market rate at the time bonds are issued.

In addition to the number of interest payments and the maturity length of the bond, both the face rate and the market rate of interest must be known to calculate the issue price of a bond. The **bond issue price** equals the *present value* of the cash flows that the bond will produce.

Bonds produce two types of cash flows for the investor:

1. Interest receipts
2. Repayment of principal (face value)

The interest receipts constitute an annuity of payments each interest period over the life of the bonds. The repayment of principal (face value) is a one-time receipt that occurs at the end of the term of the bonds. We must calculate the present value of the interest receipts (using Table 9-4 on page 457) and the present value of the principal amount (using Table 9-2 on page 455). The total of the two present value calculations represents the issue price of the bond.

Face rate of interest
The rate of interest on the bond certificate.

Alternate term: Stated rate, nominal rate, contract rate, coupon rate.

Market rate of interest
The rate that investors could obtain by investing in other bonds that are similar to the issuing firm's bonds.

Alternate term: Effective rate, bond yield.

STUDY TIP

Calculating the issue price of a bond always involves a calculation of the present value of the cash flows.

Bond issue price
The present value of the annuity of interest payments plus the present value of the principal.

Example 10-1 Calculating Bond Issuance at a Discount

Suppose that on January 1, 2012, Discount Firm wants to issue bonds with a face value of $10,000. The face, or coupon, rate of interest has been set at 8%. The bonds will pay interest annually, and the principal amount is due in four years. Also, suppose that the market rate of interest for other similar bonds is currently 10%. Because the market rate of interest exceeds the coupon rate, investors will not be willing to pay $10,000, but something less. We want to calculate the amount that will be obtained from the issuance of Discount Firm's bonds.

Discount's bond will produce two sets of cash flows for the investor:

1. An annual interest payment of $800 ($10,000 × 8%) per year for four years.
2. Repayment of the principal of $10,000 at the end of the fourth year.

(Continued)

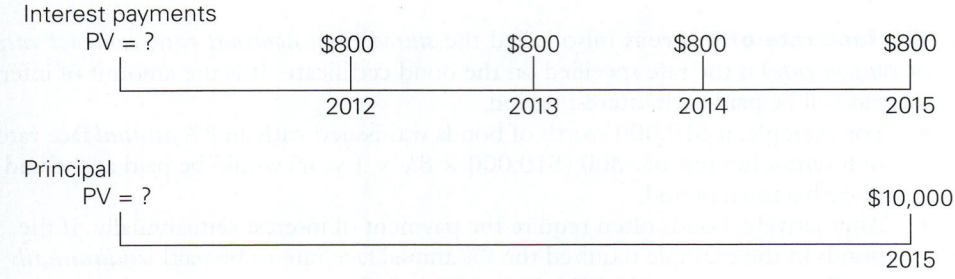

10-1

REAL WORLD PRACTICE

Reading Coca-Cola's Balance Sheet

Coca-Cola lists three items as long-term liabilities on its 2010 balance sheet. What are those items? Did they increase or decrease?

To calculate the issue price, we must calculate the present value of the two sets of cash flows. A time diagram portrays the cash flows as follows:

Interest payments

PV = ?	$800	$800	$800	$800
	2012	2013	2014	2015

Principal

PV = ?				$10,000
				2015

We can calculate the issue price by using the compound interest tables found in Chapter 9, as follows:

$800 × 3.16987 (factor from Table 9-4 for 4 periods, 10%)	$2,536
$10,000 × 0.68301 (factor from Table 9-2 for 4 periods, 10%)	6,830
Issue price	$9,366

The factors used to calculate the present value represent four periods and 10% interest. This is a key point.

> The issue price of a bond is always calculated using the market rate of interest. The face rate of interest determines the amount of the interest payments, but the market rate determines the present value of the payments and the present value of the principal (and therefore the issue price).

The example of Discount Firm reveals that the bonds with a $10,000 face value amount would be issued for $9,366. The bond markets and the financial press often state the issue price as a percentage of the face amount. The percentage for Discount's bonds can be calculated as ($9,366/$10,000) × 100, or 93.66%.

Exhibit 10-3 illustrates how bonds are actually listed in the reporting of the bond markets. The exhibit lists two types of **IBM** bonds that were traded on a particular day. The portion immediately after the company name (e.g., 6³⁄₈ 13) indicates that the face rate of interest is 6³⁄₈% and the due date of the bonds is the year 2013. The next column, (e.g., 6.5) indicates that the bond investor who purchased the bonds on that day will receive a yield of 6.5%. The column labeled "Vol" indicates the number of bonds, in thousands, that were bought and sold during the day. The column labeled "Close" indicates the market price of the bonds at the end of the day. For example, the first issue of IBM bonds closed at 98³⁄₄%, which means that the price was 98³⁄₄% of the face value of the bonds. These bonds are trading at a discount because the face rate (6³⁄₈%) is less than the market rate of 6.5%. The bonds in the second issue (7¼%) have a face rate of 7¼%; will become due in the year 2014; and closed at 101½, or at a premium. The Net Chg column indicates the change in the bond price that occurred for the day's trading.

EXHIBIT 10-3 Listing of Bonds on the Bond Market

Bonds	Cur Yld	Vol	Close	Net Chg
IBM 6³⁄₈ 13	6.5	280	98³⁄₄	−¼
IBM 7¼ 14	7.1	68	101½	+¼

LO3 Determine the issue price of a bond using compound interest techniques.

- Bonds are issued at a price that reflects the market rate of interest on the day the bond is purchased. The actual issue price of a bond represents the present value of all future cash flows related to the bond.

POD REVIEW 10.3

QUESTIONS   Answers to these questions are on the last page of the chapter.

1. On January 1, 2012, Omega Corporation issued a three-year, $1,000 bond with a nominal interest rate of 9%. At the time, the market rate of interest was 9%. The company's issue price for the bond would be

   a. $1,000.
   b. $1,300.
   c. $1,025.
   d. $700.

2. If the market rate had been 8% at the time of issuance,

   a. the bonds would have been issued at a premium.

   b. the bonds would have been issued at a discount.
   c. the bonds would have been issued at face value.
   d. there would have been 1% accrued interest at the time of issuance.

3. If the market rate had been 10% at the time of issuance,

   a. the bonds would have been issued at a premium.
   b. the bonds would have been issued at a discount.
   c. the bonds would have been issued at face value.
   d. there would have been 1% accrued interest at the time of issuance.

Premium or Discount on Bonds

OVERVIEW: A premium or discount represents the difference between the face value and the issuance price of the bond. Bonds are issued at a discount when the market rate of interest exceeds the face rate. The discount on the bond equals the face value less issue price. A discount is a deduction to the bonds payable liability and thus is a *contra* liability. Bonds are issued at a premium when the face rate exceeds the market rate. The premium on the bond equals the issue price less face value. A premium is an addition to the bonds payable liability on the balance sheet.

LO4 Show that you understand the effect on the balance sheet of the issuance of bonds.

Premium or **discount** represents the difference between the face value and the issue price of a bond. The relationship is stated as follows:

$$\text{Premium} = \text{Issue Price} - \text{Face Value}$$
$$\text{Discount} = \text{Face Value} - \text{Issue Price}$$

In other words, when issue price exceeds face value, the bonds have sold at a premium and when the face value exceeds the issue price, the bonds have sold at a discount.

We will continue with the Discount Firm in Example 10-1 to illustrate the accounting for bonds sold at a discount. Discount Firm's bonds sold at a discount calculated as follows

$$\text{Discount} = \$10,000 - \$9,366$$
$$= \$634$$

Discount Firm could identify and analyze the effect of the issuance of the bonds as follows:

Premium
The excess of the issue price over the face value of the bonds.

Discount
The excess of the face value of bonds over the issue price.

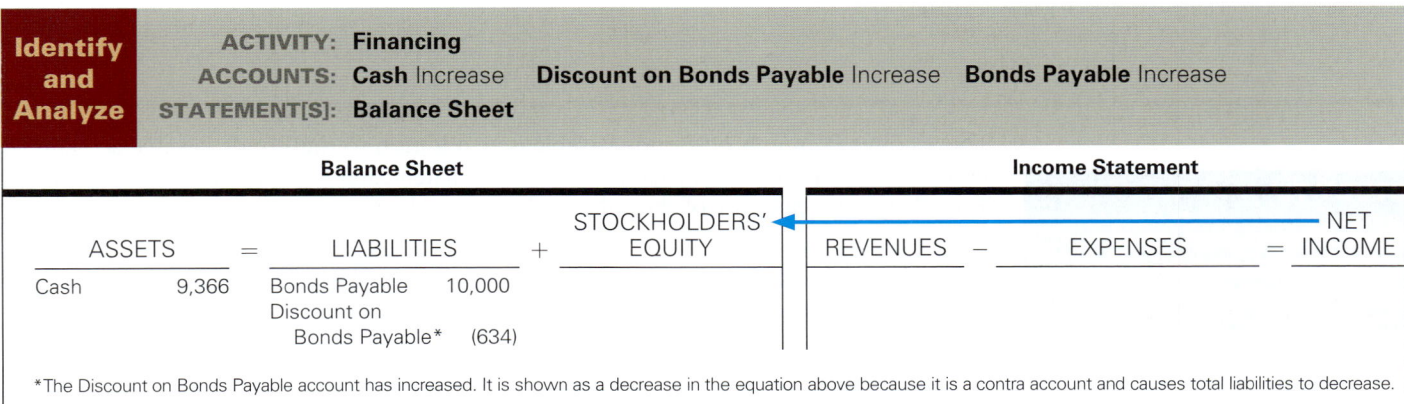

Identify and Analyze	**ACTIVITY: Financing**		
	ACCOUNTS: Cash Increase **Discount on Bonds Payable** Increase **Bonds Payable** Increase		
	STATEMENT[S]: Balance Sheet		

Balance Sheet				Income Statement		
ASSETS	=	LIABILITIES	+	STOCKHOLDERS' EQUITY	REVENUES − EXPENSES	= NET INCOME
Cash 9,366		Bonds Payable 10,000 Discount on Bonds Payable* (634)				

*The Discount on Bonds Payable account has increased. It is shown as a decrease in the equation above because it is a contra account and causes total liabilities to decrease.

The Discount on Bonds Payable account is shown as a contra liability on the balance sheet in conjunction with the Bonds Payable account and is a deduction from that account. If Discount Firm prepared a balance sheet immediately after the bond issuance, the following would appear in the Long-Term Liabilities category of the balance sheet:

Long-term liabilities:	
Bonds payable	$10,000
Less: Discount on bonds payable	634
	$ 9,366

The Discount Firm example has illustrated a situation in which the market rate of a bond issue is higher than the face rate. Now we will examine the opposite situation, when the face rate exceeds the market rate. Again, we are interested in calculating the issue price of the bonds.

Example 10-2 Calculating Bond Issuance at a Premium

Suppose that on January 1, 2012, Premium Firm wants to issue the same bonds as in Example 10-1: $10,000 face value bonds with an 8% face rate of interest and with interest paid annually each year for four years. Assume, however, that the market rate of interest is 6% for similar bonds. The issue price is calculated as the present value of the annuity of interest payments plus the present value of the principal at the market rate of interest. The calculations are as follows:

$800 × 3.46511 (factor from Table 9-4 for 4 periods, 6%)	$ 2,772
$10,000 × 0.79209 (factor from Table 9-2 for 4 periods, 6%)	7,921
Issue price	$10,693

We have calculated that the bonds would be issued for $10,693. Because the bonds would be issued at an amount that is higher than the face value amount, they would be issued at a premium. The amount of the premium is calculated as follows:

$$\text{Premium} = \$10,693 - \$10,000$$
$$= \$693$$

© Cengage Learning 2013

Premium Firm could identify and analyze the effect of the issuance of the bonds as follows:

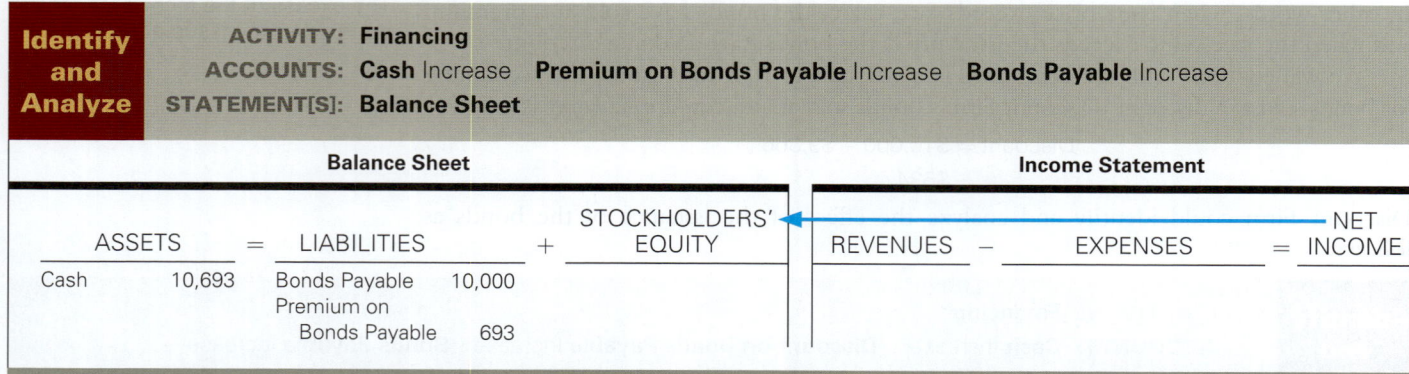

The account Premium on Bonds Payable is an addition to the Bonds Payable account. If Premium Firm presented a balance sheet immediately after the bond issuance, the Long-Term Liabilities category of the balance sheet would appear as follows:

Long-term liabilities:	
Bonds payable	$10,000
Plus: Premium on bonds payable	693
	$10,693

© Cengage Learning 2013

STUDY TIP

When interest rates increase, present values decrease. This is called an inverse relationship.

You should learn two important points from Discount Firm in Example 10-1 and Premium Firm in Example 10-2:

- **You should be able to determine whether a bond will sell at a premium or a discount by the relationship that exists between the face rate and the market rate of interest.** *Premium* and *discount* do not mean "good" and "bad," respectively. Premium or discount arises solely because of the difference that exists between the face rate and the market rate of interest for a bond issue. The same relationship always exists, so the following statements hold true:

    If Market Rate = Face Rate, THEN bonds are issued at face value amount.
    If Market Rate > Face Rate, THEN bonds are issued at a discount.
    If Market Rate < Face Rate, THEN bonds are issued at a premium.

- **The relationship between interest rates and bond prices is always inverse.** To understand the term *inverse relationship,* refer to Examples 10-1 and 10-2. The bonds of the two firms are identical in all respects except for the market rate of interest. When the market rate was 10%, the bond issue price was $9,366 (Example 10-1). When the market rate was 6%, the bond issue price increased to $10,693 (Example 10-2). These examples illustrate that as interest rates decrease, prices on the bond markets increase and that as interest rates increase, bond prices decrease.

LO4 Show that you understand the effect on the balance sheet of the issuance of bonds.

- Bonds are recorded on the balance sheet at an amount that takes into account the premium or discount associated with bonds on the date they are issued.
    - Bond premiums represent amounts paid in excess of par, and bond discounts represent amounts paid below par.

POD REVIEW 10.4

QUESTIONS   **Answers to these questions are on the last page of the chapter.**

1. The excess of the issue price over the face value of the bond is referred to as
    a. a discount.
    b. a premium.
    c. accrued interest.
    d. prepaid interest.

2. If the market rate of the bond at the time of issuance is greater than the face rate,
    a. the bonds will be issued at a premium.
    b. the bonds will be issued at a discount.
    c. a gain will occur.
    d. a loss will occur.

Bond Amortization

OVERVIEW: Amortization of premium or discount on bonds payable allocates the difference in interest rates (face and market rates) over the life of the bond so that interest expense each period reflects the effective rate, or the market rate, of the borrowing. The effective interest method calculates interest on the net liability every period at the market rate. For bonds issued at a discount, the net liability starts below face value and increases every period until the discount is fully amortized at maturity. For bonds issued at premium, the opposite is true: the net liability starts above face value and decreases every period until the premium is fully amortized at maturity.

LO5 Find the amortization of premium or discount using the effective interest method.

Purpose of Amortization

The amount of interest expense that should be reflected on a firm's income statement for bonds payable is the true, or effective, interest. The effective interest should reflect the face rate of interest as well as interest that results from issuing the bond at a premium or discount. To reflect that interest component, the amount initially recorded in the

Premium on Bonds Payable or the Discount on Bonds Payable account must be amortized, or spread over the life of the bond.

Amortization refers to the process of transferring an amount from the discount or premium account to interest expense each time period to adjust interest expense. One commonly used method of amortization is the effective interest method. This section will illustrate how to amortize a discount amount and then how to amortize a premium amount.

To illustrate amortization of a discount, we need to return to Discount Firm in Example 10-1. We have seen that the issue price of the bond could be calculated as $9,366, resulting in a contra-liability balance of $634 in the Discount on Bonds Payable account. (See the accounting transaction on page 495.) But what does the initial balance of the Discount account really represent? The discount should be thought of as additional interest that Discount Firm must pay over and above the 8% face rate. Remember that Discount received only $9,366 but must repay the full principal of $10,000 at the bond due date. For that reason, the $634 discount is an additional interest cost that must be reflected as interest expense. It is reflected as interest expense by the process of amortization. In other words, interest expense is made up of two components: cash interest and amortization. We will now consider how to amortize premium or discount.

Effective Interest Method: Impact on Expense

Effective interest method of amortization

The process of transferring a portion of the premium or discount to interest expense; this method results in a constant effective interest rate.

Alternate term: Interest method.

Carrying value

The face value of a bond plus the amount of unamortized premium or minus the amount of unamortized discount.

Alternate term: Book value.

The **effective interest method of amortization** amortizes discount or premium in a manner that produces a constant effective interest rate from period to period. The dollar amount of interest expense will vary from period to period, but the rate of interest will be constant. This interest rate is referred to as the *effective interest rate* and is equal to the market rate of interest at the time the bonds are issued.

To illustrate this point, we introduce two new terms. The **carrying value** of bonds is represented by the following:

$$\text{Carrying Value} = \text{Face Value} - \text{Unamortized Discount}$$

The carrying value of the bonds for Discount Firm in Example 10-1 as of the date of issuance of January 1, 2012, could be calculated as follows:

$$\$10,000 - \$634 = \$9,366$$

In those situations in which there is a premium instead of a discount, carrying value is represented by the following:

$$\text{Carrying Value} = \text{Face Value} + \text{Unamortized Premium}$$

The carrying value of the bonds for Premium Firm in Example 10-2 as of the date of issuance of January 1, 2012, could be calculated as follows:

$$\$10,000 + \$693 = \$10,693$$

The second term was suggested earlier. The *effective rate of interest* is represented by the following:

$$\text{Effective Rate} = \text{Annual Interest Expense/Carrying Value}$$

Effective Interest Method

The amortization table in Exhibit 10-4 illustrates effective interest amortization of the bond discount for Discount Firm in Example 10-1.

As illustrated in Exhibit 10-4, the effective interest method of amortization is based on several important concepts. The relationships can be stated in equation form as follows:

$$\text{Cash Interest (in Column 1)} = \text{Bond Face Value} \times \text{Face Rate}$$
$$\text{Interest Expense (in Column 2)} = \text{Carrying Value} \times \text{Effective Rate}$$
$$\text{Discount Amortized (in Column 3)} = \text{Interest Expense} - \text{Cash Interest}$$

Column 1 indicates that the cash interest to be paid is $800 ($10,000 × 8%). Column 2 indicates the annual interest expense at the effective rate of interest (market rate at the time of issuance). This is a constant rate of interest (10% in Example 10-1) and is calculated by multiplying the carrying value as of the beginning of the period by the market rate of interest. In 2012, the interest expense is $937 ($9,366 × 10%). Note that the amount of interest expense changes each year because the carrying value changes as discount is amortized. The amount of discount amortized each year in Column 3 is the difference between the cash interest in Column 1 and the interest expense in Column 2. Again, note that the amount of discount amortized changes in each of the four years. Finally, the carrying value in Column 4 is the previous year's carrying value plus the discount amortized in Column 3. When bonds are issued at a discount, the carrying value starts at an amount less than face value and increases each period until it reaches the face value amount.

Example 10-3 Recording Amortization of Discount

Assume that we want to record amortization for Discount Firm for 2012. Exhibit 10-4 is the basis for determining the effect of amortization on the firm's financial statements. The effect of the payment of interest and amortization of discount could be identified and analyzed as follows:

Identify and Analyze	**ACTIVITY: Operating**
	ACCOUNTS: Interest Expense Increase **Discount on Bonds Payable** Decrease **Cash** Decrease
	STATEMENT[S]: Balance Sheet and Income Statement

Balance Sheet					Income Statement			
ASSETS	=	LIABILITIES	+	STOCKHOLDERS' EQUITY	REVENUES	−	EXPENSES	= NET INCOME
Cash (800)		Discount on Bonds Payable* 137		(937)			Interest Expense 937	(937)

*The Discount on Bonds Payable account has decreased. It is shown as an increase in the equation above because it is a contra account and causes total liabilities to increase.

The balance of the Discount on Bonds Payable account as of December 31, 2012, would be calculated as follows:

Beginning balance, January 1, 2012	$634
Less: Amount amortized	137
Ending balance, December 31, 2012	$497

© Cengage Learning 2013

EXHIBIT 10-4 Discount Amortization: Effective Interest Method of Amortization

Date	Column 1 Cash Interest	Column 2 Interest Expense	Column 3 Discount Amortized	Column 4 Carrying Value
	8%	10%	Col. 2 − Col. 1	
1/1/2012	—	—	—	$ 9,366
12/31/2012	$800	$937	$137	9,503
12/31/2013	800	950	150	9,653
12/31/2014	800	965	165	9,818
12/31/2015	800	982	182	10,000

© Cengage Learning 2013

In Example 10-3, the December 31, 2012, balance represents the amount *unamortized,* or the amount that will be amortized in future time periods. On the balance sheet presented as of December 31, 2012, the unamortized portion of the discount appears as the balance of the Discount on Bonds Payable account as follows:

Long-term liabilities	
Bonds payable	$10,000
Less: Discount on bonds payable	497
	$ 9,503

The process of amortization would continue for four years, until the balance of the Discount on Bonds Payable account has been reduced to zero. By the end of 2015, all of the balance of the Discount on Bonds Payable account will have been transferred to the Interest Expense account and represents an increase in interest expense each period.

The amortization of a premium has an impact opposite that of the amortization of a discount. We will use Premium Firm from Example 10-2 to illustrate. Recall that on January 1, 2012, Premium Firm issued $10,000 face value bonds with a face rate of interest of 8%. At the time the bonds were issued, the market rate was 6%, resulting in an issue price of $10,693 and a credit balance in the Premium on Bonds Payable account of $693.

The amortization table in Exhibit 10-5 illustrates effective interest amortization of the bond premium for Premium Firm. As the exhibit illustrates, effective interest amortization of a premium is based on the same concepts as amortization of a discount. The following relationships still hold true:

Cash Interest (in Column 1) = Bond Face Value × Face Rate

Interest Expense (in Column 2) = Carrying Value × Effective Rate

Column 1 indicates that the cash interest to be paid is $800 ($10,000 × 8%). Column 2 indicates the annual interest expense at the effective rate. In 2012, the interest expense is $642 ($10,693 × 6%). Note, however, two differences between Exhibits 10-4 and 10-5. In the amortization of a premium, the cash interest in Column 1 exceeds the interest expense in Column 2. Therefore, the premium amortized is defined as follows:

Premium Amortized (in Column 3) = Cash Interest − Interest Expense

Also, note that the carrying value in Column 4 starts at an amount higher than the face value of $10,000 ($10,693) and is amortized downward until it reaches face value. Therefore, the carrying value at the end of each year is the carrying value at the beginning of the period minus the premium amortized for that year. For example, the carrying value in Exhibit 10-5 at the end of 2012 ($10,535) was calculated by subtracting the premium amortized for 2012 ($158 in Column 3) from the carrying value at the beginning of 2012 ($10,693).

EXHIBIT 10-5 Premium Amortization: Effective Interest Method of Amortization

Date	Column 1 Cash Interest	Column 2 Interest Expense	Column 3 Premium Amortized	Column 4 Carrying Value
	8%	6%	Col. 1 − Col. 2	
1/1/2012	—	—	—	$10,693
12/31/2012	$800	$642	$158	10,535
12/31/2013	800	632	168	10,367
12/31/2014	800	622	178	10,189
12/31/2015	800	611	189	10,000

Example 10-4 Recording Amortization of a Premium

Assume that we want to record amortization for Premium Firm for 2012. Exhibit 10-5 is the basis for determining the effect of amortization of a premium on the firm's financial statements. The effect of the payment of interest and amortization of premium could be identified and analyzed as follows:

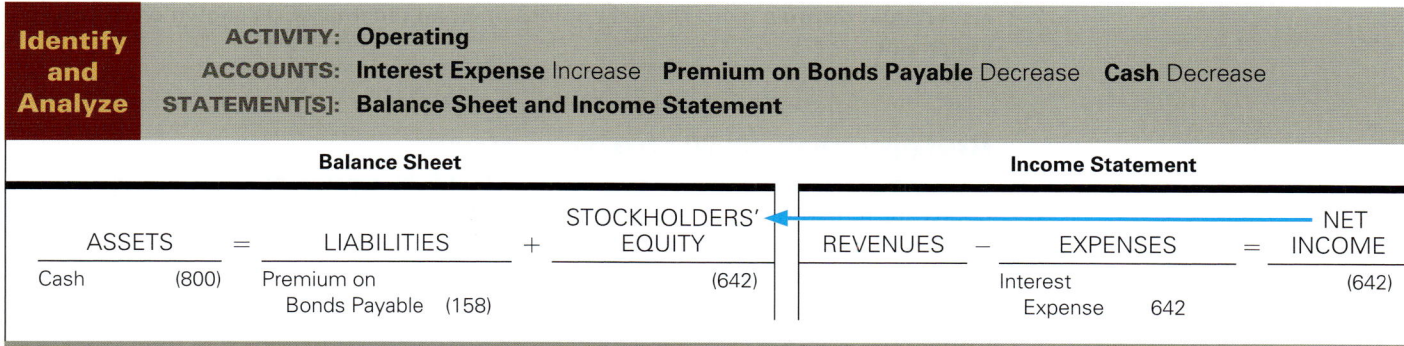

Identify and Analyze	**ACTIVITY: Operating**
	ACCOUNTS: Interest Expense Increase **Premium on Bonds Payable** Decrease **Cash** Decrease
	STATEMENT[S]: Balance Sheet and Income Statement

Balance Sheet					Income Statement			
ASSETS	=	LIABILITIES	+	STOCKHOLDERS' EQUITY	REVENUES	−	EXPENSES	= NET INCOME
Cash (800)		Premium on Bonds Payable (158)		(642)			Interest Expense 642	(642)

The balance of the Premium on Bonds Payable account as of December 31, 2012, would be calculated as follows:

Beginning balance, January 1, 2012	$693
Less: Amount amortized	158
Ending balance, December 31, 2012	$535

© Cengage Learning 2013

In Example 10-4, the December 31, 2012, balance represents the amount *unamortized*, or the amount that will be amortized in future time periods. On the balance sheet presented as of December 31, 2012, the unamortized portion of the premium appears as the balance of the Premium on Bonds Payable account as follows:

Long-term liabilities:	
Bonds payable	$10,000
Plus: Premium on bonds payable	535
	$10,535

The process of amortization would continue for four years, until the balance of the Premium on Bonds Payable account has been reduced to zero. By the end of 2015, all of the balance of the Premium on Bonds Payable account will have been transferred to the Interest Expense account and represents a reduction of interest expense each period.

LO5 Find the amortization of premium or discount using the effective interest method.

- The premium or discount on bonds must be amortized over the life of the bond to accurately reflect the interest expense.
- The effective interest method amortizes discounts or premiums in a way that produces a constant interest rate from one period to the next.

POD REVIEW 10.5

QUESTIONS   **Answers to these questions are on the last page of the chapter.**

1. When a bond is at a premium, the interest expense each year
   a. is greater than cash payment for interest.
   b. is less than the cash for interest.
   c. equals the cash payment for interest.
   d. cannot be determined without details of the bond issue.

2. When a bond is issued at a discount, the interest expense each year
   a. is greater than the cash payment for interest.
   b. is less than cash payment for interest.
   c. equals the cash payment for interest.
   d. cannot be determined without details of the bond issue.

© Cengage Learning 2013

Redemption of Bonds

LO6 Find the gain or loss on retirement of bonds.

OVERVIEW: Redemption of bonds represents repayment of the principal. If bonds are redeemed at maturity, no gain or loss occurs. If bonds are retired before maturity, a gain or loss occurs. If the redemption price is larger than the bond carrying value, the issuer must record a loss. If the carrying value is larger than the redemption price, the issuer must record a gain. The gain or loss on bond redemption is shown on the income statement.

Redemption at Maturity

The term *redemption* refers to retirement of bonds by repayment of the principal. When bonds are retired on their due date, the accounting entry is not difficult. Refer again to Discount Firm from Examples 10-1 and 10-3. If Discount Firm retires its bonds on the due date of December 31, 2015, it must repay the principal of $10,000 and Cash is reduced by $10,000. Notice that no gain or loss is incurred because the carrying value of the bond at that point is $10,000.

Retired Early at a Gain

A firm may want to retire bonds before their due date for several reasons. A firm may simply have excess cash and determine that the best use of those funds is to repay outstanding bond obligations. Bonds also may be retired early because of changing interest rate conditions. If interest rates in the economy decline, firms may find it advantageous to retire bonds that have been issued at higher rates. Of course, what is advantageous to the issuer is not necessarily so for the investor. Early retirement of callable bonds is always a possibility that must be anticipated. Large institutional investors expect such a development and merely reinvest the money elsewhere. Many individual investors are more seriously inconvenienced when a bond issue is called.

Gain or loss on redemption
The difference between the carrying value and the redemption price at the time bonds are redeemed.

Bond terms generally specify that if bonds are retired before their due date, they are not retired at the face value amount, but at a call price or redemption price indicated on the bond certificate. Also, the amount of unamortized premium or discount on the bonds must be considered when bonds are retired early. The retirement results in a **gain or loss on redemption** that must be calculated as follows:

$$\text{Gain} = \text{Carrying Value} - \text{Redemption Price}$$
$$\text{Loss} = \text{Redemption Price} - \text{Carrying Value}$$

In other words, the issuing firm must calculate the carrying value of the bonds at the time of redemption and compare it with the total redemption price. If the carrying value is higher than the redemption price, the issuing firm must record a gain. If the carrying value lower than there redemption price, the issuing firm must record a loss.

Example 10-5 Calculating a Gain on Bond Redemption

Refer to Premium Firm from Example 10-4. Assume that on December 31, 2012, Premium Firm wants to retire its bonds due in 2015. Assume, as in the previous section, that the bonds were issued at a premium of $692 at the beginning of 2012. Premium Firm has used the effective interest method of amortization and has recorded the interest and amortization entries for the year. (See page 501.) This has resulted in a balance of $535 in the Premium on Bonds Payable account as of December 31, 2012. Also, assume that Premium Firm's bond certificates indicate that the bonds may be retired early at a call price of 102 (meaning 102% of face value). Thus, the redemption price is 102% of $10,000, or $10,200.

(Continued)

Premium Firm's retirement of bonds would result in a gain. The gain can be calculated using two steps:

1. **Calculate the carrying value of the bonds as of the date they are retired.** The carrying value of Premium Firm's bonds at that date is calculated as follows:

$$\text{Carrying Value} = \text{Face Value} + \text{Unamortized Premium}$$
$$= \$10,000 + \$535$$
$$= \$10,535$$

Note that the carrying value calculated is the same amount indicated for December 31, 2012, in Column 4 of the effective interest amortization table of Exhibit 10-5.

2. **Calculate the gain:**

$$\text{Gain} = \text{Carrying Value} - \text{Redemption Price}$$
$$= \$10,535 - (\$10,000 \times 1.02)$$
$$= \$10,535 - \$10,200$$
$$= \$335$$

When bonds are retired, the balance of the Bonds Payable account and the remaining balance of the Premium on Bonds Payable account must be eliminated from the balance sheet.

Example 10-6 Calculating a Loss on Bond Redemption

Refer to Premium Firm from Example 10-4. Assume that Premium Firm retires bonds at December 31, 2012, as in the previous section. However, assume that the call price for the bonds is 107 (or 107% of face value).

Again, the calculations can be performed in two steps:

1. **Calculate the carrying value:**

$$\text{Carrying Value} = \text{Face Value} + \text{Unamortized Premium}$$
$$= \$10,000 + \$535$$
$$= \$10,535$$

2. **Compare the carrying value with the redemption price to calculate the amount of the loss:**

$$\text{Loss} = \text{Redemption Price} - \text{Carrying Value}$$
$$= (\$10,000 \times 1.07) - \$10,535$$
$$= \$10,700 - \$10,535$$
$$= \$165$$

In Example 10-6, a loss of $165 has resulted from the retirement of Premium Firm's bonds. A loss means that the company paid more to retire the bonds than the amount at which the bonds were recorded on the balance sheet.

Financial Statement Presentation of Gain or Loss

The accounts Gain on Bond Redemption and Loss on Bond Redemption are income statement accounts. A gain on bond redemption increases Premium Firm's income; a loss decreases its income. In most cases, a gain or loss should not be considered "unusual" or "infrequent" and therefore should not be placed in the section of the income statement where extraordinary items are presented. While gains and losses should be treated as part of the company's operating income, some statement users may consider them as "one-time" events and choose to exclude them when predicting a company's future income. For that reason, it would be very helpful if companies would present their gains and losses separately on the income statement so that readers could determine whether such amounts will affect future periods.

LO6 Find the gain or loss on retirement of bonds.

- Bonds are retired for various reasons, and if they are retired before their due date, the amount is different from the face value. Unamortized bond premiums or discounts may result in a gain or loss.
  - When the redemption price is less than the carrying value, a gain results. When the redemption price is greater than the carrying value, a loss results.

POD REVIEW 10.6

QUESTIONS   **Answers to these questions are on the last page of the chapter.**

1. When bonds are retired or repaid at their due date, there generally will be
   a. a gain.
   b. a loss.
   c. accrued interest.
   d. no gain or loss.

2. What does a gain on redemption of bonds indicate?
   a. The carrying value of the bond was larger than the redemption price.
   b. The carrying value of the bond was less than the redemption price.
   c. The carrying value of the bond was equal to the redemption price.
   d. The bondholders were not paid the full face value at time of redemption.

Liability for Leases

LO7 Determine whether a lease agreement must be reported as a liability on the balance sheet.

OVERVIEW: There are two types of leases: operating leases and capital leases. In an operating lease, the lessee does not account for the property as an asset or the obligation for payments as a liability. Capital leases give the lessee sufficient rights of ownership and control of the property to be considered the owner. The property is recorded as an asset for the lessee on the balance sheet. The asset is depreciated the same way as other similar assets the company owns. The present value of the lease payments is recorded as a liability. Interest expense is recorded each period based on the remaining obligation times the effective interest rate.

Long-term bonds and notes payable are important sources of financing for many large corporations and are quite prominent in the Long-Term Liability category of the balance sheet for many firms. But other important elements of that category of the balance sheet also represent long-term obligations. This section introduces you to leases because they are a major source of financing for many companies. Another liability, deferred taxes, is introduced in the appendix at the end of this chapter. In some cases, these liabilities are required to be reported on the financial statements and are important components of the Long-Term Liabilities section of the balance sheet. In other cases, the items are not required to be presented in the financial statements and can be discerned only by a careful reading of the notes to the financial statements.

Leases

A *lease*, a contractual arrangement between two parties, allows one party, the *lessee*, the right to use an asset in exchange for making payments to its owner, the *lessor*. A common example of a lease arrangement is the rental of an apartment. The tenant is the lessee, and the landlord is the lessor.

Lease agreements are a form of financing. In some cases, it is more advantageous to lease an asset than to borrow money to purchase it. The lessee can conserve cash because a lease does not require a large initial cash outlay. A wide variety of lease arrangements exists, ranging from simple to complex agreements that span a long time period. Lease arrangements are popular because of their flexibility. The terms of a lease can be structured in many ways to meet the needs of the lessee and lessor. This results in difficult accounting questions:

1. *Should the right to use property be reported as an asset by the lessee?*
2. *Should the obligation to make payments be reported as a liability by the lessee?*
3. *Should all leases be accounted for in the same manner regardless of the terms of the lease agreement?*

The answers are that some leases should be reported as an asset and a liability by the lessee and some should not. The accountant must examine the terms of the lease agreement and compare those terms with an established set of criteria.

Lease Criteria From the viewpoint of the lessee, there are two types of lease agreements: operating and capital. In an **operating lease**, the lessee acquires the right to use an asset for a limited period of time. The lessee is *not* required to record the right to use the property as an asset or to record the obligation for payments as a liability. Therefore, the lessee is able to attain a form of *off-balance-sheet financing*. That is, the lessee has attained the right to use property but has not recorded that right, or the accompanying obligation, on the balance sheet. By escaping the balance sheet, the lease does not add to debt or impair the debt-to-equity ratio that investors usually calculate. Management has a responsibility to make sure that such off-balance-sheet financing is not, in fact, a long-term obligation. The company's auditors are supposed to analyze the terms of the lease carefully to make sure that management has exercised its responsibility.

The second type of lease agreement is a **capital lease**. In this type of lease, the lessee has acquired sufficient rights of ownership and control of the property to be considered its owner. The lease is called a *capital lease* because it is capitalized (recorded) on the balance sheet by the lessee.

A lease should be considered a capital lease by the lessee when one or more of the following criteria are met:[1]

1. The lease transfers ownership of the property to the lessee at the end of the lease term.
2. The lease contains a bargain-purchase option to purchase the asset at an amount lower than its fair market value.
3. The lease term is 75% or more of the property's economic life.
4. The present value of the minimum lease payments is 90% or more of the fair market value of the property at the inception of the lease.

If none of the criteria are met, the lease agreement is accounted for as an operating lease. This is an area in which it is important for the accountant to exercise professional judgment. In some cases, firms may take elaborate measures to evade or manipulate the criteria that would require lease capitalization. The accountant should determine what is full and fair disclosure based on an unbiased evaluation of the substance of the transaction.

Operating Leases You have already accounted for operating leases in previous chapters when recording rent expense and prepaid rent. A rental agreement for a limited time period is also a lease agreement.

Operating lease
A lease that does not meet any of the four criteria and is not recorded as an asset by the lessee.

Capital lease
A lease that is recorded as an asset by the lessee.

Example 10-7 Recording an Operating Lease

Suppose that Lessee Firm wants to lease a car for a new salesperson. A lease agreement is signed with Lessor Dealer on January 1, 2012, to lease a car for the year for $4,000, payable on December 31, 2012. Typically, a car lease does not transfer title at the end of the term, does not include a bargain-purchase price, and does not last for more than 75% of the car's

(Continued)

[1] *Leasing*, ASC Topic 840.25 (formerly *Statement of Financial Accounting Standards No. 13*, "Accounting for Leases").

life. In addition, the present value of the lease payments is not 90% of the car's value. Because the lease does not meet any of the specified criteria, it should be presented as an operating lease. Lessee Firm would simply record lease expense (or rent expense) of $4,000 for the year.

Although operating leases are not recorded on the balance sheet by the lessee, they are mentioned in financial statement notes. The FASB requires note disclosure of the amount of future lease obligations for leases that are considered operating leases. Exhibit 10-6 provides a portion of the note from **Gap, Inc.**'s 2010 annual report. The note reveals that Gap, Inc., has used operating leases as an important source of financing and has significant off-balance-sheet commitments in future periods as a result. An investor might want to add this off-balance-sheet item to the debt on the balance sheet to get a conservative view of the company's obligations.

Capital Leases Capital leases are presented as assets and liabilities by the lessee because they meet one or more of the lease criteria.

Example 10-8 Calculating the Amount to Capitalize for a Lease

Suppose that Lessee Firm in Example 10-7 wanted to lease a car for a longer period of time. Assume that on January 1, 2012, Lessee signs a lease agreement with Lessor Dealer to lease a car. The terms of the agreement specify that Lessee will make annual lease payments of $4,000 per year for five years, payable each December 31. Also, assume that the lease specifies that at the end of the lease agreement, the title to the car is transferred to Lessee Firm. Lessee must decide how to account for the lease agreement.

The lease should be treated as a capital lease by Lessee because it meets at least one of the four criteria. (It meets the first criteria concerning transfer of title.) A capital lease must be recorded at its present value by Lessee as an asset and as an obligation. As of January 1, 2012, we must calculate the present value of the annual payments. If we assume an interest rate of 8%, the present value of the payments is $15,972 ($4,000 × an annuity factor of 3.99271 from Table 9-4 on page 457).

> **STUDY TIP**
>
> It is called a capital lease because the lease is capital or put on the books of the lessee as an asset.

EXHIBIT 10-6 Gap, Inc.'s 2010 Note Disclosure of Leases

Note 9. Leases

We lease most of our store premises and some of our corporate facilities and distribution centers. These operating leases expire at various dates through 2031. Most store leases are for a five year base period and include options that allow us to extend the lease term beyond the initial base period, subject to terms agreed upon at lease inception. Some leases also include early termination options, which can be exercised under specific conditions.

We also lease certain equipment under operating leases that expire at various dates through 2014.

The aggregate minimum non-cancelable annual lease payments under leases in effect on January 29, 2011, are as follows:

($ in millions) Fiscal Year	
2011	$ 997
2012	841
2013	710
2014	602
2015	483
Thereafter	1,483
Total minimum lease commitments	$5,116

The total minimum lease commitment amount above does not include minimum sublease rent income of $50 million receivable in the future under non-cancelable sublease agreements.

The contractual arrangement between Lessee Firm and Lessor Dealer is called a lease agreement, but clearly the agreement is much different than a year-to-year lease arrangement. Essentially, Lessee Firm has acquired the right to use the asset for its entire life and does not need to return it to Lessor Dealer. You may call this agreement a lease, but it actually represents a purchase of the asset by Lessee with payments made over time.

For Example 10-8, the first entry is made on the basis of the present value. The effect of the lease could be identified and analyzed as follows:

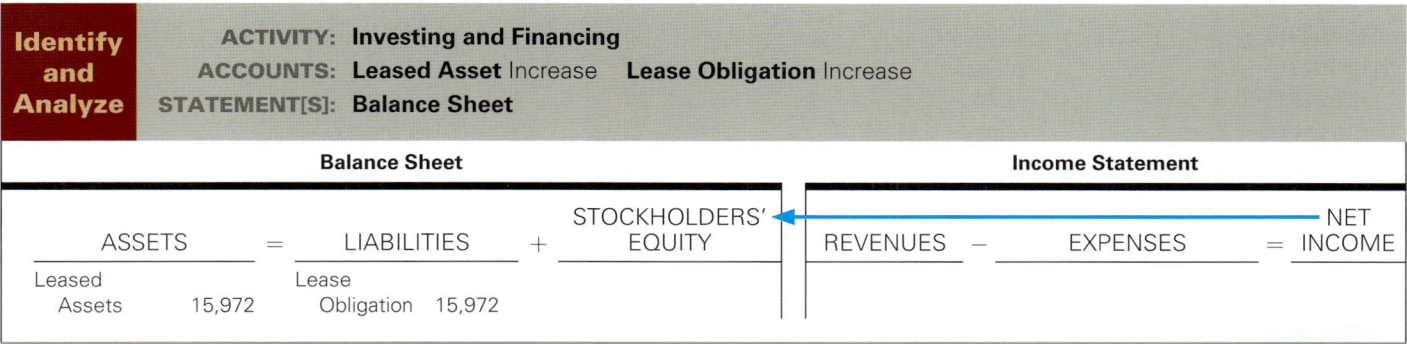

The Leased Asset account is a long-term asset similar to plant and equipment and represents the fact that Lessee has acquired the right to use and retain the asset. Because the leased asset represents depreciable property, depreciation must be reported for each of the five years of asset use as follows. On December 31, 2012, Lessee records depreciation of $3,194 ($15,972/5 years), assuming that the straight-line method is adopted. The effect of the depreciation is as follows:

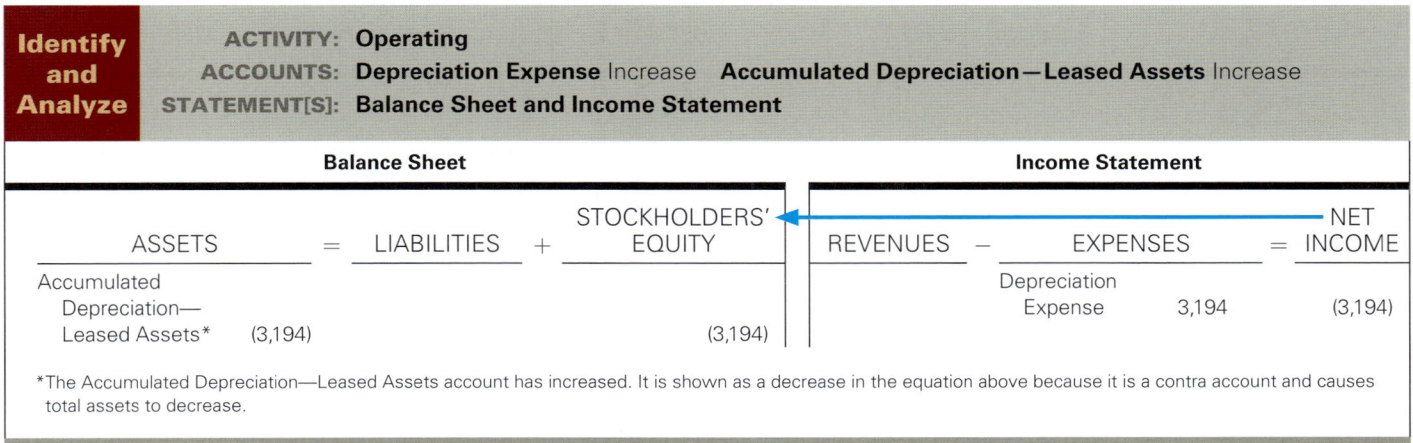

Some firms refer to depreciation of leased assets as *amortization*.

On December 31, Lessee Firm also must make a payment of $4,000 to Lessor Dealer. A portion of each payment represents interest on the obligation (loan), and the remainder represents a reduction of the principal amount. Each payment must be separated into its principal and interest components. Generally, the effective interest method is used for that purpose. An effective interest table can be established using the same concepts used to amortize a premium or discount on bonds payable.

Exhibit 10-7 illustrates the effective interest method applied to Lessee Firm in Example 10-8. Note that the table begins with an obligation amount equal to the present value of the payments of $15,972. Each payment is separated into principal and interest amounts so that the amount of the loan obligation at the end of the lease agreement equals zero. The amortization table is the basis for the amounts that are reflected on the financial statement. Exhibit 10-7 indicates that the $4,000 payment in 2012 should be considered as interest of $1,278 (8% of $15,972) and reduction of

EXHIBIT 10-7 Lease Amortization: Effective Interest Method of Amortization

Date	Column 1 Lease Payment	Column 2 Interest Expense	Column 3 Reduction of Obligation	Column 4 Lease Obligation
		8%	Col. 1 − Col. 2	
1/1/2012	—	—	—	$15,972
12/31/2012	$4,000	$1,278	$2,722	13,250
12/31/2013	4,000	1,060	2,940	10,310
12/31/2014	4,000	825	3,175	7,135
12/31/2015	4,000	571	3,429	3,706
12/31/2016	4,000	294	3,706	-0-

© Cengage Learning 2013

principal of $2,722. On December 31, 2012, Lessee Firm records an entry for the annual lease payment. The effect could be identified and analyzed as follows:

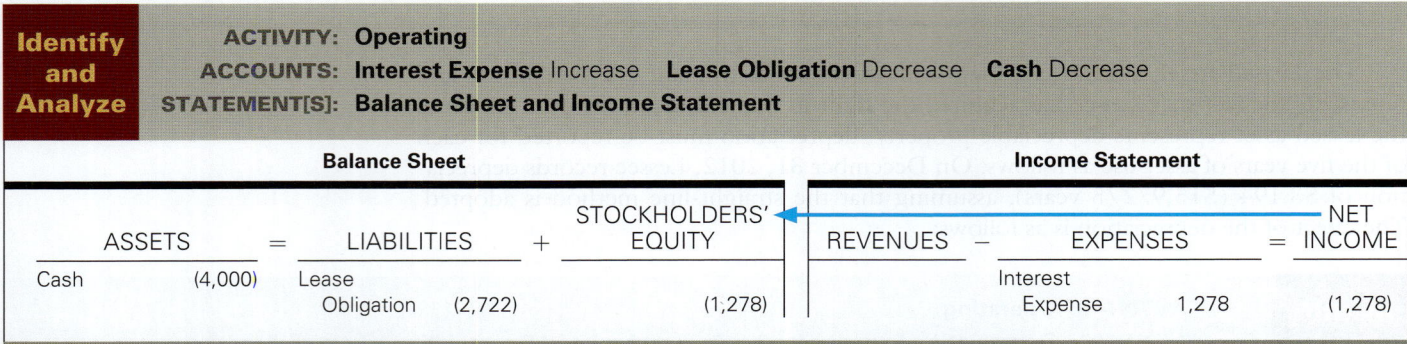

Identify and Analyze

ACTIVITY: Operating
ACCOUNTS: Interest Expense Increase   **Lease Obligation** Decrease   **Cash** Decrease
STATEMENT[S]: Balance Sheet and Income Statement

Balance Sheet					Income Statement				
ASSETS	=	LIABILITIES	+	STOCKHOLDERS' EQUITY	REVENUES	−	EXPENSES	=	NET INCOME
Cash (4,000)		Lease Obligation (2,722)		(1,278)			Interest Expense 1,278		(1,278)

Therefore, for a capital lease, Lessee Firm must record both an asset and a liability. The asset is reduced by the process of depreciation. The liability is reduced by reductions of principal using the effective interest method. According to Exhibit 10-7, the total lease obligation as of December 31, 2012, is $13,250. This amount must be separated into Current and Long-Term categories. The portion of the liability that will be paid within one year of the balance sheet should be considered a current liability. Exhibit 10-7 indicates that the liability will be reduced by $2,940 in 2013 and that amount should be considered a current liability. The remaining amount of the liability, $10,310 ($13,250 − $2,940), should be considered long-term. On the balance sheet as of December 31, 2012, Lessee Firm reports the following balances related to the lease obligation:

Assets:		
Leased assets	$15,972	
Less: Accumulated depreciation	3,194	
		$12,778
Current liabilities:		
Lease obligation		$ 2,940
Long-term liabilities:		
Lease obligation		$10,310

Notice that the depreciated asset does not equal the present value of the lease obligation. This is not unusual. For example, an automobile may be completely depreciated but still have payments due on it.

IFRS and Leasing

The accounting for leases is an excellent example of the differences in how U.S. and IFRS accounting standards are applied. Earlier in the text, we indicated that U.S. standards are often "rule-based" and international standards are "principles-based." In the United States, the criteria to determine whether a lease contract should be considered a capital lease are applied in a rather rigid way. If a lease meets any of the criteria, it must be accounted for as a capital lease. If it does not meet the criteria, even by a small margin, then it is considered an operating lease. The international accounting standards provide lease criteria that are similar to the U.S. standards. However, the criteria are used as "guidelines" rather than rigid rules. Therefore, there is much more flexibility in applying the lease standards when using the international standards. While many consider this to be a positive aspect of international accounting, it also requires more judgment by accountants in applying those standards.

The accounting for leases in the United States will be changing in some major ways. At the time of the writing of this text, the FASB had proposed changes to the accounting rules that would require many more leases to be shown on the balance sheet. Many companies may object to this new accounting because they prefer to treat leases as operating leases and not show the leased asset on the balance sheet. The new accounting rules for leases will provide more information to statement users and will also bring the U.S. accounting standards more in line with international standards.

LOOKING AHEAD

LO7 Determine whether a lease agreement must be reported as a liability on the balance sheet.

- Leases can be classified as two types: operating leases and capital leases. Capital leases imply more rights of ownership. The accounting for these two types of leases is as follows:

  - Under an operating lease, the lessee does not record the right to use the leased asset or any related obligation to make lease payments on the balance sheet.

  - Under a capital lease, the lessee records the right to use the property and the lease payments that are obligated to be paid on the balance sheet.

POD REVIEW 10.7

QUESTIONS   Answers to these questions are on the last page of the chapter.

1. When a lease is classified as an operating lease,
   a. the lease liability should be presented on the balance sheet of the lessee.
   b. the lease liability should be presented on the balance sheet of the lessor.
   c. title to the leased asset passes to the lessee at the end of the lease.
   d. the leased liability should not be presented on the balance sheet of the lessor.

2. When a lease is classified as a capital lease,
   a. the lease liability should be presented on the balance sheet of the lessee.
   b. the lease liability should be presented on the balance sheet of the lessor.
   c. title to the leased asset may not pass to the lessee at the end of the lease.
   d. the leased asset liability should be presented on the balance sheet of the lessor.

Analyzing Debt to Assess a Firm's Ability to Pay Its Liabilities

LO8 Explain how investors use ratios to evaluate long-term liabilities.

OVERVIEW: The debt-to-equity ratio measures the proportion of a company's debt to its equity. It is computed as total liabilities divided by total stockholders' equity. The times interest earned ratio measures a company's ability to meet interest obligations as they come due. It is computed as income before interest and tax divided by interest expense.

Long-term liabilities are a component of the "capital structure" of the company and are included in the calculation of the debt-to-equity ratio:

$$\text{Debt-to-Equity Ratio} = \frac{\text{Total Liabilities}}{\text{Total Stockholder's Equity}}$$

Most investors would prefer to see equity rather than debt on the balance sheet. Debt, and its interest charges, make up a fixed obligation that must be repaid in a finite period of time. In contrast, equity never has to be repaid and the dividends that are declared on it are optional. Stock investors view debt as a claim against the company that must be satisfied before they get a return on their money.

Other ratios used to measure the degree of debt obligation include the times interest earned ratio and the debt service coverage ratio:

$$\text{Times Interest Earned Ratio} = \frac{\text{Income Before Interest and Tax}}{\text{Interest Expense}}$$

$$\text{Debt Service Coverage Ratio} = \frac{\text{Cash Flow from Operations Before Interest and Tax}}{\text{Interest and principal Payment}}$$

Lenders want to be sure that borrowers can pay the interest and repay the principal on a loan. Both of the preceding ratios reflect the degree to which a company can make its debt payment out of current cash flow.

For more on these ratios for PepsiCo, Inc., and how they are used, see the following Ratio Decision Model.

USING THE RATIO DECISION MODEL

Analyzing the Debt-to-Equity and Times Interest Earned Ratios

Use the following Ratio Decision Model to evaluate the debt for PepsiCo or any other public company.

1. Formulate the Question

Long-term debt is an important element of the financing of a company. Most companies use a combination of debt and equity (stock) to finance their operations, achieve a profit, and provide a return to their investors. Investors and creditors must carefully review the financial statements to determine whether a company will be able to meet its obligations. The use of debt is a good management strategy, but sometimes a company may have too much debt. The important question to ask is:

What is the amount of debt in relation to the total equity of the company?

A second important question to ask is:

Will the company be able to meet its obligations related to the debt? That is, when an interest payment comes due, will the company have the ability to make the payment?

2. Gather the Information Needed

For those questions to be addressed, information from the balance sheet and the income statement needs to be collected and analyzed.

- Total debt and total equity: From the balance sheet
- Income before interest and tax: From the income statement (Go online to get this statement from PepsiCo.)
- Interest expense: From the income statement

3. Calculate the Ratio

$$\text{Debt-to-Equity Ratio} = \frac{\text{Total Liabilities}}{\text{Total Stockholders' Equity}}$$

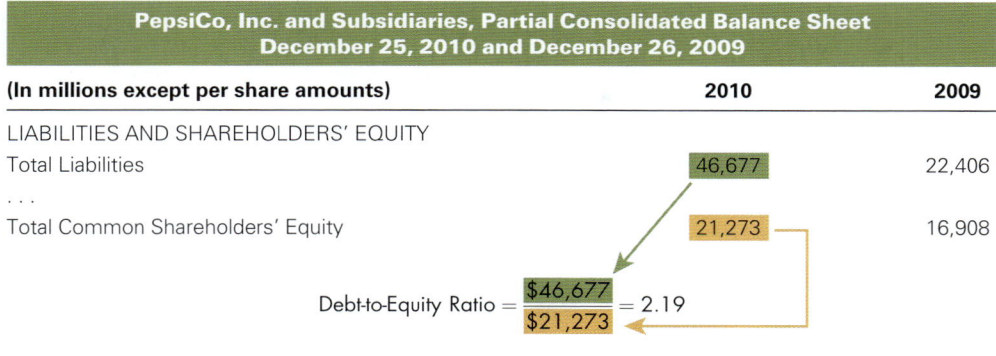

PepsiCo, Inc. and Subsidiaries, Partial Consolidated Balance Sheet **December 25, 2010 and December 26, 2009**		
(In millions except per share amounts)	2010	2009
LIABILITIES AND SHAREHOLDERS' EQUITY		
Total Liabilities	46,677	22,406
. . .		
Total Common Shareholders' Equity	21,273	16,908

$$\text{Debt-to-Equity Ratio} = \frac{\$46,677}{\$21,273} = 2.19$$

$$\text{Times Interest Earned Ratio} = \frac{\text{Income Before Interest and Tax}}{\text{Interest Expense}}$$

PepsiCo, Inc. and Subsidiaries, Partial Consolidated Statement of Income, **Fiscal years ended December 25, 2010 and December 26, 2009.**		
(In millions except per share amounts)	2010	2009
Net Revenue	$57,838	$43,232
Cost of sales	26,575	20,099
Selling, general and administrative expenses	22,814	15,026
Amortization of intangible assets	117	63
Operating Profit	8,332	8,044
Bottling equity income	735	365
Interest expense	(903)	(397)
Interest income	68	67
Income Before Income Taxes	8,232	8,079

> **Since the ratio concerns income before interest and income tax, you must add the amount of interest, $903, to $8,232 to get $9,135.**

$$\text{Times Interest Earned Ratio} = \frac{\$9,135}{\$903} = 10.12$$

4. Compare the Ratio with Others

PepsiCo's debt-to-equity ratio and times interest earned ratio should be compared to those of prior years and to those of companies in the same industry.

	PepsiCo		Coca-Cola	
	2010	**2009**	**2010**	**2009**
Debt-to-equity ratio	2.19	1.33	1.34	0.94
Times interest earned ratio	10.12	21.35	45.93	36.93

5. Interpret the Results

PepsiCo and Coca-Cola are strong companies with a very safe balance of debt to equity. PepsiCo's debt-to equity ratio increased considerably from 2009 to 2010, and Coca-Cola's also increased. Both companies have a small amount of interest obligations compared to their income available to meet those obligations. PepsiCo has 10.12 times more income than its interest expense for 2010, while Coca-Cola has 45.93. These ratios indicate that the creditors for both companies are confident that each company will be able to meet its interest obligations on its long-term debt. ∎

LO8 Explain how investors use ratios to evaluate long-term liabilities.

POD REVIEW 10.8

- Investors use the debt-to-equity ratio and the times interest earned ratio as measures of a company's abilities to meet its long-term obligations.

QUESTIONS   Answers to these questions are on the last page of the chapter.

1. When an investor views the debt-to-equity ratio of a company,
   a. it is a measure of the company's liquidity.
   b. a high value is generally viewed favorably.
   c. a low value is generally viewed favorably.
   d. it is measure of the company's ability to generate cash.

2. When an investor views the times interest earned ratio of a company,
   a. it is a measure of the company's liquidity.
   b. a high value is generally viewed favorably.
   c. a low value is generally viewed favorably.
   d. it is measure of the company's ability to generate cash.

How Long-Term Liabilities Affect the Statement of Cash Flows

LO9 Explain the effects that transactions involving long-term liabilities have on the statement of cash flows.

OVERVIEW: Long-term liabilities are generally presented in the Financing Activities section of the statement of cash flows. Decreases in a long-term liability require payments and thus decrease cash. Increases in a long-term liability represent additional funding and therefore increases in cash. One exception is the change in the Deferred Tax account, which is reported in the Operating Activities category.

Exhibit 10-8 indicates the impact that long-term liabilities have on a company's cash flow and their placement on the cash flow statement.

Most long-term liabilities are related to a firm's financing activities. Therefore, the change in the balance of each long-term liability account should be reflected in the Financing Activities category of the statement of cash flows. The decrease in a long-term liability account indicates that cash has been used to pay the liability. Therefore, in the statement of cash flows, a decrease in a long-term liability account should appear as a subtraction, or reduction. The increase in a long-term liability account indicates that the firm has obtained additional cash via a long-term obligation. Therefore, an increase in a long-term liability account should appear on the statement of cash flows as an addition.

The statement of cash flows of The Coca-Cola Company is presented in Exhibit 10-9. Note that the Financing Activities category contains two items related to long-term liabilities. In 2010, long-term debt was issued for $1,931.8 million and is an addition to cash. This indicates that Coca-Cola increased its cash position by borrowings. Second, the payment of debt is listed as a deduction of $1,147.5 million. This indicates that Coca-Cola paid long-term liabilities, resulting in a reduction of cash.

EXHIBIT 10-8 Long-Term Liabilities on the Statement of Cash Flows

Item	Statement of Cash Flows	
	Operating Activities	
Net Income		xxx
Increase in current liability		+
Decrease in current liability		−
	Investing Activities	
	Financing Activities	
Increase in long-term payable		+
Decrease in long-term payable		−

Although most long-term liabilities are reflected in the Financing Activities category of the statement of cash flows, there are exceptions. The most notable exception involves the Deferred Tax account (discussed in the appendix at the end of this chapter). The change in this a account is reflected in the Operating Activities category of the statement of cash flows. This presentation is necessary because the Deferred Tax account is related to an operating item, income tax expense. For example, in Exhibit 10-9, Coca-Cola listed a deduction of $75.7 million in the Operating Activities category of the 2010 statement of cash flows. This indicates that $75.7 million less was recorded as expense than was paid out in cash. Therefore, the amount is a negative amount in, or an addition to, the Operating Activities category

EXHIBIT 10-9 The Coca-Cola Company and Subsidiaries' 2010 Consolidated Statements of Cash Flows

Years Ended December 31,	2010	2009	2008
(In millions)			
Operating activities			
Net income	$ 4,946.3	$ 4,551.0	$ 4,313.2
Adjustments to reconcile to cash provided by operations			
Charges and credits:			
Depreciation and amortization	1,276.2	1,216.2	1,207.8
Deferred income taxes	(75.7)	203.0	101.5
Impairment and other charges (credits), net	29.1	(61.1)	6.0
Gain on sale of investment		(94.9)	(160.1)
Share-based compensation	83.1	112.9	112.5
Other	211.6	(347.1)	90.5
Changes in working capital items:			
Accounts receivable	(50.1)	(42.0)	16.1
Inventories, prepaid expenses and other current assets	(50.8)	1.0	(11.0)
Accounts payable	(39.8)	(2.2)	(40.1)
Income taxes	54.9	212.1	195.7
Other accrued liabilities	(43.2)	2.1	85.1
Cash provided by operations	6,341.6	5,751.0	5,917.2
Investing activities			
Property and equipment expenditures	(2,135.5)	(1,952.1)	(2,135.7)
Purchases of restaurant businesses	(183.4)	(145.7)	(147.0)
Sales of restaurant businesses and property	377.9	406.0	478.8
Proceeds on sale of investment		144.9	229.4
Other	(115.0)	(108.4)	(50.2)
Cash used for investing activities	(2,056.0)	(1,655.3)	(1,624.7)
Financing activities			
Net short-term borrowings	3.1	(285.4)	266.7
Long-term financing issuances	1,931.8	1,169.3	3,477.5
Long-term financing repayments	(1,147.5)	(664.6)	(2,698.5)
Treasury stock purchases	(2,698.5)	(2,797.4)	(3,919.3)
Common stock dividends	(2,408.1)	(2,235.5)	(1,823.4)
Proceeds from stock option exercises	463.1	332.1	548.2
Excess tax benefit on share-based compensation	128.7	73.6	124.1
Other	(1.3)	(13.1)	(89.8)
Cash used for financing activities	(3,728.7)	(4,421.0)	(4,114.5)
Effect of exchange rates on cash and equivalents	34.1	57.9	(95.9)
Cash and equivalents increase (decrease)	591.0	(267.4)	82.1
Cash and equivalents at beginning of year	1,796.0	2,063.4	1,981.3
Cash and equivalents at end of year	$ 2,387.0	$ 1,796.0	$ 2,063.4

© Cengage Learning 2013

LO9 Explain the effects that transactions involving long-term liabilities have on the statement of cash flows.

POD REVIEW 10.9

- Cash flows related to long-term liabilities are generally related to a firm's financing activities.

QUESTIONS   **Answers to these questions are on the last page of the chapter.**

1. If a long-term liability account increases, how should it be presented?

   a. as an increase in cash in the Operating Activities category
   b. as an increase in cash in the Financing category
   c. as a decrease in cash in the Financing category
   d. as an increase in cash in the Investing category

2. If a long-term liability account decreases, how should it be presented?

   a. as an increase in cash in the Operating Activities category
   b. as an increase in cash in the Financing category
   c. as a decrease in cash in the Financing category
   d. as an increase in cash in the Investing category

APPENDIX

Accounting Tools: Other Liabilities

This appendix will discuss another item found in the Long-Term Liabilities category of many companies: deferred taxes. The purpose here is to make you aware of its existence when you are reading financial statements.

Deferred Tax

LO10 Explain deferred taxes and calculate the deferred tax liability.

OVERVIEW: Deferred tax reconciles the difference between income for reporting purposes and income for tax purposes as a result of differing rules for each. Permanent differences result when there are differences between the tax code and GAAP that require different treatment for various items. Temporary differences affect both reporting and taxes, but not at the same time. The Deferred Tax account results from temporary, *not* permanent, differences. The deferred tax amount represents the amount of temporary differences times the company's tax rate.

The financial statements of most major firms include an item titled Deferred Income Taxes or Deferred Tax. (See PepsiCo's deferred taxes in Exhibit 10-1 and Coca-Cola's in the chapter opening.) In most cases, the account appears in the Long-Term Liabilities section of the balance sheet, and the dollar amount might be large enough to catch the user's attention. In fact, deferred income taxes represent one of the most misunderstood aspects of financial statements. This section addresses some of the questions concerning deferred taxes.

Deferred tax is an amount that reconciles the differences between the accounting done for purposes of financial reporting to stockholders ("book" purposes) and the accounting done for tax purposes. It may surprise you that U.S. firms are allowed to use accounting methods for financial reporting that differ from those used for tax calculations. The reason is that the IRS defines income and expense differently than does the FASB. As a result, companies tend to use accounting methods that minimize income for

Deferred tax
The account used to reconcile the difference between the amount recorded as income tax expense and the amount that is payable as income tax.

tax purposes but maximize income in the annual report to stockholders. This is not true in some foreign countries where financial accounting and tax accounting are more closely aligned. Firms in those countries do not report deferred tax because the difference between methods is not significant.

When differences between financial and tax reporting do occur, the differences can be classified into two types: permanent and temporary. **Permanent differences** occur when an item is included in the tax calculation and is never included for book purposes—or vice versa, when an item is included for book purposes but not for tax purposes.

Permanent difference
A difference that affects the tax records but not the accounting records, or vice versa.

For example, the tax laws allow taxpayers to exclude interest on certain investments, usually state and municipal bonds, from their income. These are generally called *tax-exempt bonds*. When a corporation buys tax-exempt bonds, it does not have to declare the interest as income for tax purposes. When the corporation develops its income statement for stockholders (book purposes), however, the interest is included and appears in the Interest Income account. Therefore, tax-exempt interest represents a permanent difference between tax and book calculations.

Temporary differences occur when an item affects both book and tax calculations but not in the same time period. A difference caused by depreciation methods is the most common type of temporary difference. In previous chapters, you learned that depreciation may be calculated using a straight-line method or an accelerated method such as the double-declining-balance method. Most firms do not use the same depreciation method for book and tax purposes, however. Generally, straight-line depreciation is used for book purposes and an accelerated method is used for tax purposes because accelerated depreciation lowers taxable income—at least in early years—and therefore reduces the tax due. The IRS refers to this accelerated method as the *Modified Accelerated Cost Recovery System (MACRS)*. It is similar to other accelerated depreciation methods in that it allows the firm to take larger depreciation deductions for tax purposes in the early years of the asset and smaller deductions in the later years. Over the life of the depreciable asset, the total depreciation using straight-line is equal to that using MACRS. Therefore, this difference is an example of a temporary difference between book and tax reporting.

Temporary difference
A difference that affects both book and tax records but not in the same time period.

Alternate term: Timing difference.

The Deferred Tax account is used to reconcile the differences between the accounting for book purposes and for tax purposes. It is important to distinguish between permanent and temporary differences because the FASB has ruled that not all differences should affect the Deferred Tax account. The Deferred Tax account should reflect temporary differences but not items that are permanent differences between book accounting and tax reporting.[2]

Example 10-9 Calculation and Reporting Deferred Tax

Assume that Startup Firm begins business on January 1, 2012. During 2012, the firm has sales of $6,000 and has no expenses other than depreciation and income tax at the rate of 40%. Startup has depreciation on only one asset. That asset was purchased on January 1, 2012, for $10,000 and has a four-year life. Startup has decided to use the straight-line depreciation method for financial reporting purposes. Startup's accountants have chosen to use MACRS for tax purposes, however, resulting in $4,000 depreciation in 2012 and a decline of $1,000 per year thereafter.

The depreciation amounts for each of the four years for Startup's asset are as follows:

Year	Tax Depreciation	Book Depreciation	Difference
2012	$ 4,000	$ 2,500	$ 1,500
2013	3,000	2,500	500
2014	2,000	2,500	(500)
2015	1,000	2,500	(1,500)
Totals	$10,000	$10,000	$ 0

(Continued)

---

[2] *Deferred Tax* ASC Topic 740 (formerly *Statement of Financial Accounting Standards No. 109*, "Accounting for the Income Taxes").

Startup's tax calculation for 2012 is based on the accelerated depreciation of $4,000, as follows:

Sales	$6,000
Depreciation expense	4,000
Taxable income	$2,000
× Tax rate	40%
Tax payable to IRS	$ 800

For 2012, Startup owes $800 of tax to the IRS. This amount is ordinarily recorded as tax payable until the time it is remitted.

Startup also wants to develop an income statement to send to the stockholders. What amount should be shown as tax expense on the income statement? You may guess that the Tax Expense account on the income statement should reflect $800 because that is the amount to be paid to the IRS. That guess is not correct in this case, however. Remember that the tax payable amount was calculated using the depreciation method that Startup chose for tax purposes. The income statement must be calculated using the straight-line method, which Startup uses for book purposes. Therefore, Startup's income statement for 2012 appears as follows:

Sales	$6,000
Depreciation expense	2,500
Income before tax	$3,500
Tax expense (40%)	1,400
Net income	$2,100

© Cengage Learning 2013

In Example 10-9, Startup must make the following accounting entry to record the amount of tax expense and tax payable for 2012. The effect is as follows:

Identify and Analyze	ACTIVITY: **Operating**		
	ACCOUNTS: **Tax Expense** Increase **Tax Payable** Increase **Deferred Tax** Increase		
	STATEMENT[S]: **Balance Sheet and Income Statement**		

Balance Sheet				Income Statement			
ASSETS	=	LIABILITIES	+	STOCKHOLDERS' EQUITY	REVENUES −	EXPENSES	= NET INCOME
		Tax Payable 800				Tax Expense 1,400	(1,400)
		Deferred Tax 600		(1,400)			

The Deferred Tax account is a balance sheet account. A balance in it reflects the fact that Startup has received a tax benefit by recording accelerated depreciation, in effect delaying the ultimate obligation to the IRS. To be sure, the amount of deferred tax still represents a liability of Startup. The Deferred Tax account balance of $600 represents the amount of the 2012 temporary difference of $1,500 times the tax rate of 40% ($1,500 × 40% = $600).

What can you learn from Startup Firm in Example 10-9?

- First, when you see a firm's income statement, the amount listed as tax expense does not represent the amount of cash paid to the government for taxes. Accrual accounting procedures require that the tax expense amount be calculated using the accounting methods chosen for book purposes.
- Second, when you see a firm's balance sheet, the amount in the Deferred Tax account reflects all of the temporary differences between the accounting

methods chosen for tax and book purposes. The accounting and financial communities are severely divided on whether the Deferred Tax account represents a "true" liability. The FASB has taken the stance that deferred tax is an amount that results in a future obligation and meets the definition of a liability.

LO10 Explain deferred taxes and calculate the deferred tax liability.

- Differences arise between the tax treatment of revenue and expense items for financial accounting (book) and tax accounting methods. Deferred taxes are those amounts that reconcile these differences.
  - Permanent differences occur when an item is included for tax purposes but not book, or vice versa.
  - Temporary differences occur when there are differences between the time an item is recognized for tax purposes and the time it is recognized for book purposes.

POD REVIEW 10.10

QUESTIONS   **Answers to these questions are on the last page of the chapter.**

1. When a company uses the straight-line depreciation method for financial reporting purposes and an accelerated depreciation method for tax purposes, what is the result?
   a. a deferred tax asset
   b. a deferred tax liability
   c. no deferred taxes
   d. a violation of GAAP

2. Items that are considered permanent differences
   a. should be reflected as deferred tax assets on the balance sheet.
   b. should be reflected as deferred tax liabilities on the balance sheet.
   c. are items that have been excluded from both tax and financial statement calculation.
   d. should not be reflected in the Deferred Tax account.

© Cengage Learning 2013

RATIO REVIEW

$$\text{Debt-to-Equity Ratio} = \frac{\text{Total Liabilities}}{\text{Total Stockholder's Equity}}$$

$$\text{Times Interest Earned Ratio} = \frac{\text{Income Before Interest and Tax}}{\text{Interest Expense}}$$

ACCOUNTS HIGHLIGHTED

Account Title	Where It Appears	In What Section	Page Number
Bonds Payable	Balance Sheet	Long-Term Liabilities	490
Premium on Bonds Payable	Balance Sheet	Long-Term Liabilities	495
Discount on Bonds Payable	Balance Sheet	Long-Term Liabilities as a contra account	495
Gain on Bond Redemption	Income Statement	Other Income/Expense	502
Loss on Bond Redemption	Income Statement	Other Income/Expense	502
Leased Asset	Balance Sheet	Property, Plant, and Equipment	505
Lease Obligation	Balance Sheet	Long-Term Liabilities	505
Deferred Income Tax	Balance Sheet	May be Asset or Liability	514

KEY TERMS QUIZ

Read each definition below and write the number of the definition in the blank beside the appropriate term. The quiz solutions appear at the end of the chapter.

_____ Long-term liability
_____ Face value
_____ Debenture bonds
_____ Serial bonds
_____ Callable bonds
_____ Face rate of interest
_____ Market rate of interest
_____ Bond issue price
_____ Premium
_____ Discount

_____ Effective interest method of
         amortization
_____ Carrying value
_____ Gain or loss on redemption
_____ Operating lease
_____ Capital lease
_____ Deferred tax (Appendix)
_____ Permanent difference (Appendix)
_____ Temporary difference (Appendix)

1. The principal amount of the bond as stated on the bond certificate.
2. Bonds that do not all have the same due date. A portion of the bonds comes due each time period.
3. The interest rate stated on the bond certificate. It is also called the _nominal_ or _coupon rate_.
4. The total of the present value of the cash flows produced by a bond. It is calculated as the present value of the annuity of interest payments plus the present value of the principal.
5. An obligation that will not be satisfied within one year.
6. The excess of the issue price over the face value of bonds. It occurs when the face rate on the bonds exceeds the market rate.
7. Bonds that are backed by the general creditworthiness of the issuer and are not backed by specific collateral.
8. The excess of the face value of bonds over the issue price. It occurs when the market rate on the bonds exceeds the face rate.
9. Bonds that may be redeemed or retired before their specified due date.
10. The process of transferring a portion of premium or discount to interest expense. This method transfers an amount resulting in a constant effective interest rate.
11. The face value of a bond plus the amount of unamortized premium or minus the amount of unamortized discount.
12. The interest rate that bondholders could obtain by investing in other bonds that are similar to the issuing firm's bonds.
13. The difference between the carrying value and the redemption price at the time bonds are redeemed. This amount is presented as an income statement account.
14. A lease that does not meet any of four criteria and is not recorded by the lessee.
15. A lease that meets one or more of four criteria and is recorded as an asset by the lessee.
16. A difference between the accounting for tax purposes and the accounting for financial reporting purposes. This type of difference affects both book and tax calculations but not in the same time period.
17. The account used to reconcile the difference between the amount recorded as income tax expense and the amount that is payable as income tax.
18. A difference between the accounting for tax purposes and the accounting for financial reporting purposes. This type of difference occurs when an item affects one set of calculations but not the other set.

ALTERNATE TERMS

bond retirement extinguishment of bonds
carrying value book value
effective interest method of amortization
   interest method
face rate of interest stated rate, nominal
   rate, contract rate, coupon rate

face value par value
market rate of interest effective rate, bond
   yield
redemption price reacquisition price
temporary difference timing difference

WARMUP EXERCISES & SOLUTIONS

Warmup Exercise 10-1   LO2

A bond due in ten years with face value of $1,000 and face rate of interest of 8% is issued when
the market rate of interest is 6%.

Required

1. What is the issue price of the bond?
2. What is the amount of premium or discount on the bond at the time of issuance?
3. What amount of interest expense will be shown on the income statement for the first year of
    the bond?
4. What amount of the premium or discount will be amortized during the first year of the
    bond?

Warmup Exercise 10-2   LO7

You have signed an agreement to lease a car for four years and will make annual payments of
$4,000 at the end of each year. (Assume that the lease meets the criteria for a capital lease.)

Required

1. Calculate the present value of the lease payments assuming an 8% interest rate.
2. Identify and analyze the effect of signing the lease.
3. When the first lease payment is made, what portion of the payment will be considered
    interest?

Solutions to Warmup Exercises

Warmup Exercise 10-1

1. The issue price of the bond would be calculated at the present value:

$80(7.36009) =	$ 589	using Table 9-4, where $i = 6\%$ and $n = 10$
$1,000(0.55839) =	558	using Table 9-2, where $i = 6\%$ and $n = 10$
Issue price	$1,147	(rounded)

2. The amount of the premium is the difference between the issue price and the face value:

$$\text{Premium} = \$1,147 - \$1,000$$
$$= \$147$$

3. The amount of interest expense can be calculated as follows:

$$\text{Interest Expense} = \$1,147 \times 0.06$$
$$= \$68.82$$

(Continued)

4. The amount that will be amortized can be calculated as follows:

$$\begin{aligned} \text{Amortized} &= \text{Cash Interest} - \text{Interest Expense} \\ &= (\$1,000 \times 0.08) - (\$1,147 \times 0.06) \\ &= \$80.00 - \$68.82 \\ &= \$11.18 \end{aligned}$$

Warmup Exercise 10-2

1. The present value of the lease payments can be calculated as follows:

$$\begin{aligned} \text{Present Value} &= \$4,000 \times (3.31213) \text{ using Table 9-4, where } i = 8\%, n = 4 \\ &= \$13,249 \end{aligned}$$

2. The effect of signing the lease agreement is as follows:

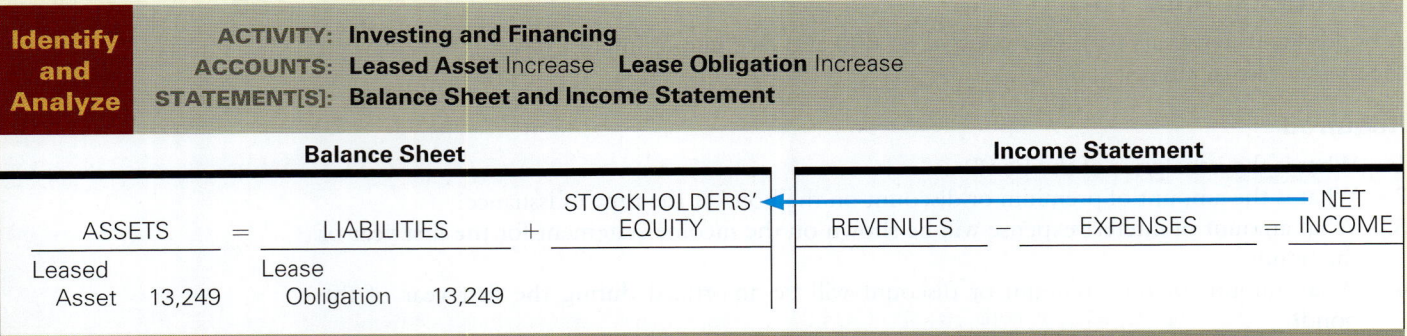

3. The amount of interest can be calculated as follows:

$$\begin{aligned} \text{Interest} &= \$13,249 \times 0.08 \\ &= \$1,059.92 \end{aligned}$$

REVIEW PROBLEM & SOLUTION

The following items pertain to the liabilities of Brent Foods. You may assume that Brent Foods began business on January 1, 2012; therefore, the beginning balance of all accounts was zero.

a. On January 1, 2012, Brent Foods issued bonds with a face value of $50,000. The bonds are due in five years and have a face interest rate of 10%. The market rate on January 1 for similar bonds was 12%. The bonds pay interest annually each December 31. Brent has chosen to use the effective interest method of amortization for any premium or discount on the bonds.

b. On December 31, 2012, Brent Foods signed a lease agreement with Cordova Leasing. The agreement requires Brent to make annual lease payments of $3,000 per year for four years, with the first payment due on January 1, 2014. The agreement stipulates that ownership of the property is transferred to Brent at the end of the four-year lease. Assume that an 8% interest rate is used for the leasing transaction.

c. On January 1, 2013, Brent redeems its bonds payable at the specified redemption price of 101. Because this item occurs in 2013, it does not affect the balance sheet prepared for year-end 2012.

Required

1. Determine the effect on the accounting equation of the December 31, 2012, interest adjustment in (a) and the signing of the lease in (b).
2. Develop the Long-Term Liabilities section of Brent Foods' balance sheet as of December 31, 2012, based on (a) and (b). You do not need to consider the notes that accompany the balance sheet.
3. Would the company prefer to treat the lease in (b) as an operating lease? Why or why not?
4. Calculate the gain or loss on the bond redemption for (c).

Solution to Review Problem

1. a. The issue price of the bonds on January 1 must be calculated at the present value of the interest payments and the present value of the principal, as follows:

$$\$5,000 \times 3.60478 \qquad \$18,024$$
$$\$50,000 \times 0.56743 \qquad \underline{28,372}$$
$$\text{Issue price} \qquad \underline{\$46,400} \quad \text{(rounded)}$$

The amount of the discount is calculated as follows:

$$\$50,000 - \$46,400 = \$3,600$$

The effect of the interest payment and amortization is as follows:

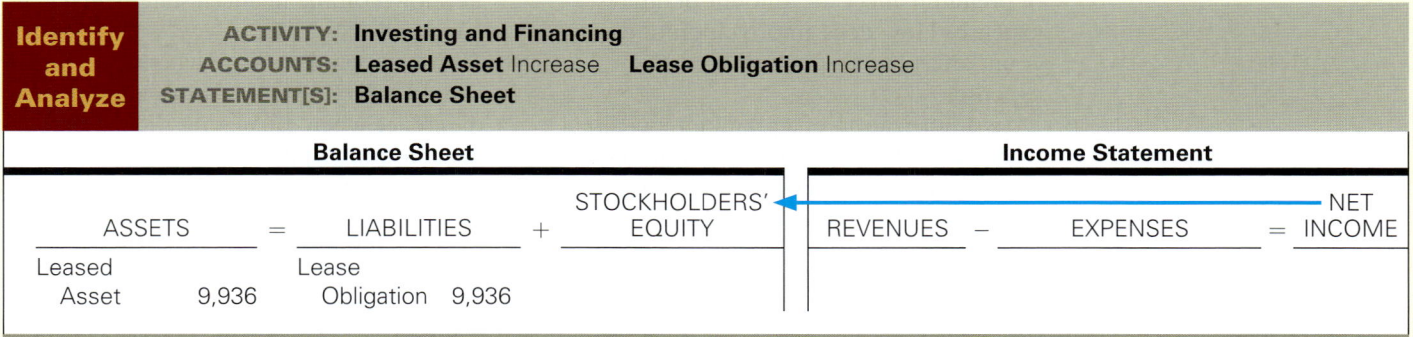

Identify and Analyze

ACTIVITY: Operating
ACCOUNTS: Interest Expense Increase   Discount on Bonds Payable Decrease   Cash Decrease
STATEMENT[S]: Balance Sheet and Income Statement

Balance Sheet					Income Statement			
ASSETS	=	LIABILITIES	+	STOCKHOLDERS' EQUITY	REVENUES	−	EXPENSES	= NET INCOME
Cash (5,000)		Discount on Bonds Payable* 568		(5,568)			Interest Expense 5,568	(5,568)

*The Discount on Bonds Payable account has decreased. It is shown as an increase in the equation above because it is a contra account and causes total liabilities to increase.

The interest expense is calculated using the effective interest method by multiplying the carrying value of the bonds times the market rate of interest ($46,400 × 12%).

Brent must show two accounts in the Long-Term Liabilities section of the balance sheet: Bonds Payable of $50,000 and Discount on Bonds Payable of $3,032 ($3,600 less $568 amortized).

  b. The lease meets the criteria to be a capital lease. Brent must report the lease as an asset and report the obligation for lease payments as a liability. The transaction should be reported at the present value of the lease payments, $9,936 (computed by multiplying $3,000 by the annuity factor of 3.31213). The effect of the lease is as follows:

Identify and Analyze

ACTIVITY: Investing and Financing
ACCOUNTS: Leased Asset Increase   Lease Obligation Increase
STATEMENT[S]: Balance Sheet

Balance Sheet					Income Statement			
ASSETS	=	LIABILITIES	+	STOCKHOLDERS' EQUITY	REVENUES	−	EXPENSES	= NET INCOME
Leased Asset 9,936		Lease Obligation 9,936						

Because the lease agreement was signed on December 31, 2012, it is not necessary to amortize the Lease Obligation account in 2012. The account should be stated in the Long-Term Liabilities section of Brent's balance sheet at $9,936.

(Continued)

2. The Long-Term Liabilities section of Brent's balance sheet for December 31, 2012, on the basis of (a) and (b) is as follows:

Brent Foods
Partial Balance Sheet
As of December 31, 2012

Long-term liabilities:		
Bonds payable	$50,000	
Less: Unamortized discount on bonds payable	3,032	$46,968
Lease obligation		9,936
Total long-term liabilities		$56,904

3. The company would prefer that the lease be an operating lease because it would not have to report the asset or liability on the balance sheet. This off-balance-sheet financing may give a more favorable impression of the company.

4. Brent must calculate the loss on the bond redemption as the difference between the carrying value of the bonds ($46,968) and the redemption price ($50,000 × 1.01). The amount of the loss is calculated as follows:

$$\$50,500 - \$46,968 = \$3,532 \text{ loss on redemption}$$

QUESTIONS

1. Which interest rate, the face rate or the market rate, should be used when calculating the issue price of a bond? Why?

2. What is the tax advantage that companies experience when bonds are issued instead of stock?

3. Does the issuance of bonds at a premium indicate that the face rate is higher or lower than the market rate of interest?

4. How does the effective interest method of amortization result in a constant rate of interest?

5. What is the meaning of the following sentence: Amortization affects the amount of interest expense. How does amortization of premium affect the amount of interest expense? How does amortization of discount affect the amount of interest expense?

6. Does amortization of a premium increase or decrease the bond carrying value? Does amortization of a discount increase or decrease the bond carrying value?

7. Is there always a gain or loss when bonds are redeemed? How is the gain or loss calculated?

8. What are the reasons that not all leases are accounted for in the same manner? Do you think it would be possible to develop a new accounting rule that would treat all leases in the same manner? Explain.

9. What is the meaning of the term *off-balance-sheet financing*? Why do some firms want to engage in off-balance-sheet transactions?

10. What are the effects on the financial statements when a lease is considered an operating lease rather than a capital lease?

11. Should depreciation be reported on leased assets? If so, over what period of time should depreciation occur?

12. Why do firms have a Deferred Tax account? Where should that account be shown on the financial statements? (Appendix)

13. How can you determine whether an item should reflect a permanent or a temporary difference when calculating the deferred tax amount? (Appendix)

14. Does the amount of income tax expense presented on the income statement represent the amount of tax actually paid? Why or why not? (Appendix)

15. Do you agree with this statement? All liabilities could be legally enforced in a court of law.

BRIEF EXERCISES

Brief Exercise 10-1 Classification of Long-Term Liabilities   LO1

Which of the following would normally be included in the Long-Term Liability category of the balance sheet?

Accounts Payable
Bonds Payable
Accrued Expenses
Current Maturities of Long-Term Debt
Accrued Income Taxes

Brief Exercise 10-2 Bond Features   LO2

Define the following terms related to bonds payable.

Debenture bonds	Face value of the bonds
Secured bonds	Face rate of interest
Convertible bonds	Issue price
Callable bonds	

Brief Exercise 10-3 Bond Issue Price   LO3

EXAMPLE 10-1, 10-2

A bond payable is dated January 1, 2012, and is issued on that date. The face value of the bond is $100,000, and the face rate of interest is 8%. The bond pays interest semiannually. The bond will mature in five years.

Required

1. What will be the issue price of the bond if the market rate of interest is 6% at the time of issuance?
2. What will be the issue price of the bond if the market rate of interest is 8% at the time of issuance?
3. What will be the issue price of the bond if the market rate of interest is 10% at the time of issuance?

Brief Exercise 10-4 Effect of Bond Issuance   LO4

EXAMPLE 10-1

A bond with a face value of $10,000 is issued at a discount of $800 on January 1, 2012. The face rate of interest on the bond is 7%.

Required

1. Was the market rate at the time of issuance greater than 7% or less than 7%?
2. If a balance sheet is presented on January 1, 2012, how will the bonds appear on the balance sheet?
3. If a balance sheet is presented on December 31, 2012, will the amount for the bonds be higher or lower than on January 1, 2012?

Brief Exercise 10-5 Amortization of Premium or Discount   LO5

EXAMPLE 10-4

Bonds payable are dated January 1, 2012, and are issued on that date. The face value of the bonds is $100,000, and the face rate of interest is 8%. The bonds pay interest semiannually. The bonds will mature in five years. The market rate of interest at the time of issuance was 6%.

Required

1. Using the effective interest amortization method, what amount should be amortized for the first six-month period? What amount of interest expense should be reported for the first six-month period?
2. Using the effective interest amortization method, what amount should be amortized for the period from July 1 to December 31, 2012? What amount of interest expense should be reported for the period from July 1 to December 31, 2012?

LO6

EXAMPLE 10-5, 10-6

Brief Exercise 10-6 Gain or Loss on Bonds

Refer to Brief Exercise 10-5. Assume that the bonds are redeemed on December 31, 2012, at 102.

Required

1. Calculate the gain or loss on bond redemption.
2. Identify and analyze the effect of the bond redemption.

LO7

EXAMPLE 10-8

Brief Exercise 10-7 Lease Classification

Dianne Company signed a ten-year lease agreement on January 1, 2012. The lease requires payments of $5,000 per year every December 31. Dianne estimates that the leased property has a life of 12 years. The interest rate that applies to the lease is 8%.

Required

1. Should Dianne Company treat the lease as an operating lease or a capital lease?
2. If a balance sheet is presented on January 1, 2012, what amounts related to the lease will appear on the balance sheet?
3. Assume that the leased asset is depreciated using the straight-line method. Assume that the lease is amortized using the effective interest method. What amounts should appear on the balance sheet of December 31, 2012?

LO8

Brief Exercise 10-8 Debt-to-Equity Ratio

Will Able Corporation's balance sheet showed the following amounts: Current Liabilities, $10,000; Bonds Payable, $3,000; Lease Obligations, $4,000; and Notes Payable, $600. Total stockholders' equity was $12,000. The debt-to-equity ratio is:

a. 0.63.
b. 0.83.
c. 1.42.
d. 1.47.

LO9

Brief Exercise 10-9 Long-Term Liabilities and Cash Flow

In what category of the statement of cash flows should the following items be shown? Should they appear as a positive or negative amount on the statement of cash flows?

Increases in long-term liabilities
Decreases in long-term liabilities
Interest expense
Depreciation expense on leased assets
Increase in deferred tax

LO10

EXAMPLE 10-9

Brief Exercise 10-10 Deferred Tax (Appendix)

On January 1, 2012, Deng Company purchased an asset for $100,000. For financial accounting purposes, the asset will be depreciated on a straight-line basis over five years with no residual value at the end of that time. For tax purposes, the asset will be depreciated as follows: 2012, $40,000; 2013, $30,000; 2014, $20,000; 2015, $10,000; and 2016, $0. Assume that the company is subject to a 40% tax rate.

Required

1. What is the amount of deferred tax at December 31, 2012?
2. Does the deferred tax represent an asset or a liability?
3. What is the amount of deferred tax at December 31, 2016?

EXERCISES

Exercise 10-1 Relationships

The following components are computed annually when a bond is issued for other than its face value:

LO2
EXAMPLE 10-3, 10-4

- Cash interest payment
- Interest expense
- Amortization of discount/premium
- Carrying value of bond

Required

State whether each component will increase (I), decrease (D), or remain constant (C) as the bond approaches maturity given the following situations:

1. Issued at a discount
2. Issued at a premium

Exercise 10-2 Issue Price

The following terms relate to independent bond issues:

LO3
EXAMPLE 10-1, 10-2

a. 500 bonds; $1,000 face value; 8% stated rate; 5 years; annual interest payments
b. 500 bonds; $1,000 face value; 8% stated rate; 5 years; semiannual interest payments
c. 800 bonds; $1,000 face value; 8% stated rate; 10 years; semiannual interest payments
d. 2,000 bonds; $500 face value; 12% stated rate; 15 years; semiannual interest payments

Required

Assuming the market rate of interest is 10%, calculate the selling price for each bond issue.

Exercise 10-3 Issue Price

Youngblood Inc. plans to issue $500,000 face value bonds with a stated interest rate of 8%. They will mature in ten years. Interest will be paid semiannually. At the date of issuance, assume that the market rate is (a) 8%, (b) 6%, and (c) 10%.

LO3
EXAMPLE 10-1, 10-2

Required

For each market interest rate, answer the following questions:

1. What is the amount due at maturity?
2. How much cash interest will be paid every six months?
3. At what price will the bond be issued?

Exercise 10-4 Impact of Two Bond Alternatives

Yung Chong Company wants to issue 100 bonds, $1,000 face value, in January. The bonds will have a ten-year life and pay interest annually. The market rate of interest on January 1 will be 9%. Yung Chong is considering two alternative bond issues: (a) bonds with a face rate of 8% and (b) bonds with a face rate of 10%.

LO4
EXAMPLE 10-1, 10-2

Required

1. Could the company save money by issuing bonds with an 8% face rate? If it chooses alternative (a), what would be the interest cost as a percentage?
2. Could the company benefit by issuing bonds with a 10% face rate? If it chooses alternative (b), what would be the interest cost as a percentage?

LO6
EXAMPLE 10-5

Exercise 10-5 Redemption of a Bond at Maturity

On March 31, 2012, Sammonds Inc. issued $250,000 face value bonds at a discount of $7,000. The bonds were retired at their maturity date, March 31, 2022.

Required

Assuming that the last interest payment and the amortization of the discount have already been recorded, calculate the gain or loss on the redemption of the bonds on March 31, 2022. Indicate the effect on the accounting equation of the redemption of the bonds.

LO6
EXAMPLE 10-5

Exercise 10-6 Redemption of Bonds

Reynolds Corporation issued $75,000 face value bonds at a discount of $2,500. The bonds contain a call price of 103. Reynolds decides to redeem the bonds early when the unamortized discount is $1,750.

Required

1. Calculate Reynolds Corporation's gain or loss on the early redemption of the bonds.
2. Describe how the gain or loss would be reported on the income statement and in the notes to the financial statements.

LO7
EXAMPLE 10-8

Exercise 10-7 Financial Statement Impact of a Lease

Benjamin's Warehouse signed a six-year capital lease on January 1, 2012, with payments due every December 31. Interest is calculated annually at 10%, and the present value of the minimum lease payments is $13,065.

Required

1. Calculate the amount of the annual payment that Benjamin's must make every December 31.
2. Calculate the amount of the lease obligation that would be presented on the December 31, 2013, balance sheet (after two lease payments have been made).

LO7
EXAMPLE 10-7, 10-8

Exercise 10-8 Leased Assets

Koffman and Sons signed a four-year lease for a forklift on January 1, 2012. Annual lease payments of $1,510, based on an interest rate of 8%, are to be made every December 31, beginning with December 31, 2012.

Required

1. Assume that the lease is treated as an operating lease.

    a. Will the value of the forklift appear on Koffman's balance sheet?
    b. What account will indicate that lease payments have been made?

2. Assume that the lease is treated as a capital lease.

    a. Identify and analyze the effect when the lease is signed. Explain why the value of the leased asset is not recorded at $6,040 ($1,510 × 4).
    b. Identify and analyze the effect of the first lease payment on December 31, 2012.
    c. Calculate the amount of depreciation expense for the year 2012.
    d. At what amount would the lease obligation be presented on the balance sheet as of December 31, 2012?

LO7
EXAMPLE 10-8

Exercise 10-9 Leased Asset

Hopper Corporation signed a ten-year capital lease on January 1, 2012. The lease requires annual payments of $8,000 every December 31.

Required

1. Assuming an interest rate of 9%, calculate the present value of the minimum lease payments.
2. Explain why the value of the leased asset and the accompanying lease obligation are not reported on the balance sheet initially at $80,000.

Exercise 10-10 Impact of Transactions Involving Capital Leases on Statement of Cash Flows

LO9

Assume that Garnett Corporation signs a lease agreement with Duncan Company to lease a piece of equipment and determines that the lease should be treated as a capital lease. Garnett records a leased asset in the amount of $53,400 and a lease obligation in the same amount on its balance sheet.

Required

1. Indicate how this transaction would be reported on Garnett's statement of cash flows.
2. In the following list of transactions relating to this lease, identify each item as operating (O), investing (I), financing (F), or not separately reported on the statement of cash flows (N).

_____ Reduction of lease obligation (principal portion of lease payment)
_____ Interest expense
_____ Depreciation expense—leased assets

Exercise 10-11 Impact of Transactions Involving Tax Liabilities on Statement of Cash Flows

LO9

In the following list, identify each item as operating (O), investing (I), financing (F), or not separately reported on the statement of cash flows (N). For items identified as operating, indicate whether the related amount would be added to or deducted from net income in determining the cash flows from operating activities.

_____ Decrease in taxes payable
_____ Increase in deferred taxes

Exercise 10-12 Impact of Transactions Involving Bonds on Statement of Cash Flows

LO9

In the following list, identify each item as operating (O), investing (I), financing (F), or not separately reported on the statement of cash flows (N).

_____ Proceeds from issuance of bonds payable
_____ Interest expense
_____ Redemption of bonds payable at maturity

Exercise 10-13 Deferred Tax (Appendix)

LO10
EXAMPLE 10-9

On January 1, 2012, Kunkel Corporation purchased an asset for $32,000. Assume that this is the only asset owned by the corporation. Kunkel has decided to use the straight-line method to depreciate it. For tax purposes, it will be depreciated over three years. It will be depreciated over five years, however, for the financial statements provided to stockholders. Assume that Kunkel Corporation is subject to a 40% tax rate.

Required

Calculate the balance to be reflected in the Deferred Tax account for Kunkel Corporation for each year 2012 through 2016.

Exercise 10-14 Temporary and Permanent Differences (Appendix)

LO10
EXAMPLE 10-9

Madden Corporation wants to determine the amount of deferred tax that should be reported on its 2012 financial statements. It has compiled a list of differences between the accounting conducted for tax purposes and the accounting used for financial reporting (book) purposes.

Required

For each of the following items, indicate whether the difference should be classified as a permanent or a temporary difference.

(Continued)

1. During 2012, Madden received interest on state bonds purchased as an investment. The interest can be treated as tax-exempt interest for tax purposes.
2. During 2012, Madden paid for a life insurance premium on two key executives. Madden's accountant has indicated that the amount of the premium cannot be deducted for income tax purposes.
3. During December 2012, Madden received money for renting a building to a tenant. Madden must report the rent as income on its 2012 tax form. For book purposes, however, the rent will be considered income on the 2013 income statement.
4. Madden owns several pieces of equipment that it depreciates using the straight-line method for book purposes. An accelerated method of depreciation is used for tax purposes, however.
5. Madden offers a warranty on the product it sells. The corporation records the expense of the warranty repair costs in the year the product is sold (the accrual method) for book purposes. For tax purposes, however, Madden is not allowed to deduct the expense until the period the product is repaired.
6. During 2012, Madden was assessed a large fine by the federal government for polluting the environment. Madden's accountant has indicated that the fine cannot be deducted as an expense for income tax purposes.

MULTI-CONCEPT EXERCISES

LO4 • 5
EXAMPLE 10-1, 10-3

Exercise 10-15 Impact of a Discount

Berol Corporation sold 20-year bonds on January 1, 2012. The face value of the bonds was $100,000, and they carry a 9% stated rate of interest, which is paid on December 31 of every year. Berol received $91,526 in return for the issuance of the bonds when the market rate was 10%. Any premium or discount is amortized using the effective interest method.

Required

1. Identify and analyze the effect of the sale of the bonds on January 1, 2012, and the proper balance sheet presentation on this date.
2. Identify and analyze the effect of the payment of interest on December 31, 2012, and the proper balance sheet presentation on this date.
3. Explain why it was necessary for Berol to issue the bonds for only $91,526 rather than $100,000.

LO4 • 5
EXAMPLE 10-2, 10-4

Exercise 10-16 Impact of a Premium

Assume the same set of facts for Berol Corporation as in Exercise 10-15 except that it received $109,862 in return for the issuance of the bonds when the market rate was 8%.

Required

1. Identify and analyze the effect of the sale of the bonds on January 1, 2012, and the proper balance sheet presentation on this date.
2. Identify and analyze the effect of the payment of interest on December 31, 2012, and the proper balance sheet presentation on this date.
3. Explain why the company was able to issue the bonds for $109,862 rather than for the face amount.

LO4 • 5
EXAMPLE 10-1, 10-2

Exercise 10-17 Issuance of a Bond at Face Value

On January 1, 2012, Whitefeather Industries issued 300, $1,000 face value bonds. The bonds have a five-year life and pay interest at the rate of 10%. Interest is paid semiannually on July 1 and January 1. The market rate of interest on January 1 was 10%.

Required

1. Calculate the issue price of the bonds and identify and analyze the effect of the issuance of the bonds on January 1, 2012.

2. Explain how the issue price would have been affected if the market rate of interest had been higher than 10%.
3. Identify and analyze the effect of the payment of interest on July 1, 2012.
4. Calculate the amount of interest accrued on December 31, 2012.

PROBLEMS

Problem 10-1 Factors That Affect the Bond Issue Price   LO3

Becca Company is considering the issue of $100,000 face value, ten-year term bonds. The bonds will pay 6% interest each December 31. The current market rate is 6%; therefore, the bonds will be issued at face value.

Required

1. For each of the following situations, indicate whether you believe the company will receive a premium on the bonds or will issue them at a discount or at face value. Without using numbers, explain your position.

   a. Interest is paid semiannually instead of annually.
   b. Assume instead that the market rate of interest is 7%; the nominal rate is still 6%.

2. For each situation in part (1), prove your statement by determining the issue price of the bonds given the changes in (a) and (b).

Problem 10-2 Amortization of Discount   LO5

Stacy Company issued five-year, 10% bonds with a face value of $10,000 on January 1, 2012. Interest is paid annually on December 31. The market rate of interest on this date is 12%, and Stacy Company receives proceeds of $9,279 on the bond issuance.

Required

1. Prepare a five-year table (similar to Exhibit 10-4) to amortize the discount using the effective interest method.
2. What is the total interest expense over the life of the bonds? cash interest payment? discount amortization?
3. Identify and analyze the effect of the payment of interest and the amortization of discount on December 31, 2014 (the third year), and determine the balance sheet presentation of the bonds on that date.

Problem 10-3 Amortization of Premium   LO5

Assume the same set of facts for Stacy Company as in Problem 10-2 except that the market rate of interest of January 1, 2012, is 8% and the proceeds from the bond issuance equal $10,799.

Required

1. Prepare a five-year table (similar to Exhibit 10-5) to amortize the premium using the effective interest method.
2. What is the total interest expense over the life of the bonds? cash interest payment? premium amortization?
3. Identify and analyze the effect of the payment of interest and the amortization of premium on December 31, 2014 (the third year), and determine the balance sheet presentation of the bonds on that date.

Problem 10-4 Redemption of Bonds   LO6

McGee Company issued $200,000 face value bonds at a premium of $4,500. The bonds contain a call provision of 101. McGee decides to redeem the bonds due to a significant decline in interest rates. On that date, McGee had amortized only $1,000 of the premium.

(Continued)

Required

1. Calculate the gain or loss on the early redemption of the bonds.
2. Calculate the gain or loss on the redemption assuming that the call provision is 103 instead of 101.
3. Indicate where the gain or loss should be presented on the financial statements.
4. Why do you suppose the call price is normally higher than 100?

LO7   Problem 10-5 Financial Statement Impact of a Lease

On January 1, 2012, Muske Trucking Company leased a semitractor and trailer for five years. Annual payments of $28,300 are to be made every December 31 beginning December 31, 2012. Interest expense is based on a rate of 8%. The present value of the minimum lease payments is $112,994 and has been determined to be greater than 90% of the fair market value of the asset on January 1, 2012. Muske uses straight-line depreciation on all assets.

Required

1. Prepare a table similar to Exhibit 10-7 to show the five-year amortization of the lease obligation.
2. Identify and analyze the effect of the lease transaction on January 1, 2012.
3. Identify and analyze the effect of all transactions on December 31, 2013 (the second year of the lease).
4. Prepare the balance sheet presentation as of December 31, 2013, for the leased asset and the lease obligation.

LO10   Problem 10-6 Deferred Tax Calculations (Appendix)

Wyhowski Inc. reported income from operations, before taxes, for 2010–2012 as follows:

2010	$210,000
2011	240,000
2012	280,000

When calculating income, Wyhowski deducted depreciation on plant equipment. The equipment was purchased January 1, 2010, at a cost of $88,000. The equipment is expected to last three years and have an $8,000 salvage value. Wyhowski uses straight-line depreciation for book purposes. For tax purposes, depreciation on the equipment is $50,000 in 2010, $20,000 in 2011, and $10,000 in 2012. Wyhowski's tax rate is 35%.

Required

1. How much did Wyhowski pay in income tax each year?
2. How much income tax expense did Wyhowski record each year?
3. What is the balance in the Deferred Income Tax account at the end of 2010, 2011, and 2012?

LO10   Problem 10-7 Deferred Tax (Appendix)

Erinn Corporation has compiled its 2012 financial statements. Included in the Long-Term Liabilities category of the balance sheet are the following amounts:

	2012	2011
Deferred tax	$180	$100

Included in the income statement are the following amounts related to income taxes:

	2012	2011
Income before tax	$500	$400
Tax expense	200	160
Net income	$300	$240

In the notes that accompany the 2012 statement are the following amounts:

	2012
Current provision for tax	$120
Deferred portion	80

Required

1. Identify and analyze the effect of the transaction in 2012 for income tax expense, deferred tax, and income tax payable.
2. Assume that a stockholder has inquired about the meaning of the numbers recorded and disclosed about deferred tax. Explain why the Deferred Tax liability account exists. Also, what do the terms *current provision* and *deferred portion* mean? Why is the deferred amount in the note $80 when the deferred amount on the 2012 balance sheet is $180?

MULTI-CONCEPT PROBLEMS

Problem 10-8 Bond Transactions   LO4 • 5

Brand Company issued $1,000,000 face value, eight-year, 12% bonds on April 1, 2012, when the market rate of interest was 12%. Interest payments are due every October 1 and April 1. Brand uses a calendar year-end.

Required

1. Identify and analyze the effect of the issuance of the bonds on April 1, 2012.
2. Identify and analyze the effect of the interest payment on October 1, 2012.
3. Explain why additional interest must be recorded on December 31, 2012. What impact does this have on the amounts paid on April 1, 2013?
4. Determine the total cash inflows and outflows that occurred on the bonds over the eight-year life.

Problem 10-9 Partial Classified Balance Sheet for Walgreens   LO1 • 8 • 10

The following items, listed alphabetically, appear on **Walgreens**'s consolidated balance sheet at August 31, 2010 (in millions):

Accrued expenses and other liabilities	$2,763
Deferred income taxes (long-term)	318
Long-term debt	2,389
Other noncurrent liabilities	1,735
Short-term borrowings	12
Trade accounts payable	4,585
Income taxes	73

Required

1. Prepare the Current Liabilities and Long-Term Liabilities sections of Walgreens's classified balance sheet at August 31, 2010.
2. Walgreens had total liabilities of $10,766 and total shareholders' equity of $14,376 at August 31, 2009. Total shareholders' equity at August 31, 2010, amounted to $14,400. (All amounts are in millions.) Compute Walgreens's debt-to-equity ratio at August 31, 2010 and 2009. As an investor, how would you react to the changes in this ratio?
3. What other related ratios would the company's lenders use to assess the company? What do these ratios measure?

ALTERNATE PROBLEMS

Problem 10-1A Factors that Affect the Bond Issue Price   LO3

Rivera Inc. is considering the issuance of $500,000 face value, ten-year term bonds. The bonds will pay 10% interest each December 31. The current market rate is 10%; therefore, the bonds will be issued at face value.

(Continued)

Required

1. For each of the following situations, indicate whether you believe the company will receive a premium on the bonds or will issue them at a discount or at face value. Without using numbers, explain your position.

    a. Interest is paid semiannually instead of annually.
    b. Assume interest is paid annually but that the market rate of interest is 8%; the nominal rate is still 10%.

2. For each situation in part (1), prove your statement by determining the issue price of the bonds given the changes in (a) and (b).

LO5   Problem 10-2A Amortization of Discount

Ortega Company issued five-year, 5% bonds with a face value of $50,000 on January 1, 2012. Interest is paid annually on December 31. The market rate of interest on this date is 8%, and Ortega Company receives proceeds of $44,011 on the bond issuance.

Required

1. Prepare a five-year table (similar to Exhibit 10-4) to amortize the discount using the effective interest method.
2. What is the total interest expense over the life of the bonds? cash interest payment? discount amortization?
3. Identify and analyze the effect of the payment of interest on December 31, 2014 (the third year), and the balance sheet presentation of the bonds on that date.

LO5   Problem 10-3A Amortization of Premium

Assume the same set of facts for Ortega Company as in Problem 10-2A except that the market rate of interest of January 1, 2012, is 4% and the proceeds from the bond issuance equal $52,227.

Required

1. Prepare a five-year table (similar to Exhibit 10-5) to amortize the premium using the effective interest method.
2. What is the total interest expense over the life of the bonds? cash interest payment? premium amortization?
3. Identify and analyze the effect of the payment of interest on December 31, 2014 (the third year), and the balance sheet presentation of the bonds on that date.

LO5   Problem 10-4A Redemption of Bonds

Elliot Company issued $100,000 face value bonds at a premium of $5,500. The bonds contain a call provision of 101. Elliot decides to redeem the bonds due to a significant decline in interest rates. On that date, Elliot had amortized only $2,000 of the premium.

Required

1. Calculate the gain or loss on the early redemption of the bonds.
2. Calculate the gain or loss on the redemption assuming that the call provision is 104 instead of 101.
3. Indicate how the gain or loss would be reported on the income statement and in the notes to the financial statements.
4. Why do you suppose the call price is normally higher than 100?

LO7   Problem 10-5A Financial Statement Impact of a Lease

On January 1, 2012, Kiger Manufacturing Company leased a factory machine for six years. Annual payments of $21,980 are to be made every December 31 beginning December 31, 2012. Interest expense is based on a rate of 9%. The present value of the minimum lease payments is $98,600 and has been determined to be greater than 90% of the fair market value of the machine on January 1, 2012. Kiger uses straight-line depreciation on all assets.

Required

1. Prepare a table similar to Exhibit 10-7 to show the six-year amortization of the lease obligation.
2. Identify and analyze the effect of the lease transaction on January 1, 2012.
3. Identify and analyze the effect of all transactions on December 31, 2013 (the second year of the lease).
4. Prepare the balance sheet presentation as of December 31, 2013, for the leased asset and the lease obligation.

Problem 10-6A Deferred Tax (Appendix)   LO10

Thad Corporation has compiled its 2012 financial statements. Included in the Long-Term Liabilities category of the balance sheet are the following amounts:

	2012	2011
Deferred tax	$180	$200

Included in the income statement are the following amounts related to income taxes:

	2012	2011
Income before tax	$500	$400
Tax expense	100	150
Net income	$400	$250

Required

1. Determine the effect on the accounting equation in 2012 for income tax expense, deferred tax, and income tax payable.
2. Assume that a stockholder has inquired about the meaning of the numbers recorded and disclosed about deferred tax. Explain why the Deferred Tax liability account exists.

Problem 10-7A Deferred Tax Calculations (Appendix)   LO10

Clemente Inc. has reported income for book purposes as follows for the past three years:

(In thousands)	Year 1	Year 2	Year 3
Income before taxes	$120	$120	$120

Clemente has identified two items that are treated differently in the financial records and in the tax records. The first one is interest income on municipal bonds, which is recognized on the financial reports to the extent of $5,000 each year but does not show up as a revenue item on the company's tax return. The other item, equipment, is depreciated using the straight-line method at the rate of $20,000 each year for financial accounting but is depreciated for tax purposes at the rate of $30,000 in Year 1, $20,000 in Year 2, and $10,000 in Year 3.

Required

1. Determine the amount of cash that Clemente paid for income taxes each year. Assume that a 40% tax rate applies to all three years.
2. Calculate the balance in the Deferred Tax account at the end of Years 1, 2, and 3. How does this account appear on the balance sheet?

ALTERNATE MULTI-CONCEPT PROBLEMS

Problem 10-8A Financial Statement Impact of a Bond   LO4 • 6

Worthington Company issued $1,000,000 face value, six-year, 10% bonds on July 1, 2012, when the market rate of interest was 12%. Interest payments are due every July 1 and January 1. Worthington uses a calendar year-end.

Required

1. Identify and analyze the effect of the issuance of the bonds on July 1, 2012.
2. Identify and analyze the effect of the entry on December 31, 2012, to accrue interest expense.

(Continued)

3. Identify and analyze the effect of the interest payment on January 1, 2013.
4. Calculate the amount of cash that will be paid for the retirement of the bonds on the maturity date.

LO1 • 8 • 10   Problem 10-9A Partial Classified Balance Sheet for Boeing

The following items appear on the consolidated balance sheet of **Boeing Inc.** at December 31, 2010 (in millions). The information in parentheses was added to aid in your understanding.

Accounts payable	$ 7,715
Accrued retiree healthcare	8,025
Accrued pension plan liability, net	9,800
Other accrued liabilities	13,802
Advances and billings in excess of related costs (current)	12,323
Deferred income taxes and income taxes payable (assume current)	607
Short-term debt and current portion of long-term debt	948
Non-current income taxes payable	418
Other long-term liabilities	592
Long-term debt	11,473

Required

1. Prepare the Current Liabilities and Long-Term Liabilities sections of Boeing's classified balance sheet at December 31, 2010.
2. Boeing had total liabilities of $59,828 and total shareholders' equity of $2,128 at December 31, 2009. Total shareholders' equity amounted to $2,766 at December 31, 2010. (All amounts are in millions.) Compute Boeing's debt-to-equity ratio at December 31, 2010 and 2009. As an investor, how would you react to the changes in this ratio?
3. What other related ratios would the company's lenders use to assess the company? What do these ratios measure?

DECISION CASES

Reading and Interpreting Financial Statements

LO1 • 8   Decision Case 10-1 Evaluating the Liabilities of General Mills

Refer to the **General Mills**'s financial statements at the end of the text and answer the following questions:

1. What are the items listed as long-term liabilities by General Mills? How did those liabilities change from 2009 to 2010?
2. Calculate the debt-to-equity ratio and the times interest earned ratio of the company for 2009 and 2010. What do those ratios reveal about the company and its ability to meet its obligations on its long-term liabilities?

LO9 • 10   Decision Case 10-2 Comparing Two Companies: General Mills and Kellogg's

Refer to **General Mills**'s balance sheet and statement of cash flows at May 30, 2010, and **Kellogg's** balance sheet and statement of cash flows at December 31, 2010. Answer the following questions:

1. Calculate the debt-to-equity ratio for the two companies. How do the ratios compare? What does that tell you about the two companies?
2. Did the long-term liabilities of each company increase or decrease during the year? What were the most important changes? What impact do the changes have on the companies' cash flows?
3. What were the most important sources and uses of cash disclosed in the financing activities portion of the statement of cash flows for each company? Kellogg's had both a positive and negative amount in the Financing Activities section related to notes payable during the year. Why does the Long-Term Liability portion of the balance sheet indicate both a decrease and an increase?

Decision Case 10-3 Reading PepsiCo's Statement of Cash Flows LO9 • 10

A portion of the Financing Activities section of **PepsiCo**'s statement of cash flows for the year ended December 25, 2010, follows (in millions):

Financing Activities

Proceeds from issuances of long-term debt	$ 6,451
Payments of long-term debt	(59)
Debt repurchase	(500)
Short-term borrowings, by original maturity	
More than three months—proceeds	227
More than three months—payments	(96)
Three months or less, net	2,351
Cash dividends paid	(2,978)
Share repurchases—common	(4,978)
Share repurchases—preferred	(5)

Required

1. Explain why proceeds from debt is shown as a positive amount and payment of debt is shown as a negative amount.
2. During 2010, interest rates remained at low levels. Explain why the company might have paid off debt during such conditions.
3. What are possible reasons why the company repurchased some of its stock?

Making Financial Decisions

Decision Case 10-4 Making a Loan Decision LO1 • 7

Assume that you are a loan officer in charge of reviewing loan applications from potential new clients at a major bank. You are considering an application from Molitor Corporation, which is a fairly new company with a limited credit history. It has provided a balance sheet for its most recent fiscal year as follows:

Molitor Corporation
Balance Sheet
December 31, 2012

Assets		Liabilities	
Cash	$ 10,000	Accounts payable	$100,000
Receivables	50,000	Notes payable	200,000
Inventory	100,000		
Equipment	500,000	**Stockholders' Equity**	
		Common stock	80,000
		Retained earnings	280,000
Total assets	$660,000	Total liabilities and stockholders' equity	$660,000

Your bank has established certain guidelines that must be met before it will make a favorable loan recommendation. These include minimum levels for several financial ratios. You are particularly concerned about the bank's policy that loan applicants must have a total-assets-to-debt ratio of at least 2 to 1 to be acceptable. Your initial analysis of Molitor's balance sheet indicates that the firm has met the minimum total-assets-to-debt ratio requirement. On reading the notes that accompany the financial statements, however, you discover the following statement:

Molitor has engaged in a variety of innovative financial techniques resulting in the acquisition of $200,000 of assets at very favorable rates. The company is obligated to make a series of payments over the next five years to fulfill its commitments in conjunction with these financial instruments. Current GAAP do not require the assets acquired or the related obligations to be reflected on the financial statements.

(Continued)

Required

1. How should this note affect your evaluation of Molitor's loan application? Calculate a revised total-assets-to-debt ratio for Molitor.
2. Do you believe that the bank's policy concerning a minimum total-assets-to-debt ratio can be modified to consider financing techniques that are not reflected on the financial statements? Write a statement that expresses your position on this issue.

LO6   **Decision Case 10-5 Bond Redemption Decision**

Armstrong Aero Ace, a flight training school, issued $100,000 of 20-year bonds at face value when the market rate was 10%. The bonds have been outstanding for ten years. The company pays annual interest on January 1. The current rate for similar bonds is 4%. On January 1, the controller would like to retire the bonds at 102 and then issue $100,000 of ten-year bonds to pay 4% annual interest.

Required

Draft a memo to the controller advising him to retire the outstanding bonds and issue new debt. Ignore taxes.

Ethical Decision Making

LO7   **Decision Case 10-6 Determination of Asset Life**

Jen Latke is an accountant for Hale's Manufacturing Company. Hale's has entered into an agreement to lease a piece of equipment from EZ Leasing. Jen must decide how to report the lease agreement on Hale's financial statements.

     Jen has reviewed the lease contract carefully. She also has reviewed the four lease criteria specified in the accounting rules. She has been able to determine that the lease does not meet three of the criteria. However, she is concerned about the criterion that indicates that if the term of the lease is 75% or more of the life of the property, the lease should be classified as a capital lease. Jen is fully aware that Hale's does not want to record the lease agreement as a capital lease, but prefers to show it as a type of off-balance-sheet financing.

     Jen's reading of the lease contract indicates that the asset has been leased for seven years. She is unsure of the life of such assets, however, and has consulted two sources to determine it. One of them states that equipment similar to that owned by Hale's is depreciated over nine years. The other, a trade publication of the equipment industry, indicates that equipment of this type will usually last for 12 years.

Required

1. How should Jen report the lease agreement in the financial statements?
2. If Jen decides to present the lease as an off-balance-sheet arrangement, has she acted ethically? Explain.

SOLUTIONS TO KEY TERMS QUIZ

5	Long-term liability		10	Effective interest method of amortization
1	Face value			
7	Debenture bonds		11	Carrying value
2	Serial bonds		13	Gain or loss on redemption
9	Callable bonds		14	Operating lease
3	Face rate of interest		15	Capital lease
12	Market rate of interest		17	Deferred tax (Appendix)
4	Bond issue price		18	Permanent difference (Appendix)
6	Premium		16	Temporary difference (Appendix)
8	Discount			

ANSWERS TO POD REVIEW

LO1	1. b	2. d	
LO2	1. c	2. b	
LO3	1. a	2. a	3. b
LO4	1. b	2. b	
LO5	1. b	2. a	

LO6	1. d	2. a
LO7	1. b	2. a
LO8	1. c	2. b
LO9	1. b	2. c
LO10	1. b	2. d

Stockholders' Equity

11

AFTER STUDYING THIS CHAPTER, YOU SHOULD BE ABLE TO:

LO1 Understand the concept of stockholders' equity and identify the components of the Stockholders' Equity category of the balance sheet and the accounts found in each component.

LO2 Show that you understand the characteristics of common and preferred stock and the differences between the classes of stock.

LO3 Determine the financial statement impact when stock is issued for cash or for other consideration.

LO4 Describe the financial statement impact of stock treated as treasury stock.

LO5 Compute the amount of cash dividends when a firm has issued both preferred and common stock.

LO6 Show that you understand the difference between cash and stock dividends and the effect of stock dividends.

LO7 Determine the difference between stock dividends and stock splits.

LO8 Show that you understand the statement of stockholders' equity and comprehensive income.

LO9 Understand how investors use ratios to evaluate stockholders' equity.

LO10 Explain the effects that transactions involving stockholders' equity have on the statement of cash flows.

LO11 Describe the important differences between the sole proprietorship and partnership forms of organization versus the corporate form (Appendix).

STUDY LINKS

A Look at Previous Chapters The previous chapter indicated how companies use long-term debt as a means of financing the company.

A Look at This Chapter This chapter concentrates on the issues concerned with the Stockholders' Equity section of the balance sheet. The use of equity is an

important source of financing for all corporations. The chapter also considers the various types of dividends paid to stockholders.

A Look at the Upcoming Chapter Chapter 12 includes an expanded discussion of the preparation and use of the statement of cash flows.

The airline industry is very volatile and has certainly experienced difficulties over the past few years. With reduced revenues, weak demand, high fixed costs, high fuel costs, and increasing expenses for security and insurance, the results for many of the airline companies have been grim. **United Airlines** and several other airlines declared bankruptcy in order to restructure, but throughout all of the bad times, **Southwest Airlines** has performed fairly well and has become the model for the future of the industry. The other airlines know that they must cut costs and become more efficient in order to compete with Southwest.

How does Southwest do it? Southwest Airlines Company provides short-haul, high-frequency, point-to-point, low-fare air transportation services. Southwest's 537 aircraft provide service between more than 72 cities in 32 states. In addition, Southwest serves many conveniently located satellite and downtown airports, such as Dallas Love Field, Houston Hobby, and Chicago Midway. The company's operating strategy also permits Southwest to achieve high-asset utilization. Aircraft are scheduled to minimize the amount of time they sit at the gate, pegged at approximately 25 minutes, consequently reducing the number of aircraft and gate facilities that would otherwise be required.

Southwest Airlines has consistently been an innovator in the industry. In January 1995, Southwest introduced a ticketless travel option, eliminating the need to print and then process a paper ticket. Recently, Southwest has resisted the move by other airlines to charge flyers for checking a bag, thereby maintaining its identity for quality, customer-friendly service at a low cost.

All of the company's efforts are consistent with its financial strategy to build shareholder value, which contributes to the Stockholders' Equity portion of the balance sheet shown here.

The company experienced a loss during the economic downturn of 2008 but until then had been consistently profitable for many years. As a result, the stockholders have benefited, and shareholder value will likely continue to grow.

Why is this chapter important to you?

- You need to know what components are presented in the Stockholders' Equity section of the balance sheet. (See pp. 540–544.)
- You need to know the types of stock that companies can issue and the advantages of each class of stock. (See pp. 545–546.)
- You need to know the importance and the meaning of treasury stock. (See pp. 548–550.)
- You need to know the types of dividends that a company might pay. (See pp. 561–566.)
- You need to know what comprehensive income is and how it differs from the net income amount a company may present. (See pp. 568–569.)

This chapter, and the accompanying financial statements of Southwest Airlines and other companies, will help you to understand the Stockholders' Equity section of the balance sheet.

Southwest Airlines Co. Partial Consolidated Balance Sheet (In millions, except share data)		
	December 31,	
	2010	**2009**
Stockholders' equity:		
Common stock, $1.00 par value: 2,000,000,000 shares authorized; 807,611,634 shares issued in 2010 and 2009	$ 808	$ 808
Capital in excess of par value	1,183	1,216
Retained earnings	5,399	4,971
Accumulated other comprehensive loss	(262)	(578)
Treasury stock, at cost: 60,177,362 and 64,820,703 shares in 2010 and 2009, respectively	(891)	(963)
Total stockholders' equity	$6,237	$5,454

An Overview of Stockholders' Equity

LO1 Understand the concept of stockholders' equity and identify the components of the Stockholders' Equity category of the balance sheet and the accounts found in each component.

OVERVIEW: Stockholders are the owners of a corporation and have a residual interest in assets after liabilities are satisfied. Stockholders' equity has two major components: contributed capital and retained earnings. Contributed capital represents the amount the corporation received from the sale of stock to the stockholders. The stock may be either common stock or preferred stock. For each class of stock, the company must indicate the number of shares authorized, issued, and outstanding. The amount received at issuance that exceeds the par value of the stock is presented as Additional Paid-In Capital. Retained earnings is the amount of net income over the life of the company not paid out as dividends. It represents an important link between the income statement and the balance sheet.

Equity as a Source of Financing

Whenever a company needs to raise money, it must choose from the alternative financing sources available. Financing can be divided into two general categories: debt (borrowing from banks or other creditors) and equity (issuing stock). The company's management must consider the advantages and disadvantages of each alternative. Exhibit 11-1 indicates a few of the factors that must be considered.

Issuing stock is a popular method of financing because of its flexibility. It provides advantages for the issuing company and the investors (stockholders). Investors are primarily concerned with the return on their investment. With stock, the return might be in the form of dividends paid to the investors but might also be the price appreciation of the stock. Stock is popular because it generally provides a higher rate of return (but also a higher degree of risk) than can be obtained by creditors who receive interest from lending money. Stock is popular with issuing companies because dividends on stock can be adjusted according to the company's profitability: higher dividends can be paid when the firm is profitable; lower dividends, when it is not. Interest on debt financing, on the other hand, is generally fixed and is a legal liability that cannot be adjusted when a company experiences lower profitability.

There are several disadvantages in issuing stock. Stock usually has voting rights, and issuing stock allows new investors to vote. Existing investors may not want to share the control of the company with new stockholders. From the issuing company's viewpoint, there is also a serious tax disadvantage to stock versus debt. As indicated in Chapter 10, interest on debt is tax-deductible and results in lower taxes. Dividends on stock, on the other hand, are not tax-deductible and do not result in tax savings to the issuing

EXHIBIT 11-1 Advantages and Disadvantages of Stock versus Debt Financing

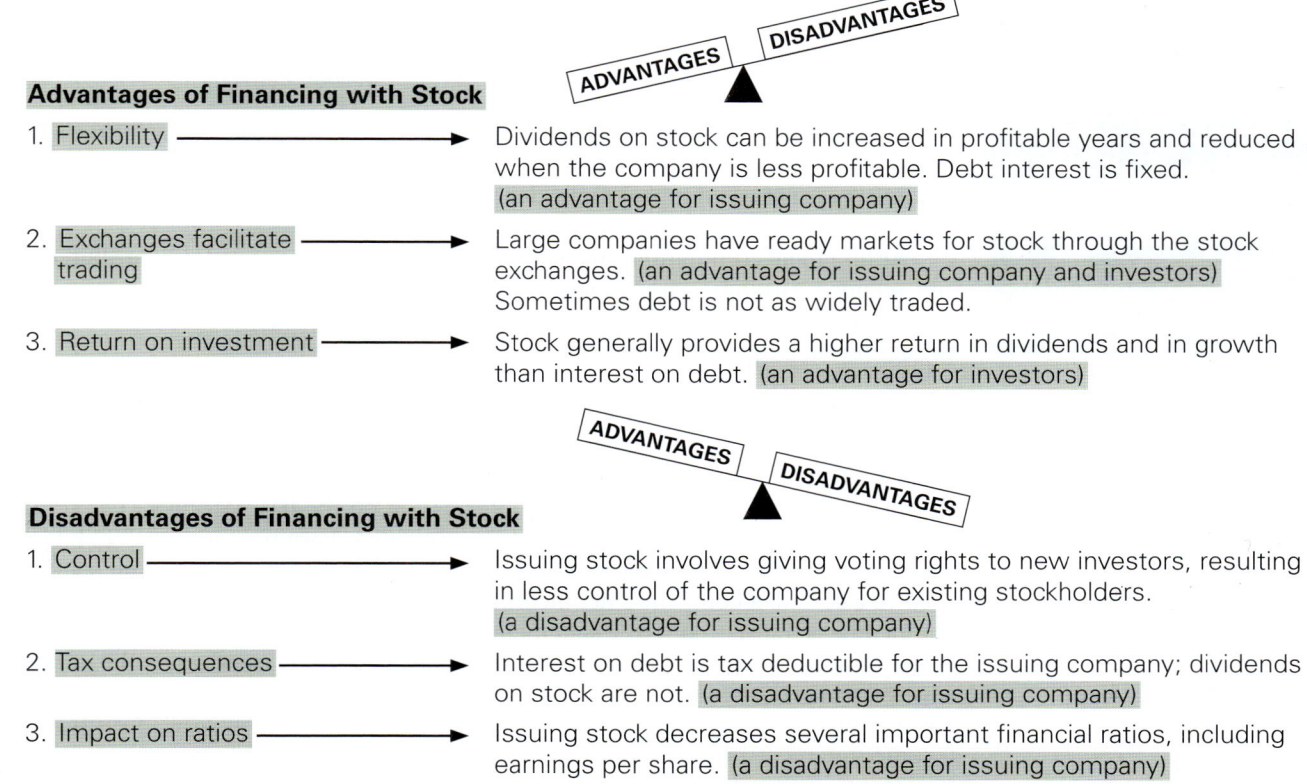

Advantages of Financing with Stock

1. Flexibility ⟶ Dividends on stock can be increased in profitable years and reduced when the company is less profitable. Debt interest is fixed. (an advantage for issuing company)

2. Exchanges facilitate trading ⟶ Large companies have ready markets for stock through the stock exchanges. (an advantage for issuing company and investors) Sometimes debt is not as widely traded.

3. Return on investment ⟶ Stock generally provides a higher return in dividends and in growth than interest on debt. (an advantage for investors)

Disadvantages of Financing with Stock

1. Control ⟶ Issuing stock involves giving voting rights to new investors, resulting in less control of the company for existing stockholders. (a disadvantage for issuing company)

2. Tax consequences ⟶ Interest on debt is tax deductible for the issuing company; dividends on stock are not. (a disadvantage for issuing company)

3. Impact on ratios ⟶ Issuing stock decreases several important financial ratios, including earnings per share. (a disadvantage for issuing company)

company. Finally, issuing stock has an impact on the company's financial statements. Issuing stock decreases several important financial ratios, such as earnings per share. Issuing debt does not have a similar effect on the earnings per share ratio.

Management must consider many other factors in deciding between debt and equity financing. The company's goal should be financing the company in a manner that results in the lowest overall cost of capital to the firm. Usually, companies attain that goal by having a reasonable balance of both debt and equity financing.

Stockholders' Equity on the Balance Sheet

The basic accounting equation is often stated as follows:

$$\text{Assets} = \text{Liabilities} + \text{Owners' Equity}$$

Owners' equity is viewed as a residual amount. That is, the owners of a corporation have a claim to all assets after the claims represented by liabilities to creditors have been satisfied.

This text concentrates on the corporate form of organization and refers to the owners' equity as *stockholders' equity*. To review, the basic accounting equation for a corporation is as follows:

$$\text{Assets} = \text{Liabilities} + \text{Stockholders' Equity}$$

The stockholders are the owners of a corporation. They have a residual interest in its assets after the claims of all creditors have been satisfied.

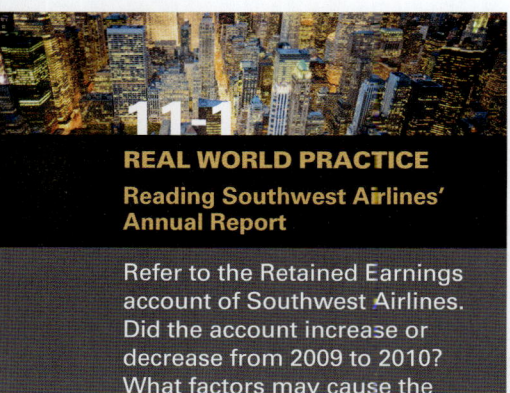

The Stockholders' Equity category of all corporations has two major components or subcategories:

$$\text{Total Stockholders' Equity} = \text{Contributed Capital}$$
$$+$$
$$\text{Retained Earnings}$$

Contributed capital represents the amount the corporation has received from the sale of stock to stockholders. Retained earnings is the amount of net income the corporation has earned but not paid as dividends. Instead, the corporation retains and reinvests the income.

Although all corporations maintain the two primary categories of contributed capital and retained earnings, within these categories, they use a variety of accounts that have several different titles. The next section examines two important items: income and dividends and their impact on the Retained Earnings account.

How Income and Dividends Affect Retained Earnings

The Retained Earnings account serves as a link between the income statement and the balance sheet. The term *articulated statements* refers to the fact that the information on the income statement is related to the information on the balance sheet. The bridge (or link) between the two statements is the Retained Earnings account. Exhibit 11-2 presents this relationship graphically. As the exhibit indicates, the income statement is used to calculate a company's net income for a given period of time. The amount of the net income is transferred to the statement of retained earnings and is added to the beginning balance of retained earnings (with dividends deducted) to calculate the ending balance of retained earnings. The ending balance of retained earnings is portrayed on the balance sheet in the Stockholders' Equity category. That is why you must prepare the income statement before the balance sheet, as you discovered when developing financial statements in previous chapters of the text.

Identifying Components of the Stockholders' Equity Section of the Balance Sheet

The Liabilities and Stockholders' Equity portion of the balance sheet of **Southwest Airlines** was presented in the chapter opener. We will focus on the Stockholders' (Shareholders') Equity category of the balance sheet. All corporations begin the Stockholders'

EXHIBIT 11-2 Retained Earnings Connects the Income Statement and the Balance Sheet

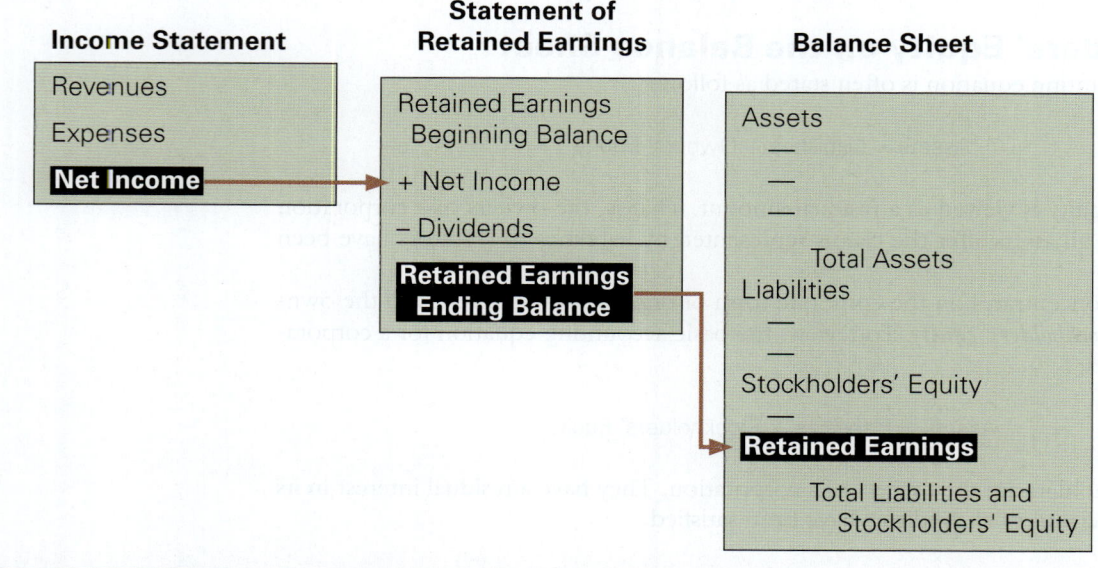

Equity category with a list of the firm's contributed capital. In some cases, there are two categories of stock: common stock and preferred stock. (The latter is discussed later in this chapter.) Common stock normally carries voting rights. The common stockholders elect the corporation's officers and establish its bylaws and governing rules. Corporations often have more than one type of common stock, each with different rights or terms.

Number of Shares It is important to determine the number of shares of stock for each stock account. Corporate balance sheets report the number of shares in three categories: **authorized**, **issued**, and **outstanding shares**.

To become incorporated, a business must develop articles of incorporation and apply to the proper state authorities for a corporate charter. The corporation must specify the maximum number of shares that it will be allowed to issue. This maximum number of shares is called the *authorized stock*. A corporation applies for authorization to issue many more shares than it will issue immediately to allow for future growth and other events that may occur over its long life. For example, Southwest Airlines has 2,000,000,000 shares of common stock authorized, but only 807,611,634 shares had been issued as of December 31, 2010.

The number of shares *issued* indicates the number of shares that have been sold or transferred to stockholders. The number of shares issued does not necessarily mean, however, that those shares are currently outstanding. The term *outstanding* indicates shares actually in the stockholders' hands. Shares that have been issued by the corporation and then repurchased are counted as shares issued but not as shares outstanding. Quite often, corporations repurchase their own stock as treasury stock (explained in more detail later in this chapter). Treasury stock reduces the number of shares outstanding. The number of Southwest Airlines' shares of common stock outstanding at December 31, 2010, could be calculated as follows:

Number of shares issued	807,611,634
Less: Treasury stock	60,177,362
Number of shares outstanding	747,434,272

Par Value: The Firm's "Legal Capital" The Stockholders' Equity category of many balance sheets refers to an amount as the *par value* of the stock. For example, Southwest Airlines' common stock has a par value of $1 per share. **Par value** is an arbitrary amount stated on the face of the stock certificate and represents the legal capital of the corporation. Most corporations set the par value of the stock at very low amounts because there are legal difficulties if stock is sold at less than par. Therefore, par value does not indicate the stock's value or the amount that is obtained when the stock is sold on the stock exchange; it is simply an arbitrary amount that exists to fulfill legal requirements. A company's legal requirement depends on its state of incorporation. Some states do not require corporations to indicate a par value; other states require corporations to designate the *stated value* of the stock. A stated value is accounted for in the same manner as a par value and appears in the Stockholders' Equity category in the same manner as a par value.

The amount of the par value is the amount that is presented in the stock account. That is, the dollar amount in a firm's stock account can be calculated as its par value per share times number of shares issued. For Southwest Airlines, the dollar amount appearing in the Common Stock account can be calculated as follows:

$1 Par Value per Share × 807,611,634 Shares Issued = $807,611,634 million

(rounded to $808 million on the balance sheet Balance in the Common Stock Account

Additional Paid-In Capital The dollar amounts of the stock accounts in the Stockholders' Equity category do not indicate the amount that was received when the stock was sold to stockholders. The Common Stock and Preferred Stock accounts indicate only the par value of the stock. When stock is issued for an amount higher than the par value, the excess is reported as **additional paid-in capital**. Several different titles

---

Authorized shares
The maximum number of shares a corporation may issue as indicated in the corporate charter.

Issued shares
The number of shares sold or distributed to stockholders.

Outstanding shares
The number of shares issued less the number of shares held as treasury stock.

STUDY TIP

Treasury stock is included in the number of shares issued. It is not part of the number of shares outstanding.

© Cengage Learning 2013

Par value
An arbitrary amount that represents the legal capital of the firm.

Additional paid-in capital
The amount received for the issuance of stock in excess of the par value of the stock.

Alternate term: Paid-in capital in excess of par.

are used for this account, including Capital in Excess of Par Value, Capital Surplus (an old term that should no longer be used), and Premium on Stock. Regardless of the title, the account represents the amount received in excess of par when stock was issued.

Southwest Airlines' balance sheet indicates paid-in capital of $1,183 million at December 31, 2010. The company, like many other corporations, presents only one amount for additional paid-in capital for all stock transactions. Therefore, we are unable to determine whether the amount resulted from the issuance of common stock or other stock transactions. As a result, it is often impossible to determine the issue price of each category of stock even with a careful analysis of the balance sheet and the accompanying notes.

Retained Earnings: The Amount Not Paid as Dividends

Retained **earnings** represents net income that the firm has earned but has *not paid* as dividends. Remember that retained earnings is an amount that is accumulated over the entire life of the corporation and does not represent the income or dividends for a specific year. A balance in retained earnings does not indicate that the company had a net income of this amount in the current year; it simply means that over the life of the corporation, the company has retained more net income than it paid out as dividends to stockholders.

It is also important to remember that the balance of the Retained Earnings account does not mean that liquid assets of that amount are available to the stockholders. Corporations decide to retain income because they have needs other than paying dividends to stockholders. The needs may include the purchase of assets, the retirement of debt, or other financial needs. Money spent for those needs usually benefits the stockholders in the long run, but liquid assets equal to the balance of the Retained Earnings account are not necessarily available to stockholders.

IFRS and Stockholders' Equity

The accounting for stockholders' equity under U.S. accounting rules is similar in most respects to the accounting under international accounting rules. However, there is one important difference regarding items that have characteristics of both debt and equity. For example, a convertible bond (discussed in Chapter 10) is in some ways similar to debt, but because it will become stock if converted, it also has the characteristics of equity. Under international accounting rules, an item such as this must be separated into two parts and one portion shown in the Liability category and another in the Stockholders' Equity category. U.S. accounting standards do not require such an item to be recorded as a separate amount. It is recorded as either a liability or an amount in stockholders' equity.

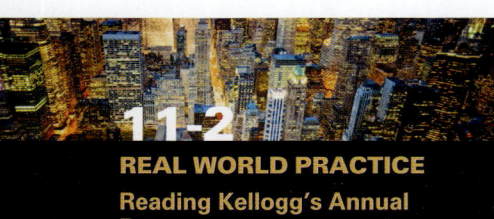

11-2

REAL WORLD PRACTICE
Reading Kellogg's Annual Report

Refer to the **Kellogg's** balance sheet for 2010 reproduced at the end of this book. Determine the number of shares of common stock authorized, issued, and outstanding at the balance sheet date.

Retained earnings
Net income that has been made by the corporation but not paid out as dividends.

Alternate term: Retained income.

LO1 Understand the concept of stockholders' equity and identify the components of the Stockholders' Equity category of the balance sheet and the accounts found in each component.

- Stockholders' equity consists of contributed capital from stockholders and retained earnings from the current and prior periods of operation that have not been paid as dividends.
  - Disclosure for stocks must include the number of shares authorized, issued, and outstanding, along with the par value.

POD REVIEW 11.1

QUESTIONS   Answers to these questions are on the last page of the chapter.

1. A company has 10,000 shares of stock authorized at January 1. During the year, 6,000 shares are issued to the stockholders and the company purchases 500 shares as treasury stock. At December 31, the number of shares outstanding is
   a. 10,000.
   b. 9,500.
   c. 6,000.
   d. 5,500.

2. Over its lifetime, ABC Company has paid out more in dividends than it has had in net income. The balances in the Stockholders' Equity section of the balance sheet would most likely reveal a
   a. negative balance in the Common Stock account.
   b. positive balance in the Common Stock account.
   c. negative balance in the Retained Earnings account.
   d. positive balance in the Retained Earnings account.

What Is Preferred Stock?

OVERVIEW: Preferred stock is flexible, with provisions tailored to a company's needs. Dividends must be distributed to preferred stockholders before common stockholders. Preferred stock may have several features or provisions. It may be cumulative, participating, or callable. All of these features are intended to make the stock more attractive to potential investors.

LO2 Show that you understand the characteristics of common and preferred stock and the differences between the classes of stock.

Many companies have a class of stock called *preferred stock*. One of the advantages of preferred stock is the flexibility it provides because its terms and provisions can be tailored to meet the firm's needs. These terms and provisions are detailed in the stock certificate. Generally, preferred stock offers holders a preference to dividends declared by the corporation. That is, if dividends are declared, the preferred stockholders must receive dividends first, before the holders of common stock.

The dividend rate on preferred stock may be stated two ways:

1. It may be stated as a percentage of the stock's par value. For example, if a stock is presented on the balance sheet as $100 par, 7% preferred stock, its dividend rate is $7 per share ($100 × 7%).
2. The dividend may be stated as a per-share amount. For example, a stock may appear on the balance sheet as $100 par, $7 preferred stock, meaning that the dividend rate is $7 per share.

Investors in common stock should note the dividend requirements of the preferred shareholder. The greater the obligation to the preferred shareholder, the less desirable the common stock becomes.

In the event that a corporation is liquidated, or dissolved, preferred stockholders have a right to the company's assets before the common stockholders. Following are additional terms and features that may be associated with preferred stock:

- *Convertible* Preferred stock may allow stockholders the right to convert the stock into common stock.
- *Redeemable* Preferred stock may allow stockholders to redeem their stock at a specified price.
- *Callable* Preferred stock may be callable at the option of the company. In this case, the company can choose to pay a specified amount to the stockholders in order to redeem or retire the stock.
- *Cumulative* The dividend on preferred stock may be cumulative. When this is the case, dividends that are not paid are considered to be *in arrears*. Before a dividend on common stock can be declared in a subsequent period, the dividends in arrears as well as the current year's dividend must be paid to the preferred stockholders.
- *Participating* When preferred stock carries a participating feature, it allows the preferred stockholders to receive a dividend in excess of the regular rate when the firm has been particularly profitable and declares an abnormally large dividend.

Preferred stock is attractive to many investors because it offers a return in the form of a dividend at a level of risk that is lower than that of most common stocks. Usually, the dividend available on preferred stock is more stable from year to year; as a result, the market price of the stock is also more stable. In fact, when preferred stock carries certain provisions, the stock is very similar to bonds and notes payable. Management must evaluate whether such securities represent debt and should be presented in the Liability category of the balance sheet or whether they represent equity and should be presented in the Equity category. Such a decision involves the concept of *substance over form*. That is, a company must look not only at the legal form but also at the economic substance of the security to decide whether it is debt or equity.

Convertible feature
Allows preferred stock to be exchanged for common stock.

Redeemable feature
Allows stockholders to sell stock back to the company.

Callable feature
Allows the firm to eliminate a class of stock by paying the stockholders a specified amount.

Cumulative feature
The right to dividends in arrears before the current-year dividend is distributed.

Participating feature
Allows preferred stockholders to share on a percentage basis in the distribution of an abnormally large dividend.

POD REVIEW 11.2

LO2 Show that you understand the characteristics of common and preferred stock and the differences between the classes of stock.

- The types of stock issued by a firm are common stock and preferred stock.
  - Preferred stock receives first preference for dividends and generally provides a more stable dividend stream to stockholders than does common stock.
  - Common stockholders have a claim to the residual interest in a company after all debtors' and preferred stockholders' claims are satisfied. Generally, only common stockholders are allowed voting rights.

QUESTIONS   **Answers to these questions are on the last page of the chapter.**

1. A company has issued both common and preferred stock. When a company pays a cash dividend to stockholders,

   a. the preferred stockholders receive a dividend before common stockholders are paid.
   b. the common stockholders receive a dividend before preferred stockholders are paid.
   c. both common and preferred stockholders share equally in any dividend that is paid.
   d. the company is legally obligated to pay a dividend to preferred and common stockholders each year.

2. What does it mean when preferred stock has a cumulative feature?

   a. A dividend must be paid to the preferred stockholders each year.
   b. A dividend cannot be paid to the common stockholders.
   c. When dividends are not paid in one period, those dividends must be paid in a subsequent period before common stockholders receive a dividend.
   d. The preferred stockholders can sue the company if a dividend is not paid.

Issuance of Stock

LO3 Determine the financial statement impact when stock is issued for cash or for other consideration.

OVERVIEW: Stock may be issued for cash or for noncash assets. When stock is issued for cash, the amount of its par value should be reported in the stock account and the amount in excess of par should be reported in the Paid-In Capital account; the total amount increases cash. When stock is exchanged for noncash items, the transaction must be recorded at the fair market value of the stock or the assets received, whichever is most readily determined.

Stock Issued for Cash

Stock may be issued in several different ways. It may be issued for cash or for noncash assets. When stock is issued for cash, the amount of its par value should be reported in the Stock account and the amount in excess of par should be reported in the Additional Paid-In Capital account.

Example 11-1 Recording Stock Issued for Cash

Assume that on July 1, a firm issued 1,000 shares of $10 par common stock for $15 per share. The effect of the stock issuance could be identified and analyzed as follows:

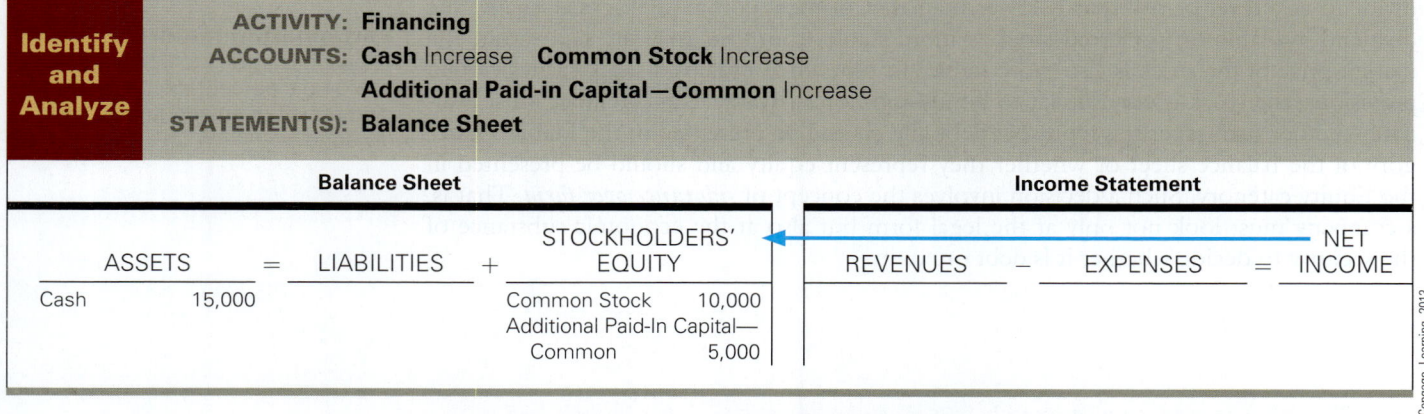

Identify and Analyze

ACTIVITY: Financing
ACCOUNTS: **Cash** Increase   **Common Stock** Increase
Additional Paid-in Capital—Common Increase
STATEMENT(S): Balance Sheet

Balance Sheet				Income Statement			
ASSETS	=	LIABILITIES	+	STOCKHOLDERS' EQUITY	REVENUES	− EXPENSES	= NET INCOME
Cash 15,000				Common Stock 10,000 Additional Paid-In Capital— Common 5,000			

As noted earlier, the Common Stock account and the Additional Paid-In Capital account are both presented in the Stockholders' Equity category of the balance sheet and represent the contributed capital component of the corporation.

If no-par stock is issued, the corporation does not distinguish between common stock and additional paid-in capital. If the firm in Example 11-1 had issued no-par stock on July 1 for $15 per share, the entire amount of $15,000 would have been presented in the Common Stock account.

Stock Issued for Noncash Consideration

Occasionally, stock is issued in return for something other than cash. For example, a corporation may issue stock to obtain land or buildings. When such a transaction occurs, the company faces the difficult task of deciding what value to place on the transaction. This is especially difficult when the market values of the elements of the transaction are not known with complete certainty. According to the general guideline, the transaction should be reported at fair market value. Market value may be indicated by the value of the consideration given (stock) or the value of the consideration received (property), whichever can be most readily determined.

Example 11-2 Recording Stock for Noncash Consideration

Assume that on July 1, a firm issued 500 shares of $10 par preferred stock to acquire a building. The stock is not widely traded, and the current market value of the stock is not evident. The building has recently been appraised by an independent firm as having a market value of $12,000. In this case, the effect of the issuance of the stock could be identified and analyzed as follows:

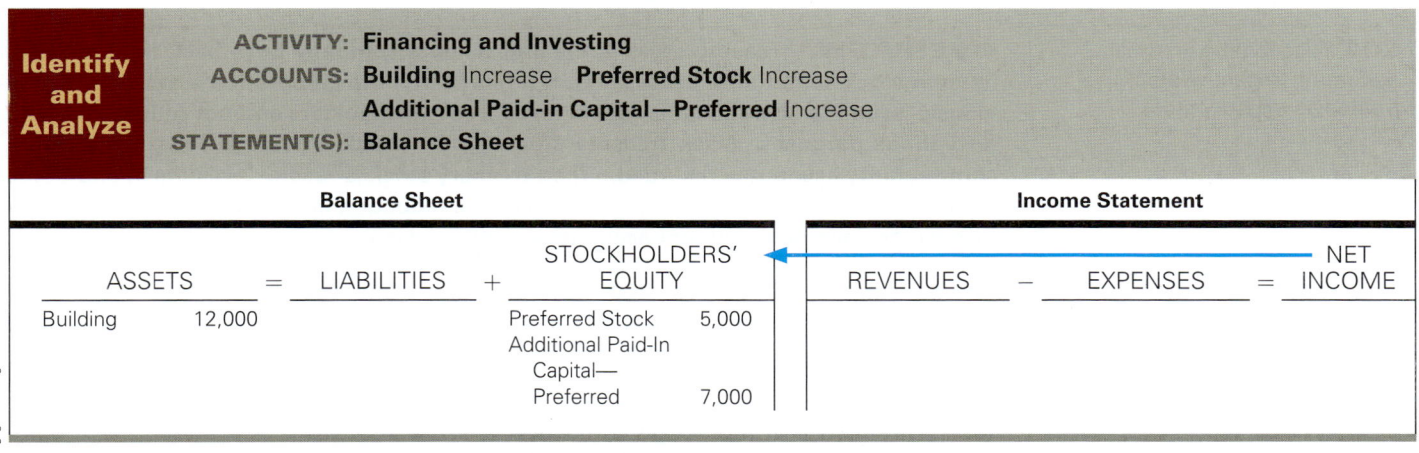

In other situations, the market value of the stock might be more readily determined and should be used as the best measure of the value of the transaction. Market value may be represented by the current stock market quotation or by a recent cash sale of the stock. The company should attempt to develop the best estimate of the market value of the noncash transaction and should neither intentionally overstate nor intentionally understate the assets received by the issuance of stock.

LO3 Determine the financial statement impact when stock is issued for cash or for other consideration.

- When stock is issued for cash or other consideration, the number of outstanding shares is increased and the par value of stock is recorded along with any amount in excess of par being recorded to the Additional Paid-In Capital account.

  - When stock is sold for cash, the asset Cash is increased. When issued for noncash consideration, other asset accounts are increased.

POD REVIEW 11.3

QUESTIONS   **Answers to these questions are on the last page of the chapter.**

1. When a company has common stock with a $10 per-share par value and the stock is issued for $15 per share,

   a. the $5 per share should be considered a gain on the stock and the amount should be shown on the income statement.

   b. the company should show $15 per share in the Common Stock account in the Stockholders' Equity section of the balance sheet.

   c. the company should show $5 per share as a debit balance in the Additional Paid-In Capital portion of stockholders' equity.

   d. the company should show $5 per share as a credit balance in the Additional Paid-In Capital portion of stockholders' equity.

2. A company has issued 1,000 shares of $10 par common stock in exchange for a machine. The company believes the machine has a fair market value of $12,000. What amount should be recorded?

   a. The company should record the machine at $12,000 if the fair market value of the stock cannot be determined.

   b. The company should record the machine at $10,000.

   c. The company should record a credit to the Common Stock account for $12,000.

   d. The company should record a debit to Additional Paid-In Capital for $2,000.

What Is Treasury Stock?

LO4 Describe the financial statement impact of stock treated as treasury stock.

OVERVIEW: Treasury stock is created when a company buys back (repurchases) its own stock sometime after issuing it. It represents the corporation's own stock, previously issued to shareholders, repurchased from stockholders and not retired, but held for various purposes. When treasury stock is purchased, a debit to Treasury Stock, a contra-equity account is recorded. When treasury stock is resold, it results in additional paid-in capital if sold for more than its cost or a reduction in equity if sold for less than its cost. No income statement accounts are affected in treasury stock transactions.

Treasury stock
Stock issued by the firm and then repurchased but not retired.

The Stockholders' Equity category of Southwest Airlines' balance sheet in the chapter opener includes **treasury stock** in the amount of $891 million. The Treasury Stock account is created when a corporation buys its own stock sometime after issuing it. For an amount to be treated as treasury stock:

1. It must be the corporation's own stock.
2. It must have been issued to the stockholders at some point.
3. It must have been repurchased from the stockholders.
4. It must not be retired, but must be held for some purpose. Treasury stock is not considered outstanding stock and does not have voting rights.

A corporation might repurchase stock as treasury stock for several reasons. The most common reason is to have stock available to distribute to employees for bonuses or to make available as part of an employee benefit plan. Firms also might buy treasury stock to maintain a favorable market price for the stock or to improve the appearance of the firm's financial ratios. More recently, firms have purchased their stock to maintain control of the ownership and to prevent unwanted takeover or buyout attempts. Of course, the lower the stock price, the more likely a company is to buy back its own stock and wait for the shares to rise in value before reissuing them.

The two methods to account for treasury stock transactions are the cost method and the par value method. We will present the more commonly used cost method.

Example 11-3 Recording the Purchase of Treasury Stock

Assume that the Stockholders' Equity section of Rezin Company's balance sheet on December 31, 2012, appears as follows:

Common stock, $10 par value,	
1,000 shares issued and outstanding	$10,000
Additional paid-in capital—Common	12,000
Retained earnings	15,000
Total stockholders' equity	$37,000

Assume that on February 1, 2013, Rezin buys 100 of its shares as treasury stock at $25 per share. The effect of the purchase of the treasury stock is as follows:

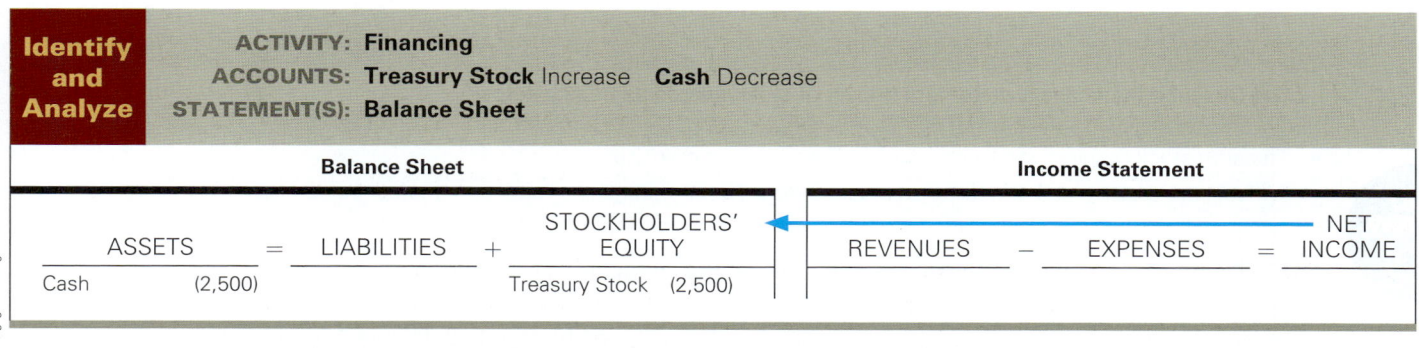

Identify and Analyze

ACTIVITY: Financing
ACCOUNTS: Treasury Stock Increase **Cash** Decrease
STATEMENT(S): Balance Sheet

Balance Sheet			Income Statement		
ASSETS	= LIABILITIES +	STOCKHOLDERS' EQUITY	REVENUES	− EXPENSES	= NET INCOME
Cash (2,500)		Treasury Stock (2,500)			

The purchase of treasury stock does not directly affect the Common Stock account. The Treasury Stock account is considered a contra account and is subtracted from the total of contributed capital and retained earnings in the Stockholders' Equity section. Treasury Stock is *not* an asset account. When a company buys its own stock, it is contracting its size and reducing the equity of stockholders. Therefore, Treasury Stock is a *contra-equity* account, not an asset.

The Stockholders' Equity section of Rezin's balance sheet on February 1, 2013, after the purchase of the treasury stock, appears as follows:

Common stock, $10 par value,	
1,000 shares issued, 900 outstanding	$10,000
Additional paid-in capital—Common	12,000
Retained earnings	15,000
Total contributed capital and retained earnings	$37,000
Less: Treasury stock, 100 shares at cost	2,500
Total stockholders' equity	$34,500

Corporations may choose to reissue stock to investors after it has been held as treasury stock. When treasury stock is resold for more than it cost, the difference between the sales price and the cost appears in the Additional Paid-In Capital—Treasury Stock account. For example, if Rezin resold 100 shares of treasury stock on May 1, 2013, for $30 per share, the Treasury Stock account would be reduced by $2,500 (100 shares times $25 per share) and the Additional Paid-In Capital—Treasury Stock account would be increased by $500 (100 shares times the difference between the purchase price of $25 and the reissue price of $30).

When treasury stock is resold for an amount less than its cost, the difference between the sales price and the cost is deducted from the Additional Paid-In Capital—Treasury Stock account. If that account does not exist, the difference should be deducted from the Retained Earnings account. For example, assume that Rezin Company had resold 100 shares of treasury stock on May 1, 2013, for $20 per share instead of $30 as in the previous example. In this example, Rezin has had no other treasury stock transactions; therefore, no balance existed in the Additional Paid-In Capital—Treasury Stock account. Rezin would then reduce the Treasury Stock account by $2,500 (100 shares times $25 per share) and would reduce Retained Earnings by $500 (100 shares times the difference between the purchase price of $25 and the reissue price of $20 per share). Thus, the Additional Paid-In Capital—Treasury Stock account may have a positive balance, but entries that result in a negative balance in the account should not be made.

Note that **income statement accounts are never involved in treasury stock transactions**. Regardless of whether treasury stock is reissued for more or less than its cost, the effect is reflected in the Stockholders' Equity accounts. It is simply not possible for a firm to engage in transactions involving its own stock and have the result affect the performance of the firm as reflected on the income statement.

POD REVIEW 11.4

LO4 Describe the financial statement impact of stock treated as treasury stock.

- Treasury stock results when a corporation buys back its own stock.
  - Treasury stock is accounted for as a contra-equity account and is a reduction of stockholders' equity.

QUESTIONS   **Answers to these questions are on the last page of the chapter.**

1. The Treasury Stock account should be considered
   a. an asset account.
   b. an income statement account.
   c. an increase in the Stockholders' Equity portion of the balance sheet.
   d. a deduction in the Stockholders' Equity portion of the balance sheet.

2. A company issued 5,000 shares of $5 par common stock for $20 per share. The company purchased 2,000 shares as treasury stock at $22 per share. Later, the company reissued 500 shares of the treasury stock at $23 per share. Which of the following is true?
   a. The company has a gain of $500 that should appear on the income statement.
   b. The company has a gain of $1,500 that should appear on the income statement.
   c. The Treasury Stock account should have a balance of $33,000.
   d. The Treasury Stock account should have a balance of $32,500.

Retirement of Stock

Retirement of stock
When the stock is repurchased with no intention of reissuing at a later date.

Retirement of stock occurs when a corporation buys back stock after it has been issued to investors and does not intend to reissue the stock. Retirement often occurs because the corporation wants to eliminate a particular class of stock or a particular group of stockholders. When stock is repurchased and retired, the balances of the Stock account and the Paid-In Capital account that were created when the stock was issued must be eliminated. When the original issue price is higher than the repurchase price of the stock, the difference is reflected in the Paid-In Capital from Stock Retirement account. When the repurchase price of the stock is more than the original issue price, the difference reduces the Retained Earnings account. The general principle for retirement of stock is the same as for treasury stock transactions. No income statement accounts are affected by the retirement. The effect is reflected in the Cash account and the Stockholders' Equity accounts.

Dividends: Distribution of Income to Shareholders

OVERVIEW: Cash dividends may be declared only if a company has sufficient cash available and adequate retained earnings. Cash dividends are not an expense on the income statement. They are a liability at the date of declaration. When more than one class of stock is outstanding, cash dividends must be allocated between them based on the provisions of the preferred stock. Stock dividends occur when a company issues its own stock. The accounting for stock dividends depends on the size of the dividend. A stock split is similar to a stock dividend but does not require an accounting entry.

LO5 Compute the amount of cash dividends when a firm has issued both preferred and common stock.

Cash Dividends

Corporations may declare and issue several different types of dividends, the most common of which is a cash dividend to stockholders. Cash dividends may be declared quarterly, annually, or at other intervals. Normally, cash dividends are declared on one date, referred to as the *date of declaration*, and are paid out on a later date, referred to as the *payment date*. The dividend is paid to the stockholders who own the stock as of a particular date, the *date of record*.

Generally, two requirements must be met before the board of directors can declare a cash dividend. First, sufficient cash must be available by the payment date to pay to the stockholders. Second, the Retained Earnings account must have a sufficient positive balance. Dividends reduce the balance of the account; therefore, Retained Earnings must have a balance before the dividend declaration. Most firms have an established policy concerning the portion of income that will be declared as dividends. The **dividend payout ratio** is calculated as the annual dividend amount divided by the annual net income. The dividend payout ratio for many firms is 50% or 60% and seldom exceeds 70%. Typically, utilities pay a high proportion of their earnings as dividends. In contrast, fast-growing companies in technology often pay nothing to stockholders. Some investors want and need the current income of a high-dividend payout, but others would rather not receive dividend income and prefer to gamble that the stock price will appreciate.

Dividend payout ratio
The annual dividend amount divided by the annual net income.

Cash dividends become a liability on the date they are declared. An accounting entry should be recorded on that date to acknowledge the liability and reduce the balance of the Retained Earnings account.

Example 11-4 Recording the Declaration of a Dividend

Assume that on July 1, the board of directors of Grant Company declared a cash dividend of $7,000 to be paid on September 1. The effect of the declaration of the dividend is as follows:

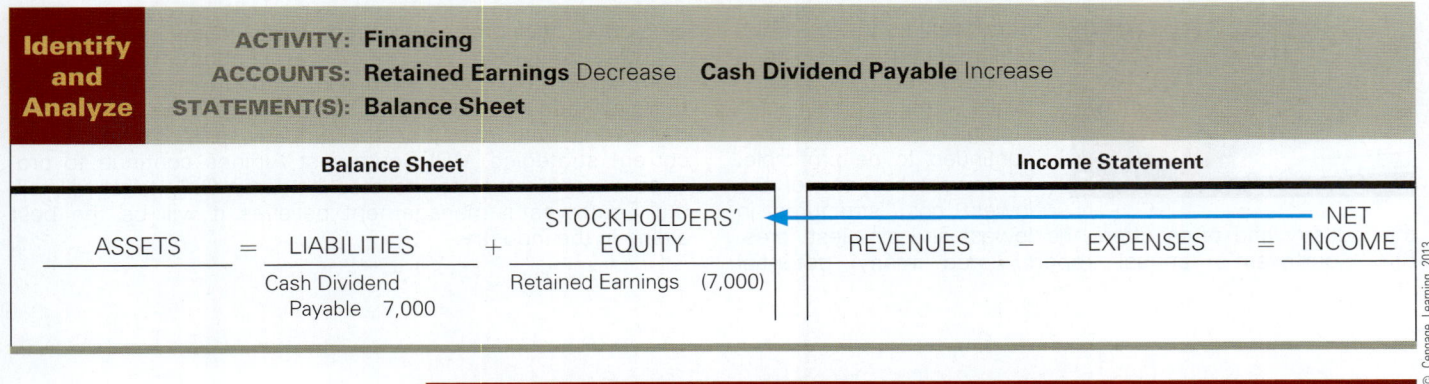

Identify and Analyze

ACTIVITY: Financing
ACCOUNTS: Retained Earnings Decrease   Cash Dividend Payable Increase
STATEMENT(S): Balance Sheet

Balance Sheet			Income Statement		
ASSETS	= LIABILITIES	+ STOCKHOLDERS' EQUITY	REVENUES	− EXPENSES	= NET INCOME
	Cash Dividend Payable 7,000	Retained Earnings (7,000)			

© Cengage Learning 2013

The Cash Dividend Payable account is a liability and is normally shown in the Current Liabilities section of the balance sheet.

The important point to remember is that dividends reduce the amount of retained earnings *when declared*. When dividends are paid, the company reduces the liability to stockholders reflected in the Cash Dividend Payable account.

Cash Dividends for Preferred and Common Stock

When cash dividends involving more than one class of stock are declared, the corporation must determine the proper amount to allocate to each class of stock. As indicated earlier, the amount of dividends to which preferred stockholders have rights depends on the terms and provisions of the preferred stock. The proper allocation of cash dividends is illustrated with an example of a firm that has two classes of stock: preferred and common.

Example 11-5 Computing Dividend Payments for Noncumulative Preferred Stock

Assume that on December 31, 2012, Stricker Company has outstanding 10,000 shares of $10 par, 8% preferred stock and 40,000 shares of $5 par common stock. Stricker was unable to declare a dividend in 2010 or 2011 but wants to declare a $70,000 dividend for 2012. The dividend is to be allocated to preferred and common stockholders in accordance with the terms of the stock agreements.

If the terms of the stock agreement indicate that the preferred stock is not cumulative, the preferred stockholders do not have a right to dividends in arrears. The dividends that were not declared in 2010 and 2011 are simply lost and do not affect the distribution of the dividend in 2012. Therefore, the cash dividend declared in 2012 is allocated between preferred and common stockholders as follows:

	To Preferred	To Common
Step 1: Distribute current-year dividend to preferred (10,000 shares × $10 par × 8% × 1 year)	$8,000	
Step 2: Distribute remaining dividend to common ($70,000 − $8,000)		$62,000
Total allocated	$8,000	$62,000
Dividend per share:		
Preferred: $8,000/10,000 shares	$ 0.80	
Common: $62,000/40,000 shares		$ 1.55

© Cengage Learning 2013

Example 11-6 Computing Dividend Payments for Cumulative Preferred Stock

If the terms of the stock agreement in Example 11-5 indicate that the preferred stock is cumulative, the preferred stockholders have a right to dividends in arrears before the current year's dividend is distributed. Therefore, Stricker performs the following steps:

	To Preferred	To Common
Step 1: Distribute dividends in arrears to preferred (10,000 shares × $10 par × 8% × 2 years)	$16,000	
Step 2: Distribute current-year dividend to preferred (10,000 shares × $10 par × 8% × 1 year)	8,000	
Step 3: Distribute remainder to common ($70,000 − $24,000)		$46,000
Total allocated	$24,000	$46,000
Dividend per share:		
Preferred: $24,000/10,000 shares	$ 2.40	
Common: $46,000/40,000 shares		$ 1.15

© Cengage Learning 2013

LO5 Compute the amount of cash dividends when a firm has issued both preferred and common stock.

- The amount of a preferred stock dividend depends on the terms of the stock agreement: cumulative, noncumulative, or cumulative and participating.

POD REVIEW 11.5

QUESTIONS Answers to these questions are on the last page of the chapter.

1. When are cash dividends a reduction from the Retained Earnings account?
   a. at the time the dividend is declared
   b. at the time the dividend is paid
   c. only if they are dividends on common stock
   d. only if they are dividends on preferred stock

2. At December 31, 2012, Rhodes Company has 10,000 shares of $10 par, 6% cumulative preferred stock outstanding and 4,000 shares of $5 par common stock

outstanding. The company did not pay a dividend in 2010 or 2011. If the company pays a dividend in 2012, how much must be paid for the common stockholders to receive a dividend?

   a. $6,000
   b. $12,000
   c. $18,000
   d. $24,000

© Cengage Learning 2013

Stock Dividends

Cash dividends are the most popular and widely used form of dividend, but at times, corporations may use stock dividends instead of or in addition to cash dividends. A **stock dividend** occurs when a corporation declares and issues additional shares of its own stock to existing stockholders. Firms use stock dividends for several reasons.

LO6 Show that you understand the difference between cash and stock dividends and the effect of stock dividends.

1. Stock dividends do not require the use of cash. A corporation may not have sufficient cash available to declare a cash dividend.
2. Stock dividends reduce the market price of the stock. The lower price may make the stock more attractive to a wider range of investors.
3. Stock dividends do not represent taxable income to recipients and may be attractive to some wealthy investors.

Stock dividend
The issuance of additional shares of stock to existing stockholders.

Similar to cash dividends, stock dividends are normally declared by the board of directors on a specific date and the stock is distributed to the stockholders at a later date. The corporation recognizes the stock dividend on the date of declaration.

Example 11-7 Recording a Small Stock Dividend

Assume that Shah Company's Stockholders' Equity category of the balance sheet appears as follows as of January 1, 2012:

Common stock, $10 par,	
5,000 shares issued and outstanding	$ 50,000
Additional paid-in capital—Common	30,000
Retained earnings	70,000
Total stockholders' equity	$150,000

Assume that on January 2, 2012, Shah declares a 10% stock dividend to common stockholders to be distributed on April 1, 2012. Small stock dividends (usually those of 20% to 25%) normally are recorded at the *market value* of the stock as of the date of declaration. Assume that Shah's common stock is selling at $40 per share on that date. Therefore, the total market value of the stock dividend is $20,000 (10% of 5,000 shares outstanding, or 500 shares, times $40 per share). Shah records the transaction on the date of declaration and the effect of the declaration is as follows:

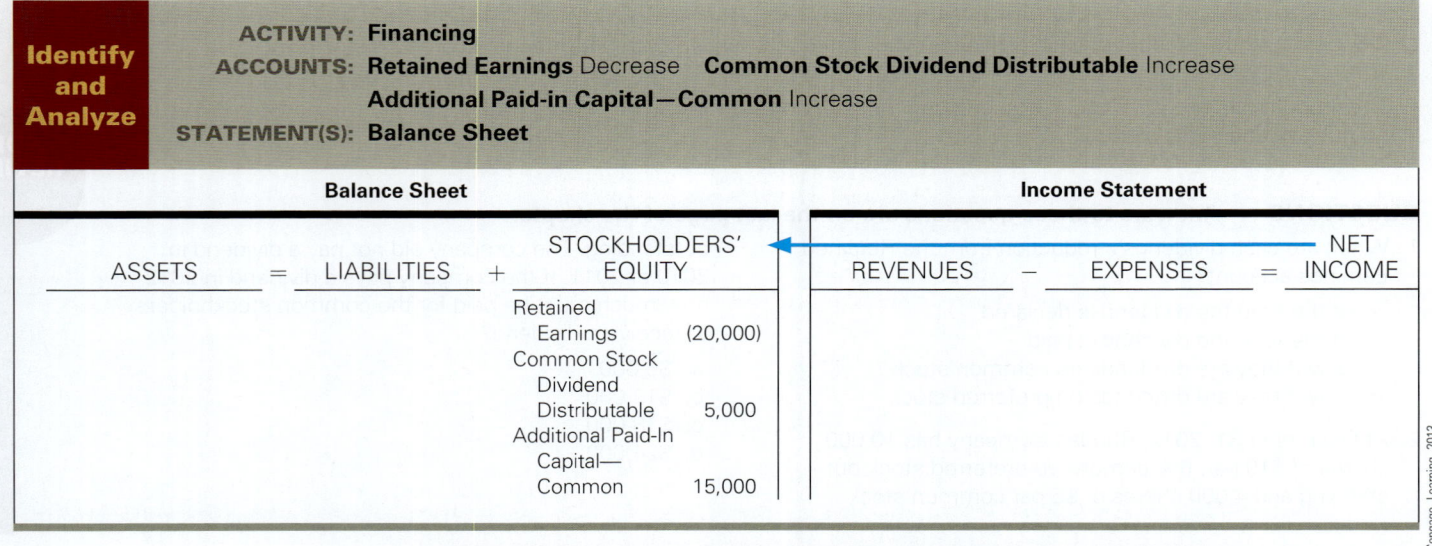

Identify and Analyze

ACTIVITY: Financing

ACCOUNTS: Retained Earnings Decrease   **Common Stock Dividend Distributable** Increase
                 Additional Paid-in Capital—Common Increase

STATEMENT(S): Balance Sheet

Balance Sheet					Income Statement				
ASSETS	=	LIABILITIES	+	STOCKHOLDERS' EQUITY	REVENUES	−	EXPENSES	=	NET INCOME
				Retained Earnings (20,000)					
				Common Stock Dividend Distributable 5,000					
				Additional Paid-In Capital—Common 15,000					

© Cengage Learning 2013

The Common Stock Dividend Distributable account represents shares of stock to be issued; it is not a liability account because no cash or assets are to be distributed to the stockholders. Thus, it should be treated as an account in the Stockholders' Equity section of the balance sheet and is a part of the contributed capital component of equity.

Note that the declaration of a stock dividend does not affect the total stockholders' equity of the corporation, although the retained earnings are reduced. That is, the Stockholders' Equity section of Shah's balance sheet on January 2, 2012, is as follows after the declaration of the dividend:

Common stock, $10 par, 5,000 shares issued and	
outstanding	$ 50,000
Common stock dividend distributable, 500 shares	5,000
Additional paid-in capital—Common	45,000
Retained earnings	50,000
Total stockholders' equity	$150,000

The account balances are different, but total stockholders' equity is $150,000 both before and after the declaration of the stock dividend. In effect, retained earnings has been capitalized (transferred permanently to the contributed capital accounts). When a corporation actually issues a stock dividend, an amount from the Stock Dividend Distributable account must be transferred to the appropriate stock account.

Example 11-7 has illustrated the general rule that stock dividends should be reported at fair market value. That is, in the transaction to reflect the stock dividend, retained earnings is decreased in the amount of the fair market value per share of the stock times the number of shares to be distributed. When a large stock dividend is declared, however, accountants do not follow the general rule we have illustrated. A large stock dividend is a stock dividend of more than 20 to 25% of the number of shares of stock outstanding. In that case, the stock dividend is reported at *par value* rather than at fair market value.

That is, Retained Earnings is decreased in the amount of the par value per share times the number of shares to be distributed.

Example 11-8 Recording the Declaration of a Large Stock Dividend

Refer to the Shah Company in Example 11-7. Assume that instead of a 10% dividend, on January 2, 2012, Shah declares a 100% stock dividend to be distributed on April 1, 2012. The stock dividend results in 5,000 additional shares being issued and certainly meets the definition of a large stock dividend. The effect of the declaration of a large stock dividend can be identified and analyzed as follows:

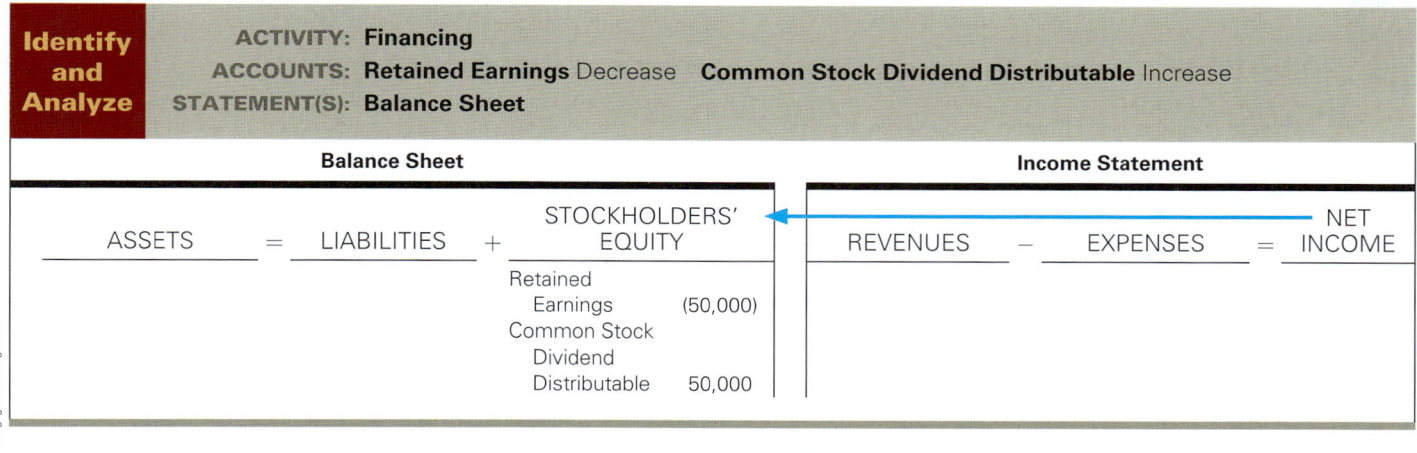

The effect when the stock dividend is actually distributed is as follows:

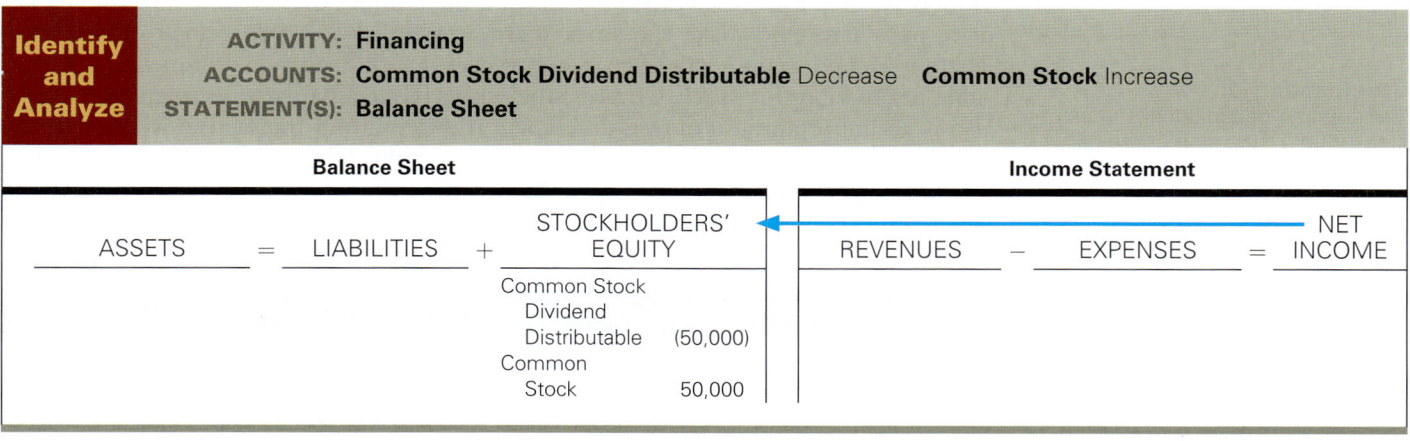

The Stockholders' Equity category of Shah's balance sheet as of April 1 after the stock dividend is as follows:

Common stock, $10 par,	
10,000 shares issued and outstanding	$100,000
Additional paid-in capital—Common	30,000
Retained earnings	20,000
Total stockholders' equity	$150,000

Again, note that the stock dividend has not affected total stockholders' equity. Shah has $150,000 of stockholders' equity both before and after the stock dividend. The difference between large and small stock dividends is the amount transferred from retained earnings to the Contributed Capital portion of equity.

LO6 Show that you understand the difference between cash and stock dividends and the effect of stock dividends.

- Stock dividends are given in lieu of cash dividends. Stockholders receive shares of stock, which do not require a current use of cash resources by the corporation.
  - Stock dividends do not affect total stockholders' equity. They reduce retained earnings and increase the amount of common stock and additional paid-in capital.

POD REVIEW 11.6

QUESTIONS   **Answers to these questions are on the last page of the chapter.**

1. What is the effect on the financial statements when a dividend in the form of stock is declared and issued?

   a. Retained earnings is not affected.
   b. Retained earnings is decreased, and total stockholders' equity is decreased.
   c. Retained earnings is decreased, and total stockholders' equity is not affected.
   d. Retained earnings is not decreased, but total stockholders' equity does decrease.

2. What is the effect of a stock dividend declared and issued versus a cash dividend declared and paid?

   a. A stock dividend does not decrease the company's total assets.
   b. A cash dividend does not decrease the company's total assets.
   c. A stock dividend does not affect retained earnings.
   d. A cash dividend does not affect retained earnings.

Stock Splits

LO7 Determine the difference between stock dividends and stock splits.

Stock split
The creation of additional shares of stock with a reduction of the par value of the stock.

A **stock split** is similar to a stock dividend in that it results in additional shares of stock outstanding and is nontaxable. In fact, firms may use a stock split for nearly the same reasons as a stock dividend: to increase the number of shares, reduce the market price per share, and make the stock more accessible to a wider range of investors. There is an important legal difference, however. Stock dividends do not affect the par value per share of the stock, whereas stock splits reduce the par value per share. There also is an important accounting difference. An accounting transaction is *not recorded* when a corporation declares and executes a stock split. None of the Stockholders' Equity accounts are affected by the split. Rather, the note information accompanying the balance sheet must disclose the additional shares and the reduction of the par value per share.

Example 11-9 Reporting a Stock Split

Refer to the Shah Company in Examples 11-7 and 11-8. Assume that on January 2, 2012, Shah issued a 2-for-1 stock split instead of a stock dividend. The split results in an additional 5,000 shares of stock outstanding but is not recorded in a formal accounting transaction. Therefore, the Stockholders' Equity section of Shah Company immediately after the stock split on January 2, 2012, is as follows:

(Continued)

Common stock, $5 par,	
10,000 shares issued and outstanding	$ 50,000
Additional paid-in capital—Common	30,000
Retained earnings	70,000
Total stockholders' equity	$150,000

© Cengage Learning 2013

Note in Example 11-9 that the par value per share has been reduced from $10 to $5 per share of stock as a result of the split. Like a stock dividend, the split does not affect total stockholders' equity because no assets have been transferred. Therefore, the split simply results in more shares of stock with claims to the same net assets of the firm.

LO7 Determine the difference between stock dividends and stock splits.

- Both stock splits and stock dividends increase the number of shares of stock outstanding although they are fundamentally different transactions.
  - Stock splits do not require an accounting transaction to be recorded, do not reduce the par value of the stock, and have no effect on retained earnings or additional paid-in capital.

POD REVIEW 11.7

QUESTIONS Answers to these questions are on the last page of the chapter.

1. What is the effect of a stock dividend declared and issued versus a stock split issued?
   a. A stock split does not affect the number of shares of stock outstanding.
   b. A stock dividend does not affect the number of shares of stock outstanding.
   c. A stock dividend does not affect retained earnings.
   d. A stock split does not affect retained earnings.

2. When a stock split is issued to the stockholders,
   a. the market price per share of the stock will likely decline.
   b. the market price per share of the stock will not likely decline.
   c. the company's total stockholders' equity will decrease.
   d. the company's total stockholders' equity will increase.

© Cengage Learning 2013

Statement of Stockholders' Equity

OVERVIEW: The purpose of the statement of stockholders' equity is to explain the difference between the beginning and ending balances of each account in the Stockholders' Equity section of the balance sheet. Comprehensive income is the net assets resulting from all transactions except for investments by owners and distributions to owners during a time period.

LO8 Show that you understand the statement of stockholders' equity and comprehensive income.

In addition to a balance sheet, an income statement, and a cash flow statement, many annual reports contain a **statement of stockholders' equity**. This statement explains the reasons for the difference between the beginning and ending balance of each account in the Stockholders' Equity category of the balance sheet. Of course, if the only changes are the result of income and dividends, a statement of retained earnings is sufficient. When other changes have occurred in Stockholders' Equity accounts, this more complete statement is necessary.

The statement of stockholders' equity of Fun Fitness, Inc., is presented in Exhibit 11-3 for the year 2012. The statement starts with the beginning balances of each of the accounts as of December 31, 2012. Fun Fitness's stockholders' equity is presented in four categories (the columns on the statement) as of December 31, 2012, as follows (in millions):

Statement of stockholders' equity
Reflects the differences between beginning and ending balances for all accounts in the Stockholders' Equity category of the balance sheet.

Number of shares	1,000,000
Common stock	$50.0
Paid-in capital	$350.0
Retained earnings	$400.0

The statement of stockholders' equity indicates the items or events that affected stockholders' equity during 2012. The items or events were as follows:

Item or Event	Effect on Stockholders' Equity
Net earnings ⟶	Increased retained earnings by $64.0 million
Dividends ⟶	Decreased retained earnings by $25.0 million
Shares issued ⟶	Increased common stock by $5.0 million and Increased paid-in capital by $39.0 million

The last line of the statement of stockholders' equity indicates the ending balances of the stockholders' equity accounts as of the balance sheet date, December 31, 2012. Note that each of the stockholders' equity accounts increased during 2012. The statement of stockholders' equity is useful in explaining the reasons for the changes that occurred.

EXHIBIT 11-3 Fun Fitness's Statement of Stockholders' Equity, 2012

Fun Fitness, Inc.
Statement of Stockholders' Equity
For the Year Ended December 31, 2012

(dollar amounts in millions)

Stockholders' Equity	Common Stock		Paid-In Capital	Retained Earnings
	Shares	Amount		
Balance, December 31, 2011	1,000,000	$50.0	$350.0	$400.0
Net earnings				64.0
Cash dividend declared				(25.0)
Issuance of stock	100,000	5.0	39.0	
Balance, December 31, 2012	1,100,000	$55.0	$389.0	$439.0

What Is Comprehensive Income?

There has always been some question about which items or transactions should be shown on the income statement and included in the calculation of net income. Generally, the accounting rule-making bodies have held that the income statement should reflect an *all-inclusive* approach. That is, all events and transactions that affect income should be shown on the income statement. This approach prevents manipulation of the income figure by those who would like to show "good news" on the income statement and "bad news" directly on the retained earnings statement or the statement of stockholders' equity. The result of the all-inclusive approach is that the income statement includes items that are not necessarily under management's control, such as losses from natural disasters, meaning that the income statement may not be a true reflection of a company's future potential.

The FASB has accepted certain exceptions to the all-inclusive approach and has allowed items to be recorded directly to the Stockholders' Equity category. This text discussed one such item: unrealized gains and losses on investment securities. Exhibit 11-4 presents several additional items that are beyond the scope of this text. Items such as these have been excluded from the income statement for various reasons. Quite often, the justification is a concern for the volatility of the net income number.

A new term has been coined to incorporate the "income-type" items that escape the income statement. **Comprehensive income** is the net assets increase resulting from all transactions during a time period (except for investments by owners and distributions to owners). Exhibit 11-4 presents the statement of comprehensive income and its relationship to the traditional income statement. It illustrates that comprehensive income encompasses all of the revenues and expenses that are presented on the income

Comprehensive income
The total change in net assets from all sources except investments by or distributions to the owners.

EXHIBIT 11-4 The Relationship between the Income Statement and the Statement of Comprehensive Income

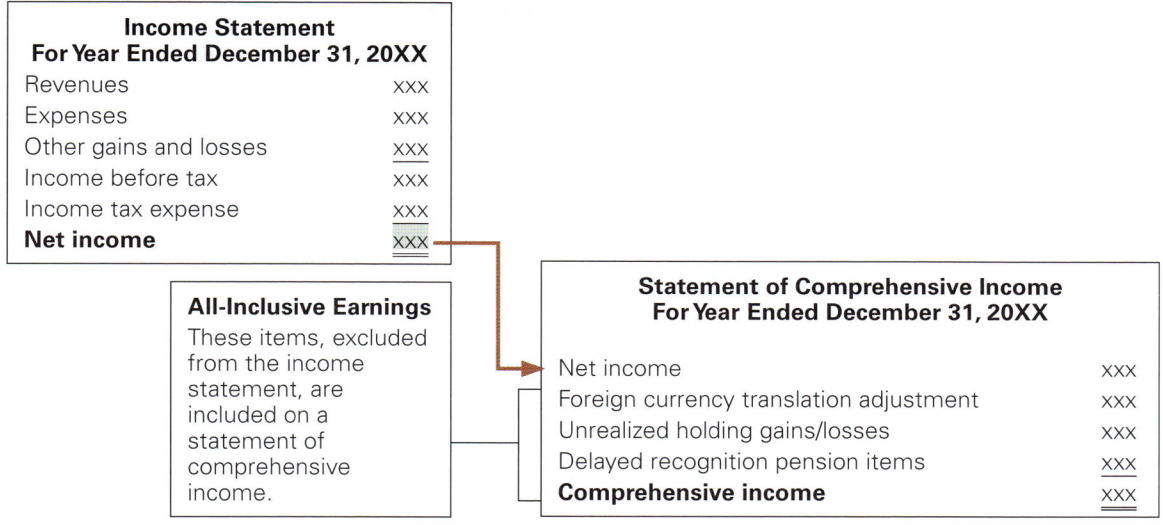

statement to calculate net income and includes items that are not presented on the income statement but that affect total stockholders' equity.[1] The comprehensive income measure is truly all-inclusive because it includes transactions such as unrealized gains that affect stockholders' equity. Firms are required to disclose comprehensive income because it provides a more complete measure of performance.

Until recently, U.S. companies had a great deal of flexibility in how they reported comprehensive income amounts in their financial statements. However, the FASB has indicated that comprehensive income must be presented in conjunction with a company's income statement. This can be done in two ways. First, companies can show the comprehensive income items at the bottom of the income statement—a so-called one-statement approach. Second, companies can follow a two-statement approach as indicated in Exhibit 11-4. Under this approach, a separate statement titled the Statement of Comprehensive Income must be presented. Either way, comprehensive income amounts will become increasingly important to investors as a measure of a company's profitability.

LOOKING AHEAD

LO8 Show that you understand the statement of stockholders' equity and comprehensive income.

- The statement of stockholders' equity shows how all of the equity accounts changed for a particular accounting period or specific periods.
- Comprehensive income is based on the notion that the income statement be inclusive of all items affecting the wealth of an entity. The calculation of comprehensive income takes into account the increase in net assets during a time period.

POD REVIEW 11.8

QUESTIONS   **Answers to these questions are on the last page of the chapter.**

1. Which of the following would be considered part of other comprehensive income?

   a. foreign currency translation adjustment items
   b. unrealized holding gains/losses on certain types of securities
   c. delayed recognition pension items
   d. all of the above

2. Which of the following would be included as an element of other comprehensive income?

   a. foreign currency translation adjustment items
   b. amounts resulting from treasury stock transactions
   c. issuance of stock for more than par value
   d. issuance of stock dividends or stock splits

---

[1] The format of Exhibit 11-4 is suggested by the FASB. The FASB also allows other possible formats of the statement of comprehensive income.

What Analyzing Stockholders' Equity Reveals About a Firm's Value

LO9 Understand how investors use ratios to evaluate stockholders' equity.

OVERVIEW: Book value per share represents the rights of each share of stock to the net assets of the company. It is calculated as the total stockholders' equity divided by the number of shares of common stock outstanding. If preferred stock is present, stockholders' equity must be adjusted to reflect its liquidation value. The stock's market value represents the price at which the stock is currently selling.

Book Value per Share

Book value per share
Total stockholders' equity divided by the number of shares of common stock outstanding.

Users of financial statements are often interested in computing the value of a corporation's stock. This is a difficult task because *value* is not a well-defined term and means different things to different users. One measure of value is the book value of the stock. **Book value per share** of common stock represents the rights that each share of common stock has to the net assets of the corporation. The term *net assets* refers to the total assets of the firm minus total liabilities. In other words, net assets equal the total stockholders' equity of the corporation. Therefore, when only common stock is present, book value per share is measured as follows:

$$\text{Book Value per Share} = \frac{\text{Total Stockholders' Equity}}{\text{Numbers of Shares of Stock Outstanding}}$$

The book value per share is the amount per share of net assets to which the company's common stockholders have the rights. It does not indicate the market value of the common stock. That is, book value per share does not indicate the price that should be paid by those who want to buy or sell the stock on the stock exchange. Book value also is an incomplete measure of value because the corporation's net assets are normally measured on the balance sheet at the original cost, not at the current value of the assets.

For more information on how investors use book value per share and what this measure means, see the Ratio Decision Model that follows.

USING THE RATIO DECISION MODEL

Analyzing Book Value per Share

Use the following Ratio Decision Model to evaluate the book value per common share of **Kellogg's** or any other public company.

1. Formulate the Question

Investors realize that several measures of the value of a company impact the stock price of a company. Investors in common stock also realize that they have a right to the company's assets only after the rights of creditors and preferred stockholders have been satisfied. Investors can determine their rights by calculating the book value per share of the stock. Normally, a company will not be liquidated, but investors still need to understand how the book value per share relates to the actual stock price for the company. The important questions are:

What price per share does an investor want to pay for a company's stock? Should that price be above or below book value per share?

2. Gather the Information from the Financial Statements

- Total stockholders' equity: From the statement of stockholders' equity
- Number of shares of stock outstanding: From the statement of stockholders' equity

3. Calculate the Ratio

$$\text{Book Value per Share} = \frac{\text{Total Stockholders' Equity}}{\text{Number of Shares of Stock Outstanding}}$$

Kellogg's Inc. Consolidated Balance Sheets (in millions, except share data)	2010	2009
Shareholders equity		
Common stock, $.25 par value, 1,000,000,000 shares authorized		
Issued: 419,272,027 shares in 2010 and 419,058,168 shares in 2009	105	105
Capital in excess of par value	495	472
Retained earnings	6,122	5,481
Treasury stock at cost:		
53,667,635 shares in 2010 and 37,678,215 shares in 2009	(2,650)	(1,820)
Accumulated other comprehensive income (loss)	(1,914)	(1,966)
TOTAL SHAREHOLDERS' EQUITY	$ 2,158	$ 2,272

$$\text{Book Value per Share} = \frac{\$2,158,000,000}{365,604,392} = \$5.90$$

© Cengage Learning 2013

Note: Shares outstanding is 419,272,027 issued less 53,667,635 treasury stock.

4. Compare the Ratio with Others

Kellogg's book value per share of common stock may be compared to prior years and to companies in the same industry.

	KELLOGG'S		GENERAL MILLS	
	December 31, 2010	December 31, 2009	May 30, 2010	May 31, 2009
Book value per share	$5.90	$5.96	$8.60	$8.26

5. Interpret the Results

For 2010, Kellogg's common stockholders have the right to $5.90 per share of net assets in the corporation. That has decreased from the $5.96 per share in 2009.

The book value per share indicates the recorded minimum value per share of the stock, but it is not a very accurate measure of the price that an investor would be willing to pay for a share of stock. The book value of a stock is often thought to be the "floor" of a stock price. When a company has a stock price that is less than its book value, it may be an indication that the stockholders would be better off if the company were liquidated rather than continue in business. ■

Calculating Book Value When Preferred Stock Is Present

The focus of the computation of book value per share is always on the value per share of the *common* stock. Therefore, the computation must be adjusted for corporations that have both preferred and common stock. The numerator of the fraction, total stockholders' equity, should be reduced by the rights that preferred stockholders have to the

EXHIBIT 11-5 Workout Wonders' Stockholders' Equity Section

Stockholders' Equity Section of Balance Sheet December 31, 2012, and December 31, 2011		
(in millions)	2012	2011
Preferred stock, no par value (liquidation value, $500)	$ 400	$ 400
Common stock, par value 1 2/3 per share (issued 1,782 shares)	30	30
Capital in excess of par value	618	548
Retained earnings	18,730	15,961
Accumulated other comprehensive loss	(886)	(1,267)
Less: Repurchased common stock, at cost (103 and 77 shares, respectively)	(4,920)	(3,376)
Total shareholders' equity	$13,972	$12,296

corporation's net assets. Normally, this can be accomplished by deducting the redemption value or liquidation value of the preferred stock along with any dividends in arrears on cumulative preferred stock. The denominator should not include the number of shares of preferred stock.

To illustrate the computation of book value per share when both common and preferred stock are present, we refer to the Stockholders' Equity category of Workout Wonders, presented in Exhibit 11-5. When calculating book value per share, we want to consider only the *common* stockholders' equity. Exhibit 11-5 indicates that the company had total stockholders' equity in 2012 of $13,972 million but also that preferred stockholders had a right to $500 million in the event of liquidation. Therefore, $500 million must be deducted to calculate the rights of the common stockholders:

$$\$13,972 - \$500 = \$13,472 \text{ million common stockholders' equity}$$

The number of shares of common stock *outstanding* for the company is 1,782 million issued less 103 million of treasury stock. Therefore, the computation of book value per share is as follows:

$$\$13,472/1,679 = \$8.02 \text{ Book Value per Share}$$

If the company was liquidated and the assets sold at their recorded values, the common stockholders would receive $8.02 per share. Of course, if the company went bankrupt and had to liquidate assets at distressed values, stockholders would receive something less than book value.

Market Value per Share

The market value of the stock is a more meaningful measure of the value of the stock to those financial statement users interested in buying or selling shares of stock. The **market value per share** is the price at which stock is currently selling. When stock is sold on a stock exchange, the price can be determined by its most recent selling price. For example, the listing for **Nike Inc.** stock on the Internet may indicate the following:

Market value per share
The selling price of the stock as indicated by the most recent transactions.

52-Week			Daily			
High	Low	Sym	High	Low	Last	Change
68.17	39.17	NKE	43.3	42.01	42.93	+0.48 (1.13%)

The two left-hand columns indicate the stock price for the last 52-week period. Nike Inc. sold as high as $68.17 and as low as $39.17 during that time period. The right-hand portion indicates the high and low for the previous day's trading and the closing price. Nike sold as high as $43.30 per share and as low as $42.01 per share and closed at $42.93. For the day, the stock increased by 1.13%, or $0.48 per share.

The market value of the stock depends on many factors. Stockholders must evaluate a corporation's earnings and liquidity as indicated in the financial statements. They also must consider a variety of economic factors and project all of the factors into the future to determine the proper market value per share of the stock. Many investors use sophisticated investment techniques, including large databases, to identify factors that affect a company's stock price.

LO9 Understand how investors use ratios to evaluate stockholders' equity.

- Ratios used to analyze stockholders' equity are designed to measure some aspect of the value of the firm held by stockholders. Some common measures include:
  - Book value per share—a measure based on balance sheet accounting amounts recorded.
  - Market value per share—a measure aimed at assessing fair market value based on the current price of stock.

POD REVIEW 11.9

QUESTIONS   Answers to these questions are on the last page of the chapter.

1. The ratio of book value per share
   a. is an indication of the market value of the stock on the stock exchange.
   b. has total assets as the denominator.
   c. has total assets as the numerator.
   d. is an indication of the rights of the common stockholders to the company's assets.

2. If a company has both common and preferred stock and wants to calculate book value per share,

   a. the rights of the preferred stockholders to the company's assets should be deducted before book value per share is calculated.
   b. the rights of the common stockholders to the company's assets should be deducted before book value per share is calculated.
   c. the amount of stock outstanding in the numerator of the fraction should represent only the preferred stock.
   d. the amount of stock outstanding in the numerator of the fraction should represent the total of the common and preferred stock.

© Cengage Learning 2013

How Changes in Stockholders' Equity Affect the Statement of Cash Flows

OVERVIEW: Issuance and repurchase of stock and payment of dividends are financing items on the statement of cash flows. The issuance of stock results in a cash inflow or increase. Repurchase or retirement of stock represents a cash outflow or decrease. Cash dividends represent a cash outflow or decrease.

LO10 Explain the effects that transactions involving stockholders' equity have on the statement of cash flows.

It is important to determine the effect that the issuance of stock, the repurchase of stock, and the payment of dividends have on the statement of cash flows. The impact that each of these business activities has on cash must be reflected on the statement. Exhibit 11-6 indicates how these stockholders' equity transactions affect cash flow and where the items should be placed on the statement of cash flows.

EXHIBIT 11-6 The Effect of Stockholders' Equity Items on the Statement of Cash Flows

Item	Statement of Cash Flows	
	Operating Activities	
Net Income		xxx
	Investing Activities	
	Financing Activities	
Issuance of Stock	⟶	+
Retirement or repurchase of stock	⟶	−
Payment of dividends	⟶	−

© Cengage Learning 2013

© Cengage Learning 2013

Name: Jeffrey K. Hanna, CFA

Education: B.B.A., B.A., Kent State University; M.A., University of Rhode Island

College Major: Economics/Spanish/Economics

Occupation: Portfolio Manager

Age: 48

Position: Vice President & Senior Portfolio Manager

Company Name: Citizens Bank

See Jeffrey Hanna's interview clip in CNOW.

SPOTLIGHT
Portfolio Manager Makes Good Use of Financial Statements

Portfolio managers of equity funds provide investors with the expertise needed to analyze the factors affecting equity investing within a very competitive environment. **Jeffrey K. Hanna**, CFA, is the vice president and senior portfolio manager for Citizens Bank; he helps clients meet their retirement, education, and general investing needs.

According to Jeffrey, the income statement and the statement of cash flows tend to be very useful in the analysis of companies because they tell the story of how a company's decisions have affected the value of that company. There is a great deal of information to be gleaned from these two statements—they provide a wealth of information to users of financial statements. Typically, he would compare the balance sheets of companies within industries and use this to measure any large differences. Some of the important ratios he reviews would be asset-related, such as current ratios, inventory ratios, and debt and equity ratios such as debt/asset and equity/assets.

Jeffrey believes the quality of financial statements has generally improved over the years. The FASB has introduced many new standards and has addressed some of the more pressing needs for transparency. In addition, the international accounting standards have also brought more transparency and conformity around the world. Accounting sets the framework for further analysis, which allows comparison among companies and industries. Changes in pronouncements will alter the interpretation—and valuation—of a company, and it is the role of the analyst to help interpret and make a judgment call on how these changes affect the company.

Jeffrey confirms that his college accounting background has taught him to think logically and develop a framework for analyzing companies and industries. This has been critical to his success as a portfolio manager.

> **Be sure to develop a good working knowledge of financial accounting. It will serve you well in all financial fields you encounter throughout your career.**

© Cengage Learning 2013

The issuance of stock is a method to finance business. Therefore, the cash *inflow* from the sale of stock to stockholders should be reflected as an inflow in the Financing Activities section of the statement of cash flows. Generally, companies do not disclose separately the amount received for the par value of the stock and the amount received in excess of par. Rather, one amount is listed to indicate the total inflow of cash.

The repurchase or retirement of stock also represents a financing activity. Therefore, the cash *outflow* should be reflected as a reduction of cash in the Financing Activities section of the statement of cash flows. Again, companies do not distinguish between the amount paid for the par of the stock and the amount paid in excess of par. One amount is generally listed to indicate the total cash outflow to retire stock.

Dividends paid to stockholders represent a cost of financing the business with stock. Therefore, dividends paid should be reflected as a cash *outflow* in the Financing Activities section of the statement of cash flows. It is important to distinguish between the declaration of dividends and the payment of dividends. The cash outflow occurs at the time the dividend is paid and should be reflected on the statement of cash flows in that period.

The 2010 partial statement of cash flows for Southwest Airlines Co., is shown in Exhibit 11-7. During 2010, the company had considerable cash outflows associated with its long-term debt and capital lease obligations of $155 million. The company had additional cash outflows for payments of credit line borrowing of $44 million and payments of dividends of $13 million.

EXHIBIT 11-7 Southwest Airlines Co.'s Partial Statement of Cash Flows

Southwest Airlines Co.			
Consolidated Statement of Cash Flows			
	Years Ended December 31,		
(in millions)	**2010**	**2009**	**2008**
CASH FLOWS FROM FINANCING ACTIVITIES:			
Issuance of long-term debt	—	455	1,000
Proceeds from credit line borrowing	—	83	91
Proceeds from revolving credit facility	—	—	400
Proceeds from sale leaseback transactions	—	381	173
Proceeds from Employee stock plans	55	20	117
Payments of long-term debt and capital lease obligations	(155)	(86)	(55)
Payments of revolving credit facility	—	(400)	—
Payment of credit line borrowing	(44)	(97)	—
Payments of cash dividends	(13)	(13)	(13)
Repurchase of common stock	—	—	(54)
Other, net	8	(13)	(5)
Net cash provided by (used in) financing activities	(149)	330	1,654

© Cengage Learning 2013

LO10 Explain the effects that transactions involving stockholders' equity have on the statement of cash flows.

- Transactions involving stockholders' equity accounts are classified as financing activities. Issuing stock produces cash inflows. Dividends and the retirement or repurchase of stock produce cash outflows.

POD REVIEW 11.10

QUESTIONS **Answers to these questions are on the last page of the chapter.**

1. On the statement of cash flows, where should the effect of the company's stock transactions be reflected?

   a. in the Operating Activities category
   b. in the Investing Activities category
   c. in the Financing Activities category
   d. none of the above

2. When treasury stock is purchased by the company, how should it appear?

   a. as a cash inflow in the Financing Activities category
   b. as a cash outflow in the Financing Activities category
   c. as a cash inflow in the Investing Activities category
   d. as a cash outflow in the Investing Activities category

© Cengage Learning 2013

APPENDIX

Accounting Tools: Unincorporated Businesses

The focus of Chapter 11, as with the rest of the text, has been on the corporate form of organization. Most of the large, influential companies in the United States are organized as corporations. They have a legal and economic existence that is separate from that of the owners of the business, the stockholders. Yet many other companies in the economy are organized as sole proprietorships or partnerships. The purpose of this appendix is to show briefly how the characteristics of such organizations affect the accounting, particularly the accounting for the Owners' Equity category of the balance sheet.

LO11 Describe the important differences between the sole proprietorship and partnership forms of organization versus the corporate form.

Sole Proprietorships

OVERVIEW: A sole proprietorship is a business owned by one person. It is not a separate entity for legal or tax purposes. For accounting purposes, the assets and liabilities of the owner must be kept separate from the business. Owners' equity is one account—the owner's capital account.

Sole proprietorship
A business with a single owner.

A **sole proprietorship** is a business owned by one person. Most sole proprietorships are small in size, with the owner serving as the operator or manager of the company. The primary advantage of the sole proprietorship form of organization is its simplicity. The Owners' Equity category of the balance sheet consists of one account, the owner's capital account. The owner answers to no one but himself or herself. A disadvantage of the sole proprietorship is that all responsibility for the success or failure of the venture attaches to the owner, who often has limited resources.

There are three important points to remember about this form of organization:

1. A sole proprietorship is not a separate entity for legal purposes. This means that the law does not distinguish between the assets of the business and those of its owner. If an owner loses a lawsuit, for example, the law does not limit an owner's liability to the amount of assets of the business, but extends liability to the owner's personal assets. Thus, the owner is said to have *unlimited liability*.

2. Accountants adhere to the *entity principle* and maintain a distinction between the owner's personal assets and the assets of the sole proprietorship. The balance sheet of a sole proprietorship should reflect only the "business" assets and liabilities, with the difference reflected as owner's capital.

3. A sole proprietorship is not treated as a separate entity for federal income tax purposes. That is, the sole proprietorship does not pay tax on its income. Rather, the business income must be declared as income on the owner's personal tax return, and income tax is assessed at the personal tax rate rather than the rate that applies to companies organized as corporations. This may or may not be advantageous depending on the amount of income involved and the owner's tax situation.

Typical Transactions

When the owners of a corporation, the stockholders, invest in the corporation, they normally do so by purchasing stock. When investing in a sole proprietorship, the owner simply contributes cash or other assets to the business.

Example 11-10 Recording Investments in a Sole Proprietorship

Assume that on January 1, 2012, Peter Tom began a new business by investing $10,000 cash. The effect of the investment by the owner is as follows:

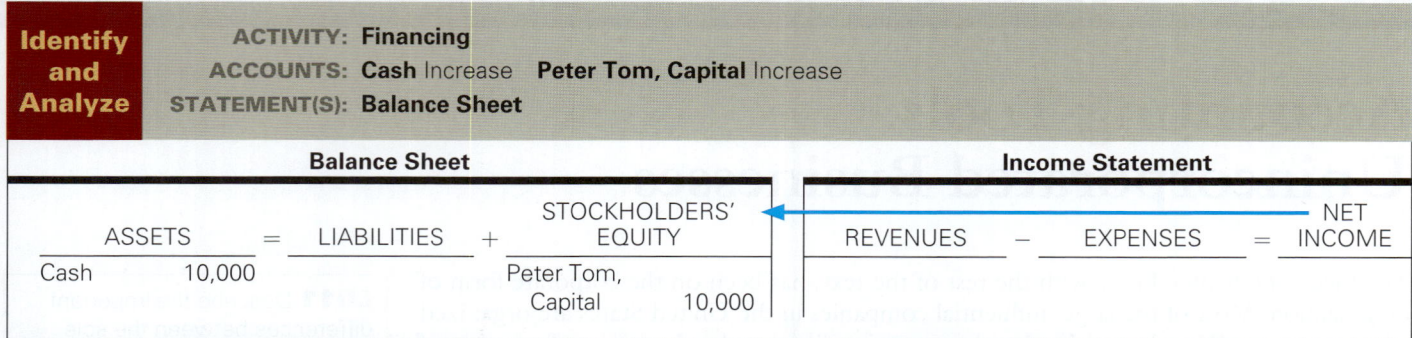

Identify and Analyze	**ACTIVITY:** Financing
	ACCOUNTS: Cash Increase Peter Tom, Capital Increase
	STATEMENT(S): Balance Sheet

Balance Sheet				Income Statement				
ASSETS	=	LIABILITIES	+	STOCKHOLDERS' EQUITY	REVENUES	−	EXPENSES	= NET INCOME
Cash 10,000				Peter Tom, Capital 10,000				

The Peter Tom, Capital account is an owner's equity account and reflects the rights of the owner to the business assets.

(Continued)

An owner's withdrawal of assets from the business is recorded as a reduction of owner's equity. Assume that on July 1, 2012, Peter Tom took an auto valued at $6,000 from the business to use as his personal auto. The effect of the withdrawal by the owner is as follows:

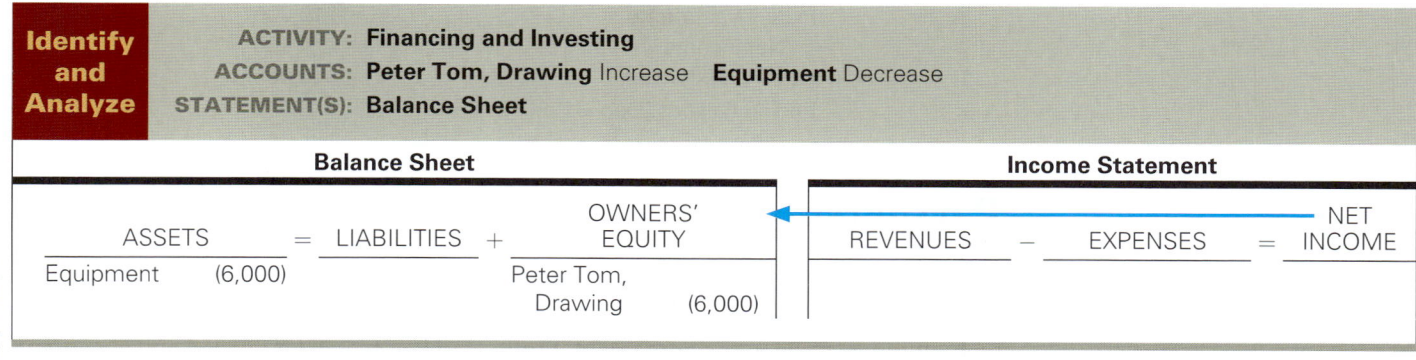

The Peter Tom, Drawing account is a contra-equity account. Sometimes a drawing account is referred to as a *withdrawals account,* as in Peter Tom, Withdrawals. An increase in the account reduces the owner's equity. At the end of the fiscal year, the drawing account should be closed to the capital account and the effect is as follows:

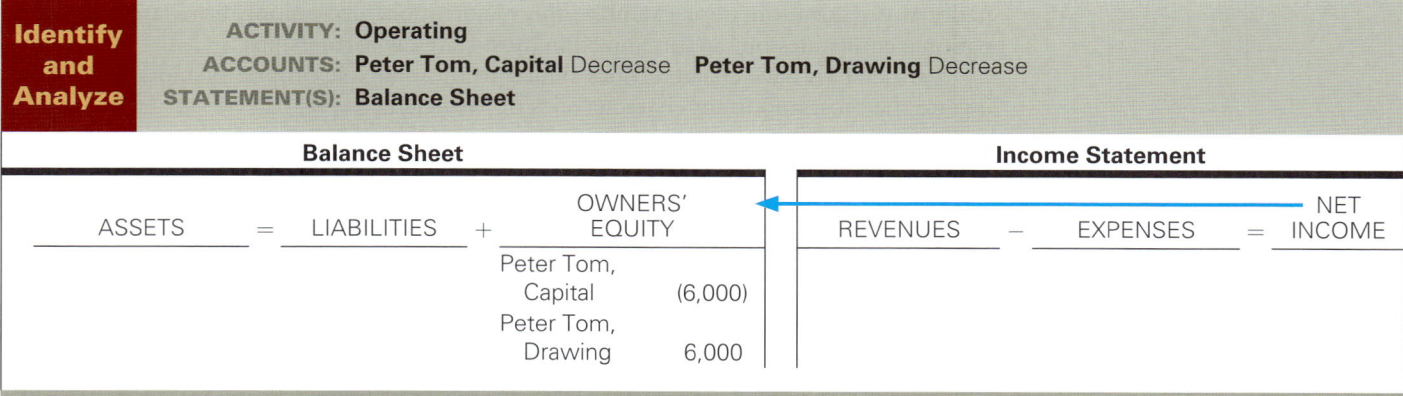

The amount of the net income of the business also should be reflected in the capital account. Assume that all revenue and expense accounts of Peter Tom Company have been closed to the Income Summary account, resulting in a balance of $4,000, the net income for the year. The Income Summary account is closed to capital and the effect is as follows:

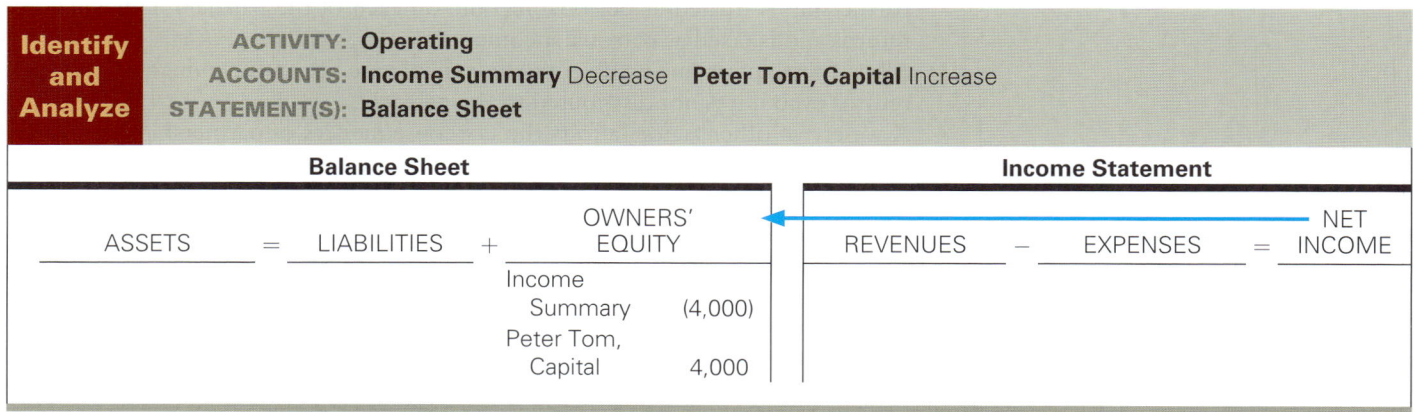

The Owner's Equity section of the balance sheet for Peter Tom Company consists of one account, the capital account, calculated as follows:

Beginning balance, Jan.1, 2012	$ 0
Plus: Investments	10,000
Net income	4,000
Less: Withdrawals	(6,000)
Ending balance, Dec. 31, 2012	$ 8,000

Partnerships

OVERVIEW: A partnership is similar to a proprietorship, but with more than one owner. The partnership agreement governs how income (losses) will be distributed. If no mention is made in the agreement, profits and losses will be divided equally among partners. A separate capital account is maintained for each partner, as well as separate drawing accounts. The partnership does not pay income tax. Instead, income of the partnership is taxed on each owner's tax return.

Partnership
A business owned by two or more individuals that has the characteristic of unlimited liability.

A **partnership** is a company owned by two or more people. Like sole proprietorships, most partnerships are fairly small businesses formed when individuals combine their capital and managerial talents for a common business purpose. Other partnerships are large, national organizations. For example, the major public accounting firms are very large, national companies but are organized in most states as partnerships.

Partnerships have characteristics similar to those of sole proprietorships. The following are the most important characteristics of partnerships:

1. Unlimited liability
    *   Legally, the assets of the business are not separate from the partners' personal assets.
    *   Each partner is personally liable for the debts of the partnership.
    *   Creditors have a legal claim first to the assets of the partnership and then to the assets of the individual partners.
2. Limited life
    *   Corporations have a separate legal existence and an unlimited life; partnerships do not. The life of a partnership exists only so long as the contract between the partners is valid.
    *   The partnership ends when a partner withdraws or a new partner is added. A new partnership must be created for the business to continue.
3. Not taxed as a separate entity
    *   Partnerships are subject to the same tax features as sole proprietorships.
    *   The partnership itself does not pay federal income tax. Rather, the income of the partnership is treated as personal income on each of the partners' individual tax returns and is taxed as personal income.
    *   All partnership income is subject to federal income tax on the individual partners' returns even if it is not distributed to the partners.
    *   A variety of other factors affects the tax consequences of partnerships versus the corporate form of organization. Those aspects are quite complex and beyond the scope of this text.

Partnership agreement
Specifies how much the owners will invest, what their salaries will be, and how profits will be shared.

A partnership is based on a **partnership agreement**. It is very important that the partners agree in writing about all aspects of the partnership. The agreement should detail items such as how much capital each partner is to invest, how much time each partner is expected to devote to the business, what the salary of each partner is, and how income of the partnership is to be divided. If a partnership agreement is not present, the courts may be forced to settle disputes between partners. Therefore, the partners should develop a partnership agreement when the firm is first established and review the agreement periodically to determine if changes are necessary.

Investments and Withdrawals

In a partnership, it is important to account separately for the capital of each partner. A capital account should be established in the Owners' Equity section of the balance sheet for each partner. Investments into the company should be credited to the partner making the investment.

Example 11-11 Recording Investments in a Partnership

Assume that on January 1, 2012, Paige Thoms and Amy Rebec begin a partnership named AP Company. Paige contributes $10,000 cash, and Amy contributes equipment valued at $5,000. The effect of the investment by the owners is as follows:

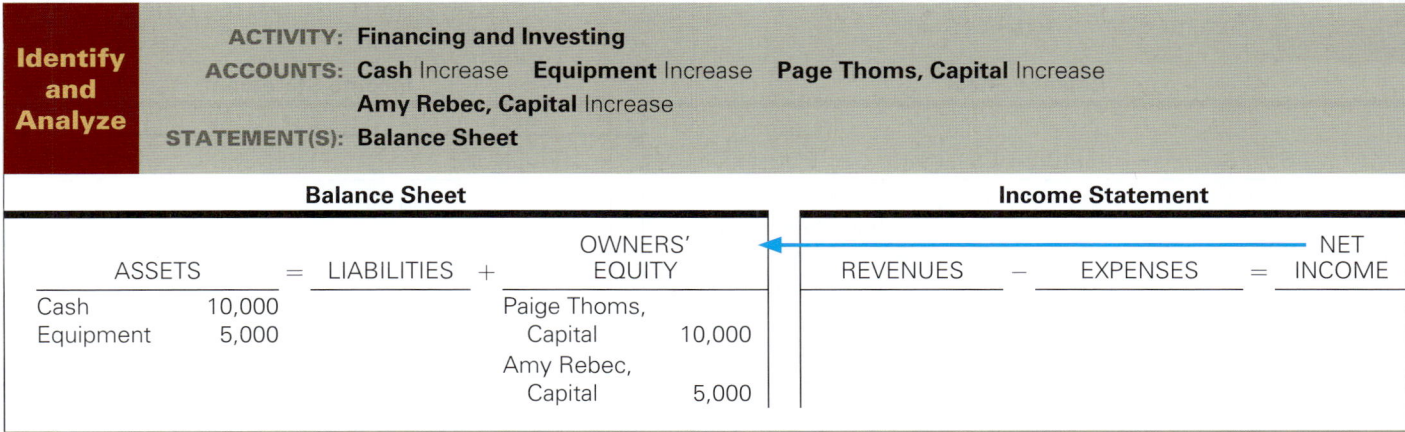

A drawing account also should be established for each owner of the company to account for withdrawals of assets. Assume that on April 1, 2012, each owner withdraws $2,000 of cash from AP Company. The effect of the withdrawal by the owner is as follows:

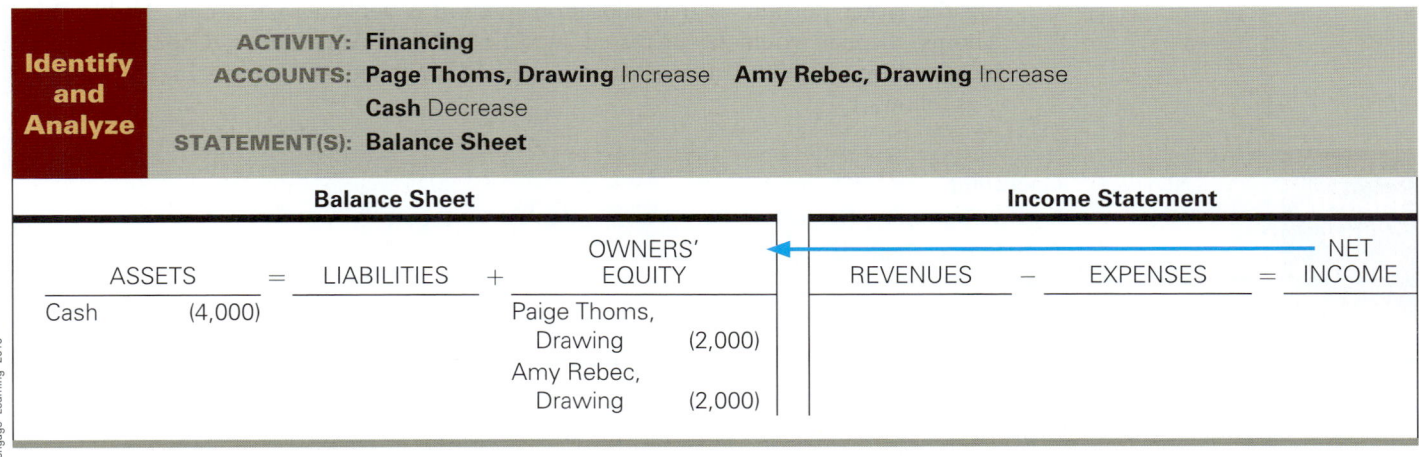

Distribution of Income

The partnership agreement governs the manner in which income should be allocated to partners. The distribution may recognize the partners' relative investment in the business, their time and effort, their expertise and talents, or other factors. Three methods of income allocation will be illustrated, but be aware that partnerships use many other allocation methods. Although these allocation methods are straightforward, partnerships often dissolve because one or more of the partners believes that the allocation is unfair. It is very difficult to devise a method that will make all partners happy.

One way to allocate income is to divide it evenly between the partners. In fact, when a partnership agreement is not present, the courts specify that an equal allocation must be applied regardless of the relative contributions or efforts of the partners. For example, assume that AP Company has $30,000 of net income for the period and has established an agreement that income should be allocated evenly between the two partners, Paige and Amy. Each capital account would be increased by $15,000. The effect of closing the Income Summary account to the capital accounts is as follows:

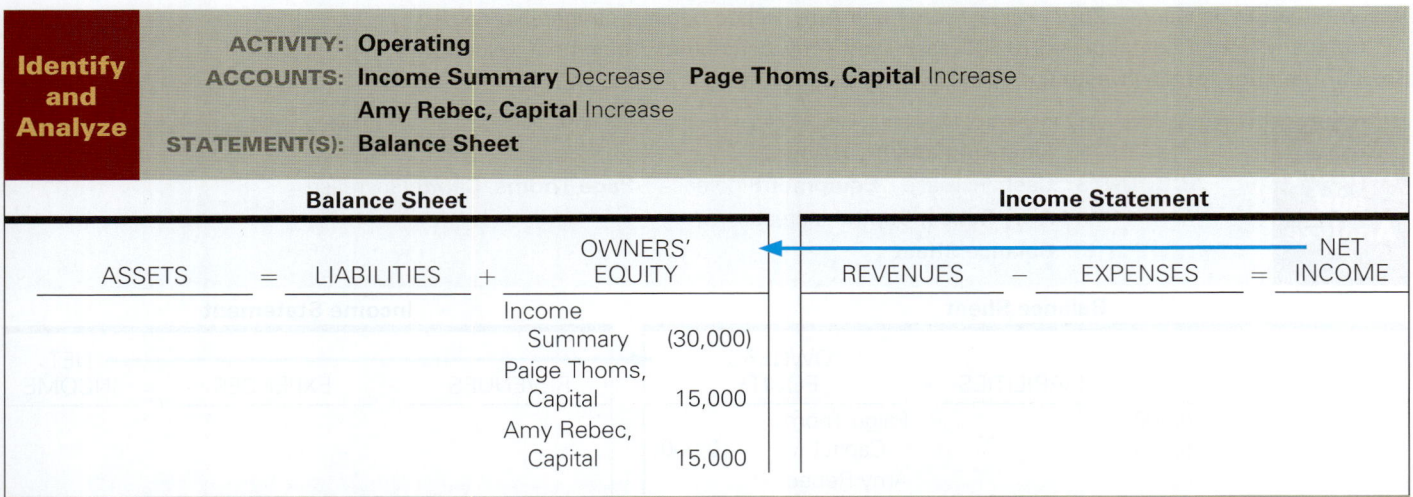

An equal distribution of income to all partners is easy to apply but is not fair to those partners who have contributed more in money or time to the partnership.

Another way to allocate income is to specify in the partnership agreement that income be allocated according to a *stated ratio*. For example, Paige and Amy may specify that all income of AP Company should be allocated in a 2-to-1 ratio, with Paige receiving the larger portion. If that allocation method is applied to Example 11-11, Paige Thoms, Capital would be increased by $20,000 and Amy Rebec, Capital would be increased by $10,000. If that allocation method is applied to Example 11-11, the effect is as follows:

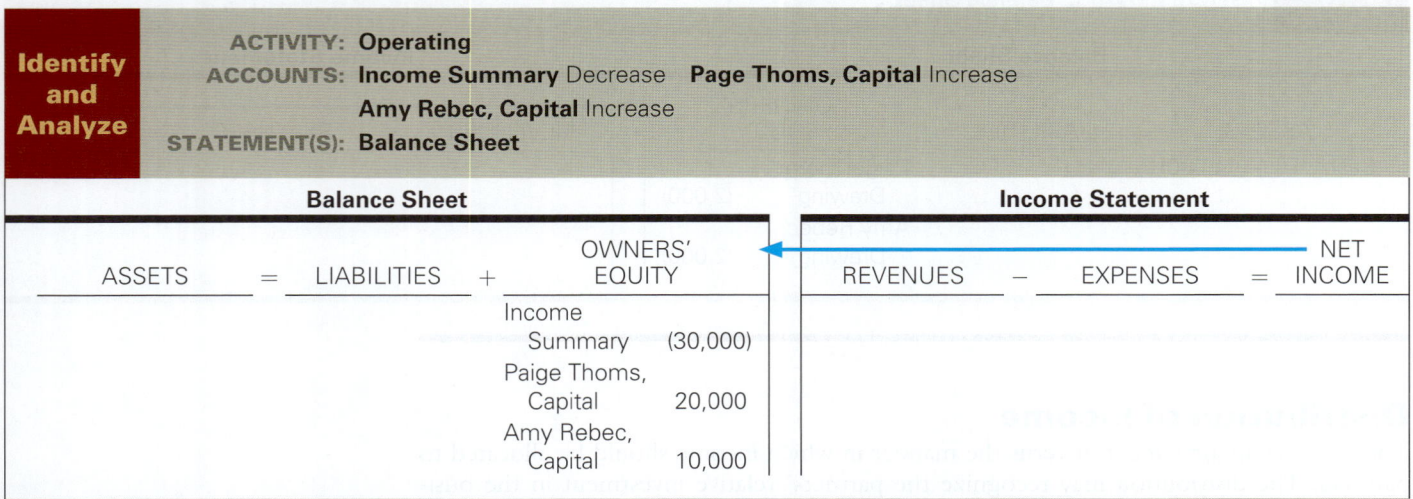

Finally, an allocation method that more accurately reflects the partners' input is illustrated. It is based on salaries, interest on invested capital, and a stated ratio. Assume that the partnership agreement of AP Company specifies that Paige and Amy be allowed a salary of $6,000 and $4,000, respectively; that each partner receive 10% on her capital balance; and that any remaining income be allocated equally. Assume that AP Company has been in operation for several years and that the capital balances of the owners at the end of 2012, before the income distribution, are as follows:

Paige Thoms, Capital	$40,000
Amy Rebec, Capital	50,000

If AP Company calculated that its 2012 net income (before partner salaries) was $30,000, income would be allocated between the partners as follows:

	Paige	Amy
Distributed for salaries:	$ 6,000	$ 4,000
Distributed for interest:		
Paige ($40,000 × 10%)	4,000	
Amy ($50,000 × 10%)		5,000
Remainder = $30,000 – $10,000 – $9,000 = $11,000		
Remainder distributed equally:		
Paige ($11,000/2)	5,500	
Amy ($11,000/2)		5,500
Total distributed	$15,500	$14,500

Paige Thoms, Capital would be increased by $15,500, and Amy Rebec, Capital, by $14,500. The effect of closing the Income Summary account to the capital accounts is as follows:

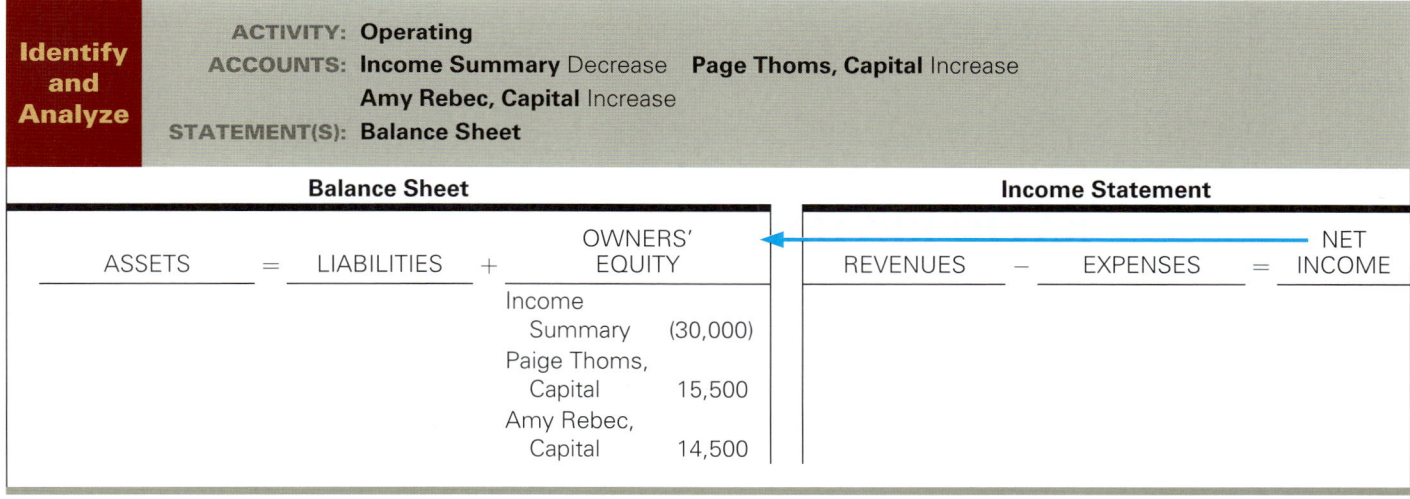

Identify and Analyze

ACTIVITY: Operating

ACCOUNTS: Income Summary Decrease   Page Thoms, Capital Increase
Amy Rebec, Capital Increase

STATEMENT(S): Balance Sheet

Balance Sheet				Income Statement			
ASSETS	=	LIABILITIES	+	OWNERS' EQUITY	REVENUES	– EXPENSES	= NET INCOME
				Income Summary (30,000)			
				Paige Thoms, Capital 15,500			
				Amy Rebec, Capital 14,500			

This indicates that the amounts of $15,500 and $14,500 were allocated to Paige and Amy, respectively. It does not indicate the amount actually paid to (or withdrawn by) the partners. However, for tax purposes, the income of the partnership is treated as personal income on the partners' individual tax returns regardless of whether the income is actually paid in cash to the partners. This aspect often encourages partners to withdraw income from the business and makes it difficult to retain sufficient capital for the business to operate profitably.

LO11 Describe the important differences between the sole proprietorship and partnership forms of organization versus the corporate form.

- Sole proprietorships are businesses that are not incorporated and are owned by one individual. The business entity and individual are not distinguished from one another for legal and tax purposes.
- Partnerships are also unincorporated entities but are owned by two or more individuals. The partners and their respective shares of the business are not distinguished from one another for legal purposes. The partnership itself is not taxed on earnings, but individual partners are taxed for their share.
- Corporations, unlike partnerships, have some of the following distinguishing characteristics: they are generally taxable entities and have an unlimited life. The corporate form has been adopted by most larger businesses and is therefore emphasized in this text.

POD REVIEW 11.11

QUESTIONS   Answers to these questions are on the last page of the chapter.

1. When a company is organized as a sole proprietorship,
   a. the assets and liabilities of the company should not be separate from the owner's assets and liabilities.
   b. the assets and liabilities of the company should be kept separate from the owner's assets and liabilities.
   c. the company must pay income tax on its income.
   d. the owner of the company is considered to have a limited liability for the actions of the company.

2. When a company is organized as a partnership,
   a. the partners share equally in the income of the company.
   b. all partners must contribute the same amount of money to establish the partnership.
   c. the partnership must pay tax on its income.
   d. each partner is personally liable for the actions of the company.

RATIO REVIEW

$$\text{Book Value per Share} = \frac{\text{Total Stockholders' Equity}^*}{\text{Number of Shares of Common Stock Outstanding}}$$

*When preferred stock is outstanding, the redemption value or liquidation value (disclosed on the preferred stock line or in the notes) of the preferred stock must be subtracted from total stockholders' equity.

ACCOUNTS HIGHLIGHTED

Account Title	Where It Appears	In What Section	Page Number
Common Stock	Balance Sheet	Contributed Capital	546
Preferred Stock	Balance Sheet	Contributed Capital	547
Additional Paid-in Capital	Balance Sheet	Contributed Capital	546
Retained Earnings	Balance Sheet	Retained Earnings	542
Treasury Stock	Balance Sheet	(bottom portion of stockholders' equity as a contra account)	548
Cash Dividend Payable	Balance Sheet	Current Liabilities	552
Stock Dividend Distributable	Balance Sheet	Contributed Capital	554

KEY TERMS QUIZ

Read each definition below and write the number of the definition in the blank beside the appropriate term. The quiz solutions appear at the end of the chapter.

_____ Authorized shares
_____ Issued shares
_____ Outstanding shares
_____ Par value
_____ Additional paid-in capital
_____ Retained earnings
_____ Cumulative feature
_____ Participating feature
_____ Convertible feature
_____ Callable feature
_____ Treasury stock
_____ Retirement of stock

_____ Dividend payout ratio
_____ Stock dividend
_____ Stock split
_____ Statement of stockholders' equity
_____ Comprehensive income
_____ Book value per share
_____ Market value per share
_____ Sole proprietorship (Appendix)
_____ Partnership (Appendix)
_____ Partnership agreement (Appendix)

1. The number of shares sold or distributed to stockholders.
2. An arbitrary amount that is stated on the face of the stock certificate and that represents the legal capital of the firm.
3. Net income that has been made by the corporation but not paid out as dividends.
4. The right to dividends in arrears before the current-year dividend is distributed.
5. Allows preferred stock to be returned to the corporation in exchange for common stock.
6. Stock issued by the firm and then repurchased but not retired.
7. The annual dividend amount divided by the annual net income.
8. A statement that reflects the differences between beginning and ending balances for all accounts in the Stockholders' Equity category.
9. Creation of additional shares of stock and reduction of the par value of the stock.
10. Total stockholders' equity divided by the number of shares of common stock outstanding.
11. The total change in net assets from all sources except investments by or distributions to the owners.
12. The selling price of the stock as indicated by the most recent stock transactions on, for example, the stock exchange.
13. The maximum number of shares a corporation may issue as indicated in the corporate charter.
14. The number of shares issued less the number of shares held as treasury stock.
15. The amount received for the issuance of stock in excess of the par value of the stock.
16. A provision allowing the preferred stockholders to share, on a percentage basis, in the distribution of an abnormally large dividend.
17. Allows the issuing firm to eliminate a class of stock by paying the stockholders a fixed amount.
18. When the stock of a corporation is repurchased with no intention of reissuing at a later date.
19. A corporation's declaration and issuance of additional shares of its own stock to existing stockholders.
20. A business owned by two or more individuals that has the characteristic of unlimited liability.
21. A document that specifies how much each owner should invest, what the salary of each owner is, and how profits are to be shared.
22. A business with a single owner.

ALTERNATE TERMS

additional paid-in capital paid-in capital in excess of par

additional paid-in capital—treasury stock paid-in capital from treasury stock transactions

callable feature redeemable

capital account owners' equity account

contributed capital paid-in capital

retained earnings retained income

small stock dividend stock dividend less than 20%

stockholders' equity owners' equity

WARMUP EXERCISES & SOLUTIONS

LO1 ## Warmup Exercise 11-1

A company has a Retained Earnings account with a January 1 balance of $500,000. The accountant has reviewed the following information for the current year:

Increase in cash balance	$50,000
Net income	80,000
Dividends declared	30,000
Dividends paid	20,000
Decrease in accounts receivable balance	10,000

Required

Calculate the ending balance of the Retained Earnings account.

Key to the Solution Cash and accounts receivable do not affect retained earnings. Also, note that dividends are deducted from retained earnings at the time they are declared rather than when they are paid.

LO2 ## Warmup Exercise 11-2

A company begins business on January 1 and issues 100,000 shares of common stock. On July 1, the company declares and issues a 2-for-1 stock split. On October 15, the company purchases 20,000 shares of stock as treasury stock and reissues 5,000 shares by the end of the month.

Required

Calculate the number of shares issued and the number of shares outstanding as of the end of the first year of operations.

LO9 ## Warmup Exercise 11-3

1. Company A has total stockholders' equity at year-end of $500,000 and has 10,000 shares of stock.
2. Company B has total stockholders' equity at year-end of $500,000 and has 10,000 shares of stock. The company also has 50,000 shares of preferred stock, which has a $1 par value and a liquidation value of $3 per share.

Required

Calculate the book value per share for Company A and Company B.

Key to the Solution Book value per share is calculated for the common stockholder. If preferred stock is present, an amount must be deducted that represents the amount the preferred stockholder would receive at liquidation.

Solutions to Warmup Exercises

Warmup Exercise 11-1

The ending balance of the Retained Earnings account should be calculated as follows:

Beginning balance	$500,000
Plus: Net income	80,000
Less: Dividends declared	(30,000)
Ending balance	$550,000

Warmup Exercise 11-2

The number of shares of stock issued is 200,000, or 100,000 times 2 because of the stock split. The number of shares outstanding is 185,000, calculated as follows:

Number of shares after split	100,000 × 2 = 200,000
Less purchase of treasury stock	(20,000)
Plus stock reissued	5,000
Total outstanding	185,000 shares

Warmup Exercise 11-3

1. Book value per share is $50, or $500,000/10,000.
2. Book value per share is $35, or ($500,000 – $150,000)/10,000.

REVIEW PROBLEM & SOLUTION

Andrew Company was incorporated on January 1, 2012, under a corporate charter that authorized the issuance of 50,000 shares of $5 par common stock and 20,000 shares of $100 par, 8% preferred stock. The following events occurred during 2012. Andrew wants to record the events and develop financial statements on December 31, 2012.

a. Issued for cash 10,000 shares of common stock at $25 per share and 1,000 shares of preferred stock at $110 per share on January 15, 2012.
b. Acquired a patent on April 1 in exchange for 2,000 shares of common stock. At the time of the exchange, the common stock was selling on the local stock exchange for $30 per share.
c. Repurchased 500 shares of common stock on May 1 at $20 per share. The corporation is holding the stock to be used for an employee bonus plan.
d. Declared a cash dividend of $1 per share to common stockholders and an 8% dividend to preferred stockholders on July 1. The preferred stock is noncumulative, nonparticipating. The dividend will be distributed on August 1.
e. Distributed the cash dividend on August 1.
f. Declared and distributed to preferred stockholders a 10% stock dividend on September 1. At the time of the dividend declaration, preferred stock was valued at $130 per share.
g. On December 31, calculated the annual net income for the year to be $200,000.

Required

1. Analyze the effect of the items (a) through (f).
2. Develop the Stockholders' Equity section of Andrew Company's balance sheet at December 31, 2012. You do not need to consider the notes that accompany the balance sheet.
3. Determine the book value per share of the common stock. Assume that the preferred stock can be redeemed at par.

Solution to Review Problem

1. The following effects will occur:

   a. The effect of the issuance of stock could be identified and analyzed as follows:

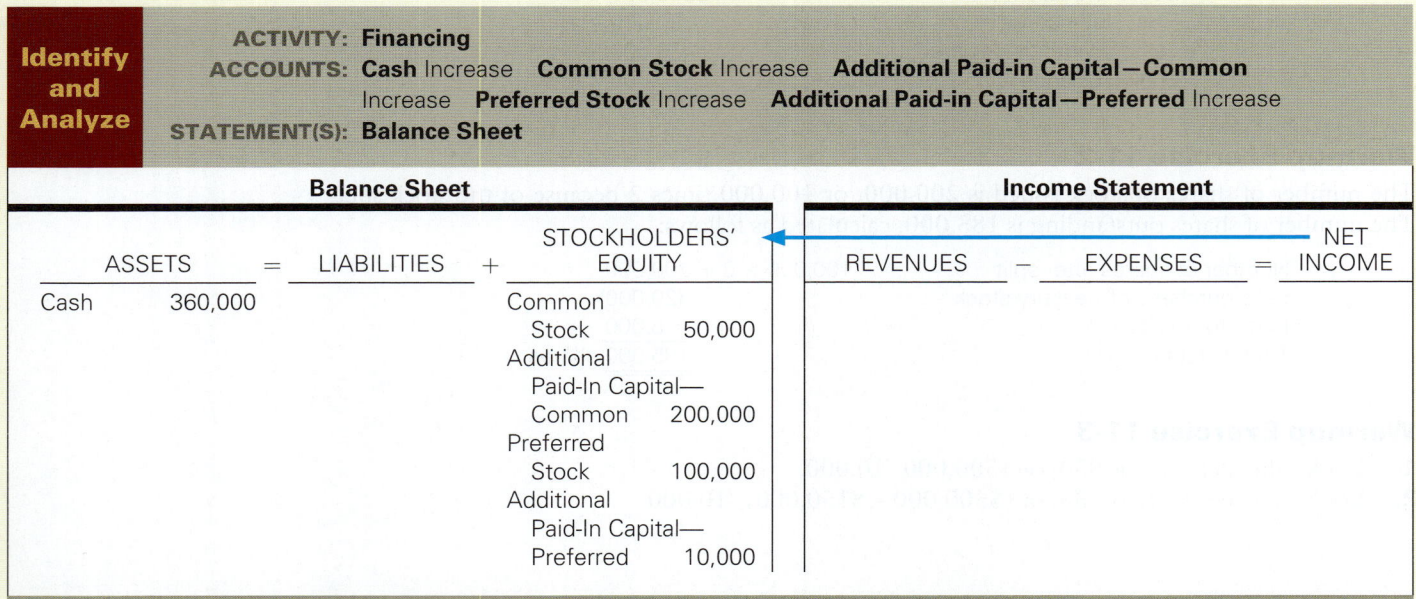

Identify and Analyze	**ACTIVITY: Financing** **ACCOUNTS: Cash** Increase **Common Stock** Increase **Additional Paid-in Capital—Common** Increase **Preferred Stock** Increase **Additional Paid-in Capital—Preferred** Increase **STATEMENT(S): Balance Sheet**				

Balance Sheet				Income Statement		
ASSETS	=	LIABILITIES	+	STOCKHOLDERS' EQUITY		
REVENUES	−	EXPENSES	=	NET INCOME		
Cash 360,000				Common Stock 50,000		
				Additional Paid-In Capital— Common 200,000		
				Preferred Stock 100,000		
				Additional Paid-In Capital— Preferred 10,000		

   b. The effect of the issuance of stock for the patent could be identified and analyzed as follows:

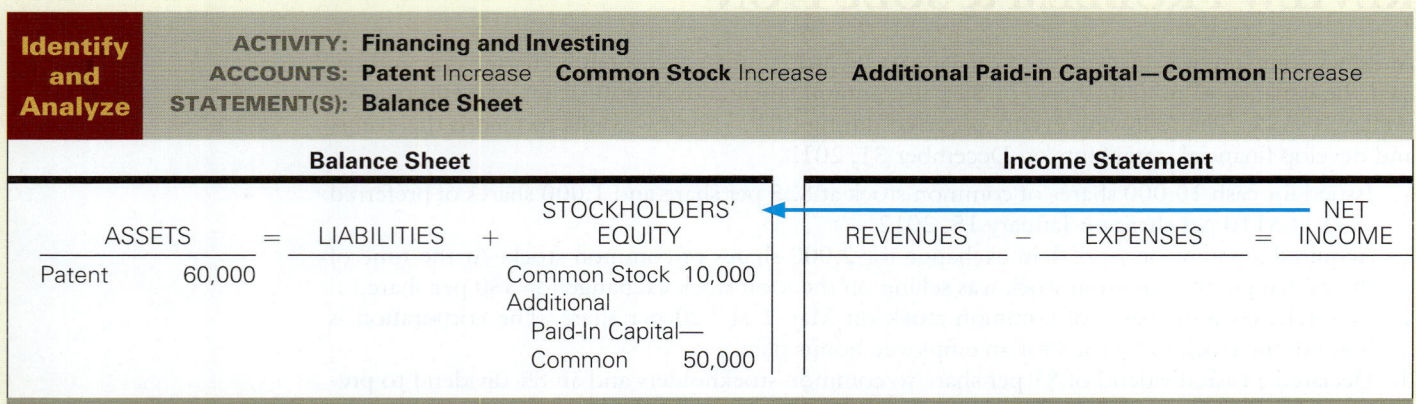

Identify and Analyze	**ACTIVITY: Financing and Investing** **ACCOUNTS: Patent** Increase **Common Stock** Increase **Additional Paid-in Capital—Common** Increase **STATEMENT(S): Balance Sheet**

Balance Sheet				Income Statement		
ASSETS	=	LIABILITIES	+	STOCKHOLDERS' EQUITY	REVENUES − EXPENSES = NET INCOME	
Patent 60,000				Common Stock 10,000		
				Additional Paid-In Capital— Common 50,000		

   c. The effect of the stock acquired as treasury stock is as follows:

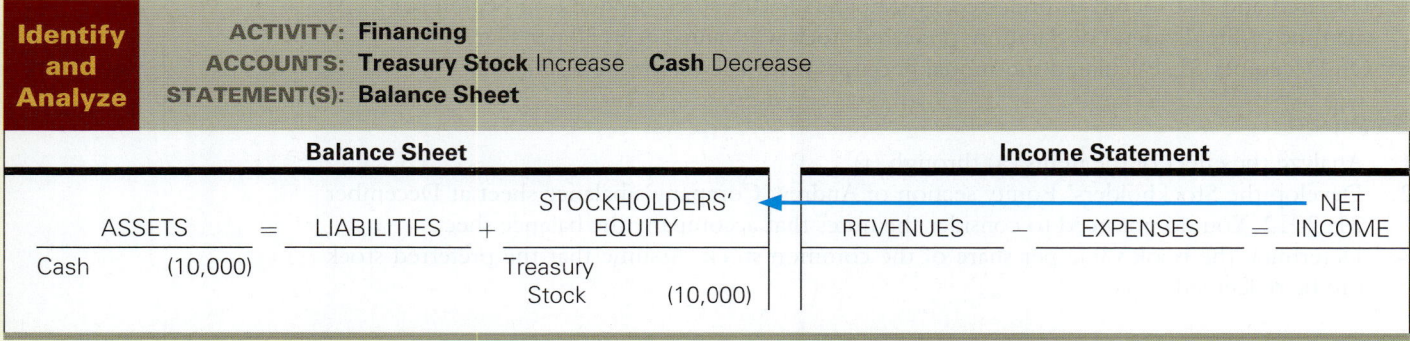

Identify and Analyze	**ACTIVITY: Financing** **ACCOUNTS: Treasury Stock** Increase **Cash** Decrease **STATEMENT(S): Balance Sheet**

Balance Sheet				Income Statement		
ASSETS	=	LIABILITIES	+	STOCKHOLDERS' EQUITY	REVENUES − EXPENSES = NET INCOME	
Cash (10,000)				Treasury Stock (10,000)		

d. A cash dividend should be declared on the number of shares of stock outstanding as of July 1. The effect is as follows:

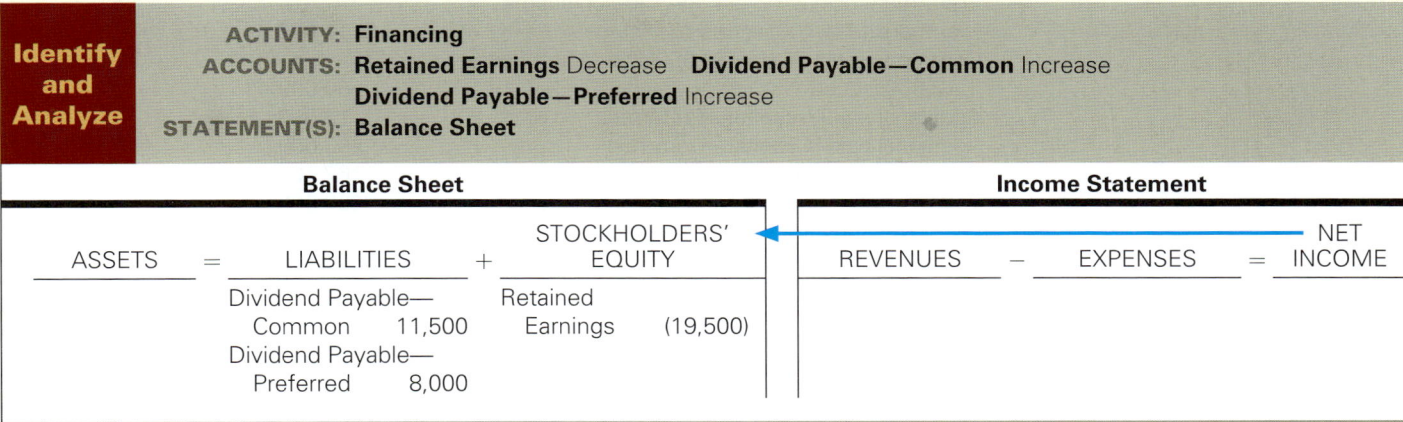

The number of common shares outstanding should be calculated as the number of shares issued (12,000) less the number of shares of treasury stock (500). The preferred stock dividend should be calculated as 1,000 shares times $100 par times 8%.

e. The effect of the distribution is as follows:

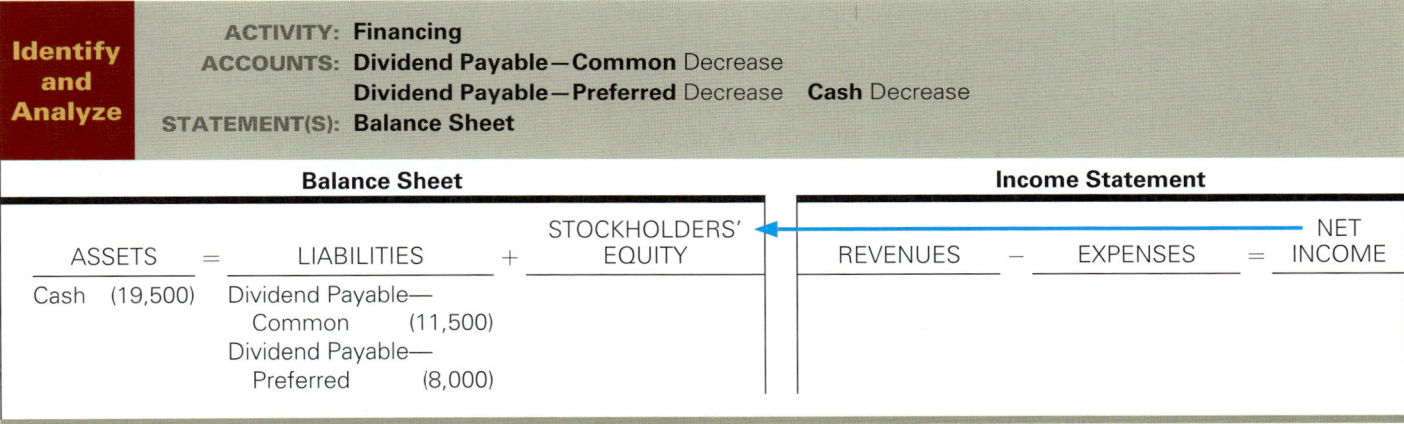

f. A stock dividend should be based on the number of shares of stock outstanding and should be declared and recorded at the market value of the stock. The effect is as follows:

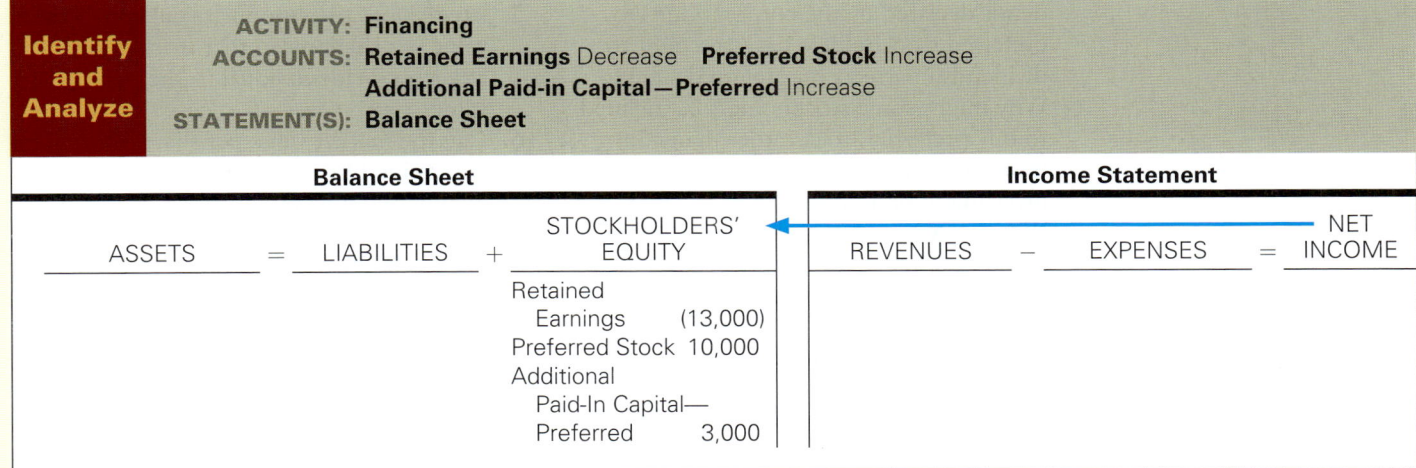

(Continued)

2. The Stockholders' Equity section for Andrew Company after completing these transactions appears as follows:

Preferred stock, $100 par, 8%, 20,000 shares authorized, 1,100 issued	$110,000
Common stock, $5 par, 50,000 shares authorized, 12,000 issued	60,000
Additional paid-in capital—Preferred	13,000
Additional paid-in capital—Common	250,000
Retained earnings	167,500*
Total contributed capital and retained earnings	$600,500
Less: Treasury stock, 500 shares, common	(10,000)
Total stockholders' equity	$590,500

*$200,000 − $19,500 − $13,000 = $167,500

3. The book value per share of the common stock is calculated as follows:

$$($590,500 − $110,000)/11,500 \text{ shares} = $41.78$$

QUESTIONS

1. What are the two major components of stockholders' equity? Which accounts generally appear in each component?
2. Corporations disclose the number of shares authorized, issued, and outstanding. What is the meaning of each of those terms? What causes a difference between the number of shares issued and the number outstanding?
3. Why do firms designate an amount as the par value of stock? Does par value indicate the selling price or market value of the stock?
4. If a firm has a net income for the year, will the balance in the Retained Earnings account equal the net income? What is the meaning of the balance of the account?
5. What is the meaning of the statement that preferred stock has a preference to dividends declared by the corporation? Do preferred stockholders have the right to dividends in arrears on preferred stock?
6. Why might some stockholders be inclined to buy preferred stock rather than common stock? What are the advantages of investing in preferred stock?
7. Why are common shareholders sometimes called *residual owners* when a company has both common and preferred stock outstanding?
8. When stock is issued in exchange for an asset, at what amount should the asset be reported? How could the fair market value be determined?
9. What is treasury stock? Why do firms use it? Where does it appear on a corporation's financial statements?
10. When treasury stock is bought and sold, the transactions do not result in gains or losses reported on the income statement. What account or accounts are used instead? Why are no income statement amounts recorded?
11. Many firms operate at a dividend payout ratio of less than 50%. Why do firms not pay a larger percentage of income as dividends?
12. What is a stock dividend? How should it be recorded?
13. Would you rather receive a cash dividend or a stock dividend from a company? Explain.
14. What is the difference between stock dividends and stock splits? How should stock splits be recorded?
15. How is the book value per share calculated? Does the amount calculated as book value per share mean that stockholders will receive a dividend equal to the book value?
16. Can the market value per share of stock be determined by the information on the income statement?
17. What is the difference between a statement of stockholders' equity and a retained earnings statement?
18. What is an advantage of organizing a company as a corporation rather than a partnership? Why don't all companies incorporate? (Appendix)
19. What are some ways that partnerships could share income among the partners? (Appendix)

BRIEF EXERCISES

Brief Exercise 11-1 Components of Stockholders' Equity

LO1

Nash Company has the following accounts among the items on its balance sheet at December 31, 2012:

Common Stock, $10 par, 10,000 shares authorized, 9,000 issued, 8,000 outstanding Preferred Stock, $100 par, 8%, cumulative, 1,000 shares authorized, issued, and outstanding

Cash Dividend Payable	$ 50,000
Retained Earnings	100,000
Additional Paid-In Capital	200,000
Investment in Common Stock of Horton Company	60,000
Treasury Stock, 1,000 shares, common stock	20,000
Accumulated Other Comprehensive Income—Unrealized	
Gain on Investment Security	5,000

Required

Develop the Stockholders' Equity section of the balance sheet for Nash Company at December 31, 2012.

Brief Exercise 11-2 Common and Preferred Stock

LO2
EXAMPLE 11-6

Fielder Company has the following accounts in the Stockholders' Equity category of the balance sheet:

Common Stock, $10 no par, 10,000 shares authorized, 9,000 issued, 8,000 outstanding

Preferred Stock, $100 par, 8%, cumulative, participating, 1,000 shares authorized, issued, and outstanding

Required

1. Explain how the issuance of stock affects the financial statements when the stock has no par value.
2. Why would preferred stockholders want to have a cumulative feature in preferred stock?
3. When a participating feature is present in preferred stock, how does it affect the amount of dividends that preferred stockholders can expect to receive?

Brief Exercise 11-3 Stock Issuance

LO3
EXAMPLE 11-1, 11-2

Morris had the following transactions during 2012:
1. Issued 2,000 shares of $10 par common stock for cash at $17 per share.
2. Issued 1,000 shares of preferred stock to acquire land. The preferred stock has a par value of $5 per share. The land has been appraised at $7,000.
3. Issued 5,000 shares of $10 par common stock as payment to a company that provided advertising for the company. The stock was selling on the stock exchange at $12 per share at the time of issuance.

Required

Identify and analyze the effect of each transaction

Brief Exercise 11-4 Treasury Stock

LO4
EXAMPLE 11-3

Indicate whether the following transactions increase, decrease, or have no effect on (a) total assets and on (b) total stockholders' equity.

_____ Issue 1,000 shares of common stock at $10 per share
_____ Purchase 500 shares of common stock as treasury stock at $15 per share
_____ Reissue 400 shares of treasury stock at $18 per share
_____ Reissue 100 shares of treasury stock at $12 per share

LO5
EXAMPLE 11-5, 11-6

Brief Exercise 11-5 Cash Dividends

At December 31, 2012, Black Company has the following:

Common Stock, $10 par, 10,000 shares authorized, 9,000 issued, 8,000 outstanding

Preferred Stock, $100 par, 8%, cumulative, 1,000 shares authorized, issued, and outstanding

The company did not pay any dividend during 2011 or 2010.

Required

Compute the amount of dividend to be received by the common and preferred stockholders in 2012 if the company declared a dividend of (a) $16,000, (b) $24,000, and (c) $60,000.

LO6
EXAMPLE 11-4, 11-7

Brief Exercise 11-6 Cash and Stock Dividends

At December 31, 2012, White Company has the following:

Common Stock, $10 par, 10,000 shares authorized, 9,000 issued, 8,000 outstanding

Required

Indicate whether the following would increase, decrease, or have no effect on (a) assets, (b) retained earnings, and (c) total stockholders' equity.

_____ A company declares and pays a cash dividend of $25,000.
_____ A company declares and issues a 10% stock dividend.

LO7
EXAMPLE 11-8, 11-9

Brief Exercise 11-7 Stock Dividends and Stock Splits

At December 31, 2012, Green Company and Blue Company have identical amounts of common stock and retained earnings as follows:

Common Stock, $10 par, 50,000 shares authorized, 9,000 issued, 9,000 outstanding

Retained Earnings, $500,000

At December 31, 2013, Green Company declares and issues a 100% stock dividend, while Blue Company declares and issues a 2-for-1 stock split.

Required

Determine for each company the following amounts as of January 1, 2013:

_____ Number of shares of common stock outstanding
_____ Par value per share of the common stock
_____ Total amount reported in Common Stock account
_____ Retained earnings

LO8
EXAMPLE 11-1, 11-3

Brief Exercise 11-8 Develop Stockholders' Equity

Nash Company has the following accounts among the items on the balance sheet at January 1, 2012:

Common Stock, $10 par, 10,000 shares authorized, 9,000 issued, 8,000 outstanding Preferred Stock, $100 par, 8%, cumulative, 1,000 shares authorized, issued, and outstanding

Retained Earnings	$100,000
Additional Paid-In Capital	200,000
Treasury Stock, 1,000 shares, common stock	20,000

During 2012, the company issued 500 shares of common stock at $14 per share and reissued 400 shares of treasury stock at $20 per share. The company reported a net income of $60,000 for 2012.

Required

Develop the Stockholders' Equity section for Nash Company at December 31, 2012.

Brief Exercise 11-9 Book Value per Share

LO9

Deer Company has the following amounts in the Stockholders' Equity category of the balance sheet at December 31, 2012:

Preferred Stock, $100 par, 8%, noncumulative (liquidation value of $110 per share)	$100,000
Paid-In Capital—Preferred	50,000
Common Stock, $5 par	400,000
Paid-In Capital—Common	40,000
Retained Earnings	200,000

Required

Determine the book value per share of the Deer Company stock.

Brief Exercise 11-10 Cash Flow Effects

LO10

For each of the following items, indicate (a) in what category of the statement of cash flows the item will be reported and (b) whether it will appear as a cash inflow, cash outflow, or neither.

Issuance of common stock for cash
Purchase of treasury stock
Issuance of a stock dividend
Reissuance of treasury stock
Issuance of common stock to acquire land

Brief Exercise 11-11 Sole Proprietorship (Appendix)

LO11
EXAMPLE 11-10

Furyk Company opened business as a sole proprietorship on January 1, 2012. The owner contributed $500,000 cash on that date. During the year, the company had a net income of $10,000. The company purchased equipment of $100,000 during the year. The owner also withdrew $60,000 to pay for personal expenses during 2012.

Required

Determine the company's owner's equity at December 31, 2012.

EXERCISES

Exercise 11-1 Solving for Stockholders' Equity Amounts

LO1

Assume that the following amounts are known for Colten Company for the current year:

Retained Earnings, beginning balance	$210,000
Retained Earnings, ending balance	250,000
Net income	115,000
Fair value of large stock dividend declared	25,000
Dividend Payable, beginning balance	75,000
Dividend Payable, ending balance	80,000

Required

1. Assume that the only other amount that affected Retained Earnings during the year was a cash dividend that was declared. Compute the amount of the cash dividend declared during the current year.
2. Compute the amount of cash dividends actually paid in cash to stockholders during the year.

Exercise 11-2 Solving for Stockholders' Equity Amounts

LO1

Assume that the following amounts are known for Miles Company for the current year:

Retained Earnings, beginning balance	$420,000
Retained Earnings, ending balance	500,000
Cash dividends declared	100,000
Fair value of large stock dividend declared	50,000
Dividend Payable, beginning balance	90,000
Dividend Payable, ending balance	80,000

(Continued)

Required

1. Assume that the only other amount that affected Retained Earnings during the year was the net income. Compute the net income for Miles Company for the current year.
2. Compute the amount of cash dividends actually paid in cash to stockholders during the year.

LO1   Exercise 11-3 Solve for Unknowns

The Stockholders' Equity category of Zache Company's balance sheet appears below.

Common stock, $10 par, 10,000 shares issued, 9,200 outstanding	$?
Additional paid-in capital	?
Total contributed capital	$350,000
Retained earnings	100,000
Treasury stock, ? shares at cost	10,000
Total stockholders' equity	$?

Required

1. Determine the missing values indicated by question marks.
2. What was the cost per share of the treasury stock?

LO1   Exercise 11-4 Stockholders' Equity Accounts

MJ Company has identified the following items. Indicate whether each item is included in an account in the Stockholders' Equity category of the balance sheet and identify the account title. Also, indicate whether the item would increase or decrease stockholders' equity.

1. Preferred stock issued by MJ
2. Amount received by MJ in excess of par value when preferred stock was issued
3. Dividends in arrears on MJ preferred stock
4. Cash dividend declared but unpaid on MJ stock
5. Stock dividend declared but unissued by MJ
6. Treasury stock
7. Amount received in excess of cost when treasury stock is reissued by MJ
8. Retained earnings

LO3   Exercise 11-5 Stock Issuance

EXAMPLE 11-1

The following transactions are for Weber Corporation in 2012:

a. On March 1, the corporation was organized and received authorization to issue 5,000 shares of 8%, $100 par value preferred stock and 2,000,000 shares of $10 par value common stock.
b. On March 10, Weber issued 5,000 shares of common stock at $35 per share.
c. On March 18, Weber issued 100 shares of preferred stock at $120 per share.
d. On April 12, Weber issued another 10,000 shares of common stock at $45 per share.

Required

1. Identify and analyze the effect of each transaction.
2. Prepare the Stockholders' Equity section of the balance sheet as of December 31, 2012.
3. Does the balance sheet indicate the market value of the stock at year-end? Explain.

LO3   Exercise 11-6 Stock Issuance

EXAMPLE 11-1, 11-2

Horace Company had the following transactions during 2012, its first year of business.

a. Issued 5,000 shares of $5 par common stock for cash at $15 per share.
b. Issued 7,000 shares of common stock on May 1 to acquire a factory building from Barkley Company. Barkley had acquired the building in 2008 at a price of $150,000. Horace estimated that the building was worth $175,000 on May 1, 2012.
c. Issued 2,000 shares of stock on June 1 to acquire a patent. The accountant has been unable to estimate the value of the patent but has determined that Horace's common stock was selling at $25 per share on June 1.

Required

1. Identify and analyze the effect of each transaction.
2. Determine the balance sheet amounts for common stock and additional paid-in capital.

Exercise 11-7 Treasury Stock Transactions

LO4
EXAMPLE 11-3

The Stockholders' Equity category of Little Joe's balance sheet on January 1, 2012, appeared as follows:

Common stock, $5 par, 40,000 shares issued and outstanding	$200,000
Additional paid-in capital	90,000
Retained earnings	100,000
Total stockholders' equity	$390,000

The following transactions occurred during 2012:

a. Reacquired 5,000 shares of common stock at $20 per share on February 1.
b. Reacquired 1,200 shares of common stock at $13 per share on March 1.

Required

1. Identify and analyze the effect of each transaction.
2. Assume that the treasury stock was reissued on October 1 at $12 per share. Did the company benefit from the treasury stock reissuance? Where is the "gain" or "loss" presented on the financial statements?
3. What effect did the two transactions to purchase treasury stock and the later reissuance of that stock have on the Stockholders' Equity section of the balance sheet?

Exercise 11-8 Treasury Stock

LO4
EXAMPLE 11-3

The Stockholders' Equity category of Bradford Company's balance sheet on January 1, 2012, appeared as follows:

Common stock, $10 par, 10,000 shares issued and outstanding	$100,000
Additional paid-in capital	50,000
Retained earnings	80,000
Total stockholders' equity	$230,000

The following transactions occurred during 2012:

a. Reacquired 2,000 shares of common stock at $20 per share on July 1.
b. Reacquired 400 shares of common stock at $18 per share on August 1.

Required

1. Identify and analyze the effect of each transaction.
2. Assume that the company resold the shares of treasury stock at $28 per share on October 1. Did the company benefit from the treasury stock transaction? If so, where is the "gain" presented on the balance sheet?

Exercise 11-9 Cash Dividends

LO5
EXAMPLE 11-5, 11-6

The Stockholders' Equity category of Jackson Company's balance sheet as of January 1, 2012, appeared as follows:

Preferred stock, $100 par, 8%, 2,000 shares issued and outstanding	$200,000
Common stock, $10 par, 5,000 shares issued and outstanding	50,000
Additional paid-in capital	300,000
Total contributed capital	$550,000
Retained earnings	400,000
Total stockholders' equity	$950,000

(Continued)

The notes that accompany the financial statements indicate that Jackson has not paid dividends for the two years prior to 2012. On July 1, 2012, Jackson declares a dividend of $100,000 to be paid to preferred and common stockholders on August 1.

Required

1. Determine the amounts of the dividends to be allocated to preferred and common stockholders assuming that the preferred stock is noncumulative, nonparticipating stock.
2. Identify and analyze the effect of the transactions on July 1 and August 1, 2012.
3. Determine the amounts of the dividends to be allocated to preferred and common stockholders assuming instead that the preferred stock is cumulative, nonparticipating stock.

LO5
EXAMPLE 11-5, 11-6

Exercise 11-10 Cash Dividends

Kerry Company has 1,000 shares of $100 par value, 9% preferred stock and 10,000 shares of $10 par value common stock outstanding. The preferred stock is cumulative and nonparticipating. Dividends were paid in 2008. Since 2008, Kerry has declared and paid dividends as follows:

2009	$ 0
2010	10,000
2011	20,000
2012	25,000

Required

1. Determine the amount of the dividends to be allocated to preferred and common stockholders for each year 2010 to 2012.
2. If the preferred stock had been noncumulative, how much would have been allocated to the preferred and common stockholders each year?

LO6
EXAMPLE 11-7

Exercise 11-11 Stock Dividends

The Stockholders' Equity category of Worthy Company's balance sheet as of January 1, 2012, appeared as follows:

Common stock, $10 par, 40,000 shares issued and outstanding	$400,000
Additional paid-in capital	100,000
Retained earnings	400,000
Total stockholders' equity	$900,000

The following transactions occurred during 2012:

a. Declared a 10% stock dividend to common stockholders on January 15. At the time of the dividend, the common stock was selling for $30 per share. The stock dividend was to be issued to stockholders on January 30, 2012.
b. Distributed the stock dividend to the stockholders on January 30, 2012.

Required

1. Identify and analyze the effect of the transactions.
2. Develop the Stockholders' Equity category of Worthy Company's balance sheet as of January 31, 2012, after the stock dividend was issued. What effect did those transactions have on total stockholders' equity?

LO7
EXAMPLE 11-7, 11-9

Exercise 11-12 Stock Dividends and Stock Splits

Whitacre Company's Stockholders' Equity section of the balance sheet on December 31, 2011, was as follows:

Common stock, $10 par value, 60,000 shares issued and outstanding	$ 600,000
Additional paid-in capital	480,000
Retained earnings	1,240,000
Total stockholders' equity	$2,320,000

On May 1, 2012, Whitacre declared and issued a 15% stock dividend, when the stock was selling for $20 per share. Then on November 1, it declared and issued a 2-for-1 stock split.

Required

1. How many shares of stock are outstanding at year-end?
2. What is the par value per share of these shares?
3. Develop the Stockholders' Equity category of Whitacre's balance sheet as of December 31, 2012.

Exercise 11-13 Stock Dividends versus Stock Splits

LO7

EXAMPLE 11-8, 11-9

Campbell Company wants to increase the number of shares of its common stock outstanding and is considering a stock dividend versus a stock split. The Stockholders' Equity section of the firm's most recent balance sheet appeared as follows:

Common stock, $10 par, 50,000 shares issued and outstanding	$ 500,000
Additional paid-in capital	750,000
Retained earnings	880,000
Total stockholders' equity	$2,130,000

If a stock dividend is chosen, the firm wants to declare a 100% stock dividend. Because the stock dividend qualifies as a "large stock dividend," it must be recorded at par value. If a stock split is chosen, Campbell will declare a 2-for-1 split.

Required

1. Compare the effects of the stock dividends and stock splits on the accounting equation.
2. Develop the Stockholders' Equity category of Campbell's balance sheet (a) after the stock dividend and (b) after the stock split.

Exercise 11-14 Comprehensive Income

LO8

Assume that you are the accountant for Ellis Corporation, which has issued its 2012 annual report. You have received an inquiry from a stockholder who has questions about several items in the annual report, including why Ellis has not shown certain transactions on the income statement. In particular, Ellis's 2012 balance sheet revealed two accounts in Stockholders' Equity (Unrealized Gain/Loss—Available-for-Sale Securities and Loss on Foreign Currency Translation Adjustments) for which the dollar amounts involved were not reported on the income statement.

Required

Draft a written response to the stockholder's inquiry that explains the nature of the two accounts and the reason the amounts involved were not recorded on the 2012 income statement. Do you think that the concept of comprehensive income would be useful to explain the impact of all events for Ellis Corporation? Why or why not?

Exercise 11-15 Reporting Changes in Stockholders' Equity Items

LO8

On May 1, 2011, Ryde Inc. had common stock of $345,000, additional paid-in capital of $1,298,000, and retained earnings of $3,013,000. Ryde did not purchase or sell any common stock during the year. The company reported net income of $556,000 and declared dividends in the amount of $78,000 during the year ended April 30, 2012.

Required

Prepare a financial statement that explains the differences between the beginning and ending balances for the accounts in the Stockholders' Equity category of the balance sheet.

LO9   Exercise 11-16 Payout Ratio and Book Value per Share

Divac Company has developed a statement of stockholders' equity for the year 2012 as follows:

	Preferred Stock	Paid-In Capital— Preferred	Common Stock	Paid-In Capital— Common	Retained Earnings
Balance, Jan. 1	$100,000	$50,000	$400,000	$40,000	$200,000
Stock issued			100,000	10,000	
Net income					80,000
Cash dividend					−45,000
Stock dividend	10,000	5,000			−15,000
Balance, Dec. 31	$110,000	$55,000	$500,000	$50,000	$220,000

Divac's preferred stock is $100 par, 8% stock. If the stock is liquidated or redeemed, stockholders are entitled to $120 per share. There are no dividends in arrears on the stock. The common stock has a par value of $5 per share.

Required

1. Determine the dividend payout ratio for the common stock.
2. Determine the book value per share of Divac's common stock.

LO10   Exercise 11-17 Determining Dividends Paid on Statement of Cash Flows

Clifford Company's comparative balance sheet included dividends payable of $80,000 at December 31, 2011, and $100,000 at December 31, 2012. Dividends declared by Clifford during 2012 amounted to $400,000.

Required

1. Calculate the amount of dividends actually paid to stockholders during 2012.
2. How will Clifford report the dividend payments on its 2012 statement of cash flows?

LO10   Exercise 11-18 Impact of Transactions Involving Dividends on Statement of Cash Flows

From the following list, identify each item as operating (O), investing (I), financing (F), or not separately reported on the statement of cash flows (N).

_____ Payment of cash dividend on common stock
_____ Payment of cash dividend on preferred stock
_____ Distribution of stock dividend
_____ Declaration of stock split

LO10   Exercise 11-19 Impact of Transactions Involving Issuance of Stock on Statement of Cash Flows

From the following list, identify each item as operating (O), investing (I), financing (F), or not separately reported on the statement of cash flows (N).

_____ Issuance of common stock for cash
_____ Issuance of preferred stock for cash
_____ Issuance of common stock for equipment
_____ Issuance of preferred stock for land and building
_____ Conversion of preferred stock into common stock

LO10   Exercise 11-20 Impact of Transactions Involving Treasury Stock on Statement of Cash Flows

From the following list, identify each item as operating (O), investing (I), financing (F), or not separately reported on the statement of cash flows (N).

_____   Repurchase of common stock as treasury stock
_____   Reissuance of common stock (held as treasury stock)
_____   Retirement of treasury stock

Exercise 11-21 Partnerships (Appendix)

LO11
EXAMPLE 11-11

Sports Central is a sporting goods store owned by Lewis, Jamal, and Lapin in partnership. On January 1, 2012, their capital balances were as follows:

Lewis, Capital	$20,000
Jamal, Capital	50,000
Lapin, Capital	30,000

During 2012, Lewis withdrew $5,000; Jamal, $12,000; and Lapin, $9,000. Income for the partnership for 2012 was $50,000.

Required

If the partners agreed to allocate income equally, what was the ending balance in each of their capital accounts on December 31, 2012?

Exercise 11-22 Sole Proprietorships (Appendix)

LO11
EXAMPLE 11-10

Terry Woods opened Par Golf as a sole proprietor by investing $50,000 cash on January 1, 2012. Because the business was new, it operated at a net loss of $10,000 for 2012. During the year, Terry withdrew $20,000 from the business for living expenses. Terry also had $4,000 of interest income from sources unrelated to the business.

Required

Present the Owner's Equity category of Par Golf's balance sheet as of December 31, 2012.

PROBLEMS

Problem 11-1 Stockholders' Equity Category

LO1

Peeler Company was incorporated as a new business on January 1, 2012. The corporate charter approved on that date authorized the issuance of 1,000 shares of $100 par, 7% cumulative, nonparticipating preferred stock and 10,000 shares of $5 par common stock. On January 10, Peeler issued for cash 500 shares of preferred stock at $120 per share and 4,000 shares of common stock at $80 per share. On January 20, it issued 1,000 shares of common stock to acquire a building site at a time when the stock was selling for $70 per share.

During 2012, Peeler established an employee benefit plan and acquired 500 shares of common stock at $60 per share as treasury stock for that purpose. Later in 2012, it resold 100 shares of the stock at $65 per share.

On December 31, 2012, Peeler determined its net income for the year to be $40,000. The firm declared the annual cash dividend to preferred stockholders and a cash dividend of $5 per share to the common stockholders. The dividends will be paid in 2013.

Required

Develop the Stockholders' Equity category of Peeler's balance sheet as of December 31, 2012. Indicate on the statement the number of shares authorized, issued, and outstanding for both preferred and common stock.

Problem 11-2 Evaluating Alternative Investments

LO2

Ellen Hays received a windfall from one of her investments. She would like to invest $100,000 of the money in Linwood Inc., which is offering common stock, preferred stock, and bonds on the open market. The common stock has paid $8 per share in dividends for the past three years, and the company expects to be able to perform as well in the current year. The current market price of the common stock is $100 per share. The preferred stock has an 8% dividend rate, cumulative and nonparticipating. The bonds are selling at par with an 8% stated rate.

(Continued)

Required

1. What are the advantages and disadvantages of each type of investment?
2. Recommend one type of investment over the others to Ellen and justify your reason.

LO5 Problem 11-3 Dividends for Preferred and Common Stock

The Stockholders' Equity category of Greenbaum Company's balance sheet as of December 31, 2012, appeared as follows:

Preferred stock, $100 par, 8%, 1,000 shares	
issued and outstanding	$ 100,000
Common stock, $10 par, 20,000 shares	
issued and outstanding	200,000
Additional paid-in capital	250,000
Total contributed capital	$ 550,000
Retained earnings	450,000
Total stockholders' equity	$1,000,000

The notes to the financial statements indicate that dividends were not declared or paid for 2010 or 2011. Greenbaum wants to declare a dividend of $59,000 for 2012.

Required

Determine the total and the per-share amounts that should be declared to the preferred and common stockholders under the following assumptions:
1. The preferred stock is noncumulative, nonparticipating.
2. The preferred stock is cumulative, nonparticipating.

LO6 Problem 11-4 Effect of Stock Dividend

Favre Company has a history of paying cash dividends on its common stock. However, the firm did not have a particularly profitable year in 2012. At the end of the year, Favre found itself without the necessary cash for a dividend and therefore declared a stock dividend to its common stockholders. A 50% stock dividend was declared to stockholders on December 31, 2012. The board of directors is unclear about a stock dividend's effect on Favre's balance sheet and has requested your assistance.

Required

1. Write a statement to indicate the effect the stock dividend has on the financial statements of Favre Company.
2. A group of common stockholders has contacted the firm to express its concern about the effect of the stock dividend and to question the effect the stock dividend may have on the market price of the stock. Write a statement to address the stockholders' concerns.

LO7 Problem 11-5 Dividends and Stock Splits

On January 1, 2012, Frederiksen Inc.'s Stockholders' Equity category appeared as follows:

Preferred stock, $80 par value, 7%, 3,000	
shares issued and outstanding	$ 240,000
Common stock, $10 par value, 15,000 shares	
issued and outstanding	150,000
Additional paid-in capital—Preferred	60,000
Additional paid-in capital—Common	225,000
Total contributed capital	$ 675,000
Retained earnings	2,100,000
Total stockholders' equity	$2,775,000

The preferred stock is noncumulative and nonparticipating. During 2012, the following transactions occurred:

a. On March 1, declared a cash dividend of $16,800 on preferred stock. Paid the dividend on April 1.

b. On June 1, declared a 5% stock dividend on common stock. The current market price of the common stock was $18. The stock was issued on July 1.

c. On September 1, declared a cash dividend of $0.50 per share on the common stock; paid the dividend on October 1.

d. On December 1, issued a 2-for-1 stock split of common stock when the stock was selling for $50 per share.

Required

1. Explain each transaction's effect on the stockholders' equity accounts and the total stockholders' equity.

2. Develop the Stockholders' Equity category of the December 31, 2012, balance sheet. Assume that the net income for the year was $650,000.

3. Write a paragraph that explains the difference between a stock dividend and a stock split.

Problem 11-6 Statement of Stockholders' Equity   LO8

Refer to all of the facts in Problem 11-1.

Required

Develop a statement of stockholders' equity for Peeler Company for 2012. The statement should start with the beginning balance of each stockholders' equity account and explain the changes that occurred in each account to arrive at the 2012 ending balances.

Problem 11-7 Wal-Mart's Comprehensive Income   LO8

Following is the consolidated statement of shareholders' equity of **Wal-Mart Stores, Inc.**, for the year ended January 31, 2010:

WAL-MART STORES, INC.

Fiscal years ended January 31,	2010	2009	2008
Comprehensive Income:			
Consolidated net income[1]	$14,848	$13,899	$13,137
Other comprehensive income:			
Currency translation[2]	2,854	(6,860)	1,226
Net change in fair values of derivatives	94	(17)	—
Minimum pension liability	(220)	(46)	138
Total comprehensive income	$17,576	$ 6,976	$14,501

Required

1. Which items were included in comprehensive income? If these items had been included on the income statement as part of net income, what would have been the effect?

2. Would the concept of comprehensive income help to explain to Wal-Mart's stockholders the impact of all events that took place in 2010? Why or why not?

Problem 11-8 Effects of Stockholders' Equity Transactions on Statement of Cash Flows   LO10

Refer to all of the facts in Problem 11-1.

Required

Indicate how each transaction affects the cash flow of Peeler Company by preparing the Financing Activities section of the 2012 statement of cash flows. Provide an explanation for the exclusion of any of these transactions from the Financing Activities section of the statement.

Problem 11-9 Sole Proprietorships (Appendix)   LO11

On May 1, Chong Yu deposited $120,000 of his own savings in a separate bank account to start a printing business. He purchased copy machines for $42,000. Expenses for the year, including depreciation on the copy machines, were $84,000. Sales for the year, all in cash, were $108,000. Chong withdrew $12,000 during the year.

(Continued)

Required

1. What is the balance in Chong's capital account at the end of the year?
2. Explain why the balance in Chong's capital account is different from the amount of cash on hand.

LO11

Problem 11-10 Partnerships (Appendix)

Kirin Nerise and Milt O'Brien agreed to form a partnership to operate a sandwich shop. Kirin contributed $25,000 cash and will manage the store. Milt contributed computer equipment worth $8,000 and $92,000 cash. Milt will keep the financial records. During the year, sales were $90,000 and expenses (including a salary to Kirin) were $76,000. Kirin withdrew $500 per month. Milt withdrew $4,000 (total). Their partnership agreement specified that Kirin would receive a salary of $7,200 for the year. Milt would receive 6% interest on his initial capital investment. All remaining income or loss would be equally divided.

Required

Calculate the ending balance in each partner's equity account.

LO11

Problem 11-11 Income Distribution of a Partnership (Appendix)

Louise Abbott and Buddie Costello are partners in a comedy club business. The partnership agreement specifies the manner in which income of the business is to be distributed. Louise is to receive a salary of $20,000 for managing the club. Buddie is to receive interest at the rate of 10% on her capital balance of $300,000. Remaining income is to be distributed at a 2-to-1 ratio.

Required

Determine the amount that should be distributed to each partner assuming the following business net incomes:

1. $15,000
2. $50,000
3. $80,000

MULTI-CONCEPT PROBLEMS

LO1 • 4

Problem 11-12 Stockholders' Equity Section of the Balance Sheet

The newly hired accountant at Ives Inc. prepared the following balance sheet:

Assets	
Cash	$ 3,500
Accounts receivable	5,000
Treasury stock	500
Plant, property, and equipment	108,000
Retained earnings	1,000
Total assets	$118,000
Liabilities	
Accounts payable	$ 5,500
Dividends payable	1,500
Stockholders' Equity	
Common stock, $1 par, 100,000 shares issued	100,000
Additional paid-in capital	11,000
Total liabilities and stockholders' equity	$118,000

Required

1. Prepare a corrected balance sheet. Write a short explanation for each correction.
2. Why does the Retained Earnings account have a negative balance?

Problem 11-13 Analysis of Stockholders' Equity

LO1 • 4

The Stockholders' Equity section of the December 31, 2012, balance sheet of Eldon Company appeared as follows:

Preferred stock, $30 par value, 5,000 shares authorized, ? shares issued	$120,000
Common stock, ? par, 10,000 shares authorized, 7,000 shares issued	70,000
Additional paid-in capital—Preferred	6,000
Additional paid-in capital—Common	560,000
Additional paid-in capital—Treasury stock	1,000
Total contributed capital	$757,000
Retained earnings	40,000
Less: Treasury stock, preferred, 100 shares	(3,200)
Total stockholders' equity	$?

Required

Determine the following items based on Eldon's balance sheet.
1. The number of shares of preferred stock issued
2. The number of shares of preferred stock outstanding
3. The average per-share sales price of the preferred stock when issued
4. The par value of the common stock
5. The average per-share sales price of the common stock when issued
6. The cost of the treasury stock per share
7. The total stockholders' equity
8. The per-share book value of the common stock assuming that there are no dividends in arrears and that the preferred stock can be redeemed at its par value

Problem 11-14 Effects of Stockholders' Equity Transactions on the Balance Sheet

LO3 • 4 • 7

The following transactions occurred at Horton Inc. during its first year of operation:

a. Issued 100,000 shares of common stock at $5 each; 1,000,000 shares are authorized at $1 par value.
b. Issued 10,000 shares of common stock for a building and land. The building was appraised for $20,000, but the value of the land is undeterminable. The stock is selling for $10 on the open market.
c. Purchased 1,000 shares of its own common stock on the open market for $16 per share.
d. Declared a dividend of $0.10 per share on outstanding common stock. The dividend is to be paid after the end of the first year of operations. Market value of the stock is $26.
e. Declared a 2-for-1 stock split. The market value of the stock was $37 before the stock split.
f. Reported $180,000 of income for the year.

Required

1. Indicate each transaction's effect on the assets, liabilities, and stockholders' equity of Horton Inc.
2. Prepare the Stockholders' Equity section of the balance sheet.
3. Write a paragraph that explains the number of shares of stock issued and outstanding at the end of the year.

ALTERNATE PROBLEMS

Problem 11-1A Stockholders' Equity Category

LO1

Kebler Company was incorporated as a new business on January 1, 2012. The corporate charter approved on that date authorized the issuance of 2,000 shares of $100 par, 7% cumulative, non-participating preferred stock and 20,000 shares of $5 par common stock. On January 10, Kebler

(Continued)

issued for cash 1,000 shares of preferred stock at $120 per share and 8,000 shares of common stock at $80 per share. On January 20, it issued 2,000 shares of common stock to acquire a building site at a time when the stock was selling for $70 per share.

During 2012, Kebler established an employee benefit plan and acquired 1,000 shares of common stock at $60 per share as treasury stock for that purpose. Later in 2012, it resold 100 shares of the stock at $65 per share.

On December 31, 2012, Kebler determined its net income for the year to be $80,000. The firm declared the annual cash dividend to preferred stockholders and a cash dividend of $5 per share to the common stockholders. The dividend will be paid in 2013.

Required

Develop the Stockholders' Equity category of Kebler's balance sheet as of December 31, 2012. Indicate on the statement the number of shares authorized, issued, and outstanding for both preferred and common stock.

LO2   ## Problem 11-2A Evaluating Alternative Investments

Rob Lowe would like to invest $100,000 in Franklin Inc., which is offering common stock, preferred stock, and bonds on the open market. The common stock has paid $1 per share in dividends for the past three years, and the company expects to be able to double the dividend in the current year. The current market price of the common stock is $10 per share. The preferred stock has an 8% dividend rate. The bonds are selling at par with a 5% stated rate.

Required

1. Explain Franklin's obligation to pay dividends or interest on each instrument.
2. Recommend one type of investment over the others to Rob and justify your reason.

LO5   ## Problem 11-3A Dividends for Preferred and Common Stock

The Stockholders' Equity category of Rausch Company's balance sheet as of December 31, 2012, appeared as follows:

Preferred stock, $100 par, 8%, 2,000 shares issued and outstanding	$ 200,000
Common stock, $10 par, 40,000 shares issued and outstanding	400,000
Additional paid-in capital	500,000
Total contributed capital	$1,100,000
Retained earnings	900,000
Total stockholders' equity	$2,000,000

The notes to the financial statements indicate that dividends were not declared or paid for 2010 or 2011. Rausch wants to declare a dividend of $118,000 for 2012.

Required

Determine the total and the per-share amounts that should be declared to the preferred and common stockholders under the following assumptions:
1. The preferred stock is noncumulative, nonparticipating.
2. The preferred stock is cumulative, nonparticipating.

LO6   ## Problem 11-4A Effect of Stock Dividend

Travanti Company has a history of paying cash dividends on its common stock. Although the firm has been profitable this year, the board of directors is planning construction of a second manufacturing plant. To reduce the amount that they must borrow to finance the expansion, the directors are contemplating replacing their usual cash dividend with a 40% stock dividend. The board is unsure about a stock dividend's effect on the company's balance sheet and has requested your assistance.

Required

1. Write a statement to explain the effect the stock dividend has on the financial statements of Travanti Company.
2. A group of common stockholders has contacted the firm to express its concern about the effect of the stock dividend and to question the effect the stock dividend may have on the market price of the stock. Write a statement to address the stockholders' concerns.

Problem 11-5A Dividends and Stock Splits

LO7

On January 1, 2012, Svenberg Inc.'s Stockholders' Equity category appeared as follows:

Preferred stock, $80 par value, 8%, 1,000 shares issued and outstanding	$ 80,000
Common stock, $10 par value, 10,000 shares issued and outstanding	100,000
Additional paid-in capital—Preferred	60,000
Additional paid-in capital—Common	225,000
Total contributed capital	$ 465,000
Retained earnings	1,980,000
Total stockholders' equity	$2,445,000

The preferred stock is noncumulative and nonparticipating. During 2012, the following transactions occurred:

a. On March 1, declared a cash dividend of $6,400 on preferred stock. Paid the dividend on April 1.
b. On June 1, declared an 8% stock dividend on common stock. The current market price of the common stock was $26. The stock was issued on July 1.
c. On September 1, declared a cash dividend of $0.70 per share on the common stock; paid the dividend on October 1.
d. On December 1, issued a 3-for-1 stock split of common stock, when the stock was selling for $30 per share.

Required

1. Explain each transaction's effect on the stockholders' equity accounts and the total stockholders' equity.
2. Develop the Stockholders' Equity category of the balance sheet. Assume that the net income for the year was $720,000.
3. Write a paragraph that explains the difference between a stock dividend and a stock split.

Problem 11-6A Statement of Stockholders' Equity

LO8

Refer to all of the facts in Problem 11-1A.

Required

Develop a statement of Stockholders' Equity for Kebler Company for 2012. The statement should start with the beginning balance of each stockholders' equity account and explain the changes that occurred in each account to arrive at the 2012 ending balances.

Problem 11-7A Costco's Comprehensive Income

LO8

Following is the consolidated statement of stockholders' equity of **Costco Wholesale Corporation** for the year ended August 29, 2010:

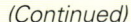

(Continued)

Costco Wholesale Corporation
Consolidated Statements of Equity
and Comprehensive Income
(dollars in millions)

	Additional Paid-in Capital	Accumulated Other Comprehensive Income	Total Costco		Noncontrolling Interests	Total
			Retained Earnings	Stockholders' Equity		
BALANCE AT AUGUST 30, 2009	3,811	110	6,101	10,024	80	10,104
Comprehensive Income:						
Net income			1,303	1,303	20	1,323
Unrealized gain on short-term investments, net of ($1) tax		3		3	0	3
Foreign currency translation adjustment and other		9		9	1	10
Comprehensive income				1,315	21	1,336
Stock options exercised and vesting of restricted stock units, including income tax benefits and other	205			205		205
Conversion of convertible notes	1			1		1
Repurchase of common stock	(92)		(476)	(568)		(568)
Stock-based compensation	190			190		190
Cash dividends			(338)	(338)		(338)
BALANCE AT AUGUST 29, 2010	$4,115	$122	$6,590	$10,829	$101	$10,930

Required

1. Costco has an item in the statement of stockholders' equity called other comprehensive income. What are the possible sources of other comprehensive income as discussed in your text?
2. Besides net income and other comprehensive income, what other items affected stockholders' equity during the period?
3. How do cash dividends affect stockholders' equity? How would a stock dividend affect stockholders' equity?

LO10 Problem 11-8A Effects of Stockholders' Equity Transactions on the Statement of Cash Flows

Refer to all of the facts in Problem 11-1A.

Required

Indicate how each transaction affects the cash flow of Kebler Company by preparing the Financing Activities section of the 2012 statement of cash flows. Provide an explanation for the exclusion of any of these transactions from the Financing Activities section of the statement.

LO11 Problem 11-9A Sole Proprietorships (Appendix)

On May 1, Chen Chien Lao deposited $150,000 of her own savings in a separate bank account to start a printing business. She purchased copy machines for $52,500. Expenses for the year, including depreciation on the copy machines, were $105,000. Sales for the year, all in cash, were $135,000. Chen withdrew $15,000 during the year.

Required

1. What is the balance in Chen's capital account at the end of the year?
2. Explain why the balance in Chen's capital account is different from the amount of cash on hand.

Problem 11-10A Partnerships (Appendix)

LO11

Karen Locke and Gina Keyes agreed to form a partnership to operate a sandwich shop. Karen contributed $35,000 cash and will manage the store. Gina contributed computer equipment worth $11,200 and $128,800 cash. Gina will keep the financial records. During the year, sales were $126,000 and expenses (including a salary for Karen) were $106,400. Karen withdrew $700 per month. Gina withdrew $5,600 (total). Their partnership agreement specified that Karen would receive a salary of $10,800 for the year. Gina would receive 6% interest on her initial capital investment. All remaining income or loss would be equally divided.

Required

Calculate the ending balance in each partner's equity account.

Problem 11-11A Income Distribution of a Partnership (Appendix)

LO11

Kay Katz and Doris Kan are partners in a dry-cleaning business. The partnership agreement specifies the manner in which income of the business is to be distributed. Kay is to receive a salary of $40,000 for managing the business. Doris is to receive interest at the rate of 10% on her capital balance of $600,000. Remaining income is to be distributed at a 2-to-1 ratio.

Required

Determine the amount that should be distributed to each partner assuming the following business net incomes:
1. $30,000
2. $100,000
3. $160,000

ALTERNATE MULTI-CONCEPT PROBLEMS

Problem 11-12A Analysis of Stockholders' Equity

LO1 • 4

The Stockholders' Equity section of the December 31, 2012, balance sheet of Carter Company appeared as follows:

Preferred stock, $50 par value,	
10,000 shares authorized, ? shares issued	$ 400,000
Common stock, ? par value, 20,000 shares	
authorized, 14,000 shares issued	280,000
Additional paid-in capital—Preferred	12,000
Additional paid-in capital—Common	980,000
Additional paid-in capital—Treasury stock	2,000
Total contributed capital	$1,674,000
Retained earnings	80,000
Less: Treasury stock, preferred, 200 shares	(12,800)
Total stockholders' equity	$?

Required

Determine the following items based on Carter's balance sheet.
1. The number of shares of preferred stock issued
2. The number of shares of preferred stock outstanding
3. The average per-share sales price of the preferred stock when issued
4. The par value of the common stock
5. The average per-share sales price of the common stock when issued
6. The cost of the treasury stock per share
7. The total stockholders' equity
8. The per-share book value of the common stock assuming that there are no dividends in arrears and that the preferred stock can be redeemed at its par value

LO1 • 4   **Problem 11-13A Stockholders' Equity Section of the Balance Sheet**

The newly hired accountant at Grainfield Inc. is considering the following list of accounts as he prepares the balance sheet. All of the accounts have positive balances. The company is authorized to issue 1,000,000 shares of common stock and 10,000 shares of preferred stock. The treasury stock was purchased at $5 per share.

Treasury stock (common)	$ 15,000
Retained earnings	54,900
Dividends payable	1,500
Common stock, $1 par	100,000
Additional paid-in capital	68,400
Preferred stock, $10 par, 5%	50,000

Required

1. Prepare the Stockholders' Equity section of the balance sheet for Grainfield.
2. Explain why some of the listed accounts are not shown in the Stockholders' Equity section.

LO3 • 4 • 7   **Problem 11-14A Effects of Stockholders' Equity Transactions on Balance Sheet**

The following transactions occurred at Hilton Inc. during its first year of operation:

a. Issued 10,000 shares of common stock at $10 each; 100,000 shares are authorized at $1 par value.
b. Issued 10,000 shares of common stock for a patent, which is expected to be effective for the next 15 years. The value of the patent is undeterminable. The stock is selling for $10 on the open market.
c. Purchased 1,000 shares of its own common stock on the open market for $10 per share.
d. Declared a dividend of $0.50 per share of outstanding common stock. The dividend is to be paid after the end of the first year of operations. Market value of the stock is $10.
e. Reported $340,000 of income for the year.

Required

1. Indicate each transaction's effect on the assets, liabilities, and stockholders' equity of Hilton Inc.
2. Hilton's president has asked you to explain the difference between contributed capital and retained earnings. Discuss the terms as they relate to Hilton.
3. Determine the book value per share of the stock at the end of the year.

DECISION CASES

Reading and Interpreting Financial Statements

LO1 • 8   **Decision Case 11-1 Comparing Two Companies in the Same Industry: Kellogg's and General Mills**

Refer to the Stockholders' Equity section of the balance sheets of **Kellogg's** as of December 31, 2010, and **General Mills** as of May 30, 2010.

Required

1. For each company, what are the numbers of shares of common stock authorized, issued, and outstanding as of the balance sheet date?
2. Did the balance of the Retained Earnings account of each company increase or decrease during the year? What factors can affect the Retained Earnings balance?
3. How does the total stockholders' equity of each company compare to that of the other company? Does the difference mean that one company's stock is more valuable than the other's? Explain your answer.

Decision Case 11-2 Reading General Mills's Statement of Cash Flows LO10

Refer to **General Mills**'s statement of cash flows for the year ending May 30, 2010.

Required

1. What sources of cash are revealed in the Financing Activities category of the statement of cash flows?
2. What was the amount of dividends paid to stockholders during the period?
3. The Financing Activities section indicates a large negative amount for the purchase of treasury stock. When treasury stock is purchased, what is the effect on the accounts of the balance sheet?

Making Financial Decisions

Decision Case 11-3 Debt versus Preferred Stock LO1 • 2

Assume that you are an analyst attempting to compare the financial structures of two companies. In particular, you must analyze the debt and equity categories of the two firms and calculate a debt-to-equity ratio for each firm. The Liability and Equity categories of First Company at year-end appeared as follows:

Liabilities	
Accounts payable	$ 500,000
Loan payable	800,000
Stockholders' Equity	
Common stock	300,000
Retained earnings	600,000
Total liabilities and equity	$2,200,000

First Company's loan payable bears interest at 8%, which is paid annually. The principal is due in five years.

The Liability and Equity categories of Second Company at year-end appeared as follows:

Liabilities	
Accounts payable	$ 500,000
Stockholders' Equity	
Common stock	300,000
Preferred stock	800,000
Retained earnings	600,000
Total liabilities and equity	$2,200,000

Second Company's preferred stock is 8%, cumulative. A provision of the stock agreement specifies that the stock must be redeemed at face value in five years.

Required

1. It appears that the loan payable of First Company and the preferred stock of Second Company are very similar. What are the differences between the two securities?
2. When calculating the debt-to-equity ratio, do you believe that the Second Company preferred stock should be treated as debt or as stockholders' equity? Write a statement expressing your position on the issue.

Decision Case 11-4 Preferred versus Common Stock LO2

Rohnan Inc. needs to raise $500,000. It is considering two options:

a. Issue preferred stock, $100 par, 8%, cumulative, nonparticipating, callable at $110. The stock could be issued at par.
b. Issue common stock, $1 par, market $10. Currently, the company has 400,000 shares outstanding distributed equally in the hands of five owners. The company has never paid a dividend.

Required

Rohnan has asked you to consider both options and make a recommendation. It is equally concerned with cash flow and company control. Write your recommendations.

Ethical Decision Making

LO9   Decision Case 11-5   Inside Information

Jim Brock was an accountant with Hubbard Inc., a large corporation with stock that was publicly traded on the New York Stock Exchange. One of Jim's duties was to manage the corporate reporting department, which was responsible for developing and issuing Hubbard's annual report. At the end of 2012, Hubbard closed its accounting records and initial calculations indicated a very profitable year. In fact, the net income exceeded the amount that had been projected during the year by the financial analysts who followed Hubbard's stock.

Jim was pleased with the company's financial performance. In January 2013, he suggested that his father buy Hubbard's stock because he was sure the stock price would increase when the company announced its 2012 results. Jim's father followed that advice and bought a block of stock at $25 per share.

On February 15, 2013, Hubbard announced its 2012 results and issued the annual report. The company received favorable press coverage about its performance, and the stock price on the stock exchange increased to $32 per share.

Required

What was Jim's professional responsibility to Hubbard Inc. concerning the issuance of the 2012 annual report? Did Jim act ethically in this situation?

LO5   Decision Case 11-6   Dividend Policy

Hancock Inc. is owned by nearly 100 shareholders. Judith Stitch owns 48% of the stock. She needs cash to fulfill her commitment to donate the funds to construct a new art gallery. Some of her friends have agreed to vote for Hancock to pay a larger-than-normal dividend to shareholders. Judith has asked you to vote for the large dividend because she knows that you also support the arts. When informed that the dividend may create a working capital hardship on Hancock, Judith responded: "There is plenty of money in Retained Earnings. The dividend will not affect the cash of the company." Respond to her comment. What ethical questions do you and Judith face? How would you vote?

SOLUTIONS TO KEY TERMS QUIZ

13	Authorized shares		18	Retirement of stock
1	Issued shares		7	Dividend payout ratio
14	Outstanding shares		19	Stock dividend
2	Par value		9	Stock split
15	Additional paid-in capital		8	Statement of stockholders' equity
3	Retained earnings		11	Comprehensive income
4	Cumulative feature		10	Book value per share
16	Participating feature		12	Market value per share
5	Convertible feature		22	Sole proprietorship (Appendix)
17	Callable feature		20	Partnership (Appendix)
6	Treasury stock		21	Partnership agreement (Appendix)

INTEGRATIVE PROBLEM

Evaluating financing options for asset acquisition and their impact on financial statements

Following are the financial statements for Griffin Inc. for the year 2012:

Griffin Inc.
Balance Sheet
December 31, 2012
(in millions)

Assets		Liabilities	
Cash	$ 1.6	Current portion of lease	
Other current assets	6.4	obligation	$ 1.0
Leased assets (net of		Other current liabilities	3.0
accumulated depreciation)	7.0	Lease obligation—Long term	6.0
Other long-term assets	45.0	Other long-term liabilities	6.0
		Total liabilities	$16.0
		Stockholders' Equity	
		Preferred stock	$ 1.0
		Additional paid-in capital—	
		Preferred	2.0
		Common stock	4.0
		Additional paid-in capital—	
		Common	16.0
		Retained earnings	21.0
		Total stockholders' equity	$44.0
		Total liabilities and	
Total assets	$60.0	stockholders' equity	$60.0

Griffin Inc.
Income Statement
For the Year Ended December 31, 2012
(in millions)

Revenues		$ 50.0
Expenses:		
Depreciation of leased asset	$ 1.0	
Depreciation—Other assets	3.2	
Interest on leased asset	0.5	
Other expenses	27.4	
Income tax (30% rate)	5.4	
Total expenses		(37.5)
Income before extraordinary loss		$ 12.5
Extraordinary loss (net of $0.9 taxes)		(2.1)
Net income		$ 10.4
EPS before extraordinary loss		$ 3.10
EPS extraordinary loss		(0.53)
EPS—Net income		$ 2.57

Additional information:

Griffin Inc. has authorized 500,000 shares of 10%, $10 par value, cumulative preferred stock. There were 100,000 shares issued and outstanding at all times during 2012. The firm also has authorized 5 million shares of $1 par common stock, with 4 million shares issued and outstanding.

(Continued)

On January 1, 2012, Griffin Inc. acquired an asset, a piece of specialized heavy equipment, for $8 million with a capital lease. The lease contract indicates that the term of the lease is eight years. Payments of $1.5 million are to be made each December 31. The first lease payment was made December 31, 2012, and consisted of $1 million principal and $0.5 million of interest expense. The capital lease is depreciated using the straight-line method over eight years with zero salvage value.

Required

1. Assuming that the equipment was acquired using a capital lease, identify and analyze the effect of the acquisition, depreciation, and lease payment.
2. The management of Griffin Inc. is considering the financial statement impact of methods of financing, other than the capital lease, that could have been used to acquire the equipment. For each alternative (a), (b), and (c), indicate the effect on the accounting equation and prepare revised 2012 financial statements. Calculate, as revised, the following amounts or ratios:

   Current ratio
   Debt-to-equity ratio
   Net income
   EPS—Net income

Assume that the following alternative actions would have taken place on January 1, 2012:

a. Instead of acquiring the equipment with a capital lease, the company negotiated an operating lease to use the asset. The lease requires annual year-end payments of $1.5 million and results in "off-balance-sheet" financing. (*Hint:* The $1.5 million should be treated as rental expense.)
b. Instead of acquiring the equipment with a capital lease, Griffin Inc. issued bonds for $8 million and purchased the equipment with the proceeds of the bond issue. Assume that the bond interest of $0.5 million was accrued and paid on December 31, 2012. A portion of the principal also is paid each year for eight years. On December 31, 2012, the company paid $1 million of principal and anticipated another $1 million of principal to be paid in 2013. Assume that the equipment would have an eight-year life and would be depreciated on a straight-line basis with zero salvage value.
c. Instead of acquiring the equipment with a capital lease, Griffin Inc. issued 200,000 additional shares of 10% preferred stock to raise $8 million and purchased the equipment for $8 million with the proceeds from the stock issue. Dividends on the stock are declared and paid annually. Assume that a dividend payment was made on December 31, 2012. Assume that the equipment would have an eight-year life and would be depreciated on a straight-line basis with zero salvage value.

ANSWERS TO POD REVIEW

LO1	1. d	2. c		**LO7**	1. d	2. a
LO2	1. a	2. c		**LO8**	1. d	2. a
LO3	1. d	2. a		**LO9**	1. d	2. a
LO4	1. d	2. c		**LO10**	1. c	2. b
LO5	1. a	2. c		**LO11**	1. b	2. d
LO6	1. c	2. a				

The Statement of Cash Flows

12

AFTER STUDYING THIS CHAPTER, YOU SHOULD BE ABLE TO:

LO1 Understand the concept of cash flows and accrual accounting, and explain the purpose of a statement of cash flows.

LO2 Explain what cash equivalents are and how they are treated on the statement of cash flows.

LO3 Describe operating, investing, and financing activities and give examples of each.

LO4 Describe the difference between the direct and indirect methods of computing cash flow from operating activities.

LO5 Prepare a statement of cash flows using the direct method to determine cash flow from operating activities.

LO6 Prepare a statement of cash flows using the indirect method to determine cash flow from operating activities.

LO7 Use cash flow information to help analyze a company.

LO8 Use a work sheet to prepare a statement of cash flows using the indirect method to determine cash flow from operating activities (Appendix).

STUDY LINKS

A Look at Previous Chapters Previous chapters showed that assets and liabilities involve important cash flows to a business at one time or another. Chapter 2 introduced the statement of cash flows along with the other financial statements.

Chapter 11 completed examination of the accounting and reporting issues for a company's various assets, liabilities, and equities. Specifically, that chapter considered how companies account for stockholders' equity.

A Look at This Chapter Now that we have a fuller appreciation of how to account for the various assets and liabilities of a business, we turn our attention in this chapter to an in-depth examination of the statement of cash flows.

A Look at the Upcoming Chapter Stockholders, creditors, and other groups use financial statements, including the statement of cash flows, to analyze a company. Earlier chapters called attention to various ratios often used to aid in these analyses. The final chapter discusses the use of ratios and other types of analysis to ensure a better understanding of the financial strength and health of companies.

MAKING BUSINESS DECISIONS
BEST BUY

"Cash is king" is an expression you have undoubtedly heard. After learning the basics of accounting in this course, you now have a good idea of the meaning of that expression. Cash is the one universally recognized medium of exchange in today's world. Currencies vary—from the U.S dollar to the Mexican peso to the European community euro—but cash is what bankers and other creditors expect when it comes time to settle outstanding obligations. And it's what stockholders expect if dividends are going to be paid.

Best Buy, North America's leading specialty retailer for a wide variety of consumer electronics, computers, and appliances, understands the supremacy of cash as well as any company does. A glance at the Operating Activities section of Best Buy's statement of cash flows on the next page shows a business that not only earned $1.366 billion in fiscal 2011 but also generated $1.19 billion in cash from its operations.

What a company does with its cash is central to its long-term success. And a statement of cash flows provides a clear picture of what the company has done historically with this most liquid of all assets. Best Buy invested in its future by spending $744 million on additions to its property and equipment, which for a merchandiser means expansion of its retail stores. The Financing Activities section of the statement reveals that Best Buy borrowed $3.021 billion and repaid $3.12 billion of debt. Finally, note that Best Buy also returned cash to its stockholders, $237 million in dividends and another $1.193 billion to buy back common stock.

Company management, creditors, and stockholders are interested not only in what a company's bottom line is but also in where the company's cash comes from and where it goes. Why do you need to study this chapter?

- You need to understand why net earnings are not the same as cash provided by operating activities. (See pp. 605–608.)

- You need to understand how accountants reconcile the difference between these two amounts. (See pp. 615–618.)

- You need to know what are the various sources and uses of cash in a company's investing and financing activities. (See pp. 610–613.)

- You need to know how you can use information about a company's cash flows to analyze its performance. (See pp. 633–636.)

Best Buy
Consolidated Statements of Cash Flows
$ in millions

Fiscal Years Ended	February 26, 2011	February 27, 2010	February 28, 2009
Operating Activities			
Net earnings including noncontrolling interests	$ 1,366	$ 1,394	$ 1,033
Adjustments to reconcile net earnings to total cash provided by operating activities:			
Depreciation	896	838	730
Amortization of definite-lived intangible assets	82	88	63
Asset impairments	10	4	177
Restructuring charges	222	52	78
Stock-based compensation	121	118	110
Deferred income taxes	(134)	(30)	(43)
Excess tax benefits from stock-based compensation	(11)	(7)	(6)
Other, net	1	(4)	12
Changes in operating assets and liabilities, net of acquired assets and liabilities:			
Receivables	(371)	(63)	(419)
Merchandise inventories	(400)	(609)	258
Other assets	40	(98)	(175)
Accounts payable	(443)	141	139
Other liabilities	(156)	279	(75)
Income taxes	(33)	103	(5)
Total cash provided by operating activities	1,190	2,206	1,877
Investing Activities			
Additions to property and equipment, net of $81, $9 and $42 non-cash capital expenditures in fiscal 2011, 2010 and 2009, respectively	(744)	(615)	(1,303)
Purchases of investments	(267)	(16)	(81)
Sales of investments	415	56	246
Acquisitions of businesses, net of cash acquired	—	(7)	(2,170)
Proceed from sale of business, net of cash transferred	21	—	—
Change in restricted assets	(2)	18	(97)
Settlement of net investment hedges	12	40	—
Other, net	(4)	(16)	(22)
Total cash used in investing activities	(569)	(540)	(3,427)
Financing Activities			
Repurchase of common stock	(1,193)	—	—
Issuance of common stock under employee stock purchase plan and for the exercise of stock options	179	138	83
Dividends paid	(237)	(234)	(223)
Repayments of debt	(3,120)	(5,342)	(4,712)
Proceeds from issuance of debt	3,021	5,132	5,606
Acquisition of noncontrolling interests	(21)	(34)	(146)
Excess tax benefits from stock-based compensation	11	7	6
Other, net	3	(15)	(23)
Total cash (used in) provided by financing activities	(1,357)	(348)	591
Effect of Exchange Rate Changes on Cash	13	10	19
(Decrease) increase in Cash and Cash Equivalents	(723)	$ 1,328	(940)
Cash and Cash Equivalents at Beginning of Year	1,826	498	$ 1,438
Cash and Cash Equivalents at End of Year	$ 1,103	$ 1,826	$ 498
Supplemental Disclosure of Cash Flow Information			
Income taxes paid	$ 882	$ 732	$ 766
Interest paid	68	78	83

Annotations:
- Earnings of $1.366 billion
- Includes cost to open new stores
- Cash from operations less than net earnings
- Unlike prior years, no new business acquired in current year
- About the same amount of debt repaid as the amount borrowed

See Notes to Consolidated Financial Statements.

© Cengage Learning 2013

Cash Flows and Accrual Accounting

OVERVIEW: A statement of cash flows complements an accrual-based income statement by providing information on a company's cash flows from operating, investing, and financing activities.

LO1 Understand the concept of cash flows and accrual accounting, and explain the purpose of a statement of cash flows.

All external parties have an interest in a company's cash flows.

- Stockholders need some assurance that enough cash is being generated from operations to pay dividends and to invest in the company's future.
- Creditors want to know if cash from operations is sufficient to repay their loans along with interest.

This chapter will show you how to read, understand, and prepare the statement of cash flows, which is perhaps the key financial statement for the survival of every business.

The *bottom line* is a term used many different ways in today's society. "I wish politicians would cut out all of the rhetoric and get to the bottom line." "The bottom line is that the manager was fired because the team wasn't winning." "Our company's bottom line is twice what it was last year." This last use of the term, in reference to a company's net income, is probably the way in which *bottom line* was first used. In recent years, managers, stockholders, creditors, analysts, and other users of financial statements have become more wary of focusing on any one number as an indicator of a company's overall performance. Most experts now agree that there has been a tendency to rely far too heavily on net income and its companion, earnings per share, and in many cases to ignore a company's cash flows. As you know by now from your study of accounting, you can't pay bills with net income; you need cash!

To understand the difference between a company's bottom line and its cash flow, consider the case of **Best Buy** in its 2011 fiscal year. Best Buy reported net earnings (income) of $1,366 million. However, as shown in the chapter opener, during this same time period, its cash actually decreased by $723 million. How is this possible? First, net income is computed on an accrual basis, not a cash basis. Second, the income statement primarily reflects events related to the operating activities of a business, that is, selling products or providing services.

A company's cash position can increase or decrease over a period, and it can report a net profit or a net loss. If you think about it, one of four combinations is possible:

1. A company can report an increase in cash and a net profit.
2. A company can report a decrease in cash and a net profit.
3. A company can report an increase in cash and a net loss.
4. A company can report a decrease in cash and a net loss.

Exhibit 12-1 illustrates this point by showing the performance of four companies, including Best Buy. **Apple** is the only one of the four companies that improved its cash position *and* reported a net profit. Best Buy reported a net profit but saw its cash decline. **AMR** reported a net loss but improved its cash position. Finally, **U.S. Steel** experienced a net loss *and* saw its cash decline. To summarize, a company with a profitable year does not necessarily increase its cash position, nor does a company with an unprofitable year always experience a decrease in cash.

Purpose of the Statement of Cash Flows

The **statement of cash flows** is an important complement to the other major financial statements. It summarizes the operating, investing, and financing activities of a business over a period of time. The balance sheet summarizes the cash on hand and the balances in other assets, liabilities, and owners' equity accounts, providing a snapshot at a specific point in time. **The statement of cash flows reports the changes in cash over a period of time and, most importantly,** *explains those changes.*

Statement of cash flows
The financial statement that summarizes an entity's cash receipts and cash payments during the period from operating, investing, and financing activities.

EXHIBIT 12-1 Cash Flows and Net Income for Four Companies (all amounts in millions of dollars)

Company	Beginning Balance in Cash	Ending Balance in Cash	Increase (Decrease) in Cash	Net Income (Loss)
Apple, Inc. (fiscal year ended September 25, 2010)	$5,263	$11,261	$5,998	$14,013
Best Buy Co., Inc. (fiscal year ended February 26, 2011)	1,826	1,103	(723)	1,366
AMR Corporation (principal subsidiary is American Airlines—fiscal year ended December 31, 2010)	153	168	15	(471)
U.S. Steel Corporation (fiscal year ended December 31, 2010)	1,218	578	(640)	(482)

© Cengage Learning 2013

The income statement summarizes performance on an accrual basis. Income on this basis is a better indicator of *future* cash inflows and outflows than is a statement limited to current cash flows. The statement of cash flows complements the accrual-based income statement by allowing users to assess a company's performance on a cash basis. As you will see in Example 12-1, however, it also goes beyond presenting data related to operating performance and looks at other activities that affect a company's cash position.

Reporting Requirements for a Statement of Cash Flows

Accounting standards specify both the basis for preparing the statement of cash flows and the classification of items on the statement.[1] First, the statement must be prepared on a cash basis. Second, the cash flows must be classified into three categories:

- Operating activities
- Investing activities
- Financing activities

We now take a closer look at each of these important requirements in preparing a statement of cash flows.

Example 12-1 Preparing a Statement of Cash Flows

Consider the following discussion between the owner of Fox River Realty and the company accountant. After a successful first year in business in 2011 in which the company earned a profit of $100,000, the owner reviews the income statement for the second year, as presented below.

Fox River Realty
Income Statement
For the Year Ended December 31, 2012

Revenues	$400,000
Depreciation expense	$ 50,000
All other expenses	100,000
Total expenses	$150,000
Net income	$250,000

The owner is pleased with the results and asks to see the balance sheet. Comparative balance sheets for the first two years are presented on the next page.

(Continued)

---

[1] *Statement of Cash Flows*, ASC Topic 230 (formerly *Statement of Cash Flows*, Statement of Financial Accounting Standards No. 95).

Fox River Realty
Comparative Balance Sheets
December 31

	2012	2011
Cash	$ 50,000	$ 150,000
Plant and equipment	600,000	350,000
Accumulated depreciation	(150,000)	(100,000)
Total assets	$ 500,000	$ 400,000
Notes payable	$ 100,000	$ 150,000
Common stock	250,000	200,000
Retained earnings	150,000	50,000
Total equities	$ 500,000	$ 400,000

Where Did the Cash Go? At first glance, the owner is surprised to see the significant decline in the Cash account. She immediately presses the accountant for answers. With such a profitable year, where has the cash gone? Specifically, why has cash decreased from $150,000 to $50,000 even though income rose from $100,000 in the first year to $250,000 in the second year?

The accountant points out that income on a cash basis is even higher than the reported $250,000. Because depreciation expense is an expense that does not use cash (cash is used when the plant and equipment are purchased, not when they are depreciated), cash provided from operating activities is calculated as follows:

Net income	$250,000
Add back: Depreciation expense	50,000
Cash provided by operating activities	$300,000

Further, the accountant reminds the owner of the additional $50,000 that she invested in the business during the year. Now the owner is even more bewildered: with cash from operations of $300,000 and her own infusion of $50,000, why did cash *decrease* by $100,000? The accountant refreshes the owner's memory about three major outflows of cash during the year. First, even though the business earned $250,000, she withdrew $150,000 in dividends during the year. Second, the comparative balance sheets indicate that notes payable with the bank were reduced from $150,000 to $100,000, requiring the use of $50,000 in cash. Finally, the comparative balance sheets show an increase in plant and equipment for the year from $350,000 to $600,000—a sizable investment of $250,000 in new long-term assets.

Statement of Cash Flows To summarize what happened to the cash, the accountant prepares a statement of cash flows, shown below.

Fox River Realty
Statement of Cash Flows
For the Year Ended December 31, 2012

Cash provided (used) by operating activities	
Net income	$ 250,000
Add back: Depreciation expense	50,000
Net cash provided (used) by operating activities	$ 300,000
Cash provided (used) by investing activities	
Purchase of new plant and equipment	$(250,000)
Cash provided (used) by financing activities	
Additional investment by owner	$ 50,000
Cash dividends paid to owner	(150,000)
Repayment of notes payable to bank	(50,000)
Net cash provided (used) by financing activities	$(150,000)
Net increase (decrease) in cash	$(100,000)
Cash balance at beginning of year	150,000
Cash balance at end of year	$ 50,000

(Continued)

© Cengage Learning 2013

Although the owner is not particularly happy with the decrease in cash for the year, she is satisfied with the statement as an explanation of where the cash came from and how it was used. The statement summarizes the important cash activities for the year and fills a void created with the presentation of just an income statement and a balance sheet.

POD REVIEW 12.1

LO1 Understand the concept of cash flows and accrual accounting, and explain the purpose of a statement of cash flows.

- The statement of cash flows helps investors understand cash inflows and outflows of an entity based on its operating, investing, and financing activities. It provides complementary information to the accrual-based income statement.

QUESTIONS   Answers to these questions are on the last page of the chapter.

1. Which of the following is a correct statement about the relationship between net income and cash flow?

   a. Cash will increase during a year in which a company reports net income.
   b. Cash will decrease during a year in which a company reports a net loss.
   c. Cash can increase or decrease during a year in which a company reports net income.
   d. None of the above is correct.

2. What are the three categories into which cash flows are classified?

   a. operating, investing, and producing
   b. operating, investing, and financing
   c. operating, nonoperating, and financing
   d. none of the above

© Cengage Learning 2013

The Definition of Cash: Cash and Cash Equivalents

LO2 Explain what cash equivalents are and how they are treated on the statement of cash flows.

OVERVIEW: Cash equivalents are assets readily convertible to a determinable amount of cash, with a maturity date of three months or less. They are combined with cash on a statement of cash flows.

The purpose of the statement of cash flows is to provide information about a company's cash inflows and outflows. Thus, it is essential to have a clear understanding of what the definition of *cash* includes. According to accounting standards, certain items are recognized as being equivalent to cash and are combined with cash on the balance sheet and the statement of cash flows.

Commercial paper (short-term notes issued by corporations), money market funds, and Treasury bills are examples of cash equivalents. To be classified as a **cash equivalent**, an item must be readily convertible to a known amount of cash and have a maturity *to the investor* of three months or less. For example, a three-year Treasury note purchased two months before its maturity is classified as a cash equivalent. However, the same note purchased two years before maturity would be classified as an investment.

Cash equivalent
An item readily convertible to a known amount of cash with a maturity to the investor of three months or less.

Example 12-2 Determining What Is a Cash Equivalent

To understand why cash equivalents are combined with cash when a statement of cash flows is prepared, assume that a company has a cash balance of $10,000 and no assets that qualify

(Continued)

as cash equivalents. Further assume that the $10,000 is used to purchase 90-day Treasury bills. The effect of the transaction can be identified and analyzed as follows:

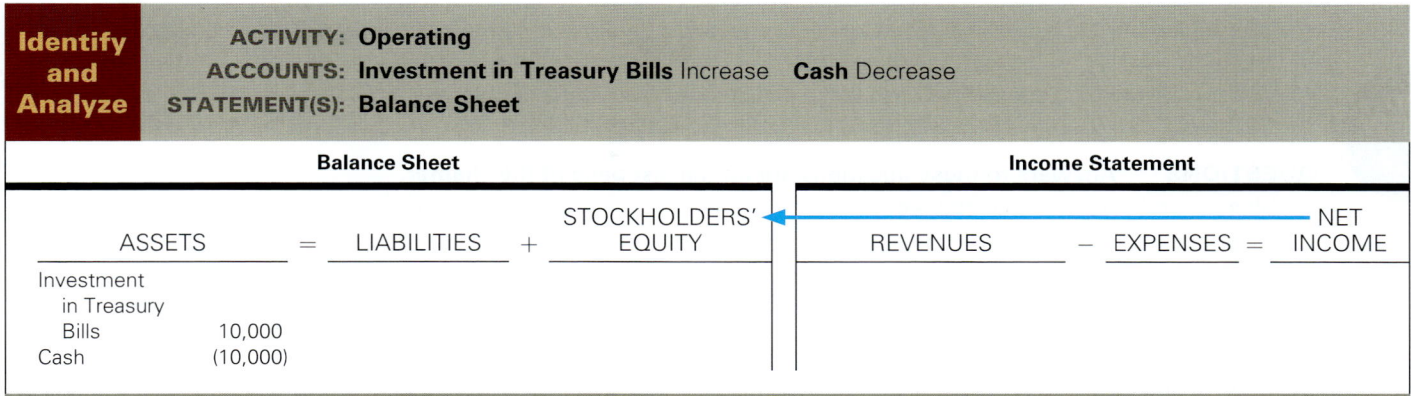

For record-keeping purposes, it is important to recognize this transaction as a transfer between cash in the bank and an investment in a government security. In the strictest sense, the investment represents an outflow of cash. The purchase of a security with such a short maturity does not, however, involve any significant degree of risk in terms of price changes and thus is not reported on the statement of cash flows as an outflow. Instead, for purposes of classification on the balance sheet and the statement of cash flows, this is merely a transfer *within* the cash and cash equivalents category. The point is that before the purchase of the Treasury bills, the company had $10,000 in cash and cash equivalents and that after the purchase, it still had $10,000 in cash and cash equivalents. *Because nothing changed, the transaction is not reported on the statement of cash flows.* Finally, the purchase of treasury bills is assumed to be a use of temporary excess operating funds and is therefore classified as "operating" in the "Identify and Analyze" section above.

Now consider a different transaction in which a company purchases shares of GM common stock for cash. This transaction can be identified and analyzed as follows:

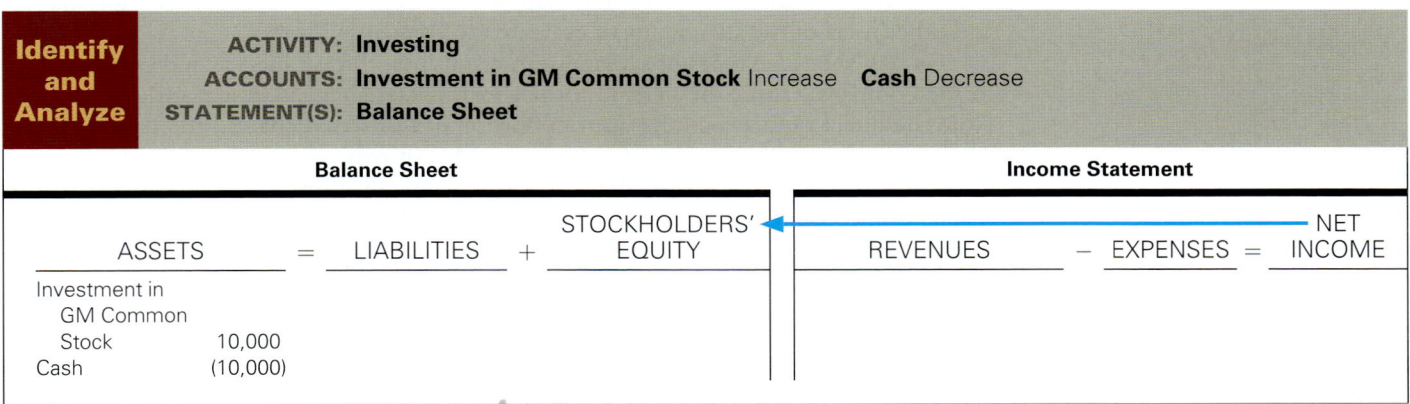

This purchase involves a certain amount of risk for the company making the investment. The GM stock is not convertible to a known amount of cash because its market value is subject to change. Thus, for balance sheet purposes, the investment is not considered a cash equivalent; therefore, it is not combined with cash but is classified as either a short- or long-term investment depending on the company's intent in holding the stock. **The investment in stock of another company is considered a significant activity and thus is reported on the statement of cash flows.**

POD REVIEW 12.2

LO2 Explain what cash equivalents are and how they are treated on the statement of cash flows.

- Cash equivalents are assets that are readily convertible to a determinable amount of cash, having a maturity date of three months or less.
- The term *cash* in the statement of cash flows includes cash and cash equivalents.

QUESTIONS   Answers to these questions are on the last page of the chapter.

1. Where are cash equivalents reported?

   a. in the Operating Activities section of the statement of cash flows
   b. in the Financing Activities section of the statement of cash flows
   c. on neither the balance sheet nor the statement of cash flows
   d. none of the above

2. Which of the following is a cash equivalent?

   a. an investment in the common stock of another company
   b. an investment in the bonds of another company
   c. a money market account
   d. none of the above

Classification of Cash Flows

LO3 Describe operating, investing, and financing activities and give examples of each.

OVERVIEW: Operating activities involve cash flows related to the production of goods or services for customers. Investing activities arise from acquiring and disposing of long-term assets, and financing activities relate to generating funds through debt and equity securities and making payments related to those securities.

For the statement of cash flows, companies are required to classify activities into three categories: operating, investing, or financing. These categories represent the major functions of an entity, and classifying activities in this way allows users to look at important relationships. For example, one important financing activity for many businesses is borrowing money. Grouping the cash inflows from borrowing money during the period with the cash outflows from repaying loans during the period makes it easier for analysts and other users of the statements to evaluate the company.

Each of the three types of activities can result in both cash inflows and cash outflows to the company. Thus, the general format for the statement is shown in Exhibit 12-2. Note the direct tie between the bottom portion of this statement and the balance sheet. The beginning and ending balances in cash and cash equivalents, shown as the last two lines on the statement of cash flows, are taken directly from the comparative balance sheets. Some companies end their statement of cash flows with the figure for the net increase or decrease in cash and cash equivalents and do not report the beginning and ending balances in cash and cash equivalents directly on the statement of cash flows. Instead, the reader must turn to the balance sheet for those amounts.

Operating activities
Activities concerned with the acquisition and sale of products and services.

Operating Activities **Operating activities** involve acquiring and selling products and services. The specific activities of a business depend on its type. For example, the purchase of raw materials is an important operating activity for a manufacturer. For a retailer, the purchase of inventory from a distributor constitutes an operating activity. For a realty company, the payment of a commission to a salesperson is an operating activity. All three types of businesses sell either products or services, and their sales are important operating activities.

A statement of cash flows reflects the cash effects, either inflows or outflows, associated with each of these activities. For example, the manufacturer's payment for purchases of raw materials results in a cash outflow. The receipt of cash from collecting an account receivable results in a cash inflow. The income statement reports operating activities on an accrual basis. The statement of cash flows reflects a company's operating activities on a cash basis.

EXHIBIT 12-2 Format for the Statement of Cash Flows

Smith Corporation Statement of Cash Flows For the Year Ended December 31, 2012		
Cash flows from operating activities		
Inflows	$ xxx	
Outflows	(xxx)	
Net cash provided (used) by operating activities		$xxx
Cash flows from investing activities		
Inflows	$ xxx	
Outflows	(xxx)	
Net cash provided (used) by investing activities		xxx
Cash flows from financing activities		
Inflows	$ xxx	
Outflows	(xxx)	
Net cash provided (used) by financing activities		xxx
Net increase (decrease) in cash and cash equivalents		$xxx
Cash and cash equivalents at beginning of year		xxx
Cash and cash equivalents at end of year		$xxx

© Cengage Learning 2013

Investing Activities **Investing activities** involve acquiring and disposing of long-term assets. Replacing worn-out plant and equipment and expanding the existing base of long-term assets are essential to all businesses. Cash is paid for these acquisitions, often called *capital expenditures*. The following excerpt from Best Buy's 2011 statement of cash flows (also shown in the chapter opener) indicates that the company spent $744 million for ❶ additions to property and equipment during fiscal 2011. (All amounts are in millions of dollars.)

> **Investing activities**
> Activities concerned with the acquisition and disposal of long-term assets.

Investing Activities	
❶ Additions to property and equipment, net of $81 non-cash capital expenditures in fiscal 2011	(744)
❷ Purchases of investments	(267)
❸ Sales of investments	415
❹ Acquisitions of businesses, net of cash acquired	—
Proceeds from sale of business, net of cash transferred	21
Change in restricted assets	(2)
Settlement of net investment hedges	12
Other, net	(4)
Total cash used in investing activities	(569)

Sales of long-term assets such as plant and equipment are not generally a significant source of cash. These assets are acquired to be used in producing goods and services or to support this function, rather than to be resold, as is true for inventory. Occasionally, however, plant and equipment may wear out or no longer be needed and are offered for sale. Best Buy does not separately report any sales of property and equipment during 2011.

Chapter 7 explained why companies sometimes invest in the stocks and bonds of other companies. During 2011, Best Buy spent $267 million to ❷ invest in other companies and generated $415 million ❸ from selling investments. Finally, the acquisition of one company by another is an important investing activity; however, Best Buy did not buy any other businesses in 2011.

Financing Activities All businesses rely on internal financing, external financing, or a combination of the two in meeting their needs for cash. Initially, a new business

HOT TOPICS
Returning Cash to the Stockholders

In the two years leading up to its 2011 fiscal year, Best Buy didn't buy back any of its own stock. That changed dramatically in 2011, when the electronics retailer reported that it used $1.193 billion of its cash to repurchase common stock. Interestingly, this was a similar amount to the $1.190 billion Best Buy generated from its operating activities in that year. What would prompt a company to spend such large amounts of cash generated from its operations on the repurchase of its own stock?

Companies buy treasury stock for a variety of reasons. Sometimes it is purchased to have available for employee benefit plans. At other times, it is done to maintain a favorable market price for the stock. Or, it may simply be a way to keep control over the company and prevent unwanted takeover attempts. Periodically, Best Buy announces its plans to buy back stock, something it calls a "share repurchase program." Four months into its 2012 fiscal year, the company's board of directors authorized a new $5 billion repurchase program. In a press release, the company explained the program as a sign that it was committed to enhancing returns to its shareholders. As a further signal of its commitment, the board approved a 7% increase in the quarterly dividend.

Companies use the cash generated from operations for various purposes, including capital expenditures and the repayment of debt. Sometimes, as in the case of Best Buy, the cash is returned to owners, whether through cash dividends or the buyback of some of the existing shares.

Source: Best Buy Co., Inc., 2011 annual report and June 21, 2011, press release.

Financing activities
Activities concerned with the raising and repaying of funds in the form of debt and equity.

must have a certain amount of investment by the owners to begin operations. After this, many companies use notes, bonds, and other forms of debt to provide financing. Issuing stock and various forms of debt results in cash inflows that appear as **financing activities** on the statement of cash flows. On the other side, the repurchase of a company's own stock and the repayment of borrowings are important cash outflows to be reported in the Financing Activities section of the statement. The payment of cash dividends is listed in this section as well. Best Buy's 2011 statement of cash flows lists many of the common cash inflows and outflows from financing activities (amounts in millions of dollars):

Financing Activities	
❺ Repurchase of common stock	(1,193)
❹ Issuance of common stock under employee stock purchase plan and for the exercise of stock options	179
❸ Dividends paid	(237)
❷ Repayments of debt	(3,120)
❶ Proceeds from issuance of debt	3,021
Acquisition of noncontrolling interests	(21)
Excess tax benefits from stock based compensation	11
Other, net	3
Total cash (used in) provided by financing activities	(1,357)

In 2011, Best Buy generated $3,021 million from ❶ issuing new debt and paid $3,120 million to ❷ retire existing debt. Another $237 million was paid in ❸ dividends to stockholders. Also, during the year, the company raised $179 million by ❹ issuing common stock. Finally, Best Buy spent $1,193 million to ❺ buy back its own common stock.

Summary of the Three Types of Activities   To summarize the categorization of the activities of a business as operating, investing, and financing, refer to Exhibit 12-3. The exhibit lists examples of each of the three activities along with the related balance sheet accounts and the account classifications on the balance sheet.

STUDY TIP

Later in the chapter, you will learn a technique to use in preparing the statement of cash flows. Recall then the observations made here regarding what types of accounts affect each of the three activities.

© Cengage Learning 2013

EXHIBIT 12-3 Classification of Items on the Statement of Cash Flows

Activity	Examples	Effect on Cash	Related Balance Sheet Account	Classification on Balance Sheet
Operating	Collection of customer accounts	Inflow	Accounts receivable	Current asset
	Payment to suppliers for	Outflow	Accounts payable	Current liability
	inventory		Inventory	Current asset
	Payment of wages	Outflow	Wages payable	Current liability
	Payment of taxes	Outflow	Taxes payable	Current liability
Investing	Capital expenditures	Outflow	Plant and equipment	Long-term asset
	Purchase of another company	Outflow	Long-term investment	Long-term asset
	Sale of plant and equipment	Inflow	Plant and equipment	Long-term asset
	Sale of another company	Inflow	Long-term investment	Long-term asset
Financing	Issuance of capital stock	Inflow	Capital stock	Stockholders' equity
	Issuance of bonds	Inflow	Bonds payable	Long-term liability
	Issuance of bank note	Inflow	Notes payable	Long-term liability
	Repurchase of stock	Outflow	Treasury stock	Stockholders' equity
	Retirement of bonds	Outflow	Bonds payable	Long-term liability
	Repayment of notes	Outflow	Notes payable	Long-term liability
	Payment of dividends	Outflow	Retained earnings	Stockholders' equity

© Cengage Learning 2013

In the exhibit, operating activities center on the acquisition and sale of products and services and related costs, such as wages and taxes. Two important observations can be made about the cash flow effects from the operating activities of a business:

1. **The cash flows from operating activities are the cash effects of transactions that enter into the determination of net income.** For example, the sale of a product enters into the calculation of net income. The cash effect of this transaction—that is, the collection of the account receivable—results in a cash inflow from operating activities.

2. **Cash flows from operating activities usually relate to an increase or decrease in a current asset or in a current liability.** For example, the payment of taxes to the government results in a decrease in taxes payable, which is a current liability on the balance sheet.

Note that investing activities normally relate to long-term assets on the balance sheet. For example, the purchase of new plant and equipment increases long-term assets, and the sale of those same assets reduces long-term assets on the balance sheet.

Finally, **note that financing activities usually relate to either long-term liabilities or stockholders' equity accounts.** There are exceptions to these observations about the type of balance sheet account involved with each of the three types of activities, but these rules of thumb are useful as you begin to analyze transactions and attempt to determine their classification on the statement of cash flows.

Noncash Investing and Financing Activities

Occasionally, companies engage in important investing and financing activities that do not affect cash.

Example 12-3 Determining Noncash Investing and Financing Activities

Assume that at the end of the year, Wolk Corp. issues capital stock to an inventor in return for the exclusive rights to a patent. Although the patent has no ready market value, the stock could have been sold on the open market for $25,000. The effect of this transaction can be identified and analyzed as follows:

(Continued)

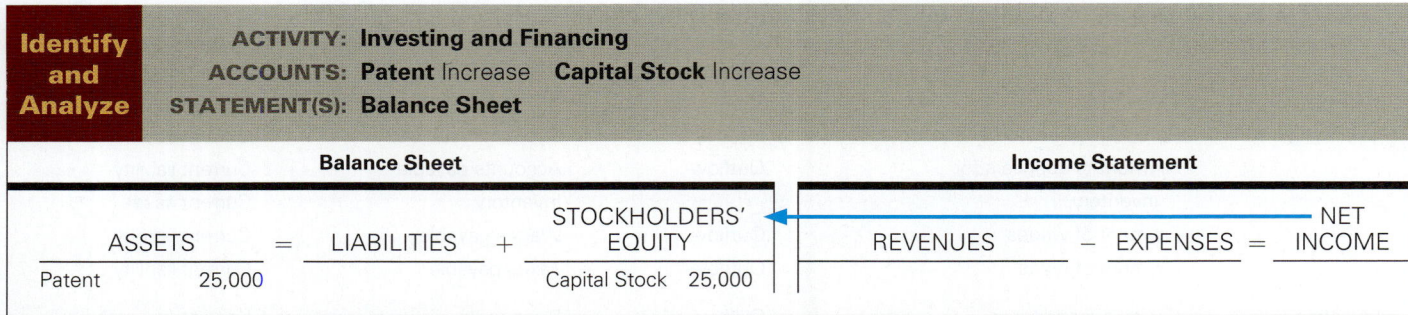

Identify and Analyze

ACTIVITY: Investing and Financing
ACCOUNTS: **Patent** Increase   **Capital Stock** Increase
STATEMENT(S): Balance Sheet

Balance Sheet					Income Statement			
ASSETS	=	LIABILITIES	+	STOCKHOLDERS' EQUITY	REVENUES	−	EXPENSES =	NET INCOME
Patent 25,000				Capital Stock 25,000				

This transaction does not involve cash and therefore is not reported on the statement of cash flows. However, what if the scenario was changed slightly? Assume that Wolk wants the patent but the inventor is not willing to accept stock in return for it. So, instead, Wolk sells stock on the open market for $25,000 and then pays this amount in cash to the inventor for the rights to the patent. Consider the effects of these two transactions. First, the issuance of the stock increases Cash and Stockholders' Equity and can be identified and analyzed as follows:

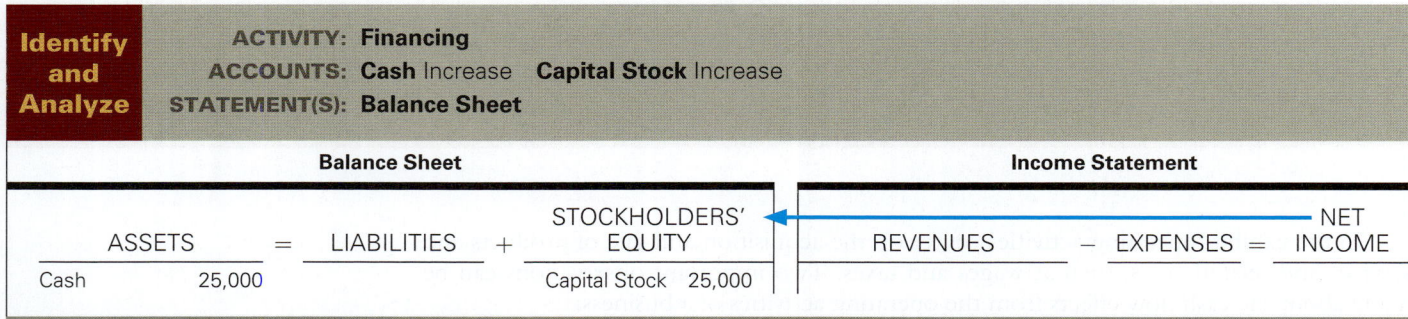

Identify and Analyze

ACTIVITY: Financing
ACCOUNTS: **Cash** Increase   **Capital Stock** Increase
STATEMENT(S): Balance Sheet

Balance Sheet					Income Statement			
ASSETS	=	LIABILITIES	+	STOCKHOLDERS' EQUITY	REVENUES	−	EXPENSES =	NET INCOME
Cash 25,000				Capital Stock 25,000				

Next, the acquisition of the patent can be identified and analyzed as follows:

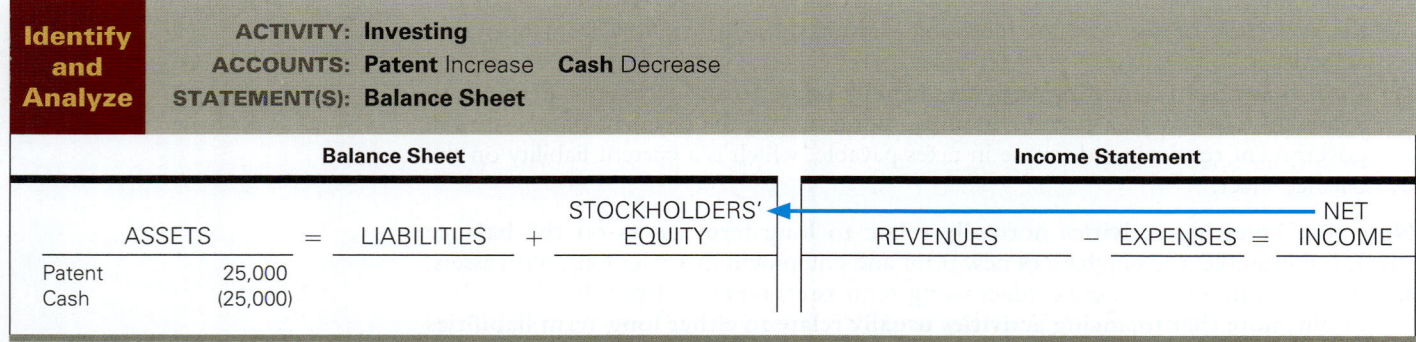

Identify and Analyze

ACTIVITY: Investing
ACCOUNTS: **Patent** Increase   **Cash** Decrease
STATEMENT(S): Balance Sheet

Balance Sheet					Income Statement			
ASSETS	=	LIABILITIES	+	STOCKHOLDERS' EQUITY	REVENUES	−	EXPENSES =	NET INCOME
Patent 25,000								
Cash (25,000)								

How would these two transactions be reported on a statement of cash flows? The first transaction appears as a cash inflow in the Financing Activities section of the statement; the second is reported as a cash outflow in the Investing Activities section. Even though the *form* of this arrangement (with stock sold for cash and then the cash paid to the inventor) differs from the form of the first arrangement (with stock exchanged directly for the patent), the *substance* of the two arrangements is the same. That is, both involve a significant financing activity, the issuance of stock, and an important investing activity, the acquisition of a patent. Because the substance is what matters, accounting standards require that any significant noncash transactions be reported in a separate schedule or in a note to the financial statements. For the transaction in which stock was issued directly to the inventor, presentation in a schedule is as follows:

Supplemental schedule of noncash investing and financing activities

Acquisition of patent in exchange for capital stock $25,000

LO3 Describe operating, investing, and financing activities and give examples of each.

- Activities that generate or consume cash are classified into three categories for the statement of cash flows.
  - Operating activities usually involve cash flows related to the production of goods or services for customers.
  - Investing activities relate to acquiring and disposing of long-term assets.
  - Financing activities relate to raising funds through debt and equity securities and making payments related to those securities.

POD REVIEW 12.3

QUESTIONS   Answers to these questions are on the last page of the chapter.

1. Which of the following should be classified as an investing activity on the statement of cash flows?

   a. issuance of capital stock
   b. payment of dividends
   c. payment to suppliers for inventory
   d. none of the above

2. How should the repurchase of a company's own stock be reported on the statement of cash flows?

   a. as an operating activity
   b. as an investing activity
   c. as a financing activity
   d. Repurchase of a company's own stock is not reported on the statement of cash flows.

© Cengage Learning 2013

Two Methods of Reporting Cash Flow from Operating Activities

OVERVIEW: A statement of cash flows prepared using the direct method reports cash receipts and cash payments in the Operating Activities section. Under the indirect method, net income is adjusted for the effects of accruals and deferrals. The amount of net cash provided by operating activities is the same regardless of which method is used.

LO4 Describe the difference between the direct and indirect methods of computing cash flow from operating activities.

Companies use one of two methods to report the amount of cash flow from operating activities. The first approach, called the **direct method**, involves reporting major classes of gross cash receipts and cash payments. For example, cash collected from customers is reported separately from any interest and dividends received. Each of the major types of cash payments related to the company's operations follows, such as cash paid for inventory, for salaries and wages, for interest, and for taxes. Under the **indirect method**, net cash flow from operating activities is computed by adjusting net income to remove the effect of all deferrals of past operating cash receipts and payments and all accruals of future operating cash receipts and payments.

The FASB prefers the direct method, but it is used much less frequently than the indirect method. To compare and contrast the two methods, assume that Boulder Company begins operations as a corporation on January 1, 2012, with the owners' investment of $10,000 in cash. An income statement for 2012 and a balance sheet as of December 31, 2012, are presented in Exhibits 12-4 and 12-5, respectively.

Direct method
For preparing the Operating Activities section of the statement of cash flows, the approach in which cash receipts and cash payments are reported.

Indirect method
For preparing the Operating Activities section of the statement of cash flows, the approach in which net income is reconciled to net cash flow from operations.

EXHIBIT 12-4 Boulder Company's Income Statement

Boulder Company Income Statement For the Year Ended December 31, 2012	
Revenues	$ 80,000
Operating expenses	(64,000)
Income before tax	$ 16,000
Income tax expense	(4,000)
Net income	$ 12,000

© Cengage Learning 2013

EXHIBIT 12-5 Boulder Company's Balance Sheet

Boulder Company Balance Sheet As of December 31, 2012			
Assets		**Liabilities and Stockholders' Equity**	
Cash	$15,000	Accounts payable	$ 6,000
Accounts receivable	13,000	Capital stock	10,000
		Retained earnings	12,000
Total	$28,000	Total	$28,000

© Cengage Learning 2013

Example 12-4 Determining Cash Flows from Operating Activities—Direct Method

To report cash flow from operating activities under the direct method, we look at each of the items on the income statement and determine how much cash each of those activities generated or used. Revenues for the period were $80,000. The balance sheet at the end of the period shows a balance in Accounts Receivable of $13,000; however, Boulder collected only $80,000 − $13,000, or $67,000, from its sales of the period. Thus, the first line on the statement of cash flows in Exhibit 12-6 reports $67,000 in cash collected from customers. Remember that the *net increase* in Accounts Receivable must be deducted from sales to find cash collected. For a new company, this is the same as the ending balance because the company starts the year without a balance in Accounts Receivable.

The same logic can be applied to determine the amount of cash expended for operating purposes. Operating expenses on the income statement are reported at $64,000. According to the balance sheet, however, $6,000 of the expense is unpaid at the end of the period as evidenced by the balance in Accounts Payable. Thus, the amount of cash expended for operating purposes as reported on the statement of cash flows in Exhibit 12-6 is $64,000 − $6,000, or $58,000. The other cash payment in the Operating Activities section of the statement is $4,000 for income taxes. Because no liability for income taxes is reported on the balance sheet, we know that $4,000 represents both the income tax expense of the period and the amount paid to the government. The only other item on the statement of cash flows in Exhibit 12-6 is the cash inflow from financing activities for the amount of cash invested by the owner in return for capital stock.

EXHIBIT 12-6 Statement of Cash Flows Using the Direct Method

Boulder Company Statement of Cash Flows For the Year Ended December 31, 2012	
Cash flows from operating activities	
Cash collected from customers	$ 67,000
Cash payments for operating purposes	(58,000)
Cash payments for taxes	(4,000)
Net cash inflow from operating activities	$ 5,000
Cash flows from financing activities	
Issuance of capital stock	$ 10,000
Net increase in cash	$ 15,000
Cash balance, beginning of period	0
Cash balance, end of period	$ 15,000

© Cengage Learning 2013

Example 12-5 Determining Cash Flows from Operating Activities—Indirect Method

When the indirect method is used, the first line in the Operating Activities section of the statement of cash flows as shown in Exhibit 12-7 is the net income of the period. Net income is then adjusted to reconcile it to the amount of cash provided by operating activities. As reported on the income statement, this net income figure includes sales of $80,000 for the period. As we know, however, the amount of cash collected was $13,000 less than this because not all customers paid Boulder the amount due. **The increase in Accounts Receivable for the period is deducted from net income on the statement because the increase indicates that the company sold more during the period than it collected in cash.**

The logic for the addition of the increase in Accounts Payable is similar, although the effect is the opposite. The amount of operating expenses deducted on the income statement was $64,000. We know, however, that the amount of cash paid was $6,000 less than this, as the balance in Accounts Payable indicates. **The increase in Accounts Payable for the period is added back to net income on the statement because the increase indicates that the company paid less during the period than it recognized in expense on the income statement.** Because this is Boulder's first year of operations, we wouldn't be too concerned that accounts receivable is increasing faster than accounts payable. If this becomes a trend, however, we would try to improve the accounts receivable collections process.

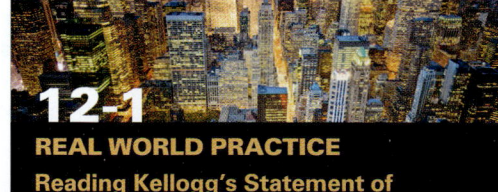

12-1

REAL WORLD PRACTICE

Reading Kellogg's Statement of Cash Flows

Does Kellogg's use the direct or indirect method in the Operating Activities section of its statement of cash flows? How can you tell?

EXHIBIT 12-7 Statement of Cash Flows Using the Indirect Method

Boulder Company Statement of Cash Flows For the Year Ended December 31, 2012	
Cash flows from operating activities	
Net income	$ 12,000
Adjustments to reconcile net income to net cash from operating activities:	
Increase in accounts receivable	(13,000)
Increase in accounts payable	6,000
Net cash inflow from operating activities	$ 5,000
Cash flows from financing activities	
Issuance of capital stock	$ 10,000
Net increase in cash	$ 15,000
Cash balance, beginning of period	0
Cash balance, end of period	$ 15,000

Two important observations should be made in comparing the two methods illustrated in Examples 12-4 and 12-5:

1. The amount of cash provided by operating activities is the same under the two methods: $5,000; they simply use different computational approaches to arrive at the cash generated from operations.

2. The remainder of the statement of cash flows is the same regardless of which method is used.

The only difference between the two methods is in the Operating Activities section of the statement.

To this point, we have concentrated on the purpose of a statement of cash flows and the major reporting requirements related to it. We turn next to a methodology used in preparing the statement.

LO4 Describe the difference between the direct and indirect methods of computing cash flow from operating activities.

- The indirect method derives cash flows from operating activities by starting with net income and then making adjustments for the effects of accruals and deferrals resulting from accrual-based accounting.
- The direct method reports cash receipts and cash disbursements related to operations.

POD REVIEW 12.4

QUESTIONS   **Answers to these questions are on the last page of the chapter.**

1. The first line on a company's statement of cash flows is net income. Which method does the company use to prepare its statement?
   a. direct
   b. indirect
   c. operating
   d. It is not possible to tell from the information provided.

2. Oak began the year with a balance of $5,000 in Accounts Receivable and ended the year with $8,000 in the account. Revenues for the period amounted to $37,000. Under the direct method, Oak will report cash collected from customers of
   a. $34,000.
   b. $37,000.
   c. $40,000.
   d. $42,000.

How the Statement of Cash Flows Is Put Together

LO5 Prepare a statement of cash flows using the direct method to determine cash flow from operating activities.

OVERVIEW: A systematic approach can be used to provide the information necessary to prepare a statement of cash flows. In this section, we illustrate the direct method of presenting cash provided by operating activities.

Two interesting observations can be made about the statement of cash flows. First, the "answer" to a statement of cash flows is known before it is prepared. That is, the change in cash for the period is known by comparing two successive balance sheets. Thus, it is not the change in cash that is emphasized on the statement of cash flows but the *explanations* for the change in cash. That is, each item on a statement of cash flows helps to explain why cash changed by the amount it did during the period. The second important observation relates even more specifically to how this statement is prepared. An income statement and a balance sheet are prepared by taking the balances in each of the various accounts in the general ledger and putting them in the right place on the right statement. In preparing the statement of cash flows, the transactions during the period must be analyzed to (1) determine which of them affected cash and (2) classify each of the cash effects into one of the three categories.

So far in this chapter, the statements of cash flows have been prepared without the use of any special tools. In more complex situations, however, some type of methodology is needed. We will review the basic accounting equation and then illustrate a systematic approach for preparing the statement. The chapter appendix presents a worksheet approach to the preparation of the statement of cash flows.

The Accounting Equation and the Statement of Cash Flows

The basic accounting equation is as follows:

$$\text{Assets} = \text{Liabilities} + \text{Stockholders' Equity}$$

Next, consider this refinement of the equation:

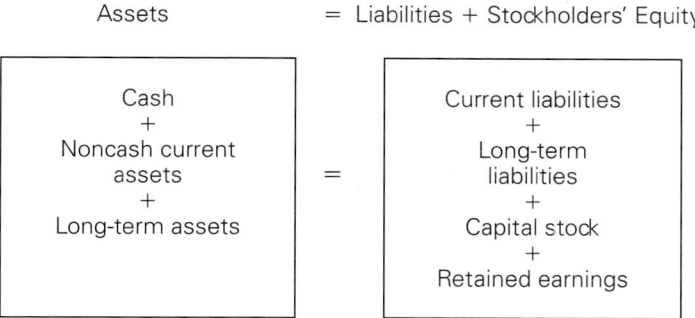

The equation can be rearranged so that only cash is on the left side and all other items are on the right side:

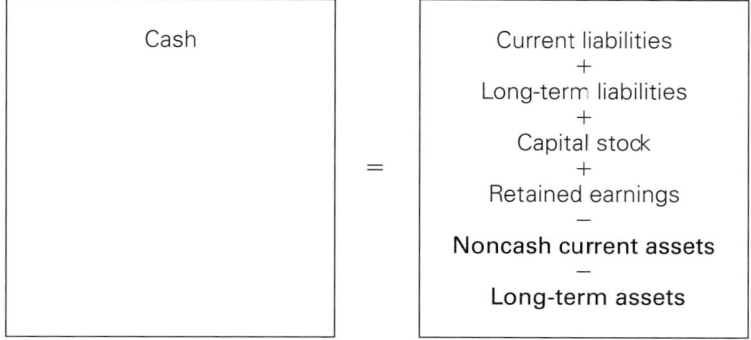

Therefore, any changes in cash must be accompanied by a corresponding change in the right side of the equation. For example, an increase or inflow of cash could result from an increase in long-term liabilities in the form of issuing bonds payable, an important financing activity for many companies. Or an increase in cash could come from a decrease in long-term assets in the form of a sale of fixed assets. The various possibilities for inflows (+) and outflows (−) of cash can be summarized by activity as follows:

Activity	Left Side	Right Side	Example
Operating			
	+ Cash	− Noncash current assets	Collect accounts receivable
	− Cash	+ Noncash current assets	Prepay insurance
	+ Cash	+ Current liabilities	Collect customer's deposit
	− Cash	− Current liabilities	Pay suppliers
	+ Cash	+ Retained earnings	Make a cash sale
Investing			
	+ Cash	− Long-term assets	Sell equipment
	− Cash	+ Long-term assets	Buy equipment
Financing			
	+ Cash	+ Long-term liabilities	Issue bonds
	− Cash	− Long-term liabilities	Retire bonds
	+ Cash	+ Capital stock	Issue capital stock
	− Cash	− Capital stock	Buy capital stock
	− Cash	− Retained earnings	Pay dividends

Those examples show that inflows and outflows of cash relate to increases and decreases in the various balance sheet accounts. We now turn to analyzing these accounts as a way to assemble a statement of cash flows.

An Approach to Preparing the Statement of Cash Flows: Direct Method

The following steps can be used to prepare a statement of cash flows:

1. **Set up three schedules with the following headings:**
   a. Cash Flows from Operating Activities
   b. Cash Flows from Investing Activities
   c. Cash Flows from Financing Activities

   As we analyze the transactions that affect each of the noncash balance sheet accounts, any cash effects are entered on the appropriate master schedule. When completed, the three master schedules contain all of the information needed to prepare a statement of cash flows.

2. **Determine the cash flows from operating activities.** Generally, this requires analyzing each item on the *income statement* and in the *Current Asset* and *Current Liability accounts*. As cash flows are identified in this analysis, they are entered on the schedule of cash flows from operating activities.

3. **Determine the cash flows from investing activities.** Generally, this requires analyzing the *Long-Term Asset* accounts and any additional information provided. As cash flows are identified in this analysis, they are entered on the schedule of cash flows from investing activities. Any significant noncash activities are entered on a supplemental schedule.

4. **Determine the cash flows from financing activities.** Generally, this requires analyzing the *Long-Term Liability* and *Stockholders' Equity* accounts and any additional information provided. As cash flows are identified and analyzed in this analysis, they are entered on the schedule of cash flows from financing activities. Any significant noncash activities are entered on a supplemental schedule.

In general, the cash effects of changes in current accounts are reported in the Operating section; changes relating to long-term asset accounts are reported in the Investing section; and changes relating to long-term liabilities and stockholders' equity are reported in the Financing section. The general rules for classification of activities have a few exceptions, but they will not be covered here.

To illustrate this approach, we will refer to the income statement in Exhibit 12-8 and to the comparative balance sheets and the additional information provided for Julian

EXHIBIT 12-8 Julian Corp.'s Income Statement

<table>
<tr><td colspan="3" align="center">**Julian Corp.**
Income Statement
For the Year Ended December 31, 2012</td></tr>
<tr><td>Revenues and gains:</td><td></td><td></td></tr>
<tr><td>Sales revenue</td><td>$670,000</td><td></td></tr>
<tr><td>Interest revenue</td><td>15,000</td><td></td></tr>
<tr><td>Gain on sale of machine</td><td>5,000</td><td></td></tr>
<tr><td>Total revenues and gains</td><td></td><td>$690,000</td></tr>
<tr><td>Expenses and losses:</td><td></td><td></td></tr>
<tr><td>Cost of goods sold</td><td>$390,000</td><td></td></tr>
<tr><td>Salaries and wages</td><td>60,000</td><td></td></tr>
<tr><td>Depreciation</td><td>40,000</td><td></td></tr>
<tr><td>Insurance</td><td>12,000</td><td></td></tr>
<tr><td>Interest</td><td>15,000</td><td></td></tr>
<tr><td>Income taxes</td><td>50,000</td><td></td></tr>
<tr><td>Loss on retirement of bonds</td><td>3,000</td><td></td></tr>
<tr><td>Total expenses and losses</td><td></td><td>570,000</td></tr>
<tr><td>Net income</td><td></td><td>$120,000</td></tr>
</table>

Corp. in Exhibit 12-9. Assuming we have already set up the three schedules for operating, investing, and financing activities (step 1), we outline the preparation of the statement of cash flows starting with step 2.

Step 2: Determine the Cash Flows from Operating Activities

To do this, you need to consider each of the items on the income statement and any related current assets or liabilities from the balance sheet.

Sales Revenue and Accounts Receivable Sales as reported on the income statement in Exhibit 12-8 amounted to $670,000. Based on the beginning and ending balances in Exhibit 12-9, Accounts Receivable increased by $6,000, from $57,000 to $63,000. *This indicates that Julian had $6,000 more in sales to its customers than it*

EXHIBIT 12-9 Julian Corp.'s Comparative Balance Sheets

Julian Corp. Comparative Balance Sheets	December 31	
	2012	2011
Cash	$ 35,000	$ 46,000
Accounts receivable	63,000	57,000
Inventory	84,000	92,000
Prepaid insurance	12,000	18,000
Total current assets	$ 194,000	$213,000
Long-term investments	$ 120,000	$ 90,000
Land	150,000	100,000
Property and equipment	320,000	280,000
Accumulated depreciation	(100,000)	(75,000)
Total long-term assets	$ 490,000	$395,000
Total assets	$ 684,000	$608,000
Accounts payable	$ 38,000	$ 31,000
Salaries and wages payable	7,000	9,000
Income taxes payable	8,000	5,000
Total current liabilities	$ 53,000	$ 45,000
Notes payable	$ 85,000	$ 35,000
Bonds payable	200,000	260,000
Total long-term liabilities	$ 285,000	$295,000
Capital stock	$ 100,000	$ 75,000
Retained earnings	246,000	193,000
Total stockholders' equity	$ 346,000	$268,000
Total liabilities and stockholders' equity	$ 684,000	$608,000

Additional Information

1. Long-term investments were purchased for $30,000. The securities are classified as available for sale.
2. Land was purchased by issuing a $50,000 note payable.
3. Equipment was purchased for $75,000.
4. A machine with an original cost of $35,000 and a book value of $20,000 was sold for $25,000.
5. Bonds with a face value of $60,000 were retired by paying $63,000 in cash.
6. Capital stock was issued in exchange for $25,000 in cash.
7. Dividends of $67,000 were paid.

collected in cash from them (assuming that all sales are on credit). Thus, cash collections must have been $670,000 − $6,000, or $664,000. Another way to look at this is as follows:

Beginning accounts receivable	$ 57,000
+ Sales revenue	670,000
− Cash collections	(X)
= Ending accounts receivable	$ 63,000

Solving for X, we can find cash collections:

$$\$57,000 + \$670,000 - X = \$\ 63,000$$
$$X = \underline{\$664,000}$$

At this point, note the inflow of Cash for $664,000 as shown in the Schedule of Cash Flows from Operating Activities in Exhibit 12-10.

Interest Revenue Julian reported interest revenue on the income statement of $15,000. Did the company actually receive that amount of cash, or was it merely an accrual of revenue earned but not yet received? The answer can be found by examining the Current Assets section of the balance sheet. Because there is no Interest Receivable account, the amount of interest earned was the amount of cash received.

The amount of cash received should be entered in the Schedule of Cash Flows from Operating Activities, as shown in Exhibit 12-10.

Gain on Sale of Machine A gain on the sale of machine of $5,000 is reported as the next line on the income statement. Any cash received from the sale of a long-term asset is reported in the Investing Activities section of the statement of cash flows. Thus, we ignore the gain when reporting cash flows from operating activities under the direct method.

Cost of Goods Sold, Inventory, and Accounts Payable Cost of goods sold, as reported on the income statement, amounts to $390,000. Recall that $390,000 is not the amount of cash expended to pay suppliers of inventory. First, cost of goods sold represents the cost of the inventory sold during the period, not the amount purchased. Thus, we must analyze the Inventory account to determine the purchases of the period. Second, the amount of purchases is not the same as the cash paid to suppliers because purchases are normally on account. Therefore, we must analyze the Accounts Payable account to determine the cash payments.

Based on the beginning and ending balances in Exhibit 12-9, inventory decreased during the year by $8,000, from $92,000 to $84,000. *This means that the cost of*

EXHIBIT 12-10 Schedule of Cash Flows from Operating Activities

Cash Flows from Operating Activities	
Cash receipts from:	
Sales on account	664,000
Interest	15,000
Cash payments for:	
Inventory purchases	(375,000)
Salaries and wages	(62,000)
Insurance	(6,000)
Interest	(15,000)
Taxes	(47,000)

inventory sold was $8,000 more than the purchases of the period. Another way to look at this is as follows:

Beginning inventory	$ 92,000
+ Purchases	X
− Cost of goods sold	(390,000)
= Ending inventory	$ 84,000

Solving for X, we can find purchases:

$$\$92,000 + X - \$390,000 = \$ 84,000$$
$$X = \$382,000$$

Note from Exhibit 12-9 that Accounts Payable increased during the year by $7,000. *This means that Julian's purchases were $7,000 more during the period than its cash payments.* Thus, cash payments must have been $382,000 – $7,000, or $375,000. Another way to look at this is as follows:

Beginning accounts payable	$ 31,000
+ Purchases	382,000
− Cash payments	(X)
= Ending accounts payable	$ 38,000

Solving for X, we can find cash payments:

$$\$31,000 + \$382,000 - X = \$ 38,000$$
$$X = \$375,000$$

At this point, we indicate in the schedule in Exhibit 12-10 that the cash payments for inventory total $375,000.

Salaries and Wages Expense and Salaries and Wages Payable

The second expense listed on the income statement in Exhibit 12-8 is salaries and wages of $60,000. However, did Julian *pay* this amount to employees during the year? The answer can be found by examining the Salaries and Wages Payable account in the balance sheet in Exhibit 12-9. From the balance sheet, we note that the liability account decreased by $2,000, from $9,000 to $7,000.

This means that the amount of cash paid to employees was $2,000 more than the amount of expense accrued. Another way to look at the cash payments of $60,000 + $2,000, or $62,000, is as follows:

Beginning salaries and wages payable	$ 9,000
+ Salaries and wages expense	60,000
− Cash payments to employees	(X)
= Ending salaries and wages payable	$ 7,000

Solving for X, we can find cash payments:

$$\$9,000 + \$60,000 - X = \$ 7,000$$
$$X = \$62,000$$

As you can see in Exhibit 12-10, the cash paid of $62,000 appears as a cash outflow in the Schedule of Cash Flows from Operating Activities.

Depreciation Expense

The next item on the income statement is depreciation of $40,000. Depreciation of tangible long-term assets, amortization of intangible assets, and depletion of natural resources are different from most other expenses in that they have no effect on cash flow. The only related cash flows are from the purchase and sale of these long-term assets, and these are reported in the Investing Activities section of the statement of cash flows. Thus, depreciation is not reported on the Schedule of Cash Flows from Operating Activities when the direct method is used.

Insurance Expense and Prepaid Insurance According to the income statement in Exhibit 12-8, Julian recorded insurance expense of $12,000 during 2012. This amount is not the cash payments for insurance, however, because Julian has a Prepaid Insurance account on the balance sheet. Recall from Chapter 4 that as a company buys insurance, it increases its Prepaid Insurance account. As the insurance expires, this account is reduced and an expense is recognized. Note from the balance sheet in Exhibit 12-9 that the Prepaid Insurance account decreased during the period by $6,000, from $18,000 to $12,000. *This means that the amount of cash paid for insurance was $6,000 less than the amount of expense recognized.* Thus, the cash payments must have been $12,000 – 6,000, or $6,000. Another way to look at the cash payments is as follows:

Beginning prepaid insurance	$ 18,000
+ Cash payments for insurance	X
– Insurance expense	(12,000)
= Ending prepaid insurance	$ 12,000

Solving for X, we can find the amount of cash paid:

$$\$18,000 + X - \$12,000 = \$12,000$$
$$X = \underline{\$\ 6,000}$$

Note the cash outflow of $6,000 as entered in Exhibit 12-10 in the Schedule of Cash Flows from Operating Activities.

Interest Expense The amount of interest expense reported on the income statement is $15,000. Because the balance sheet does not report an accrual of interest owed but not yet paid (an Interest Payable account), we know that $15,000 is also the amount of cash paid. The schedule in Exhibit 12-10 reflects the cash outflow of $15,000 for interest.

Whether interest paid is properly classified as an operating activity is subject to considerable debate. The FASB decided in favor of classification of interest as an operating activity because, unlike dividends, it appears on the income statement. This, it was argued, provides a direct link between the statement of cash flows and the income statement. Many argue, however, that it is inconsistent to classify dividends paid as a financing activity but interest paid as an operating activity. After all, both represent returns paid to providers of capital: interest to creditors and dividends to stockholders.

Income Taxes Expense and Income Taxes Payable The income statement in Exhibit 12-8 reports income tax expense of $50,000. We know, however, that this is not necessarily the amount paid to the government during the year. In fact, note the increase in the Income Taxes Payable account on the balance sheets in Exhibit 12-9. The liability increased by $3,000, from $5,000 to $8,000. *This means that the amount of cash paid to the government in taxes was $3,000 less than the amount of expense accrued.* Another way to look at the cash payments of $50,000 – $3,000, or $47,000, is as follows:

Beginning income taxes payable	$ 5,000
+ Income tax expense	50,000
– Cash payments for taxes	(X)
= Ending income taxes payable	$ 8,000

Solving for X, we can find the amount of cash paid:

$$\$5,000 + \$50,000 - X = \$\ 8,000$$
$$X = \underline{\$47,000}$$

As you can see by examining Exhibit 12-10, the cash payments for taxes is the last item on the Schedule of Cash Flows from Operating Activities.

Loss on Retirement of Bonds A $3,000 loss on the retirement of bonds is reported as the last item under expenses and losses on the income statement in

Exhibit 12-8. Any cash paid to retire a long-term liability is reported in the Financing Activities section of the statement of cash flows. Thus, we ignore the loss when reporting cash flows from operating activities under the direct method.

Compare Net Income with Net Cash Flow from Operating Activities

At this point, all of the items on the income statement have been analyzed, as have all of the current asset and current liability accounts. All of the information needed to prepare the Operating Activities section of the statement of cash flows has been gathered.

To summarize, **preparation of the Operating Activities section of the statement of cash flows requires the conversion of each item on the income statement to a cash basis. The Current Asset and Current Liability accounts are analyzed to discover the cash effects of each item on the income statement.** Exhibit 12-11 summarizes this conversion process.

EXHIBIT 12-11 Conversion of Income Statement Items to Cash Basis

Income Statement	Amount	Adjustments	Cash Flows
Sales revenue	$670,000		$670,000
		+ Decreases in accounts receivable	0
		− Increases in accounts receivable	(6,000)
		Cash collected from customers	$664,000
Interest revenue	15,000		$ 15,000
		+ Decreases in interest receivable	0
		− Increases in interest receivable	0
		Cash collected in interest	$ 15,000
Gain on sale of machine	5,000	*Not an operating activity*	$ 0
Cost of goods sold	390,000		$390,000
		+ Increases in inventory	0
		− Decreases in inventory	(8,000)
		+ Decreases in accounts payable	0
		− Increases in accounts payable	(7,000)
		Cash paid to suppliers	$375,000
Salaries and wages	60,000		$ 60,000
		+ Decreases in salaries and wages payable	2,000
		− Increases in salaries and wages payable	0
		Cash paid to employees	$ 62,000
Depreciation	40,000	*No cash flow effect*	$ 0
Insurance	12,000		$ 12,000
		+ Increases in prepaid insurance	0
		− Decreases in prepaid insurance	(6,000)
		Cash paid for insurance	$ 6,000
Interest	15,000		$ 15,000
		+ Decreases in interest payable	0
		− Increases in interest payable	0
		Cash paid for interest	$ 15,000
Income taxes	50,000		$ 50,000
		+ Decreases in income taxes payable	0
		− Increases in income taxes payable	(3,000)
		Cash paid for taxes	$ 47,000
Loss on retirement of bonds	3,000	*Not an operating activity*	$ 0
Net income	$120,000	Net cash flow from operating activities	$174,000

Note in the exhibit the various adjustments made to put each income statement item on a cash basis. For example, the $6,000 increase in accounts receivable for the period is deducted from sales revenue of $670,000 to arrive at cash collected from customers. Similar adjustments are made to each of the other income statement items with the exception of depreciation, the gain, and the loss. Depreciation is ignored because it does not have an effect on cash flow. The gain relates to the sale of a long-term asset, and any cash effect is reflected in the Investing Activities section of the statement of cash flows. Similarly, the loss resulted from the retirement of bonds and any cash flow effect is reported in the Financing Activities section. The bottom of the exhibit highlights an important point: Julian reported net income of $120,000, but generated $174,000 in cash from operations.

Step 3: Determine the Cash Flows from Investing Activities

We now turn our attention to the Long-Term Asset accounts and any additional information available about these accounts. Julian has three long-term assets on its balance sheet: Long-Term Investments, Land, and Property and Equipment.

Long-Term Investments Item 1 in the additional information in Exhibit 12-9 indicates that Julian purchased $30,000 of investments during the year. The $30,000 net increase in the Long-Term Investments account confirms this. (No mention is made of the sale of any investments during 2012.) The purchase of investments requires the use of $30,000 of cash, as indicated on the Schedule of Cash Flows from Investing Activities in Exhibit 12-12.

Land Note the $50,000 net increase in land. Item 2 in the additional information indicates that Julian purchased land by issuing a $50,000 note payable. This transaction obviously does not involve cash. The transaction has an important financing element and an investing component, however. The issuance of the note is a financing activity, and the acquisition of land is an investing activity. Because no cash was involved, the transaction is reported in a separate schedule instead of directly on the statement of cash flows:

Supplemental schedule of noncash investing and financing activities	
Acquisition of land in exchange for note payable	$50,000

Property and Equipment Property and equipment increased by $40,000 during 2012. However, Julian acquired equipment and sold a machine (item 3 and item 4, respectively, in the additional information in Exhibit 12-9). As was discussed earlier in the chapter, acquisitions of new plant and equipment are important investing activities for most businesses. Thus, the $75,000 expended to acquire new plant and equipment appears in the schedule in Exhibit 12-12 as a cash outflow.

As reported in the balance sheets in Exhibit 12-9, the Property and Equipment account increased during the year by only $40,000, from $280,000 to $320,000. Since Julian *added* to this account $75,000, however, we know that it must have disposed of some assets as well. In fact, item 4 in the additional information in Exhibit 12-9 reports

EXHIBIT 12-12 Schedule of Cash Flows from Investing Activities

Cash Flows from Investing Activities	
Cash inflows from:	
Sale of machine	25,000
Cash outflows for:	
Purchase of investments	(30,000)
Purchase of property and equipment	(75,000)

the sale of a machine with an original cost of $35,000. An analysis of the Property and Equipment account confirms this amount:

Beginning property and equipment	$280,000
+ Acquisitions	75,000
− Disposals	(X)
= Ending property and equipment	$320,000

Solving for X, we can find the *cost* of the fixed assets sold during the year:

$$\$280,000 + \$75,000 - X = \$320,000$$
$$X = \$\ 35,000$$

The additional information also indicates that the book value of the machine sold was $20,000. This means that if the original cost was $35,000 and the book value was $20,000, the Accumulated Depreciation on the machine sold must have been $35,000 − $20,000, or $15,000. An analysis similar to the one we just looked at for Property and Equipment confirms this amount:

Beginning accumulated depreciation	$ 75,000
+ Depreciation expense [entry (i)]	40,000
− Accumulated depreciation on assets sold	(X)
= Ending accumulated depreciation	$100,000

Solving for X, we can find the accumulated depreciation on the assets disposed of during the year:

$$\$75,000 + \$40,000 - X = \$100,000$$
$$X = \$\ 15,000$$

Finally, we are told in the additional information that the machine was sold for $25,000. *If the selling price was $25,000 and the book value was $20,000, Julian reports a gain on the sale of $5,000, an amount that is confirmed on the income statement in Exhibit 12-8.* To summarize, the machine was sold for $25,000, an amount that exceeded its book value of $20,000, thus generating a gain of $5,000. The cash inflow of $25,000 is entered on the Schedule of Cash Flows from Investing Activities in Exhibit 12-12.

Step 4: Determine the Cash Flows from Financing Activities

These activities generally involve long-term liabilities and stockholders' equity. First, we consider Julian's two long-term liabilities: Notes Payable and Bonds Payable; then, the two stockholders' equity accounts: Capital Stock and Retained Earnings.

Notes Payable Recall that item 2 in the additional information reported that Julian purchased land in exchange for a $50,000 note payable. This amount is confirmed on the balance sheets, which show an increase in notes payable of $50,000, from $35,000 to $85,000. In the discussion of investing activities, we already entered this transaction on a supplemental schedule of noncash activities because it was a significant financing activity but did not involve cash.

Bonds Payable The balance sheets in Exhibit 12-9 report a decrease in bonds payable of $60,000, from $260,000 to $200,000. Item 5 in the additional information in Exhibit 12-9 indicates that bonds with a face value of $60,000 were retired by paying $63,000 in cash. The book value of the bonds retired is the same as the face value of $60,000 because there is no unamortized discount or premium on the records. *When a company has to pay more in cash ($63,000) to settle a debt than the book value of the debt ($60,000), it reports a loss.* Recall the $3,000 loss reported on the income statement in Exhibit 12-8. For purposes of preparing a statement of cash flows with the direct method, however, the important amount is the $63,000 in cash paid to retire the bonds.

EXHIBIT 12-13 Schedule of Cash Flows from Financing Activities

Cash Flows from Financing Activities	
Cash inflows from:	
Issuance of stock	25,000
Cash outflows for:	
Retirement of bonds	(63,000)
Payment of cash dividends	(67,000)

© Cengage Learning 2013

This amount appears as a cash outflow in the Schedule of Cash Flows from Financing Activities shown in Exhibit 12-13.

Capital Stock Exhibit 12-9 indicates an increase in capital stock of $25,000, from $75,000 to $100,000. Julian issued capital stock in exchange for $25,000 in cash, according to item 6 in the additional information in Exhibit 12-9. Some companies issue additional stock after the initial formation of the corporation to raise needed capital.

The increase in Cash from this issuance is presented as a cash inflow in the Schedule of Cash Flows from Financing Activities shown in Exhibit 12-13.

Retained Earnings This account increased during the year by $53,000, from $193,000 to $246,000. Because we know from Exhibit 12-8 that net income was $120,000, however, the company must have declared some dividends.

We can determine the amount of cash dividends for 2012 in the following manner:

Beginning retained earnings	$193,000
+ Net income	120,000
− Cash dividends	(X)
= Ending retained earnings	$246,000

Solving for X, we can find the amount of cash dividends paid during the year.[2]

$$\$193,000 + \$120,000 - X = \$246,000$$
$$X = \$\ 67,000$$

Item 7 in the additional information confirms that this was in fact the amount of dividends paid during the year. The dividends paid appear in the Schedule of Cash Flows from Financing Activities presented in Exhibit 12-13.

Using the Three Schedules to Prepare a Statement of Cash Flows

All of the information needed to prepare a statement of cash flows is now available in the three schedules, along with the supplemental schedule prepared earlier. From the information gathered in Exhibits 12-10, 12-12, and 12-13, a completed statement of cash flows appears in Exhibit 12-14.

What does Julian's statement of cash flows tell us? Cash flow from operations totaled $174,000. Cash used to acquire investments and equipment amounted to $80,000 after $25,000 was received from the sale of a machine. A net amount of $105,000 was used for financing activities. Thus, Julian used more cash than it generated, which is why the cash balance declined. That's okay for a year or two, but if this continues, the company won't be able to pay its bills.

---

[2] Any decrease in Retained Earnings represents the dividends *declared* during the period rather than the amount paid. If there had been a Dividends Payable account, we would have analyzed it to find the amount of dividends paid. The lack of a balance in such an account at the beginning or end of the period tells us that Julian paid the same amount of dividends that it declared during the period.

LO5 Prepare a statement of cash flows using the direct method to determine cash flow from operating activities.

- Using the approach illustrated in this section, it is possible to determine the cash flow from the major operating activities, such as sales, purchases, salaries and wages, and operating expenses, and from investing and financing activities.

POD REVIEW 12.5

QUESTIONS   Answers to these questions are on the last page of the chapter.

1. Baxter began the year with a balance of $15,000 in Salaries and Wages Payable and ended the year with $10,000 in the account. Salaries and Wages Expense for the period amounted to $98,000. Under the direct method, Baxter will report cash payments for salaries and wages of
   a. $93,000.
   b. $98,000.
   c. $103,000.
   d. $108,000.

2. How is depreciation expense treated under the direct method?
   a. as an outflow in the Operating Activities section of the statement
   b. as an outflow in the Investing Activities section of the statement
   c. as an addition to net income in the Operating Activities section of the statement
   d. Depreciation expense does not appear on the statement of cash flows when the direct method is used.

© Cengage Learning 2013

EXHIBIT 12-14 Completed Statement of Cash Flows for Julian Corp.

Julian Corp. Statement of Cash Flows For the Year Ended December 31, 2012	
Cash flows from operating activities	
Cash receipts from:	
Sales on account	$ 664,000
Interest	15,000
Total cash receipts	$ 679,000
Cash payments for:	
Inventory purchases	$(375,000)
Salaries and wages	(62,000)
Insurance	(6,000)
Interest	(15,000)
Taxes	(47,000)
Total cash payments	$(505,000)
Net cash provided by operating activities	$ 174,000
Cash flows from investing activities	
Purchase of investments	$ (30,000)
Purchase of property and equipment	(75,000)
Sale of machine	25,000
Net cash used by investing activities	$ (80,000)
Cash flows from financing activities	
Retirement of bonds	$ (63,000)
Issuance of stock	25,000
Payment of cash dividends	(67,000)
Net cash used by financing activities	$(105,000)
Net decrease in cash	$ (11,000)
Cash balance, December 31, 2011	46,000
Cash balance, December 31, 2012	$ 35,000
Supplemental schedule of noncash investing and financing activities	
Acquisition of land in exchange for note payable	$ 50,000

© Cengage Learning 2013

An Approach to Preparing the Statement of Cash Flows: Indirect Method

LO6 Prepare a statement of cash flows using the indirect method to determine cash flow from operating activities.

OVERVIEW: A systematic approach can be used to provide the information necessary to prepare a statement of cash flows. In this section, we illustrate the indirect method of presenting cash provided by operating activities.

Reconcile Net Income to Net Cash Flows from Operating Activities

The purpose of the Operating Activities section of the statement changes when the indirect method is used. Instead of reporting cash receipts and cash payments, **the objective is to reconcile net income to net cash flow from operating activities.** The other two sections of the completed statement in Exhibit 12-14, the Investing and Financing sections, are unchanged.

An approach similar to that used for the direct method can be used to prepare the Operating Activities section of the statement of cash flows under the indirect method.

Net Income Recall that the first line in the Operating Activities section of the statement under the indirect method is net income. That is, we start with the assumptions that all revenues and gains reported on the income statement increase cash flow and that all expenses and losses decrease cash flow. Julian's net income of $120,000, as reported on its income statement in Exhibit 12-8, is reported as the first item in the Operating Activities section of the statement of cash flows shown in Exhibit 12-15.

Accounts Receivable Recall from the balance sheets in Exhibit 12-9 the net increase in Accounts Receivable of $6,000. Because net income includes sales (as opposed to cash collections), the $6,000 *net increase* must be *deducted* to adjust net income to cash from operations as shown in Exhibit 12-15.

Gain on Sale of Machine The gain itself did not generate any cash, but the sale of the machine did. And as we found earlier, the cash generated by selling the machine was reported in the Investing Activities section of the statement. The cash proceeds included the gain. Because the gain is included in the net income figure, it must be *deducted* to determine cash from operations. Also note that the gain is included twice in

EXHIBIT 12-15 Indirect Method for Reporting Cash Flows from Operating Activities

Julian Corp. Partial Statement of Cash Flows For the Year Ended December 31, 2012	
Net cash flows from operating activities	
Net income	$120,000
Adjustments to reconcile net income to net cash provided by operating activities:	
Increase in accounts receivable	(6,000)
Gain on sale of machine	(5,000)
Decrease in inventory	8,000
Increase in accounts payable	7,000
Decrease in salaries and wages payable	(2,000)
Depreciation expense	40,000
Decrease in prepaid insurance	6,000
Increase in income taxes payable	3,000
Loss on retirement of bonds	3,000
Net cash provided by operating activities	$174,000

cash inflows if it is not deducted from the net income figure in the Operating Activities section. Note the deduction of $5,000 in Exhibit 12-15.

Inventory As the $8,000 net decrease in the Inventory account indicates, Julian liquidated a portion of its stock of inventory during the year. A net decrease in this account indicates that the company sold more products than it purchased during the year. As shown in Exhibit 12-15, the *net decrease* of $8,000 is *added back* to net income.

Accounts Payable According to Exhibit 12-9, Julian owed suppliers $31,000 at the start of the year. By the end of the year, the balance had grown to $38,000. Effectively, the company saved cash by delaying the payment of some of its outstanding accounts payable. The *net increase* of $7,000 in this account is *added back* to net income, as shown in Exhibit 12-15.

Salaries and Wages Payable Salaries and Wages Payable decreased during the year by $2,000. The rationale for *deducting* the $2,000 *net decrease* in this liability in Exhibit 12-15 follows from what was just said about an increase in Accounts Payable. The payment to employees of $2,000 more than the amount included in expense on the income statement requires an additional deduction under the indirect method.

Depreciation Expense Depreciation is a noncash expense. Because it was deducted to arrive at net income, we must *add back* $40,000, the amount of depreciation, to find cash from operations. The same holds true for amortization of intangible assets and depletion of natural resources.

Prepaid Insurance This account decreased by $6,000, according to Exhibit 12-9. A decrease in this account indicates that Julian deducted more on the income statement for the insurance expense of the period than it paid in cash for new policies. That is, the cash outlay for insurance protection was not as large as the amount of expense reported on the income statement. Thus, the *net decrease* in the account is *added back* to net income in Exhibit 12-15.

Income Taxes Payable Exhibit 12-9 reports a net increase of $3,000 in Income Taxes Payable. The *net increase* of $3,000 in this liability is *added back* to net income in Exhibit 12-15 because the payments to the government were $3,000 less than the amount included on the income statement.

Loss on Retirement of Bonds The $3,000 loss from retiring bonds was reported on the income statement as a deduction. There are two parts to the explanation for adding back the loss to net income to eliminate its effect in the Operating Activities section of the statement. First, any cash outflow from retiring bonds is properly classified as a financing activity, not an operating activity. The entire cash outflow should be reported in one classification rather than being allocated between two classifications. Second, the amount of the cash outflow is $63,000, not $3,000. To summarize, to convert net income to a cash basis, the loss is added back in the Operating Activities section to eliminate its effect. The actual use of cash to retire the bonds is shown in the Financing section of the statement.

Summary of Adjustments to Net Income under the Indirect Method Following is a list of the most common adjustments to net income when the indirect method is used to prepare the Operating Activities section of the statement of cash flows:

Additions to Net Income	Deductions from Net Income
Decrease in accounts receivable	Increase in accounts receivable
Decrease in inventory	Increase in inventory
Decrease in prepayments	Increase in prepayments
Increase in accounts payable	Decrease in accounts payable
Increase in accrued liabilities	Decrease in accrued liabilities
Losses on sales of long-term assets	Gains on sales of long-term assets
Losses on retirements of bonds	Gains on retirements of bonds
Depreciation, amortization, and depletion	

STUDY TIP

Notice in this list how changes in current assets and current liabilities are treated on the statement. For example, because accounts receivable and accounts payable are on opposite sides of the balance sheet, increases in each of them are handled in opposite ways. But an increase in one and a decrease in the other are treated the same way.

© Cengage Learning 2013

12-3

REAL WORLD PRACTICE

Reading Best Buy's Statement of Cash Flows

According to the supplemental disclosure at the bottom of Best Buy's statement of cash flow, what amount did the company pay in income taxes in the most recent year? Would this necessarily be the same amount that the company reported as income tax expense on its income statement? Explain your answer.

Comparison of the Indirect and Direct Methods

The amount of cash provided by operating activities is the same under the direct and indirect methods. The relative merits of the two methods, however, have stirred considerable debate in the accounting profession. The FASB has expressed a strong preference for the direct method but allows companies to use the indirect method.

If a company uses the indirect method, it must separately disclose two important cash payments: income taxes paid and interest paid. Thus, if Julian uses the indirect method, it reports the following at the bottom of the statement of cash flows or in a note to the financial statements:

Income taxes paid	$47,000
Interest paid	15,000

Advocates of the direct method believe that the information provided with this approach is valuable in evaluating a company's operating efficiency. For example, use of the direct method allows the analyst to follow any trends in cash receipts from customers and compare them with cash payments to suppliers. The information presented in the Operating Activities section of the statement under the direct method is certainly user-friendly. Someone without a technical background in accounting can easily tell where cash came from and where it went during the period.

Advocates of the indirect method argue two major points: (1) The direct method reveals too much about a business by telling readers the amount of cash receipts and cash payments from operations. (2) The indirect method focuses attention on the differences between income on an accrual basis and a cash basis. In fact, this reconciliation of net income and cash provided by operating activities is considered to be important enough that **if a company uses the direct method, it must present a separate schedule to reconcile net income to net cash from operating activities.** This schedule, in effect, is the same as the Operating Activities section for the indirect method.

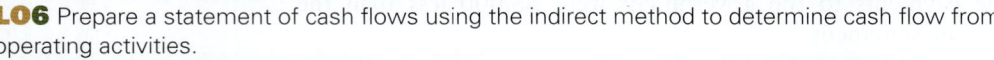

LO6 Prepare a statement of cash flows using the indirect method to determine cash flow from operating activities.

POD REVIEW

12.6

• The approach illustrated in this section uses the changes in current asset and liability accounts related to accruals and deferrals to adjust net income to cash flows from operating activities.

QUESTIONS   Answers to these questions are on the last page of the chapter.

1. Which of the following is an addition to net income when the indirect method is used?

   a. increase in inventory
   b. decrease in accounts payable
   c. loss on sale of equipment
   d. None of the above is an addition to net income under the indirect method.

2. How is depreciation expense treated under the indirect method?

   a. as an outflow in the Operating Activities section of the statement
   b. as an outflow in the Investing Activities section of the statement
   c. as an addition to net income in the Operating Activities section of the statement
   d. Depreciation expense does not appear on the statement of cash flows when the indirect method is used.

If the proposals in a joint project of the FASB and the IASB are adopted, financial statements would look significantly different than they do today. The two groups are looking specifically at how the three major financial statements—the statement of financial position, the statement of comprehensive income, and the statement of cash flows—could be constructed to be more useful. The project focuses specifically on the organization and presentation of information in the financial statements.

LOOKING AHEAD

Tetra Images/Getty Images

One of the two major concerns of the groups is cohesiveness, that is, how the items on each of the financial statements relate to one another. The consensus is that, as currently constructed, items are not cohesive across the statements. For example, the major sections on a balance sheet, or statement of financial position, are assets, liabilities, and equity. Yet, a statement of cash flows presents information in three completely different sections: operating, investing, and financing. If the current proposal is adopted, the balance sheet of the future would have sections similar to what are currently on a statement of cash flows, with operating and investing subcategories within a business section, and debt and equity subcategories within a financing section.

Another of the most important changes under the proposal is that companies would be required to use the direct method in the Operating Activities section of the statement of cash flows. Both the FASB and the IASB currently state a strong preference for the direct method, but allow companies to use the indirect method. So not only might the balance sheet look significantly different in the future, but the statement of cash flows for a vast majority of companies would also have a very different appearance in the Operating section, reflecting the cash receipts and cash payments for the period.

Source: "Financial Statement Presentation," Staff Draft of Exposure Draft, July 2010, International Accounting Standards Board and Financial Accounting Standards Board.

The Use of Cash Flow Information

OVERVIEW: Analysts use information from the statement of cash flows to evaluate companies. One commonly used measure is a company's cash flow adequacy.

LO7 Use cash flow information to help analyze a company.

The statement of cash flows is a critical disclosure to a company's investors and creditors. Many investors focus on cash flow from operations rather than net income as their key statistic. Similarly, many bankers are as concerned with cash flow from operations as they are with net income because they care about a company's ability to pay its bills. There is the concern that accrual accounting can mask cash flow problems. For example, a company with smooth earnings could be building up accounts receivable and inventory. This may not become evident until the company is in deep trouble.

The statement of cash flows provides investors, analysts, bankers, and other users with a valuable starting point as they attempt to evaluate a company's financial health. They pay particular attention to the relationships among various items on the statement, as well as to other financial statement items. In fact, many large banks have their own cash flow models, which typically involve a rearrangement of the items on the statement of cash flows to suit their needs. We now consider two examples of how various groups use cash flow information.

Creditors and Cash Flow Adequacy

Bankers and other creditors are especially concerned with a company's ability to meet its principal and interest obligations. *Cash flow adequacy* is a measure intended to help in this regard.[3] It gauges the cash that a company has available to meet future debt obligations after paying taxes and interest costs and making capital expenditures. Because

---

[3] An article appearing in the January 10, 1994, edition of *The Wall Street Journal* reported that **Fitch Investors Service Inc.** has published a rating system to compare the cash flow adequacy of companies that it rates single-A in its credit ratings. The rating system is intended to help corporate bond investors assess the ability of these companies to meet their maturing debt obligations. Lee Berton, "Investors Have a New Tool for Judging Issuers' Health: 'Cash-Flow Adequacy,'" p. C1.

capital expenditures on new plant and equipment are a necessity for most companies, analysts are concerned with the cash available to repay debt *after* the company has replaced and updated its existing base of long-term assets.

$$\text{Cash Flow Adequacy} = \frac{\text{Cash Flow from Operating Activities} - \text{Capital Expenditures}}{\text{Average Amount of Debt Maturing over Next Five Years}}$$

How could you use the information in an annual report to measure a company's cash flow adequacy? First, whether a company uses the direct or indirect method to report cash flow from operating activities, this number represents cash flow after interest and taxes are paid. The numerator of the ratio is determined by deducting capital expenditures, as they appear in the Investing Activities section of the statement, from cash flow from operating activities. A disclosure required by the SEC provides the information needed to calculate the denominator of the ratio. This regulatory body requires companies to report the annual amount of long-term debt maturing over each of the next five years. For more on the cash flow adequacy of Best Buy, see the Ratio Decision Model that follows.

Best Buy's Cash Flow Adequacy To calculate this ratio, consider the following amounts from Best Buy's statement of cash flows for the year ended February 26, 2011 (amounts in millions of dollars):

Total cash provided by operating activities	$1,190
Additions to property and equipment	$ 744

Note 6 in Best Buy's 2011 annual report provides the following information:

At February 26, 2011, the future maturities of long-term debt, including capitalized leases, consisted of the following:

Fiscal Year	
2012[1]	$ 441
2013	37
2014	537
2015	36
2016	29
Thereafter	72
Total long-term debt	$1,152[4]

[1]Holders of our convertible debentures may require us to purchase all or a portion of their debentures on January 15, 2012. The table above assumes that all holders exercise their redemption right on that date.

USING THE RATIO DECISION MODEL

Analyzing Cash Flow Adequacy

Use the following Ratio Decision Model to evaluate the cash flow adequacy of Best Buy or any other public company.

1. Formulate the Question
Managers, investors, and creditors are all interested in a company's cash flows. They must be able to answer the following question:

Did the company generate enough cash this year from its operations to pay for its capital expenditures and meet its maturing debt obligations?

[4] Best Buy 2011 10K, p. 104.

2. Gather the Information from the Financial Statements

- Total cash from operating activities: From the statement of cash flows
- Necessary capital expenditures: From the statement of cash flows
- Average debt maturing over next five years: From the note disclosures

3. Calculate the ratio

$$\text{Cash Flow Adequacy} = \frac{\text{Cash Flow from Operating Activities} - \text{Capital Expenditures}}{\text{Average Amount of Debt Maturing over Next Five Years}}$$

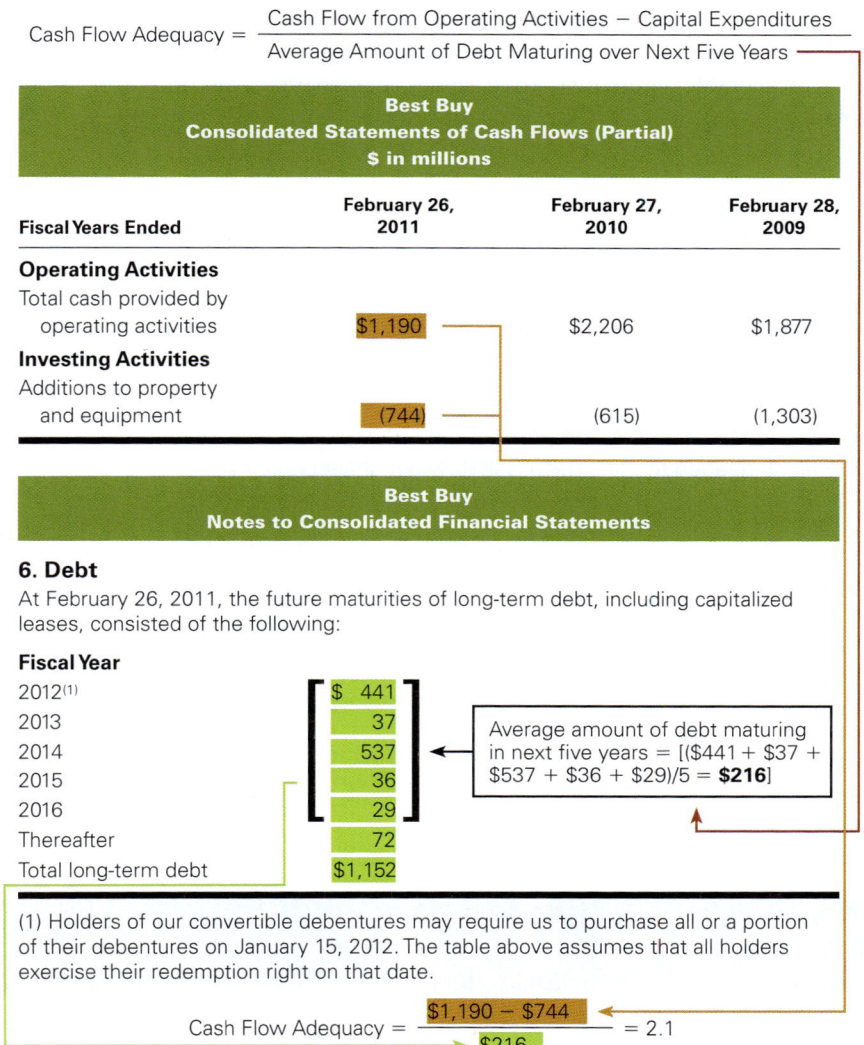

Best Buy
Consolidated Statements of Cash Flows (Partial)
$ in millions

Fiscal Years Ended	February 26, 2011	February 27, 2010	February 28, 2009
Operating Activities			
Total cash provided by operating activities	$1,190	$2,206	$1,877
Investing Activities			
Additions to property and equipment	(744)	(615)	(1,303)

Best Buy
Notes to Consolidated Financial Statements

6. Debt

At February 26, 2011, the future maturities of long-term debt, including capitalized leases, consisted of the following:

Fiscal Year

2012[1]	$ 441
2013	37
2014	537
2015	36
2016	29
Thereafter	72
Total long-term debt	$1,152

Average amount of debt maturing in next five years = [($441 + $37 + $537 + $36 + $29)/5 = **$216**]

(1) Holders of our convertible debentures may require us to purchase all or a portion of their debentures on January 15, 2012. The table above assumes that all holders exercise their redemption right on that date.

$$\text{Cash Flow Adequacy} = \frac{\$1,190 - \$744}{\$216} = 2.1$$

4. Compare the Ratio with Others

Best Buy's cash flow adequacy may be compared to that of prior years and to that of companies of similar size in the same industry.

	Best Buy		Radio Shack	
	Year Ended February 26, 2011	Year Ended February 27, 2010	Year Ended December 31, 2010	Year Ended December 31, 2009
Cash Flow Adequacy	2.1	7.6	0.5	1.2

5. Interpret the Results

Best Buy's ratio decreased in the most recent year; however, the ratio in both years indicates that the company's cash flow was sufficient to repay its average annual debt over the next five years. Radio Shack's ratio was also higher in the prior year than it was in the current year. ■

Stockholders and Cash Flow per Share

One measure of the relative worth of an investment in a company is the ratio of the stock's market price per share to the company's earnings per share (that is, the price/earnings ratio). But many stockholders and Wall Street analysts are even more interested in the price of the stock in relation to the company's cash flow per share. Cash flow for purposes of this ratio is normally limited to cash flow from operating activities. These groups have used this ratio to evaluate investments—even though the accounting profession has expressly forbidden the reporting of cash flow per share information in the financial statements. The accounting profession's belief is that this type of information is not an acceptable alternative to earnings per share as an indicator of company performance.

LO7 Use cash flow information to help analyze a company.

POD REVIEW 12.7

- Cash flow per share and cash flow adequacy are two measures that investors and creditors can use to evaluate the financial health of an entity.

QUESTIONS   Answers to these questions are on the last page of the chapter.

1. Where would a person find the information needed to compute the cash flow adequacy ratio?

   a. the statement of cash flows only
   b. the income statement only
   c. the statement of cash flows and the notes to the statements
   d. the balance sheet only

2. Cash flow per share is

   a. the same as earnings per share.
   b. computed by dividing cash on the balance sheet by the number of shares outstanding.
   c. an acceptable alternative to earnings per share according to the accounting profession.
   d. not an acceptable alternative to earnings per share according to the accounting profession.

APPENDIX

Accounting Tools: A Work-Sheet Approach to the Statement of Cash Flows

LO8 Use a work sheet to prepare a statement of cash flows using the indirect method to determine cash flow from operating activities.

OVERVIEW: A work sheet is a useful device to help in the preparation of a statement of cash flows.

The chapter illustrated a systematic approach to aid in the preparation of a statement of cash flows. We now consider the use of a work sheet as an alternative tool to organize the information needed to prepare the statement. We will use the information given in the chapter for Julian Corp. (Refer to Exhibits 12-8 and 12-9 for the income statement and comparative balance sheets, respectively.) Although it is possible to use a work sheet to prepare the statement when the Operating Activities section is prepared under the direct method, we illustrate the use of a work sheet using the more popular indirect method.

A work sheet for Julian Corp. is presented in Exhibit 12-16. The following steps were taken to prepare the work sheet:

Step 1: The balances in each account at the end and the beginning of the period are entered in the first two columns of the work sheet. For Julian, these balances can be found in its comparative balance sheets in Exhibit 12-9. Note that credit balances are shown in parentheses on the work sheet. Because the work sheet lists all balance sheet accounts, the total of the debit balances must equal the total of the credit balances; thus, the totals at the bottom for these first two columns equal $0.

Step 2: The additional information listed at the bottom of Exhibit 12-9 is used to record the various investing and financing activities on the work sheet. (The item numbers that follow correspond to the superscript numbers on the work sheet in Exhibit 12-16.)

EXHIBIT 12-16 Julian Corp. Statement of Cash Flows Work Sheet

Julian Corp.
Statement of Cash Flows Work Sheet (Indirect Method)
(all amounts in thousands of dollars)

| | Balances | | | Cash inflows (Outflows) | | | Noncash |
Accounts	12/31/12	12/31/11	Changes	Operating	Investing	Financing	Activities
Cash	35	46	$(11)^{16}$				
Accounts Receivable	63	57	6^{10}	$(6)^{10}$			
Inventory	84	92	$(8)^{11}$	8^{11}			
Prepaid Insurance	12	18	$(6)^{12}$	6^{12}			
Long-Term Investments	120	90	30^1		$(30)^1$		
Land	150	100	50^2				$(50)^2$
Property and Equipment	320	280	75^3		$(75)^3$		
			$(35)^4$		25^4		
Accumulated Depreciation	(100)	(75)	15^4				
			$(40)^9$	40^9			
Accounts Payable	(38)	(31)	$(7)^{13}$	7^{13}			
Salaries and Wages Payable	(7)	(9)	2^{14}	$(2)^{14}$			
Income Taxes Payable	(8)	(5)	$(3)^{15}$	3^{15}			
Notes Payable	(85)	(35)	$(50)^2$				50^2
Bonds Payable	(200)	(260)	$(60)^6$			$(63)^5$	
Capital Stock	(100)	(75)	$(25)^6$			25^6	
Retained Earnings	(246)	(193)	67^7	$(5)^4$		$(67)^7$	
				3^5			
			$(120)^8$	120^8			
Totals	0	0	0	174	(80)	(105)	0
Net decrease in cash				$(11)^{16}$			

Source: The authors are grateful to Jeannie Folk for the development of this work sheet.

1. Long-term investments were purchased for $30,000. Because this transaction required the use of cash, it is entered in parentheses in the Investing column and in the Changes column as an addition to the Long-Term Investments account.

2. Land was acquired by issuing a $50,000 note payable. This transaction is entered on two lines on the work sheet. First, $50,000 is added to the Changes column for Land and as a corresponding deduction in the Noncash column (the last column on the work sheet). Likewise, $50,000 is added to the Changes column for Notes Payable and to the Noncash column.

3. Item 3 in the additional information indicates the acquisition of equipment for $75,000. This amount appears on the work sheet as an addition to Property and Equipment in the Changes column and as a deduction (cash outflow) in the Investing column.

4. A machine with an original cost of $35,000 and a book value of $20,000 was sold for $25,000, resulting in four entries on the work sheet. First, the amount of cash received, $25,000, is entered as an addition in the Investing column on the line for property and equipment. On the same line, the cost of the machine, $35,000, is entered as a deduction in the Changes column. The difference between the cost of the machine, $35,000, and its book value, $20,000, is its accumulated depreciation of $15,000. This amount is shown as a deduction from this account in the Changes column. Because the gain of $5,000 is included in net income, it is deducted in the Operating column (on the Retained Earnings line).

5. Bonds with a face value of $60,000 were retired by paying $63,000 in cash, resulting in the entry of three amounts on the work sheet. The face value of the bonds, $60,000, is entered as a reduction of Bonds Payable in the Changes column. The amount paid to retire the bonds, $63,000, is entered on the same line in the Financing column. The loss of $3,000 is added in the Operating column because it was a deduction to arrive at net income.

6. Capital stock was issued for $25,000. This amount is entered on the Capital Stock line under the Changes column (as an increase in the account) and under the Financing column as an inflow.

7. Dividends of $67,000 were paid. This amount is entered as a reduction in Retained Earnings in the Changes column and as a cash outflow in the Financing column.

Step 3: Because the indirect method is being used, net income of $120,000 for the period is entered as an addition to Retained Earnings in the Operating column of the work sheet [entry (8)]. The amount is also entered as an increase (in parentheses) in the Changes column.

Step 4: Any noncash revenues or expenses are entered on the work sheet on the appropriate lines. For Julian, depreciation expense of $40,000 is added (in parentheses) to Accumulated Depreciation in the Changes column and in the Operating column. This entry is identified on the work sheet as entry (9).

Step 5: Each of the changes in the noncash current asset and current liability accounts is entered in the Changes column and in the Operating column. These entries are identified on the work sheet as entries (10) through (15).

Step 6: Totals are determined for the Operating, Investing, and Financing columns and entered at the bottom of the work sheet. The total for the final column, Noncash Activities, of $0, is also entered.

Step 7: The net cash inflow (outflow) for the period is determined by adding the totals of the Operating, Investing, and Financing columns. For Julian, the net cash *outflow* is $11,000, shown as entry (16) at the bottom of the statement. This same amount is then transferred to the line for Cash in the Changes column. Finally, the total of the Changes column at this point should net to $0.

LO8 Use a work sheet to prepare a statement of cash flows using the indirect method to determine cash flow from operating activities.

- A work sheet is an alternative tool to help in the preparation of a statement of cash flows.

QUESTIONS   Answers to these questions are on the last page of the chapter.

1. On the work sheet illustrated in this appendix, what should be the total of the Changes column?
   a. zero
   b. the same number as total assets
   c. the same number as net income
   d. A Changes column does not appear on the work sheet.

2. What if the Changes column on the type of work sheet illustrated in this chapter shows a negative $50,000 for bonds payable? What will the work sheet also show?
   a. $50,000 inflow in the Operating column
   b. $50,000 inflow in the Investing column
   c. $50,000 inflow in the Financing column
   d. $50,000 outflow in the Financing column

RATIO REVIEW

$$\text{Cash Flow Adequacy} = \frac{\begin{array}{c}\text{Cash Flow from Operating Activities} - \text{Capital Expenditures} \\ \text{(Statement of Cash Flows)}\end{array}}{\begin{array}{c}\text{Average Amount of Debt Maturing over Next Five Years} \\ \text{(Notes to the Financial Statements)}\end{array}}$$

KEY TERMS QUIZ

Read each definition below and write the number of the definition in the blank beside the appropriate term. The quiz solutions appear at the end of the chapter.

_____ Statement of cash flows
_____ Cash equivalent
_____ Operating activities
_____ Investing activities

_____ Financing activities
_____ Direct method
_____ Indirect method

1. Activities concerned with the acquisition and sale of products and services.
2. For preparing the Operating Activities section of the statement of cash flows, the approach in which net income is reconciled to net cash flow from operations.
3. The financial statement that summarizes an entity's cash receipts and cash payments during the period from operating, investing, and financing activities.
4. An item readily convertible to a known amount of cash with a maturity to the investor of three months or less.
5. Activities concerned with the acquisition and disposal of long-term assets.
6. For preparing the Operating Activities section of the statement of cash flows, the approach in which cash receipts and cash payments are reported.
7. Activities concerned with the raising and repaying of funds in the form of debt and equity.

ALTERNATE TERMS

bottom line net income
cash flow from operating activities cash flow from operations

statement of cash flows cash flows statement

WARMUP EXERCISES & SOLUTIONS

LO1 **Warmup Exercise 12-1 Purpose of the Statement of Cash Flows**

Most companies begin the statement of cash flows by indicating the amount of net income and ending it with the beginning and ending cash balances. Why is the statement necessary if net income already appears on the income statement and the cash balances can be found on the balance sheet?

Key to the Solution Recall the purpose of the statement of cash flows as described in the beginning of the chapter.

LO3 **Warmup Exercise 12-2 Classification of Activities**

For each of the following activities, indicate whether it should appear on the statement of cash flows as an operating (O), investing (I), or financing (F) activity. Assume that the company uses the direct method of reporting in the Operating Activities section.

_____ 1. New equipment is acquired for cash.
_____ 2. Thirty-year bonds are issued.
_____ 3. Cash receipts from the cash register are recorded.
_____ 4. The biweekly payroll is paid.
_____ 5. Common stock is issued for cash.
_____ 6. Land that was being held for future expansion is sold at book value.

Key to the Solution Recall the general rules for each of the categories: operating activities involve acquiring and selling products and services, investing activities deal with acquiring and disposing of long-term assets, and financing activities are concerned with the raising and repaying of funds in the form of debt and equity.

LO6 **Warmup Exercise 12-3 Adjustments to Net Income with the Indirect Method**

Assume that a company uses the indirect method to prepare the Operating Activities section of the statement of cash flows. For each of the following items, indicate whether it would be added to net income (A), be deducted from net income (D), or not be reported in this section of the statement under the indirect method (NR).

_____ 1. Decrease in accounts payable
_____ 2. Increase in accounts receivable
_____ 3. Decrease in prepaid insurance
_____ 4. Purchase of new factory equipment
_____ 5. Depreciation Expense
_____ 6. Gain on retirement of bonds

Key to the Solution Refer to the summary of adjustments to net income under the indirect method on page 631.

Solutions to Warmup Exercises

Warmup Exercise 12-1

The statement of cash flows is a complement to the other statements in that it summarizes the operating, investing, and financing activities over a period of time. Even though the net income and cash balances are available on other statements, the statement of cash flows explains to the reader why net income is different from cash flow from operations and why cash changed by the amount it did during the period.

Warmup Exercise 12-2

1. I   2. F   3. O   4. O   5. F   6. I

Warmup Exercise 12-3

1. D   2. D   3. A   4. NR   5. A   6. D

REVIEW PROBLEM & SOLUTION

An income statement and comparative balance sheets for Dexter Company follow.

Dexter Company
Income Statement
For the Year Ended December 31, 2012

Sales revenue	$89,000
Cost of goods sold	57,000
Gross profit	$32,000
Depreciation expense	$ 6,500
Advertising expense	3,200
Salaries expense	12,000
Total operating expenses	$21,700
Operating income	$10,300
Loss on sale of land	2,500
Income before tax	$ 7,800
Income tax expense	2,600
Net income	$ 5,200

Dexter Company
Comparative Balance Sheets
December 31

	December 31	
	2012	**2011**
Cash	$ 12,000	$ 9,500
Accounts receivable	22,000	18,400
Inventory	25,400	20,500
Prepaid advertising	10,000	8,600
Total current assets	$ 69,400	$ 57,000
Land	$120,000	$ 80,000
Equipment	190,000	130,000
Accumulated depreciation	(70,000)	(63,500)
Total long-term assets	$240,000	$146,500
Total assets	$309,400	$203,500
Accounts payable	$ 15,300	$ 12,100
Salaries payable	14,000	16,400
Income taxes payable	1,200	700
Total current liabilities	$ 30,500	$ 29,200
Capital stock	$200,000	$100,000
Retained earnings	78,900	74,300
Total stockholders' equity	$278,900	$174,300
Total liabilities and stockholders' equity	$309,400	$203,500

Additional Information:

1. Land was acquired during the year for $70,000.
2. An unimproved parcel of land was sold during the year for $27,500. Its original cost to Dexter was $30,000.

(Continued)

3. A specialized piece of equipment was acquired in exchange for capital stock in the company. The value of the capital stock was $60,000.
4. In addition to the capital stock issued in (3), stock was sold for $40,000.
5. Dividends of $600 were paid.

Required

Prepare a statement of cash flows for 2012 using the direct method in the Operating Activities section of the statement. Include supplemental schedules to report any noncash investing and financing activities and to reconcile net income to net cash provided by operating activities.

Solution to Review Problem

Dexter Company
Statement of Cash Flows
For the Year Ended December 31, 2012

Cash flows from operating activities		
Cash collections from customers		$ 85,400
Cash payments:		
To suppliers	$(58,700)	
For advertising	(4,600)	
To employees	(14,400)	
For income taxes	(2,100)	
Total cash payments		$(79,800)
Net cash provided by operating activities		$ 5,600
Cash flows from investing activities		
Purchase of land		$(70,000)
Sale of land		27,500
Net cash used by investing activities		$(42,500)
Cash flows from financing activities		
Issuance of capital stock		$ 40,000
Payment of cash dividends		(600)
Net cash provided by financing activities		$ 39,400
Net increase in cash		$ 2,500
Cash balance, December 31, 2011		9,500
Cash balance, December 31, 2012		$ 12,000
Supplemental schedule of noncash investing and financing activities		
Acquisition of specialized equipment in exchange for capital stock		$ 60,000
Reconciliation of net income to net cash provided by operating activities		
Net income		$ 5,200
Adjustments to reconcile net income to net cash provided by operating activities:		
Increase in accounts receivable		(3,600)
Increase in inventory		(4,900)
Increase in prepaid advertising		(1,400)
Increase in accounts payable		3,200
Decrease in salaries payable		(2,400)
Increase in income taxes payable		500
Depreciation expense		6,500
Loss on sale of land		2,500
Net cash provided by operating activities		$ 5,600

QUESTIONS

1. What is the purpose of the statement of cash flows? As a flows statement, explain how it differs from the income statement.

2. What is a cash equivalent? Why is it included with cash for purposes of preparing a statement of cash flows?

3. Preston Corp. acquires a piece of land by signing a $60,000 promissory note and making a down payment of $20,000. How should this transaction be reported on the statement of cash flows?

4. Hansen Inc. made two purchases during December. One was a $10,000 Treasury bill that matures in 60 days from the date of purchase. The other was a $20,000 investment in Motorola common stock that will be held indefinitely. How should each purchase be treated for purposes of preparing a statement of cash flows?

5. Companies are required to classify cash flows as operating, investing, or financing. Which of these three categories do you think will most likely have a net cash outflow over a number of years? Explain your answer.

6. A fellow student says to you: "The statement of cash flows is the easiest of the basic financial statements to prepare because you know the answer before you start. You compare the beginning and ending balances in cash on the balance sheet and compute the net inflow or outflow of cash. What could be easier?" Do you agree? Explain your answer.

7. What is your evaluation of the following statements? Depreciation is responsible for providing some of the highest amounts of cash for capital-intensive businesses. This is obvious by examining the Operating Activities section of the statement of cash flows. Other than the net income of the period, depreciation is often the largest amount reported in this section of the statement.

8. Which method for preparing the Operating Activities section of the statement of cash flows, the direct or the indirect method, do you believe provides more information to users of the statement? Explain your answer.

9. Assume that a company uses the indirect method to prepare the Operating Activities section of the statement of cash flows. Why would a decrease in accounts receivable during the period be added back to net income?

10. Why is it necessary to analyze both inventory and accounts payable in trying to determine cash payments to suppliers when the direct method is used?

11. A company has a very profitable year. What explanations might there be for a decrease in cash?

12. A company reports a net loss for the year. Is it possible that cash could increase during the year? Explain your answer.

13. What effect does a decrease in income taxes payable for the period have on cash generated from operating activities? Does it matter whether the direct or the indirect method is used?

14. Why do accounting standards require a company to separately disclose income taxes paid and interest paid if it uses the indirect method?

15. Is it logical that interest paid is classified as a cash outflow in the Operating Activities section of the statement of cash flows but that dividends paid are included in the Financing Activities section? Explain your answer.

16. Jackson Company prepays the rent on various office facilities. The beginning balance in Prepaid Rent was $9,600, and the ending balance was $7,300. The income statement reports Rent Expense of $45,900. Under the direct method, what amount would appear for cash paid in rent in the Operating Activities section of the statement of cash flows?

17. Baxter Inc. buys as treasury stock 2,000 shares of its own common stock at $20 per share. How is this transaction reported on the statement of cash flows?

18. Duke Corp. sold a delivery truck for $9,000. Its original cost was $25,000, and the book value at the time of the sale was $11,000. How does the transaction to record the sale appear on a statement of cash flows prepared under the indirect method?

19. Billings Company has a patent on its books with a balance at the beginning of the year of $24,000. The ending balance for the asset was $20,000. The company did not buy or sell any patents during the year, nor does it use an Accumulated Amortization account. Assuming that the company uses the indirect method in

preparing a statement of cash flows, how is the decrease in the Patents account reported on the statement?

20. Ace Inc. declared and distributed a 10% stock dividend during the year. Explain how, if at all, you think this transaction should be reported on a statement of cash flows.

21. Explain where to find the information needed to determine a company's cash flow adequacy.

BRIEF EXERCISES

LO1

Brief Exercise 12-1 Purpose of the Statement of Cash Flows

You have been studying accounting for nearly a semester now and have become convinced of the value of determining a company's net income on an accrual basis. Why do you think the accounting profession requires companies also to prepare a statement of cash flows, especially since you can look at two successive balance sheets to see the change in cash?

LO2

EXAMPLE 12-2

Brief Exercise 12-2 Cash Equivalents

A friend in your class is confused and asks for your help in understanding cash equivalents: "Say a company invests $50,000 in a 60-day certificate of deposit. Since the company obviously used cash to buy the CD, why is this not classified as an investing activity on the statement of cash flows?" How would you respond to your friend's question?

LO3

EXAMPLE 12-1

Brief Exercise 12-3 Three Types of Activities

For each of the following transactions on the statement of cash flows, indicate whether it would appear in the Operating Activities section (O), in the Investing Activities section (I), or in the Financing Activities section (F). Assume the use of the direct method in the Operating Activities section.

_____ 1. Repayment of long-term debt
_____ 2. Purchase of equipment
_____ 3. Collection of customer's account
_____ 4. Issuance of common stock
_____ 5. Purchase of another company
_____ 6. Payment of dividends
_____ 7. Payment of income taxes
_____ 8. Sale of equipment

LO4

EXAMPLE 12-4, 12-5

Brief Exercise 12-4 Direct versus Indirect Method

For each of the following items, indicate whether it would appear on a statement of cash flows prepared using the direct method (D) or the indirect method (I).

_____ 1. Net income
_____ 2. Increase in accounts receivable
_____ 3. Collections on accounts receivable
_____ 4. Payments on accounts payable
_____ 5. Decrease in accounts payable
_____ 6. Depreciation expense
_____ 7. Gain on early retirement of bonds
_____ 8. Cash sales

LO5

Brief Exercise 12-5 Direct Method

Fill in the blank for each of the following situations.

Balance Sheet	Beginning	Ending	Income Statement	Cash Inflow (Outflow)
1. Accounts receivable	$2,000	$5,000	Sales on account, $15,000	$_____
2. Prepaid insurance	$4,000	$3,000	Insurance expense, $7,000	$_____
3. Income taxes payable	$6,000	$9,000	Income tax expense, $20,000	$_____
4. Wages payable	$5,000	$3,000	Wages expense, $25,000	$_____

Brief Exercise 12-6 Indirect Method

LO6
EXAMPLE 12-1, 12-5

For each of the following items, indicate whether it would be added to (A) or deducted from (D) net income to arrive at net cash flow provided by operating activities under the indirect method.

_____ 1. Increase in accounts receivable
_____ 2. Decrease in prepaid rent
_____ 3. Decrease in inventory
_____ 4. Decrease in accounts payable
_____ 5. Increase in income taxes payable
_____ 6. Depreciation expense
_____ 7. Gain on sale of equipment
_____ 8. Loss on early retirement of bonds

Brief Exercise 12-7 Cash Flow Adequacy

LO7

A company generated $1,500,000 from its operating activities and spent $900,000 on additions to its plant and equipment during the year. The total amount of debt that matures in the next five years is $750,000. Compute the company's cash flow adequacy ratio for the year.

Brief Exercise 12-8 Work Sheet

LO8

Assume that a company uses a work sheet as illustrated in Exhibit 12-16 to prepare its statement of cash flows and that it uses the indirect method in the Operating Activities section of the statement. For each of the following changes in balance sheet accounts, indicate in one of the three columns whether it is an addition (A) or a deduction (D). Assume that the change in (2) and (6) includes a corresponding change in cash.

	Type of Activity		
Balance Sheet Change	**Operating**	**Investing**	**Financing**
1. Accounts receivable increased	_____	_____	_____
2. Land increased	_____	_____	_____
3. Inventory decreased	_____	_____	_____
4. Accounts payable decreased	_____	_____	_____
5. Income taxes payable increased	_____	_____	_____
6. Capital stock increased	_____	_____	_____

EXERCISES

Exercise 12-1 Cash Equivalents

LO2
EXAMPLE 12-2

Metropolis Industries invested its excess cash in the following instruments during December 2012:

Certificate of deposit, due January 31, 2013	$ 35,000
Certificate of deposit, due June 30, 2013	95,000
Investment in City of Elgin bonds, due May 1, 2014	15,000
Investment in Quantum Data stock	66,000
Money market fund	105,000
90-day Treasury bills	75,000
Treasury note, due December 1, 2013	200,000

Required

Determine the amount of cash equivalents that should be combined with cash on the company's balance sheet at December 31, 2012, and for purposes of preparing a statement of cash flows for the year ended December 31, 2012.

LO3

EXAMPLE 12-1, 12-5

Exercise 12-2 Classification of Activities for Carnival Corporation

Carnival Corporation & plc is one of the largest cruise companies in the world with such well-known brands as Carnival Cruise Lines, Holland America Line, and Princess Cruises. Classify each of the following items found on the company's 2010 statement of cash flows according to whether it would appear in the Operating Activities section (O), in the Investing Activities section (I), or in the Financing Activities section (F). The company uses the indirect method in the Operating Activities section of its statement.

_____ 1. Dividends paid
_____ 2. Proceeds from issuance of other long-term debt
_____ 3. Depreciation and amortization
_____ 4. Additions to property and equipment
_____ 5. Purchases of treasury stock
_____ 6. Net income

LO3

EXAMPLE 12-1, 12-3

Exercise 12-3 Cash Flows from Investing and Financing Activities and Noncash Activities

For each of the following transactions, indicate whether they would be reported in the Investing Activities section of the statement of cash flows (I) or the Financing Activities section (F). Put an S in the blank if the transaction does not affect cash but is reported in a supplemental schedule of noncash activities.

_____ 1. Issued capital stock for cash.
_____ 2. Issued a five-year note payable in exchange for a patent.
_____ 3. Acquired land for cash.
_____ 4. Issued bonds payable for cash.
_____ 5. Issued capital stock in exchange for a trademark.
_____ 6. Acquired equipment for cash.

LO3

Exercise 12-4 Retirement of Bonds Payable on the Statement of Cash Flows—Indirect Method

Redstone Inc. has the following debt outstanding on December 31, 2012:

10% bonds payable, due 12/31/16	$500,000	
Discount on bonds payable	(40,000)	$460,000

On this date, Redstone retired the entire bond issue by paying cash of $510,000.

Required

1. Identify and analyze the transaction to record the bond retirement.
2. Describe how the bond retirement would be reported on the statement of cash flows assuming that Redstone uses the indirect method.

LO3

EXAMPLE 12-1, 12-3, 12-4

Exercise 12-5 Classification of Activities

For each of the following transactions reported on a statement of cash flows, indicate whether it would appear in the Operating Activities section (O), in the Investing Activities section (I), or in the Financing Activities section (F). Put an S in the blank if the transaction does not affect cash but is reported in a supplemental schedule of noncash activities. Assume that the company uses the direct method in the Operating Activities section.

_____ 1. A company purchases its own common stock in the open market and immediately retires it.
_____ 2. A company issues preferred stock in exchange for land.
_____ 3. A six-month bank loan is obtained.
_____ 4. Twenty-year bonds are issued.
_____ 5. A customer's open account is collected.
_____ 6. Income taxes are paid.
_____ 7. Cash sales for the day are recorded.

_____   8. Cash dividends are declared and paid.
_____   9. A creditor is given shares of common stock in the company in return for cancel-
                 lation of a long-term loan.
_____   10. A new piece of machinery is acquired for cash.
_____   11. Stock of another company is acquired as an investment.
_____   12. Interest is paid on a bank loan.
_____   13. Factory workers are paid.

Exercise 12-6 Working Backward: Dividends on the Statement of Cash Flows   LO5

Stanton Corp. began operations on January 1, 2012. The statement of cash flows for the first year reported dividends paid of $160,000. The balance sheet at the end of the first year reported $40,000 in dividends payable and $580,000 in ending retained earnings. Determine Stanton's net income for its first year of operations.

Exercise 12-7 Dividends on the Statement of Cash Flows   LO5

The following selected account balances are available from the records of Lewistown Company:

	December 31	
	2012	2011
Dividends payable	$ 30,000	$ 20,000
Retained earnings	375,000	250,000

Other information available for 2012 is as follows:

a. Lewistown reported net income of $285,000 for the year.
b. It declared and distributed a stock dividend of $50,000 during the year.
c. It declared cash dividends at the end of each quarter and paid them within the next 30 days of the following quarter.

Required

1. Determine the amount of cash dividends *paid* during the year for presentation in the Financing Activities section of the statement of cash flows.
2. Should the stock dividend described in part (b) appear on a statement of cash flows? Explain your answer.

Exercise 12-8 Determination of Missing Amounts—Cash Flow from Operating Activities   LO5

The computation of cash provided by operating activities requires analysis of the noncash current asset and current liability accounts. Determine the missing amounts for each of the following independent cases:

Case 1

Accounts receivable, beginning of year	$150,000
Accounts receivable, end of year	100,000
Credit sales for the year	175,000
Cash sales for the year	60,000
Write-offs of uncollectible accounts	35,000
Total cash collections for the year (from cash sales and collections on account)	?

Case 2

Inventory, beginning of year	$ 80,000
Inventory, end of year	55,000
Accounts payable, beginning of year	25,000
Accounts payable, end of year	15,000
Cost of goods sold	175,000
Cash payments for inventory (assume all purchases of inventory are on account)	?

Case 3

Prepaid insurance, beginning of year	$ 17,000
Prepaid insurance, end of year	20,000
Insurance expense	15,000
Cash paid for new insurance policies	?

Case 4

Income taxes payable, beginning of year	$ 95,000
Income taxes payable, end of year	115,000
Income tax expense	300,000
Cash payments for taxes	?

LO5   Exercise 12-9   Operating Activities Section—Direct Method

The following account balances for the noncash current assets and current liabilities of Labrador Company are available:

	December 31	
	2012	2011
Accounts receivable	$ 4,000	$ 6,000
Inventory	32,000	25,000
Office supplies	7,000	10,000
Accounts payable	7,500	4,500
Salaries and wages payable	1,500	2,500
Interest payable	500	1,000
Income taxes payable	4,500	3,000

In addition, the income statement for 2012 is as follows:

	2012
Sales revenue	$100,000
Cost of goods sold	75,000
Gross profit	$ 25,000
General and administrative expense	$ 8,000
Depreciation expense	3,000
Total operating expenses	$ 11,000
Income before interest and taxes	$ 14,000
Interest expense	3,000
Income before tax	$ 11,000
Income tax expense	5,000
Net income	$ 6,000

Required

1. Prepare the Operating Activities section of the statement of cash flows using the direct method.
2. What does the use of the direct method reveal about a company that the indirect method does not?

LO5   Exercise 12-10   Working Backward: Cash Payments—Direct Method

Homeier Heating reported the following amounts on its comparative balance sheets:

	12/31/12	12/31/11
Current Assets:		
Inventories	$66,000	$55,000
Current Liabilities:		
Accounts payable	33,000	24,000

The company uses the direct method on its statement of cash flows and reported that it spent $44,000 during 2012 to acquire inventory. Determine cost of goods sold expense for 2012.

Exercise 12-11 Cash Payments—Direct Method   LO5

Lester Enterprises' comparative balance sheets included inventory of $90,200 at December 31, 2011, and $70,600 at December 31, 2012. Lester's comparative balance sheets also included accounts payable of $57,700 at December 31, 2011, and $39,200 at December 31, 2012. Lester's accounts payable balances are composed solely of amounts due to suppliers for purchases of inventory on account. Cost of goods sold, as reported by Lester on its 2012 income statement, amounted to $770,900. What is the amount of cash payments for inventory that Lester will report in the Operating Activities section of its 2012 statement of cash flows assuming that the direct method is used?

Exercise 12-12 Cash Payments—Direct Method   LO5

Wolf's comparative balance sheets included inventory of $45,000 at December 31, 2011, and $63,000 at December 31, 2012. The comparative balance sheets also included accounts payable of $33,000 at December 31, 2011, and $39,000 at December 31, 2012. Wolf's accounts payable balances are composed solely of amounts due to suppliers for purchases of inventory on account. Cost of goods sold, as reported on the 2012 income statement, amounted to $120,000. What is the amount of cash payments for inventory that Wolf will report in the Operating Activities section of its 2012 statement of cash flows assuming that the direct method is used?

Exercise 12-13 Working Backward: Cash Collections—Direct Method   LO5

Butler Corp. reported the following in the Current Assets section of its comparative balance sheets:

	12/31/12	12/31/11
Current Assets:		
Accounts receivable	$12,500	$15,300

The company uses the direct method on its statement of cash flows and reported that it collected $45,200 during 2012 from its customers. Determine sales revenue for 2012.

Exercise 12-14 Cash Collections—Direct Method   LO5

Stanley Company's comparative balance sheets included accounts receivable of $80,800 at December 31, 2011, and $101,100 at December 31, 2012. Sales reported by Stanley on its 2012 income statement amounted to $1,450,000. What is the amount of cash collections that Stanley will report in the Operating Activities section of its 2012 statement of cash flows assuming that the direct method is used?

Exercise 12-15 Cash Collections—Direct Method   LO5

Spencer Corp. reported accounts receivable of $28,000 on its December 31, 2011, balance sheet. On December 31, 2012, accounts receivable had decreased to $22,000. Sales for the year amounted to $55,000. What is the amount of cash collections that Spencer will report in the Operating Activities section of its 2012 statement of cash flows assuming that the direct method is used?

Exercise 12-16 Operating Activities Section—Indirect Method   LO6

The following account balances for the noncash current assets and current liabilities of Suffolk Company are available:

	December 31	
	2012	2011
Accounts receivable	$43,000	$35,000
Inventory	30,000	40,000
Prepaid rent	17,000	15,000
Totals	$90,000	$90,000

	December 31	
	2012	**2011**
Accounts payable	$26,000	$19,000
Income taxes payable	6,000	10,000
Interest payable	15,000	12,000
Totals	$47,000	$41,000

Net income for 2012 is $40,000. Depreciation expense is $20,000. Assume that all sales and all purchases are on account.

Required

1. Prepare the Operating Activities section of the statement of cash flows using the indirect method.
2. Provide a brief explanation as to why cash flow from operating activities is more or less than the net income of the period.

LO6 **Exercise 12-17 Cash Payments for Income Taxes—Indirect Method**

Timber Corp. began the year with a balance in its Income Taxes Payable account of $10,000. The year-end balance in the account was $15,000. The company uses the indirect method in the Operating Activities section of the statement of cash flows. Therefore, it presents the amount of income taxes paid at the bottom of the statement as a supplemental disclosure. The amount of taxes paid during the year was $12,000.

What amount of income tax expense will appear on Timber's income statement?

LO6 **Exercise 12-18 Adjustments to Net Income with the Indirect Method**

EXAMPLE 12-1, 12-5

Assume that a company uses the indirect method to prepare the Operating Activities section of the statement of cash flows. For each of the following items, indicate whether it would be added to net income (A), deducted from net income (D), or not reported in this section of the statement under the indirect method (NR).

_____ 1. Depreciation expense
_____ 2. Gain on sale of used delivery truck
_____ 3. Increase in accounts receivable
_____ 4. Increase in accounts payable
_____ 5. Purchase of new delivery truck
_____ 6. Loss on retirement of bonds
_____ 7. Increase in prepaid rent
_____ 8. Decrease in inventory
_____ 9. Issuance of note payable due in three years
_____ 10. Amortization of patents

LO7 **Exercise 12-19 Cash Flow Adequacy**

On its most recent statement of cash flows, a company reported net cash provided by operating activities of $12,000,000. Its capital expenditures for the same year were $2,000,000. A note to the financial statements indicated that the total amount of debt that would mature over the next five years was $20,000,000.

Required

1. Compute the company's cash flow adequacy ratio.
2. If you were a banker considering loaning money to this company, why would you be interested in knowing its cash flow adequacy ratio? Would you feel comfortable making a loan based on the ratio you computed in part (1)? Explain your answer.

MULTI-CONCEPT EXERCISES

Exercise 12-20 Classification of Activities

LO2 • 3
EXAMPLE 12-1, 12-2

Use the following legend to indicate how each transaction would be reported on the statement of cash flows. (Assume that the stocks and bonds of other companies are classified as long-term investments.)

II = Inflow from investing activities
OI = Outflow from investing activities
IF = Inflow from financing activities
OF = Outflow from financing activities
CE = Classified as a cash equivalent and included with cash for purposes of preparing the statement of cash flows

_____	1.	Purchased a six-month certificate of deposit
_____	2.	Purchased a 60-day Treasury bill
_____	3.	Issued 1,000 shares of common stock
_____	4.	Purchased 1,000 shares of stock in another company
_____	5.	Purchased 1,000 shares of its own stock to be held in the treasury
_____	6.	Invested $1,000 in a money market fund
_____	7.	Sold 500 shares of stock of another company
_____	8.	Purchased 20-year bonds of another company
_____	9.	Issued 30-year bonds
_____	10.	Repaid a six-month bank loan

Exercise 12-21 Working Backward: Financing Activities on the Statement of Cash Flows

LO3 • 6

The Operating Activities section of Washburn Company's 2012 statement of cash flows reported an adjustment for a gain on the retirement of bonds of $5,000. The Financing Activities section of the statement reported a cash outflow of $95,000 from the retirement of the bonds.

Required

1. Is the gain on the retirement of the bonds added or deducted in the Operating Activities section of the statement of cash flows?
2. What was the book value of the bonds retired?

Exercise 12-22 Classification of Activities

LO3 • 5
EXAMPLE 12-1, 12-3, 12-4

Use the following legend to indicate how each transaction would be reported on the statement of cash flows. (Assume that the company uses the direct method in the Operating Activities section.)

IO = Inflow from operating activities
OO = Outflow from operating activities
II = Inflow from investing activities
OI = Outflow from investing activities
IF = Inflow from financing activities
OF = Outflow from financing activities
NR = Not reported in the body of the statement of cash flows but included in a supplemental schedule

_____	1.	Collected $10,000 in cash from customers' open accounts for the period
_____	2.	Paid one of the company's inventory suppliers $500 in settlement of an open account
_____	3.	Purchased a new copier for $6,000; signed a 90-day note payable
_____	4.	Issued bonds at face value of $100,000
_____	5.	Made $23,200 in cash sales for the week
_____	6.	Purchased an empty lot adjacent to the factory for $50,000; the seller of the land agrees to accept a five-year promissory note as consideration

	7.	Renewed the property insurance policy for another six months; cash of $1,000 is paid for the renewal
	8.	Purchased a machine for $10,000
	9.	Paid cash dividends of $2,500
	10.	Reclassified as short-term a long-term note payable of $5,000 that is due within the next year
	11.	Purchased 500 shares of the company's own stock on the open market for $4,000
	12.	Sold 500 shares of Nike stock for book value of $10,000 (they had been classified as long-term investments)

LO3 • 6   Exercise 12-23 Long-Term Assets on the Statement of Cash Flows— Indirect Method

The following account balances are taken from the records of Martin Corp. for the past two years.

	December 31	
	2012	**2011**
Plant and equipment	$750,000	$500,000
Accumulated depreciation	160,000	200,000
Patents	92,000	80,000
Retained earnings	825,000	675,000

Other information available for 2012 is as follows:

a. Net income for the year was $200,000.
b. Depreciation expense on plant and equipment was $50,000.
c. Plant and equipment with an original cost of $150,000 were sold for $64,000. (You will need to determine the book value of the assets sold.)
d. Amortization expense on patents was $8,000.
e. Both new plant and equipment and patents were purchased for cash during the year.

Required

Indicate, with amounts, how all items related to these long-term assets would be reported in the 2012 statement of cash flows, including any adjustments in the Operating Activities section of the statement. Assume that Martin uses the indirect method.

LO3 • 6   Exercise 12-24 Working Backward: Investing Activities on the Statement of Cash Flows

The Operating Activities section of Miller Corp.'s 2012 statement of cash flows reported an adjustment for depreciation expense of $25,000, as well as another for a loss on the sale of equipment of $5,000 (the equipment was sold on the last day of the year). The equipment was Miller's only long-term asset, and it had a book value of $80,000 at the beginning of 2012.

Required

1. Is the depreciation expense added or deducted in the Operating Activities section of the statement of cash flows? Is the loss added or deducted in this section?
2. What other section of the statement of cash flows will be affected by the sale of the equipment? What amount will appear in this section?

LO1 • 5   Exercise 12-25 Income Statement, Statement of Cash Flows (Direct Method), and Balance Sheet

The following events occurred at Handsome Hounds Grooming Company during its first year of business:

a. To establish the company, the two owners contributed a total of $50,000 in exchange for common stock.

b. Grooming service revenue for the first year amounted to $150,000, of which $40,000 was on account.
c. Customers owe $10,000 at the end of the year from the services provided on account.
d. At the beginning of the year, a storage building was rented. The company was required to sign a three-year lease for $12,000 per year and make a $2,000 refundable security deposit. The first year's lease payment and the security deposit were paid at the beginning of the year.
e. At the beginning of the year, the company purchased a patent at a cost of $100,000 for a revolutionary system to be used for dog grooming. The patent is expected to be useful for ten years. The company paid 20% down in cash and signed a four-year note at the bank for the remainder.
f. Operating expenses, including amortization of the patent and rent on the storage building, totaled $80,000 for the first year. No expenses were accrued or unpaid at the end of the year.
g. The company declared and paid a $20,000 cash dividend at the end of the first year.

Required

1. Prepare an income statement for the first year.
2. Prepare a statement of cash flows for the first year using the direct method in the Operating Activities section.
3. Did the company generate more or less cash flow from operations than it earned in net income? Explain why there is a difference.
4. Prepare a balance sheet as of the end of the first year.

PROBLEMS

Problem 12-1 Year-End Balance Sheet and Statement of Cash Flows— Indirect Method   LO6

The balance sheet of Terrier Company at the end of 2011 is presented here, along with certain other information for 2012:

	December 31, 2011
Cash	$ 140,000
Accounts receivable	155,000
Total current assets	$ 295,000
Land	$ 300,000
Plant and equipment	500,000
Accumulated depreciation	(150,000)
Investments	100,000
Total long-term assets	$ 750,000
Total assets	$1,045,000
Current liabilities	$ 205,000
Bonds payable	$ 300,000
Common stock	$ 400,000
Retained earnings	140,000
Total stockholders' equity	$ 540,000
Total liabilities and stockholders' equity	$1,045,000

Other information is as follows:

a. Net income for 2012 was $70,000.
b. Included in operating expenses was $20,000 in depreciation.
c. Cash dividends of $25,000 were declared and paid.
d. An additional $150,000 of bonds was issued for cash.
e. Common stock of $50,000 was purchased for cash and retired.
f. Cash purchases of plant and equipment during the year were $200,000.
g. An additional $100,000 of bonds was issued in exchange for land.

h. During the year, sales exceeded cash collections on account by $10,000. All sales are on account,

i.   The amount of current liabilities remained unchanged during the year.

Required

1.   Prepare a statement of cash flows for 2012 using the indirect method in the Operating Activities section. Include a supplemental schedule for noncash activities.
2.   Prepare a balance sheet at December 31, 2012.
3.   Provide a possible explanation as to why Terrier decided to issue additional bonds for cash during 2012.

LO8   Problem 12-2 Statement of Cash Flows Using a Work Sheet—Indirect Method (Appendix)

Refer to all of the facts in Problem 12-1.

Required

1.   Prepare a balance sheet at December 31, 2012.
2.   Using the format in the chapter's appendix, prepare a statement of cash flows work sheet.
3.   Prepare a statement of cash flows for 2012 using the indirect method in the Operating Activities section.
4.   Provide a possible explanation as to why Terrier decided to issue additional bonds for cash during 2012.

LO5   Problem 12-3 Statement of Cash Flows—Direct Method

The income statement for Astro Inc. for 2012 is as follows:

	For the Year Ended December 31, 2012
Sales revenue	$ 500,000
Cost of goods sold	400,000
Gross profit	$ 100,000
Operating expenses	180,000
Loss before interest and taxes	$ (80,000)
Interest expense	20,000
Net loss	$(100,000)

Presented here are comparative balance sheets:

	December 31 2012	December 31 2011
Cash	$ 95,000	$ 80,000
Accounts Receivable	50,000	75,000
Inventory	100,000	150,000
Prepayments	55,000	45,000
Total current assets	$ 300,000	$ 350,000
Land	$ 475,000	$ 400,000
Plant and equipment	870,000	800,000
Accumulated depreciation	(370,000)	(300,000)
Total long-term assets	$ 975,000	$ 900,000
Total assets	$1,275,000	$1,250,000
Accounts payable	$ 125,000	$ 100,000
Other accrued liabilities	35,000	45,000
Interest payable	15,000	10,000
Total current liabilities	$ 175,000	$ 155,000
Long-term bank loan payable	$ 340,000	$ 250,000

(Continued)

	December 31	
	2012	**2011**
Common stock	$ 450,000	$ 400,000
Retained earnings	310,000	445,000
Total stockholders' equity	$ 760,000	$ 845,000
Total liabilities and stockholders' equity	$1,275,000	$1,250,000

Other information is as follows:

a. Dividends of $35,000 were declared and paid during the year.
b. Operating expenses include $70,000 of depreciation.
c. Land and plant and equipment were acquired for cash, and additional stock was issued for cash. Cash also was received from additional bank loans.

The president has asked you some questions about the year's results. He is disturbed with the $100,000 net loss for the year. He notes, however, that the cash position at the end of the year is improved. He is confused about what appear to be conflicting signals: "How could we have possibly added to our bank accounts during such a terrible year of operations?"

Required

1. Prepare a statement of cash flows for 2012 using the direct method in the Operating Activities section.
2. On the basis of your statement in part (1), draft a brief memo to the president to explain why cash increased during such an unprofitable year. Include in your memo your recommendations for improving the company's bottom line.

Problem 12-4 Statement of Cash Flows—Indirect Method   LO6

Refer to all of the facts in Problem 12-3.

Required

1. Prepare a statement of cash flows for 2012 using the indirect method in the Operating Activities section.
2. On the basis of your statement in part (1), draft a brief memo to the president to explain why cash increased during such an unprofitable year. Include in your memo your recommendations for improving the company's bottom line.

Problem 12-5 Statement of Cash Flows Using a Work Sheet—Indirect   LO8
Method (Appendix)

Refer to all of the facts in Problem 12-3.

Required

1. Using the format in the chapter's appendix, prepare a statement of cash flows work sheet.
2. Prepare a statement of cash flows for 2012 using the indirect method in the Operating Activities section.
3. On the basis of your statement in part (2), draft a brief memo to the president to explain why cash increased during such an unprofitable year. Include in your memo your recommendations for improving the company's bottom line.

Problem 12-6 Statement of Cash Flows—Direct Method   LO5

Peoria Corp. just completed another successful year, as indicated by the following income statement:

	For the Year Ended December 31, 2012
Sales revenue	$1,250,000
Cost of goods sold	700,000
Gross profit	$ 550,000
Operating expenses	150,000

(Continued)

	For the Year Ended December 31, 2012
Income before interest and taxes	$ 400,000
Interest expense	25,000
Income before taxes	$ 375,000
Income tax expense	150,000
Net income	$ 225,000

Presented here are comparative balance sheets:

	December 31	
	2012	2011
Cash	$ 52,000	$ 90,000
Accounts receivable	180,000	130,000
Inventory	230,000	200,000
Prepayments	15,000	25,000
Total current assets	$ 477,000	$ 445,000
Land	$ 750,000	$ 600,000
Plant and equipment	700,000	500,000
Accumulated depreciation	(250,000)	(200,000)
Total long-term assets	$1,200,000	$ 900,000
Total assets	$1,677,000	$1,345,000
Accounts payable	$ 130,000	$ 148,000
Other accrued liabilities	68,000	63,000
Income taxes payable	90,000	110,000
Total current liabilities	$ 288,000	$ 321,000
Long-term bank loan payable	$ 350,000	$ 300,000
Common stock	$ 550,000	$ 400,000
Retained earnings	489,000	324,000
Total stockholders' equity	$1,039,000	$ 724,000
Total liabilities and stockholders' equity	$1,677,000	$1,345,000

Other information is as follows:

a. Dividends of $60,000 were declared and paid during the year.
b. Operating expenses include $50,000 of depreciation.
c. Land and plant and equipment were acquired for cash, and additional stock was issued for cash. Cash also was received from additional bank loans.

The president has asked you some questions about the year's results. She is very impressed with the profit margin of 18% (net income divided by sales revenue). She is bothered, however, by the decline in the company's cash balance during the year. One of the conditions of the existing bank loan is that the company maintain a minimum cash balance of $50,000.

Required

1. Prepare a statement of cash flows for 2012 using the direct method in the Operating Activities section.
2. On the basis of your statement in part (1), draft a brief memo to the president to explain why cash decreased during such a profitable year. Include in your explanation any recommendations for improving the company's cash flow in future years.

LO6   Problem 12-7 Statement of Cash Flows—Indirect Method

Refer to all of the facts in Problem 12-6.

Required

1. Prepare a statement of cash flows for 2012 using the indirect method in the Operating Activities section.
2. On the basis of your statement in part (1), draft a brief memo to the president to explain why cash decreased during such a profitable year. Include in your explanation any recommendations for improving the company's cash flow in future years.

Problem 12-8 Statement of Cash Flows Using a Work Sheet—Indirect Method (Appendix)   LO8

Refer to all of the facts in Problem 12-6.

Required

1. Using the format in the chapter's appendix, prepare a statement of cash flows worksheet.
2. Prepare a statement of cash flows for 2012 using the indirect method in the Operating Activities section.
3. On the basis of your statement in part (2), draft a brief memo to the president to explain why cash decreased during such a profitable year. Include in your explanation any recommendations for improving the company's cash flow in future years.

Problem 12-9 Statement of Cash Flows—Indirect Method   LO6

The following balances are available for Chrisman Company:

	December 31	
	2012	**2011**
Cash	$ 8,000	$ 10,000
Accounts receivable	20,000	15,000
Inventory	15,000	25,000
Prepaid rent	9,000	6,000
Land	75,000	75,000
Plant and equipment	400,000	300,000
Accumulated depreciation	(65,000)	(30,000)
Totals	$462,000	$401,000
Accounts payable	$ 12,000	$ 10,000
Income taxes payable	3,000	5,000
Short-term notes payable	35,000	25,000
Bonds payable	75,000	100,000
Common stock	200,000	150,000
Retained earnings	137,000	111,000
Totals	$462,000	$401,000

Bonds were retired during 2012 at face value, plant and equipment were acquired for cash, and common stock was issued for cash. Depreciation expense for the year was $35,000. Net income was reported at $26,000.

Required

1. Prepare a statement of cash flows for 2012 using the indirect method in the Operating Activities section.
2. Did Chrisman generate sufficient cash from operations to pay for its investing activities? How did it generate cash other than from operations? Explain your answers.

Problem 12-10 Statement of Cash Flows Using a Work Sheet—Indirect Method (Appendix)   LO8

Refer to all of the facts in Problem 12-9.

Required

1. Using the format in the chapter's appendix, prepare a statement of cash flows worksheet.
2. Prepare a statement of cash flows for 2012 using the indirect method in the Operating Activities section.
3. Did Chrisman generate sufficient cash from operations to pay for its investing activities? How did it generate cash other than from operations? Explain your answers.

MULTI-CONCEPT PROBLEMS

L04 • 5 **Problem 12-11 Statement of Cash Flows—Direct Method**

Glendive Corp. is in the process of preparing its statement of cash flows for the year ended June 30, 2012. An income statement for the year and comparative balance sheets are as follows:

	For the Year Ended June 30, 2012
Sales revenue	$550,000
Cost of goods sold	350,000
Gross profit	$200,000
General and administrative expenses	$ 55,000
Depreciation expense	75,000
Loss on sale of plant assets	5,000
Total expenses and losses	$135,000
Income before interest and taxes	$ 65,000
Interest expense	15,000
Income before taxes	$ 50,000
Income tax expense	17,000
Net income	$ 33,000

	June 30	
	2012	**2011**
Cash	$ 31,000	$ 40,000
Accounts receivable	90,000	75,000
Inventory	80,000	95,000
Prepaid rent	12,000	16,000
Total current assets	$ 213,000	$ 226,000
Land	$ 250,000	$ 170,000
Plant and equipment	750,000	600,000
Accumulated depreciation	(310,000)	(250,000)
Total long-term assets	$ 690,000	$ 520,000
Total assets	$ 903,000	$ 746,000
Accounts payable	$ 155,000	$ 148,000
Other accrued liabilities	32,000	26,000
Income taxes payable	8,000	10,000
Total current liabilities	$ 195,000	$ 184,000
Long-term bank loan payable	$ 100,000	$ 130,000
Common stock	$ 350,000	$ 200,000
Retained earnings	258,000	232,000
Total stockholders' equity	$ 608,000	$ 432,000
Total liabilities and stockholders' equity	$ 903,000	$ 746,000

Dividends of $7,000 were declared and paid during the year. New plant assets were purchased during the year for $195,000 in cash. Also, land was purchased for cash. Plant assets were sold during the year for $25,000 in cash. The original cost of the assets sold was $45,000, and their book value was $30,000. Additional stock was issued for cash, and a portion of the bank loan was repaid.

Required

1. Prepare a statement of cash flows for 2012 using the direct method in the Operating Activities section.

2. Evaluate the following statement: Whether a company uses the direct or indirect method to report cash flows from operations is irrelevant because the amount of cash flow from operating activities is the same regardless of which method is used.

Problem 12-12 Statement of Cash Flows—Indirect Method   LO4 • 6

Refer to all of the facts in Problem 12-11.

Required

1. Prepare a statement of cash flows for 2012 using the indirect method in the Operating Activities section.
2. Evaluate the following statement: Whether a company uses the direct or indirect method to report cash flows from operations is irrelevant because the amount of cash flow from operating activities is the same regardless of which method is used.

Problem 12-13 Statement of Cash Flows—Direct Method   LO2 • 5

Lang Company has not yet prepared a formal statement of cash flows for 2012. Following are comparative balance sheets as of December 31, 2012 and 2011, and a statement of income and retained earnings for the year ended December 31, 2012:

Lang Company
Balance Sheet
December 31
(thousands omitted)

Assets	2012	2011
Current assets:		
Cash	$ 60	$ 100
U.S. Treasury bills (six-month)	0	50
Accounts receivable	610	500
Inventory	720	600
Total current assets	$1,390	$1,250
Long-term assets:		
Land	$ 80	$ 70
Buildings and equipment	710	600
Accumulated depreciation	(180)	(120)
Patents (less amortization)	105	130
Total long-term assets	$ 715	$ 680
Total assets	$2,105	$1,930
Liabilities and Owners' Equity		
Current liabilities:		
Accounts payable	$ 360	$ 300
Taxes payable	25	20
Notes payable	400	400
Total current liabilities	$ 785	$ 720
Term notes payable—due 2016	200	200
Total liabilities	$ 985	$ 920
Owners' equity:		
Common stock outstanding	$ 830	$ 700
Retained earnings	290	310
Total owners' equity	$1,120	$1,010
Total liabilities and owners' equity	$2,105	$1,930

(Continued)

Lang Company
Statement of Income and Retained Earnings
For the Year Ended December 31, 2012
(thousands omitted)

Sales		$2,408
Less expenses and interest:		
Cost of goods sold	$1,100	
Salaries and benefits	850	
Heat, light, and power	75	
Depreciation	60	
Property taxes	18	
Patent amortization	25	
Miscellaneous expense	10	
Interest	55	2,193
Net income before income taxes		$ 215
Income taxes		105
Net income		$ 110
Retained earnings—January 1, 2012		310
		$ 420
Stock dividend distributed		130
Retained earnings—December 31, 2012		$ 290

Required

1. For purposes of a statement of cash flows, are the U.S. Treasury bills cash equivalents? If not, how should they be classified? Explain your answers.
2. Prepare a statement of cash flows for 2012 using the direct method in the Operating Activities section.   (CMA adapted)

ALTERNATE PROBLEMS

LO5 **Problem 12-1A Statement of Cash Flows—Direct Method**

The income statement for Pluto Inc. for 2012 is as follows:

	For the Year Ended December 31, 2012
Sales revenue	$350,000
Cost of goods sold	150,000
Gross profit	$200,000
Operating expenses	250,000
Loss before interest and taxes	$ (50,000)
Interest expense	10,000
Net loss	$ (60,000)

Presented here are comparative balance sheets:

	December 31	
	2012	2011
Cash	$ 25,000	$ 10,000
Accounts receivable	30,000	80,000
Inventory	100,000	100,000
Prepayments	36,000	35,000
Total current assets	$191,000	$225,000
Land	$300,000	$200,000
Plant and equipment	500,000	250,000
Accumulated depreciation	(90,000)	(50,000)
Total long-term assets	$710,000	$400,000
Total assets	$901,000	$625,000

	December 31	
	2012	**2011**
Accounts payable	$ 50,000	$ 10,000
Other accrued liabilities	40,000	20,000
Interest payable	22,000	12,000
Total current liabilities	$112,000	$ 42,000
Long-term bank loan payable	$450,000	$100,000
Common stock	$300,000	$300,000
Retained earnings	39,000	183,000
Total stockholders' equity	$339,000	$483,000
Total liabilities and stockholders' equity	$901,000	$625,000

Other information is as follows:

a. Dividends of $84,000 were declared and paid during the year.
b. Operating expenses include $40,000 of depreciation.
c. Land and plant and equipment were acquired for cash. Cash was received from additional bank loans.

The president has asked you some questions about the year's results. He is disturbed with the net loss of $60,000 for the year. He notes, however, that the cash position at the end of the year is improved. He is confused about what appear to be conflicting signals: "How could we have possibly added to our bank accounts during such a terrible year of operations?"

Required

1. Prepare a statement of cash flows for 2012 using the direct method in the Operating Activities section.
2. On the basis of your statement in part (1), draft a brief memo to the president to explain why cash increased during such an unprofitable year. Include in your memo your recommendations for improving the company's bottom line.

Problem 12-2A Statement of Cash Flows—Indirect Method   LO6

Refer to all of the facts in Problem 12-1A.

Required

1. Prepare a statement of cash flows for 2012 using the indirect method in the Operating Activities section.
2. On the basis of your statement in part (1), draft a brief memo to the president to explain why cash increased during such an unprofitable year. Include in your memo your recommendations for improving the company's bottom line.

Problem 12-3A Statement of Cash Flows Using a Work Sheet—Indirect   LO8
Method (Appendix)

Refer to all of the facts in Problem 12-1A.

Required

1. Using the format in the chapter's appendix, prepare a statement of cash flows work sheet.
2. Prepare a statement of cash flows for 2012 using the indirect method in the Operating Activities section.
3. On the basis of your statement in part (2), draft a brief memo to the president to explain why cash increased during such an unprofitable year. Include in your memo your recommendations for improving the company's bottom line.

LO6 Problem 12-4A Statement of Cash Flows—Indirect Method

The following balances are available for Madison Company:

	December 31	
	2012	2011
Cash	$ 12,000	$ 10,000
Accounts receivable	10,000	12,000
Inventory	8,000	7,000
Prepaid rent	1,200	1,000
Land	75,000	75,000
Plant and equipment	200,000	150,000
Accumulated depreciation	(75,000)	(25,000)
Totals	$231,200	$230,000
Accounts payable	$ 15,000	$ 15,000
Income taxes payable	2,500	2,000
Short-term notes payable	20,000	22,500
Bonds payable	75,000	50,000
Common stock	100,000	100,000
Retained earnings	18,700	40,500
Totals	$231,200	$230,000

Bonds were issued during 2012 at face value, and plant and equipment were acquired for cash. Depreciation expense for the year was $50,000. A net loss of $21,800 was reported.

Required

1. Prepare a statement of cash flows for 2012 using the indirect method in the Operating Activities section.
2. Briefly explain how Madison was able to increase its cash balance during a year in which it incurred a net loss.

LO8 Problem 12-5A Statement of Cash Flows Using a Work Sheet—Indirect Method (Appendix)

Refer to all of the facts in Problem 12-4A.

Required

1. Using the format in the chapter's appendix, prepare a statement of cash flows work sheet.
2. Prepare a statement of cash flows for 2012 using the indirect method in the Operating Activities section.
3. Briefly explain how Madison was able to increase its cash balance during a year in which it incurred a net loss.

LO5 Problem 12-6A Statement of Cash Flows—Direct Method

Wabash Corp. just completed another successful year, as indicated by the following income statement:

	For the Year Ended December 31, 2012
Sales revenue	$2,460,000
Cost of goods sold	1,400,000
Gross profit	$1,060,000
Operating expenses	460,000
Income before interest and taxes	$ 600,000
Interest expense	100,000
Income before taxes	$ 500,000
Income tax expense	150,000
Net income	$ 350,000

Presented here are comparative balance sheets:

| | December 31 | |
	2012	2011
Cash	$ 140,000	$ 210,000
Accounts receivable	60,000	145,000
Inventory	200,000	180,000
Prepayments	15,000	25,000
Total current assets	$ 415,000	$ 560,000
Land	$ 600,000	$ 700,000
Plant and equipment	850,000	600,000
Accumulated depreciation	(225,000)	(200,000)
Total long-term assets	$1,225,000	$1,100,000
Total assets	$1,640,000	$1,660,000
Accounts payable	$ 140,000	$ 120,000
Other accrued liabilities	50,000	55,000
Income taxes payable	80,000	115,000
Total current liabilities	$ 270,000	$ 290,000
Long-term bank loan payable	$ 200,000	$ 250,000
Common stock	$ 450,000	$ 400,000
Retained earnings	720,000	720,000
Total stockholders' equity	$1,170,000	$1,120,000
Total liabilities and stockholders' equity	$1,640,000	$1,660,000

Other information is as follows:

a. Dividends of $350,000 were declared and paid during the year.
b. Operating expenses include $25,000 of depreciation.
c. Land was sold for its book value, and new plant and equipment were acquired for cash.
d. Part of the bank loan was repaid, and additional common stock was issued for cash.

The president has asked you some questions about the year's results. She is very impressed with the profit margin of 14% (net income divided by sales revenue). She is bothered, however, by the decline in the company's cash balance during the year. One of the conditions of the existing bank loan is that the company maintain a minimum cash balance of $100,000.

Required

1. Prepare a statement of cash flows for 2012 using the direct method in the Operating Activities section.
2. On the basis of your statement in part (1), draft a brief memo to the president to explain why cash decreased during such a profitable year. Include in your explanation any recommendations for improving the company's cash flow in future years.

Problem 12-7A Statement of Cash Flows—Indirect Method   LO6

Refer to all of the facts in Problem 12-6A.

Required

1. Prepare a statement of cash flows for 2012 using the indirect method in the Operating Activities section.
2. On the basis of your statement in part (1), draft a brief memo to the president to explain why cash decreased during such a profitable year. Include in your explanation any recommendations for improving the company's cash flow in future years.

Problem 12-8A Statement of Cash Flows Using a Work Sheet—Indirect   LO8
Method (Appendix)

Refer to all of the facts in Problem 12-6A.

(Continued)

Required

1. Using the format in the chapter's appendix, prepare a statement of cash flows work sheet.
2. Prepare a statement of cash flows for 2012 using the indirect method in the Operating Activities section.
3. On the basis of your statement in part (2), draft a brief memo to the president to explain why cash decreased during such a profitable year. Include in your explanation any recommendations for improving the company's cash flow in future years.

LO6 **Problem 12-9A** **Year-End Balance Sheet and Statement of Cash Flows—Indirect Method**

The balance sheet of Poodle Company at the end of 2011 is presented here, along with certain other information for 2012:

	December 31, 2011
Cash	$ 155,000
Accounts receivable	140,000
Total current assets	$ 295,000
Land	$ 100,000
Plant and equipment	700,000
Accumulated depreciation	(175,000)
Investments	125,000
Total long-term assets	$ 750,000
Total assets	$1,045,000
Current liabilities	$ 325,000
Bonds payable	$ 100,000
Common stock	$ 500,000
Retained earnings	120,000
Total stockholders' equity	$ 620,000
Total liabilities and stockholders' equity	$1,045,000

Other information is as follows:

a. Net income for 2012 was $50,000.
b. Included in operating expenses was $25,000 in depreciation.
c. Cash dividends of $40,000 were declared and paid.
d. An additional $50,000 of common stock was issued for cash.
e. Bonds payable of $100,000 were purchased for cash and retired at no gain or loss.
f. Cash purchases of plant and equipment during the year were $60,000.
g. An additional $200,000 of land was acquired in exchange for a long-term note payable.
h. During the year, sales exceeded cash collections on account by $15,000. All sales are on account.
i. The amount of current liabilities decreased by $20,000 during the year.

Required

1. Prepare a statement of cash flows for 2012 using the indirect method in the Operating Activities section. Include a supplemental schedule for noncash activities.
2. Prepare a balance sheet at December 31, 2012.
3. What primary uses did Poodle make of the cash it generated from operating activities?

LO8 **Problem 12-10A** **Statement of Cash Flows Using a Work Sheet—Indirect Method (Appendix)**

Refer to all of the facts in Problem 12-9A.

Required

1. Prepare a balance sheet at December 31, 2012.
2. Using the format in the chapter's appendix, prepare a statement of cash flows work sheet.

3. Prepare a statement of cash flows for 2012 using the indirect method in the Operating Activities section.
4. Provide a possible explanation as to why Poodle decided to purchase and retire bonds during 2012.

ALTERNATE MULTI-CONCEPT PROBLEMS

Problem 12-11A Statement of Cash Flows—Direct Method

LO4 • 5

Bannack Corp. is in the process of preparing its statement of cash flows for the year ended June 30, 2012. An income statement for the year and comparative balance sheets are as follows:

	For the Year Ended June 30, 2012
Sales revenue	$400,000
Cost of goods sold	240,000
Gross profit	$160,000
General and administrative expenses	$ 40,000
Depreciation expense	80,000
Loss on sale of plant assets	10,000
Total expenses and losses	$130,000
Income before interest and taxes	$ 30,000
Interest expense	15,000
Income before taxes	$ 15,000
Income tax expense	5,000
Net income	$ 10,000

	June 30	
	2012	2011
Cash	$ 25,000	$ 40,000
Accounts receivable	80,000	69,000
Inventory	75,000	50,000
Prepaid rent	2,000	18,000
Total current assets	$ 182,000	$ 177,000
Land	$ 60,000	$ 150,000
Plant and equipment	575,000	500,000
Accumulated depreciation	(310,000)	(250,000)
Total long-term assets	$ 325,000	$ 400,000
Total assets	$ 507,000	$ 577,000
Accounts payable	$ 145,000	$ 140,000
Other accrued liabilities	50,000	45,000
Income taxes payable	5,000	15,000
Total current liabilities	$ 200,000	$ 200,000
Long-term bank loan payable	$ 75,000	$ 150,000
Common stock	$ 100,000	$ 100,000
Retained earnings	132,000	127,000
Total stockholders' equity	$ 232,000	$ 227,000
Total liabilities and stockholders' equity	$ 507,000	$ 577,000

Dividends of $5,000 were declared and paid during the year. New plant assets were purchased during the year for $125,000 in cash. Also, land was sold for cash at its book value. Plant assets were sold during the year for $20,000 in cash. The original cost of the assets sold was $50,000, and their book value was $30,000. A portion of the bank loan was repaid.

(Continued)

Required

1. Prepare a statement of cash flows for 2012 using the direct method in the Operating Activities section.
2. Evaluate the following statement: Whether a company uses the direct or indirect method to report cash flows from operations is irrelevant because the amount of cash flow from operating activities is the same regardless of which method is used.

LO4 • 6 **Problem 12-12A Statement of Cash Flows—Indirect Method**

Refer to all of the facts in Problem 12-11A.

Required

1. Prepare a statement of cash flows for 2012 using the indirect method in the Operating Activities section.
2. Evaluate the following statement: Whether a company uses the direct or indirect method to report cash flows from operations is irrelevant because the amount of cash flow from operating activities is the same regardless of which method is used.

LO2 • 5 **Problem 12-13A Statement of Cash Flows—Direct Method**

Shepard Company has not yet prepared a formal statement of cash flows for 2012. Comparative balance sheets as of December 31, 2012 and 2011, and a statement of income and retained earnings for the year ended December 31, 2012, appear below and on the following page.

Shepard Company
Balance Sheet
December 31
(thousands omitted)

Assets	2012	2011
Current assets:		
Cash	$ 50	$ 75
U.S. Treasury bills (six-month)	25	0
Accounts receivable	125	200
Inventory	525	500
Total current assets	$ 725	$ 775
Long-term assets:		
Land	$ 100	$ 80
Buildings and equipment	510	450
Accumulated depreciation	(190)	(150)
Patents (less amortization)	90	110
Total long-term assets	$ 510	$ 490
Total assets	$1,235	$1,265
Liabilities and Owners' Equity		
Current Liabilities:		
Accounts payable	$ 370	$ 330
Current assets:		
Taxes payable	10	20
Notes payable	300	400
Total current liabilities	$ 680	$ 750
Term notes payable—due 2016	200	200
Total liabilities	$ 880	$ 950
Owners' equity:		
Common stock outstanding	$ 220	$ 200
Retained earnings	135	115
Total owners' equity	$ 355	$ 315
Total liabilities and owners' equity	$1,235	$1,265

Shepard Company
Statement of Income and Retained Earnings
For the Year Ended December 31, 2012
(thousands omitted)

Sales		$1,416
Less expenses and interest:		
Cost of goods sold	$990	
Salaries and benefits	195	
Heat, light, and power	70	
Depreciation	40	
Property taxes	2	
Patent amortization	20	
Miscellaneous expense	2	
Interest	45	1,364
Net income before income taxes		$ 52
Income taxes		12
Net income		$ 40
Retained earnings—January 1, 2012		115
		$ 155
Stock dividend distributed		20
Retained earnings—December 31, 2012		$ 135

Required

1. For purposes of a statement of cash flows, are the U.S. Treasury bills cash equivalents? If not, how should they be classified? Explain your answers.
2. Prepare a statement of cash flows for 2012 using the direct method in the Operating Activities section. (CMA adapted)

DECISION CASES

Reading and Interpreting Financial Statements

Decision Case 12-1 Comparing Two Companies in the Same Industry: LO3 • 4
Kellogg's and General Mills

Refer to the statement of cash flows for both **Kellogg's** and **General Mills** for the most recent year and any other pertinent information reprinted at the back of this book.

Required

1. Which method, direct or indirect, does each company use in preparing the Operating Activities section of their statements of cash flows? Explain.
2. By what amount did net cash provided by operating activities increase or decrease from the prior year for each company? What is the largest adjustment to reconcile net income to net cash provided by operating activities for each company?
3. What amount did each company spend during the most recent year to acquire property and equipment? How does this amount compare with the amount that each company spent in the prior year?
4. What is the primary source of financing for each of the two companies? Did either or both companies buy back some of their own shares during the most recent year? If so, what might be some reasons for doing this?

Decision Case 12-2 Comparing Two Companies in the Same Industry: LO7
Kellogg's and General Mills Cash Flow Adequacy

Refer to the statement of cash flows for both **Kellogg's** and **General Mills** for the most recent year and any other pertinent information reprinted at the back of this book.

(Continued)

Required

1. Compute each company's cash flow adequacy ratio for the most recent year.
2. What do the ratios computed in part (1) tell you about each company's cash flow adequacy? Which company's ratio is higher?

LO2 • 3   Decision Case 12-3 Reading and Interpreting Best Buy's Statement of Cash Flows

Refer to **Best Buy's** statement of cash flows shown in the chapter opener and answer the following questions for the most recent year.

Required

1. Which method, direct or indirect, does Best Buy use in preparing the Operating Activities section of its statement of cash flows? Explain how you know which method is being used.
2. By what amount does total cash provided by operating activities differ from net earnings? What are the two largest adjustments to reconcile the two numbers? Explain the nature of these adjustments. Why is one added and the other deducted?
3. What is the largest source of cash in the Investing Activities section of the statement? What is the largest use in this section? What was the other large use of cash in this section?
4. What is the largest source of cash in the Financing Activities section of the statement? What is the largest use of cash in this section? Explain how these two items are related.

Making Financial Decisions

LO1 • 5   Decision Case 12-4 Dividend Decision and the Statement of Cash Flows—Direct Method

Bailey Corp. just completed the most profitable year in its 25-year history. Reported earnings of $1,020,000 on sales of $8,000,000 resulted in a very healthy profit margin of 12.75%. Each year before releasing the financial statements, the board of directors meets to decide on the amount of dividends to declare for the year. For each of the past nine years, the company has declared a dividend of $1 per share of common stock, which has been paid on January 15 of the following year.

Presented here are the income statement for the year and the comparative balance sheets as of the end of the last two years. Additional information follows:

	For the Year Ended December 31, 2012
Sales revenue	$8,000,000
Cost of goods sold	4,500,000
Gross profit	$3,500,000
Operating expenses	1,450,000
Income before interest and taxes	$2,050,000
Interest expense	350,000
Income before taxes	$1,700,000
Income tax expense (40%)	680,000
Net income	$1,020,000

	December 31	
	2012	**2011**
Cash	$ 480,000	$ 450,000
Accounts receivable	250,000	200,000
Inventory	750,000	600,000
Prepayments	60,000	75,000
Total current assets	$ 1,540,000	$ 1,325,000
Land	$ 3,255,000	$ 2,200,000
Plant and equipment	4,200,000	2,500,000
Accumulated depreciation	(1,250,000)	(1,000,000)
Long-term investments	500,000	900,000
Patents	650,000	750,000
Total long-term assets	$ 7,355,000	$ 5,350,000
Total assets	$ 8,895,000	$ 6,675,000
Accounts payable	$ 350,000	$ 280,000
Other accrued liabilities	285,000	225,000
Income taxes payable	170,000	100,000
Dividends payable	0	200,000
Notes payable due within next year	200,000	0
Total current liabilities	$ 1,005,000	$ 805,000
Long-term notes payable	$ 300,000	$ 500,000
Bonds payable	2,200,000	1,500,000
Total long-term liabilities	$ 2,500,000	$ 2,000,000
Common stock, $10 par	$ 2,500,000	$ 2,000,000
Retained earnings	2,890,000	1,870,000
Total stockholders' equity	$ 5,390,000	$ 3,870,000
Total liabilities and stockholders' equity	$ 8,895,000	$ 6,675,000

Additional information follows:

a. All sales are on account, as are all purchases.
b. Land was purchased through the issuance of bonds. Additional land (beyond the amount purchased through the issuance of bonds) was purchased for cash.
c. New plant and equipment were acquired during the year for cash. No plant assets were retired during the year. Depreciation expense is included in operating expenses.
d. Long-term investments were sold for cash during the year.
e. No new patents were acquired, and none were disposed of during the year. Amortization expense is included in operating expenses.
f. Notes payable due within the next year represents the amount reclassified from long term to short term.
g. Fifty thousand shares of common stock were issued during the year at par value.

As Bailey's controller, you have been asked to recommend to the board whether to declare a dividend this year and, if so, whether the precedent of paying a $1-per-share dividend can be maintained. The president is eager to keep the dividend at $1 in view of the successful year just completed. He is also concerned, however, about the effect of a dividend on the company's cash position. He is particularly concerned about the large amount of notes payable that comes due next year. He further notes the aggressive growth pattern in recent years, as evidenced this year by large increases in land and plant and equipment.

Required

1. Using the format in Exhibit 12-11, convert the income statement from an accrual basis to a cash basis.
2. Prepare a statement of cash flows using the direct method in the Operating Activities section.

(Continued)

3. What do you recommend to the board of directors concerning the declaration of a cash dividend? Should the $1-per-share dividend be declared? Should a smaller amount be declared? Should no dividend be declared? Support your answer with any necessary computations. From a cash flow perspective, include in your response your concerns about the following year.

LO1 • 6 **Decision Case 12-5 Equipment Replacement Decision and Cash Flows from Operations**

Conrad Company has been in operation for four years. The company is pleased with the continued improvement in net income but is concerned about a lack of cash available to replace existing equipment. Land, buildings, and equipment were purchased at the beginning of Year 1. No subsequent fixed asset purchases have been made, but the president believes that equipment will need to be replaced in the near future. The following information is available. (All amounts are in millions of dollars.)

| | Year of Operation | | | |
	Year 1	Year 2	Year 3	Year 4
Net income (loss)	$(10)	$ (2)	$15	$20
Depreciation expense	30	25	15	14
Increase (decrease) in:				
Accounts receivable	32	5	12	20
Inventories	26	8	5	9
Prepayments	0	0	10	5
Accounts payable	15	3	(5)	(4)

Required

1. Compute the cash flow from operations for each of Conrad's first four years of operation.
2. Write a memo to the president explaining why the company is not generating sufficient cash from operations to pay for the replacement of equipment.

Ethical Decision Making

LO1 • 6 **Decision Case 12-6 Loan Decision and the Statement of Cash Flows—Indirect Method**

Mega Enterprises is in the process of negotiating an extension of its existing loan agreements with a major bank. The bank is particularly concerned with Mega's ability to generate sufficient cash flow from operating activities to meet the periodic principal and interest payments. In conjunction with the negotiations, the controller prepared the following statement of cash flows to present to the bank:

Mega Enterprises
Statement of Cash Flows
For the Year Ended December 31, 2012
(all amounts in millions of dollars)

Cash flows from operating activities	
Net income	$ 65
Adjustments to reconcile net income to net cash provided by operating activities:	
Depreciation and amortization	56
Increase in accounts receivable	(19)
Decrease in inventory	27
Decrease in accounts payable	(42)
Increase in other accrued liabilities	18
Net cash provided by operating activities	$ 105

Cash flows from investing activities

Acquisitions of other businesses	$(234)
Acquisitions of plant and equipment	(125)
Sale of other businesses	300
Net cash used by investing activities	$ (59)

Cash flows from financing activities

Additional borrowings	$ 150
Repayments of borrowings	(180)
Cash dividends paid	(50)
Net cash used by financing activities	$ (80)
Net decrease in cash	$ (34)
Cash balance, January 1, 2012	42
Cash balance, December 31, 2012	$ 8

During 2012, Mega sold one of its businesses in California. A gain of $150 million was included in 2012 income as the difference between the proceeds from the sale of $450 million and the book value of the business of $300 million. The effect of the sale can be identified and analyzed as follows (amounts are in millions of dollars):

Identify and Analyze

ACTIVITY: Investing

ACCOUNTS: Cash Increase   **California Properties** Decrease   **Gain on Sale** Increase

STATEMENT(S): Balance Sheet and Income Statement

Balance Sheet						Income Statement				
ASSETS		=	LIABILITIES	+	STOCKHOLDERS' EQUITY	REVENUES		−	EXPENSES =	NET INCOME
Cash	450				150	Gain on Sale	150			150
California Properties	(300)									

Required

1. Comment on the presentation of the sale of the California business on the statement of cash flows. Does the way in which the sale was reported violate GAAP? Regardless of whether it violates GAAP, does the way in which the transaction was reported on the statement result in a misstatement of the net decrease in cash for the period? Explain your answers.
2. Prepare a revised statement of cash flows for 2012 with the proper presentation of the sale of the California business.
3. Has the controller acted in an unethical manner in the way the sale was reported on the statement of cash flows? Explain your answer.

Decision Case 12-7 Cash Equivalents and the Statement of Cash Flows   LO2 • 3

In December 2012, Rangers Inc. invested $100,000 of idle cash in U.S. Treasury notes. The notes mature on October 1, 2013, at which time Rangers expects to redeem them at face value of $100,000. The treasurer believes that the notes should be classified as cash equivalents because of the plans to hold them to maturity and receive face value. He also wants to avoid presentation of the purchase as an investing activity because the company made sizable capital expenditures during the year. The treasurer realizes that the decision about classification of the Treasury notes rests with you as controller.

Required

1. According to GAAP, how should the investment in U.S. Treasury notes be classified for purposes of preparing a statement of cash flows for the year ended December 31, 2012? Explain your answer.

(Continued)

2. If the purchase of the notes is classified as an operating rather than an investing activity, is the information provided to outside readers free from bias? Explain.

3. As controller for Rangers, what would you do in this situation? What would you tell the treasurer?

SOLUTIONS TO KEY TERMS QUIZ

3	Statement of cash flows	7	Financing activities
4	Cash equivalent	6	Direct method
1	Operating activities	2	Indirect method
5	Investing activities		

ANSWERS TO POD REVIEW

LO1	1. c	2. b		**LO5**	1. c	2. d
LO2	1. d	2. c		**LO6**	1. c	2. c
LO3	1. d	2. c		**LO7**	1. c	2. d
LO4	1. b	2. a		**LO8**	1. a	2. c

Financial Statement Analysis

13

AFTER STUDYING THIS CHAPTER, YOU SHOULD BE ABLE TO:

LO1 Explain the various limitations and considerations in financial statement analysis.

LO2 Use comparative financial statements to analyze a company over time (horizontal analysis).

LO3 Use common-size financial statements to compare various financial statement items (vertical analysis).

LO4 Compute and use various ratios to assess liquidity.

LO5 Compute and use various ratios to assess solvency.

LO6 Compute and use various ratios to assess profitability.

LO7 Explain how to report on and analyze other income statement items (Appendix).

STUDY LINKS

A Look at Previous Chapters Chapter 2 introduced a few key financial ratios and explained how investors and creditors use them to better understand a company's financial statements. Many of the subsequent chapters introduced ratios relevant to the particular topic being discussed.

A Look at This Chapter Ratio analysis is one important type of analysis used to interpret financial statements. This chapter expands the discussion of ratio analysis and introduces other valuable techniques used by investors, creditors, and analysts in making informed decisions. The chapter shows that ratios and other forms of analyses can provide additional insight beyond that available from merely reading the financial statements.

Star Wars®. The Old Republic®. NCAA Football 2012®. Batman: Arkham City Collector's Edition®. What does each of these popular video games have in common? They are just a few of the thousands of games carried in the more than 6,500 **GameStop** stores in the United States and 17 countries around the world. Billing itself as the world's largest video game and entertainment software retailer in the world, GameStop had its humble beginnings as Babbage's, a small software retailer in Dallas. Through a series of mergers, the company has grown to employ over 45,000 team members and even has its own magazine, *Game Informer*.

GameStop's stock first traded on the New York Stock Exchange on February 13, 2002. In an amazingly short time span, the company reported record sales in its 2010 fiscal year of nearly $9.5 billion and net income of over $400 million. This translates to a profit margin of 4.3%. Given the economic recession now gripping the world, this type of performance is enviable for any company, even more so for one so closely tied to the disposable income of consumers.

How did GameStop achieve these results? The table reproduced on the following page provides at least a partial answer to this question. Note that the three-year comparative income statements are not reported in dollars, but rather in percentages, with each line item stated as a percentage of sales. As we will see later in this chapter,

these "common-size financial statements" allow the user to focus on the relationships between statement items rather than on absolute dollar amounts. For example, cost of goods sold as a percentage of sales for the two most recent years was the same at 73.2%. This means that about three-fourths of every dollar generated in sales goes to pay for the products GameStop sells. Note that this is one percentage point lower than in the first of the three years. Thus, gross margin was up in the two most recent years to 26.8% from 25.8% in the first of the three years.

Why do you need to study this chapter? Earlier chapters looked at various ratios; this last chapter examines these ratios in more detail and considers other tools you can use to judge the financial health and performance of companies:

- You need to know what tools you can use to assess the performance of a company over time. (See pp. 702–707.)

- You need to know how you can use common-size financial statements to assess a company's performance in any one period. (See pp. 707–709.)

- You need to know what ratios are available to judge a company's liquidity, solvency, and profitability. (See pp. 710–726.)

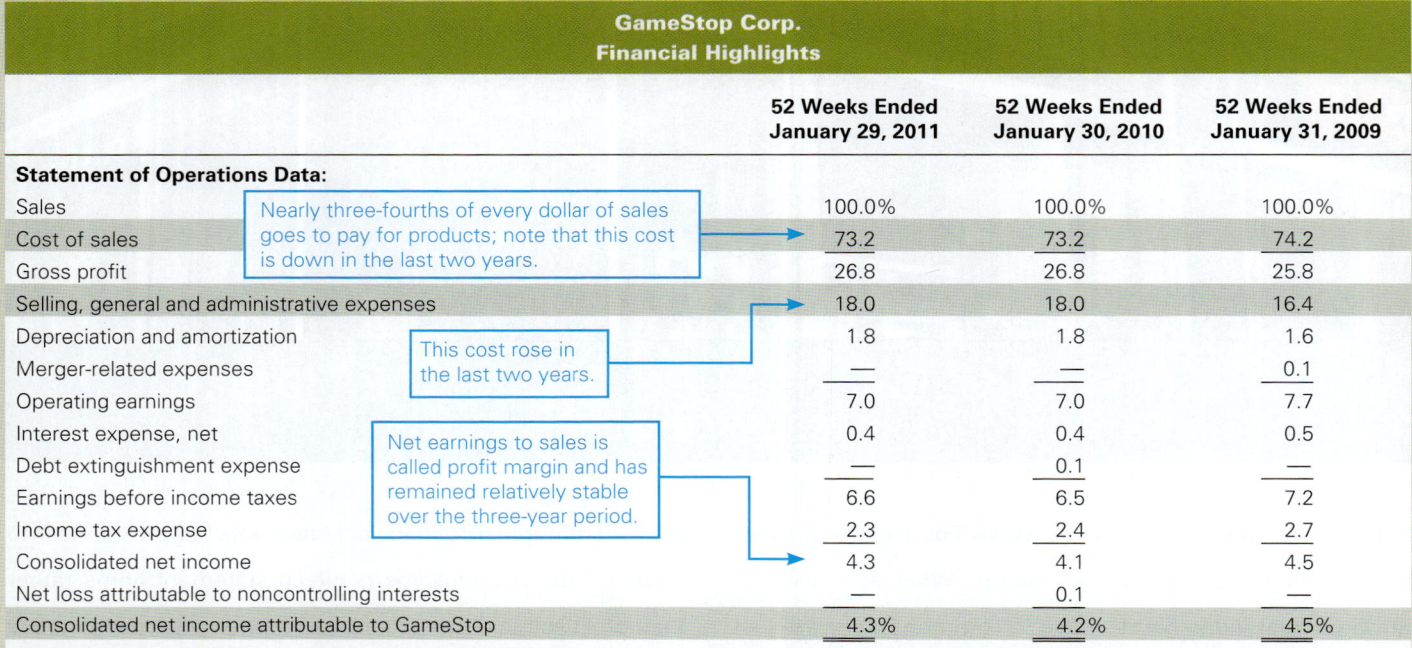

GameStop Corp. Financial Highlights			
	52 Weeks Ended January 29, 2011	**52 Weeks Ended January 30, 2010**	**52 Weeks Ended January 31, 2009**
Statement of Operations Data:			
Sales	100.0%	100.0%	100.0%
Cost of sales	73.2	73.2	74.2
Gross profit	26.8	26.8	25.8
Selling, general and administrative expenses	18.0	18.0	16.4
Depreciation and amortization	1.8	1.8	1.6
Merger-related expenses	—	—	0.1
Operating earnings	7.0	7.0	7.7
Interest expense, net	0.4	0.4	0.5
Debt extinguishment expense	—	0.1	—
Earnings before income taxes	6.6	6.5	7.2
Income tax expense	2.3	2.4	2.7
Consolidated net income	4.3	4.1	4.5
Net loss attributable to noncontrolling interests	—	0.1	—
Consolidated net income attributable to GameStop	4.3%	4.2%	4.5%

Callout annotations in the table:
- Nearly three-fourths of every dollar of sales goes to pay for products; note that this cost is down in the last two years.
- This cost rose in the last two years.
- Net earnings to sales is called profit margin and has remained relatively stable over the three-year period.

Source: GameStop Corp. Web site and 2010 annual report

Precautions in Statement Analysis

LO1 Explain the various limitations and considerations in financial statement analysis.

OVERVIEW: The use of alternative accounting principles and the effects of inflation are just two of the factors that must be considered when analyzing financial statements.

Various groups have different purposes for analyzing a company's financial statements. For example, a banker is interested primarily in the likelihood that a loan will be repaid. Certain ratios indicate the ability to repay principal and interest. A stockholder, on the other hand, is concerned with a fair return on the amount invested in the company. Again, certain ratios are helpful in assessing the return to the stockholder. The managers of a business also are interested in the tools of financial statement analysis because various outside groups judge managers by using certain key ratios. Fortunately, most financial statements provide information about financial performance. Publicly held corporations are required to include in their annual reports a section that reviews the past year, with management's comments on its performance as measured by selected ratios and other forms of analysis.

Before turning to various techniques commonly used in the financial analysis of a company, you must understand some limitations and other considerations in statement analysis.

Watch for Alternative Accounting Principles

Every set of financial statements is based on various assumptions. For example, a cost-flow method must be assumed in valuing inventory and recognizing cost of goods sold. The accountant chooses FIFO, LIFO, or one of the other acceptable methods. Analysts or other users find this information in the financial statement notes. The selection of a particular inventory valuation method has a significant effect on certain key ratios.

Recognition of the acceptable alternatives is especially important in comparing two or more companies. Changes in accounting methods, such as a change in the depreciation method, also make comparing results for a given company over time more difficult.

Take Care When Making Comparisons

Users of financial statements often place too much emphasis on summary indicators and key ratios such as the current ratio and the earnings per share amount. No single ratio is capable of telling the user everything there is to know about a particular company. The calculation of various ratios for a company is only a starting point. One technique discussed is the comparison of ratios for different periods of time. Has the ratio gone up or down from last year? What is the percentage of increase or decrease in the ratio over the last five years? Recognizing trends in ratios is important when analyzing any company.

The potential investor also must recognize the need to compare one company with others in the same industry. For example, a particular measure of performance may cause an investor to conclude that the company is not operating efficiently. Comparison with an industry standard, however, might indicate that the ratio is normal for companies in that industry. Various organizations publish summaries of selected ratios organized by industry for a sample of U.S. companies.

Although industry comparisons are useful, caution is necessary in interpreting the results of such analyses. Few companies in today's economy operate in a single industry. Exceptions exist, but most companies cross the boundaries of a single industry. *Conglomerates,* companies operating in more than one industry, present a special challenge to the analyst. Also, it is not unusual to find companies in the same industry using different inventory valuation techniques or depreciation methods.

Finally, many corporate income statements contain nonoperating items such as extraordinary items and gains and losses from discontinued operations. When these items exist, the reader must exercise extra caution in making comparisons. To assess the future prospects of a group of companies, you may want to compare income statements *before* taking into account the effects these items have on income.

Understand the Possible Effects of Inflation

Inflation, or an increase in the level of prices, is another important consideration in analyzing financial statements. The statements, to be used by outsiders, are based on historical costs and are not adjusted for the effects of increasing prices. For example, consider the following trend in a company's sales for the past three years:

	2012	2011	2010
Net sales	$121,000	$110,000	$100,000

As measured by the actual dollars of sales, sales have increased by 10% each year. Caution is necessary in concluding that the company is better off in each succeeding year because of the increase in sales *dollars*. Assume, for example, that 2010 sales of $100,000 are the result of selling 100,000 units at $1 each. Are 2011 sales of $110,000 the result of selling 110,000 units at $1 each or of selling 100,000 units at $1.10 each? Although on the surface knowing which result accounts for the sales increase may seem unimportant, the answer can have significant ramifications. If the company found it necessary to increase selling price to $1.10 in the face of increasing costs, it may be no better off than it was in 2010 in terms of gross profit. On the other hand, if the company is able to increase sales revenue by 10% based primarily on growth in unit sales, its performance would be considered stronger than if the increase were due merely to a price increase. Published financial statements are stated in historical costs and therefore have not been adjusted for the effects of inflation.

LO1 Explain the various limitations and considerations in financial statement analysis.

- Financial statement analysis can be a powerful and useful tool in assessing various characteristics of a firm's operations, but the following factors should be considered when conducting this analysis:
  - Alternative accounting principles may sometimes be used.
  - Comparisons must consider inflation, trends over time, and industry norms.
  - Ratios from financial statements tell only part of the story about a firm's performance.

POD REVIEW 13.1

QUESTIONS   Answers to these questions are on the last page of the chapter.

1. Which of the following should be taken into account when a company's performance is analyzed?

   a. the effects of inflation
   b. trends over time
   c. industry norms
   d. All of the above should be considered.

2. Suppose two companies in the same industry use different methods to value inventory.

   a. This makes comparisons easier.
   b. This makes it impossible to compare the two companies.
   c. This makes comparisons more difficult but not impossible.
   d. This will never happen because all companies in a particular industry must use the same method.

Analysis of Comparative Statements: Horizontal Analysis

LO2 Use comparative financial statements to analyze a company over time (horizontal analysis).

OVERVIEW: Comparative financial statements can be used to analyze a company over time (horizontal analysis).

We are now ready to analyze a set of financial statements. We will begin by looking at the comparative statements of a company for a two-year period. The analysis of the statements over a series of years is often called **horizontal analysis**. We will then see how the statements can be recast in what are referred to as *common-size statements*. The analysis of common-size statements is called **vertical analysis**. Finally, we will consider the use of a variety of ratios to analyze a company.

Horizontal analysis
A comparison of financial statement items over a period of time.

Vertical analysis
A comparison of various financial statement items within a single period with the use of common-size statements.

Example 13-1 Preparing Comparative Balance Sheets—Horizontal Analysis

Comparative balance sheets for a hypothetical entity, Henderson Company, are presented below.

Read from earlier year to later year. Usually, this is from right to left.

Henderson Company
Comparative Balance Sheets
December 31, 2012 and 2011
(all amounts in thousands of dollars)

The base year is normally on the right.

	December 31		Increase (Decrease)	
	2012	**2011**	**Dollars**	**Percent**
Cash	$ 320	$ 1,350	$ (1,030) ❶	(76)%
Accounts receivable	5,500	4,500	1,000	22
Inventory	4,750	2,750	2,000 ❷	73
Prepaid insurance	150	200	(50)	(25)
Total current assets	$10,720	$ 8,800	$ 1,920	22

Dollar change from year to year.

Percentage change from one year to the next year.

(Continued)

Land	$ 2,000	$ 2,000	$ 0	0	
Buildings and equipment	6,000	4,500	1,500	33	
Accumulated depreciation	(1,850)	(1,500)	(350)	(23)	
Total long-term assets	$ 6,150	$ 5,000	$ 1,150	23	
Total assets	$16,870	$13,800	$ 3,070	22	
Accounts payable	$ 4,250	$ 2,500	$ 1,750 ❸	70	
Taxes payable	2,300	2,100	200	10	
Notes payable	600	800	(200)	(25)	
Current portion of bonds	100	100	0	0	
Total current liabilities	$ 7,250	$ 5,500	$ 1,750	32	
Bonds payable	700	800	(100)	(13)	
Total liabilities	$ 7,950	$ 6,300	$ 1,650	26	
Preferred stock, $5 par	$ 500	$ 500	$ 0	0	
Common stock, $1 par	1,000	1,000	0	0	
Retained earnings	7,420	6,000	1,420	24	
Total stockholders' equity	$ 8,920	$ 7,500	$ 1,420	19	
Total liabilities and stockholders' equity	$16,870	$13,800	$ 3,070	22	

In **horizontal analysis**, read right to left to compare one year's results with the next as a dollar amount of change and as a percentage of change from year to year.

Note: Referenced amounts are boldfaced for convenience.

The increase or decrease in each of the major accounts on the balance sheet is shown in absolute dollars and as a percentage. The base year for computing the percentage increase or decrease in each account is the first year, 2011, and is normally shown on the right side. By reading across from right to left (thus the term *horizontal analysis*), the analyst can quickly spot any unusual changes in accounts from the previous year. Three accounts stand out: ❶ Cash decreased by 76%, ❷ Inventory increased by 73%, and ❸ Accounts Payable increased by 70%. (These lines are also boldfaced for convenience.) Individually, each of these large changes is a red flag. Taken together, these changes send the financial statement user the warning that the business may be deteriorating. Each of these large changes should be investigated further.

© Cengage Learning 2013

Example 13-2 Preparing Comparative Statements of Income and Retained Earning—Horizontal Analysis

Shown below are comparative statements of income and retained earnings for Henderson for 2012 and 2011.

Henderson Company
Comparative Statements of Income and Retained Earnings
For the Years Ended December 31, 2012 and 2011
(all amounts in thousands of dollars)

	December 31		Increase (Decrease)		
	2012	**2011**	**Dollars**	**Percent**	
Net sales	$24,000	$20,000	$ 4,000 ❶	20%	
Cost of goods sold	18,000	14,000	4,000 ❷	29	These three increases in revenue and expenses resulted in an operating income *decrease* of 25%.
Gross profit	$ 6,000	$ 6,000	$ 0	0	
Selling, general, and administrative expense	3,000	2,000	1,000 ❸	50	
Operating income	$ 3,000	$ 4,000	$(1,000) ❹	(25)	
Interest expense	140	160	(20)	(13)	
Income before tax	$ 2,860	$ 3,840	$ (980)	(26)	
Income tax expense	1,140	1,540	(400)	(26)	
Net income	$ 1,720	$ 2,300	$ (580)	(25)	

(Continued)

Preferred dividends	50	50
Income available to common	$ 1,670	$ 2,250
Common dividends	250	250
To retained earnings	$ 1,420	$ 2,000
Retained earnings, 1/1	6,000	4,000
Retained earnings, 12/31	$ 7,420	$ 6,000

Note: Referenced amounts are boldfaced for convenience.

At first glance, ❶ the 20% increase in sales to $24 million appears promising; but management was not able to limit the increase in ❷ cost of goods sold or ❸ selling, general, and administrative expense to 20%. The analysis indicates that cost of goods sold increased by 29% and selling, general, and administrative expense increased by 50%. The increases in these two expenses more than offset the increase in sales and resulted in a ❹ decrease in operating income of 25%.

© Cengage Learning 2013

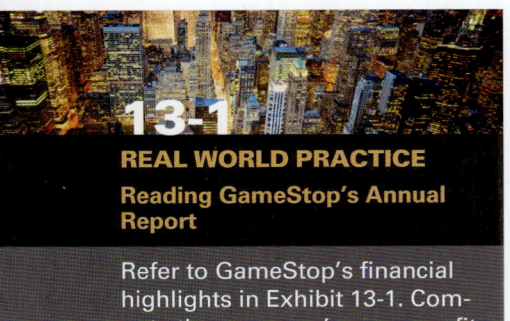

13-1

REAL WORLD PRACTICE

Reading GameStop's Annual Report

Refer to GameStop's financial highlights in Exhibit 13-1. Compute the company's gross profit ratio for each of the five years. Is there a noticeable upward or downward trend in the ratio over this time period?

© Nikada/istockphoto.com

Companies that experience sales growth often become lax about controlling expenses. Their managements sometimes forget that the bottom line is what counts, not the top line. Perhaps the salespeople are given incentives to increase sales without considering the costs of the sales. Maybe management is spending too much on overhead, including its own salaries. Business owners must address these concerns if they want to get a reasonable return on their investment.

Horizontal analysis can be extended to include more than two years of results. At a minimum, publicly held companies are required to include income statements and statements of cash flows for the three most recent years and balance sheets as of the end of the two most recent years. Many annual reports include, as supplementary information, financial summaries of operations for extended periods of time. As illustrated in Exhibit 13-1, **GameStop** includes a five-year summary of selected financial data, such as gross profit, net income, working capital, and total assets. Note the increase in both sales and gross profit in every year over the five-year period. Also note, however, that GameStop does not include in the summary the gross profit ratio (gross profit divided by sales), although it can easily be found by dividing the third line on the exhibit by the first line. A comparison of the trend in this ratio would help to determine whether the company has effectively controlled the cost to manufacture its products.

EXHIBIT 13-1 GameStop Financial Summary

Our selected financial data set forth below should be read in conjunction with "Management's Discussion and Analysis of Financial Condition and Results of Operations" and the consolidated financial statements and notes thereto included elsewhere in this Form 10-K.

	52 Weeks Ended, January 29, 2011	52 Weeks Ended, January 30, 2010	52 Weeks Ended, January 31, 2009	52 Weeks Ended, February 2, 2008	53 Weeks Ended, February 3, 2007
	(In millions, except per share data and statistical data)				
Statement of Operations Data:					
Sales	$ 9,473.7	$ 9,078.0	$ 8,805.9	$ 7,094.0	$ 5,318.9
Cost of sales	6,936.1	6,643.3	6,535.8	5,280.3	3,847.5
Gross profit	2,537.6	2,434.7	2,270.1	1,813.7	1,471.4
Selling, general and administrative expenses	1,700.3	1,635.1	1,445.4	1,182.0	1,021.1
Depreciation and amortization	174.7	162.6	145.0	130.3	109.8
Merger-related expenses(1)	—	—	4.6	—	6.8

> Both sales and gross profit have increased each year for four consecutive years.

EXHIBIT 13-1 GameStop Financial Summary (Continued)

Operating earnings	662.6	637.0	675.1	501.4	333.7
Interest expense (income), net	35.2	43.2	38.8	47.7	73.3
Debt extinguishment expense	6.0	5.3	2.3	12.6	6.1
Earnings before income taxes expenses	621.4	588.5	634.0	441.1	254.3
Income tax expense	214.6	212.8	235.7	152.8	96.0
Consolidated net income	406.8	375.7	398.3	288.3	158.3
Net loss attributable to noncontrolling interest	1.2	1.6	—	—	—
Consolidated net income attributable to GameStop	$ 408.0	$ 377.3	$ 398.3	$ 288.3	$ 158.3
Basic net income per common share (2)	$ 2.69	$ 2.29	$ 2.44	$ 1.82	$ 1.06
Diluted net income per common share (2)	$ 2.65	$ 2.25	$ 2.38	$ 1.75	$ 1.00
Weighted average shares outstanding — basic (2)	151.6	164.5	163.2	158.2	149.9
Weighted average shares outstanding — diluted (2)	154.0	167.9	167.7	164.8	158.3
Store Operating Data:					
Number of stores by segment					
United States	4,536	4,429	4,331	4,061	3,799
Canada	345	337	325	287	267
Australia	405	388	350	280	219
Europe	1,384	1,296	1,201	636	493
Total	6,670	6,450	6,207	5,264	4,778
Comparable store sales increase (decrease)(3)	1.1%	(7.9)%	12.3%	24.7%	11.9%
Inventory turnover	5.1	5.2	5.8	6.0	5.2
Balance Sheet Data:					
Working capital	$ 407.0	$ 471.6	$ 255.3	$ 534.2	$ 353.3
Total assets	5,063.8	4,955.3	4,483.5	3,775.9	3,349.6
Total debt, net	249.0	447.3	545.7	574.5	855.5
Total liabilities	2,167.9	2,232.3	2,212.9	1,913.4	1,973.7
Total equity	2,895.9	2,723.0	2,270.6	1,862.4	1,375.9

(1) The Company's results of operations for fiscal 2008 and the 53 weeks ended February 3, 2007 ("fiscal 2006") include expenses believed to be of a one-time or short-term nature associated with the Micromania acquisition (fiscal 2008) and the EB merger (fiscal 2006), which included $4.6 million and $6.8 million, respectively, considered in operating earnings. In fiscal 2008, the $4.6 million included $3.5 million related to foreign currency losses on funds used to purchase Micromania. In fiscal 2006, the $6.8 million included $1.9 million in charges associated with assets of the Company considered to be impaired as a result of the EB merger and $ 4.9 million in costs associated with integrating the operations of GameStop and EB.

(2) Weighted average shares outstanding and earnings per common share have been adjusted to reflect the conversion of Class B common stock that was outstanding proir to its conversion into Class A common stock on a one-for-one basis on February 7, 2007 and two-for-one stock split on March 16, 2007. The Company's Class B common stock was traded on the NYSE under the symbol "GME.B" until February 7, 2007.

(3) Stores are included in our comparable store sales base beginning in the 13th month of operation.

Source: GameStop Corp. 2010 10-K, pp. 27–28.

Tracking items over a series of years, a practice called *trend analysis,* can be a very powerful tool for the analyst. Advanced statistical techniques are available for analyzing trends in financial data and, most importantly, for projecting those trends to future periods. Some of the techniques, such as time series analysis, have been used extensively in forecasting sales trends.

Historically, attention has focused on the balance sheet and income statement in analyzing a company's position and results of operation. Only recently have analysts and other users begun to appreciate the value in incorporating the statement of cash flows into their analyses.

Example 13-3 Preparing Comparative Statements of Cash Flow—Horizontal Analysis

Comparative statements of cash flows for Henderson are shown below.

Henderson Company
Comparative Statements of Cash Flows
For the Years Ended December 31, 2012 and 2011
(all amounts in thousands of dollars)

	2012	2011	Increase (Decrease) Dollars	Increase (Decrease) Percent
Net Cash Flows from Operating Activities				
❷ Net income	$ 1,720	$ 2,300	$ (580)	(25)%
Adjustments:				
Depreciation expense	350	300		
Changes in:				
❸ Accounts receivable	(1,000)	500		
❹ Inventory	(2,000)	(300)		
Prepaid insurance	50	50		
Accounts payable	1,750	(200)		
Taxes payable	200	300		
Net cash provided by operating activities ❶ Unfavorable	$ 1,070 ←	$ 2,950	$(1,880)	(64)%
Net Cash Flows from Investing Activities				
Purchase of buildings	$(1,500)	$(2,000)	$ (500)	(25)%
Net Cash Flows from Financing Activities				
Repayment of notes	$ (200)	$ (200)	0	0
Retirement of bonds	(100)	(100)	0	0
Cash dividends—preferred	(50)	(50)	0	0
Cash dividends—common	(250)	(250)	0	0
Net cash used by financing activities	$ (600)	$ (600)	0	0
Net increase (decrease) in cash	$ (1,030)	$ 350		
Beginning cash balance	1,350	1,000		
Ending cash balance	$ 320	$ 1,350		
Supplemental Information				
Interest paid	$ 140	$ 160		
Income taxes paid	$ 940	$ 1,440		

Note: Referenced amounts are boldfaced for convenience.

Henderson's financing activities remained constant over the two-year period. Each year, the company paid $200,000 on notes, another $100,000 to retire bonds, and $300,000 to stockholders in dividends. Cash outflow from investing activities slowed down somewhat in 2012 with the purchase of $1.5 million in new buildings compared with $2 million the year before.

The most noticeable difference between Henderson's statements of cash flows for the two years is in the Operating Activities section. Operations ❶ generated almost $2 million less in cash in 2012 than in 2011 ($1.07 million in 2012 versus $2.95 million in 2011). The decrease in ❷ net income was partially responsible for this reduction in cash from operations. However, the increases in ❸ accounts receivable and ❹ inventory in 2012 had a significant impact on the decrease in cash generated from operating activities.

LO2 Use comparative financial statements to analyze a company over time (horizontal analysis).

- Amounts appearing on comparative financial statements may be used to perform horizontal analysis.

POD
REVIEW
13.2

QUESTIONS Answers to these questions are on the last page of the chapter.

1. A comparison of financial statement items for a single company over a period of time is called

   a. horizontal analysis.
   b. vertical analysis.
   c. operational analysis.
   d. none of the above.

2. What is the minimum number of years for which publicly traded companies must include the following statements in their annual report filed with the SEC?

   a. two years for income statements and statements of cash flows and three years for balance sheets
   b. three years for income statements and statements of cash flows and two years for balance sheets
   c. three years for income statements, statements of cash flows, and balance sheets
   d. one year for income statements, statements of cash flows, and balance sheets

Analysis of Common-Size Statements: Vertical Analysis

OVERVIEW: Common-size financial statements are useful to compare various items (vertical analysis).

LO3 Use common-size financial statements to compare various financial statement items (vertical analysis).

Often, it is easier to examine comparative financial statements when they have been standardized. *Common-size statements* recast all items on the statement as a percentage of a selected item on the statement. This excludes size as a relevant variable in the analysis. This type of analysis could be used to compare **Wal-Mart** with the smaller **Target** or to compare **IBM** with the smaller **Apple Computer**. It is also a convenient way to compare the same company from year to year.

Example 13-4 Preparing Common-Size Balance Sheets—Vertical Analysis

Vertical analysis involves looking at the relative size and composition of various items on a particular financial statement. Common-size comparative balance sheets for Henderson Company are presented below.

Henderson Company
Common-Size Comparative Balance Sheets
December 31, 2012 and 2011
(all amounts in thousands of dollars)

	December 31, 2012		December 31, 2011		
	Dollars	**Percent**	**Dollars**	**Percent**	
Cash	$ 320	1.9%	$ 1,350	9.8%	Compare percentages across years to spot year-to-year trends.
Accounts receivable	5,500	32.6	4,500	32.6	
Inventory	4,750	28.1	2,750	19.9	In **vertical analysis**, compare each line item as a percentage of total (100%) to highlight a company's overall condition.
Prepaid insurance	150	0.9	200	1.5	
Total current assets	$ 10,720	63.5%	$ 8,800	63.8%	
Land	$ 2,000	11.9%	$ 2,000	14.5%	
Buildings and equipment, net	4,150	24.6	3,000	21.7	
Total long-term assets	$ 6,150	36.5%	$ 5,000	36.2%	
Total assets	$16,870	100.0%	$13,800	100.0%	

(Continued)

Accounts payable	$ 4,250	25.2%	$ 2,500	18.1%
Taxes payable	2,300	13.6	2,100	15.2
Notes payable	600	3.6	800	5.8
Current portion of bonds	100	0.6	100	0.7
Total current liabilities	$ 7,250	❹ 43.0%	$ 5,500	39.8%
Bonds payable	700	❺ 4.1	800	5.8
Total liabilities	$ 7,950	47.1%	$ 6,300	45.6%
Preferred stock, $5 par	$ 500	3.0%	$ 500	3.6%
Common stock, $1 par	1,000	5.9	1,000	7.3
Retained earnings	7,420	44.0	6,000	43.5
Total stockholders' equity	$ 8,920	❻ 52.9%	$ 7,500	54.4%
Total liabilities and stockholders' equity	$16,870	100.0%	$13,800	100.0%

Note: Referenced amounts are boldfaced for convenience.

Note that all asset accounts are stated as a percentage of total assets. Similarly, all liability and stockholders' equity accounts are stated as a percentage of total liabilities and stockholders' equity. The combination of the comparative balance sheets for the two years and the common-size feature allows the analyst to spot critical changes in the composition of the assets. We noted in Example 13-1 that cash had decreased by 76% over the two years. The decrease of ❶ cash from 9.8% of total assets to only 1.9% is highlighted here.

You can also observe that ❷ total current assets have continued to represent just under two-thirds (63.5%) of total assets. If cash has decreased significantly in terms of the percentage of total assets, what accounts have increased to maintain current assets at two-thirds of total assets? We can quickly determine from these data that although ❸ inventory represented 19.9% of total assets at the end of 2011, the percentage is up to 28.1% at the end of 2012. This change in the relative composition of current assets between cash and inventory may signal that the company is having trouble selling inventory.

Total ❹ current liabilities represent a slightly higher percentage of total liabilities and stockholders' equity at the end of 2012 than at the end of 2011. The increase is balanced by a slight decrease in the relative percentages of ❺ long-term debt (the bonds) and ❻ stockholders' equity. We will return later to further analysis of the composition of both the current and the noncurrent accounts.

13-2

REAL WORLD PRACTICE

Reading Kellogg's Income Statement

Refer to Kellogg's three-year comparative income statements reprinted in the back of this book. For each of the three years presented, compute the gross profit and profit margin ratios. Also, compute the percentage increase or decrease of each ratio for each of the last two years. What conclusions can you draw from your analysis?

Example 13-5 Preparing Common-Size Income Statements—Vertical Analysis

Common-size comparative income statements for Henderson are presented below.

Henderson Company
Common-Size Comparative Income Statements
For the Years Ended December 31, 2012 and 2011
(all amounts in thousands of dollars)

	2012		2011		
	Dollars	Percent	Dollars	Percent	
Net sales	$24,000	❶ 100.0%	$20,000	100.0%	
Cost of goods sold	❸ 18,000	75.0	14,000	70.0	Gross profit as a percentage of sales
Gross profit	$ 6,000	❷ 25.0%	$ 6,000	30.0%	is the **gross profit** ratio.
Selling, general, and administrative expense	3,000	12.5	2,000	10.0	

(Continued)

Operating income	$ 3,000	12.5%	$ 4,000	20.0%
Interest expense	140	0.6	160	0.8
Income before tax	$ 2,860	11.9%	$ 3,840	19.2%
Income tax expense	1,140	4.8	1,540	7.7
Net income	**$ 1,720**	❹ 7.1%	**$ 2,300**	11.5%

The ratio of net income to net sales is the **profit margin ratio.**

Note: Referenced amounts are boldfaced for convenience.

The *base*, or benchmark, on which all other items in the income statement are compared is ❶ net sales. Again, observations from the comparative statements alone are further confirmed by examining the common-size statements. Although the **gross profit ratio**—gross profit as a percentage of net sales—was 30.0% in 2011, the same ratio for 2012 is only 25.0% ❷. Recall the earlier observation that although sales increased by 20% from one year to the next, ❸ cost of goods sold increased by 29%.

In addition to the gross profit ratio, an important relationship from this example is the ratio of net income to net sales, or **profit margin ratio**. The ratio, an overall indicator of management's ability to control expenses, reflects the amount of income for each dollar of sales. Some analysts prefer to look at income before tax rather than at final net income because taxes are not typically an expense that can be controlled. Further, if the company does not earn a profit before tax, it will incur no tax expense. Note the decrease in Henderson's ❶ profit margin: from 11.5% in 2011 to 7.1% in 2012 (or from 19.2% to 11.9% on a before-tax basis).

Gross profit ratio
Gross profit to net sales

Profit margin ratio
Net income to net sales.

© Cengage Learning 2013

LO3 Use common-size financial statements to compare various financial statement items (vertical analysis).

- Common-size statements recast all items as a percentage of a selected item on the statement, such as sales on the income statement.
- The use of common-size financial statements, also known as vertical analysis, facilitates comparisons between companies in addition to comparisons between different periods for the same company.

POD REVIEW

13.3

QUESTIONS **Answers to these questions are on the last page of the chapter.**

1. If you were concerned about whether selling and administrative expenses were reasonable this past year given the level of sales, which type of analysis would you perform?

   a. horizontal analysis
   b. trend analysis
   c. vertical analysis
   d. none of the above

2. On common-size comparative income statements, all line items are stated as a percentage of

   a. net sales.
   b. net income.
   c. total assets.
   d. none of the above.

© Cengage Learning 2013

HOT TOPICS
Another Take on Vertical Analysis

Richard Levine/Alamy

Investors don't rely solely on the information provided in annual reports to make decisions. The quarterly report, or 10Q, filed with the SEC contains information on a timelier basis. Companies often use the 10Q, and its accompanying press release, to provide investors with more than just the numbers contained in the financial statements.

In its first quarter report for the 2011 fiscal year, GameStop's income statement reported both record sales and earnings. Two accompanying schedules, titled "Sales Mix" and "Gross Profit Mix," provide additional insights, reporting both dollar amounts and

percentages. For example, the first schedule shows that nearly 60% of GameStop's first quarter sales came from new video game hardware and software, while about 27% was from used products (the remaining 13% of sales is labeled "other"). The gross profit schedule is nearly inverted. New products accounted for only 26% of gross profit, but used video game products generated 48% of the retailer's gross profit. This type of feedback is useful both to management for planning purposes and also to analysts trying to project the future in an industry as fluid as video game sales. Often, some of the most valuable information is found outside the basic financials.

Source: GameStop Corp., May 19, 2011, press release.

Liquidity Analysis and the Management of Working Capital

LO4 Compute and use various ratios to assess liquidity.

OVERVIEW: Various ratios can be used to analyze a company's liquidity, that is, the ability to repay current liabilities as they come due.

Two ratios were discussed in the last section: the *gross profit ratio* and the *profit margin ratio*. A ratio is simply the relationship, normally stated as a percentage, between two financial statement amounts. This section considers a wide range of ratios that management, analysts, and others use for a variety of purposes. The ratios are classified in three main categories according to their use in performing (1) liquidity analysis, (2) solvency analysis, and (3) profitability analysis.

Liquidity
The nearness to cash of the assets and liabilities.

Liquidity is a relative measure of the nearness to cash of the assets and liabilities of a company. Nearness to cash deals with the length of time before cash is realized. Various ratios are used to measure liquidity, and they concern basically the company's ability to pay its debts as they come due. Recall the distinction between the current and long-term classifications on the balance sheet. Current assets are assets that will be converted into cash or consumed within one year or within the operating cycle if the cycle is longer than one year. The operating cycle for a manufacturing company is the length of time between the purchase of raw materials and the eventual collection of any outstanding account receivable from the sale of the product. Current liabilities are a company's obligations that require the use of current assets or the creation of other current liabilities to satisfy the obligations.

The nearness to cash of the current assets is indicated by their placement on the balance sheet. Current assets are listed on the balance sheet in descending order of their nearness to cash. Liquidity is, of course, a matter of degree, with cash being the most liquid of all assets. With few exceptions, such as prepaid insurance, most current assets are convertible into cash. However, accounts receivable is closer to being converted into cash than is inventory. An account receivable need only be collected to be converted to cash. An item of inventory must first be sold; then assuming that sales of inventory are on account, the account must be collected before cash is realized.

Working Capital

Working capital
Current assets minus current liabilities.

Working capital is the excess of current assets over current liabilities at a point in time:

$$\text{Working Capital} = \text{Current Assets} - \text{Current Liabilities}$$

Example 13-6 Computing Working Capital

Reference to Henderson's comparative balance sheets in Example 13-1 indicates the following:

	December 31	
	2012	**2011**
Current assets	$10,720,000	$8,800,000
Current liabilities	7,250,000	5,500,000
Working capital	$ 3,470,000	$3,300,000

The management of working capital is an extremely important task for any business. A comparison of Henderson's working capital at the end of each of the two years indicates a slight increase in the degree of protection for short-term creditors of the company. Management must strive for the ideal balance of current assets and current liabilities. However, working capital is limited in its informational value. It reveals nothing about the composition of the current accounts. Also, the dollar amount of working capital may not be useful for comparison with other companies of different sizes in the same industry. Working capital of $3,470,000 may be adequate for Henderson Company, but it might signal impending bankruptcy for a much larger company.

Current Ratio

The **current ratio**, one of the most widely used financial statement ratios, is calculated as follows:

$$\text{Current Ratio} = \frac{\text{Current Assets}}{\text{Current Liabilities}}$$

Current ratio
The ratio of current assets to current liabilities.

Example 13-7 Computing the Current Ratio

For Henderson Company, the ratio at each year-end is as follows:

	December 31	
2012		**2011**
$\dfrac{\$10,720,000}{\$7,250,000} = 1.48 \text{ to } 1$		$\dfrac{\$8,000,000}{\$5,500,000} = 1.60 \text{ to } 1$

At the end of 2012, Henderson had $1.48 of current assets for every $1 of current liabilities. Is this current ratio adequate, or is it a sign of impending financial difficulties? Some analysts use a general rule of thumb of 2 to 1 for the current ratio as a sign of short-term financial health. However, companies in certain industries have historically operated with current ratios much less than 2 to 1.

Interpreting the current ratio also involves the composition of the current assets. Cash is usually the only acceptable means of payment for most liabilities. Therefore, it is important to consider the makeup, or *composition*, of the current assets. Refer to Example 13-4 and Henderson's common-size balance sheets. Not only did the current ratio decline during 2012, but the proportion of the total current assets made up by inventory increased, whereas the proportion made up by accounts receivable remained the same. Recall that accounts receivable is only one step removed from cash, whereas inventory requires both sale and collection of the subsequent account.

> **STUDY TIP**
>
> Some of the ratios discussed in this chapter, such as the current ratio, were introduced in earlier chapters. Use the information here as a review of those earlier introductions.

© Cengage Learning 2013

© Cengage Learning 2013

Acid-Test Ratio

The **acid-test or quick ratio** is a stricter test of a company's ability to pay its current debts as they are due. Specifically, it is intended to deal with the composition problem because it *excludes* inventories and prepaid assets from the numerator of the fraction:

$$\text{Acid-Test or Quick Ratio} = \frac{\text{Quick Assets}}{\text{Current Liablities}}$$

Acid-test or quick ratio
A stricter test of liquidity than the current ratio; excludes inventory and prepayments from the numerator.

where

$$\text{Quick Assets} = \text{Cash} + \text{Marketable Securities} + \text{Current Receivables}$$

Example 13-8 Computing the Acid-Test Ratio

Henderson's quick assets consist of only cash and accounts receivable, and its quick ratios are as follows:

	December 31	
2012		**2011**
$\dfrac{\$320,000 + \$5,500,000}{\$7,250,000} = 0.80 \text{ to } 1$		$\dfrac{\$1,350,000 + \$4,500,000}{\$5,500,000} = 1.06 \text{ to } 1$

Does the quick ratio of less than 1 to 1 at the end of 2012 mean that Henderson will be unable to pay creditors on time? **For many companies, an acid-test ratio below 1 is not desirable because it may signal the need to liquidate marketable securities to pay bills, regardless of the current trading price of the securities**. (Recall that Henderson has no marketable securities.) Although the quick ratio is a better indication of short-term debt-paying ability than

(Continued)

the current ratio, it is still not perfect. Henderson's own normal credit terms and the credit terms that it receives from its suppliers would answer this question.

Assume that Henderson requires its customers to pay their accounts within 30 days and that its suppliers allow payment anytime within 60 days. The relatively longer credit terms extended by Henderson's suppliers give the company some cushion in meeting its obligations. The due date of the $2,300,000 in taxes payable also could have a significant effect on the company's ability to remain in business.

Cash Flow from Operations to Current Liabilities

Cash flow from operations to current liabilities ratio
A measure of the ability to pay current debts from operating cash flows.

Two limitations exist with either the current ratio or the quick ratio as a measure of liquidity. First, almost all debts require the payment of cash. Thus, a ratio that focuses on cash is more useful. Second, both ratios focus on liquid assets at a *point in time*. Cash flow from operating activities, as reported on the statement of cash flows, can be used to indicate the flow of cash during the year to cover the debts due. The **cash flow from operations to current liabilities ratio** is computed as follows:

$$\text{Cash Flow from Operations to Current Liabilities Ratio} = \frac{\text{Net Cash Provided by Operating Activities}}{\text{Average Current Liabilities}}$$

Note the use of *average* current liabilities in the denominator. Because we need to calculate the *average* current liabilities for both years, Henderson's ending balance sheet on December 31, 2010, is given in Exhibit 13-2.

EXHIBIT 13-2 Henderson Company's Balance Sheet, End of 2010

Henderson Company Balance Sheet December 31, 2010 (all amounts in thousands of dollars)	
Cash	$ 1,000
Accounts receivable	5,000
Inventory	2,450
Prepaid insurance	250
Total current assets	$ 8,700
Land	$ 2,000
Buildings and equipment, net	1,300
Total long-term assets	$ 3,300
Total assets	$12,000
Accounts payable	$ 2,700
Taxes payable	1,800
Notes payable	1,000
Current portion of bonds	100
Total current liabilities	$ 5,600
Bonds payable	900
Total liabilities	$ 6,500
Preferred stock, $5 par	$ 500
Common stock, $1 par	1,000
Retained earnings	4,000
Total stockholders' equity	$ 5,500
Total liabilities and stockholders' equity	$12,000

Example 13-9 Computing Cash Flow from Operations to Current Liabilities

Henderson's cash flow from operations to current liabilities ratio each year is as follows:

2012	2011
$\dfrac{\$1,070,000}{(\$7,250,000 + \$5,500,000)/2} = 16.8\%$	$\dfrac{\$2,950,000}{(\$5,500,000 + \$5,600,000)/2} = 53.2\%$

Two factors are responsible for the large decrease in this ratio from 2011 to 2012. First, cash generated from operations during 2012 was less than half what it was during 2011 (the numerator). Second, average current liabilities were smaller in 2011 than in 2012 (the denominator). An analysis of the company's health in terms of its liquidity would concentrate on the reason for these decreases.

Accounts Receivable Analysis

The analysis of accounts receivable is an important component in the management of working capital. A company must be willing to extend credit terms that are liberal enough to attract and maintain customers, but at the same time, management must continually monitor the accounts to ensure collection on a timely basis. One measure of the efficiency of the collection process is the **accounts receivable turnover ratio**:

$$\text{Accounts Receivable Turnover Ratio} = \frac{\text{Net Credit Sales}}{\text{Average Accounts Receivable}}$$

Accounts receivable turnover ratio
A measure of the number of times accounts receivable are collected in a period.

   Both the current and the quick ratios measure liquidity at a point in time and all numbers come from the balance sheet, but a turnover ratio is an *activity* ratio and consists of an activity (sales in this case) divided by a base to which it is naturally related (accounts receivable). Because an activity such as sales is for a period of time (a year in this case), the base should be stated as an average for that same period of time.

Example 13-10 Computing Accounts Receivable Turnover and Number of Day's Sales in Receivable

The accounts receivable turnover ratios for both years for Henderson follow. (We will assume that all sales are on account.)

2012	2011
$\dfrac{\$24,000,000}{(\$5,500,000 + \$4,500,000/2)} = 4.8\,\text{times}$	$\dfrac{\$20,000,000}{(\$4,500,000 + \$5,000,000)/2} = 4.2\,\text{times}$

Accounts turned over, on average, 4.2 times in 2011, compared with 4.8 times in 2012. What does this mean about the average length of time that an account was outstanding? Another way to measure efficiency in the collection process is to calculate the **number of days' sales in receivables**:

Number of days' sales in receivables
A measure of the average age of accounts receivable.

$$\text{Number of Days' Sales in Receivables} = \frac{\text{Number of Days in the Period}}{\text{Accounts Receivable Turnover}}$$

For simplicity, we assume 360 days in a year:

2012	2011
$\dfrac{360\ \text{days}}{4.8\ \text{times}} = 75\ \text{days}$	$\dfrac{360\ \text{days}}{4.2\ \text{times}} = 86\ \text{days}$

The average number of days an account is outstanding, or the average collection period, is 75 days in 2012, down from 86 days in 2011. Is this acceptable? The answer depends on the company's credit policy. If Henderson's normal credit terms require payment within 60 days, further investigation is needed even though the number of days outstanding has decreased from the previous year.

© Cengage Learning 2013

Management needs to be concerned with both the collectibility of an account as it ages and the cost of funds tied up in receivables. For example, a $1 million average receivable balance that requires an additional month to collect suggests that the company is forgoing $10,000 in lost profits assuming that the money could be reinvested in the business to earn 1% per month, or 12% per year.

Inventory Analysis

Inventory turnover ratio
A measure of the number of times inventory is sold during a period.

A similar set of ratios can be calculated to analyze the efficiency in managing inventory. The **inventory turnover ratio** is as follows:

$$\text{Inventory Turnover Ratio} = \frac{\text{Cost of Goods Sold}}{\text{Average Inventory}}$$

Example 13-11 Computing Inventory Turnover and Number of Days Sales in Inventory

The inventory turnover ratio for each of the two years for Henderson is as follows:

2012	2011
$\dfrac{\$18,000,000}{(\$4,750,000 + \$2,750,000)/2} = 4.8 \text{ times}$	$\dfrac{\$14,000,000}{(\$2,750,000 + \$2,450,000)/2} = 5.4 \text{ times}$

Number of days' sales in inventory
A measure of how long it takes to sell inventory.

Henderson was slightly more efficient in 2011 in moving its inventory. The number of "turns" each year varies widely for different industries. For example, a wholesaler of perishable fruits and vegetables may turn over inventory at least 50 times per year. An airplane manufacturer, however, may turn over its inventory once or twice a year. What does the number of turns per year reveal about the average length of time it takes to sell an item of inventory? The **number of days' sales in inventory** is an alternative measure of the company's efficiency in managing inventory. It is the number of days between the date an item of inventory is purchased and the date it is sold:

$$\text{Number of Days' Sales in Inventory} = \frac{\text{Number of Days in the Period}}{\text{Inventory Turnover}}$$

The number of days' sales in inventory for Henderson is as follows:

2012	2011
$\dfrac{360 \text{ days}}{4.8 \text{ times}} = 75 \text{ days}$	$\dfrac{360 \text{ days}}{5.4 \text{ times}} = 67 \text{ days}$

© Cengage Learning 2013

This measure can reveal a great deal about inventory management. An unusually low turnover (and, of course, a high number of days in inventory) may signal a large amount of obsolete inventory or problems in the sales department, or it may indicate that the company is pricing its products too high and the market is reacting by reducing demand for the company's products.

Cash Operating Cycle

Cash-to-cash operating cycle
The length of time from the purchase of inventory to the collection of any receivable from the sale.

The **cash-to-cash operating cycle** is the length of time between the purchase of merchandise for sale, assuming a retailer or wholesaler, and the eventual collection of the cash from the sale. One method to approximate the number of days in a company's operating cycle involves combining two measures:

Cash-to-Cash Operating Cycle = Number of Days' Sales in Inventory
                               + Number of Days' Sales in Receivables

Example 13-12 Computing the Cash-to-Cash Operating Cycle

Henderson's operating cycles for 2012 and 2011 are as follows:

2012	2011
75 days + 75 days = 150 days	67 days + 86 days = 153 days

The average length of time between the purchase of inventory and the collection of cash from sale of the inventory was 150 days in 2012. Note that although the length of the operating cycle did not change significantly from 2011 to 2012, the composition did change: the increase in the average number of days in inventory was offset by the decrease in the average number of days in receivables.

© Cengage Learning 2013

L04 Compute and use various ratios to assess liquidity.

- Liquidity is a measure of the relative ease with which assets can be converted to cash. Several ratios may be used to assess different aspects of liquidity, including:
  - Current, acid-test (quick), cash from operations to current liabilities, accounts receivable turnover, and inventory turnover ratios.
  - The cash-to-cash operating cycle measures the average length of time between the purchase of inventory and collection of cash after a sale takes place.

POD REVIEW 13.4

QUESTIONS **Answers to these questions are on the last page of the chapter.**

1. Which of the following current assets are excluded from the numerator used to compute the acid-test or quick ratio?

   a. inventories
   b. accounts receivable
   c. prepaid assets
   d. Both inventories and prepaid assets are excluded.

2. What numerators are used in the computation of the accounts receivable turnover ratio and the inventory turnover ratio, respectively?

   a. net credit sales and cost of goods sold
   b. cost of goods sold and net credit sales
   c. net credit sales for both
   d. cost of goods sold for both

© Cengage Learning 2013

Solvency Analysis

OVERVIEW: Various ratios can be used to analyze a company's solvency, that is, the ability to remain in business over the long term.

L05 Compute and use various ratios to assess solvency.

Solvency refers to a company's ability to remain in business over the long term. It is related to liquidity but differs in time. Although liquidity relates to the firm's ability to pay next year's debts as they come due, solvency concerns the ability of the firm to stay financially healthy over the period of time that existing debt (short- and long-term) is outstanding.

Solvency
The ability of a company to remain in business over the long term.

Debt-to-Equity Ratio

Capital structure is the focal point in solvency analysis. This refers to the composition of the right side of the balance sheet and the mix between debt and stockholders' equity. The composition of debt and equity in the capital structure is an important determinant of the cost of capital to a company. We will have more to say later about the effects that the mix of debt and equity has on profitability. For now, consider the **debt-to-equity ratio**:

Debt-to-equity ratio
The ratio of total liabilities to total stockholders' equity.

$$\text{Debt-to-Equity Ratio} = \frac{\text{Total Liabilities}}{\text{Total Stockholders' Equity}}$$

Example 13-13 Computing the Debt-to-Equity Ratio

Henderson's debt-to-equity ratio at each year-end is as follows:

December 31	
2012	**2011**
$\dfrac{\$7,950,000}{\$8,920,000} = 0.89 \text{ to } 1$	$\dfrac{\$6,300,000}{\$7,500,000} = 0.84 \text{ to } 1$

The 2012 ratio indicates that for every $1.00 of capital that stockholders provided, creditors provided $0.89. Variations of the debt-to-equity ratio are sometimes used to assess solvency. For example, an analyst might calculate the ratio of total liabilities to the sum of total liabilities and stockholders' equity. This results in a ratio that differs from the debt-to-equity ratio, but the objective of the measure is the same—to determine the degree to which the company relies on outsiders for funds.

What is an acceptable ratio of debt to equity? As with all ratios, the answer depends on the company, the industry, and many other factors. **You should not assume that a lower debt-to-equity ratio is better.** Certainly, taking on additional debt is risky. Many companies are able to benefit from borrowing money, however, by putting the cash raised to good use in their businesses. Later in the chapter, we discuss the concept of leverage: using borrowed money to benefit the company and its stockholders.

The recent recession has focused more attention on the debt-to-equity ratio. Investors and creditors are increasingly wary of companies that have taken on large amounts of debt relative to the amounts of capital provided by owners.

Times Interest Earned

Times interest earned ratio
An income statement measure of the ability of a company to meet its interest payments.

The debt-to-equity ratio is a measure of the company's overall long-term financial health. Management must also be aware of its ability to meet current interest payments to creditors. The **times interest earned ratio** indicates the company's ability to meet the current year's interest payments out of the current year's earnings:

$$\text{Times Interest Earned Ratio} = \frac{\text{Net Income} + \text{Interest Expense} + \text{Income Tax Expense}}{\text{Interest Expense}}$$

Both interest expense and income tax expense are added back to net income in the numerator because interest is a deduction in arriving at the amount of income subject to tax. If a company had just enough income to cover the payment of interest, tax expense would be zero. As far as lenders are concerned, the greater the interest coverage, the better. Bankers often place more importance on the times interest earned ratio than on earnings per share.

Example 13-14 Computing the Times Interest Earned Ratio

The times interest earned ratio for Henderson for 2012 and 2011 can be computed as follows:

2012	**2011**
$\dfrac{\$1,720,000 + \$140,000 + \$1,140,000}{\$140,000}$	$\dfrac{\$2,300,000 + \$160,000 + \$1,540,000}{\$160,000}$
$= 21.4 \text{ to } 1$	$= 25.0 \text{ to } 1$

The ratios for both years indicate that Henderson's earnings are more than ample to cover its interest.

Debt Service Coverage

Two problems exist with the times interest earned ratio as a measure of the ability to pay creditors. First, the denominator of the fraction considers only *interest*. Management must also be concerned with the *principal* amount of loans maturing in the next year. The second problem deals with the difference between the cash and accrual bases of accounting. The numerator of the times interest earned ratio is not a measure of the *cash* available to repay loans. Keep in mind the various noncash adjustments, such as depreciation, that enter into the determination of net income. Also, recall that the denominator of the times interest earned ratio is a measure of interest expense, not interest payments. The **debt service coverage ratio** is a measure of the amount of cash that is generated from operating activities during the year and that is available to repay interest due and any maturing principal amounts (i.e., the amount available to "service" the debt):

$$\text{Debt Service Coverage Ratio} = \frac{\text{Cash Flow from Operations Before Interest and Tax Payments}}{\text{Interest and Principal Payments}}$$

Debt service coverage ratio
A statement of cash flows measure of the ability of a company to meet its interest and principal payments.

Some analysts use an alternative measure in the numerator of this ratio called EBITDA, which stands for earnings before interest, taxes, depreciation, and amortization. Whether EBITDA is a good substitute for cash flow from operations before interest and tax payments depends on whether there were significant changes in current assets and current liabilities during the period. If significant changes in these accounts occurred during the period, cash flow from operations before interest and tax payments is a better measure of a company's ability to cover interest and debt payments.

Example 13-15 Computing the Debt Service Coverage Ratio

Cash flow from operations is available on the comparative statement of cash flows in Example 13-3. As was the case with the times interest earned ratio, the net cash provided by operating activities is adjusted to reflect the amount available before paying interest and taxes.

The income statement in Example 13-2 reflects the *expense* for interest and taxes each year. The amounts of interest and taxes paid each year are shown as supplemental information at the bottom of the statement of cash flows in Example 13-3 and are relevant in computing the debt service coverage ratio.

Any principal payments must be included with interest paid in the denominator of the debt service coverage ratio. According to the Financing Activities section of the statements of cash flows in Example 13-3, Henderson repaid $200,000 each year on the notes payable and $100,000 each year on the bonds. The debt service coverage ratios for the two years are calculated as follows:

2012

$$\frac{\$1{,}070{,}000 + \$140{,}000 + \$940{,}000}{\$140{,}000 + \$200{,}000 + \$100{,}000} = 4.89 \text{ times}$$

2011

$$\frac{\$2{,}950{,}000 + \$160{,}000 + \$1{,}440{,}000}{\$160{,}000 + \$200{,}000 + \$100{,}000} = 9.89 \text{ times}$$

Like Henderson's times interest earned ratio, its debt service coverage ratio decreased during 2012. According to the calculations, however, Henderson still generated almost $5 of cash from operations during 2012 to "cover" every $1 of required interest and principal payments.

© Cengage Learning 2013

Cash Flow from Operations to Capital Expenditures Ratio

One final measure is useful in assessing the solvency of a business. The **cash flow from operations to capital expenditures ratio** measures a company's ability to use operations to finance its acquisitions of productive assets. To the extent that a company is able to do this, it should rely less on external financing or additional contributions

Cash flow from operations to capital expenditures ratio
A measure of the ability of a company to finance long-term asset acquisitions with cash from operations.

by the owners to replace and add to the existing capital base. The ratio is computed as follows:

$$\text{Cash Flow from Operations to Capital Expenditures Ratio} = \frac{\text{Cash Flow from Operations} - \text{Total Dividends Paid}}{\text{Cash Paid for Acquisitions}}$$

Note that the numerator of the ratio measures the cash flow *after* all dividend payments are met.[1]

Example 13-16 Computing the Cash Flow from Operations to Capital Expenditures Ratio

The calculation of the ratios for Henderson follows:

2012	2011
$\dfrac{\$1,070,000 - \$300,000}{\$1,500,000} = 51.3\%$	$\dfrac{\$2,950,000 - \$300,000}{\$2,000,000} = 132.5\%$

Although the amount of capital expenditures was less in 2012 than in 2011, the company generated considerably less cash from operations in 2012 to cover these acquisitions. In fact, the ratio of less than 100% in 2012 indicates that Henderson was not able to finance all of its capital expenditures from operations *and* cover its dividend payments.

© Cengage Learning 2013

LO5 Compute and use various ratios to assess solvency.

- Solvency measures a company's ability to maintain its financial health over the long term. Several ratios may be used to assess different aspects of solvency, including:
  - Debt-to-equity, times interest earned, debt service coverage, and cash flow from operations to capital expenditures ratios.

POD REVIEW 13.5

QUESTIONS   **Answers to these questions are on the last page of the chapter.**

1. Which of the following measures of solvency focuses specifically on the extent to which a company relies on outsiders for funds?

   a. debt-to-equity ratio
   b. times interest earned ratio
   c. debt service coverage ratio
   d. cash flow from operations to capital expenditures ratio

2. Solvency is concerned with the ability of a company to

   a. pay next year's debts as they come due.
   b. remain in business over the long term.
   c. provide a reasonable return to stockholders.
   d. do none of the above.

© Cengage Learning 2013

Profitability Analysis

LO6 Compute and use various ratios to assess profitability.

OVERVIEW: Various ratios can be used to measure a company's profitability, that is, how well management is using resources to earn a return on the funds provided by creditors and stockholders.

Liquidity analysis and solvency analysis deal with management's ability to repay short- and long-term creditors. Creditors are concerned with a company's profitability because

---

[1] Dividends paid are reported on the statement of cash flows in the Financing Activities section. The amount *paid* should be used for this calculation rather than the amount declared, which appears on the statement of retained earnings.

a profitable company is more likely to be able to make principal and interest payments. Of course, stockholders care about a company's profitability because it affects the market price of the stock and the ability of the company to pay dividends. Various measures of **profitability** indicate how well management is using the resources at its disposal to earn a return on the funds invested by various groups. Two frequently used profitability measures, the gross profit ratio and the profit margin ratio, were discussed earlier in the chapter. We now turn to other measures of profitability.

Profitability
How well management is using company resources to earn a return on the funds invested by various groups.

Rate of Return on Assets

Before computing the rate of return, we must answer an important question: *return to whom?* **Every return ratio is a measure of the relationship between the income earned by the company and the investment made in the company by various groups.** The broadest rate of return ratio is the **return on assets ratio** because it considers the investment made by *all* providers of capital, from short-term creditors to bondholders to stockholders. Therefore, the denominator, or base, for the return on assets ratio is average total liabilities and stockholders' equity—which, of course, is the same as average total assets.

Return on assets ratio
A measure of a company's success in earning a return for all providers of capital.

The numerator of a return ratio will be some measure of the company's income for the period. The income selected for the numerator must match the investment or base in the denominator. For example, if average total assets is the base in the denominator, it is necessary to use an income number that is applicable to all providers of capital.

Therefore, the income number used in the rate of return on assets is income *after* interest expense is added back. This adjustment considers creditors as one of the groups that has provided funds to the company. In other words, we want the amount of income before creditors or stockholders have been given any distributions (i.e., interest to creditors or dividends to stockholders). Interest expense must be added back on a net-of-tax basis. Because net income is on an after-tax basis, for consistency purposes, interest must also be placed on a net, or after-tax, basis.

The return on assets ratio is as follows:

$$\text{Return on Assets Ratio} = \frac{\text{Net Income} + \text{Interest Expense, Net of Tax}}{\text{Average Total Assets}}$$

Example 13-17 Computing the Return on Assets Ratio

If we assume a 40% tax rate (which is the actual ratio of income tax expense to income before tax for Henderson), its return on assets ratios will be as follows:

		2012		2011
Net income		$ 1,720,000		$ 2,300,000
Add back:				
Interest expense	$ 140,000		$ 160,000	
× (1 − tax rate)	× 0.6	84,000	× 0.6	96,000
Numerator		$ 1,804,000		$ 2,396,000
Assets, beginning of year		$13,800,000		$12,000,000
Assets, end of year		16,870,000		13,800,000
Total		$30,670,000		$25,800,000
Denominator:				
Average total assets (total above divided by 2)		$15,335,000		$12,900,000
		$ 1,804,000		$ 2,396,000
		$15,335,000		$12,900,000
Return on assets ratio		= 11.76%		= 18.57%

Components of Return on Assets

Return on sales ratio
A variation of the profit margin ratio; measures earnings before interest expense.

What caused Henderson's return on assets to decrease so dramatically from the previous year? The answer can be found by considering the two components that make up the return on assets ratio. The first of these components is the **return on sales ratio** and is calculated as follows:

$$\text{Return on Sales Ratio} = \frac{\text{Net Income} + \text{Interest Expense, Net of Tax}}{\text{Net Sales}}$$

Example 13-18 Computing the Return on Sales Ratio

The return on sales ratios for Henderson for the two years are as follows:

2012	2011
$\dfrac{\$1,720,000 + \$84,000}{\$24,000,000} = 7.52\%$	$\dfrac{\$2,300,000 + \$96,000}{\$20,000} = 11.98\%$

The ratio for 2012 indicates that for every $1.00 of sales, the company was able to earn a profit (before the payment of interest) of between $0.07 and $0.08, as compared with a return of almost $0.12 on the dollar in 2011.

© Cengage Learning 2013

Asset turnover ratio
The relationship between net sales and average total assets.

The other component of the rate of return on assets is the **asset turnover ratio**. The ratio is similar to both the inventory turnover and the accounts receivable turnover ratios because it is a measure of the relationship between some activity (net sales in this case) and some investment base (average total assets):

$$\text{Asset Turnover Ratio} = \frac{\text{Net Sales}}{\text{Average Total Assets}}$$

Example 13-19 Computing the Asset Turnover Ratio

For Henderson, the ratio for each of the two years follows:

2012	2011
$\dfrac{\$24,000,000}{\$15,335,000} = 1.57\text{ times}$	$\dfrac{\$20,000,000}{\$12,900,000} = 1.55\text{ times}$

© Cengage Learning 2013

The explanation for the decrease in Henderson's return on assets lies in the drop in the return on sales since the asset turnover ratio was almost the same. To summarize, note the relationship among the three ratios:

$$\text{Return on Assets} = \text{Return on Sales} \times \text{Asset Turnover}$$

For 2012, Henderson's return on assets consists of the following:

$$\frac{\$1,804,000}{\$24,000,000} \times \frac{\$24,000,000}{\$15,335,000} = 7.52\% \times 1.57 = 11.8\%$$

Finally, notice that net sales cancels out of both ratios, leaving the net income adjusted for interest divided by average assets as the return on assets ratio.

Return on Common Stockholders' Equity

Reasoning similar to that used to calculate return on assets can be used to calculate the return on capital provided by the common stockholder. Because we are interested in the return to the common stockholder, our base is no longer average total assets, but average common stockholders' equity. Similarly, the appropriate income figure for the numerator is net income less preferred dividends because we are interested in the return to the common stockholder after all claims have been settled. Income taxes and interest expense have already been deducted in arriving at net income, but preferred dividends have not been because dividends are a distribution of profits, not an expense.

The **return on common stockholders' equity ratio** is computed as follows:

$$\text{Return on Common Stockholders' Equity Ratio} = \frac{\text{Net Income} - \text{Preferred Dividends}}{\text{Average Common Stockholders' Equity}}$$

Return on common stockholders' equity ratio
A measure of a company's success in earning a return for the common stockholders.

Example 13-20 Computing the Return on Common Stockholders' Equity

The average common stockholders' equity for Henderson is calculated using information from Example 13-1 and Exhibit 13-2:

	Account Balances at December 31		
	2012	**2011**	**2010**
Common stock, $1 par	$1,000,000	$1,000,000	$1,000,000
Retained earnings	7,420,000	6,000,000	4,000,000
Total common equity	$8,420,000	$7,000,000	$5,000,000

Average common equity:
  2011: ($7,000,000 + $5,000,000)/2 = $6,000,000
  2012: ($8,420,000 + $7,000,000)/2 = $7,710,000

Net income less preferred dividends—or "income available to common" as it is called—can be found by referring to net income on the income statement and to preferred dividends on the statement of retained earnings. The combined statement of income and retained earnings in Example 13-2 gives the relevant amounts for the numerator. Henderson's return on equity for the two years is as follows:

2012	**2011**
$\dfrac{\$1,720,000 - \$50,000}{\$7,710,000} = 21.66\%$	$\dfrac{\$2,300,000 - \$50,000}{\$6,000,000} = 37.50\%$

Even though Henderson's return on stockholders' equity ratio decreased significantly from one year to the next, most stockholders would be very happy to achieve these returns on their money. Very few investments offer more than 10% return unless substantial risk is involved.

© Cengage Learning 2013

Return on Assets, Return on Equity, and Leverage

The return on assets for 2012 was 11.8%. But the return to the common stockholders was much higher: 21.7%. How do you explain this phenomenon? Why are the stockholders receiving a higher return on their money than all of the providers of money combined are getting? A partial answer to those questions can be found by reviewing the cost to Henderson of the various sources of capital.

Example 13-1 indicates that notes, bonds, and preferred stock are the primary sources of capital other than common stock. (Accounts payable and taxes payable are *not* included because they represent interest-free loans to the company from suppliers and the government.) These sources and the average amount of each outstanding during 2012 follow:

	Account Balances at December 31		
	2012	**2011**	**Average**
Notes payable	$ 600,000	$ 800,000	$ 700,000
Current portion of bonds	100,000	100,000	100,000
Bonds payable—Long term	700,000	800,000	750,000
Total liabilities	$1,400,000	$1,700,000	$1,550,000
Preferred stock	$ 500,000	$ 500,000	$ 500,000

What was the cost to Henderson of each of these sources? The cost of the money provided by the preferred stockholders is clearly the amount of dividends of $50,000. The cost as a percentage is $50,000/$500,000, or 10%. The average cost of the borrowed money can be approximated by dividing the 2012 interest expense of $140,000 by the average of the notes payable and bonds payable of $1,550,000. The result is an average cost of these two sources of $140,000/$1,550,000, or approximately 9%.

The concept of **leverage** refers to the practice of using borrowed funds and amounts received from preferred stockholders in an attempt to earn an overall return that is higher than the cost of these funds. Recall the rate of return on assets for 2012: 11.8%. Because this return is on an after-tax basis, it is necessary for comparative purposes to convert the average cost of borrowed funds to an after-tax basis. Although we computed an average cost for borrowed money of 9%, the actual cost of the borrowed money is 5.4% [9% × (100% − 40%)] after taxes. Because dividends are *not* tax-deductible, the cost of the money provided by preferred stockholders is 10%, as calculated earlier.

Has Henderson successfully employed favorable leverage? That is, has it been able to earn an overall rate of return on assets that is higher than the amounts that it must pay creditors and preferred stockholders? Henderson has been successful in using outside money: neither of the sources must be paid a rate in excess of the 11.8% overall rate on assets used. Henderson has also been able to borrow some amounts on an interest-free basis. As mentioned earlier, the accounts payable and taxes payable represent interest-free loans from suppliers and the government, although the loans are typically for a short period of time, such as 30 days.

In summary, the excess of the 21.7% return on equity over the 11.8% return on assets indicates that Henderson's management has been successful in employing leverage; that is, there is favorable leverage. Is it possible to be unsuccessful in this pursuit; that is, can there be unfavorable leverage? If the company must pay more for the amounts provided by creditors and preferred stockholders than it can earn overall, as indicated by the return on assets, there will, in fact, be unfavorable leverage. This may occur when interest requirements are high and net income is low. A company would likely have a high debt-to-equity ratio as well when there is unfavorable leverage.

leverage
The use of borrowed funds and amounts contributed by preferred stockholders to earn an overall return higher than the cost of these funds.

Earnings per Share

Earnings per share (EPS)
A company's bottom line stated on a per-share basis.

Earnings per share (EPS) is one of the most quoted statistics for publicly traded companies. Stockholders and potential investors want to know what their share of profits is, not just the total dollar amount. Presentation of profits on a per-share basis also allows the stockholder to relate earnings to what he or she paid for a share of stock or to the current trading price of a share of stock.

In simple situations, earnings per share is calculated as follows:

$$\text{Earnings per Share} = \frac{\text{Net Income} - \text{Preferred Dividends}}{\text{Weighted Average Number of Common Shares Outstanding}}$$

Example 13-21 Computing Earnings per Share

Because Henderson had 1,000,000 shares of common stock outstanding throughout both 2011 and 2012, its EPS for each of the two years is as follows:

2012	2011
$\frac{\$1,720,000 - \$50,000}{1,000,000 \text{ shares}} = \$1.67$ per share	$\frac{\$2,300,000 - \$50,000}{1,000,000 \text{ shares}} = \$2.25$ per share

© Cengage Learning 2013

A number of complications can arise in the computation of EPS, and the calculations can become exceedingly complex for a company with many different types of securities in its capital structure. These complications are beyond the scope of this book and are discussed in more advanced accounting courses.

Price/Earnings Ratio

Earnings per share is an important ratio for an investor because of its relationship to dividends and market price. Stockholders hope to earn a return by receiving periodic dividends or eventually selling the stock for more than they paid for it or both. Although earnings are related to dividends and market price, the latter two are of primary interest to the stockholder.

Mentioned earlier was the desire of investors to relate the earnings of the company to the market price of the stock. Now that we have stated Henderson's earnings on a per-share basis, we can calculate the **price/earnings (P/E) ratio**. What market price is relevant? Should we use the market price that the investor paid for a share of stock, or should we use the current market price? Because earnings are based on the most recent evaluation of the company for accounting purposes, it seems logical to use current market price, which is based on the stock market's current assessment of the company. Therefore, the ratio is computed as follows:

$$\text{Price/Earnings Ratio} = \frac{\text{Current Market Price}}{\text{Earnings per Share}}$$

Price/earnings (P/E) ratio
The relationship between a company's performance according to the income statement and its performance in the stock market.

Example 13-22 Computing the Price/Earnings Ratio

Assume that the current market price for Henderson's common stock is $15 per share at the end of 2012 and $18 per share at the end of 2011. The price/earnings ratio for each of the two years is as follows:

2012	2011
$\dfrac{\$\,15 \text{ per share}}{\$\,1.67 \text{ per share}} = 9 \text{ to } 1$	$\dfrac{\$18 \text{ per share}}{\$2.25 \text{ per share}} = 8 \text{ to } 1$

© Cengage Learning 2013

What is normal for a P/E ratio? As is the case for all other ratios, it is difficult to generalize as to what is good or bad. The P/E ratio compares the stock market's assessment of a company's performance with the company's success as reflected on the income statement. A relatively high P/E ratio may indicate that a stock is overpriced by the market; a P/E ratio that is relatively low could indicate that a stock is underpriced.

The P/E ratio is often thought to indicate the "quality" of a company's earnings. For example, assume that two companies have identical EPS ratios of $2 per share. Why should investors be willing to pay $20 per share (or 10 times earnings) for the stock of one company but only $14 per share (or 7 times earnings) for the stock of the other company? First, we must realize that many factors in addition to the reported earnings of the company affect market prices. General economic conditions, the outlook for the particular industry, and pending lawsuits are just three factors that can affect the trading price of a company's stock. The difference in P/E ratios for the two companies may reflect the market's assessment of the accounting practices of the companies, however. Assume that the company with a market price of $20 per share uses LIFO in valuing inventory and that the company trading at $14 per share uses FIFO. The difference in prices may indicate that investors believe that even though the companies have the same EPS, the LIFO company is "better off" because it will have a lower amount of taxes to pay. (Recall that in a period of inflation, the use of LIFO results in more cost of goods sold, less income, and therefore lower income taxes.) Finally, aside from the way investors view the accounting practices of different companies, also consider the fact that, to a large extent, earnings reflect the use of historical costs, as opposed to fair market values, in assigning values to assets. Investors must consider the extent to which a company's assets are worth more than what was paid for them.

Dividend Ratios

Dividend payout ratio
The percentage of earnings paid out as dividends.

Two ratios are used to evaluate a company's dividend policies: the *dividend payout ratio* and the *dividend yield ratio*. The **dividend payout ratio** is the ratio of the common dividends per share to the earnings per share:

$$\text{Dividend Payout Ratio} = \frac{\text{Common Dividends per Share}}{\text{Earnings per Share}}$$

Example 13-23 Computing the Dividend Payout Ratio

Example 13-2 indicates that Henderson paid $250,000 in common dividends each year, or with 1 million shares outstanding, $0.25 per share. The two payout ratios are as follows:

2012	2011
$\dfrac{\$0.25}{\$1.67} = 15.0\%$	$\dfrac{\$0.25}{\$2.25} = 11.1\%$

Henderson's management was faced with an important financial policy decision in 2012. Should the company maintain the same dividend of $0.25 per share even though EPS dropped significantly? Many companies prefer to maintain a level dividend pattern, hoping that a drop in earnings is only temporary.

© Cengage Learning 2013

Dividend yield ratio
The relationship between dividends and the market price of a company's stock.

The second dividend ratio of interest to stockholders is the **dividend yield ratio**. It is the ratio of common dividends per share to the market price per share.

$$\text{Dividend Yield Ratio} = \frac{\text{Common Dividends per Share}}{\text{Market Price per Share}}$$

Example 13-24 Computing the Dividend Yield Ratio

The yield to Henderson's stockholders would be calculated as follows:

2012	2011
$\dfrac{\$0.25}{\$15} = 1.7\%$	$\dfrac{\$0.25}{\$18} = 1.4\%$

As shown, Henderson common stock does not provide a high yield to its investors. The relationship between the dividends and the market price indicates that investors buy the stock for reasons other than the periodic dividend return.

© Cengage Learning 2013

The dividend yield is very important to investors who depend on dividend checks to pay their living expenses. Utility stocks are popular among retirees because these shares have dividend yields as high as 5%. That is considered a good investment with relatively low risk and some opportunity for gains in the stock price. On the other hand, investors who want to put money into growing companies are willing to forego dividends if it means the potential for greater price appreciation.

Summary of Selected Financial Ratios

We have completed our review of the various ratios used to assess a company's liquidity, solvency, and profitability. For ease of reference, Exhibit 13-3 summarizes the ratios discussed in this chapter. Keep in mind that this list is not all-inclusive and that certain ratios used by analysts and others may be specific to a particular industry or type of business.

EXHIBIT 13-3 Summary of Selected Financial Ratios

Liquidity Analysis

Working capital — Current Assets − Current Liabilities

Current ratio — $\dfrac{\text{Current Assets}}{\text{Current Liabilities}}$

Acid-test ratio (quick ratio) — $\dfrac{\text{Cash} + \text{Marketable Securities} + \text{Current Receivables}}{\text{Current Liabilities}}$

Cash flow from operations to current liabilities ratio — $\dfrac{\text{Net Cash Provided by Operating Activities}}{\text{Average Current Liabilities}}$

Accounts receivable turnover ratio — $\dfrac{\text{Net Credit Sales}}{\text{Average Accounts Receivable}}$

Number of days' sales in receivables — $\dfrac{\text{Number of Days in the Period}}{\text{Accounts Receivable Turnover}}$

Inventory turnover ratio — $\dfrac{\text{Cost of Goods Sold}}{\text{Average Inventory}}$

Number of days' sales in inventory — $\dfrac{\text{Number of Days in the Period}}{\text{Inventory Turnover}}$

Cash-to-cash operating cycle — Number of Days' Sales in Inventory + Number of Days' Sales in Receivables

Solvency Analysis

Debt-to-equity ratio — $\dfrac{\text{Total Liabilities}}{\text{Total Stockholders' Equity}}$

Times interest earned ratio — $\dfrac{\text{Net Income} + \text{Interest Expense} + \text{Income Tax Expense}}{\text{Interest Expense}}$

Debt service coverage ratio — $\dfrac{\text{Cash Flow from Operations before Interest and Tax Payments}}{\text{Interest and Principal Payments}}$

Cash flow from operations to capital expenditures ratio — $\dfrac{\text{Cash Flow from Operations} - \text{Total Dividends Paid}}{\text{Cash Paid for Acquisitions}}$

Profitability Analysis

Gross profit ratio — $\dfrac{\text{Gross Profit}}{\text{Net Sales}}$

Profit margin ratio — $\dfrac{\text{Net Income}}{\text{Net Sales}}$

Return on assets ratio — $\dfrac{\text{Net Income} + \text{Interest Expense, Net of Tax}}{\text{Average Total Assets}}$

Return on sales ratio — $\dfrac{\text{Net Income} + \text{Interest Expense, Net of Tax}}{\text{Net Sales}}$

Asset turnover ratio — $\dfrac{\text{Net Sales}}{\text{Average Total Assets}}$

Return on common stockholders' equity ratio — $\dfrac{\text{Net Income} - \text{Preferred Dividends}}{\text{Average Common Stockholders' Equity}}$

Earnings per share — $\dfrac{\text{Net Income} - \text{Preferred Dividends}}{\text{Weighted Average Number of Common Shares Outstanding}}$

Price/earnings ratio — $\dfrac{\text{Current Market Price}}{\text{Earnings per Share}}$

Dividend payout ratio — $\dfrac{\text{Common Dividends per Share}}{\text{Earnings per Share}}$

Dividend yield ratio — $\dfrac{\text{Common Dividends per Share}}{\text{Market Price per Share}}$

LOOKING AHEAD

Earlier chapters have described the efforts of the FASB and IASB to usher in a new era in financial statement presentation. If statements in the future take on a different look, what does this mean for statement analysis? One of the principles guiding the efforts of the two groups is cohesiveness, that is, the financial statements should complement each other. For example, the statement of cash flows currently classifies activities in three categories: operating, investing, and financing. To complement it, the balance sheet of the future would classify assets and liabilities into two major categories: business and financing. Within the business section, assets and liabilities would be further divided into operating and investing categories. Assets and liabilities within each category would still be identified as either short or long term. So, the information needed to determine a company's current ratio would still be available, but it might require more effort than is currently required.

Financial statements of the future are likely to spawn new forms of analysis. Vertical and horizontal analyses will continue, but with different line items being compared on balance sheets and income statements. New ratios are likely to be devised to take advantage of the improvements in statement presentation. All of these changes present opportunities for new professionals willing to "look ahead" in serving the needs of the investing public.

Source: "Financial Statement Presentation," Staff Draft of Exposure Draft, July 2010, International Accounting Standards Board and Financial Accounting Standards Board.

Tetra Images/Getty Images

LO6 Compute and use various ratios to assess profitability.

- Profitability concerns the ability of management to use a company's resources to earn a return on funds invested. Measures of profitability include:

  - Return on assets, return on common stockholders' equity, earnings per share, price/earnings, dividend payout, and dividend yield ratios.

POD REVIEW 13.6

QUESTIONS   Answers to these questions are on the last page of the chapter.

1. The multiplication of which two ratios yields the return on assets ratio?

   a. return on sales and asset turnover
   b. profit margin and return on sales
   c. profit margin and asset turnover
   d. return on common stockholders' equity and asset turnover

2. Which of the following is an indication that a company has successfully employed leverage?

   a. The return on assets exceeds the return on common stockholders' equity.
   b. The return on common stockholders' equity exceeds the return on assets.
   c. The return on common stockholders' equity exceeds the price/earnings ratio.
   d. None of the above

APPENDIX

Accounting Tools: Reporting and Analyzing Other Income Statement Items

OVERVIEW: In any one year, a company might report either or both discontinued operations and extraordinary items on the income statement.

LO7 Explain how to report on and analyze other income statement items.

Not all companies have income statements that are as easy to understand and interpret as GameStop's statement. Some companies report either or both discontinued operations and extraordinary items on their income statements. Although the nature of these two items is very distinct, the two do share some common characteristics. First, they are all reported near the end of the income statement, after income from continuing operations. Second, they are reported separately on the income statement to call the reader's attention to their unique nature and to the fact that any additions to or deductions from income they give rise to may not necessarily reoccur in future periods. Finally, each of these items is shown net of their tax effects. This means that any additional taxes due because of them or any tax benefits from them are deducted from the items themselves. Following is a brief description of each item.

Discontinued Operations

When a company decides to sell or otherwise dispose of one of its operations, it must report separately on that division or segment of the business on its income statement. This includes any gain or loss from the disposal of the business as well as any net income or loss from operating the business until the disposal date. Because the discontinued segment of the business will not be part of the company's future operations, **discontinued operations** are disclosed separately on the income statement. Analysts and other users would normally consider only income from continuing operations in making decisions.

Discontinued operations
A line item on the income statement to reflect any gains or losses from the disposal of a segment of the business as well as any net income or loss from operating that segment.

Extraordinary Items

According to accounting standards, certain events that give rise to gains or losses are deemed to be extraordinary and are thus disclosed separately on the income statement. To qualify for extraordinary treatment, the gain or loss must be due to an event that is both unusual in nature and infrequent in occurrence.[2] Under current accounting standards, an **extraordinary item** is relatively rare, for example, when a natural catastrophe such as a tornado destroys a plant in an area not known for tornadoes. As is the case for discontinued operations, analysts and others often ignore the amount of such gains and losses since they are aware that these items are not likely to reoccur in the future.

Extraordinary item
A line item on the income statement to reflect any gains or losses that arise from an event that is both unusual in nature and infrequent in occurrence.

---

[2] *Income Statement Extraordinary and Unusual Items*, ASC Topic 225-20 (formerly *Reporting the Results of Operations*, APB Opinion No. 30).

LO7 Explain how to report on and analyze other income statement items.

- Two components of the income statement are reported after income from operations or are reported separately because of their unique nature. These items include:
  - Discontinued operations and extraordinary items.

POD REVIEW 13.7

QUESTIONS   Answers to these questions are on the last page of the chapter.

1. Which of the following items are reported on the income statement net of their tax effects?
   a. discontinued operations
   b. extraordinary items
   c. Neither of the above are reported net of their tax effects.
   d. Both (a) and (b) are reported net of their tax effects.

2. What conditions are necessary for a gain or loss to qualify for extraordinary treatment on the income statement?
   a. It must be unusual in nature and never have occurred before.
   b. It must be unusual in nature and infrequent in occurrence.
   c. It must be nonoperating in nature and infrequent in occurrence.
   d. Extraordinary gains and losses are not reported on the income statement.

KEY TERMS QUIZ

Because of the number of terms introduced in this chapter, there are two quizzes on key terms. For each quiz, read each definition below and write the number of that definition in the blank beside the appropriate term. The quiz solutions appear at the end of the chapter.

Quiz 1:

_____ Horizontal analysis
_____ Vertical analysis
_____ Gross profit ratio
_____ Profit margin ratio
_____ Liquidity
_____ Working capital
_____ Current ratio
_____ Acid-test or quick ratio
_____ Cash flow from operations to current liabilities ratio

_____ Accounts receivable turnover ratio
_____ Number of days' sales in receivables
_____ Inventory turnover ratio
_____ Number of days' sales in inventory
_____ Cash-to-cash operating cycle

1. A stricter test of liquidity than the current ratio; excludes inventory and prepayments from the numerator.
2. Current assets minus current liabilities.
3. The ratio of current assets to current liabilities.
4. A measure of the average age of accounts receivable.
5. A measure of the ability to pay current debts from operating cash flows.
6. A measure of the number of times accounts receivable are collected in a period.
7. A measure of how long it takes to sell inventory.
8. The length of time from the purchase of inventory to the collection of any receivable from the sale.
9. A measure of the number of times inventory is sold during a period.
10. Gross profit to net sales.
11. A comparison of various financial statement items within a single period with the use of common-size statements.
12. Net income to net sales.
13. The nearness to cash of the assets and liabilities.
14. A comparison of financial statement items over a period of time.

Quiz 2:

_____ Solvency	_____ Return on common stockholders'
_____ Debt-to-equity ratio	equity ratio
_____ Times interest earned ratio	_____ Leverage
_____ Debt service coverage ratio	_____ Earnings per share (EPS)
_____ Cash flow from operations to	_____ Price/earnings (P/E) ratio
capital expenditures ratio	_____ Dividend payout ratio
_____ Profitability	_____ Dividend yield ratio
_____ Return on assets ratio	_____ Discontinued operations
_____ Return on sales ratio	(Appendix)
_____ Asset turnover ratio	_____ Extraordinary item (Appendix)

1. A measure of a company's success in earning a return for the common stockholders.
2. The relationship between a company's performance according to the income statement and its performance in the stock market.
3. The ability of a company to remain in business over the long term.
4. A variation of the profit margin ratio; measures earnings before payments to creditors.
5. A company's bottom line stated on a per-share basis.
6. The percentage of earnings paid out as dividends.
7. The ratio of total liabilities to total stockholders' equity.
8. A measure of the ability of a company to finance long-term asset acquisitions with cash from operations.
9. A measure of a company's success in earning a return for all providers of capital.
10. The relationship between net sales and average total assets.
11. The relationship between dividends and the market price of a company's stock.
12. The use of borrowed funds and amounts contributed by preferred stockholders to earn an overall return higher than the cost of these funds.
13. An income statement measure of the ability of a company to meet its interest payments.
14. A statement of cash flows measure of the ability of a company to meet its interest and principal payments.
15. How well management is using company resources to earn a return on the funds invested by various groups.
16. A line item on the income statement to reflect any gains or losses that arise from an event that is both unusual in nature and infrequent in occurrence.
17. A line item on the income statement to reflect any gains or losses from the disposal of a segment of the business as well as any net income or loss from operating that segment.

ALTERNATE TERMS

acid-test ratio quick ratio	**number of days' sales in receivables**
horizontal analysis trend analysis	average collection period
	price/earnings ratio P/E ratio

WARMUP EXERCISES

Warmup Exercise 13-1 Types of Ratios   LO4 • 5 • 6

Fill in the blanks to indicate whether each of the following ratios is concerned with a company's liquidity (L), its solvency (S), or its profitability (P).

_____   1.   Return on assets ratio
_____   2.   Current ratio
_____   3.   Debt-to-equity ratio

(Continued)

_____ 4. Earnings per share
_____ 5. Inventory turnover ratio
_____ 6. Gross profit ratio

Key to the Solution Review the summary of selected ratios in Exhibit 13-3.

LO4   Warmup Exercise 13-2 Accounts Receivable Turnover

Company A reported sales during the year of $1,000,000. Its average accounts receivable balance during the year was $250,000. Company B reported sales during the same year of $400,000 and had an average accounts receivable balance of $40,000.

Required

1. Compute the accounts receivable turnover for both companies.
2. What is the average length of time each company takes to collect its receivables?

Key to the Solution Review the summary of selected ratios in Exhibit 13-3.

LO6   Warmup Exercise 13-3 Earnings per Share

A company reported net income during the year of $90,000 and paid dividends of $15,000 to its common stockholders and $10,000 to its preferred stockholders. During the year, 20,000 shares of common stock were outstanding and 10,000 shares of preferred stock were outstanding.

Required

Compute earnings per share for the year.

Key to the Solution Recall that earnings per share has relevance only to the common stockholders; therefore, it is a measure of the earnings per common share outstanding, after taking into account any claims of preferred stockholders.

Solutions to Warmup Exercises

Warmup Exercise 13-1

1. P   2. L   3. S   4. P   5. L   6. P

Warmup Exercise 13-2

1. On average, Company A turns over its accounts receivable four times during the year ($1,000,000/$250,000); Company B, ten times during the year ($400,000/$40,000).
2. Assuming 360 days in a year, Company A takes, on average, 90 days to collect its accounts receivable; Company B takes, on average, 36 days.

Warmup Exercise 13-3

Earnings per share: ($90,000 – $10,000)/20,000 shares = $4 per share

REVIEW PROBLEM

On pages 707–709 are three comparative financial statements for **GameStop Corp.**, as shown in its 2010 annual report. Note that the 2010 fiscal year ends on January 29, 2011, and the 2009 fiscal year ends on January 30, 2010.

Required

1. Compute the following ratios for the years ended January 29, 2011, and January 30, 2010, or as of the end of those two years, as appropriate. Beginning balances for the year ended January 30, 2010, are not available; that is, you do not have a balance sheet as of January 31, 2009. Therefore, to be consistent, use year-end balances for both years where you would normally use average amounts for the year. To compute the return on assets ratio, you need

to find the tax rate. Use the relationship between income tax expense and earnings before income tax expense to find the rate for each year.

   a. Current ratio
   b. Quick ratio
   c. Cash flow from operations to current liabilities ratio
   d. Number of days' sales in receivables
   e. Number of days' sales in inventory
   f. Debt-to-equity ratio
   g. Times interest earned ratio
   h. Return on assets ratio
   i. Return on common stockholders' equity ratio

2. Comment on GameStop's liquidity. Has it improved or declined over the two-year period?
3. Does Game Stop appear to be solvent to you? Explain your answer.
4. Comment on GameStop's profitability. Would you buy stock in the company? Why or why not?

GameStop Corp.
Consolidated Balance Sheets

	January 29, 2011	January 30, 2010
	(In millions)	
ASSETS		
Current assets:		
Cash and cash equivalents	$ 710.8	$ 905.4
Receivables, net	65.5	64.0
Merchandise inventories, net	1,257.5	1,053.6
Deferred income taxes—current	28.8	21.2
Prepaid expenses	75.7	59.4
Other current assets	16.5	23.7
Total current assets	2,154.8	2,127.3
Property and equipment:		
Land	24.0	11.5
Buildings and leasehold improvements	577.2	523.0
Fixtures and equipment	817.8	711.5
Total property and equipment	1,419.0	1,246.0
Less accumulated depreciation and amortization	805.2	661.8
Net properly and equipment	613.8	584.2
Goodwill, net	1,996.3	1,946.5
Other intangible assets	254.6	259.9
Other noncurrent assets	44.3	37.4
Total noncurrent assets	2,909.0	2,828.0
Total assets	$5,063.8	$4,955.3
LIABILITIES AND STOCKHOLDERS' EQUITY		
Current liabilities:		
Accounts payable	$1,028.1	$ 961.7
Accrued liabilities	657.0	632.1
Taxes payable	62.7	61.9
Total current liabilities	1,747.8	1,655.7
Senior notes payable, long-term portion, net	249.0	447.3
Deferred taxes	74.9	25.5
Other long-term liabilities	96.2	103.8
Total long-term liabilities	420.1	576.6
Total liabilities	2,167.9	2,232.3

(Continued)

	January 29, 2011	January 30, 2010
	(In millions)	
Commitments and contingencies (Notes 10 and 11)		
Stockholders' equity:		
Preferred stock—authorized 5.0 shares; no shares issued or outstanding	—	—
Class A common stock—$.001 par value; authorized 300.0 shares; 146.0 and 158.7 shares outstanding, respectively	0.1	0.2
Additional paid-in-capital	928.9	1,210.5
Accumulated other comprehensive income	162.5	114.7
Retained earnings	1,805.8	1,397.8
Equity attributable to GameStop Corp. stockholders	2,897.3	2,723.2
Equity (deficit) attributable to noncontrolling interest	(1.4)	(0.2)
Total equity	2,895.9	2,723.0
Total liabilities and stockholders' equity	$5,063.8	$4,955.3

See accompanying notes to consolidated financial statements.

GameStop Corp.
Consolidated Statements of Operations

	52 Weeks Ended January 29, 2011	52 Weeks Ended January 30, 2010	52 Weeks Ended January 31, 2009
	(In millions, except per share data)		
Sales	$9,473.7	$9,078.0	$8,805.9
Cost of sales	6,936.1	6,643.3	6,535.8
Gross profit	2,537.6	2,434.7	2,270.1
Selling, general and administrative expenses	1,700.3	1,635.1	1,445.4
Depreciation and amortization	174.7	162.6	145.0
Merger-related expenses	—	—	4.6
Operating earnings	662.6	637.0	675.1
Interest income	(1.8)	(2.2)	(11.6)
Interest expense	37.0	45.4	50.4
Debt extinguishment expense	6.0	5.3	2.3
Earnings before income tax expense	621.4	588.5	634.0
Income tax expense	214.6	212.8	235.7
Consolidated net income	406.8	375.7	398.3
Net loss attributable to noncontrolling interests	1.2	1.6	—
Consolidated net income attributable to GameStop	$ 408.0	$ 377.3	$ 398.3
Basic net income per common share[1]	$ 2.69	$ 2.29	$ 2.44
Diluted net income per common share[1]	$ 2.65	$ 2.25	$ 2.38
Weighted average shares of common stock—basic	151.6	164.5	163.2
Weighted average shares of common stock—diluted	154.0	167.9	167.7

[1]Basic net income per share and diluted net income per share are calculated based on consolidated net income attributable to GameStop.

See accompanying notes to consolidated financial statements.

GameStop Corp.
Consolidated Statements of Cash Flows

	52 Weeks Ended January 29, 2011	52 Weeks Ended January 30, 2010	52 Weeks Ended January 31, 2009
	(In millions)		
Cash flows from operating activities:			
Consolidated net income	$ 406.8	$ 375.7	$ 398.3
Adjustments to reconcile net earnings to net cash flows provided by operating activities:			
Depreciation and amortization (including amounts in cost of sales)	176.8	164.1	146.4
Provision for inventory reserves	27.5	48.9	43.0
Amortization and retirement of deferred financing fees and issue discounts	5.0	5.0	3.7
Stock-based compensation expense	29.6	37.8	35.4
Deferred income taxes	38.2	(1.2)	(24.7)
Excess tax (benefits) expense realized from exercise of stock-based awards	(18.6)	0.4	(34.2)
Loss on disposal of property and equipment	7.6	4.4	5.2
Changes in other long-term liabilities	(7.2)	7.6	7.4
Changes in operating assets and liabilities, net			
Receivables, net	0.2	4.2	(2.9)
Merchandise inventories	(227.2)	29.6	(209.5)
Prepaid expenses and other current assets	(10.5)	2.3	(16.4)
Prepaid income taxes and accrued income taxes payable	22.3	54.6	43.9
Accounts payable and accrued liabilities	140.7	(89.2)	153.6
Net cash flows provided by operating activities	591.2	644.2	549.2
Cash flows from investing activities:			
Purchase of property and equipment	(197.6)	(163.8)	(183.2)
Acquisitions, net of cash acquired	(38.1)	(8.4)	(630.7)
Other	(4.4)	(15.0)	(7.0)
Net cash flows used in investing activities	(240.1)	(187.2)	(820.9)
Cash flows from financing activities:			
Repurchase of notes payable	(200.0)	(100.0)	(30.0)
Purchase of treasury shares	(381.2)	(58.4)	—
Borrowings from the revolver	120.0	115.0	—
Repayment of revolver borrowings	(120.0)	(115.0)	—
Borrowings for acquisition	—	—	425.0
Repayments of acquisition borrowings	—	—	(425.0)
Issuance of shares relating to stock options	10.8	4.5	28.9
Excess tax benefits (expense) realized from exercise of stock-based awards	18.6	(0.4)	34.2
Other	(3.8)	(0.1)	(3.5)
Net cash flows provided by (used in) financing activities	(555.6)	(154.4)	29.6
Exchange rate effect on cash and cash equivalents	9.9	24.7	(37.2)
Net increase (decrease) in cash and cash equivalents	(194.6)	327.3	(279.3)
Cash and cash equivalents at beginning of period	905.4	578.1	857.4
Cash and cash equivalents at end of period	$ 710.8	$ 905.4	$ 578.1

See accompanying notes to consolidated financial statements.

Solution to Review Problem

1. Ratios:

    Notes: 2010 is the fiscal year ended January 29, 2011, and 2009 is the fiscal year ended January 30, 2010. Consolidated net income rather than Consolidated net income attributable to GameStop was used for all computations requiring net income amount.

    a.   2010: $2,154.8/$1,747.8 = 1.23
         2009: $2,127.3/$1,655.7 = 1.28
    b.   2010: ($710.8 + $65.5)/$1,747.8 = 0.44
         2009: ($905.4 + $64.0)/$1,655.7 = 0.59
    c.   2010: $591.2/$1,747.8 = 0.34
         2009: $644.2/$1,655.7 = 0.39
    d.   2010: 360 days/($9,473.7/$65.5) = 2.49 days
         2009: 360 days/($9,078.0/$64.0) = 2.54 days
    e.   2010: 360 days/($6,936.1/$1,257.5) = 65.27 days
         2009: 360 days/($6,643.3/$1,053.6) = 57.09 days
    f.   2010: $2,167.9/$2,895.9 = 0.75
         2009: $2,232.3/$2,723.0 = 0.82
    g.   2010: ($406.8 + $37.0 + $214.6)/$37.0 = 17.79 times
         2009: ($375.7 + $45.4 + $212.8)/$45.4 = 13.96 times
    h.   2010: {$406.8 + [$37.0(1 − 0.35*)]}/$5,063.8 = 8.51%
         2009: {$375.7 + [$45.4(1 − 0.36*)]}/$4,955.3 = 8.17%
    i.   2010: $406.8/$2,895.9 = 14.05%
         2009: $375.7/$2,723.0 = 13.80%

    *Tax rate for each of the two years:
      2010: $214.6/$621.4 = 0.35
      2009: $212.8/$588.5 = 0.36

2. Both the current ratio and the quick ratio declined slightly over the two-year period. Cash flow from operations to current liabilities also declined a small percentage. The number of days' sales in inventory at the end of 2010 of 65.27 days means that the company turns its inventory over about every two months. GameStop appears to be liquid and able to meet its short-term obligations.

3. The debt-to-equity ratios indicate that GameStop's reliance on debt decreased slightly over the two-year period, with $0.75 of liabilities for every $1 of stockholders' equity at the end of 2010. The times interest earned ratio improved, from about $14 of earnings before interest and taxes for every $1 of interest to a ratio in 2010 of about 18 to 1. GameStop appears to be solvent with a relatively healthy mix of debt and equity in its capital structure.

4. The return on assets for 2010 is 8.51%, and the return on common stockholders' equity is 14.05%. Both of these return ratios are slightly higher than in the prior year, which is commendable given the current economic environment. It should be noted that the company did not pay dividends in either of the two years and therefore would not be a good investment for those who want periodic dividend receipts. GameStop appears to be a very sound investment, but many other factors, including information on the current market price of the stock, should be considered before making a decision.

QUESTIONS

1. Two companies are in the same industry. Company A uses the LIFO method of inventory valuation, and Company B uses FIFO. What difficulties does this present when comparing the two companies?

2. You are told to compare the company's results for the year, as measured by various ratios, with one of the published surveys that arranges information by industry classification. What difficulties might you encounter when making comparisons using industry standards?

3. What types of problems does inflation cause when financial statements are analyzed?

4. Distinguish between horizontal and vertical analyses. Why is the analysis of common-size statements called *vertical* analysis? Why is horizontal analysis sometimes called *trend* analysis?

5. A company experiences a 15% increase in sales over the previous year. However, gross profit actually decreased by 5% from the previous year. What are some of the possible causes for an increase in sales but a decline in gross profit?

6. A company's total current assets have increased by 5% over the prior year. Management is concerned, however, about the composition of the current assets. Why is the composition of current assets important?

7. Ratios were categorized in the chapter according to their use in performing three different types of analysis. What are the three types of ratios?

8. Describe the operating cycle for a manufacturing company. How would the cycle differ for a retailer?

9. What accounts for the order in which current assets are presented on a balance sheet?

10. A company has a current ratio of 1.25 but an acid-test (or quick) ratio of only 0.65. How can this difference in the two ratios be explained? What concerns might you have about this company?

11. Explain the basic concept underlying all turnover ratios. Why is it advisable in computing a turnover ratio to use an average in the denominator (for example, average inventory)?

12. Sanders Company's accounts receivable turned over nine times during the year. The credit department extends terms of 2/10, n/30. Does the turnover ratio indicate any problems that management should investigate? Explain.

13. The turnover of inventory for Ace Company has slowed from 6.0 times per year to 4.5. What are some possible explanations for this decrease?

14. How does the operating cycle for a manufacturer differ from the operating cycle for a service company (e.g., an airline)?

15. What is the difference between liquidity analysis and solvency analysis?

16. Why is the debt service coverage ratio a better measure of solvency than the times interest earned ratio?

17. A friend tells you that the best way to assess solvency is by comparing total debt to total assets. Another friend says that solvency is measured by comparing total debt to total stockholders' equity. Which friend is correct?

18. A company is in the process of negotiating with a bank for an additional loan. Why will the bank be interested in the company's debt service coverage ratio?

19. What is the rationale for deducting dividends when computing the ratio of cash flow from operations to capital expenditures?

20. The rate of return on assets ratio is computed by dividing net income and interest expense, net of tax, by average total assets. Why is the numerator net income and interest expense, net of tax, rather than just net income?

21. A company has a return on assets of 14% and a return on common stockholders' equity of 11%. The president of the company has asked you to explain the reason for this difference. What causes the difference? How is the concept of financial leverage involved?

22. What is meant by the "quality" of a company's earnings? Explain why the price/earnings ratio for a company may indicate the quality of earnings.

23. Some ratios are more useful for management, whereas others are better suited to the needs of outsiders, such as stockholders and bankers. What is an example of a ratio that is primarily suited to management use? What ratio is more suited to use by outsiders?

24. The needs of service-oriented companies in analyzing financial statements differ from those of product-oriented companies. Why is this true? Give an example of a ratio that is meaningless to a service business.

25. What is the reason for reporting discontinued operations and extraordinary items in a separate section of an income statement? (Appendix)

BRIEF EXERCISES

LO1

Brief Exercise 13-1 Limitations in Ratio Analysis

A supplier is thinking of extending credit to a company but decides not to because the company's current ratio is only 0.50. Do you agree with the supplier's decision? What other factors need to be considered in drawing any conclusions about a company's liquidity?

LO2

EXAMPLE 13-1, 13-2, 13-3

Brief Exercise 13-2 Horizontal Analysis

Fill in the blanks for each of the following statements.

A comparison of financial statement items within a single period is called _____ analysis.
A comparison of financial statement items over a period of time is called _____ analysis.

LO3

EXAMPLE 13-4, 13-5

Brief Exercise 13-3 Vertical Analysis

Assume that your boss has asked you to prepare common-size financial statements. All accounts on the balance sheet should be stated as a percentage of which number? All accounts on the income statement should be stated as a percentage of which number?

LO4

EXAMPLE 13-7, 13-8, 13-10, 13-11

Brief Exercise 13-4 Liquidity Analysis

For each of the following ratios, fill in the missing numerator.

Ratio	
Current:	$\dfrac{}{\text{Current Liabilities}}$
Acid-Test:	$\dfrac{}{\text{Current Liabilities}}$
Accounts Receivable Turnover:	$\dfrac{}{\text{Average Accounts Receivable}}$
Inventory Turnover:	$\dfrac{}{\text{Average Inventory}}$

LO5

EXAMPLE 13-14, 13-15, 13-16

Brief Exercise 13-5 Solvency Analysis

Fill in the blank with the name of the ratio that would be used for each of the following situations.

Ratio	Measures the ability of the company to
_____	Meet its interest and principal payments
_____	Finance long-term asset acquisitions with cash from operations
_____	Meet its interest payments

LO6

EXAMPLE 13-17, 13-18, 13-20, 13-21

Brief Exercise 13-6 Profitability Analysis

For each of the following ratios, indicate what adjustment must be made to net income in the numerator and whether the adjustment is an addition to (A) or a deduction from (D) net income.

Ratio	Adjustment to Net Income in Numerator (A) or (D)
Return on assets	_____
Return on common stockholders' equity	_____
Earnings per share	_____
Return on sales	_____

LO7

Brief Exercise 13-7 Other Income Statement Items (Appendix)

Fill in the blank to indicate the line item that would appear on the income statement for each of the following events.

Item on Income Statement	Event
_____	Disposed of a segment of the business
_____	Incurred a loss from an event that was unusual and infrequently occurring

EXERCISES

Exercise 13-1 Liquidity Analyses for McDonald's and Wendy's/Arby's Group

LO4
EXAMPLE 13-6, 13-7, 13-8

The following information was summarized from the balance sheets of **McDonald's Corporation** at December 31, 2010, and **Wendy's/Arby's Group, Inc.**, at January 2, 2011.

	McDonald's (in millions)	Wendy's/Arby's Group (in thousands)
Current Assets:		
Cash and cash equivalents	$ 2,387.0	$ 512,508
Accounts receivable and notes receivable, net	1,179.1	84,258
Inventories	109.9	22,694
Prepaid expenses and other current assets	692.5	24,386
Deferred income tax benefit	0	34,389
Advertising funds restricted assets		76,553
Total current assets	$ 4,368.5	$ 754,788
Current liabilities	$ 2,924.7	$ 421,486
Noncurrent liabilities	$14,416.3	$2,147,994
Shareholders' equity	$14,634.2	$2,163,174

Required

1. Using the information provided, compute the following for each company at year-end:

   a. Working capital
   b. Current ratio
   c. Quick ratio

2. Comment briefly on the liquidity of each of these two companies. Which appears to be more liquid?

Exercise 13-2 Accounts Receivable and Inventory Analyses for Coca-Cola and PepsiCo

LO4
EXAMPLE 13-10, 13-11, 13-12

The following information was obtained from the 2010 and 2009 financial statements of **The Coca-Cola Company and Subsidiaries** and **PepsiCo, Inc., and Subsidiaries**. (Year-ends for PepsiCo are December 25, 2010, and December 26, 2009.) Assume all sales are on credit for both companies.

(in millions)		Coca-Cola	PepsiCo
Accounts and notes receivable, net[a]	12/31/10	$ 4,430	$ 6,323
	12/31/09	3,758	4,624
Inventories	12/31/10	2,650	3,372
	12/31/09	2,354	2,618
Net revenue[b]	2010	35,119	57,838
	2009	30,990	43,232
Cost of goods sold[c]	2010	12,693	26,575
	2009	11,088	20,099

[a]Described as "trade accounts receivable, less allowances" by Coca-Cola.
[b]Described as "net operating revenues" by Coca-Cola.
[c]Described as "cost of sales" by PepsiCo.

Required

1. Using the information provided, compute the following for each company for 2010:

   a. Accounts receivable turnover ratio
   b. Number of days' sales in receivables
   c. Inventory turnover ratio
   d. Number of days' sales in inventory
   e. Cash-to-cash operating cycle

2. Comment briefly on the liquidity of each of these two companies.

LO4
EXAMPLE 13-11

Exercise 13-3 Inventory Analysis

The following account balances are taken from the records of Lewis Inc., a wholesaler of fresh fruits and vegetables:

	December 31		
	2012	**2011**	**2010**
Merchandise inventory	$200,000	$150,000	$120,000

	2012	**2011**
Cost of goods sold	$7,100,000	$8,100,000

Required

1. Compute Lewis's inventory turnover ratio for 2012 and 2011.
2. Compute the number of days' sales in inventory for 2012 and 2011. Assume 360 days in a year.
3. Comment on your answers in parts (1) and (2) relative to the company's management of inventory over the two years. What problems do you see in its inventory management?

LO4
EXAMPLE 13-10

Exercise 13-4 Accounts Receivable Analysis

The following account balances are taken from the records of the Faraway Travel Agency:

	December 31		
	2012	**2011**	**2010**
Accounts receivable	$150,000	$100,000	$80,000

	2012	**2011**
Net credit sales	$600,000	$540,000

Faraway extends credit terms requiring full payment in 60 days, with no discount for early payment.

Required

1. Compute Faraway's accounts receivable turnover ratio for 2012 and 2011.
2. Compute the number of days' sales in receivables for 2012 and 2011. Assume 360 days in a year.
3. Comment on the efficiency of Faraway's collection efforts over the two-year period.

LO4
EXAMPLE 13-10

Exercise 13-5 Working Backward: Accounts Receivable Analysis

Adair Corp. is concerned because the average time to collect its accounts receivable was 15 days longer than its normal credit terms of net 30. Adair reported the following in the Current Assets section of its comparative balance sheets:

	12/31/12	12/31/11
Current Assets:		
Accounts receivable	$115,000	$85,000

Assuming 360 days in a year, determine Adair's net credit sales for 2012.

LO4
EXAMPLE 13-7, 13-8, 13-9

Exercise 13-6 Liquidity Analyses for Coca-Cola and PepsiCo

The following information was summarized from the balance sheets of the **The Coca-Cola Company and Subsidiaries** at December 31, 2010, and **PepsiCo, Inc., and Subsidiaries** at December 25, 2010:

(in millions)	Coca-Cola	PepsiCo
Cash and cash equivalents	$ 8,517	$ 5,943
Short-term investments	2,682	426
Marketable securities	138	—

(in millions)	Coca-Cola	PepsiCo
Accounts and notes receivables, net*	4,430	6,323
Inventories	2,650	3,372
Prepaid expenses and other current assets	3,162	1,505
Total current assets	$21,579	$17,569
Current liabilities	$18,508	$15,892

*Described as "trade accounts receivable, less allowances" by Coca-Cola.

Required

1. Using the information provided, compute the following for each company at the end of 2010:

   a. Current ratio
   b. Quick ratio

2. Coca-Cola reported cash flow from operations of $9,532 million during 2010. PepsiCo reported cash flow from operations of $8,448 million. Current liabilities reported by Coca-Cola at December 31, 2009, and PepsiCo at December 26, 2009, were $13,721 million and $8,756 million, respectively. Compute the cash flow from operations to current liabilities ratio for each company for 2010.

3. Comment briefly on the liquidity of each of these two companies. Which appears to be more liquid?

4. What other ratios would help you more fully assess the liquidity of these companies?

Exercise 13-7 **Working Backward: Current Ratio**

LO4
EXAMPLE 13-7

Cass Corp.'s December 31, 2011, balance sheet reported current assets of $120,000 and current liabilities of $100,000. The current ratio increased by 25% one year later, on December 31, 2012. Current liabilities on this date were $140,000. Determine current assets on December 31, 2012.

Exercise 13-8 **Working Backward: Debt Service Coverage**

LO5
EXAMPLE 13-15

Madison Corp. reported the following in the Current Assets section of its comparative balance sheets:

	December 31, 2012	December 31, 2011
Current Liabilities:		
Current portion of notes payable	$400,000	$600,000

Supplemental information at the bottom of Madison's 2012 statement of cash flows was as follows:

	2012	2011
Interest paid	$135,000	$155,000
Income taxes paid	550,000	425,000

Madison's 2012 debt service coverage ratio was 20 to 1. Determine Madison's cash flow from operations for 2012.

Exercise 13-9 **Solvency Analyses for IBM**

LO5
EXAMPLE 13-13, 13-14,
13-15, 13-16

The following information was obtained from the comparative financial statements included in **IBM**'s 2010 annual report. (All amounts are in millions of dollars.)

	December 31, 2010	December 31, 2009
Total liabilities	$90,279	$86,267
Total equity	23,172	22,755

(Continued)

	For the Years Ended December 31	
	2010	2009
Interest expense	$ 368	$ 402
Interest paid on debt	951	1,240
Provision for income taxes	4,890	4,713
Income taxes paid—net of refunds received	3,238	1,567
Net income	14,833	13,425
Net cash provided by operating activities	19,549	20,773
Cash dividends paid	3,177	2,860
Payments for plant, rental machines and other property	4,185	3,447
Payments to settle debt	6,522	13,495

Required

1. Using the information provided, compute the following for 2010 and 2009:

   a. Debt-to-equity ratio (at each year-end)
   b. Times interest earned ratio
   c. Debt service coverage ratio
   d. Cash flow from operations to capital expenditures ratio

2. Comment briefly on the company's solvency.

LO5
EXAMPLE 13-13, 13-14, 13-15

Exercise 13-10 Solvency Analysis

The following information is available from the balance sheets at the ends of the two most recent years and the income statement for the most recent year of Impact Company:

	December 31	
	2012	2011
Accounts payable	$ 65,000	$ 50,000
Accrued liabilities	25,000	35,000
Taxes payable	60,000	45,000
Short-term notes payable	0	75,000
Bonds payable due within next year	200,000	200,000
Total current liabilities	$ 350,000	$ 405,000
Bonds payable	$ 600,000	$ 800,000
Common stock, $10 par	$1,000,000	$1,000,000
Retained earnings	650,000	500,000
Total stockholders' equity	$1,650,000	$1,500,000
Total liabilities and stockholders' equity	$2,600,000	$2,705,000

	2012
Sales revenue	$1,600,000
Cost of goods sold	950,000
Gross profit	$ 650,000
Selling and administrative expense	300,000
Operating income	$ 350,000
Interest expense	89,000
Income before tax	$ 261,000
Income tax expense	111,000
Net income	$ 150,000

Other Information

a. Short-term notes payable represents a 12-month loan that matured in November 2012. Interest of 12% was paid at maturity.

b. One million dollars of serial bonds had been issued ten years earlier. The first series of $200,000 matured at the end of 2012, with interest of 8% payable annually.

c. Cash flow from operations was $185,000 in 2012. The amounts of interest and taxes paid during 2012 were $89,000 and $96,000, respectively.

Required

1. Compute the following for Impact Company:

   a. The debt-to-equity ratio at December 31, 2012, and December 31, 2011
   b. The times interest earned ratio for 2012
   c. The debt service coverage ratio for 2012

2. Comment on Impact's solvency at the end of 2012. Do the times interest earned ratio and the debt service coverage ratio differ in their indication of Impact's ability to pay its debts? Explain.

Exercise 13-11 Return Ratios and Leverage

LO6

EXAMPLE 13-17, 13-18, 13-19, 13-20

The following selected data are taken from the financial statements of Evergreen Company:

Sales revenue	$ 650,000
Cost of goods sold	400,000
Gross profit	$ 250,000
Selling and administrative expense	100,000
Operating income	$ 150,000
Interest expense	50,000
Income before tax	$ 100,000
Income tax expense (40%)	40,000
Net income	$ 60,000
Accounts payable	$ 45,000
Accrued liabilities	70,000
Income taxes payable	10,000
Interest payable	25,000
Short-term loans payable	150,000
Total current liabilities	$ 300,000
Long-term bonds payable	$ 500,000
Preferred stock, 10%, $100 par	$ 250,000
Common stock, no par	600,000
Retained earnings	350,000
Total stockholders' equity	$1,200,000
Total liabilities and stockholders' equity	$2,000,000

Required

1. Compute the following ratios for Evergreen Company:

   a. Return on sales
   b. Asset turnover (Assume that total assets at the beginning of the year were $1,600,000.)
   c. Return on assets
   d. Return on common stockholders' equity (Assume that the only changes in stockholders' equity during the year were from the net income for the year and dividends on the preferred stock.)

2. Comment on Evergreen's use of leverage. Has it successfully employed leverage? Explain.

Exercise 13-12 Profitability Analysis for Carnival Corp.

LO6

EXAMPLE 13-20

Carnival Corporation & plc is one of the largest cruise companies in the world with such well-known brands as Carnival Cruise Lines, Holland America Line, and Princess Cruises. For the year ended November 30, 2010, the company reported net income of $1,978 million. Total shareholders' equity on this date was $23,031 million, and on November 30, 2009, it was $22,039 million. No preferred stock was outstanding in either year.

(Continued)

Required

1. Compute Carnival's return on common stockholders' equity for the year ended November 30, 2010.
2. What other ratio would you want to compute to decide whether Carnival is successfully employing leverage? Explain your answer.

LO6
EXAMPLE 13-19

Exercise 13-13 Working Backward: Profitability Analysis

Murphy Company's total liabilities on December 31, 2012, amounted to $1,500,000. The debt-to-equity ratio on this date was 1.5 to 1. Net income for 2012 was $250,000, and the profit margin was 5%.

Required

1. Determine Murphy's net sales for 2012.
2. Determine Murphy's total assets on December 31, 2012.
3. Determine Murphy's asset turnover ratio for 2012, using year-end total assets, rather than average total assets.

LO6
EXAMPLE 13-17, 13-18,
13-19

Exercise 13-14 Relationships among Return on Assets, Return on Sales, and Asset Turnover

A company's return on assets is a function of its ability to turn over its investment (asset turnover) and earn a profit on each dollar of sales (return on sales). For each of the following independent cases, determine the missing amounts. *(Note:* Assume in each case that the company has no interest expense; that is, net income is used as the definition of income in all calculations.)

Case 1

Net income	$ 10,000
Net sales	$ 80,000
Average total assets	$ 60,000
Return on assets	?

Case 2

Net income	$ 25,000
Average total assets	$ 250,000
Return on sales	2%
Net sales	?

Case 3

Average total assets	$ 80,000
Asset turnover	1.5 times
Return on sales	6%
Return on assets	?

Case 4

Return on assets	10%
Net sales	$ 50,000
Asset turnover	1.25 times
Net income	?

Case 5

Return on assets	15%
Net income	$ 20,000
Return on sales	5%
Average total assets	?

LO6
EXAMPLE 13-21, 13-22,
13-23, 13-24

Exercise 13-15 EPS, P/E Ratio, and Dividend Ratios

The Stockholders' Equity section of the balance sheet for Cooperstown Corp. at the end of 2012 appears as follows:

8%, $100 par, cumulative preferred stock, 200,000 shares authorized, 50,000 shares issued and outstanding	$ 5,000,000
Additional paid-in capital on preferred	2,500,000

Common stock, $5 par, 500,000 shares authorized, 400,000	
shares issued and outstanding	2,000,000
Additional paid-in capital on common	18,000,000
Retained earnings	37,500,000
Total stockholders' equity	$65,000,000

Net income for the year was $1,300,000. Dividends were declared and paid on the preferred shares during the year, and a quarterly dividend of $0.40 per share was declared and paid each quarter on the common shares. The closing market price for the common shares on December 31, 2012, was $24.75 per share.

Required

1. Compute the following ratios for the common stock:
   a. Earnings per share
   b. Price/earnings ratio
   c. Dividend payout ratio
   d. Dividend yield ratio

2. Assume that you are an investment adviser. What other information would you want to have before advising a client regarding the purchase of Cooperstown stock?

Exercise 13-16 Return on Stockholders' Equity

LO6

EXAMPLE 13-20

Rogers Inc. had 500,000 shares of $2 par common stock outstanding at the end of both 2011 and 2012. Retained earnings at the end of 2011 amounted to $1,800,000. No dividends were paid during 2012, and net income for the year was $400,000. Determine Rogers' return on stockholders' equity for 2012.

MULTI-CONCEPT EXERCISES

Exercise 13-17 Earnings per Share and Extraordinary Items (Appendix)

LO6 • 7

EXAMPLE 13-21

The Stockholders' Equity section of the balance sheet for Lahey Construction Company at the end of 2012 is as follows:

9%, $10 par, cumulative preferred stock, 500,000 shares	
authorized, 200,000 shares issued and outstanding	$ 2,000,000
Additional paid-in capital on preferred	7,500,000
Common stock, $1 par, 2,500,000 shares authorized,	
1,500,000 shares issued and outstanding	1,500,000
Additional paid-in capital on common	21,000,000
Retained earnings	25,500,000
Total stockholders' equity	$57,500,000

The lower portion of the 2012 income statement indicates the following:

Net income before tax		$ 9,750,000
Income tax expense (40%)		(3,900,000)
Income before extraordinary items		$ 5,850,000
Extraordinary loss from flood	$(6,200,000)	
Less related tax effect (40%)	2,480,000	(3,720,000)
Net income		$ 2,130,000

Assume that the number of shares outstanding did not change during the year.

Required

1. Compute earnings per share *before* extraordinary items.
2. Compute earnings per share *after* the extraordinary loss.
3. Which of the two EPS ratios is more useful to management? Explain your answer. Would your answer be different if the ratios were to be used by an outsider(e.g., by a potential stockholder)? Why or why not?

LO2 • 3
EXAMPLE 13-2, 13-5

Exercise 13-18 Common-Size Income Statements and Horizontal Analysis

Income statements for Mariners Corp. for the past two years are as follows:

	(amounts in thousands of dollars)	
	2012	2011
Sales revenue	$60,000	$50,000
Cost of goods sold	42,000	30,000
Gross profit	$18,000	$20,000
Selling and administrative expense	9,000	5,000
Operating income	$ 9,000	$15,000
Interest expense	2,000	2,000
Income before tax	$ 7,000	$13,000
Income tax expense	2,000	4,000
Net income	$ 5,000	$ 9,000

Required

1. Using the format in Example 13-5, prepare common-size comparative income statements for the two years for Mariners Corp.
2. What observations can you make about the common-size statements? List at least four observations.
3. Using the format in Example 13-2, prepare comparative income statements for Mariners Corp., including columns for the dollars and for the percentage increase or decrease in each item on the statement.
4. Identify the two items on the income statement that experienced the largest change from one year to the next. For each of these items, explain where you would look to find additional information about the change.

LO2 • 3
EXAMPLE 13-1, 13-4

Exercise 13-19 Common-Size Balance Sheets and Horizontal Analysis

Comparative balance sheets for Farinet Company for the past two years are as follows:

	December 31	
	2012	2011
Cash	$ 16,000	$ 20,000
Accounts receivable	40,000	30,000
Inventory	30,000	50,000
Prepaid rent	18,000	12,000
Total current assets	$ 104,000	$112,000
Land	$ 150,000	$150,000
Plant and equipment	800,000	600,000
Accumulated depreciation	(130,000)	(60,000)
Total long-term assets	$ 820,000	$690,000
Total assets	$ 924,000	$802,000
Accounts payable	$ 24,000	$ 20,000
Income taxes payable	6,000	10,000
Short-term notes payable	70,000	50,000
Total current liabilities	$ 100,000	$ 80,000
Bonds payable	$ 150,000	$200,000
Common stock	$ 400,000	$300,000
Retained earnings	274,000	222,000
Total stockholders' equity	$ 674,000	$522,000
Total liabilities and stockholders' equity	$ 924,000	$802,000

Required

1. Using the format in Example 13-4, prepare common-size comparative balance sheets for the two years for Farinet Company.
2. What observations can you make about changes in the relative composition of Farinet's accounts from the common-size balance sheets? List at least five observations.
3. Using the format in Example 13-1, prepare comparative balance sheets for Farinet Company, including columns for the dollars and for the percentage increase or decrease in each item on the statement.
4. Identify the five items on the balance sheet that experienced the largest change from one year to the next. For each of these items, explain where you would look to find additional information about the change.

PROBLEMS

Problem 13-1 Effect of Transactions on Working Capital, Current Ratio, and Quick Ratio

LO4

(*Note:* Consider completing Problem 13-2 after this problem to ensure that you obtain a clear understanding of the effect of various transactions on these measures of liquidity.) The following account balances are taken from the records of Liquiform Inc.:

Cash	$ 70,000
Short-term investments	60,000
Accounts receivable	80,000
Inventory	100,000
Prepaid insurance	10,000
Accounts payable	75,000
Taxes payable	25,000
Salaries and wages payable	40,000
Short-term loans payable	60,000

Required

1. Use the information provided to compute the amount of working capital and Liquiform's current and quick ratios (round to three decimal points).
2. Determine the effect that each of the following transactions will have on Liquiform's working capital, current ratio, and quick ratio by recalculating each and then indicating whether the measure is increased, decreased, or not affected by the transaction. (For the ratios, round to three decimal points.) Consider each transaction independently; that is, assume that it is the *only* transaction that takes place.

	Effect of Transaction on		
Transaction	**Working Capital**	**Current Ratio**	**Quick Ratio**
a. Purchased inventory on account, $20,000			
b. Purchased inventory for cash, $15,000			
c. Paid suppliers on account, $30,000			
d. Received cash on account, $40,000			
e. Paid insurance for the following year, $20,000			
f. Made sales on account, $60,000			
g. Repaid short-term loans at bank, $25,000			
h. Borrowed $40,000 at bank for 90 days			
i. Declared and paid $45,000 cash dividend			
j. Purchased $20,000 of short-term investments			
k. Paid $30,000 in salaries			
l. Accrued additional $15,000 in taxes			

LO4 Problem 13-2 Effect of Transactions on Working Capital, Current Ratio, and Quick Ratio

(*Note:* Consider completing this problem after Problem 13-1 to ensure that you obtain a clear understanding of the effect of various transactions on these measures of liquidity.) The following account balances are taken from the records of Veriform Inc.:

Cash	$ 70,000
Short-term investments	60,000
Accounts receivable	80,000
Inventory	100,000
Prepaid insurance	10,000
Accounts payable	75,000
Taxes payable	25,000
Salaries and wages payable	40,000
Short-term loans payable	210,000

Required

1. Use the information provided to compute the amount of working capital and Veriform's current and quick ratios (round to three decimal points).
2. Determine the effect that each of the following transactions will have on Veriform's working capital, current ratio, and quick ratio by recalculating each and then indicating whether the measure is increased, decreased, or not affected by the transaction. (For the ratios, round to three decimal points.) Consider each transaction independently; that is, assume that it is the *only* transaction that takes place.

	Effect of Transaction on		
Transaction	**Working Capital**	**Current Ratio**	**Quick Ratio**
a. Purchased inventory on account, $20,000			
b. Purchased inventory for cash, $15,000			
c. Paid suppliers on account, $30,000			
d. Received cash on account, $40,000			
e. Paid insurance for the following year, $20,000			
f. Made sales on account, $60,000			
g. Repaid short-term loans at bank, $25,000			
h. Borrowed $40,000 at bank for 90 days			
i. Declared and paid $45,000 cash dividend			
j. Purchased $20,000 of short-term investments			
k. Paid $30,000 in salaries			
l. Accrued additional $15,000 in taxes			

LO6 Problem 13-3 Goals for Sales and Return on Assets

The president of Blue Skies Corp. and his vice presidents are reviewing the operating results of the year just completed. Sales increased by 15% from the previous year to $60,000,000. Average total assets for the year were $40,000,000. Net income, after adding back interest expense, net of tax, was $5,000,000.

The president is happy with the performance over the past year but is never satisfied with the status quo. He has set two specific goals for next year: (1) a 20% growth in sales and (2) a return on assets of 15%.

To achieve the second goal, the president has stated his intention to increase the total asset base by 12.5% over the base for the year just completed.

Required

1. For the year just completed, compute the following ratios:
   a. Return on sales
   b. Asset turnover
   c. Return on assets

2. Compute the necessary asset turnover for next year to achieve the president's goal of a 20% increase in sales.
3. Calculate the income needed next year to achieve the goal of a 15% return on total assets. *(Note: Assume that income is defined as net income plus interest, net of tax.)*
4. Based on your answers to parts (2) and (3), comment on the reasonableness of the president's goals. On what must the company focus to attain these goals?

Problem 13-4 Goals for Sales and Income Growth

LO6

Sunrise Corp. is a major regional retailer. The chief executive officer (CEO) is concerned with the slow growth both of sales and of net income and the subsequent effect on the trading price of the common stock. Selected financial data for the past three years follow.

Sunrise Corp.
(in millions)

		2012	2011	2010
1.	Sales	$200.0	$192.5	$187.0
2.	Net income	6.0	5.8	5.6
3.	Dividends declared and paid	2.5	2.5	2.5
December 31 balances:				
4.	Owners' equity	70.0	66.5	63.2
5.	Debt	30.0	29.8	30.3
Selected year-end financial ratios				
	Net income to sales	3.0%	3.0%	3.0%
	Asset turnover	2 times	2 times	2 times
6.	Return on owners' equity*	8.6%	8.7%	8.9%
7.	Debt to total assets	30.0%	30.9%	32.4%

*Based on year-end balances in owners' equity.

The CEO believes that the price of the stock has been adversely affected by the downward trend of the return on equity, the relatively low dividend payout ratio, and the lack of dividend increases. To improve the price of the stock, she wants to improve the return on equity and dividends.

She believes that the company should be able to meet these objectives by (1) increasing sales and net income at an annual rate of 10% a year and (2) establishing a new dividend policy that calls for a dividend payout of 50% of earnings or $3,000,000, whichever is larger.

The 10% annual sales increase will be accomplished through a new promotional program. The president believes that the present net income to sales ratio of 3% will be unchanged by the cost of this new program and any interest paid on new debt. She expects that the company can accomplish this sales and income growth while maintaining the current relationship of total assets to sales. Any capital that is needed to maintain this relationship and that is not generated internally would be acquired through long-term debt financing. The CEO hopes that debt would not exceed 35% of total liabilities and owners' equity.

Required

1. Using the CEO's program, prepare a schedule that shows the appropriate data for the years 2013, 2014, and 2015 for the items numbered 1 through 7 on the preceding schedule.
2. Can the CEO meet all of her requirements if a 10% per-year growth in income and sales is achieved? Explain your answer.
3. What alternative actions should the CEO consider to improve the return on equity and to support increased dividend payments?
4. Explain the reasons that the CEO might have for wanting to limit debt to 35% of total liabilities and owners' equity.

(CMA adapted)

MULTI-CONCEPT PROBLEMS

LO4 • 5 • 6 Problem 13-5 Comparison with Industry Averages

Heartland Inc. is a medium-size company that has been in business for 20 years. The industry has become very competitive in the last few years, and Heartland has decided that it must grow if it is going to survive. It has approached the bank for a sizable five-year loan, and the bank has requested Heartland's most recent financial statements as part of the loan package.

The industry in which Heartland operates consists of approximately 20 companies relatively equal in size. The trade association to which all of the competitors belong publishes an annual survey of the industry, including industry averages for selected ratios for the competitors. All companies voluntarily submit their statements to the association for this purpose.

Heartland's controller is aware that the bank has access to this survey and is very concerned about how the company fared this past year compared with the rest of the industry. The ratios included in the publication and the averages for the past year are as follows:

Ratio	Industry Average
Current ratio	1.23
Acid-test (quick) ratio	0.75
Accounts receivable turnover	33 times
Inventory turnover	29 times
Debt-to-equity ratio	0.53
Times interest earned	8.65 times
Return on sales	6.57%
Asset turnover	1.95 times
Return on assets	12.81%
Return on common stockholders' equity	17.67%

The financial statements to be submitted to the bank in connection with the loan follow.

Heartland Inc.
Statement of Income and Retained Earnings
For the Year Ended December 31, 2012
(thousands omitted)

Sales revenue	$ 542,750
Cost of goods sold	(435,650)
Gross profit	$ 107,100
Selling, general, and administrative expenses	$ (65,780)
Loss on sales of securities	(220)
Income before interest and taxes	$ 41,100
Interest expense	(9,275)
Income before taxes	$ 31,825
Income tax expense	(12,730)
Net income	$ 19,095
Retained earnings, January 1, 2012	58,485
	$ 77,580
Dividends paid on common stock	(12,000)
Retained earnings, December 31, 2012	$ 65,580

Heartland Inc.
Comparative Statements of Financial Position
(thousands omitted)

	December 31, 2012	December 31, 2011
Assets		
Current assets:		
Cash	$ 1,135	$ 750
Marketable securities	1,250	2,250
Accounts receivable, net of allowances	15,650	12,380
Inventories	12,680	15,870
Prepaid items	385	420
Total current assets	$ 31,100	$ 31,670
Long-term investments	$ 425	$ 425
Property, plant, and equipment:		
Land	$ 32,000	$ 32,000
Buildings and equipment, net of accumulated depreciation	216,000	206,000
Total property, plant, and equipment	$248,000	$238,000
Total assets	$279,525	$270,095
Liabilities and Stockholders' Equity		
Current liabilities:		
Short-term notes	$ 8,750	$ 12,750
Accounts payable	20,090	14,380
Salaries and wages payable	1,975	2,430
Income taxes payable	3,130	2,050
Total current liabilities	$ 33,945	$ 31,610
Long-term bonds payable	$ 80,000	$ 80,000
Stockholders' equity:		
Common stock, no par	$100,000	$100,000
Retained earnings	65,580	58,485
Total stockholders' equity	$165,580	$158,485
Total liabilities and stockholders' equity	$279,525	$270,095

Required

1. Prepare a columnar report for the controller of Heartland Inc. comparing the industry averages for the ratios published by the trade association with the comparable ratios for Heartland. For Heartland, compute the ratios as of December 31, 2012, or for the year ending December 31, 2012, whichever is appropriate.
2. Briefly evaluate Heartland's ratios relative to the industry averages.
3. Do you think that the bank will approve the loan? Explain your answer.

Problem 13-6 Basic Financial Ratios   LO4 • 5 • 6

The accounting staff of CCB Enterprises has completed the financial statements for the 2012 calendar year. The statement of income for the current year and the comparative statements of financial position for 2012 and 2011 follow.

CCB Enterprises
Statement of Income
For the Year Ended December 31, 2012
(thousands omitted)

Revenue:	
Net sales	$800,000
Other	60,000
Total revenue	$860,000

(Continued)

Expenses:

Cost of goods sold	$540,000
Research and development	25,000
Selling and administrative	155,000
Interest	20,000
Total expenses	$740,000
Income before income taxes	$120,000
Income taxes	48,000
Net income	$ 72,000

CCB Enterprises
Comparative Statements of Financial Position
December 31, 2012 and 2011
(thousands omitted)

	2012	2011
Assets		
Current assets:		
Cash and short-term investments	$ 26,000	$ 21,000
Receivables, less allowance for doubtful accounts ($1,100 in 2012 and $1,400 in 2011)	48,000	50,000
Inventories, at lower of FIFO cost or market	65,000	62,000
Prepaid items and other current assets	5,000	3,000
Total current assets	$144,000	$136,000
Other assets:		
Investments, at cost	$106,000	$106,000
Deposits	10,000	8,000
Total other assets	$116,000	$114,000
Property, plant, and equipment:		
Land	$ 12,000	$ 12,000
Buildings and equipment, less accumulated depreciation ($126,000 in 2012 and $122,000 in 2011)	268,000	248,000
Total property, plant, and equipment	$280,000	$260,000
Total assets	$540,000	$510,000

	2012	2011
Liabilities and Owners' Equity		
Current liabilities:		
Short-term loans	$ 22,000	$ 24,000
Accounts payable	72,000	71,000
Salaries, wages, and other	26,000	27,000
Total current liabilities	$120,000	$122,000
Long-term debt	$160,000	$171,000
Total liabilities	$280,000	$293,000
Owners' equity:		
Common stock, at par	$ 44,000	$ 42,000
Paid-in capital in excess of par	64,000	61,000
Total paid-in capital	$108,000	$103,000
Retained earnings	152,000	114,000
Total owners' equity	$260,000	$217,000
Total liabilities and owners' equity	$540,000	$510,000

Required

1. Calculate the following financial ratios for 2012 for CCB Enterprises:

   a. Times interest earned
   b. Return on total assets
   c. Return on common stockholders' equity
   d. Debt-to-equity ratio (at December 31, 2012)
   e. Current ratio (at December 31, 2012)
   f. Quick (acid-test) ratio (at December 31, 2012)
   g. Accounts receivable turnover ratio (Assume that all sales are on credit.)
   h. Number of days' sales in receivables
   i. Inventory turnover ratio (Assume that all purchases are on credit.)
   j. Number of days' sales in inventory
   k. Number of days in cash operating cycle

2. Prepare a few brief comments on the overall financial health of CCB Enterprises. For each comment, indicate any information that is not provided in the problem that you would need to fully evaluate the company's financial health.

(CMA adapted)

Problem 13-7 Projected Results to Meet Corporate Objectives   LO5 • 6

Tablon Inc. is a wholly owned subsidiary of Marbel Co. The philosophy of Marbel's management is to allow the subsidiaries to operate as independent units. Corporate control is exercised through the establishment of minimum objectives for each subsidiary, accompanied by substantial rewards for success and penalties for failure. The time period for performance review is long enough for competent managers to display their abilities.

Each quarter, the subsidiary is required to submit financial statements. The statements are accompanied by a letter from the subsidiary president explaining the results to date, a forecast for the remainder of the year, and the actions to be taken to achieve the objectives if the forecast indicates that the objectives will not be met.

Marbel management, in conjunction with Tablon management, had set the objectives listed below for the year ending May 31, 2013. These objectives are similar to those set in previous years.

- Sales growth of 20%
- Return on stockholders' equity of 15%
- A long-term debt-to-equity ratio of not more than 1.0
- Payment of a cash dividend of 50% of net income, with a minimum payment of at least $400,000

Tablon's controller has just completed the financial statements for the six months ended November 30, 2012, and the forecast for the year ending May 31, 2013. The statements follow.

After a cursory glance at the financial statements, Tablon's president concluded that not all objectives would be met. At a staff meeting of the Tablon management, the president asked the controller to review the projected results and recommend possible actions that could be taken during the remainder of the year so that Tablon would be more likely to meet the objectives.

Tablon Inc.
Income Statement
(thousands omitted)

	Year Ended May 31, 2012	Six Months Ended November 30, 2012	Forecast for Year Ending May 31, 2013
Sales	$25,000	$15,000	$30,000
Cost of goods sold	$13,000	$ 8,000	$16,000
Selling expenses	5,000	3,500	7,000
Administrative expenses and interest	4,000	2,500	5,000
Income taxes (40%)	1,200	400	800
Total expenses and taxes	$23,200	$14,400	$28,800

(Continued)

	Year Ended May 31, 2012	Six Months Ended November 30, 2012	Forecast for Year Ending May 31, 2013
Net income	$ 1,800	$ 600	$ 1,200
Dividends declared and paid	600	0	600
Income retained	$ 1,200	$ 600	$ 600

Tablon Inc.
Statement of Financial Position
(thousands omitted)

	May 31, 2012	November 30, 2012	Forecast for May 31, 2013
Assets			
Cash	$ 400	$ 500	$ 500
Accounts receivable (net)	4,100	6,500	7,100
Inventory	7,000	8,500	8,600
Plant and equipment (net)	6,500	7,000	7,300
Total assets	$18,000	$22,500	$23,500
Liabilities and Equities			
Accounts payable	$ 3,000	$ 4,000	$ 4,000
Accrued taxes	300	200	200
Long-term borrowing	6,000	9,000	10,000
Common stock	5,000	5,000	5,000
Retained earnings	3,700	4,300	4,300
Total liabilities and equities	$18,000	$22,500	$23,500

Required

1. Calculate the projected results for each of the four objectives established for Tablon Inc. State which results will not meet the objectives by year-end.
2. From the data presented, identify the factors that seem to contribute to the failure of Tablon Inc. to meet all of its objectives.
3. Explain the possible actions that the controller could recommend in response to the president's request.

(CMA adapted)

ALTERNATE PROBLEMS

LO6 **Problem 13-1A Goals for Sales and Return on Assets**

The president of Blue Moon Corp. and her department managers are reviewing the operating results of the year just completed. Sales increased by 12% from the previous year to $750,000. Average total assets for the year were $400,000. Net income, after adding back interest expense, net of tax, was $60,000.

The president is happy with the performance over the past year but is never satisfied with the status quo. She has set two specific goals for next year: (1) a 15% growth in sales and (2) a return on assets of 20%.

To achieve the second goal, the president has stated her intention to increase the total asset base by 10% over the base for the year just completed.

Required

1. For the year just completed, compute the following ratios:
   a. Return on sales
   b. Asset turnover
   c. Return on assets

2. Compute the necessary asset turnover for next year to achieve the president's goal of a 15% increase in sales.
3. Calculate the income needed next year to achieve the goal of a 20% return on total assets. (Note: Assume that *income* is defined as net income plus interest, net of tax.)
4. Based on your answers to parts (2) and (3), comment on the reasonableness of the president's goals. On what must the company focus to attain these goals?

Problem 13-2A Effect of Transactions on Debt-to-Equity Ratio   LO5

(*Note:* Consider completing Problem 13-3A after this problem to ensure that you obtain a clear understanding of the effect of various transactions on this measure of solvency.) The following account balances are taken from the records of Monet's Garden Inc.:

Current liabilities	$150,000
Long-term liabilities	375,000
Stockholders' equity	400,000

Required

1. Use the information provided to compute Monet's debt-to-equity ratio (round to three decimal points).
2. Determine the effect that each of the following transactions will have on Monet's debt-to-equity ratio by recalculating the ratio and then indicating whether the ratio is increased, decreased, or not affected by the transaction. (Round to three decimal points.) Consider each transaction independently; that is, assume that it is the *only* transaction that takes place.

Transaction	Effect of Transaction on Debt-to Equity Ratio
a. Purchased inventory on account, $20,000	
b. Purchased inventory for cash, $15,000	
c. Paid suppliers on account, $30,000	
d. Received cash on account, $40,000	
e. Paid insurance for the following year, $20,000	
f. Made sales on account, $60,000	
g. Repaid short-term loans at bank, $25,000	
h. Borrowed $40,000 at bank for 90 days	
i. Declared and paid $45,000 cash dividend	
j. Purchased $20,000 of short-term investments	
k. Paid $30,000 in salaries	
l. Accrued additional $15,000 in taxes	

Problem 13-3A Effect of Transactions on Debt-to-Equity Ratio   LO5

(*Note:* Consider completing this problem after Problem 13-2A to ensure that you obtain a clear understanding of the effect of various transactions on this measure of solvency.) The following account balances are taken from the records of Degas Inc.:

Current liabilities	$ 25,000
Long-term liabilities	125,000
Stockholders' equity	400,000

Required

1. Use the information provided to compute Degas's debt-to-equity ratio (round to three decimal points).
2. Determine the effect that each of the following transactions will have on Degas's debt-to-equity ratio by recalculating the ratio and then indicating whether the ratio is increased, decreased, or not affected by the transaction. (Round to three decimal points.) Consider each transaction independently; that is, assume that it is the *only* transaction that takes place.

Transaction	Effect of Transaction on Debt-to-Equity Ratio
a. Purchased inventory on account, $20,000	
b. Purchased inventory for cash, $15,000	
c. Paid suppliers on account, $30,000	
d. Received cash on account, $40,000	
e. Paid insurance for the following year, $20,000	
f. Made sales on account, $60,000	
g. Repaid short-term loans at bank, $25,000	
h. Borrowed $40,000 at bank for 90 days	
i. Declared and paid $45,000 cash dividend	
j. Purchased $20,000 of short-term investments	
k. Paid $30,000 in salaries	
l. Accrued additional $15,000 in taxes	

LO6

Problem 13-4A Goals for Sales and Income Growth

Sunset Corp. is a major regional retailer. The chief executive officer (CEO) is concerned with the slow growth both of sales and of net income and the subsequent effect on the trading price of the common stock. Selected financial data for the past three years follow.

Sunset Corp.
(in millions)

	2012	2011	2010
1. Sales	$100.0	$96.7	$93.3
2. Net income	3.0	2.9	2.8
3. Dividends declared and paid	1.2	1.2	1.2
December 31 balances:			
4. Stockholders' equity	40.0	38.2	36.5
5. Debt	10.0	10.2	10.2
Selected year-end financial ratios			
Net income to sales	3.0%	3.0%	3.0%
Asset turnover	2 times	2 times	2 times
6. Return on stockholders' equity*	7.5%	7.6%	7.7%
7. Debt to total assets	20.0%	21.1%	21.8%

*Based on year-end balances in stockholders' equity.

The CEO believes that the price of the stock has been adversely affected by the downward trend of the return on equity, the relatively low dividend payout ratio, and the lack of dividend increases. To improve the price of the stock, he wants to improve the return on equity and dividends.

He believes that the company should be able to meet these objectives by (1) increasing sales and net income at an annual rate of 10% a year and (2) establishing a new dividend policy that calls for a dividend payout of 60% of earnings or $2,000,000, whichever is larger.

The 10% annual sales increase will be accomplished through a product enhancement program. The president believes that the present net income to sales ratio of 3% will be unchanged by the cost of this new program and any interest paid on new debt. He expects that the company can accomplish this sales and income growth while maintaining the current relationship of total assets to sales. Any capital that is needed to maintain this relationship and that is not generated internally would be acquired through long-term debt financing. The CEO hopes that debt would not exceed 25% of total liabilities and stockholders' equity.

Required

1. Using the CEO's program, prepare a schedule that shows the appropriate data for the years 2013, 2014, and 2015 for the items numbered 1 through 7 on the preceding schedule.
2. Can the CEO meet all of his requirements if a 10% per-year growth in income and sales is achieved? Explain your answers.
3. What alternative actions should the CEO consider to improve the return on equity and to support increased dividend payments?

(CMA adapted)

ALTERNATE MULTI-CONCEPT PROBLEM

Problem 13-5A Basic Financial Ratios

LO4 • 5 • 6

The accounting staff of SST Enterprises has completed the financial statements for the 2012 calendar year. The statement of income for the current year and the comparative statements of financial position for 2012 and 2011 follow.

SST Enterprises
Statement of Income
Year Ended December 31, 2012
(thousands omitted)

Revenue:	
Net sales	$600,000
Other	45,000
Total revenue	$645,000
Expenses:	
Cost of goods sold	$405,000
Research and development	18,000
Selling and administrative	120,000
Interest	15,000
Total expenses	$558,000
Income before income taxes	$ 87,000
Income taxes	27,000
Net income	$ 60,000

SST Enterprises
Comparative Statements of Financial Position
December 31, 2012 and 2011
(thousands omitted)

	2012	2011
Assets		
Current assets:		
Cash and short-term investments	$ 27,000	$ 20,000
Receivables, less allowance for doubtful accounts ($1,100 in 2012 and $1,400 in 2011)	36,000	37,000
Inventories, at lower of FIFO cost or market	35,000	42,000
Prepaid items and other current assets	2,000	1,000
Total current assets	$100,000	$100,000
Property, plant, and equipment:		
Land	$ 9,000	$ 9,000
Buildings and equipment, less accumulated depreciation ($74,000 in 2012 and $62,000 in 2011)	191,000	186,000
Total property, plant, and equipment	$200,000	$195,000
Total assets	$300,000	$295,000

(Continued)

	2012	2011
Liabilities and Stockholders' Equity		
Current liabilities:		
Short-term loans	$ 20,000	$ 15,000
Accounts payable	80,000	68,000
Salaries, wages, and other	5,000	7,000
Total current liabilities	$105,000	$ 90,000
Long-term debt	15,000	40,000
Total liabilities	$120,000	$130,000
Stockholders' equity:		
Common stock, at par	$ 50,000	$ 50,000
Paid-in capital in excess of par	25,000	25,000
Total paid-in capital	$ 75,000	$ 75,000
Retained earnings	105,000	90,000
Total stockholders' equity	$180,000	$165,000
Total liabilities and stockholders' equity	$300,000	$295,000

Required

1. Calculate the following financial ratios for 2012 for SST Enterprises:

    a. Times interest earned
    b. Return on total assets
    c. Return on common stockholders' equity
    d. Debt-to-equity ratio (at December 31, 2012)
    e. Current ratio (at December 31, 2012)
    f. Quick (acid-test) ratio (at December 31, 2012)
    g. Accounts receivable turnover ratio (Assume that all sales are on credit.)
    h. Number of days' sales in receivables
    i. Inventory turnover ratio (Assume that all purchases are on credit.)
    j. Number of days' sales in inventory
    k. Number of days in cash operating cycle

2. Prepare a few brief comments on the overall financial health of SST Enterprises. For each comment, indicate any information that is not provided in the problem that you would need to fully evaluate the company's financial health.

(CMA adapted)

LO4 • 5 • 6   Problem 13-6A Comparison with Industry Averages

Midwest Inc. is a medium-size company that has been in business for 20 years. The industry has become very competitive in the last few years, and Midwest has decided that it must grow if it is going to survive. It has approached the bank for a sizable five-year loan, and the bank has requested Midwest's most recent financial statements as part of the loan package.

The industry in which Midwest operates consists of approximately 20 companies relatively equal in size. The trade association to which all of the competitors belong publishes an annual survey of the industry, including industry averages for selected ratios for the competitors. All companies voluntarily submit their statements to the association for this purpose.

Midwest's controller is aware that the bank has access to this survey and is very concerned about how the company fared this past year compared with the rest of the industry. The ratios included in the publication and the averages for the past year are as follows:

Ratio	Industry Average
Current ratio	1.20
Acid-test (quick) ratio	0.50
Inventory turnover	35 times
Debt-to-equity ratio	0.50
Times interest earned	25 times
Return on sales	3%
Asset turnover	3.5 times
Return on common stockholders' equity	20%

The financial statements to be submitted to the bank in connection with the loan follow.

Midwest Inc.
Statement of Income and Retained Earnings
For the Year Ended December 31, 2012
(thousands omitted)

Sales revenue	$ 420,500
Cost of goods sold	(300,000)
Gross profit	$ 120,500
Selling, general, and administrative expenses	(85,000)
Income before interest and taxes	$ 35,500
Interest expense	(8,600)
Income before taxes	$ 26,900
Income tax expense	(12,000)
Net income	$ 14,900
Retained earnings, January 1, 2012	12,400
	$ 27,300
Dividends paid on common stock	(11,200)
Retained earnings, December 31, 2012	$ 16,100

Midwest Inc.
Comparative Statements of Financial Position
(thousands omitted)

	December 31, 2012	December 31, 2011
Assets		
Current assets:		
Cash	$ 1,790	$ 2,600
Marketable securities	1,200	1,700
Accounts receivable, net of allowances	400	600
Inventories	8,700	7,400
Prepaid items	350	400
Total current assets	$ 12,440	$ 12,700
Long-term investments	$ 560	$ 400
Property, plant, and equipment:		
Land	$ 12,000	$ 12,000
Buildings and equipment, net of accumulated depreciation	87,000	82,900
Total property, plant, and equipment	$ 99,000	$ 94,900
Total assets	$112,000	$108,000
Liabilities and Stockholders' Equity		
Current liabilities:		
Short-term notes	$ 800	$ 600
Accounts payable	6,040	6,775
Salaries and wages payable	1,500	1,200
Income taxes payable	1,560	1,025
Total current liabilities	$ 9,900	$ 9,600
Long-term bonds payable	$ 36,000	$ 36,000
Stockholders' equity:		
Common stock, no par	$ 50,000	$ 50,000
Retained earnings	16,100	12,400
Total stockholders' equity	$ 66,100	$ 62,400
Total liabilities and stockholders' equity	$112,000	$108,000

(Continued)

Required

1. Prepare a columnar report for the controller of Midwest Inc. comparing the industry averages for the ratios published by the trade association with the comparable ratios for Midwest. For Midwest, compute the ratios as of December 31, 2012, or for the year ending December 31, 2012, whichever is appropriate.
2. Briefly evaluate Midwest's ratios relative to the industry averages.
3. Do you think that the bank will approve the loan? Explain your answer.

LO5 • 6 Problem 13-7A Projected Results to Meet Corporate Objectives

Grout Inc. is a wholly owned subsidiary of Slait Co. The philosophy of Slait's management is to allow the subsidiaries to operate as independent units. Corporate control is exercised through the establishment of minimum objectives for each subsidiary, accompanied by substantial rewards for success and penalties for failure. The time period for performance review is long enough for competent managers to display their abilities.

Each quarter, the subsidiary is required to submit financial statements. The statements are accompanied by a letter from the subsidiary president explaining the results to date, a forecast for the remainder of the year, and the actions to be taken to achieve the objectives if the forecast indicates that the objectives will not be met.

Slait management, in conjunction with Grout management, had set the objectives listed below for the year ending September 30, 2013. These objectives are similar to those set in previous years.

- Sales growth of 10%
- Return on stockholders' equity of 20%
- A long-term debt-to-equity ratio of not more than 1.0
- Payment of a cash dividend of 50% of net income, with a minimum payment of at least $500,000

Grout's controller has just completed preparing the financial statements for the six months ended March 31, 2013, and the forecast for the year ending September 30, 2013. The statements are presented below.

After a cursory glance at the financial statements, Grout's president concluded that not all objectives would be met. At a staff meeting of the Grout management, the president asked the controller to review the projected results and recommend possible actions that could be taken during the remainder of the year so that Grout would be more likely to meet the objectives.

Grout Inc.
Income Statement
(thousands omitted)

	Year Ended September 30, 2012	Six Months Ended March 31, 2013	Forecast for Year Ending September 30, 2013
Sales	$10,000	$6,000	$12,000
Cost of goods sold	$ 6,000	$4,000	$ 8,000
Selling expenses	1,500	900	1,800
Administrative expenses and interest	1,000	600	1,200
Income taxes	500	300	600
Total expenses and taxes	$ 9,000	$5,800	$11,600
Net income	$ 1,000	$ 200	$ 400
Dividends declared and paid	500	0	400
Income retained	$ 500	$ 200	$ 0

Grout Inc.
Statement of Financial Position
(thousands omitted)

	September 30, 2012	March 31, 2013	Forecast for September 30, 2013
Assets			
Cash	$ 400	$ 500	$ 500
Accounts receivable (net)	2,100	3,400	2,600
Inventory	7,000	8,500	8,400
Plant and equipment (net)	2,800	2,500	3,200
Total assets	$12,300	$14,900	$14,700
Liabilities and Equities			
Accounts payable	$ 3,000	$ 4,000	$ 4,000
Accrued taxes	300	200	200
Long-term borrowing	4,000	5,500	5,500
Common stock	4,000	4,000	4,000
Retained earnings	1,000	1,200	1,000
Total liabilities and equities	$12,300	$14,900	$14,700

Required

1. Calculate the projected results for each of the four objectives established for Grout Inc. State which results will not meet the objectives by year-end.
2. From the data presented, identify the factors that seem to contribute to the failure of Grout Inc. to meet all of its objectives.
3. Explain the possible actions that the controller could recommend in response to the president's request.

(CMA adapted)

DECISION CASES

Reading and Interpreting Financial Statements

Decision Case 13-1 Horizontal Analysis for Kellogg's

LO2

Refer to the financial statement information of **Kellogg's** reprinted at the back of the book.

Required

1. Prepare a work sheet with the following headings:

	Increase (Decrease) from			
	2009 to 2010		2008 to 2009	
Income Statement Accounts	Dollars	Percent	Dollars	Percent

2. Complete the work sheet using each of the account titles on Kellogg's income statement. Round all percentages to the nearest one-tenth of a percent.
3. What observations can you make from this horizontal analysis? What is your overall analysis of operations? Have the company's operations improved over the three-year period?

LO3   Decision Case 13-2 **Vertical Analysis for Kellogg's**

Refer to the financial statement information of **Kellogg's** reprinted at the back of the book.

Required

1. Using the format in Example 13-5, prepare common-size comparative income statements for 2010 and 2009. Use as the base "Net sales." Round all percentages to the nearest one-tenth of a percent.
2. What changes do you detect in the income statement relationships from 2009 to 2010?
3. Using the format in Example 13-4, prepare common-size comparative balance sheets at the end of 2010 and 2009. Round all percentages to the nearest one-tenth of a percent.
4. What observations can you make about the relative composition of Kellogg's assets from the common-size statements? What observations can be made about the changes in the relative composition of liabilities and stockholders' equity accounts?

LO3   Decision Case 13-3 **Comparing Two Companies in the Same Industry: Kellogg's and General Mills**

This case should be completed after responding to the requirements in Decision Case 13-2. Refer to the financial statement information of **Kellogg's** and **General Mills** reprinted at the back of the book.

Required

1. Using the format in Example 13-5, prepare common-size comparative income statements for the years ending May 30, 2010, and May 31, 2009, for General Mills. Round all percentages to the nearest one-tenth of a percent.
2. The common-size comparative income statements indicate the relative importance of items on the statement. Compare the common-size income statements of General Mills and Kellogg's. What are the most important differences between the two companies' income statements?
3. Using the format in Example 13-4, prepare common-size comparative balance sheets on May 30, 2010, and May 31, 2009, for General Mills. Round all percentages to the nearest one-tenth of a percent.
4. The common-size comparative balance sheets indicate the relative importance of items on the statement. Compare the common-size balance sheets of General Mills and Kellogg's. What are the most important differences between the two companies' balance sheets?

LO4 • 5 • 6   Decision Case 13-4 **Ratio Analysis for General Mills**

Refer to the financial statement information of **General Mills** reprinted at the back of the book.

Required

1. Compute the following ratios and other amounts for each of the two years, ending May 30, 2010, and May 31, 2009. Because only two years of data are given on the balance sheets, to be consistent, you should use year-end balances for each year in lieu of average balances. Assume 360 days to a year. State any other necessary assumptions in making the calculations. Round all ratios to the nearest one-tenth of a percent.

    a. Working capital
    b. Current ratio
    c. Acid-test ratio
    d. Cash flow from operations to current liabilities
    e. Debt-to-equity ratio
    f. Cash flow from operations to capital expenditures
    g. Asset turnover
    h. Return on sales
    i. Return on assets
    j. Return on common stockholders' equity

2. What is your overall analysis of the financial health of General Mills?

Making Financial Decisions

Decision Case 13-5 Acquisition Decision

LO4 • 5 • 6 • 7

Diversified Industries is a large conglomerate that is continually in the market for new acquisitions. The company has grown rapidly over the last ten years through buyouts of medium-size companies. Diversified does not limit itself to companies in any one industry, but looks for firms with a sound financial base and the ability to stand on their own financially.

The president of Diversified recently told a meeting of the company's officers: "I want to impress two points on all of you. First, we are not in the business of looking for bargains. Diversified has achieved success in the past by acquiring companies with the ability to be a permanent member of the corporate family. We don't want companies that may appear to be a bargain on paper but can't survive in the long run. Second, a new member of our family must be able to come in and make it on its own—the parent is not organized to be a funding agency for struggling subsidiaries."

Ron Dixon is the vice president of acquisitions for Diversified, a position he has held for five years. He is responsible for making recommendations to the board of directors on potential acquisitions. Because you are one of his assistants, he recently brought you a set of financials for a manufacturer, Heavy Duty Tractors Inc. Dixon believes that Heavy Duty is a "can't-miss" opportunity for Diversified and asks you to confirm his hunch by performing basic financial statement analysis on the company. The most recent comparative balance sheets and income statement for the company follow.

Heavy Duty Tractors Inc.
Comparative Statements of Financial Position
(thousands omitted)

	December 31, 2012	December 31, 2011
Assets		
Current assets:		
Cash	$ 48,500	$ 24,980
Marketable securities	3,750	0
Accounts receivable, net of allowances	128,420	84,120
Inventories	135,850	96,780
Prepaid items	7,600	9,300
Total current assets	$324,120	$215,180
Long-term investments	$ 55,890	$ 55,890
Property, plant, and equipment:		
Land	$ 45,000	$ 45,000
Buildings and equipment, less accumulated depreciation of $385,000 in 2012 and $325,000 in 2011	545,000	605,000
Total property, plant, and equipment	$590,000	$650,000
Total assets	$970,010	$921,070
Liabilities and Stockholders' Equity		
Current liabilities:		
Short-term notes	$ 80,000	$ 60,000
Accounts payable	65,350	48,760
Salaries and wages payable	14,360	13,840
Income taxes payable	2,590	3,650
Total current liabilities	$162,300	$126,250
Long-term bonds payable, due 2019	$275,000	$275,000
Stockholders' equity:		
Common stock, no par	$350,000	$350,000
Retained earnings	182,710	169,820
Total stockholders' equity	$532,710	$519,820
Total liabilities and stockholders' equity	$970,010	$921,070

(Continued)

Heavy Duty Tractors Inc.
Statement of Income and Retained Earnings
For the Year Ended December 31, 2012
(thousands omitted)

Sales revenue	$875,250
Cost of goods sold	542,750
Gross profit	$332,500
Selling, general, and administrative expenses	264,360
Operating income	$ 68,140
Interest expense	45,000
Net income before taxes and extraordinary items	$ 23,140
Income tax expense	9,250
Income before extraordinary items	$ 13,890
Extraordinary gain, less taxes of $6,000	9,000
Net income	$ 22,890
Retained earnings, January 1, 2012	169,820
	$192,710
Dividends paid on common stock	10,000
Retained earnings, December 31, 2012	$182,710

Required

1. How liquid is Heavy Duty Tractors? Support your answer with any ratios that you believe are necessary to justify your conclusion. Also indicate any other information that you would want to have in making a final determination on its liquidity.
2. In light of the president's comments, should you be concerned about the solvency of Heavy Duty Tractors? Support your answer with the necessary ratios. How does the maturity date of the outstanding debt affect your answer?
3. Has Heavy Duty demonstrated the ability to be a profitable member of the Diversified family? Support your answer with the necessary ratios.
4. What will you tell your boss? Should he recommend to the board of directors that Diversified put in a bid for Heavy Duty Tractors?

LO3   Decision Case 13-6   Pricing Decision

BPO's management believes the company has been successful at increasing sales because it has not increased the selling price of its products even though its competition has increased prices and costs have increased. Price and cost relationships in Year 1 were established because they represented industry averages. The following income statements are available for BPO's first three years of operation:

	Year 3	Year 2	Year 1
Sales	$125,000	$110,000	$100,000
Cost of goods sold	62,000	49,000	40,000
Gross profit	$ 63,000	$ 61,000	$ 60,000
Operating expenses	53,000	49,000	45,000
Net income	$ 10,000	$ 12,000	$ 15,000

Required

1. Using the format in Example 13-5, prepare common-size comparative income statements for the three years.
2. Explain why net income has decreased while sales have increased.
3. Prepare an income statement for Year 4. Sales volume in units is expected to increase by 10%, and costs are expected to increase by 8%.
4. Do you think BPO should raise its prices or maintain the same selling prices? Explain your answer.

Ethical Decision Making

Decision Case 13-7 Provisions in a Loan Agreement   LO4 • 5

As controller of Midwest Construction Company, you are reviewing with your assistant, Dave Jackson, the financial statements for the year just ended. During the review, Jackson reminds you of an existing loan agreement with Southern National Bank. Midwest has agreed to the following conditions:

- The current ratio will be maintained at a minimum level of 1.5 to 1.0 at all times.
- The debt-to-equity ratio will not exceed 0.5 to 1.0 at any time.

Jackson has drawn up the following preliminary condensed balance sheet for the year just ended:

Midwest Construction Company
Balance Sheet
December 31
(in millions of dollars)

Current assets	$16	Current liabilities	$10
Long-term assets	64	Long-term debt	15
		Stockholders' equity	55
Total	$80	Total	$80

Jackson wants to discuss two items with you. First, long-term debt currently includes a $5 million note payable to Eastern State Bank that is due in six months. The plan is to go to Eastern before the note is due and ask it to extend the maturity date of the note for five years. Jackson doesn't believe that Midwest needs to include the $5 million in current liabilities because the plan is to roll over the note.

Second, in December of this year, Midwest received a $2 million deposit from the state for a major road project. The contract calls for the work to be performed over the next 18 months. Jackson recorded the $2 million as revenue this year because the contract is with the state; there shouldn't be any question about being able to collect.

Required

1. Based on the balance sheet that Jackson prepared, is Midwest in compliance with its loan agreement with Southern? Support your answer with any necessary computations.
2. What would you do with the two items in question? Do you see anything wrong with the way Jackson has handled each of them? Explain your answer.
3. Prepare a revised balance sheet based on your answer to part (2). Also, compute a revised current ratio and debt-to-equity ratio. Based on the revised ratios, is Midwest in compliance with its loan agreement?

Decision Case 13-8 Inventory Turnover   LO4

Garden Fresh Inc. is a wholesaler of fresh fruits and vegetables. Each year, it submits a set of financial ratios to a trade association. Even though the association doesn't publish the individual ratios for each company, the president of Garden Fresh thinks it is important for public relations that his company look as good as possible. Due to the nature of the fresh fruits and vegetables business, one of the major ratios tracked by the association is inventory turnover. Garden Fresh's inventory stated at FIFO cost was as follows:

	Year Ending December 31	
	2012	**2011**
Fruits	$10,000	$ 9,000
Vegetables	30,000	33,000
Totals	$40,000	$42,000

Sales revenue for the year ending December 31, 2012, is $3,690,000. The company's gross profit ratio is normally 40%.

Based on these data, the president thinks the company should report an inventory turnover ratio of 90 times per year.

(Continued)

Required

1. Using the necessary calculations, explain how the president came up with an inventory turn-over ratio of 90 times.
2. Do you think the company should report a turnover ratio of 90 times? If not, explain why you disagree and explain, with calculations, what you think the ratio should be.
3. Assume that you are the controller for Garden Fresh. What will you tell the president?

SOLUTIONS TO KEY TERMS QUIZ

Quiz 1:

14	Horizontal analysis	5	Cash flow from operations to current
11	Vertical analysis		liabilities ratio
10	Gross profit ratio	6	Accounts receivable turnover ratio
12	Profit margin ratio	4	Number of days' sales in receivables
13	Liquidity	9	Inventory turnover ratio
2	Working capital	7	Number of days' sales in inventory
3	Current ratio	8	Cash-to-cash operating cycle
1	Acid-test or quick ratio		

Quiz 2:

3	Solvency	1	Return on common stockholders'
7	Debt-to-equity ratio		equity ratio
13	Times interest earned ratio	12	Leverage
14	Debt service coverage ratio	5	Earnings per share (EPS)
8	Cash flow from operations to capital	2	Price/earnings (P/E) ratio
	expenditures ratio	6	Dividend payout ratio
15	Profitability	11	Dividend yield ratio
9	Return on assets ratio	17	Discontinued operations (Appendix)
4	Return on sales ratio	16	Extraordinary item (Appendix)
10	Asset turnover ratio		

INTEGRATIVE PROBLEM

Presented here are a statement of income and retained earnings and comparative balance sheets for Gallagher, Inc., which operates a national chain of sporting goods stores.

Gallagher, Inc.
Statement of Income and Retained Earnings
For the Year Ended December 31, 2012
(all amounts in thousands of dollars)

Net sales	$48,000
Cost of goods sold	36,000
Gross profit	$12,000
Selling, general, and administrative expense	6,000
Operating income	$ 6,000
Interest expense	280
Income before tax	$ 5,720
Income tax expense	2,280
Net income	$ 3,440
Preferred dividends	100
Income available to common	$ 3,340
Common dividends	500
To retained earnings	$ 2,840
Retained earnings, 1/1	12,000
Retained earnings, 12/31	$14,840

Gallagher, Inc.
Comparative Balance Sheets
December 31, 2012 and 2011
(all amounts in thousands of dollars)

	December 31	
	2012	**2011**
Cash	$ 840	$ 2,700
Accounts receivable	12,500	9,000
Inventory	8,000	5,500
Prepaid insurance	100	400
Total current assets	$21,440	$17,600
Land	$ 4,000	$ 4,000
Buildings and equipment	12,000	9,000
Accumulated depreciation	(3,700)	(3,000)
Total long-term assets	$12,300	$10,000
Total assets	$33,740	$27,600
Accounts payable	$ 7,300	$ 5,000
Taxes payable	4,600	4,200
Notes payable	2,400	1,600
Current portion of bonds	200	200
Total current liabilities	$14,500	$11,000
Bonds payable	1,400	1,600
Total liabilities	$15,900	$12,600
Preferred stock, $5 par	$ 1,000	$ 1,000
Common stock, $1 par	2,000	2,000
Retained earnings	14,840	12,000
Total stockholders' equity	$17,840	$15,000
Total liabilities and stockholders' equity	$33,740	$27,600

Required

1. Prepare a statement of cash flows for Gallagher, Inc., for the year ended December 31, 2012, using the *indirect* method in the Operating Activities section of the statement.
2. Gallagher's management is concerned with its short-term liquidity and its solvency over the long run. To help management evaluate these, compute the following ratios, rounding all answers to the nearest one-tenth of a percent:

    a. Current ratio
    b. Acid-test ratio
    c. Cash flow from operations to current liabilities ratio
    d. Accounts receivable turnover ratio
    e. Number of days' sales in receivables
    f. Inventory turnover ratio
    g. Number of days' sales in inventory
    h. Debt-to-equity ratio
    i. Debt service coverage ratio
    j. Cash flow from operations to capital expenditures ratio

3. Comment on Gallagher's liquidity and its solvency. What additional information do you need to fully evaluate the company?

ANSWERS TO POD REVIEW

LO1	1. d	2. c		**LO5**	1. a	2. b
LO2	1. a	2. b		**LO6**	1. a	2. b
LO3	1. c	2. a		**LO7**	1. d	2. b
LO4	1. d	2. a				

International Financial Reporting Standards

IFRS

AFTER STUDYING THIS APPENDIX, YOU SHOULD BE ABLE TO:

LO1 Explain why accounting standards currently differ among countries around the world.

LO2 Explain the benefits from a single set of accounting standards.

LO3 Describe the role of the International Accounting Standards Board in setting accounting standards and be familiar with the time frame for the convergence of U.S. GAAP and IFRS standards.

LO4 Describe the most significant differences between U.S. GAAP and IFRS.

LO5 Understand how differences in format and terminology affect the appearance of financial statements in various countries.

STUDY LINKS

You have $1,000 to invest and are trying to decide between the common shares of three car makers: **Ford Motor Company** in the United States, **Daimler AG** in Germany, and **Hyundai Motor Company** in the Republic of Korea. As part of your analysis, you read the notes to the financial statements for each company and realize that the accounting standards used by the three companies might not necessarily be the same. Not surprisingly, Ford's statements are prepared in accordance with U.S. generally accepted accounting principles (U.S. GAAP) as determined by the Financial Accounting Standards Board (FASB). On the other hand, Daimler follows a set of international accounting standards that we will describe later in this appendix. Finally, Hyundai's financial statements reflect standards generally accepted in the Republic of Korea. When you compare the net income of the three companies, can you be assured that you are comparing "apples to apples"? Or could it be that differences in accounting standards are responsible for some of the differences in the earnings of the three companies?

The objective of this appendix is to give you an appreciation for the differences in accounting standards around the world and an understanding of efforts to develop a unified set of standards that all companies would use, regardless of their home country. **Because these efforts are in continual development, we will use the web site that accompanies this textbook to keep you updated on the progress being made.**

Why do you need to study this appendix?

- You need to know why accounting standards differ across countries. (See pp. A-2–A-4.)
- You need to know whether accounting standards should be the same in all countries. Or put another way, you need to know what benefits there would be if all companies used the same standards, regardless of their home country. (See pp. A-4–A-6.)
- You need to know who is responsible for developing a single set of global standards. (See pp. A-6–A-7.)
- You need to know the *major differences* between IFRS and U.S. GAAP. (See pp. A-7–A-11.)
- You need to know when international standards will be adopted in the United States and when it is likely that a single set of standards will be used by all companies. (See pp. A-6–A-7.)
- You need to know if there is a standard format and set of terms used on financial statements around the world. (See pp. A-11–A-13.)

Regardless of your career path, these issues will be important to your future in business. With the rapid development of global business, your need to understand the movement toward a unified set of accounting standards will only increase in importance.

LO1 Explain why accounting standards currently differ among countries around the world.

Why Do Accounting Standards Differ?

No single explanation can be given for the divergence of accounting standards. However, the following are among the most important reasons why they differ:

1. Legal System

The two primary legal systems used around the world are the *common law system* and the *code law system*. The common law system has its roots in the United Kingdom and, because of historical ties, is also the system used in the United States. In common law countries, there are generally fewer statutes written into the laws and thus more reliance on interpretation by the courts. In code law countries, such as Germany, there are more detailed rules written into the statutes. But what does this difference have to do with accounting standards? Because less detailed laws are written into the statutes of common law countries such as the United States, nongovernmental bodies such as the Financial Accounting Standards Board (FASB) have developed more detailed rules. In contrast, the accounting standards in Germany are much briefer.

2. Taxation

Countries differ in terms of how similar or different the rules are for determining accounting income and taxable income. For example, in the United States significant differences exist between the two because the computation of accounting income is based on the rules of the FASB whereas taxable income is based on the rules as set forth by the Internal Revenue Service. In many other countries, including Japan and much of Europe, fewer differences exist between the amount of income reported to stockholders and that reported to the taxing authorities.

3. Financing

Corporations in the United States receive most of their financing from two sources: creditors and stockholders. Because stockholders and creditors such as bondholders and banks are not privy to the internal records of the corporation, accountability to the public is of paramount importance. In some other countries, more of the financing may come from families, banks, and even the government. In these cases, there has been less need to develop detailed rules for disclosure.

4. Inflation

In some countries, notably those in Latin America and South America, inflation has been much more rampant than in other parts of the world. Because of the instability of the measuring unit that is the currency in those countries, companies have been required to adjust their financial statements to take into account the effects of inflation. At one time, the FASB developed rules for companies in the United States to use to adjust for inflation. As inflation has subsided in this country, U.S. companies no longer present financial information adjusted for the effects of inflation.

5. Relationships Between Countries

Countries that have strong political and economic ties often share similar accounting practices. For example, the roots of accounting systems in Canada and Australia, two former British colonies, can be traced to those found in the United Kingdom.

6. State of Economic Development

At any one time, all countries around the world are at different stages in the development of their economies. For example, the free-market systems used in the United Kingdom and in the United States have been in place for many years. Complex business arrangements such as leases and pension plans necessitate relatively detailed accounting rules to deal with them. In contrast, the economies in some countries, such as those that made up the former Soviet Union, are just beginning to develop and thus so are the accounting standards in those countries.

We have now seen that accounting standards differ around the world for a variety of reasons, some of which are interrelated. For example, the legal system in the United States, coupled with a highly advanced economy, has resulted in a lengthy and complex set of accounting standards. Although the Securities and Exchange Commission has ultimate authority to set accounting standards, it has delegated much of the responsibility to the non-governmental FASB. As a private-sector, independent body the FASB gathers information from a variety of sources, including the multi-billion-dollar corporations that dominate business in this country. The influence of these companies in setting accounting standards is considerable. In some of the less-developed countries of the world, especially those in which the forces of capitalism are less prevalent, accounting standards have developed at a much slower pace.

LO1 Explain why accounting standards currently differ among countries around the world.

- Accounting standards vary around the world for a variety of reasons, including:
  - Some countries follow a common law system and others rely more heavily on code law.
  - In some countries, accounting standards follow the tax law more closely than in other countries.
  - The source of financing can affect how accounting standards are developed.
  - Significant inflation may result in accounting rules to adjust the statements for its effects.
  - The standards in some countries are influenced by those in other countries.
  - The state of economic development can affect accounting standards.

POD REVIEW A.1

QUESTIONS   **Answers to these questions are on the last page of the appendix.**

1. Which of the following countries use a common law system?
   a. Germany
   b. United Kingdom
   c. United States
   d. both the United Kingdom and the United States

2. Which of the following statements is true about accounting standards in the United States?
   a. They are the same as the taxation rules.
   b. Minor differences exist between accounting standards and taxation rules.
   c. Significant differences exist between accounting standards and taxation rules.
   d. Accounting standards are set by the Internal Revenue Service.

LO2 Explain the benefits from a single set of accounting standards.

Benefits from a Single Set of Standards

Consider the case of **General Mills**. According to the company's web site, it sells its products in more than 100 countries and has offices or manufacturing facilities in more than 30 countries, and its international business accounts for $2.7 billion in annual sales. And it operates a joint venture with **Nestlé**, a Swiss company, called **Cereal Partners Worldwide**. Like a vast majority of publicly traded U.S. corporations, General Mills truly is a global company. So what would be some of the advantages to General Mills and its stockholders if a single set of accounting standards were used around the world?

1. Save on Accounting Costs

The development of accounting systems, their maintenance, and the eventual preparation of financial statements are major costs to most businesses, especially those with significant international operations. For example, the financial statements of General Mills's foreign subsidiaries must be consolidated with those of the parent corporation. The income from the company's joint venture with Nestlé must be accounted for prior to presenting the company's net income. Both of these tasks are that much more costly to General Mills if accounting principles differ in those other countries. A single set of worldwide accounting standards would save companies considerable money in accounting fees.

2. Make It Easier to Acquire Foreign Companies

Consider the following from the notes to **Kellogg's** 2010 annual report:

> *In June 2008, the Company acquired a majority interest in the business of Zhenghang Food Company Ltd. (Navigable Foods) for approximately $36 million (net of cash received). Navigable Foods, a manufacturer of cookies and crackers in the northern and northeastern regions of China, included approximately 1,800 employees, two manufacturing facilities and a sales and distribution network.*[1]

Certainly, Kellogg's took a close look at the financial statements of this Chinese company prior to acquiring it. But what if those statements were prepared using different standards than those used in the United States? A single set of standards would make it much easier to decide whether to acquire a foreign company.

3. Make It Easier to Access Foreign Capital Markets

Assume that a U.S. company wants to borrow money from a bank in Japan. With the current differences in accounting standards between the two countries, the Japanese bank might require the U.S. borrower to present financial statements prepared in accordance with Japanese standards. Or conversely, consider the case of a Japanese company that wants to list its stock on the New York Stock Exchange (a subsidiary of NYSE Euronext). It would likely need to adjust its financial statements so that they were in conformity with U.S. accounting practices. Both the U.S. company looking to borrow money abroad and the Japanese company wanting to access the U.S. capital markets could save considerable time and money if a single set of standards were used universally.

4. Facilitate Comparisons

Recall the dilemma presented at the beginning of this appendix: you are deciding whether to invest in Ford Motor Company in this country, Daimler AG in Germany, or Hyundai Motor Company in Korea. Just as it would be easier for one corporation to evaluate alternative investments if those companies all used the same accounting rules, so would it be easier for analysts and individual investors to compare companies if a single set of standards were used by all of them.

To a large extent, corporations are the primary beneficiaries of a unified set of accounting standards. They save accounting costs and can more easily make acquisition decisions and access foreign capital markets. Thus, stockholders, as the owners of corporations, have a vested interest in the development of common standards. However, not all companies and their stockholders are convinced that unified standards are in their best interests. For example, the argument has been made that U.S. corporations may find themselves more susceptible to lawsuits in a principles-based system that relies on fewer detailed rules. Considerable costs will be incurred in training accountants under a new set of standards. Ultimately, it will be the responsibility of the Securities and Exchange Commission in this country to decide if the advantages outweigh the disadvantages.

---

[1] Kellogg's 2010 annual report, p. 35.

LO2 Explain the benefits from a single set of accounting standards.

- Certain benefits would result from a uniform set of accounting standards, including:
  - Save on accounting costs.
  - Make it easier to acquire foreign companies.
  - Make it easier to access foreign capital markets.
  - Facilitate comparisons.

POD REVIEW A.2

QUESTIONS   Answers to these questions are on the last page of the appendix.

1. Which of the following statements is true?
   a. A single set of accounting standards would make it easier to compare Ford, Daimler, and Hyundai since they currently do not use the same standards.
   b. Ford, Daimler, and Hyundai operate in different parts of the world, and thus there is no need for them to have the same accounting standards.
   c. Ford, Daimler, and Hyundai all currently use the same accounting standards because they are in the same industry.
   d. None of these is a true statement.

2. Which of the following is a reason for a single set of accounting standards?
   a. A company could more easily decide whether to buy a competitor in another country.
   b. A company could reduce the cost to consolidate a foreign subsidiary.
   c. Any differences between accounting income and taxable income would be eliminated, saving on accounting costs.
   d. Both a. and b. are true.

LO3 Describe the role of the International Accounting Standards Board in setting accounting standards and be familiar with the time frame for the convergence of U.S. GAAP and IFRS standards.

Who Is Responsible for Developing Global Accounting Standards?

The IFRS Foundation includes among its principal objectives:

> to develop a single set of high quality, understandable, enforceable and globally accepted international financial reporting standards (IFRSs) through its standard-setting body, the IASB.[2]

The International Accounting Standards Committee was established in 1973 to develop worldwide standards and was replaced in 2001 by the IASB. With headquarters in London, the IASB not only issues new accounting standards (called *International Financial Reporting Standards* or *IFRS*), but it also works with national accounting groups such as the FASB towards convergence of standards.

According to the IASB, approximately 120 countries now either require or permit the use of IFRS. In fact use of IFRS is now mandatory in all member states of the economic and political organization known as the European Union. Outside Europe, other countries have formally announced their convergence plans. For example, China has substantially reached convergence with IFRS. Beginning in 2011, all Canadian listed companies were required to use IFRS. Companies in Mexico must begin using IFRS by 2012. Japan expects to make a decision in 2012 about mandatory adoption.

Where does this leave the United States? In recent years, groups in this country have given signals that the United States is moving toward convergence. First, in 2007, the SEC dropped its longstanding rule that required foreign companies who filed financial statements with it to adjust those statements to conform with U.S. GAAP. The only stipulation is that the statements must follow the standards of the IASB. Second, in 2008, the SEC indicated that it would give a limited number of U.S. corporations the option of adopting IFRS as early as 2009.

In 2002, the IASB and the FASB formalized their commitment to the union of U.S. and international standards with the Norwalk agreement. Since that time, the two

---

[2] IFRS Foundation web site.

groups have continued their efforts in this regard. For example, in October 2009, the FASB and the IASB reaffirmed their commitment to achieving convergence. As part of this agreement, the two bodies set 2011 as the deadline for completion of a number of joint projects they are currently working on. It is possible that the United States will simply require companies to use IFRS. It is more likely that the United States will continue working to eliminate differences between U.S. and international standards.

Throughout this book, we have focused our attention on the fundamental concepts underlying financial reporting and the standards that have been developed in this country to support those concepts. Many of the differences between U.S. GAAP and IFRS deal with complex issues beyond the scope of this book. In the next section, we consider the major differences between the two sets of rules, emphasizing those topics that have been discussed in each of the chapters.

LO3 Describe the role of the International Accounting Standards Board in setting accounting standards and be familiar with the time frame for the convergence of U.S. GAAP and IFRS standards.

- The International Accounting Standards Board is the group responsible for the development of a single set of worldwide accounting standards.
- The FASB and similar accounting bodies in other countries are currently working with the IASB to achieve the goal of a single set of standards.

POD REVIEW
A.3

QUESTIONS　　**Answers to these questions are on the last page of the appendix.**

1. The group with primary responsibility for development of a single set of accounting standards around the world is the
   a. FASB.
   b. IASC.
   c. IASB.
   d. No single group has assumed this responsibility.

2. Which of the following statements accurately represents the adoption by U.S. companies of IFRS?
   a. U.S. companies currently follow IFRS.
   b. U.S. companies currently have the option of using either U.S. GAAP or IFRS.
   c. No date has yet been set for the adoption of IFRS by all U.S. companies.
   d. None of these is a true statement.

© Cengage Learning 2013

Major Differences Between U.S. GAAP and IFRS

LO4 Describe the most significant differences between U.S. GAAP and IFRS.

Chapter 1: Accounting as a Form of Communication

By July 1, 2009, when the codification of accounting standards took effect, the FASB had issued 168 standards, in addition to various interpretations and other documents that comprise what is considered to be U.S. GAAP. In contrast, during a very similar time period, the IASB and its predecessor body had released only about 50 standards. Additionally, FASB statements are generally much more detailed than those of the IASB. Because there are significantly more standards in the United States and they are more detailed, standard setting in the United States has often been characterized as *rule based,* whereas the approach used by the international body is said to be more *principle based.* Because less-detailed guidance is usually provided in international standards, it stands to reason that more disclosures are warranted. Thus, it is common to see significantly more disclosures in notes to the financial statements of companies that follow IFRS than for those companies following U.S. GAAP. These differences are summarized as follows:

	U.S. GAAP	IFRS
Type of standards	Rule based	Principle based
Number of standards	More	Fewer
Level of detail in standards	More detailed	Less detailed
Level of disclosure required	Less	More

Chapter 2: Financial Statements and the Annual Report

As another indication of the cooperation between the FASB and the IASB, in September 2010, the two groups released a joint statement titled "Conceptual Framework for Financial Reporting." With this statement, both the objectives of financial reporting and the qualitative characteristics that make accounting information useful are the same for the two groups. These concepts are discussed in detail in Chapter 2.

Both U.S. GAAP and IFRS require a complete set of financial statements to include a balance sheet, a statement of stockholders' equity, an income statement, and a statement of cash flows. The FASB and the IASB are currently working on a joint project to provide guidance on the presentation of the information in each of these statements.

Chapter 3: Processing Accounting Information

How accounting information is processed is largely a function of the technology available to implement an accounting system rather than the result of any specific accounting standards in a particular country. The technology available in less developed countries may influence the development of accounting systems in those countries. The double-entry system devised in 15th-century Italy is still used almost universally today.

Chapter 4: Income Measurement and Accrual Accounting

The accrual accounting system is used almost universally and is the basis for financial statements prepared using both U.S. GAAP and IFRS.

Chapter 5: Inventories and Cost of Goods Sold

The LIFO inventory method is popular in the United States, to some extent due to the fact that it allows companies to minimize income taxes during a period of rising prices. Recall from Chapter 5 that the LIFO conformity rule requires that a company that wants to use the LIFO method for reporting cost of goods sold on its tax return must also use LIFO on its books. Many countries do not allow LIFO for either tax or financial reporting purposes. In fact, the IASB strictly prohibits the use of LIFO by companies that follow its standards. There has been considerable discussion in the United States about the repeal of LIFO for tax purposes. If this were to happen, it is likely that its use for financial reporting purposes would be eliminated as well.

Both U.S. GAAP and IFRS require use of the lower-of-cost-or-market rule to value inventories. However, the two sets of standards differ in two respects. First, U.S. GAAP defines market value as *replacement cost*, subject to a maximum and minimum amount. In contrast, IFRS uses *net realizable value* as the measure of the market value of inventory, and no upper or lower limits are imposed. Second, under U.S. GAAP, if inventory is written down to a new, lower market value, this amount becomes the basis for that inventory. Future write-downs of the inventory use this new amount to compare with market value. However, under IFRS, write-downs of inventory can be reversed in later periods. That is, a gain is recognized when the value of the inventory goes back up.

Chapter 6: Cash and Internal Control

The Sarbanes-Oxley Act of 2002 (SOX) placed strict reporting requirements on companies that want to list their securities on U.S. stock exchanges. The initial costs to comply with the act and the annual requirements to maintain an effective system of internal control have been substantial for these companies. No such reporting requirements exist for companies that report using IFRS. It will be interesting to see whether convergence of U.S. GAAP with IFRS results in any additional requirements similar to those now imposed in this country under SOX.

Chapter 7: Receivables and Investments

No significant differences exist in the accounting for receivables in this country and internationally. U.S. GAAP and IFRS both require that investments be carried at fair value rather than historical cost, although there are minor differences in the rules for application of fair value accounting.

Chapter 8: Operating Assets: Property, Plant, and Equipment, and Intangibles

While the accounting for operating assets is similar under IFRS and U.S. GAAP standards, there are several important differences.

The same depreciation methods are available for long-term assets under both sets of standards, but the estimates of residual values and the depreciable lives of assets may be assessed differently. Under IFRS, estimates of the life of assets and the residual value of assets must be reviewed at least annually, and if the estimates have changed, then the company should treat the change as a change in estimate. U.S. GAAP requires companies to assess the estimate of residual value and life only when circumstances have changed and the accountant believes a change in estimate is necessary. Also, the treatment of interest to be capitalized on self-constructed assets varies between IFRS and U.S. GAAP. U.S. GAAP requires that a company **must** capitalize interest on such assets, while IFRS permits capitalization but does not require it.

There are also differences in the reporting for particular operating assets. Both IFRS and U.S. GAAP require companies to report an amount for goodwill and record a write down of the goodwill if the asset has been "impaired." However, the methods of evaluating impairment differ between the two sets of standards. The treatment of research and development (R&D) costs also differs. U.S. GAAP requires all internally generated research and development costs to be treated as an expense. IFRS requires research costs to be recognized as an expense but does allow certain development costs to be accounted for as an asset.

Perhaps the most significant difference in the accounting for operating assets concerns the use of fair values. Generally, both sets of standards require operating assets to be carried at their historical cost. However, IFRS allows companies to revalue the assets at fair value (either up or down from historical cost) if reliable measures are available. U.S. GAAP does not allow companies to revalue to fair value except in cases where an impairment of an asset has occurred and the asset must be written down to a lower value.

Chapter 9: Current Liabilities, Contingencies, and the Time Value of Money

You may be surprised to learn that U.S. GAAP does not require companies to present a balance sheet with classifications for current and long-term liabilities, or any other classifications. Many companies do, however, present a classified balance sheet in order to present information that balance sheet readers consider to be important. In contrast to U.S. GAAP, IFRS does require companies to present current and noncurrent classifications of assets and liabilities.

The IFRS and U.S. GAAP standards differ significantly on what we have referred to as contingencies in Chapter 9. For reporting in the United States, liabilities for which the outcome is dependent upon a future event must be recorded if the unfavorable outcome is probable and the amount can be reasonably estimated. If the outcome is at least reasonably possible, then the liability should be disclosed, usually in the notes to the financial statements. For IFRS, the term *contingent liabilities* is used only for items that are not recorded on the financial statements. The liabilities that are considered probable and are recorded are referred to as *provisions*. Also, the two sets of standards differ somewhat on what should be considered as "probable."

Finally, the standards differ on the reporting of liabilities where a range of values is available as a possible outcome. U.S. GAAP requires that a company report the low end of the range if the outcome is probable, and disclose the upper end of the range in the notes. IFRS, however, requires companies to record the midpoint of the range as a provision if the unfavorable outcome is probable.

Chapter 10: Long-Term Liabilities

The accounting for leases is an excellent example of the differences between IFRS and U.S. GAAP. Often, the difference is not in the rules themselves, but in the application of the rules and the degree of judgment or flexibility allowed in the application of the rules. The criteria concerning whether a lease is a capital lease are similar for IFRS and U.S. GAAP. However, the criteria are considered more like "guidelines" for IFRS reporting, and companies may deviate from the criteria. For U.S. GAAP reporting, the lease criteria are applied in a more rigid manner.

There are also differences in some of the more technical aspects of the accounting for deferred taxes, a topic covered in the appendix to Chapter 10. In particular, the guidelines for whether deferred taxes should be treated as current or long-term amounts differ between IFRS and U.S. GAAP. Also, the treatment of amounts that are considered deferred tax assets differs between the two sets of standards.

Chapter 11: Stockholders' Equity

In general, the accounting for stockholders' equity is the same for IFRS and U.S. GAAP. The most significant difference concerns financial instruments that have both debt and equity characteristics (a convertible bond is one example). IFRS requires the portion of the instrument that represents debt to be presented in the Liability category and the portion of the instrument that represents equity to be in stockholders' equity. U.S. GAAP does not always require such instruments to be separately reported as debt and equity.

Also, both IFRS and U.S. GAAP require the presentation of comprehensive income amounts in the Stockholders' Equity category. However, the manner of reporting comprehensive income amounts as income on the income statement or statement of comprehensive income varies between the two sets of standards. These variations are beyond the scope of this text book.

Chapter 12: The Statement of Cash Flows

Both U.S. GAAP and IFRS require the inclusion of a statement of cash flows in a complete set of financial statements. Each set of standards also mandates that activities be classified into three categories: operating, investing, and financing. Some differences in classification exist. For example, interest (either received or paid) is always classified as an operating activity under U.S. GAAP. IFRS allows flexibility; cash receipts may be classified as either operating or investing activities and cash payments as either operating or financing. Similarly, dividends paid are always classified as financing activities under U.S. GAAP, but they may be classified as either operating or financing activities under IFRS. Recall from Chapter 12 that significant noncash activities may be presented in either a separate schedule on the face of the statement of cash flows or in the notes to the statements. Under IFRS, these noncash activities must be presented in the notes.

Chapter 13: Financial Statement Analysis

The IASB prohibits the presentation of items on the income statement as extraordinary. This is in contrast to U.S. GAAP, which requires gains and losses that are both unusual in nature and infrequent in occurrence to be classified as extraordinary in a separate section of the income statement.

Both U.S. GAAP and IFRS require separate presentation on the income statement for discontinued operations. The two sets of standards differ in some respects, particularly with regard to how a discontinued operation is defined.

LO4 Describe the most significant differences between U.S. GAAP and IFRS.

- Although U.S. GAAP and IFRS are similar in many respects, significant differences still exist.
  - U.S. GAAP is much more detailed.
  - The FASB has issued many more standards than has the IASB.
  - IFRS requires more disclosures in the notes to the financial statements.

POD REVIEW A.4

QUESTIONS   **Answers to these questions are on the last page of the appendix.**

1. Which of the following is true regarding the valuation of inventory?
   a. IFRS permits but does not require the use of LIFO.
   b. IFRS does not allow the use of LIFO.
   c. U.S. GAAP no longer allows the use of LIFO.
   d. None of these is a true statement.

2. Which of the following is true regarding the valuation of operating assets?
   a. U.S. GAAP allows companies to use fair value.
   b. IFRS allows companies to use fair value.
   c. Neither U.S. GAAP nor IFRS allows companies to use fair value.
   d. IFRS requires companies to use fair value.

© Cengage Learning 2013

Format and Terminology Differences

LO5 Understand how differences in format and terminology affect the appearance of financial statements in various countries.

Up to this point, the focus has been on the differing accounting standards used in the preparation of financial statements around the world. But what about the *format* for the statements and the *terms* used for the various statement items? It should come as no surprise that significant differences exist in how financial statements are presented and the names given to various accounts. For example, consider the partial *statement of financial position* (balance sheet) for Daimler AG shown in Exhibit A-1. (We show only the first two columns on the statement titled "Consolidated"—the entire statement also displays columns for its divisions: "Industrial Business" and "Daimler Financial Services.")

Note that amounts are stated in millions of euros, the common currency for members of the European Union. Also, a vast majority of the statement items are referenced to notes to the financial statements. As mentioned earlier in this appendix, because IFRS is less rules based, it is common to see more disclosures in notes to the financial statements (recall that Daimler AG uses IFRS in preparing its statements). In fact, Daimler AG's 2010 annual report includes 70 pages devoted to covering 38 notes to the financial statements.

One of the most striking differences is the *ordering* of both the assets and the equity and liabilities on the statement. For example, long-term assets are presented first, followed by current assets. Also, note that three common current assets are listed in reverse order of liquidity: inventories first, followed by trade receivables and then cash and cash equivalents. Similarly, equity items are presented before liabilities, with current liabilities as the last category on the statement. *Essentially, the entire statement of financial position is inverted compared to what is commonly seen in the United States.*

Significant differences in terminology are also evident in looking at Daimler AG's statement. For example, consider the Equity section. *Share Capital* is the name the company uses for what would normally be referred to as Capital Stock by a U.S. company. *Capital Reserves* is the equivalent of Additional Paid-In Capital. Daimler AG's noncurrent and current liabilities both contain an item called *Provisions for Other Risks*. This is what most U.S. companies would refer to as Contingent Liabilities. Financial statement users need to be aware of these differences in format and terminology. However, these differences should not impede the ability to analyze and make effective use of foreign statements.

EXHIBIT A-1 Daimler AG's Balance Sheet

		Consolidated	
		At December 31,	
In millions of euros	Note	2010	2009
Assets			
Intangible assets	10	7,504	6,753
Property, plant and equipment	11	17,593	15,965
Equipment on operating leases	12	19,925	18,532
Investments accounted for using the equity method	13	3,960	4,295
Receivables from financial services	14	22,864	22,250
Marketable debt securities	15	766	1,224
Other financial assets	16	3,194	2,793
Deferred tax assets	9	2,613	2,233
Other assets	17	408	496
Total non-current assets		78,827	74,541
Inventories	18	14,544	12,845
Trade receivables	19	7,192	5,285
Receivables from financial services	14	18,166	16,228
Cash and cash equivalents		10,903	9,800
Marketable debt securities	15	1,330	5,118
Other financial assets	16	2,247	2,342
Other assets	17	2,621	2,352
Sub-total current assets		57,003	53,970
Assets held for sale from non-automotive leasing portfolios	3	—	310
Total current assets		57,003	54,280
Total assets		135,830	128,821
Equity and liabilities			
Share capital		3,058	3,045
Capital reserves		11,905	11,864
Retained earnings		20,553	16,163
Other reserves		864	632
Treasury shares		−7	−1,443
Equity attributable to shareholders of Daimler AG		36,373	30,261
Minority interest		1,580	1,566
Total equity	20	37,953	31,827
Provisions for pensions and similar obligations	22	4,329	4,082
Provisions for income taxes		2,539	2,774
Provisions for other risks	23	5,548	4,696
Financing liabilities	24	27,861	33,258
Other financial liabilities	25	1,883	2,148
Deferred tax liabilities	9	675	509
Deferred income		1,824	1,914
Other liabilities	26	79	75
Total non-current liabilities		44,738	49,456

Callout boxes:
- Non-current assets listed before current assets
- Same as Capital Stock
- Same as Additional Paid-in Capital
- Equity listed first
- Non-current liabilities listed before current liabilities

(Continued)

EXHIBIT A-1 Daimler AG's Balance Sheet (Continued)

	Note	Consolidated At December 31, 2010	2009
Trade payables		7,657	5,622
Provisions for income taxes		1,229	509
Provisions for other risks	23	6,992	6,311
Financing liabilities	24	25,821	25,036
Other financial liabilities	25	8,626	7,589
Deferred income		1,269	1,397
Other liabilities	26	1,545	1,074
Total current liabilities		53,139	47,538
Total equity and liabilities		135,830	128,821

The accompanying notes are an integral part of these consolidated financial statements.

LO5 Understand how differences in format and terminology affect the appearance of financial statements in various countries.

- In some countries, long-term assets are listed before current assets on the balance sheet and long-term liabilities before current liabilities. It is also common to see the stockholders' equity accounts displayed above the liability accounts.
- Users must be alert to differing terms to describe the same items on financial statements.

POD REVIEW A.5

QUESTIONS   **Answers to these questions are on the last page of the appendix.**

1. Which of the following is a true statement about classification on a balance sheet?
   a. Current assets are listed before noncurrent assets in all countries.
   b. Current assets are listed after noncurrent assets in all countries.
   c. The United States is the only country in which assets are categorized as current or noncurrent.
   d. None of the other statements is true.

2. Which of the following is a true statement about the terms used on the balance sheet?
   a. Neither IFRS nor U.S. GAAP requires a standard set of terms on the balance sheet.
   b. Terminology is consistent across all countries.
   c. IFRS requires a standard set of terms on the balance sheet.
   d. U.S. GAAP requires a standard set of terms on the balance sheet.

QUESTIONS

1. What are at least four reasons that accounting standards currently differ between countries?
2. How have accounting standards developed differently in countries that use a common law system as opposed to those using code law?
3. Why might you expect the accounting standards in Australia to be similar to those in the United Kingdom?
4. What are at least three advantages in all companies around the world using the same accounting standards?
5. How would you describe the current role of the IASB in setting accounting standards?
6. How would you evaluate the following statement: "All of the other major industrialized countries of the world have now adopted IFRS and the United States has

set a date for adoption by all companies that currently follow FASB standards"?

7. You are considering investing in the airline industry and are looking specifically at buying shares of either **Southwest Airlines**, **British Airways**, or **Korean Airlines**. Would you expect the financial statements of these three companies to be prepared using the same accounting principles? Explain your answer.

8. How does the application of the lower-of-cost-or-market rule differ between U.S. GAAP and IFRS?

9. How would you evaluate the following statement: "Both the tax laws in the United States and IFRS allow the use of LIFO for tax purposes but only if the method is also used for financial reporting purposes"?

10. How are research and development costs accounted for differently under U.S. GAAP and IFRS?

11. Do either or both U.S. GAAP and IFRS allow operating assets to be carried on the balance sheet at fair value?

12. How does the meaning of the term *contingent liabilities* differ between U.S. GAAP and IFRS?

13. How does the application of the criteria for accounting for leases differ between U.S. GAAP and IFRS?

14. What differences are there in classification of interest received and interest paid under U.S. GAAP and IFRS?

15. How are extraordinary items presented on the income statement of a company following U.S. GAAP? How does this differ if the company follows IFRS?

16. Is there a standard format used in all countries for the statement of financial position? Explain.

EXERCISES

LO4 Exercise A-1 U.S. GAAP versus IFRS

Fill in the blanks below with either "more" or "less" to indicate the differences in U.S. GAAP and IFRS:

	U.S. GAAP	IFRS
Number of standards	_____	_____
Level of detail in standards	_____	_____
Level of disclosure required	_____	_____

LO4 Exercise A-2 Lower-of-Cost-or-Market Rule

The cost of Baxter's inventory at the end of the year was $50,000. Due to obsolescence, the cost to replace the inventory was only $40,000. Net realizable value—what the inventory could be sold for—is $42,000.

Required

Determine the amount Baxter should report on its year-end balance sheet for inventory assuming the company follows (a) U.S. GAAP and (b) IFRS.

LO4 Exercise A-3 Valuation of Operating Assets

Maple Corp. owns a building with an original cost of $1,000,000 and accumulated depreciation at the balance sheet date of $200,000. Based on a recent appraisal, the fair value of the building is $850,000.

Required

1. At what amount will the building be reported on the year-end balance sheet if Maple follows U.S. GAAP?
2. Does Maple have a choice in the amount to report for the building if instead it follows IFRS? What are those choices?

Exercise A-4 Statement of Cash Flows

LO4

During the most recent year, Butler paid $95,000 in interest to its lenders and $80,000 in dividends to its stockholders.

Required

1. In which category of the statement of cash flows (operating, investing, or financing) should each of these amounts be shown if Butler follows U.S. GAAP? If more than one category is acceptable, indicate what the choices are.
2. In which category of the statement of cash flows (operating, investing, or financing) should each of these amounts be shown if Butler follows IFRS? If more than one category is acceptable, indicate what the choices are.

Exercise A-5 Format and Terminology Differences

LO5

Refer to the statement of financial position for **Daimler AG** as shown on pages A-12–A-13.

Required

1. What is the currency used in preparing this statement?
2. Identify at least three differences in the format of the statement compared to what would normally be seen on a statement of financial position for a U.S. company.
3. Refer to the Equity section of the statement. What account titles would normally be used in the United States for the first two items in this section?

Answers to Pod Review

LO1	1. d	2. c		LO4	1. b	2. b
LO2	1. a	2. d		LO5	1. d	2. a
LO3	1. c	2. c				

Excerpts from Kellogg's Form 10-K for the Fiscal Year Ended January 1, 2011 [2010]

UNITED STATES SECURITIES AND EXCHANGE COMMISSION
Washington, D.C. 20549

FORM 10-K

☑ **ANNUAL REPORT PURSUANT TO SECTION 13 OR 15(d) OF THE SECURITIES EXCHANGE ACT OF 1934**

For the Fiscal Year Ended January 1, 2011

☐ **TRANSITION REPORT PURSUANT TO SECTION 13 OR 15(d) OF THE SECURITIES EXCHANGE ACT OF 1934**

For The Transition Period From   To

Commission file number 1-4171

Kellogg Company
(Exact name of registrant as specified in its charter)

Delaware	**38-0710690**
(State or other jurisdiction of Incorporation or organization)	(I.R.S. Employer Identification No.)

One Kellogg Square
Battle Creek, Michigan 49016-3599

(Address of Principal Executive Offices)

Registrant's telephone number: (269) 961-2000

Securities registered pursuant to Section 12(b) of the Securities Act:

Title of each class:	Name of each exchange on which registered:
Common Stock, $.25 par value per share	**New York Stock Exchange**

Securities registered pursuant to Section 12(g) of the Securities Act: None

---

Indicate by a check mark if the registrant is a well-known seasoned issuer, as defined in Rule 405 of the Securities Act.   Yes ☑   No ☐

Indicate by check mark if the registrant is not required to file reports pursuant to Section 13 or Section 15 (d) of the Act.   Yes ☐   No ☑

Note — Checking the box above will not relieve any registrant required to file reports pursuant to Section 13 or 15(d) of the Exchange Act from their obligations under those Sections.

Indicate by check mark whether the registrant: (1) has filed all reports required to be filed by Section 13 or 15(d) of the Securities Exchange Act of 1934 during the preceding 12 months (or for such shorter period that the registrant was required to file such reports), and (2) has been subject to such filing requirements for the past 90 days.   Yes ☑   No ☐

Indicate by check mark whether the registrant has submitted electronically and posted on its website, if any, every Interactive Data File required to be submitted and posted pursuant to Rule 405 of Regulation S-T during the preceding 12 months (or for such shorter period that the registrant was required to submit and post such files).   Yes ☑   No ☐

Indicate by check mark if disclosure of delinquent filers pursuant to Item 405 of Regulation S-K is not contained herein, and will not be contained, to the best of the registrant's knowledge in definitive proxy or information statements incorporated by reference in Part III of this Form 10-K or any amendment to this Form 10-K.   ☐

Indicate by check mark whether the registrant is a large accelerated filer, an accelerated filer, a non-accelerated filer or a smaller reporting company. See the definitions of "large accelerated filer," "accelerated filer" and "smaller reporting company" in Rule 12b-2 of the Exchange Act. (Check one)

Large accelerated filer ☑   Accelerated filer ☐   Non-accelerated filer ☐   Smaller reporting company ☐

Indicate by check mark whether the registrant is a shell company (as defined in Rule 12b-2 of the Act).   Yes ☐   No ☑

The aggregate market value of the common stock held by non-affiliates of the registrant (assuming for purposes of this computation only that the W. K. Kellogg Foundation Trust, directors and executive officers may be affiliates) as of the close of business on July 3, 2010 was approximately $13.7 billion based on the closing price of $50.67 for one share of common stock, as reported for the New York Stock Exchange on that date.

As of January 29, 2011, 365,098,153 shares of the common stock of the registrant were issued and outstanding.

Parts of the registrant's Proxy Statement for the Annual Meeting of Shareowners to be held on April 29, 2011 are incorporated by reference into Part III of this Report.

ITEM 8. FINANCIAL STATEMENTS AND SUPPLEMENTARY DATA

Kellogg Company and Subsidiaries

Consolidated Statement of Income

(millions, except per share data)	2010	2009	2008
Net sales	**$12,397**	$12,575	$12,822
Cost of goods sold	**7,108**	7,184	7,455
Selling, general and administrative expense	**3,299**	3,390	3,414
Operating profit	**$ 1,990**	$ 2,001	$ 1,953
Interest expense	**248**	295	308
Other income (expense), net	**—**	(22)	(14)
Income before income taxes	**1,742**	1,684	1,631
Income taxes	**502**	476	485
Net income	**$ 1,240**	$ 1,208	$ 1,146
Net loss attributable to noncontrolling interests	**(7)**	(4)	(2)
Net income attributable to Kellogg Company	**$ 1,247**	$ 1,212	$ 1,148
Per share amounts:			
Basic	**$ 3.32**	$ 3.17	$ 3.01
Diluted	**$ 3.30**	$ 3.16	$ 2.99
Dividends per share	**$ 1.560**	$ 1.430	$ 1.300

Refer to Notes to Consolidated Financial Statements.

Kellogg Company and Subsidiaries

Consolidated Balance Sheet

(millions, except share data)	2010	2009
Current assets		
Cash and cash equivalents	$ 444	$ 334
Accounts receivable, net	1,190	1,093
Inventories	1,056	910
Other current assets	225	221
Total current assets	2,915	2,558
Property, net	3,128	3,010
Goodwill	3,628	3,643
Other intangibles, net	1,456	1,458
Other assets	720	531
Total assets	$11,847	$11,200
Current liabilities		
Current maturities ofl ong-term debt	$ 952	$ 1
Notes payable	44	44
Accounts payable	1,149	1,077
Other current liabilities	1,039	1,166
Total current liabilities	3,184	2,288
Long-term debt	4,908	4,835
Deferred income taxes	697	425
Pension liability	265	430
Other liabilities	639	947
Commitments and contingencies		
Equity		
Common stock, $.25 par value, 1,000,000,000 shares authorized		
Issued: 419,272,027 shares in 2010 and 419,058,168 shares in 2009	105	105
Capital in excess of par value	495	472
Retained earnings	6,122	5,481
Treasury stock at cost		
53,667,635 shares in 2010 and 37,678,215 shares in 2009	(2,650)	(1,820)
Accumulated other comprehensive income (loss)	(1,914)	(1,966)
Total Kellogg Company equity	2,158	2,272
Noncontrolling interests	(4)	3
Total equity	2,154	2,275
Total liabilities and equity	$11,847	$11,200

Refer to Notes to Consolidated Financial Statements.

Kellogg Company and Subsidiaries

Consolidated Statement of Equity

(millions)	Common stock shares	Common stock amount	Capital in excess of par value	Retained earnings	Treasury stock shares	Treasury stock amount	Accumulated other comprehensive income (loss)	Total Kellogg Company equity	Non-controlling interests	Total equity	Total comprehensive income (loss)
Balance, December 29, 2007	419	$105	$388	$4,217	29	$(1,357)	$ (827)	$ 2,526	$ 2	$ 2,528	$ 1,321
Common stock repurchases					13	(650)		(650)		(650)	
Business acquisitions								—	7	7	
Net income (loss)				1,148				1,148	(2)	1,146	$ 1,146
Dividends				(495)				(495)		(495)	
Other comprehensive income							(1,314)	(1,314)		(1,314)	$(1,314)
Stock compensation			51					51		51	
Stock options exercised and other			(1)	(34)	(5)	217		182		182	
Balance, January 3, 2009	419	$105	$438	$4,836	37	$(1,790)	$(2,141)	$ 1,448	$ 7	$ 1,455	$ (168)
Common stock repurchases					4	(187)		(187)		(187)	
Net income (loss)				1,212				1,212	(4)	1,208	$ 1,208
Dividends				(546)				(546)		(546)	
Other comprehensive income							175	175		175	175
Stock compensation			37					37		37	
Stock options exercised and other			(3)	(21)	(3)	157		133		133	
Balance, January 2, 2010	419	$105	$472	$5,481	38	$(1,820)	$(1,966)	$ 2,272	$ 3	$ 2,275	$ 1,383
Common stock repurchases					21	(1,057)		(1,057)		(1,057)	
Net income (loss)				1,247				1,247	(7)	1,240	1,240
Dividends				(584)				(584)		(584)	
Other comprehensive income							52	52		52	52
Stock compensation			19					19		19	
Stock options exercised and other			4	(22)	(5)	227		209		209	
Balance, January 1, 2011	**419**	**$105**	**$495**	**$6,122**	**54**	**$(2,650)**	**$(1,914)**	**$ 2,158**	**$(4)**	**$ 2,154**	**$ 1,292**

Refer to Notes to Consolidated Financial Statements.

Kellogg Company and Subsidiaries

Consolidated Statement of Cash Flows

(millions)	2010	2009	2008
Operating activities			
Net income	$ 1,240	$ 1,208	$1,146
Adjustments to reconcile net income to operating cash flows:			
Depreciation and amortization	392	384	375
Deferred income taxes	266	(40)	157
Other	97	13	121
Pension and other postretirement benefit contributions	(643)	(100)	(451)
Changes in operating assets and liabilities:			
Trade receivables	59	(75)	48
Inventories	(146)	(13)	41
Accounts payable	72	(59)	32
Accrued income taxes	(192)	112	(85)
Accrued interest expense	9	(5)	3
Accrued and prepaid advertising, promotion and trade allowances	(12)	91	(10)
Accrued salaries and wages	(169)	42	(47)
All other current assets and liabilities	35	85	(63)
Net cash provided by operating activities	$ 1,008	$ 1,643	$1,267
Investing activities			
Additions to properties	$ (474)	$ (377)	$ (461)
Acquisitions of businesses, net of cash acquired	—	—	(213)
Other	9	7	(7)
Net cash used in investing activities	$ (465)	$ (370)	$ (681)
Financing activities			
Net increase (reduction) of notes payable, with maturities less than or equal to 90 days	$ (1)	$(1,284)	$ 23
Issuances of notes payable, with maturities greater than 90 days	—	10	190
Reductions of notes payable, with maturities greater than 90 days	—	(70)	(316)
Issuances ofl ong-term debt	987	1,241	756
Reductions ofl ong-term debt	(1)	(482)	(468)
Net issuances of common stock	204	131	175
Common stock repurchases	(1,052)	(187)	(650)
Cash dividends	(584)	(546)	(495)
Other	8	5	5
Net cash used in financing activities	$ (439)	$(1,182)	$ (780)
Effect of exchange rate changes on cash and cash equivalents	6	(12)	(75)
Increase (decrease) in cash and cash equivalents	$ 110	$ 79	$ (269)
Cash and cash equivalents at beginning of year	334	255	524
Cash and cash equivalents at end of year	$ 444	$ 334	$ 255

Refer to Notes to Consolidated Financial Statements.

Kellogg Company and Subsidiaries

Notes to Consolidated Financial Statements

NOTE 1
ACCOUNTING POLICIES

Basis of presentation
The consolidated financial statements include the accounts of Kellogg Company and its majority-owned subsidiaries (Kellogg or the Company). Intercompany balances and transactions are eliminated.

The Company's fiscal year normally ends on the Saturday closest to December 31 and as a result, a 53rd week is added approximately every sixth year. The Company's 2010 and 2009 fiscal years each contained 52 weeks and ended on January 1, 2011 and January 2, 2010, respectively. The Company's 2008 fiscal year ended on January 3, 2009, and included a 53rd week. While quarters normally consist of 13-week periods, the fourth quarter of fiscal 2008 included a 14th week.

Use of estimates
The preparation of financial statements in conformity with accounting principles generally accepted in the United States of America requires management to make estimates and assumptions that affect the reported amounts of assets and liabilities, the disclosure of contingent liabilities at the date of the financial statements and the reported amounts of revenues and expenses during the periods reported. Actual results could differ from those estimates.

Cash and cash equivalents
Highly liquid investments with remaining stated maturities of three months or less when purchased are considered cash equivalents and recorded at cost.

Accounts receivable
Accounts receivable consists principally of trade receivables, which are recorded at the invoiced amount, net of allowances for doubtful accounts and prompt payment discounts. Trade receivables do not bear interest. The allowance for doubtful accounts represents management's estimate of the amount of probable credit losses in existing accounts receivable, as determined from a review of past due balances and other specific account data. Account balances are written off against the allowance when management determines the receivable is uncollectible. The Company does not have off-balance sheet credit exposure related to its customers.

Inventories
Inventories are valued at the lower of cost or market. Cost is determined on an average cost basis.

Property
The Company's property consists mainly of plants and equipment used for manufacturing activities. These assets are recorded at cost and depreciated over estimated useful lives using straight-line methods for financial reporting and accelerated methods, where permitted, for tax reporting. Major property categories are depreciated over various periods as follows (in years): manufacturing machinery and equipment 5-20; office equipment 4-5; computer equipment and capitalized software 3-5; building components 15-30; building structures 50. Cost includes interest associated with significant capital projects. Plant and equipment are reviewed for impairment when conditions indicate that the carrying value may not be recoverable. Such conditions include an extended period of idleness or a plan of disposal. Assets to be disposed of at a future date are depreciated over the remaining period of use. Assets to be sold are written down to realizable value at the time the assets are being actively marketed for sale and a sale is expected to occur within one year. As of year-end 2010 and 2009, the carrying value of assets held for sale was insignificant.

Goodwill and other intangible assets
Goodwill and indefinite-lived intangibles are not amortized, but are tested at least annually for impairment. An intangible asset with a finite life is amortized on a straight-line basis over the estimated useful life.

For the goodwill impairment test, the fair value of the reporting units are estimated based on market multiples. This approach employs market multiples based on earnings before interest, taxes, depreciation and amortization, earnings for companies that are comparable to the Company's reporting units and discounted cash flow. The assumptions used for the impairment test are consistent with those utilized by a market participant performing similar valuations for the Company's reporting units.

Similarly, impairment testing of other intangible assets requires a comparison of carrying value to fair value of that particular asset. Fair values of non-goodwill intangible assets are based primarily on projections of future cash flows to be generated from that asset. For instance, cash flows related to a particular trademark would be based on a projected royalty stream attributable to branded product sales, discounted at rates consistent with rates used by market participants.

These estimates are made using various inputs including historical data, current and anticipated market conditions, management plans, and market comparables.

Revenue recognition

The Company recognizes sales upon delivery of its products to customers. Revenue, which includes shipping and handling charges billed to the customer, is reported net of applicable provisions for discounts, returns, allowances, and various government withholding taxes. Methodologies for determining these provisions are dependent on local customer pricing and promotional practices, which range from contractually fixed percentage price reductions to reimbursement based on actual occurrence or performance. Where applicable, future reimbursements are estimated based on a combination of historical patterns and future expectations regarding specific in-market product performance.

Advertising and promotion

The Company expenses production costs of advertising the first time the advertising takes place. Advertising expense is classified in selling, general and administrative (SGA) expense.

The Company classifies promotional payments to its customers, the cost of consumer coupons, and other cash redemption offers in net sales. The cost of promotional package inserts is recorded in cost of goods sold (COGS). Other types of consumer promotional expenditures are recorded in SGA expense.

Research and development

The costs of research and development (R&D) are expensed as incurred and are classified in SGA expense. R&D includes expenditures for new product and process innovation, as well as significant technological improvements to existing products and processes. The Company's R&D expenditures primarily consist of internal salaries, wages, consulting, and supplies attributable to time spent on R&D activities. Other costs include depreciation and maintenance of research facilities and equipment, including assets at manufacturing locations that are temporarily engaged in pilot plant activities.

Stock-based compensation

The Company uses stock-based compensation, including stock options, restricted stock and executive performance shares, to provide long-term performance incentives for its global workforce.

The Company classifies pre-tax stock compensation expense principally in SGA expense within its corporate operations. Expense attributable to awards of equity instruments is recorded in capital in excess of par value in the Consolidated Balance Sheet.

Certain of the Company's stock-based compensation plans contain provisions that accelerate vesting of awards upon retirement, disability, or death of eligible employees and directors. A stock-based award is considered vested for expense attribution purposes when the employee's retention of the award is no longer contingent on providing subsequent service. Accordingly, the Company recognizes compensation cost immediately for awards granted to retirement-eligible individuals or over the period from the grant date to the date retirement eligibility is achieved, if less than the stated vesting period.

The Company recognizes compensation cost for stock option awards that have a graded vesting schedule on a straight-line basis over the requisite service period for the entire award.

Corporate income tax benefits realized upon exercise or vesting of an award in excess of that previously recognized in earnings ("windfall tax benefit") is recorded in other financing activities in the Consolidated Statement of Cash Flows. Realized windfall tax benefits are credited to capital in excess of par value in the Consolidated Balance Sheet. Realized shortfall tax benefits (amounts which are less than that previously recognized in earnings) are first offset against the cumulative balance of windfall tax benefits, if any, and then charged directly to income tax expense. The Company currently has sufficient cumulative windfall tax benefits to absorb arising shortfalls, such that earnings were not affected during the periods presented. Correspondingly, the Company includes the impact of pro forma deferred tax assets (i.e., the "as if" windfall or shortfall) for purposes of determining assumed proceeds in the treasury stock calculation of diluted earnings per share.

Pension benefits, nonpension postretirement and postemployment benefits

The Company sponsors a number of U.S. and foreign plans to provide pension, health care, and other welfare benefits to retired employees, as well as salary continuance, severance, and long-term disability to former or inactive employees.

The recognition of benefit expense is based on actuarial assumptions, such as discount rate, long-term rate of compensation increase, long-term rate of return on plan assets and health care cost trend rate, and is reported in COGS and SGA expense on the Consolidated Statement of Income.

Pension and nonpension postretirement benefits. Variances between the expected and actual rates of return on plan assets are recognized in the calculated value of plan assets over a five-year period. Once recognized, experience gains and losses are amortized using a declining-balance method over the average remaining service period of active plan participants. Management reviews the Company's expected long-term rates of return annually; however, the benefit trust investment performance for one particular year does not, by itself, significantly influence this evaluation. The expected rates of return are not revised provided these rates fall between the 25th and 75th percentile of expected long-term returns, as determined by the Company's modeling process.

Pension obligation related experience gains or losses are amortized using a straight-line method over the average remaining service period of active plan participants. Health care claims cost related experience gains or losses are recognized in the calculated amount of claims experience over a four year period and once recognized, are amortized using a straight-line method over 15 years.

For defined benefit pension and postretirement plans, the Company records the net overfunded or underfunded position as a pension asset or pension liability on the Consolidated Balance Sheet. The change in funded status for the year is reported as a component of other comprehensive income (loss), net of tax, in equity.

Postemployment benefits. The Company recognizes an obligation for postemployment benefit plans that vest or accumulate with service. Obligations associated with the Company's postemployment benefit plans, which are unfunded, are included in other current liabilities and other liabilities on the Consolidated Balance Sheet. All gains and losses are recognized over the average remaining service period of active plan participants.

Postemployment benefits that do not vest or accumulate with service or benefits to employees in excess of those specified in the respective plans are expensed as incurred.

Income taxes
The Company recognizes uncertain tax positions based on a benefit recognition model. Provided that the tax position is deemed more likely than not of being sustained, the Company recognizes the largest amount of tax benefit that is greater than 50 percent likely of being ultimately realized upon settlement. The tax position is derecognized when it is no longer more likely than not of being sustained. The Company classifies income tax-related interest and penalties as interest expense and SGA expense, respectively, on the Consolidated Statement of Income. The current portion of the Company's unrecognized tax benefits is presented in the Consolidated Balance Sheet in other current assets and other current liabilities, and the amounts expected to be settled after one year are recorded in other assets and other liabilities.

Income taxes are provided on the portion of foreign earnings that is expected to be remitted to and taxable in the United States.

Derivative Instruments
The fair value of derivative instruments is recorded in other current assets, other assets, other current liabilities or other liabilities. Gains and losses representing either hedge ineffectiveness, hedge components excluded from the assessment of effectiveness, or hedges of translational exposure are recorded in the Consolidated Statement of Income in other income (expense), net. In the Consolidated Statement of Cash Flows, settlements of cash flow and fair value hedges are classified as an operating activity; settlements of all other derivatives are classified as a financing activity.

Cash flow hedges. Qualifying derivatives are accounted for as cash flow hedges when the hedged item is a forecasted transaction. Gains and losses on these instruments are recorded in other comprehensive income until the underlying transaction is recorded in earnings. When the hedged item is realized, gains or losses are reclassified from accumulated other comprehensive income (loss) (AOCI) to the Consolidated Statement of Income on the same line item as the underlying transaction.

Fair value hedges. Qualifying derivatives are accounted for as fair value hedges when the hedged item is a recognized asset, liability, or firm commitment. Gains and losses on these instruments are recorded in earnings, offsetting gains and losses on the hedged item.

Net investment hedges. Qualifying derivative and nonderivative financial instruments are accounted for as net investment hedges when the hedged item is a nonfunctional currency investment in a subsidiary. Gains and losses on these instruments are included in foreign currency translation adjustments in AOCI.

Other contracts. The Company also periodically enters into foreign currency forward contracts and options to reduce volatility in the translation of foreign currency earnings to U.S. dollars. Gains and losses on these instruments are recorded in other income (expense), net, generally reducing the exposure to translation volatility during a full-year period.

Foreign currency exchange risk. The Company is exposed to fluctuations in foreign currency cash flows related primarily to third-party purchases, intercompany transactions and when applicable, nonfunctional currency denominated third-party debt. The Company is also exposed to fluctuations in the value of foreign currency investments in subsidiaries and cash flows related to repatriation of these investments. Additionally, the Company is exposed to volatility in the translation of foreign currency denominated earnings to U.S. dollars. Management assesses foreign currency risk based on transactional cash flows and translational volatility and may enter into forward contracts, options, and currency swaps to reduce fluctuations in long or short currency positions. Forward contracts and options are generally less than 18 months duration. Currency swap agreements are established in conjunction with the term of underlying debt issues.

For foreign currency cash flow and fair value hedges, the assessment of effectiveness is generally based on changes in spot rates. Changes in time value are reported in other income (expense), net.

Interest rate risk. The Company is exposed to interest rate volatility with regard to future issuances of fixed rate debt. The Company periodically uses interest rate swaps, including forward-starting swaps, to reduce interest rate volatility and funding costs associated with certain debt issues, and to achieve a desired proportion of variable versus fixed rate debt, based on current and projected market conditions.

Fixed-to-variable interest rate swaps are accounted for as fair value hedges and the assessment of effectiveness is based on changes in the fair value of the underlying debt, using incremental borrowing rates currently available on loans with similar terms and maturities.

Price risk. The Company is exposed to price fluctuations primarily as a result of anticipated purchases of raw and packaging materials, fuel, and energy. The Company has historically used the combination ofl ong-term contracts with suppliers, and exchange-traded futures and option contracts to reduce price fluctuations in a desired percentage of forecasted raw material purchases over a duration of generally less than 18 months.

Commodity contracts are accounted for as cash flow hedges. The assessment of effectiveness for exchange-traded instruments is based on changes in futures prices. The assessment of effectiveness for over-the-counter transactions is based on changes in designated indices.

New accounting standards
Business combinations and noncontrolling interests. In December 2007, the FASB (Financial Accounting Standards Board) issued separate standards on business combinations and noncontrolling interests in consolidated financial statements. These standards were adopted by the Company at the beginning of its 2009 fiscal year.

For business combinations, the underlying fair value concepts of previous guidance was retained, but the method for applying the acquisition method changed in a number of significant respects including 1) the requirement to expense transaction fees and expected restructuring costs as incurred, rather than including these amounts in the allocated purchase price, 2) the requirement to recognize the fair value of contingent

consideration at the acquisition date, rather than the expected amount when the contingency is resolved, 3) the requirement to recognize the fair value of acquired in-process research and development assets at the acquisition date, rather than immediately expensing them, and 4) the requirement to recognize a gain in relation to a bargain purchase price, rather than reducing the allocated basis ofl ong-lived assets. In addition, changes in deferred tax asset valuation allowances and acquired income tax uncertainties after the measurement period are recognized in net income rather than as adjustments to the cost of an acquisition, including changes that relate to business combinations completed prior to 2009. The impact of adoption of this standard on the Company's financial statements was not significant.

For noncontrolling interests, the consolidated financial statements are presented as if the parent company investors (controlling interests) and other minority investors (noncontrolling interests) in partially-owned subsidiaries have similar economic interests in a single entity. As a result, investments in noncontrolling interests are reported as equity in the consolidated financial statements. Furthermore, the consolidated financial statements include 100% of a controlled subsidiary's earnings, rather than only the Company's share. Lastly, transactions between the Company and noncontrolling interests are reported in equity as transactions between shareholders provided that these transactions do not create a change in control. Previously, acquisitions of additional interests in a controlled subsidiary generally resulted in remeasurement of assets and liabilities acquired; dispositions of interests resulted in a gain or loss. The impact of adoption of this standard on the Company's financial statements was not significant.

Variable interest entities. In December 2009, the FASB amended the Accounting Standards Codification related to the consolidation provisions that apply to variable interest entities. This guidance was effective for fiscal years beginning after November 15, 2009 and was adopted by the Company on a prospective basis as of January 3, 2010 without material impact to its consolidated financial statements.

NOTE 2
ACQUISITIONS, GOODWILL AND OTHER INTANGIBLE ASSETS

Acquisitions
During 2008, the Company made acquisitions in order to expand its presence geographically and increase its manufacturing capacity.

Results of operations of the acquired businesses have been included in the Company's consolidated financial statements beginning on the dates of acquisition; such amounts were insignificant to the Company's consolidated results of operations when considered individually or in the aggregate.

Specialty Cereals. In September 2008, the Company acquired Specialty Cereals of Sydney, Australia, a manufacturer and distributor of natural ready-to-eat cereals. The Company paid $37 million cash in connection with the transaction, including approximately $5 million to the seller's lenders to settle debt of the acquired entity. This acquisition is included in the Asia Pacific operating segment.

IndyBake Products/Brownie Products. In August 2008, the Company acquired certain assets and liabilities of the business of IndyBake Products and Brownie Products (collectively, IndyBake), located in Indiana and Illinois. IndyBake, a contract manufacturing business that produced cracker, cookie and frozen dough products, had been a partner to Kellogg for many years as a snacks contract manufacturer.

The Company paid approximately $42 million cash in connection with the transaction, including approximately $8 million to the seller's lenders to settle debt of the acquired entity. This acquisition is included in the North America operating segment.

Navigable Foods. In June 2008, the Company acquired a majority interest in the business of Zhenghang Food Company Ltd. (Navigable Foods) for approximately $36 million (net of cash received). Navigable Foods, a manufacturer of cookies and crackers in the northern and northeastern regions of China, included approximately 1,800 employees, two manufacturing facilities and a sales and distribution network.

During 2008, the Company paid $31 million cash in connection with the acquisition, including approximately $22 million to lenders and other third parties to settle debt and other obligations of the acquired entity. Additional purchase price payable in June 2011 amounts to $5 million and is recorded on the Company's Consolidated Balance Sheet in other current liabilities. This acquisition is included in the Asia Pacific operating segment.

In conjunction with acquisition of Navigable Foods, the Company obtained the option to purchase the noncontrolling interest of Navigable Foods beginning June 30, 2011. The noncontrolling interest holder also obtained the option to cause the Company to purchase its remaining interest. The options, which have similar terms, include an exercise price that is expected to approximate fair value on the date of exercise.

United Bakers In January 2008, subsidiaries of the Company acquired substantially all of the equity interests in OJSC Kreker (doing business as United Bakers) and consolidated subsidiaries, a leading producer of cereal, cookie, and cracker products in Russia. United Bakers had approximately 4,000 employees, six manufacturing facilities, and a broad distribution network.

The Company paid $110 million cash (net of $5 million cash acquired), including approximately $67 million to settle debt and other assumed obligations of the acquired entities. Of the total cash paid, $5 million was spent prior to 2008 for transaction fees and advances. This acquisition is included in the Europe operating segment.

The purchase agreement between the Company and the seller provided for payment of contingent consideration under a calculation based primarily on sales, capital expenditures and earnings before income taxes, depreciation and amortization for the three-year period ended December 31, 2010. Based on the calculation, the Company is not required to provide contingent consideration to the seller.

Goodwill and other intangible assets

For the periods presented, the Company's intangible assets consisted of the following:

Intangible assets subject to amortization

(millions)	Gross carrying amount 2010	2009	Accumulated amortization 2010	2009
Trademarks	$19	$19	$16	$15
Other	41	41	31	30
Total	$60	$60	$47	$45

	2010	2009
Amortization expense (a)	$2	$3

(a) The currently estimated aggregate amortization expense for each of the next five succeeding fiscal periods is approximately $2 million per year.

Intangible assets not subject to amortization

(millions)	Total carrying amount 2010	2009
Trademarks	$1,443	$1,443

Changes in the carrying amount of goodwill

(millions)	North America	Europe	Latin America	Asia Pacific (a)	Consolidated
January 3, 2009	$3,539	$61	$—	$ 37	$3,637
Currency translation adjustment	—	1	—	5	6
January 2, 2010	$3,539	$62	$—	$ 42	$3,643
Impairment charge	—	—	—	(20)	(20)
Currency translation adjustment	—	—	—	5	5
January 1, 2011	**$3,539**	**$62**	**$—**	**$ 27**	**$3,628**

(a) Includes Australia, Asia and South America.

Impairment charges

In the fourth quarter of 2010, the Company recorded impairment charges totaling $29 million in connection with the Navigable Foods business in China, which was purchased by the Company in 2008.

The charges included $20 million representing the goodwill recorded in conjunction with the 2008 acquisition. The China business has been generating operating losses since the acquisition and that trend is expected to continue. As a result, management determined in the fourth quarter of 2010 that the current business has not proven to be the right vehicle for entry into the Chinese marketplace and began exploring various strategic alternatives to reduce operating losses in the future. The impairment charge was recorded in SGA expense in the Asia Pacific operating segment.

Prior to assessing the goodwill for impairment, the Company determined that the long-lived assets of the China reporting unit were impaired and should be written down to their estimated fair value of $10 million. This resulted in a fixed asset impairment charge of $9 million in 2010 that was recorded in the Asia Pacific operating segment, of which $8 million was recorded in COGS, and $1 million was recorded in SGA expense.

NOTE 3
EXIT OR DISPOSAL ACTIVITIES

The Company views its continued spending on cost-reduction initiatives as part of its ongoing operating principles to provide greater visibility in achieving its long-term profit growth targets. Initiatives undertaken are currently expected to recover cash implementation costs within a five-year period of completion. Upon completion (or as each major stage is completed in the case of multi-year programs), the project begins to deliver cash savings and/or reduced depreciation.

Cost summary
During 2010, the Company recorded $19 million of costs associated with exit or disposal activities. $6 million represented severance, $5 million was for pension costs, $7 million for other costs including relocation of assets and employees and $1 million for asset write-offs. $4 million of the charges were recorded in cost of goods sold (COGS) in the Europe operating segment. $15 million of the charges were recorded in selling, general and administrative (SGA) expense in the following operating segments (in millions): North America—$11; Europe—$2; and Asia Pacific—$2.

The Company recorded $65 million of costs in 2009 associated with exit or disposal activities. $44 million represented severance and other cash costs, $3 million was for pension costs, $6 million for asset write offs, and $12 million for other costs including relocation of assets and employees. $40 million of the charges were recorded in cost of goods sold (COGS) in the following operating segments (in millions): North America—$14;

Europe—$16; Latin America—$9; and Asia Pacific—$1. $25 million of the charges were recorded in selling, general and administrative (SGA) expense in the following operating segments (in millions): North America—$10; Europe—$13; Latin America—$1; and Asia Pacific—$1.

For 2008, the Company recorded charges of $27 million, comprised of $7 million of asset write-offs, $17 million for severance and other cash costs and $3 million related to pension costs. $23 million of the 2008 charges were recorded in COGS within the Europe operating segment, with the balance recorded in SGA expense in the Latin America operating segment.

At January 1, 2011, exit cost reserves were $5 million, related to severance payments which will be made in 2011. Exit cost reserves at January 2, 2010 were $25 million related to severance payments.

Specific initiatives
2010 activities
During 2010, the Company incurred costs related to two ongoing programs which will result in COGS and SGA expense savings. The COGS program relates to Kellogg's lean, efficient, and agile network (K LEAN). The SGA programs focus on the efficiency and effectiveness of various support functions.

The Company commenced K LEAN in 2009. K LEAN seeks to optimize the Company's global manufacturing network, reduce waste, and develop best practices on a global basis. The Company incurred $4 million of costs in the Europe operating segment for 2010 which included cash payments for severance and other cash costs for asset removal and relocation at various global manufacturing facilities.

The following table presents the total program costs through January 1, 2011.

(millions)	Employee severance	Other cash costs (a)	Asset write-offs	Retirement benefits (b)	Total
For the year ended, January 2, 2010	$15	$ 6	$—	$ 3	$24
For the year ended, January 1, 2011	3	—	1	—	4
Total program costs	$18	$ 6	$ 1	$ 3	$28

(a) Includes cash costs for equipment removal and relocation.

(b) Pension plan curtailment losses and special termination benefits.

The above costs impacted operating segments, as follows (in millions): North America—$14; Europe—$13; and Asia Pacific—$1. The cost and cash outlay in 2011 for these programs is estimated to be an additional $3 million.

The following table presents a reconciliation of the severance reserve for this program.

(millions)	Beginning of period	Accruals	Payments	End of period
For the year ended, January 2, 2010	$—	$15	$ (9)	$6
For the year ended, January 1, 2011	6	3	(7)	2
Total project to date		**$18**	**$(16)**	

In 2009, the Company commenced various SGA programs which will result in an improvement in the efficiency and effectiveness of various support functions. The programs realign these functions to provide greater consistency across processes, procedures and capabilities in order to support the global organization. The Company incurred $15 million of costs for 2010 which included cash payments for severance and other cash costs associated with the elimination of salaried positions. The above costs impacted operating segments for the year-to-date period, as follows (in millions): North America—$11; Europe—$2; and Asia Pacific—$2.

The following table presents the total program costs through January 1, 2011.

(millions)	Employee severance	Other cash costs (a)	Retirement benefits (b)	Total
For the year ended, January 2, 2010	$17	$ 8	$—	$25
For the year ended, January 1, 2011	3	7	5	15
Total program costs	**$20**	**$15**	**$ 5**	**$40**

(a)   Includes cash costs for equipment removal and relocation.

(b)   Pension plan curtailment losses and special termination benefits.

The above costs impacted operating segments, as follows (in millions): North America—$21; Europe—$15; Latin America—$1; and Asia Pacific—$3. The cost and cash outlay for these programs in 2011 is estimated to be an additional $10 million.

The following table presents a reconciliation of the severance reserve for this program.

(millions)	Beginning of period	Accruals	Payments	End of period
For the year ended, January 2, 2010	$—	$17	$ (5)	$12
For the year ended, January 1, 2011	12	3	(12)	3
Total project to date		**$20**	**$(17)**	

Prior year activities
During 2009, in addition to the COGS and SGA programs above, the Company incurred costs related to a European manufacturing optimization program in Bremen, Germany and a supply chain network rationalization program in Latin America.

The Company incurred $7 million of costs during the year, representing cash payments for severance, related to a manufacturing optimization program in Bremen, Germany. The program will result in future cash savings through the elimination of employee positions and were recorded within COGS in the Europe operating segment. The program was substantially complete as of the end of the third quarter, 2009. Severance reserves were $7 million as of January 2, 2010 and were paid out during 2010.

The Company incurred $9 million of costs related to a supply chain rationalization in Latin America which resulted in the closing of a plant in Guatemala. The charges represent $3 million of cash payments for severance and other cash costs associated with the elimination of employee positions and $6 million for asset removal and relocation costs as well as non-cash asset write offs. Efficiencies gained in other plants in the Latin America network allow the Company to service the Guatemala market from those plants. The costs were recorded in COGS in the Latin America operating segment and there were no severance reserves as of January 2, 2010.

In 2008, the Company executed a cost-reduction initiative in Latin America that resulted in the elimination of salaried positions. The cost of the program was $4 million and was recorded in Latin America's SGA expense. The charge related primarily to severance benefits which were paid in 2008. There were no reserves as of January 3, 2009 related to this program.

The Company commenced a multi-year European manufacturing optimization plan in 2006 to improve utilization of its facility in Manchester, England and to better align production in Europe. The project resulted in an elimination of hourly and salaried positions from the Manchester facility through voluntary early retirement and severance programs. The Company incurred $8 million of expense in 2008, $19 million in 2007 and $28 million in 2006. The pension trust funding requirements of these early retirements exceeded the recognized benefit expense by $5 million which was funded in 2006. During this program certain manufacturing equipment was removed from service. All of the costs for the European manufacturing optimization plan have been recorded in COGS within the Company's Europe operating segment. All other cash costs were paid in the period incurred. The project was completed in 2008.

NOTE 4
EQUITY

Earnings per share

Basic net earnings per share is determined by dividing net income attributable to Kellogg Company by the weighted-average number of common shares outstanding during the period. Diluted net earnings per share is similarly determined, except the denominator is increased to include the number of additional common shares that would have been outstanding if all the dilutive potential common shares had been issued. Dilutive potential common shares are comprised principally of employee stock options issued by the Company. Basic net earnings per share is reconciled to diluted net earnings per share in the following table:

(millions, except per share data)	Net income attributable to Kellogg Company	Average shares outstanding	Net earnings per share
2010			
Basic	**$1,247**	**376**	**$ 3.32**
Dilutive potential common shares	—	**2**	**(0.02)**
Diluted	**$1,247**	**378**	**$ 3.30**
2009			
Basic	$1,212	382	$ 3.17
Dilutive potential common shares	—	2	(0.01)
Diluted	$1,212	384	$ 3.16
2008			
Basic	$1,148	382	$ 3.01
Dilutive potential common shares	—	3	(0.02)
Diluted	$1,148	385	$ 2.99

The total number of anti-dilutive potential common shares excluded from the reconciliation for each period was (in millions): 2010–4.9; 2009–12.2; 2008–2.6.

Stock transactions

The Company issues shares to employees and directors under various equity-based compensation and stock purchase programs, as further discussed in Note 7. The number of shares issued during the periods presented was (in millions): 2010–5; 2009–3; 2008–5. The Company issued shares totaling less than one million in each of the years presented under *Kellogg Direct*™ , a direct stock purchase and dividend reinvestment plan for U.S. shareholders.

On April 23, 2010, the Company's board of directors authorized a $2.5 billion three-year repurchase program for 2010 through 2012. During 2010, the Company repurchased approximately 21 million shares of common stock for a total of $1,057 million, of which $1,052 was paid during the year and $5 million was payable at January 1, 2011. During 2009, the Company repurchased 4 million shares of common stock at a total cost of $187 million. During 2008, the Company repurchased 13 million shares of common stock at a total cost of $650 million.

Comprehensive income

Comprehensive income includes net income and all other changes in equity during a period except those resulting from investments by or distributions to shareholders. Other comprehensive income for all years presented consists of foreign currency translation adjustments, fair value adjustments associated with cash flow hedges and adjustments for net experience losses and prior service cost related to employee benefit plans.

During 2010, the Company amended its U.S. postretirement healthcare benefit plan, which resulted in a $17 million decrease of a deferred tax asset and is included in tax expense with prior service credit (cost) arising during the period. During 2008, the assets of the Company's postretirement and postemployment benefit plans suffered losses of over $1 billion due to the substantial allocation of assets in the equity market.

(millions)	Pre-tax amount	Tax (expense) benefit	After-tax amount
2010			
Net income			$ 1,240
Other comprehensive income:			
Foreign currency translation adjustments	$ (18)	$ —	(18)
Cash flow hedges:			
Unrealized gain (loss) on cash flow hedges	51	(21)	30
Reclassification to net earnings	34	(9)	25
Postretirement and postemployment benefits:			
Amounts arising during the period:			
Net experience gain (loss)	(71)	30	(41)
Prior service credit (cost)	(8)	(13)	(21)
Reclassification to net earnings:			
Net experience loss	102	(32)	70
Prior service cost	11	(4)	7
	$ 101	$ (49)	52
Total comprehensive income			$ 1,292
2009			
Net income			$ 1,208
Other comprehensive income:			
Foreign currency translation adjustments	$ 65	$ —	65
Cash flow hedges:			
Unrealized gain (loss) on cash flow hedges	(6)	3	(3)
Reclassification to net earnings	(3)	—	(3)
Postretirement and postemployment benefits:			
Amounts arising during the period:			
Net experience gain (loss)	161	(72)	89
Prior service credit (cost)	(33)	11	(22)
Reclassification to net earnings:			
Net experience loss	63	(21)	42
Prior service cost	11	(4)	7
	$ 258	$ (83)	175
Total comprehensive income			$ 1,383
2008			
Net income			$ 1,146
Other comprehensive income:			
Foreign currency translation adjustments	$ (431)	$ —	(431)
Cash flow hedges:			
Unrealized gain (loss) on cash flow hedges	(33)	12	(21)
Reclassification to net earnings	5	(2)	3
Postretirement and postemployment benefits:			
Amounts arising during the period:			
Net experience gain (loss)	(1,402)	497	(905)
Prior service credit (cost)	3	(1)	2
Reclassification to net earnings:			
Net experience loss	49	(17)	32
Prior service cost	9	(3)	6
	$(1,800)	$486	(1,314)
Total comprehensive income			$ (168)

Accumulated other comprehensive income (loss) at January 1, 2011 and January 2, 2010 consisted of the following:

(millions)	**2010**	2009
Foreign currency translation adjustments	$ (789)	$ (771)
Cash flow hedges — unrealized net gain (loss)	25	(30)
Postretirement and postemployment benefits:		
Net experience loss	(1,075)	(1,104)
Prior service cost	(75)	(61)
Total accumulated other comprehensive income (loss)	$(1,914)	$(1,966)

NOTE 5
LEASES AND OTHER COMMITMENTS

The Company's leases are generally for equipment and warehouse space. Rent expense on all operating leases was (in millions): 2010-$154; 2009-$150; 2008-$145. During 2008, the Company entered into approximately $3 million in capital lease agreements to finance the purchase of equipment. The Company did not enter into any capital lease agreements during 2009 and 2010.

At January 1, 2011, future minimum annual lease commitments under non-cancelable operating and capital leases were as follows:

(millions)	Operating leases	Capital leases
2011	$149	$ 1
2012	126	1
2013	94	1
2014	66	1
2015	47	—
2016 and beyond	103	1
Total minimum payments	$585	$ 5
Amount representing interest		(1)
Obligations under capital leases		4
Obligations due within one year		(1)
Long-term obligations under capital leases		$ 3

The Company has provided various standard indemnifications in agreements to sell and purchase business assets and lease facilities over the past several years, related primarily to pre-existing tax, environmental, and employee benefit obligations. Certain of these indemnifications are limited by agreement in either amount and/or term and others are unlimited. The Company has also provided various "hold harmless" provisions within certain service type agreements. Because the Company is not currently aware of any actual exposures associated with these indemnifications, management is unable to estimate the maximum potential future payments to be made. At January 1, 2011, the Company had not recorded any liability related to these indemnifications.

NOTE 6
DEBT

The following table presents the components of notes payable at year end January 1, 2011 and January 2, 2010:

(millions)	2010	2009
Bank borrowings	$44	$44

Long-term debt at year end consisted primarily of issuances of U.S. Dollar Notes, as follows:

(millions)	2010	2009
(a) 7.45% U.S. Dollar Debentures due 2031	$1,090	$1,089
(b) 4.0% U.S. Dollar Notes due 2020	991	—
(a) 6.6% U.S. Dollar Notes due 2011	951	951
(c) 4.25% U.S. Dollar Notes due 2013	800	787
(d) 5.125% U.S. Dollar Notes due 2012	768	749
(e) 4.45% U.S. Dollar Notes due 2016	748	748
(f) 4.15% U.S. Dollar Notes due 2019	498	498
Other	14	14
	5,860	4,836
Less current maturities	(952)	(1)
Balance at year end	$4,908	$4,835

(a) In March 2001, the Company issued $4.6 billion ofl ong-term debt instruments, primarily to finance the acquisition of Keebler Foods Company. The preceding table reflects the remaining principal amounts outstanding as of year-end 2010 and 2009. The effective interest rate as of January 1, 2011 on the Notes due 2011, reflecting issuance discount, hedge settlement and interest rate swaps, was 6.54%. The effective interest rate as of January 1, 2011 on the Debentures due 2031, reflecting issuance discount and hedge settlement, was 7.62%. Initially, these instruments were privately placed, or sold outside the United States, in reliance on exemptions from registration under the Securities Act of 1933, as amended (the 1933 Act). The Company then exchanged new debt securities for these initial debt instruments, with the new debt securities being substantially identical in all respects to the initial debt instruments, except for being registered under the 1933 Act. These debt securities contain standard events of default and covenants. The Notes due 2011 and the Debentures due 2031 may be redeemed in whole or in part by the Company at any time at prices determined under a formula (but not less than 100% of the principal amount plus unpaid interest to the redemption date). The Company redeemed $72 million of the Notes due 2011 in December 2007 and another $482 million in December 2009. The Company incurred $35 million of interest expense and $3 million of accelerated losses on interest rate swaps previously recorded in accumulated other comprehensive income in connection with the 2009 tender offer. In May 2009, the Company entered into interest rate swaps with notional amounts totaling $400 million, which effectively converted a portion of the Notes due 2011 from a fixed rate to a floating rate obligation for the remainder of the ten-year term. These derivative instruments were designated as fair value hedges of the debt obligation. The fair value adjustment for the interest rate swaps was $6 million, and was recorded as an increase in the hedged debt balance at January 1, 2011.

(b) On December 8, 2010, the Company issued $1.0 billion of ten-year 4.0% fixed rate U.S. Dollar Notes, using net proceeds from these Notes for incremental pension and postretirement benefit plan contributions and to retire a portion of its commercial paper. The effective interest rate on these Notes, reflecting issuance discount and hedge settlement, was 3.42%. The Notes contain customary covenants that limit the ability of the Company and its restricted subsidiaries (as defined) to incur certain liens or enter into certain sale and lease-back transactions. The customary covenants also contain a change of control provision.

(c) On March 6, 2008, the Company issued $750 million of five-year 4.25% fixed rate U.S. Dollar Notes, using the proceeds from these Notes to retire a portion of its U.S. commercial paper. These Notes were issued under an existing shelf registration statement. The effective interest rate as of January 1, 2011 on these Notes, reflecting issuance discount, hedge settlement and interest rate swaps, was 1.20%. The Notes contain customary covenants that limit the ability of the Company and its restricted subsidiaries (as defined) to incur certain liens or enter into certain sale and lease-back transactions. The customary covenants also contain a change of control provision. In conjunction with this debt issuance, the Company entered into interest rate swaps with notional amounts totaling $750 million, which effectively converted this debt from a fixed rate to a floating rate obligation for the duration of the five-year term. These derivative instruments were designated as fair value hedges of the debt obligation. The fair value adjustment for the interest rate swaps was $50 million, and was recorded as an increase in the hedged debt balance at January 1, 2011.

(d) In December 2007, the Company issued $750 million of five-year 5.125% fixed rate U.S. Dollar Notes, using the proceeds from these Notes to replace a portion of its U.S. commercial paper. These Notes were issued under an existing shelf registration statement. The effective interest rate as of January 1, 2011 on these Notes, reflecting issuance discount, hedge settlement and interest rate swaps, was 3.45%. The Notes contain customary covenants that limit the ability of the Company and its restricted subsidiaries (as defined) to incur certain liens or enter into certain sale and lease-back transactions. The customary covenants also contain a change of control provision. In May 2009, the Company entered into interest rate swaps with notional amounts totaling $750 million, which effectively converted these Notes from a fixed rate to a floating rate obligation for the remainder of the five-year term. These derivative instruments were designated as fair value hedges of the debt obligation. The fair value adjustment for the interest rate swaps was $18 million, and was recorded as an increase in the hedged debt balance at January 1, 2011.

(e) On May 18, 2009, the Company issued $750 million of seven-year 4.45% fixed rate U.S. Dollar Notes, using net proceeds from these Notes to retire a portion of its commercial paper. The effective interest rate on these Notes, reflecting issuance discount and hedge settlement, was 4.46%. The Notes contain customary covenants that limit the ability of the Company and its restricted subsidiaries (as defined) to incur certain liens or enter into certain sale and lease-back transactions. The customary covenants also contain a change of control provision.

(f) On November 15, 2009, the Company issued $500 million of ten-year 4.15% fixed rate U.S. Dollar Notes, using net proceeds from these Notes to retire a portion of its 6.6% U.S. Dollar Notes due 2011. The effective interest rate on these Notes, reflecting issuance discount and hedge settlement, was 4.23%. The Notes contain customary covenants that limit the ability of the Company and its restricted subsidiaries (as defined) to incur certain liens or enter into certain sale and lease-back transactions. The customary covenants also contain a change of control provision.

In February 2007, the Company and two of its subsidiaries (the Issuers) established a program under which the Issuers may issue euro-commercial paper notes up to a maximum aggregate amount outstanding at any time of $750 million or its equivalent in alternative currencies. The notes may have maturities ranging up to 364 days and will be senior unsecured obligations of the applicable Issuer. Notes issued by subsidiary Issuers will be guaranteed by the Company. The notes may be issued at a discount or may bear fixed or floating rate interest or a coupon calculated by reference to an index or formula. As of January 1, 2011 and January 2, 2010, no notes were outstanding under this program.

At January 1, 2011, the Company had $2.3 billion of short-term lines of credit, virtually all of which were unused and available for borrowing on an unsecured basis. These lines were comprised principally of an unsecured Five-Year Credit Agreement, which the Company entered into during November 2006 and expires in 2011. The Company plans to renew the agreement during 2011. The agreement allows the Company to borrow, on a revolving credit basis, up to $2.0 billion, to obtain letters of credit in an aggregate amount up to $75 million, and to provide a procedure for lenders to bid on short-term debt of the Company. The agreement contains customary covenants and warranties, including specified restrictions on indebtedness, liens, sale and leaseback transactions, and a specified interest coverage ratio. If an event of default occurs, then, to the extent permitted, the administrative agent may terminate the commitments under the credit facility, accelerate any outstanding loans, and demand the deposit of cash collateral equal to the lender's letter of credit exposure plus interest.

Scheduled principal repayments on long-term debt are (in millions): 2011–$946; 2012–$750; 2013–$752; 2014–$8; 2015–$1; 2016 and beyond–$3,351.

Interest paid was (in millions): 2010–$244; 2009–$302; 2008–$305. Interest expense capitalized as part of the construction cost of fixed assets was (in millions): 2010–$2; 2009–$3; 2008–$6.

NOTE 7
STOCK COMPENSATION

The Company uses various equity-based compensation programs to provide long-term performance incentives for its global workforce. Currently, these incentives consist principally of stock options, and to a lesser extent, executive performance shares and restricted stock grants. The Company also sponsors a discounted stock purchase plan in the United States and matching-grant programs in several international locations. Additionally, the Company awards restricted stock to its outside directors. These awards are administered through several plans, as described within this Note.

The 2009 Long-Term Incentive Plan (2009 Plan), approved by shareholders in 2009, permits awards to employees and officers in the form of incentive and non-qualified stock options, performance units, restricted stock or restricted stock units, and stock appreciation rights. The 2009 Plan, which replaced the 2003 Long-Term Incentive Plan (2003 Plan), authorizes the issuance of a total of (a) 27 million shares; plus (b) the total number of shares as to which awards granted under the 2009 Plan or the 2003 or 2001 Incentive Plans expire or are forfeited, terminated or settled in cash. No more than 5 million shares can be issued in satisfaction of performance units, performance-based restricted shares and other awards (excluding stock options and stock appreciation rights). There are additional annual limitations on awards or payments to individual participants. Options granted under the 2009 Plan generally vest over three years while options granted under the 2003 Plan vest over two years. At January 1, 2011, there were 23 million remaining authorized, but unissued, shares under the 2009 Plan.

The Non-Employee Director Stock Plan (2009 Director Plan) was approved by shareholders in 2009 and allows each eligible non-employee director to receive shares of the Company's common stock annually. The number of shares granted pursuant to each annual award will be determined by the Nominating and Governance Committee of the Board of Directors. The 2009 Director Plan, which replaced the 2000 Non-Employee Director Stock Plan (2000 Director Plan), reserves 500,000 shares for issuance, plus the total number of shares as to which awards granted under the 2009 Director Plan or the 2000 Director Plans expire or are forfeited, terminated or settled in cash. The 2000 Director Plan allowed each eligible non-employee director to receive 2,100 shares of the Company's common stock annually and annual grants of options to purchase 5,000 shares of the Company's common stock. Under both the 2009 and 2000 Director Plans, shares (other than stock options) are placed in the Kellogg Company Grantor Trust for Non-Employee Directors (the Grantor Trust). Under the terms of the Grantor Trust, shares are available to a director only upon termination of service on the Board. Under the 2009 Director Plan, 26,000 shares were awarded in 2010 and 32,510 shares were awarded in 2009. Under the 2000 Director Plan, 54,465 options and 19,964 shares were awarded in 2008.

The 2002 Employee Stock Purchase Plan was approved by shareholders in 2002 and permits eligible employees to purchase Company stock at a discounted price. This plan allows for a maximum of

2.5 million shares of Company stock to be issued at a purchase price equal to 95% of the fair market value of the stock on the last day of the quarterly purchase period. Total purchases through this plan for any employee are limited to a fair market value of $25,000 during any calendar year. At January 1, 2011, there were approximately 0.8 million remaining authorized, but unissued, shares under this plan. Shares were purchased by employees under this plan as follows (approximate number of shares): 2010–123,000; 2009–159,000; 2008–157,000. Options granted to employees to purchase discounted stock under this plan are included in the option activity tables within this note.

Additionally, during 2002, an international subsidiary of the Company established a stock purchase plan for its employees. Subject to limitations, employee contributions to this plan are matched 1:1 by the Company. Under this plan, shares were granted by the Company to match an equal number of shares purchased by employees as follows (approximate number of shares): 2010–66,000; 2009–74,000; 2008–78,000.

Compensation expense for all types of equity-based programs and the related income tax benefit recognized were as follows:

(millions)	2010	2009	2008
Pre-tax compensation expense	$29	$48	$74
Related income tax benefit	$10	$17	$26

Pre-tax compensation expense for 2008 included $4 million of expense related to the modification of certain stock options to eliminate the accelerated ownership feature (AOF) and $13 million representing cash compensation to holders of modified stock options to replace the value of the AOF, which is discussed in the section, "Stock options."

As of January 1, 2011, total stock-based compensation cost related to nonvested awards not yet recognized was approximately $33 million and the weighted-average period over which this amount is expected to be recognized was approximately 2 years.

Cash flows realized upon exercise or vesting of stock-based awards in the periods presented are included in the following table. Tax benefits realized upon exercise or vesting of stock-based awards generally represent the tax benefit of the difference between the exercise price and the strike price of the option.

Cash used by the Company to settle equity instruments granted under stock-based awards was insignificant.

(millions)	2010	2009	2008
Total cash received from option exercises and similar instruments	$204	$131	$175
Tax benefits realized upon exercise or vesting of stock-based awards:			
Windfall benefits classified as financing cash flow	8	4	12
Other amounts classified as operating cash flow	20	12	17
Total	$ 28	$ 16	$ 29

Shares used to satisfy stock-based awards are normally issued out of treasury stock, although management is authorized to issue new shares to the extent permitted by respective plan provisions. Refer to Note 4 for information on shares issued during the periods presented to employees and directors under various long-term incentive plans and share repurchases under the Company's stock repurchase authorizations. The Company does not currently have a policy of repurchasing a specified number of shares issued under employee benefit programs during any particular time period.

Stock options

During 2010 and 2009, non-qualified stock options were granted to eligible employees under the 2009 Plan with exercise prices equal to the fair market value of the Company's stock on the grant date, a contractual term of ten years, and a three-year graded vesting period.

During 2008, non-qualified stock options were granted to eligible employees under the 2003 Plan with exercise prices equal to the fair market value of the Company's stock on the grant date, a contractual term of ten years, and a two-year graded vesting period. Grants to outside directors under the Director Plan included similar terms, but vested immediately.

Effective April 25, 2008, the Company eliminated the AOF from all outstanding stock options. Stock options that contained the AOF feature included the vested pre-2004 option awards and all reload options. Reload options are the stock options awarded to eligible employees and directors to replace previously owned Company stock used by those individuals to pay the exercise price, including related employment taxes, of vested pre-2004 options awards containing the AOF. The reload options were immediately vested with an expiration date which was the same as the original option grant. Apart from removing the AOF, the stock options were not otherwise affected. Holders of the stock options received cash compensation to replace the value of the AOF.

The Company accounted for the elimination of the AOF as a stock option modification, which required the Company to record a charge equal to the difference between the value of the modified stock options on the date of modification and their values immediately prior to modification. Since the modified stock options were 100% vested and had relatively short remaining contractual terms of one to five years, the Company used a Black-Scholes model to value the awards for the purpose of calculating the modification charge. The total fair value of the modified stock options increased by $4 million due to an increase in the expected term.

As a result of this action, pre-tax compensation expense for 2008 included $4 million of expense related to the modification of stock options and $13 million representing cash compensation paid to holders of the stock options to replace the value of the AOF. Approximately 900 employees were holders of the modified stock options.

Management estimates the fair value of each annual stock option award on the date of grant using a lattice-based option valuation model. Composite assumptions are presented in the following table. Weighted-average values are disclosed for certain inputs which incorporate a range of assumptions. Expected volatilities are based principally on historical volatility of the Company's stock, and to a lesser extent, on implied volatilities from traded options on the Company's stock. Historical volatility corresponds to the contractual term of the options granted. The Company uses historical data to estimate option exercise and employee termination within the valuation models; separate groups of employees that have similar historical exercise behavior are considered separately for valuation purposes. The expected term of options granted represents the period of time that options granted are expected to be outstanding; the weighted-average expected term for all employee groups is presented in the following table. The risk-free rate for periods within the contractual life of the options is based on the U.S. Treasury yield curve in effect at the time of grant.

Stock option valuation model assumptions for grants within the year ended:	2010	2009	2008
Weighted-average expected volatility	20.00%	24.00%	20.75%
Weighted-average expected term (years)	4.94	5.00	4.08
Weighted-average risk-free interest rate	2.54%	2.10%	2.66%
Dividend yield	2.80%	3.40%	2.40%
Weighed-average fair value of options granted	$ 7.90	$ 6.33	$ 7.90

A summary of option activity for the year ended January 1, 2011 is presented in the following table:

Employee and director stock options	Shares (millions)	Weighted-average exercise price	Weighted-average contractual term (years)	Aggregate intrinsic value (millions)
Outstanding, beginning of year	26	$45		
Granted	4	53		
Exercised	(4)	43		
Outstanding, end of year	26	$47	6.3	$125
Exercisable, end of year	20	$46	5.5	$100

Additionally, option activity for the comparable prior year periods is presented in the following table:

(millions, except per share data)	2009	2008
Outstanding, beginning of year	26	26
Granted	4	5
Exercised	(3)	(5)
Forfeitures and expirations	(1)	—
Outstanding, end of year	26	26
Exercisable, end of year	22	20
Weighted-average exercise price:		
Outstanding, beginning of year	$45	$44
Granted	40	51
Exercised	41	42
Forfeitures and expirations	48	—
Outstanding, end of year	$45	$45
Exercisable, end of year	$45	$44

The total intrinsic value of options exercised during the periods presented was (in millions): 2010–$45; 2009–$25; 2008–$55.

Other stock-based awards
Other stock-based awards consisted principally of executive performance shares and restricted stock granted under the 2009 Plan during 2009 and 2010 and the 2003 Plan during 2008.

In 2010, 2009 and 2008, the Company made performance share awards to a limited number of senior executive-level employees, which entitles these employees to receive a specified number of shares of the Company's common stock on the vesting date, provided cumulative three-year targets are achieved. The cumulative three-year targets involved operating profit and internal net sales growth for the 2010 grant, cost savings for the 2009 grant and operating profit for the 2008 grant. Management estimates the fair value of performance share awards based on the market price of the underlying stock on the date of grant, reduced by the present value of estimated dividends foregone during the performance period. The 2010, 2009 and 2008 target grants (as revised for non-vested forfeitures and other adjustments) currently correspond to approximately 204,000, 170,000 and 160,000 shares, respectively, with a grant-date fair value of approximately $48, $36, and $47 per share. The actual number of shares issued on the vesting date could range from zero to 200% of target, depending on actual performance achieved. Based on the market price of the Company's common stock at year-end 2010, the maximum future value that could be awarded on the vesting date was (in millions): 2010 award–$21; 2009 award–$17; and 2008 award–$10. The 2007 performance share award, payable in stock, was settled at 150% of target in February 2010 for a total dollar equivalent of $14 million.

The Company also periodically grants restricted stock and restricted stock units to eligible employees. The Company awarded grants under the 2009 Plan during 2009 and 2010 and under the 2003 Plan during 2008. Restrictions with respect to sale or transferability generally lapse after three years and the grantee is normally entitled to receive shareholder dividends during the vesting period. Management estimates the fair value of restricted stock grants based on the market price of the underlying stock on the date of grant. A summary of restricted stock activity for the year ended January 1, 2011, is presented in the following table:

Employee restricted stock and restricted stock units	Shares (thousands)	Weighted-average grant-date fair value
Non-vested, beginning of year	256	$48
Granted	121	53
Vested	(67)	47
Forfeited	(6)	49
Non-vested, end of year	304	$49

Grants of restricted stock and restricted stock units for comparable prior-year periods were: 2009–68,000; 2008–162,000.

The total fair value of restricted stock and restricted stock units vesting in the periods presented was (in millions): 2010–$3; 2009–$3; 2008–$7.

NOTE 8
PENSION BENEFITS

The Company sponsors a number of U.S. and foreign pension plans to provide retirement benefits for its employees. The majority of these plans are funded or unfunded defined benefit plans, although the Company does participate in a limited number of multiemployer or other defined contribution plans for certain employee groups. Defined benefits for salaried employees are generally based on salary and years of service, while union employee benefits are generally a negotiated amount for each year of service.

Obligations and funded status
The aggregate change in projected benefit obligation, plan assets, and funded status is presented in the following tables.

(millions)	2010	2009
Change in projected benefit obligation		
Beginning of year	$3,605	$3,110
Service cost	88	79
Interest cost	200	196
Plan participants' contributions	2	4
Amendments	8	30
Actuarial gain (loss)	241	264
Benefits paid	(203)	(183)
Curtailment and special termination benefits	—	3
Foreign currency adjustments	(11)	102
End of year	$3,930	$3,605
Change in plan assets		
Fair value beginning of year	$3,323	$2,563
Actual return on plan assets	480	719
Employer contributions	350	87
Plan participants' contributions	2	4
Benefits paid	(177)	(158)
Foreign currency adjustments	(11)	108
Fair value end of year	$3,967	$3,323
Funded status	$ 37	$ (282)
Amounts recognized in the Consolidated Balance Sheet consist of		
Other assets	$ 333	$ 160
Other current liabilities	(43)	(12)
Other liabilities	(253)	(430)
Net amount recognized	$ 37	$ (282)
Amounts recognized in accumulated other comprehensive income consist of		
Net experience loss	$1,277	$1,287
Prior service cost	96	102
Net amount recognized	$1,373	$1,389

The accumulated benefit obligation for all defined benefit pension plans was $3.61 billion and $3.32 billion at January 1, 2011 and January 2, 2010, respectively. Information for pension plans with accumulated benefit obligations in excess of plan assets were:

(millions)	2010	2009
Projected benefit obligation	$248	$2,759
Accumulated benefit obligation	207	2,601
Fair value of plan assets	11	2,317

Expense
The components of pension expense are presented in the following table. Pension expense for defined contribution plans relates principally to multiemployer plans in which the Company participates on behalf of certain unionized workforces in the United States. The 2010 and 2009 defined contribution plan expense includes $5 million and $12 million, respectively, related to curtailment and special termination benefits related to multi-employer plans. The final calculation of these liabilities are pending full-year 2011 and 2010

contribution base units, respectively, and are therefore subject to adjustment. The associated cash obligation is payable over a maximum 20-year period; management has not determined the actual period over which the payments will be made.

(millions)	2010	2009	2008
Service cost	$ 88	$ 79	$ 85
Interest cost	200	196	197
Expected return on plan assets	(316)	(315)	(300)
Amortization of unrecognized prior service cost	14	13	12
Recognized net loss	81	46	36
Curtailment and special termination benefits—net loss	—	6	12
Pension expense:			
Defined benefit plans	67	25	42
Defined contribution plans	32	38	22
Total	$ 99	$ 63	$ 64

The estimated net experience loss and prior service cost for defined benefit pension plans that will be amortized from accumulated other comprehensive income into pension expense over the next fiscal year are approximately $104 million and $14 million, respectively.

Certain of the Company's subsidiaries sponsor 401(k) or similar savings plans for active employees. Expense related to these plans was $37 million in 2010, 2009 and 2008. These amounts are not included in the preceding expense table. Company contributions to these savings plans approximate annual expense. Company contributions to multiemployer and other defined contribution pension plans approximate the amount of annual expense presented in the preceding table.

Beginning in 2010, new U.S. salaried and non-union hourly employees were not eligible to participate in the defined benefit pension plan. These employees are eligible to participate in an enhanced defined contribution plan. The change does not impact employees with a hire date before December 31, 2009.

Assumptions

The worldwide weighted-average actuarial assumptions used to determine benefit obligations were:

	2010	2009	2008
Discount rate	5.4%	5.7%	6.2%
Long-term rate of compensation increase	4.2%	4.1%	4.2%

The worldwide weighted-average actuarial assumptions used to determine annual net periodic benefit cost were:

	2010	2009	2008
Discount rate	5.7%	6.2%	6.2%
Long-term rate of compensation increase	4.1%	4.2%	4.4%
Long-term rate of return on plan assets	8.9%	8.9%	8.9%

To determine the overall expected long-term rate of return on plan assets, the Company models expected returns over a 20-year investment horizon with respect to the specific investment mix of its major plans. The return assumptions used reflect a combination of rigorous historical performance analysis and forward-looking views of the financial markets including consideration of current yields on long-term bonds, price-earnings ratios of the major stock market indices, and long-term inflation. The U.S. model, which corresponds to approximately 69% of consolidated pension and other postretirement benefit plan assets, incorporates a long-term inflation assumption of 2.5% and an active management premium of 1% (net of fees) validated by historical analysis. Similar methods are used for various foreign plans with invested assets, reflecting local economic conditions. The expected rate of return for 2010 of 8.9% equated to approximately the 62nd percentile expectation. Refer to Note 1.

To conduct the annual review of discount rates, the Company selected the discount based on a cash-flow matching analysis using Towers Watson's proprietary RATE:Link tool and projections of the future benefit payments that constitute the projected benefit obligation for the plans. RATE:Link establishes the uniform discount rate that produces the same present value of the estimated future benefit payments, as is generated by discounting each year's benefit payments by a spot rate applicable to that year. The spot rates used in this process are derived from a yield curve created from yields on the 40th to 90th percentile of U.S. high quality bonds. A similar methodology is applied in Canada and Europe, except the smaller bond markets imply that yields between the 10th and 90th percentiles are preferable. The measurement dates for the defined benefit plans are consistent with the Company's fiscal year end. Accordingly, the Company selected discount rates to measure our benefit obligations consistent with market indices during December of each year.

Plan assets

The Company categorized Plan assets within a three level fair value hierarchy described as follows:

Investments stated at fair value as determined by quoted market prices (Level 1) include:

Cash and cash equivalents: Value based on cost, which approximates fair value.

Corporate stock, common: Value based on the last sales price on the primary exchange.

Mutual funds: Valued at the net asset value of shares held by the Plan at year end.

Investments stated at estimated fair value using significant observable inputs (Level 2) include:

Cash and cash equivalents: Institutional short-term investment vehicles valued daily.

Collective trusts: Value based on the net asset value of units held at year end.

Bonds: Value based on matrices or models from pricing vendors.

Investments stated at estimated fair value using significant unobservable inputs (Level 3) include:

Real Estate: Value based on the net asset value of units held at year end. The fair value of real estate holdings is based on market data including earnings capitalization, discounted cash flow analysis, comparable sales transactions or a combination of these methods.

Bonds: Value based on matrices or models from brokerage firms. A limited number of the investments are in default.

The preceding methods described may produce a fair value calculation that may not be indicative of net realizable value or reflective of future fair values. Furthermore, although the Company believes its valuation methods are appropriate and consistent with other market participants, the use of different methodologies or assumptions to determine the fair value of certain financial instruments could result in a different fair value measurement at the reporting date.

The Company's practice regarding the timing of transfers between levels is to measure transfers in at the beginning of the month and transfers out at the end of the month. For the year ended January 1, 2011, the Company had no transfers between Levels 1 and 2.

The fair value of Plan assets as of January 1, 2011 summarized by level within the fair value hierarchy are as follows:

(millions)	Total Level 1	Total Level 2	Total Level 3	Total
Cash and cash equivalents	$ 169	$ 38	$—	$ 207
Corporate stock, common:				
Domestic	645	—	—	645
International	185	—	—	185
Mutual funds:				
Domestic equity	44	—	—	44
International equity	419	—	—	419
Collective trusts:				
Domestic equity	—	539	—	539
International equity	—	1,020	—	1,020
Domestic debt	—	13	—	13
International debt	—	275	—	275
Bonds, corporate	—	350	1	351
Bonds, government	—	180	—	180
Bonds, other	—	29	—	29
Real estate	—	—	58	58
Other	—	(5)	7	2
Total	**$1,462**	**$2,439**	**$66**	**$3,967**

The fair value of Plan assets at January 2, 2010 are summarized as follows:

(millions)	Total Level 1	Total Level 2	Total Level 3	Total
Cash and cash equivalents	$ 55	$ 116	$—	$ 171
Corporate stock, common	713	—	—	713
Mutual funds:				
Equity investments	489	—	—	489
Collective trusts:				
Equity investments	—	1,145	—	1,145
Debt investments	—	281	—	281
Bonds, corporate	—	278	3	281
Bonds, government	—	78	—	78
Government mortgage backed securities	—	74	—	74
Bonds, other	—	57	4	61
Real estate	—	—	32	32
Other	—	—	(2)	(2)
Total	$1,257	$2,029	$37	$3,323

There were no unfunded commitments to purchase investments at January 1, 2011 or January 2, 2010.

The Company's investment strategy for its major defined benefit plans is to maintain a diversified portfolio of asset classes with the primary goal of meeting long-term cash requirements as they become due. Assets are invested in a prudent manner to maintain the security of funds while maximizing returns within the Plan's investment policy. The investment policy specifies the type of investment vehicles appropriate for the Plan, asset allocation guidelines, criteria for the selection of investment managers, procedures to monitor overall investment performance as well as investment manager performance. It also provides guidelines enabling Plan fiduciaries to fulfill their responsibilities.

The current weighted-average target asset allocation reflected by this strategy is: equity securities–75%; debt securities–23%; other–2%. Investment in Company common stock represented 1.3% and 1.6% of consolidated plan assets at January 1, 2011 and January 2, 2010, respectively. Plan funding strategies are influenced by tax regulations and funding requirements. The Company currently expects to contribute approximately $180 million to its defined benefit pension plans during 2011.

Level 3 gains and losses
Changes in the fair value of the Plan's Level 3 assets are summarized as follows:

(millions)	Bonds, corporate	Bonds, other	Real estate	Other	Total
January 3, 2009	$11	$11	$27	$ 3	$ 52
Net purchases, sales and other	(4)	(6)	—	(4)	(14)
Realized and unrealized gain (loss)	1	1	5	(1)	6
Transfer out	(5)	(2)	—	—	(7)
January 2, 2010	$ 3	$ 4	$32	$(2)	$ 37
Net purchases, sales and other	(2)	(4)	19	6	19
Realized and unrealized gain	—	—	7	1	8
Transfer out	—	—	—	2	2
January 1, 2011	$ 1	$—	$58	$ 7	$ 66

The net change in Level 3 assets includes a gain of less than $1 million attributable to the change in unrealized holding gains or losses related to Level 3 assets held at January 1, 2011.

Benefit payments
The following benefit payments, which reflect expected future service, as appropriate, are expected to be paid (in millions): 2011–$233; 2012–$202; 2013–$212; 2014–$217; 2015–$226; 2016 to 2020–$1,286.

NOTE 9
NONPENSION POSTRETIREMENT AND POSTEMPLOYMENT BENEFITS

Postretirement
The Company sponsors a number of plans to provide health care and other welfare benefits to retired employees in the United States and Canada, who have met certain age and service requirements. The majority of these plans are funded or unfunded defined benefit plans, although the Company does participate in a limited number of multiemployer or other defined contribution plans for certain employee groups. The Company contributes to voluntary employee benefit association (VEBA) trusts to fund certain U.S. retiree health and welfare benefit obligations.

In the first quarter of 2010, the Patient Protection and Affordable Care Act (PPACA) was signed into law. There are various provisions which will impact the Company, however, the Company has determined that the Act did not have a material impact on the accumulated benefit obligation as of January 1, 2011 for nonpension postretirement benefit plans.

Obligations and funded status
The aggregate change in accumulated postretirement benefit obligation, plan assets, and funded status is presented in the following tables.

(millions)	2010	2009
Change in accumulated benefit obligation		
Beginning of year	$1,162	$1,108
Service cost	20	18
Interest cost	64	65
Actuarial loss	36	25
Benefits paid	(60)	(61)
Foreign currency adjustments	2	7
End of year	$1,224	$1,162
Change in plan assets		
Fair value beginning of year	$ 672	$ 553
Actual return on plan assets	108	170
Employer contributions	293	13
Benefits paid	(65)	(64)
Fair value end of year	$1,008	$ 672
Funded status	$ (216)	$ (490)
Amounts recognized in the Consolidated Balance Sheet consist of		
Other current liabilities	$ (2)	$ (2)
Other liabilities	(214)	(488)
Net amount recognized	$ (216)	$ (490)
Amounts recognized in accumulated other comprehensive income consist of		
Net experience loss	$ 315	$ 340
Prior service credit	(9)	(11)
Net amount recognized	$ 306	$ 329

Expense
Components of postretirement benefit expense were:

(millions)	2010	2009	2008
Service cost	$ 20	$ 18	$ 17
Interest cost	64	65	67
Expected return on plan assets	(64)	(68)	(63)
Amortization of unrecognized prior service credit	(3)	(2)	(3)
Recognized net loss	17	13	9
Postretirement benefit expense:			
Defined benefit plans	34	26	27
Defined contribution plans	2	1	2
Total	$ 36	$ 27	$ 29

The estimated net experience loss for defined benefit plans that will be amortized from accumulated other comprehensive income into nonpension postretirement benefit expense over the next fiscal year is expected to be approximately $20 million, partially offset by amortization of prior service credit of $3 million.

Assumptions

The weighted-average actuarial assumptions used to determine benefit obligations were:

	2010	2009	2008
Discount rate	5.3%	5.7%	6.1%

The weighted-average actuarial assumptions used to determine annual net periodic benefit cost were:

	2010	2009	2008
Discount rate	5.7%	6.1%	6.4%
Long-term rate of return on plan assets	8.9%	8.9%	8.9%

The Company determines the overall discount rate and expected long-term rate of return on VEBA trust obligations and assets in the same manner as that described for pension trusts in Note 8.

The assumed health care cost trend rate is 6.6% for 2011, decreasing gradually to 4.5% by the year 2015 and remaining at that level thereafter. These trend rates reflect the Company's recent historical experience and management's expectations regarding future trends. A one percentage point change in assumed health care cost trend rates would have the following effects:

(millions)	One percentage point increase	One percentage point decrease
Effect on total of service and interest cost components	$ 10	$ (8)
Effect on postretirement benefit obligation	131	(109)

Plan assets

The fair value of Plan assets as of January 1, 2011 summarized by level within the fair value hierarchy described in Note 8, are as follows:

(millions)	Total Level 1	Total Level 2	Total Level 3	Total
Cash and cash equivalents	$ 17	$ 31	$—	$ 48
Corporate stock, common:				
Domestic	184	—	—	184
International	12	—	—	12
Mutual funds:				
Domestic equity	76	—	—	76
International equity	97	—	—	97
Domestic debt	73	—	—	73
Collective trusts:				
Domestic equity	—	241	—	241
International equity	—	137	—	137
Bonds, corporate	—	99	—	99
Bonds, government	—	34	—	34
Bonds, other	—	7	—	7
Total	$459	$549	$—	$1,008

The fair value of Plan assets at January 2, 2010 are summarized as follows:

(millions)	Total Level 1	Total Level 2	Total Level 3	Total
Cash and cash equivalents	$ —	$ 31	$—	$ 31
Corporate stock, common	132	4	—	136
Mutual funds:				
Equity investments	122	—	—	122
Debt investments	45	—	—	45
Collective trusts:				
Equity investments	—	202	—	202
Debt investments	—	28	—	28
Bonds, corporate	—	73	—	73
Bonds, government	—	14	—	14
Government mortgage backed securities	—	13	—	13
Bonds, other	—	7	1	8
Total	$299	$372	$ 1	$672

The Company's asset investment strategy for its VEBA trusts is consistent with that described for its pension trusts in Note 8. The current target asset allocation is 75% equity securities and 25% debt securities. The Company currently expects to contribute approximately $16 million to its VEBA trusts during 2011.

Level 3 gains and losses

The change in the fair value of the Plan's Level 3 assets is summarized as follows:

(millions)	Bonds, other
January 3, 2009	$ 6
Net purchases, sales and other	(2)
Gain	1
Transfer out	(4)
January 2, 2010	$ 1
Net purchases, sales and other	(1)
January 1, 2011	**$—**

Postemployment

Under certain conditions, the Company provides benefits to former or inactive employees in the United States and several foreign locations, including salary continuance, severance, and long-term disability. The Company's postemployment benefit plans are unfunded. Actuarial assumptions used are generally consistent with those presented for pension benefits in Note 8. The aggregate change in accumulated postemployment benefit obligation and the net amount recognized were:

(millions)	2010	2009
Change in accumulated benefit obligation		
Beginning of year	**$ 74**	$ 65
Service cost	**6**	6
Interest cost	**4**	4
Actuarial loss	**8**	8
Benefits paid	**(7)**	(10)
Foreign currency adjustments	**—**	1
End of year	**$ 85**	$ 74
Funded status	**$(85)**	$(74)
Amounts recognized in the Consolidated Balance Sheet consist of		
Other current liabilities	**$ (8)**	$ (7)
Other liabilities	**(77)**	(67)
Net amount recognized	**$(85)**	$(74)
Amounts recognized in accumulated other comprehensive income consist of		
Net experience loss	**$ 43**	$ 39
Net amount recognized	**$ 43**	$ 39

Components of postemployment benefit expense were:

(millions)	2010	2009	2008
Service cost	**$ 6**	$ 6	$ 5
Interest cost	**4**	4	4
Recognized net loss	**4**	4	4
Postemployment benefit expense	**$14**	$14	$13

The estimated net experience loss that will be amortized from accumulated other comprehensive income into postemployment benefit expense over the next fiscal year is approximately $4 million.

Benefit payments

The following benefit payments, which reflect expected future service, as appropriate, are expected to be paid:

(millions)	Postretirement	Postemployment
2011	$ 70	$ 8
2012	76	9
2013	78	9
2014	80	10
2015	81	10
2016-2020	423	58

NOTE 10
INCOME TAXES

The components of income before income taxes and the provision for income taxes were as follows:

(millions)	2010	2009	2008
Income before income taxes			
United States	**$1,271**	$1,207	$1,030
Foreign	**471**	477	601
	1,742	1,684	1,631
Income taxes			
Currently payable			
Federal	**97**	331	135
State	**10**	39	3
Foreign	**129**	146	190
	236	516	328
Deferred			
Federal	**239**	(8)	173
State	**26**	(3)	22
Foreign	**1**	(29)	(38)
	266	(40)	157
Total income taxes	**$ 502**	$ 476	$ 485

The difference between the U.S. federal statutory tax rate and the Company's effective income tax rate was:

	2010	2009	2008
U.S. statutory income tax rate	**35.0%**	35.0%	35.0%
Foreign rates varying from 35%	**–4.1%**	–4.2	–5.0
State income taxes, net of federal benefit	**1.4%**	1.4	1.0
Cost (benefit) of remitted and unremitted foreign earnings	**0.9%**	–0.8	1.6
Tax audit activity	**–1.6%**	–0.9	–1.5
Net change in valuation allowances	**0.5%**	0.4	—
U.S. deduction for qualified production activities	**–1.1%**	–1.6	—
Other	**–2.2%**	–1.1	–1.4
Effective income tax rate	**28.8%**	28.2%	29.7%

As presented in the preceding table, the Company's 2010 consolidated effective tax rate was 28.8%, as compared to 28.2% in 2009 and 29.7% in 2008. The 2010 effective income tax rate was impacted primarily by the remeasurement ofl iabilities for uncertain tax positions. Current authoritative guidance related to liabilities for uncertain tax positions requires the Company to remeasure its liabilities for uncertain tax positions based on new information during the period, including interactions with tax authorities. Based on our interactions with tax authorities in various state and foreign jurisdictions, we reduced certain liabilities for uncertain tax positions by $42 million and increased others by $13 million in 2010. The other line item contains the benefit from an immaterial correction of an item related to prior years that was booked in the first quarter of 2010, as well as the U.S. research and development tax credit.

During 2010, the Company provided $15 million on both remitted and unremitted foreign earnings, which represents the actual or expected tax effect of remitting foreign earnings net of available foreign tax credits. This includes a benefit of $18 million on earnings remitted in 2010 and a charge of $33 million on unremitted earnings not considered indefinitely reinvested. $17 million of this expense relates to current year earnings, while $16 million relates to prior year earnings.

As of January 1, 2011, the Company had recorded a deferred tax liability of $57 million related to $300 million of earnings. Accumulated foreign earnings of approximately $1.5 billion, primarily in Europe, were considered indefinitely reinvested. Accordingly, deferred income taxes have not been provided on these earnings and it is not practical to estimate the deferred tax impact of those earnings.

The 2009 effective tax rate reflected the favorable impact of various audit settlements as well as a U.S. deduction for qualified production activities as defined by the Internal Revenue Code. The deduction is based on U.S. manufacturing activities. During 2009, the Company finalized its assessment of foreign earnings and capital to be repatriated under the prior year repatriation plan resulting in a favorable impact to the cost of remitted and unremitted foreign earnings.

The 2008 effective tax rate reflected the favorable impact of various tax audit settlements. In conjunction with a planned international legal restructuring, management recorded a total charge of $42 million on $1 billion of unremitted foreign earnings and capital. During 2008, $710 million of these earnings and capital were repatriated. The total charge in the year included a provision of $18 million for deferred taxes related to the remaining $290 million of unremitted foreign earnings.

Changes in valuation allowances on deferred tax assets and the corresponding impacts on the effective income tax rate result from management's assessment of the Company's ability to utilize certain future tax deductions, operating losses and tax credit carryforwards prior to expiration. Valuation allowances were recorded to reduce deferred tax assets to an amount that will, more likely than not, be realized in the future. The total tax benefit of carryforwards at year-end 2010 and 2009 were $60 million and $37 million, respectively, with related valuation allowances at year-end 2010 and 2009 of approximately $35 and $22 million. Of the total carryforwards at year-end 2010, $2 million expire in 2011; $4 million expire in 2014 with the remainder expiring after five years.

The following table provides an analysis of the Company's deferred tax assets and liabilities as of year-end 2010 and 2009. Operating loss and credit

carryforwards related to certain foreign operations increased in 2010. The increase in the deferred tax asset was partially offset by a corresponding increase in valuation allowances. The significant decrease in the employee benefits caption of the Company's deferred tax asset was due to pension contributions made at the end of 2010. The deferred tax liability for unremitted foreign earnings increased by $37 million; $33 million of this change is attributable to tax expense recorded in 2010, while $4 million relates to remeasurement for foreign currency changes.

(millions)	Deferred tax assets		Deferred tax liabilities	
	2010	2009	**2010**	2009
U.S. state income taxes	$ **7**	$ 8	$ **77**	$ 60
Advertising and promotion-related	**24**	26	**3**	4
Wages and payroll taxes	**25**	30	—	—
Inventory valuation	**28**	22	—	—
Employee benefits	**187**	393	**65**	42
Operating loss and credit carryforwards	**60**	37	—	—
Hedging transactions	**1**	15	**16**	—
Depreciation and asset disposals	**25**	18	**311**	313
Capitalized interest	**7**	7	**9**	11
Trademarks and other intangibles	—	—	**472**	467
Deferred compensation	**48**	50	—	—
Stock options	**52**	51	—	—
Unremitted foreign earnings	—	—	**57**	20
Other	**51**	67	**8**	12
	515	724	**1,018**	929
Less valuation allowance	**(36)**	(28)	—	—
Total deferred taxes	**$ 479**	$ 696	**$1,018**	$929
Net deferred tax asset (liability)	**$(539)**	$(233)		
Classified in balance sheet as:				
Other current assets	**$ 110**	$ 128		
Other current liabilities	**(13)**	(7)		
Other assets	**61**	71		
Other liabilities	**(697)**	(425)		
Net deferred tax asset (liability)	**$(539)**	$(233)		

The change in valuation allowance reducing deferred tax assets was:

(millions)	**2010**	2009	2008
Balance at beginning of year	**$28**	$22	$22
Additions charged to income tax expense	**11**	14	6
Reductions credited to income tax expense	**(2)**	(7)	(3)
Currency translation adjustments	**(1)**	(1)	(3)
Balance at end of year	**$36**	$28	$22

Cash paid for income taxes was (in millions): 2010–$409; 2009–$409; 2008–$397. Income tax benefits realized from stock option exercises and deductibility of other equity-based awards are presented in Note 7.

Uncertain tax positions

The Company is subject to federal income taxes in the U.S. as well as various state, local, and foreign jurisdictions. The Company's annual provision for U.S. federal income taxes represents approximately 70% of the Company's consolidated income tax provision. The Company was chosen to participate in the Internal Revenue Service (IRS) Compliance

Assurance Program (CAP) beginning with the 2008 tax year. As a result, with limited exceptions, the Company is no longer subject to U.S. federal examinations by the IRS for years prior to 2010. The Company is under examination for income and non-income tax filings in various state and foreign jurisdictions, most notably: 1) a U.S.-Canadian transfer pricing issue pending international arbitration (Competent Authority) with a related advanced pricing agreement for years 1997-2008 for which an extension through 2011 has been requested; 2) an on-going examination of 2002-2008 U.K. income tax filings which is expected to be finalized in 2011; 3) Mexico for years 2003 and forward; and 4) Spain for years 2005 to 2006.

As of January 1, 2011, the Company has classified $43 million of unrecognized tax benefits as a current liability. Management's estimate of reasonably possible changes in unrecognized tax benefits during the next twelve months is comprised of the current liability balance expected to be settled within one year, offset by approximately $10 million of projected additions related primarily to ongoing intercompany transfer pricing activity. Management is currently unaware of any issues under review that could result in significant additional payments, accruals, or other material deviation in this estimate.

Following is a reconciliation of the Company's total gross unrecognized tax benefits as of the years ended January 1, 2011, January 2, 2010 and January 3, 2009. For the 2010 year, approximately $83 million represents the amount that, if recognized, would affect the Company's effective income tax rate in future periods.

(millions)	2010	2009	2008
Balance at beginning of year	$130	$132	$169
Tax positions related to current year:			
Additions	12	17	24
Tax positions related to prior years:			
Additions	13	4	2
Reductions	(42)	(9)	(56)
Settlements	(6)	(8)	(3)
Lapses in statutes ofl imitation	(3)	(6)	(4)
Balance at end of year	$104	$130	$132

For the year ended January 1, 2011, the company recognized an increase of $2 million of tax-related interest and penalties and had $26 million accrued at year end. For the year ended January 2, 2010, the Company recognized a reduction of $1 million of tax-related interest and penalties and had approximately $25 million accrued at January 2, 2010. For the year ended January 3, 2009, the Company recognized a reduction of $2 million of tax-related interest and penalties and had approximately $29 million accrued at January 3, 2009.

NOTE 11
DERIVATIVE INSTRUMENTS AND FAIR VALUE MEASUREMENTS

The Company is exposed to certain market risks such as changes in interest rates, foreign currency exchange rates, and commodity prices, which exist as part of its ongoing business operations. Management uses derivative financial and commodity instruments, including futures, options, and swaps, where appropriate, to manage these risks. Instruments used as hedges must be effective at reducing the risk associated with the exposure being hedged and must be designated as a hedge at the inception of the contract.

The Company designates derivatives as cash flow hedges, fair value hedges, net investment hedges, or other contracts used to reduce volatility in the translation of foreign currency earnings to U.S. dollars. As a matter of policy, the Company does not engage in trading or speculative hedging transactions.

Total notional amounts of the Company's derivative instruments as of January 1, 2011 and January 2, 2010 were as follows:

(millions)	2010	2009
Foreign currency exchange contracts	$1,075	$1,588
Interest rate contracts	1,900	1,900
Commodity contracts	379	213
Total	$3,354	$3,701

Following is a description of each category in the fair value hierarchy and the financial assets and liabilities of the Company that were included in each category at January 1, 2011 and January 2, 2010, measured on a recurring basis.

Level 1 — Financial assets and liabilities whose values are based on unadjusted quoted prices for identical assets or liabilities in an active market. For the Company, level 1 financial assets and liabilities consist primarily of commodity derivative contracts.

Level 2 — Financial assets and liabilities whose values are based on quoted prices in markets that are not active or model inputs that are observable either directly or indirectly for substantially the full term of the asset or liability.

For the Company, level 2 financial assets and liabilities consist of interest rate swaps and over-the-counter commodity and currency contracts.

The Company's calculation of the fair value of interest rate swaps is derived from a discounted cash flow analysis based on the terms of the contract and the interest rate curve. Commodity derivatives are valued using an income approach based on the commodity index prices less the contract rate multiplied by the notional amount. Foreign currency contracts are valued using an income approach based on forward rates less the contract rate multiplied by the notional amount. The Company's calculation of the fair value ofl evel 2 financial assets and liabilities takes into consideration the risk of nonperformance, including counterparty credit risk.

Level 3 — Financial assets and liabilities whose values are based on prices or valuation techniques that require inputs that are both unobservable and significant to the overall fair value measurement. These inputs reflect management's own assumptions about the assumptions a market participant would use in pricing the asset or liability. The Company did not have any level 3 financial assets or liabilities as of January 1, 2011 or January 2, 2010.

The following table presents assets and liabilities that were measured at fair value in the Consolidated Balance Sheet on a recurring basis as of January 1, 2011 and January 2, 2010:

(millions)	Level 1 2010	Level 1 2009	Level 2 2010	Level 2 2009	Total 2010	Total 2009
Assets:						
Foreign currency exchange contracts:						
Other current assets	$—	$—	$ 7	$ 7	$ 7	$ 7
Interest rate contracts:						
Other current assets	—	—	5	—	5	—
Other assets	—	—	69	44	69	44
Commodity contracts:						
Other current assets	23	4	—	—	23	4
Total assets	**$23**	$ 4	**$ 81**	$ 51	**$104**	$ 55
Liabilities:						
Foreign currency exchange contracts:						
Other current liabilities	$—	$—	**$(27)**	$(31)	**$ (27)**	$(31)
Interest rate contracts:						
Other liabilities	—	—	—	(1)	—	(1)
Commodity contracts:						
Other current liabilities	—	—	**(10)**	(6)	**(10)**	(6)
Other liabilities	—	—	**(29)**	(14)	**(29)**	(14)
Total liabilities	**$—**	$—	**$(66)**	$(52)	**$ (66)**	$(52)

The effect of derivative instruments on the Consolidated Statement of Income for the years ended January 1, 2011 and January 2, 2010 was as follows:

Derivatives in fair value hedging relationships	Location of gain (loss) recognized in income	Gain (loss) recognized in income	
(millions)		**2010**	2009
Foreign currency exchange contracts	Other income (expense), net	**$(51)**	$(46)
Interest rate contracts	Interest expense	**39**	28
Total		**$(12)**	$(18)

Derivatives in cash flow hedging relationships	Gain (loss) recognized in AOCI		Location of gain (loss) reclassified from AOCI	Gain (loss) reclassified from AOCI into income		Location of gain (loss) recognized in income (a)	Gain (loss) recognized in income(a)	
(millions)	**2010**	2009		**2010**	2009		**2010**	2009
Foreign currency exchange contracts	**$(19)**	$(23)	COGS	**$(25)**	$19	Other income (expense), net	**$ (1)**	$ (8)
Foreign currency exchange contracts	**—**	3	SGA expense	**(1)**	(3)	Other income (expense), net	**—**	—
Interest rate contracts	**67**	—	Interest expense	**(4)**	(8)	N/A	**—**	—
Commodity contracts	**3**	14	COGS	**(4)**	(5)	Other income (expense), net	**(1)**	(2)
Total	**$51**	$(6)		**$(34)**	$3		**$ (2)**	$(10)

Derivatives not designated as hedging instruments	Location of gain (loss) recognized in income	Gain (loss) recognized in income	
(millions)		**2010**	2009
Foreign currency exchange contracts	Other income (expense), net	**$ —**	$ 1
Total		**$ —**	$ 1

(a)   Includes the ineffective portion and amount excluded from effectiveness testing.

Certain of the Company's derivative instruments contain provisions requiring the Company to post collateral on those derivative instruments that are in a liability position if the Company's credit rating falls below BB+ (S&P), or Baa1 (Moody's). The fair value of all derivative instruments with credit-risk-related contingent features in a liability position on January 1, 2011 was $36 million. If the credit-risk-related contingent features were triggered as of January 1, 2011, the Company would be required to post collateral of $36 million. In addition, certain derivative instruments contain provisions that would be triggered in the event the Company defaults on its debt agreements. There were no collateral posting requirements as of January 1, 2011 triggered by credit-risk-related contingent features.

Other fair value measurements

Level 3 assets measured on a nonrecurring basis at January 1, 2011 and January 2, 2010 consisted ofl ong-lived assets and goodwill.

The Company's calculation of the fair value ofl ong-lived assets is based on market comparables, market trends and the condition of the assets. Long-lived assets with a carrying amount of $19 million were written down to their fair value of $10 million at January 1, 2011, resulting in an impairment charge of $9 million, which was included in earnings for the period.

Goodwill with a carrying amount of $20 million was written off at January 1, 2011 to reflect its implied fair value, resulting in an impairment charge of $20 million, which was included in earnings for the period. Please refer to the impairment discussion in Note 2.

The following table presents assets that were measured at fair value on the Consolidated Balance Sheet on a nonrecurring basis as of January 1, 2011 and January 2, 2010:

	Fair value		Level 3		Total gains (losses)	
(millions)	**2010**	2009	**2010**	2009	**2010**	2009
Description:						
Long-lived assets	**$10**	$—	**$10**	$—	**$ (9)**	$—
Goodwill	—	—	—	—	**(20)**	—
Total	**$10**	$—	**$10**	$—	**$(29)**	$—

Financial instruments

The carrying values of the Company's short-term items, including cash, cash equivalents, accounts receivable, accounts payable and notes payable approximated fair value. The fair value of the Company's long-term debt is calculated based on broker quotes and was as follows at January 1, 2011:

(millions)	Fair Value	Carrying Value
Current maturities ofl ong-term debt	$ 961	$ 952
Long-term debt	5,361	4,908
Total	$6,322	$5,860

Credit risk concentration

The Company is exposed to credit loss in the event of nonperformance by counterparties on derivative financial and commodity contracts. Management believes a concentration of credit risk with respect to derivative counterparties is limited due to the credit ratings of the counterparties and the use of master netting and reciprocal collateralization agreements.

Master netting agreements apply in situations where the Company executes multiple contracts with the same counterparty. Certain counterparties represent a concentration of credit risk to the Company. If those counterparties fail to perform according to the terms of derivative contracts, this would result in a loss to the Company of $50 million as of January 1, 2011.

For certain derivative contracts, reciprocal collateralization agreements with counterparties call for the posting of collateral in the form of cash, treasury securities or letters of credit if a fair value loss position to the Company or our counterparties exceeds a certain amount. There were no collateral balance requirements at January 1, 2011.

Management believes concentrations of credit risk with respect to accounts receivable is limited due to the generally high credit quality of the Company's major customers, as well as the large number and geographic dispersion of smaller customers. However, the Company conducts a disproportionate amount of business with a small number ofl arge multinational grocery retailers, with the five largest accounts encompassing approximately 30% of consolidated trade receivables at January 1, 2011.

NOTE 12
PRODUCT WITHDRAWALS

During 2010, 2009 and 2008, the Company recorded charges in connection with product withdrawals. The Company recorded estimated customer returns and consumer rebates as a reduction of net sales, costs associated with returned product and the disposal and write-off of inventory as COGS, and other recall costs as SGA expense.

On June 25, 2010, the Company announced a recall of select packages of Kellogg's cereal primarily in the U.S. due to an odor from waxy resins found in the package liner. The following table presents a summary of related charges for the year ended January 1, 2011:

(millions, except per share amount)	2010
Reduction of net sales	$ 29
COGS	16
SGA expense	1
Total	$ 46
Impact on earnings per diluted share	$(0.09)

In addition to charges recorded in connection with the withdrawal, the Company also lost sales of the impacted products that are not included in the table above.

On January 16, 2009, the Company announced a recall of certain *Austin* and *Keebler* branded peanut butter sandwich crackers and certain *Famous Amos* and *Keebler* branded peanut butter cookies. The recall was expanded in February 2009 to include certain *Bear Naked*, *Kashi* and *Special K* products. The decision to recall the products was made following an investigation by the United States Food and Drug Administration concerning a salmonella outbreak thought to be caused by tainted peanut related products. The products subject to the recall contained peanut based ingredients manufactured by the Peanut Corporation of America whose Blakely, Georgia plant was found to contain salmonella. The following table presents a summary of related charges for the years ended January 2, 2010 and January 3, 2009:

(millions, except per share amount)	2009	2008	Total
Reduction of net sales	$ 12	$ 12	$24
COGS	18	21	39
SGA expense	1	1	2
Total	$ 31	$ 34	$65
Impact on earnings per diluted share	$(0.06)	$(0.06)	

In addition to charges recorded in connection with the withdrawal, the Company also lost sales of the impacted products that are not included in the table above.

NOTE 13
CONTINGENCIES

The Company is subject to various legal proceedings, claims, and governmental inspections or investigations in the ordinary course of business covering matters such as general commercial, governmental regulations, antitrust and trade regulations, product liability, environmental, intellectual property, workers' compensation, employment and other actions. These matters are subject to uncertainty and the outcome is not predictable with assurance. The Company uses a combination of insurance and self-insurance for a number of risks, including workers' compensation, general liability, automobile liability and product liability.

The Company has established accruals for certain matters where losses are deemed probable and reasonably estimable. There are other claims and legal proceedings pending against the Company for which accruals have not been established. It is reasonably possible that some of these matters could result in an unfavorable judgment against the Company and could require payment of claims in amounts that cannot be estimated at January 1, 2011. Based upon current information, management does not expect any of the claims or legal proceedings pending against the Company to have a material impact on the Company's consolidated financial statements.

NOTE 14
QUARTERLY FINANCIAL DATA (unaudited)

	Net sales		Gross profit	
(millions, except per share data)	2010	2009	2010	2009
First	$ 3,318	$ 3,169	$1,425	$1,302
Second	3,062	3,229	1,305	1,404
Third	3,157	3,277	1,369	1,440
Fourth	2,860	2,900	1,190	1,245
	$12,397	$12,575	$5,289	$5,391

	Net income attributable to Kellogg Company		Per share amounts	
	2010	2009	2010	2009
			Basic Diluted	Basic Diluted
First	$ 418	$ 321	$1.10 $1.09	$.84 $.84
Second	302	354	.80 .79	.93 .92
Third	338	361	.91 .90	.94 .94
Fourth	189	176	.51 .51	.46 .46
	$1,247	$1,212		

The principal market for trading Kellogg shares is the New York Stock Exchange (NYSE). At year-end 2010, the closing price (on the NYSE) was $51.08 and there were 40,527 shareholders of record.

Dividends paid per share and the quarterly price ranges on the NYSE during the last two years were:

2010 — Quarter	Dividend per share	Stock price High	Low
First	$ .3750	$55.45	$51.70
Second	.3750	56.00	49.75
Third	.4050	52.58	47.28
Fourth	.4050	51.62	48.51
	$1.5600		
2009 — Quarter			
First	$ .3400	$45.94	$35.64
Second	.3400	47.72	37.84
Third	.3750	49.90	45.58
Fourth	.3750	54.10	48.15
	$1.4300		

NOTE 15
OPERATING SEGMENTS

Kellogg Company is the world's leading producer of cereal and a leading producer of convenience foods, including cookies, crackers, toaster pastries, cereal bars, fruit snacks, frozen waffles, and veggie foods. Kellogg products are manufactured and marketed globally. Principal markets for these products include the United States and United Kingdom. The Company currently manages its operations in four geographic operating segments, comprised of North America and the three International operating segments of Europe, Latin America, and Asia Pacific.

The measurement of operating segment results is generally consistent with the presentation of the Consolidated Statement of Income and Consolidated Balance Sheet. Intercompany transactions between operating segments were insignificant in all periods presented.

(millions)	2010	2009	2008
Net sales			
North America	$ 8,402	$ 8,510	$ 8,457
Europe	2,230	2,361	2,619
Latin America	923	963	1,030
Asia Pacific (a)	842	741	716
Consolidated	$12,397	$12,575	$12,822
Operating profit			
North America	$ 1,554	$ 1,569	$ 1,447
Europe	364	348	390
Latin America	153	179	209
Asia Pacific (a)	74	86	92
Corporate	(155)	(181)	(185)
Consolidated	$ 1,990	$ 2,001	$ 1,953
Depreciation and amortization			
North America	$ 257	$ 256	$ 249
Europe	53	60	72
Latin America	17	28	24
Asia Pacific (a)	53	22	23
Corporate	12	18	7
Consolidated	$ 392	$ 384	$ 375
Interest expense			
North America	$ —	$ —	$ 1
Europe	1	1	2
Latin America	—	—	—
Asia Pacific (a)	1	—	—
Corporate	246	294	305
Consolidated	$ 248	$ 295	$ 308
Income taxes			
North America	$ 482	$ 474	$ 418
Europe	23	22	25
Latin America	29	32	38
Asia Pacific (a)	19	16	16
Corporate	(51)	(68)	(12)
Consolidated	$ 502	$ 476	$ 485
Total assets			
North America	$ 8,623	$ 8,465	$ 8,443
Europe	1,700	1,630	1,545
Latin America	784	585	515
Asia Pacific (a)	596	535	408
Corporate	3,006	3,354	4,305
Elimination entries	(2,862)	(3,369)	(4,270)
Consolidated	$11,847	$11,200	$10,946
Additions to long-lived assets			
North America	$ 327	$ 236	$ 262
Europe	57	50	172
Latin America	43	58	70
Asia Pacific (a)	45	30	66
Corporate	2	3	6
Consolidated	$ 474	$ 377	$ 576

(a) Includes Australia, Asia and South Africa.

The Company's largest customer, Wal-Mart Stores, Inc. and its affiliates, accounted for approximately 21% of consolidated net sales during 2010, 21% in 2009, and 20% in 2008, comprised principally of sales within the United States.

Supplemental geographic information is provided below for net sales to external customers and long-lived assets:

(millions)	2010	2009	2008
Net sales			
United States	$ 7,786	$ 7,946	$ 7,866
United Kingdom	870	906	1,026
Other foreign countries	3,741	3,723	3,930
Consolidated	$12,397	$12,575	$12,822
Long-lived assets			
United States	$ 1,993	$ 1,916	$ 1,922
United Kingdom	272	278	260
Other foreign countries	863	816	751
Consolidated	$ 3,128	$ 3,010	$ 2,933

Supplemental product information is provided below for net sales to external customers:

(millions)	2010	2009	2008
North America			
Retail channel cereal	$ 2,947	$ 3,080	$ 3,038
Retail channel snacks	4,048	4,012	3,960
Frozen and specialty channels	1,407	1,418	1,459
International			
Cereal	3,309	3,326	3,547
Convenience foods	686	739	818
Consolidated	$12,397	$12,575	$12,822

NOTE 16
SUPPLEMENTAL FINANCIAL STATEMENT DATA

Consolidated Statement of Income

(millions)	2010	2009	2008
Research and development expense	$ 187	$ 181	$ 181
Advertising expense	$1,130	$1,091	$1,076

Consolidated Balance Sheet

(millions)	2010	2009
Trade receivables	$ 893	$ 951
Allowance for doubtful accounts	(10)	(9)
Refundable income taxes	189	23
Other receivables	118	128
Accounts receivable, net	$ 1,190	$ 1,093
Raw materials and supplies	$ 224	$ 214
Finished goods and materials in process	832	696
Inventories	$ 1,056	$ 910
Deferred income taxes	$ 110	$ 128
Other prepaid assets	115	93
Other current assets	$ 225	$ 221
Land	$ 107	$ 106
Buildings	1,842	1,750
Machinery and equipment (a)	5,462	5,383
Construction in progress	407	291
Accumulated depreciation	(4,690)	(4,520)
Property, net	$ 3,128	$ 3,010
Other intangibles	$ 1,503	$ 1,503
Accumulated amortization	(47)	(45)
Other intangibles, net	$ 1,456	$ 1,458
Pension	$ 333	$ 160
Other	387	371
Other assets	$ 720	$ 531
Accrued income taxes	$ 60	$ 33
Accrued salaries and wages	153	322
Accrued advertising and promotion	405	409
Other	421	402
Other current liabilities	$ 1,039	$ 1,166
Nonpension postretirement benefits	$ 214	$ 488
Other	425	459
Other liabilities	$ 639	$ 947

(a) Includes an insignificant amount of capitalized internal-use software.

Allowance for doubtful accounts

(millions)	2010	2009	2008
Balance at beginning of year	$ 9	$10	$ 5
Additions charged to expense	2	3	6
Doubtful accounts charged to reserve	(1)	(4)	(1)
Balance at end of year	$10	$ 9	$10

Management's Responsibility for Financial Statements

Management is responsible for the preparation of the Company's consolidated financial statements and related notes. We believe that the consolidated financial statements present the Company's financial position and results of operations in conformity with accounting principles that are generally accepted in the United States, using our best estimates and judgments as required.

The independent registered public accounting firm audits the Company's consolidated financial statements in accordance with the standards of the Public Company Accounting Oversight Board and provides an objective, independent review of the fairness of reported operating results and financial position.

The board of directors of the Company has an Audit Committee composed of five non-management Directors. The Committee meets regularly with management, internal auditors, and the independent registered public accounting firm to review accounting, internal control, auditing and financial reporting matters.

Formal policies and procedures, including an active Ethics and Business Conduct program, support the internal controls and are designed to ensure employees adhere to the highest standards of personal and professional integrity. We have a rigorous internal audit program that independently evaluates the adequacy and effectiveness of these internal controls.

Management's Report on Internal Control over Financial Reporting

Management is responsible for designing, maintaining and evaluating adequate internal control over financial reporting, as such term is defined in Rule 13a-15(f) under the Securities Exchange Act of 1934, as amended. Our internal control over financial reporting is designed to provide reasonable assurance regarding the reliability of financial reporting and the preparation of the financial statements for external purposes in accordance with U.S. generally accepted accounting principles.

We conducted an evaluation of the effectiveness of our internal control over financial reporting based on the framework in Internal Control — Integrated Framework issued by the Committee of Sponsoring Organizations of the Treadway Commission.

Because of its inherent limitations, internal control over financial reporting may not prevent or detect misstatements. Also, projections of any evaluation of effectiveness to future periods are subject to the risk that controls may become inadequate because of changes in conditions or that the degree of compliance with the policies or procedures may deteriorate.

Based on our evaluation under the framework in Internal Control — Integrated Framework, management concluded that our internal control over financial reporting was effective as of January 1, 2011. The effectiveness of our internal control over financial reporting as of January 1, 2011 has been audited by PricewaterhouseCoopers LLP, an independent registered public accounting firm, as stated in their report which follows.

John A. Bryant
President and Chief Executive Officer

Ronald L. Dissinger
Senior Vice President and Chief Financial Officer

Report of Independent Registered Public Accounting Firm

To the Shareholders and Board of Directors of Kellogg Company

In our opinion, the consolidated financial statements listed in the index appearing under Item 15(a)(1) present fairly, in all material respects, the financial position of Kellogg Company and its subsidiaries at January 1, 2011 and January 2, 2010, and the results of their operations and their cash flows for each of the three years in the period ended January 1, 2011 in conformity with accounting principles generally accepted in the United States of America. Also in our opinion, the Company maintained, in all material respects, effective internal control over financial reporting as of January 1, 2011, based on criteria established in *Internal Control — Integrated Framework* issued by the Committee of Sponsoring Organizations of the Treadway Commission (COSO). The Company's management is responsible for these financial statements, for maintaining effective internal control over financial reporting and for its assessment of the effectiveness of internal control over financial reporting, included in the accompanying Management's Report on Internal Control over Financial Reporting. Our responsibility is to express opinions on these financial statements and on the Company's internal control over financial reporting based on our integrated audits. We conducted our audits in accordance with the standards of the Public Company Accounting Oversight Board (United States). Those standards require that we plan and perform the audits to obtain reasonable assurance about whether the financial statements are free of material misstatement and whether effective internal control over financial reporting was maintained in all material respects. Our audits of the financial statements included examining, on a test basis, evidence supporting the amounts and disclosures in the financial statements, assessing the accounting principles used and significant estimates made by management, and evaluating the overall financial statement presentation. Our audit of internal control over financial reporting included obtaining an understanding of internal control over financial reporting, assessing the risk that a material weakness exists, and testing and evaluating the design and operating effectiveness of internal control based on the assessed risk. Our audits also included performing such other procedures as we considered necessary in the circumstances. We believe that our audits provide a reasonable basis for our opinions.

A company's internal control over financial reporting is a process designed to provide reasonable assurance regarding the reliability of financial reporting and the preparation of financial statements for external purposes in accordance with generally accepted accounting principles. A company's internal control over financial reporting includes those policies and procedures that (i) pertain to the maintenance of records that, in reasonable detail, accurately and fairly reflect the transactions and dispositions of the assets of the company; (ii) provide reasonable assurance that transactions are recorded as necessary to permit preparation of financial statements in accordance with generally accepted accounting principles, and that receipts and expenditures of the company are being made only in accordance with authorizations of management and directors of the company; and (iii) provide reasonable assurance regarding prevention or timely detection of unauthorized acquisition, use, or disposition of the company's assets that could have a material effect on the financial statements.

Because of its inherent limitations, internal control over financial reporting may not prevent or detect misstatements. Also, projections of any evaluation of effectiveness to future periods are subject to the risk that controls may become inadequate because of changes in conditions, or that the degree of compliance with the policies or procedures may deteriorate.

PricewaterhouseCoopers LLP

Battle Creek, Michigan
February 25, 2011

Excerpts from General Mills's Form 10-K for the Fiscal Year Ended May 30, 2010 [2010]

UNITED STATES
SECURITIES AND EXCHANGE COMMISSION
Washington, D.C. 20549
FORM 10-K

☒ ANNUAL REPORT PURSUANT TO SECTION 13 OR 15(d) OF THE SECURITIES EXCHANGE ACT OF 1934

FOR THE FISCAL YEAR ENDED May 30, 2010

☐ TRANSITION REPORT PURSUANT TO SECTION 13 OR 15(d) OF THE SECURITIES EXCHANGE ACT OF 1934

FOR THE TRANSITION PERIOD FROM _____ TO _____

Commission file number: 001-01185

GENERAL MILLS, INC.
(Exact name of registrant as specified in its charter)

Delaware	41-0274440
(State or other jurisdiction of	(I.R.S. Employer
incorporation or organization)	Identification No.)
Number One General Mills Boulevard	55426
Minneapolis, Minnesota	(Zip Code)
(Address of principal executive offices)	

(763) 764-7600

(Registrant's telephone number, including area code)

Securities registered pursuant to Section 12(b) of the Act:

Title of each class	Name of each exchange on which registered
Common Stock, $.10 par value	New York Stock Exchange

Securities registered pursuant to Section 12(g) of the Act: None

Indicate by check mark if the registrant is a well-known seasoned issuer, as defined in Rule 405 of the Securities Act. Yes ☒ No ☐

Indicate by check mark if the registrant is not required to file reports pursuant to Section 13 or Section 15(d) of the Act. Yes ☐ No ☒

Indicate by check mark whether the registrant (1) has filed all reports required to be filed by Section 13 or 15(d) of the Securities Exchange Act of 1934 during the preceding 12 months (or for such shorter period that the registrant was required to file such reports), and (2) has been subject to such filing requirements for the past 90 days. Yes ☒ No ☐

Indicate by check mark whether the registrant has submitted electronically and posted on its corporate website, if any, every Interactive Data File required to be submitted and posted pursuant to Rule 405 of Regulation S-T during the preceding 12 months (or for such shorter period that the registrant was required to submit and post such files). Yes ☒ No ☐

Indicate by check mark if disclosure of delinquent filers pursuant to Item 405 of Regulation S-K is not contained herein, and will not be contained, to the best of registrant's knowledge, in definitive proxy or information statements incorporated by reference in Part III of this Form 10-K or any amendment to this Form 10-K. ☒

Indicate by check mark whether the registrant is a large accelerated filer, an accelerated filer, a non-accelerated filer, or a smaller reporting company. See the definitions of "large accelerated filer," "accelerated filer" and "smaller reporting company" in Rule 12b-2 of the Exchange Act. (Check one):

Large accelerated filer	☒	Accelerated filer	☐
Non-accelerated filer	☐ (Do not check if a smaller reporting company)	Smaller reporting company	☐

Indicate by check mark whether the registrant is a shell company (as defined in Rule 12b-2 of the Act).

Yes ☐ No ☒

Aggregate market value of Common Stock held by non-affiliates of the registrant, based on the closing price of $34.05 per share as reported on the New York Stock Exchange on November 27, 2009 (the last business day of the registrant's most recently completed second fiscal quarter): $22,384.1 million.

Number of shares of Common Stock outstanding as of June 18, 2010: 651,216,065 (excluding 103,397,263 shares held in the treasury).

DOCUMENTS INCORPORATED BY REFERENCE

Portions of the registrant's Proxy Statement for its 2010 Annual Meeting of Stockholders are incorporated by reference into Part III.

ITEM 8   Financial Statements and Supplementary Data

REPORT OF MANAGEMENT RESPONSIBILITIES

The management of General Mills, Inc. is responsible for the fairness and accuracy of the consolidated financial statements. The statements have been prepared in accordance with accounting principles that are generally accepted in the United States, using management's best estimates and judgments where appropriate. The financial information throughout this Annual Report on Form 10-K is consistent with our consolidated financial statements.

Management has established a system of internal controls that provides reasonable assurance that assets are adequately safeguarded and transactions are recorded accurately in all material respects, in accordance with management's authorization. We maintain a strong audit program that independently evaluates the adequacy and effectiveness of internal controls. Our internal controls provide for appropriate separation of duties and responsibilities, and there are documented policies regarding use of our assets and proper financial reporting. These formally stated and regularly communicated policies demand highly ethical conduct from all employees.

The Audit Committee of the Board of Directors meets regularly with management, internal auditors, and our independent registered public accounting firm to review internal control, auditing, and financial reporting matters. The independent registered public accounting firm, internal auditors, and employees have full and free access to the Audit Committee at any time.

The Audit Committee reviewed and approved the Company's annual financial statements. The Audit Committee recommended, and the Board of Directors approved, that the consolidated financial statements be included in the Annual Report. The Audit Committee also appointed KPMG LLP to serve as the Company's independent registered public accounting firm for fiscal 2011, subject to ratification by the stockholders at the annual meeting.

/s/ K. J. Powell   /s/ D. L. Mulligan

K. J. Powell   D. L. Mulligan
Chairman of the Board   Executive Vice President
and Chief Executive Officer   and Chief Financial Officer

July 9, 2010

Report of Independent Registered Public Accounting Firm

The Board of Directors and Stockholders

General Mills, Inc.:

We have audited the accompanying consolidated balance sheets of General Mills, Inc. and subsidiaries as of May 30, 2010, and May 31, 2009, and the related consolidated statements of earnings, total equity and comprehensive income, and cash flows for each of the fiscal years in the three-year period ended May 30, 2010. In connection with our audits of the consolidated financial statements, we have audited the accompanying financial statement schedule. We also have audited General Mills Inc.'s internal control over financial reporting as of May 30, 2010, based on criteria established in *Internal Control — Integrated Framework* issued by the Committee of Sponsoring Organizations of the Treadway Commission (COSO). General Mills, Inc.'s management is responsible for these consolidated financial statements and financial statement schedule, for maintaining effective internal control over financial reporting, and for its assessment of the effectiveness of internal control over financial reporting, included in Management's Report on Internal Control over Financial Reporting. Our responsibility is to express an opinion on these consolidated financial statements and financial statement schedule and an opinion on the Company's internal control over financial reporting based on our audits.

We conducted our audits in accordance with the standards of the Public Company Accounting Oversight Board (United States). Those standards require that we plan and perform the audits to obtain reasonable assurance about whether the financial statements are free of material misstatement and whether effective internal control over financial reporting was maintained in all material respects. Our audits of the consolidated financial statements included examining, on a test basis, evidence supporting the amounts and disclosures in the financial statements, assessing the accounting principles used and significant estimates made by management, and evaluating the overall financial statement presentation. Our audit of internal control over financial reporting included obtaining an understanding of internal control over financial reporting, assessing the risk that a material weakness exists, and testing and evaluating the design and operating effectiveness of internal control based on the assessed risk. Our audits also included performing such other procedures as we considered necessary in the circumstances. We believe that our audits provide a reasonable basis for our opinions.

A company's internal control over financial reporting is a process designed to provide reasonable assurance regarding the reliability of financial reporting and the preparation of financial statements for external purposes in accordance with generally accepted accounting principles. A company's internal control over financial reporting includes those policies and procedures that (1) pertain to the maintenance of records that, in reasonable detail, accurately and fairly reflect the transactions and dispositions of the assets of the company; (2) provide reasonable assurance that transactions are recorded as necessary to permit preparation of financial statements in accordance with generally accepted accounting principles, and that receipts and expenditures of the company are being made only in accordance with authorizations of management and directors of the company; and (3) provide reasonable assurance regarding prevention or timely detection of unauthorized acquisition, use, or disposition of the company's assets that could have a material effect on the financial statements.

Because of its inherent limitations, internal control over financial reporting may not prevent or detect misstatements. Also, projections of any evaluation of effectiveness to future periods are subject to the risk that controls may become inadequate because of changes in conditions, or that the degree of compliance with the policies or procedures may deteriorate.

In our opinion, the consolidated financial statements referred to above present fairly, in all material respects, the financial position of General Mills, Inc. and subsidiaries as of May 30, 2010, and May 31, 2009, and the results of their operations and their cash flows for each of the fiscal years in the three-year period ended May 30, 2010, in conformity with U.S. generally accepted accounting principles. Also in our opinion, the accompanying financial statement schedule, when considered in relation to the basic consolidated financial statements taken as a whole, presents fairly, in all material respects, the information set forth therein. Also in our opinion, General Mills, Inc. maintained, in all material respects, effective internal control over financial reporting as of May 30, 2010, based on criteria established in *Internal Control — Integrated Framework* issued by the Committee of Sponsoring Organizations of the Treadway Commission.

As disclosed in Note 1 to the Consolidated Financial Statements, the Company changed its method of accounting for noncontrolling interests in fiscal year 2010.

/s/ KPMG LLP

Minneapolis, Minnesota

July 9, 2010

Consolidated Statements of Earnings

GENERAL MILLS, INC. AND SUBSIDIARIES

(In Millions, Except per Share Data)

	Fiscal Year		
	2010	2009	2008
Net sales	$ 14,796.5	$ 14,691.3	$ 13,652.1
Cost of sales	8,922.9	9,457.8	8,778.3
Selling, general, and administrative expenses	3,236.1	2,951.8	2,623.6
Divestitures (gain), net	—	(84.9)	—
Restructuring, impairment, and other exit costs	31.4	41.6	21.0
Operating profit	2,606.1	2,325.0	2,229.2
Interest, net	401.6	382.8	399.7
Earnings before income taxes and after-tax earnings from joint ventures	2,204.5	1,942.2	1,829.5
Income taxes	771.2	720.4	622.2
After-tax earnings from joint ventures	101.7	91.9	110.8
Net earnings, including earnings attributable to noncontrolling interests	1,535.0	1,313.7	1,318.1
Net earnings attributable to noncontrolling interests	4.5	9.3	23.4
Net earnings attributable to General Mills	$ 1,530.5	$ 1,304.4	$ 1,294.7
Earnings per share - basic	$ 2.32	$ 1.96	$ 1.93
Earnings per share - diluted	$ 2.24	$ 1.90	$ 1.85
Dividends per share	$ 0.96	$ 0.86	$ 0.78

See accompanying notes to consolidated financial statements.

Consolidated Balance Sheets

GENERAL MILLS, INC. AND SUBSIDIARIES

(In Millions, Except Par Value)

	May 30, 2010	May 31, 2009
ASSETS		
Current assets:		
Cash and cash equivalents	$ 673.2	$ 749.8
Receivables	1,041.6	953.4
Inventories	1,344.0	1,346.8
Deferred income taxes	42.7	15.6
Prepaid expenses and other current assets	378.5	469.3
Total current assets	3,480.0	3,534.9
Land, buildings, and equipment	3,127.7	3,034.9
Goodwill	6,592.8	6,663.0
Other intangible assets	3,715.0	3,747.0
Other assets	763.4	895.0
Total assets	$ 17,678.9	$ 17,874.8
LIABILITIES AND EQUITY		
Current liabilities:		
Accounts payable	$ 849.5	$ 803.4
Current portion of long-term debt	107.3	508.5
Notes payable	1,050.1	812.2
Other current liabilities	1,762.2	1,481.9
Total current liabilities	3,769.1	3,606.0
Long-term debt	5,268.5	5,754.8
Deferred income taxes	874.6	1,165.3
Other liabilities	2,118.7	1,932.2
Total liabilities	12,030.9	12,458.3
Stockholders' equity:		
Common stock, 754.6 shares issued, $0.10 par value	75.5	75.5
Additional paid-in capital	1,307.1	1,212.1
Retained earnings	8,122.4	7,235.6
Common stock in treasury, at cost, shares of 98.1 and 98.6	(2,615.2)	(2,473.1)
Accumulated other comprehensive loss	(1,486.9)	(877.8)
Total stockholders' equity	5,402.9	5,172.3
Noncontrolling interests	245.1	244.2
Total equity	5,648.0	5,416.5
Total liabilities and equity	$ 17,678.9	$ 17,874.8

See accompanying notes to consolidated financial statements.

Consolidated Statements of Total Equity and Comprehensive Income

GENERAL MILLS, INC. AND SUBSIDIARIES

(In Millions, Except per Share Data)

| | $.10 Par Value Common Stock (One Billion Shares Authorized) | | | | | | | | |
| | Issued | | | Treasury | | | Accumulated Other | | |
	Shares	Par Amount	Additional Paid-In Capital	Shares	Amount	Retained Earnings	Comprehensive Income (Loss)	Noncontrolling Interests	Total
Balance as of May 27, 2007	1,004.6 $	100.5 $	5,791.0	(323.4) $	(6,198.0) $	5,745.3 $	(120.1) $	1,139.2	$ 6,457.9
Comprehensive income:									
Net earnings, including earnings attributable to noncontrolling interests						1,294.7		23.4	1,318.1
Other comprehensive income							293.2	3.2	296.4
Total comprehensive income									1,614.5
Cash dividends declared ($0.78 per share)						(529.7)			(529.7)
Stock compensation plans (includes income tax benefits of $55.7)			121.0	13.0	261.6				382.6
Shares purchased				(47.8)	(1,384.6)				(1,384.6)
Retirement of treasury shares	(250.0)	(25.0)	(5,055.8)	250.0	5,080.8				—
Shares issued under forward purchase contract			168.2	28.6	581.8				750.0
Unearned compensation related to restricted stock unit awards			(104.1)						(104.1)
Adoption of FIN 48			57.8			8.4			66.2
Repurchase of Series B-1 limited membership interests in General Mills Cereals, LLC (GMC)						(8.0)		(835.0)	(843.0)
Repurchase of GM Capital Inc. Series A preferred stock								(150.0)	(150.0)
Sale of GMC Class A limited membership interests in GMC								92.3	92.3
Distributions to noncontrolling interest holders								(26.5)	(26.5)
Earned compensation			133.2						133.2
Balance as of May 25, 2008	754.6	75.5	1,111.3	(79.6)	(1,658.4) $	6,510.7	173.1	246.6	6,458.8
Comprehensive income:									
Net earnings, including earnings attributable to noncontrolling interests						1,304.4		9.3	1,313.7
Other comprehensive loss							(1,050.9)	(1.2)	(1,052.1)
Total comprehensive income									261.6
Cash dividends declared ($0.86 per share)						(579.5)			(579.5)
Stock compensation plans (includes income tax benefits of $94.0)			23.0	19.6	443.1				466.1
Shares purchased				(40.4)	(1,296.4)				(1,296.4)
Shares issued for acquisition			16.4	1.8	38.6				55.0
Unearned compensation related to restricted stock unit awards			(56.2)						(56.2)
Distributions to noncontrolling interest holders								(10.5)	(10.5)
Earned compensation			117.6						117.6
Balance as of May 31, 2009	754.6	75.5	1,212.1	(98.6)	(2,473.1)	7,235.6	(877.8)	244.2	5,416.5
Comprehensive income:									
Net earnings, including earnings attributable to noncontrolling interests						1,530.5		4.5	1,535.0
Other comprehensive income (loss)							(609.1)	0.2	(608.9)
Total comprehensive income									926.1
Cash dividends declared ($0.96 per share)						(643.7)			(643.7)
Stock compensation plans (includes income tax benefits of $114.0)			53.3	21.8	549.7				603.0
Shares purchased				(21.3)	(691.8)				(691.8)
Unearned compensation related to restricted stock unit awards			(65.6)						(65.6)
Distributions to noncontrolling interest holders								(3.8)	(3.8)
Earned compensation			107.3						107.3
Balance as of May 30, 2010	754.6 $	75.5 $	1,307.1	(98.1) $	(2,615.2) $	8,122.4 $	(1,486.9) $	245.1	$ 5,648.0

See accompanying notes to consolidated financial statements.

Consolidated Statements of Cash Flows

GENERAL MILLS, INC. AND SUBSIDIARIES

(In Millions)

	Fiscal Year		
	2010	2009	2008
Cash Flows - Operating Activities			
Net earnings, including earnings attributable to noncontrolling interests	$ 1,535.0 $	1,313.7 $	1,318.1
Adjustments to reconcile net earnings to net cash provided by operating activities:			
Depreciation and amortization	457.1	453.6	459.2
After-tax earnings from joint ventures	(101.7)	(91.9)	(110.8)
Stock-based compensation	107.3	117.7	133.2
Deferred income taxes	22.3	215.8	98.1
Tax benefit on exercised options	(114.0)	(89.1)	(55.7)
Distributions of earnings from joint ventures	88.0	68.5	108.7
Pension and other postretirement benefit plan contributions	(17.2)	(220.3)	(14.2)
Pension and other postretirement benefit plan (income) expense	(37.9)	(27.5)	5.5
Divestitures (gain), net	—	(84.9)	—
Gain on insurance settlement	—	(41.3)	—
Restructuring, impairment, and other exit costs (income)	23.4	31.3	(1.7)
Changes in current assets and liabilities	143.4	176.9	(126.7)
Other, net	75.5	5.7	(83.8)
Net cash provided by operating activities	2,181.2	1,828.2	1,729.9
Cash Flows - Investing Activities			
Purchases of land, buildings, and equipment	(649.9)	(562.6)	(522.0)
Acquisitions	—	—	0.6
Investments in affiliates, net	(130.7)	5.9	64.6
Proceeds from disposal of land, buildings, and equipment	7.4	4.1	25.9
Proceeds from divestiture of product lines	—	244.7	—
Proceeds from insurance settlement	—	41.3	—
Other, net	52.0	(22.3)	(11.5)
Net cash used by investing activities	(721.2)	(288.9)	(442.4)
Cash Flows - Financing Activities			
Change in notes payable	235.8	(1,390.5)	946.6
Issuance of long-term debt	—	1,850.0	1,450.0
Payment of long-term debt	(906.9)	(370.3)	(1,623.4)
Settlement of Lehman Brothers forward purchase contract	—	—	750.0
Repurchase of Series B-1 limited membership interests in GMC	—	—	(843.0)
Repurchase of General Mills Capital, Inc. preferred stock	—	—	(150.0)
Proceeds from sale of Class A limited membership interests in GMC	—	—	92.3
Proceeds from common stock issued on exercised options	388.8	305.2	191.4
Tax benefit on exercised options	114.0	89.1	55.7
Purchases of common stock for treasury	(691.8)	(1,296.4)	(1,432.4)
Dividends paid	(643.7)	(579.5)	(529.7)
Other, net	—	(12.1)	(0.5)
Net cash used by financing activities	(1,503.8)	(1,404.5)	(1,093.0)
Effect of exchange rate changes on cash and cash equivalents	(32.8)	(46.0)	49.4
Increase (decrease) in cash and cash equivalents	(76.6)	88.8	243.9
Cash and cash equivalents - beginning of year	749.8	661.0	417.1
Cash and cash equivalents - end of year	$ 673.2 $	749.8 $	661.0
Cash Flow from Changes in Current Assets and Liabilities:			
Receivables	$ (121.1) $	81.8 $	(94.1)
Inventories	(16.7)	(28.1)	(165.1)
Prepaid expenses and other current assets	53.5	30.2	(65.9)
Accounts payable	69.6	(116.4)	125.1
Other current liabilities	158.1	209.4	73.3
Changes in current assets and liabilities	$ 143.4 $	176.9 $	(126.7)

See accompanying notes to consolidated financial statements.

Notes to Consolidated Financial Statements

GENERAL MILLS, INC. AND SUBSIDIARIES

NOTE 1. BASIS OF PRESENTATION AND RECLASSIFICATIONS

Basis of Presentation

Our Consolidated Financial Statements include the accounts of General Mills, Inc. and all subsidiaries in which we have a controlling financial interest. Intercompany transactions and accounts are eliminated in consolidation.

Our fiscal year ends on the last Sunday in May. Fiscal 2010 and 2008 each consisted of 52 weeks, and fiscal 2009 consisted of 53 weeks.

In December 2007, the Financial Accounting Standards Board (FASB) issued new guidance on noncontrolling interests in financial statements. The guidance establishes accounting and reporting standards that require: the ownership interest in subsidiaries held by parties other than the parent to be clearly identified and presented in the Consolidated Balance Sheets within equity, but separate from the parent's equity; the amount of consolidated net earnings attributable to the parent and the noncontrolling interest to be clearly identified and presented on the face of the Consolidated Statements of Earnings; and changes in a parent's ownership interest while the parent retains its controlling financial interest in its subsidiary to be accounted for consistently.

We adopted the guidance at the beginning of fiscal 2010. To conform to the current period presentation, we made the following reclassifications to net earnings attributable to noncontrolling interests in our Consolidated Statements of Earnings:

| | Fiscal Year | |
In Millions	2009	2008
From interest, net	$ 7.2	$ 22.0
From selling, general, and administrative (SG&A) expenses	2.1	1.4
Total net earnings attributable to noncontrolling interests	$ 9.3	$ 23.4

Also, noncontrolling interests previously reported as minority interests have been reclassified to a separate section in equity on the Consolidated Balance Sheets as a result of the adoption. In addition, certain other reclassifications to our previously reported financial information have been made to conform to the current period presentation.

In May 2010, our Board of Directors approved a two-for-one stock split to be effected in the form of a 100 percent stock dividend to stockholders of record on May 28, 2010. The Company's stockholders received one additional share of common stock for each share of common stock in their possession on that date. The additional shares were distributed on June 8, 2010. This did not change the proportionate interest that a stockholder maintained in the Company. All shares and per share amounts have been adjusted for the two-for-one stock split throughout this report.

Change in Reporting Period

As part of a long-term plan to conform the fiscal year ends of all our operations, we have changed the reporting period of certain countries within our International segment from an April fiscal year end to a May fiscal year end to match our fiscal calendar. Accordingly, in the year of change, our results include 13 months of results from the affected operations compared to 12 months in previous fiscal years. In fiscal 2010, we changed many of the countries in our Asia/Pacific region, and in fiscal 2009 we changed most countries in our Latin America region. The impact of these changes was not material to our results of operations and, therefore, we did not restate prior period financial statements for comparability. Countries within the International segment that remain on an April fiscal year end include our European operations and China.

NOTE 2. SUMMARY OF SIGNIFICANT ACCOUNTING POLICIES

Cash and Cash Equivalents

We consider all investments purchased with an original maturity of three months or less to be cash equivalents.

Inventories

All inventories in the United States other than grain and certain organic products are valued at the lower of cost, using the last-in, first-out (LIFO) method, or market. Grain inventories and all related cash contracts and derivatives are valued at market with all net changes in value recorded in earnings currently.

Inventories outside of the United States are valued at the lower of cost, using the first-in, first-out (FIFO) method, or market.

Shipping costs associated with the distribution of finished product to our customers are recorded as cost of sales, and are recognized when the related finished product is shipped to and accepted by the customer.

Land, Buildings, Equipment, and Depreciation

Land is recorded at historical cost. Buildings and equipment, including capitalized interest and internal engineering costs, are recorded at cost and depreciated over estimated useful lives, primarily using the straight-line method. Ordinary maintenance and repairs are charged to cost of sales. Buildings are usually depreciated over 40 to 50 years, and equipment, furniture, and software are usually depreciated over 3 to 10 years. Fully depreciated assets are retained in buildings and equipment until disposal. When an item is sold or retired, the accounts are relieved of its cost and related accumulated depreciation; the resulting gains and losses, if any, are recognized in earnings. As of May 30, 2010, assets held for sale were insignificant.

Long-lived assets are reviewed for impairment whenever events or changes in circumstances indicate that the carrying amount of an asset (or asset group) may not be recoverable. An impairment loss would be recognized when estimated undiscounted future cash flows from the operation and disposition of the asset group are less than the carrying amount of the asset group. Asset groups have identifiable cash flows and are largely independent of other asset groups. Measurement of an impairment loss would be based on the excess of the carrying amount of the asset group over its fair value. Fair value is measured using a discounted cash flow model or independent appraisals, as appropriate.

Goodwill and Other Intangible Assets
Goodwill is not subject to amortization and is tested for impairment annually and whenever events or changes in circumstances indicate that impairment may have occurred. Impairment testing is performed for each of our reporting units. We compare the carrying value of a reporting unit, including goodwill, to the fair value of the unit. Carrying value is based on the assets and liabilities associated with the operations of that reporting unit, which often requires allocation of shared or corporate items among reporting units. If the carrying amount of a reporting unit exceeds its fair value, we revalue all assets and liabilities of the reporting unit, excluding goodwill, to determine if the fair value of the net assets is greater than the net assets including goodwill. If the fair value of the net assets is less than the net assets including goodwill, impairment has occurred. Our estimates of fair value are determined based on a discounted cash flow model. Growth rates for sales and profits are determined using inputs from our annual long-range planning process. We also make estimates of discount rates, perpetuity growth assumptions, market comparables, and other factors.

We evaluate the useful lives of our other intangible assets, mainly brands, to determine if they are finite or indefinite-lived. Reaching a determination on useful life requires significant judgments and assumptions regarding the future effects of obsolescence, demand, competition, other economic factors (such as the stability of the industry, known technological advances, legislative action that results in an uncertain or changing regulatory environment, and expected changes in distribution channels), the level of required maintenance expenditures, and the expected lives of other related groups of assets.

Our indefinite-lived intangible assets, mainly intangible assets primarily associated with the *Pillsbury*, *Totino's*, *Progresso*, *Green Giant*, *Old El Paso*, and *Häagen-Dazs* brands, are also tested for impairment annually and whenever events or changes in circumstances indicate that their carrying value may not be recoverable. We performed our fiscal 2010 assessment of our brand intangibles as of December 1, 2009. Our estimate of the fair value of the brands was based on a discounted cash flow model using inputs which included: projected revenues from our annual long-range plan; assumed royalty rates that could be payable if we did not own the brands; and a discount rate. As of our assessment date, there was no impairment of any of our intangibles as their related fair values were substantially in excess of the carrying values.

Investments in Joint Ventures
Our investments in companies over which we have the ability to exercise significant influence are stated at cost plus our share of undistributed earnings or losses. We receive royalty income from certain joint ventures, incur various expenses (primarily research and development), and record the tax impact of certain joint venture operations that are structured as partnerships. In addition, we make advances to our joint ventures in the form of loans or capital investments. We also sell certain raw materials, semi-finished goods, and finished goods to the joint ventures, generally at market prices.

Variable Interest Entities
As of May 30, 2010, we had invested in three variable interest entities (VIEs). We have an interest in a contract manufacturer at our former facility in Geneva, Illinois. We are the primary beneficiary (PB) and have consolidated this entity. This entity had property and equipment with a carrying value of $19.4 million and long-term debt of $20.9 million as of May 30, 2010. The liabilities recognized as a result of consolidating this entity do not represent additional claims on our general assets. We also have an interest in a contract manufacturer in Greece that is a VIE. Although we are the PB, we have not consolidated this entity because it is not practical to do so and it is not material to our results of operations, financial condition, or liquidity as of and for the year ended May 30, 2010. This entity had assets of $6.7 million and liabilities of $1.4 million as of May 30, 2010. We are not the PB of the remaining VIE. Our maximum exposure to loss from the three VIEs is limited to the $20.9 million of long-term debt of the contract manufacturer in Geneva, Illinois and our $2.2 million equity investment in the VIE of which we are not the PB. We have not provided financial or other support to these VIEs during the current period nor are there arrangements related to these VIEs that could require us to provide financial support in the future.

Revenue Recognition
We recognize sales revenue when the shipment is accepted by our customer. Sales include shipping and handling charges billed to the customer and are reported net of consumer coupon redemption, trade promotion and other costs, including estimated allowances for returns, unsalable product, and prompt pay discounts. Sales, use, value-added, and other excise taxes are not recognized in revenue. Coupons are recorded when distributed, based on estimated redemption rates. Trade promotions are recorded based on estimated participation and performance levels for offered programs at the time of sale. We generally do not allow a right of return. However, on a limited case-by-case basis with prior approval, we may allow customers to return product. In limited circumstances, product returned in saleable condition is resold to other customers or outlets. Receivables from customers generally do not bear interest. Terms and collection patterns vary around the world and by channel. The allowance for doubtful accounts represents our estimate of probable non-payments and credit losses in our existing receivables, as determined based on a review of past due balances and other specific account data. Account balances are written off against the allowance when we deem the amount is uncollectible.

Environmental

Environmental costs relating to existing conditions caused by past operations that do not contribute to current or future revenues are expensed. Liabilities for anticipated remediation costs are recorded on an undiscounted basis when they are probable and reasonably estimable, generally no later than the completion of feasibility studies or our commitment to a plan of action.

Advertising Production Costs

We expense the production costs of advertising the first time that the advertising takes place.

Research and Development

All expenditures for research and development (R&D) are charged against earnings in the year incurred. R&D includes expenditures for new product and manufacturing process innovation, and the annual expenditures are comprised primarily of internal salaries, wages, consulting, and other supplies attributable to time spent on R&D activities. Other costs include depreciation and maintenance of research facilities, including assets at facilities that are engaged in pilot plant activities.

Foreign Currency Translation

For all significant foreign operations, the functional currency is the local currency. Assets and liabilities of these operations are translated at the period-end exchange rates. Income statement accounts are translated using the average exchange rates prevailing during the year. Translation adjustments are reflected within accumulated other comprehensive loss in stockholders' equity. Gains and losses from foreign currency transactions are included in net earnings for the period except for gains and losses on investments in subsidiaries for which settlement is not planned for the foreseeable future and foreign exchange gains and losses on instruments designated as net investment hedges. These gains and losses are recorded in accumulated other comprehensive loss.

Derivative Instruments

All derivatives are recognized on the Consolidated Balance Sheets at fair value based on quoted market prices or our estimate of their fair value, and are recorded in either current or noncurrent assets or liabilities based on their maturity. Changes in the fair values of derivatives are recorded in net earnings or other comprehensive income, based on whether the instrument is designated and effective as a hedge transaction and, if so, the type of hedge transaction. Gains or losses on derivative instruments reported in accumulated other comprehensive loss are reclassified to earnings in the period the hedged item affects earnings. If the underlying hedged transaction ceases to exist, any associated amounts reported in accumulated other comprehensive loss are reclassified to earnings at that time. Any ineffectiveness is recognized in earnings in the current period.

We use derivatives to manage our exposure to changes in commodity prices. We do not perform the assessments required to achieve hedge accounting for commodity derivative positions. Accordingly, the changes in the values of these derivatives are recorded currently in cost of sales in our Consolidated Statements of Earnings.

Although we do not meet the criteria for cash flow hedge accounting, we nonetheless believe that these instruments are effective in achieving our objective of providing certainty in the future price of commodities purchased for use in our supply chain. Accordingly, for purposes of measuring segment operating performance these gains and losses are reported in unallocated corporate items outside of segment operating results until such time that the exposure we are managing affects earnings. At that time we reclassify the gain or loss from unallocated corporate items to segment operating profit, allowing our operating segments to realize the economic effects of the derivative without experiencing any resulting mark-to-market volatility, which remains in unallocated corporate items.

Stock-based Compensation

We generally recognize compensation expense for grants of restricted stock units using the value of a share of our stock on the date of grant. We estimate the value of stock option grants using the Black-Scholes valuation model. Stock compensation is recognized straight line over the vesting period. All of our stock compensation expense is recorded in SG&A in the Consolidated Statement of Earnings and in unallocated corporate items in our segment results.

Certain equity-based compensation plans contain provisions that accelerate vesting of awards upon retirement, disability, or death of eligible employees and directors. We consider a stock-based award to be vested when the employee's retention of the award is no longer contingent on providing subsequent service. Accordingly, the related compensation cost is recognized immediately for awards granted to retirement-eligible individuals or over the period from the grant date to the date retirement eligibility is achieved, if less than the stated vesting period.

We report the benefits of tax deductions in excess of recognized compensation cost as a financing cash flow, thereby reducing net operating cash flows and increasing net financing cash flows.

Defined Benefit Pension, Other Postretirement, and Postemployment Benefit Plans
We sponsor several domestic and foreign defined benefit plans to provide pension, health care, and other welfare benefits to retired employees. Under certain circumstances, we also provide accruable benefits to former or inactive employees in the United States and Canada and members of our Board of Directors, including severance and certain other benefits payable upon death. We recognize an obligation for any of these benefits that vest or accumulate with service. Postemployment benefits that do not vest or accumulate with service (such as severance based solely on annual pay rather than years of service) are charged to expense when incurred. Our postemployment benefit plans are unfunded.

We recognize the underfunded or overfunded status of a defined benefit postretirement plan as an asset or liability and recognize changes in the funded status in the year in which the changes occur through accumulated other comprehensive loss.

Use of Estimates
Preparing our Consolidated Financial Statements in conformity with accounting principles generally accepted in the United States requires us to make estimates and assumptions that affect reported amounts of assets and liabilities, disclosures of contingent assets and liabilities at the date of the financial statements, and the reported amounts of revenues and expenses during the reporting period. These estimates include our accounting for promotional expenditures, valuation of long-lived assets, intangible assets, stock-based compensation, income taxes, and defined benefit pension, post-retirement and post-employment benefits. Actual results could differ from our estimates.

Other New Accounting Standards
In fiscal 2010, we adopted new accounting guidance on employer's disclosures for post-retirement benefit plan assets. The guidance requires an employer to disclose information on the investment policies and strategies and the significant concentrations of risk in plan assets. An employer must also disclose the fair value of each major category of plan assets as of each annual reporting date together with the information on the inputs and valuation techniques used to develop such fair value measurements. The adoption of the guidance did not have an impact on our results of operations or financial condition. See Note 13.

In fiscal 2010, we adopted new accounting guidance on accounting for equity method investments. The guidance addresses the impact of the issuance of the noncontrolling interests and business combination guidance on accounting for equity method investments. The adoption of the guidance did not have a material impact on our results of operations or financial condition.

In fiscal 2010, we adopted new accounting guidance issued to assist in determining whether instruments granted in share-based payment transactions are participating securities. The guidance provides that unvested share-based payment awards that contain non-forfeitable rights to dividends or dividend equivalents (whether paid or unpaid) are participating securities and shall be included in the computation of EPS pursuant to the two-class method. The adoption of the guidance did not have a material impact on our basic or diluted EPS.

In fiscal 2010, we adopted new accounting guidance on convertible debt instruments. The guidance requires issuers to account separately for the liability and equity components of convertible debt instruments that may be settled in cash or other assets. The adoption of the guidance did not have a material impact on our results of operations or financial condition.

In fiscal 2009, we adopted the measurement date provisions of new accounting guidance related to defined benefit pension and other postretirement plans. The guidance requires the funded status of a plan to be measured as of the date of the year-end statement of financial position and requires additional disclosures in the notes to consolidated financial statements. The guidance also requires employers recognize on a prospective basis the funded status of their defined benefit pension and other postretirement plans in their consolidated balance sheets and recognize as a component of other comprehensive income, net of income tax, the gains or losses and prior service costs or credits that arise during the period but are not recognized as components of net periodic benefit cost. The adoption of the measurement date provisions did not have a material impact on our results of operations or financial condition.

In fiscal 2009, we adopted new accounting guidance on fair value measurements. The guidance provides a single definition of fair value, a framework for measuring fair value, and expanded disclosures about fair value measurements. The guidance applies to instruments accounted for under previously issued pronouncements that prescribe fair value as the relevant measure of value. We adopted the guidance at the beginning of fiscal 2009 for all instruments valued on a recurring basis, and the adoption did not have a material impact on our financial statements. The FASB deferred the effective date of the guidance until the beginning of fiscal 2010 as it relates to fair value measurement requirements for nonfinancial assets and liabilities that are not remeasured at fair value on a recurring basis. This includes fair value calculated in impairment assessments of goodwill, indefinite-lived intangible assets, and other long-lived assets. We adopted the guidance at the beginning of fiscal 2010 for all fair value measurements of nonfinancial assets and liabilities that are not remeasured at fair value on a recurring basis, and the adoption did not have a material impact on our financial statements.

In fiscal 2009, we adopted new accounting guidance on share-based payment awards. The guidance requires that tax benefits from dividends paid on unvested restricted shares be charged directly to stockholders' equity instead of benefiting income tax expense. The adoption of the guidance did not have a material impact on our results of operations or financial condition.

NOTE 3. ACQUISITIONS AND DIVESTITURES

There were no acquisitions or divestitures in fiscal 2010.

In fiscal 2009, we sold our bread concentrates product line within our Bakeries and Foodservice segment, including a plant in Cedar Rapids, Iowa, for $8.3 million in cash. We recorded a pre-tax loss of $5.6 million on the transaction. We also sold a portion of the assets of the frozen unbaked bread dough product line within our Bakeries and Foodservice segment, including plants in Bakersfield, California; Hazleton, Pennsylvania; Montreal, Canada; and Vinita, Oklahoma, for $43.9 million in cash, an $11.9 million note receivable, and contingent future payments based on the post-sale performance of the product line. Certain assets sold were shared with a frozen dinner roll product line within our U.S. Retail segment, and we exited this product line as a result of the asset sale. We recorded a pre-tax loss of $38.3 million. In fiscal 2010, we recorded cash proceeds of $3.2 million related to the repayment of the note. Additional cash proceeds will be recognized in the future as the note is repaid and if the buyer is required to make any performance-based contingent payments. In fiscal 2009, we sold our *Pop•Secret* microwave popcorn product line from our U.S. Retail segment for $192.5 million in cash, and we recorded a pre-tax gain of $128.8 million. We received cash proceeds of $158.9 million after repayment of a lease obligation and transaction costs. In fiscal 2009, we also acquired Humm Foods, Inc. (Humm Foods), the maker of *Lärabar* fruit and nut energy bars. We issued 1.8 million shares of our common stock with a value of $55.0 million to the shareholders of Humm Foods as consideration for the acquisition. We recorded the purchase price less tangible and intangible net assets acquired as goodwill of $41.6 million. The pro forma effect of this acquisition was not material.

During fiscal 2008, the 8th Continent soymilk business was sold. Our 50 percent share of the after-tax gain on the sale was $2.2 million, of which we recognized $1.7 million in after-tax earnings from joint ventures in fiscal 2008. In fiscal 2010, we recorded an additional gain of $0.6 million when certain conditions related to the sale were satisfied. Also during fiscal 2008, we acquired a controlling interest in HD Distributors (Thailand) Company Limited. Prior to acquiring the controlling interest, we accounted for our investment as a joint venture. The purchase price, net of cash acquired, resulted in a $1.3 million cash inflow classified in acquisitions on the Consolidated Statements of Cash Flows.

NOTE 4. RESTRUCTURING, IMPAIRMENT, AND OTHER EXIT COSTS

We view our restructuring activities as a way to meet our long-term growth targets. Activities we undertake must meet internal rate of return and net present value targets. Each restructuring action normally takes one to two years to complete. At completion (or as each major stage is completed in the case of multi-year programs), the project begins to deliver cash savings and/or reduced depreciation. These activities result in various restructuring costs, including asset write-offs, exit charges including severance, contract termination fees, and decommissioning and other costs. Depreciation associated with restructured assets as used in the context of our disclosures regarding restructuring activity refers to the increase in depreciation expense caused by shortening the useful life or updating the salvage value of depreciable fixed assets to coincide with the end of production under an approved restructuring plan. Any impairment of the asset is recognized immediately in the period the plan is approved.

In fiscal 2010, we recorded restructuring, impairment, and other exit costs pursuant to approved plans as follows:

Expense (Income), in Millions	
Discontinuation of kids' refrigerated yogurt beverage and microwave soup product lines	$ 24.1
Discontinuation of the breadcrumbs product line at Federalsburg, Maryland plant	6.2
Sale of Contagem, Brazil bread and pasta plant	(0.6)
Charges associated with restructuring actions previously announced	1.7
Total	$ 31.4

In fiscal 2010, we decided to exit our kids' refrigerated yogurt beverage product line at our Murfreesboro, Tennessee plant and our microwave soup product line at our Vineland, New Jersey plant to rationalize capacity for more profitable items. Our decisions to exit these U.S. Retail segment products resulted in a $24.1 million non-cash charge against the related long-lived assets. No employees were affected by these actions. We expect to recognize $2.1 million of other exit costs related to these actions, which we anticipate will be completed by the end of the second quarter of fiscal 2011. We also decided to exit our breadcrumbs product line at our Federalsburg, Maryland in our Bakeries and Foodservice segment. As a result of this decision, we concluded that the future cash flows generated by these products were insufficient to recover the net book value of the associated long-lived assets. Accordingly, we recorded a non-cash charge of $6.2 million primarily related to the impairment of these long-lived assets and in the fourth quarter of fiscal 2010, we sold our breadcrumbs manufacturing facility in Federalsburg for $2.9 million. In fiscal 2010, we also recorded a $0.6 million net gain on the sale of our previously closed Contagem, Brazil bread and pasta plant for cash proceeds of $5.9 million, and recorded $1.7 million of costs related to previously announced restructuring actions. In fiscal 2010, we paid $8 million in cash related to restructuring actions taken in fiscal 2010 and previous years.

In fiscal 2009, we recorded restructuring, impairment, and other exit costs pursuant to approved plans as follows:

Expense, in Millions		
Closure of Contagem, Brazil bread and pasta plant	$	16.8
Discontinuation of product line at Murfreesboro, Tennessee plant		8.3
Charges associated with restructuring actions previously announced		16.5
Total	$	41.6

In fiscal 2009, due to declining financial results, we approved the restructuring of our International segment's business in Brazil. We discontinued the production and marketing of *Forno De Minas* cheese bread and *Frescarini* pasta brands in Brazil and closed our Contagem, Brazil manufacturing facility. These actions affected 556 employees in our Brazilian operations. Our other product lines in Brazil were not affected by the decision. As a result of this decision, we incurred a charge of $16.8 million in the fourth quarter of fiscal 2009, consisting primarily of $5.3 million of employee severance, a $10.2 million non-cash impairment charge to write down assets to their net realizable value, and $1.3 million of other costs associated with this restructuring action. This restructuring action was completed in the second quarter of fiscal 2010.

In fiscal 2009, due to declining net sales and to improve manufacturing capacity for other product lines, we decided to exit our U.S. Retail segment's *Perfect Portions* refrigerated biscuits product line at our manufacturing facility in Murfreesboro, Tennessee. We recorded an $8.0 million non-cash impairment charge against long lived assets used for this product line and $0.3 million of other costs associated with this restructuring action. Our other product lines at Murfreesboro were not affected by the decision, and no employees were affected by this action, which was completed in the second quarter of fiscal 2010.

In fiscal 2009, we also incurred $16.5 million of incremental plant closure expenses related to previously announced restructuring activities, including $10.3 million for the remainder of our lease obligation at our previously closed facility in Trenton, Ontario.

In fiscal 2008, we recorded restructuring, impairment, and other exit costs pursuant to approved plans as follows:

Expense, in Millions		
Closure of Poplar, Wisconsin plant	$	2.7
Closure and sale of Allentown, Pennsylvania frozen waffle plant		9.4
Closure of leased Trenton, Ontario frozen dough plant		10.9
Restructuring of production scheduling and discontinuation of cake product line at Chanhassen, Minnesota plant		1.6
Gain on sale of previously closed Vallejo, California plant		(7.1)
Charges associated with restructuring actions previously announced		3.5
Total	$	21.0

The roll forward of our restructuring and other exit cost reserves, included in other current liabilities, is as follows:

In Millions	**Severance**		**Contract Termination**	**Other Exit Costs**		**Total**	
Reserve balance as of May 27, 2007	$	3.4	$ —	$	0.9	$	4.3
2008 charges, including foreign currency translation		20.9	—		—		20.9
Utilized in 2008		(16.7)	—		(0.6)		(17.3)
Reserve balance as of May 25, 2008		7.6	—		0.3		7.9
2009 charges, including foreign currency translation		5.5	10.3		—		15.8
Utilized in 2009		(4.7)	—		(0.2)		(4.9)
Reserve balance as of May 31, 2009		8.4	10.3		0.1		18.8
2010 charges, including foreign currency translation		0.2	0.8		—		1.0
Utilized in 2010		(6.0)	(3.0)		—		(9.0)
Reserve balance as of May 30, 2010	$	2.6	$ 8.1	$	0.1	$	10.8

The charges recognized in the roll forward of our reserves for restructuring and other exit costs do not include items charged directly to expense (e.g., asset impairment charges, the gain or loss on the sale of restructured assets, and the write-off of spare parts) and other periodic exit costs recognized as incurred, as those items are not reflected in our restructuring and other exit cost reserves on our Consolidated Balance Sheets.

NOTE 5. INVESTMENTS IN JOINT VENTURES

We have a 50 percent equity interest in Cereal Partners Worldwide (CPW), which manufactures and markets ready-to-eat cereal products in more than 130 countries and republics outside the United States and Canada. CPW also markets cereal bars in several European countries and manufactures private label cereals for customers in the United Kingdom. We have guaranteed a portion of CPW's debt and its pension obligation in the United Kingdom.

We also have a 50 percent equity interest in Häagen-Dazs Japan, Inc. (HDJ). This joint venture manufactures, distributes, and markets *Häagen-Dazs* ice cream products and frozen novelties.

Results from our CPW and HDJ joint ventures are reported for the 12 months ended March 31.

During fiscal 2008, the 8th Continent soy milk business was sold, and our 50 percent share of the after-tax gain on the sale was $2.2 million, of which $1.7 million was recorded in fiscal 2008. In fiscal 2010 we recorded an additional gain of $0.6 million when certain conditions related to the sale were satisfied.

Joint venture balance sheet activity follows:

In Millions		May 30, 2010		May 31, 2009
Cumulative investments	$	398.1	$	283.3
Goodwill and other intangibles		512.6		593.9
Aggregate advances		238.2		114.8

Joint venture earnings and cash flow activity follows:

				Fiscal Year		
In Millions		2010		2009		2008
Sales to joint ventures	$	10.7	$	14.2	$	12.8
Net advances (repayments)		128.1		(8.2)		(75.2)
Dividends received		88.0		68.5		108.7

Summary combined financial information for the joint ventures on a 100 percent basis follows:

				Fiscal Year		
In Millions		2010		2009		2008
Net sales	$	2,360.0	$	2,280.0	$	2,207.7
Gross margin		1,053.2		873.5		906.6
Earnings before income taxes		251.2		234.7		231.7
Earnings after income taxes		202.3		175.3		190.4

In Millions		May 30, 2010		May 31, 2009
Current assets	$	731.7	$	835.4
Noncurrent assets		907.3		895.0
Current liabilities		1,322.0		1,394.6
Noncurrent liabilities		112.1		66.9

CPW reclassified certain expenses as a reduction to net sales. To conform to the current period presentation, CPW reduced its previously reported net sales by approximately $150 million in fiscal 2009 and $200 million in 2008. There was no effect on after-tax earnings from joint ventures in our Consolidated Statements of Earnings.

NOTE 6. GOODWILL AND OTHER INTANGIBLE ASSETS

The components of goodwill and other intangible assets are as follows:

In Millions	May 30, 2010	May 31, 2009
Goodwill	$ 6,592.8	$ 6,663.0
Other intangible assets:		
Intangible assets not subject to amortization:		
Brands	3,679.6	3,705.3
Intangible assets subject to amortization:		
Patents, trademarks, and other finite-lived intangibles	54.4	56.1
Less accumulated amortization	(19.0)	(14.4)
Intangible assets subject to amortization	35.4	41.7
Other intangible assets	3,715.0	3,747.0
Total	$ 10,307.8	$ 10,410.0

The changes in the carrying amount of goodwill for fiscal 2008, 2009, and 2010 are as follows:

In Millions	U.S. Retail	International	Bakeries and Foodservice	Joint Ventures	Total
Balance as of May 27, 2007	$ 5,202.9	$ 142.2	$ 981.8	$ 508.5	$6,835.4
Finalization of purchase accounting	—	(0.3)	—	(16.3)	(16.6)
Adoption of FIN 48	(110.9)	(10.6)	(30.4)	—	(151.9)
Other activity, primarily foreign currency translation	15.0	15.1	4.3	84.8	119.2
Balance as of May 25, 2008	5,107.0	146.4	955.7	577.0	6,786.1
Acquisition of Humm Foods	41.6	—	—	—	41.6
Divestitures	(17.8)	(0.1)	(23.7)	—	(41.6)
Deferred tax adjustment related to divestitures	(46.5)	(4.5)	(12.8)	—	(63.8)
Deferred tax adjustment resulting from change in acquisition-related income tax liabilities	14.0	1.3	3.8	—	19.1
Other activity, primarily foreign currency translation	—	(19.8)	—	(58.6)	(78.4)
Balance as of May 31, 2009	5,098.3	123.3	923.0	518.4	6,663.0
Other activity, primarily foreign currency translation	—	(1.3)	—	(68.9)	(70.2)
Balance as of May 30, 2010	$ 5,098.3	$ 122.0	$ 923.0	$ 449.5	$6,592.8

The changes in the carrying amount of other intangible assets for fiscal 2008, 2009, and 2010 are as follows:

In Millions	U.S. Retail	International	Joint Ventures	Total
Balance as of May 27, 2007	$ 3,175.2	$ 460.9	$ 57.9	$ 3,694.0
Finalization of purchase accounting	—	15.6	16.3	31.9
Other activity, primarily foreign currency translation	—	42.3	9.0	51.3
Balance as of May 25, 2008	3,175.2	518.8	83.2	3,777.2
Acquisition of Humm Foods	19.4	—	—	19.4
Other activity, primarily foreign currency translation	14.3	(56.2)	(7.7)	(49.6)
Balance as of May 31, 2009	3,208.9	462.6	75.5	3,747.0
Other activity, primarily foreign currency translation	(2.3)	(17.3)	(12.4)	(32.0)
Balance as of May 30, 2010	$ 3,206.6	$ 445.3	$ 63.1	$ 3,715.0

NOTE 7. FINANCIAL INSTRUMENTS, RISK MANAGEMENT ACTIVITIES, AND FAIR VALUES

FINANCIAL INSTRUMENTS

The carrying values of cash and cash equivalents, receivables, accounts payable, other current liabilities, and notes payable approximate fair value. Marketable securities are carried at fair value. As of May 30, 2010, and May 31, 2009, a comparison of cost and market values of our marketable debt and equity securities is as follows:

In Millions	Cost Fiscal Year		Market Value Fiscal Year		Gross Gains Fiscal Year		Gross Losses Fiscal Year	
	2010	2009	2010	2009	2010	2009	2010	2009
Available for sale:								
Debt securities	$ 11.8	$ 35.1	$ 11.9	$ 35.0	$ 0.1	$ 0.1	$ —	$ (0.2)
Equity securities	6.1	6.1	15.5	13.8	9.4	7.7	—	—
Total	$ 17.9	$ 41.2	$ 27.4	$ 48.8	$ 9.5	$ 7.8	$ —	$ (0.2)

Earnings include insignificant realized gains from sales of available-for-sale marketable securities. Gains and losses are determined by specific identification. Classification of marketable securities as current or noncurrent is dependent upon management's intended holding period, the security's maturity date, or both. The aggregate unrealized gains and losses on available-for-sale securities, net of tax effects, are classified in AOCI within stockholders' equity. Scheduled maturities of our marketable securities are as follows:

In Millions	Available for Sale	
	Cost	Market Value
Under 1 year (current)	$ 4.8	$ 4.8
From 1 to 3 years	0.8	0.8
From 4 to 7 years	4.1	4.1
Over 7 years	2.1	2.2
Equity securities	6.1	15.5
Total	$ 17.9	$ 27.4

Marketable securities with a market value of $2.3 million as of May 30, 2010, were pledged as collateral for certain derivative contracts.

The fair values and carrying amounts of long-term debt, including the current portion, were $5,958.8 million and $5,375.8 million as of May 30, 2010. The fair value of long-term debt was estimated using market quotations and discounted cash flows based on our current incremental borrowing rates for similar types of instruments.

RISK MANAGEMENT ACTIVITIES

As a part of our ongoing operations, we are exposed to market risks such as changes in interest rates, foreign currency exchange rates, and commodity prices. To manage these risks, we may enter into various derivative transactions (e.g., futures, options, and swaps) pursuant to our established policies.

COMMODITY PRICE RISK

Many commodities we use in the production and distribution of our products are exposed to market price risks. We utilize derivatives to manage price risk for our principal ingredients and energy costs, including grains (oats, wheat, and corn), oils (principally soybean), non-fat dry milk, natural gas, and diesel fuel. Our primary objective when entering into these derivative contracts is to achieve certainty with regard to the future price of commodities purchased for use in our supply chain. We manage our exposures through a combination of purchase orders, long-term contracts with suppliers, exchange-traded futures and options, and over-the-counter options and swaps. We offset our exposures based on current and projected market conditions and generally seek to acquire the inputs at as close to our planned cost as possible.

As discussed in Note 2, we do not perform the assessments required to achieve hedge accounting for commodity derivative positions. Pursuant to this policy, unallocated corporate items for fiscal 2010 and fiscal 2009 included:

| | Fiscal Year | | |
In Millions	2010	2009	2008
Net gain (loss) on mark-to-market valuation of commodity positions	$ (54.7)	$ (249.6)	$ 115.3
Net loss (gain) on commodity positions reclassified from unallocated corporate items to segment operating profit	55.7	134.8	(55.7)
Net mark-to-market revaluation of certain grain inventories	(8.1)	(4.1)	(2.6)
Net mark-to-market valuation of certain commodity positions recognized in unallocated corporate items	$ (7.1)	$ (118.9)	$ 57.0

As of May 30, 2010, the net notional value of commodity derivatives was $464.2 million, of which $295.2 million related to agricultural inputs and $169.0 million related to energy inputs. These contracts relate to inputs that generally will be utilized within the next 12 months.

INTEREST RATE RISK

We are exposed to interest rate volatility with regard to future issuances of fixed-rate debt, and existing and future issuances of floating-rate debt. Primary exposures include U.S. Treasury rates, LIBOR, and commercial paper rates in the United States and Europe. We use interest rate swaps and forward-starting interest rate swaps to hedge our exposure to interest rate changes, to reduce the volatility of our financing costs, and to achieve a desired proportion of fixed-rate versus floating-rate debt, based on current and projected market conditions. Generally under these swaps, we agree with a counterparty to exchange the difference between fixed-rate and floating-rate interest amounts based on an agreed upon notional principal amount.

Floating Interest Rate Exposures — Except as discussed below, floating-to-fixed interest rate swaps are accounted for as cash flow hedges, as are all hedges of forecasted issuances of debt. Effectiveness is assessed based on either the perfectly effective hypothetical derivative method or changes in the present value of interest payments on the underlying debt. Effective gains and losses deferred to AOCI are reclassified into earnings over the life of the associated debt. Ineffective gains and losses are recorded as net interest. The amount of hedge ineffectiveness was less than $1 million in each of fiscal 2010, 2009 and 2008.

Fixed Interest Rate Exposures — Fixed-to-floating interest rate swaps are accounted for as fair value hedges with effectiveness assessed based on changes in the fair value of the underlying debt and derivatives, using incremental borrowing rates currently available on loans with similar terms and maturities. Ineffective gains and losses on these derivatives and the underlying hedged items are recorded as net interest. The amount of hedge ineffectiveness was less than $1 million in each of fiscal 2010, 2009 and 2008.

In advance of a planned debt financing in fiscal 2011, we entered into $500 million of treasury lock derivatives with an average fixed rate of 4.3 percent. All of these treasury locks were cash settled for $17.1 million coincident with the issuance of our $500 million 30-year fixed-rate notes, which settled subsequent to our fiscal 2010 year end, on June 1, 2010. As of May 30, 2010, a $16.8 million pre-tax loss remained in AOCI, which will be reclassified to earnings over the term of the underlying debt.

During the second quarter of fiscal 2010 we entered into $700 million of swaps to convert $700 million of 5.65 percent fixed-rate notes due September 10, 2012, to floating rates. In May 2010, we repurchased $179.2 million of our 5.65 percent notes, and as a result, we received $2.7 million to settle a portion of these swaps that related to the repurchased debt.

In anticipation of our acquisition of The Pillsbury Company (Pillsbury) and other financing needs, we entered into pay-fixed interest rate swap contracts during fiscal 2001 and 2002 totaling $7.1 billion to lock in our interest payments on the associated debt. As of May 30, 2010, we still owned $1.6 billion of Pillsbury-related pay-fixed swaps that were previously neutralized with offsetting pay-floating swaps in fiscal 2002.

In advance of a planned debt financing in fiscal 2007, we entered into $700.0 million pay-fixed, forward-starting interest rate swaps with an average fixed rate of 5.7 percent. All of these forward-starting interest rate swaps were cash settled for $22.5 million coincident with our $1.0 billion 10-year fixed-rate note offering on January 24, 2007. As of May 30, 2010, a $14.9 million pre-tax loss remained in AOCI, which will be reclassified to earnings over the term of the underlying debt.

The following table summarizes the notional amounts and weighted-average interest rates of our interest rate swaps. As discussed above, we have neutralized all of our Pillsbury-related pay-fixed swaps with pay-floating swaps; however, we cannot present them on a net basis in the following table because the offsetting occurred with different counterparties. Average floating rates are based on rates as of the end of the reporting period.

In Millions	May 30, 2010		May 31, 2009
Pay-floating swaps — notional amount	$	2,155.6	$ 1,859.3
Average receive rate		4.8%	5.7%
Average pay rate		0.3%	0.3%
Pay-fixed swaps — notional amount	$	1,600.0	$ 2,250.0
Average receive rate		0.3%	0.5%
Average pay rate		7.3%	6.4%

The swap contracts mature at various dates from fiscal 2011 to 2013 as follows:

	Fiscal Year Maturity Date			
In Millions		Pay Floating		Pay Fixed
2011	$	17.6	$	—
2012		1,603.3		850.0
2013		534.7		750.0
Total	$	2,155.6	$	1,600.0

FOREIGN EXCHANGE RISK

Foreign currency fluctuations affect our net investments in foreign subsidiaries and foreign currency cash flows related to foreign-denominated commercial paper, third party purchases, intercompany loans, and product shipments. We are also exposed to the translation of foreign currency earnings to the U.S. dollar. Our principal exposures are to the Australian dollar, British pound sterling, Canadian dollar, Chinese renminbi, euro, Japanese yen, and Mexican peso. We mainly use foreign currency forward contracts to selectively hedge our foreign currency cash flow exposures. We also generally swap our foreign-denominated commercial paper borrowings and nonfunctional currency intercompany loans back to U.S. dollars or the functional currency; the gains or losses on these derivatives offset the foreign currency revaluation gains or losses recorded in earnings on the associated borrowings. We generally do not hedge more than 18 months forward.

The amount of hedge ineffectiveness was less than $1 million in each of fiscal 2010, 2009 and 2008.

We also have many net investments in foreign subsidiaries that are denominated in euros. We hedged a portion of these net investments by issuing euro-denominated commercial paper and foreign exchange forward contracts. As of May 30, 2010, we had deferred net foreign currency transaction losses of $95.7 million in accumulated other comprehensive loss (AOCI) associated with hedging activity.

FAIR VALUE MEASUREMENTS AND FINANCIAL STATEMENT PRESENTATION

We categorize assets and liabilities into one of three levels based on the assumptions (inputs) used in valuing the asset or liability. Level 1 provides the most reliable measure of fair value, while Level 3 generally requires significant management judgment. The three levels are defined as follows:

Level 1: Unadjusted quoted prices in active markets for identical assets or liabilities.

Level 2: Observable inputs other than quoted prices included in Level 1, such as quoted prices for similar assets or liabilities in active markets or quoted prices for identical assets or liabilities in inactive markets.

Level 3: Unobservable inputs reflecting management's assumptions about the inputs used in pricing the asset or liability.

The fair values of our assets, liabilities, and derivative positions recorded at fair value as of May 30, 2010, were as follows:

In Millions	Fair Values of Assets				Fair Values of Liabilities			
	Level 1	Level 2	Level 3	Total	Level 1	Level 2	Level 3	Total
Derivatives designated as hedging instruments:								
Interest rate contracts (a) (d)	$ —	$ 5.8	$ —	$ 5.8	$ —	$ (17.1)	$ —	$ (17.1)
Foreign exchange contracts (b) (c)	—	8.6	—	8.6	—	(12.5)	—	(12.5)
Total	—	14.4	—	14.4	—	(29.6)	—	(29.6)
Derivatives not designated as hedging instruments:								
Interest rate contracts (a) (d)	—	124.3	—	124.3	—	(163.1)	—	(163.1)
Foreign exchange contracts (b)	—	9.5	—	9.5	—	(1.0)	—	(1.0)
Commodity contracts (b) (f)	—	7.4	—	7.4	(5.6)	—	—	(5.6)
Total	—	141.2	—	141.2	(5.6)	(164.1)	—	(169.7)
Other assets and liabilities reported at fair value:								
Marketable investments (a) (e)	15.5	11.9	—	27.4	—	—	—	—
Grain contracts (b) (f)	—	11.9	—	11.9	—	(13.0)	—	(13.0)
Long-lived assets (g)	—	0.4	—	0.4	—	—	—	—
Total	15.5	24.2	—	39.7	—	(13.0)	—	(13.0)
Total assets, liabilities, and derivative positions recorded at fair value	$ 15.5	$ 179.8	$ —	$ 195.3	$ (5.6)	$ (206.7)	$ —	$ (212.3)

(a)   These contracts and investments are recorded as other assets or as other liabilities, as appropriate, based on whether in a gain or loss position. Certain marketable investments are recorded as cash and cash equivalents.

(b)   These contracts are recorded as prepaid expenses and other current assets or as other current liabilities, as appropriate, based on whether in a gain or loss position.

(c)   Based on observable market transactions of spot currency rates and forward currency prices.

(d)   Based on LIBOR and swap rates.

(e)   Based on prices of common stock and bond matrix pricing.

(f)   Based on prices of futures exchanges and recently reported transactions in the marketplace.

(g)   We recorded a $6.6 million non-cash impairment charge in fiscal 2010 to write down certain long-lived assets to their fair value of $0.4 million. Fair value was based on recently reported transactions for similar assets in the marketplace. These assets had a book value of $7.0 million and were associated with the exit activities described in Note 4.

We did not significantly change our valuation techniques from prior periods.

Information related to our cash flow hedges, net investment hedges, and other derivatives not designated as hedging instruments for the fiscal years ended May 30, 2010, and May 31, 2009, follows:

In Millions	Interest Rate Contracts Fiscal Year		Foreign Exchange Contracts Fiscal Year		Equity Contracts Fiscal Year		Commodity Contracts Fiscal Year		Total Fiscal Year	
	2010	2009	2010	2009	2010	2009	2010	2009	2010	2009
Derivatives in Cash Flow Hedging Relationships:										
Amount of gain (loss) recognized in OCI (a)	$ (11.7)	$ (1.1)	$ (13.3)	$ 9.1	$ —	$ —	$ —	$ —	$ (25.0)	$ 8.0
Amount of gain (loss) reclassified from AOCI into earnings (a) (b)	(18.0)	(15.8)	(26.4)	27.7	—	—	—	—	(44.4)	11.9
Amount of gain (loss) recognized in earnings (c) (d)	(0.3)	(0.1)	(0.5)	0.3	—	—	—	—	(0.8)	0.2
Derivatives in Fair Value Hedging Relationships:										
Amount of net gain recognized in earnings (d)	0.2	—	—	—	—	—	—	—	0.2	—
Derivatives in Net Investment Hedging Relationships:										
Amount of gain recognized in OCI (a)	—	—	—	6.0	—	—	—	—	—	6.0
Derivatives Not Designated as Hedging Instruments:										
Amount of gain (loss) recognized in earnings (e)	0.2	3.3	13.3	(70.2)	0.2	0.2	(54.7)	(249.6)	(41.0)	(316.3)

(a)   Effective portion.

(b)   Gain (loss) reclassified from AOCI into earnings is reported in interest, net for interest rate swaps and in cost of sales and SG&A expenses for foreign exchange contracts.

(c)   All gain (loss) recognized in earnings is related to the ineffective portion of the hedging relationship. No amounts were reported as a result of being excluded from the assessment of hedge effectiveness.

(d)   Net gain recognized in earnings is related to the ineffective portion of the hedging relationship and the related hedged items. No amounts were reported as a result of being excluded from the assessment of hedge effectiveness.

(e)   Gain (loss) recognized in earnings is reported in interest, net for interest rate contracts, in cost of sales for commodity contracts, and in SG&A expenses for equity contracts.

AMOUNTS RECORDED IN ACCUMULATED OTHER COMPREHENSIVE LOSS

Unrealized losses from interest rate cash flow hedges recorded in AOCI as of May 30, 2010, totaled $25.1 million after tax. These deferred losses are primarily related to interest rate swaps we entered into in contemplation of future borrowings and other financing requirements and are being reclassified into net interest over the lives of the hedged forecasted transactions. As of May 30, 2010, we had no amounts from commodity derivatives recorded in AOCI. Unrealized losses from foreign currency cash flow hedges recorded in AOCI as of May 30, 2010, were $3.8 million after-tax. The net amount of pre-tax gains and losses in AOCI as of May 30, 2010, that we expect to be reclassified into net earnings within the next 12 months is $17.5 million of expense.

CREDIT-RISK-RELATED CONTINGENT FEATURES

Certain of our derivative instruments contain provisions that require us to maintain an investment grade credit rating on our debt from each of the major credit rating agencies. If our debt were to fall below investment grade, the counterparties to the derivative instruments could request full collateralization on derivative instruments in net liability positions. The aggregate fair value of all derivative instruments with credit-risk-related contingent features that were in a liability position on May 30, 2010, was $16.3 million. We have not posted any collateral associated with these contracts. If the credit-risk-related contingent features underlying these agreements were triggered on May 30, 2010, we would be required to post an additional $16.3 million of collateral to the counterparties.

CONCENTRATIONS OF CREDIT AND COUNTERPARTY CREDIT RISK

During fiscal 2010, Wal-Mart Stores, Inc. and its affiliates (Wal-Mart) accounted for 23 percent of our consolidated net sales and 30 percent of our net sales in the U.S. Retail segment. No other customer accounted for 10 percent or more of our consolidated net sales. Wal-Mart also represented 5 percent of our net sales in the International segment and 7 percent of our net sales in the Bakeries and Foodservice segment. As of May 30, 2010, Wal-Mart accounted for 28 percent of our U.S. Retail receivables, 4 percent of our International receivables, and 7 percent of our Bakeries and Foodservice receivables. The five largest customers in our U.S. Retail segment accounted for 54 percent of its fiscal 2010 net sales, the five largest customers in our International segment accounted for 23 percent of its fiscal 2010 net sales, and the five largest customers in our Bakeries and Foodservice segment accounted for 45 percent of its fiscal 2010 net sales.

We enter into interest rate, foreign exchange, and certain commodity and equity derivatives, primarily with a diversified group of highly rated counterparties. We continually monitor our positions and the credit ratings of the counterparties involved and, by policy, limit the amount of credit exposure to any one party. These transactions may expose us to potential losses due to the risk of nonperformance by these counterparties; however, we have not incurred a material loss. We also enter into commodity futures transactions through various regulated exchanges.

The amount of loss due to the credit risk of the counterparties, should the counterparties fail to perform according to the terms of the contracts, is $60.1 million against which we hold $20.0 million of collateral. Under the terms of master swap agreements, some of our transactions require collateral or other security to support financial instruments subject to threshold levels of exposure and counterparty credit risk. Collateral assets are either cash or U.S. Treasury instruments and are held in a trust account that we may access if the counterparty defaults.

NOTE 8. DEBT

Notes Payable

The components of notes payable and their respective weighted-average interest rates at the end of the periods were as follows:

In Millions		May 30, 2010				May 31, 2009	
		Notes Payable	Weighted-Average Interest Rate			Notes Payable	Weighted-Average Interest Rate
U.S. commercial paper	$	973.0	0.3%		$	401.8	0.5%
Euro commercial paper		—	—			275.0	0.5
Financial institutions		77.1	10.6			135.4	12.9
Total	$	1,050.1	1.1%		$	812.2	2.6%

To ensure availability of funds, we maintain bank credit lines sufficient to cover our outstanding short-term borrowings. Commercial paper is a continuing source of short-term financing. We issue commercial paper in the United States and Europe. Our commercial paper borrowings are supported by $2.9 billion of fee-paid committed credit lines, consisting of a $1.8 billion facility expiring in October 2012 and a $1.1 billion facility expiring in October 2010. We also have $278.9 million in uncommitted credit lines that support our foreign operations. As of May 30, 2010, there were no amounts outstanding on the fee-paid committed credit lines and $76.5 was drawn on the uncommitted lines. The credit facilities contain several covenants, including a requirement to maintain a fixed charge coverage ratio of at least 2.5. We were in compliance with all credit facility covenants as of May 30, 2010.

Long-Term Debt

In May 2010, we paid $437.0 million to repurchase in a cash tender offer $400.0 million of our previously issued debt. We repurchased $220.8 million of our 6.0 percent notes due 2012 and $179.2 million of our 5.65 percent notes due 2012. As a result of the repurchase, we recorded interest expense of $40.1 million which represented the premium paid in the tender offer, the write-off of the remaining discount and unamortized fees, and the settlement of related swaps. We issued commercial paper to fund the repurchase.

During fiscal 2010, we repaid $88.0 million of long-term bank debt held by wholly owned foreign subsidiaries.

In January 2009, we issued $1.2 billion aggregate principal amount of 5.65 percent notes due 2019. In August 2008, we issued $700.0 million aggregate principal amount of 5.25 percent notes due 2013. The proceeds of these notes were used to repay a portion of our outstanding commercial paper. Interest on these notes is payable semi-annually in arrears. These notes may be redeemed at our option at any time for a specified make-whole amount. These notes are senior unsecured, unsubordinated obligations that include a change of control repurchase provision.

In June 2010, subsequent to our fiscal 2010 year end, we issued $500.0 million aggregate principal amount of 5.4 percent notes due 2040. The significant terms of these notes are similar to our previously issued notes.

Certain of our long-term debt and noncontrolling interests agreements contain restrictive covenants. As of May 30, 2010, we were in compliance with all of these covenants.

As of May 30, 2010, the $40.6 million pre-tax loss recorded in AOCI associated with our previously designated interest rate swaps will be reclassified to net interest over the remaining lives of the hedged transactions. The amount expected to be reclassified from AOCI to net interest in fiscal 2011 is $13.1 million pre-tax.

A summary of our long-term debt is as follows:

In Millions		May 30, 2010		May 31, 2009
5.65% notes due February 15, 2019	$	1,150.0	$	1,150.0
6% notes due February 15, 2012		1,019.5		1,240.3
5.7% notes due February 15, 2017		1,000.0		1,000.0
5.2% notes due March 17, 2015		750.0		750.0
5.25% notes due August 15, 2013		700.0		700.0
5.65% notes due September 10, 2012		520.8		700.0
Medium-term notes, 4.8% to 9.1%, due fiscal 2011 or later		204.4		204.4
Debt of consolidated contract manufacturer		20.9		26.5
Floating-rate notes due January 22, 2010		—		500.0
Other, including capital leases		10.2		(7.9)
		5,375.8		6,263.3
Less amount due within one year		(107.3)		(508.5)
Total long-term debt	$	5,268.5	$	5,754.8

Principal payments due on long-term debt in the next five years based on stated contractual maturities, our intent to redeem, or put rights of certain note holders are $107.3 million in fiscal 2011, $1,031.3 million in fiscal 2012, $633.6 million in fiscal 2013, $702.6 million in fiscal 2014, and $750.1 million in fiscal 2015.

NOTE 9. NONCONTROLLING INTERESTS

As discussed in Note 1, at the beginning of fiscal 2010, we adopted new accounting guidance on noncontrolling interests in financial statements. As a result of this adoption, noncontrolling interests, previously reported primarily as minority interests, were reclassified to a separate section in equity on the Consolidated Balance Sheets.

Our principal noncontrolling interest relates to our subsidiary GMC. GMC issued a managing membership interest and limited preferred membership interests to certain of our wholly owned subsidiaries. We continue to hold the entire managing membership interest, and therefore direct the operations of GMC. We currently hold all interests in GMC other than Class A Limited Membership Interests (Class A Interests) which are held by an unrelated third-party investor. As of May 30, 2010, the carrying value of all outstanding Class A Interests was $242.3 million, classified as noncontrolling interests on our Consolidated Balance Sheets.

The holder of the Class A Interests receives quarterly preferred distributions from available net income based on the application of a floating preferred return rate, currently equal to the sum of three-month LIBOR plus 65 basis points, to the holder's capital account balance established in the most recent mark-to-market valuation (currently $248.1 million).

For financial reporting purposes, the assets, liabilities, results of operations, and cash flows of GMC are included in our Consolidated Financial Statements. The return to the third-party investor is reflected in net earnings attributable to noncontrolling interests in the Consolidated Statements of Earnings.

In addition, we have 7 foreign subsidiaries that have minority interests totaling $2.8 million as of May 30, 2010.

Our noncontrolling interests contain restrictive covenants. As of May 30, 2010, we were in compliance with all of these covenants.

NOTE 10. STOCKHOLDERS' EQUITY

Cumulative preference stock of 5.0 million shares, without par value, is authorized but unissued.

All common stock share and per share amounts have been adjusted for the two-for-one stock split on May 28, 2010.

During fiscal 2010, we repurchased 21.3 million shares of common stock for an aggregate purchase price of $691.8 million. During fiscal 2009, we repurchased 40.4 million shares of common stock for an aggregate purchase price of $1,296.4 million. During fiscal 2008, we repurchased 47.8 million shares of common stock for an aggregate purchase price of $1,384.6 million.

On December 10, 2007, our Board of Directors approved the retirement of 250.0 million shares of common stock in treasury. This action reduced common stock by $25.0 million, reduced additional paid-in capital by $5,055.8 million, and reduced common stock in treasury by $5,080.8 million on our Consolidated Balance Sheets.

In fiscal 2007, our Board of Directors authorized the repurchase of up to 150 million shares of our common stock. On June 28, 2010, our Board of Directors authorized the repurchase of up to 100 million shares of our common stock. The fiscal 2011 authorization terminated and replaced the fiscal 2007 authorization. Purchases under the authorization can be made in the open market or in privately negotiated transactions, including the use of call options and other derivative instruments, Rule 10b5-1 trading plans, and accelerated repurchase programs. The authorization has no specified termination date.

In October 2004, Lehman Brothers Holdings Inc. (Lehman Brothers) issued $750.0 million of notes, which were mandatorily exchangeable for shares of our common stock. In connection with the issuance of those notes, an affiliate of Lehman Brothers entered into a forward purchase contract with us, under which we were obligated to deliver to such affiliate between 28.0 million and 34.0 million shares of our common stock, subject to adjustment under certain circumstances. We delivered 28.6 million shares in October 2007, in exchange for $750.0 million in cash from Lehman Brothers. We used the cash to reduce outstanding commercial paper balances.

The following table provides details of total comprehensive income:

In Millions	Fiscal 2010		
	Pretax	Tax	Net
Net earnings attributable to General Mills			$ 1,530.5
Net earnings attributable to noncontrolling interests			4.5
Net earnings, including earnings attributable to noncontrolling interests			$ 1,535.0
Other comprehensive income (loss):			
Foreign currency translation	$ (163.3)	$ —	$ (163.3)
Net actuarial loss arising during period	(786.3)	314.8	(471.5)
Other fair value changes:			
Securities	1.9	(0.7)	1.2
Hedge derivatives	(25.0)	10.6	(14.4)
Reclassification to earnings:			
Hedge derivatives	44.4	(17.0)	27.4
Amortization of losses and prior service costs	19.1	(7.6)	11.5
Other comprehensive income (loss) in accumulated other comprehensive loss	(909.2)	300.1	(609.1)
Other comprehensive income attributable to noncontrolling interests	0.2	—	0.2
Other comprehensive income (loss)	$ (909.0)	$ 300.1	$ (608.9)
Total comprehensive income			$ 926.1

In Millions	Fiscal 2009		
	Pretax	Tax	Net
Net earnings attributable to General Mills			$ 1,304.4
Net earnings attributable to noncontrolling interests			9.3
Net earnings, including earnings attributable to noncontrolling interests			$ 1,313.7
Other comprehensive income (loss):			
Foreign currency translation	$ (286.6)	$ —	$ (286.6)
Net actuarial loss arising during period	(1,254.0)	477.8	(776.2)
Other fair value changes:			
Securities	(0.6)	0.2	(0.4)
Hedge derivatives	8.0	(3.4)	4.6
Reclassification to earnings:			
Hedge derivatives	(11.9)	4.6	(7.3)
Amortization of losses and prior service costs	24.2	(9.2)	15.0
Other comprehensive income (loss) in accumulated other comprehensive loss	(1,520.9)	470.0	(1,050.9)
Other comprehensive loss attributable to noncontrolling interests	(1.2)	—	(1.2)
Other comprehensive income (loss)	$ (1,522.1)	$ 470.0	$ (1,052.1)
Total comprehensive income			$ 261.6

In Millions	Fiscal 2008		
	Pretax	Tax	Net
Net earnings attributable to General Mills			$ 1,294.7
Net earnings attributable to noncontrolling interests			23.4
Net earnings, including earnings attributable to noncontrolling interests			$ 1,318.1
Other comprehensive income (loss):			
Foreign currency translation	$ 243.1	$ —	$ 243.1
Minimum pension liability	61.4	(22.0)	39.4
Other fair value changes:			
Securities	1.5	(0.6)	0.9
Hedge derivatives	59.6	(21.3)	38.3
Reclassification to earnings:			
Hedge derivatives	(64.5)	23.5	(41.0)
Amortization of losses and prior service costs	20.6	(8.1)	12.5
Other comprehensive income (loss) in accumulated other comprehensive income	321.7	(28.5)	293.2
Other comprehensive income attributable to noncontrolling interests	3.2	—	3.2
Other comprehensive income (loss)	$ 324.9	$ (28.5)	$ 296.4
Total comprehensive income			$ 1,614.5

During fiscal 2009, we incurred unrecognized losses in excess of $1.1 billion on assets, primarily equity securities, in our defined benefit pension and other postretirement benefit plans. These losses were recognized in other comprehensive income. In fiscal 2010 and future years, the losses are reflected in pension expense using the market-related value of the plan assets over a five year period and amortized using a declining balance method over the average remaining service period of active plan participants.

In fiscal 2010, 2009, and 2008, except for reclassifications to earnings, changes in other comprehensive income (loss) were primarily non-cash items.

Accumulated other comprehensive loss balances, net of tax effects, were as follows:

In Millions		May 30, 2010		May 31, 2009
Foreign currency translation adjustments	$	194.9	$	358.2
Unrealized gain (loss) from:				
Securities		5.6		4.4
Hedge derivatives		(28.9)		(41.9)
Pension, other postretirement, and postemployment benefits:				
Net actuarial loss		(1,611.0)		(1,168.2)
Prior service costs		(47.5)		(30.3)
Accumulated other comprehensive loss	$	(1,486.9)	$	(877.8)

NOTE 11. STOCK PLANS

All shares and per share amounts have been adjusted for the two-for-one stock split on May 28, 2010.

We use broad-based stock plans to help ensure that management's interests are aligned with those of our stockholders. As of May 30, 2010, a total of 24,337,402 shares were available for grant in the form of stock options, restricted shares, restricted stock units, and shares of common stock under the 2009 Stock Compensation Plan (2009 Plan) and the 2006 Compensation Plan for Non-Employee Directors (2006 Director Plan). On September 21, 2009, our stockholders approved the 2009 Plan, replacing the 2007 Stock Compensation Plan (2007 Plan). Restricted shares and restricted stock units may also be granted under our Executive Incentive Plan (EIP) through September 25, 2010. The 2009 Plan and EIP also provide for the issuance of cash-settled share-based units. Stock-based awards now outstanding include some granted under the 1995, 1996, 1998 (senior management), 1998 (employee), 2001, 2003, 2005, and 2007 stock plans, under which no further awards may be granted. The stock plans provide for full vesting of options, restricted shares, restricted stock units, and cash-settled share-based units upon completion of specified service periods or in certain circumstances, following a change of control.

Stock Options
The estimated fair values of stock options granted and the assumptions used for the Black-Scholes option-pricing model were as follows:

		Fiscal Year				
		2010		2009		2008
Estimated fair values of stock options granted	$	3.20	$	4.70	$	5.28
Assumptions:						
Risk-free interest rate		3.7%		4.4%		5.1%
Expected term		8.5 years		8.5 years		8.5 years
Expected volatility		18.9%		16.1%		15.6%
Dividend yield		3.4%		2.7%		2.7%

The valuation of stock options is a significant accounting estimate which requires us to use judgments and assumptions that are likely to have a material impact on our financial statements. Annually, we make predictive assumptions regarding future stock price volatility, employee exercise behavior, dividend yield, and the forfeiture rate.

We estimate the fair value of each option on the grant date using the Black-Scholes option-pricing model, which requires us to make predictive assumptions regarding future stock price volatility, employee exercise behavior, and dividend yield. We estimate our future stock price volatility using the historical volatility over the expected term of the option, excluding time periods of volatility we believe a marketplace participant would exclude in estimating our stock price volatility. For fiscal 2010 and all future grants, we have excluded historical volatility for fiscal 2002 and prior, primarily because volatility driven by our acquisition of Pillsbury does not reflect what we believe to be expected future volatility. We also have considered, but did not use, implied volatility in our estimate, because trading activity in options on our stock, especially those with tenors of greater than 6 months, is insufficient to provide a reliable measure of expected volatility.

Our expected term represents the period of time that options granted are expected to be outstanding based on historical data to estimate option exercise and employee termination within the valuation model. Separate groups of employees have similar historical exercise behavior and therefore were aggregated into a single pool for valuation purposes. The weighted-average expected term for all employee groups is presented in the table above. The risk-free interest rate for periods during the expected term of the options is based on the U.S. Treasury zero-coupon yield curve in effect at the time of grant.

Any corporate income tax benefit realized upon exercise or vesting of an award in excess of that previously recognized in earnings (referred to as a windfall tax benefit) is presented in the Consolidated Statements of Cash Flows as a financing cash flow.

Realized windfall tax benefits are credited to additional paid-in capital within the Consolidated Balance Sheets. Realized shortfall tax benefits (amounts which are less than that previously recognized in earnings) are first offset against the cumulative balance of windfall tax benefits, if any, and then charged directly to income tax expense, potentially resulting in volatility in our consolidated effective income tax rate. We calculated a cumulative memo balance of windfall tax benefits from post-1995 fiscal years for the purpose of accounting for future shortfall tax benefits.

Options may be priced at 100 percent or more of the fair market value on the date of grant, and generally vest four years after the date of grant. Options generally expire within 10 years and one month after the date of grant.

Information on stock option activity follows:

	Options Exercisable (Thousands)		Weighted-Average Exercise Price Per Share	Options Outstanding (Thousands)		Weighted-Average Exercise Price Per Share
Balance as of May 27, 2007	79,011.8	$	20.58	107,546.4	$	21.54
Granted				10,998.8		29.38
Exercised				(12,270.2)		18.75
Forfeited or expired				(232.6)		25.21
Balance as of May 25, 2008	76,389.2		21.23	106,042.4		22.68
Granted				6,495.4		31.74
Exercised				(17,548.4)		19.60
Forfeited or expired				(382.4)		27.50
Balance as of May 31, 2009	67,619.2		21.96	94,607.0		23.84
Granted				6,779.4		27.99
Exercised				(20,013.6)		19.87
Forfeited or expired				(268.2)		24.82
Balance as of May 30, 2010	**47,726.6**	**$**	**22.89**	**81,104.6**	**$**	**25.17**

Stock-based compensation expense related to stock option awards was $34.4 million in fiscal 2010, $40.0 million in fiscal 2009, and $52.8 million in fiscal 2008.

Net cash proceeds from the exercise of stock options less shares used for withholding taxes and the intrinsic value of options exercised were as follows:

	Fiscal Year		
In Millions	**2010**	2009	2008
Net cash proceeds	$ **388.5**	$ 305.9	$ 192.0
Intrinsic value of options exercised	$ **271.8**	$ 226.7	$ 134.4

Restricted Stock, Restricted Stock Units, and Cash-Settled Share-Based Units

Stock and units settled in stock subject to a restricted period and a purchase price, if any (as determined by the Compensation Committee of the Board of Directors), may be granted to key employees under the 2009 Plan. Restricted shares and restricted stock units, up to 50 percent of the value of an individual's cash incentive award, may also be granted through the EIP. Certain restricted stock and restricted stock unit awards require the employee to deposit personally owned shares (on a one-for-one basis) during the restricted period. Restricted stock and restricted stock units generally vest and become unrestricted four years after the date of grant. Participants are entitled to dividends on such awarded shares and units, but only receive those amounts if the shares or units ultimately vest. The sale or transfer of these shares and units is restricted during the vesting period. Participants holding restricted stock, but not restricted stock units, are entitled to vote on matters submitted to holders of common stock for a vote.

Information on restricted stock unit and cash-settled share-based units activity follows:

	Equity Classified		Liability Classified			
	Share-Settled Units (Thousands)	**Weighted-Average Grant-Date Fair Value**	**Share-Settled Units (Thousands)**	**Weighted-Average Grant-Date Fair Value**	**Cash-Settled Share-Based Units (Thousands)**	**Weighted-Average Grant-Date Fair Value**
Non-vested as of May 31, 2009	8,782.1 $	28.35	317.6 $	28.98	1,749.9 $	31.70
Granted	2,494.3	28.12	141.0	27.92	2,110.4	27.92
Vested	(898.3)	26.02	(17.2)	28.95	(74.3)	29.85
Forfeited or expired	(168.3)	29.13	(17.1)	28.85	(82.3)	28.86
Non-vested as of May 30, 2010	**10,209.8 $**	**28.49**	**424.3 $**	**28.64**	**3,703.7 $**	**29.65**

	Fiscal Year		
	2010	2009	2008
Number of units granted (thousands)	**4,745.7**	4,348.0	3,904.4
Weighted average price per unit	$ **28.03**	$ 31.70	$ 29.31

The total grant-date fair value of restricted stock unit awards that vested during fiscal 2010 was $26.1 million, and restricted stock unit awards with a grant-date fair value of $79.9 million vested during fiscal 2009.

As of May 30, 2010, unrecognized compensation expense related to non-vested stock options and restricted stock units was $187.2 million. This expense will be recognized over 21 months, on average.

Stock-based compensation expense related to restricted stock units and cash-settled share-based payment awards was $131.0 million for fiscal 2010, $101.4 million for fiscal 2009, and $80.4 million for fiscal 2008.

NOTE 12. EARNINGS PER SHARE

All shares and per share amounts have been adjusted for the two-for-one stock split on May 28, 2010.

Basic and diluted earnings per share (EPS) were calculated using the following:

In Millions, Except per Share Data	Fiscal Year		
	2010	2009	2008
Net earnings attributable to General Mills	$ 1,530.5	$ 1,304.4	$ 1,294.7
Capital appreciation paid on Series B-1 Interests in GMC (a)	—	—	(8.0)
Net earnings for basic and diluted EPS calculations	$ 1,530.5	$ 1,304.4	$ 1,286.7
Average number of common shares — basic EPS	659.6	663.7	665.9
Incremental share effect from:			
Stock options (b)	17.7	17.9	21.3
Restricted stock, restricted stock units, and other (b)	6.0	5.5	5.6
Forward purchase contract (c)	—	—	1.0
Average number of common shares — diluted EPS	683.3	687.1	693.8
Earnings per share — basic	$ 2.32	$ 1.96	$ 1.93
Earnings per share — diluted	$ 2.24	$ 1.90	$ 1.85

(a)   On August 7, 2007, we repurchased all of the Series B-1 limited membership interests in GMC for $843 million, of which $8 million related to capital appreciation paid to the third-party holders of the interests and reduced net earnings available to common stockholders in our basic and diluted EPS calculations.

(b)   Incremental shares from stock options and restricted stock units are computed by the treasury stock method. Stock options and restricted stock units excluded from our computation of diluted EPS because they were not dilutive were as follows:

In Millions	Fiscal Year		
	2010	2009	2008
Anti-dilutive stock options and restricted stock units	6.3	14.2	9.4

(c)   On October 15, 2007, we settled a forward purchase contract with Lehman Brothers by issuing 28.6 million shares of common stock.

NOTE 13. RETIREMENT BENEFITS AND POSTEMPLOYMENT BENEFITS

Defined Benefit Pension Plans

We have defined benefit pension plans covering most domestic, Canadian, and United Kingdom employees. Benefits for salaried employees are based on length of service and final average compensation. Benefits for hourly employees include various monthly amounts for each year of credited service. Our funding policy is consistent with the requirements of applicable laws. We made $200.0 million of voluntary contributions to our principal domestic plans in fiscal 2009. We did not make any contributions in fiscal 2010, and we do not expect to be required to make any contributions in fiscal 2011. Our principal domestic retirement plan covering salaried employees has a provision that any excess pension assets would be allocated to active participants if the plan is terminated within five years of a change in control.

Other Postretirement Benefit Plans

We also sponsor plans that provide health care benefits to the majority of our domestic and Canadian retirees. The salaried health care benefit plan is contributory, with retiree contributions based on years of service. We make decisions to fund related trusts for certain employees and retirees on an annual basis. We did not make voluntary contributions to these plans in fiscal 2010 or fiscal 2009.

Health Care Cost Trend Rates

Assumed health care costs trends are as follows:

	Fiscal Year	
	2010	2009
Health care cost trend rate for next year	**9.0% and 9.0%**	9.0% and 9.5%
Rate to which the cost trend rate is assumed to decline (ultimate rate)	**5.2%**	5.2%
Year that the rate reaches the ultimate trend rate	**2019**	2018

We review our health care cost trend rates annually. Our review is based on data we collect about our health care claims experience and information provided by our actuaries. This information includes recent plan experience, plan design, overall industry experience and projections, and assumptions used by other similar organizations. Our initial health care cost trend rate is adjusted as necessary to remain consistent with this review, recent experiences, and short-term expectations. Our initial health care cost trend rate assumption is 9.0 percent for all retirees. Rates are graded down annually until the ultimate trend rate of 5.2 percent is reached in 2019 for all retirees. The trend rates are applicable for calculations only if the retirees' benefits increase as a result of health care inflation. The ultimate trend rate is adjusted annually, as necessary, to approximate the current economic view on the rate of long-term inflation plus an appropriate health care cost premium. Assumed trend rates for health care costs have an important effect on the amounts reported for the other postretirement benefit plans.

A one percentage point change in the health care cost trend rate would have the following effects:

In Millions	One Percentage Point Increase	One Percentage Point Decrease
Effect on the aggregate of the service and interest cost components in fiscal 2011	$ 7.9	$ (6.8)
Effect on the other postretirement accumulated benefit obligation as of May 30, 2010	96.7	(85.0)

The Patient Protection and Affordable Care Act, as amended by the Health Care and Education Reconciliation Act of 2010 (collectively, the Act) was signed into law in March 2010. The Act codifies health care reforms with staggered effective dates from 2010 to 2018. Estimates of the future impacts of several of the Act's provisions are incorporated into our postretirement benefit liability including the elimination of lifetime maximums and the imposition of an excise tax on high cost health plans. These changes resulted in a $24.0 million increase in our postretirement benefit liability as of May 30, 2010.

Postemployment Benefit Plans

Under certain circumstances, we also provide accruable benefits to former or inactive employees in the United States, Canada, and Mexico, and members of our Board of Directors, including severance and certain other benefits payable upon death. We recognize an obligation for any of these benefits that vest or accumulate with service. Postemployment benefits that do not vest or accumulate with service (such as severance based solely on annual pay rather than years of service) are charged to expense when incurred. Our postemployment benefit plans are unfunded.

We use our fiscal year end as the measurement date for all our defined benefit pension and other postretirement benefit plans.

Summarized financial information about defined benefit pension, other postretirement, and postemployment benefits plans is presented below:

In Millions	Defined Benefit Pension Plans Fiscal Year		Other Postretirement Benefit Plans Fiscal Year		Postemployment Benefit Plans Fiscal Year	
	2010	2009	2010	2009	2010	2009
Change in Plan Assets:						
Fair value at beginning of year	$ 3,157.8	$ 4,128.7	$ 235.6	$ 349.6		
Actual return on assets	535.9	(1,009.1)	41.0	(94.4)		
Employer contributions	17.1	220.2	0.1	0.1		
Plan participant contributions	3.5	3.1	11.3	11.0		
Benefits payments	(182.6)	(177.4)	(3.7)	(30.7)		
Foreign currency	(1.9)	(7.7)	—			
Fair value at end of year	$ 3,529.8	$ 3,157.8	$ 284.3	$ 235.6		
Change in Projected Benefit Obligation:						
Benefit obligation at beginning of year	$ 3,167.3	$ 3,224.1	$ 852.0	$ 911.3	$ 112.5	$ 104.6
Service cost	70.9	76.5	12.9	14.2	7.2	6.5
Interest cost	230.3	215.4	61.6	61.2	5.6	4.9
Plan amendment	25.8	0.3	7.5	(1.3)	—	2.3
Curtailment/other	—	—	—	—	10.6	8.4
Plan participant contributions	3.5	3.1	11.3	11.0	—	—
Medicare Part D reimbursements	—	—	4.7	4.7	—	—
Actuarial loss (gain)	716.4	(166.8)	168.1	(92.0)	11.8	1.6
Benefits payments	(182.6)	(177.4)	(57.5)	(57.8)	(17.6)	(15.6)
Foreign currency	(1.6)	(7.9)	—	0.7	0.2	(0.2)
Projected benefit obligation at end of year	$ 4,030.0	$ 3,167.3	$ 1,060.6	$ 852.0	$ 130.3	$ 112.5
Plan assets less than benefit obligation as of fiscal year end	$ (500.2)	$ (9.5)	$ (776.3)	$ (616.4)	$ (130.3)	$ (112.5)

The accumulated benefit obligation for all defined benefit plans was $3,620.3 million as of May 30, 2010, and $2,885.3 million as of May 31, 2009.

Amounts recognized in accumulated other comprehensive loss as of May 30, 2010, and May 31, 2009, are as follows:

In Millions	Defined Benefit Pension Plans Fiscal Year		Other Postretirement Benefit Plans Fiscal Year		Postemployment Benefit Plans Fiscal Year		Total Fiscal Year	
	2010	2009	2010	2009	2010	2009	2010	2009
Net actuarial loss	$ (1,369.9)	$ (1,028.2)	$ (225.2)	$ (130.3)	$ (15.9)	$ (9.7)	$ (1,611.0)	$ (1,168.2)
Prior service (costs) credits	(41.3)	(29.6)	1.0	6.8	(7.2)	(7.5)	(47.5)	(30.3)
Amounts recorded in accumulated other comprehensive loss	$ (1,411.2)	$ (1,057.8)	$ (224.2)	$ (123.5)	$ (23.1)	$ (17.2)	$ (1,658.5)	$ (1,198.5)

Plans with accumulated benefit obligations in excess of plan assets are as follows:

In Millions	Defined Benefit Pension Plans Fiscal Year		Other Postretirement Benefit Plans Fiscal Year		Postemployment Benefit Plans Fiscal Year	
	2010	2009	2010	2009	2010	2009
Projected benefit obligation	$299.6	$ 225.2	$ —	$ —	$ —	$ —
Accumulated benefit obligation	252.5	194.4	1,060.6	852.0	130.3	112.5
Plan assets at fair value	17.3	15.9	284.3	235.6	—	—

Components of net periodic benefit (income) costs are as follows:

In Millions	Defined Benefit Pension Plans Fiscal Year			Other Postretirement Benefit Plans Fiscal Year			Postemployment Benefit Plans Fiscal Year		
	2010	2009	2008	2010	2009	2008	2010	2009	2008
Service cost	$ 70.9	$ 76.5	$ 80.1	$ 12.9	$ 14.2	$ 16.4	$ 7.2	$ 6.5	$ 5.4
Interest cost	230.3	215.4	196.7	61.6	61.2	58.8	5.7	4.9	3.7
Expected return on plan assets	(400.1)	(385.8)	(360.6)	(29.2)	(30.0)	(30.3)	—	—	—
Amortization of losses	8.4	7.8	22.7	2.0	7.2	15.3	1.0	1.0	(0.2)
Amortization of prior service costs (credits)	6.9	7.4	7.5	(1.6)	(1.4)	(1.4)	2.4	2.2	2.2
Other adjustments	—	—	—	—	—	—	10.6	8.4	2.3
Settlement or curtailment losses	—	—	0.3	—	—	—	—	—	—
Net (income) expense	$ (83.6)	$ (78.7)	$ (53.3)	$ 45.7	$ 51.2	$ 58.8	$ 26.9	$ 23.0	$ 13.4

We expect to recognize the following amounts in net periodic benefit (income) costs in fiscal 2011:

In Millions	Defined Benefit Pension Plans	Other Postretirement Benefit Plans	Postemployment Benefit Plans
Amortization of losses	$ 81.2	$ 14.4	$ 2.1
Amortization of prior service costs (credits)	9.0	(0.6)	2.4

Assumptions
Weighted-average assumptions used to determine fiscal year-end benefit obligations are as follows:

	Defined Benefit Pension Plans Fiscal Year		Other Postretirement Benefit Plans Fiscal Year		Postemployment Benefit Plans Fiscal Year	
	2010	2009	2010	2009	2010	2009
Discount rate	5.85%	7.49%	5.80%	7.45%	5.12%	7.06%
Rate of salary increases	4.93	4.92	—	—	4.93	4.93

Weighted-average assumptions used to determine fiscal year net periodic benefit (income) costs are as follows:

	Defined Benefit Pension Plans Fiscal Year			Other Postretirement Benefit Plans Fiscal Year			Postemployment Benefit Plans Fiscal Year		
	2010	2009	2008	**2010**	2009	2008	**2010**	2009	2008
Discount rate	**7.49%**	6.88%	6.18%	**7.45%**	6.90%	6.15%	**7.06%**	6.64%	6.05%
Rate of salary increases	**4.92**	4.93	4.39	—	—	—	**4.93**	4.93	4.39
Expected long-term rate of return on plan assets	**9.55**	9.55	9.56	**9.33**	9.35	9.33	**—**	—	—

Discount Rates

Our discount rate assumptions are determined annually as of the last day of our fiscal year for all of our defined benefit pension, other postretirement, and postemployment benefit plan obligations. We also use the same discount rates to determine defined benefit pension, other postretirement, and postemployment benefit plan income and expense for the following fiscal year. We work with our actuaries to determine the timing and amount of expected future cash outflows to plan participants and, using the top quartile of AA-rated corporate bond yields, to develop a forward interest rate curve, including a margin to that index based on our credit risk. This forward interest rate curve is applied to our expected future cash outflows to determine our discount rate assumptions.

Fair Value of Plan Assets

In the fourth quarter of fiscal 2010, we adopted new accounting guidance requiring additional disclosures for plan assets of defined benefit pension and other postretirement benefit plans. This guidance requires that we categorize plan assets within a three level fair value hierarchy as described in Note 7.

The fair values of our pension and postretirement benefit plan assets at May 30, 2010, by asset category are as follows:

In Millions	Level 1	Level 2	Level 3	Total Assets
Fair value measurement of pension plan assets:				
Equity (a)	$ 744.5 $	716.6 $	512.8 $	1,973.9
Fixed income (b)	700.0	206.0	3.9	909.9
Real asset investments (c)	72.4	75.8	298.7	446.9
Other investments (d)	—	39.9	0.3	40.2
Cash and accruals	158.9	—	—	158.9
Total fair value measurement of pension plan assets	$ 1,675.8 $	1,038.3 $	815.7 $	3,529.8
Fair value measurement of postretirement benefit plan assets:				
Equity (a)	$ 10.1 $	81.4 $	25.7 $	117.2
Fixed income (b)	1.1	46.1	1.7	48.9
Real asset investments (c)	0.1	3.7	14.6	18.4
Other investments (d)	—	71.4	—	71.4
Cash and accruals	28.4	—	—	28.4
Fair value measurement of postretirement benefit plan assets	$ 39.7 $	202.6 $	42.0 $	284.3

(a) Primarily publicly traded common stock and private equity partnerships for purposes of total return and to maintain equity exposure consistent with policy allocations. Investments include: i) United States and international equity securities, mutual funds and equity futures valued at closing prices from national exchanges; and ii) commingled funds, privately held securities and private equity partnerships valued at unit values or net asset values provided by the investment managers, which are based on the fair value of the underlying investments. Various methods are used to determine fair values and may include the cost of the investment, most recent financing, and expected cash flows. For some of these investments, realization of the estimated fair value is dependent upon transactions between willing sellers and buyers.

(b) Primarily government and corporate debt securities for purposes of total return and managing fixed income exposure to policy allocations. Investments include: i) fixed income securities and bond futures generally valued at closing prices from national exchanges, fixed income pricing models and/or independent financial analysts; and ii) fixed commingled funds valued at unit values provided by the investment managers, which are based on the fair value of the underlying investments.

(c) Publicly traded common stock and limited partnerships in the energy and real estate sectors for purposes of total return. Investments include: i) energy and real estate securities generally valued at closing prices from national exchanges; and ii) commingled funds, private securities, and limited partnerships valued at unit values or net asset values provided by the investment managers, which are generally based on the fair value of the underlying investments.

(d) Global balanced fund of equity, fixed income and real estate securities for purposes of meeting Canadian pension plan asset allocation policies and insurance and annuity contracts for purposes of providing a stable stream of income for retirees and to fund postretirement medical benefits. Fair values are derived from unit values provided by the investment managers, which are generally based on the fair value of the underlying investments and contract fair values from the providers.

The following table is a roll forward of the Level 3 investments of our pension and postretirement benefit plan assets during the year ended May 30, 2010:

In Millions	Balance as of May 31, 2009	Transfers In/(Out)	Purchases, Sales Issuances, and Settlements (Net)	Net Gain/(Loss)	Balance as of May 30, 2010
Pension benefit plan assets:					
Equity	$ 423.9 $	— $	17.0 $	71.9 $	**512.8**
Fixed income	4.2	—	(1.2)	0.9	**3.9**
Real asset investments	275.2	—	25.0	(1.5)	**298.7**
Other investments	0.5	—	(0.3)	0.1	**0.3**
Fair value activity of pension level 3 plan assets	$ 703.8 $	— $	40.5 $	71.4 $	**815.7**
Postretirement benefit plan assets:					
Equity	$ 23.8 $	— $	(1.5) $	3.4 $	**25.7**
Fixed income	1.5	—	—	0.2	**1.7**
Real asset investments	17.0	—	(0.6)	(1.8)	**14.6**
Fair value activity of postretirement benefit level 3 plan assets:	$ 42.3 $	— $	(2.1) $	1.8 $	**42.0**

The net change in Level 3 assets attributable to unrealized gains at May 30, 2010, were $72.2 million for our pension plan assets, and $1.2 million for our postretirement plan assets.

Expected Rate of Return on Plan Assets
Our expected rate of return on plan assets is determined by our asset allocation, our historical long-term investment performance, our estimate of future long-term returns by asset class (using input from our actuaries, investment services, and investment managers), and long-term inflation assumptions. We review this assumption annually for each plan, however, our annual investment performance for one particular year does not, by itself, significantly influence our evaluation.

Weighted-average asset allocations for the past two fiscal years for our defined benefit pension and other postretirement benefit plans are as follows:

	Defined Benefit Pension Plans Fiscal Year		Other Postretirement Benefit Plans Fiscal Year	
	2010	2009	**2010**	2009
Asset category:				
United States equities	**32.6%**	29.5%	**37.3%**	32.6%
International equities	**17.1**	19.1	**18.3**	18.4
Private equities	**14.7**	13.6	**9.9**	12.0
Fixed income	**22.4**	24.4	**28.1**	28.4
Real assets	**13.2**	13.4	**6.4**	8.6
Total	**100.0%**	100.0%	**100.0%**	100.0%

The investment objective for our defined benefit pension and other postretirement benefit plans is to secure the benefit obligations to participants at a reasonable cost to us. Our goal is to optimize the long-term return on plan assets at a moderate level of risk. The defined benefit pension and other postretirement portfolios are broadly diversified across asset classes. Within asset classes, the portfolios are further diversified across investment styles and investment organizations. For the defined benefit pension and other postretirement benefit plans, the long-term investment policy allocations are: 30 percent to equities in the United States; 20 percent to international equities; 10 percent to private equities; 30 percent to fixed income; and 10 percent to real assets (real estate, energy, and timber). The actual allocations to these asset classes may vary tactically around the long-term policy allocations based on relative market valuations.

Contributions and Future Benefit Payments

We do not expect to make contributions to our defined benefit, other postretirement, and postemployment benefits plans in fiscal 2011. Actual fiscal 2011 contributions could exceed our current projections, as influenced by our decision to undertake discretionary funding of our benefit trusts and future changes in regulatory requirements. Estimated benefit payments, which reflect expected future service, as appropriate, are expected to be paid from fiscal 2011-2020 as follows:

In Millions	Defined Benefit Pension Plans		Other Postretirement Benefit Plans Gross Payments		Medicare Subsidy Receipts		Postemployment Benefit Plans
2011	$	194.8	$	56.5	$	5.4	$	18.4
2012		202.8		60.9		5.8		18.4
2013		211.9		64.0		6.4		17.2
2014		221.4		66.1		6.9		15.9
2015		231.4		69.6		7.5		15.0
2016-2020		1,331.7		394.8		45.4		67.0

Defined Contribution Plans

The General Mills Savings Plan is a defined contribution plan that covers domestic salaried, hourly, nonunion, and certain union employees. This plan is a 401(k) savings plan that includes a number of investment funds, including a Company stock fund, and an Employee Stock Ownership Plan (ESOP). We sponsor another money purchase plan for certain domestic hourly employees with net assets of $16.8 million as of May 30, 2010, and $15.6 million as of May 31, 2009. We also sponsor defined contribution plans in many of our foreign locations. Our total recognized expense related to defined contribution plans was $64.5 million in fiscal 2010, $59.5 million in fiscal 2009, and $61.9 million in fiscal 2008.

We matched a percentage of employee contributions to the General Mills Savings Plan with a base match plus a variable year-end match that depended on annual results. Effective April 1, 2010, the company match is directed to investment options of the participant's choosing. Prior to April 1, 2010, the company match was invested in company stock in the ESOP fund. The number of shares of our common stock allocated to participants in the ESOP was 5.9 million as of May 30, 2010, and 5.6 million as of May 31, 2009.

The ESOP originally purchased our common stock principally with funds borrowed from third parties and guaranteed by us. The ESOP shares are included in net shares outstanding for the purposes of calculating our EPS. The ESOP's third-party debt was repaid on June 30, 2007. The ESOP's only assets are our common stock and temporary cash balances. The ESOP's share of the total defined contribution expense was $53.7 million in fiscal 2010, $50.6 million in fiscal 2009, and $52.3 million in fiscal 2008. The ESOP's expense was calculated by the "shares allocated" method.

The Company stock fund and the ESOP had $610.3 million and $425.3 million of General Mills common stock as of May 30, 2010, and May 31, 2009.

NOTE 14. INCOME TAXES

The components of earnings before income taxes and after-tax earnings from joint ventures and the corresponding income taxes thereon are as follows:

		Fiscal Year	
In Millions	**2010**	2009	2008
Earnings before income taxes and after-tax earnings from joint ventures:			
United States	$ **2,060.4** $	1,717.5 $	1,646.5
Foreign	**144.1**	224.7	183.0
Total earnings before income taxes and after-tax earnings from joint ventures	$ **2,204.5** $	1,942.2 $	1,829.5
Income taxes:			
Currently payable:			
Federal	$ **616.0** $	457.8 $	447.7
State and local	**87.4**	37.3	52.9
Foreign	**45.5**	9.5	23.5
Total current	**748.9**	504.6	524.1
Deferred:			
Federal	**38.5**	155.7	65.9
State and local	**(4.9)**	36.3	24.2
Foreign	**(11.3)**	23.8	8.0
Total deferred	**22.3**	215.8	98.1
Total income taxes	$ **771.2** $	720.4 $	622.2

The Patient Protection and Affordable Care Act, as amended by the Health Care and Education Reconciliation Act of 2010 (collectively, the Act) was signed into law in March 2010. The federal government currently provides a subsidy, on a tax-free basis, to companies that provide certain retiree prescription drug benefits (the Medicare Part D subsidy). The Act reduces the tax deductibility of retiree health cost to the extent of any Medicare Part D subsidy received beginning in 2013. As a result of this change in tax treatment, we recorded a non-cash income tax charge and a decrease to our deferred tax assets of $35.0 million in fiscal 2010 as of the enactment date of the Act.

The following table reconciles the United States statutory income tax rate with our effective income tax rate:

	Fiscal Year		
	2010	2009	2008
United States statutory rate	35.0%	35.0%	35.0%
State and local income taxes, net of federal tax benefits	2.5	2.9	3.5
Foreign rate differences	(1.8)	(2.3)	(1.2)
Enactment date effect of health care reform	1.3	—	—
Federal court decisions, including interest	—	2.7	(1.7)
Domestic manufacturing deduction	(1.8)	(1.1)	(1.0)
Other, net	(0.2)	(0.1)	(0.6)
Effective income tax rate	35.0%	37.1%	34.0%

The tax effects of temporary differences that give rise to deferred tax assets and liabilities are as follows:

In Millions	May 30, 2010		May 31, 2009
Accrued liabilities	$	190.4	$	160.0
Restructuring, impairment, and other exit charges		—		0.4
Compensation and employee benefits		680.6		559.9
Pension liability		76.5		—
Unrealized hedge losses		15.6		18.4
Unrealized losses		248.6		221.7
Capital losses		93.1		165.7
Net operating losses		119.8		94.6
Other		134.5		95.4
Gross deferred tax assets		1,559.1		1,316.1
Valuation allowance		392.0		440.4
Net deferred tax assets		1,167.1		875.7
Brands		1,279.5		1,286.6
Depreciation		307.6		308.1
Prepaid pension asset		—		81.3
Intangible assets		107.4		102.2
Tax lease transactions		68.7		72.6
Other		235.8		174.6
Gross deferred tax liabilities		1,999.0		2,025.4
Net deferred tax liability	$	831.9	$	1,149.7

We have established a valuation allowance against certain of the categories of deferred tax assets described above as current evidence does not suggest we will realize sufficient taxable income of the appropriate character (e.g., ordinary income versus capital gain income) within the carry forward period to allow us to realize these deferred tax benefits.

Of the total valuation allowance of $392.0 million, $168.8 million relates to a deferred tax asset for losses recorded as part of the Pillsbury acquisition. Of the remaining valuation allowance, $93.1 million relates to capital loss carryforwards and $119.8 million relates to state and foreign operating loss carryforwards. As of May 30, 2010, we believe it is more likely than not that the remainder of our deferred tax asset is realizable.

The carryforward periods on our foreign loss carryforwards are as follows: $81.2 million do not expire; $9.8 million expire between fiscal 2011 and fiscal 2012; and $19.7 million expire between fiscal 2013 and fiscal 2019.

We have not recognized a deferred tax liability for unremitted earnings of $2.1 billion from our foreign operations because our subsidiaries have invested or will invest the undistributed earnings indefinitely, or the earnings will be remitted in a tax-free transaction. It is impractical for us to determine the amount of unrecognized deferred tax liabilities on these indefinitely reinvested earnings. Deferred taxes are recorded for earnings of our foreign operations when we determine that such earnings are no longer indefinitely reinvested.

Annually we file more than 350 income tax returns in approximately 100 global taxing jurisdictions. A number of years may elapse before an uncertain tax position is audited and finally resolved. While it is often difficult to predict the final outcome or the timing of resolution of any particular uncertain tax position, we believe that our liabilities for income taxes reflect the most likely outcome. We adjust these liabilities, as well as the related interest, in light of changing facts and circumstances. Settlement of any particular position would usually require the use of cash.

The number of years with open tax audits varies depending on the tax jurisdiction. Our major taxing jurisdictions include the United States (federal and state) and Canada. We are no longer subject to United States federal examinations by the IRS for fiscal years before 2002.

The IRS has concluded its field examination of our 2006 and prior federal tax years, which resulted in payments of $17.6 million in fiscal 2009 and $56.5 million in fiscal 2008 to cover the additional U.S. income tax liability plus interest related to adjustments during these audit cycles. The IRS also proposed additional adjustments for the fiscal 2002 to 2006 audit cycles related to the amount of capital loss and depreciation and amortization we reported as a result of our sale of noncontrolling interest in our GMC subsidiary. The IRS has proposed adjustments that effectively eliminate most of the tax benefits associated with this transaction. We believe our positions are supported by substantial technical authority and are vigorously defending our positions. We are currently in negotiations with the IRS Appeals Division for fiscal 2002 to 2006. We have determined that a portion of this matter should be included as a tax liability and have accordingly included it in our total liabilities for uncertain tax positions. The IRS initiated its audit of our fiscal 2007 and 2008 tax years during fiscal 2009.

In the third quarter of fiscal 2008, we recorded an income tax benefit of $30.7 million as a result of a favorable U.S. district court decision on an uncertain tax matter. In the third quarter of fiscal 2009, the U.S. Court of Appeals for the Eighth Circuit issued an opinion reversing the district court decision. As a result, we recorded $52.6 million (including interest) of income tax expense related to the reversal of cumulative income tax benefits from this uncertain tax matter recognized in fiscal years 1992 through 2008. We expect to make cash tax and interest payments of approximately $31.7 million in connection with this matter.

Various tax examinations by United States state taxing authorities could be conducted for any open tax year, which vary by jurisdiction, but are generally from 3 to 5 years. Currently, several state examinations are in progress. The Canada Revenue Agency is conducting an audit of our income tax returns in Canada for fiscal years 2003 (which is our earliest tax year still open for examination) through 2005. We do not anticipate that any United States state tax or Canadian tax adjustments will have a significant impact on our financial position or results of operations.

We apply a more-likely-than-not threshold to the recognition and derecognition of uncertain tax positions. Accordingly we recognize the amount of tax benefit that has a greater than 50 percent likelihood of being ultimately realized upon settlement. Future changes in judgment related to the expected ultimate resolution of uncertain tax positions will affect earnings in the quarter of such change.

The following table sets forth changes in our total gross unrecognized tax benefit liabilities, excluding accrued interest, for fiscal 2010. Approximately $206.4 million of this total represents the amount that, if recognized, would affect our effective income tax rate in future periods. This amount differs from the gross unrecognized tax benefits presented in the table because certain of the liabilities below would impact deferred taxes if recognized or are the result of stock compensation items impacting additional paid-in capital. We also would record a decrease in U.S. federal income taxes upon recognition of the state tax benefits included therein.

	Fiscal Year		
In Millions	2010		2009
Balance, beginning of year	$	570.1	$ 534.6
Tax position related to current year:			
Additions		19.7	66.8
Tax positions related to prior years:			
Additions		7.1	48.9
Reductions		(37.6)	(63.7)
Settlements		(1.9)	(13.0)
Lapses in statutes of limitations		(4.5)	(3.5)
Balance, end of year	$	552.9	$ 570.1

As of May 30, 2010, we have classified $299.0 million of the unrecognized tax benefits as a current liability as we expect to pay these amounts within the next 12 months, including a portion of our potential liability for the matter resolved by the U.S. Court of Appeals, as discussed above. While fiscal years 2007 and 2008 are currently under examination by the Internal Revenue Service (IRS), we are not able to reasonably estimate the timing of future cash flows beyond 12 months due to uncertainties in the timing of this and other tax audit outcomes. The remaining amount of our unrecognized tax liability was classified in other liabilities.

We report accrued interest and penalties related to unrecognized tax benefits in income tax expense. For fiscal 2010, we recognized a net $16.2 million of tax-related net interest and penalties, and had $174.8 million of accrued interest and penalties as of May 30, 2010.

NOTE 15. LEASES AND OTHER COMMITMENTS

An analysis of rent expense by type of property for operating leases follows:

	Fiscal Year		
In Millions	**2010**	2009	2008
Warehouse space	$ **55.7**	$ 51.4	$ 49.9
Equipment	**30.6**	39.1	28.6
Other	**51.6**	49.5	43.2
Total rent expense	$ **137.9**	$ 140.0	$ 121.7

Some operating leases require payment of property taxes, insurance, and maintenance costs in addition to the rent payments. Contingent and escalation rent in excess of minimum rent payments and sublease income netted in rent expense were insignificant.

Noncancelable future lease commitments are:

In Millions	**Operating Leases**	**Capital Leases**
2011	$ 87.4	$ 1.7
2012	63.9	1.3
2013	46.8	1.1
2014	31.5	0.3
2015	22.4	0.2
After 2015	63.3	—
Total noncancelable future lease commitments	$ 315.3	$ 4.6
Less: interest		(0.5)
Present value of obligations under capital leases		$ 4.1

These future lease commitments will be partially offset by estimated future sublease receipts of $16 million. Depreciation on capital leases is recorded as depreciation expense in our results of operations.

As of May 30, 2010, we have issued guarantees and comfort letters of $537.5 million for the debt and other obligations of consolidated subsidiaries, and guarantees and comfort letters of $301.6 million for the debt and other obligations of non-consolidated affiliates, mainly CPW. In addition, off-balance sheet arrangements are generally limited to the future payments under non-cancelable operating leases, which totaled $315.3 million as of May 30, 2010.

We are involved in various claims, including environmental matters, arising in the ordinary course of business. In the opinion of management, the ultimate disposition of these matters, either individually or in aggregate, will not have a material adverse effect on our financial position or results of operations.

NOTE 16. BUSINESS SEGMENT AND GEOGRAPHIC INFORMATION

We operate in the consumer foods industry. We have three operating segments by type of customer and geographic region as follows: U.S. Retail, 69.8 percent of our fiscal 2010 consolidated net sales; International, 18.2 percent of our fiscal 2010 consolidated net sales; and Bakeries and Foodservice, 12.0 percent of our fiscal 2010 consolidated net sales.

Our U.S. Retail segment reflects business with a wide variety of grocery stores, mass merchandisers, membership stores, natural food chains, and drug, dollar and discount chains operating throughout the United States. Our major product categories in this business segment are ready-to-eat cereals, refrigerated yogurt, ready-to-serve soup, dry dinners, shelf stable and frozen vegetables, refrigerated and frozen dough products, dessert and baking mixes, frozen pizza and pizza snacks, grain, fruit and savory snacks, and a wide variety of organic products including soup, granola bars, and cereal.

In Canada, our major product categories are ready-to-eat cereals, shelf stable and frozen vegetables, dry dinners, refrigerated and frozen dough products, dessert and baking mixes, frozen pizza snacks, and grain, fruit and savory snacks. In markets outside North America, our product categories include super-premium ice cream, grain snacks, shelf stable and frozen vegetables, dough products, and dry dinners. Our International segment also includes products manufactured in the United States for export, mainly to Caribbean and Latin American markets, as well as products we manufacture for sale to our international joint ventures. Revenues from export activities are reported in the region or country where the end customer is located. These international businesses are managed through 34 sales and marketing offices.

In our Bakeries and Foodservice segment our major product categories are cereals, snacks, yogurt, unbaked and fully baked frozen dough products, baking mixes, and flour. Many products we sell are branded to the consumer and nearly all are branded to our customers. We sell to distributors and operators in many customer channels including foodservice, convenience stores, vending, and supermarket bakeries. Following our fiscal 2009 divestitures, substantially all of this segment's operations are located in the United States.

Operating profit for these segments excludes unallocated corporate items, restructuring, impairment, and other exit costs, and divestiture gains and losses. Unallocated corporate items include variances to planned corporate overhead expenses, variances to planned domestic employee benefits and incentives, all stock-based compensation costs, annual contributions to the General Mills Foundation, and other items that are not part of our measurement of segment operating performance. These include gains and losses arising from the revaluation of certain grain inventories and gains and losses from mark-to-market valuation of certain commodity positions until passed back to our operating segments in accordance with our policy as discussed in Note 2. These items affecting operating profit are centrally managed at the corporate level and are excluded from the measure of segment profitability reviewed by executive management. Under our supply chain organization, our manufacturing, warehouse, and distribution activities are substantially integrated across our operations in order to maximize efficiency and productivity. As a result, fixed assets and depreciation and amortization expenses are neither maintained nor available by operating segment.

As discussed in Note 1, we adopted new accounting guidance on noncontrolling interests at the beginning of fiscal 2010. To conform to the current year's presentation, earnings attributable to noncontrolling interests in foreign subsidiaries of $2.1 million in fiscal 2009, and $1.4 million in fiscal 2008, which were previously deducted from the International segment's operating profit, have been reclassified to net earnings attributable to noncontrolling interests.

Our operating segment results were as follows:

In Millions		Fiscal Year				
		2010		2009		2008
Net sales:						
U.S. Retail	$	10,323.5	$	10,052.1	$	9,072.0
International		2,702.5		2,591.4		2,558.8
Bakeries and Foodservice		1,770.5		2,047.8		2,021.3
Total	$	14,796.5	$	14,691.3	$	13,652.1
Operating profit:						
U.S. Retail	$	2,392.0	$	2,208.5	$	1,971.2
International		219.2		263.5		270.3
Bakeries and Foodservice		250.1		171.0		165.4
Total segment operating profit		2,861.3		2,643.0		2,406.9
Unallocated corporate items		223.8		361.3		156.7
Divestitures (gain), net		—		(84.9)		—
Restructuring, impairment, and other exit costs		31.4		41.6		21.0
Operating profit	$	2,606.1	$	2,325.0	$	2,229.2

The following table provides financial information by geographic area:

In Millions		Fiscal Year				
		2010		2009		2008
Net sales:						
United States	$	12,077.6	$	12,057.4	$	11,036.7
Non-United States		2,718.9		2,633.9		2,615.4
Total	$	14,796.5	$	14,691.3	$	13,652.1

In Millions		May 30, 2010		May 31, 2009
Land, buildings, and equipment:				
United States	$	2,619.7	$	2,555.6
Non-United States		508.0		479.3
Total	$	3,127.7	$	3,034.9

NOTE 17. SUPPLEMENTAL INFORMATION

The components of certain Consolidated Balance Sheet accounts are as follows:

In Millions	May 30, 2010		May 31, 2009
Receivables:			
From customers	$ 1,057.4	$	971.2
Less allowance for doubtful accounts	(15.8)		(17.8)
Total	$ 1,041.6	$	953.4

In Millions	May 30, 2010		May 31, 2009
Inventories:			
Raw materials and packaging	$ 247.5	$	273.1
Finished goods	1,131.4		1,096.1
Grain	107.4		126.9
Excess of FIFO or weighted-average cost over LIFO cost (a)	(142.3)		(149.3)
Total	$ 1,344.0	$	1,346.8

(a) Inventories of $958.3 million as of May 30, 2010, and $908.3 million as of May 31, 2009, were valued at LIFO.

In Millions	May 30, 2010		May 31, 2009
Prepaid expenses and other current assets:			
Prepaid expenses	$ 127.5	$	197.5
Accrued interest receivable, including interest rate swaps	64.9		73.4
Derivative receivables, primarily commodity-related	48.8		32.0
Other receivables	101.4		87.6
Current marketable securities	4.8		23.4
Miscellaneous	31.1		55.4
Total	$ 378.5	$	469.3

In Millions	May 30, 2010		May 31, 2009
Land, buildings, and equipment:			
Land	$ 58.0	$	55.2
Buildings	1,653.8		1,571.8
Buildings under capital lease	19.6		25.0
Equipment	4,405.6		4,324.0
Equipment under capital lease	25.0		27.7
Capitalized software	318.7		268.0
Construction in progress	469.0		349.2
Total land, buildings, and equipment	6,949.7		6,620.9
Less accumulated depreciation	(3,822.0)		(3,586.0)
Total	$ 3,127.7	$	3,034.9

In Millions	May 30, 2010		May 31, 2009
Other assets:			
Pension assets	$ 2.2	$	195.1
Investments in and advances to joint ventures	398.1		283.3
Life insurance	88.2		89.8
Non-current derivative receivables	130.1		189.8
Miscellaneous	144.8		137.0
Total	$ 763.4	$	895.0

In Millions	May 30, 2010		May 31, 2009
Other current liabilities:			
Accrued payroll	$ 331.4	$	338.2
Accrued interest	136.5		182.1
Accrued trade and consumer promotions	555.2		473.5
Accrued taxes	440.2		168.0
Derivative payable	18.1		25.8
Accrued customer advances	25.5		19.3
Miscellaneous	255.3		275.0
Total	$ 1,762.2	$	1,481.9

In Millions	May 30, 2010	May 31, 2009
Other noncurrent liabilities:		
Interest rate swaps	$ 180.2	$ 258.7
Accrued compensation and benefits, including obligations for underfunded other postretirement and postemployment benefit plans	1,588.1	1,051.0
Accrued income taxes	276.3	541.5
Miscellaneous	74.1	81.0
Total	$2,118.7	$1,932.2

Certain Consolidated Statements of Earnings amounts are as follows:

In Millions	Fiscal Year		
	2010	2009	2008
Depreciation and amortization	$ 457.1	$ 453.6	$ 459.2
Research and development expense	218.3	208.2	204.7
Advertising and media expense (including production and communication costs)	908.5	732.1	587.2

The components of interest, net are as follows:

Expense (Income), in Millions	Fiscal Year		
	2010	2009	2008
Interest expense	$ 374.5	$ 409.5	$ 432.0
Capitalized interest	(6.2)	(5.1)	(5.0)
Interest income	(6.8)	(21.6)	(27.3)
Loss on debt repurchase	40.1	—	—
Interest, net	$ 401.6	$ 382.8	$ 399.7

Certain Consolidated Statements of Cash Flows amounts are as follows:

In Millions	Fiscal Year		
	2010	2009	2008
Cash interest payments	$ 384.1	$ 292.8	$ 436.6
Cash paid for income taxes	672.5	395.3	444.4

In fiscal 2009, we acquired Humm Foods by issuing 1.8 million shares of our common stock to its shareholders, with a value of $55.0 million, as consideration. This acquisition is treated as a non-cash transaction in our Consolidated Statement of Cash Flows.

NOTE 18. QUARTERLY DATA (UNAUDITED)

In May 2010, our Board of Directors approved a two-for-one stock split to be effected in the form of a 100 percent stock dividend to stockholders of record on May 28, 2010. The Company's stockholders received one additional share of common stock for each share of common stock in their possession on that date. The additional shares were distributed on June 8, 2010. This did not change the proportionate interest that a stockholder maintained in the Company. All shares and per share amounts have been adjusted for the two-for-one stock split.

Summarized quarterly data for fiscal 2010 and fiscal 2009 follows:

In Millions, Except Per Share Amounts	First Quarter Fiscal Year		Second Quarter Fiscal Year		Third Quarter Fiscal Year		Fourth Quarter Fiscal Year	
	2010	2009	2010	2009	2010	2009	2010	2009
Net sales	$ 3,518.8	$ 3,497.3	$ 4,078.2	$ 4,010.8	$ 3,629.1	$ 3,537.4	$ 3,570.4	$ 3,645.7
Gross margin	1,458.7	1,191.7	1,746.1	1,219.6	1,377.5	1,277.5	1,291.3	1,544.6
Net earnings attributable to General Mills (a)	420.6	278.5	565.5	378.2	332.5	288.9	211.9	358.8
EPS:								
Basic	$ 0.64	$ 0.41	$ 0.86	$ 0.57	$ 0.50	$ 0.44	$ 0.32	$ 0.54
Diluted	$ 0.62	$ 0.40	$ 0.83	$ 0.54	$ 0.48	$ 0.42	$ 0.31	$ 0.53
Dividends per share	$ 0.24	$ 0.22	$ 0.23	$ 0.21	$ 0.25	$ 0.21	$ 0.24	$ 0.22
Market price of common stock:								
High	$ 30.20	$ 33.85	$ 34.56	$ 35.08	$ 36.18	$ 32.39	$ 36.96	$ 27.75
Low	$ 25.59	$ 29.94	$ 28.99	$ 29.06	$ 34.00	$ 27.52	$ 34.74	$ 23.61

(a) Net earnings in the fourth quarter of fiscal 2010 included interest expense of $40.1 million related to the repurchase of certain notes and a non-cash income tax charge of $35.0 million resulting from a change in deferred tax assets (see Note 14).

Glossary

AOCI. Accumulated other comprehensive income (loss).

Average total capital. Used for calculating return on average total capital. Notes payable, long-term debt including current portion, noncontrolling interests, and stockholders' equity, excluding accumulated other comprehensive income (loss) and certain after-tax earnings adjustments. The average is calculated using the average of the beginning of fiscal year and end of fiscal year Consolidated Balance Sheet amounts for these line items.

Core working capital. Accounts receivable plus inventories less accounts payable, all as of the last day of our fiscal year.

Depreciation associated with restructured assets. The increase in depreciation expense caused by updating the salvage value and shortening the useful life of depreciable fixed assets to coincide with the end of production under an approved restructuring plan, but only if impairment is not present.

Derivatives. Financial instruments such as futures, swaps, options, and forward contracts that we use to manage our risk arising from changes in commodity prices, interest rates, foreign exchange rates, and stock prices.

Fixed charge coverage ratio. The sum of earnings before income taxes and fixed charges (before tax), divided by the sum of the fixed charges (before tax) and interest.

Generally Accepted Accounting Principles (GAAP). Guidelines, procedures, and practices that we are required to use in recording and reporting accounting information in our financial statements.

Goodwill. The difference between the purchase price of acquired companies and the related fair values of net assets acquired.

Hedge accounting. Accounting for qualifying hedges that allows changes in a hedging instrument's fair value to offset corresponding changes in the hedged item in the same reporting period. Hedge accounting is permitted for certain hedging instruments and hedged items only if the hedging relationship is highly effective, and only prospectively from the date a hedging relationship is formally documented.

Interest bearing instruments. Notes payable, long-term debt, including current portion, cash and cash equivalents, and certain interest bearing investments classified within prepaid expenses and other current assets and other assets.

LIBOR. London Interbank Offered Rate.

Mark-to-market. The act of determining a value for financial instruments, commodity contracts, and related assets or liabilities based on the current market price for that item.

Net mark-to-market valuation of certain commodity positions. Realized and unrealized gains and losses on derivative contracts that will be allocated to segment operating profit when the exposure we are hedging affects earnings.

Net price realization. The impact of list and promoted price changes, net of trade and other price promotion costs.

Noncontrolling interests. Interests of subsidiaries held by third parties.

Notional principal amount. The principal amount on which fixed-rate or floating-rate interest payments are calculated.

OCI. Other comprehensive income (loss).

Operating cash flow to debt ratio. Net cash provided by operating activities, divided by the sum of notes payable and long-term debt, including current portion.

Reporting unit. An operating segment or a business one level below an operating segment.

Return on average total capital. Net earnings attributable to General Mills, excluding after-tax net interest, and adjusted for certain items affecting year-over-year comparability, divided by average total capital.

Segment operating profit margin. Segment operating profit divided by net sales for the segment.

Supply chain input costs. Costs incurred to produce and deliver product, including ingredient and conversion costs, inventory management, logistics, warehousing, and others.

Total debt. Notes payable and long-term debt, including current portion.

Transaction gains and losses. The impact on our Consolidated Financial Statements of foreign exchange rate changes arising from specific transactions.

Translation adjustments. The impact of the conversion of our foreign affiliates' financial statements to U.S. dollars for the purpose of consolidating our financial statements.

Variable interest entities (VIEs). A legal structure that is used for business purposes that either (1) does not have equity investors that have voting rights and share in all the entity's profits and losses or (2) has equity investors that do not provide sufficient financial resources to support the entity's activities.

Working capital. Current assets and current liabilities, all as of the last day of our fiscal year.

ITEM 9   Changes in and Disagreements With Accountants on Accounting and Financial Disclosure

None.

ITEM 9A   Controls and Procedures

We, under the supervision and with the participation of our management, including our Chief Executive Officer and Chief Financial Officer, have evaluated the effectiveness of the design and operation of our disclosure controls and procedures (as defined in Rule 13a-15(e) under the 1934 Act). Based on that evaluation, our Chief Executive Officer and Chief Financial Officer have concluded that, as of May 30, 2010, our disclosure controls and procedures were effective to ensure that information required to be disclosed by us in reports that we file or submit under the 1934 Act is (1) recorded, processed, summarized, and reported within the time periods specified in applicable rules and forms, and (2) accumulated and communicated to our management, including our Chief Executive Officer and Chief Financial Officer, in a manner that allows timely decisions regarding required disclosure.

There were no changes in our internal control over financial reporting (as defined in Rule 13a-15(f) under the 1934 Act) during our fiscal quarter ended May 30, 2010, that have materially affected, or are reasonably likely to materially affect, our internal control over financial reporting.

MANAGEMENT'S REPORT ON INTERNAL CONTROL OVER FINANCIAL REPORTING

The management of General Mills, Inc. is responsible for establishing and maintaining adequate internal control over financial reporting, as such term is defined in Rule 13a-15(f) under the 1934 Act. The Company's internal control system was designed to provide reasonable assurance to our management and the Board of Directors regarding the preparation and fair presentation of published financial statements. Under the supervision and with the participation of management, including our Chief Executive Officer and Chief Financial Officer, we conducted an assessment of the effectiveness of our internal control over financial reporting as of May 30, 2010. In making this assessment, management used the criteria set forth by the Committee of Sponsoring Organizations of the Treadway Commission (COSO) in Internal Control — Integrated Framework.

Based on our assessment using the criteria set forth by COSO in Internal Control — Integrated Framework, management concluded that our internal control over financial reporting was effective as of May 30, 2010.

KPMG LLP, our independent registered public accounting firm, has issued a report on the effectiveness of the Company's internal control over financial reporting.

/s/ K. J. Powell   /s/ D. L. Mulligan

K. J. Powell   D. L. Mulligan
Chairman of the Board and Chief   Executive Vice President and Chief
Executive Officer   Financial Officer

July 9, 2010

Our registered public accounting firm's attestation report on our internal control over financial reporting is included in the "Report of Independent Registered Public Accounting Firm" in Item 8 of this report.

Glossary

A

Accelerated depreciation A higher amount of depreciation is recorded in the early years and a lower amount in the later years. (p. 384)

Account A record used to accumulate amounts for each individual asset, liability, revenue, expense, and component of stockholders' equity. (p. 113)

Account receivable A receivable arising from the sale of goods or services with a verbal promise to pay. (p. 332)

Accounting The process of identifying, measuring, and communicating economic information to various users. (p. 11)

Accounting controls Procedures concerned with safeguarding the assets or the reliability of the financial statements. (p. 306)

Accounting cycle A series of steps performed each period and culminating with the preparation of a set of financial statements. (p. 184)

Accounting system Methods and records used to accurately report an entity's transactions and to maintain accountability for its assets and liabilities. (p. 305)

Accounts payable Amounts owed for inventory, goods, or services acquired in the normal course of business. (p. 431)

Accounts receivable turnover ratio A measure of the number of times accounts receivable are collected in a period. (p. 689)

Accrual Cash has not yet been paid or received but expense has been incurred or revenue earned. (p. 178)

Accrual basis A system of accounting in which revenues are recognized when earned and expenses are recognized when incurred. (p. 162)

Accrued asset An asset resulting from the recognition of a revenue before the receipt of cash. (p. 178)

Accrued liability A liability resulting from the recognition of an expense before the payment of cash. (pp. 178, 437)

Acid-test or Quick ratio A stricter test of liquidity than the current ratio; excludes inventory and prepayments from the numerator. (p. 687)

Acquisition cost The amount that includes all of the cost normally necessary to acquire an asset and prepare it for its intended use. (p. 380)

Additional paid-in capital The amount received for the issuance of stock in excess of the par value of the stock. (p. 543)

Adjusting entries Journal entries made at the end of a period by a company using the accrual basis of accounting. (p. 168)

Administrative controls Procedures concerned with efficient operation of the business and adherence to managerial policies. (p. 306)

Aging schedule A form used to categorize the various individual accounts receivable according to the length of time each has been outstanding. (p. 339)

Allowance for doubtful accounts A contra-asset account used to reduce accounts receivable to its net realizable value. (p. 336)

Allowance method A method of estimating bad debts on the basis of either the net credit sales of the period or the accounts receivable at the end of the period. (p. 336)

American Institute of Certified Public Accountants (AICPA) The professional organization of certified public accountants. (p. 25)

Annuity A series of payments of equal amounts. (p. 450)

Asset A future economic benefit. (p. 9)

Asset turnover ratio The relationship between net sales and average total assets. (p. 696)

Audit committee A board of directors subset that acts as a direct contact between the stockholders and the independent accounting firm. (p. 305)

Auditing The process of examining the financial statements and the underlying records of a company to render an opinion as to whether the statements are fairly presented. (p. 26)

Auditors' report The opinion rendered by a public accounting firm concerning the fairness of the presentation of the financial statements. (p. 81)

Authorized shares The maximum number of shares a corporation may issue as indicated in the corporate charter. (p. 543)

B

Balance sheet The financial statement that summarizes the assets, liabilities, and owners' equity at a specific point in time. (p. 15)

Bank reconciliation A form used by the accountant to reconcile or resolve any differences between the balance shown on the bank statement for a particular account with the balance shown in the accounting records. (p. 299)

Bank statement A detailed list, provided by the bank, of all activity for a particular account during the month. (p. 298)

Blind receiving report A form used by the receiving department to account for the quantity and condition of merchandise received from a supplier. (p. 314)

Board of directors A group composed of key officers of a corporation and outside members responsible for general oversight of the affairs of the entity. (p. 305)

Bond A certificate that represents a corporation's promise to repay a certain amount of money and interest in the future. (p. 7)

Bond issue price The present value of the annuity of interest payments plus the present value of the principal. (p. 493)

Book value The original cost of an asset minus the amount of accumulated depreciation. (p. 383)

Book value per share Total stockholders' equity divided by the number of shares of common stock outstanding. (p. 560)

Business All of the activities necessary to provide the members of an economic system with goods and services. (p. 4)

Business entity An organization operated to earn a profit. (p. 6)

C

Callable bonds Bonds that may be redeemed or retired before their specified due date. (p. 492)

Callable feature Allows the firm to eliminate a class of stock by paying the stockholders a specified amount. (p. 545)

Capital expenditure A cost that improves the asset and is added to the asset account. (p. 389)

Capital lease A lease that is recorded as an asset by the lessee. (p. 505)

Capital stock Indicates the owners' contributions to a corporation. (p. 9)

Capitalization of interest Interest on constructed assets is added to the asset account. (p. 382)

Carrying value The face value of a bond plus the amount of unamortized premium or minus the amount of unamortized discount. (p. 498)

Cash basis A system of accounting in which revenues are recognized when cash is received and expenses are recognized when cash is paid. (p. 162)

Cash equivalent An investment that is readily convertible to a known amount of cash and has an original maturity to the investor of three months or less. (p. 294)

Cash flow from operations to capital expenditures ratio A measure of the ability of a company to finance long-term asset acquisitions with cash from operations. (p. 693)

Cash flow from operations to current liabilities ratio A measure of the ability to pay current debts from operating cash flows. (p. 688)

Cash-to-cash operating cycle The length of time from the purchase of inventory to the collection of any receivable from the sale. (p. 690)

Certified Public Accountant (CPA) The designation for an individual who has passed a uniform exam administered by the AICPA and has met other requirements as determined by individual states. (p. 25)

Change in estimate A change in the life of the asset or in its residual value. (p. 388)

Chart of accounts A numerical list of all accounts used by a company. (p. 114)

Closing entries Journal entries made at the end of the period to return the balance in all nominal accounts to zero and transfer the net income or loss and the dividends to Retained Earnings. (p. 185)

Comparability For accounting information, the quality that allows a user to analyze two or more companies and look for similarities and differences. (p. 59)

Compound interest Interest calculated on the principal plus previous amounts of interest. (p. 446)

Comprehensive income Total change in net assets from all sources except investments by or distributions to the owners. (p. 558)

Conservatism The practice of using the least optimistic estimate when two estimates of amounts are about equally likely. (p. 60)

Consistency For accounting information, the quality that allows a user to compare two or more accounting periods for a single company. (p. 60)

Contingent asset An existing condition for which the outcome is not known but by which the company stands to gain. (p. 443)

Contingent liability An existing condition for which the outcome is not known but depends on some future event. (p. 440)

Contra account An account with a balance that is opposite that of a related account. (p. 170)

Control account The general ledger account that is supported by a subsidiary ledger. (p. 334)

Convertible feature Allows preferred stock to be exchanged for common stock. (p. 545)

Corporation A form of entity organized under the laws of a particular state; ownership evidenced by shares of stock. (p. 7)

Cost of goods available for sale Beginning inventory plus cost of goods purchased. (p. 226)

Cost of goods sold Cost of goods available for sale minus ending inventory. (p. 226)

Cost principle Assets are recorded at the cost to acquire them. (p. 23)

Credit An entry on the right side of an account. (p. 118)

Credit card draft A multiple-copy document used by a company that accepts a credit card for a sale. (p. 347)

Credit memoranda Additions on a bank statement for such items as interest paid on the account and notes collected by the bank for the customer. (p. 299)

Creditor Someone to whom a company or person has a debt. (p. 9)

Cumulative feature The right to dividends in arrears before the current-year dividend is distributed. (p. 545)

Current asset An asset that is expected to be realized in cash or sold or consumed during the operating cycle or within one year if the cycle is shorter than one year. (p. 63)

Current liability An obligation that will be satisfied within the next operating cycle or within one year if the cycle is shorter than one year. (pp. 65, 431)

Current maturities of long-term debt The portion of a long-term liability that will be paid within one year. (p. 435)

Current ratio Current assets divided by current liabilities. (p. 67)

Current value The amount of cash or its equivalent that could be received by selling an asset currently. (p. 160)

D

Debenture bonds Bonds that are not backed by specific collateral. (p. 492)

Debit An entry on the left side of an account. (p. 118)

Debit memoranda Deductions on a bank statement for items such as NSF checks and various service charges. (p. 299)

Debt securities Securities issued by corporations and governmental bodies as a form of borrowing. (p. 349)

Debt service coverage ratio A statement of cash flows measure of the ability of a company to meet its interest and principal payments. (p. 693)

Debt-to-equity ratio The ratio of total liabilities to total stockholders' equity. (p. 691)

Deferral Cash has been paid or received but expense or revenue has not yet been recognized. (p. 177)

Deferred expense An asset resulting from the payment of cash before the incurrence of expense. (p. 177)

Deferred revenue A liability resulting from the receipt of cash before the recognition of revenue. (p. 177)

Deferred tax The account used to reconcile the difference between the amount recorded as income tax expense and the amount that is payable as income tax. (p. 514)

Deposit in transit A deposit recorded on the books but not yet reflected on the bank statement. (p. 299)

Depreciation The process of allocating the cost of a long-term tangible asset over its useful life. (pp. 59, 382)

Direct method For preparing the Operating Activities section of the statement of cash flows, the approach in which cash receipts and cash payments are reported. (p. 615)

Direct write-off method The recognition of bad debts expense at the point an account is written off as uncollectible. (p. 335)

Discontinued operations A line item on the income statement to reflect any gains or losses from the disposal of a segment of the business as well as any net income or loss from operating that segment. (p. 703)

Discount The excess of the face value of bonds over the issue price. (p. 495)

Discount on notes payable A contra liability that represents interest deducted from a loan in advance. (p. 434)

Discounting The process of selling a promissory note. (p. 348)

Dividend payout ratio The annual dividend amount divided by the annual net income; or the percentage of earnings paid out as dividends. (pp. 551, 700)

Dividend yield ratio The relationship between dividends and the market price of a company's stock. (p. 700)

Dividends A distribution of the net income of a business to its owners. (p. 17)

Double-declining-balance method Depreciation is recorded at twice the straight-line rate, but the balance is reduced each period. (p. 384)

Double-entry system A system of accounting in which every transaction is recorded with equal debits and credits and the accounting equation is kept in balance. (p. 120)

E

Earnings per share (EPS) A company's bottom line stated on a per-share basis. (p. 698)

Economic entity concept The assumption that a single, identifiable unit must be accounted for in all situations. (p. 6)

Effective interest method of amortization The process of transferring a portion of the premium or discount to interest expense; this method results in a constant effective interest rate. (p. 498)

Equity securities Securities issued by corporations as a form of ownership in the business. (p. 349)

Estimated liability A contingent liability that is accrued and reflected on the balance sheet. (p. 440)

Event A happening of consequence to an entity. (p. 107)

Expense(s) Outflows of assets or incurrences of liabilities resulting from delivering goods, rendering services, or carrying out other activities. (pp. 9, 168)

External event An event involving interaction between an entity and its environment. (p. 107)

Extraordinary item A line item on the income statement to reflect any gains or losses that arise from an event that is both unusual in nature and infrequent in occurrence. (p. 703)

F

Face rate of interest The rate of interest on the bond certificate. (p. 493)

Face value The principal amount of the bond as stated on the bond certificate. (p. 491)

Faithful representation The quality of information that makes it complete, neutral, and free from error. (p. 59)

FIFO method An inventory costing method that assigns the most recent costs to ending inventory. (p. 240)

Financial accounting The branch of accounting concerned with the preparation of financial statements for outsider use. (p. 11)

Financial Accounting Standards Board (FASB) The group in the private sector with authority to set accounting standards. (p. 25)

Financing activities Activities concerned with the raising and repaying of funds in the form of debt and equity. (p. 612)

Finished goods A manufacturer's inventory that is complete and ready for sale. (p. 222)

FOB destination point Terms that require the seller to pay for the cost of shipping the merchandise to the buyer. (p. 231)

FOB shipping point Terms that require the buyer to pay for the shipping costs. (p. 231)

Future value of a single amount Amount accumulated at a future time from a single payment or investment. (p. 447)

Future value of an annuity The amount accumulated in the future when a series of payments is invested and accrues interest. (p. 450)

G

Gain on sale of asset The excess of the selling price over the asset's book value. (p. 393)

Gain or loss on redemption The difference between the carrying value and the redemption price at the time bonds are redeemed. (p. 502)

General journal The journal used in place of a specialized journal. (p. 124)

General ledger A book, a file, a hard drive, or another device containing all of the accounts. (p. 115)

Generally accepted accounting principles (GAAP) The various methods, rules, practices, and other procedures that have evolved over time in response to the need to regulate the preparation of financial statements. (p. 24)

Going concern The assumption that an entity is not in the process of liquidation and that it will continue indefinitely. (p. 23)

Goodwill The excess of the purchase price to acquire a business over the value of the individual net assets acquired. (p. 395)

Gross profit Sales less cost of goods sold. (pp. 70, 223)

Gross profit ratio Gross profit divided by net sales. (p. 233)

H

Historical cost The amount paid for an asset and used as a basis for recognizing it on the balance sheet and carrying it on later balance sheets. (p. 160)

Horizontal analysis A comparison of financial statement items over a period of time. (p. 678)

I

Income statement A statement that summarizes revenues and expenses. (p. 15)

Indirect method For preparing the Operating Activities section of the statement of cash flows, the approach in which net income is reconciled to net cash flow from operations. (p. 615)

Intangible assets Assets with no physical properties. (p. 395)

Interim statements Financial statements prepared monthly, quarterly, or at other intervals less than a year in duration. (p. 185)

Internal audit staff The department responsible for monitoring and evaluating the internal control system. (p. 307)

Internal control report A report required by Section 404 of the Sarbanes-Oxley Act to be included in a company's annual report in which management assesses the effectiveness of the internal control structure. (p. 303)

Internal control system Policies and procedures necessary to ensure the safeguarding of an entity's assets, the reliability of its accounting records, and the accomplishment of overall company objectives. (p. 302)

Internal event An event occurring entirely within an entity. (p. 107)

International Accounting Standards Board (IASB) The organization formed to develop worldwide accounting standards. (p. 25)

Inventory profit The portion of the gross profit that results from holding inventory during a period of rising prices. (p. 245)

Inventory turnover ratio A measure of the number of times inventory is sold during the period. (p. 253)

Investing activities Activities concerned with the acquisition and disposal of long-term assets. (p. 611)

Invoice A form sent by the seller to the buyer as evidence of a sale. (p. 313)

Invoice approval form A form the accounting department uses before making payment to document the accuracy of all information about a purchase. (p. 314)

Issued shares The number of shares sold or distributed to stockholders. (p. 543)

J

Journal A chronological record of transactions. (p. 123)

Journalizing The act of recording journal entries. (p. 123)

K

Key terms for promissory notes These terms, with their definitions in the text, are important for your understanding. (p. 344)

L

Land improvements Costs that are related to land but that have a limited life. (p. 382)

Leverage The use of borrowed funds and amounts contributed by preferred stockholders to earn an overall return higher than the cost of these funds. (p. 698)

Liability An obligation of a business. (p. 8)

LIFO conformity rule The IRS requirement that when LIFO is used on a tax return, it must also be used in reporting income to stockholders. (p. 244)

LIFO liquidation The result of selling more units than are purchased during the period, which can have negative tax consequences if a company is using LIFO. (p. 244)

LIFO method An inventory method that assigns the most recent costs to cost of goods sold. (p. 241)

LIFO reserve The excess of the value of a company's inventory stated at FIFO over the value stated at LIFO. (p. 244)

Liquidity The ability of a company to pay its debts as they come due. (p. 67)

Long-term liability An obligation that will not be satisfied within one year or the current operating cycle. (p. 488)

Loss on sale of asset The amount by which selling price is less than book value. (p. 394)

Lower-of-cost-or-market (LCM) rule A conservative inventory valuation approach that is an attempt to anticipate declines in the value of inventory before its actual sale. (p. 250)

M

Maker The party that agrees to repay the money for a promissory note at some future date. (p. 344)

Management accounting The branch of accounting concerned with providing management with information to facilitate planning and control. (p. 11)

Market rate of interest The rate that investors could obtain by investing in other bonds that are similar to the issuing firm's bonds. (p. 493)

Market value per share The selling price of the stock as indicated by the most recent transactions. (p. 562)

Matching principle The association of revenue of a period with all of the costs necessary to generate that revenue. (p. 167)

Materiality The magnitude of an accounting information omission or misstatement that will affect the judgment of someone relying on the information. (p. 60)

Merchandise Inventory The account wholesalers and retailers use to report inventory held for resale. (p. 221)

Monetary unit The yardstick used to measure amounts in financial statements; the dollar in the United States. (p. 23)

Moving average The name given to an average cost method when a weighted average cost assumption is used with a perpetual inventory system. (p. 259)

Multiple-step income statement An income statement that shows classifications of revenues and expenses as well as important subtotals. (p. 70)

N

Net income The excess of revenues over expenses. (p. 16)

Net sales Sales revenue less sales returns and allowances and sales discounts. (p. 224)

Nominal accounts The name given to revenue, expense, and dividend accounts because they are temporary and are closed at the end of the period. (p. 185)

Nonbusiness entity An organization operated for some purpose other than to earn a profit. (p. 7)

Note payable A liability resulting from the signing of a promissory note. (pp. 344, 432)

Note receivable An asset resulting from the acceptance of a promissory note from another company. (p. 344)

Number of days' sales in inventory A measure of how long it takes to sell inventory. (pp. 254, 690)

Number of days' sales in receivables A measure of the average age of accounts receivable. (p. 689)

O

Operating activities Activities concerned with the acquisition and sale of products and services. (p. 610)

Operating cycle The period of time between the purchase of inventory and the collection of any receivable from the sale of the inventory. (p. 62)

Operating lease A lease that does not meet any of the four criteria and is not recorded as an asset by the lessee. (p. 505)

Outstanding check A check written by a company but not yet presented to the bank for payment. (p. 298)

Outstanding shares The number of shares issued less the number of shares held as treasury stock. (p. 543)

Owners' equity The owners' claims on the assets of an entity. (p. 14)

P

Par value An arbitrary amount that represents the legal capital of the firm. (p. 543)

Participating feature Allows preferred stockholders to share on a percentage basis in the distribution of an abnormally large dividend. (p. 545)

Partnership A business owned by two or more individuals; the organization form often used by accounting firms and law firms. (p. 6)

Partnership agreement Specifies how much the owners will invest, what their salaries will be, and how profits will be shared. (p. 568)

Payee The party that will receive the money from a promissory note at some future date. (p. 344)

Periodic system A system in which the Inventory account is updated only at the end of the period. (p. 227)

Permanent difference A difference that affects the tax records but not the accounting records, or vice versa. (p. 515)

Perpetual system A system in which the Inventory account is increased at the time of each purchase and decreased at the time of each sale. (p. 227)

Petty cash fund Money kept on hand for making minor disbursements in coin and currency rather than by writing checks. (p. 301)

Posting The process of transferring amounts from a journal to the ledger accounts. (p. 123)

Premium The excess of the issue price over the face value of the bonds. (p. 495)

Present value of a single amount The amount at a present time that is equivalent to a payment or an investment at a future time. (p. 449)

Present value of an annuity The amount at a present time that is equivalent to a series of payments and interest in the future. (p. 451)

Price/earnings (P/E) ratio The relationship between a company's performance according to the income statement and its performance in the stock market. (p. 699)

Profit margin Net income divided by sales. (p. 72)

Profit margin ratio Net income to net sales. (p. 685)

Profitability How well management is using company resources to earn a return on the funds invested by various groups. (p. 695)

Promissory note A written promise to repay a definite sum of money on demand or at a fixed or determinable date in the future. (p. 344)

Public Company Accounting Oversight Board (PCAOB) The five-member body created by the Sarbanes-Oxley Act that was given the authority to set auditing standards in the United States. (p. 305)

Purchase Discounts A contra-purchases account used to record reductions in purchase price for early payment to a supplier. (p. 231)

Purchase order A form sent by the purchasing department to the supplier. (p. 312)

Purchase requisition form A form a department uses to initiate a request to order merchandise. (p. 310)

Purchase Returns and Allowances A contra-purchases account used in a periodic inventory system when a refund is received from a supplier or a reduction is given in the balance owed to a supplier. (p. 230)

Purchases An account used in a periodic inventory system to record acquisitions of merchandise. (p. 229)

R

Raw materials The inventory of a manufacturer before the addition of any direct labor or manufacturing overhead. (p. 222)

Real accounts The name given to balance sheet accounts because they are permanent and are not closed at the end of the period. (p. 185)

Recognition The process of recording an item in the financial statements as an asset, a liability, a revenue, an expense, or the like. (p. 158)

Redeemable feature Allows stockholders to sell stock back to the company. (p. 545)

Relevance The capacity of information to make a difference in a decision. (p. 58)

Replacement cost The current cost of a unit of inventory. (p. 245)

Research and development costs Costs incurred in the discovery of new knowledge. (p. 396)

Retained earnings The part of owners' equity that represents the income earned less dividends paid over the life of an entity. (p. 15)

Retirement of stock When the stock is repurchased with no intention of reissuing at a later date. (p. 550)

Return on assets ratio A measure of a company's success in earning a return for all providers of capital. (p. 695)

Return on common stockholders' equity ratio A measure of a company's success in earning a return for the common stockholders. (p. 697)

Return on sales ratio A variation of the profit margin ratio; measures earnings before interest expense. (p. 696)

Revenue expenditure A cost that keeps an asset in its normal operating condition and is treated as an expense. (p. 389)

Revenue recognition principle Revenues are recognized in the income statement when they are realized, or realizable, and earned. (p. 165)

Revenue(s) Inflows of assets or settlements of liabilities from delivering or producing goods, rendering services, or conducting other activities. (pp. 9, 165)

S

Sales Discounts A contra-revenue account used to record discounts given to customers for early payment of their accounts. (p. 225)

Sales Returns and Allowances Contra-revenue account used to record refunds to customers and reductions of their accounts. (p. 224)

Sales revenue A representation of the inflow of assets. (p. 224)

Sarbanes-Oxley Act An act of Congress in 2002 intended to bring reform to corporate accountability and stewardship in the wake of a number of major corporate scandals. (pp. 30, 302)

Securities and Exchange Commission (SEC) The federal agency with ultimate authority to determine the rules for preparing statements for companies whose stock is sold to the public. (p. 25)

Serial bonds Bonds that do not all have the same due date; a portion of the bonds comes due each time period. (p. 492)

Share of stock A certificate that acts as evidence of ownership in a corporation. (p. 7)

Simple interest Interest is calculated on the principal amount only. (p. 445)

Single-step income statement An income statement in which all expenses are added together and subtracted from all revenues. (p. 69)

Sole proprietorship A form of organization with a single owner. (p. 6)

Solvency The ability of a company to remain in business over the long term. (p. 691)

Source document A piece of paper that is used as evidence to record a transaction. (p. 108)

Specific identification method An inventory costing method that relies on matching unit costs with the actual units sold. (p. 238)

Statement of cash flows The financial statement that summarizes an entity's cash receipts and cash payments during the period from operating, investing, and financing activities. (pp. 17, 605)

Statement of retained earnings The statement that summarizes the income earned and dividends paid over the life of a business. (p. 17)

Statement of stockholders' equity Reflects the differences between beginning and ending balances for all accounts in the Stockholders' Equity category of the balance sheet. (p. 557)

Stock dividend The issuance of additional shares of stock to existing stockholders. (p. 553)

Stock split The creation of additional shares of stock with a reduction of the par value of the stock. (p. 556)

Stockholder One of the owners of a corporation. (p. 9)

Stockholders' equity The owners' equity in a corporation. (p. 14)

Straight-line method The assignment of an equal amount of depreciation to each period. (pp. 170, 383)

Subsidiary ledger The detail for a number of individual items that collectively make up a single general ledger account. (p. 334)

T

Temporary difference A difference that affects both book and tax records but not in the same time period. (p. 515)

Time period An artificial segment on the calendar used as the basis for preparing financial statements. (p. 24)

Time value of money An immediate amount should be preferred over an amount in the future. (p. 444)

Times interest earned ratio An income statement measure of the ability of a company to meet its interest payments. (p. 692)

Transaction Any event that is recognized in a set of financial statements. (p. 107)

Transportation-In An adjunct account used to record freight costs paid by the buyer. (p. 229)

Treasury stock Stock issued by the firm and then repurchased but not retired. (p. 548)

Trial balance A list of each account and its balance; used to prove equality of debits and credits. (p. 126)

U

Understandability The quality of accounting information that makes it comprehensible to those willing to spend the necessary time. (p. 58)

Units-of-production method Depreciation is determined as a function of the number of units the asset produces. (p. 383)

V

Vertical analysis A comparison of various financial statement items within a single period with the use of common-size statements. (p. 678)

W

Weighted average cost method An inventory costing method that assigns the same unit cost to all units available for sale during the period. (p. 239)

Work in process The cost of unfinished products in a manufacturing company. (p. 222)

Work sheet A device used at the end of the period to gather the information needed to prepare financial statements without actually recording and posting adjusting entries. (p. 185)

Working capital Current assets minus current liabilities. (p. 67)

Index

Real company names and key terms appear in boldfaced type, and any page numbers of where definitions appear are also in bold.

Ethics and Accounting: A Decision-Making Model

IDENTIFICATION

1. **Recognize an ethical dilemma.**

   - Conflicting accounting rules.
   - No GAAP to follow.
   - Fraud or other questionable actions have occurred.

ANALYSIS

2. **Analyze the key elements in the situation.**

   - Who benefits?
   - Who is harmed?
   - What are their rights and claims?
   - What are the conflicting interests?
   - What are the accountant's responsibilities?

3. **List alternatives and evaluate the impacts on those affected.**

   - Most useful and timely information for decisions?
   - Most faithful representation for decision makers?
   - Most accurate information?
   - Is the information free from bias?
   - Most likely impact on those affected?

RESOLUTION

4. **Select the best alternative.**

   - Which alternative is most relevant, most complete, most neutral, and most free from error?

Financial Decision Framework

1. Formulate the Question.

2. Gather the Information from the Financial Statements and Other Sources.

3. Analyze the Financials.

4. Make the Decision.

5. Interpret the Results.

Ratio Decision Model

1. Formulate the Question.

2. Gather the Information from the Financial Statements.

3. Calculate the Ratio.

4. Compare the Ratio with Others.

5. Interpret the Results.

SUMMARY OF SELECTED FINANCIAL RATIOS

RATIO NAME	FORMULA	PAGE REFERENCE*
Liquidity Analysis		
Working capital	Current Assets − Current Liabilities	67, 686
Current ratio	$\dfrac{\text{Current Assets}}{\text{Current Liabilities}}$	68, **78**, 687
Acid-test ratio (quick ratio)	$\dfrac{\text{Cash} + \text{Marketable Securities} + \text{Current Receivables}}{\text{Current Liabilities}}$	687
Cash flow from operations to current liabilities ratio	$\dfrac{\text{Net Cash Provided by Operating Activities}}{\text{Average Current Liabilities}}$	688
Accounts receivable turnover ratio	$\dfrac{\text{Net Credit Sales}}{\text{Average Accounts Receivable}}$	341, **342–343**, 689
Number of days' sales in receivables	$\dfrac{\text{Number of Days in the Period}}{\text{Accounts Receivable Turnover}}$	689
Inventory turnover ratio	$\dfrac{\text{Cost of Goods Sold}}{\text{Average Inventory}}$	**253–254**, 690
Number of days' sales in inventory	$\dfrac{\text{Number of Days in the Period}}{\text{Inventory Turnover}}$	690
Cash-to-cash operating cycle	Number of Days' Sales in Inventory + Number of Days' Sales in Receivables	690
Solvency Analysis		
Debt-to-equity ratio	$\dfrac{\text{Total Liabilities}}{\text{Total Stockholders' Equity}}$	**510–511**, 691
Times interest earned ratio	$\dfrac{\text{Net Income} + \text{Interest Expense} + \text{Income Tax Expense}}{\text{Interest Expense}}$	**510–511**, 692
Debt service coverage ratio	$\dfrac{\text{Cash Flow from Operations before Interest and Tax Payments}}{\text{Interest and Principal Payments}}$	693
Cash flow from operations to capital expenditures ratio	$\dfrac{\text{Cash Flow from Operations} - \text{Total Dividends Paid}}{\text{Cash Paid for Acquisitions}}$	694
Profitability Analysis		
Gross profit ratio	$\dfrac{\text{Gross Profit}}{\text{Net Sales}}$	233, **234–235**, 684
Profit margin ratio	$\dfrac{\text{Net Income}}{\text{Net Sales}}$	**79–80**, 685
Return on assets ratio	$\dfrac{\text{Net Income} + \text{Interest Expense, Net of Tax}}{\text{Average Total Assets}}$	695
Return on sales ratio	$\dfrac{\text{Net Income} + \text{Interest Expense, Net of Tax}}{\text{Net Sales}}$	696
Asset turnover ratio	$\dfrac{\text{Net Sales}}{\text{Average Total Assets}}$	403, **404–406**, 696
Return on common stockholders' equity ratio	$\dfrac{\text{Net Income} - \text{Preferred Dividends}}{\text{Average Common Stockholders' Equity}}$	697
Earnings per share	$\dfrac{\text{Net Income} - \text{Preferred Dividends}}{\text{Weighted Average Number of Common Shares Outstanding}}$	698
Price/earnings ratio	$\dfrac{\text{Current Market Price}}{\text{Earnings per Share}}$	699
Dividend payout ratio	$\dfrac{\text{Common Dividends per Share}}{\text{Earnings per Share}}$	551, 700
Dividend yield ratio	$\dfrac{\text{Common Dividends per Share}}{\text{Market Price per Share}}$	700
Cash flow adequacy	$\dfrac{\text{Cash Flow from Operating Activities} - \text{Capital Expenditures}}{\text{Average Amount of Debt Maturing over Next Five Years}}$	**634–635**

*boldface = Ratio Decision Model

The Accounting Equation

The accounting equation is the foundation for the entire accounting system:

Assets = Liabilities + Owners' Equity
or
Assets = Liabilities + Stockholders' Equity

Accounting Equation and the Balance Sheet

Assets	=	Liabilities	+	Owners' Equity
Economic resources Examples: • Cash • Accounts receivable • Land		**Creditors' claims to the assets** Examples: • Accounts payable • Notes payable		**Owners' claims to the assets** Examples: • Capital stock • Retained earnings

The Financial Statements

Balance Sheet *shows* assets, liabilities, and stockholders' equity at a certain date.

Income Statement *shows* revenues and expenses for the period.

Statement of Retained Earnings *shows* changes in retained earnings during the period.

Statement of Cash Flows *shows* cash flow effects of operating, investing, and financing activities for a period.

Relationships among the Financial Statements

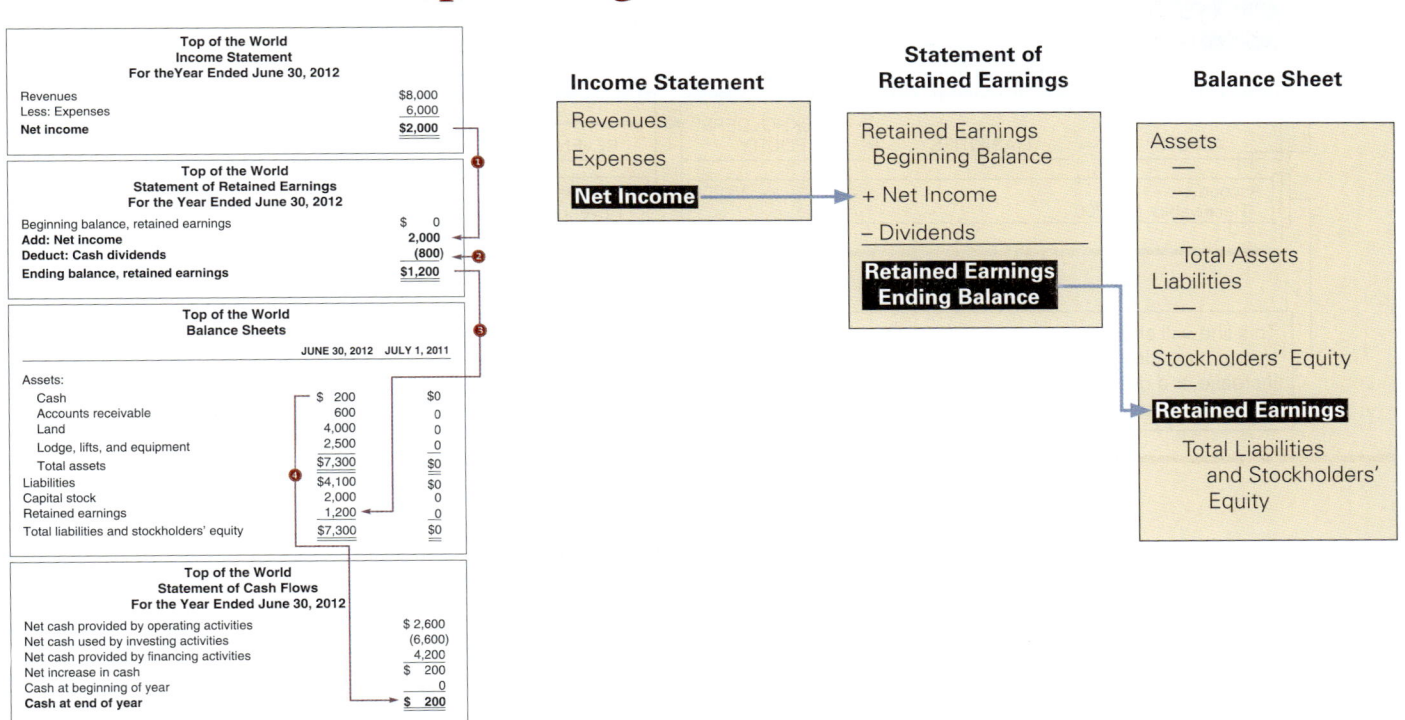

Top of the World
Income Statement
For the Year Ended June 30, 2012

Revenues	$8,000
Less: Expenses	6,000
Net income	$2,000

Top of the World
Statement of Retained Earnings
For the Year Ended June 30, 2012

Beginning balance, retained earnings	$ 0
Add: Net income	2,000
Deduct: Cash dividends	(800)
Ending balance, retained earnings	$1,200

Top of the World
Balance Sheets

	JUNE 30, 2012	JULY 1, 2011
Assets:		
Cash	$ 200	$0
Accounts receivable	600	0
Land	4,000	0
Lodge, lifts, and equipment	2,500	0
Total assets	$7,300	$0
Liabilities	$4,100	$0
Capital stock	2,000	0
Retained earnings	1,200	0
Total liabilities and stockholders' equity	$7,300	$0

Top of the World
Statement of Cash Flows
For the Year Ended June 30, 2012

Net cash provided by operating activities	$ 2,600
Net cash used by investing activities	(6,600)
Net cash provided by financing activities	4,200
Net increase in cash	$ 200
Cash at beginning of year	0
Cash at end of year	$ 200

Income Statement

Revenues
Expenses
Net Income

Statement of Retained Earnings

Retained Earnings Beginning Balance
+ Net Income
– Dividends
Retained Earnings Ending Balance

Balance Sheet

Assets
—
—
—
Total Assets
Liabilities
—
Stockholders' Equity
Retained Earnings
Total Liabilities and Stockholders' Equity

Transaction Analysis*

	Assets					=	Liabilities		+	Stockholders' Equity	
Transaction Number	Cash	Accounts Receivable	Equipment	Building	Land		Accounts Payable	Notes Payable		Capital Stock	Retained Earnings

*The accounts shown here are one possible set of accounts; other accounts are introduced in later chapters.

EXHIBIT 3-5 Introducing the Identify and Analyze Transaction Format

Example: Transaction 4, p.109 : Sale of monthly memberships on account:

Transaction Analysis Format (used in **Ch. 3**)

- Shows how transactions are analyzed in account names (**Cash, Accounts Receivable**, etc., as shown below) and accounting equation categories (**Assets, Liabilities, Stockholders' Equity**). (Amounts are eventually reflected in the financial statements.)

Transaction Number	Cash	Accounts Receivable	Equipment	Building	Land	Accounts Payable	Notes Payable	Capital Stock	Retained Earnings
		Assets			=	Liabilities		+ Stockholders' Equity	
4		$15,000							$15,000

Identify and Analyze Format (used in **Chs. 4–13**)

- Answers the three questions for each transaction:
  - What type of *Activity* does the transaction reflect?
  - What *Accounts* are affected?
  - Which *Financial Statement(s)* are affected?
- Shows how the balance sheet and the income statement are affected by the transaction, listing account names and amounts recorded under each accounting equation category.

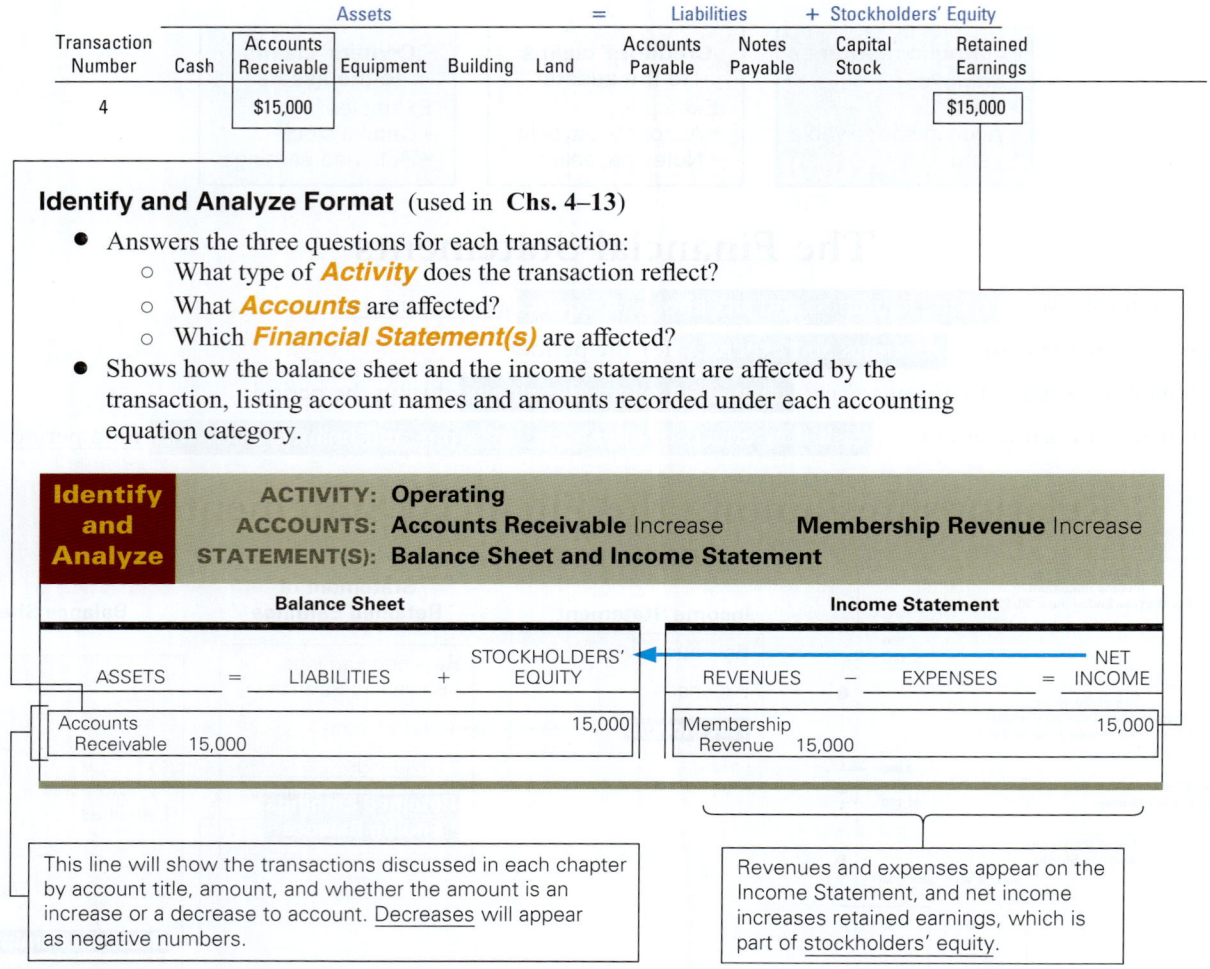

Identify and Analyze	**ACTIVITY:** Operating
	ACCOUNTS: Accounts Receivable Increase **Membership Revenue** Increase
	STATEMENT(S): Balance Sheet and Income Statement

Balance Sheet				Income Statement			
ASSETS	=	LIABILITIES	+	STOCKHOLDERS' EQUITY	REVENUES	−	EXPENSES	=	NET INCOME
Accounts Receivable 15,000				15,000	Membership Revenue 15,000				15,000

This line will show the transactions discussed in each chapter by account title, amount, and whether the amount is an increase or a decrease to account. Decreases will appear as negative numbers.

Revenues and expenses appear on the Income Statement, and net income increases retained earnings, which is part of stockholders' equity.

Cost of Goods Sold

	Beginning inventory	What is on hand to start the period
+	Cost of goods purchased	What was acquired for resale during the period
=	Cost of goods available for sale	The "pool" of costs to be distributed
−	Ending inventory	What was not sold during the period and therefore is on hand to start the next period
=	Cost of goods sold	What was sold during the period

Components of Stockholders' Equity

Assets = Liabilities + Stockholders' Equity

Total Stockholders' Equity = Contributed Capital
+
Retained Earnings